INTERNATIONAL PRIVATE LAW:
A SCOTS PERSPECTIVE

THIRD EDITION

INTERNATIONAL PRIVATE LAW: A SCOTS PERSPECTIVE

THIRD EDITION

Elizabeth B. Crawford, LLB (Hons), PhD,
Solicitor
Professor of International Private Law,
University of Glasgow

and

Janeen M. Carruthers, LLB (Hons), Dip LP, PhD,
Solicitor
Professor of Private Law,
University of Glasgow

W. GREEN  THOMSON REUTERS

First edition   1998
Second edition   2006

Published in 2010 by
Thomson Reuters (Legal) Limited
(Registered in England and Wales,
Company No 1679046.
Registered office and address for service
100 Avenue Road, Swiss Cottage,
London, NW3 3PF) trading as W. Green

Typeset by LBJ Typesetting Ltd, Kingsclere
Printed and bound in the UK by CPI William Clowes, Beccles, MR34 7TL

No natural forests were destroyed to make this product;
only farmed timber was used and re-planted.

A catalogue record for this title is available from
the British Library

ISBN 978–0–414–01775–7

Thomson Reuters and the Thomson Reuters logo are
trademarks of Thomson Reuters.

To our families, respectively and respectfully.

PREFACE TO THE THIRD EDITION

Earlier than anticipated, we deliver the third edition of "IPL in Scotland", now as a freestanding volume rather than as part of Greens Concise Law Series, and under the title *International Private Law: A Scots Perspective*. In view of the pace of the EU programme of harmonisation of conflict of laws of Member States, a new edition is timely.

The new title is intended to convey the changed and changing nature of international private law rules, as applicable in Scotland. Many, but by no means all, of these rules are held in common with the rest of the UK and with fellow EU Member States. What is offered here, therefore, is a treatment of the intrinsically Scottish rules of international private law, together with an account and critique of those UK and EU/Hague harmonised rules which increasingly dominate the subject. The whole is viewed through the lens of Scots law, paying full respect to Scots private law and international private law sources and authorities, early and modern. Yet in the 21st century there is a notable degree of comity and mutual reliance among "UK" conflict lawyers, who work together to secure what jointly is conceived to be in the best interests of UK citizens (or domiciliaries) in a rapidly changing legal situation in which civilian practices and modes of thinking are inevitably pre-eminent.

There are few chapters unaffected by European changes, which in recent years have encompassed matters of jurisdiction, choice of law, recognition and enforcement of judgments, and related procedural topics. EU judicial co-operation in civil matters now rests upon the Treaty on the functioning of the European Union (the Lisbon Treaty). Where EU legislation already is in force, our policy has been to begin the relevant chapter with that material, on the rationale that this is the most useful manner of presentation for the reader, enabling immediate reference to the law in force. Where the EU instrument is merely proposed (as, for example, in relation to choice of law in divorce ("Rome III"), or Succession ("Rome V")), we have favoured a chronological approach.

The most active and most difficult area is that concerning the rules of civil and commercial jurisdiction. A pressing matter for Scots lawyers is to examine the extent of operation of the Brussels regime of jurisdiction and judgments, to draw a line of demarcation between "Brussels" and "non-Brussels" cases, and to keep abreast of what may be proposed as regards the relationship, in terms of jurisdiction and judgment recognition, between Member States and Third States. Also, importantly, the revised Lugano Convention ("Lugano II") has come into being, and its provisions are addressed, together with its relationship with the Brussels I Regulation. Likewise, the relationship between the rules of jurisdiction of the Brussels regime, on the one hand, and arbitration as a means of resolving international commercial disputes, on the other, has required attention. In procedure, full account is taken of the development of yet more rapid judgment enforcement procedures within the EU: Regulation 1896/2006 creating a European Order for Payment Procedure, and Regulation 861/2007 creating a European Small Claims Procedure.

In choice of law, Chapter 13 (Proprietary and Financial Consequences of Marriage and Other Adult Relationships) takes full account of the Maintenance Regulation (Regulation 4/2009); Chapters 15 (Contractual Obligations) and 16 (Non-contractual Obligations) include, respectively, analysis of the Rome I Regulation (Regulation 593/2008) and Rome II Regulation (Regulation 864/2007). In addition to applicable law rules for delict, the latter instrument contains applicable law rules for unjust enrichment, *negotiorum gestio* and *culpa in contrahendo*, which, as laid down in statutory form, are a novelty in Scots law.

Early discussion, on an EU basis, concerning the principle of *iura novit curia*, and the implications of more widespread acceptance of this principle in legal systems favouring the adversarial process (such as our own), may portend significant change as part of the project to transform national sets of conflict rules into a corpus of harmonised rules. Though the UK approach to proof of foreign law has been criticised on the ground, *inter alia*, that it curbs development of the subject, causing the conflict potential of a case to remain unfulfilled, the case law cited in this edition is more voluminous even than before. This is attributable partly to the lively state of the conflict branch of law generally, but also to the need for interpretative direction, by domestic courts and/or the CJEU, which new legislative instruments, national and European, demand. Amidst the rigour and sobriety, perhaps there is time for the *faux-naïf*:

> *"I'm not going to argue with Maud" says Horace. "She's a girl. What's the real answer?"*
> *"Oh, the Correctional Court at Lille found for the railway company. Payelle had to reimburse them."*
> *"I won!" shouts Horace. "Maud got it wrong."*
> *"No one got it wrong," George replies, "The case could have gone either way. That's why things go to court in the first place."*[1]

To this complex and rewarding branch of law has been added the complexity of seeking to ascertain the ranking *inter se*, and respective application of, different sets of rules (national, European and international; and in and across those categories), which operate within the same subject area. Unappealing though at first sight it may be, we think that the term "demarcation law", suggested as a title for the subject early in its development, has become apposite to describe a crucial part of the conflict lawyer's expertise.

Detailed, clear and accurate statement of the law is a discipline and first duty demanded of the writer. Wit and elegance of expression have to take a subordinate role, but we have enjoyed searching for *le mot juste* and the felicitous phrase, as we have enjoyed the writing task as a whole. As a reversal of the adage that any age is younger when one achieves it than when it is viewed in advance, the writing of each chapter has proved to be a lengthier exercise than expected; there have been many more par 5s on this golf course than usually are encountered, and lengthy ones at that, making it a challenge to get up in regulation, Regulation by Regulation.

As with the second edition, this work is entirely jointly authored, and at its completion we report our continuing enjoyment of the subject, and pleasure in the company.

We express our appreciation to the commissioning, editorial and marketing sections of W. Green, and record, in particular, our thanks to Janet Campbell, Kathy Pauline, and Alan Bett.

We are grateful to our families for their patience and their support of a demanding endeavour.

We have sought to state the law as at July 31, 2010.

EBC and JMC
Glasgow, August 2010.

---

[1] Julian Barnes, *Arthur & George* (London: Vintage reissue, 2006), p.72

PREFACE TO THE SECOND EDITION

Many changes have occurred in Scots conflict rules since publication of the first edition of this book at the end of 1998.

In the first place, the development by the European Union of an "area of freedom, security and justice" has justified and necessitated, *inter alia*, the assimilation of the conflict rules of Member States across an increasing number of areas of private law. The European programme affects all aspects of the conflict of laws, viz. jurisdiction, choice of law, and recognition and enforcement of judgments, as well as procedural matters.

A programme of work was set for the period 1999 to 2004 at an Extraordinary European Council Meeting at Tampere, Finland. Important legislative reform under the Tampere agenda includes the conversion of the 1968 Brussels Convention on jurisdiction and the enforcement of judgments in civil and commercial matters into Council Regulation (EC) No 44/2001; Council Regulation (EC) No. 1346/2000 on Insolvency Proceedings; and, significantly, moving into Family Law, Council Regulation (EC) No 2201/2003 ("Brussels II Bis") concerning jurisdiction and the recognition and enforcement of judgments in matrimonial matters and matters of parental responsibility. These are weighty changes concerning substantive conflict rules. There have been also a number of changes to procedural conflict rules, including those relating to service of documents, and taking of evidence abroad.

This programme is to be pursued without pause under the Hague Programme, adopted by the European Council in 2004, for the period 2005–2009. Negotiations continue on the conversion into a Regulation of the 1980 Rome Convention on the Law Applicable to Contractual Obligations; and upon a Proposal for a Regulation on the Law Applicable to Non-Contractual Obligations ("Rome II"). Green Papers recently have been presented by the European Commission on applicable law and jurisdiction in divorce matters; on succession and wills; and on maintenance.

Secondly, a number of important changes have been made to Scottish and English domestic law, requiring concomitant conflict rules. Where such rules are lacking, expert commentary must be provided. The prime examples in this category arise in Family Law, in particular with regard to the creation of the new status of civil partner under the Civil Partnership Act 2004; and the statutory regulation in Scots law of certain aspects of *de facto* cohabitation.

Thirdly, the Family Law (Scotland) Act 2006 has placed on a statutory basis for the first time a number of Scots conflict rules in Family Law, such as those relating to validity of marriage, and matrimonial property, thereby crystallising them, and in so doing changing conflict rules by seemingly foreclosing the operation of certain options which existed at common law. The Act has added rules on a number of particular points of conflict significance, including a new provision concerning void marriages, and a different rule for ascribing the domicile of persons under 16. It is fortunate that the publication schedule of this book has permitted us to take full account of this major new Act.

The material has been re-ordered, and the book is presented now in two parts. Part A deals with matters such as methodology; connecting factors; and the pre-eminent subject of civil and commercial jurisdiction, including full analysis of UK and ECJ case law such as *Gasser v Misat, Turner v Grovit and Owusu*. The subjects of evidence and procedure and foreign decree enforcement, included in Part A, reflect the importance of these rules, and their inter-relationship with jurisdictional rules. Part B gives a full account of the conflict rules of Scots law in all major areas of private law. Substantial re-writing has occurred, particularly in the chapters on marriage and other adult relationships; consistorial causes; property and financial consequences of adult relationships; children; contractual obligations; non-contractual obligations; and insolvency.

It has been our aim to provide a comprehensive account of Scots conflict rules in all major areas of private law. This must be done within reasonable compass, and the decision was made to excise chapters on company law and criminal law to compensate for the increase in text which the changes outlined above demand.

We wish to record our thanks to our research assistant, Michael Thomson, who ably assisted us during the summer of 2005.

As is obvious, this book is now a co-authored composition. EBC expresses her gratitude to JMC for joining her in this venture. Our friends will know that differences of opinion between us are seldom found (the most profound being Burns's/Burns' poems; by great forbearance EBC has allowed the case of *Dinwoodie's Executrix v Carruthers' Executor* to pass unchanged, in deference to Dr Carruthers's opinion). There has been no division of labour or writing tasks; the work is entirely jointly authored.

At the University of Glasgow in recent years the authors have greatly expanded the conflict of laws teaching provision. We are privileged to teach in an area which is that of our prime research interest; teaching and writing are best when they are interlinked. The authors acknowledge the benefit which accrues to them through teaching, and trust that the mutual advantage is apparent also from the student perspective.

This book is dedicated to David M. Walker, *Regius Professor Emeritus of Law in the University of Glasgow*, whose contribution to legal scholarship in Scots law and legal education is immense. For EBC, Professor Walker was an inspirational teacher; for JMC, of the next generation, a mentor in her early research; to both of us, a friend whose kind interest and encouragement we appreciate. We are honoured that Professor Walker has accepted this dedication. We have endeavoured to state the law as at 8 June 2006, although it has been possible to take account of some later developments.

EBC
JMC
University of Glasgow

June 2006

PREFACE TO THE FIRST EDITION

This book is the product of the Printed Notes provided annually for the class of International Private Law at Glasgow University. Originally, and for many years, they were the work of Alex Donaldson, my predecessor as lecturer in that class. Thereafter they were updated and enlarged by me until there came a time at which it seemed appropriate to develop them further into book form. The text is intended principally for students, but I hope that it may be of wider use and interest. I have sought to state the law as at the date of this Preface.

The account presented is of Scottish conflict rules. A Scots forum is assumed, and accordingly the substantive domestic legal background as well as the system of conflict rules is that of Scottish private law. Nevertheless, since in my view much in the conflict of laws is held in common with England, many English conflict cases are cited, for interest and by way of illustration. They may be persuasive. Differences between Scots conflict rules and English conflict rules, in common law or statute, in substance or procedure, in emphasis or in nuance, I have tried to identify at appropriate points in the text.

I am grateful to my colleagues in the Stair building for their advice and expertise in many areas of law; to my researchers—successively, Paul Sheehan, Susan Mitchell, Shaheed Fatima and Jacqueline Donald—for their help; and to the editorial team at W. Green for bringing the book to publication.

Above all, I thanks Moira Smith, who has converted many versions of this text into its final form, and without whose great skill and patience the book would not have been completed.

Finally I record my gratitude to all the students over the years to whom I have had the pleasure and the privilege of speaking on the subject of International Private Law. The classes have been a joy to me, as I know they were to Alex Donaldson. Mr Donaldson's death occurred in April 1998, after the completion of the text but before production of the book. International Private Law in Scotland is dedicated to him, by a pupil to a teacher.

Elizabeth B. Crawford
University of Glasgow

30 September 1998

CONTENTS

TABLE OF CASES

Table of Cases

TABLE OF STATUTES

ACTS OF THE SCOTTISH PARLIAMENT

TABLE OF STATUTORY INSTRUMENTS

TABLE OF INTERNATIONAL CONVENTIONS

TABLE OF EUROPEAN LEGISLATION

TREATIES

SELECT BIBLIOGRAPHY

GENERAL

Anton, A.E., *Private International Law: A treatise from the standpoint of Scots law*, 1st edn (Edinburgh: SULI/W. Green, 1967).

Binchy, W., *Irish Conflict of Laws*, 2nd edn, (London: Bloomsbury Professional, 2011).

Briggs, A., *The Conflict of Laws*, 2nd edn, (Oxford: Oxford University Press, 2008).

Briggs, A. and Rees, P., *Civil Jurisdiction and Judgments*, 5th edn (London: Lloyds of London Press, 2009).

Cheshire, North and Fawcett: Private International Law, edited by J.J. Fawcett and J.M. Carruthers, 14th edn (Oxford: Oxford University Press, 2008).

Clarkson, C.M.V. and Hill, J., *The Conflict of Laws*, 3rd edn (Oxford: Oxford University Press, 2006).

Crawford, E.B. and Carruthers, J.M., *Avizandum Legislation on International Private Law*, 2nd edn (Edinburgh: Avizandum, 2010).

Dicey, Morris and Collins on the Conflict of Laws, edited by L. Collins, 14th edn (London: Sweet & Maxwell, 2006).

Graveson, R.H., *Private International Law*, 7th edn (London: Sweet & Maxwell, 1974).

Hill, J., *International Commercial Disputes in English Courts*, 3rd edn (Oxford: Hart, 2005).

Morris, J.C.H., *The Conflict of Laws*, edited by D. McClean and K. Beevers, 7th edn (London: Sweet & Maxwell, 2009).

von Savigny, F.C., *A Treatise on the Conflict of Laws*, translated by W. Guthrie, 2nd edn (Edinburgh: T&T Clark, 1880).

von Bar, C.L., *The Theory and Practice of Private International Law*, translated by G.R. Gillespie, 2nd edn (Edinburgh: W. Green & Sons, 1892).

Westlake, J., *A Treatise on Private International Law*, edited by N. Bentwich, 7th edn (London: Sweet & Maxwell, 1925).

Wolff, M., *Private International Law*, 2nd edn (Oxford: Clarendon Press, 1950).

REFLECTIVE/SPECIFIC

Ahern, J. and Binchy, W. (eds), *The Rome II Regulation on the Law Applicable to Non-contractual Obligations* (Leiden: Martinus Nijhoff, 2009).

Ahern, J. and Binchy, W. (eds), *The Rome I Regulation: Implications for International Commercial Litigation* (Brill, 2010).

Beaumont, P.R. and McEleavy, P.E., *The Hague Convention on International Child Abduction* (Oxford: Oxford University Press, 1999).

Bell, A., *Forum Shopping and Venue in Transnational Litigation* (Oxford: Oxford University Press, 2003).

Briggs, A., *Agreements on Jurisdiction and Choice of Law* (Oxford: Oxford University Press, 2008).

Carruthers, J.M., *The Transfer of Property in the Conflict of Laws* (Oxford: Oxford University Press, 2005).

Cavers, D.F, *The Choice of Law Process* (Michigan: Ann Arbor, University of Michigan Press, 1966).

Cook, W.W., *The Logical and Legal Bases of the Conflict of Laws* (Cambridge, Massuchusetts: Harvard University Press, 1942).

Currie, B., *Selected Essays on the Conflict of Laws* (Duke University Press, 1963).

Dickinson, A., *The Rome II Regulation: The Law Applicable to Non-contractual Obligations* (Oxford: Oxford University Press, 2008); Supplement (2010).

Edwards, L. and Waelde, C. (eds), *Law and the Internet* (Oxford: Hart, 2009).

Einhorn, T. and Siehr, K. (eds), *Intercontinental Cooperation through Private International Law: Essays in Memory of Peter E Nygh* (Hague: TMC Asser Press, 2004).

Falconbridge, J., *Essays on the Conflict of Laws* (Canada Law Book Co Ltd, 1954).

Fawcett, J.J. (ed.), *Reform and Development of Private International Law: Essays in Honour of Sir Peter North* (Oxford: Oxford University Press, 2002).

Fawcett, J.J., Harris, J.M. and Bridge, M., *International Sale of Goods in the Conflict of Laws* (Oxford: Oxford University Press, 2005).

Fawcett, J.J. and Torremans, P., *Intellectual Property and Private International Law* (Oxford: Oxford University Press, 1998).

Fentiman, R., *Foreign Law in English Courts* (Oxford: Oxford University Press, 1998).

Fentiman, R., *International Commercial Litigation* (Oxford: Oxford University Press, 2010).

Ferrari, F. and Leible, S. (eds), *Rome I Regulation: The Law Applicable to Contractual Obligations in Europe* (Munich: Sellier, 2009).

Fletcher, I.F., *Insolvency in Private International Law: National and International Approaches*, 2nd edn (Oxford: Oxford University Press, 2005).

Geeroms, S., *Foreign Law in Civil Litigation: A Comparative and Functional Analysis* (Oxford: Oxford University Press, 2004).

Gillies, L.E., *Electronic Commerce and International Private Law* (Aldershot: Ashgate, 2008).

Harris, J.M., *The Hague Trusts Convention: The Private International Law of Trusts* (Oxford: Hart Publishing, 2002).

Hill, J., *Cross-Border Consumer Contracts* (Oxford: Oxford University Press, 2009).

Hood, K.J., *Conflict of Laws within the UK* (Oxford: Oxford University Press, 2007).

Kadner Graziano, T. with Grant, E., *The Law Applicable to Non-contractual Obligations in Europe: A Guide to the Rome II Regulation* (Oxford: Hart Publishing, 2011).

Kahn-Freund, O., *General Problems of Private International Law* (Leyden: Sijthoff and Noordhoff, 1980).

Kennett, W., *The Enforcement of Judgments in Europe* (Oxford: Oxford University Press, 2000).

Kruger, T., *Civil Jurisdiction Rules of the EU and their Impact on Third States* (Oxford: Oxford University Press, 2008).

Lalive, P., *The Transfer of Chattels in the Conflict of Laws* (London: OUP, 1955).

Magnus, U. and Mankowski, P., *Brussels I Regulation* (Munch: Sellier, 2007).

Meston, M.C., *The Succession (Scotland) Act 1964*, 5th edn (Edinburgh: W. Green, 2002).

Mills, A., *The Confluence of Public and Private International Law* (Cambridge: Cambridge University Press, 2009).

Morse, C.G.J., *Torts in Private International Law* (Amsterdam: North-Holland Publishing Co, 1978).

Moss, G., Fletcher, I. and Isaacs, S., *The EC Regulation on Insolvency Proceedings: A Commentary and Annotated Guide* (Oxford: Oxford University Press, 2009).

North, P.M., *Essays in Private International Law* (Kluwer, 1993).

North, P.M., *Private International Law Problems in Common Law Jurisdictions* (1993).

Nygh, P.E., *Autonomy in International Contracts* (Oxford: Clarendon Press, 1998).

Ooi, M., *Shares and other Securities in the Conflict of Laws* (Oxford: Oxford University Press, 2003).

Panagopoulos, G., *Restitution in Private International Law* (Oxford: Hart, 2000).

Raphael, T., *The Anti-Suit Injunction* (Oxford: Oxford University Press, 2008).

Robertson, A.H., *Characterization in the Conflict of Laws* (Cambridge: Massachusetts: Harvard University Press, 1940).

Tang, Z. S., *Electronic Consumer Contracts in the Conflict of Laws* (Oxofrd: Hart, 2009).

Zaphiriou, G.A, *The Transfer of Chattels in Private International Law: A Comparative Study* (London: University of London, The Athlone Press, 1956).

CHAPTER 1

NATURE OF THE SUBJECT

NATURE

International private law is also known as conflict of laws and its rules are **1–01** known as conflict rules. Although the process of assimilation of conflict rules among the Member States of the European Community, and beyond, is well under way, nonetheless it must be understood that each legal system has its own body of conflict rules in every substantive private law area to deal with conflict cases arising in its courts, and for jurisdictional and procedural matters, and means of foreign judgment enforcement. Conflict cases are those which contain a foreign element, but not all cases containing a foreign element are necessarily "conflict"; they may reveal themselves on the facts to be domestic,[1] or they may be treated as domestic cases if no offer,[2] or no timeous offer,[3] is made to prove foreign law. In such an event, the court may proceed on the basis that the content of the foreign law is the same as its own.[4]

Generally, therefore, international private law is that branch of the law of any system which is applied to determine questions which involve foreign elements. More particularly, it is the branch of the private law of any legal system which consists of the rules which enable its courts to determine the following matters:

(a) the rules of jurisdiction to be followed by its courts;
(b) the system of law which is to be applied by those courts to determine the rights of the parties in cases involving foreign elements ("choice of law"); and
(c) the extent to which recognition is to be given by those courts to decrees of foreign courts, and the manner of enforcement of such recognised decrees, if enforcement be necessary; and conversely, the extent to which recognition of its own decrees and, if need be, enforcement thereof is to be accorded elsewhere.

Thus, in cases involving relevant foreign elements, a legal system's conflict rules determine which court has jurisdiction, which law is applicable and whether or not decrees can be recognised and/or enforced beyond the legal system from which they emanate. A key element in the last of these topics is the consideration of whether the foreign court had jurisdiction, in the view of the forum's conflict rules; clearly, the foreign court itself thought it had jurisdiction.

---

[1] *William Grant & Sons Ltd v Glen Catrine Bonded Warehouse Ltd*, 1995 S.L.T. 936.
[2] *Pryde v Proctor & Gamble Ltd*, 1971 S.L.T. (Notes) 18.
[3] *Bonnor v Balfour Kilpatrick Ltd*, 1974 S.L.T. 187; 1975 S.L.T. (Notes) 3.
[4] *De Reneville v De Reneville* [1948] P. 100; see also *Rodden v Whatlings Ltd*, 1960 S.L.T. (Notes) 96. See paras 8–17—18–20.

The subject, therefore, is concerned with the relationship among different systems of private law, not with the relationship among sovereign states as political units. Only occasionally will the subjects of public international law (which in its nature is international, and not peculiar to each legal system) and international private law meet[5]; they will not usually clash with each other, pursuing, rather, parallel courses, with the result that it will usually be found that their approaches to a problem common to both differ.[6]

Even if viewed originally as akin to public international law, international private law is truly a branch of the private law of a legal system. This means that different legal systems' rules of international private law will differ from one another, unless and until the harmonisation process supervenes in any given area and to a full or limited extent. It means also that there is no affront to the sovereignty of the forum in entertaining the notion of upholding foreign acquired rights because the matter is regulated by a branch of the forum's own law.

1–02   As the twentieth century progressed, legislation in the United Kingdom showed an increasing awareness of conflict issues and of the matter of territorial application of rules. Since 1970, the subject of Scots and English international private law has been transformed from one largely regulated by common law to one largely regulated by legislation. Some statutes have been required to enable the UK to ratify international conventions; others are the result of domestic initiatives. These legislative interventions have been concerned with all areas of the subject, personal,[7] commercial,[8] and procedural.[9]

---

[5] e.g. sovereign immunity; international personality; jurisdiction (not, perhaps, as that word is understood in a domestic or conflict of laws sense, but used to express locus standi, the legality of expression of interest by a state in an incident which takes place within its own borders, or to one of its nationals outside its own borders or otherwise outside its borders). Sometimes, the two branches are involved jointly in a question: an example is the extent to which English and Scots law should recognise private law "events", such as the celebration or termination of a marriage, the conclusion of a contract, and rights which would normally flow therefrom, if the event has taken place within a state the government of which is not formally recognised by the UK ("the problem of unrecognised governments"). See Robert Leslie, "The Existence of Governments and the Conflict of Laws: The Republic of Somalia Case", 1997 Jur. Rev. 110. See *Sierra Leone Telecommunications Co Ltd v Barclays Bank Plc* [1998] 2 All E.R. 820; see also (incidentally) *Bank of Credit and Commerce International (Overseas) Ltd (In Liquidation) v Price Waterhouse* [1997] 4 All E.R. 108. Cf. Foreign Corporations Act 1991. For a modern examination of the relationship between public and private international law, see Alex Mills, *The Confluence of Public and Private International Law: justice, pluralism and subsidiarity in the international constitutional ordering of private law* (Cambridge: Cambridge University Press, 2009).

[6] e.g. *Kuwait Airways Corp v Iraqi Airways Co (No.6)* [2002] UKHL 19; [2002] 3 All E.R. 209, discussed in Janeen M. Carruthers and Elizabeth B. Crawford, (2003) 52 I.C.L.Q. 761. The subject of cultural property is notable for attracting international private law and public international law attention: see Janeen M. Carruthers, *The Transfer of Property in the Conflict of Laws* (Oxford: Oxford University Press, 2005), paras 5.23–5.32; and *Cheshire, North and Fawcett: Private International Law*, edited by J.J. Fawcett and J.M. Carruthers, 14th edn (Oxford: Oxford University Press, 2008), pp.1223, 1224.

[7] e.g. Recognition of Divorces and Legal Separations Act 1971, superseded by Family Law Act 1986; Domicile and Matrimonial Proceedings Act 1973; Matrimonial and Family Proceedings Act 1984; Child Abduction and Custody Act 1985; Civil Partnership Act 2004; Family Law (Scotland) Act 2006; and Adoption and Children (Scotland) Act 2007.

[8] e.g. Contracts (Applicable Law) Act 1990; Private International Law (Miscellaneous Provisions) Act 1995; Civil Jurisdiction and Judgments Act 1982; Civil Jurisdiction and Judgments Act 1991; and Recognition of Trusts Act 1987.

[9] e.g. Prescription and Limitation (Scotland) Act 1973, as amended; and Evidence (Proceedings in Other Jurisdictions) Act 1975.

Traditionally, UK statutes do not have extraterritorial operation unless this is express, or necessarily implied,[10] and this is especially strongly held in certain branches such as criminal law,[11] but in recent years there have been more examples of express extraterritorial application, *especially* in criminal law.[12] Moreover, it must always be remembered that British statutes have a silent or implicit extraterritorial dimension by virtue of our conflict choice of law rules, as later explained. If Scots or English law is the law governing the substance of the question (the *lex causae*), the relevant Scots or English law, common law or statutory, will apply, e.g. if the deceased died domiciled in Scotland, the distribution, testate or intestate, of his moveable estate, *wherever situated*, will be subject to the provisions of the Succession (Scotland) Act 1964.

Technological and electronic advances pose immense difficulties of jurisdiction and choice of law, particularly in matters of intellectual property, and copyright,[13] and with regard to the dissemination of defamatory[14] or otherwise offensive material. In 1996, negotiations took place in Geneva under the auspices of the World Intellectual Property Organisation, with the aim of reaching agreement to extend the copyright protection of the 1886 Berne Convention for the Protection of Literary and Artistic Work, to material transmitted over the internet, which resulted in the 1996 Geneva Copyright Treaty. Generally, however, technology is well in advance of legal thinking. Similar difficulties arise in relation to electronic commerce and related property problems, e.g. the transfer of securities held with an intermediary, where modern holding practice typically is "dematerialised" and "immobilised".[15]

Therefore, the subject of conflict of laws, which hitherto has been characterised by respect for territorial boundaries, must continue to respond to the challenge of finding appropriate solutions to the growing number of legal

---

[10] V.C.R.A.C. Crabbe, *Understanding Statutes* (London: Cavendish, 1994), pp.176–177; *Cross on Statutory Interpretation*, edited by John Bell and Sir George Engel, 3rd edn (Edinburgh: Butterworths, 1995), pp.5, 6; Francis A.R. Bennion, *Statutory Interpretation* (London: Butterworths, 1984), pp.453 et seq. (and 5th edn, 2008). The position seems to be that UK statutes apply geographically intraterritorially and bind British subjects and aliens within the Realm, but whether an Act binds British subjects in their activities abroad depends upon the intention of the legislature in each instance, there being no presumption either way except that criminal statutes in the main are local. See, e.g. *Att Gen for Alberta v Huggard Assets Ltd* [1953] A.C. 420, per Lord Asquith of Bishopstone at 441; *CEB Draper & Son Ltd v Edward Turner & Son Ltd* [1964] 3 All E.R. 148, per Lord Denning at 150; *Yorke v British & Continental Steamship Co* (1945) 78 Ll. L.Rep. 181. The terms of a statute may have the effect that a foreigner is entitled to take advantage of UK legislation even if not subject to it: *Krzus v Crow's Nest Pass Coal Co Ltd* [1912] A.C. 590.

[11] Most conflict of laws textbooks are chary of including within their treatment the subject of criminal law. An exception is the first edition of this work: Crawford, *International Private Law in Scotland* (Edinburgh: W.Green, 1998), Ch.20.

[12] e.g. Sexual Offences (Conspiracy and Incitement) Act 1996 s 6; Criminal Justice and Immigration Act 2008; *Serious Fraud Office v King* [2009] 2 All E.R. 223. See Crawford, *International Private Law in Scotland*, 1998, para.20.06; and now, in relation to the EU JHA criminal justice programme: *http://ec.europa.eu/justice_home/fsj/criminal/wai/fsj_criminal_intro_en.htm* [Accessed June 3, 2010].

[13] cf. *Shetland Times Ltd v Wills*, 1997 S.L.T. 669.

[14] See paras 7–21 and 16–55.

[15] Efforts have been made to address in a harmonised way (i.e. among the Member States of the EC, and also across the rules of jurisdiction and applicable law) problems arising, e.g. in consumer contracts. See paras 15–28 and 17–35.

problems, of jurisdiction and choice of law, prompted by technological and electronic advances.

THE NAME

1–03 The names "international private law", "private international law" and "conflict of laws" are each suitable descriptions of this branch of law, but conflict lawyers, being particularly fond of disputation, tend to disagree first on the name of their subject of study.[16] It has been said of the subject that "dispute starts from the title page". In this treatment of the subject, we shall use the term international private law, as it is believed to be the name tradition-ally used in Scotland, and it brings to mind more quickly and aptly the nature of the subject.

TERMINOLOGY

1–04 Traditionally, but more rarely in modern instruments, treatments of interna-tional private law are characterised by the use of Latin terminology. The following is a list of expressions frequently used:

Lex fori	The *internal* (or local or domestic) law of the country in which an action is raised.
Lex causae	The legal system which governs the subject matter of an action or the rights of parties, that is, the law in accordance with which the substance of a legal ques-tion is to be determined.
Lex domicilii	The law of a person's domicile.
Lex patriae	The law of a person's nationality.
Lex loci celebrationis	The law of the country where a marriage is celebrated.
Lex situs and lex loci rei sitae	The law of the country in which immoveable property or moveable assets are situated: the latter term used to be considered the correct one with regard to moveables, but nowadays *lex situs* is used in all property cases.
Lex loci actus	The law of the country where a legal act or transaction takes place.
Lex actus	The law with which a legal act or transaction has the most real connection. This may or may not be also the *lex loci actus*: in many cases the two coincide.
Lex loci contractus	The law of the country in which a contract technically is said to have been made.
Lex loci solutionis	The law of the country in which performance of a contract is to take place.

---

[16] Martin Wolff, *Private International Law*, 2nd edn (Oxford: Clarendon Press, 1950), p.10, rightly predicted that the German suggestion of "demarcation law" was unlikely to become popular. He notes that Baty considered the term "polarized law".

Lex loci delicti   The law of the country where a delict or tort allegedly has been committed.

Lex successionis   The law in accordance with which rights of succession to the estate of a deceased are to be determined.

THE LAW OF A COUNTRY

The expression "the law of a country" is ambiguous because its meaning may **1–05** be construed in either of the following ways:

(a) *Narrow sense*: in this sense it means the purely internal, or domestic, law of a country, excluding all conflict rules providing for the recognition of foreign elements and rights under foreign laws.
(b) *Wide sense*: in this sense it means the internal law as above, together with the conflict rules of the country in question.

The term "country" should be taken to mean law unit, or legal system, having an independent body of law.[17] The expression "law of a country" will be used in this work in its narrow sense, except in the context of discussion of the methodological problems of *renvoi* and the incidental question.[18]

The term "Scots law", therefore, in its wide sense, includes that body of Scots private law rules in use to decide questions which raise foreign issues, of jurisdiction, choice of law, and/or extraterritorial recognition and enforcement of judgments. While it is true to say that each body of conflict rules is peculiar to its own legal system, each is affected now more than ever before by international legal, commercial and political developments, and by technological advances.

HARMONISATION

The subject has undergone fundamental change. The nature of Scots and **1–06** English conflict rules until as late as the end of the twentieth century were, paradoxically, national in nature, despite their international purpose and despite the provision in the twentieth century of certain examples of international co-operation in the treatment of private law problems which cross the boundaries of legal systems, e.g. commercial codes on carriage,[19] such

---

[17] Hence in the UK there are three separate law units, namely, England and Wales, Scotland and Northern Ireland; and in the "British Islands" there are, in addition, Jersey, Guernsey, Alderney and Sark (the latter often subsumed under Guernsey), and the Isle of Man. *Dicey, Morris and Collins on the Conflict of Laws*, edited by L. Collins, 14th edn (London: Sweet & Maxwell, 2006), para.1–064. Similarly, there are Canadian provinces and Australian States. For some purposes, e.g. consistorial causes or company law, the law may be the same for all the component parts and so the meaning of "country" in that context is the composite unit. The situation in the USA is doubly complex, since there may be State/Federal and US/international conflicts.

[18] See Chs 4 and 5, below.

[19] See generally Jason C.T. Chuah, *Law of International Trade: Cross-Border Commercial Transactions*, 4th edn (London: Sweet & Maxwell, 2009).

as the conventions on the carriage of goods by sea,[20] by air,[21] by rail,[22] or by road.[23]

The outstanding feature of the modern age is the creation and development of a supranational body of conflict rules, as evidenced by intra-EU and international co-operation in the harmonisation of conflict rules. The impetus comes principally from the EU and the Hague Conference on Private International Law.

EUROPEAN HARMONISATION

1–07 The most striking change in the nature and content of the conflict rules of Scotland and England has been occasioned by the ambitious and wide-ranging programme of harmonisation of law undertaken by the EU in its Justice and Home Affairs portfolio, with the aim of creating an "Area of Freedom, Security and Justice". The central policy is the removal of barriers to the free movement of persons, goods, services and capital. The legal basis for the development of this area is founded upon the Treaty of Amsterdam arts 61–67. Measures in the field of judicial co-operation in civil matters having cross-border implications are authorised by art.65, "insofar as necessary for the proper functioning of the internal market".[24]

---

[20] Athens Convention relating to the Carriage of Passengers and their Luggage by Sea 1974 (Merchant Shipping Act 1995); Hague-Visby Rules on Carriage of Goods by Sea (Carriage of Goods by Sea Act 1971); UN Convention on the Carriage of Goods by Sea 1978 ("the Hamburg Rules"); and UN Convention on Contracts for the International Carriage of Goods Wholly or Partly By Sea 2008 (multimodal carriage of goods: "the Rotterdam Rules").

[21] Warsaw Convention for the Unification of Certain Rules relating to International Carriage by Air 1929, as amended at The Hague, 1955, supplemented by the Guadalajara Convention 1961 (Carriage by Air Act 1961), and modernised by the Montreal Convention for the Unification of Certain Rules relating to International Carriage by Air 1999. *Abnett v British Airways Plc*, 1997 S.L.T. 492 HL (no remedy available except under convention). See also *Reid v Ski Independence*, 1999 S.L.T. (Sh. Ct.) 62; *Western Digital Corp v British Airways Plc* [1999] 2 Lloyd's Rep. 380; *Phillips v Air New Zealand Ltd* [2002] 2 Lloyd's Rep. 408; *Quantum Corp Inc v Plane Trucking Ltd* [2002] 2 Lloyd's Rep. 25; *King v Bristow Helicopters Ltd*, 2002 S.L.T. 378; *Disley v Levine (t/a Airtrack Levine Paragliding)* [2002] 1 W.L.R. 785; *Morris v KLM Royal Dutch Airlines* [2002] Q.B. 100; *GKN Westland Helicopters Ltd v Korean Airlines Co Ltd* [2003] 2 Lloyd's Rep. 629; *Re Deep Vein Thrombosis and Air Travel Group Litigation* [2006] 1 All E.R. 786; *Laroche v Spirit of Adventure (UK) Ltd* [2009] 2 All E.R. 175; *Barclay v British Airways Plc* [2009] 1 All E.R. 871; and *Société Kenya Airways v Airbus SAS* [2009] I.L.Pr. 3 Cour d'Appel Orleans, France ((High) ranking of Warsaw Convention jurisdiction rules).

[22] Berne Convention concerning International Carriage by Rail 1980 (International Transport Conventions Act 1983), revised 1999. See Railways and Transport Safety Act 2003 s.103.

[23] Geneva Convention on the Contract for the International Carriage of Goods by Road 1956 (Carriage of Goods by Road Act 1965); *Hatzl v XL Insurance Co Ltd* [2009] EWCA Civ 223.

[24] See Protocol No.4 on the position of the UK and Ireland [1997] OJ C340/99, in terms of which the default position for the UK and Ireland is one of opt-out, but within three months of presentation of a proposal under Title IIIa of the Treaty establishing the European Community, either country may intimate the wish to opt in. On exercise of the opt-in mechanism, see House of Lords, European Union Committee, *2nd Report of Session 2008–09, Enhanced scrutiny of EU legislation with a United Kingdom opt-In* (The Stationery Office, 2009), HL Paper No.25 (Session 2008/09). Under the Lisbon Treaty, qv, see Protocol No.21 on the position of the UK and Ireland in respect of the area of freedom, security and justice [2008] OJ C115/295. Contrast Protocol No.5 on the position of Denmark [1997] OJ C340/101, in terms of which Denmark shall not take part in the adoption of proposed measures pursuant to Title IIIa of the Treaty establishing the European Community. In the particular matter of rules of civil and commercial jurisdiction and judgment enforcement, see the Agreement between the European Community and the Kingdom of Denmark on jurisdiction and the recognition and enforcement of judgments in civil and commercial matters [2005] OJ L299/62 (see Ch.7, below).

The Treaty establishing a Constitution for Europe, signed on October 29, 2004, sought further to entrench the establishment of the European common judicial area, confirming the purpose and accelerating the pace of achieving it, but the Treaty was rejected by voters in France and Holland. In consequence, the Treaty of Lisbon amending the Treaty on European Union and the Treaty establishing the European Community (known initially as "the Reform Treaty") was produced, and was signed on December 13, 2007 by all European Member States. After protracted negotiations,[25] the ratification process was completed in all 27 Member States on November 3, 2009, and the Treaty came into force on December 1, 2009.

The Lisbon Treaty is shorthand for two new treaties, viz. The Treaty on the Functioning of the European Union ("TFEU")[26] and The Treaty on European Union ("TEU"). The TFEU contains a number of new provisions pertaining to justice and home affairs. The provision on judicial co-operation in civil matters is contained in art.81 (ex TEC art.65), viz.:

"1. The Union shall develop judicial cooperation in civil matters having cross-border implications, based on the principle of mutual recognition of judgments and of decisions in extrajudicial cases. Such cooperation may include the adoption of measures for the approximation of the laws and regulations of thc Mcmber States.

2. For the purposes of paragraph 1, the European Parliament and the Council, acting in accordance with the ordinary legislative procedure, shall adopt measures, *particularly when necessary for the proper functioning of the internal market*,[27] aimed at ensuring:

   (a) the mutual recognition and enforcement between Member States of judgments and of decisions in extrajudicial cases;
   (b) the cross-border service of judicial and extrajudicial documents;
   (c) the compatibility of the rules applicable in the Member States concerning conflict of laws and of jurisdiction;
   (d) cooperation in the taking of evidence;
   (e) effective access to justice;
   (f) the elimination of obstacles to the proper functioning of civil proceedings, if necessary by promoting the compatibility of the rules on civil procedure applicable in the Member States;
   (g) the development of alternative methods of dispute settlement;
   (h) support for the training of the judiciary and judicial staff.

3. Notwithstanding paragraph 2, measures concerning family law with cross-border implications shall be established by the Council, acting in accordance with a special legislative procedure. The Council shall act unanimously after consulting the European Parliament.

   The Council, on a proposal from the Commission, may adopt a decision determining those aspects of family law with cross-border

---

[25] Due to problems particularly in Ireland, Germany, the Czech Republic and Poland. See, for detail, *The Treaty of Lisbon after the Second Irish Referendum* (The Stationery Office, 2009), HC Research Paper 09/75.

[26] Which amends and replaces the old Treaty establishing the European Community ("TEC"). See also Protocol No.21 on the position of the UK and Ireland in respect of the area of freedom, security and justice [2008] OJ C115/295 (default opt-out).

[27] Emphasis added. Note the change of wording from Treaty of Amsterdam art.65.

implications which may be the subject of acts adopted by the ordinary legislative procedure. The Council shall act unanimously after consulting the European Parliament. The proposal referred to in the second subparagraph shall be notified to the national Parliaments. If a national Parliament makes known its opposition within six months of the date of such notification, the decision shall not be adopted. In the absence of opposition, the Council may adopt the decision."

The TFEU increases the number of subject areas in respect of which voting in the European Parliament and the Council no longer must be unanimous, and in respect of which it is sufficient to have "qualified majority voting" ("QMV"). The entry into force of the Treaty of Lisbon has certain consequences for ongoing, inter-institutional decision-making procedures.[28] Moreover, it makes changes to the organisation and jurisdiction of the Court of Justice of the European Union ("CJEU"). The CJEU has acquired general jurisdiction to give preliminary rulings in the area of freedom, security and justice.[29]

In detail, with regard to the European agenda,[30] the aims in the period 1999 to 2004 were pursued under the heading of the "Tampere Agenda". 2005 marked the beginning of the follow-up, "second generation" agenda, the "Hague Programme",[31] for the period until 2009. The Commission has stated that the strength of the Hague Programme lay in its longer term perspective.[32]

Strategic priorities for the period 2010 to 2014 have been agreed sub nom. the "Stockholm Programme",[33] and include revision of Regulation 44/2001,[34]

---

[28] See Communication from the Commission to the European Parliament and the Council COM/2009/065 final.

[29] For earlier position, see Elizabeth B. Crawford and Janeen M. Carruthers, "Conflict of Loyalties in the Conflict of Laws: the Cause, the Means and the Cost of Harmonisation", 2005 Jur. Rev. 251, 252. See, for current procedure, Information note on references from national courts for a preliminary ruling [2009] OJ C297/1.

[30] See continuing progress on the "scoreboard" at *http://ec.europa.eu/justice_home/doc_centre/ scoreboard_en.htm* [Accessed June 4, 2010].

[31] The Hague Programme: Strengthening Freedom, Security and Justice in the European Union [2005] OJ C53/1; and the Council and Commission Action Plan Implementing the Hague Programme Strengthening Freedom, Security and Justice in the European Union [2005] OJ C198/1. See, eg, Communication from the Commission to the Council and the European Parliament: Report on Implementation of the Hague Programme for 2007 COM(2008) 373 final. See, more generally, Crawford and Carruthers, "Conflict of Loyalties in the Conflict of Laws", 2005 Jur. Rev. 251.

[32] See Communication from the Commission to the Council, the European Parliament, the European Economic and Social Committee and the Committee of the Regions—Justice, Freedom and Security in Europe since 2005: An Evaluation of the Hague Programme and Action Plan COM(2009) 263 final, para.VI. See also Implementation Scoreboard SEC(2009) 756 final; Extended Report on the Evaluation of the Programme SEC(2009)766 final; and Institutional Scoreboard SEC(2009) 767 final.

[33] Communication from the Commission to the European Parliament, the Council, the European Economic and Social Committee and the Committee of the Regions: Delivering an Area of Freedom, Security & Justice for Europe's Citizens: Action Plan Implementing the Stockholm Programme COM(2010) 175 final. See also Draft Presidency Note Multiannual Programme for an Area of Freedom, Security and Justice Serving the Citizen: the Stockholm Programme 14449/09 JAI 679.

[34] Regulation 44/2001 on jurisdiction and the recognition and enforcement of judgments in civil and commercial matters [2001] OJ L12/1 ("Brussels I Regulation"). See Ch.7, below.

review of certain provisions of the Rome I Regulation,[35] and of the Rome II Regulation,[36] revision of the Brussels II *bis* Regulation,[37] and development of applicable law rules concerning wills and succession[38] and matrimonial property.[39] The details of these, and other, proposed developments will be discussed at appropriate points throughout the text.

Instruments (actual and proposed) to achieve implementation of the European harmonisation agenda

The European Regulation is the legislative tool of choice in order to achieve **1–08** the harmonisation of European conflict laws, in view of the desired speed of change and the benefits which the Regulation affords, namely, uniform date of entry into force, uniform application, and automatic right of appeal to the Court of Justice of the European Union on points of interpretation.

Although the basis of European actings in the area of harmonisation of law is regional, instruments typically adopt a principle of universality, meaning that in the forum of an EU Member State the harmonised rules must apply, even though the result of applying them is to identify as applicable the law of a non-EU Member State. One of the political priorities for the 2010–2014 period is "Europe in a Global World": the external dimension of freedom, security and justice. It is said that this dimension is crucial to the successful implementation of the objectives of the Stockholm Programme. As far as judicial co-operation in civil matters is concerned, the operation of the Brussels rules in the international legal order (a subject under which is subsumed the task of setting the geographical and legal boundaries of the so-called Brussels regime, and the resolution of difficult issues regarding the relationship between the EU and non-EU Member States, referred to as "Third States", including, in particular, the debate as to what should be the rights in civil litigation of European citizens against defendants resident in Third States) is a topic of growing controversy and concern, both to those within and those outside the regime.[40] It seems impossible to contain the European programme; or to effect its ambitious aims without seeping into the area beyond Europe, and without affecting non-EU citizens. One of the principal concerns for the next period of development and implementation of the European programme is to manage this relationship.

The instruments which are concerned with the allocation of jurisdiction and the enforcement of judgments fall under the "Brussels" family name, since in philosophy and detail they stem from the 1968 Brussels Convention on Jurisdiction and the Enforcement of Judgments in Civil and Commercial

---

[35] Regulation 593/2008 on the law applicable to contractual obligations (Rome I) [2008] OJ L177/6. See Ch.15, below.

[36] Regulation 864/2007 on the law applicable to non-contractual obligations (Rome II) [2007] OJ L199/40. See Ch.16, below.

[37] Regulation 2201/2003 concerning jurisdiction and the recognition and enforcement of judgments in matrimonial matters and in matters of parental responsibility [2003] OJ L338/1. See Ch.12, below.

[38] See Ch.18, below.

[39] See Ch.13, below.

[40] See para.7–64, below.

Matters[41] (henceforth "Brussels I").[42] The principle of mutual recognition of judgments, which is founded upon agreement as to acceptable grounds of jurisdiction within the EU, is said to be the cornerstone of judicial co-operation in civil matters. In 2001, certain amendments were made to the text of Brussels I upon its conversion into a Regulation (the Brussels I Regulation).[43] This foundation instrument currently is subject to review, and a further legislative proposal is expected.[44]

As well as dealing with jurisdiction and judgment enforcement, the EU has enacted a number of important procedural law instruments, pertaining to civil and commercial litigation, such as Regulations on the taking of evidence abroad,[45] and the service of documents.[46] Additionally, in recent years, regulations have been enacted with the aim of accelerating enforcement of Member State decrees which in their nature are uncontroversial, such as small claims[47] and uncontested claims.[48] One of the primary aims is to complete the already advanced implementation of mutual recognition and enforcement of judgments, by abolishing all intermediate measures in the Member State where the decree is to be enforced; this is termed removal of the "*exequatur*" procedure.

Measures have been introduced in family law, following the commercial model, to govern jurisdiction and the recognition of judgments emanating from Member States. The most important instrument in this area is Regulation 2201/2003 ("Brussels II *bis*").[49]

The instruments which are concerned with choice of law fall under the "Rome" patronymic. The most significant instrument in choice of law was the 1980 Rome Convention on the Law Applicable to Contractual Obligations ("Rome I"), now replaced by the Rome I Regulation.[50] This Regulation, in

---

[41] Entry into force in 1973 among the original six (Belgium, France, Germany, Italy, Luxembourg and the Netherlands). See also Accession Convention 1978, signed by the UK, Denmark and Ireland (into effect for the UK by Civil Jurisdiction and Judgments Act 1982); Greek Accession Convention 1982; Spanish and Portuguese Accession Convention 1989 (the San Sebastian Convention, bringing certain substantive changes). The Lugano Convention 1988 made parallel provision for the EFTA bloc (then Austria, Finland, Iceland, Norway, Sweden and Switzerland). Lugano was implemented for the UK by Civil Jurisdiction and Judgments Act 1991. The Lugano Convention was revised in 2007 in order to align it with the Brussels I Regulation: [2007] OJ L339/3. Since Austria, Finland and Sweden have become EU members, the revised Lugano Convention applies only in relation to Iceland, Norway and Switzerland. Liechtenstein, although an EFTA state, is not a party to the Lugano Convention.

[42] Implemented in the UK by means of the Civil Jurisdiction and Judgments Act 1982. See Ch.7, below.

[43] See also the Civil Jurisdiction and Judgments Order 2001 (SI 2001/3929).

[44] See Ch.7, below.

[45] Regulation 1206/2001 on cooperation between the courts of the Member States in the taking of evidence in civil or commercial matters [2001] OJ L174/1. See Ch.8, below.

[46] Regulation 1393/2007 on the service in the Member States of judicial and extrajudicial documents in civil or commercial matters [2007] OJ L324/79 (replacing Regulation 1348/2000 on the service in the Member States of judicial and extrajudicial documents in civil or commercial matters [2000] OJ L160/37). See Ch.8, below.

[47] Regulation 861/2007 creating a European small claims procedure [2007] OJ L199/1.

[48] Regulation 805/2004 creating a European Enforcement Order for uncontested claims [2004] OJ L143/15; and Regulation 1896/2006 creating a European order for payment procedure [2006] OJ L399/1.

[49] Repealing Regulation 1347/2000 on jurisdiction and the recognition and enforcement of judgments in matrimonial matters and in matters of parental responsibility for children of both spouses ("Brussels II") [2000] OJ L160/19.

[50] See Ch.15, below.

combination with the Rome II Regulation[51] (concerning non-contractual obligations arising out of tort, delict, unjust enrichment, *negotiorum gestio*, and *culpa in contrahendo*), means that there is now in place a harmonised corpus of rules applicable to the great majority of conflict disputes arising in the law of obligations before EU Member State courts.

During the period of the Hague Programme, an instrument provisionally termed "Rome III", and comprising proposals pertaining to jurisdiction and choice of law in divorce,[52] was the subject of debate in and among Member States. On that occasion, however, since compromise could not be reached, the project as originally planned lapsed, though impetus remains for "enhanced co-operation" in this area.

Some instruments deal with multiple aspects of the conflict of laws, namely, jurisdiction, applicable law, recognition and enforcement of decisions, and co-operative measures. A recent example is Regulation 4/2009 concerning maintenance obligations.[53] The subjects of matrimonial property[54] and succession[55] look set to be dealt with similarly.

The European Council recently has emphasised the importance of starting work on codification of the instruments adopted so far in the area of judicial co-operation in civil matters. Technically, it would seem to be satisfactory to have multiple instruments in cognate areas brought into a streamlined, single instrument. In terms of historical perspective on the subject, the hope expressed by the Council that work on the codification of private international law should begin as soon as possible heralds the next development in a profoundly changed landscape.

GLOBAL HARMONISATION

The EU operates at a regional level among its Member States, but the Hague **1–09** Conference on Private International Law functions at a global level. The Hague Conference is an inter-governmental body, founded in 1893, dedicated to the harmonisation of the conflict rules of different legal systems, and the development and service of multilateral legal instruments. In 1955 the Conference was put on a statutory footing, and now has 69 Member States and Regional Economic Integration Organisations ("REIO") from all continents. A REIO is defined[56] as an international organisation that is constituted solely by sovereign States and to which its Member States have transferred competence over a range of matters,[57] including the authority to make decisions binding on its Member States in respect of those matters.[58] Competence having been transferred, the REIO has the rights and objections of a Contracting State.

---

[51] See Ch.16, below.
[52] EU Green Paper on applicable law and jurisdiction in divorce matters COM(2005) 82 final. See Ch.12, below.
[53] Regulation 4/2009 on jurisdiction, applicable law, recognition and enforcement of decisions and cooperation in matters relating to maintenance obligations [2009] OJ L7/1. See Ch.13, below.
[54] See Ch.13, below.
[55] See Ch.18, below.
[56] The 1955 Statute of the Hague Conference on Private International Law, as amended, art.3.9.
[57] i.e. including, for this purpose, matters of private international law.
[58] The 1955 Statute of the Hague Conference on Private International Law, as amended, provides in art.3 that the Member States of the Conference may decide to admit to membership any REIO which has submitted an application.

The main participation by the United Kingdom in Hague Conference projects has been in the period after 1951.[59] Significantly, on April 3, 2007, the European Community was admitted to membership of the Hague Conference as an REIO.[60] With the entry into force of the Treaty of Lisbon on December 1, 2009, the European Union replaces and succeeds the European Community as from that date. Although the EU's membership of the Hague Conference does not supplant the membership thereof of individual EU Member States, nevertheless by dint of shared competence in projects which fall within the expanding EU remit, participation by individual EU Member States in Hague Conference projects is correspondingly inhibited,[61] because each EU Member State, as a result of opting-in to the European harmonisation scheme, has lost its capacity to act autonomously in any matter concerning judicial co-operation in civil law which falls within EU competence.[62]

The Hague Conference's chosen mode of proceeding is by multilateral treaty or convention, to which Member States may accede, occasionally under reservation as to particular provisions. Conventions may deal only with jurisdiction or with choice of law; or they may deal with jurisdiction and with recognition and enforcement of judgments ("double"); or possibly with all three aspects ("triple"), or even four ("quadruple").[63]

Since 1955 36 conventions and 2 protocols have been finalised, notable examples of which are: 1961 Convention on the Conflict of Laws relating to the Form of Testamentary Dispositions; 1970 Convention on the Taking of Evidence Abroad in Civil or Commercial Matters; 1980 Convention on the Civil Aspects of International Child Abduction; 1985 Convention on the Law Applicable to Trusts and on their Recognition; 1996 Convention on Jurisdiction, Applicable Law, Recognition, Enforcement and Cooperation in respect of Parental Responsibility Measures for the Protection of Children; 2002 Convention on the Law Applicable to Certain Rights in Respect of Securities Held with an Intermediary; 2005 Convention on Choice of Court Agreements; and 2007 Convention on the International Recovery of Child Support and other forms of Family Maintenance. A true measure of the success of a convention is the extent

---

[59] See K. Lipstein, "One Hundred Years of Hague Conferences on Private International Law" (1993) 42 I.C.L.Q. 553. For background information, and detail of conventions, see *http://www.hcch.net* [Accessed June 4, 2010].

[60] See Andrea Schulz, "The Accession of the European Community to the Hague Conference on Private International Law" (2007) 56 I.C.L.Q. 939. Cf. negotiations, begun in 2010, to permit accession by EU to ECHR.

[61] See para.1–07, above. It is for the REIO to indicate the extent that it has subject matter competence, and for the REIO and its constituent States to consider whether any subsequent action has to be taken by those States in relation to other matters.

[62] For example, the entry by the EU into family law regulation has removed from EC Member States their autonomy in the signature and ratification of Hague instruments concerning family law. See, e.g. in relation to 1996 Hague Convention, Ch.14, below. Council Note 15226/08 JUSTCIV 235 entitled, "Accession by the European Community to Conventions of The Hague Conference on Private International Law" sets out a letter from the European Commission and Council to the Hague Conference on Private International Law, outlining the intended European approach to existing Hague Conventions, using the classification (a) Conventions which the European Community should join; (b) Conventions requiring further reflection; (c) Conventions which should be left aside; and (d) Conventions which should be left for the Member States to join.

[63] See, e.g. the cumbrously named 1996 Convention on Jurisdiction, Applicable Law, Recognition, Enforcement and Cooperation in respect of Parental Responsibility Measures for the Protection of Children.

to which it is acceptable internationally, as expressed in the number of states acceding to the instrument, an excellent example being the 1980 Convention on the Civil Aspects of International Child Abduction.

Engines for law reform—potential for duplication and rivalry

Clearly there is potential for over-regulation and duplication where different **1–10** law reform agencies operate in the same subject area. The relationship between the Hague Conference, on the one hand, and the EU Council and Commission and EU Member States, on the other, is of moment.[64] It can be seen that the same subject area within the conflict of laws has been addressed at differing points in time by the Hague Conference and by the EU. A complicating feature of modern conflict of laws is the "layering phenomenon", which is seen most plainly where international instruments overlap, in terms of substance and geography, giving rise to the need to rank potentially applicable sets of rules.[65] The layering phenomenon also is seen in demarcation questions which necessitate a decision as to whether or not the factual matrix of the instance is to be governed by one or other potentially applicable body of rules, each of which is concerned with the same general subject matter.[66] Likewise, where the United Kingdom decides against opting-in to an EU instrument on a given area of law, a UK forum must apply the pre-existing national rule, giving rise to a layered system within Europe. In the case of wills and succession, if the UK continues to hold its position against opting-in to the proposed Regulation,[67] the pre-existing Scots and English national rules will continue to apply. Finally, a problem may arise in the EU context concerning the application within the United Kingdom (or within any other multi-legal system Member State) of a particular set of harmonised conflict rules, i.e. in intra-UK cases, should the harmonised rules apply? It is usual for the UK to be given the opportunity to elect not to have the harmonised rule apply in disputes arising between or among its constituent legal systems,[68] but equally, it is usual for the UK to decline to exercise this option.

When the modern configuration of the conflict of laws is viewed in the light of this layering phenomenon, it is clear that a key skill for the modern conflict lawyer is sensitivity to the importance of selecting, and if necessary justifying

---

[64] H. van Loon and A. Schulz, "The European Community and the Hague Conference on Private International Law" in Bernd Martenczuk and Sarvaas van Thiel (eds), *Justice, Liberty, Security: New Challenges for the External Relations of the European Union* (Brussels: Institute for European Studies of the Free University of Brussels, 2007).

[65] While ranking of provisions may give rise to problems of hierarchy within instruments, the ranking of different instruments *inter se* in the same subject area normally is set out in a "disconnection clause" within the later instrument, as in Brussels II *bis* art.60. For example, certain provisions of Brussels II *bis* have provided a significant overlay, in qualifying cases of intra-EC child abduction, on the operation of the scheme of rules put in place by the 1980 Hague Convention on the Civil Aspects of International Child Abduction (see Ch.14, below). Similarly, the operation of the 1970 Hague Convention on the Taking of Evidence Abroad in Civil or Commercial Matters, implemented in the UK by means of the Evidence (Proceedings in Other Jurisdictions) Act 1975, has been overtaken, in qualifying cases, by Regulation 1206/2001. For an example of co-operative symbiosis in the law of maintenance, see para.13–33.

[66] e.g. In the matter of choice of law in contract, whether the case falls to be regulated by the Rome I Regulation, or by residual national rules, as a result of being excluded, by reason of its nature, from the scope of the Regulation (art.1).

[67] See Ch.18, below.

[68] e.g. Rome I Regulation art.22 and Rome II Regulation art.25.

as applicable, a particular set of rules from several potentially applicable sets of rules. The subject has passed beyond the simple layer analogy to one of millefeuille confection.

Insofar as efforts by the European Council and Commission and the Hague Conference have as their goal the harmonisation of *choice of law* (conflict) rules, they aim to produce the result that the courts of all Member/Contracting States will agree as to which law shall apply in any given situation. The purpose of harmonisation of the *substantive* rules of legal systems would have the result that the issue of choice of law would matter less, because the substantive content of each law which potentially could be chosen would be identical.[69] Both harmonisation aims can be viewed as facilitating large-scale legal, political and economic objectives. Harmonisation of substantive rules is a longer-term and more ambitious goal. Even if harmonisation of conflict of laws is "achieved" in major areas of private law, the interpretation of harmonisation instruments will vary from Member/Contracting State to Member/Contracting State. The degree of interpretative guidance differs from instrument to instrument, depending upon the availability and status of accompanying expert reports,[70] and upon the rules concerning appeal to an international court.[71] Therefore, notwithstanding the harmonisation at some future date of conflict rules across all major areas, and within a particular political grouping such as the EU, conflict problems would continue to arise, as to interpretation of the rules and the extent of application thereof.

---

[69] There was issued in January 2009 by a body of academics an Academic Common Frame of Reference, containing "Principles, Definitions and Model Rules of European Private Law". This is intended to provide a "bank" of principles and definitions which may be adopted at a national legislative level, or by contracting parties at an individual level. See *Report on the Draft Common Frame of Reference*, prepared for the Scottish Government by Laura Macgregor (*http://www.scotland.gov.uk/Publications/2009/03/05095153/0*), and House of Lords, European Union Committee, *Report on European Contract Law: The Draft Common Frame of Reference* (The Stationery Office, 2009), HL Paper No.95 (Session 2008/09). There are earlier examples of attempts to achieve substantive harmonisation, e.g. agreement on a uniform law on the international sale of goods available for selection by parties (under the Uniform Laws on International Sales Act 1967). For a consideration of the problems arising from the interaction of the two types of harmonisation: see S. Knöfel, "EC Legislation on Conflict of Laws: Interactions and Incompatabilities between Conflict Rules" (1998) 47 I.C.L.Q. 439. See generally, James Fawcett, Jonathan M. Harris and Michael Bridge, *International Sale of Goods in the Conflict of Laws* (Oxford: Oxford University Press, 2005).

[70] As regards interpretation of the Rome I Convention, the Giuliano and Lagarde Report may be relied upon by the courts (M. Giuliano and P. Lagarde, "Report on the Convention on the Law Applicable to Contractual Obligations" [1980] OJ C282/23), and authoritative interpretative rulings may be handed down by the Court of Justice of the European Union (Contracts (Applicable Law) Act 1990 s.3; and the Contracts (Applicable Law) Act 1990 (Commencement No.2) Order 2004 (SI 2004/3448), bringing into force in the United Kingdom on March 1, 2005 the 1988 Brussels Protocol, enables appellate courts to refer cases to the European Court of Justice for interpretative rulings on the Rome I Convention). For the position under the Rome I Regulation, see Ch.15, below. Contrast the position concerning, e.g. 1980 Hague Convention on the Civil Aspects of International Child Abduction, for which there is no central court of over-arching authority. The national courts may derive assistance from the Perez-Vera Report (*Actes et Documents*, Fourteenth Session of the Hague Conference) and the INCADAT database of decisions maintained by the Hague Conference on Private International Law.

[71] A question in each case is by which national court(s) reference may be made. For interpretation of the Brussels I Regulation, reference may be made only by a national court, "against whose decisions there is no judicial remedy under national law" (i.e. in the UK, only the House of Lords Supreme Court). See generally, "New Rules on Civil Jurisdiction", 2002 S.L.T. (News) 39.

CHAPTER 2

HISTORY

One of the earliest examples of a system of conflict rules is to be found, **2–01**
preserved in the Louvre Museum, carved on a black pillar: it is the Code of
Hammurabi, King of Babylon. He became king in 2400 BC. The code includes
rules of international private law in the areas of property law, family law and
the law of contract. Hammurabi distinguished between persons and things, and
applied different choice of law rules to each; thus Hammurabi law governed all
contracts made in Babylon regardless of the personal law of the parties,
whereas capacity to marry was governed by the law of the religion provided
that the religion was that of the God of the sun or the God of justice. Where
the religion was neither, Hammurabi law applied: in the earliest days, as now,
the forum preferred to keep overall control. Whatever religion, the form of
marriage, if celebrated in Babylon, was governed by the *lex loci celebrationis*
(a normal choice of law rule down the years). The distinction between that
which pertains to persons (deemed to be "permanent", that is of long term
consequence, and calling for a governing law which would transcend territorial
connections as they might change from time to time) and that which pertains
to things (often thought to be "transient", that is of short/medium term consequence, and in respect of which a localised governing law might be thought
appropriate) is a most useful starting point in any consideration of choice of
law and forms the basis of the distinction drawn in the early Middle Ages by
the post-Glossator, Bartolus, who distinguished between statutes personal and
statutes real. By the sixth century Hammurabi's Kingdom drew a different
distinction—that between Islam and infidel. The personal law of the Muslim
was to be the law of Islam, no matter where s/he might be domiciled.

Roman law is not a fertile source of conflict rules or thinking. Martin Wolff[1]
notes that the *Corpus Juris Civilis*, that repository of answers to "practically
every conceivable legal question", says little on the subject of the application
of foreign laws. Rome's promising circumstances, of legal ability and extensive empire, produced little from the perspective of the conflict of laws, as
Graveson points out,[2] largely because Roman law was so dominant that if one
party to a dispute was a Roman citizen, the application of no other system of
law would be considered. Roman citizens alone had the privilege of being
governed by the *jus civile* of Rome: provincials were subject to their own
provincial laws. Hence, the *jus civile* governed the rights *inter se* (and against
the world) of Roman citizens; where the dispute was between provincials from

---

[1] Wolff, *Private International Law*, 2nd edn, 1950, p.19.
[2] Ronald H. Graveson, *Private International Law*, 7th edn (London: Sweet & Maxwell,
1974), p.30.

different provinces the *jus gentium*, the law of nations, "which bore little relation to the provincial laws of either party",[3] would regulate the outcome.

In AD 212, by the Edict of Caracalla, which increased greatly the number
of persons entitled to the status of Roman citizen and liable to pay citizens'
taxes, the ambit of the civil law of Rome was extended to include all people
living within the Roman Empire. Hence, that system of private law became
territorial—that is to say, it was the same for all people, of whatever race,
living within the rule of Rome.

Next came the barbarian invasion, which overthrew the Roman Empire, and
settled different tribes in territories previously Roman. Law became personal,
and those few who travelled took their personal laws with them like a cloak.
This era of personal law, existing from about the sixth to tenth centuries, was
succeeded by a period (eleventh to twelfth centuries) when territorial laws
prevailed. The meaningful development was the emergence of the powerful
Italian city states in the thirteenth century. As these cities (of Bologna,
Florence, Genoa, Padua, Milan, Modena, Venice and others) developed, they
began to pass their own statutes or legal codes which applied over and above
the common law. Problems arose in conflicts between the statutes of different
cities or between statutes and the common law and the true origin of conflict
of laws is to be found in such problems, and in the necessity to identify the
applicable law.

Even before this, it is thought that the presence of a number of races in Italy
had resulted in the practice of expressing a choice of law in contract. Trade has
always fostered the development of conflict rules. So too has scholarship.[4] In
the thirteenth century, the subject was exciting interest among scholars. Of the
Glossators, and post-Glossators[5] the greatest contribution to the development
of thinking in the conflict of laws was made by Bartolus of Saxoferrato
(1314–1357). He made the distinction, in his "Statute Theory", between
statutes personal (affecting a person in his personal and domestic life wherever he might go), and *statutes real* (concerning *things*: such laws applied only
within the territory of the enacting state, and would affect also all persons
transacting with things within that state, but might extend also to moveable
property outside the jurisdiction but belonging to subjects of that state).
However difficult it may be in a particular case to make this classification, the
distinction which Bartolus drew is essential to an understanding of the nature
and content of orthodox conflict rules and methodology. It is essential to grasp
that the law which one may expect to have applied to one's situation in the
fundamental things of life is not necessarily the appropriate law to govern that
which is commercial and/or relatively transient.

2–02   The Statute Theory was applied by the French jurists of the sixteenth
century, with varying approaches. D'Argentré, of the Breton (territorial) background, favoured the extension of the scope of the statute real, and the ascription of doubtful cases to that category, while Dumoulin (Molinaeus) advocated

---

[3] Graveson, *Private International Law*, 7th edn, 1974, p.30.
[4] Wolff, *Private International Law*, 2nd edn, 1950, p.21: "Private International Law was a product
  of the Italian Universities of the thirteenth century".
[5] Or better, "Commentators": Wolfgang Kunkel, *Roman Legal and Constitutional History*
  (London: Clarendon Press, 1966), pp.171, 172. Kunkel argues that the work of putting a
  gloss on the Roman texts was creative work and a significant contribution, not merely "laborious
  erudition".

what we now call "party autonomy", a permissive attitude towards choice of law by parties.

The developments in France were followed by a corresponding development in the Netherlands by jurists of the Dutch School, such as Burgundus (d. 1649), Paul Voet (d. 1677), his son, John Voet (1647–1714), and Huber (1636–94). The last mentioned was a professor and judge from Friesland, whose treatise on the subject, entitled *De Conflictu Legum* (1689) was only five quarto pages in length but immensely influential. By Huber's time, political considerations and notions of sovereignty had begun to impinge. Why should a sovereign admit the application within his kingdom of the laws of another sovereign? Huber provided the following guide and explanation in his maxims:

(1) The laws of each state have force within the limits of that government, and bind all subject to it, but not beyond.
(2) All persons within the limits of a government, whether they live there permanently or temporarily, are deemed to be subjects thereof.
(3) Sovereigns will so act by way of comity that rights acquired within the limits of a government retain their force everywhere so far as they do not cause prejudice to the power or rights of such government or of its subjects.

It should be noted that in his third maxim, Huber made two suggestions to explain the extraterritorial application of law. The first is comity, which may be translated as international goodwill into which is mixed a measure of reciprocity and mutual advantage, and the second is the use of the phrase "rights acquired". The second concept later gave support to that theory (called the "Vested Rights Theory") which is based upon the proposition that it is not foreign law per se, but a right acquired under a foreign legal system, which is enforced *extra territorium*.

In England, there is little trace of any attempt to apply conflict rules and principles before 1603. There could be little private law conflict between England and Scotland because the gates were closed: the Scots Act of 1431 (c.128) made it treason to live in England without permission of the King of Scotland, that of 1436 (c.145) forbade Scots from buying English goods "under pain of escheat", and that of 1587 (c.105) prohibited a Scot from marrying an Englishwoman. (When the gates were opened, the differences in the domestic laws of persons of the neighbouring countries made the conflict cases particularly interesting.)[6] In addition, England had not the beneficial exposure to the influence of the continental jurists. The English practice was to apply English law to all disputes coming before English courts, whether or not the case contained a foreign element.

When the Crowns were unified in 1603, a problem was posed for Huber's sovereignty theory in that the king was sovereign of two legal systems. Previously, the English courts had applied English law to all disputes whether or not foreign elements were involved: surely some validity now must be

---

[6] Andrew D. Gibb, *Law from Over The Border* (Edinburgh: W. Green, 1950), p.89. See, more recently, Kirsty J. Hood, *Conflict of Laws within the UK* (Oxford: Oxford University Press, 2007).

accorded in England to the King's law in/of Scotland? In *Calvin's Case*,[7] it was held by the Exchequer Chamber in England that Scots born after the accession of James to the throne of England did not have the status of aliens in England. Many would consider this a constitutional, or international, case rather than a conflict case. One of the earliest reported conflict cases is that of *Dungannon*,[8] upon the question of which law should govern the rate of interest under an Irish bond. It indicates the beginning of a readiness to accept that some law, other than that of the English law of the forum might apply.

In the 1760s, the great Anglo-Scottish lawyer, Lord Mansfield, made valuable contributions to early conflict of laws thinking, for example in the identification of the law which should govern substantive questions pertaining to a contract, where no choice of law has been made.[9] In these early days—for despite Hammurabi's black pillar, the subject is not old[10]—English courts were troubled by the taking of jurisdiction in a case of alleged civil wrongdoing where the actings complained of had been committed abroad. They devised, therefore, the fiction of "local venue", and would accept the plea that the event had taken place, "in the Parish of St Mary le Bow" (laying the venue).[11] This fiction also tended to lead the English courts to the view that the *lex fori* was the natural law to apply. The consequences of this were far reaching both for England and Scotland, and even after the revision of conflict rules in tort/delict by the Private International Law (Miscellaneous Provisions) Act 1995, the influence of the *lex fori* was not extinguished.[12] The fiction of "local venue" was abandoned in English law, and was never present in Scots law which found no difficulty in assuming jurisdiction in a case relating to a foreign delict so long as a personal link would justify it.[13]

Since 1707 the systems of Scotland and England have grown together in all areas, including international private law, and in truth are closer in their conflict rules than in many other areas. The English rules in this area were slower to emerge, and developed later in a typically pragmatic and remedy-based manner (although Morris[14] was of the view that the attention paid in the

---

[7] *Calvin's Case* (1608) 7 Co. Rep. 1; 2 St. Tr. 559.

[8] *Dungannon v Hackett* (1702) 1 Eq. Cas. Abr. 289. See also *Cottington's Case* (1678) 2 Swans. 326, and (1607) *Wiers Case* 1 Rolle, Abridgmt. 530, 12, admitting the obligation in principle to recognise and give effect to foreign judgments: Wolff, *Private International Law*, 2nd edn, 1950, p.30.

[9] *Robinson v Bland* (1760) 2 Burr. 1077.

[10] Still something of a teenager: C.G.J. Morse, "Retention of Title in English Private International Law" [1993] J.B.L. 168. One might comment in 2010 that the conflict rules of Scotland and England have been required to grow up, and adapt, fast since 1993.

[11] *Mostyn v Fabrigas* (1774) 1 Coup. 161; 1 S.L.C. 615, in which Lord Mansfield again brought the law forward by taking the view that a justification by the *lex loci delicti* could be pleaded as a defence to an action in England. But see Graveson, *Private International Law*, 7th edn, 1974, p.135, on the matter of taking jurisdiction where the conduct complained of related to immovable property in Nova Scotia (a "local" (land) action as opposed to a "transitory" (with the potential to arise anywhere) action, in English parlance). Morse, *Torts in Private International Law* (Oxford: North-Holland Publishing Company, 1978), p.9.

[12] The common law "rule of double actionability" is retained by s.13 in relation to actions pertaining to defamation, and in other less obvious ways, and survives also the introduction of the Rome II Regulation. See Ch.16, below.

[13] And until 1971 (when this requirement was removed by the Law Reform (Jurisdiction in Delict) (Scotland) Act 1971) so long as the defender was served within the jurisdiction.

[14] J.H.C. Morris, *The Conflict of Laws*, edited by David McClean, 4th ed (London: Sweet & Maxwell, 1993), p.6. A.V. Dicey's *Digest of the law of England with reference to the conflict of laws* (London: Stevens, 1896) is regarded as the first systematic English treatment.

decision of cases to the writings of jurists was unusual in English law). Of the Anglo-American school the greatest debt is owed to the jurist Joseph Story (1779–1845)[15] who drew the strands together. He was followed by Dicey and Westlake, a long line of learned writers[16] and a wealth of nineteenth and twentieth-century case law.

DEVELOPMENT OF CONFLICT RULES IN SCOTLAND

In consequence of the close ties between Scotland and France before the **2–03** Reformation and between Scotland and the Netherlands after the Reformation, the Scots courts had to deal with conflict problems at an earlier date than the English courts.[17] The dictionaries of Morison, Kilkerran and others contain reports of Scots conflict cases[18] a century ahead of English cases.

Knowledge of conflict thinking grew through scholarship[19] and through trade, the latter perhaps, in the view of Gibb,[20] even more valuable. It is gratifyingly evident in the early case of *Stranger from Middleburg v Executors of Smith*,[21] a case concerning a bond which the deceased Smith, a Scot, had made in Flanders, but had failed to honour, and from whose estate in Scotland the Flemish creditor had been obliged to seek satisfaction. The Scots court upheld the bond as valid, though it lacked witnesses, "because the pursuer offered to prove that it was the custom of the country that such bonds, albeit wanting witnesses, yet were effectual against the subscribers thereof"[22]—a matter to be proved, not by declarations of witnesses, but by a testimonial by the judges of the country. In *A Frenchman against an Englishman*[23] it was held that the Scottish Lords of Council were competent judges between stranger and stranger, in all civil actions "even concerning transactions outside the realm", and should decide according to, "the common law, and not after the municipal law of this realme": the applicable law therefore was not to be Scots law, despite the fact that Scotland was the forum. Possibly what was intended was the application of the "Law of Nations", that is, principles of right reason generally accepted internationally.

---

[15] Joseph Story, *Commentaries on the Conflict of Laws* (Boston: Hilliaid, Gray and Co, 1834).
[16] Through Cheshire, Graveson, Morris and Anton, the distinguished list continues up to the expertise of the present day.
[17] Gibb, "International Private Law in Scotland in the 16th and 17th Centuries" (1927) 39 J.R. 369; A. Donaldson, "Some Conflict Rules of Scots Law" in The Grotius Society (London: Longmans, Green and Co), *Problems of Public and Private International Law* (1953) Vol.39, pp.145–148.
[18] See Alexander E. Anton with Paul R. Beaumont, *Private International Law: A Treatise from the Standpoint of Scots Law*, 2nd edn (Edinburgh: W. Green, 1990), pp.9–13. But also in the later Victorian years, Scotland produced significant and helpful cases: see Lachlan MacKinnon, *Leading Cases in the International Private Law of Scotland* (Edinburgh: W. Green, 1934); and see Gibb, *Law from Over The Border*, 1950, pp.89–91.
[19] It is well established that many Scottish students resorted to European universities in the Low Countries such as Franeker and Leyden: David M. Walker, *The Scottish Legal System*, 8th edn revised (Edinburgh: W. Green, 2001), p.163.
[20] Gibb, "International Private Law in Scotland in the 16th and 17th Centuries" (1927) 39 J.R. 369, 373.
[21] (1626) Mor. 12420.
[22] This accords with the modern practice: Rome I Regulation art.11(1). See Ch.13, below.
[23] (1550) Mor. 7323.

The links achieved as a result of trade demonstrated at an early date some of the problems which international private law exists to try to solve. It was the practice in Scotland to confer upon one town in the Low Countries a monopoly of trade: this was the "Scottish Staple", established at various times at Middleburg, Campvere, Antwerp, Bruges, and from 1541, at Vere. All Scots merchants had to use the favoured town, and in return it would keep the channel safe, and provide warehouse accommodation and wharfage.[24] Hence, there grew up a little Scottish colony which had a Governor, the Lord Conservator of the Scottish privileges, with jurisdiction to hear disputes between Scots litigants and to apply Scots law. Gibb notes how remarkable it is to find a judge exercising exclusive jurisdiction and using his own law in a foreign country.[25] The Scots community *lege Scotica viverunt*. There was appeal to the Scots courts. Where the parties were Scots and Dutch, a mixed court of local magistrates and arbiters appointed by the Conservator would decide the issue, but it is uncertain according to which law. We know that when a Scotsman married a Dutchwoman, she came under the jurisdiction of the Conservator and became subject to Scots law. It has been pointed out,[26] however, that there was a loophole (closed in 1696) which gave advantages for the potentially insolvent Scots merchant: if he became bankrupt, his property would escape safe to his wife.

When a community is transferred out of its usual abode, it is compelled to consider the conflict of laws. Conversely, when the gates are closed between neighbours, conditions do not encourage development of conflict thinking.

Donaldson[27] concluded that, although Scotland by the end of the seventeenth century could not be said to be furnished with a complete set of conflict rules, certain principles were clearly established, namely, the pre-eminence of the *lex situs* in property matters,[28] and of the *lex fori* in procedure, and the universality of bankruptcy.

HOW SCOTTISH ARE OUR CONFLICT RULES?

2–04   In contrast with the early days, for many years there has been a spirit of co-operation and sympathy between English and Scots law and between their law reform agencies in the matters of the aims and content of their conflict rules. Not only can there be identified swathes of conflict rules which long have been similar in content and mutually supportive,[29] there is now also, in an increasing

---

[24] Gibb, "International Private Law in Scotland in the 16th and 17th Centuries" (1927) 39 J.R. 369, 375, who comments that English merchants were never other than private adventurers.

[25] Though the Scottish court, in 1992, in the person of Lord Milligan transported itself, with the co-operation of the Lithuanian Supreme Court, to Vilnius, in Latvia, to hear a case concerning alleged war crimes. This was done in view of the age and infirmity of the witnesses (although the original pursuer, alleged to be a war criminal, participated in the proceedings by satellite telephone link from Edinburgh, in view of his age and infirmity). Similarly, in 1999, the High Court of Justiciary sat, with its usual powers, at Camp Zeist, Netherlands, in the cause *HM Advocate v Al Megrahi*.

[26] Gibb, "International Private Law in Scotland in the 16th and 17th Centuries" (1927) 39 J.R. 369, 377.

[27] Donaldson, "Some Conflict Rules of Scots Law" in *Problems of Public and Private International Law*, 1953, p.147.

[28] *Lamb v Heath* (1624) Mor. 4812.

[29] e.g. in family law, obligations, property and succession (while there remain many differences between the domestic laws of Scotland and England in these areas).

number of areas, uniformity attributable to the Europeanisation of the subject.[30] Further, there is within the UK mutual recognition of consistorial decrees,[31] of parental responsibility orders and adoption orders,[32] and of confirmation and probate/letters of administration.[33] Strictly speaking, conflict decisions of one legal system of the UK are merely persuasive in the other, but the conflict decisions of the one jurisdiction are likely to be followed in the other if on a point common to both sets of conflict rules. If the decision is of the House of Lords on a matter of general principle, Anton[34] notes that for all practical purposes the decisions will be of equal authority in both countries: in this way there have become "naturalised" in England, Scottish House of Lords cases and vice versa. The twin Victorian domicile pillars of *Udny v Udny*[35] and *Bell v Kennedy*[36] (both Scottish House of Lords cases) represent a very British view of domicile.[37] A caveat perhaps should be inserted: where a substantial body of interpretative case law has been developed in Scotland in a particular subject matter, e.g. concerning the 1980 Hague Convention on the Civil Aspects of International Child Abduction, there is less need and less inclination to refer to English authority. The approach taken in this book is that the conflict rules of Scots and English law in many areas have more to unite them than to divide them: where there are differences, or have been differences, these will be mentioned in the text. This is not intended to detract in any way from the status of the body of Scots conflict rules as a complete and independent system, capable of providing an answer to any conflict problem.

Account must be taken of the fundamental constitutional change effected by the Scotland Act 1998, as a result of which matters of Scottish civil law fall within the legislative competence of the Scottish Parliament.[38] Section 126(4)(a) interprets the civil law of Scotland as a reference to the general principles of private law, including private international law.[39] An Act of the Scottish Parliament is not law insofar as any provision thereof is outside the legislative competence of the Parliament; reserved matters are expressly excluded from the legislative competence of the Scottish Parliament. The question whether a provision relates to a reserved matter is to be determined by reference to the purpose of the provision.[40] Although international private law generally is a devolved matter falling within the legislative competence of the Scottish Parliament, the private international law aspects of reserved matters likewise are reserved (s.29(4)(b); e.g. the international private law rules concerning intellectual property).

---

[30] See Ch.1, above. Consider, in the context of the EU JHA harmonisation programme, the lack of development, by design one assumes, of special intra-UK conflict rules: see para.1–10, above.

[31] See Ch.12, below.

[32] See Ch.14, below.

[33] See Ch.18, below.

[34] Anton with Beaumont, *Private International Law*, 2nd edn, 1990, p.9.

[35] (1869) 7 M. (H.L.) 89.

[36] (1868) 6 M. (H.L.) 69.

[37] Subject now to the divergence wrought by the Scottish Parliament in s.22 of the Family Law (Scotland) Act 2006.

[38] Scotland Act 1998 s.29 (legislative competence) establishes what the Scottish Parliament may not do rather than what it may do. Section 29(2)(b) provides that reserved matters (s.30, Sch.5) are outside Scottish Parliamentary competence.

[39] Family Law (Scotland) Act 2006 s.38 serves as an example of Holyrood utilisation of this competence.

[40] Scotland Act 1998 s.29(3).

In terms of s.57 ("Community law and Convention rights"), despite the transfer to the Scottish Ministers of functions in relation to implementing obligations under Community law, any function of a Minister of the Crown in relation to any matter shall continue to be exercisable by him as regards Scotland for the purposes of s.2(2) of the European Communities Act 1972. In this context, therefore, there is "shared power" between Scottish and UK Ministers. Furthermore, Sch.5 Pt 1 para.7 "reserves" foreign affairs, including relations with the EC, but excepting implementation of obligations under Community law.[41] Moreover, it is intended[42] that the Scottish Government will be involved closely in policy formation and negotiation of European legislation.

With regard to participation in and ratification of initiatives of the Hague Conference on Private International Law, it remains the case that the United Kingdom is the Hague Conference Contracting State. Nevertheless, on occasion, as a result of differences in the content of certain areas of domestic law of Scotland and England, it may happen that the United Kingdom will sign a Hague Convention on behalf of one constituent legal system only.[43]

By constitutional convention,[44] it is possible for the UK Parliament, with consent of the Scottish Parliament, to legislate for Scotland in devolved matters. In the context of the conflict of laws, particularly in family law, there may be perceivable benefits from having the UK Parliament legislate for the entire UK, thus lessening the likelihood of intra-UK conflict problems. The resultant UK legislation may contain separate provision for each legal system within the UK, but even if that is the case, it is hoped that the legislation will demonstrate internal UK coherence.[45]

Even in the post-devolution era, therefore, the relationship between Scots and English conflict of laws and their continuing development (independently, intra-UK, intra-EU and vis-à-vis third states) still is characterised by a subtle interaction and interdependence.

---

[41] Secondary legislation is likely to be required separately in Scotland and in England, e.g. pertaining to Regulation 2201/2003; European Communities (Jurisdiction and Judgments in Matrimonial and Parental Responsibility Matters) Regulations 2005 (SI 2005/265) (England and Wales); and European Communities (Matrimonial and Parental Responsibility Jurisdiction and Judgments) (Scotland) Regulations 2005 (SSI 2005/42).

[42] Scottish Office, *Scotland's Parliament* (HMSO, 1997), Cm.3658, Ch.8.

[43] e.g. 2000 Hague Convention on International Protection of Adults, signed by the UK separately for Scotland and for England, and ratified by Scotland. For England and Wales, see Mental Capacity Act 2005.

[44] Originally a "Sewel motion", and now properly a "legislative consent motion". See generally Noreen Burrows, "This is Scotland's Parliament; Let Scotland's Parliament Legislate", 2002 Jur. Rev. 213.

[45] The Civil Partnership Act 2004, which affects reserved matters as well as devolved matters, was referred to Westminster by means of a Sewel motion. The Act, however, makes bespoke provision for the different legal systems within the UK. See Ch.11, below. Cf. Matrimonial and Family Proceedings Act 1984 Pt 3 (England) and Pt 4 (Scotland): see Ch 13, below.

CHAPTER 3

OPERATION OF FOREIGN LAW: THEORIES OF INCLUSION AND RULES OF EXCLUSION

Why should the domestic law of one legal system be recognised and given **3–01** effect to in another? It is surely a sufficient reply that there is in each developed legal system a system of rules, known as its international private law, or conflict of laws, rules, which regulates these matters: the operation of the rules of one legal system within the bounds of another stems from the law of the latter. There is therefore no affront to sovereignty.

However, over the course of the relatively young life of the subject, various theories have been advanced to explain the extraterritorial effect of a rule:

(1) The international theory (comity) finds the nature of the subject in the notion of international goodwill or reciprocity, a "do as you would be done by" spirit of international co-operation,[1] which indeed is present in many modern international legislative exercises,[2] as well as in longer-established bodies of rules based on mutual assistance,[3] the more so if the legal systems involved are each members of a supranational body.[4]

(2) The statutory or neo-statutory theory is derived from the distinction made by Bartolus[5] between statutes real (affecting only property situated within the enacting state) and statutes personal (affecting the individual in his personal life wherever he or she might go). The distinction remains illuminating.

(3) Savigny's theory of the natural seat of an obligation[6] holds that every relationship is by its nature connected more strongly with one legal

---

[1] See L. Collins, "Comity in Modern Private International Law" in James Fawcett (ed.), *Reform and Development in Private International Law: Essays in Honour of Sir Peter North* (Oxford: Oxford University Press, 2002), Ch.4.

[2] e.g. 1980 Hague Convention on the Civil Aspects of International Child Abduction and 1996 Hague Convention on Jurisdiction, Applicable Law, Recognition, Enforcement and Cooperation in respect of Parental Responsibility Measures for the Protection of Children.

[3] e.g. in foreign judgment enforcement: Administration of Justice Act 1920 and Foreign Judgments (Reciprocal Enforcement) Act 1933; and Civil Jurisdiction and Judgments Acts 1982 and 1991.

[4] See Ch.1, above.

[5] See para.2–01, above.

[6] Friedrich Carl von Savigny, translated by Sheriff William Guthrie, *A Treatise on the Conflict of Laws* (Edinburgh: T&T Clark, 1869); cf. in similar vein, American view expressed by Holmes and Cardozo JJ. that foreign law constitutes an *obligatio* which, "follows the person and may be enforced wherever the person may be found": *Slater v Mexican National Railway* (1904) 194 U.S. 120 at 126.

system than with any other. That legal system, therefore, being the source of rights and obligations, should determine the outcome wherever it is litigated.

Savigny's view was "universalist" and supranational, seeking uniformity in the treatment of conflict cases. Savigny's work (adapted)[7] had a Scottish follower in James Lorimer (1818–90), writer on international law (favouring the law of nature).[8]

(4) Mancini's theory of nationality. The movements for political unification of Italy and Germany in the latter part of the nineteenth century brought with them a natural enthusiasm for nationality as the most suitable choice of personal law. Mancini argued that nationality was the basis of international law (propounding this at a famous lecture at the University of Turin in 1851) and that a person should be entitled, under limited exceptions, to be governed by the law of his nationality even when abroad.

(5) The territorial theory originated in the writings of the Dutch jurists and in particular those of Huber.[9] This theory, which reflects the concerns of the time at which Huber was writing (1689), and which is founded upon the dignity of sovereigns, and their power and authority within their own realms, continues to influence many areas of the subject, e.g. matters of title to property, immoveable or moveable, in respect of which the *lex situs*[10] is the pre-eminently applicable law. In effect the theory means that a state has complete power over all persons and property within its territory, that within its territory only its own law applies, and that it has no power over persons and property outside its own territory: "The Laws of a foreign State have no coercive force extra territorium."[11] It follows from this that, if foreign rights are to be recognised and enforced in Scotland, they must be regarded as being part of Scots law and/or as acquiring recognition, and justifying enforcement, under Scots conflict rules.

(6) The local law theory, which arose from the observations and writings of the American jurist Cook,[12] suggests that the forum, when asked to lend its aid to enforce a foreign right which has originated in a foreign system, does not apply foreign law, but uses an analogous right of its own domestic law to achieve the same end.[13]

(7) The theory of Justice. It may be that the true basis of the subject is simply the desire and necessity to ensure that the ends of justice are served and in particular that justice is done to the individual whose personal or business life has led him or her to experience the conflict of laws. "Conflicts justice" would seem to include considerations such as seeking to meet reasonable party expectations, and to achieve

[7] David M. Walker, *The Scottish Jurists* (Edinburgh: W. Green, 1985), p.369.
[8] Walker, *The Scottish Jurists*, 1985, p.370.
[9] See para.2–02, above.
[10] As to meaning of which, see Ch.17, below.
[11] *Morison's Dictionary*, 4453.
[12] Walter W. Cook, *The Logical and Legal Bases of the Conflict of Laws* (Cambridge, Massachusetts: Harvard University Press, 1942).
[13] Cases may be found in which the theory seems to be borne out by the circumstances and outcome, e.g. *Re Bettinson's Question* [1956] Ch. 67.

certainty, predictability and uniformity of result. Graveson writes that this is the major basis of the subject.[14] It is doubtful whether the grand aim of uniformity of result regardless of forum is ever capable of being accomplished, but many agree that the pursuit of "private law justice" is the main aim and raison d'être of the subject.

(8) American policy evaluation theories, discussed and debated in the USA since the 1930s (termed "The American Revolution")[15], constitute a fundamental change in thinking, both as to theory and as to method.

There are many approaches, and there has been much writing.[16] Essentially policy evaluation thinking seeks to depart from the traditional jurisdiction-selecting[17] approach of "blind" or "blinkered" selection of the law to be applied which is appropriate in the abstract (in the view of the forum) to adjudicate upon the type of problem in question, and instead to have regard to the nature and desirability (in the view of the forum, presumably) of the particular outcome, i.e. to consider the effect in the concrete case of the application of such law. Every forum has to struggle against the view, conscious or subconscious, that its own law is best. Commentators and courts must be alert to incidence of "homeward trend" on the part of the forum, that is to say, a tendency of the forum to favour its own law and/or its "own" litigant. It has been suggested that often the effect of the policy evaluation theories—or, properly, methods—is that the forum wends its way home, albeit by a circuitous route.

Examples of the policy evaluation methods include the theories of "Government Interest Analysis" (can the policies of the competing laws be ascertained? How reasonable is it for each respective state to assert an interest in the application of its law?), "Comparative Impairment" (if policies conflict, there should be applied the law of the state whose interest would be more/most gravely impaired if not

---

[14] Graveson, *Private International Law*, 7th edn, 1974, p.7. He cites at p.9 the *National Bank of Greece and Athens SA v Metliss* [1958] A.C. 509, per Viscount Simonds at 525. This case, together with *Adams v National Bank of Greece and Athens SA* [1961] A.C. 255, narrates a lengthy story, at the end of which English creditors under an English bond made with Greek debtors were held by the House of Lords to be entitled to enforce their debt in England against the debtor's successors, Greek moratoriums notwithstanding.

[15] See Morris, *Conflict of Laws*, 6th edn, 2005, Ch.21; and P.M. North, "Family Law and the American Revolution" in Peter M. North, *Essays in Private International Law* (Oxford: Clarendon Press, 1993), Ch.6.

[16] Though the writing may be said to be concerned particularly with inter-state conflicts. See, in particular, Brainerd Currie, *Selected Essays on the Conflict of Laws* (Durham, North Carolina: Duke University Press, 1963); D.F. Cavers, *The Choice of Law Process* (Ann Arbor: University of Michigan Press, 1965); and A. Shapira, *The Interest Approach to Choice of Law* (The Hague: Martinus Nijhoff, 1970). The federal structure, wherever found (but especially in the USA) is likely to produce conflict disputes. The American Law Institute brought together, in a Restatement, the most important principles. The Restatement is persuasive, not binding on states, but has been influential for good. The first Restatement (1934, with Reporter Beale) was certain in tone and favoured the Vested Rights approach (*q.v.*); the second Restatement (1971, with Reporter Reese) is more open to the new theories and methods.

[17] This is a term used to describe the orthodox choice of law process which seeks to apply the law indicated as applicable, category by category, according to the forum's choice of law rules. This method is not intended to take account of the outcome in the instant case. The term is confusing because "jurisdiction" in this context must be interpreted, unusually, as a reference to application of the rules of a particular legal system and does not pertain to the allocation or exercise of civil jurisdiction by a particular forum.

applied), "Principles of Preference"[18] and "Choice Influencing Factors", which proceed on the basis that agreement on certain general aims, for example protection of justified expectations, or uniformity of result, should aid choice of law.

All such policy evaluation methods involve "rule-selection", that is, "looking up to see the finishing tape", which is at odds with the orthodox or classical "jurisdiction-selection" method traditionally held to provide the benefits of neutrality and distance. Quite apart from the question of acceptability in principle of such a rule-selection approach, it is thought unsuitable in an international, as opposed to an inter-state, context.[19]

The European Community's ambitious programme of harmonisation of private international law in many private law subject areas is predicated on the basis that the emerging corpus of assimilated conflict rules derives from, and demonstrates, jurisdiction-selection methodology.

(9) The theory of the vested or acquired right, based on the territorial theory, was advocated by Dicey. The effect of the theory is that, if a question should arise in Scotland as to the enforcement of a "foreign right", in solving the problem the Scots court must determine the origin of the foreign right and ascertain whether it is a right which has been validly acquired under its own law. If that is so, the right will be enforceable in Scotland provided that its enforcement does not fall within any of the exceptions, discussed in paras 3–02 et seq., below. Whatever the merits and standing of the theory (or of any theory of extraterritorial validity and enforceability of rights), at least the exceptions or limitations are well known, well understood, and well vouched[20]: no Scots or English court will recognise or give effect to a foreign right if this would involve:

(a) the enforcement of foreign revenue laws;
(b) the enforcement of foreign penal laws;
(c) the enforcement of foreign confiscatory laws; or
(d) making a decision inconsistent with the public policy or morality of the United Kingdom, or detrimental to its political and judicial institutions.

The procedure available by Scots law must be appropriate for the enforcement of the right, and a foreign right, which is otherwise valid, will not be enforced if its enforcement would involve any question of discretion or some other element which would be exercised more appropriately by a foreign court.[21]

---

[18] Cavers's suggestions are concerned principally with the law of obligations, offering guidance to the forum on grounds of general policy (the higher standard of required conduct being usually, but not always, preferred) in choosing between or among the rules of interested states.

[19] Morris, *Conflict of Laws*, 7th edn, 2009, para.21–015 (re principles of preference): "[H]ow could a judge express a preference for the rules adopted by one country or another when those countries are not component parts of a federal system but are linked only by diplomatic relations or (perhaps) by a common cultural heritage?"

[20] Though nowadays, while the core of the exceptions holds firm, the edges, as a result of harmonisation and globalisation, are not so well defined. For a modern discussion of the topic generally, see *Iran v Barakat Galleries Ltd* [2009] Q.B. 22, per Lord Phillips at [95] et seq.

[21] cf. *Phrantzes v Argenti* [1960] 2 Q.B. 19; contrast *Shahnaz v Rizwan* [1965] 1 Q.B. 390.

The vested rights theory has been the subject of trenchant criticism.[22] The germ of the theory (as well as of the comity theory) can be found in Huber's third maxim (see para.2–02, above). The premise is that it is not the foreign law per se which is being enforced *extra territorium*, but rights acquired *under* the foreign law; but it is difficult to see how the rights conferred by a legal system can be dissociated from the law which created them. Moreover, if the forum is to set itself to implement foreign acquired rights, so far as its own public policy and procedure allow, it must ascertain the law by which the right is to be tested to determine whether it has vested or has been acquired. The theory contains no choice of law rules. The forum cannot start from the right and work backwards, assuming/supposing that the right should be enforced; that law which is the origin of the right may not be (in the view of the forum) the correct choice of law to apply.[23] Therefore, if the acquired rights theory is to be used at all, it seems suitable only for simpler cases where all seemingly relevant factors (apart from the identity of the forum) pertain to one legal system, and the remedy available in the legal system of origin is sought elsewhere: a number of cases in the conflict of laws catalogue satisfy this test,[24] but a much greater number do not. However, there is no doubt that the vested rights theory, as encapsulated in a form of words as a guide, instils the correct attitude of international co-operation and open-mindedness.[25] Novelty in itself should be no bar to the enforcement of a foreign acquired right,[26] nor to the recognition of a foreign status unknown but unexceptionable.[27]

(10) Economic analysis of the conflict of laws.[28] A further and more modern lens through which to view the subject is that of the economic analysis theory, which examines the interrelationship of systems of private law, particularly in the law of obligations. The analysis is part of what may be called the "Law and Economics Movement". It requires the expertise of the economist and the conflict lawyer, not as yet a commonly found combination of talents. This modern debate

---

[22] Supporters are Clive M. Schmitthoff, *The English Conflict of Laws* (London: Stevens & Sons Ltd, 1954), pp.32 and 35 et seq., and J.H. Beale, *Treatise on the Conflict of Laws* (New York: Baker, Voorhis & Co, 1935). The theory has been criticised by Cheshire, various editions, and see *Cheshire, North and Fawcett: Private International Law*, 14th edn, 2008, pp.24–26, Wolff, *Private International Law*, 2nd edn, 1950, p.2, moderately by Graveson, *Private International Law*, 7th edn, 1974, p.38 and others.

[23] cf. Guthrie's translation of Savigny: Anton with Beaumont, *Private International Law*, 2nd edn, 1990, p.28.

[24] e.g. *Dalrymple v Dalrymple* (1811) 2 Hag. Con. 54 at 58; *Caldwell v Van Vlissengen* (1851) 9 Hare 415 at 425; *Hooper v Gumm* (1867) L.R. 2 Ch. 282, per Turner L.J. at 289, 290; *Slater v Mexican National Railroad Co* (1904) 194 U.S. 120 at 125; *Re Bettinson's Question* [1956] Ch. 67; *Phrantzes v Argenti* [1960] 2 Q.B. 19; *Shahnaz v Rizwan* [1965] 1 Q.B. 390.

[25] See *Cheshire, North and Fawcett: Private International Law*, 14th edn, 2008, p.26.

[26] *Shahnaz v Rizwan* [1965] 1 Q.B. 390: contrast *Phrantzes v Argenti* [1960] 2 Q.B. 19.

[27] *Bumper Development Corp v Commissioner of Police of the Metropolis* [1991] 1 W.L.R. 1362.

[28] See, generally, Michael J. Whincop and Mary Keyes, *Policy and Pragmatism in the Conflict of Laws* (Aldershot: Ashgate, 2001); Basedow and Kono (eds) (in cooperation with Rühl), *An Economic Analysis of Private International Law* (Tübingen: Mohr Siebeck, 2006); and Erin A. O'Hara (ed.), *Economics of Conflict of Laws* (Cheltenham: Edward Elgar Publishing, 2007). For further secondary literature, see *Cheshire, North and Fawcett: Private International Law*, 14th edn, 2008, p.36.

seeks to bring an economic efficiency perspective to bear on issues of jurisdiction and choice of law, but within the new approach there seems to be no consensus of opinion as to whether the focus should be on state interests, or individual interests. The purpose has been to ascertain whether or not such an approach can provide "more scientific, objective foundations to the discipline of private international law"[29] and promote global and individual economic welfare in the determination of conflict cases. For example, the forces of competition might be thought capable of improving the value to individual litigants of the outcome of a given dispute in that both in jurisdiction and choice of law states would have an incentive, through their laws, to attract parties and their business[30]—always assuming that conflict rules permit a degree of party freedom to choose the court and the law.

THE EXCEPTIONS TO THE ENFORCEMENT OF FOREIGN RIGHTS (THE EXCLUSION OF FOREIGN LAW)

REVENUE LAWS

3–02   As a general rule, the revenue laws of a foreign country are not enforceable in the United Kingdom because such laws are regarded as being essentially local in their application and not appropriate for enforcement in any other country.[31] In principle the exception applies as regards the revenue laws of all other countries whatsoever, including those of the British Commonwealth,[32] but increasingly one requires to make special mention of the intra-EC situation, where exceptions to the exception can be identified.[33] Nonetheless, in *QRS 1 ApS v Frandsen*,[34] the Court of Appeal ruled that the principle of "the revenue law

---

[29] Michaels, in Basedow and Kono (eds), *Economic Analysis of Private International Law*, 2006, p.144.

[30] O'Hara (ed.), *Economics of Conflict of Laws*, 2007, p.xxii.

[31] See *Holman v Johnson* (1775–1802) All E.R. Rep. 98, per Lord Mansfield C.J. at 99: "no country ever takes note of the revenue laws of another"; *The Eva* [1921] P. 454; *Re Visser* [1928] Ch. 877; *Rossano v Manufacturers' Life Insurance Co* [1963] 2 Q.B. 352; and *Lord Advocate v Tursi*, 1998 S.L.T. 1035. The principal authority is *India v Taylor* [1955] A.C. 491.

[32] *Att Gen for Canada v William Schulze & Co*, 1901 9 S.L.T. 4, per Lord Stormonth-Darling at 5. See also *India v Taylor* [1955] A.C. 491.

[33] e.g. in terms of Regulation 1346/2000 on insolvency proceedings [2000] OJ L160/1 art.39, any creditor who has his habitual residence, domicile or registered office in a Member State, other than the State of the opening of insolvency proceedings, including the tax authorities and social security authorities of Member States, shall have the right to lodge claims in the insolvency proceedings in writing. There is also the concept of the "Community duty or tax", enforceable across boundaries of Member States (Directive 76/308 on mutual assistance on recovery of claims (OJ 1976 L73/18), as amended by Directive 79/1071 (OJ 1979 L331/10) and Directive 2001/44 (OJ 2001 L175/17), implemented by Directive 2002/94 (OJ 2002 L337/41); implemented in the UK by the Recovery of Duties and Taxes Etc. Due in Other Member States (Corresponding UK Claims, Procedure and Supplementary) Regulations 2004 (SI 2004/674)). In terms of Criminal Justice Act 1993 s.71, a person who in the UK assists in, or induces, any conduct outside the UK which contravenes inter alia the determination, discharge or enforcement of any liability for any of the following Community duties or taxes commits an offence (that is to say, any Community customs duty, agricultural levy, value added tax under the law of any Member State, excise duty in another Member State or any duty or tax which is imposed by or in pursuance of any Community instrument or the movement of goods into or out of any Member State).

[34] [1999] 3 All E.R. 289.

exception", as a fundamental of English law, could be objectively justified and was not, therefore, incompatible with European Community law.

Within the United Kingdom, as a result of the overarching jurisdiction of the Westminster Parliament and the common exchequer, revenue laws are enforceable throughout the UK. However, in view of s.73 of the Scotland Act 1998, which confers upon the Scottish Parliament tax-varying power,[35] the Scottish Parliament has power to vary, "for Scottish taxpayers",[36] the basic rate of income tax by up to 3 per cent.[37] The question which in time may require to be answered is whether the Inland Revenue in Scotland may pursue a claim against a Scottish taxpayer, later resident in England, for any unpaid tax due by him/her, arising under a provision made by the Scottish Parliament. While it may be anomalous that it should not be able to do so, by reason of the "revenue law exception", this may indeed be the case since a distinction can still be drawn between tax legislation passed on a UK basis by the Westminster Parliament under its superior authority, and that passed by the Scottish Parliament under its tax-varying powers.

When considering a claim the forum will categorise its nature as "revenue", or not. It does not matter in what light the claim is viewed in its legal system of "origin". Lord Cameron stated in *Metal Industries (Salvage) Ltd v ST Harle (Owners)*[38]:

> "It is a general rule of law that no state will act as a tax gatherer for another or permit its courts to be used for that purpose, and it is a corollary of that rule that what is a revenue or fiscal claim is to be determined by the Courts of the country where the claim is sought to be enforced and in accordance with the lex fori."

Hence the important point should be noted that classification of the nature of a claim is a matter for the forum.[39]

The forum will not knowingly be deluded by the manner in which the claim comes to court, or by its form, but rather will seek to ascertain its true nature.[40] A claim for local rates has been classified as "revenue"[41]; so too has been a claim in a Scottish multiplepoinding for employers' contributions, unpaid, to a French government benefit scheme for seamen.[42] However, where the *lex causae* has the effect of permitting its exchange control laws to discharge a contractual obligation, the contract will be discharged according to Scots and English conflict rules.[43] Nor will UK courts connive at an attempt to deprive a

---

[35] Scotland Act 1998 Pt IV ss.73–79.
[36] Scotland Act 1998 s.75 defines "Scottish taxpayer" essentially on the basis of the proportion of days during which a person has resided in Scotland in the tax year in question.
[37] Scotland Act 1998 s.73(1)(b).
[38] 1962 S.L.T. 114 at 116.
[39] See *Tasarruf Mevduati Sigorta Fonu v Demirel* [2006] EWHC 3354 (Ch) at [65]; affirmed without discussion of this point [2007] 1 W.L.R. 2508, with leave to appeal to the House of Lords refused.
[40] *Peter Buchanan Ltd v McVey* [1955] A.C. 516; [1954] I.R. 89; cf. *QRS 1 ApS v Frandsen* [1999] 3 All E.R. 289. See also *Brokaw v Seatrain UK Ltd* [1971] 2 All E.R. 98, per Lord Denning at 100, citing *Holman v Johnson* [1775–1802] All E.R. Rep. 98 at 99. Cf. *Revenue and Customs Commissioners v Total Network SL* [2008] 2 All E.R. 413 (HL).
[41] *Sydney Municipal Council v Bull* [1909] 1 K.B. 7.
[42] *Metal Industries (Salvage) Ltd v ST Harle (Owners)*, 1962 S.L.T. 114.
[43] See *Re Claim by Helbert Wagg & Co Ltd* [1956] Ch. 323 and *Kahler v Midland Bank Ltd* [1950] A.C. 24.

foreign government of its revenue.[44] A most instructive example is provided by the case of *Re Norway's Application*,[45] a tax investigation into the affairs of the late AJ, a Norwegian domiciliary. With the agreement of the late AJ's family, the Norwegian tax authorities sought to have evidence taken in England from two merchant bankers for use in a tax litigation in Norway. This was done by means of "letters of request" under the Evidence (Proceedings in Other Jurisdictions) Act 1975.[46] The House of Lords permitted the application on the view that this was not an attempt to collect foreign revenue but rather a request for assistance in a tax investigation. As to the warring principles of banker/client confidentiality on the one hand, and the demands of international comity on the other, the court favoured the latter, while protecting the former by a careful monitoring of the terms of the questions to be asked. Moreover, trustees or executors who decide to pay foreign inheritance tax may be exonerated (though the foreign government could not stand in UK courts to claim the sum), if by their action they have taken the only means of giving effect to the wishes of the testator or testatrix.[47]

The revenue law exception applies only to the collection of money, with the result that foreign revenue laws may be recognised and receive effect indirectly. Foreign revenue laws therefore have received effect as regards currency laws,[48] sufficiency of stamp duty, or forgery of coins or banknotes. Double taxation treaties exist with the aim of ensuring that the income of corporate bodies or individuals is subjected to taxation only by one of the signatory states: they provide the detailed regulation required to assess the income according to its source.

Therefore, there are exceptions to the revenue law exception, or limitations on it.

PENAL LAWS

3–03   Penal laws are regarded also as being strictly local and therefore they are not enforceable in another state.[49] In the sense of this rule, a penal law is a measure

---

[44] e.g. by affording a party, who for tax reasons had divested himself in America of shares in favour of his wife, the opportunity to attempt to prove the true position by trying to rebut the presumption of gift: *Re Emery's Investment Trusts* [1959] Ch. 410.

[45] *Re Norway's Application (Nos 1 and 2)* [1989] 1 All E.R. 745.

[46] With regard to the classification of a fiscal case as being of a "civil or commercial" nature, in order to satisfy the 1975 Act s.1, the House of Lords held that classification of the proceedings was to be referred to the laws of both states (the requesting state and the state addressed), since there was no internationally acceptable classification. Lord Goff, giving the leading speech, concluded that the 1975 Act would apply only if both states agreed that the proceedings were to be categorised as civil. A dual approach to classification is unusual.

[47] *Scottish National Orchestra Society Ltd v Thomson's Executor*, 1969 S.L.T. 325; *Re Lord Cable deceased* [1976] 3 All E.R. 417.

[48] *Re Claim by Helbert Wagg & Co Ltd* [1956] Ch. 323; *Kahler v Midland Bank Ltd* [1950] A.C. 24; *Zivnostenska Banka National Corp v Frankman* [1950] A.C. 57; contrast *Indian & General Investment Trust Co v Borax Consolidated Ltd* [1920] 1 K.B. 539 and *Rossano v Manufacturers Life Insurance Co* [1963] 2 Q.B. 352.

[49] "The courts of no country execute the penal laws of another", *The Antelope*, 10 Wheaton 123, per Marshall C.J. quoted in *Huntington v Attrill* [1893] A.C. 150. *Ogden v Folliot* (1790) 3 T.R. 726; affirming sub nom. *Folliot v Ogden* (1789) 1 Ll.Bl. 123. See more recently *Pocket Kings Ltd v Safenames Ltd* [2009] EWHC 2529. For the problems which may arise in modern electronic conditions, see *Yahoo! Inc v La Ligue Contra Le Racisme et L'Antisemitisme*, 433 F 3d.; 2006 U.S. App. Lexis 668. Cf. *King v Serious Fraud Office* [2009] 1 W.L.R. 718.

directed by a state against a particular individual or group of individuals. Hence it does not include a penalty in a private contract,[50] nor does it include a general enactment confiscating all property, such an enactment falling under the heading of "confiscatory laws" below.

The classic definition was given by the Privy Council in *Huntington v Attrill*[51]: the "penal law exception" refers to "a penalty imposed by the State for some criminal violation of its rules". The (excluded) proceeding:

> ". . . must be in the nature of a suit in favour of the State whose law has been infringed, and the penalties must be recoverable at the instance of the State, or a State official, or a member of the public acting in the public interest".

This means that criminal law is intraterritorial. A person should face trial (if necessary following extradition) in the legal system where he allegedly committed the offence. There can be no conviction in Scotland on the ground of breach of a foreign criminal law, nor enforcement of a judgment given in foreign criminal proceedings.[52]

Sometimes the question of where an offence has taken place becomes of essential importance for the purpose of the meaning and operation of a statute. With regard to British statutes, there is a strong, though weakening,[53] presumption against extraterritorial effect in the case of criminal statutes. Thus, on interpretation of the (English) Theft Act 1968, in circumstances where a criminal plan had been devised to bring stolen cars into Britain from Germany, it has been held that since the statutory crime of theft is a "once and for all" and not a "continuing" act, there could be no conviction in England, the criminal activity having been completed abroad.[54] It may be possible to sever the civil from the criminal aspect of a foreign award granted in a legal system which has a unified procedure, and there is no objection to enforcing the award of civil damages.[55]

To classify the nature of the foreign law as penal, or not, is the function of the forum.[56] In *Huntington v Attrill*, the question was whether the New York-imposed liability on promoters for making misrepresentations in company reports was penal (criminal) in nature, or remedial (protective of private interests). The Privy Council, exercising the power of classification on appeal from the Court of Ontario, found it was not penal within the relevant conflict rule (or exception). A modern instance of the same point is provided by *United States Securities & Exchange Commission v Manterfield*,[57] in which the Court

---

[50] *SA Consortium General Textiles v Sun & Sand Agencies Ltd* [1978] Q.B. 279, per Lord Denning at 299, 300.

[51] [1893] A.C. 150.

[52] Though an instance of account being taken in Scotland, for the purpose of sentencing, of an individual's criminal history in England is to be found in the case of *Herd v HM Advocate*, 1993 G.W.D. 24-1503; cf. shrieval jurisdiction in relation to a statutory offence allegedly committed abroad: *McCarron (George Wallace) v HM Advocate*, 2001 S.L.T. 866.

[53] See para.1–02, above.

[54] *R. v Atakpu (Austin)* [1993] 4 All E.R. 215; and *R. (on the application of Purdy) v DPP* [2009] UKHL 45 (Suicide Act 1961). See para.3–07, below.

[55] *Raulin v Fischer* [1911] 2 K.B. 93.

[56] See, e.g., exercise of this function by the Irish court in *Larkins v National Union of Mineworkers* [1985] I.R. 671. *Iran v Barakat Galleries Ltd* [2009] Q.B. 22 at [106].

[57] [2009] 1 Lloyd's Rep 399.

of Appeal dismissed the argument that a freezing order[58] made by an English court in support of United States proceedings amounted to the enforcement of US penal law. The approach was taken that the forum would ascertain which part of the foreign judgment it was being asked to enforce, having regard to the substance of the relief. In the circumstances the Court of Appeal concluded that what was sought was the disgorgement of the alleged proceeds of fraud for the benefit of investors, i.e. that it was remedial in nature, and so enforceable, rather than penal. Moreover, the court held that comity required the English court to lend its assistance to thwart international fraudulent activity, notwithstanding that the fraud did not take place in the UK, nor were British interests directly affected.

In this connection, therefore, "penal" should be understood as meaning "criminal" rather than unfair or discriminatory.[59] A case may arise in which a foreign law can be regarded as "penal" in both senses, as illustrated by *Banco de Vizcaya v Don Alfonso De Borbon y Austria*.[60] The Spanish Republican Government purported to confiscate the property in England of the former King Alfonso, founding on a Spanish decree declaring the King guilty of high treason and an outlaw. The English forum refused to entertain the Spanish claim (which came to court in the form of a claim by the Spanish bank). In whatever form it appeared, it was an attempt to have enforced extraterritorially a foreign "penal" (and confiscatory) law. Again, in *United States v Inkley*,[61] the attempt by the US Government to recover an "appearance bond" (security for appearance in forthcoming American criminal proceedings), granted by Inkley when in America, was irrecoverable from him when resident in England, because in the view of the English court the bond was inextricably linked with American public, criminal procedure.

Certain foreign statutory provisions, such as prohibitions on export without licence of historic artefacts, may be difficult to classify. In the leading case of *Att Gen of New Zealand v Ortiz*,[62] Maori carvings having been removed from New Zealand without the requisite certificate under the (New Zealand) Historic Articles Act 1962, the plaintiff sought to restrain the sale of these articles in London. Two principal questions arose: (1) the nature of the New Zealand statutory provision; and (2) interpretation of the wording of the provision, and in particular of the word "forfeit". In the Court of Appeal[63] the majority view was that the provision was "penal" (in the sense of criminal), although Lord Denning placed it in a broad grouping which he termed "other public law" (and hence concurred with his brother judges in finding it not enforceable *extra territorium*).[64] The speeches in the House of Lords were concerned only with interpretation of the word "forfeit", and the view taken of

---

[58] See para.7–75, below.
[59] Though early cases used it in this way: *Wolff v Oxholm* (1817) 6 M. & S. 92; see also *Re Fried Krupp AG* [1917] 2 Ch. 188.
[60] [1935] 1 K.B. 140.
[61] [1989] Q.B. 255. See also *United States v A Ltd* [2003] C.L.Y.B. 621.
[62] [1983] 2 All E.R. 93. Cf. *Iran v Barakat Galleries Ltd* [2009] Q.B. 22.
[63] [1982] 3 All E.R. 432.
[64] cf. *Att Gen v Heinemann Publishers Australia PTY Ltd* [1988] C.L.Y. 1982; and *United States v A Ltd* [2003] C.L.Y.B. 621.

the proper meaning was that the carvings fell into the ownership of the Crown in right of New Zealand only if seized within the territorial bounds of New Zealand; on interpretation, there could be no notional forfeiture upon seizure following export from New Zealand without a licence.[65] Hence, to have acceded to the Attorney General's claim would have amounted to giving effect extraterritorially to a foreign penal law.

CONFISCATORY LAWS

There are three manifestations of confiscatory law: **3–04**

(a) *expropriation or confiscation*: the taking by a state of property belonging to a private individual or body for public purposes without adequate compensation;

(b) *nationalisation*: the taking of private property for public purposes in the same circumstances as in (a) above, but upon payment of compensation;

(c) *requisitioning*: the taking of private property for public purposes with compensation for a limited period such as the duration of a war.[66]

Modern instances tend to concern the first of these.

The general principle is that the act of any recognised government[67] is accepted as being effective as regards all property situated within its territory, but as having no effect on property situated outside such territory. Hence, a confiscatory act directed against an individual or a class of individuals will be deemed to be completely effective as regards property belonging to such persons within the territory of the "confiscating" state,[68] but will not receive any effect in the view of Scots law as regards assets situated outside that territory.[69] The question, therefore, may simply be one as to the location of property, the territorial limits of the state which has purported to confiscate,[70] or as to the effective completion[71] of the purported confiscation within those

---

[65] cf. and contrast *Spain v Christie, Manson & Woods Ltd* [1986] 1 W.L.R. 1120.

[66] As to which see anomalous wartime case of *Lorentzen v Lydden & Co Ltd* [1942] 2 K.B. 202.

[67] See Robert Leslie, "The Existence of Governments and the Conflict of Laws: the Republic of Somalia Case", 1997 Jur. Rev. 110.

[68] *AM Luther Co v James Sagor & Co* [1921] 3 K.B. 532; *Princess Paley Olga v Weisz* [1929] 1 K.B. 718; *Frankfurther v WL Exner Ltd* [1947] Ch. 629; *Novello & Co Ltd v Hinrichsen Edition Ltd* [1951] Ch. 1026.

[69] *Bank voor Handel en Scheepvaart NV v Slatford* [1953] 1 Q.B. 248.

[70] *The Jupiter (No.3)* [1927] P. 122; [1927] P. 250.

[71] In *Iran v Barakat Galleries Ltd* [2009] Q.B. 22, Lord Phillips at [148] opines that where a foreign sovereign state has occasion to claim in England property to which it alleges it has acquired ownership through confiscation or compulsory process, this can be done only where the foreign state had taken the property in question into its possession. In his Lordship's view a different situation arose in the instant proceedings in that Iran did not assert a claim based on compulsory acquisition, but rather put forward a patrimonial claim based upon legislation. Insofar as Lord Phillips took the view that, in the latter circumstances, success in an English claim does not depend on a state having reduced the property in question into its possession, one can detect a departure from the reasoning in *Ortiz*.

limits.[72] The suggestion made in *Anglo-Iranian Oil Co v Jaffrate (The Rose Mary)*,[73] that another requirement of an effective confiscation was that the persons divested of their property must be nationals of the confiscating state, was shortlived, and was disapproved in *Re Helbert Wagg*.[74] Intraterritorial compulsory acquisitions by recognised governments therefore are recognised.

Should a state purport to confiscate property beyond its territorial bounds, there will be a question of interpretation as to the intended extent of the confiscatory order; but even if extraterritorial ambit is intended, it is unlikely to receive effect. In *Lecouturier v Rey*[75] a French confiscation was interpreted by the House of Lords as having been intended to be only of intraterritorial effect. However, in the words of Lord Macnaghten:

> "To me it seems perfectly plain that it must be beyond the power of any foreign Court or any foreign legislature to prevent the monks from availing themselves in England of the benefit of the reputation which the liqueurs of their manufacture have acquired here".

It may be asked whether any inquiry can be made by the forum of the "immoral" quality of intraterritorial confiscation,[76] so as to provide justification for the forum in refusing recognition; or, in the obverse situation, whether a "benevolent" quality of an extraterritorial confiscation should permit recognition thereof.[77] It is thought that each of these submissions is only superficially attractive. There is found in *Oppenheimer v Cattermole*[78] condemnation of Nazi removal of Jewish German citizenship.[79] Morris[80] raises the possibility that if a confiscation be regarded as discriminatory and unfair, there might be some means of circumventing the established conflict rule as to title to property if the confiscated property should find its way to Britain. However, on the

---

[72] *Williams & Humbert Ltd v W&H Trade Marks (Jersey) Ltd* [1986] A.C. 368: in complex circumstances, it was held by the House of Lords that a Spanish compulsory acquisition had in fact been completed within the territorial boundaries of Spain. But see F.A. Mann, "The Effect in England of the Compulsory Acquisition by a Foreign State of the Shares in a Foreign Company", 1987 L.Q.R. 191.

[73] [1953] 1 W.L.R. 246.

[74] [1956] Ch. 323.

[75] [1910] A.C. 262 at 265.

[76] Consider the attempt made by Nourse J. in *Williams & Humbert Ltd*, at first instance, to categorise governmental decrees according to degrees of unacceptability on moral grounds: [1985] 2 All E.R. 208 at 213–215; and see per Sir John Donaldson M.R. in *Settebello Ltd v Banco Totta and Acores* [1985] 1 W.L.R. 1050 at 1056, 1057.

[77] See *Peer International Corp v Termidor Music Publishers Ltd* [2004] Ch. 212; Morris, *Conflict of Laws*, 7th edn, 2009, para.15–051. Contrast the clear decision against extraterritorial effect of a New Zealand statute of reasonable intent in *Att Gen of New Zealand v Ortiz* [1983] 2 All E.R. 93.

[78] [1975] 1 All E.R. 538 HL.

[79] The majority of their Lordships were in agreement with Wolff, *Private International Law*, 2nd edn, 1950, p.129: e.g. *Oppenheimer v Cattermole* [1975] 1 All E.R. 538, per Lord Hodson at 557: "The courts of this country are not in my opinion obliged to shut their eyes to the shocking nature of such legislation as the 1941 decree if and when it falls for consideration." Yet in the circumstances the removal of citizenship was held to be effective; in consequence, in this tax case, the taxpayer was not entitled to tax relief under the relevant double taxation agreement.

[80] Morris, *Conflict of Laws*, 7th edn, 2009, para.15–045. But see *Frankfurther v WL Exner Ltd* [1947] Ch. 629, per Romer J. at 644 (strict territorial approach), and conclusion in Morris, *Conflict of Laws*, 7th edn, 2009, para.15–051.

whole it has to be concluded that there seems to be little support in case authority for this suggestion.[81] The House of Lords in *Williams & Humbert Ltd* took the view that expropriation is a common occurrence and that the forum should be concerned only with the territoriality principle.[82] The position is regulated in the general case by the principle of territoriality, and by the resultant principle found in moveable property that he who takes a good title by the *lex situs* obtains a good title against the world.[83]

It has been established above that extraterritorial purported confiscations will not be viewed by courts in the UK as effective[84]; intraterritorial governmental confiscations will be regarded by courts in the UK as valid. An important difficulty arises in some cases where it is not clear whether the purported confiscation took place extraterritorially or intraterritorially, the most notable example being *Kuwait Airways Corp v Iraqi Airways Co*,[85] which contained human rights arguments, and the facts of which gave rise to concerted opprobrium from the international community.

Kuwait Airways Corp v Iraqi Airways Co illustrates various points: the meaning of intraterritoriality; the application of the rule of intraterritoriality; the appropriate use of public policy to recognise or not intraterritorial confiscations; the appropriate use of public policy to exclude the application of an otherwise applicable foreign law in terms of the choice of law rule in tort; application of the common law choice of law rule of double actionability in tort; application of the choice of law rule in property; and interaction of international private law and public international law. The student of the rules of jurisdiction might also note the lack of close connection between the forum and the circumstances of the alleged tort. The first three of these issues shall be discussed in this chapter, and the remaining issues at relevant points throughout the book.

The case arose out of the circumstances of the 1990 Gulf War. After lengthy **3–05** litigation, including a trial of jurisdictional issues, it came before the House of Lords in the form of an action laid in the English tort of conversion (wrongful interference with the property of another). Iraqi military forces having occupied Kuwait, the Iraqi authorities passed resolutions proclaiming Iraqi

---

[81] However, in the case of Nazi confiscations, the pressure of international opinion seems likely to result in compensation, disbursement and/or restoration of property. The Holocaust (Return of Cultural Objects) Act 2009 confers power on named bodies within the UK such as the Trustees of the British Museum and the Board of Trustees for the National Galleries of Scotland to transfer objects from their collections if the designated advisory panel (the functions of which are to consider claims made in respect of objects, and relating to events occurring during the Nazi era 1933–1945) has recommended the transfer and the panel's recommendation has been approved by the Secretary of State (with the consent of the Scottish Ministers if the object forms part of the collection of a Scottish body). See Carruthers, *The Transfer of Property in the Conflict of Laws*, 2005, Ch.5, on the treatment of cultural property. As to the criminal aspects of illicit trafficking in cultural goods, see, e.g., European Council Conclusions of November 27, 2008 on Preventing and Combating Illicit Trafficking in Cultural Goods.

[82] *Williams & Humbert Ltd* [1986] A.C. 368, per Lord Templeman at 427, 428 and 431. As to human rights infringement and condemnation by the opinion of the international community, see *Kuwait Airways Corp v Iraqi Airways Co (No.6)* [2002] 3 All E.R. 209.

[83] *Cammell v Sewell* (1860) 5 H. & M. 728 (Exchequer Chamber); *Princess Paley Olga v Weisz* [1929] 1 K.B. 718. See Ch.17, below.

[84] *Spain v National Bank of Scotland*, 1939 S.C. 413.

[85] [2002] 3 All E.R. 209. See Crawford and Carruthers, *"Kuwait Airways Corporation v Iraqi Airways Company"*, 2003 (52) I.C.L.Q. 761.

sovereignty over Kuwait, and seized from Kuwait airport and removed to Iraq, a number of commercial aircraft belonging to Kuwait Airways Corp ("KAC"). One month later, the Revolutionary Command Council of Iraq passed Resolution 369 dissolving KAC, and purporting to transfer all of its property, wherever situated, to the Iraqi Airways Co ("IAC"). Early in 1991, KAC began litigation against IAC and the Republic of Iraq, seeking return of the aircraft, or payment of the value, and damages.

The question of fundamental importance at the outset was whether the seizure of the aircraft was to be regarded as *intra territorium* Iraq, in light of Iraq's purported annexation of Kuwait. The purported annexation was universally condemned, and United Nations Security Council resolutions called on Member States to give no recognition, directly or indirectly, to the annexation.

Many conflict confiscation cases arose from turbulent events of the twentieth century, such as the Russian Revolution, the Spanish Civil War, and seizure of property by the Nazi regime. An important strand in the conflict reasoning of any Scots or English forum called upon to adjudicate upon such cases was whether the UK recognised the authority of the government which performed the confiscation in question, or which subsequently ratified the confiscatory actings, as de jure or de facto[86] in control of the territory in question.[87] A summary of twentieth century cases must conclude that the courts in Scotland and England recognised the actings of a governing body subsequently recognised (politically) by the UK Government, and all the private law consequences which flowed from such initial confiscation, without commenting upon the "morality" of the confiscatory event.

On this reasoning, had Kuwait been recognised, sooner or later, as Iraqi territory, then precedent suggests that a Scottish or English court would have recognised the confiscation and its private law consequences.[88] Conversely, the annexation of Kuwait not having been accorded recognition, had the litigation presented as a confiscation one, precedent would have required that the confiscation be refused recognition as an extraterritorial purported seizure. But the litigation presented in tort, and there was little discussion of these important anterior points. On the facts, the House of Lords, by application of the common law rule of double actionability in delict,[89] decided that KAC had not been divested of its property, and therefore had a claim for compensation.

A final point which may be relevant in this area of law is the position with regard to taking suit against a foreign government.[90] Historically, a Scots or

---

[86] As a result of a parliamentary announcement in 1980 the British Government stated that it would no longer give formal recognition to new governments, although it would continue formally to recognise new states where appropriate. Henceforward, the status of a new regime must be inferred from the manner of the British Government's dealings with it, as to which the Foreign and Commonwealth Office will provide information. See Leslie, "The Existence of Governments and the Conflict of Laws", 1997 Jur. Rev. 110, 112.

[87] *Princess Paley Olga v Weisz* [1929] 1 K.B. 718.

[88] Subject to a scintilla of doubt about the proper reaction to "immoral"/evil conduct.

[89] See paras 16–56—16–59, below.

[90] See *Cheshire, North and Fawcett: Private International Law*, 14th edn, 2008, p.491 et seq. See Ch.7, below. The question whether a shipyard was a sufficiently state-owned entity so as to come within the definition of a state for the purposes of the 1978 Act was answered in the negative in *Wilhelm Finance Inc v Ente Administrador del Astillero Rio Santiago* [2009] EWHC 1074 (Comm).

English court could not proceed with an action against a foreign government in cases such as these if the foreign government had been recognised (politically) by the UK government as the de jure or de facto government, and was in peaceful possession of the property in question.[91] The subject of sovereign immunity was placed on a statutory basis following the European Convention on State Immunity (1972), resulting in the passing of the State Immunity Act 1978.

> "The basic principle of the 1978 Act is that a foreign state is immune from the jurisdiction of the English courts and effect is to be given to that immunity whether or not the state appears in the proceedings."[92]

Hence, a state is immune from the jurisdiction of the UK courts, unless it submits to the jurisdiction thereof,[93] but there are certain important exceptions from immunity.[94]

Where the foreign government is the pursuer, no question of immunity from suit arose at common law, or arises under statute.[95] However, in terms of substance, a foreign state or its official representative will not be able to secure from a Scottish or English court an order which gives effect extraterritorially to a foreign governmental act.[96]

PUBLIC POLICY

It is a well-settled principle that UK courts will not apply a foreign rule if its **3–06** terms, or the result which follows from the application thereof, would be contrary to British conceptions of public policy, notwithstanding that the right which is sought to be enforced is enforceable under the *lex causae*. This bar to

---

[91] *Compania Naviera Vascongada v The Cristina* [1938] A.C. 485; *Spain v Owners of the Arantzazu Mendi* [1939] A.C. 256; *The Abodi Mendi* [1939] P. 178; *Zarine v Ramava* [1942] I.R. 148. See Leslie, "The Existence of Governments and the Conflict of Laws", 1997 Jur. Rev. 110, 110.

[92] *Cheshire, North and Fawcett: Private International Law*, 14th edn, 2008, p.494. As to sovereigns and heads of state, in public and private capacities, see *Bank of Credit and Commerce International (Overseas) Ltd (In Liquidation) v Price Waterhouse* [1997] 4 All E.R. 108; *Mbasogo v Logo Ltd (No.1)* [2007] Q.B. 846; and *Korea National Insurance Co v Allianz Global Corporate & Specialty AG* [2008] EWCA Civ 1355.

[93] ss.1–2. See *NML Capital Ltd v Argentina* [2010] EWCA Civ 41.

[94] Thus the following are justiciable: s.3—commercial transactions and contracts to be performed in the UK (see *Alcom v Columbia* [1984] 2 All E.R. 6); s.4—contracts of employment between the state and an individual; s.5—proceedings in respect of personal injury, death or damage to property; s.6—proceedings relating to property in the UK; s.7—proceedings relating to patents and trade marks; s.8—proceedings relating to a state's membership of a body corporate incorporated under the law of the UK; s.9—proceedings relating to agreement to submit to arbitration; s.10—admiralty proceedings; and s.11—state liability for value added tax, customs duty or excise duty. The subject of the extent of immunity, where not expressly excluded by the 1978 Act, arose in *Jones v Saudi Arabia* [2004] EWCA Civ 1394, with regard to the question whether or not an implied exception to immunity exists in the case of alleged torture by a foreign state and its officials.

[95] State Immunity Act 1978 s.2.

[96] See *Att Gen of New Zealand v Ortiz* [1983] 2 All E.R. 93. Cf. *Equatorial Guinea v Royal Bank of Scotland International* [2006] UKPC 7; and *Mbasogo v Logo Ltd (No.1)* [2007] Q.B. 846.

the enforcement of a foreign right may derive from policy enshrined in or capable of being inferred from legislation, or existing at common law:

(a) Legislation

A British Act of Parliament directly or indirectly may render a foreign right void as regards its enforcement in this country[97]; so too may a British act of indemnity or government declaration.[98]

(b) Public policy at common law

Public policy in this sense means British conceptions of morality and justice. In practice, the courts have applied this restraint in the following circumstances[99]:

(1) where the fundamental conceptions of British justice have been disregarded[100];
(2) where British conceptions of morality have been infringed;
(3) where the enforcement of a transaction would prejudice the interests of the United Kingdom or its good relations with foreign powers[101];
(4) where the recognition of a penal[102] condition of status or its incidents would offend British conceptions of human liberty and freedom of action.

It is accepted that the use of public policy in the conflict of laws should be more restricted than in domestic law, its scope narrower. The conflict of laws does not promote conflict, but is concerned with the resolution of disputes in as fair-minded and non-partisan a manner as can be achieved by any given forum. This (even) more restrictive attitude towards public policy in the international private law context is termed "external public policy". There is a particular danger of public policy making mischief and running counter to the aims of the subject. Nevertheless, public policy must exist as a tool or a mechanism, available for use by the forum in any subject area of the conflict of

---

[97] *Phillips v Eyre* (1870–71) L.R. 6 Q.B. 1; *Poll v Lord Advocate* (1899) 1 F. 823.

[98] *Dobree v Napier* (1836) 2 Bing. N.C. 781; *Buron v Denman* (1848) 2 Ex. 167; *Carr v Fracis Times & Co* [1902] A.C. 176; *Nissan v Att Gen* [1967] 3 W.L.R. 1044.

[99] See P.B. Carter, "The Role of Public Policy in English Private International Law", 1993 (42) I.C.L.Q. 1; and Robert Leslie, "The Relevance of Public Policy in Legal Issues Involving Other Countries and Their Laws", 1995 Jur. Rev. 477.

[100] *Re Hope* (1857) 8 De G.M. & G. 731 (collusive divorce); contrast *Crowe v Crowe* [1937] 2 All E.R. 723; *Grell v Levy* (1864) 16 C.B. (N.S.) 73 (*pactum de quota litis*); *Kaufman v Gerson* [1904] 1 K.B. 591 (*pactum illicitum*, unenforceable in England, even if acceptable by its French proper law); *Roussillon v Roussillon* (1880) L.R. 14 Ch.D. 51. Contrast *Addison v Brown* [1954] 1 W.L.R. 779. See more recently *Mohamed v Alaga & Co* [1998] 2 All E.R. 720 (domestic case with foreign aspects).

[101] *Foster v Driscoll* [1929] 1 K.B. 470; *Regazzione v KC Sethia (1944) Ltd* [1958] A.C. 301 (refusal of English court to allow the normal contractual remedies where the terms of the contract, to the knowledge of both parties, contravened Indian legislation prohibiting export of jute to South Africa); *Re Emery's Investment Trusts* [1959] Ch. 410.

[102] In this sense, "penal" should be taken to mean (excessively) punitive, unfair or discriminatory. Examples arise in relation to prohibitions on marriage out of religion or out of caste: *Chetti v Chetti* [1909] P. 67; *MacDougall v Chitnavis*, 1937 S.C. 390. See para.11–19, below.

laws, in order that the forum may avoid a result which, though identified as the "correct" result by its appropriate conflict rule, is nevertheless fundamentally unacceptable. One question which arose from the case of *Kuwait Airways Corp v Iraqi Airways Co*[103] was whether it was justifiable for the forum to ignore part of the *lex loci delicti*.[104] The dissenting speech of Lord Scott proceeded on the basis that the forum must accept and apply the whole content of the *lex loci delicti* as it stood in the eyes of Iraqi law, but the majority held that the Iraqi Resolution 369[105] constituted a fundamental breach of international law, this view strengthened by background circumstances of public international law as expressed in condemnatory UN Security Council resolutions. In this way, the Resolution could be excised and a thereby modified *lex loci delicti* applied.

In this matter of policy objection, we should remember that the domestic policy of the forum upon a certain matter may change from time to time, e.g. in relation to contingent fees, perhaps, or recognition of same-sex relationships, or gaming contracts,[106] and further that the forum must strive so far as possible, temporal issues aside, to be consistent within and across subject areas.[107] However, in conflict cases, the ranking of policies may vary according to context and period of history.[108] The right of any forum to act in the light of its own conscience is an essential part of its conflict rules, and the availability of exercise of such discretion by the forum serves to secure participation by contracting states in international co-operative projects, since the international instruments to date invariably contain a public policy discretion. Normally this discretion may be used only where the rule in question is "manifestly contrary to public policy"; while this phrase has become formulaic, it is undeniable that it contains a warning against over-use. Since its exercise is a manifestation of individual state discretion, attempts to formulate a fixed, predetermined, regionally-harmonised view on a matter sub nom. public policy are inappropriate and paradoxical.[109]

---

[103] *Kuwait Airways Corp v Iraqi Airways Co (No.6)* [2002] 3 All E.R. 209.

[104] See Carruthers and Crawford, "*Kuwait Airways Corporation v Iraqi Airways Company*", 2003 (52) I.C.L.Q. 761, 770.

[105] See para.3–05, above.

[106] *Ferguson v Littlewoods Pools Ltd*, 1997 S.L.T. 309. See now Gambling Act 2005 s.335.

[107] It can be shown that consistency is not always achieved: 100 years after refusing to recognise the status of slaves (*Sommerset v Stewart* (1772) 20 St. Tr. 1; *Knight v Wedderburn* (1778) Mor. 14545), the English courts enforced a contract for the sale of slaves, because the contract was valid by its Brazilian proper law (*Santos v Illidge* (1860) 8 C.B. (N.S.) 861). See also *Corbett v Corbett* [1957] 1 All E.R. 621 in the matter of foreign prohibition of marriage between Jew and Gentile.

[108] See Carruthers and Crawford, "*Kuwait Airways Corporation v Iraqi Airways Company*", 2003 (52) I.C.L.Q. 761, 768, fn.57.

[109] In the drafting of Rome II, negotiation took place on the insertion of a "Community public policy" provision; the provision was dropped from the final Regulation, but a hint of the approach can be seen in recital (32). See Elizabeth B. Crawford and Janeen M. Carruthers, "Variations on a theme of Rome II. Reflections on proposed choice of law rules for non-contractual obligations: Part 1" (2005) 9(1) Edin. L.R. 65. The harmonisation exercise of the European regime may require the suppression of the normally available freedom to refuse to recognise a judgment on the ground of differing substantive law (Brussels II *bis* art.25) and therefore represents a further incursion into independent judgment.

It is possible to employ flexibility. The court in Scotland might accept a foreign status without being obliged to accept all its incidents, or to recognise a foreign divorce without accepting all the terms imposed by the foreign court.[110]

The effect of a successful plea to public policy in any given forum is normally negative, that is to say, it operates to exclude application of the rule of the otherwise applicable *lex causae*, and thereby to revert to the default position of application of the *lex fori*. But a positive use also can be envisaged, that is, where the public policy of the forum insists upon application of the domestic *lex fori*, overriding the otherwise applicable foreign law in order to supply a remedy or fill a gap. There is a further consideration, concerning the effect of the forum's public policy upon the extent to which it might, contrary to what has been explained above, permit the operation in its territory of a "public law" of a foreign sovereign state. Until very recently, the term "other public law" of a foreign state has been used as a protective residual category of exception to the vested rights theory, in order to justify the forum's non-application of a law which it found difficult to characterise as penal, revenue or confiscatory, but which could be regarded as ejusdem generis, the genus being laws which purport to exercise sovereign authority beyond the territory of the enacting state. It was in this sense that Lord Denning used the term in *Ortiz* in the Court of Appeal.[111] However, in *Iran v Barakat Galleries Ltd*,[112] in which there is a review of the exclusion of operation of foreign law in British courts, Lord Phillips examines the "other public law" exception in order to ascertain whether or not a court in the UK is bound to find that there is a rule which prevents the enforcement in the UK of all foreign sovereign rights.[113] His Lordship favours an interpretation which permits the enforcement of foreign sovereign rights where the state owns property in the same way as a private citizen, and so may be said to be exercising property rights akin to those of such a person and acting effectively in a "private" capacity. If the matter can be viewed in this light, the conclusion may be that it is a matter of positive policy for a UK court to uphold the right, rather than the more neutral position that there is no reason not to do so. Indeed Lord Phillips considered that it would certainly be contrary to public policy for such a quasi-private claim to be excluded. This important amplification of UK public policy as exercised by the courts takes place against a backdrop of growing international acceptance of the desirability of preserving cultural heritage and, arguably, may be particular to that area.

The presence and use of public policy will be discussed in context throughout this work.

---

[110] e.g. *Wood v Wood* [1957] P. 254.

[111] *Att Gen of New Zealand v Ortiz* [1982] 3 W.L.R. 570, per Lord Denning M.R. at 585. Contrast Ackner and O'Connor L.JJ., in whose view the provision was categorised as penal, the former doubting the existence of the residual category. For background, see *Iran v Barakat Galleries Ltd* [2009] Q.B. 22, per Lord Phillips at [112] et seq. This line of reasoning was used by the High Court of Australia in *AG(UK) v Heinemann Publishers Australia Pty Ltd (No.2)* (1988) 165 C.L.R. 30 to block enforcement in Australia of obligations owed to the UK Government, this principle rendering unenforceable actions to enforce the governmental interests of a foreign state. See also *Equatorial Guinea v Royal Bank of Scotland International* [2006] UKPC 7; and *Mbasogo v Logo Ltd (No.1)* [2007] Q.B. 846.

[112] [2009] Q.B. 22.

[113] *Iran v Barakat Galleries Ltd* [2009] Q.B. 22 at [125] et seq.

THE OPERATION OF STATUTE LAW AND THE CONFLICT OF LAWS: AMBIT OF STATUTES

Both British[114] and foreign statutes are presumed to have a strictly limited **3–07** territorial effect so that in general they apply respectively only to persons and property in British or foreign territory.[115] In many conflict cases it will be found that the answer to a problem depends upon the scope of a statute[116] and that the real question is one of interpretation as to whether or not a particular statute is intended to apply, e.g. only to persons domiciled or resident in a particular country, or to contracts made or to be performed in, or to actings which took place in, some particular country.[117] In order to resolve a cross-border instance, a question of statutory interpretation may arise of a statute which Parliament did not consciously enact as a conflict of laws provision[118]; the problem is one of extent of operation as established when necessary by judicial interpretation. Traditionally, the UK Parliament passed Acts with intended extraterritorial operation only in relation to nationality, status and capacity,[119] and exchange control,[120] but it is notable that many incursions have been made into the principle of intraterritoriality of Scottish or English statutes pertaining to criminal law.[121] British courts apply equivalent principles to the operation of foreign statutes[122]: it is probable that a foreign statute dealing with a matter of nationality, status and capacity, or exchange control

---

[114] *Tomalin v S Pearson and Son Ltd* [1909] 2 K.B. 61; *Yorke v British & Continental Steamship Co Ltd* (1945) 78 Ll. L. Rep. 181 (Digest 144). It may happen, however, that foreigners may be entitled to benefits under British statutory provisions—*Davidsson v Hill* [1901] 2 K.B. 606; *Krzus v Crow's Nest Pass Coal Co Ltd* [1912] A.C. 590; *Cox v Owners of the Esso Malaysia (The Esso Malaysia)* [1974] 3 W.L.R. 341.

[115] Contrast the situation in which British forces occupy foreign territory in order to maintain security: *R. (on the application of Al-Skeini) v Secretary of State for Defence* [2008] 1 A.C. 153.

[116] Statutes imposing licensing requirements are particularly likely to be intraterritorial. *Dublin Finance Corp v Rowe* [1943] N.I. 1; *Goetschuis v Brightman*, 245 N.Y. 186, 156 N.E. 660 (1927). And see *Dulaney v Merry & Son* [1901] 1 Q.B. 536.

[117] Consider, e.g., the scope of the Age of Legal Capacity (Scotland) Act 1991; see David I. Nichols, "Can They or Can't They? Children and the Age of Legal Capacity (Scotland) Act 1991", 1991 S.L.T. (News) 395. As to the territorial scope of UK employment law, see conjoined House of Lords decision *Serco Ltd v Lawson* [2006] UKHL 3; *Masri v Consolidated Contractors International (UK) (No.4)* [2009] UKHL 43; and *Ravat v Halliburton Manufacturing & Services Ltd* [2010] CSIH 52.

[118] *Fox v Lawson* [1974] A.C. 803; *Cox v Army Council* [1963] A.C. 48; and *Duncan v Motherwell Bridge Engineering Co Ltd*, 1952 S.L.T. 433. See also *R. v Atakpu* [1993] 4 All E.R. 215; *Re Seagull Manufacturing Co Ltd (In Liquidation)* [1993] 2 All E.R. 980; *Re Paramount Airways Ltd (No.2)* [1992] 3 All E.R. 1. Further, *Lawson v Serco Ltd* [2006] 1 All E.R. 823; *Diggins v Condor Marine Crewing Services Ltd* [2009] I.C.R. 609; *Tradition Securities and Futures SA v X* [2009] I.C.R. 88; and *Dolphin Drilling Personnel PTE Ltd v Alan Winks and Dolphin Drilling Ltd* [2009] EATS/0049/08/BI. As to territorial extent of Human Rights Act 1998 as it applies to British military personnel serving abroad, see *R. (on the application of Smith) v Oxfordshire Assistant Deputy Coroner* [2010] UKSC 29.

[119] e.g. *Sussex Peerage Case* (1884) 11 Cl. & F. 85; and *Pugh v Pugh* [1951] P. 482.

[120] *Boissevain v Weil* [1950] A.C. 327.

[121] In respect of which see Elizabeth B. Crawford, *International Private Law*, 1st edn (Edinburgh: W. Green / Sweet & Maxwell, 1998), Ch.20.

[122] *Bank voor Handel en Scheepvaart NV v Slatford (No.2)* [1953] 1 Q.B. 248: a decree of the Dutch government in wartime exile in England was not capable, in the view of the English court of the *lex fori* and *lex situs*, of affecting gold physically in England. Contrast *Lorentzen v Lydden & Co Ltd* [1942] 2 K.B. 202, now discredited. See also *F&K Jabbour v Custodian of Israeli Absentee Property* [1954] 1 W.L.R. 139.

would receive extraterritorial effect in Scotland,[123] subject to the forum's public policy.

It is important to appreciate that the corpus of Scots and English conflict rules, specifically so designated, now is largely statutory. These statutes may be entirely "conflict" law,[124] or may be general statutes, containing particular provisions of conflict of laws implication, which intentionally[125] (or possibly inadvertently)[126] adhere to or cut across pre-existing conflict rules or reasoning.

The final point to make at this juncture is that as a matter of technical or orthodox conflict reasoning in a Scots or English forum, any rule, common law or statutory, of the applicable law (*lex causae*) must apply, if it is substantive in nature and in its terms does not offend the policy of the forum. A more complex point is that modern conflict of laws instruments employ as a drafting device the concept of "mandatory rules".[127] Since the forum must give effect to these mandatory provisions of its own law or of a third law,[128] the result is that rules, usually statutory, of legal systems over and above the *lex causae*, sometimes must be applied by the forum. Hence, by reason of conflict of laws methodology, a Scots or English forum in a suitable case, potentially in any branch of law, may be required to give effect to a foreign statutory provision.

THE OPERATION OF ECHR AND THE CONFLICT OF LAWS

3–08 In conflict cases, as in all other cases, arising before UK courts, the implications of the European Convention on Human Rights (ECHR) are potentially relevant as a result of the incorporation of the Convention into the law of the UK by the Human Rights Act 1998. The effect of s.6(1) of the 1998 Act is that courts must not act in a manner which is incompatible with Convention rights, and must take into account relevant jurisprudence of the European Court of Human Rights. To date within the conflict of laws ECHR concerns have manifested themselves principally in questions of access to court, that is, in the area of jurisdiction and judgments,[129] although instances have arisen also in family law (e.g. in the matters of same-sex "marriage"[130] and international child abduction[131]) and in relation to the protection of property.[132] Specifically,

---

[123] cf. *Starkowski v Att Gen* [1954] A.C. 155; and *Re Claim by Helbert Wagg & Co Ltd* [1956] Ch. 323.

[124] e.g. Matrimonial and Family Proceedings Act 1984; Family Law Act 1986; Contracts (Applicable Law) Act 1990; Private International Law (Miscellaneous Provisions) Act 1995.

[125] Unfair Contract Terms Act 1977 (*Trident Turboprop (Dublin) Ltd v First Flight Couriers Ltd* [2009] EWCA Civ 290); Family Law (Scotland) Act 2006.

[126] Timeshare Act 1992.

[127] These are specific rules, as opposed to general policy attitudes, the application of which the parties may not by their own agreement avoid. See further Ch.15, below.

[128] See Ch.15, below.

[129] J. Fawcett, "The Impact of Article 6(1) of the ECHR on Private Intenational Law" (2007) 56 I.C.L.Q. 1; and Gavin Ward, "Protection of the Right to a Fair Trial and Civil Jurisdiction: the Institutional Legitimacy in Permitting Delay" 2008 Jur. Rev. 15.

[130] *Wilkinson v Kitzinger* [2006] EWHC 2022 (Fam).

[131] e.g. *Sylvester v Austria* [2003] 2 F.L.R. 210; *Monory v Romania* (2005) 41 E.H.R.R. 37; and *Maire v Portugal* [2004] 2 F.L.R. 653, (2006) 43 E.H.R.R. 13.

[132] *Orams v Apostolides* [2006] EWHC 2226 (QB) (and see also *Apostolides v Orams* (C-420/07) [2010] 1 All E.R. (Comm) 950 and 992).

questions have arisen in relation to the operation of the Brussels regime of *jurisdiction* and judgment enforcement,[133] in the light of art.6 of the ECHR which confers the right to a fair and public hearing within a reasonable time by an independent and impartial tribunal established by law. The priority of process system of jurisdiction allocation within the Brussels regime (*lis pendens*)[134] secures for the court first seised the unassailable right to decide upon its own competence; until this decision is made any other interested court must stay its proceedings. The ECJ so far has not been receptive to the argument that lengthy delays in the court first seised amount to a breach of the art.6 rights of the litigants.[135] Notably, negotiations were begun in 2010 to permit the EU to accede to the ECHR.

SUMMARY 3

A foreign right validly acquired under its proper/applicable law (that is, by the law which in the view of a Scottish forum is the *lex causae*) will be enforceable in Scotland provided that the form of procedure available under Scots law is not inappropriate to the enforcement of the right, and the right does not fall within any of the areas where the operation of foreign law is excluded. **3–09**

---

[133] *Marie Brizzard et Roger International SA v William Grant & Sons Ltd (No.2)*, 2002 S.L.T. 1365; *Maronier v Larmer* [2003] Q.B. 620; and *Krombach v Bamberski* [2001] Q.B. 709.
[134] See Ch.7, below.
[135] *Erich Gasser GmbH v MISAT Srl* (C-116/02) [2005] Q.B. 1.

CHAPTER 4

METHOD

THE STAGES IN A CONFLICT CASE

4–01

(1) *Jurisdiction* over both the subject matter and the defender is always determined by the *lex fori*, in accordance with the rules applicable in any given situation (in many civil and commercial cases as directed by Regulation 44/2001).[1]

(2) The *form of action* is decided by the *lex fori*.

(3) *Characterisation* of the issue is also decided by the *lex fori*.[2]

(4) The *choice of law rule* is indicated by the *lex fori* after characterisation of the nature of the point at issue has been determined as in (3) above. It may be that the question has several strands, each of which properly may be referred by the forum, in the exercise of its conflict rules, to a different law. This is termed dépeçage or, by the Americans, "picking and choosing"—an "issue by issue", segregated approach.[3]

(5) The *connecting factor* or point of contact is indicated by the choice of law rule. The connecting factor is a legal concept or localising agent, such as domicile, habitual residence, *locus celebrationis*, or situation of property, upon which a choice of law rule is based. It is the link between an event or transaction or person, on the one hand, and a legal system, on the other. The connecting factor is determined by the *lex fori* with two exceptions:

(a) the nature of property as moveable or immoveable is always decided by the *lex situs*[4];

(b) nationality (except in time of war) is always decided by the law of the country the nationality of which is in question.[5]

(6) *Procedure*. Foreign rules of a purely procedural nature are not applicable in a Scots forum and so must be identified and excluded. The possibly applicable laws therefore are classified by the forum as

---

[1] See Ch.7, below.

[2] At least in practice. For doubts and theories, see below.

[3] See the Canadian case of *Reed v Reed* (1969) 6 D.L.R. (3d.) 617 in which legal capacity to marry (consanguinity) was referred only to the British Columbian ante-nuptial domiciles, and the requirement of parental consent only to the Washington State *lex loci celebrationis*, thereby producing, as it happened, the positive result of a valid marriage. Dépeçage is seen most clearly in the context of choice of law rules concerning the law of obligations, and its application will be discussed in Chs 15 and 16, below.

[4] *Macdonald v Macdonald*, 1932 S.C. (H.L.) 79.

[5] *Oppenheimer v Cattermole* [1973] Ch. 264, reversed [1975] 2 W.L.R. 347; [1975] 1 All E.R. 538 HL.

pertaining to procedure or substance: foreign rules of procedure are denied effect and domestic rules applied.[6]

(7) *Substance*. The existence and extent of the rights of the parties are determined in accordance with the *lex causae*, by applying the substantive law indicated by the forum's choice of law rule. Strictly, the function of the conflict lawyer is complete when he or she has answered the question of which law applies. If the *lex causae* happens to be the law of the forum, the outcome will be determined by the forum's domestic law on the point; if the *lex causae* is a foreign law, the onus lies upon the interested party to aver and prove foreign law to the satisfaction of the Scots court.

(8) *Proof of foreign law*.[7] Foreign law is a question of fact in a British court and therefore it must be proved by the party seeking to rely on it.[8] There is a presumption[9] in Scots and English law that the law of a foreign country is the same as the *lex fori* and the onus is on a person who maintains otherwise to aver the foreign law and to prove it.[10] If no evidence is led of foreign law, the court is entitled to proceed on the basis that it is the same as its own law. This rule has fundamental implications for the conduct of litigation, and arguably stunts the development of UK conflict rules, for it means that a case will proceed as a purely domestic case if neither litigant offers to plead and prove foreign law. By inadvertence, negligence or complicity between the adversaries, the conflict dimension of a case may be lost. While Scots judges have judicial knowledge of Scots law, including its conflict rules, a judge cannot of his own initiative order proof of the content of foreign law. Hence although the court will apply the appropriate conflict rule (even if the parties fail to plead it), in the absence of proof of foreign law, operation of the conflict rule effectively will be frustrated. However even where the foreign law is "proved", it should not be supposed that a forum proceeds always on an accurate understanding or application of its content. If it is not "proved", there are recent indications that the result that the forum will apply the domestic law on the point may be displaced by the dismissal of the claim or the defence which has been advanced but not proved.[11]

---

[6] *Re Wilks* [1935] 1 Ch. 645; *Re Goenaga* [1949] P. 367.

[7] See, for detail, Ch.8, below.

[8] See Richard Fentiman, *Foreign Law in English Courts: pleading, proof and choice of law* (Oxford: Oxford University Press, 1998), which begins: "How foreign law is pleaded and proved is the crux of the conflict of laws".

[9] But see Adrian Briggs, *The Conflict of Laws* (Oxford: Oxford University Press, 2008), p.6.

[10] *De Reneville v De Reneville* [1948] P. 100. See also *Pryde v Proctor & Gamble Ltd*, 1971 S.L.T. (Notes) 18; *Bonnor v Balfour Kilpatrick Ltd*, 1975 S.L.T. (Notes) 3; *Faulkner (Michael Stanislaus) v Hill*, 1942 J.C. 20; *Scottish National Orchestra Society Ltd v Thomson's Executor*, 1969 S.L.T. 325; *Armour v Thyssen Edelstahlwerke AG*, 1989 S.L.T. 182; 1990 S.L.T. 891 HL; *Rodden v Whatlings Ltd*, 1960 S.L.T. (Notes) 96; and *Kraus's Administrators v Sullivan*, 1998 S.L.T. 963.

[11] See *Global Multimedia International Ltd v ARA Media Services* [2006] EWHC 3107 (Ch), per Sir Andrew Morritt C. at [38]: following the view expressed in Dicey and Morris, *The Conflict of Laws*, 13th edn, 2000, that it is inaccurate to refer to a presumption of identity of content of foreign law with English law, his Lordship continued: "The true proposition, I believe, is that as foreign law is in most cases a question of fact to be proved by evidence, in the absence of such evidence the court has no option but to apply English law. But if the facts alleged demonstrate that, for example, the proper law of a contract is not the law of England then as the law

The UK approach to proof of foreign law may be described as occupying one end of a spectrum[12] of judicial approaches to the matter. At the opposite end, under the maxim *jura novit curia*,[13] the judge of his own accord must seek to be informed on the content of any foreign law which seems to him to be relevant. There are signs that as part of the EU private international law harmonisation project, and in order to ensure compliance by Member States with harmonised provisions which are intended to be mandatory,[14] the European legislators may require from Member States a uniform approach to proof of foreign law, at least in specific subject areas.[15]

CHARACTERISATION

4–02 The problem or method (or method, with problems) of characterisation, or classification, is as old as law itself. It is the natural inclination of the lawyer to categorise a legal problem. In domestic law, the matter must be placed under a particular *nomen juris*, or more than one. Of course, the issue may cross juridical boundaries, and the problem as a whole will be likely to do so. For example, in domestic law a grievance may find its legal basis in contract or delict or both (travel accident), or in property and contract (loss of or mistaken re-sale of property entrusted for repair), or matrimonial law and succession (testamentary provisions rendered inoperative through occurrence of subsequent marriage by testator).[16] In domestic cases, advice will be offered to the potential litigant whether to sue, for example, in contract or delict (assuming both bases of action are available) based upon perceived financial or tactical advantage, e.g. a head of damage may be available in delict but not in contract.

The characterisation exercise in the conflict of laws has a much deeper significance than in domestic law. In the first place, the rules of jurisdiction of the proposed forum must be satisfied, and these will vary in content according to the nature of the action, as personal or commercial, and within the many subdivisions of the latter, as, for example, pertaining to contract, delict or property.

When the forum is seised of jurisdiction, it must decide upon its characterisation of the problem, for upon that characterisation will depend the choice of

---

of England includes the principles of private international law those principles may demonstrate that some other system of law is applicable to the claim and if the relevant principles of that system of law are not sufficiently proved the claim may fail for that reason."

[12] See Trevor C. Hartley, "Pleading and Proof of Foreign Law: the Major European Systems Compared", 1996 45 I.C.L.Q. 271.

[13] While the principle in all relevant legal systems may be that the court in the person of the judge(s) has knowledge of the law (domestic and conflict), the question is whether or not the court is empowered, entitled, or indeed obliged to ascertain the content of the law which, under its own conflict rules, it is enjoined to apply.

[14] e.g. Rome I Regulation Ch.II; and Rome II, Ch.II. In the formulation of harmonised applicable law rules in any given instrument, typically the draftsmen employ the directive "shall be" [governed].

[15] e.g. the EC Commission is bound under art.30(1) of the Rome II Regulation to produce not later than August 20, 2011 a study on the manner of treatment of proof of foreign law in the Member States and the extent to which Member State courts apply foreign law in terms of that instrument.

[16] By English domestic law, though not by Scots domestic law, later marriage revokes earlier will unless the will was made in contemplation of the later marriage. See Ch.18, below.

law rule to be applied, upon which, in turn, will depend availability (in principle) of remedy, and all further substantive matters concerning constitution of the claim, defences and heads of damage. As observed above, one of the most important demarcations which the forum must draw is between that which is substantive and that which is procedural.[17]

Traditionally—though less so in the era of harmonisation and Europeanisation—the choice of law rule is likely to differ from forum to forum, a fact which brings to its proper prominence the importance of the identity of the forum. Moreover, even if the conflict rule of different legal systems should appear to be the same, the characterisation of issues adopted by different courts in the interpretation and application of the rule may differ. There may be wide agreement that in respect of marriage, matters of formal validity must be referred to the *lex loci celebrationis*, and matters of capacity, essentials, or substance are governed by the personal law—but is there any reason to suppose that these courts will assign a particular problem, such as lack of parental consent, to the same legal category?[18] How many courts would characterise the matter as relating to form, and how many as relating to essence? It might be argued that the only view which matters is that of the legal system in which the case is litigated, given that decree enforcement internationally is now well regulated, but in matters of family law, there are further aspects to be considered: not only nowadays is more than one court likely to be competent (leading to potential conflicts as to jurisdiction), but the outcome, if competent courts should disagree on the choice of law rule to be applied and/or upon characterisation of issues within that choice, is likely to be limping status.

If competent courts should agree that a matter is governed by an individual's personal law, will they agree upon the identity of that law? Nationality, domicile, and habitual residence each may be contenders. If courts should agree upon the application of habitual residence, will their rules for determining habitual residence, and the application thereof, be identical? Where the connecting factor is ostensibly the same, differences in interpretation thereof may give rise to what are known as "latent conflicts".[19] If, on the other hand, the choice of law rules, or the connecting factors ex facie be different, the conflict is more clearly seen and therefore is said to be "patent".

It becomes apparent that the hopes of success of litigants will vary according to forum, and that in a conflict case the problem of classification is more acute, and the importance and complexity of the task is much greater than in a domestic case. The importance of the characterisation exercise in traditional conflict methodology cannot be overstated.

In Scots and English courts, the characterisation exercise in practice is performed by the forum in accordance with its own law, but taking an "international" or "enlightened" view.[20] Very few inroads upon this practice have

---

[17] See, e.g, Chs.8 and para.16–44, below.

[18] *Bliersbach v McEwen*, 1959 S.L.T. 81 at 85: after careful consideration, a Dutch rule requiring parental consent to marriage of a Dutch subject under 21 years was categorised by a Scots court as a (mere) prohibitive rather than an irritant (fundamental) impediment (in the canon law terminology).

[19] *Re Annesley* [1926] Ch. 692.

[20] cf. *Re Bonacina* [1912] 2 Ch. 394; Private International Law (Miscellaneous Provisions) Act 1995 s.9(2).

been made,[21] but in terms of theory, there are other views on the proper solution of the characterisation problem.[22] The literature on the subject is immense.[23]

<h2 style="text-align:center">WHAT IS CHARACTERISED?</h2>

4–03 Additionally, one must ask what it is that the forum must characterise: facts, issues, and/or rules of law? Generally, one might say that it is the facts which lead the court to the categorisation of the issue. In complex cases,[24] judges may disagree about the issue(s) presenting, and may look behind the form in which the case is pleaded to ascertain the true character of the problem(s). Possibly the most helpful explanation is that there are different stages in the conflict of law process, and it seems that what the forum must characterise varies according to the stage it has reached. In the initial question of jurisdiction, the putative forum may be required to make a provisional characterisation.[25] Thereafter, with regard to choice of law, the forum must allocate the question raised by the factual situation to what it deems to be the correct legal category,[26] and later in the process, one might say that the subject of identification of a choice of law rule is a legal question arising from a factual situation and that the focus of characterisation is a legal matter, being the determination of the question to which the rule of law relates. The relationship of fact and law in this exercise is interdependent.

Wolff noted that, "each general conception has a firm and stable nucleus but an indistinct periphery, and it would be practically impossible for any legislator or court to establish a rigid and precise delimitation."[27] In more recent years, Mance L.J. has called for a "more nuanced analysis":

---

[21] Though see Family Law Act 1986 s.46(5). See also Prescription and Limitation (Scotland) Act 1973, as amended, and Foreign Limitation Periods Act 1984, directing a Scots or English court, subject to public policy, to apply the limitation period prescribed by the *lex causae*, without reference to the characterisation of the foreign rule, as substantive or procedural, by the *lex causae* or by the *lex fori*. See also, exceptionally, characterisation by the *lex situs* of the nature of property, and by the putative *lex patria* of the meaning of nationality.

[22] Most prominently the *lex causae* theory, as upheld by Wolff, *Private International Law*, 2nd edn, 1950, at pp.154–156, that characterisation be performed according to the applicable law, though this has an obvious difficulty of circularity of reasoning. For an example of characterisation by the *lex causae*, see *Maldonado* [1954] P. 223. A refinement on the forum-centred approach was urged by Robertson, to the effect that the court must initially characterise according to its own law (primary characterisation), but having been led by its own choice of law rule to the foreign law which it considers relevant, it must thereafter adopt the classification by the foreign law (secondary characterisation) (Arthur H. Robertson, *Characterization in the Conflict of Laws* (Cambridge, Massachusetts, Harvard University Press, 1940)).

[23] A distinguished sample comprises Robertson, *Characterization in the Conflict of Laws*, 1940; Falconbridge, *Selected Essays on the Conflict of Laws*, 2nd edn (Toronto: Canada Law Book Company, 1954), Chs 3–5; and Lederman, "Classification in Private International Law", 29 Can. Bar Rev. 3.

[24] e.g. *Macmillan Inc v Bishopsgate Investment Trust plc (No.3)* [1996] 1 All E.R. 585, per Staughton L.J. at 589, endorsed by Mance L.J. in *Raiffeisen Zentralbank Osterreich AG v Five Star General Trading LLC (The Mount I)* [2001] I Lloyd's Rep. 597; *Atlantic Telecom GmbH, Noter*, 2004 S.L.T. 1031, per Lord Brodie at 1041.

[25] See Elizabeth B. Crawford, "The Uses of Putativity and Negativity in the Conflict of Laws", 2005 54 I.C.L.Q. 829. Also *Burke v Uvex Sports GmbH* [2005] I.L.Pr. 26.

[26] *Cheshire, North and Fawcett: Private International Law*, 14th edn, 2008, term this "classification of the cause of action" (p.42).

[27] Wolff, *Private International Law*, 2nd edn, 1950, p.150.

". . . the overall aim is to identify the most appropriate law to govern a particular issue. The classes or categories of issue which the law recognises . . . are man-made, not natural. They have no inherent value, beyond their purpose in assisting to select the most appropriate law."[28]

The characterisation task must be undertaken with perceptiveness, and a sensitivity to the goal of the choice of law process, which is to identify and apply to the problem the appropriate law in the view of the forum.

FALSE CONFLICTS

The conflict lawyer should be alert to the presence of "false conflicts" that is, **4–04** to note that there is only a conflict problem if there is a conflict, and that there is no conflict if there would be a coincidence of outcome, no matter which of the potentially applicable laws were applied. Three examples can be provided.

First, there is a false conflict if the result of application of different connecting factors, e.g. domicile and habitual residence, by the different choice of law rules of different legal systems would be to apply the *same* law. This is the opposite of the latent conflict outlined above; it is rather latent harmony.

Secondly, there is a false conflict where, of two contending legal systems, only one has an "interest" in the application of its own law in the particular case. If the outcome were that neither law was applied, both would be frustrated, for the two laws have a common interest that one of the laws be applied. An example of the second type of false conflict is as follows: if, by the law of country A, the loan of a car in A were to impose on the owner liability for negligent driving by the borrower, but only if the negligent driving occurred within country A, and if the borrower drove the car negligently in country B, which imposed the same liability as did A but only if the contract of loan had been made in country B.[29] If by the process of conflict reasoning neither A law nor B law would apply, arguably the purpose of both would be frustrated, for both appear to adhere in principle to the imposition of liability on the car owner.

A third example of false conflict results from the interaction of certain sets of rules, choice of law and/or domestic: e.g., where, by the Arcadian *locus delicti* there is inter-spousal immunity in tort, but by the Utopian *lex fori* there is a policy objection to such immunity, and where by Utopian law parties involved in a road accident in Arcadia are husband and wife, but by Arcadian law they are not deemed to be validly married. There is no reason by either law why the woman, injured through the negligent driving of the man, should not sue him for damages in Utopia or in Arcadia. A similar situation arises where the principal point at issue is whether a will has been revoked by a subsequent marriage[30]: the same concatenation of circumstances is present if by the *lex causae* (the *lex successionis*, being the law which contains the revocation rule) the marriage is invalid, but by the *lex fori* (which has no such revocation rule) the marriage is valid. The forum should note the coincidence of outcome despite the different paths of reasoning, and heed should be paid to what lies

---

[28] *Raiffeisen Zentralbank Osterreich AG v Five Star General Trading LLC (The Mount I)* [2001] I Lloyd's Rep. 597 at [27], [28].
[29] This example is taken from Morris, *Conflict of Laws*, 4th edn, 1993, p.422.
[30] cf. *Re Swan's Will* (1871) 2 V.L.R. (I.E.&M.) 47.

in common rather than to what divides. While these circumstances otherwise might have given rise to an "Incidental Question" (*q.v.*), the identity of result is justification for aborting that question.

MANIPULATIVE CHARACTERISATION

4–05 Where a conflict rule is inflexible (by pointing to a "hard" single-contact connecting factor, such as nationality) and is viewed by the forum as unsatisfactory, the forum may chafe under its restrictions and may be tempted to reclassify the problem, by taking it out of its natural category and placing it in another category, thereby delivering a different and more palatable result. This is termed "manipulative characterisation". It may be argued, for example, that a rule presented as delictual in its legal system of origin, which prohibits litigation between spouses, is overlaid with a family law purpose; and further, that it might be reasonable to argue that it was not intended to apply to a married couple passing through the enacting legal system, who are strangers to that legal system.[31] If a wife should choose to sue her husband for damages arising out of his culpable lack of care in a forum which has a choice of law rule in delict of strict application of the *lex loci delicti*, re-characterisation by the forum of the inter-spousal immunity rule of the *locus delicti* as one pertaining to family law and not to delict, may permit circumvention by the claimant of the prohibition.

To summarise:

(a) Different legal systems may classify the same set of facts, or the same issue arising therefrom, in different ways, e.g. breach of promise of marriage.[32]

(b) Different legal systems may attach different meanings to the same legal terms, e.g. domicile, or habitual residence.[33] It is not to be thought that one meaning is correct and another wrong; rather the forum must ascertain which definition ought to apply in a given case. This is the problem of "latent conflict".

---

[31] This is the type of factual scenario against which American conflict theorists tested their policy evaluation theories (see Ch.3, above). A traditional solution in such a case may arise not through identification of a false conflict but in a threshold "disapplication" of the *lex loci delicti* as applicable law in tort (cf. Private International Law (Miscellaneous Provisions) Act 1995 s.12), or through exclusion of the foreign rule by operation of the forum's public policy (s.14). See Ch.16, below. In Scots domestic law, the prohibition upon spouse suing spouse in delict was removed by the Law Reform (Husband and Wife) Act 1962 s.2(1), except where, in the view of the court, it appears that no substantial benefit would accrue to either party from the continuation of the action (s.2(2)). See *Kozikowska v Kozikowski (No.1)*, 1996 S.L.T. 386.

[32] Though breach of promise of marriage might be regarded in France as civil wrongdoing, if sued upon in Scotland or England the case would have proceeded as an action founded in breach of contract, no matter what the pursuer might be "French". However, all such suits in British forums now are barred, by overriding legislation of Scotland (Law Reform (Husband and Wife) (Scotland) Act 1984 s.1) and England (Law Reform (Miscellaneous Provisions) Act 1970 s.1) which provides that no action will lie, whatever the law applicable to the promise or agreement.

[33] cf. Kahn Freund's "hidden homonym". The English or Scots forum will insist upon deciding, according to its own rules, what is the domicile of an individual: *Re Annesley* [1926] Ch. 692 (though see Family Law Act 1986 s.46(5)). This problem is particularly acute with regard to the connecting factor of habitual residence, in respect of which increasingly it may be said that different meanings and different attributes attend the concept, depending on judge and context: see Ch.6, below.

(c) Some legal systems contain legal rights or remedies which are unknown in others.

(d) The conflict rules of two legal systems may be the same and yet the two systems may classify the same legal issue in different ways so as to produce entirely different results, e.g. whether the requirement of parental consent to marriage is one of essential or formal validity; or whether a wife's rights in property upon her husband's death should be categorised as rights of succession or rights arising out of the matrimonial relationship.[34]

APPLICATIONS OF CHARACTERISATION

This central matter of characterisation is most easily understood through examples. **4–06**

From the law of marriage, the cases of *Apt v Apt*[35] and *Ponticelli v Ponticelli*[36] demonstrate the orthodox, jurisdiction selection approach to solving a conflict problem. If a Scots domiciliary be party (the absent party) to a proxy marriage celebrated abroad, and the question of validity of the marriage comes before a Scots court, the Scots forum must categorise the problem. Once the problem has been accommodated within a legal category (formal validity of marriage), the relevant choice of law rule is applied. The connecting factor to govern the formal validity of marriage indicated by the choice of law rule under English and Scots conflict rules is the *lex loci celebrationis*. If, by the *lex loci celebrationis*, a proxy marriage is acceptable, the marriage will be regarded as valid in Scotland, subject only to public policy, even though by domestic Scots law marriages cannot be validly celebrated by proxy. An English court has held that the foreign *lex loci celebrationis* governs validity of marriage where *neither* party was present, though this may be doubted, because though a celebration took place abroad, the better view would seem to be that the true place of celebration of marriage (constituted by the exchange of consent) was the English *lex loci contractus*.[37]

From the law of property, an example may be cited in which a man of Russian domicile, a patient in a London hospital, transferred in contemplation of death, money and jewellery to his mistress and one month later died. The claims on his estate of his widow and sons, brought to an English court, depended on whether the court viewed the matter as one of succession (to be referred to the Russian last domicile of the deceased as the long-established connecting factor in the view of the forum), or as one of transfer of moveable

---

[34] As in the notable case of *Anton v Bartolo* (the "Maltese Marriage case") (1891) Clunet 1171. A question famously arose in this area for decision by the House of Lords: *De Nicols v Curlier (No.1)* [1900] A.C. 21. Clear evidence was led of French law that the community of property established by the French Civil Code transcended any change of domicile during the marriage. The court abided by the French rule that community rights were not disturbed by a change of domicile. See further, para.13–02, below. In many cases presenting a problem of characterisation, as in *De Nicols* itself, the word characterisation may not be explicitly mentioned, and the determinative rôle of the forum hardly or not expressly noticed.

[35] [1948] P. 83.

[36] [1958] P. 204.

[37] *McCabe v McCabe* [1994] 1 F.C.R. 257 CA; *The Independent*, September 3, 1993. R.D. Leslie, "Foreign Consensual Marriages", 1994 S.L.T. (News) 87.

property (in which case the connecting factor would be the English *lex situs* of the property at the time of the purported transfer). The court characterised the point as one of property, and applied English domestic law qua *lex situs*, by which the gift was valid.[38]

From the law of succession, the case of *Re Martin*[39] concerned the classification of the English domestic rule that marriage revokes a will, unless the will is made in express contemplation of a particular marriage which subsequently takes place. Does this rule belong to the rules of marriage or of succession? The testatrix, of French domicile, made a will in England in English form. Later she married a professor of French origin, a fugitive from French justice. When the French criminal prescriptive period expired, he returned to France without her. They were not divorced, and since unity of domicile between spouses then prevailed, she, predeceasing him, died possessed of the French domicile of her husband. Had her will been revoked by her marriage? The English court held that the matter was one of marriage law, to be referred to the connecting factor of her domicile immediately after marriage (surprisingly, held to be English) and not to her French domicile at death (being the applicable law in succession).

In *Re Cohn*,[40] Uthwatt J. held that a rule governing sequence of death in a common calamity was a matter of substantive succession law of the German *lex causae*, qua *lex successionis*. Its characterisation as substantive under English succession law did not matter because the parties having died domiciled in Germany, the rule of the German *lex causae* necessarily prevailed in relation to substantive issues. Similarly in *In the Estate of Fuld (Deceased) (No.3)*,[41] the effect of "undue influence" (however termed) upon a testator was a matter of substantive succession law to be governed by Peter Fuld's (German) domicile at the relevant date.[42] Scarman J. assigned rules of burden of proof, in this instance at least, to the category of procedure.[43]

In the Estate of Maldonado[44] is unusual in that the Court of Appeal accepted the Spanish characterisation of the nature of the Spanish government's claim to ownerless property. Spanish law was the *lex causae*, qua *lex successionis*: "it has been found (and the Crown has accepted the finding) that the State of Spain is, in the eye of Spanish law, the true heir",[45] and not the fiscal recipient of ownerless property.

These examples serve to give an indication of traditional conflict of laws methodology. It can be seen that the connecting factor constitutes a link, and a justification, between forum and outcome. In jurisdiction selection systems, the forum must act within the constraints of this methodology. Operating within this approach, therefore, the forum is precluded from choosing directly what it perceives to be, in terms of content or application, the "best" or "better" rule from home and foreign contenders.

---

[38] *Re Korvine's Trust* [1921] 1 Ch. 343.

[39] [1900] P. 211.

[40] [1945] Ch. 5. See Ch.8, below.

[41] [1968] P. 675.

[42] That is, the date of testing, presumably, rather than the date of death—though this cannot be stated with absolute certainty, as Fuld was held by the English court never at any point in his life to have lost his German domicile of origin.

[43] *Fuld (No.3)* [1968] P. 675, per Scarman J. at 696–697. However, the categorisation of burden of proof generally is not uncontroversial. See Ch.8, below.

[44] [1954] P. 223.

[45] *Maldonado* [1954] P. 223, per Jenkins L.J. at 250. See further, Ch.18, below.

TIME

Time may be a relevant factor in the forum's resolution of a conflict problem.[46] **4–07**
The temporal dimension may be important as a result of one of a number of
eventualities:

   (a) *The content of the forum's choice of law rule may change* (*le conflit*
       transitoire), e.g. the choice of law rule applicable in a Scots court in
       a matter of delict will vary according to the date of the act or omis-
       sion giving rise to the claim. If this occurred prior to May 1, 1996, the
       rule of double actionability must operate[47]; conversely, if after that
       date, but before January 11, 2009, the case will be governed by the
       Private International Law (Miscellaneous Provisions) Act 1995; and
       if the event giving rise to damage occurred after January 11, 2009, the
       case will be governed by the Rome II Regulation.[48]
          Where change in the choice of law rule of the forum is effected by
       legislative means, transitional provisions as a matter of good drafting
       practice normally will be found, but these too may give rise to inter-
       pretative difficulty.[49]
   (b) *The connecting factor may require to be defined by time.*[50]
       Connecting factors may be fixed, constant or static, on the one hand,
       or variable/dynamic on the other. Examples of the former are the *lex*
       situs of immoveable property,[51] *lex loci contractus*,[52] *lex loci actus*,[53]
       and *lex loci celebrationis*.[54] Examples of the variable/dynamic
       connecting factors are the *lex situs* of moveables, and domicile/
       habitual residence/nationality of persons. *Locus delicti* (place of
       occurrence of harm) may be a fixed connecting factor depending on
       the circumstances, e.g. a road accident, but in more complex cases of
       multi-locational harm the case is more likely to be regarded as
       "spread over" space and time. Delicts, therefore, may have a contin-
       uing quality, on the facts or in their constituent elements, and may
       display both spatial and temporal problems.[55]
          Within the category of variable/dynamic factors, a subtle distinction
       perhaps can be drawn between a connecting factor such as the *situs* of
       moveable property which, by nature, may change from time to time,

---

[46] See F. Mann, "The Time Element in the Conflict of Laws" (1954) 31 B.Y.B.I.L. 217.
[47] cf. *Kuwait Airways Corp v Iraqi Airways Co (No.6)* [2002] 3 All E.R. 209.
[48] Rome II Regulation arts 31, 32.
[49] e.g. unity of domicile between husband and wife was thought to have been removed by the
     Domicile and Matrimonial Proceedings Act 1973 s.1(1) and (2), but the case of *Inland Revenue*
     Commissioners v Duchess of Portland [1982] Ch. 314 reveals an imperfection in the drafting of
     the rule governing the domicile after January 1, 1974 of women married before January 1, 1974.
     See Ch.6, below.
[50] For the purposes of jurisdiction and/or choice of law and/or recognition of decrees.
[51] The *situs* of land obviously can never change, unless politically by means of territorial realign-
     ment, a rare occurrence.
[52] Rome I Regulation art.11: see Ch.15, below.
[53] See e.g. Wills Act 1963 s.1, which, however, also exemplifies the use, in the alternative, of the
     variable connecting factors of domicile or habitual residence or nationality, each qualified in
     terms of time. See Ch.18, below.
[54] Except perhaps in relation to marriage by cohabitation with habit and repute: see Ch.11, below.
[55] *Soutar v Peters*, 1912 1 S.L.T. 111; *Henderson v Jaouen* [2002] 2 All E.R. 705.

but in respect of the identification of which at any one time (*tempus inspiciendum*), only that time is relevant[56]; and a connecting factor such as domicile which also by nature may change from time to time, but in respect of the identification of which at any one time, review will have to be made of earlier (but not later) events.[57] The domicile or habitual residence of the *propositus* is a "variable" as opposed to "static" connecting factor, and is useless as a guide unless the rule of choice of law, or jurisdiction,[58] specifies the date at which domicile or habitual residence is to be determined. Thus, legal capacity to marry is referred to the law of the domicile *immediately before marriage*[59]; legal testamentary capacity (age, sanity) to the law of the domicile *at the date of testing*[60]; and proprietary testamentary capacity (freedom to disinherit one's family) to the law of the deceased's domicile *at death*.[61] It is necessary therefore to determine the domicile or habitual residence of the *propositus* at a particular point in time for the purpose of resolving the particular conflict problem before the court.

Various examples can be presented to demonstrate that the temporal aspect of a conflict rule may be significant.

With regard to choice of law in annulment of marriage, for example, the court, if it chooses to apply the law of the domicile (a variable connecting factor) of either or both parties, should make explicit whether it seeks to apply the domicile at the date of the purported marriage or at the date of litigation. Principle suggests that the former is the correct approach,[62] but in jurisdictional terms, it has happened that the parties have benefited from a change in the legal nature of their marriage (most commonly from potentially polygamous to monogamous) by the date of consistorial litigation in a UK forum.[63]

In matrimonial property questions, there is a divergence between those legal systems which adhere to the immutability approach, which is that parties' rights in moveable property are fixed, being regulated by whatever touchstone is preferred (as to which time again

---

[56] See *Winkworth v Christie, Manson & Woods Ltd* [1980] 1 Ch. 496; see Ch.17, below.

[57] cf. *Bell v Kennedy* (1868) 6 M. (H.L.) 69. The crucial year being 1838 for the establishment of Bell's domicile, the House of Lords could not look forward to view Bell's life thereafter, which clearly showed adoption of Scots domicile. On the other hand, investigation had to be made of Bell's life up to 1838 and of his father's life in order to reach a conclusion as to Bell's domicile at the relevant date.

[58] cf. *Canada Trust v Stolzenburg (No.2)* [2000] 4 All E.R. 481.

[59] *Brook v Brook* (1861) 9 H.L. Cas. 193; *Mette v Mette* (1859) 1 Sw. & Tr. 416; *Re Paine* [1940] Ch. 46; *Re Bozzelli Settlement* [1902] 1 Ch. 751; *Re De Wilton* [1900] 2 Ch. 481; see Ch.11, below and now Family Law (Scotland) Act 2006 s.38(2).

[60] As noted above, this point is not completely vouched but see *Fuld (No.3)* [1968] P. 675; Scottish Law Commission, *Some Miscellaneous Topics in the Law of Succession* (HMSO, 1986), Scot. Law Com. Memo. No.71, para.6.14 and Scottish Law Commission, *Report on Succession* (HMSO, 1990), Scot. Law Com. No.124 (heritage and moveables).

[61] *Re Groos* [1915] 1 Ch. 572. The very idea of an instrument being "inchoate" is interesting. A will is inchoate: one cannot say that it is the last will of the testator until his death occurs (assuming lucidity to the end). Similarly, one cannot say whether its provisions are essentially valid until that date, because its essential validity will be judged by the law of his last domicile, which can be ascertained with certainty only at the date of death.

[62] cf. *Szechter v Szechter* [1971] P. 286.

[63] cf. *Cheni v Cheni* [1965] P. 85, and *Parkasho v Singh* [1968] P. 233. But see now Matrimonial Proceedings (Polygamous Marriages) Act 1972 s.2; see Ch.11, below.

may be relevant)[64]; and those, principally in the USA, which consider that parties' rights in moveables may change with changes in the domicile of the spouses during the marriage.

A variation upon this theme concerns competing titles to moveable property, where identification of the *lex situs* is not necessarily conclusive if rights to that property traceable to different legal bases should conflict. For example, security rights over moveables are governed in principle by the *lex situs*; but should the governing law be the situation of the moveables when the terms of the contract and relevant security are concluded, e.g. Germany, or the *situs*, e.g. Scotland, of the moveables when an issue of bankruptcy arises and the validity of rights in security become commercially and practically important?[65] This, for the forum, is rather an issue of ranking its own choice of law rules in order of importance in a particular case. In the contest between Scots choice of law rules of property and choice of law rules of contract, the property rules have been given precedence.[66]

Elsewhere, but rarely, a choice of law rule may contain within it a cumulative reference to more than one *tempus inspiciendum*.[67]

(c) *The substantive content of the lex causae may change*, in such a way as to have significance for the case (*le conflit mobile dans le temps*). Parties' choice of applicable law to govern their contract is a choice of that body of law as it may prevail from time to time.[68] It follows that the passage of time may bring about supervening illegality of contractual terms.[69] In other cases the choice falls upon the domestic content at a defined date, e.g. in distribution of an estate in accordance with the domiciliary law at death.[70] A consequence of change of content of the applicable law may be positive, in that defects in formalities of marriage may be removed by subsequent retrospective legislation or government decree, recognised by Scots conflict rules.[71]

(d) *Innominate cases*. Divorce yields interesting examples of the significance of time. If the forum has jurisdiction, according to current law it will apply its own domestic law to the grounds on which divorce

---

[64] *Re Egerton's Will Trusts* [1956] Ch. 593.

[65] Stewart, "Romalpa Clauses", 1985 S.L.T. (News) 149, and see Ch.17, below.

[66] See Ch.17, below.

[67] e.g. the English choice of law rule concerning legitimation by subsequent marriage, which prevailed before the Legitimacy Act 1926, and which required legal capacity in the father to legitimate by this manner by his personal law both at the date of the birth of the child, and at the date of the marriage: see *Re Goodman's Trusts* (1881) L.R. 17 Ch.D. 266.

[68] Though consider in the area of trusts and truster's intentions *Wright's Trustees v Callander*, 1993 S.L.T. 556 and *Crawford*, 1994 S.L.T. (News) 225.

[69] cf. *Ralli Bros v Compania Naviera Sota y Aznar* [1920] 2 K.B. 287.

[70] *Lynch v Provisional Government of Paraguay* (1871) L.R. 2 P. & D. 268 in which the English court, concerned to address an application for a grant of probate to the universal legatee of moveable property, situated in England, of the deceased, Lopez, who died domiciled in Paraguay, did not give effect to Paraguayan legislation which purported to confiscate all his property, wherever situate, after his death. It is fair to say, however, that this case equally could be explained as a refusal to give extraterritorial effect to foreign expropriatory legislation, or on policy grounds, or as a simple affirmation of our choice of ultimate domicile as *lex successionis*. But see *Nelson v Bridport* (1846) 8 Beav. 547, where the necessity to defer at all times to the *lex situs* is affirmed. Practicalities on which the theory of the supremacy of the *lex situs* is based may require recognition of even post-death changes.

[71] cf. *Starkowski v Att Gen* [1954] A.C. 155. See Ch.11, below.

may be obtained.[72] Consequently, it does not matter whether the acts complained of were of legal significance as grounds of marriage dissolution when and/or where committed.[73] It does not matter that they took place before a change of domicile, the divorce court having taken jurisdiction on the basis of a new domicile.[74] Grounds of annulment are quite different as they are necessarily linked as a matter of temporal and legal priority to principles relating to the essential or formal constitution of marriage.

The significance of time is easy to see when the matter is pointed out. However, though all the points made above may be valid considerations, the "primary dimension" of conflict problems is spatial.

THE INCIDENTAL QUESTION

4–08 An incidental or preliminary question may arise in a conflict problem if the choice of law rule of the forum relating to a matter refers to a foreign law, but, before the main question can be answered, it is necessary to obtain an answer to another question also containing foreign elements. The problem which arises is whether this incidental question is to be solved by application of the choice of law rules of that same foreign law as applies to the main question, or by application of the choice of law rules of the *lex fori* as to the incidental question. Should the forum permit its chosen law to regulate not only the main, but also the preliminary question?

This problem arises only[75] if the following conditions are present:

(a) the main question must be referred to a foreign law under the choice of law rule of the forum;
(b) the main question cannot be answered until an incidental question has been answered;
(c) the choice of law rules of the (normally foreign) *lex causae* pertaining to the main question and those of the forum produce different results as to the answer to the incidental question.

---

[72] *Zanelli v Zanelli* [1948] W.N. 381. See choice of law in divorce and nullity contrasted, Ch.12, below.

[73] Contrast *Ali v Ali* [1968] P. 564 where in specialised circumstances the English court was unwilling to take into consideration any alleged matrimonial offences pre-dating the unilateral conversion by Ali, through change of domicile from Indian to English, of the nature of the marriage from potentially polygamous to monogamous.

[74] *Carswell v Carswell* (1881) 8 R. 901 (alleged desertion took place in Canada: divorce forum in Scotland); *Morton v Morton* (1897) 5 S.L.T. 222 (divorce forum in Scotland: place of alleged adultery probably Ireland but report does not specify). But equally (*Stavert v Stavert* (1882) 9 R. 519) commission of the offence within the forum is not enough! Jurisdiction cannot be founded in such cases *ratione delicti*.

[75] The problem does not arise frequently, or at least is not discussed often. But see *Shaw v Gould* (1868) L.R. 3 H.L. 55; *Re Johnson* [1903] 1 Ch. 821; *Re Stirling* [1908] 2 Ch. 344; *Re Bischoffscheim* [1948] Ch. 79; *Haque v Haque* (1962) 108 C.L.R. 230; *Schwebel v Ungar* (1963) 42 D.L.R. (2d) 622 (Ont.C.A.); affirmed (1964) 48 D.L.R. (2d) 644 (Sup. Ct. Can.); *R. v Brentwood Superintendent Registrar of Marriages Ex p. Arias* [1968] 2 Q.B. 956 (approach superseded by legislative intervention per Recognition of Divorces and Legal Separations Act 1971 s.7, itself superseded by Family Law Act 1986 s.50).

It may be that the problem of the incidental question is present in a case, but is ignored or overlooked by the court.[76] The problem seems to be an unavoidable one in certain sets of circumstances.[77]

This deeper mystery of the conflict of laws is most readily understood if set in narrative form. The classic exposition concerns the distribution by a Scots court (qua forum) of that part of the intestate moveable estate situated in Scotland belonging to the deceased, X, who died domiciled in Attica. Since by Scots choice of law rules the distribution of moveable estate is governed by the law of the deceased's last domicile, the *lex causae* in this example is the law of Attica. But Attican law has choice of law rules of its own, which are likely to differ from those of the Scots *lex fori*.

How is the matter to be decided if by Attican law a portion of moveables falls to the widow of the deceased; but it is discovered that X had a complex matrimonial history, and that she who on first sight appears to be X's widow, is X's second[78] "wife", and that the marriage to the earlier wife has been terminated by divorce or annulment, as to the validity of which the choice of law rules of Scotland and of Attica do not agree? Should the Scottish forum permit the law of Attica to regulate not only the intestate moveable succession with regard to its (Attican) domiciliary,[79] but also to answer the incidental or preliminary question of, "*who* is X's widow?" If prepared to cede to Attican law the decision upon *both* questions, the Scots court would be said to follow the *lex causae* theory in its approach to the incidental question. If it prefers to apply its own choice of law rule on recognition of overseas consistorial decrees, it would be said to adopt the *lex fori* theory. If it should happen that the divorce between X and his first wife had been obtained from a Scots court, a later Scots court is likely to find it difficult in effect to deny its own decree.[80]

There is no definitive answer to the manner in which the incidental question should be addressed. There is general agreement upon the pursuit of the aims of justice and expediency, but which manner of proceeding best serves the case and produces a positive outcome (and for whom?) is a matter of conjecture.

Parliament, in removing one related problem,[81] left unanswered the question of what is to happen when the Scots court has to consider the legal capacity to marry of an individual who is deemed to have such capacity by the law of his domicile, but who has been divorced by a decree not recognised by Scots law. No such case appears yet to have presented itself to a Scots forum, but is exactly the situation in the classic incidental question found in the case of *Schwebel v Ungar*.[82] A husband and wife, both Jews domiciled in Hungary, decided to emigrate to Israel. En route, in Italy, they were divorced by ghet

---

[76] Consider, e.g. *Shaw v Gould* (1868) L.R. 3 H.L. 55; *Perrini v Perrini* [1979] 2 All E.R. 323; *Lawrence v Lawrence* [1985] 2 All E.R. 733.

[77] Morris, *Conflict of Laws*, 7th edn, 2009, para.20–015.

[78] Or third or subsequent "wife", giving rise to the possibility of multiple incidental questions.

[79] Who the law of Attica may not consider to be its domiciliary; and in any case the law of Attica may consider the law of the last nationality to be the appropriate *lex successionis*—but that is another story, told in Ch.5 and Ch.18, below.

[80] But see *R. v Brentwood Superintendent Registrar of Marriages Ex p. Arias* [1968] 2 Q.B. 956.

[81] See Family Law Act 1986 s.50. See Ch.12, below.

[82] (1963) 42 D.L.R. (2d) 622 (Ont. C.A.); affirmed (1964) 48 D.L.R. (2d) 644 (Sup. Ct. Can.).

(Jewish religious divorce).[83] Such a divorce was worthy of recognition by the law of Israel, but not by the law of Hungary which was the personal law of the parties at the relevant time. Each party later acquired a domicile of choice in Israel. Thereafter, the woman removed to Canada where, being still of Israeli domicile, she purported to re-marry in Toronto. Her new "husband" later sought annulment of the later "marriage" in a Canadian court.

The law of Ontario referred the woman's capacity to marry to the Israeli law of her ante-nuptial domicile, but in the matter of the incidental question—of the validity of the antecedent divorce, which was capable of having its own conflict rule—the Ontarian court was not willing by its *own* conflict rules on the particular issue of religious divorces to recognise the ghet as valid (since it was not valid by the Hungarian law of the husband's domicile at the time).[84]

The dilemma is clear to see. The decision by the Supreme Court of Canada, affirming the Ontario Court of Appeal, was to have the Israeli law governing the main question of capacity to marry, regulate also the incidental question of validity of antecedent divorce. The case therefore provides an example of the *lex causae* approach to resolving the incidental question. But one might say that overall control was still with the forum, which chose to take that path, the conflict rules of Ontario containing the possibility, at the option of the Ontarian forum, to defer to the conflict rules of the foreign system which the Canadian court itself had selected to answer the main question.

Writers are divided in approach. The *lex causae* approach, as well as being internationally minded, has an attraction. It concedes that a foreign law has a conflict of laws dimension (and that that dimension is equipped with detailed conflict rules), and is willing to remit the entirety of the problem to the entirety of that foreign law, which the forum itself has selected in the first place: perhaps that is what "application" of the *lex causae* entails.[85]

It may be that the natural approach of the Scots lawyer is to refer the entire matter to the *lex causae*. Such an approach is preferable in the interests of international harmony and universality of status, unless the price in terms of internal dissonance is too high.[86] Few, however, would advise a rigid, predetermined attitude in this area where instances in any event are rare. *Potior et utilior*, we might say, had we not let go of the Latin.

THE END OF THE BEGINNING

4–09 The aim of each system of choice of law rules is to identify the appropriate law to govern a question which has arisen for decision in the court of that system, and which contains foreign elements. The content of the choice of law rules of systems of law will vary from system to system, though as the years go on, the "harmonisation" impetus will bring about a measure of agreement among consenting states, ex facie, if not necessarily in interpretation and application of harmonised choice of law rules.

---

[83] As to Scots and English conflict rules on recognition of religious (extrajudicial) divorces, see Ch.12, below.
[84] This also would have been the Scottish view at this date: see *Makouipour v Makouipour*, 1967 S.L.T. 101 (form of divorce valid by Iranian law of the husband). See Ch.12, below.
[85] See Ch.5, below.
[86] Wolff, *Private International Law*, 2nd edn, 1950, p.209. Cf. fn.80, above.

That which remains to be considered is the meaning of the word "law", as used in the expression "choice of law". For if every developed legal system has both domestic law and conflict law, its law "flat", and its law "in the round"— then when the Scots forum chooses, e.g. "French" law to govern an issue, should it be within the Scots court's contemplation that French *conflict* law should be proved and followed? This is the celebrated problem of *renvoi*, the pleasures of which next will be tasted.

SUMMARY 4

1. The forum having accepted jurisdiction, the *lex fori* governs: **4–10**

   (a) the form of action;
   (b) characterisation of the point at issue;
   (c) selection of the choice of law rule, including definition, identification and ascertainment of the connecting factor;
   (d) application of the choice of law rule; and
   (e) matters of procedure.[87]

2. For foreign law to apply, it must be averred and its content proved.
3. The element of time may be relevant.
4. The circumstances may present an incidental question.

---

[87] See Ch.8, below.

CHAPTER 5

RENVOI

NATURE OF THE SUBJECT

5–01 *Renvoi* means a dismissal, a sending away, or sending back. The word denotes a mystery which lies at the heart of the conflict of laws. The problem springs from the dual meaning of the expression *"the law of a country"*. This term may be used in a narrow sense or in a wide sense. It may mean the law of country X in its narrow domestic sense or the law of country X "in the round", including its conflict rules. Hence, in suggesting a choice of the law of country X as the applicable law in a given problem, one may be criticised for lack of specification.

The natural home of *renvoi* is the law of succession.[1] A classic example of the *renvoi* problem concerns the question of succession to the moveable estate in Scotland of a British subject who died domiciled in a foreign country, by the law of which succession to moveables is governed by the law of the nationality (instead of by the law of the domicile). If, according to the Scots choice of law rule governing succession to moveable property, the estate of the deceased is to be distributed according to the French law of his domicile, ought we to include within our understanding of "the law of the domicile", the French choice of law rule concerning succession to moveable estate, so as to secure the outcome that the distribution of the moveables in Scotland will be effected according to the law of the nationality?[2]

The *renvoi* problem in general may be said to arise whenever, within the permitted scope of operation of *renvoi* as noted below, a question of law is referred notionally by one law (the *lex fori*) to another law (the *lex causae*) in its entirety, and that other law either refers it back to the original law (*renvoi* remission) or refers it to still another law (*renvoi* transmission).[3] The narrow range of potentially usable connecting factors in any given problem probably accounts for the small number of instances of *renvoi* transmission.

---

[1] The *renvoi* process was used without success in *Fuld (No.3)* [1968] P. 675 to attempt to save two (of the four) codicils from a finding of formal invalidity.

[2] It seems, however, that we are never prepared fully to put ourselves into the position of the foreign law: there is always a holding-back in that the deceased's domicile is identified according to the rules of the *lex fori. Re Annesley* [1926] Ch. 692; and see *Re Askew* [1930] 2 Ch. 259, per Maugham J. at 273.

[3] *Re Trufort* (1887) L.R. 36 Ch.D. 600; *Secretary of State for Foreign Affairs v Charlesworth Pilling & Co* [1901] A.C. 372; *Armitage v Att Gen* [1906] P. 135; *Sasson v Sasson* [1924] A.C. 1007; *Bartlett v Bartlett* [1925] A.C. 377; and *Re Achillopoulos* [1928] 1 Ch. 433. These are cases decided in the era in which the English courts adopted the single *renvoi* theory, *q.v.* A more modern example is *R. v Brentwood Superintendent Registrar of Marriages Ex p. Arias* [1968] 3 All E.R. 279.

HISTORY OF THE PROBLEM

The problem of *renvoi* entered the consciousness of the English judiciary as a **5–02** means of circumventing the rigid rule then operative concerning formal validity of wills, which required that in order to be formally valid, a will had to satisfy the formal validity rules of the legal system of the last domicile of the testator.[4] The courts were reluctant to strike down a will on a point of form if, by reference to the "total" law of a country in which the deceased died domiciled, a positive outcome might be obtained by permitting onward reference to another law, thereby enlarging the number of potentially applicable laws governing formal validity. "The fountain-head of authority is *Collier v Rivaz*"[5]: "the court sitting here . . . must consider itself sitting in Belgium."[6] The English court, by so doing, rendered itself able to come to the view that codicils formally invalid by the Belgian law of the domicile but valid under English law, could be admitted to probate in England, for Belgian law "in the round" would have referred the matter to the English law of the nationality.

A grand Scottish *renvoi* case is there none, though there is evidence that the Scots courts will accept the concept of transmission, that is to say, that they would be prepared to apply the law of a third country if referred thereto by the foreign law identified by the Scottish choice of law rule.[7]

If there is value in the *renvoi* exercise, there is no reason in principle for its exclusion from areas other than succession, although there may be persuasive reasons of time, expense, complexity and uncertainty, as well as incontrovertible reasons of prohibition contained in statute, convention or regulation.

THE THEORIES

There is much writing on this acclaimed subject.[8] The following is an outline **5–03** of three basic approaches.

---

[4] See, for example, early cases such as: *Collier v Rivaz* (1841) 2 Curt. 855; *Laneuville v Anderson* (1860) 2 Sw. & Tr. 24; *Bremer v Freeman* (1857) 10 Moo. P.C. 306; *Frere v Frere* (1847) 5 Notes of Cases 593; *In the Goods of Lacroix* (1877) 2 P.D. 94. *Collier* was disapproved firmly but on no easily decipherable grounds in *Bremer*.

[5] *Dicey, Morris and Collins on the Conflict of Laws*, 14th edn, 2006, para.4–010.

[6] *Collier v Rivaz* (1841) 2 Curt. 855, per Sir Herbert Jenner at 859.

[7] See, e.g. *McKay v Walls*, 1951 S.L.T. (Notes) 6; *Armitage v Att Gen* [1906] P. 135; *Mountbatten v Mountbatten* [1959] 1 All E.R. 99. Reference to the personal law of the institute on a question of status, as opposed to the law of the testator, shows the same "open" attitude: *Mitchell's Trustee v Rule* (1908) 16 S.L.T. 189; *Smith's Trustees v Macpherson's Trustees*, 1926 S.C. 983; cf. *Wright's Trustees v Callander*, 1992 S.L.T. 498 Ex Div; 1993 S.L.T. 556 HL. Contrast *Re Fergusson's Will* [1902] 1 Ch. 483. See generally the "recognition by" mode of reasoning used to extend the range of courts considered by UK common law rules to be competent to grant divorce: cf. Family Law Act 1986 ss.46(2)(b)(ii), 51(3)(b)(ii). See also Marriage (Scotland) Act 1977 s.3(5): certificate of legal capacity required for a foreign domiciliary intending to marry in Scotland will be acceptable if issued by a competent authority in a state other than the domicile if by the law of the latter the law of that other state is the personal law.

[8] e.g. J.P. Bate, *Note on the Doctrine of Renvoi* (London: Stevens and Sons Ltd, 1904); Griswold, "Renvoi Revisited", 51 Harv. L.R. 1165; Falconbridge, *Conflict of Laws*, 2nd edn, 1954, Chs 6–10; Munro, "The Magic Roundabout of the Conflict of Laws", 1978 J.R. 65; G. Sauveplanne, *International Encyclopaedia of Comparative Law* (Mohr Siebeck and Martinus Nijhoff, 1990), Vol.III, Ch.6; Adrian Briggs, "In Praise and Defence of Renvoi" (1998) 47 I.C.L.Q. 877.

(1) INTERNAL LAW THEORY

5–04 The question should be solved by the simple application of the forum-identi-
fied *lex causae*, in its narrow domestic sense. This is not so much a theory of
renvoi as a refusal to entertain it. There is little doubt that the internal law
approach was taken in early cases.[9] In *Re Annesley*[10] its use was expressly
commended as avoiding the "endless oscillation"[11] which other theories entail.

(2) PARTIAL *RENVOI*, OR SINGLE *RENVOI* THEORY

5–05 The starting point is the *lex fori* in its wide sense from which the question is
referred (*envoi*) to another law, the *lex causae* (usually the law of the domicile), which in turn may refer it back (*renvoi*) to the *lex fori* (usually qua
lex patriae). If the *lex fori* accepts the *renvoi* or reference back, at that stage
the court applies its own law in its narrow sense. The essentials of this theory
are that:

    (a) the starting point for the forum is the *lex fori*, the conflict rules of
        which enable identification of the (foreign) *lex causae*;
    (b) proof is required of the choice of law rules of the foreign *lex causae*;
        and
    (c) at the third stage the application is always of a law in its narrow
        domestic sense.

The effect of applying this theory is that one legal system defers to another
legal system's choice of law rules.[12] At one time the single *renvoi* theory was
approved in England,[13] but it is not now applied by the English courts. There
seems no particular logic in stopping the game at this point, but once having
started down the road of *renvoi* reasoning, it would be hard to say when it is
logical to stop.

L'Affaire Forgo[14] provides an example of the French attitude to the problem.
Forgo was a national of Bavaria who had lived in France since the age of five
and who had a de facto domicile there. He was illegitimate. He died intestate.
Under the Code Napoleon his whole estate fell to the French government
because of his illegitimate status, but under the law of Bavaria it passed to his
collaterals. The French *lex fori*, holding that the question was referred by
French choice of law rules to the Bavarian law of the nationality, found that
that law referred the question back to French law, as the law of the domicile or

---

[9] See *Re Askew* [1930] 2 Ch. 259, per Maugham J. at 264.
[10] [1926] Ch. 692.
[11] *Re Annesley* [1926] Ch. 692, per Russell J. at 708, 709. However, this preference for the simple
approach was obiter, for *Annesley* marks the beginning of the favour shown by English law to
the double *renvoi* theory, *q.v.* The effect of applying the internal law theory and the double
renvoi theory may often be the same.
[12] But it depends what one means by the forum's choice of "law"; it might reasonably mean a
choice of the foreign law in its entirety. On a simple view, however, the "British" preference for
domicile to govern matters of status and succession represents a conscious policy decision. See
Ch.6, below.
[13] *Re Johnson* [1903] 1 Ch. 821.
[14] (1833) 10 Clunet 64.

habitual residence: at that point France accepted the *renvoi* or reference back and applied its own domestic law.

(3) FOREIGN COURT THEORY OR TOTAL *RENVOI* OR DOUBLE *RENVOI* THEORY

The forum endeavours to place itself at the outset notionally in the position of **5–06** the foreign court and to decide the question as that court would decide it.[15] In succession cases, according to the Scottish choice of law rule, the relevant notional foreign court normally will be the court of the domicile of the deceased as regards moveables and will be the court of the *lex situs* as regards immoveables. The notional first reference is therefore from that foreign court applying its law in the wide sense, to the law thereby indicated; and, if the latter law notionally would refer the matter back to the law of the foreign court, the question is whether the foreign court will accept the *renvoi*. The essentials of this theory are that:

(a) the starting point is (notionally) the foreign court;
(b) it is necessary to know not only the choice of law rule of the foreign law, but also whether or not the foreign law recognises the *renvoi* doctrine and would accept a *renvoi* remission; and
(c) at the third stage the application is always of a law in its narrow sense.

If the foreign court accepts the principle of *renvoi*, it will accept (notionally) the reference back and the forum will consider itself entitled to apply that foreign law in its narrow sense[16]; but if it will not accept a *renvoi*,[17] there can be no reference back. In such a case, an English court applies, in its narrow sense, the law indicated by the foreign choice of law rule which is usually the law of the nationality. Where the country of nationality comprises territorial units with different legal systems, the English courts have applied the law of the territorial unit in which the deceased had his domicile of origin. It has often been remarked that a *renvoi* remission may cause difficulty because there is no "British" law, nor "English" nationality. *Re O'Keefe (Deceased)*[18] provides an example of difficulties which may be encountered if the link with the *lex patriae* is tenuous and there has been a change of political status of the territory in which the *propositus* had her domicile of origin. However, the problem of ascribing the law of the nationality where the state is not unitary, and the problems of proof of foreign law, are secondary problems: one must first decide whether one is going to have any truck with the *renvoi* dimension.

A major stumbling block with regard to the foreign court theory of *renvoi* is that it "works" only if the foreign court is not applying the same theory. If it should do so, the forum should have to seek to impersonate a foreign court

---

[15] *Armitage v Att Gen* [1906] P. 135; *Bartlett v Bartlett* [1925] A.C. 377; *Re Achillopoulos* [1928] 1 Ch. 433; *Re Annesley* [1926] Ch. 692; *Re Ross* [1930] 1 Ch. 377; *Re Askew* [1930] 2 Ch. 259; *Re O'Keefe (Deceased)* [1940] Ch. 124; *Re Duke of Wellington* [1947] Ch. 506; affirmed [1948] Ch. 118; *Jaber Elias Kotia v Katr Bint Jiryes Nahas* [1941] A.C. 403; *Fuld (No.3)* [1968] P. 675.
[16] *Re Annesley* [1926] Ch. 692 (France).
[17] *Re Ross* [1930] 1 Ch. 377 (Italy).
[18] [1940] Ch. 124.

which is seeking to impersonate the forum: this is a problem too far even for the enthusiasts to solve. But this theoretical objection to the theory remains theoretical; there are few *renvoi* cases, and none it seems in which the English court has found the foreign court to be playing the same double *renvoi* game. The foreign court has been found to be playing single *renvoi* (France and Germany), or not to be playing at all (Italy), or not to know whether it is playing or not (Spain). Hence, the "mirror effect", or the "after you, Claud; no, after you, Montmorency"[19] scenario, or *circulus inextricabilis* has not arisen. The Scots attitude to *renvoi*, in principle and in practice, is a matter of conjecture.[20]

THE SCOPE OF OPERATION OF *RENVOI*

SUCCESSION

5–07 The doctrine of *renvoi* in English conflict of laws jurisprudence has been applied to questions involving intestacy, legal rights, formal and essential validity of wills, succession to immoveables, title to moveables, formal validity of marriage and other aspects of status, in particular legitimation. Even in the area of succession, however, archetypically appropriate for the operation of *renvoi*, the trend has been expressly to exclude it.[21] The Wills Act 1963 s.1, provides that a will shall be treated as properly executed if its execution conformed to the *internal* law of the various possibly applicable laws regulating execution. The effect of this is to eliminate *renvoi* in questions relating to formal validity of wills. As to matters of essential validity of wills, the effect of harmonisation of choice of law rules at a European level, "will obviate the need for renvoi where all the connecting factors are situated in a Member State."[22] The Hague Trusts Convention (given effect in Scots and English law by the Recognition of Trusts Act 1987) by art.17 excludes *renvoi*.[23]

CONTRACT

5–08 From time to time, there have been suggestions, which have not been taken up, that *renvoi* might also be applied in other branches of law—as for example in

---

[19] A reference to the officers' eternal bowing to one another at the Battle of Fontenoy; cf. *Re Askew* [1930] 2 Ch. 259, per Maugham J. at 267.

[20] Wm Binchy, *Irish Conflict of Laws* (Butterworth (Ireland) Ltd, 1988), p.38, speculates that the dearth of Irish *renvoi* cases may be due to the trend for Irish emigration to take place to countries such as Canada, USA, Australia, New Zealand, South Africa and Argentina, which belong to the family of "domicile" countries. By inference, therefore, where there are personal connections with civilian countries, there is greater potential for *renvoi* problems. Binchy suggests that there may be cases in the future as a result of greater interaction between continental Europe and Ireland.

[21] The query then arises whether the express exclusion of *renvoi* in any instrument means that incidental questions presenting within the ambit of such an instrument must be determined by the forum adopting a *lex fori* approach (see Ch.4, above).

[22] Proposal for a Regulation of the European Parliament and of the Council on jurisdiction, applicable law, recognition and enforcement of decisions and authentic instruments in matters of succession and the creation of a European Certificate of Succession COM(2009) 154 final (2009/0157 COD), art.26; and earlier Green Paper, Succession and Wills COM(2005) 65 final, para.2.7. See generally Ch.18, below.

[23] In instruments of the Hague Conference *renvoi* will operate unless explicitly excluded.

contract,[24] bills of exchange[25] and enforcement of arbitral awards.[26] However, in *Re United Railways of Havana and Regla Warehouses Ltd*,[27] the Court of Appeal made it clear that, "the principle of renvoi finds no place in the field of contract",[28] and the matter has been put beyond doubt by the Contracts (Applicable Law) Act 1990, bringing into United Kingdom law the Rome Convention on the law applicable to contractual obligations, art.15 of which excludes the application of *renvoi*. Likewise, art.20 of the Rome I Regulation excludes *renvoi*.

DELICT

Similarly, in delict, *renvoi* was not thought to be applicable at common law.[29] The **5–09** point is now regulated by art.24 of the Rome II Regulation and, in residual cases arising in Scots and English courts, by s.9(5) of the Private International Law (Miscellaneous Provisions) Act 1995, both of which exclude the operation of *renvoi*. In Australia, the decision of the High Court in *Neilson v Overseas Projects Corp of Victoria Ltd*[30] excited much comment in light of its acceptance of the application of *renvoi* in a case litigated in Australia, arising from a tort which occurred in the People's Republic of China. It may be conjectured that in this instance *renvoi* was perceived to be a useful device to circumvent the inflexibility of the Australian choice of law rule in tort.The injured party was an Australian citizen, domiciled in Western Australia, who had been living in China as a consequence of her husband's employment there. The couple had been billeted in accommodation in Wuhan, China, which took the form of a two storey apartment connected by an internal staircase with no banister. The Neilsons complained about the dangerous state of the staircase to Mr Neilson's employer, which owned the apartment, but nothing was done to remedy the situation. Thereafter Mrs Neilson was injured when she was descending the stairs. She was treated in a Chinese hospital for three weeks before being advised to return to Australia.

Subsequently, Mrs Neilson sued her husband's employer in contract and tort (under the head of occupiers' liability) in Western Australia. The employer's insurance company, incorporated in New South Wales, was joined as a third party. The Australian choice of law rule in tort directed strict application of the

---

[24] *Vita Food Products Inc v Unus Shipping Co Ltd (In Liquidation)* [1939] A.C. 277. Cf. *Amin Rasheed Shipping Corp v Kuwait Insurance Co (The Al Wahab)* [1983] 2 All E.R. 884, per Lord Diplock at 888; and *Musawi v RE International (UK) Ltd* [2007] EWHC 2981 (Ch) at [20].

[25] *Alcock v Smith* [1892] 1 Ch. 238; *Embiricos v Anglo-Austrian Bank* [1905] 1 K.B. 677; *F Koechlin et Cie v Kestenbaum Bros* [1927] 1 K.B. 889.

[26] e.g. *Dallah Real Estate & Tourism Holding Co v Pakistan* [2008] EWHC 1901 (Comm), per Aikens J. at [78] (for the purposes of the Arbitration Act 1996 s.103(2)(b)).

[27] [1960] Ch. 52 CA; [1961] A.C. 1007 HL.

[28] *Re United Railways of Havana and Regla Warehouses Ltd* [1960] Ch. 52, per Jenkins L.J. at 96, 97, Willmer L.J. dissenting at 115. The glancing reference made by Christopher Clarke J. in *Cherney v Deripaska* [2008] EWHC 1530 (Comm) at [136] to the use of *renvoi* in determining the applicable law of a contract seems, therefore, misguided.

[29] *McElroy v McAllister*, 1949 S.C. 110, per Lord Russell at 126.

[30] [2005] HCA 54, discussed by M. Keyes, "The Doctrine of Renvoi in International Torts: Mercantile Mutual Insurance v Neilson" (2005) 13 *Torts Law Journal* 1; A. Lu and L. Carroll, "Ignored No More—Renvoi and International Torts Litigated in Australia" (2005) 1 J. Priv. Int. L. 35; and R. Mortensen, "Troublesome and Obscure: The Renewal of Renvoi in Australia" (2006) 2 J. Priv. Int. L. 1.

lex loci delicti (Chinese law) to govern questions of substance. However, by Chinese conflict of laws rules contained in the Law of Civil Relations involving Foreigners, a remission to Australian law, being the law of the common nationality or common domicile of the claimant and defendant, might be made. The point which precipitated the discussion of *renvoi* was the question whether or not the claim in tort was time-barred. By Chinese law there was a one-year limitation period for personal injury actions, in contrast to the more generous six-year period prevailing under Australian law. Since the date of litigation was almost six years after the accident, clearly a notional remission to Australian law was crucial for the claimant. While the judge at first instance was sympathetic to *renvoi* reasoning, his decision was reversed by the Full Court, which held that a reference to foreign law (Chinese law) in this regard must be a reference to its substantive domestic law only. But by a clear majority, the High Court of Australia, on appeal from the Full Court, preferred to adopt *renvoi* reasoning in the application of the Australian choice of law rules in tort, so as to enable the foreign law indicated by the rules to be interpreted as a reference to the whole of that law. A majority of five judges accepted the doctrine of double *renvoi*. This is a remarkable decision. In legal systems which follow a more flexible choice of law rule in delict (as for example provided by Rome II), there would seem to be less need and less justification for taking this unusual line.

UNJUSTIFIED ENRICHMENT

5–10 Interestingly, elsewhere in the law of obligations, in relation to unjustified enrichment, an argument was made in *Barros Mattos Junior v MacDaniels Ltd*[31] that the applicable law should be understood as meaning the applicable law in its totality, but this argument was rejected as premature. Insofar as unjust enrichment now is governed by Rome II,[32] there is no scope for the application of *renvoi* in any relevant case arising in a European forum.[33] In this (exclusion of *renvoi*) aspect, as in other important aspects of conflict of laws rules within the law of obligations as operated in Member State courts, there is now a uniform approach.

PROPERTY

5–11 With regard to property problems, Dicey, Morris and Collins[34] considers that *renvoi* should be available in cases involving title to land abroad, because if there is one certainty in the conflict of laws, it is that, in matters pertaining to land, effectiveness of the conflict rule requires that the *lex situs* be entirely satisfied. Hence, choice of the *lex situs* may in the end mean choice of the entirety of that law.[35]

---

[31] [2005] I.L.Pr. 45, per Collins J. at [121].
[32] Rome II Ch.III: unjust enrichment, *negotiorum gestio* and *culpa in contrahendo*.
[33] Rome II art.24.
[34] *Dicey, Morris and Collins on the Conflict of Laws*, 14th edn, 2006, para.4–024.
[35] Though see *Re Ross* [1930] 1 Ch. 377: the effect of application of the Italian *lex situs* "in the round" led to the application, by the English forum, of the English law of succession.

As regards moveable property, it can be noted that in *Winkworth v Christie, Manson & Woods Ltd*,[36] counsel argued strongly for a departure from the *lex situs* rule in problems of ownership of moveable property. The judge of first instance, though unconvinced, expressly made it clear that, at the trial, use might be made of *renvoi* reasoning to suggest that the Italian *lex situs* itself might not consider that Italian (domestic) law should apply. However, such a hint of openness to the *renvoi* argument is to be contrasted with the dictum of Staughton L.J. in *Macmillan Inc v Bishopsgate Investment Trust Plc (No.3)*,[37] a case concerning ownership of intangible moveables, namely, shares.

More recently, the question of *renvoi* was raised in *Iran v Berend*[38] in the determination of title to a fragment of fifth century BC limestone relief from Persepolis. The case contains a useful consideration by Eady J. of the policy considerations affecting a judicial decision whether or not to admit the operation of *renvoi* in the resolution of a case.[39] Eady J., concerned to decide a matter of ownership of tangible property, saw no reason to depart from the resistant attitude displayed by the court in *Macmillan*: "I can find no reason to differ from Millett J. and to hold, for the first time, that public policy requires English law to introduce the notion of renvoi into the determination of title to movables."[40]

In 2009 further opportunity was afforded to visit the topic in the complex Admiralty cause, *Dornoch Ltd v Westminster International BV*.[41] It was necessary to determine the precise meaning of *"lex situs"* in the context of determining proprietary interests in a vessel. In identifying the law of Thailand as the *lex situs*, the question remained whether, in this context, the reference to Thai law should include Thai choice of law rules. After consideration, Tomlinson J. preferred to maintain a cautious line by construing Thai law in its narrow, domestic sense. However, his Lordship declined to give a definitive answer on the question whether the expression *"lex situs"*, in the context of moveable property generally, necessarily includes or excludes the rules of international private law.[42] The essence of his judgment is captured as follows:

"If therefore I were to decide that as a matter of English common law reference to the *lex situs* as being the law governing the incidence of proprietary rights in moveable property includes reference to the choice of law or private international law rules of the situs, I would I think be rowing against a strong tide. Moreover, in the commercial context in which the question arises here I should be loath to assimilate the law to that hitherto applicable only in fields such as the formal and intrinsic validity of wills, intestate succession and legitimation by subsequent marriage when in the fields of contract, tort, restitution and trusts a

---

[36] [1980] 1 Ch. 496. See also *Glencore Internationl AG v Metro Trading International Inc (No.2)* [2001] 1 Lloyd's Rep. 284, per Moore-Bick J. at [41].
[37] [1996] 1 W.L.R. 387 at 405.
[38] [2007] EWHC 132 (QB).
[39] *Iran v Berend* [2007] EWHC 132 (QB) at [22]–[33].
[40] *Iran v Berend* [2007] EWHC 132 (QB), per Eady J. at [26].
[41] Also termed *The WD Fairway* [2009] EWHC 889 (Admlty).
[42] *Dornoch Ltd v Westminster International BV (The WD Fairway)* [2009] EWHC 889 (Admlty) at [28].

deliberate decision has apparently been taken to eschew the doctrine of renvoi."[43]

Further useful lengthy consideration of the operation of *renvoi* in the context of property rights is provided by *Blue Sky One Ltd v Mahan Air*,[44] a complex litigation concerning the property implications of the sanctions imposed by the United States government preventing the sale or lease of US aircraft manufactured in the US to Iranian individuals or companies. Beatson J. in *Blue Sky*, in pondering counsel's submissions in favour of the application of the *renvoi* doctrine,[45] on a case by case analysis, depending upon identification of the policy underlying the private international law rule in question, concluded that, despite the attractiveness of the suggestion, the consequence would be the construction of a very uncertain legal regime: "[I]ndeed it could lead to a Tennysonian wilderness of single instances".[46] For this and other more practical reasons, Beatson J. inclined to follow the line traced by Millet J. in *Macmillan Inc*, Eady J. in *Berend*, and Tomlinson J. in *Dornoch Ltd*, and decided that the reference to the *lex situs* in the case of a transfer of title to tangible movables such as aircraft means the domestic law of the place of the *situs* of the aircraft on the relevant date, and not the entirety of that law.

FAMILY LAW

5–12 In family law, the Law Commissions commented[47] that *renvoi* reasoning may be useful when referring to the *lex loci celebrationis* (formal validity of marriage),[48] with the aim of promoting greater uniformity of status (to avoid "limping marriages") and of allowing a greater number of marriages to be upheld.

> "On the whole, we think that these arguments should prevail [against those of inconvenience, delay and cost in litigation, and theoretical problems]. Our provisional recommendation is that the reference made by our choice of law rules to the law of the country of celebration should in the case of marriages celebrated abroad be construed as a reference to the whole law of that country (including its choice of law rules) and not merely to its domestic rules."[49]

Similarly,[50] in the matter of capacity to marry, the Law Commissions were amenable to the *renvoi* argument.

---

[43] *The WD Fairway* [2009] EWHC 889 (Admlty) at [87].

[44] [2010] EWHC 631 (Comm).

[45] *Blue Sky One Ltd v Mahan Air* [2010] EWHC 631 (Comm) at [157]–[185].

[46] *Blue Sky One Ltd v Mahan Air* [2010] EWHC 631 (Comm) at [172].

[47] Law Commission and Scottish Law Commission, *Private International Law: Choice of Law Rules in Marriage* (HMSO, 1985), Law Com. Working Paper No.89; Scot. Law Com. Memo. No.64, paras 2.12, 2.13, 2.39–2.42.

[48] See *Taczanowska v Taczanowski* [1957] P. 301; and *Hooper v Hooper* [1959] 1 W.L.R. 1021.

[49] Law Commission and Scottish Law Commission, *Choice of Law Rules in Marriage*, 1985, Law Com. Working Paper No.89; Scot. Law Com. Memo. No.64, para.2.39.

[50] Law Commission and Scottish Law Commission, *Choice of Law Rules in Marriage*, 1985, Law Com. Working Paper No.89; Scot. Law Com. Memo. No.64, para.3.39.

Where *renvoi* is not expressly excluded by legislation or precedent, care must be taken, if advantageous to the litigant, to construct a reasoned view as to the possible application of *renvoi* in the given situation. It is a rule of Hague Convention drafting that the word "law" includes rules of private international law and that reference is to internal rules only if that is explicitly stated.[51] In other legislation, the reasonable conclusion is that, if not expressly excluded, *renvoi* is available by default. Thus, for example, in the Family Law (Scotland) Act 2006, which contains certain provisions of conflict of laws significance, there is contained in s.38 (validity of marriages) a rule concerning the treatment in a Scots court of a foreign rule requiring parental consent to marriage, viz.:

"If the law of the place in which a person is domiciled requires a person under a certain age to obtain parental consent before entering into a marriage, that requirement shall not be taken to affect the capacity of a person to enter into a marriage in Scotland unless failure to obtain such consent would render invalid any marriage that the person purported to enter into in any form anywhere in the world."

It would appear that the reference to the, "law of the place in which such a person is domiciled" must encompass the choice of law rules of that legal system.[52]

PERSPECTIVE

The *renvoi* process may be seen as the antithesis of the certainty and speed **5–13** that business requires. Therein must lie the explanation for its exclusion generally from the commercial sphere, because if there is any validity in principle in *renvoi* thinking, surely it should apply across the whole range of private law subjects. Yet the effect of judicial openness to *renvoi* normally is positive.[53] It has been a notable claim of *renvoi* proponents that the operation of the doctrine is capable of producing uniformity of result regardless of forum, i.e. harmony of decision, but a brief analysis of an hypothetical problem of intestate moveable succession reveals that diversity of result often may emerge, depending upon the approach to *renvoi* taken in each of the "forums" where is situated moveable estate of the deceased requiring to be distributed. As Munro demonstrates,[54] where one forum (the situation of the bulk of the deceased's moveable estate)

---

[51] The Peréz-Vera Report on the 1980 Hague Abduction Convention emphasised that the applicable law includes rules of private international law, so as to expand the potential reach of the Convention.

[52] The provenance of this provision is the Scottish Law Commission, *Report on Family Law* (HMSO, 1992), Scot. Law Com. No.135, paras 14.8–14.10, recommendation 70(a). Notably the Civil Partnership Act 2004 s.124(10) provides that, in testing the validity of civil partnerships registered outside Scotland, where reference is made to the "relevant law", that means "the law of the country or territory where the overseas relationship was registered (including its rules of private international law)".

[53] Though it may be productive of mischief: see *Re JB (Child Abduction) (Rights of Custody: Spain)* [2004] 1 F.L.R. 796 (English forum permitted application of Spanish law "in the round", resulting in a remission to English law in terms of which the unmarried, bereft father, had no parental rights such as to justify a petition for return of the child under the 1980 Hague Convention on the grounds of wrongful removal). See K. Beevers and J. Perez Milla, "Convention 'Rights of Custody'—Who Decides? An Anglo-Spanish Perspective" (2007) 3 J. Priv. Int. L. 201.

[54] See Munro, "The Magic Roundabout of the Conflict of Laws", 1978 J.R. 65, 78–80.

favours the internal law theory, and the other (which qua *situs* is required to distribute the remainder of the deceased's moveable estate) favours the partial *renvoi* theory, a uniform approach to the distribution of the whole estate appears likely to be the outcome. Where, however, both systems favour the partial *renvoi* approach, the result would be diversity. Where both systems prefer the double *renvoi* approach, there would be an impasse. Moreover, results other than these may eventuate in a particular case, by reason of different approaches which legal systems may take to characterisation and interpretation, and which have the potential to act as obstacles to achieving a uniform result. The simple point can be made that the legal systems involved may differ in their definition of their preferred connecting factor(s)[55]; and there is the more complex point that an incidental question may arise which affects the validity of the claim of an heir, especially qua widow.[56]

In any case of this type, the search for uniformity of treatment by the interested forums is said to be worth attempting. However, in argumentative mode, one might ask whether uniformity of treatment of a deceased's estate is always absolutely desirable. If the deceased had significant legal links with two legal systems, one of which strongly endorses the principle of family protection, and the other the principle of freedom of testation, advocates of harmony of decision, by seeking to secure a uniform distribution, necessarily would exclude the policy of one of those laws. Moreover, it must be queried how often these transnational succession problems arise. The EU in its harmonisation programme proceeds on the basis that there is a need for harmonisation of approach within Member States to govern such trans-European cases, and proposes a system of harmonised choice of law rules in succession, asserting that if this were achieved, the need for *renvoi* in these cases at Community level would fall away.

While the status of *renvoi* as an intellectual plaything in the subject is renowned, its potential use as a tool, to positive effect (i.e. in providing a legitimate escape route to a more positive result), or as a corrective (i.e. to seek to neutralise the effects of forum-shopping)[57] also should be recognised.

RENVOI CASES

5–14   The following is a summary of important English cases in which the foreign court theory of *renvoi* has been applied.

Re Annesley [1926] Ch. 692

Mrs Annesley, an Englishwoman, lived in France from 1866 until her death there in 1924. By the date of her death, she had not taken the steps prescribed by the French Civil Code to acquire French domicile; the requisite form, not completed, was found among her papers. She made a will in France in English form in which she declared that she intended to remain a British subject, and that she had not any intention of abandoning her English domicile. By the will she left the residue of her estate to one daughter absolutely, but she had another child who was excluded from the will. By English law she could dispose of all

---

[55] *Re Annesley* [1926] Ch. 692.
[56] See Ch.4, above.
[57] See Adrian Briggs, "In Praise and Defence of Renvoi" (1998) 47 I.C.L.Q. 877.

her estate as she wished, but by French law she could dispose by will of only one-third of her moveable estate, and the question at issue was whether her will had effectively conveyed the whole of the residue to the favoured daughter.

The question giving rise to the *renvoi* issue was the devolution of her moveable property, and the essential validity of her testamentary provisions pertaining thereto, which, by the choice of law rule of English law, is determined by the law of the domicile. Russell J. arrived at his decision that Mrs Annesley's freedom of testation was governed by French law, by the following reasoning:

(a) The connecting factor was domicile, which must be interpreted and identified by the English law of the forum, no matter what any other law might provide as to domicile.

(b) By English law, Mrs Annesley died domiciled in France.

(c) Applying the law of France as the law of the domicile, the English court must endeavour notionally to place itself in the same position as a French court and decide the matter as a French court would decide it. Starting then from French law as the law of the domicile in its wide sense, that law referred the matter (i.e. the essential validity of the will) to "British law" as the law of the nationality and the only meaning which could be given to "British law" in the circumstances was English law, which, in turn, would refer the matter back to the law of France. According to expert evidence preferred by Russell J., French law accepted a reference back and so the English court sitting, as it were, in the position of the French court, accepted the *renvoi* and applied French law in its narrow sense, with the result that it was held that Mrs Annesley's will could dispose of only one-third of her estate.

(d) It would have been possible to have arrived at the same result by ignoring *renvoi* and simply applying French law directly in its narrow sense as the law of the domicile. Indeed Russell J. commended this route, although single-handedly, it seems, he introduced into English conflict rules by this decision the double *renvoi* approach.

Re Ross [1930] 1 Ch. 377

Mrs Ross was a British subject of English domicile of origin, who died **5–15** domiciled in Italy leaving English and Italian wills. By those wills, she bequeathed the residue of her (moveable) estate in England to a niece and her (moveable and immoveable) estate in Italy to a grand-nephew, and in so doing she excluded her son from the succession. He raised an action in England for payment of the indefeasible rights of succession due to him under Italian law. Luxmoore J. decided as follows:

(a) As regards moveables, the connecting factor was domicile and the case must be decided in the same way as an Italian court would decide it, because in the view of the English forum the deceased died domiciled in Italy.

(b) Starting with Italian law (in its wide sense), that law referred the question to "British law" as the law of the nationality which, as in *Annesley*, could mean only English law, because the testatrix had her domicile of origin in England and had no other connection with Britain. English law would refer the question back to the law of Italy. The expert evidence, however, showed that the law of Italy could *not* accept a *renvoi*, so the matter could not proceed beyond the reference from Italian law, as the starting point, to "British law". As the Italian court could not accept a *renvoi*, it would insist upon applying "British law", and so the English court accepted the remission and applied English law in its narrow or domestic sense. In effect, therefore, the English court perforce applied the law of the domicile of origin in preference to the law of the last domicile. Was this the result of excessive care and politeness, or did the English court thereby truly give effect to its conception of Italian law?

(c) As regards immoveable property in Italy, the same decision was arrived at by the same reasoning, the starting point again being the law of Italy, this time qua *lex situs*.[58]

NOTE that the essential difference between *Annesley* and *Ross* lies simply in the fact that French law accepted the doctrine of *renvoi* whereas Italian law did not do so.

Re Askew [1930] 2 Ch. 259

5–16   Under an English marriage contract the husband, who was domiciled in England, had a power of appointment of a trust fund among the children of his marriage and of any subsequent marriage which he might make. Later he went to Germany where he acquired a domicile and became the father of an illegitimate daughter. He divorced his wife and married the child's mother. Subsequently, he purported to appoint the income upon trust after his death to be paid to his second wife, and after her death, to the children of the second marriage. A question having been raised about the propriety of the exercise of the power in relation to the daughter above-mentioned (a matter which depended on her status being established as a child legitimated by subsequent marriage), the court followed the reasoning set out below:

(a) The question at issue was one of status, and so the connecting factor was domicile. The father was taken by the English court to have a German domicile at the date of birth of the daughter in question.

(b) Starting with German law in its wide sense, that law referred the matter to the law of the nationality, "British law", which, once again, could mean only English law.

(c) English law referred the matter back to the law of Germany, which accepted *renvoi*, and so German law was applied in its narrow sense; as the child had been legitimated by that law, it could succeed despite its adulterine status in the eyes of English law. This was a positive outcome for the child, the more so because by English domestic law at the time the child, being an "adulterine bastard", was not capable of being legitimated.

---

[58] This produced the extremely unusual result that rights of succession to land in Italy were governed by the law of England; cf. with regard to the devolution of immoveables in Spain, *Re Duke of Wellington* [1947] Ch. 506; affirmed [1948] Ch. 118.

Re O'Keefe (Deceased) [1940] Ch. 124

This case is often cited to demonstrate that the operation of *renvoi* may have **5–17** artificial results.

Miss O'Keefe died intestate in Italy in 1937. Her father was born in County Clare, Ireland, and he lived first in India for many years and then in other countries. Miss O'Keefe, born in Calcutta, lived in India, France, England, Spain, Tangier and the Channel Islands, but for the last 47 years of her life in Italy, where she had acquired a domicile. Her domicile of origin was in Ireland, in the part which became Eire (now the Republic of Ireland), but she had not been in Ireland since a holiday visit when she was 18 years of age. At the time of her death she was a British—not Irish—subject. This case concerned the intestate succession to her estate, in respect of which the law of Ireland was applied, by the same reasoning as in *Ross*, as follows:

(a) English law as the law of the forum (where the assets were situated) decided that domicile was the connecting factor and that Miss O'Keefe had died domiciled in Italy.

(b) Italian law in its wide sense referred the matter to "British law" as the law of the nationality. "British law" would refer the matter back to the law of Italy, but Italian law could not accept a *renvoi*, and so the question had to be decided according to "British law", whatever that might mean.

(c) Following Ross, the judge held that the law of the domicile of origin, the law of Ireland, was the only law which could be applied (though Miss O'Keefe was not a citizen of Ireland). An alternative in such a case would have been to hold the deceased domiciled in that part of the British Commonwealth in which he or she last had a domicile before acquiring a foreign domicile. The case attracts comment because in lay terms the choice of Irish law had little connection with the facts of the deceased's life, and in technical terms the English court could hardly be said to be applying the law of her nationality as was the rule of Italian law. Nevertheless, the unusual outcome reflects the unusual personal and political circumstances of the case and it is submitted that the task of applying the law of the nationality in relation to a multi-legal system state will not normally be productive of such difficulty.

Re Duke of Wellington [1947] Ch. 506; affirmed [1948] Ch. 118

The sixth Duke of Wellington, domiciled in England, left assets in England **5–18** and Spain and made two wills dealing respectively with those assets. By the Spanish will he left his land in Spain to the person who was to succeed jointly to the English dukedom and the Spanish dukedom. He died unmarried and it transpired that, while his uncle succeeded to the English title, it was his sister who succeeded to the Spanish title, with the result that the destination in the Spanish will failed because there was no one beneficiary to succeed to both titles. The question arose at first instance and on appeal in England as to the determination of the manner in which the Spanish estate, moveable and immoveable, should devolve. By Spanish law succession to moveables and immoveables was governed by the law of the nationality. Wynn-Parry J. held that in these circumstances (of application of English law), the Spanish property, moveable and immoveable, ineffectually disposed of by the Spanish will, fell to be distributed in accordance with the English will which the sixth Duke had made in order to dispose of the remainder of his property, specifically excepting the property competently disposed of under the Spanish will. The court at first instance dealt with the case of moveable property on the simple view that it would descend in accordance with the English law of the ultimate domicile of the deceased. Therefore, by inference, it can be deduced that the English court felt under no obligation to dwell upon the consequences of the Spanish preference for a unity of succession rule and for application of the *lex patriae*.

The significance of the case resides in the treatment of the succession to immoveables which provoked a notable *renvoi* discussion. In relation to immoveable property, Wynn-Parry J., starting with Spanish law as the *lex situs*, held that the law referred the matter to "British law" as the law of the nationality, which could mean only English law. English law would refer the matter back to the *lex situs*, but each side produced conflicting expert evidence as to whether or not Spanish law would accept *renvoi*. One of the experts died before the hearing, but no objection was taken to his affidavit being read and relied on on behalf of the current Duke. The judge had to decide the point for himself and held, on balance, that Spanish law did not accept the reference back, and so he applied English law. In the Court of Appeal the only matters raised pertain to the construction and effect of the two wills in English law; by application of English law the seventh Duke was entitled under the English will to succeed to the Spanish property, moveable and immoveable, comprised in, but ineffectually disposed of by, the Spanish will. English law regulated the devolution of Spanish immoveable property, and in the view of the English court, the Spanish courts would be bound to register the title of the seventh Duke as the absolute owner of the Spanish immoveable property.[59]

The judgment of Wynn-Parry J. contains a very well-known conflict of laws lament:

> "[I]t would be difficult to imagine a harder task than that which faces me, namely, of expounding for the first time either in this country or in Spain the relevant law of Spain as it would be expounded by the Supreme Court of Spain, which up to the present time has made no pronouncement on the subject, and having to base that exposition on evidence which satisfies me that on this subject there exists a profound cleavage of legal opinion in Spain, and two conflicting decisions of courts of inferior jurisdiction".[60]

---

[59] See *Re Duke of Wellington* [1947] Ch. 506, per Wynn-Parry J. at 524. Normally, the *lex situs* is authoritative in matters pertaining to immoveable property (see Ch.17, below). Note, however, that certain incursions into this principle are identifiable, from which it can be seen that the *lex situs* sometimes is required to be compliant: see Carruthers, *Transfer of Property in the Conflict of Laws*, 2005, paras 2.76–2.86.

[60] *Re Duke of Wellington* [1947] Ch. 506 at 515.

SUMMARY 5

Renvoi: remission and transmission

1. The classic example of the *renvoi* problem is a question of succession to moveable estate in Scotland belonging to a British subject who has died intestate and domiciled in a foreign country, the law of which refers questions of succession to the law of the nationality.

2. Theories:

   (a) internal law theory
   (b) single *renvoi* theory
   (c) foreign court theory—which requires knowledge of
      (i) the choice of law rule of the foreign law; and
      (ii) whether or not the foreign law accepts a *renvoi* remission.

3. English courts apply the foreign court theory. The starting point notionally is the foreign court: if the foreign law accepts *renvoi*, that foreign law in the narrow sense is applied by the English court; if not, in the reported cases the forum reverts to application of its own domestic law.

4. The Scottish view of *renvoi* is untested in case law.

5. The doctrine has been applied principally in succession cases, and also to questions of status. Where benefit can be conferred on a party, modern English litigators apparently do not feel precluded from seeking to employ *renvoi* arguments,[61] where such arguments are not expressly prohibited by legislation. As a matter of drafting practice, European instruments typically exclude *renvoi* by stipulating that the application of the law of any country specified by the instrument means the rules of law in force in that country other than its rules of private international law.

---

[61] See, e.g. *Iran v Berend* [2007] EWHC 132 (QB), per Eady J. at [22]; and *The WD Fairway* [2009] EWHC 889 (Admlty). Cf. *Neilson v Overseas Projects Corp of Victoria Ltd* [2005] HCA 54.

CHAPTER 6

DOMICILE AND OTHER PERSONAL LAW CONNECTING FACTORS

THE NATURE OF DOMICILE

6–01 Every person in the course of his life becomes concerned in matters with legal implications, some of which are transient or temporary, and others of a more permanent nature. It is necessary to find a sufficiently weighty connecting factor for the regulation of the latter. The country to which a person "belongs" suggests itself as suitable. In continental European countries such matters have tended, in the past at least, to be governed by the law of the nationality, but in English speaking countries, which usually contain various states, provinces or units, each with its own legal system, there is no such thing as the "law of nationality". As a result, the laws of English speaking countries generally, and some others, e.g. Scandinavia, provide that questions of status and personal law, in general, are to be governed by the law of a person's domicile,[1] which is the place where he has his permanent home in the legal sense. It has been estimated that allegiance to the factors of nationality and domicile, respectively, is equally divided,[2] but it should be noted that the scope of operation of both factors is diminishing in view of the fact that all European states now must employ principally the connecting factor of habitual residence, as a result of the high incidence of its use in modern harmonisation instruments.

In the case of *Udny v Udny*,[3] which, with *Bell v Kennedy*,[4] forms the twin pillars on which the Scots and English rules of domicile are built, there is found the following explanation:

> "The law of England, and of almost all civilised countries, ascribes to each individual at his birth two distinct legal states or conditions; one by virtue of which he becomes the subject of some particular country, binding him by the tie of natural allegiance, which may be called his political status; another by virtue of which he has ascribed to him the character of a citizen of some particular country, and as such is possessed of certain municipal rights, and subject to certain obligations, which latter character is the civil status or condition of the individual, and may be quite different from his political status, for the political status may depend upon different laws in different countries, whereas the civil status

---

[1] See, e.g. K. Norrie, "Personal Law: Concept and Development", 1983 S.L.T. (News) 53.
[2] Norrie, "Personal Law: Concept and Development", 1983 S.L.T. (News) 53, 54.
[3] (1869) 7 M. (H.L.) 89, per Lord Westbury at 99.
[4] (1868) 6 M. (H.L.) 69.

is governed universally by one specific principle. Domicile or the place of settled residence of an individual is the criterion established by law for the purpose of determining the legal condition of the person, for it is on this basis that the personal rights of the parties—that is, the law which determines his majority or minority, marriage, succession, testacy or intestacy—must depend."

DOMICILE, NATIONALITY AND RESIDENCE COMPARED

Domicile is the tie or connection between an individual and an area or a terri- **6–02** torial unit governed by a common body of law. It is a relationship between an individual and a system of law. Because domicile implies a connection between a person and a territory having a common body of law, it follows that there is no such thing as British, Canadian, Australian or American domicile. A person may have a domicile only in a territory subject to a single system of law such as Scotland, England (and Wales), the Provinces of Quebec or Ontario, etc. in Canada, the States of New South Wales, Victoria, etc. in Australia,[5] New York, Ohio, etc. in USA or one of the Channel Islands.[6]

Domicile is a personal rather than administrative matter and may be changed without state authorisation. Cases of doubt can be resolved only by adjudication of the court, for there is no paper "evidence" of a person's domicile.

It is notoriously difficult to define domicile. Broadly, in its classic, i.e. common law, sense, the domicile of any person is the legal system which is considered by law to be his "permanent", i.e. established, home. It is, in general, the country which is in fact his home, but in some cases it is the country which, whether it is in fact his home or not, is determined to be such by rule of law.

Nationality is the tie of allegiance which binds an individual to a state and involves reciprocal duties of obedience and protection. State authorisation is required before nationality may be changed.[7]

Residence is a mere physical fact independent of will or intention, but it may involve legal consequences such as liability to pay income tax or rendering oneself subject to the jurisdiction of a particular court.

Habitual residence is a modern contender for the role of personal law.[8] It might be thought that the use of the adjective "habitual" denotes substantial

---

[5] By way of exception, for certain purposes (e.g. divorce), legislation within a non-unitary state may speak of, say, "Australian domicile", *Cheshire, North and Fawcett: Private International Law*, 14th edn, 2008, p.156.

[6] As the rules stand at present, an emigrant from Scotland to USA cannot be said to have acquired a new domicile until he has settled in a particular state. The Law Commissions proposed a change: *Private International Law: The Law of Domicile* (HMSO, 1987), Law Com. No.168; Scot. Law Com. No.107, para.7.8.

[7] i.e. for a person desiring change of nationality, the outcome (acquisition of the new; continuance of the old?) will depend on the laws of the states involved, including their attitudes to dual nationality. Further, the decision on who is a national of a state is a matter for the law of the state the nationality of which is in question: *Oppenheimer v Cattermole* [1975] 1 All E.R. 538.

[8] See, e.g. Child Abduction and Custody Act 1985; Family Law Act 1986 ss.26, 46; Children (Scotland) Act 1995 s.14; Regulation 2201/2003 ("Brussels II *bis*"); and the 1996 Hague Convention on the Protection of Children.

factual connection, not only more than sojourn,[9] but also more than mere "residence" or "ordinary residence". This, however, may be too simplistic a thought, for there is absence of agreement on the definition of habitual residence. Moreover, its meaning is likely to vary according to context. This will be examined in detail later in the chapter.

STATUTORY DEFINITION OF DOMICILE

6–03 The concept of domicile in its classic sense and its rules remain the same wherever they are encountered—marriage, succession, legitimacy or other area of personal law: the single conception theory.

However, "domicile" may be given a special meaning, defined by statute for a particular purpose. This is a modern occurrence. An artificial conception of domicile was introduced by the Finance Act 1975 s.45 (now repealed) for Inland Revenue purposes only. This is now contained in the Inheritance Tax Act 1984 s.267,[10] which provides that a person who is not domiciled in the UK at any given time shall be treated for inheritance tax purposes as if he were domiciled in the UK (and not elsewhere) at the relevant time if either:

(a) he was domiciled in the United Kingdom within the three years immediately preceding the relevant time; or
(b) he was resident in the United Kingdom in not less than 17 of the 20 years of assessment ending with the year of assessment in which the relevant time falls.

In this connection, exceptionally, domicile is that of the "United Kingdom", or not.

A much more important example of a particular statutory meaning of "domicile" is its use for the purpose of ascertaining jurisdiction in terms of the Civil Jurisdiction and Judgment Acts 1982 and 1991, and the Brussels I Regulation.[11] "Domicile" in this context bears no relation to domicile in its classic meaning. The definition or indicia of domicile in its classic sense, including capacity to acquire domicile, is the prerogative of the forum to decide. But a Member State forum's role with regard to the meaning of domicile within the Brussels regime is different. If the individual is not domiciled in the forum, art.59(2) of the Brussels I Regulation requires the forum (if need be) to ascertain if the individual is domiciled in another Member State by application of the rules of "domicile" of that other Member State.

---

[9] Wolff, *Private International Law*, 2nd edn, 1950, p.110 defines residence as, "habitual physical presence in a place . . . more than sojourn (physical presence) and less than domicile. It is a purely factual conception and requires no legal capacity". In *Winans v Att Gen (No.1)* [1904] A.C. 287, Lord Macnaghten at 298 described Winans as "a sojourner and stranger" when he came to England, and "a sojourner and a stranger in it" when he died, i.e. not domiciled in England at death, though resident there.

[10] See also Income Tax Act 2007 Ch.2 (Residence), and s.831 in particular (as amended by Finance Act 2008), and guidance on residence and domicile contained in HM Revenue and Customs, *Residence, Domicile and the Remittance Basis* (The Stationery Office, 2010), HMRC 6 (replacing IR20).

[11] Civil Jurisdiction and Judgments Act 1982 ss.41–46; and now Civil Jurisdiction and Judgments Order 2001 (SI 2001/3929), reg.9. See Ch.7, below.

Family Law (Scotland) Act 2006

The development of the rules of domicile in Scots and English law has been **6–04** characterised by steady common law progression, punctuated by legislative intervention on particular matters. It is important to note at this juncture that s.22 of the Family Law (Scotland) Act 2006 ("the 2006 Act") effects a change in the domicile rules of Scots law concerning the domicile of persons under 16 years of age. This provision has the potential to undermine long-established rules of domicile, and its influence will be further reaching, and its consequences more radical, than the name of the section ("domicile of persons under 16") and its ostensible purpose suggests. The rules to be set out in this chapter therefore must be read against the potential for change which s.22 contains.[12]

Unless otherwise indicated, the remainder of this chapter is concerned with domicile in its classic sense.[13]

THE RULES OF DOMICILE—A PRÉCIS

Knowledge of the subject of domicile requires a grasp of its technical rules and **6–05** familiarity with the case authorities in which the topic is rich. The rules of domicile are a construct of the common law. Statutory reform of the classic domicile rules, though significant in content, is late in date and specific in nature.

A summary of the rules is set out below. Full discussion of the principles follows later in the chapter.

(a) No person can be without a domicile, though they may lack a home in fact[14] and/or may have no knowledge of the concept of a legal home. Equally, where an individual has two or more homes, the fact that his chief and favourite residence is situated in country A may not dissuade the court from finding him to be domiciled, by application of the forum's rules, in country B.[15]

(b) No person can have more than one domicile (in the classic sense) at any one time.

(c) *Domicile of origin* is ascribed according to fixed rules. Prior to the coming into force of the 2006 Act, these rules rested on the distinction between legitimacy and illegitimacy. The Law Reform (Parent and Child) (Scotland) Act 1986, by s.9(1)(a),[16] retained the rule of law whereby a child born outside marriage took as a domicile of

---

[12] See, in detail, para.6–08, below.

[13] See regarding its use in jurisdiction, Ch.7, below.

[14] Thus, where the *propositus* was found to have led a nomadic existence, living in lodgings or with friends, she was held not to have lost her Scots domicile of origin: *Arnott v Groom* (1846) 9 D. 142.

[15] *Marchioness of Huntly v Gaskell* (1905) 8 F. (H.L.) 4 (affirming sub nom. *Brooks v Brooks's Trustees* (1902) 4 F. 1014 in Court of Session); also *Donaldson v McClure* (1857) 20 D. 207. *Re Clore (Deceased) (No.2)* [1984] S.T.C. 609. See also the special circumstances and dual residence decision in *Plummer v Inland Revenue Commissioners* [1988] 1 All E.R. 97.

[16] Repealed by Family Law (Scotland) Act 2006 Sch.3.

origin the domicile possessed by his mother at the date of his birth, affirming therefore the common law rule (applying still in England), that domicile of origin is ascribed according to status as legitimate or illegitimate.

One of the aims of the 2006 Act was to complete the process of removal from the law of Scotland of the status of illegitimacy. Abolition of the status was effected by s.21.[17] In consequence, a new rule for the ascription of domicile at birth was provided by s.22. The implications of this section are considered fully below, but essentially the new general rule is that if a child's parents are domiciled in the same country as each other, and the child has a home with either or both parent(s), the child shall be domiciled in the same country as his parents.

(d) Every person sui juris[18] may acquire a *domicile of choice* by a combination of a change of residence to a different legal system and the intention to reside in that system for as long as can be seen ahead. Any circumstances, even the seemingly trivial,[19] which seem to bear upon residence and/or intention may be considered by the court in assessing domicile, and it is the duty of counsel to bring all potentially relevant matters to the attention of the court.[20]

(e) Domicile of choice is lost by a combination of loss of residence in, *and* loss of intention for, a legal system. Retention of *either* residence[21] or intention[22] will result in retention of domicile of choice.

(f) There is a presumption in favour of an existing domicile. The onus of proof of change of domicile lies on the party arguing that change has taken place.[23] This is likely to have a crucial effect on the outcome of litigation.[24]

(g) In all types of case in which the connecting factor of domicile is used, there is a *tempus inspiciendum* according to the choice of law rule in question, e.g. capacity to marry—*ante-nuptial* domicile of each party, cumulatively applied; succession to moveables—deceased's domicile *at death*. In the ascertainment of intention, the court is precluded from taking into account factors pertaining to residence or deemed intention which post-date that time.[25]

---

[17] In cases where the person's status is governed by Scots law. See further Chs 14, especially para.14–01, and 18, below.

[18] That is, of full legal capacity, unaffected by a legal disability caused, e.g. by nonage or insanity.

[19] *Drevon v Drevon* (1834) 34 L.J. Ch. 129, per Kindersley V.C. at 133.

[20] *Brown v Brown*, 1928 S.L.T. 339, per Lord President Clyde at 341.

[21] *Re Raffenel* (1863) 3 Sw. & Tr. 49 (loss of intention, but no sufficient loss of residence).

[22] *Re Lloyd Evans* [1947] Ch. 695 (loss of residence, but continuing intention for Belgium); and *Morgan v Cilento* [2004] EWHC 188 (Ch).

[23] *Bell v Kennedy* (1868) 6 M. (H.L.) 69; *Vincent v Earl of Buchan* (1889) 16 R. 637; *Lord Advocate v Brown's Trustees*, 1907 S.C. 333; *Casey v Casey*, 1968 S.L.T. 56; *Spence v Spence*, 1995 S.L.T. 335; *Reddington v Riach's Executor*, 2002 S.L.T. 537; and *Morgan v Cilento* [2004] EWHC 188 (Ch).

[24] See *Moynihan v Moynihan* [1997] 1 F.L.R. 59; *Cyganik v Agulian* [2006] EWCA Civ 129; *Munro v Munro* [2007] EWHC 3315 (Fam); *Gaines-Cooper v Revenue and Customs Commissioners* [2007] EWHC 2617 (Ch); *Re N (Jurisdiction)* [2009] I.L.Pr. 8.

[25] *Lynch v Provisional Government of Paraguay* (1871) L.R. 2 P.&D. 268; *Bell v Kennedy* (1868) 6 M. (H.L.) 69; *Morgan v Cilento* [2004] EWHC 188 (Ch); and *Cyganik v Agulian* [2006] EWCA Civ 129, per Mummery L.J. at [46].

(h) In Scots law prior to the 2006 Act, and in English law still, an individual's domicile, during nonage, would/will be dependent upon the domicile of his father or mother, depending on the child's status, and the application if appropriate of s.4 of the Domicile and Matrimonial Proceedings Act ("DMPA") 1973 (*q.v.*), in terms of which the domicile of an under-age party will change if a change should occur in the domicile of the relevant parent.[26] By virtue of s.22 of the 2006 Act, an individual's domicile at any given point under the age of 16 will be determined by application of that section. It is important to note that the 2006 Act, in Sch.3, repeals (for Scotland only) s.4 of the DMPA 1973.

Prior to the 2006 Act, and still in English law, it was/is thought that the domicile of persons under the age of 16 both of whose parents are dead, probably cannot be changed. Though the 2006 Act is silent on the point, the situation would appear to fall within s.22(3), permitting the court to find the child domiciled in the country with which he has for the time being the closest connection.

(i) Legal capacity in Scots law to have an independent domicile depends upon having attained the age of 16[27] and upon being of sufficient mental capacity to form the requisite intention.

(j) Until January 1, 1974 the domicile of married women was dependent upon the domicile of their husbands, but s.1 of the DMPA 1973 abolished the "unity of domicile" rule in the case of persons married after that date.[28]

(k) In questions which have arisen in the courts of Scotland and England, domicile is always ascertained in accordance with the rules thereon of the *lex fori*.[29] This will include determination of legal capacity to acquire a new domicile, even though it may seem preferable for an individual's capacity to acquire a new domicile to be determined by the law of his pre-existing domicile.[30] In domicile cases before a Scots or English forum, no question ever arises of the individual's legal capacity to change his domicile throughout his life being determined by the conflict rules of any system other than that of the forum. Such conjecture would add greatly to the cost and complexity of the case, and would increase uncertainty.

---

[26] The rules of dependent domicile in Scots law rested upon statute (DMPA 1973 s.4), and common law where the circumstances fell outside the terms of s.4.

[27] Authority for this rests now not on the Age of Legal Capacity (Scotland) Act 1991 s.7 (repealed by 2006 Act Sch.3), but rather on the 2006 Act s.22(4). For English law, see DMPA 1973 s.3(a): capacity is conferred at age 16, or upon marriage before that age by a party who necessarily must not be of English domicile, since by English law persons do not have legal capacity to marry before 16.

[28] See para.6–29, below.

[29] *Re Annesley* [1926] Ch. 692. See, however, exceptionally Family Law Act 1986 s.46(5) concerning recognition of a foreign court as competent to dissolve a marriage: in extending such recognition to the foreign court of the domicile, s.46(5) permits "domicile" to be understood in either the forum's or foreign meaning.

[30] See Graveson, *Private International Law*, 7th edn, 1974, p.193.

CLASSES OF DOMICILE

Introduction

6–06   Every person sui juris (the *"propositus"*) has a domicile which may be either a "domicile of origin" or a "domicile of choice". A domicile of origin is ascribed by law to every person at birth and is involuntary. Even if it is superseded by the acquisition of a new domicile, the domicile of origin is never entirely extinguished and, if the new domicile subsequently is lost, the domicile of origin will revive. Domicile of choice is the domicile which a person sui juris may acquire by a change of residence and intention. A person who is not sui juris may acquire a derivative or dependent domicile, according to rules outlined below governing the years of legal incapacity.

The 2006 Act makes no reference to the terms "domicile of origin" and "domicile of choice". The express purpose of s.22 is to effect the ascription of domicile of persons under 16. By inference, therefore, the rules contained in s.22 cease to be applicable to a person once he attains the age of 16. In the absence of further statutory intervention, it is presumed that in any domicile litigation occurring in Scotland concerning the domicile of someone over the age of 16, the Scots court is entitled to hold that such a person has legal capacity to change his under-16 domicile to a different domicile (of choice), or any number of subsequent changes of domicile of choice. It is assumed that where the individual has made no such change after he has attained 16 years, he will be held to have retained his under-16 domicile.[31]

It is regrettable that full consideration has not been given to the implications of this ad hoc statutory incursion into the framework of the domicile rules. The silence about the name of the under-16 domicile, and its place in the general scheme, is damaging to the coherence of the domicile rules. As will be explained below, in Scots law prior to the 2006 Act, and still in English law, the domicile of origin so termed acted/acts as an "anchor" domicile, providing certainty at times of uncertainty. It is an essential part of an evolved system of rules of personal law.

DOMICILE OF ORIGIN

Scots law prior to the Family Law (Scotland) Act 2006[32]

6–07   A domicile of origin is the domicile ascribed by law to every person at birth[33] in accordance with the following rules:

(1) *Legitimate child*—The domicile is that of the child's father as at the date of the child's birth.[34] Place of birth has no necessary relevance. On the argument that a child is legitimate by English[35] and Scots[36]

---

[31] cf. *Harrison v Harrison* [1953] 1 W.L.R. 865; and *Henderson v Henderson* [1967] P. 77.
[32] And current rules of English Law.
[33] *Woodbury v Sutherland's Trustees*, 1939 S.L.T. 93. *Re Craignish* [1892] 3 Ch. 180. The only example of the ascribing of domicile of origin at a date later than birth is that of adoption.
[34] *Udny v Udny* (1869) 7 M. (H.L.) 89.
[35] *Bromley's Family Law*, edited by N.V. Lowe and G. Douglas, 10th edn (Oxford: Oxford University Press, 2007), pp.341, 342.
[36] Eskine, I, 6, 49.

domestic law if his parents were married at the time of his conception or the time of his birth, it is certainly arguable[37] that a child conceived during marriage, but born after the divorce of his parents, must take his father's domicile as a domicile of origin. However, if thereafter the child has his home with his mother, he will take his mother's domicile of dependency.[38].

(2) *Illegitimate or posthumous child*—The domicile is that of the child's mother as at the date of the child's birth.[39] Changes brought about in Scottish domestic rules concerning illegitimacy and legal equality of children by the Law Reform (Parent and Child) (Scotland) Act 1986 were not accompanied by any alteration in the rules governing the ascribing of domicile of origin or dependence.[40]

(3) *Child legitimated per subsequens matrimonium*—The domicile of origin is that of the mother as at the date of the child's birth, but the child takes the domicile of the father as from the date of the marriage as a derivative or dependent domicile.

(4) *Child of putative marriage*—The domicile is that of the innocent party to the "marriage".[41]

(5) *Adopted child*—It is thought that an adopted child will acquire from the date of the adoption the domicile of the adoptive father and that on the latter's death the domicile of the child will follow that of the adoptive mother. Generally, since an adopted child is treated as the legitimate child of the adoptive parent(s), his domicile should be determined in accordance with the legitimate child rule.

It may be found on occasion (though less commonly nowadays) that a court must trace a family history in order to provide a reasoned judgment as to the domicile of origin of the *propositus*.[42]

Family Law (Scotland) Act 2006

The aim of the legislation is that there shall, "no longer be a link between a **6–08** child's domicile and that of his parent's marital status in relation to both the domicile of origin and dependant [sic] domicile."[43]

In terms of s.22, the domicile of a person under 16 is ascribed according to the following rules:

A child shall be domiciled in the same country as his parents where:

(a) his parents are domiciled in the same country as each other; and
(b) he has a home with a parent or a home (or homes) with both of them.

---

[37] However, *Dicey, Morris and Collins on the Conflict of Laws*, 14th edn, 2006, para.6–028, say that this is an open question, and that such a child may be thought to take as his domicile of origin the domicile of his mother.

[38] See in English law (and in Scots law until the advent of the 2006 Act) DMPA 1973 s.4.

[39] *Udny v Udny* (1869) 7 M. (H.L.) 89.

[40] Law Reform (Parent and Child) (Scotland) Act 1986 s.9(1)(a); and DMPA 1973 s.4.

[41] *Smijth v Smijth*, 1918 1 S.L.T. 156. But see Alexander E. Anton, *Private International Law: A treatise from the standpoint of Scots law*, 1st edn (Edinburgh: SULI/W. Green, 1967), pp.343, 344.

[42] *Grant v Grant*, 1931 S.C. 238; *Re Flynn (No.1)* [1968] 1 W.L.R. 103.

[43] Explanatory notes to Family Law (Scotland) Bill, para.30.

Where these conditions are not satisfied, the child shall be domiciled in the country with which he has for the time being the closest connection.

The following observations may be made:

(a) Section 22 is much terser than its antecedent (cl.16 of the Bill, which contained a number of rebuttable presumptions, and gave a misleading impression of comprehensive treatment). The use of presumptions has been abandoned.

(b) Reliance is placed on the test "having a home with", which may suggest an emotional tie, rather than, or in addition to, a purely factual tie based on ordinary residence. One would assume that where a child is sent away from his parents' home to another country for education, or for reasons of safety, his "home" (notional) must yet be held to be with his parents. Speculation would suggest that, on the basis of s.22, such a child would be held to "have his home with" his parents, although he may not generally reside with them on a day-to-day basis, and so his domicile will follow that of his parents, who may or may not be domiciled in the place to which they have been posted. This example underlines the importance of interpretation of the key test of "having a home with".[44] However, it is by no means clear why the requirement of "having a home with" one or both parents is engrafted as an additional requirement upon the condition of common domicile of the child's parents.

(c) Domicile of origin has been in Scotland, and remains in England, the default position to which recourse is had in cases of doubt and uncertainty. Seeking to legislate under the heading of "domicile of persons under 16", without appreciating the repercussions thereof in relation to the ascertainment of domicile at subsequent points in the individual's life, is ill-advised. It must be remembered that rules of domicile exist to supply an appropriate legal system to govern important matters of status and capacity which may arise at any point in the life of the *propositus*. The difficulty of establishing, at the time of death of a nonagenarian, for the purpose of distribution of his estate, his domicile of origin according to these proposed rules, does not seem to have been appreciated[45]; identification of the childhood "home" of such a person in many cases may be impossible to prove.

The Law Commissions' 1987 proposals, whatever view one takes of their desirability, contained a suggested *corpus* of rules on domicile, including the abolition of domicile of origin,[46] whereas that which is contained in the 2006 Act purports to be restricted to the alteration of the rules in a particular area. The problem is that domicile at the start of life is fundamental, and has pivotal importance throughout the legal life of the *propositus*.[47]

---

[44] cf. *Williams, Petitioner*, 1977 S.L.T. (Notes) 2.

[45] cf. *Cyganik v Agulian* [2006] EWCA Civ 129, per Mummery L.J., at para.46, who quotes Kierkegaard: "[l]ife must be lived forwards, but can only be understood backwards".

[46] *Private International Law: The Law of Domicile*, 1987, Law Com. No.168; Scot. Law Com. No.107, para.4.24.

[47] See *Bell v Kennedy* (1868) 6 M. (H.L.) 69.

(d) The tacit assumption is that the new rule will apply, not only for the purposes of ascription of domicile at birth, but at any time during the first 16 years of the *propositus's* life, if an issue of domicile should arise. Express repeal of the statutory amendment to dependent domicile effected by DMPA 1973 s.4, means that s.22 governs situations which previously in a Scots court were governed by s.4. This provides a shifting test according to changing factual circumstances. One must seek to identify factual and legal scenarios (capacity of the "minor" to succeed to land or moveables; to make a will; to marry) in which the domicile of an under 16 person may be called upon, before assessing the extent of the detrimental effect of the new rule on the old. These are temporal issues, of *tempus inspiciendum*; but a much larger issue of time is the absence of any legislative provision for transitional arrangements.

(e) The question as to the time at which the new rule is to take effect is one in respect of which the Act is silent. One would have hoped that it would take effect from its date of commencement forward,[48] to regulate the domiciles of those who, at the date of coming into force of the Act, are under 16 and those at that date not yet born. Regrettably, however, by inference of the Family Law (Scotland) Act 2006 (Commencement, Transitional Provisions and Savings) Order 2006, litigation to determine the ultimate domicile of an octogenarian *propositus* who dies after commencement of the Act, may require to be carried out according to the new rules contained in the Act.[49] The point is yet untested.

(f) In seeking equality of treatment of children in this matter, certainty has been lost. A wiser approach, and one capable of application to all children regardless of status, would have been to ascribe to a child as his domicile of origin, the domicile of his mother at the date of birth, capable of rebuttal only in exceptional cases.[50] Favouring the matrilineal line has an ancient pedigree. Alternatively, absent a common domicile of the parents at the date of birth, the child, in the general case, could have taken the domicile of the mother at the date of birth as his domicile of origin. In this way, a new rule could have been devised, which in its content did not discriminate among children according to the marital status of their parents, but which would have been certain in application, and would not have damaged the overall structure of rules.

---

[48] Though this is by no means borne out by the Family Law (Scotland) Act 2006 (Commencement, Transitional Provisions and Savings) Order 2006 (SSI 2006/212), which in art.4 merely enacts that the provisions of s.22, inter alia, shall not apply in relation to any proceedings which commenced before May 4, 2006. Cf. suggested approach to transitional matters contained in Law Commission 1987 proposals, *Private International Law: The Law of Domicile*, 1987, Law Com. No.168; Scot. Law Com. No.107, para.8.7 and cll.1(2), 2(3), mentioned at para.6–29, below.

[49] See McEleavy, "Regression and Reform in the Law of Domicile" (2007) 56(2) I.C.L.Q. 453.

[50] e.g. cases of death of mother in childbirth, or adopted children, in respect of whom the pre-existing rule would still apply. The 2006 Act does not provide a special rule for adopted children; nor, in s.22, does the Act make it clear whether the word "parent" includes adoptive parent.

It is a matter of regret that the rules of domicile, in Scots law on the one hand, and in the law of England and Wales, on the other, now diverge. As a matter of necessity, the preferred personal law connecting factor within UK law, has been domicile not nationality, and a common approach to the ascription of domicile surely is desirable. What, if any, change will be made in this matter by English law is a legitimate enquiry.

DOMICILE OF CHOICE

6–09 Every person who is sui juris[51] may acquire a domicile of choice in any country (other than the country of his domicile of origin) which has a system of law of its own, only by a combination of residence (*factum*) and intention (*animus*) to reside there for as long as can be seen ahead.

Acquisition of a domicile of choice requires a change of *both* residence *and* intention.[52]

Retention of a domicile of choice is maintained by retention of *either* residence *or* intention.

Loss of a domicile of choice requires a change of *both* residence *and* intention.

The acquisition of a domicile of choice merely supersedes the domicile of origin, but does not obliterate it because, if the former is lost, the latter will revive.[53] Hence, if, in the view of the court, the *propositus* has established a domicile of choice *animo et facto* in legal system A, a change of heart or mind the next day will change nothing: the change must be acted upon sufficiently, that is, by departure in a final manner beyond the territorial limits of legal system A.[54]

It cannot be emphasised too strongly that departure in a final manner from the domicile of origin effects no change unless and until domicile of choice is established clearly elsewhere.[55] In this context only, there is a "continuance" rule, i.e. continuance of domicile of origin until displaced. In contrast, where a domicile of choice is lost *animo et facto*, the domicile of origin revives to fill any gap. This is the rule of revival of domicile of origin, which has been favoured in the UK. It is *not* the case that one domicile of choice subsists until

---

[51] See para.6–06, above.

[52] "[W]here intention is absolutely clear, a minimum of residence in the ordinary case at any rate is enough": *Willar v Willar*, 1954 S.C. 144, per Lord Justice-Clerk Thomson at 147; and *King v Foxwell* (1876) L.R. 3 Ch. D. 518. Consider the extreme circumstances of *White v Tennant*, 31 W.Va. 790, 8 S.E. 596 (1888) in which "residence" of a few hours' duration, as evidenced by deposit of belongings in the new house in the new US state, was sufficient for the *propositus* to have acquired domicile in that state, although that night, having returned to the state of his previous residence to lodge with relatives, he died there. See also the special circumstances of *Plummer v Inland Revenue Commissioners* [1988] 1 All E.R. 97 (chief residence was not moved to new country).

[53] The Family Law (Scotland) Act 2006 makes no overt change to this fundamental rule, but in future, when a Scots forum seeks to ascertain the domicile of origin of an individual whose domicile at the outset of life will have been affected by that Act, it will be required to apply s.22 to ascertain the first domicile of the *propositus*, i.e. at date of birth.

[54] cf. *Re Raffenel* (1863) 3 Sw. & Tr. 49.

[55] *Bell v Kennedy* (1868) 6 M. (H.L.) 69.

a new one is acquired.[56] Although the revival rule has been criticised, it has not been removed.

PROOF OF ACQUISITION OF DOMICILE OF CHOICE

A person averring a change of domicile either of himself or of a third party   **6–10** must show that there has been a change of *both residence* and *intention*. All relevant factors regarding these two matters must be considered.[57] Residence may throw light on intention and expressed intention may throw light on residence; for example, intention may grow as residence lengthens. The two factors are interconnected,[58] but should be considered separately, at least in the first instance.

Standard of proof

The standard of proof of change of domicile is the normal civil standard of   **6–11** the balance of probabilities. Nevertheless, a variation in difficulty of proof can be seen in relation to different types of domicile. It is relatively easy for an individual to shed, after 16, the domicile of dependence (so too, presumably, the "under-16" domicile) that he has acquired perforce through a change of domicile on the part of the person on whom his domicile was dependent.[59] At the other extreme, the most striking feature of the current rules is the "limpet-like quality" of the domicile of origin, and the difficulty of discharging the burden of showing that a domicile of choice has replaced it.[60] Scrutiny of decisions suggests that the standard of proof in such a case may go beyond "a mere balance of probabilities".[61] Stronger evidence is required to establish a change from a domicile of origin to a domicile of choice than from one domicile of

---

[56] Contrast US rule in *Re Jones' Estate* (1921) 182 N.W. 227 Supreme Court of Iowa. The difference between the two systems (USA and UK), as John G. Collier suggests at *Conflict of Laws*, 3rd edn (Cambridge: Cambridge University Press, 2001), p.51, stems from the different attitudes of a country whose sons went out to travel the world and were expected to return, and those of an immigrant country from which people were not expected to depart. See also Canadian decision, *Re Foote Estate*, 2009 ABQB 654, which evidences a desire for Canadian law of domicile to permit the court to be more flexible in its application of the rule of revival of domicile of origin.

[57] The case of *Brooks v Brooks's Trustees* (1902) 4 F. 1014 is a useful example which has been set in poetic form by William M. Gloag, *Carmina Legis* (Glasgow: Maclehose, Jackson and Co, 1920): "A domicile at birth we all acquire, True, we may change it if we so desire . . .".

[58] cf. *Haldane v Eckford (No.2)* (1869) L.R. 8 Eq. 631, as expressed in the rubric derived from Lord Westbury's judgment in *Udny*: "Residence originally temporary, and intended for a limited period, may afterwards become general and unlimited, and in such a case, so soon as the change of purpose, or animus manendi, can be inferred, the fact of domicil is established." See also *Re Foote Estate*, 2009 ABQB 654.

[59] *Harrison v Harrison* [1953] 1 W.L.R. 865. See also *Henderson v Henderson* [1967] P. 77, per Sir Jocelyn Simon, at pp.82, 83: "[t]he abandonment of a domicile of choice acquired dependently in favour of a domicile of origin reacquired by personal volition must, in the nature of things, generally be of all changes of domicile, the one the least onerous of proof."

[60] *Cyganik v Agulian* [2006] EWCA Civ 129. See at shrieval level *Williamson v Williamson*, 2009 G.W.D. 14–220.

[61] *Munro v Munro* [2007] EWHC 3315 (Fam), per Bennett J. at [32]. But see also *Re N (Jurisdiction)* [2009] I.L.Pr. 8, per Hedley J. at [8].

choice to a new domicile of choice. In all cases it is possibly easier to establish a change from one law unit to another in the same political state than to a legal system in which one will be an alien.[62]

Value of authorities

6–12   Domicile cases make a review of the life of an individual, sometimes at a particular point in the course of it,[63] and frequently at the end of that life. Since all lives are unique, it is said that the corpus of domicile cases does not form a body of precedent in the normal way and that each decision is a guide only.[64] Yet, common themes recur and similar mind-sets[65] are found, and so a wide knowledge of domicile decisions is the foundation of a convincing domicile opinion.

Residence

6–13   Actual physical residence of some kind is necessary, but residence by itself, no matter for how long, is ineffective without intention.[66] Graveson remarked[67] that the word does not command its Victorian meaning of a 10-roomed villa. Nourse, J. in *Inland Revenue Commissioners v Duchess of Portland*[68] said that: "Residence in a country for the purposes of the law of domicile is physical presence in that country as an inhabitant of it."

Lawfulness of residence

6–14   In the case of *Puttick*[69] the view was expressed firmly by Sir George Baker, President of the Family Division, that acquisition of domicile of choice in a country cannot be founded upon residence which is unlawful by the law of that country. This statement now is qualified by the unanimous decision of the House of Lords in *Mark v Mark*,[70] a divorce jurisdiction case, in which the parties were Nigerian. The wife issued a divorce petition in an English forum, relying initially for jurisdiction solely upon her habitual residence in England over the previous 12 months, but her petition was later amended so as to include the claim that she had acquired a domicile of choice in England.

---

[62] cf. *Reddington v Riach's Executor*, 2002 S.L.T. 537.

[63] See, e.g. *Bell v Kennedy* (1868) 6 M. (H.L.) 69.

[64] Per Lord McLaren in *Lord Advocate v Brown's Trustees*, 1907 S.C. 333 at 338: "In view of the weight which is so often attributed to authorities in such questions it may not be superfluous that I should begin by stating what is almost a truism, that every question of domicile is essentially a question of fact. Judicial expositions, I need hardly say, may be of great value as guides to the relative weights to be attributed to different elements of a life history in the question of domicile; but in the determination of the whole question of the domicile, each case, as I think, must be considered by itself and in the light of the facts proved."

[65] Compare the fervour for Canada of the *propositus* in each of *Inland Revenue Commissioners v Duchess of Portland* [1982] 1 All E.R. 784 and *Inland Revenue Commissioners v Bullock* [1976] 3 All E.R. 353, and contrast the decisions.

[66] *Jopp v Wood* (1865) 34 L.J. Ch. 212; *Brooks v Brooks's Trustees* (1902) 4 F. 1014; *Re Almeda* (1902) 18 T.L.R. 414; *Winans v Att Gen (No.1)* [1904] A.C. 287; *Ross v Ross*, 1930 S.C. (H.L.) 1; *Liverpool Royal Infirmary v Ramsay*, 1930 S.C. (H.L.) 83; *Grant v Grant*, 1931 S.C. 238; *Willar v Willar*, 1954 S.C. 144.

[67] Graveson, *Private International Law*, 7th edn, 1974, p.201.

[68] *Inland Revenue Commissioners v Duchess of Portland* [1982] 1 Ch. 314 at 318, 319.

[69] *Puttick v Att Gen* [1979] 3 All E.R. 463.

[70] [2005] 3 All E.R. 912.

Having first admitted that the English court had jurisdiction, the husband later changed his mind on the point, and applied for a stay of the English proceedings, on the basis that he had already commenced proceedings in Nigeria. The husband argued that the habitual residence of the wife in England for 12 months prior to the petition could not clothe the court with jurisdiction because the wife's presence in England was unlawful.She was classed as an "overstayer", i.e. a person whose leave to remain in the UK had expired. The judge at first instance held that while the wife could not be regarded as habitually resident in England, by reason of the unlawfulness of her presence, she could rely upon presence in England as a basis for the acquisition of a domicile of choice. The Court of Appeal dismissed the husband's appeal, finding that the wife had not only acquired an English domicile of choice by the time of litigation, but also had been habitually resident in England for the previous 12 months. In the House of Lords, on the residence point, Baroness Hale held that for the purpose of the 1973 Act s.5(2) (but not necessarily for other statutory provisions), the residence of the petitioner need not be lawful residence.

On the question of domicile, her Ladyship found that there was little English case authority until *Puttick*, though she drew on authorities from other Commonwealth jurisdictions. Treating the matter, therefore, as one of principle, and having regard to the object of the rules of domicile (which, in her Ladyship's view, is to discover the system of law with which the *propositus* is most closely connected for a range of purposes), Baroness Hale concluded that there was no reason in principle why a person whose presence in England is unlawful cannot there acquire a domicile of choice. She took a purposive approach; recognising the appropriateness of England as a divorce forum in the instant case did not offend, in her Ladyship's view, any general principle that a person cannot be allowed to benefit from his own criminal conduct. Lady Hale took the view that in the circumstances presented, the state had no particular interest, one way or another.[71] As a matter of fact, the wife's position was precarious, and comparable to the situations of the petitioner *Boldrini*[72] and *Cruh*.[73] In view of this decision, which was unanimous, previously held views based upon *Puttick* must be regarded now with caution. A more nuanced approach may be expected.

Intention

There must be an intention to settle in a new country having a separate body **6–15** of law. Although a person must regard his new home as being in that country for the foreseeable future, such an intention need not be irrevocable or everlasting because an everlasting intention cannot reasonably be required of anybody. However, there will not be a change of domicile if the person always had at the back of his mind the intention to leave the country at some indefinite future date, for example on retiral or death of a spouse, and to go back to his original country.[74] The decision in *Re Capdevielle*[75] in 1864 marked the

---

[71] *Mark v Mark* [2005] 3 All E.R. 912 at [44]. Contrast peerage claim *Re Barony of Moynihan* [2000] 1 F.L.R. 113.
[72] *Boldrini v Boldrini* [1932] P. 9 (re illegal alien).
[73] *Cruh v Cruh* [1945] 2 All E.R. 545 (re party subject to deportation order).
[74] *Inland Revenue Commissioners v Bullock* [1976] 3 All E.R. 353; cf. *Re De Hosson* [1937] I.R. 467. Contrast the outcome in *Inland Revenue Commissioners v Duchess of Portland* [1982] 1 Ch. 314.
[75] (1864) 2 H. & C. 985.

change to a stricter test; from that date the Scots and English courts have required what may be termed "conscious adoption" of the new legal system as home, whereas before that date residence of indefinite duration would suffice. Hence, lingering doubts and wishes are important, and may preclude acquisition of a domicile of choice.[76] *Motive* is not a bar to change of domicile so long as the *propositus*, for whatever reason, had the requisite intention to settle in the new country.[77] The individual must be capable mentally of forming that intention, though no specialised knowledge of the significance of forming such intention is necessary.

The court will not draw the inference of sufficient intention for acquisition of a domicile of choice if it appears that an individual lives "between" legal systems, and if "his complex hesitant mind" has not decided between them[78]: in such a case, domicile of origin remains. In technical terms, the burden of proof of change will not have been discharged to the satisfaction of the court. It must not be thought that the test for acquisition of a domicile of choice is impossibly high nor that it cannot be satisfied in a relatively short time.[79] In the Scots decision of *Spence v Spence*,[80] a nicely balanced case, the court took the view that a period of 10 years residence in Spain and connections through business and family (though without social connection) was not sufficient to justify a finding of acquisition of a Spanish domicile of choice. However, in *Reddington v Riach's Executor*[81] the domicile of the deceased (who died in Bournemouth, England, at the age of 95) was held to have been changed by him to that of an English domicile of choice. His domicile of origin had been Scottish, but from 1976 he had been resident in Bournemouth, continuing to reside there after the death of his wife in 1987, visiting Scotland only once or twice after 1976 and never having expressed a desire to return. A distinguishing factor between *Spence* and *Reddington* is that the alleged change of domicile in *Reddington* was between legal systems of one territorial unit of the UK to another. The similarity of circumstance and difference of outcome between the cases of *Liverpool Royal Infirmary v Ramsay*[82] and *Reddington v Riach's Executor* is striking, and may be explicable not only in terms of the differing states of mind of the *propositus* in each case, but also by reason of the elapse in time between the two decisions, perhaps exemplifying a softening in the attitude of the courts.

---

[76] *Whicker v Hume* (1858) 7 H.L. Cas. 124; *Winans v Att Gen (No.1)* [1904] A.C. 287; *Liverpool Royal Infirmary v Ramsay*, 1930 S.C. (H.L.) 83; *Gulbenkian v Gulbenkian* [1937] 4 All E.R. 618; *Re Clore (Deceased) (No.2)* [1984] S.T.C. 609 (English domicile (of origin) retained); *Inland Revenue Commissioners v Bullock* [1976] 3 All E.R. 353; *Lord v Colvin* (1859) 4 Drew 366 at 376; *Re Sillar* [1956] I.R. 344; and *Re Furse (Deceased)* [1980] 3 All E.R. 838.

[77] Intention is not compromised by the reason for entertaining the intention; *Carswell v Carswell* (1881) 8 R. 901; *Stavert v Stavert* (1882) 9 R. 519; *Morton v Morton* (1897) 5 S.L.T. 222; *Sellars v Sellars*, 1942 S.C. 206; *McLelland v McLelland*, 1943 S.L.T. 66; *Marchant v Marchant*, 1948 S.L.T. 143.

[78] *Fuld (No.3)* [1968] P. 675, per Scarman J. at 689.

[79] *McNeill v McNeill*, 1919 2 S.L.T. 127; *Elmquist v Elmquist*, 1961 S.L.T. (Notes) 71; *Rankin v Rankin*, 1960 S.L.T. 308; *Gould v Gould (No.2)*, 1968 S.L.T. 98; *McEwan v McEwan*, 1969 S.L.T. 342; contrast *Brown v Brown*, 1967 S.L.T. (Notes) 44.

[80] 1995 S.L.T. 335. Also *Marsh v Marsh*, 2002 S.L.T. (Sh.Ct.) 87; and *A v L* [2009] EWHC 1448 (Fam).

[81] 2002 S.L.T. 537.

[82] [1930] A.C. 588.

Factors which have to be considered in assessing intention

(1) Nationality

There is no necessary link between domicile and nationality.[83] Peter Fuld **6–16**
died domiciled in Germany, a Canadian citizen.[84] William Swanton died domiciled in Ireland, a US citizen.[85] In *Wahl*,[86] the enthusiasm evident in the application by the *propositus* for British citizenship did not persuade the English
forum that he was of English domicile. The proposed US citizenship of the
Chief of the Clan Ross[87] was a matter separate from his (Scottish) domicile,
and was likely to have been desired tactically for tax reasons. Nonetheless in
Munro v Munro,[88] the fact that the *propositus* had never contemplated applying
for Spanish citizenship was persuasive in a finding that he had not acquired a
domicile of choice in Spain.

(2) Residence

Residence may be "colourless"; but perhaps more often the nature of resi- **6–17**
dence may throw light on the *propositus's* intention to settle "permanently" or
otherwise.[89] Taking lodgings is less positive a step than renting, and renting
less strong than purchase.[90]

(3) Exercise of political rights, entry into social life, custom

Wholehearted entry into the political and social life of a new country is a **6–18**
significant factor in acquisition of domicile there.[91] One may contrast the
adoption by a Frenchman of the customs of an English village, in the old case
of *Drevon*, with Winans' enforced and aloof residence in Brighton. The
propositus in *Lord Advocate v Brown's Trustees* was "at home" in the social
life of Ceylon: *contra*, Lord Cullen noted in *Spence*,[92] that the pursuer's
uncontradicted evidence was that her husband's social circles in Spain were
made up of British and (in particular, Scottish) people. Nevertheless, a person
who has entered into the local community may remain, in law, a stranger in a
strange land, and may not be held to be domiciled there.[93]

---

[83] *Hamilton v Dallas* (1875) 1 Ch.D. 257; *Doucet v Geoghegan* (1879) L.R. 9 Ch. D. 441; *Bell v Bell* [1992] 2 I.R. 152; *Ross*, 1930 S.C. (H.L.) 1; *Haldane v Eckford (No.2)* (1869) L.R. 8 Eq. 631; *Brunel v Brunel* (1871) L.R. 12 Eq. 298; *Drevon* (1834) 34 L.J. Ch. 129; *Wahl v Att Gen* (1932) 147 L.T. 382; *Casey*, 1968 S.L.T. 56.
[84] *Fuld (No.3)* [1968] P. 675.
[85] *Bradfield v Swanton* [1931] I.R. 446.
[86] *Wahl v Att Gen* (1932) 147 L.T. 382.
[87] *Ross*, 1930 S.C. (H.L.) 1.
[88] *Munro v Munro* [2007] EWHC 3315 (Fam).
[89] *Aitchison v Dixon* (1870) L.R. 10 Eq. 589; *Haldane v Eckford (No.2)* (1869) L.R. 8 Eq. 631; *Platt v Att Gen of New South Wales* (1877–1888) L.R. App. Cas. 336; *Re Garden (Deceased)* (1895) 11 T.L.R. 167; *Hope, Todd and Kirk v Bruce* (1899) 6 S.L.T. 310; *Att Gen v Yule and Mercantile Bank of India* (1931) 145 L.T. 9; *Wahl v Att Gen* (1932) 147 L.T. 382; *Willar*, 1954 S.C. 144.
[90] *Re Capdevielle* (1864) 2 H. & C. 985 (29 years lodging in Manchester); see also Winans.
[91] *Drevon* (1834) 34 L.J. Ch. 129; compare generally *Doucet* (1879) L.R. 9 Ch. D. 441.
[92] *Spence*, 1995 S.L.T. 335 at 338. See also *Cyganik v Agulian* [2006] EWCA Civ 129.
[93] *Sellars*, 1942 S.C. 206; contrast *Haldane v Eckford (No.2)* (1869) L.R. 8 Eq. 631, where intention had grown as residence lengthened.

(4) Declaration of intention

6–19   A declaration as to domicile or as to intention to settle in a particular
country may be relevant, but too much reliance should not be placed on such
a declaration without first considering any possible motive behind it. In many
cases declarations have been disregarded. Moreover, it is not the prerogative
of the individual, but rather the court, to pronounce conclusively upon domicile.[94] The dictum of Lord Buckmaster in *Ross* is often quoted:

> "Declarations as to intention are rightly regarded in determining the ques-
> tion of a change of domicile, but they must be examined by considering
> the person to whom, the purposes for which, and the circumstances in
> which they are made, and they must further be fortified and carried into
> effect by conduct and action consistent with the declared intention."[95]

In many cases, declarations assert the acquisition of a new domicile, but in
others,[96] declarations profess retention of an old domicile. Declarations may
be made inter vivos, or *mortis causa*, usually as the last clause in a will,[97] but
in no case can they be regarded as more than a dubious guide for the court.
Declarations may be tactical, or tactful, to please the listener. They may be
contradictory (to please different listeners), and the court may consider some
to be persuasive and others not. If made many years previously, by a speaker
now dead, there is the problem of incomplete recollection or bias in the
listener/witness.[98] Their value as dispassionate assessments of domicile is
diminished by perceived self-interest,[99] or by ignorance of the law, the author
or speaker using the term domicile where he may not be aware of the technical

---

[94] Though see *Re M* [1937] N.I. 151 where the highly unusual step in unusual circumstances was
taken of permitting the petitioner to choose whether his domicile was that of the Irish Free State
or of Northern Ireland. He chose the latter, thereby clothing the court with jurisdiction to hear
his petition of divorce.

[95] *Ross*, 1930 S.C. (H.L.) 1 at 6; see also *De Bonneval* (1838) 1 Curt. 856; *Whicker v Hume* (1858)
7 H.L. Cas. 124; *Crookenden v Fuller* (1859) 1 Sw. & Tr. 441; *Woodbury v Sutherland's
Trustees*, 1939 S.L.T. 93; *Latta, Petitioner*, 1954 S.L.T. (Notes) 74—declarations in favour of
Glasgow vague, those in favour of Manchester convincing; *Scappaticci v Att Gen* [1955] P.47;
Re Sillar [1956] I.R. 344; *Tennekoon v Duraisamy* [1958] A.C. 354; *Rev. Comms. v Matthews*
(1958) 92 I.T.L.R. 44.

[96] *Re Steer* (1858) 3 H. & N. 594; *Re Liddell-Grainger's Will Trusts* [1936] 3 All E.R. 173; *Re
Sillar* [1956] I.R. 344.

[97] In *Reddington v Riach's Executor*, the court accepted evidence that the deceased had made
repeated remarks that his move to England was to be his last move, and noted the fact that the
deceased directed in his will that his remains should be buried in Bournemouth. Lord Clarke
took the view that a declaration in a will dated 1996, the testator's death occurring in 1999, that
the *propositus* was domiciled in Scotland, "was a statement carried over from previous wills
without, perhaps, any clear thought being given to its purpose and meaning", relying also on the
fact that the circumstances did not pass the test set in *Ross*.

[98] *Cyganik v Agulian* [2006] EWCA Civ 129. However, it is in the nature of domicile cases that
persons are found who can report significant remarks, e.g. *Haldane v Eckford (No.2)* (1869)
L.R. 8 Eq. 631, where evidence was offered of what the *propositus* had said about whether the
burial vault could accommodate him when the time came.

[99] Though few have been regarded as dismissively as the statements of the *propositus* in *Puttick v
Att Gen* [1979] 3 All E.R. 463: ". . . evidence by a person himself of his or her intentions is
treated with reserve, even where the truth of the evidence is undoubted. Here the petitioner's
evidence is all suspect, if only because she is a woman who would tell any lie, use any deceit,
to achieve her end . . ." (per Sir George Baker, President of the Family Division, at 18).

meaning and legal implications thereof. Nevertheless, on occasion,[100] declarations may tip the balance.

(5) Depositing cash or valuables

Depositing moveables in a particular place or leaving them there in a time **6–20** of emergency may indicate a mental attitude displaying "permanent" attachment to that place.[101]

In his flight from the Nazi invasion of the Channel Islands, Captain Clarke[102] left his home in Sark, furnished, and his proposed home in Guernsey not yet complete, and in the war years lived briefly in Devon and then in Mull before his death in Scotland. It was held that he died domiciled in Sark.

In *Willar*[103] it was held significant in establishing a soldier's domicile that he kept his belongings and his dog in a house in Glasgow belonging to the mother of a friend.

(6) Newspapers

Attention was paid in *Liverpool Royal Infirmary v Ramsay*[104] to the fact that **6–21** the *propositus*, George Bowie, a Glasgow-born long-time resident of Liverpool, had taken a Glasgow weekly newspaper; the order by an expatriate of a newspaper from "home" indicates at the least an emotional attachment to that community and a continuing interest in it.

(7) Old age

Care must be exercised in the consideration of this factor. An individual **6–22** may be compelled to remain in a place as a result of old age or infirmity.

If the view be taken that the *propositus* lived (and died) in the legal system of his domicile of origin, wishful thinking for life in another country can avail nothing.

If being of Scots domicile of origin, the *propositus* lived abroad without an intention to acquire a domicile of choice there, the occurrence of death abroad will not alter retention at death of the domicile of origin.

However if being of, say, French domicile of choice, the *propositus* living in France wished fervently to return to Scotland (the place of his domicile of origin) and was unable physically to do so, his French domicile will remain at death.[105]

---

[100] *Woodbury v Sutherland's Trustees*, 1939 S.L.T. 93; see also *Reddington v Riach's Executor*, 2002 S.L.T. 537.

[101] *Curling v Thornton* (1823) 2 Add. 6; *Att Gen v Dunn* (1840) 6 M. & W. 511; *Willar*, 1954 S.C. 144; *Rev. Comms. v Matthews* (1958) 92 I.T.L.R. 44; and *Haldane v Eckford (No.2)* (1869) L.R. 8 Eq. 631.

[102] *Rev. Comms v Matthews* (1958) 92 I.T.L.R. 44.

[103] *Willar*, 1954 S.C. 144.

[104] 1930 S.C. (H.L.) 83.

[105] *Re Raffenel* (1863) 3 Sw. & Tr. 49. See, generally, *Ramsay v Liverpool Royal Infirmary*, 1930 S.C. (H.L.) 83 and *Winans* [1904] A.C. 287. Contrast *Re Furse* [1980] 3 All E.R. 838 where Fox J. at 843 concluded that the deceased's intention was to return to the US from Sussex only when he was physically unable to continue an active life on the farm. He intended to live out his days in England subject to a contingency so vaguely expressed that it could not limit his intention (at 848).

If the *propositus* should set up conditions for his departure from the country which arguably is his domicile of choice, in order to return "home", and seems loath to see these fulfilled, not only may such a condition (ever less likely to be satisfied) not preclude a finding of domicile of choice in that system, but also such a finding, once made, will mean that the *propositus* would be required physically to leave the system of his adoption before domicile of origin could revive.[106]

Domicile of choice, loss of which is later rued, cannot be reinstated except on the usual rules.[107]

(8) Bequests from a particular source

6–23   If, in his will, the *propositus* has directed that a specific item situated in a certain room in a particular house be the subject of a bequest to X, then the view may be taken that the *propositus* did not contemplate departure from that house and, at least while the will remained unaltered, had "intention" for the legal system in which that house was situated.[108] But even in formalising such a commonplace thought, one can see its limitations. On a "proper" interpretation,[109] the domicile in any event may be elsewhere. Further, a man may change his domicile without changing his will. This factor, therefore, like each of those on these pages, is only a factor, and one factor among many.

(9) Lairs and directions for burial or cremation

6–24   Such directions may be relevant in so far as they show that the person contemplated burial or a scattering of ashes in a particular district, but the whole surrounding circumstances must be considered including the time interval between the direction and the date of death.[110]

LOSS OF DOMICILE OF CHOICE

6–25   A domicile of origin (and presumably, though not expressly so stated in the 2006 Act, an "under-16" domicile) is retained until a domicile of choice has been acquired. In accordance with the best established rule of all, departure from the domicile of origin, whether under duress or not, effects no change unless or until a new domicile is acquired.

A domicile of choice is retained unless and until it is abandoned by a change of *both* residence and intention, whereupon either:

---

[106] *Re Furse* [1980] 3 All E.R. 838.

[107] *Fleming v Horniman* (1928) 44 T.L.R. 315.

[108] *Re Sillar* [1956] I.R. 344.

[109] cf., e.g. *Winans* [1904] A.C. 287 and *Ramsay v Liverpool Royal Infirmary*, 1930 S.C. (H.L.) 83.

[110] *Hodgson v De Beauchesne* (1858) 12 Moore. P.C. 285; *Drevon* (1834) 34 L.J. Ch. 129; *Haldane v Eckford (No.2)* (1869) L.R. 8 Eq. 631; *Brunel* (1871) L.R. 12 Eq. 298; *Douglas v Douglas* (1871) L.R. 12 Eq. 617; *Kerr v Richardson's Trustees*, 1898 6 S.L.T. 245; *Re Garden (Deceased)* (1895) 11 T.L.R. 167; *Re Baron Emanuel de Almeda* (1902) 18 T.L.R. 414; *Liverpool Royal Infirmary v Ramsay*, 1930 S.C. (H.L.) 83; *Bradfield v Swanton* [1931] I.R. 446; *Munster and Leinster Bank Ltd v O'Connor* [1937] L.R. 462; *Latta, Petitioner*, 1954 S.L.T. (Notes) 74; *Spence*, 1995 S.L.T. 335; *Reddington v Riach's Executor*, 2002 S.L.T. 537.

(1) a new domicile of choice is acquired; or
(2) the domicile of origin revives.[111]

Loss of both elements, physical and mental, is required.[112] A domicile of choice is lost by leaving a country *animo non revertendi*[113] (or possibly *sine animo revertendi*).[114] How clear a negative is required? Megarry J. obiter in *Re Flynn*[115] took the view that a "withering away" of intention would suffice to demonstrate loss of intention, and this view finds support.[116] The difficulty arises where the *tempus inspiciendum* is found to be at a point before death. In many other cases, the whole life will be laid before the court and the *propositus's* intention will then be clear.[117] However, nice questions can arise. At what point can domicile of choice be said to be lost in a situation in which the enthusiasm of the *propositus* for the adopted country is waning, and he has established a residence in more than one legal system? Such a case was *Morgan v Cilento*,[118] where the deceased, of English domicile of origin, had acquired a domicile of choice in Queensland, Australia, but whose links with England persisted. He was found by Lewison J. to be domiciled at death in Queensland:

"I must attempt to assess [the *propositus's*] state of mind up to the day he died. To use the language of Megarry J., it may be that his intention to return to Queensland was withering. But I do not consider that it died before Anthony did. I conclude that Anthony died domiciled in Queensland."[119]

Hence, if a significant event such as death occurs when the *propositus* has an ambivalent attitude towards the adopted legal system and before the *animus* for the domicile of choice can be said to have disappeared, that domicile of choice will remain in place at the point of death.

DEATH *IN ITINERE*

In the unlikely event of death occurring on the very journey to the legal system   **6–26**
which the *propositus* intends to adopt as his new domicile of choice (death *in*

---

[111] i.e. in cases arising in future in Scotland, the "under-16" domicile revives (presumably the domicile ascribed at birth, and not any subsequent domicile acquired in terms of s.22 up to the age of 16). It must be emphasised that the 2006 Act makes no such express provision; in the absence of abolition by statute of the rule of revival, that rule must be held to continue to operate in Scots law.
[112] *Re Raffenel* (1863) 3 Sw. & Tr. 49; *Re Marrett* (1887) 36 Ch. D. 400.
[113] i.e with the (definite) intention of not returning. See *Labacianskas v Labacianskas*, 1949 S.C. 280 in which the relevant date of domicile for the purpose of declarator of presumed death was the last date on which the husband was known to be alive. Since departure from Scotland merely to look for work was held not to be sufficient to establish an intention to abandon Scots domicile, the deceased was held to have retained at the relevant date his Scottish domicile of choice.
[114] i.e. without the intention of returning (a less definite frame of mind).
[115] *Re Flynn (No.1)* [1968] 1 W.L.R. 103 at 113. See also *Tee v Tee* [1974] 1 W.L.R. 213.
[116] *Dicey, Morris and Collins on the Conflict of Laws*, 14th edn, 2006, para.6–075 *Cheshire, North and Fawcett: Private International Law*, 14th edn, 2008, p.172.
[117] Graveson, *Private International Law*, 7th edn, 1974, p.207.
[118] [2004] EWHC 188 (Ch).
[119] *Morgan v Cilento* [2004] EWHC 188 (Ch) at [76].

itinere), there may or may not be a change of domicile. If a person leaves a domicile of choice *animo non revertendi*, and death occurs before leaving the territorial bounds of the country of departure, the domicile of choice remains. If death occurs outside the territorial waters of that country, the domicile of origin will revive.[120] If, however, death occurs inside the territorial waters of the destination country, then it can be argued that domicile of choice in the new country has been established.

PERSONS NOT SUI JURIS

6–27   A person who is not sui juris does not have the legal capacity to acquire a new domicile, but his domicile may be changed through the actings of a parent. Because such a change in domicile results from the actings of another person and is involuntary on the part of the *incapax*, it is known as a derivative or dependent domicile. Such a domicile is acquired, therefore, quite independently of the residence and intention of the *propositus*.

(1) Mental *incapaces*

6–28   There is little authority, but the rule appears to be that a mentally *incapax* person retains the domicile which he had at the date when he became mentally incapacitated. His domicile can be changed only through the actings of a parent, not through the actings of a non-related guardian,[121] and even then probably only if the *incapax* became incapacitated before attaining majority. The cases are few,[122] and the law here seems to be unsatisfactory and speculative. Where the *propositus* has fluctuating periods of lucidity and incapacity, this legal problem increases. It seems likely that, in a modern case, the court would concern itself with ascertaining the degree of mental incapacity to find out if the *incapax* was capable of forming the requisite intention at the relevant time, and would seek to act in what it perceived to be the best interests of the *incapax*.

The Law Commissions suggested new rules in 1987,[123] to the effect that:

(a)   A person who has reached the age of 16, but who lacks the mental capacity to acquire a domicile of choice should be domiciled in the country with which he is for the time being most closely connected.[124]

---

[120] *In the Goods of Luigi Bianchi* (1862) 3 Sw. & Tr. 16; contrast *Re Raffenel* (1863) 3 Sw. & Tr. 49 in which the *propositus* was compelled by ill health to disembark from a boat which was to carry her to England, and then died in France, domiciled there. In this specialised aspect, as in all aspects of domicile, the forum follows its own law. The American rule is one of continuance in these cases: see *Re Jones' Estate* (1921) 182 N.W. 227 Supreme Court of Iowa. For facts and musing on *Jones*, see Collier, *Conflict of Laws*, 3rd edn, 2001, pp.52, 53.

[121] Appointed, e.g. under the Adults with Incapacity (Scotland) Act 2000.

[122] *Sharpe v Crispin* (1869) L.R. 1 P.&D. 611; *Crumpton's Judicial Factor v Finch-Noyes*, 1918 S.C. 378.

[123] The Law Commissions produced recommendations contained in *Private International Law: The Law of Domicile*, 1987, Law Com. No.168; Scot. Law Com. No.107.

[124] *Private International Law: The Law of Domicile*, 1987, Law Com. No.168; Scot. Law Com. No.107, para.6.6; r.4(1).

(b) An adult who lacked the capacity to acquire a domicile should, on restoration of that capacity, retain the domicile he had before his capacity was restored.[125]

(c) Whether a person has the mental capacity to acquire a domicile of choice should be a question of fact in each case.[126]

(d) No special protective provisions are required to qualify the recommendation that the domicile of a mentally incapable person should be in the country with which he has for the time being the closest connection.[127]

The Adults with Incapacity (Scotland) Act 2000 makes no provision with regard to the domicile of incapable persons, within the meaning of the Act.[128] The Family Law (Scotland) Act 2006 governs the domicile of all persons under 16, but makes no further or specific provision for the domicile of *incapaces* in their lives thereafter.

(2) Married women

The law was changed by the DMPA 1973. In order to appreciate the effect   **6–29** of the Act, it is helpful to state the law up to December 31, 1973 which still affects questions relating to the domicile of women married before January 1, 1974:

(a) If the marriage was valid, a wife's domicile followed that of her husband as a matter of law.[129] If the marriage was void, her domicile did not become that of her alleged husband, but she might acquire a new domicile of choice, in the same way as a single woman, in the legal system in which she was living with him. If the marriage was voidable, the wife's domicile changed with that of the husband, and she would retain that domicile even after pronouncement of a nullity decree, unless and until she changed it, *animo et facto*.[130]

(b) Separation. The domicile of a wife changed with that of the husband after a separation whether the separation was voluntary or judicial.[131]

(c) Widows and divorcées. In this case a woman, being sui juris, might acquire a new domicile, in the usual way, by a change of residence and intention, upon the termination of the marriage. However,

---

[125] *Private International Law: The Law of Domicile*, 1987, Law Com. No.168; Scot. Law Com. No.107, para.6.7; r.4(2).

[126] *Private International Law: The Law of Domicile*, 1987, Law Com. No.168; Scot. Law Com. No.107, para.6.9.

[127] *Private International Law: The Law of Domicile*, 1987, Law Com. No.168; Scot. Law Com. No.107, para.6.12.

[128] As to other matters, see Ch.10, below (status and capacity).

[129] *Re Cooke's Trustees* (1887) 56 L.T. 737; *Low v Low* (1891) 19 R. 115; *Le Mesurier v Le Mesurier* [1895] A.C. 517; *Re Mackenzie* [1911] 1 Ch. 578; *Mackinnon's Trustees v Lord Advocate*, 1920 S.C. (H.L.) 171; *Att Gen for Alberta v Cook* [1926] A.C. 444; *Dunne v Saban* [1955] P. 178; *Re Scullard* [1957] Ch. 107; *Faye v Inland Revenue Commissioners* (1961) 40 T.C. 103.

[130] *De Reneville* [1948] P. 100.

[131] *Att Gen for Alberta v Cook* [1926] A.C. 444; *Mackinnon's Trustees v Lord Advocate*, 1920 S.C. (H.L.) 171.

there would be no change if she continued to live in "his" legal system.[132]

(d) As domicile is determined by the *lex fori*, it was irrelevant that a wife might have been able to acquire a domicile separate from her husband according to the law of the country where she resided.[133]

Cases may yet arise in which it is necessary to apply the common law rules in order to ascertain the domicile of a married woman for the purpose before the court.[134]

By s.1 of the 1973 Act the position now is as follows:

"(1) Subject to subsection (2) below, the domicile of a married woman as at any time after the coming into force of this section shall, instead of being the same as her husband's by virtue only of marriage, be ascertained by reference to the same factors as in the case of any other individual capable of having an independent domicile.

(2) Where immediately before this section came into force a woman was married and then had her husband's domicile by dependence, she is to be treated as retaining that domicile (as a domicile of choice, if it is not also her domicile of origin) unless and until it is changed by acquisition or revival of another domicile, either on or after the coming into force of this section.

(3) This section extends to England and Wales, Scotland and Northern Ireland."

This change, expected to be the last word on the matter, proved not to be so. Where a woman was married before January 1, 1974, her domicile would change, on the interpretation of s.1(2) given in *Inland Revenue Commissioners v Duchess of Portland*,[135] only in accordance with the usual rules for loss of domicile of choice. There is to be no more lenient rule.[136] Hence, in the case

---

[132] *Re Raffenel* (1863) 3 Sw. & Tr. 49; *Re Wallach (Deceased)* [1950] 1 All E.R. 199. But see *Re Scullard* [1957] Ch. 107, in which the separated spouses had been living in different jurisdictions; upon the death of the husband, albeit unknown to the wife, she became sui juris and her newly validated intention when added to her residence in Guernsey created acquisition of Guernsey domicile of choice which she held at her death six weeks later. Until two weeks before her death she retained all her mental faculties. Sufficient mental capacity being present, her status as a widow rendered her intention effective.

[133] *Att Gen for Alberta v Cook* [1926] A.C. 444.

[134] e.g. *Breuning v Breuning* [2002] EWHC 236 (divorce).

[135] [1982] Ch. 314.

[136] *Inland Revenue Commissioners v Duchess of Portland* [1982] Ch. 314, per Nourse J. at 318: "I will now attempt some general observations on section 1(2) of the Act of 1973. First, it is a deeming provision. Secondly, that which is deemed in a case where the domicile of dependency is not the same as the domicile of origin is the retention of the domicile of dependency as a domicile of choice. I think that that must mean that the effect of the subsection is to reimpose the domicile of dependency as a domicile of choice. The concept of an imposed domicile of choice is not one which it is very easy to grasp, but the force of the subsection requires me to do the best I can. It requires me to treat the taxpayer as if she had acquired an English domicile of choice, even though the facts found by the commissioners tell me that that would have been an impossibility in the real world. In my judgment it necessarily follows that the question whether, after January 1, 1974, the taxpayer abandoned her deemed English domicile of choice must be determined by reference to the test appropriate to the abandonment of a domicile of

of the Duchess, while it was always clear that her intention was to return ulti-mately to Canada, her practice of taking long holidays in Quebec did not mean, after January 1, 1974 upon a proper construction of the Act, that she had ceased to reside in England.

It was suggested that in any future alteration to the rules of domicile, a different approach should be taken in the drafting of the transitional provi-sions,[137] to the effect that changes in the rules of domicile should apply to determine the domicile of a person as at any time *after* the legislation comes into force; those rules should *also* apply to times *before* the legislation comes into force, but only for the purpose of determining where, at a time *after* the legislation comes into force, a person is domiciled. Were this approach to be applied to the transitional problems associated with s.22 of the Family Law (Scotland) Act 2006,[138] it seems that the new rules for ascription of first domicile could apply in the matter of determining the domicile at death of an individual born in 1920 and dying in 2007.

(3) Under-age parties

Such persons may acquire a derivative or dependent domicile as explained **6–30** below.[139]

The DMPA 1973 s.4 (which until the coming into force of the 2006 Act on May 4, 2006 applied to Scotland, England and Northern Ireland, but now applies only to the latter two jurisdictions), provides as follows:

(1) when his father and mother are alive, but living apart, a child's domi-cile shall be that of his mother if:

    (a) he then has his home with her and has no home with his father,[140] or

    (b) he has at any time had his mother's domicile under rule (a) above and has not since had a home with his father;

(2) if a child's mother is dead, his domicile shall be the domicile which she had at her death, if he then had her domicile under rule (a) above and has not since had a home with his father.

---

choice and not by reference to the more lenient test appropriate to the abandonment of one of dependency." See Wade, "Domicile: A Re-examination of Certain Rules" (1983) 32 I.C.L.Q. 1. Presumably, though, the physical return to her domicile of origin with or without her husband must mean the resumption by a woman married before January 1, 1974 of her domi-cile of origin, unless the mental element does not support this (s.1(2)).

[137] 1987 Law Commission proposals, *Private International Law: The Law of Domicile*, Law Com. No.168; Scot. Law Com. No.107, para.8.7 and cll.1(2), 2(3).

[138] See paras 6–06 and 6–08, above.

[139] *Harrison* [1953] 1 W.L.R. 865 but consider the case of *Plummer v Inland Revenue Commissioners* [1988] 1 All E.R. 97, which examines the difficult subject of dual residence in this area of the topic.

[140] "Home": see *Williams, Petitioner*, 1977 S.L.T. (Notes) 2. The word "home" is c~~ ~~ ~~ ~~tral to this provision and was used by the Law Commissions in their 1987 proposal: the domicile rules affecting children. A curious result was produced in *Willi* having been removed from his mother's care in England to the house of his Scotland, the Lord Ordinary in subsequent custody proceedings found hi Scotland. In interpreting s.4, he held the *tempus inspiciendum* to be the "prese the date of separation: the latter was merely the requisite precondition for the c of s.4. Thus the term child's "home" was satisfied by a possibly temporary h had spent at the date of litigation only two months.

This statutory change was limited to domicile of dependence and applied only to legitimate and adopted children.

In England and Northern Ireland, the common law rules governing the domicile of persons of nonage remain applicable to those children to whom s.4 does not apply.

The Family Law (Scotland) Act 2006 repeals s.4, on the rationale that the domicile rule for persons under 16 inserted by s.22 of that Act, shall cover all questions pertaining to the domicile of such persons, without making the distinction between domicile of origin and domicile of dependence.

Prior to the 2006 Act, on attaining legal capacity a young person retained the domicile, of origin or dependence, which he had at that date, until such time as he acquired a domicile of choice. The domicile held by the young adult emerging into legal maturity hitherto has been the easiest domicile to lose.[141] Subsequent to the 2006 Act, it is thought that if the domicile of the person under 16 has been established by use of the fixed rule in s.22(1), there is no reason why the pre-existing approach should not continue. If the under-16 domicile has been established by means of s.22(3) (the flexible exception), the outcome will depend upon the strength of connection of the individual with a legal system at the *tempus inspiciendum*.

PARTICULAR CASES

6–31 Particular cases are governed by the general rules, but bearing in mind that the specialties of a situation may have an effect upon the extent to which the *propositus* is able to exercise free will as to place of residence.

(1) Prisoners[142]

6–32   If a party's freedom to choose his residence for the time being is constrained by reason of the fact that he has been imprisoned, residence in the place of incarceration is involuntary and this is likely to preclude acquisition of a domicile of choice insofar as the nature of the residence will tend to indicate absence of intention to settle in that country.

(2) Debtors[143]

6–33   Flight from creditors may be a sufficient reason to doubt that free will prompts the actings of the *propositus*, yet in *Udny*, there is no suggestion that

---

[141] If the *propositus's* dependent domicile has followed that of his parent to a foreign land, but he has not followed in person, his domicile of origin will easily be found to have revived, or he may take steps to acquire a domicile of choice: *Henderson* [1967] P. 77, where, however, Sir Jocelyn Simon held that the *propositus* retained his English dependent domicile "of quasi-choice". See also, and contrast, *Harrison* [1953] 1 W.L.R. 865.

[142] *Burton v Fisher* (1828) Milward's Rep. 183; *Dunstan v Dunstan* (1858) 28 L.J.C.P. 97. The judgment in *Re the late Emperor Napoleon Bonaparte* (1853) 2 Rob. Ecc. 606, concerning the custody of Napoleon's will and codicils, concluded, not surprisingly, that he formed no voluntary intention to settle in the British territory of St Helena, and that he died domiciled in France. Napoleon was born in Corsica; after his defeat at Leipzig, he abdicated and was given the right to rule Elba. Having escaped from Elba he advanced on Paris and ruled for the "100 days" ending at Waterloo. Then he was conveyed to St Helena as a prisoner of war and died there six years later, perhaps as a result of poison ("Scheele's Green", arsenic dye) leaking out of the wallpaper (or perhaps not).

Udny v Udny (1869) 7 M. (H.L.) 89.

Colonel Udny retained his English domicile of choice (if indeed he had acquired such a domicile) because of the enforced nature of his departure from England.[144] Udny's departure from England was final, and "voluntary", in a sense; but equally no attempt was made to persuade the court that in these circumstances he had acquired a domicile of choice in his place of refuge, France. This scenario prompted Lord Westbury's classic dictum that: "There must be a residence freely chosen, and not prescribed or dictated by any external necessity, such as the duties of office, the demand of creditors, or the relief from illness."[145]

(3) Persons seeking asylum[146]

Where the *propositus* has fled his *domicile of origin*, it will survive his **6–34** departure, and will remain until clearly superseded, on the principle of *Bell v Kennedy*.[147] Where the *propositus* is forced to leave his *domicile of choice*, the enforced nature of his leaving will mean that he retains that domicile by *animus* alone; political or other conditions in his domicile of choice will explain his departure therefrom and may explain his disinclination to return.[148] Strictly, in all such cases where lack of free will is a factor, there is no need to justify failure to return, for the onus of proof lies on the party averring change from pre-existing established domicile. However, it may be necessary to try to refute the argument that the intention of the *propositus* for his domicile of choice has "withered away".[149] Continuing spiritual attachment to the domicile of choice may be easier to show, against a background of hostile political conditions.

A refugee has had the option of remaining in difficult circumstances, or of flight; the state of mind of the *propositus* might be one of desire positively to adopt the legal system of refuge, or one simply of seeking a safe haven, careless of the legal system in which such refuge might be found. In the latter case, domicile of choice will not be acquired. In *Martin*[150] the deceased's husband, Louis Guillard, a professor of French and a fugitive from French justice, married her in England during the period of the French criminal prescription. Upon its expiry, he returned to France, leaving his wife in England. In certain cases, of which this was one, the court must judge the state of intention at a particular point in time and is not permitted to reflect on the life as a whole. The Court of Appeal (Lindley M.R. dissenting) found Professor Guillard to be domiciled in England at the time of his marriage.

---

[144] cf. *Re Lloyd Evans* [1947] Ch. 695; *Rev. Comms v Matthews* (1958) 92 I.T.L.R. 44; (even) *Labacianskas*, 1949 S.C. 280.

[145] *Udny v Udny* (1869) 7 M. (H.L.) 89 at 99.

[146] *De Bonneval* (1838) 1 Curt. 856; *Re Martin* [1900] P. 211; *Boldrini* [1932] P. 9; *May v May* [1943] 2 All E.R. 146; *Cruh* [1945] 2 All E.R. 545; *Zanelli* [1948] 64 T.L.R. 556; *Re Lloyd Evans* [1947] Ch. 695; *Rev. Comms v Matthews* (1958) 92 I.L.T.R. 44; *Puttick v Att Gen* [1979] 3 All E.R. 463. See para.6–14, above.

[147] (1868) 6 M. (H.L.) 69.

[148] *Re Lloyd Evans* [1947] Ch. 695: *propositus* did not return to his beloved Belgium during the war years, and died, domiciled of choice in Belgium, in 1944. See also *Rev. Comms v Matthews* (1958) 92 I.L.T.R. 44: war precluded return to Sark. Deceased died in Scotland domiciled in Sark. See Binchy, *Irish Conflicts of Law*, 1988, p.76.

[149] *Re Flynn (No.1)* [1968] 1 W.L.R. 103; *Tee* [1974] 1 W.L.R. 213; *Morgan v Cilento* [2004] EWHC 188 (Ch).

[150] [1900] P. 211.

Liability to be deported does not preclude the acquisition of a domicile in the country where the *propositus's* residence is subject to termination,[151] nor even does the grant of a deportation order until it is carried out.[152] Such residence would be "precarious", and the *propositus* could entertain validly the intention of remaining so long as the authorities permit. It was held in *Puttick*[153] that illegal residence based on illegal entry cannot found residence—or intention—for the purpose of domicile acquisition. As explained above,[154] this statement now is qualified by the unanimous decision of the House of Lords in *Mark v Mark*,[155] in the context of consistorial jurisdiction, that a wife's unlawful presence in England, as an "overstayer" was not a bar in the circumstances to acquisition by her of a domicile of choice in England.

(4) Diplomatic and service personnel

6–35   A member of the diplomatic corps[156] or armed forces may acquire a domicile in a country to which he has been posted if there is the necessary change of intention as well as residence[157]:

> "... there may co-exist with a residence, which has begun and is continued under military orders, facts and circumstances which establish a residence voluntary in character and chosen by the soldier, although it is a residence in the place in which he is stationed by the order of his military superiors."[158]

In principle, the same reasoning is applicable to posted workers.[159]

---

[151] *May* [1943] 2 All E.R. 146.
[152] *Cruh* [1945] 2 All E.R. 545, per Lord Denning at 546. One must conclude, therefore, that, in this specialised area, and in the absence of more modern authority, retention of intention alone will not suffice, apparently, for the *propositus* to retain a domicile of choice in the place of erstwhile asylum. Contrast *Re Lloyd Evans* [1947] Ch. 695.
[153] [1979] 3 All E.R. 463.
[154] See para.6–14, above.
[155] *Mark v Mark* [2005] 3 All E.R. 912. See para.6–14, above.
[156] *Heath v Samson* (1851) 14 Beav. 441; *Att Gen v Kent* (1862) 1 H. & C. 12; *Sharpe v Crispin* (1869) L.R. 1 P. & D. 611; *Niboyet v Niboyet* (1878) L.R. 4 P.D. 1; *Udny* (1869) 7 M. (H.L.) 89 (the father of Col. Udny was British Consul at Leghorn (Livorno) in Italy at the time of his son's birth, but Col. Udny had Scottish domicile of origin).
[157] *Yelverton v Yelverton* (1859) 1 Sw. & Tr. 574; *Campbell v Campbell* (1861) 23 D. 256; *Brown v Smith* (1852) 15 Beav. 444; *Re Mitchell Ex p. Cunningham* (1884) L.R. 13 Q.B.D. 418; *Re Patience* (1885) L.R. 29 Ch. D. 976; *Re Macreight* (1885) L.R. 30 Ch. D. 165; *Sellars*, 1942 S.C. 206; *Donaldson v Donaldson* [1949] P. 363 (acquisition by RAF officer posted to Florida of domicile of choice there); *Willar*, 1954 S.C. 144; *Cruickshanks v Cruickshanks* [1957] 1 W.L.R. 564; *Stone v Stone* [1958] 1 W.L.R. 1287 (acquisition by American soldier, Ohio domiciled of origin, of English domicile of choice).
[158] *Sellars*, 1942 S.C. 206, per Lord President Normand at 211.
[159] cf. Old cases concerning servants and officials such as government officials: *Inland Revenue Commissioners v Gordon's Executors* (1850) 12 D. 657; *Att Gen v Pottinger* (1861) 6 H. & N. 733; *Att Gen v Rowe* (1862) 1 H. & C. 31; *Fairbairn v Neville* (1897) 25 R. 192; *Cooney v Cooney*, 1950 S.L.T. (Notes) 1; *Clarke v Newmarsh* (1836) 14 S. 488 (in which an English officer, appointed lieutenant governor of Fort Augustus in 1746 after the second Jacobite rebellion, remained there for 51 years until his death in 1797, married a Scots woman, cultivated a farm, and was held to have acquired a Scottish domicile of choice).

(5) Invalids—health residence

Each case must be considered on its own merits, but the test, in the words **6–36** of Turner L.J. in *Hoskins v Matthews*,[160] is whether the person acted upon a necessity or merely exercised a preference. The intention to stay for an indefinite time in a beneficial climate may transmute into the *animus* requisite for a change of domicile and, if so, that change will occur when *animus manendi* (intention to remain for as long as can be seen ahead) is established.

(6) Old age and infirmity

This area is potentially difficult and requires care. Place of death may be **6–37** found to have a significance in domicile litigation which place of birth rarely has. Diminishing physical strength may preclude departure from a country and therefore much may rest upon the state of mind of the *propositus*.[161]

REFORM

The Scots and English rules of domicile, often criticised, provide a delicate **6–38** tool to aid the securing of an appropriate result in certain important areas of status, family law and succession. In 1985, proposals were made to reform the rules,[162] and after consultation, the Law Commissions produced in 1987 recommendations contained in *Private International Law: The Law of Domicile*. The Commissions concluded that domicile should be retained as a connecting factor in the international private law of England and Wales, Scotland and Northern Ireland. However, they suggested the making of substantial changes in the detail of the then law of domicile. These changes were not implemented.[163]

As has been seen above, the domicile change effected in Scots law by the Family Law (Scotland) Act 2006, prompted by the desire to treat all children equally, in domicile as in other matters, has weakened, by inadvertence or

---

[160] *Hoskins v Matthews* (1855) 25 L.T. (O.S.) 78: on the death of the *propositus* after 12 years' residence in Florence, a choice of residence beneficial but not essential, prompted by a spinal complaint, the English court found him domiciled at his death at the age of 60, in Tuscany. The *propositus* "was exercising a preference, and not acting upon a necessity". *Johnstone v Beattie* (1843) 10 Cl. & F. 42, at 139; *Moorhouse v Lord* (1863) 10 H.L. Cas. 272; *Lauderdale Peerage Case* (1885) 10 App. Cas. 692 at 740; *Re Garden (Deceased)* (1895) 11 T.L.R. 167; *Winans* [1904] A.C. 287; *Re James* (1908) 98 L.T. 438.

[161] See para.6–22, above.

[162] Law Commission and Scottish Law Commission, *Private International Law: The Law of Domicile* (HMSO, 1985), Law Com. Working Paper No.88; Scot. Law Com. Memo. No.63. There had been earlier attempts to reform the rules. The report of the Wynn-Parry Committee (HMSO, 1954), Cmd. 9068 had recommended abolition of domicile of origin, a continuance rule, independent domicile for judicially separated wives, and the dependence of a child's domicile upon that of the party having custody. Domicile Bills had been introduced in 1958 and 1959, but each was withdrawn. Further thoughts on domicile were contained in the Private International Law Committee, *Seventh Report of the Lord Chancellor's Private International Law Committee, 1963* (HMSO, 1963), Cmnd.1955, the chief proposal of which was a shift in the onus of proof: a person would be presumed to be domiciled in the place where he lived. The recommendations were not taken up.

[163] *Private International Law: The Law of Domicile*, 1987, Law Com. No.168; Scot. Law Com. No.107, para.8.7.

design, the previously strong structure of the domicile rules. This factor, combined with the expanding European conflict of laws family law programme, which favours the connecting factor of habitual residence (*q.v.*), may mean that the failure to adopt the Law Commissions' recommendations to "modernise" the rules of domicile is less significant than would have been thought, because the area in which domicile in its traditional sense is used as a connecting factor is subject to erosion.[164] But if that is the case, there will be a need for the rules of acquisition and loss of *habitual residence* to be more firmly drawn.

DOMICILE AND NATIONALITY

6–39 Although in English speaking countries the law of domicile applies generally in questions of personal law, nationality is a connecting factor employed by the conflict rules of many other countries. Historically, domicile was pre-eminent, but nationality was substituted as the preferred personal law in France by the Code Napoleon 1804, and this approach was adopted in Belgium and Luxembourg, with similar provisions following in Austria and Holland.

Chauvinism is out of place; different rules suit different systems. It is clear though that each factor has disadvantages:

DOMICILE

6–40   (a) A person's domicile may be in a place which has little or no connection with his home in the colloquial sense.
(b) It is difficult to supersede domicile of origin.
(c) Revival of domicile of origin may produce anomalies.
(d) Long residence in a country in itself is of no avail (leading to unpredictability).
(e) Intention is difficult to prove (also leading to unpredictability).
(f) Consequently, in a complex case, uncertainty exists in the absence of judicial decision. Judicial consideration of the life in question will be sensitive and careful, but lengthy and expensive.
(g) The effect of s.22 of the 2006 Act is destabilising.

NATIONALITY

6–41   (a) A person's nationality may have no connection with the country where he lives.

---

[164] Though there is a seam of cases arising as a result of claims under the Inheritance (Provision for Family and Dependants) Act 1975, such claims being competent only where the deceased died domiciled in England and Wales. These cases afford the opportunity for the writing of fine domicile judgments: *Morgan v Cilento* [2004] EWHC 188 (Ch); *Cyganik v Agulian* [2006] EWCA Civ 129; and *Holliday v Musa* [2010] EWCA Civ 335.

    (b) The possibility of dual nationality means that the apposite connecting factor may not be obvious.

    (c) The problem of statelessness[165] means that a person may be deemed to be without a personal law.

    (d) Nationality cannot be applied to questions of personal law in countries such as the UK, which contain different units each having a different system of law.

Each country has its own rules as to nationality and when any question arises as to whether a person is a subject of a particular state, the matter is determined by the law of that state and (unlike domicile) not by the law of the forum.[166] This is subject only to the exception that changes of nationality are not regarded as being effective during times of war,[167] although they become effective on the termination of war.

BRITISH NATIONALITY[168]

The rules regarding British nationality were based on two principles: **6–42**

    (a) birth within the territory of Great Britain; and
    (b) descent.[169]

The modern period of the law on this subject might be said to begin with the British Nationality Act 1948 which introduced the status of citizen of the United Kingdom and Colonies. The position is governed now by the British Nationality Act 1981,[170] which abolished that citizenship and substituted three categories of citizenship, namely:

    (a) British citizenship[171];
    (b) citizenship of British Dependent Territories; and
    (c) British Overseas citizenship.[172]

---

[165] *Kramer v Att Gen* [1923] A.C. 528; *Re Chamberlain's Settlement* [1921] 2 Ch. 533.

[166] *Stoeck v Public Trustee* [1921] 2 Ch. 67.

[167] *Oppenheimer v Cattermole* [1975] 1 All E.R. 538.

[168] *R. v Lynch* [1903] 1 K.B. 444; *R. v Commanding Officer of the 30th Battalion Middlesex Regiment Ex p. Freyberger* [1917] 2 K.B. 129; *Joyce v DPP* [1946] A.C. 347; *R. v Secretary of State for the Home Department Ex p. L* [1945] K.B. 7; *Lowenthal v Att Gen* [1948] 1 All E.R. 295; *Oppenheimer v Cattermole* [1975] 1 All E.R. 538.

[169] See *Stair Memorial Encyclopaedia*, Reissue (Edinburgh: Law Society of Scotland/Butterworths, 2003), Vol.14, "Nationality and Citizenship", R.M. White.

[170] For a full review of earlier authorities, see *Att Gen v HRH Prince Ernest Augustus of Hanover* [1957] A.C. 436 (affirming [1956] Ch. 188; reversing [1955] Ch. 440).

[171] See generally A.W. Bradley and K.D. Ewing, *Constitutional and Administrative Law*, 14th edn (Harlow: Pearon Longman, 2007), pp.445–448. The 1981 Act also provided for two residual categories of citizenship, viz. British subjects under the Act, and British protected persons.

[172] See also now British Nationality (Hong Kong) Act 1997; British Overseas Territories Act 2002; Nationality, Immigration and Asylum Act 2002; Immigration, Asylum and Nationality Act 2006; and Borders, Citizenship and Immigration Act 2009 Pt 2.

RESIDENCE

6–43 Residence increasingly is found to be a useful connecting factor in legislation. From the mid-twentieth century onwards,[173] its importance has tended to assert itself in the area of consistorial jurisdiction, and consequently in the rules of recognition of foreign decrees, where the granting court had assumed jurisdiction on a corresponding basis.[174] In some instances Parliament has specified the length of time necessary to satisfy the residence rule in question[175]; in such cases the main problem likely to arise is the necessary qualifying period and the extent to which interruptions can be tolerated.[176] Such time specifications ensure the existence of what is thought to be a sufficient link between the petitioner and the court to which he seeks access, or the decree which he wishes to have enforced.[177]

HABITUAL RESIDENCE

6–44 Frequently in modern conflict rules, the connecting factor of *habitual residence* is employed, particularly in family law (divorce and nullity jurisdiction and recognition; custody and abduction; guardianship and protection of children; and adoption), but it has a role also in the commercial sphere. There cannot, however, yet be said to be agreement on its meaning.[178] The concept has been left to judicial interpretation, by domestic court, or ECJ, as appropriate in the individual case.[179] To date there has been a deliberate absence of definition of the term in the legislative instruments in which it is employed, allowing great scope for judicial freedom within the bounds of the rules of precedent.[180]

There is a wealth of academic discussion upon the meaning and nature of "habitual residence",[181] debates upon whether its meaning differs from that of

---

[173] e.g. Matrimonial Causes Act 1937 s.13; Law Reform (Miscellaneous Provisions) Act 1949 ss.1, 2 (clothing the court in England or Scotland with jurisdiction to grant a consistorial decree to a wife whose foreign-domiciled husband had deserted her, on the ground of her ordinary residence in the jurisdiction for three years). Crawford, "A Day is Not Enough", 2000 J.R. 89, 90.

[174] *Travers v Holley* [1953] P. 246.

[175] DMPA 1973, ss.5, 7, 9 (consistorial jurisdiction).

[176] *Land v Land*, 1962 S.L.T. 316 (cf. *Hopkins v Hopkins* [1951] P. 116); contrast *Cabel v Cabel*, 1974 S.L.T. 295 (cf. *Stransky v Stransky* [1954] P. 428).

[177] Family Law Act 1986 s.46(2)(b).

[178] See Crawford, " 'Habitual Residence of the Child' as the Connecting Factor in Child Abduction Cases: A Consideration of Recent Cases", 1992 J.R. 177; Crawford "A Day is Not Enough: Further Views on the Meaning of Habitual Residence", 2000 J.R. 89; Crawford, "Case Analysis: *Gingi v Secretary of State for Work and Pensions*" (2003) 10 J.S.S.L. 52; R. Leslie, "Recent Scottish Cases on Habitual Residence", 1996 S.L.T. (News) 145; E. Clive, "The Concept of Habitual Residence", 1997 J.R. 137; "The New Hague Convention on Children", 1998 J.R. 169; and P. Rogerson, "Habitual Residence: The New Domicile?" (2000) 49 I.C.L.Q. 86.

[179] As to the extent to which the domestic court is bound by the ECJ definition, see *Gingi*, above, and Crawford (2003), above.

[180] There may also be a conflict aspect to the rules of binding precedent, as evidenced in *Gingi*, above.

[181] It has been said that there is no evidence in reported cases of duration longer than one year being rejected as insufficiently long to be habitual, and even that projected future residence might be relevant. See Clive, "The Concept of Habitual Residence", 1997 J.R. 137 and "The New Hague Convention on Children", 1998 J.R. 169; Crawford, " 'Habitual Residence of the Child' as the Connecting Factor in Child Abduction Cases", 1992 J.R. 177; Leslie, "Recent Scottish Cases on Habitual Residence", 1996 S.L.T. (News) 145; and Rogerson, "Habitual Residence: The New Domicile?" (2000) 49 I.C.L.Q. 86, 96–99.

"residence" or "ordinary residence", and upon its indicia generally in matters such as the necessity for "voluntariness" (at the outset? or throughout?); for "settled intention"; for "lawfulness" of residence[182]; the conditions required for its acquisition and loss; the hunt for guidelines as to how long residence takes to qualify as habitual as opposed to ordinary; whether a person can be without an habitual residence, or whether he can have more than one habitual residence simultaneously.[183] In other words, it seems necessary to furnish this connecting factor with a number of fixed rules,[184] of the type of which "domicile" has been possessed for more than a century; and this despite the fact it is the vaunted characteristic of habitual residence that it is a factual, common sense notion, readily understandable by the man in the street.

In addition to this it must be asked whether, unlike domicile, the meaning of habitual residence varies according to context.[185] One must assume that its meaning is likely to vary from one national forum to another, and may be the subject of disagreement within the judicial hierarchy of one legal system. But it may be that the same forum is required to adopt a different interpretation of the term according to the context in which it arises. Lastly, one must be aware of the favoured status of this factor in international instruments; it is a favourite of convention and regulation, and as a matter of deliberate intent has been left undefined in such instruments. Nonetheless, where the term is used in European instruments, there seems to be a growing view that an autonomous Community meaning is intended.[186] Therefore, a difference may be discernible between national forum and ECJ favoured "definitions" of the term, even where it is used in the same broad area of law, e.g. social security legislation.[187] But it cannot be said that a Community meaning for one purpose, e.g. jurisdiction in parental responsibility matters, can necessarily be transposed to another context, e.g. expatriation allowance.

International child abduction

The impetus for the upsurge in the use of habitual residence as a connecting **6–45** factor can be traced to the 1980 Hague Convention on the Civil Aspects of

---

[182] There was a tendency to consider that lawfulness of presence was not a prerequisite of a finding of habitual residence. This has received support in the most recent House of Lords decision *Mark v Mark* [2005] 3 All E.R. 912 at least with regard to its meaning for the purposes of s.5 of the DMPA 1973. The view that acquisition of domicile, on the other hand, could not be founded upon illegal residence, is now in doubt following the unanimous decision of their Lordships in *Mark*.

[183] *C v FC* [2004] 1 F.L.R. 362.

[184] Crawford, "A Day is Not Enough", 2000 J.R. 89, 94, 95.

[185] Crawford, "Case Analysis: *Gingi v Secretary of State for Work and Pensions*" (2003) 10 J.S.S.L. 52. It is suggested that there is no unitary concept; contrast domicile. See Rogerson, "Habitual Residence: The New Domicile?" (2000) 49 I.C.L.Q. 86, 87. See judicial interpretation of HMRC IR20 rules on residency for tax purposes in *R. (on the application of Davies) v Revenue and Customs Commissioners* and *R. (on the application of Gaines-Cooper) v Revenue and Customs Commissioners* [2010] EWCA Civ 83.

[186] *Proceedings Brought by A*, Case C-523/07 (Reference for a preliminary ruling by the ECJ from the Korkein hallinto-oikeus (Finland)).

[187] *Gingi v Secretary of State for Work and Pensions* [2001] EWCA Civ 1685. See *Nessa v Chief Adjudication Officer* [1999] 1 W.L.R. 1937 and contrast *Swaddling v Adjudication Officer* (C90/97) [1999] E.C.R. I-1075. See, in the context of divorce jurisdiction, *Moore v Moore* [2006] I.L.Pr. 29.

International Child Abduction, where the "habitual residence of the child" is the key factor, prompting in many forums a consideration of the characteristics of habitual residence, and in particular how it may be lost and may be gained.[188] A foreign finding as to habitual residence is not binding on the English court.[189]

Since it is not usual for a child to be financially independent, his residence is almost always dependent (factually; and therefore legally?) upon the wishes and actings of the parent upon whom he is dependent. Where wrongful removal or retention[190] is said to have occurred, the question whether the removing parent may establish for the child an habitual residence in the "new" country is a crucial one. Examples can be found of legislative provisions designed to secure (for a limited period, by means of a "deeming" provision)[191] in favour of the court of the abandoned legal system, continuing jurisdiction to adjudicate upon the case. The existence of such legislative devices does not mean that the point is conceded that a change of habitual residence may be effected by wrongful actings.[192]

The rule that the court addressed must take account of the fact that the child may have "settled" in its new environment, and also of factors such as alleged acquiescence by the bereft parent, means that provisions of the 1980 Hague Convention may operate to produce a situation in which the elapse of time produces a new status quo, resulting effectively in a (potentially) unwelcome incursion into the principle that a child's habitual residence may not be affected by wrongful actings. Examples taken from the context of international child abduction lead to a more general conclusion that it may plausibly be argued that a finding of habitual residence in any context ultimately depends upon the facts laid before the court, and on credibility of witnesses. It would seem to be agreed that there will come a point in a life history at which it would be perverse to regard a person as habitually resident at any place other than that of his established physical presence, whatever view be taken of the need for free will at the outset (inception of residence). This would mean that habitual residence initially brought about by coercion of any kind must take longer to establish, but must be capable of being established.

---

[188] *Re J (A Minor) (Abduction: Custody Rights)* [1990] 2 A.C. 562 at 578, 579; *Re N (Child Abduction: Habitual Residence)* [1993] 2 F.L.R. 124; *Re R (Wardship: Child Abduction) (No.2)* [1993] 1 F.L.R. 249; *Al-H v F* [2001] EWCA Civ 186; [2001] 1 F.L.R. 951; *Re R (Abduction: Habitual Residence)* [2003] EWHC 1968; [2004] 1 F.L.R. 216; *Re D (Abduction: Habitual Residence)* [2005] EWHC 518; [2005] 2 F.L.R. 403; *Re A (Abduction: Consent: Habitual Residence: Consent)* [2005] EWHC 2998; [2006] 2 F.L.R. 1; *E v E* [2007] EWHC 276; [2007] Fam. Law 480; and *W v F* [2007] EWHC 779 (Fam); (2007) 104(18) L.S.G. 28.

[189] *Re B (A Minor) (Child Abduction: Habitual Residence)* [1994] 2 F.L.R. 915.

[190] See Ch.14, below.

[191] Either that the child will be deemed still to be habitually resident, or that the jurisdiction of the "former" habitual residence will be clothed with a continuing (but usually limited) jurisdiction to hear the substance of the case. See, e.g. Family Law Act 1986 s.41(1)(b) and Regulation 2201/2003 art.10. See Ch.14, below.

[192] Crawford, " 'Habitual residence of the Child' as the Connecting Factor in Child Abduction Cases", 1992 J.R. 177. See *Re J (A Minor) (Abduction: Custody Rights)* [1990] 2 A.C. 562, per Lord Donaldson M.R. at 572.

Consistorial proceedings

Habitual residence now is the pivotal connecting factor in the context of **6–46** jurisdiction and recognition of overseas consistorial decrees.[193] In relation to jurisdiction and recognition of decrees of divorce, legal separation and marriage annulment among EU Member States, almost total reliance has been placed upon the concept of habitual residence as a basis. For example,[194] in matrimonial matters it is enacted that jurisdiction shall lie with the court of the Member State in which, inter alia, there is joint spousal habitual residence, or recent habitual residence by both spouses with continuing residence by one spouse, or habitual residence of either. This founding rule of jurisdiction contains examples where, in particular situations, draftsmen have added a time requirement, e.g. where the applicant is habitually resident if he or she resided there for at least a year before the application was made.[195] Such provisions exemplify the use to which, in a modern context, the factor of habitual residence can be put, and its versatility. It is not the concept itself which varies as to meaning in a list such as that contained in the Brussels II *bis* Regulation art.3,[196] but rather that the draftsmen, seeking justice in each situation, make different demands in different circumstances.

Social security

A significant case is *Nessa v Chief Adjudication Officer*,[197] in which the **6–47** point at issue was whether or not Mrs Nessa, recently arrived in the UK from Bangladesh, was entitled to claim an income support payment from the British authorities. She was considered to be entitled only if "habitually resident in the UK". The House of Lords held that, for the purpose of the Income Support (General) Regulations 1987 (SI 1987/1967), residence *for a period* is required to constitute habitual residence. Within the same subject area, the later case of *Gingi v Secretary of State for Work and Pensions*[198] demonstrates that the European Community interpretation of habitual residence in the area of social law may vary from the interpretation favoured domestically in the UK. If the issue were to be regarded as affected by Regulation 1408/71 (concerning social security payments to persons moving within the Community), Miss Gingi's case would be affected by the ECJ decision of *Swaddling v Adjudication Officer*[199] (which held in the interpretation of art.10a.1 of Regulation 1408/71, that length of residence in the Member State cannot be regarded as an intrinsic element of the concept of residence). The Court of

---

[193] Which may elicit interesting discussion of the concept: See Ch.12, below, and cases such as *Ikimi v Ikimi* [2001] 3 W.L.R. 672; *Breuning v Breuning* [2002] EWHC 236 (Fam); *Armstrong v Armstrong* [2003] EWHC 777; [2003] 2 F.L.R. 375; *Mark v Mark* [2005] UKHL 42; [2006] 1 A.C. 98; *L-K v K (No.2)* [2006] EWHC 3280 (Fam); *Witkowska v Kaminski* [2006] EWHC 1940 (Ch); [2007] 1 F.L.R. 1547; and *Marinos v Marinos* [2007] EWHC 2047 (Fam). See for purposes of Family Law (Scotland) Act 2006 s.29: *Chebotareva v Khandro (King's Executrix)*, 2008 Fam. L.R. 66.

[194] Regulation 2201/2003 art.3. See Ch.12, below.

[195] Regulation 2201/2003 art.3 indent 5.

[196] See para.12–06, below.

[197] [1999] 4 All E.R. 677. See also *Abdirahman v Secretary of State for Work and Pensions* [2007] 4 All E.R. 882.

[198] [2001] EWCA Civ 1685.

[199] (C90/97) [1999] E.C.R. I-1075; Regulation 1408/71 on the application of social security schemes to employed persons and their families moving within the Community [1971] OJ L149/2.

Appeal, having decided that Miss Gingi's situation was *not* governed by
Regulation 1408/71, was free to follow the domestic interpretation of habitual
residence set down by the House of Lords in *Nessa*.

Such cases illustrate the divergence of opinion in the matter of interpretation of
the term habitual residence which may arise between the ECJ and UK national
courts in the area of social law. Conceivably also, the term may require to be interpreted differently as between different types of social security allowance.[200]

The commercial sphere

6–48   Habitual residence has some application in the commercial sphere.[201] In
contract, under the Rome I Convention, the principal presumption to establish
the applicable law in the absence of choice was the habitual residence of the
party whose performance was characteristic of the contract.[202] The factor is a
favoured criterion in contract on policy grounds, usually with protective
purposes.[203] An innovation is contained in the Rome I Regulation, in that art.19
defines, for the purposes of the Regulation, the habitual residence of companies
and other bodies, corporate or unincorporated, as the place of central administration. Further, it defines the habitual residence of a natural person acting in
the course of his business activity as his principal place of business. Likewise,
in art.23 of the Rome II Regulation concerning non-contractual obligations, a
definition is provided of the habitual residence of companies and other bodies
corporate or unincorporated (the same as that in art.19 of Rome I, mutatis
mutandis). Separately, in Rome II, one can note the use of "commonality" (i.e.
the fact that claimant and defendant have a common habitual residence at the
time of occurrence of damage) as a principal exception to application of the
main rule proposed (e.g. place of occurrence of damage).[204]

THE RULES OF HABITUAL RESIDENCE—A PRÉCIS

6–49   Examination of the connecting factor of habitual residence reveals the degree
to which opinion varies on the topic, and serves to identify the various contexts
in which increasingly the concept is used. Though use of the concept normally
is authorised by statute, convention or regulation, its meaning typically is
undefined.

British judges on occasion have attempted to define the concept, e.g. "a
regular physical presence which must endure for some time".[205] "In our
opinion a habitual residence is one which is being enjoyed voluntarily for the

---

[200] e.g. *P Magdalena Fernández v Commission* (C-452/93) [1994] ECR I-4295 (meaning of
habitual residence for the purpose of the expatriation allowance exigible under EC Staff
Regulations); and *Patmalniece v Secretary of State for Work and Pensions* [2009] EWCA
Civ 621.
[201] e.g. Rome I Regulation arts 4.2, 5, 6, 10, 13, 19; Rome I Convention arts 4.2, 8, 11; and Rome
II Regulation arts 4.2, 5.1, 10.2, 11.2, 12.2, 23.
[202] Rome I Convention art.4.2. In this connection litigation has tended to concern identification of
the performance which is characteristic of the contract, rather than of the habitual residence of
the party effecting such performance. See now Rome I Regulation art.4.2; and Ch.15, below.
[203] See e.g. Rome I Regulation arts 4.1, 5, 6, 7, 8, 10.2; and Rome I Convention arts 5.2, 8.2.
[204] See Rome II art.4.2. See Ch.16, below.
[205] *Cruse v Chittum* [1974] 2 All E.R. 940.

time being and with the settled intention that it should continue for some time".[206] "An appreciable period of time and a settled intention will be necessary to enable him or her to become [habitually resident]."[207] There is agreement that the words habitual residence should bear their ordinary and natural meaning; it is said that the term is not a term of art, but rather a matter of fact.[208] However it can be seen that it is usually necessary for the purpose in hand to require of the undefined concept some characteristics of a term of art.

A summary of that which, with reasonable confidence, can be said to be agreed, is as follows:

(a) A person may cease to be habitually resident in country A in a single day if there is settled intention not to return to A.[209]

(b) Many would agree that such a person, having left country A with the settled intention not to return, cannot become habitually resident in country B in a single day.[210] The favoured adjective to qualify "period of time" is "appreciable".[211]

(c) While acquisition of a new habitual residence in most cases will extinguish an earlier habitual residence, concurrent habitual residence—and variations thereof, such as alternating habitual residence—seems possible in some contexts.

(d) Nowadays case authority can be found, for example, in child abduction cases[212] to the effect that a person can acquire habitual residence in the place where he is sent for a *short-term* secondment, in circumstances where he certainly does not appear to have abandoned his earlier habitual residence. Residence in such circumstances is almost bound to be on a trial or provisional basis, with corresponding intention. This could be a case of alternating or consecutive habitual residence; or perhaps less likely, joint or concurrent habitual residence, depending on the facts.

(e) A person can be without an habitual residence. There is no rule of continuance of habitual residence.[213] The loss of an existing habitual residence may leave a vacuum.

---

[206] Lord President Hope in *Dickson v Dickson*, 1990 S.C.L.R. 692 at 703, agreeing with Lord Scarman in *R. v Barnet LBC Ex p. Shah* [1983] 2 A.C. 309 at 342, 343, that the concept is the same for all practical purposes as ordinary residence. Contrast Lane J. in *Cruse v Chittum* [1974] 2 All E.R. 940, who considered that habitual residence is something more than ordinary residence. This difference of opinion (tending now to settle in favour of the former view) is symptomatic of the controversies which underlie this apparently simple term.

[207] *Re J (A Minor) (Abduction: Custody Rights)* [1990] 2 A.C. 562 (in the House of Lords sub nom. *C v S* [1990] 2 All E.R. 961 HL, per Lord Brandon at 965).

[208] Rogerson, "Habitual Residence: The New Domicile?" (2000) 49 I.C.L.Q. 86, 89.

[209] *C v S* [1990] 2 All E.R. 961 HL, per Lord Brandon at 965. His Lordship added in that example that the settled intention not to return to A was replaced with a settled intention to take up long-term residence in country B. It is not obvious, however, why there should be any need to demonstrate an intention to settle elsewhere in order to rid oneself of an habitual residence.

[210] *C v S* [1990] 2 All E.R. 961 HL, per Lord Brandon at 965.

[211] See Rogerson, "Habitual Residence: The New Domicile?" (2000) 49 I.C.L.Q. 86, 91–93. See also per Lord Donaldson in *C v S* [1990] 2 All E.R. 961 HL, in the Court of Appeal at [1990] 2 All E.R. 449 at 454; sub nom. *Re J (A Minor) (Abduction: Custody Rights)* [1990] 2 A.C. 562 at 571.

[212] e.g. *Re R (Abduction: Habitual; Residence)* [2003] EWHC 1968.

[213] Contrast *Bell v Kennedy* (1868) 6 M. (H.L.) 69.

(f) "Voluntariness" is a question of degree.[214] While free will may be necessary at the outset to establish residence, and while a complete lack of consent may preclude "settled intention", it is certainly arguable that, over time, factual residence "overwhelms all other, subjective, arguments".[215]

(g) In the specialised context of rules pertaining to children, habitual residence of a child cannot normally be lost through unilateral wrongful actings of a parent.[216]

It is not conceded that in light of the above, the advantages of the connecting factor of habitual residence are self-evident. Unless rules governing, at minimum, its acquisition and loss, are formulated (generally or in particular contexts), the factor will be flawed. It is not sufficiently robust to bear the edifice which is sought to be built upon it. While its incidence is certain to increase, its intrinsic merit has not been proved.

SUMMARY 6

6–50

1. Domicile is a relationship between a person and a territory with a common body of law: every person must have a domicile, but cannot have more than one operative domicile for the same purpose at any one time. There are no formalities for acquisition of domicile.

2. Prior to the Family Law (Scotland) Act 2006, and still in England, a domicile of origin was/is acquired at birth from a person's father's domicile at that date if the child is legitimate. Otherwise, and if posthumous, it was/is acquired from his mother's domicile at that date. Domicile at birth is ascribed now in Scots law in accordance with s.22 of the 2006 Act.

3. Onus of proof of a change of domicile rests on the person averring a change.

4. Domicile of choice is acquired by a combination of residence and intention, and is lost by a change of the same two factors.

5. Prior to the Family Law (Scotland) Act 2006, and still in England, a derivative or dependent domicile was/is acquired from the actings of another person and was independent of the *propositus's* intention. Domicile up to 16 years is ascribed now in Scots law in accordance with s.22 of the 2006 Act. In English law the matter is governed by a combination of DMPA 1973 s.4, and the common law.

6. An individual becomes sui juris with regard to domicile at the age of 16 (Scots law by inference of s.22(4) of the 2006 Act; English law per DMPA 1973 s.3).

---

[214] See Rogerson, "Habitual Residence: The New Domicile?" (2000) 49 I.C.L.Q. 86, 94, 95.

[215] Clive, "The Concept of Habitual Residence", 1997 J.R. 137, wherein it is stated, at 141, that the author had not come across any case where a person had been found not to be habitually resident in a country where he or she had lived for a year or more. See Rogerson, "Habitual Residence: The New Domicile?" (2000) 49 I.C.L.Q. 86, 94, 95.

[216] See *Re J (A Minor) (Abduction: Custody Rights)* [1990] 2 A.C. 562, per Lord Donaldson M.R. at 572. See also Ch.14, below relating to the Family Law Act 1986 s.41(1)(b) and Regulation 2201/2003 art.10.

7. Married women became sui juris with regard to domicile with effect from January 1, 1974, within the terms of DMPA 1973 s.1(1), (2).

8. Special meanings exist for domicile for the purposes of Inland Revenue law and the Civil Jurisdiction and Judgments Acts 1982 and 1991 (jurisdiction in civil and commercial matters falling within the Brussels regime).

9. Reform of domicile rules has been effected piecemeal by legislation. Wholesale reform has not come about. Yet so widespread is the use today of the connecting factor of habitual residence in modern instruments that, though the classic rules of domicile may remain largely intact, the ambit of operation of these rules seems likely to be cut down.

10. Rules for the acquisition and loss of habitual residence can be stated with less confidence, and may differ according to context, and according to definition by national courts and the ECJ, respectively.

CHAPTER 7

JURISDICTION IN CIVIL AND COMMERCIAL MATTERS

INTRODUCTION

7–01 This chapter deals with that area of the conflict of laws which is of greatest moment to litigants and their advisers. The subject of conflict of laws is built upon the three pillars of jurisdiction, choice of law, and recognition of foreign decrees. Although all three areas are likely to contribute to the securing of a remedy in a conflict dispute, attention at the outset is directed to securing the most advantageous forum, and enforcement[1] of the remedy there granted.

Rules of jurisdiction clothe the forum with its significant powers to classify the nature of the problem, segregate the substantive from the procedural, provide pre-trial safeguards, identify the applicable law, and exercise its policy discretion, most of which will be utilised in justifying the exercise of its ultimate power, to provide or withhold a remedy.

OVERVIEW

7–02 Jurisdiction means the entitlement of a court to hear an action and make a decision. The power is conferred by common law or statute of the legal system of which the putative forum forms part, augmented in the UK, by the rules of civil and commercial jurisdiction[2] contained in Council Regulation (EC) No.44/2001 on jurisdiction and the recognition and enforcement of judgments in civil and commercial matters (henceforth "the Brussels I Regulation"), which are operative where the defender is "domiciled" in an EU Member State, or, regardless of the domicile of the defender, if the court of a Member State has special jurisdiction under art.5 (by nature of the subject matter of the dispute), or exclusive jurisdiction in terms of art.22, or jurisdiction by choice of the parties under art.23, or by their submission under art.24.

In a conflict of laws context, the subject of jurisdiction connotes the allocation of jurisdiction between courts, internationally, or between the constituent legal systems of a multi-legal system state, but problems of ascertainment and allocation of jurisdiction arise also in domestic law, as, for example, in Scotland, geographically among sheriffdoms, or hierarchically, in civil and criminal matters, between the lower and higher courts.

In general terms, the grounds upon which UK courts exercise jurisdiction depend on three basic principles:

---

[1] In respect of which, see Ch.9, below.
[2] As to consistorial jurisdiction, see Ch.12, below.

(a) *actor sequitur forum rei*[3];
(b) effectiveness of any decree which may be pronounced; and/or
(c) submission, that is, that the defender has agreed to submit to the jurisdiction.

Forum actoris rules of jurisdiction, based upon a personal link between the *pursuer* and the court, have no place in "national"[4] Scots rules of jurisdiction.

In general and in theory (and usually borne out in practice), there must be a connection between the defender, or the subject matter of the dispute, and the court before which it is heard. If the connection is fragile, a rule of jurisdiction based upon it may be regarded internationally as objectionable.[5] Outside the ambit of the Brussels I Regulation, the effect of such jurisdictional rules may be mitigated by rules of *forum non conveniens* conferring on the court seised the discretion to cede jurisdiction to a court which it is persuaded is more appropriate. Nevertheless, it is not always necessary that the defender be resident in the jurisdiction in question for the case to proceed there, for there are certain rules, based on the subject matter of the litigation, which permit the identification of a different court(s) as (equally) suitable, a fact which may afford the pursuer an alternative forum in which to sue.[6]

Broadly, the subject of jurisdiction must be examined in three aspects:

(a) jurisdiction over the parties to litigation and restrictions thereon;
(b) jurisdiction over the subject matter of litigation and restrictions thereon;
(c) power/duty of a court to decline jurisdiction.

---

[3] Literally, that the pursuer must have recourse to the court where the subject matter of the dispute is situated; and broadly, that the pursuer must seek out the defender in the place of the latter's place of residence or business.

[4] i.e. those rules of jurisdiction of Scots law existing before, and continuing to co-exist with, the system of jurisdictional rules put in place by the 1968 Brussels Convention, *q.v.*, largely replaced by the Brussels I Regulation. The Brussels system contains examples of *forum actoris* rules where these are considered justified to protect disadvantaged parties (sections 3, 4, 5), but in principle such rules, being classed as "exorbitant", are not permitted under the regime to operate against persons domiciled in an EU Contracting/Member State (art.3). Nevertheless, if used, the general prohibition of review of the jurisdiction of the court of origin (Brussels I Regulation art.35.2, 35.3) renders it impossible for a court in an EU Member State in which enforcement is sought, to refuse enforcement on that ground alone: see *Krombach v Bamberski* [2001] All E.R. (EC) 584.

[5] See, e.g. the "national" English rules of jurisdiction which permit "service out of the jurisdiction" in non-Brussels cases, upon a defendant resident abroad, if the subject matter of the litigation and the facts of the case, in the discretion of the English court, warrant this. This is an example of "long arm" jurisdiction. See also ground of "temporary presence" in England only long enough for the service of a writ: *Maharanee Seethadevi Gaekwar of Baroda v Wildenstein* [1972] 2 Q.B. 283.

[6] The Brussels regime provides special or exclusive grounds of jurisdiction in addition to, although in derogation from, the principal ground of personal jurisdiction (that a defender domiciled in an EU Member State shall be sued in that State). See paras 7–16 and 7–34, below.

116   *International Private Law*

Restrictions on parties (to sue or be sued)

7–03   The following restrictions may apply:

(a) Immunity from suit may be claimed by[7] foreign sovereigns, govern-
    ments,[8] and government departments,[9] diplomatic agents and agents of
    foreign sovereigns.[10] Ambassadors, their agents, their household, and
    staff in course of duty, are immune so long as they act in their respective
    "official" capacities.[11] Upon their functions coming to an end, privileges
    and immunities normally will cease when they leave the receiving
    country, or on expiry of a reasonable period in which to do so.[12]

    The matter of state immunity is governed in the UK by the State
    Immunity Act 1978, which provides generally for state immunity
    from suit in the UK,[13] subject to the principle of submission to the
    jurisdiction of the UK courts,[14] and with exceptions on certain
    grounds,[15] e.g. in respect of "commercial transactions".[16] The crucial
    distinction latterly at common law was between a state's actions in
    the exercise of its sovereign authority (*acta jure imperii*), and its
    actions in the course of its commercial activities (*acta jure gestionis*).
    The 1978 Act takes the same approach, but the distinction is less
    clear-cut. It has been held in England that the Brussels I Regulation

---

[7] Though it may be waived, expressly or impliedly. See generally Malcolm N. Shaw, *International Law*, 6th edn (Cambridge: Cambridge University Press, 2008). Institution of proceedings by a state is an implied waiver. Waiver of diplomatic immunity must be express, and by the state, not the individual: *Al-Fayed v Al-Tajir* [1987] 2 All E.R. 396.

[8] See *Parlement Belge* (1879–1880) L.R. 5 P.D. 197; *Compania Naviera Vascongada v The Cristina* [1938] A.C. 485; *Spain v National Bank of Scotland*, 1939 S.C. 413; *Kahan v Pakistan Federation* [1951] 2 K.B. 1003; *United States v Dollfus Mieg et Cie SA* [1952] A.C. 582; *Sayce v Ameer Ruler Sadig Mohammed Abbasi Bahawalpur State* [1952] 2 Q.B. 390; and *Rahimtoola v Nizam of Hyderabad* [1958] A.C. 379 HL (though, per Lord Denning: "it is more in keeping with the dignity of a foreign sovereign to submit himself to the rule of law than to claim to be above it"). Contrast *Juan Ysmael & Co Inc v Indonesia* [1955] A.C. 72; *Baccus Srl v Servicio Nacional del Trigo* [1957] 1 Q.B. 438; and *Thai-Europe Tapioca Service Ltd v Pakistan Directorate of Agricultural Supplies (The Harmattan)* [1975] 1 W.L.R. 1485. See also *Jones v Ministry of the Interior Al-Mamlaka Al-Arabiya AS Saudiya* [2006] UKHL 26.

[9] *Krajina v Tass Agency* [1949] 2 All E.R. 274; *Baccus Srl v Servicio Nacional del Trigo* [1957] 1 Q.B. 438. Contrast *Owners of the The Philippine Admiral v Wallem Shipping (Hong Kong) Ltd (The Phillipine Admiral)* [1977] A.C. 373; *Trendtex Trading Corp v Central Bank of Nigeria* [1977] Q.B. 529; *Owners of Cargo Lately on Board the Playa Larga v Owners of the I Congreso del Partido* [1981] 2 All E.R. 1064; and *Alcom Ltd v Colombia* [1984] 2 All E.R. 6.

[10] *Re C (An Infant)* [1959] Ch. 363; and *Ghosh v D'Rozario* [1963] 1 Q.B. 106. Consuls and their staff have immunity from suit in respect of official (not private) acts by virtue of the Consular Relations Act 1968, as amended by the Diplomatic and Other Privileges Act 1971.

[11] However, a foreign state's unilateral action in purporting to confer some similar status upon an individual did not bind the court in England to accept that such a person had diplomatic status and immunity from suit: *R. v Governor of Pentonville Prison Ex p. Teja* [1971] 2 Q.B. 274; and *R. v Secretary of State for Home Department Ex p. Bagga* [1991] 1 Q.B. 485.

[12] See *Shaw v Shaw* [1979] 3 All E.R. 1.

[13] *Jones v Saudi Arabia* [2007] 1 A.C. 270 HL; contrast *Donegal International Ltd v Zambia* [2007] 1 Lloyd's Rep. 397.

[14] See s.2. See *NML Capital Ltd v Argentina* [2010] EWCA Civ 41.

[15] See ss.3–11.

[16] Defined in 1978 Act s.3(3). See *Alcom Ltd v Colombia* [1984] 2 All E.R. 6, per Lord Diplock at 8; *Bank of Credit and Commerce International (Overseas) Ltd (In Liquidation) v Price Waterhouse (No.1)* [1997] 4 All E.R. 108; *Kuwait Airways Corp v Iraqi Airways Co* [1995] 1 W.L.R. 1147 HL, per Lord Goff at 1156; *AIG Capital Partners Inc v Kazakhstan* [2006] 1 All E.R. 284; and *ETI Euro Telecom International NV v Bolivia* [2009] 1 W.L.R. 665.

should be read as subject to the international law of state immunity, and therefore as not precluding reliance upon state immunity.[17]

(b) By virtue of the Visiting Forces Act 1952, visiting forces may not be tried in UK courts.

(c) Enemy aliens may not be pursuers in a Scots forum,[18] unless resident in Scotland,[19] but it is open to such persons to defend actions.

(d) A foreign pursuer may be called upon to "sist a mandatory" as security for expenses. The function of a mandatory, appointed by the foreign party on the instruction of the court, is to perform any order of the court made during the litigation, and to be personally liable for the expenses of the action. The matter is within the discretion of the court.[20]

Alternatively, provision of caution (security) may be ordered. A balance must be kept between taking reasonable precautions to ensure that any decree pronounced against a foreign party can be satisfied, and avoiding the imposition of unreasonably onerous conditions not applicable to native litigants. While it is true that a party who chooses a British jurisdiction must take the procedural, conflict and substantive law of the forum as he finds it, it is axiomatic that he should not be subject to a disadvantage not imposed on a native litigant; nor should he enjoy an advantage not available to such a party.[21] Case law in Scotland suggests that where there is no reason to doubt the financial standing of the foreign parties, caution will not be required.[22] The imposition of a requirement to sist a mandatory arguably may be discriminatory and unjustified in terms of the Brussels jurisdiction and judgments regime.[23] Security or caution is not appropriate in respect of enforcement proceedings under the Brussels I Regulation.[24]

These cases apart, the court in Scotland or England will not be restrictive in attitude, nor offended by novelty, but rather will seek to act in accordance with the principles of comity, so far as public policy permits.[25] With regard to the status of international organisations, and their capacity to sue, reference may be made to *Arab Monetary Fund v Hashim (No.3)*,[26] and *Westland Helicopters*

[17] *Grovit v De Nederlandsche Bank* [2006] 1 All E.R. (Comm) 397.

[18] *Weber's Trustees v Riemer*, 1947 S.L.T. 295; *Netz v Ede* [1946] Ch. 224; and *R. v Bottrill Ex p. Kuechenmeister* [1947] K.B. 41.

[19] *Schulze Gow & Co v Bank of Scotland*, 1914 2 S.L.T. 455; *Weiss v Weiss*, 1940 S.L.T. 447; and *Sovfracht (V/O) v Van Udens Scheepvaart en Agentuur Maatschappij (NV Gebr)* [1943] A.C. 203.

[20] See *Renfrew and Brown v Magistrates of Glasgow* (1861) 23 D. 1003; *Gunn and Co v Couper* (1871) 10 M. 116; *NV Ondix International v Landay Ltd*, 1963 S.L.T. (Notes) 68; *Masinimport v Scottish Medical Light Industries Ltd*, 1972 S.L.T. (Notes) 76; *Re Little Olympian Each Ways Ltd (No.2)* [1994] 4 All E.R. 561, per Lindsay J. at 576; and *Rossmeier v Mounthooly Transport*, 2000 S.L.T. 208.

[21] cf. *De la Vega v Vianna* (1830) 1 B. & Ad. 284. As to the position of the native litigant see, e.g. *Merrick Homes Ltd v Duff (No.1)*, 1996 S.L.T. 932.

[22] *Kaiser Bautechnik GmbH v GA Group Ltd*, 1993 S.L.T. 826; and *Medicopharma (UK) BV v Cairns*, 1993 S.L.T. 386.

[23] See *Rossmeier v Mounthooly Transport*, 2000 S.L.T. 208; *Nguyen v Searchnet Associates Ltd*, 2000 S.L.T. (Sh. Ct.) 83; *De Beer v Kanaar & Co (No.1)* [2003] 1 W.L.R. 38; and *Bell Electric Ltd v Aweco Appliance Systems GmbH & Co KG* [2003] 1 All E.R. 344.

[24] See art.51; cf. Brussels Convention art.45.

[25] e.g. *Bumper Development Corp Ltd v Commissioner of Police of the Metropolis* [1991] 4 All E.R. 638, where the Court of Appeal permitted a Hindu temple to sue in England to recover its property, the temple having legal personality under the law where it was situated. It was entitled to sue in the person of the officer properly appointed under its own law.

[26] [1991] 1 All E.R. 871.

Ltd v Arab Organisation for Industrialisation,[27] and also to the International Organisations Act 2005.

SCOTS COMMON LAW RULES OF JURISDICTION

7–04 At common law, the grounds upon which the Scots courts assumed jurisdiction were, with only a few exceptions, grounds which generally were recognised in other countries. The likely result was that a Scots decree would be recognised and enforced internationally. The grounds were as follows:

(a) domicile of succession[28] (for use in consistorial actions and actions involving status);
(b) domicile of citation (i.e. residence);
(c) in relation to itinerants, presence of defender in Scotland, if personally cited[29];
(d) place of performance of contract[30] (*ratione contractus*)[31];
(e) place of occurrence of delict (*ratione delicti*)[32];
(f) moveables situated in Scotland[33] (*ratione rei sitae*).

At common law, the courts of the *situs* alone had jurisdiction in questions relating to immoveable property because they alone have power to grant effective decrees. In English law, the Civil Jurisdiction and Judgments Act 1982 s.30, abolished the rule in *British South Africa Co v Companhia de Mocambique*[34] which had excluded (though there were always certain exceptions) the jurisdiction of the English court to entertain an action concerning damages for trespass to foreign land, though no question of title was involved. Under s.30, the court in England and Wales or Northern Ireland has jurisdiction to hear proceedings for trespass to immoveable property situated outside that part of the UK (and hence in another part of the UK, as well as outside the UK), unless the proceedings principally are concerned with title to, or right to possession of, the property.

---

[27] [1995] 2 All E.R. 387.
[28] i.e. domicile in the classic sense. See Ch.6, above.
[29] This ground was not always recognised internationally. See now Civil Jurisdiction and Judgment Act 1982 Sch.8 r.2(a) re persons of no fixed residence.
[30] *Dallas & Co (Transport Ltd) v McArdle*, 1949 S.L.T. 375, per Lord President Cooper at 378.
[31] Jurisdiction *ratione contractus* (regarded as meaning that either the place of execution or the place of performance of the contract was within the jurisdiction) was subject to the essential condition that there had to be personal service within Scotland or within the sheriffdom: Sheriff Courts (Scotland) Act 1907 s.6(f) (now repealed to the extent that it determines jurisdiction in respect of any matter to which the Civil Jurisdiction and Judgments Act 1982 Sch.8 applies).
[32] The need for personal citation was removed by the Law Reform (Jurisdiction in Delict) (Scotland) Act 1971; also *Russell v FW Woolworth & Co Ltd*, 1982 S.L.T. 428. But see *Wendel v Moran*, 1993 S.L.T. 44.
[33] *Muir v Matassa*, 1935 S.L.T. (Sh. Ct.) 55.
[34] [1893] A.C. 602. Upheld by the House of Lords in *Hesperides Hotels Ltd v Muftizade* [1978] 3 W.L.R. 378. See, for Scotland, *Hewit's Trustees v Lawson* (1891) 18 R. 793 and *Cathcart v Cathcart* (1902) 12 S.L.T. 182.

(g) prorogation (party choice of forum)[35];

(h) reconvention[36];

(i) interdict to prevent the commission of a wrong in Scotland, on that ground alone, or a wrong abroad, if possessed of jurisdiction over the defender on another ground[37]; and

(j) in relation to trusts, the place of the domicile of a trust.

The following grounds of jurisdiction did not receive approval internationally:

(a) possession of heritage in Scotland in an action unrelated to the heritage[38];

(b) arrestment of moveable property of the defender in Scotland in order to found jurisdiction[39]; and

(c) temporary presence of the defender within the jurisdiction.[40]

At the behest of the Maxwell Committee,[41] the "residual" rules of jurisdiction now in use in Scotland[42] are set out in Sch.8 of the Civil Jurisdiction and Judgments Act 1982, as amended.[43] By reason of the 1968 Brussels Convention, and the Brussels I Regulation, the ambit of operation of these native Scots rules is much attenuated.

LEGISLATIVE OVERVIEW OF RULES OF JURISDICTION APPLICABLE IN SCOTLAND

There are four legislative regimes regulating the rules in use in Scotland **7–05** concerning civil and commercial jurisdiction, namely:

(a) The Brussels regime, which may be said to comprise the 1968 Brussels Convention, the Brussels I Regulation, and the EC-Denmark Agreement,[44] with auxiliary primary legislation in the UK in the form of the Civil Jurisdiction and Judgments Act 1982, as amended by secondary legislation;

---

[35] Agreement supplies a lack of jurisdiction over the *person*, not the type of action or subject matter.

[36] Jurisdiction which a foreign litigant, by raising an action in Scotland, is held to call down upon himself, in order to permit the defender to raise a counter-action, if the latter is necessary to do justice between the parties.

[37] David M. Walker, *Principles of Scottish Private Law*, 4th edn (Oxford: Clarendon, 1988), p.157; and see Sch.8 r.2(10).

[38] *Baron Hume's Lectures, 1786–1822*, edited by G. Campbell H. Paton (Edinburgh: Stair Society, 1939–1958), Vol.V, p.249. Cf. In English law *Emanuel v Symon* [1908] 1 K.B. 302.

[39] *Baron Hume's Lectures*, Vol.V, p.250. *Agnew v Norwest Construction Co Ltd*, 1935 S.C. 771.

[40] Not a feature of Scots common law jurisdictional rules (the jurisdiction over itinerants, that is, persons of no fixed abode, being different in purpose and nature), but found in English law, famously in *Maharanee of Baroda v Wildenstein* [1972] 2 Q.B. 283.

[41] Scottish Committee on Jurisdiction and Enforcement, *Report of the Scottish Committee on Jurisdiction and Enforcement* (HMSO, 1980).

[42] i.e. subject to the Brussels I Regulation and Civil Jurisdiction and Judgments Act 1982 Sch.4.

[43] See para.7–69, below.

[44] Agreement between the European Community and Denmark on jurisdiction and the recognition and enforcement of judgments in civil and commercial matters [2005] OJ L299/62.

(b) The Lugano Convention,[45] with auxiliary primary legislation in the UK in the form of the Civil Jurisdiction and Judgments Act 1991; and replaced by the Lugano II Convention;

(c) Civil Jurisdiction and Judgments Act 1982 Sch.4: the Modified Convention, allocating jurisdiction within the UK[46]; and

(d) Civil Jurisdiction and Judgments Act 1982 Sch.8, being the residual, "national", Scottish rules.[47]

Each of these regimes will be examined in turn in this Chapter, as well as the interrelationships between and among them.

THE BRUSSELS REGIME

1968 Brussels Convention on jurisdiction and the enforcement of judgments in civil and commercial matters

7–06   The 1968 Convention was intended to regulate both the jurisdiction of courts of Contracting States, and the enforcement in one Contracting State of judgments given in another. It is known for this reason as a "double" Convention, the two sets of rules having an interdependent relationship.[48]

The committee of experts engaged in drafting the Convention identified certain grounds of jurisdiction used in Contracting States which were unlikely to meet international standards of acceptability. These "exorbitant" grounds (e.g. the nationality of the pursuer—a *forum actoris* rule; service during temporary presence of the defendant in the UK; presence within the UK of property belonging to the defendant in actions not concerning such property) could not be used against "persons domiciled in a Contracting State",[49] a category which includes a defendant "domiciled" elsewhere in the UK, and a defender "domiciled" in Scotland. In addition to proscribing exorbitant rules, the Brussels Convention prescribed the only grounds of jurisdiction, as from time to time interpreted and amended, which could be used against such persons. Other grounds, however, could be used against defenders not domiciled in a Contracting State.[50]

---

[45] See para.7–65, below.

[46] See para.7–68, below.

[47] See para.7–69, below.

[48] See P. Jenard, Report on the Convention on Jurisdiction and the Enforcement of Judgments in Civil and Commercial Matters OJ C59 5.3.79 (henceforth "the Jenard Report"). The enforcement provisions have proved less productive of litigation than have the jurisdiction provisions.

[49] 1968 Convention art.3.

[50] If a judgment emanates from a court in a Contracting State, seised on a non-Brussels ground because the defendant was/is a non-EU domiciliary, the enforcement procedures of the Convention may be used against assets situated in a Contracting State belonging to such a person. Non-Contracting States, especially USA, expressed concern about this matter. For this reason, art.59 exists to enable non-Contracting States to make bilateral arrangements with Contracting States to protect their nationals; relevant treaties have been concluded between the UK and Canada (Reciprocal Enforcement of Foreign Judgments (Canada) Order 1987 (SI 1987/468) and Reciprocal Enforcement of Foreign Judgments (Canada) (Amendment) Order 1995 (SI 1995/2708)), and the UK and Australia (Reciprocal Enforcement of Foreign Judgments (Australia) Order 1994 (SI 1994/1901)). Treaties made under art.59 are honoured in art.72 of the Brussels I Regulation.

Civil Jurisdiction and Judgments Act 1982[51]

The 1982 Act gave the force of law within the UK to the 1968 Brussels **7–07**
Convention. The scheme of the Act is:

> Part 1: Implementation of the 1968 Convention (in terms of international
> allocation).
> Part 2: Jurisdiction, and recognition and enforcement of judgments,
> within the United Kingdom (i.e. subordinate to the 1968
> Convention; Sch.4, "Modified" Convention).
> Part 3: Jurisdiction in Scotland (subordinate to Pts 1 and 2; Sch.8).

The text of the Brussels Convention changed over the years as more countries
were admitted to membership of the EU.[52] Thus, in any dispute thought to fall
within the Brussels Convention, it was necessary to find the date of
commencement of proceedings to ascertain which version of the Convention
applied.[53]

BRUSSELS I REGULATION[54]

The completion and implementation of the 1968 Brussels Convention and **7–08**
subsequent Conventions was a signal achievement. Although certain of the
rules of the Brussels Convention, particularly those concerning jurisdiction,
generated much interpretative litigation (both domestically, within the UK and
in other Contracting States, and also as a result of references to the ECJ for
preliminary rulings),[55] when the Convention was succeeded by the Brussels I
Regulation, with effect from March 1, 2002, there was no fundamental change
in its structure or provisions, but rather a process of refinement in the light of
experience.

European Union Member State rules of jurisdiction and judgment enforcement are contained primarily in the Brussels I Regulation, the preamble to
which states that in order to attain the objective of free movement of judgments in civil and commercial matters, it is necessary and appropriate that the
rules be governed by a Community instrument which is binding and directly
applicable in Member States. Where a rule in the Regulation replicates in
wording, identical or very similar, a provision contained in the Brussels
Convention, the principle of *continuity of interpretation* will operate.[56]

---

[51] Henceforth "CJJA 1982".
[52] UK, Danish and Irish Accession Convention 1978 [1978] OJ L304/1 (see Schlosser Report
[1979] OJ C59/71); Greek Accession Convention 1982 [1982] OJ L388/1; Spanish and
Portuguese Accession Convention 1989 [1989] OJ L285/1; and Austrian, Finnish and Swedish
Accession Convention 1996 [1997] OJ C15/1.
[53] Brussels Convention art.54.
[54] Regulation 44/2001.
[55] See 1971 Protocol on Interpretation of the Brussels Convention.
[56] Brussels I Regulation recital (19): "Continuity between the Brussels Convention and this
Regulation should be ensured, and transitional provisions should be laid down to that end. The
same need for continuity applies as regards the interpretation of the Brussels Convention by the
Court of Justice of the European Communities and the 1971 Protocol should remain applicable
also to cases already pending when this Regulation enters into force". Cf. Rome I Regulation
recital (17).

It was a feature of the 1968 Convention that certain key terms were allotted a "Community" or autonomous definition for use in all Contracting States. Definition and interpretation of certain other provisions were left to the discretion of individual states, in accordance with their own conflict rules. As might be expected, the incidence of ascription of Community meanings to particular terms has increased in the Regulation.[57]

Civil Jurisdiction and Judgments Order 2001[58]

7–09   Necessary changes to the CJJA 1982, pursuant to the Brussels I Regulation, were implemented in the UK by means of the Civil Jurisdiction and Judgments Order 2001.[59]

The EC-Denmark Agreement

7–10   Denmark did not participate in the adoption of the Brussels I Regulation,[60] and therefore is not bound by it. Thus, the allocation of jurisdiction and enforcement of judgments vis-à-vis Denmark continued to be governed by the 1968 Convention until the conclusion of an Agreement between the European Community and Denmark on Jurisdiction and the Recognition and Enforcement of Judgments in Civil and Commercial Matters,[61] which extended as between the EC and Denmark the provisions of the Brussels I Regulation, with certain amendments of a fairly minor nature.[62] Accordingly, the function of the 1968 Convention is almost spent. The Brussels I Regulation, by virtue of its nature as a Regulation, will apply to new EU Member States automatically upon their entry to the EU.

Ongoing refinement of the Brussels I Regulation

7–11   Recital (28) of the Brussels I Regulation states that no later than five years after its entry into force, the Commission will present a report on its application and, if need be, submit proposals for its adaptation. Such a report was issued in April 2009,[63] accompanied by a Green Paper.[64] The Green Paper

---

[57] e.g. arts 5.1(b), 60.

[58] Civil Jurisdiction and Judgments Order 2001 (SI 2001/3929). See also the Civil Jurisdiction and Judgments Regulations 2009 (SI 2009/3131), para.7–65, below.

[59] Henceforth, "CJJO 2001".

[60] Danish citizens having rejected the Maastricht Treaty in 1992, Denmark does not participate in the adoption of measures under the head of judicial co-operation in civil and commercial matters. See now Treaty of Lisbon, Protocol No.22 on the position of Denmark [2010] OJ C/83/299.

[61] [2005] OJ L299/62. See further Council of the European Union Press Release 8402/06 (re Luxembourg meeting, April 2006), noting agreement concerning the extension to Denmark of the Brussels I Regulation (Decision 6922/06).

[62] For date of entry into force, see art.12.

[63] Report on the Application of Council Regulation (EC) No 44/2001 on jurisdiction and the recognition and enforcement of judgments in civil and commercial matters COM(2009) 174 final.

[64] Green Paper on the Review of Council Regulation (EC) No 44/2001 on jurisdiction and the recognition and enforcement of judgments in civil and commercial matters COM(2009) 175 final.

posed a number of questions, the detail of which will be examined at appropriate points throughout this Chapter, and invited responses from stakeholders, with a view to the further refinement and improvement of the operation of the instrument. From the UK perspective, the most significant response was that of the House of Lords EU Committee.[65] At the time of writing, a draft proposal amending the Regulation is awaited.[66]

BRUSSELS I REGULATION—PROVISIONS OF CENTRAL IMPORTANCE[67]

Scope

Article 1

The Regulation applies in civil and commercial matters, whatever the nature **7–12** of the court or tribunal. It shall not extend, in particular, to revenue, customs or administrative matters.

Specifically excluded from its scope are:

(a) the status or legal capacity of natural persons, rights in property arising out of a matrimonial relationship,[68] wills and succession;
(b) bankruptcy, proceedings related to the winding up of insolvent companies or other legal persons,[69] judicial arrangements, compositions and analogous proceedings;
(c) social security;
(d) arbitration.[70]

An important term at the outset is "civil and commercial matters". One aid to interpreting this phrase is the negative one of noting specific exclusions from

---

[65] House of Lords European Union Committee, *21st Report of Session 2008/09, Green Paper on the Brussels I Regulation: Report with Evidence* (The Stationery Office, 2009), HL Paper No.148 (Session 2008/09). The Report is full and informative, but clearly amounts to only one body of evidence submitted to the Commission.

[66] The proposal will be informed and assisted, in particular, by Burkhard Hess, Thomas Pfeiffer and Peter Schlosser, *Report on the Application of Regulation Brussels I in the Member States* (Study JLS/2004/C4/03) (Ruprecht-Karls Universitat Heidelberg, 2007) (henceforth "the Heidelberg Report"); and Arnaud Nuyts et al, *Study on Residual Jurisdiction (Review of the Member States' rules concerning the "Residual Jurisdiction" of their courts in civil and commercial matters, pursuant to the Brussels I and II Regulations): General Report* (JLS/C4/2005/07-30-CE) (Universite Libre de Bruxelles, 2007) (henceforth "the Nuyts Study"). See also EU Parliament Committee on Legal Affairs, *Draft Report on the Brussels I Regulation* (2009/2140/INI).

[67] See, for line-by-line commentary, Ulrich Magnus and Peter Mankowski (eds), *European Commentaries on Private International Law: Brussels I Regulation* (Munich: Sellier, 2007).

[68] Note particular problem with regard to the categorisation of maintenance: para.7–23, below.

[69] e.g. *SCT Industri AB i likvidation v Alpenblume AB* (C-111/08), OJ 2009 C205/8.

[70] See as to the "exclusion" of arbitration from the scope of the Brussels I Regulation, para.7–59, below, re *West Tankers Inc v RAS Riunione Adriatica di Securta SpA (The Front Comor)* [2007] UKHL 4, and *West Tankers Inc v Allianz SpA* [2009] 1 A.C. 1138. For examples of earlier authorities, see *Marc Rich & Co AG v Societa Italiana Impianti SpA* (C190-89) [1992] 1 Lloyd's Rep. 342; *Navigation Maritime Bulgare v Rustal Trading Ltd (The Ivan Zagubanski)* [2002] 1 Lloyd's Rep. 106; *Electronic Arts CB v CTO SpA* [2003] EWHC 1020; and *Through Transport Mutual Insurance Association (Eurasia) Ltd v New India Assurance Co Ltd (The Hari Bhum)* [2004] 1 Lloyd's Rep. 206; [2005] 1 Lloyd's Rep. 67.

the scope of the Regulation, of revenue, customs or administrative matters. Apart from such expressly excluded cases, ECJ concern has been to distinguish, and exclude, public law from private law cases, and to ensure that this is done according to a distinction made by the Community, rather than by individual legal systems. The test has been said to be "functional", rather than "institutional",[71] and classification of potentially "public law" cases depends upon whether a public authority is or is not acting in exercise of its public law powers.[72]

General rule

Article 2

7–13   "(1) Subject to this Regulation, persons domiciled in a Member State shall, whatever their nationality, be sued in the courts of that Member State.

(2) Persons who are not nationals of the Member State in which they are domiciled shall be governed by the rules of jurisdiction applicable to nationals of that State."[73]

Article 2 is the pre-eminent jurisdictional provision, to which all others are derogations. Moreover, should other optional grounds of jurisdiction fail for any reason, Article 2 remains.[74]

Recital (11) of the preamble to the Regulation states that rules of jurisdiction in the Regulation should be highly predictable. Jurisdiction must always be available on the ground of defendant's domicile, except in a few well defined situations (*q.v.*), where the subject matter of the dispute, or the exercise of party autonomy, warrants a different (alternative) linking factor.

The 1968 Brussels Convention left the definition of the "domicile" of natural persons to the discretion of individual States. For the UK, the definition of domicile of individuals now is to be found in CJJO 2001 Sch.1 para.9,[75] in the manner of a cascade provision: a definition is created first for the domicile of an individual in the UK[76]; next, for the domicile of an individual in a particular part of the UK[77]; and then in a particular place within the UK.[78] These definitions are to the effect that the requirements for domicile in the UK, etc. are satisfied if and only if the individual is resident in the UK (or a part of the UK; or the part of the UK in which that place is situated), and the nature and circumstances of his residence indicate that he has a substantial connection with the UK. Most importantly, the requirement of a substantial connection shall be presumed to be fulfilled, unless the contrary is proved, if

---

[71] Jonathan Hill, *International Commercial Disputes in English Courts*, 3rd edn (Oxford: Hart, 2005), p.337.

[72] Reference should be made to *Lufttransportunternehmen GmbH & Co KG v Organisation Européenne pour la Securité de la Navigation Aérienne (Euro-Control)* (29–76) [1976] E.C.R. 1541, distinguished in *R. v Harrow Crown Court Ex p. Unic Centre Sarl* [2000] 1 W.L.R. 2112.

[73] See Jenard Report, p.19.

[74] *Kleinwort Benson Ltd v Glasgow City Council (No.2)* [1997] 4 All E.R. 641.

[75] Amending CJJA 1982 s.41. See Ch.6, above.

[76] See para.9(2).

[77] See para.9(3).

[78] See para.9(4).

the individual has been resident in the UK, part thereof, or place therein, for the last[79] three months or more.[80] Analysis of these terms would suggest, however, that there is no reason in law why an individual might not be found "domiciled" in the UK, etc. before the elapse of a three month period. The purpose of ascribing domicile in this connection is to clothe the court with jurisdiction in a civil or commercial matter, as opposed to a matter of status, and therefore it is desirable and reasonable that the criterion should be presumptively established after the expiry of a short period of time.

The exercise of the discretion of the Scots and English courts in applying the definition of domicile is exemplified by a relatively small number of cases given the importance of the jurisdictional ground. Decisions have been required on matters such as the *tempus inspiciendum*, the effect of interruption of the running of the period, the significance of enforced residence, and the fact of dual residence. These issues represent the type of interpretative problem which always arises when a jurisdictional requirement is tied to a specific length of time.

The House of Lords in *Canada Trust Ltd v Stolzenberg (No.2)*,[81] in addressing itself[82] to the interpretation of the word "sued" as it appeared in art.2 of the Brussels Convention, was sensible of the fact that the formulation of the art.2 rule potentially subjects the claimant to the task of "shooting at a moving target". The House held that it was in accordance with reasonable canons of interpretation to construe "sued" as a reference to the date of initiation of proceedings, which, translated into English procedure rules, is the date of issue of the writ. Therefore, the domicile of the main defendant was to be ascertained at the date of issue of the writ, and not at the later date on which the proceedings were served on him.

Where residence is coerced, as e.g. where an individual was bailed to remain in the UK until trial, domicile in the place of effective imprisonment will not normally be found.[83]

In *Daniel v Foster*,[84] Sheriff Palmer assumed jurisdiction, in a Sch.4 ("Modified Convention") case where jurisdiction was at issue as a result of the defendant's pattern of life, which was such that he spent regular, but intermittent, periods of time within the sheriffdom attending to his business interests, and the remainder at his principal residence in Sussex, without it being able to be shown that he was resident continuously within the sheriffdom. The sheriff in effect held that the requisite period of three months' residence need not be continuous. Hence, dual "domicile" or even multiple "domicile" is a

---

[79] An undefined term, but meaning the period ending on the date on which the court is seised, which must be taken to be the date of initiation of proceedings; see now Brussels I Regulation art.30.
[80] See para.9(6).
[81] [2000] 4 All E.R. 481.
[82] In advance of the Community definition of "date at which a court shall be deemed to be seised", provided by art.30, (*q.v.*).
[83] *Petrotrade Inc v Smith* [1999] 1 W.L.R. 457. This proposition raises interesting questions of the factual nature of the connecting factor, and its purpose. Compare and contrast *Mark v Mark* [2005] 3 All E.R. 912, per speech of Lady Hale, considered at para.6–14, above.
[84] 1989 S.L.T. (Sh. Ct.) 90 (Sch.4 case). See also *Relfo Ltd (In Liquidation) v Varsani* [2010] EWCA Civ 560.

possibility in this context.[85] An abundance of residences may produce the effect that the owner thereof is not "domiciled" for the purpose of civil jurisdiction under the Brussels regime in any of them; and if so, he may be beyond the reach of the Brussels regime, which is something of an achievement.[86]

Article 59.1 of the Brussels I Regulation provides that in order to determine whether a party is domiciled in a Member State whose courts are seised of the matter, the court shall apply its internal law. Article 59.2, by contrast, provides that if a party is (alleged) not to be domiciled in the Member State of the forum, then in order to determine whether the party is domiciled in another Member State, the forum shall apply the law of that other Member State.[87]

The definition of the "domicile" of juristic persons has received a Community definition, found in art.60 of the Regulation, viz. that a company or other legal person is domiciled where it has its (a) statutory seat[88]; (b) its central administration; or (c) principal place of business.[89]

Significance of defendant's domicile

Article 3

7–14   "(1) Persons domiciled in a Member State may be sued in the courts of another Member State only by virtue of the rules set out in Sections 2 to 7 of this chapter.

(2) In particular the rules of national jurisdiction set out in Annex I shall not be applicable as against them."

Annex I of the Regulation details the exorbitant "national" grounds of jurisdiction of Member States. Unacceptable "UK" grounds are rules which enable jurisdiction to be founded on:

(a) service of the document instituting the proceedings on the defendant during his temporary presence in the UK; or

(b) the presence within the UK of property belonging to the defendant; or

(c) the seizure by the claimant of property situated in the UK.

---

[85] See *Gruppo Torras SA v Al-Sabah (No.1)* [1995] 1 Lloyd's Rep. 374 at 444–446; and *Haji-Ioannou v Frangos* [1999] 2 All E.R. (Comm) 865, where the question arose, inter alia, of the application of the Brussels Convention art.2, in circumstances where the defendant was resident in Monaco, a non-Contracting State, but arguably might also have been considered to have a special business domicile in Greece, by Greek law, as to which expert evidence was offered.

[86] *Cherney v Deripaska* [2007] I.L.Pr. 49.

[87] e.g. *Haji-Ioannou v Frangos* [1999] 2 All E.R. (Comm) 865. This is worthy of remark from the perspective also that in the usage of classic domicile, the forum applies its own law to all determinations of domicile: *Re Annesley* [1926] Ch. 692.

[88] See art.60.2: for the purposes of the UK and Ireland, "statutory seat" means the registered office or where there is no such office anywhere, the place of incorporation or, where there is no such place anywhere, the place under the law of which the formation of the entity took place.

[89] *King v Crown Energy Trading AG* [2003] EWHC 163; and *889457 Alberta Inc v Katanga Mining Ltd* [2009] I.L.Pr. 14. See also CJJO 2001 Sch.1 para.10 (seat of company or other legal person or association for purposes of art.22.2).

Article 4

"(1) If the defendant is not domiciled in a Member State, the jurisdiction **7–15** of the courts of each Member State shall, subject to Articles 22 and 23, be determined by the law of that Member State.[90]

(2) As against such a defendant, any person domiciled in a Member State may, whatever his nationality, avail himself in that State of the rules of jurisdiction there in force, and in particular those specified in Annex I[91] in the same way as nationals of that State."

The subject of residual, or subsidiary, national jurisdiction is a controversial and complex one, considered in detail later in this Chapter.[92]

Special jurisdictions

In Article 5, the Regulation permits a claimant to pursue his claim in a **7–16** forum other than that of the defendant's domicile, in certain specified circumstances, according to the nature of the litigation. These derogations from art.2 provide a useful alternative at the disposal of the claimant. There might be patent or latent procedural or substantive law advantages to the claimant of suing in a particular forum.

It must be remembered that the options available under art.5 are available only where the defendant is a person domiciled in a Member State. The most important special jurisdictions concern contract and delict, respectively.

Article 5.1—matters relating to a contract

An optional, "special" jurisdiction under the 1968 Brussels Convention is **7–17** found in art.5.1, concerning disputes relating to a contract. According to that provision:

"A person domiciled in a Contracting State may, in another Contracting State be sued: 1.(a) in matters relating to a contract, in the courts for the place of performance of the obligation in question."

The neighbouring phrases, "matters relating to a contract"[93] and "obligation in question"[94] received "Community" definitions. Regarding interpretation of the

---

[90] i.e. the residual national rules of the Member State. One consequence of this provision is that it enables a UK court to defer to another Member State court, sub nom. *forum non conveniens*, so long as the defendant is not domiciled in a Member State, even though in principle the plea of *forum non conveniens* has no place within the Brussels regime: *The Xin Yang and The An Kang Jiang* [1996] 2 Lloyd's Rep. 217.

[91] i.e. the exorbitant jurisdictions.

[92] See para.7–64, below.

[93] e.g. *Martin Peters Bauunternehmung GmbH v Zuid Nederlandse Aannemers Vereniging* [1983] E.C.R. 987; *Arcado SPRL v Haviland SA* (9/87) [1988] E.C.R. 1539; *Engdiv Ltd v G Percy Trentham Ltd*, 1990 S.L.T. 617; *Powell Duffryn Plc v Petereit* [1992] E.C.R. I-1745; *Jakob Handte & Co GmbH v Traitements Mecano-Chimiques des Surfaces SA (TCMS)* [1992] E.C.R. I-3967; *Boss Group Ltd v Boss France SA* [1996] 4 All E.R. 970; cf. *Halki Shipping Corp v Sopex Oils Ltd (The Halki)* [1997] 3 All E.R. 833 (arbitration); *Source v TUV Rhineland Holding*, The Times, March 28, 1997 CA; *Belgian International Insurance Group SA v McNicoll*, 1999 G.W.D. 22–1065; *Eddie v Alpa Srl*, 2000 S.L.T. 1062; and *Assitalia SpA v Frahuil SA* (C265/02) [2004] All E.R. (EC) 373 ECJ (ostensible authority to enter into contract).

[94] e.g. *A De Bloos SPRL v Bouyer SA* (C-14/76) [1976] E.C.R. 1497; *Medway Packaging Ltd v Meurer Maschinen GmbH & Co KG* [1990] 2 Lloyd's Rep. 112; *Union Transport Group Plc v*

former phrase, it should be noted that the disputed existence of a contract is a "matter relating to a contract" so long as the claimant can satisfy the court that there is a "good arguable case" that a matter relating to a contract is in issue between the parties. Similarly, repudiation of a contract is a "matter relating to a contract".[95] This has an obvious tactical implication in a *lis pendens* system (*q.v.*), which tolerates the use of negative actings to initiate litigation in an available jurisdiction of choice, even of a party who wishes to deny the existence of a contract.[96] Where the parties to a contract have agreed to refer "disputes arising therefrom, or in connection therewith", to arbitration, any subsequent claim made by one of the parties in relation to the contract, which the other does not admit, is a relevant dispute which the claimant is both entitled and bound to refer to arbitration. The belief or contention by the claimant that the defendant has no arguable defence does not take the matter out of the category of "dispute between the parties".[97]

In contrast, each forum putatively seised was directed to use its own conflict rules to interpret the phrase "place of performance".[98] This necessitated the putative forum adopting a two-step method of reasoning: (i) the applicable law of the contract was ascertained by means of application of the 1980 Rome Convention; (ii) the law thereby identified was used to identify the place of performance. If the place of performance so determined was the legal system of the forum, the forum concluded that it had jurisdiction in terms of art.5.1.[99]

Continental Lines SA [1992] 1 All E.R. 161 (where there are several obligations, the "obligation in question" is the principal one); *Agnew v Lansforsakringbolagens AB* [1996] 4 All E.R. 978 (no express distinction between obligations arising during negotiation of a contract, and those arising under or after the contract); *AIG Group (UK) Ltd v Ethniki* [2000] 2 All E.R. 566; *Raiffeisen Zentralbank Osterreich AG v National Bank of Greece SA* [1999] 1 Lloyd's Rep. 408; and *RPS Prodotti Sidrurgici Srl v Owners of the Sea Maas (The Sea Maas)* [2000] 1 All E.R. 536; and *Bitwise Ltd v CPS Broadcast Products BV*, 2003 S.L.T. 455.

[95] *Boss Group Ltd v Boss France SA* [1996] 4 All E.R. 970.

[96] See para.7–50, below.

[97] *Boss Group Ltd v Boss France SA* [1996] 4 All E.R. 970; *The Halki* [1997] 3 All E.R. 833; and *Benincasa v Dentalkit Srl* (C-269/95) [1998] All E.R. (EC) 135. However, as will be seen, the ostensible, and indeed contractually evidenced, desire to refer disputes to arbitration may prove incapable of standing against adroit use of such of the Regulation's grounds of jurisdiction as are available in the circumstances: see *West Tankers Inc v Allianz SpA* [2009] 1 A.C. 1138, para.7–59, below.

[98] e.g. *Industrie Tessili Italiana Como v Dunlop AG* (12/76) [1976] E.C.R. 1473; *Ivenel v Schwab* (133/81) [1982] E.C.R. 1891; *Shenavai v Kreischer* (266/85) [1987] E.C.R. 239; *Bank of Scotland v Investment Managment Regulatory Organisation Ltd*, 1989 S.L.T. 432; *Custom Made Commercial Ltd v Stawa Metallbau GmbH* [1994] I.L.Pr. 516; *Fisher v Unione Italiana de Riassicurazione Spa* [1998] 8 C.L. 71 (denial of obligation to perform); *Viskase Ltd v Paul Kiefel GmbH* [1999] 3 All E.R. 362; *MBM Fabri-clad Ltd v Eisen und Huttenwerke Thale AG* [2000] C.L.Y.B. 739; *Barry v Bradshaw* [2000] I.L.Pr. 706; *GIE Groupe Concorde v Master of the Vessel Suhadiwarno Panjan* (C-440/97) [2000] All E.R. (EC) 865; *Montagu Evans (A Firm) v Young*, 2000 S.L.T. 1083; *Ennstone Building Products Ltd v Stanger (No.1)* [2002] C.L.Y.B. 624; *Besix SA v Wasserreinigungsbau Alfred Kretzschmar GmbH & Co KG (WABAG)* (C256/00) [2003] 1 W.L.R. 1113 ECJ; *Prifti v Musini Sociedad Anonima de Suguros y Reaseguros* [2003] EWHC 2796; and *Engler v Janus Versand GmbH* (27/02) [2005] 7 C.L. 76 ECJ.

[99] See *William Grant & Sons International Ltd v Marie Brizard Espana SA*, 1998 S.C. 536; *Ferguson Shipbuilders Ltd v Voith Hydro GmbH & Co KG*, 2000 S.L.T. 229; and *Societe Thai Kitchen v Societe TWF* [2009] I.L.Pr. 10 *Cour de Cassation* (France) (Lugano I).

In the special jurisdiction in contract as it appears in the Brussels I Regulation,[100] a Community meaning has been ascribed to the phrase "place of performance", to remove the complexities which arose under the Convention version of the text. There is a large bank of cases interpretative of art.5.1, but pre-Regulation authorities must be viewed in the light of this important change. Thus, in terms of art.5.1 of the Regulation:

"A person domiciled in a Member State may, in another Member State, be sued:

    (a) in matters relating to a contract, in the courts for the place of performance of the obligation in question[101];

    (b) for the purpose of this provision, and unless otherwise agreed, the place of performance of the obligation in question shall be:

       — in the case of the sale of goods, the place in a Member State where, under the contract, the goods were delivered or should have been delivered,

       — in the case of the provision of services,[102] the place in a Member State where, under the contract, the services were provided or should have been provided,

    (c) if subparagraph (b) does not apply then subparagraph (a) applies."

The re-casting of art.5.1 and insertion of a Community definition of "place of performance" constitutes an improvement. However, if the case does not fall within art.5.1(b), art.5.1(c) directs that art.5.1(a) applies, which means that the default position and reasoning remains the same as the original Brussels Convention approach. One cautionary comment[103] is that while, under earlier authority,[104] the place of performance of a debtor's obligation to pay was held to be the creditor's place of business (clothing his home court with jurisdiction if an unpaid British seller should pursue a claim for payment against a foreign purchaser), under the Regulation, it is more likely that the forum will be that of the place of delivery of the goods, which usually will be the legal system of the purchaser.[105]

In the case of sale of goods, if there is more than one place of delivery within one Member State, and the national court cannot determine the principal place of delivery, the ECJ has ruled that the claimant may bring proceedings in whichever of those places he wishes.[106] Where the place of delivery of goods is identified in the contract, reference shall be made to that place.[107] Where delivery is to be made on the basis of an FOB contract, the place of

---

[100] Note that in Sch.4 (the Modified Convention) para.3(a), wording equivalent to the Brussels Convention art.5.1 remains: *JS Swan (Printing) Ltd v Kall Kwik UK Ltd*, 2009 G.W.D. 27–431; and *Commercial Marine Piling Ltd v Pierse Contracting Ltd* [2009] 2 Lloyd's Rep. 659.

[101] *Mora Shipping Inc v Axa Corporate Solutions Assurance SA* [2005] EWCA Civ 1069.

[102] As to the meaning of which, see *Falco Privatstiftung v Weller-Lindhorst* (C-533/07) [2010] Bus. L.R. 210.

[103] Morris, *Conflict of Laws*, 7th edn, 2009, para.4–026.

[104] *Bank of Scotland v Seitz*, 1990 S.L.T. 584.

[105] cf. *Continuity Promotions Ltd v O'Connor's Nenagh Shopping Centre Ltd* [2005] EWHC 3462, QBD.

[106] *Color Drack GmbH v Lexx International Vertriebs GmbH* (C-386/05) [2008] All E.R. (EC) 1044.

[107] *DPT(Duroplast Technik Verwaltungs) GmbH v Chemiplastica SpA* [2009] I.L.Pr. 15 Court of Cassation (Italy).

delivery is the port of shipment[108]—but, exceptionally, the court may look behind the technical terms of the contract in order to discover the true state of contractual affairs.[109]

With regard to "provision of services", where services are provided in several EU Member States, the place of performance is the place of the main provision of services.[110] The decision of the ECJ in *Rehder v Air Baltic Corp*[111] is to the effect that when an air passenger who intended to travel from one Member State to another suffered the cancellation of his flight, he could bring proceedings for compensation either in the court of the jurisdiction of the Member State place of departure, or that of the place of arrival. The rationale offered is that, where services are provided in different Member States, the jurisdiction must be found which has the closest linking factor with the contract, and in that scenario each place was deemed to be equally closely linked.

Inevitably, there soon arose circumstances in which obligations for the provision of services *and* for the sale of goods presented. No doubt there will be many such examples, each of which will turn on its own facts. For example, in *Societe ND Conseil SA v Societe le Meridien Hotels et Resorts World Headquarters*,[112] the service element of the contract trumped the sale of goods element; whereas in *Car Trim GmbH v KeySafety Systems Srl*,[113] the dominant characteristic of the "mixed" contract was the supply of goods, even though the purchaser had given detailed specifications with regard to his requirements as to the components to be produced.

Nullity of contract

7–18   Perhaps surprisingly, no bespoke special jurisdiction in unjust enrichment cases was created in the revised rules of special jurisdiction contained in the Regulation,[114] nor is any proposed in the Green Paper. As will be seen in the examination of choice of law rules in contract, the interface between contract and unjust enrichment (particularly cases where the enrichment results from a pre-existing contract between the parties) presents difficulties, both in domestic and conflict terms.[115]

---

[108] *Re Place of Performance of an FOB Contract* [2010] I.L.Pr. 17 Federal Supreme Court (Germany).

[109] *Scottish & Newcastle International Ltd v Othon Ghalanos Ltd* [2008] UKHL 11.

[110] *Wood Floor Solutions Andreas Domberger GmbH v Silva Trade SA* (C-19/09) [2010] I.L.Pr. 21.

[111] (C-204/08) [2009] I.L.Pr. 44.

[112] [2007] I.L.Pr. 39: the French *Cour de Cassation* accepted the reasoning of the Versailles *Cour d'Appel* that the contractual obligation consisted of the provision of intellectual services and the delivery of goods in the form of advertising material, and that the latter was merely an accessory obligation to the provision of services; the whole constituted a single obligation, led by the services component which, having been provided in London, conferred jurisdiction on the English court.

[113] [2009] I.L.Pr. 33.

[114] Contrast the choice of law position in Rome II Ch.III of which deals with non-contractual obligations arising out of unjust enrichment, *negotiorum gestio*, and *culpa in contrahendo*, discussed in Ch.16, below.

[115] See Ch.15, below.

The House of Lords held in *Kleinwort Benson Ltd v City of Glasgow City Council (No.2)*[116] that a claim arising in restitution from a *void* contract does not fall under the art.5.1 special jurisdiction in contract. On the other hand, as has been seen, matters relating to a contract can include matters relating to a disputed contract.[117] *Kleinwort* is not an ECJ decision,[118] and the CJEU might take a different view of art.5.1 of the Regulation. Arguably (especially from a European perspective), the consequences of nullity of a contract *should* be characterised as contractual for the purposes of jurisdiction, chiming with the Rome I Regulation for choice of law. It is hoped that the matter will be considered by the CJEU in such a way as to place a restitutionary claim of this sort under art.5.1. It seems not unreasonable that in all Member State courts the remedy for such claims be regulated by the content of what must be the putative applicable law of the void contract, and that the court properly seised to implement this remedy be, as it were, the "putative court" under art.5.1. To say that claims resulting from *void* contracts fall outside the ambit of art.5.1, but those which arise out of *voidable or unenforceable* contracts fall within its ambit, is not a helpful dividing line, and is one which is likely to be productive of uncertainty, and also to deprive of jurisdiction to award a restitutionary payment a forum which has just decided that the alleged contract is void.[119]

Culpa in contrahendo

As to the jurisdiction aspect of pre-contractual obligations (a matter left **7–19** open in *Kleinwort*), the House of Lords in *Agnew*[120] was prepared to hold that the art.5.1 special jurisdiction in contract applied. The justification for utilising art.5.1 is likely to be strongly fact-dependent. While a misrepresentation on the way to the conclusion of a contract might justify engaging art.5.1, allegations of breach of a "duty" not to use undue influence or duress, or other negative obligation, would seem to be a less persuasive case for special jurisdiction in contract[121] (but surely would not altogether foreclose an argument for the engagement of art.5.3 (*q.v.*), assuming that the forum putatively seised was that of the occurrence of actual or anticipated harm). For example, where it was alleged that a party unjustifiably broke off negotiations, the ECJ held in *Fonderie Officine Meccaniche Tacconi SpA*[122] that no obligation having been

---

[116] [1999] 1 A.C. 153 (a case under CJJA 1982 Sch.4). Lord Goff, delivering the leading speech, further stated that such a claim could not fall under art.5.3 (*q.v.*), since, in general, unjust enrichment does not presuppose a harmful event or a threatened wrong. Ante-dating this decision is a shrieval decision, *Strathaird Farms Ltd v GA Chattaway Co*, 1993 S.L.T. (Sh. Ct.) 36 that a claim under the *condictio indebiti* does not qualify as a "matter relating to a contract".

[117] *Boss Group Ltd v Boss Group France SA* [1996] 4 All E.R. 970; *The Halki* [1997] 3 All E.R. 833; *Belgian International Insurance Group SA v McNicoll*, 1999 G.W.D. 22–1065.

[118] The question whether restitution was to be regarded as falling under quasi-delict was referred by the Court of Appeal to the ECJ in *Barclays Bank Plc v City of Glasgow DC*; sub nom. *Kleinwort Benson Ltd v Glasgow City Council (No.1)* [1994] 2 W.L.R. 466, but the ECJ held that it had no jurisdiction to give a ruling on the interpretation of the Modified Convention (Sch.4): *Kleinwort Benson Ltd v Glasgow City Council* (C346/93) [1995] All E.R. (EC) 514.

[119] See Hill, *International Commercial Disputes in English Courts*, 3rd edn, 2005, para.5.6.16, paraphrasing the views of Lord Nicholls (dissenting) in *Kleinwort*.

[120] *Agnew v Lansforsakringsbolagens AB* [2001] 1 A.C. 223 (a Lugano case).

[121] Cheshire, North and Fawcett: *Private International Law*, 14th edn, 2008, pp.231, 232.

[122] *Fonderie Officine Meccaniche Tacconi SpA v Heinrich Wagner Sinto Machinenfabrik GmbH* (C-334/00) [2002] E.C.R. I-7357.

assumed by one party to another, there was no obligation assumed by the defendant which could justify application of art.5.1. Any alleged breach of the duty of good faith imposed by the Italian Civil Code upon which the claimant sought to rely would require to be placed in jurisdictional terms under art.5.3. In *Fonderie*, no contract resulted, and so *Agnew* might be distinguished on that ground. These are very nice distinctions.

Article 5.3—matters relating to tort, delict or quasi-delict

7–20   A person domiciled in a Member State may, in another Member State, be sued:

> "3. in matters relating to tort, delict or quasi-delict,[123] in the courts for the place where the harmful event occurred or may occur".[124]

Interpretative difficulties have arisen in jurisdiction (and in choice of law)[125] in identifying the locus of double or multi-locality delicts, i.e. where elements of the delict occur in different legal systems, most commonly where the place of acting differs from the place of effect, but also where an act or omission giving rise to injury in one jurisdiction, is followed in another legal system by deterioration of the victim's condition.[126] The point was famously discussed in *Bier BV v Mines de Potasse d'Alsace SA*[127] (in circumstances where the pollution of the Rhine in France harmed the plants of a market gardener in Holland),[128] to the effect that art.5.3 confers jurisdiction on the courts *both* for the place of acting, *and* the place where the effect(s) is/are felt, affording an option (within the option of special jurisdictions) to the aggrieved party.

The ECJ has clarified the meaning further in *Zuid Chemie BV v Philippo's Mineralenfabriek NV/SA*,[129] against a complex factual background, in response to a reference from the Dutch Hoge Raad asking whether the initial damage would be the damage which arose by virtue of delivery of a defective

---

[123] Tort, etc. has an independent Community meaning: *Kalfelis v Bankhaus Schroder Munchmeyer Hengst & Co (t/a HEMA Beteiligungsgesellschaft GmbH)* [1988] E.C.R. 5565; and *Burke v Uvex Sports GmbH* [2005] I.L.Pr. 26. See also *Swithenbank Food Ltd v Bowers* [2002] 2 All E.R. (Comm) 974; *Verein fur Konsumenteninformation v Henkel* (C-167/00) [2003] All E.R. (EC) 311 ECJ; and *Danmarks Rederiforening v Landsorganisationen i Sverige* (C18/02) [2004] All E.R. (EC) 845 ECJ.

[124] cf. Under Sch.4, *Bonnier Media Ltd v Kestral Trading Corp*, 2002 S.C.L.R. 977. See also *Reference from German Federal Court of Justice to the ECJ: eDate Advertising GmbH v X* (Case C-509/09) OJ 2010 C134/14.

[125] See Ch.16, below.

[126] e.g. *Henderson v Jaouen* [2002] 2 All E.R. 705; and *Dolphin Maritime & Aviation Services Ltd v Sveriges Angfartygs Assurans Forening* [2009] I.L.Pr. 52.

[127] [1976] E.C.R. 1735.

[128] See also *Mecklermedia Corp v DC Congress GmbH* [1998] 1 All E.R. 148; *Reunion Europeene SA v Spliethoff's Bevrachtingskantoor BV* (C51/97) [1998] CLYB 769; *Raiffeisen Zentral Bank Osterreich AG v Tranos* [2001] I.L.Pr. 9; *Casio Computer Co Ltd v Sayo (No.3)* [2001] I.L.Pr. 43; *Dexter Ltd (In Administrative Receivership) v Harley* [2001] C.L.Y.B. 810; *Alfred Dunhill Ltd v Diffusion Internationale di Maroquinerie de Prestige Sarl* [2001] C.L.Y.B. 812; *Ennstone Building Products Ltd v Stanger (No.1)* [2002] C.L.Y.B. 624; *Cronos Containers NV v Palatin* [2003] 2 Lloyd's Rep. 489; *Bus Berzelius Umwelt Service AG v Chemconserve BV Reakt Ltd* (C99/245 HR) [2004] I.L.Pr. 9 Hoge Raad (NL); *Kronhofer v Maier* (C168/02) [2004] All E.R. (EC) 939; *Mackie (t/a 197 Aerial Photography) v Askew*, 2009 S.L.T. (Sh. Ct.) 146; and *Future Investments SA v Federation Internationale de Football Association* [2010] EWHC 1019 Ch.

[129] (C-189/08) [2009] OJ C220/11.

product, or the damage which arose when normal use was made of the product. The ECJ held, in the circumstances presented, the place where the product was used for the purpose for which it was intended (and thereby caused damage) was the place of initial damage.

Whether an event is harmful is to be decided by the domestic law of the legal system chosen to govern the issue by the conflict rules of the court seised.[130] So long as some primary harm occurs within the jurisdiction, that will suffice,[131] but consequential, tangential or secondary economic loss suffered in a Member State will not be enough to confer art.5.3 jurisdiction upon it.[132]

Defamation claims

Shevill v Presse Alliance SA[133] is authority for the proposition that a **7–21** claimant may sue a publisher, under art.2, for defamation, in the publisher's place of business for all damage, wherever it is alleged to have been suffered. Alternatively, the defendant may be sued (using *Bier* reasoning) in the jurisdiction where any (even small) circulation of the allegedly defamatory matter occurred, but only to the extent of the damage allegedly suffered by the claimant in that jurisdiction. This "separate" or "pluralist" or "mosaic" approach, rather than "global" or "universal" approach, has been favoured also in non-EU cases.[134]

Relationship between article 5.1 and 5.3

The ECJ's significant decision in *Kalfelis v Bankhaus Schroder* **7–22** *Munchmeyer Hengst & Co*,[135] that the phrase "matters relating to tort, delict or quasi-delict" in art.5.3 of the Brussels Convention must be regarded as an, "independent concept covering all actions which seek to establish the liability of a defendant and which are not related to a 'contract' within the meaning of Article 5(1)", has had the consequence that an important distinction must be made in the advice given to a litigant who potentially has a claim arising both under contract and under delict, from the same circumstances, according to

---

[130] *Kitechnology BV v Unicor GmbH Plastmaschininen* [1994] I.L.Pr. 568; and *Dumez France and Tracoba v Hessische Landesbank* (C220/88) [1990] E.C.R. I–49. See R.D. Leslie, "Jurisdiction in Tort or Delict", 1997 S.L.T. (News) 133.

[131] *Minster Investments Ltd v Hyundai Precision & Industry Co Ltd* [1988] 2 Lloyd's Rep. 621 and *Equitas Ltd v Wave City Shipping Co Ltd* [2005] 2 All E.R. (Comm) 301.

[132] *Marinari v Lloyd's Bank Plc* [1996] All E.R. (EC) 84.

[133] [1996] 3 All E.R. 929.

[134] cf. *Barclay v Sweeney* [1999] I.L.Pr. 288 Court of Appeal (Paris); and *Berezovsky v Michaels (No.1)* [2000] 1 W.L.R. 1004. Contrast *Domicrest Ltd v Swiss Bank Corp* [1998] 3 All E.R. 577. See, for England and Wales, Law Commission, *Defamation and the Internet: A Preliminary Investigation* (The Stationery Office, 2002), Scoping Study No.2. Also *Godfrey v Demon Internet Ltd* [2001] Q.B. 201; *Bonnier Media Ltd v Smith*, 2003 S.C. 36; *King v Lewis* [2004] I.L.Pr. 31; *Applause Stores Ltd v Raphael* [2008] EWHC 1781 QB; *Lockton Companies International v Persons Unknown* [2009] EWHC 3423 QB; and *Martinez v Societe MGN Ltd* (Case C-161/10) OJ 2010 C148/21. As to the position in Australia, see *Gutnick v Dow Jones* [2002] HCA 56; and in Canada, *Bangoura v Washington Post*, 2005 (25) T.L.W.D. 2522–006 (CA (Ont) [2005] O.J. No.5428).

[135] (189/87) [1988] E.C.R. 5565; [1989] E.C.C. 407 (a case under the Brussels Convention). See also *Source Ltd v TUV Rheinland Holding AG* [1998] Q.B. 54.

whether the litigation in contemplation can be said to be purely domestic or having a conflict of laws dimension. In the former case, an aggrieved party is quite likely to be entitled to sue in the alternative, or at least to have a free choice as to the category of law under which he wishes to proceed to his best advantage. In contrast, in a cross-border case, the supremacy of art.5.1 of the Brussels I Regulation over art.5.3, appears to preclude suit under the head of tort/delict if there exists a contractual link between the parties.

The decision of the Irish High Court in *Burke v Uvex Sports GmbH*[136] arose from simple facts: Burke claimed for personal injuries to his face caused when his motorcycle helmet visor broke when he skidded and struck the roadside in Tipperary, Ireland. His claim was framed solely in tort against two defendants, both domiciled in Germany: first, the manufacturer, and secondly, the party from whom Burke had bought the helmet and visor. With regard to the second defendant, there was perforce a contractual relationship with Burke. The court could not overlook the existence of that contractual element,[137] with the result that it could not properly take jurisdiction over the second defendant on the basis of art.5.3 (occurrence of the delict in Ireland). It did not matter that in these circumstances, by the national law of Ireland, the contractual element of the claim did not foreclose the claim in tort; nor could account be taken of the possible detriment to the claimant (Burke) if, as a result of time limit rules, he was unable to sue the second defendant in Germany under art.2.

If art.2 jurisdiction is used, presumably one advantage for the claimant is that he may frame his action in contract *or* delict in the alternative, to hedge his risk or better his chances. Moreover, art.2 is available where the circumstances cannot be said to fall into any of the special categories, in particular neither within contract nor tort/delict. But if art.5.1 or 5.3 special jurisdiction be used, then the claimant's case would appear to be limited to an argument in contract or delict, respectively.

Other special jurisdictions

7–23   "A person domiciled in a Member State may, in another Member State, be sued:

   2. [in matters relating to maintenance][138] ...
   4. as regards a civil claim for damages or restitution which is based on an act giving rise to criminal proceedings, in the courts seised of

---

[136] [2005] I.L.Pr. 26 High Court (Ireland) (a Brussels Regulation case). See *contra, Re Mail Order Promise of Win in a Draw* [2003] I.L.Pr. 46 Federal Supreme Court (Germany).

[137] It was agreed between the parties, and accepted by Herbert J., that the contract between Burke and the second defendant was *not* a consumer contract within the provisions of arts 15–17 of the Brussels I Regulation (*Burke v UVEX Sports GmbH* [2005] I.L.Pr. 26 at [31]).

[138] Under the Brussels Convention, and the Brussels I Regulation as currently drafted, the special treatment accorded to maintenance obligations by art.5.2 suggests that this subject is intended to be included in the scope of the instrument as a civil and commercial matter (despite the exclusion in art.1.2(a)), only peripherally connected with status: *De Cavel v De Cavel* (120/79) [1980] E.C.R. 731; *Van den Boogaard v Laumen* (C220/95) [1997] E.C.R. I-1147; and *Farrell v Long* [1997] All E.R. (EC) 449. With effect from June 18, 2011, Regulation 4/2009 shall apply in EU Member States. Recital (44) of the Maintenance Regulation explains that the rule contained in art.5.2 of the Brussels I Regulation shall be replaced by those set out in Ch.II of the Maintenance Regulation. See para.13–27, below.

those proceedings, to the extent that that court has jurisdiction under its own law to entertain civil proceedings;
5. as regards a dispute arising out of the operations of a branch, agency or other establishment, in the courts for the place in which the branch, or agency or other establishment is situated . . .[139]
6. as settlor, trustee or beneficiary of a trust . . . in the courts of the Member State in which the trust is domiciled".[140]

Related actions

Article 6

A person domiciled in a Member State may also be sued: **7–24**

"1. where he is one of a number of defendants, in the courts for the place where any one of them is domiciled, provided the claims are so closely connected that it is expedient to hear and determine them together to avoid the risk of irreconcilable judgments resulting from separate proceedings[141];
2. as a third party in an action on a warranty or guarantee or in any other third party proceedings,[142] in the court seised of the original proceedings, unless these were instituted solely with the object of removing him from the jurisdiction of the court which would be competent in his case;
3. on a counter-claim arising from the same contract or facts on which the original claim was based, in the court in which the original claim is pending;
4. in matters relating to a contract, if the action may be combined with an action against the same defendant in matters relating to rights in rem in immovable property, in the court of the Member State in which the property is situated."

Of the special jurisdiction rules in art.6, that which has given rise to most litigation is art.6.1.[143] An instructive early example is *Gascoine v Pyrah*,[144] in which the Court of Appeal considered it reasonable to permit the claimants, who had brought an action in England against the first defendant (domiciled in

[139] cf. *Latchin (T/A Dinkha Latchin Associates) v General Mediterranean Holdings SA* [2003] C.L.Y.B. 601; and *Anton Durbeck GmbH v Den Norske Bank ASA* [2003] Q.B. 1160. Although this provision expands the claimant's options, it must be noted that art.5 begins with the words: "A person domiciled in a Member State may, in another Member State be sued . . .". Therefore, art.5.5 cannot be regarded as an extension of the reach of the regime in the same way as arts 9.2, 15.2 and 18.2, below, i.e. under art.5.5, the "branch" must be situated in a Member State.
[140] e.g. *Gomez v Gomez-Monche Vives* [2008] EWHC 259 (Ch). For details of this specialist area, see Jonathan Harris, *The Hague Trusts Convention: scope, application and preliminary issues* (Oxford: Hart, 2002).
[141] *Gascoine v Pyrah* [1994] I.L.Pr. 82; *Canada Trust v Stolzenberg (No.2)* [2000] 4 All E.R. 481; *Watson v First Choice Holidays & Flights Ltd* [2001] 2 Lloyd's Rep. 339; *Daly v Irish Group Travel Ltd (t/a Crystal Holidays)* [2003] I.L.Pr. 38; *Andrew Weir Shipping Ltd v Wartsila UK Ltd* [2004] 2 Lloyd's Rep. 377; *Et Plus SA v Welter* [2005] EWHC 2115 and *Masri v Consolidated Contractors International (UK) Ltd* [2006] 1 W.L.R. 830.
[142] See, e.g. *Kinnear v Falconfilms MV* [1994] 3 All E.R. 42.
[143] cf. Under Lugano II *Gard Marine & Energy Ltd v Tunnicliffe* [2009] EWHC 2388 (Comm).
[144] [1994] I.L.Pr. 82.

England) claiming financial loss resulting from negligent professional advice in the matter of the purchase of a showjumping horse, to conjoin with the first defendant, a second defendant, a veterinary expert domiciled in Germany, whose advice by telephone allegedly endorsed the wisdom of the purchase. Article 6.1 applied so as to avoid the risk of irreconcilable judgments resulting from separate proceedings. The contents of the telephone conversation between the first and second defendants were a vital issue of fact upon which courts might easily have differed were separate proceedings to ensue.

The ECJ has held that the risk of irreconcilability of judgments is the principal consideration when applications under art.6.1 are in issue.[145] It is not necessary, however, that the actions in question have identical legal bases and art.6.1 may apply where the actions have different legal bases.[146] The question whether there is such a risk of irreconcilability must be tested objectively.[147]

Disadvantaged parties

7–25   A feature of the Brussels I Regulation is the inclusion of rules providing grounds of jurisdiction protective of potentially disadvantaged parties. While the 1968 Convention afforded special protection to consumers and to insured parties, and the Lugano Convention contained a provision favouring employees, the Brussels I Regulation has gathered these provisions together, creating a protective framework for insured parties (including, under the Regulation, the beneficiaries under insurance policies, if different from the policyholder), consumers, and employees, respectively.[148] These sets of rules share common characteristics, for example, in restrictions on parties' ability to contract out of them to their (perceived) detriment; and in the principle that the "weak" party may be sued only in his domicile, whereas he may sue the "strong" party in his own domicile, as an alternative to suing in the state where the "strong" defendant is domiciled.

A significant protection afforded to "weak" parties is contained in Ch.3 (recognition and enforcement) art.35.1, to the effect that a judgment shall not be recognised if the jurisdictional provisions contained in sections 3 (insured parties), 4 (consumers) or 6 (exclusive jurisdictions) (*q.v.*) have not been met. One rationale of the Brussels regime is that at the enforcement stage the jurisdiction of the court of the Member State of origin may not be reviewed,[149] and

---

[145] cf. art.28, below.

[146] *Freeport Plc v Arnoldsson* (C-98/06) [2008] Q.B. 634.

[147] *FKI Engineering Ltd v De Wind Holdings Ltd* [2007] I.L.Pr. 17. However, in *Glaxosmithkline v Rouard* (C-462/06) [2008] E.C.R. I-3965 (reference from *Cour de Cassation*), the ECJ held firmly that in the interests of upholding the protective purpose of the special rules concerning employees contained in Ch.II section 5, it is not appropriate to permit parties to avail themselves of art.6.1. See paras 7–30—7–33, below.

[148] cf. Special choice of law rules for such contracts in Rome I Regulation arts 6, 7, 8. See Crawford and Carruthers, "Connection and Coherence Between and Among European Private International Law Instruments in the Law of Obligations" in Binchy and Ahern (eds), *Rome I Regulation: Implications for International Commercial Litigation* (Leiden: Brill, forthcoming).

[149] See art.35.3. For it is understood that the grounds of jurisdiction are intrinsically acceptable, and that each Member State will apply them competently and in good faith. This is the paradigm example of the mutual trust and confidence with which the Brussels system is imbued. The edifice of agreed jurisdictional grounds including a strict system of rules to treat the problem of conflicting jurisdictions, is constructed to avoid an outcome, among Member States, of irreconcilable judgments (though in that unwelcome event, art.34.3 and 34.4 will provide a solution).

to this principle the "weaker parties" protections are the only exceptions. The permission to contest jurisdiction contained in art.35.1 does not extend to cases falling under section 5 (jurisdiction over individual contracts of employment). It is unlikely that this occurred through simple oversight; rather that a distinction was drawn between employment contracts and the other "weaker party" cases insofar as the applicant in the former case is more likely to be the employee, and any re-visiting of the jurisdictional competence would favour the employer not the employee, who is the perceived weaker party, whom these rules are designed to protect.[150]

Disadvantaged parties are not protected from the effect of art.24 (*q.v.*), which is to confer entitlement to hear the action upon a court of a Member State to which a party has submitted (other than merely to contest the jurisdiction thereof).[151]

Articles 8–14 (jurisdiction in matters relating to insurance)

Article 9

"1. An insurer domiciled in a Member State may be sued: **7–26**
   (a) in the courts of the Member State where he is domiciled, or
   (b) in another Member State, in the case of actions brought by the policyholder, the insured or a beneficiary, in the courts for the place where the plaintiff is domiciled,
   (c) if he is a co-insurer, in the courts of a Member State in which proceedings are brought against the leading insurer.
2. An insurer who is not domiciled in a Member State, but has a branch, agency or other establishment in one of the Member States shall, in disputes arising out of the operations of the branch, agency or establishment, be deemed to be domiciled in that Member State."[152]

The victim of an accident has been assisted by creative interpretation of art.9. In its decision in *FBTO Shadeverzekeringen NV v Odenbreit*[153] the ECJ effectively added to the categories of specially protected parties under art.9.1(b), by extending its *forum actoris* benefits to the injured party in an accident, thereby allowing him to sue, in his own legal system, the wrongdoer's insurance company, so long as that is permitted by the national law of the court in question. Looking more closely at this condition, it was held in *Jones v Assurances Generales de France (AGF) SA*[154] that, on the issue of whether a direct action against the insurer is permitted, the law to be referred to was the law applicable to the insurance contract binding the defendant, i.e. the insurance contract between the insurer and the insured party. It is not, therefore, the internal law of the forum, but in effect the private international law of the forum by which

---

[150] See Hill, *International Commercial Disputes in English Courts*, 3rd edn, 2005, para.13.3.5.
[151] Hill, *International Commercial Disputes in English Courts*, 3rd edn, 2005, paras 5.2.1, 5.8.24.
[152] The concept of "deemed domicile" in this provision, built upon the agency framework, operates potentially to draw into the regime a defendant domiciled in a Third State.
[153] (C-463/06) [2007] E.C.R. I-11321; [2008] I.L.Pr. 12. See also *Re Jurisdiction in a Direct Action against an Insurer* (VI ZR 200/05) [2008] I.L.Pr. 52; *Thwaites v Aviva Assurances* Unreported December 16, 2009, Mayors and City of London Court.
[154] [2010] I.L.Pr. 4.

will be identified the applicable law of the insurance contract, viz. Rome I Regulation art.7.[155]

Article 10 lays down special provisions in respect of liability insurance,[156] and insurance of immoveable property.

Article 12 completes, with art.13, the protective structure which the Regulation provides for insurance cases. In terms of art.12.1, an insurer may bring proceedings only in the courts of the Member State in which the defendant is domiciled, irrespective of whether he is the policyholder, the insured or a beneficiary. Article 12.2 states that the provisions of section 3 shall not affect the right to bring a counter-claim in the court in which, in accordance with the section, the original claim is pending.

There follow in art.13 rules concerning the extent to which the "beneficiaries" of the provisions of section 3 may depart from them,[157] namely, only by an agreement which:

> "1.   . . . is entered into after the dispute has arisen; or
> 2.   . . . allows the policyholder, the insured or a beneficiary to bring proceedings in courts other than those indicated in this Section; or
> 3.   . . . is concluded between a policyholder and an insurer, both of whom are at the time of conclusion of the contract domiciled or habitually resident in the same Member State, and . . . has the effect of conferring jurisdiction on the courts of that State even if the harmful event were to occur abroad, provided that such an agreement is not contrary to the law of that State; or
> 4.   . . . is concluded with a policyholder who is not domiciled in a Member State, except in so far as the insurance is compulsory or relates to immoveable property in a Member State; or
> 5.   . . . relates to a contract of insurance in so far as it covers one or more of the risks set out in Article 14."

Article 14 excludes certain categories of risk, such as loss to seagoing ships, and "large" risks,[158] because certain specific risks are governed by sector-specific instruments.

Articles 15–17 (jurisdiction over consumer contracts)

Article 15

7–27   "1. In matters relating to a contract concluded by a person, the consumer,[159] for a purpose which can be regarded as being outside his

---

[155] See para.15–29, below.

[156] In respect of which, see also art.11.

[157] *Societe Financiere et Industrielle du Peloux v Axa Belgium* [2006] Q.B. 251 ECJ.

[158] As defined in Directive 73/239/EEC on the coordination of laws, regulations and administrative provisions relating to the taking-up and pursuit of the business of direct insurance other than life insurance [1973] OJ L228/3, as amended.

[159] See *Benincasa v Dentalkit Srl* (C-269/95) [1998] All E.R. (EC) 135, and *Engler v Janus Versand GmbH* (C27/02) [2005] 7 C.L. 76 ECJ. Contrast *Chris Hart (Business Sales) Ltd v Niven*, 1992 S.L.T. (Sh. Ct.) 53; *BJ Mann (Advertising) Ltd v Ace Welding & Fabrications Ltd*, 1994 S.C.LR. 763; *Standard Bank London Ltd v Apostolakis (No.1)* [2000] I.L.Pr. 766; *Davies v Rayner* [2002] 1 All E.R. (Comm) 620; *Semple Fraser WS v Quayle*, 2002 S.L.T. (Sh. Ct.) 33; *Prostar Management Ltd v Twaddle*, 2003 S.L.T. (Sh. Ct.) 11; and *Verein fur Konsumenteninformation v Henkel* (C-167/00) [2003] All E.R. (EC) 311 ECJ.

trade or profession, jurisdiction shall be determined by this Section, without prejudice to Article 4 and point 5 of Article 5, if:
 (a) it is a contract for the sale of goods on instalment credit terms; or
 (b) it is a contract for a loan repayable by instalments, or for any other form of credit, made to finance the sale of goods; or
 (c) in all other cases the contract has been concluded with a person who pursues commercial or professional activities in the Member State of the consumer's domicile or, by any means, directs[160] such activities to that Member State or to several States including that Member State, and the contract falls within the scope of such activities.
 2. Where a consumer enters into a contract with a party who is not domiciled in the Member State but has a branch, agency or other establishment in one of the Member States, that party shall, in disputes arising out of the operations of the branch, agency or establishment, be deemed to be domiciled in that State.[161]
 3. This Section shall not apply to a contract of transport other than a contract which, for an inclusive price, provides for a combination of travel and accommodation."

The question has arisen as to whether the advantageous consumer jurisdiction provisions are triggered in a situation in which an individual has received from a mail order company a letter, the terms of which suggest that she has won a prize, which can be claimed simply by returning a signed and numbered voucher. This question was referred to the ECJ for a preliminary ruling in *Ilsinger*.[162]

The facts of *Ilsinger*, which was a reference from the Austrian court, were on all fours with the prior case of *Engler v Janus*,[163] decided by the ECJ upon the meaning and scope of application of art.13.1.3 of the Brussels Convention, a provision which is substantially re-enacted in the Regulation art.15.1(c). Although the threshold wording in the Regulation is somewhat simpler, both instruments demand that a contract shall have been *concluded* by the consumer with a commercial or professional party. The ECJ in *Engler* delivered, in answer to a question identical to that posed in *Ilsinger*, the decision that since the vendor's initiative was not followed by the conclusion of a contract between the (admitted) consumer and the vendor, the litigation brought by the disappointed party could *not* be regarded as being (consumer) contractual for the purposes of art.13.1.3 of the Brussels Convention.[164]

---

[160] See *Pammer v Reederei Karl Schlüter GmbH & Co KG* (C-585/08) [2009] OJ C44/40; and *Hotel Alpenhof GesmbH v Heller* (C-144/09) [2009] OJ C153/26. Agreement on these words was hard to obtain, the consumer and the supplier lobbies being opposed in the matter of the crafting of jurisdiction rules which would be apt to cover internet trading. The same form of words has been adopted for choice of law in the Rome I Regulation art.6.1(b).

[161] Note again use of the concept of "deemed domicile", having the micro effect of assisting the consumer, and the macro effect of extending the reach of the provisions of the regime.

[162] *Ilsinger v Dreschers* (C-180/06) [2009] OJ C153/3. See Crawford, "Ilsinger v Dreschers" (2009) 4 European Journal of Consumer Law (2009) Vol 4.

[163] *Engler v Janus Versand GmbH* (C-27/02) [2005] E.C.R. I-481. See however *Re Mail Order Promise of Win in a Draw* [2003] I.L.Pr. 46 Federal Supreme Court (Germany).

[164] Although it was accepted that the circumstances were sufficient to satisfy art.5.1 (*Engler v Janus Versand GmbH* (C-27/02) [2005] E.C.R. I-481 at [60]).

In *Ilsinger*, it was necessary to decide whether art.15.1(c) of the Brussels I Regulation must be interpreted in the same way, or whether that provision might be interpreted differently by reason of its partially different wording.[165] In the particular instance, when the old and the new consumer jurisdiction provisions were compared, it could be seen that there is no substantive difference. The important point, as noted above, is that a contract shall have been concluded between the parties. In *Ilsinger*, the court[166] observed that, since the Brussels I Regulation largely replaces the Brussels Convention, the court's interpretation of the Convention extends also to the Regulation, where its provisions and those of the Brussels Convention may be treated as equivalent.

Article 16

7–28   "1. A consumer may bring proceedings against the other party to a contract either in the courts of the Member State in which that party is domiciled or in the courts for the place where the consumer is domiciled.
2. Proceedings may be brought against a consumer by the other party to the contract only in the courts of the Member State in which the consumer is domiciled.
3. This Article shall not affect the right to bring a counter-claim in the court in which, in accordance with this Section, the original claim is pending."

Article 17

7–29   "The provisions of this Section may be departed from only by an agreement:
1. which is entered into after the dispute has arisen; or
2. which allows the consumer to bring proceedings in courts other than those indicated in this Section; or
3. which is entered into by the consumer and the other party to the contract, both of whom are at the time of conclusion of the contract domiciled or habitually resident in the same Member State, and which confers jurisdiction on the courts of that Member State, provided that such an agreement is not contrary to the law of that Member State."

Articles 18–21 (jurisdiction over individual contracts of employment)[167]

7–30   Section 5 governs individual contracts of employment, including the situation (art.18.2) where an employee enters into an individual contract of employment with an employer who is not domiciled in a Member State, but has a branch, agency or other establishment in one of the Member States. In such cases, the employer shall be deemed,[168] in disputes arising out of the operations of the branch, agency, or establishment, to be domiciled in that Member State. Thus:

---

[165] See *Ilsinger v Dreschers* (C-180/06) [2009] OJ C153/3, opinion of the Advocate General at [36], [37].
[166] *Ilsinger v Dreschers* (C-180/06) [2009] OJ C153/3 at [41].
[167] cf. Under 1968 Convention, *Weber v Universal Ogden Services Ltd* (C-37/00) [2002] Q.B. 1189 (ECJ).
[168] Note again use of the concept of "deemed domicile".

Article 19

"An employer domiciled in a Member State may be sued: **7–31**
1. in the courts of the Member State where he is domiciled; or
2. in another Member State:
    (a) in the courts for the place where the employee habitually carries
        out his work or in the courts for the last place where he did so; or
    (b) if the employee does not or did not habitually carry out his work
        in any one country, in the courts for the place where the business
        which engaged the employee is or was situated."

Article 20

"1. An employer may bring proceedings only in the courts of the **7–32**
     Member State in which the employee is domiciled.
2.   The provisions of this Section shall not affect the right to bring a
     counter-claim in the court in which, in accordance with this Section,
     the original claim is pending."

Article 21

"The provisions of this Section may be departed from only by an agree- **7–33**
ment on jurisdiction:
1. which is entered into after the dispute has arisen; or
2. which allows the employee to bring proceedings in courts other than
    those indicated in this Section."

Exclusive jurisdiction

Article 22
"The following courts shall have exclusive jurisdiction, regardless of **7–34**
domicile:

1. in proceedings which have as their object rights in rem[169] in immove-
    able property,[170] or tenancies[171] of immoveable property, the courts of
    the Member State in which the property is situated.[172]

---

[169] See, e.g. *Barratt International Resorts Ltd v Martin*, 1994 S.L.T. 434; *Webb v Webb* [1994]
Q.B. 696; *Lieber v Gobel* (C292/93) [1994] I.L. Pr. 590; *Re Hayward (Deceased)* [1997] 1 All
E.R. 32; *Cambridge Bionutritional Ltd v VDC Plc*, 2000 G.W.D. 6–230; *Gaillard v Chekili*
(C518/99) [2001] I.L.Pr. 33 ECJ; *Dansommer A/S v Gotz* (C8/98) [2001] 1W.L.R. 1069 ECJ;
Ashurst v Pollard [2001] 2 W.L.R. 722; *Prazic v Prazic* [2007] I.L.Pr. 31; *R v R (Bankruptcy
Jurisdiction concerning Real Property Abroad: Setting Aside Consent Order: Estoppel)* [2007]
EWHC 2589 (Fam); *Wellington Pub Co Plc v Hancock* [2009] 48 E.G. 108; *Depfa Bank Plc v
Provincia di Pisa* [2010] EWHC 1148 (Comm); and *JP Morgan Chase Bank NA v Berliner
Verkehrsbetriebe (BVG) Anstalt des Offentlichen Rechts* [2010] EWCA Civ 390.
[170] e.g. *Reichert v Dresdner Bank* (C115/88) [1990] E.C.R. I-27; *Webb v Webb* [1994] Q.B. 696;
and *Barratt International Resorts Ltd v Martin*, 1994 S.L.T. 434.
[171] *Sanders v Van der Putte* (73/77) [1977] E.C.R. 2383; and *Klein v Rhodos Management Ltd*
[2005] I.L.Pr. 17; *Klein v Rhodos Management Ltd* (C73–04) [2006] I.L.Pr. 2.
[172] See *Rosler v Rottwinkel* [1986] Q.B. 33; *Scherrens v Maenhout* (158/87) [1988] E.C.R. 3791;
Hacker v Euro-Relais GmbH [1992] E.C.R. I-1111; and *Jarrett v Barclays Bank Plc* [1997] 2
All E.R. 484.

However, in proceedings which have as their object tenancies of immovable property concluded for temporary private use for a maximum period of six consecutive months, the courts of the Member State in which the defendant is domiciled shall also have jurisdiction, provided that the tenant is a natural person and that the landlord and the tenant are domiciled in the same Member State[173];

2. in proceedings which have as their object the validity of the constitution, the nullity or the dissolution of companies or other legal persons or associations of natural or legal persons, or of the validity of the decisions of their organs, the courts of the Member State in which the company, legal person or association has its seat. In order to determine that seat, the court shall apply its rules of private international law[174];

3. in proceedings which have as their object the validity of entries in public registers, the courts of the Member State in which the register is kept;

4. in proceedings concerned with the registration or validity of patents, trade marks, designs, or other similar rights required to be deposited or registered, the courts of the Member State in which the deposit or registration has been applied for, has taken place or is under the terms of a Community instrument or an international convention deemed to have taken place.

Without prejudice to the jurisdiction of the European Patent Office . . .;

5. in proceedings concerned with the enforcement of judgments, the courts of the Member State in which the judgment has been or is to be enforced."

Exclusive jurisdiction is mandatory in nature; jurisdiction conferred by this provision cannot be excluded by the voluntary submission by a defendant to the courts of another Member State, nor by agreement of the parties. Article 22 applies only where the subject matter of the action is connected with a Member State.[175]

Article 22.1 is the exclusive jurisdiction provision which has generated most litigation. Exclusive jurisdiction under art.22.1 pertains only in proceedings which have as their object[176] rights in rem, rendering significant the distinction between rights in rem and rights in personam.[177]

---

[173] The wording of art.22.1 of Lugano II (para.7–66, below) has been aligned with that of the Brussels I Regulation.

[174] For this purpose, the seat is to be determined by national conflict rules. For the UK, see CJJA 1982 s.43 (and s.43A re Lugano II), and CJJO 2001 Sch.1 para.10; cf. art.60 of the Regulation. See *Bambino Holdings Ltd v Speed Investments Ltd* [2004] EWCA Civ 1512.

[175] Though see para.7–63, below (*effet reflexe*).

[176] *Sanders v Van der Putte* (73/77) [1977] E.C.R. 2383; *Barratt International Resorts Ltd v Martin*, 1994 S.L.T. 434; and *Land Oberosterreich v CEZ AS* (C-343/04) [2006] I.L.Pr. 25 ECJ. Note also art.25: "Where a court of a Member State is seised of a claim which is principally concerned with a matter over which the courts of another Member State have exclusive jurisdiction by virtue of Article 22, it shall declare of its own motion that it has no jurisdiction." Article 35 regulates the limited extent to which the jurisdiction of the Member State court of origin may be reviewed by the Member State court addressed. Article 35.1 provides that a judgment shall not be recognised if it conflicts, inter alia, with section 6 of Ch.II (art.22).

[177] *Webb v Webb* [1994] 3 All E.R. 911; *Re Hayward (Deceased)* [1997] 1 All E.R. 32; *Ashurst v Pollard* [2001] 2 W.L.R. 722; *R v R (Bankruptcy Jurisdiction concerning Real Property Abroad: Setting Aside Consent Order: Estoppel)* [2007] EWHC 2589 (Fam); *Byers v Yacht Bull Corp* [2010] EWHC 133 (Ch). See, on the "in personam" loophole, Carruthers, *The Transfer of Property in the Conflict of Laws*, 2005, paras 2.39–2.50.

It can be seen from the current (and earlier) versions of the short-term tenancy provision contained in art.22.1 that liberties have been taken with use of the word "exclusive". It is clear on the face of the provision that "exclusive" in this context does not mean "unique".[178]

CHOICE OF COURT CLAUSES

If parties, one or more of whom is domiciled in a Member State, have agreed **7–35** that the court of a Member State is to have jurisdiction in any dispute arising between them, it is provided by art.23 of the Brussels I Regulation that that court shall have jurisdiction, which jurisdiction shall be exclusive unless the parties have agreed otherwise. The article provides certain requirements, set out below, as to form, which must be complied with before the agreement will qualify as a valid prorogation.

Prorogation of jurisdiction

Article 23[179]

> "1. If the parties, one or more of whom is domiciled in a Member State, **7–36**
> have agreed[180] that a court or the courts of a Member State are to have
> jurisdiction to settle any disputes which have arisen or which may
> arise in connection with a particular legal relationship, that court or
> those courts shall have jurisdiction. Such jurisdiction shall be exclu-
> sive unless the parties have agreed otherwise.[181] Such an agreement
> conferring jurisdiction shall be either:

---

[178] This is the explanation for art.29 (*lis pendens*), which allocates jurisdiction among courts with "exclusive" jurisdiction on a priority in date basis.

[179] *Siboti K/S v BP France SA* [2003] 2 Lloyd's Rep. 364; contrast *OT Africa Line Ltd v Hijazy (The Kribi) (No.1)* [2001] 1 Lloyd's Rep. 76; *Comsite Projects Ltd v Andritz AG* [2003] EWHC 958; and *Standard Steamship Owners Protection & Indemnity Association (Bermuda) Ltd v GIA Vision Bail* [2005] 1 All E.R. (Comm) 618.

[180] *Deutsche Bank AG v Asia Pacific Broadband Wireless Communications Inc* [2009] I.L.Pr. 36 addresses the question of the extent to which the appearance of consensus on the face of the deed is conclusive. See also *UBS AG v HSH Nordbank AG* [2009] EWCA Civ 585; *AP Moller-Maersk AS (t/a Maersk Line) v Sonaec Villas Cen Sad Fadoul* [2010] EWHC 355 (Comm); and *Deutsche Bank AG v Sebastian Holdings Inc* [2009] EWHC 3069 (Comm). See also L. Merrett, "Article 23 of the Brussels I Regulation: A Comprehensive Code for Jurisdiction Agreements?" (2009) 58 I.C.L.Q. 545, concluding, at 564, that the requirements laid down in art.23 are both necessary and sufficient conditions for the material validity of jurisdiction agreements under the Brussels I Regulation, i.e. in favour of holding parties to the objective appearance of agree-ment. But see *Thomas Cook Tour Operations Ltd v Hotel Kaya* [2009] EWHC 720 (QB); and *Nursaw v Dansk Jersey Eksport* [2009] I.L.Pr. 19.

[181] When, under the Brussels Convention, there was no presumption of exclusivity, a number of authorities demonstrate the drafting difficulty of securing that end: *Dresser UK Ltd v Falcongate Freight Management Ltd (The Duke of Yare)* [1992] 2 All E.R. 450; *MT Group v James Howden & Co Ltd*, 1993 S.L.T. 409; *Barratt International Resorts Ltd v Martin*, 1994 S.L.T. 434; *Morrison v Panic Link Ltd*, 1994 S.L.T. 232; *Continental Bank NA v Aeakos Compania Naviera SA* [1994] 2 All E.R. 540; *Agrafax Public Relations v United Scottish Society Inc* [1995] C.L.Y.B. 703; *Bank of Scotland v SA Banque Nationale de Paris*, 1996 S.L.T. 103; *Mainshiffarts Genossenschaft eG (MSG) v Les Gravieres Rhenanes Sarl* (C-106/95) [1997] All E.R. (EC) 385; *Hough v P&O Containers Ltd* [1998] 2 All E.R. 978; *AIG Europe (UK) Ltd v Ethniki* [2000] 2 All E.R. 566. *McGowan v Summit at Lloyds*, 2002 S.L.T. 1258; *Fratelli Babbini Di Lionello Babbini & Co SAS v BF Engineering SpA* [2005] 1 All E.R. (Comm) 55; and *Astrazeneca UK Ltd v Albemarle International Corp* [2010] EWHC 1028 (Comm).

(a) in writing or evidenced in writing[182]; or
(b) in a form which accords with practices which the parties have established between themselves; or
(c) in international trade or commerce, in a form which accords with a usage of which the parties are or ought to have been aware and which in such trade or commerce is widely known to, and regularly observed by, parties to contracts of the type involved in the particular trade or commerce concerned.[183]

2. Any communication by electronic means which provides a durable record of the agreement shall be equivalent to "writing".
3. Where such an agreement is concluded by parties, none of whom is domiciled in a Member State, the courts of other Member States shall have no jurisdiction over their disputes unless the court or courts chosen have declined jurisdiction.
4. The court or courts of a Member State on which a trust instrument has conferred jurisdiction shall have exclusive jurisdiction in any proceedings brought against a settlor, trustee or beneficiary, if relations between these persons or their rights or obligations under the trust are involved.
5. Agreements or provisions of a trust instrument conferring jurisdiction shall have no legal force if they are contrary to Articles 13, 17 or 21, or if the courts whose jurisdiction they purport to exclude have exclusive jurisdiction by virtue of Article 22."

Exclusivity of choice

7–37 One distinction between the prorogation rules contained in the Regulation and those in Sch.4 (the Modified Convention, *q.v.*)[184] is that in the former, art.23 provides a rebuttable presumption of exclusivity of jurisdiction.[185] While this is advantageous both in terms of certainty and clarity, in that it should operate to exclude doubt as to whether parties intended their chosen court to be additional to those generally available, or (as is now the case) in substitution therefor,[186] the limits of the advantage which it confers should be appreciated.[187]

---

[182] *Rolf Barkmann GmbH v Innova House Ltd*, 2008 G.W.D. 33–490; *Franke GmbH v Fallimento Rubinetterie Rapetti SpA* [2009] I.L.Pr. 13: the Italian Court of Cassation held that the requirement of written form is satisfied, where a jurisdiction clause featured among the standard general conditions of one of the contracting parties, only if that documentation is signed by both of the parties, and contains an express reference to those general conditions; and further that the requirement is not satisfied where a clause is inserted in a form signed by only one of the contracting parties. Cf. In England, *Polskie Ratownictwo Okretowe v Rallo Vito & C SNC* [2009] EWHC 2249 (Comm); and *Calyon v Wytwornia Sprzetu Komunikacynego PZL Swidnik SA* [2009] EWHC 1914 (Comm.).

[183] cf. *Coreck Maritime GmbH v Handelsveen BV* (C387/98) [2001] C.L.Y.B. 795; and *Erich Gasser Gmbh v Misat Srl* [2005] Q.B. 1.

[184] Schedule 4 (r.12) choice of court clause cases include: *Scotmotors (Plant Hire) Ltd v Dundee Petrosea Ltd*, 1982 S.L.T. 181; *British Steel Corp v Allivane International Ltd*, 1989 S.L.T. (Sh. Ct.) 57; *Jenic Properties Ltd v Andy Thornton Architectural Antiques*, 1992 S.L.T. (Sh. Ct.) 5; and *McCarthy v Abowall (Trading) Ltd*, 1992 S.L.T. (Sh. Ct.) 65.

[185] *Breitenbucher v Wittke* [2008] CSOH 145.

[186] cf. *Morrison v Panic Link Ltd*, 1994 S.L.T. 232; and *Scotmotors (Plant Hire) Ltd v Dundee Petrosea Ltd*, 1982 S.L.T. 181.

[187] See para.7–49, below.

The promise of exclusivity must bow before the provisions of arts 22 and 24; and the extent to which disadvantaged parties may depart by agreement from what is provided for their benefit in the Regulation is circumscribed.[188] Moreover, as will be seen, the strength of the *lis pendens* system, as interpreted by the ECJ, is such that a choice of court clause cannot prevail against the claim to jurisdiction of a different court which has been seised first by either party.[189] That first-seised court has jurisdiction to decide, by reason of the jurisdiction clause, or otherwise, that it has or has not jurisdiction. Nowhere in art.23, or elsewhere in the Regulation, is it provided that, as a matter of principle, in the face of proof of the existence of a choice of court clause in favour of a different court, the court first seised need defer to that court earlier "chosen"; it may be argued, in the court first seised, that a particular prorogation clause is not formally valid, or is inapplicable in the circumstances. There is an absence in the civilian tradition, nor is there any indication in the Regulation, of any justification for the court first seised deferring to a Member State court having an allegedly stronger claim (in the view of the court first seised) to hear the case. Nevertheless, following the principle of mutual trust and confidence, it is assumed that the courts of each Member State are equally competent to judge on jurisdiction, and that the court first seised, if persuaded that a valid and applicable exclusive choice of court clause exists, will defer thereto. The length of time spent by the first forum pondering jurisdiction will not affect the rightness and acceptability[190] of the principle of priority of process.[191] If the alternative court (that court selected by the parties in a choice of court agreement) is that of a non-Member State, the problem of the relationship of the Brussels regime with Third States (i.e. the extent of the reach of the regime)[192] arises.

Prorogation clauses are found also outside the Brussels regime. These will usually,[193] but not always,[194] be enforced, if necessary, by means of English or Scots court order[195] enjoining one party to desist from conducting legal proceedings in defiance of the clause. Under the Brussels regime, in light of *Turner v Grovit*,[196] the use by an English or Scottish forum of an anti-suit

---

[188] See further paras 7–51—7–53, below.

[189] *Erich Gasser Gmbh v Misat Srl* [2005] Q.B. 1. See para.7–49, below.

[190] Even though the effect of such a process may be to "torpedo" the initial cause: *Transporti Castellatti Spedizioni Internazionali SpA v Hugo Trumpy SpA* (C-159/97) [1999] E.C.R. I-1597. Frequently, in these situations, the natural claimant is required to turn defendant.

[191] T.C. Hartley, "The European Union and the Systematic Dismantling of the Common Law of Conflict of Laws" (2005) 54 I.C.L.Q. 813, 815. Cf. *Erich Gasser Gmbh v Misat Srl* [2005] Q.B. 1 at [24].

[192] *Re Harrods (Buenos Aires) Ltd (No.2)* [1992] Ch. 72. See Hill, *International Commercial Disputes in English Courts*, 3rd edn, 2005, paras 9.5.13 et seq. See paras 7–62—7–63.

[193] *Continental Bank NA v Aeakos Compania Naviera SA* [1994] 2 All E.R. 540; *Reichhold Norway ASA v Goldman Sachs International* [2000] 1 W.L.R. 173; *Messier Dowty Ltd v Sabena SA* [2000] 1 W.L.R. 2040; *The Kribi (No.1)* [2001] 1 Lloyd's Rep. 76; *Import Export Metro Ltd v Compania Sud Americana de Vapores SA* [2003] 1 All E.R. (Comm) 703; *Sabah Shipyard (Pakistan) Ltd v Pakistan* [2003] 2 Lloyd's Rep. 571; and *Beazley v Horizon Offshore Contractors Inc* [2005] I.L.Pr. 11.

[194] *Standard Bank London Ltd v Apostolakis (No.2)* [2001] Lloyd's Rep. Bank. 240; *Donohue v Armco Inc* [2002] 1 All E.R. 749; *Deutsche Bank AG v Highland Crusader Offshore Partners LP* [2009] EWCA Civ 725; and *Morgan Stanley & Co International Plc v China Haisheng Juice Holdings Co Ltd* [2009] EWHC 2409 (Comm).

[195] Order restraining foreign proceedings/anti-suit injunction: see para.7–57, below.

[196] [2005] 1 A.C. 101.

injunction to seek to prevent a party from reneging on an agreement by suing in a different Member State, in defiance of the prorogation clause, now has been confirmed as inappropriate. The Brussels regime does not purport, at least on the surface of things, to intervene where parties have prorogued the jurisdiction of a court in a non-Member State.[197] Article 23 envisages that choice of court thereunder will be made by parties, one or more of whom is domiciled in a Member State. However, art.23.3 provides that where such a choice of court agreement is concluded by parties none of whom is domiciled in a Member State, the courts of other Member States shall have no jurisdiction over their disputes unless the court(s) chosen have declined jurisdiction.

2005 Hague Convention on Choice of Court Agreements[198]

7–38   This Convention[199] represents that which could be salvaged of international co-operation and agreement generated in advance of the collapse of negotiations instigated by the Hague Conference on Private International Law to achieve a "worldwide" convention on jurisdiction and the enforcement of judgments. It was admitted in 2003 that the ambitious "worldwide" project should be laid aside. Thereafter the more restricted aim was to build upon a basis of what could be agreed at the broadest level of generality. What emerged is a Convention, the provisions of which seek to ensure the effectiveness of exclusive choice of court agreements between parties to commercial transactions, and which govern the recognition and enforcement thereof.

Although the rationale of the Hague rules is in striking contrast to the position which has emerged as confirmation of the nature of the system operating under the Brussels regime, as expressed in the judgments of the ECJ in *Gasser v Misat*[200] and *Turner v Grovit*,[201] the EU took a leading part in negotiations prior to the creation of the 2005 Convention. In the strict system of *lis pendens* under the Brussels regime, the initiative lies with the court first seised to adjudge its own jurisdiction, both generally and in light of argument that the parties had made an exclusive choice of court in favour of another jurisdiction. By contrast, the Hague Convention, after setting out[202] a lengthy list of excluded matters to which its provisions shall not apply, defines[203] "exclusive choice of court agreement" (with a presumption of exclusivity) and provides, usefully, that an exclusive choice of court agreement that forms part of a contract shall be treated as

---

[197] But see paras 7–62—7–64 concerning the inter-relationship of the Brussels regime and Third State jurisdiction.

[198] See Trevor Hartley and Masato Dogauchi, "Explanatory Report on the Convention of 30 June 2005 on Choice of Court Agreements" (The Hague, Permanent Bureau of the Hague Conference, 2007) (hereafter "Hartley and Dogauchi Report"); and Marta Pertegas, "The Brussels I Regulation and the Hague Convention on Choice of Court Agreements" (2010) 11(1) *ERA-Forum* 19.

[199] The Convention has been acceded to by Mexico, and signed by the USA and by the EU on behalf of Member States, but is not yet in force. It shall enter into force on the first day of the month following the expiration of three months after the deposit of the second instrument of ratification, acceptance, approval or accession (art.31). By declaration of the EU under art.30 of the Convention, the Member States of the EU will not sign, ratify, accept or approve the Convention, but shall be bound by it by virtue of its conclusion by the EC.

[200] *Erich Gasser Gmbh v Misat Srl* [2005] Q.B. 1.

[201] *Turner v Grovit* [2005] 1 A.C. 101. See para.7–58, below.

[202] See art.2.

[203] See art.3.

an agreement independent of the other terms of the contract.[204] The validity of the choice of court agreement cannot be contested solely on the ground that the "principal" contract is not valid.[205] The rules of the Brussels regime do not necessarily differ from this,[206] but it is useful to have the point made explicit. The essential differences introduced by this Convention are that it places the court selected by the parties in a position of authority, even though that authority sometimes is shared with the court "first seised but not chosen". These important provisions are contained in arts 5 and 6.

Article 5 (Jurisdiction of the chosen court)

"1. The court or courts of a Contracting State designated in an exclusive **7–39** choice of court agreement shall have jurisdiction to decide a dispute to which the agreement applies, unless the agreement is null and void under the law of that State.

2. A court that has jurisdiction under paragraph 1 shall not decline to exercise jurisdiction on the ground that the dispute should be decided in a court of another State."

These provisions therefore set down the power and the duty[207] of the court selected.

Article 6 (Obligations of a court not chosen)

"A court in a Contracting State other than that of the chosen court shall **7–40** suspend or dismiss proceedings to which an exclusive choice of court agreement applies unless:

a) the agreement is null and void under the law of the State of the chosen court;

b) a party lacked the capacity to conclude the agreement under the law of the State of the court seised[208];

c) giving effect to the agreement would lead to a manifest injustice or would be manifestly contrary to the public policy of the State of the court seised[209];

---

[204] See doubts which can arise in this area: *Mackender v Feldia AG* [1967] 2 Q.B. 590; *Zapata Offshore Co v Bremen and Unterweser Reederei Gmbh (The Chaparral)* [1968] 2 Lloyd's Rep. 158; [1972] 2 Lloyd's Rep. 315 (US Sup. Ct.); *Belgian International Insurance Group SA v McNicoll*, 1999 G.W.D. 22–1065; *Astilleros v Zamakona SA v MacKinnons*, 2002 S.L.T. 1206; and *Cavell USA Inc v Seaton Insurance Co* [2009] EWCA Civ 1363. See Elizabeth B. Crawford, "The Uses of Putativity and Negativity in the Conflict of Laws" (2005) 54 I.C.L.Q. 829.

[205] See art.3(d).

[206] *Benincasa v Dentalkit Srl* (C-269/95) [1997] E.C.R. I-3767. See also *Knorr-Bremse Systems for Commercial Vehicles Ltd v Haldex Brake Products GmbH* [2008] I.L.Pr. 26; and *Skype Technologies SA v Joltid Ltd* [2009] EWHC 2783 (Ch).

[207] See Hill, *International Commercial Disputes in English Courts*, 3rd edn, 2005, para.9.3.2.

[208] Note that the question of capacity (mental and legal, presumably) is to be governed by the law of the court seised, but not chosen. Contrast, at the stage of judgment recognition, the rule under art.9(b) that one reason for the requested state's refusal to recognise or enforce a resulting judgment is that a party lacked capacity to conclude the choice of court agreement under the law of the requested state.

[209] Note the power which the public policy discretion gives to the court seised.

> d) for exceptional reasons beyond the control of the parties, the agreement cannot reasonably be performed; or
>
> e) the chosen court has decided not to hear the case."

Articles 19 ("Declarations limiting jurisdiction") and 20 ("Declarations limiting recognition and enforcement") lay open the possibility of state reservations. Article 19 is remarkable in permitting a state to declare that its courts may refuse to determine disputes to which an exclusive choice of court agreement applies if, except for the location of the chosen court, there is no connection between that state and the parties or the dispute. If a state were to enter such a reservation, it would effectively be adding a mandatory rule of its own to the principal jurisdiction provision contained in art.5.1, and would be curtailing party autonomy in choice of court to an unprecedented degree. Choice of neutral court and neutral law have always been regarded in UK conflict rules as explicable and not intrinsically unreasonable.

The 2005 Convention does not deal with interim measures of protection.[210]

Recognition and enforcement under the 2005 Convention

7–41 With regard to recognition and enforcement of judgments, art.8 of the Convention provides that a judgment given by a court of a Contracting State designated in an exclusive choice of court agreement shall be recognised in other Contracting States, and may be refused effect only on the grounds specified in the Convention. In general, there shall be no review of the merits of the judgment, except insofar as necessary for the application of the provisions of the Convention. The court addressed shall be bound by the findings of fact on which the court of origin based its jurisdiction, unless that judgment was given by default. A number of the grounds of refusal of recognition rest upon natural justice, but the relationship of power between the chosen court and the court seised, as expressed in arts 6(a) and (b) and 9(a) and (b), repays study.[211] It is important, additionally, to note the possibility of state reservation offered by art.20, namely, that the courts of a state may refuse to recognise or enforce a judgment given by a court in another Contracting State if the parties were resident in the requested state, and the relationship of the parties and all other elements relevant to the dispute, other than the location of the chosen court, were connected only with the requested state.[212]

Relationship between the Brussels regime and the 2005 Hague Convention

7–42 Article 26 of the 2005 Convention ("Relationship with other international instruments") should be considered. This "disconnection clause", which is lengthy and opaque, begins, aspirationally, and in very general terms, by stating in art.26.1 that the Convention shall be interpreted so far as possible to

---

[210] See art.7.

[211] i.e. validity of agreement is determined by the law of the chosen court, at the stages both of jurisdiction allocation and judgment recognition; but the question of capacity is referred, at the stage of jurisdiction allocation, to the law of the court seised, and at the stage of judgment recognition, to the law of the court requested.

[212] This is an interesting insight into the anticipated objection by some states to parties' unfettered choice of court. It militates against forum shopping, and in spirit has something in common with the anti-avoidance provision in the Rome I Regulation art.3.3, which inhibits complete freedom of choice of law in contract.

be compatible with other treaties in force for Contracting States, whether concluded before or after this Convention. Thereafter, art.26.2 provides that the Convention shall not affect the application by a Contracting State of a treaty, whether concluded before or after the Convention, in cases where none of the parties is resident in a Contracting State that is not a party to the treaty. The effect is that where all parties to the litigation are residents of EU Member States, application of the Brussels I Regulation will not be affected. Similarly, the Brussels Regulation prevails where one party is an EU resident and the other resident in a Third State which is not party to the Hague Convention. But, where one party is an EU resident and the other resident in a Third State which is a party to the Hague Convention, the Hague Convention shall prevail.[213]

With regard to the provisions in each instrument concerning recognition and enforcement of judgments, the Convention is in keeping with the rules contained in the Regulation, but certain peculiarities have been appended in view of the particular purpose of the Convention. Article 26.4 provides, in effect, that for the purposes of obtaining recognition or enforcement of a judgment given by a court of a Contracting State which is also an EU State, the Regulation shall apply; however, it further provides that the judgment shall not be recognised or enforced to a lesser extent than it would be under the Convention.[214]

By art.26.6(b) (concerning Regional Economic Integration Organisations generally), the Regulation shall operate as regards the recognition or enforcement of judgments between EU Member States.[215]

Hartley and Dogauchi, noting[216] that since the Brussels I Regulation is a piece of EC legislation that covers much the same ground as the Convention, the most important conflicts which are likely to occur between these two instruments concern the *lis pendens* rule, proceed to provide many examples of the difficulties which may arise. Pertegas opines that now that the EU is a signatory to the Convention, EU policymakers should ensure that co-ordination is achieved between the Convention and the Brussels I Regulation in its future revised form,[217] but that even if alignment between the two

---

[213] Hartley and Dogauchi Report, para.271 ("First 'give-way' rule"); and Pertegas, "The Brussels I Regulation and the Hague Convention on Choice of Court Agreements" (2010) 11(1) *ERA-Forum* 19, 22, 23.

[214] Hartley and Dogauchi Report, paras 286, 287, explain the "Third 'give-way' rule" thus: "This rule is of significance only when both States concerned are Parties to both the Convention and the other treaty: the Convention would not apply unless both States were Parties to it and the other treaty would not apply unless both were Parties to it. The purpose of the rule is to promote the recognition and enforcement of judgments. If the other treaty does this more efficiently, or to a greater extent, it would be better to allow its application. It is only where the judgment would be recognised or enforced to a lesser extent under the other treaty that the Convention should apply. Unless the law of the requested provides otherwise, the judgment creditor can choose whether to enforce the judgment under the Convention or under the other treaty." Also Pertegas, "The Brussels I Regulation and the Hague Convention on Choice of Court Agreements" (2010) 11(1) *ERA-Forum* 19, 23.

[215] Hartley and Dogauchi Report, para.305, explain that the "Second REIO 'give-way' rule" is similar to the "Third 'give-way' rule" discussed above.

[216] Hartley and Dogauchi Report, paras 295 et seq.

[217] Pertegas, "The Brussels I Regulation and the Hague Convention on Choice of Court Agreements" (2010) 11(1) *ERA-Forum* 19, 25. See re Green Paper, para.7–11, above.

instruments is not achieved, nonetheless, they can operate harmoniously side by side.

SUBMISSION TO THE JURISDICTION

7–43 The Brussels I Regulation honours the well-established principle of founding jurisdiction upon the basis of submission.

Article 24

7–44 "Apart from jurisdiction derived from other provisions of this Regulation, a court of a Member State before which a defendant enters an appearance shall have jurisdiction. This rule shall not apply where appearance was entered to contest the jurisdiction, or where another court has exclusive jurisdiction by virtue of Article 22."

It is an important principle of the Regulation that a defendant must be allowed to appear, without prejudice, to argue for its proper application in his case, which includes allowing him to challenge or contest jurisdiction if he thinks the court has been wrongly seised. If the defendant argues in the alternative (i.e. he avers, first, that there is no jurisdiction over him, and further that, even if there is, he did not break the contract), then it seems that the defendant is not deemed to have submitted to the jurisdiction.[218] But a defendant cannot append challenges to the jurisdiction to what is essentially a defence on the merits, merely in order to evade the operation of art.24. For the defendant to evade the suggestion of submission, it must be clear to the claimant and to the court from the outset of the defence that the defendant intends to challenge the court's jurisdiction under art.24.[219] The ECJ, in *Elefanten Schuh GmbH*, held on a reference from the Belgian Court of Cassation that the simultaneous raising by the defendant of a complaint as to the jurisdiction (i.e. not later than the submission of its first substantive defence) prevented the defendant's appearance in the Belgian court from being regarded as submission thereto; consequently, effect ought to be given to the parties' choice of court clause in favour of Germany.

The principle of submission under art.24 does not apply where another Member State court has exclusive jurisdiction by virtue of art.22. In contrast, art.23 is subservient to art.24; the defendant's submission to the courts of a Member State under art.24 would appear to override an art.23 agreement.[220] This is logical: a subsequent selection of jurisdiction by means of submission trumps an earlier agreed jurisdiction.

---

[218] *Marc Rich & Co AG v Societa Italiana Impianti pA (The Atlantic Emperor) (No.2)* [1992] 1 Lloyd's Rep. 624 at 633.
[219] *Harada Ltd (t/a Chequepoint UK) v Turner (No.2)* [2003] EWCA Civ 1695 at [29]. See also *Maple Leaf Macro Volatility Master Fund v Rouvroy* [2009] 1 W.L.R. 475; [2009] EWCA Civ 1334.
[220] *Elefanten Schuh GmbH v Jacqmain* [1981] E.C.R. 1671.

CONFLICTING JURISDICTIONS AND APPROPRIATE FORUM

Conflicts of jurisdiction under the Brussels I Regulation

Lis pendens

Article 27

"1. Where proceedings involving the same cause of action[221] and **7–45** between the same parties[222] are brought in the courts of different Member States,[223] any court other than the court first seised[224] shall of its own motion stay its proceedings until such time as the jurisdiction of the court first seised is established.[225]

2. Where the jurisdiction of the court first seised is established, any court other than the court first seised shall decline jurisdiction in favour of that court."

The *lis pendens* system of jurisdiction allocation, though striking in its apparent simplicity, has generated a significant body of interpretative case law. Lord Bingham, in *Haji-Ioannou v Frangos*,[226] ruled that actions have the same cause if they have the same facts and rule of law as their basis, or if they have the same end in view. As regards the parties to the action, it was held in *The Tatry*[227] that on a proper construction of art.21 of the Brussels Convention

---

[221] e.g. *Gubisch Maschinenfabrik KG v Palumbo* [1987] E.C.R. 4861 (in which the ECJ held that an action for the rescission or discharge of a contract involved the same cause of action as an action to enforce the same contract); *Bank of Scotland v SA Banque Nationale de Paris*, 1996 S.L.T. 103; *Mecklermedia Corp v DC Congress GmbH* [1998] 1 All E.R. 148; *Owners of Cargo Lately Laden on Board the Tatry v Owners of the Maciej Rataj* [1999] Q.B. 515; *Haji-Ioannou v Frangos* [1999] 2 All E.R. (Comm) 865; *Winter Maritime Ltd v North End Oil Ltd (The Winter)* [2000] 2 Lloyd's Rep. 298; *Carnoustie Universal SA v International Transport Workers Federation* [2002] 2 All E.R. (Comm) 657 (Lugano); *Gantner Electronic GmbH v Basch Exploitatie Maatschappij BV* (C-111/01) [2003] I.L.Pr. 37 ECJ; *Bank of Tokyo-Mitsubishi Ltd v Baskan Gida Sanayi Ve Pazarlama AS* [2004] 2 Lloyd's Rep. 395; and *Royal & Sun Alliance Insurance Plc v MK Digital FZE (Cyprus) Ltd* [2005] EWHC 1408.

[222] e.g. *Drouot Assurances SA v Consolidated Metallurgical Industries (CMI Industrial Sites)* [1998] All E.R. (EC) 483: there may be such a degree of identity between the interests of insurer and insured that they must be considered to be the same party for the purposes of Brussels Convention art.21. Contrast *Mecklermedia Corp v DC Congress GmbH* [1998] 1 All E.R. 148; *Glencore International AG v Metro Trading International Inc (No.1)* [1999] 2 All E.R. (Comm) 899; *Glencore International AG v Shell International Trading & Shipping Co Ltd* [1999] 2 All E.R. (Comm) 922; *The Tatry* [1999] Q.B. 515; *Tavoulareas v Alexander G Tsavliris & Sons Maritime Co (No.2)* [2005] EWHC 2643 (Comm); *Re Claim by a German Lottery Company* [2005] I.L.Pr. 35; *JP Morgan Europe Ltd v Primacom AG* [2005] 2 All E.R. (Comm) 764; and *Kolden Holdings Ltd v Rodette Commerce Ltd* [2008] 3 All E.R. 612.

[223] The question is whether the courts in the different Member States have jurisdiction on a Brussels ground, not (necessarily, therefore) whether either or both party(ies) is/are domiciled in a Member State: *Overseas Union Insurance Ltd v New Hampshire Insurance Co* [1992] 2 All E.R. 138.

[224] As to which, see art.30. See operation of *lis pendens* system per Court of Appeal in *Royal & Sun Alliance Insurance Plc v MK Digital FZE (Cyprus) Ltd* [2006] EWCA Civ 629.

[225] However, the ECJ decision in *Overseas Union Insurance Ltd v New Hampshire Insurance Co* [1992] 2 All E.R. 138, to the effect that the rule that one Member State may not examine the jurisdiction of the court of another Member State which has been first seised, nevertheless held that this was without prejudice to the case where the court second seised has exclusive jurisdiction.

[226] [1999] 2 Lloyd's Rep. 337 at 351.

[227] [1999] Q.B. 515.

(now art.27), where two actions involve the same cause of action and some but not all of the parties to the second action are the same as the parties to the action commenced earlier in another Contracting State, the second court seised is required to decline jurisdiction only to the extent to which the parties to the proceedings before it are also parties to the action previously commenced; it does not prevent the proceedings from continuing between any other parties.

Article 28

7–46   "1. Where related[228] actions are pending in the courts of different Member States, any court other than the court first seised may stay its proceedings.

2. Where these actions are pending at first instance, any court other than the court first seised may also, on the application of one of the parties, decline jurisdiction if the court first seised has jurisdiction over the actions in question and its law permits the consolidation thereof.[229]

3. For the purposes of this Article, actions are deemed to be related where they are so closely connected that it is expedient to hear and determine them together to avoid the risk of irreconcilable judgments resulting from separate proceedings."

This manner of drafting provides a type of autonomous definition, but one in which a great deal is left to the discretion of the individual state forum.[230] The discretion conferred is two-fold; first, the value judgment to decide whether or not the two sets of proceedings are "related"; and separately, if they are related, the discretion conferred on the forum to stay its own (i.e. the later) proceedings.[231]

Article 28 effectively covers circumstances which fall outside art.27. It is not necessary under art.28 that the parties in the related actions, or even the subject matter, be identical.[232]

Article 30

7–47   "For the purposes of this Section, a court shall be deemed to be seised:

1. at the time when the document instituting the proceedings or an equivalent document is lodged with the court, provided that the plaintiff has not subsequently failed to take the steps he was required to take to have service effected on the defendant, or

---

[228] *Haji-Ioannou v Frangos* [1999] 2 All E.R. (Comm) 865; *Bank of Scotland v SA Banque Nationale de Paris*, 1996 S.L.T. 103; *Mecklermedia Corp v DC Congress GmbH* [1998] 1 All E.R. 148; *Blue Nile Shipping Co Ltd v Iguana Shipping & Finance Inc (The Happy Fellow)* [1998] 1 Lloyd's Rep. 13; *Abkco Music & Records Inc v Jodorowsky* [2003] C.L.Y.B. 598; *Evialis SA v SIAT* [2003] 2 Lloyd's Rep. 377; *Miles Platt Ltd v Townroe Ltd* [2003] 1 All E.R. (Comm) 561; *Sony Computer Entertainment Ltd v RH Freight Services Ltd* [2007] EWHC 302 (Comm); *Research in Motion UK Ltd v Visto Corp* [2008] EWCA Civ 153; *Trademark Licensing Co Ltd v Leofelis SA* [2010] I.L.Pr. 16; and *FKI Engineering Ltd v Stribog Ltd* [2010] EWHC 1160 (Comm).
[229] See, e.g. *Jacobs & Turner Ltd v Celsius Sarl*, 2007 S.L.T. 722.
[230] *Jacobs & Turner Ltd v Celsius Sarl*, 2007 S.L.T. 722; and *Cooper Tire & Rubber Co Europe Ltd v Shell Chemicals UK Ltd* [2009] EWHC 1529 (Comm).
[231] *Trademark Licensing Co Ltd v Leofelis SA* [2010] I.L.Pr. 16, per Sir William Blackburne at [38].
[232] *Sarrio SA v Kuwait Investment Authority* [1999] 1 A.C. 32.

2. if the document has to be served before being lodged with the court, at the time when it was received by the authority responsible for service, provided that the plaintiff has not subsequently failed to take the steps he was required to take to have the document lodged with the court."

Article 30 provides an autonomous definition of the date at which a court shall be deemed to be seised. It is essential in a priority of process system that there be clarity on this matter.[233] The rule is bifurcated to reflect two differing modes of practice among Member States.

Interpretation

A number of interpretative questions continues to arise about the meaning **7–48** of terms of the Regulation, and/or the ranking of its provisions inter se. The ECJ (now CJEU) responds to such references as it receives (with regard to the UK, from the Supreme Court), but its interpretative rulings are restricted to the issues in question and the questions asked, and so inevitably the body of jurisprudence can accrue only incrementally.

Erich Gasser GmbH v Misat Srl[234]

Misat, an Italian company, based in Rome, and Gasser, an Austrian **7–49** company, had done business together for a number of years in the supply by Gasser, and purchase by Misat, of children's clothing. In April 2000, Misat brought proceedings against Gasser in a court in Rome (arguing apparently that, in the circumstances, its jurisdiction was available under art.2 of the 1968 Brussels Convention), seeking, essentially, "negative declarations" to the effect that the contract between the parties had terminated by operation of law, or as a result of disagreement between the two companies; and further, a finding that Misat had not failed to perform the contract; and seeking also an order for damages plus expenses against Gasser in relation to its failure to fulfil its obligations of good faith.

In December 2000, Gasser brought an action against Misat in the Regional Court in Austria for payment of outstanding invoices, asserting that the jurisdiction of the Austrian court was established, not only on the basis of 1968 Brussels Convention art.5.1, but also on the basis that the parties had agreed a choice of court for Austria, as evidenced by a prorogation clause appearing on the back of all invoices sent by Gasser to Misat without any objection having been raised in that matter by Misat.[235] Misat denied this, contending that there had been no choice of court agreement, and further, that the litigation in Italy, being earlier in time, must take precedence.

---

[233] Identification of the point at which the court is seised proved contentious under the 1968 Brussels Convention: *Neste Chemicals SA v DK Line SA (The Sargasso)* [1994] 3 All E.R. 180; *The Duke of Yare* [1992] 1 Q.B. 502, overtaken by *Canada Trust v Stolzenberg (No.2)* [2000] 4 All E.R. 481; and *Zelger v Salinitri* [1984] E.C.R. 2397. As to the Lugano Convention, see *Phillips v Symes (A Bankrupt)* [2006] I.L.Pr. 9. Lugano II art.30 is framed in terms identical to art.30 of the Brussels I Regulation.

[234] *Erich Gasser Gmbh v Misat Srl* [2005] Q.B. 1. See application of *Gasser* ratio in *JP Morgan Europe Ltd v Primacom AG* [2005] 2 All E.R. (Comm) 764.

[235] cf. *MSG v Les Gravières Rhenanes Sarl* (C106/95) [1997] All E.R. (EC) 385.

The Austrian court decided of its own motion to stay its proceedings until the jurisdiction of the Italian court had been established. The Austrian court's view was that it had jurisdiction under art.5.1 as the court for the place of performance of the contract, but it did not rule upon the question whether there had been an agreement to confer jurisdiction on the Austrian court. On appeal against that decision by Gasser, the Oberlandsgericht Innsbruck referred these questions of interpretation to the ECJ for a preliminary ruling. In essence, this was a request for a ranking of art.17 of the Brussels Convention (prorogation of jurisdiction)[236] and art.21 (court first seised).[237]

It was decided that a national court could refer to the ECJ a request for interpretation even where the basis for the reference, factual and legal, relied upon submissions the merits of which had not yet been examined, i.e. in this case, that the choice of court clause printed on the back of the invoices, neither acknowledged nor denied by Misat, was sufficient to satisfy art.17 as a choice of court which was in accordance with the parties' practice and trade usage prevailing between Austria and Italy.[238]

But more importantly, the decision of the ECJ, which has provoked stern comment in the UK,[239] is that the system set in place by the *lis pendens* rule is pre-eminent. Therefore, where a court had been first seised, any court second seised, even one the jurisdiction of which the parties had prorogued in terms of art.17, must stay its proceedings until the court first seised has ruled upon its own jurisdiction. If the court first seised decides that it has jurisdiction, the court second seised must decline jurisdiction in favour of that court. This is the case even where the proceedings before the court first seised are protracted.

The initiative taken by Misat took the form of actings of a negative nature. A system of priority of process lends itself to such behaviour.[240]

Negative declarations

7–50   The *lis pendens* system places in an advantageous position a party who is able to initiate the process in a forum of his choice, so far as the facts admit choice of (another) Member State forum within the rules of the regime. It is necessary to attempt to assess the extent to which it is reasonable for a litigant to seize the initiative by seising a forum in which to seek a declaration of a negative nature, e.g. that he has not breached the contract: a declaration of non-liability.

Initiation of litigation by means of negative proceedings was a feature of *Gasser v Misat*.[241] The ECJ accepted[242] that the cause of action later brought

---

[236] cf. Brussels I Regulation art.23.

[237] cf. Brussels I Regulation art.27.

[238] See *Erich Gasser Gmbh v Misat Srl* [2005] Q.B. 1 at [42]. Also Crawford, "The Uses of Putativity and Negativity in the Conflict of Laws" (2005) 54 I.C.L.Q. 829.

[239] e.g. Hartley, "The European Union and the Systematic Dismantling of the Common Law of Conflict of Laws" (2005) 54 I.C.L.Q. 813.

[240] See Andrew S. Bell, *Forum Shopping and Venue in Transnational Litigation* (Oxford: Oxford University Press, 2002), Ch.4 ("Reverse Forum Shopping").

[241] One which attracted comment from Advocate General Léger: *Erich Gasser Gmbh v Misat Srl* [2005] Q.B. 1 at [68], [69]. The ECJ in its judgment ([53]; also at [68]) declined to engage with the problem.

[242] *Erich Gasser Gmbh v Misat Srl* [2005] Q.B. 1 at [46]. Hartley, "The European Union and the Systematic Dismantling of the Common Law of Conflict of Laws" (2005) 54 I.C.L.Q. 813, explains that the ruling effectively condones the use of delaying tactics by means of seeking a negative declaration in a legal system which is available under the Brussels I Regulation and which is known to be slow: *Transporti Castellatti v Hugo Trumpy* (C-159/97) [1999] E.C.R. I-1597.

before the Austrian court involved the same cause of action as the action brought previously in Rome, although the latter was for a negative declaration.

The device seems to be indulged, or tolerated, so long as, in the view of the instant forum, there has not been a gross abuse of process. But what is an abuse of process?[243] The English courts in their operation of the English residual rules (*q.v.*),[244] are not inexperienced in dealing with this matter. Increasingly, while advocating caution, the effect of recent pronouncements has been to suggest that negative actings in litigation should not necessarily be viewed negatively. Sometimes justice requires acceptance of the seeking of a negative declaration in order to avoid further, perhaps indefinite, delay and prevarication.[245] It is difficult to avoid the conclusion that the matter must be treated on a case-by-case basis. It was noted per Morison J. in *Bristow Helicopters Ltd v Sikorsky Aircraft Corp*[246] that whether such a claim is proper or not proper is not to be determined by the form of the claim, but by its substance. Where the "defendant" (i.e. the "natural" claimant) had been "temporising", the seeking of such a negative declaration was appropriate.

Such toleration within the Brussels regime is supported by a decision of Collins J., in *Bank of Tokyo-Mitsubishi Ltd v Baskan Gida Sanayi Ve Pazarlama*,[247] stating that: "Pre-emptive proceedings for a negative declaration in a preferred jurisdiction are entirely legitimate."[248] Hence the paradoxical situation has resulted that, even within EU, forum shopping by the use of actions for negative declarations has been encouraged[249]; forum shopping is not eradicated by the use of a *lis pendens* system, though the choice of forum is necessarily limited by the rules contained in sections 1–7 (arts 1–23) of the Brussels I Regulation.

RANKING OF THE JURISDICTIONAL RULES IN THE BRUSSELS I REGULATION

Choice of court agreements and *lis pendens*

The ECJ decision in *Gasser* is one of great importance as regards the ranking **7–51** or hierarchy of the provisions of the Brussels I Regulation inter se. Its effect, as has been seen, is to subordinate art.23 to art.27. The ECJ held that the pre-eminent position of the court first seised shall not be dislodged by a choice of court agreement between the parties which selects a different court (unless and

---

[243] *Messier Dowty Ltd v Sabena SA* [2000] 1 W.L.R. 2040; and *Toropdar v D* [2009] EWHC 567 (QB).

[244] Use of negative tactics to initiate litigation is not limited to the Brussels scheme: see *Bristow Helicopters Ltd v Sikorsky Aircraft Corp* [2004] 2 Lloyd's Rep. 150; *Swiss Reinsurance Co Ltd v United India Insurance Co* (Jurisdiction) [2004] I.L.Pr. 4; and *Ark Therapeutics Plc v True North Capital Ltd* [2006] 1 All E.R. (Comm) 138.

[245] *Swiss Reinsurance Co Ltd v United India Insurance Co* (Jurisdiction) [2004] I.L.Pr. 4.

[246] [2004] 2 Lloyd's Rep. 150.

[247] [2004] 2 Lloyd's Rep. 395. Also *Boss Group Ltd v Boss France SA* [1996] 4 All E.R. 970; *Benincasa v Dentalkit Srl* (C-269/95) [1998] All E.R. (EC) 135; and *Equitas Ltd v Wave City Shipping Co Ltd* [2005] 2 All E.R. (Comm) 301.

[248] *Bank of Tokyo-Mitsubishi Ltd v Baskan Gida Sanayi Ve Pazarlama AS* [2004] 2 Lloyd's Rep. 395 at [114].

[249] [2004] 2 Lloyd's Rep. 395 at [198].

until the court first seised should decide, for whatever reason—including the existence and application of the apparently flouted jurisdiction clause—that it has no jurisdiction). The principle of mutual trust and confidence demands that trust be reposed in the court of the Member State first seised to adjudicate upon its jurisdiction, competently and in good faith, and to defer to the court exclusively chosen, if persuaded that the prorogation clause is valid and applicable. There is, however, no requirement that the court first seised should arrive at its decision with reasonable speed[250]—and there's the rub.

Future position

7-52   The European Commission Report[251] acknowledges that, following the decision in *Gasser*, there is concern that the Brussels I Regulation does not sufficiently protect so-called exclusive choice of court agreements. It is further admitted that after *Turner v Grovit* (*q.v.*) national procedural devices to strengthen choice of court agreements have been proscribed, as incompatible with the Regulation. Accordingly, the Green Paper[252] advances certain possible solutions to the problem which emerges when the court first seised is not the court chosen, or allegedly chosen, in the art.23 choice of court agreement: hard law solutions, that the court chosen by the parties be released from its obligation to stay proceedings under the *lis pendens* rule; or, as a variation, that the priority of process rule would remain, but would be reversed in these circumstances, so that, in effect, the court chosen would have priority over the court first seised to determine its jurisdiction; a "softer" solution such as greater communication and co-operation between the two courts, together with a deadline for the court first seised to determine its own jurisdiction; and tangential solutions such as the availability of damages for breach of choice of court agreements. It could be that the *lis pendens* rule would be waived where the conflicting parallel proceedings are, on the one hand, on the merits, and, on the other, proceedings for negative declaratory relief; or that the competing actions be consolidated by use of art.6. Generally, with regard to operation of the *lis pendens* system, a call has gone out for greater co-operation between the courts involved.

The House of Lords EU Committee[253] responded by affirming the need to reform the current rules on *lis pendens*. While the UK has become inured to the *lis pendens* system, accepting it on the basis of the avoidance of parallel proceedings (though being of the view that the risk of irreconcilable judgments sometimes is overstated), there is great concern about abuse of the system by "torpedo-ing" litigation. Evidence offered to the committee was to the effect that the neatest solution would be to give priority to the named (i.e. chosen) court, and to impose an obligation on the court in which the torpedo is launched to stay its proceedings, while the court chosen determines any issue regarding its jurisdiction, i.e. reversing the ranking of arts 23 and 27 established in *Gasser*. On the point that a great deal depends on the view which the court takes on the existence, validity and application of the choice of court clause, it is suggested

---

[250] See para.7–49, above.
[251] Report on the application of Regulation 44/2001 COM(2009)174 final, para.3.7.
[252] Green Paper on the Review of Regulation 44/2001 COM(2009)175 final, para.3.
[253] *Green Paper on the Brussels I Regulation: Report with Evidence*, 2009, HL Paper No.148 (Session 2008/09), para.66.

that reversal should occur when a party maintains, on arguable grounds, that the issue is governed by the choice of court clause. The committee emphasised that the objectives should be to discourage the use of tactical pre-emptive claims, and expressed a preference for a general rule to ameliorate the situation (as opposed, for example, to a more particular rule framed with reference to negative declaratory relief), either by favouring the court chosen with true exclusive jurisdiction, or by reversing the priority of process rule in these cases.

Ranking of other rules

As regards other provisions of the Brussels I Regulation, art.23 (prorogation **7–53** of jurisdiction) yields to art.24 (submission to the jurisdiction), on the rationale that submission by a party, other than merely to contest the jurisdiction, amounts to acquiescence in the jurisdiction of that court. When submission post-dates the making of a choice of court agreement, the appearance in a different court by both parties, or by one party at the behest of the other, is taken to constitute later agreement (the latest indication) of a party's intentions as to choice of court, superseding earlier (even written) agreement.[254]

Neither an agreement under art.23, nor submission under art.24, can override the jurisdiction conferred "exclusively" on certain courts by art.22.

With regard to the relationship between art.6[255] and the protective jurisdictions, the ECJ has held that when the special jurisdictional rules concerning employees are engaged, and an action is brought by an employee against companies established in different Member States, which the employee considered to be his joint employers, the provisions of Ch.II section 5 of the Brussels I Regulation (jurisdiction over individual contracts of employment), because of their specific and exhaustive nature, could not be supplemented by art.6 or other rules of jurisdiction contained in the Regulation, unless this were specifically authorised.[256] Since there is no such authorisation in section 5, use of art.6.1 is not justified. This is an interesting example of the fact that certain provisions of the Regulation are interdependent, and other bodies of rules within the Regulation are hermetically sealed. It would seem reasonable to assume that this ECJ decision would apply equally to sections 3 (insurance) and 4 (consumers). The ECJ decision was reached on a literal construction of the instrument, but the court additionally took the view that the sound administration of justice would imply that art.6.1 ought to be open to both employees and employers (a policy conclusion which would be at odds with the general policy pertaining to the protection of weaker parties) (an example of conflicting policies of justice; when should adjustment not be made, and when should it be made?). Hence, the rule of special jurisdiction provided for in art.6.1 could not be applied to a dispute under Ch.II section 5.

Finally, on the theme of the interrelationship of articles within one instrument, one might query the relationship between Ch.II section 7 (arts 23 and 24) with sections 3, 4 and 5. Although there is no overt indication in the Regulation that section 7 is outranked by the sections containing protective

---

[254] *Elefanten Schuh GmbH v Jacqmain* (C-150/80) [1981] E.C.R. 1671.

[255] Jurisdiction over multiple defendants through the domicile of the "anchor" defendant.

[256] *Glaxosmithkline v Rouard* (C-462/06) [2008] E.C.R. I-3965 (reference from *Cour de Cassation*).

provisions for disadvantaged persons,[257] nor any authoritative ECJ interpretation thereon, it must surely be the case that agreements made under art.23 have no legal force if they are contrary to the protective rules enshrined in arts 13 (insured persons), 17 (consumers) and 21 (employees). In contrast, it is generally thought that the principle of submission without protest as found in art.24 applies with full force to disadvantaged parties.[258] The rationale of art.24 is that, since it represents a later choice by a party, it supersedes any choice of court made earlier; and if art.24 affects disadvantaged parties in like manner, this must mean that no account is taken, upon the later eventuality of submission, of such parties' lack of full freedom to choose in the first instance.[259] No special treatment is afforded on the second occasion. It must be presumed that to provide otherwise would be seen as benefiting the disadvantaged twice—a benefit too far, there being no intention, seemingly, to buttress such parties' pre-existing protection. Weaker parties enjoy benevolent, *forum actoris*, jurisdiction provisions. Should they find themselves in a court other than their own, they and their advisers are equipped by these special rules[260] to make an effective challenge (provided that the litigant can prove his membership of the ranks of the disadvantaged, and that the facts otherwise justify application of the protective provisions). The situation is explicable also on the argument that, after the dispute has arisen,[261] weaker parties, it would appear, are treated as not being in need of special protection, and therefore it is consistent to regard them as fully *capax* and so they "completely regain their freedom"[262] in the matter of choice of jurisdiction,[263] whether that choice be made expressly (arts 13.1, 17.1 or 21.1), or tacitly through actings (per art.24).

CONFLICTS OF JURISDICTION OUTSIDE THE BRUSSELS REGIME: THE PLEA OF *FORUM NON CONVENIENS*[264]

7-54 Choice of forum is a fiercely fought issue because the same forum is unlikely to be in the best interests of all the parties. The starting point for Scots conflict

---

[257] Contrast the specific exception from the application of art.24 of art.22.

[258] See Hill, *International Commercial Disputes in English Courts*, 3rd edn, 2005, paras 5.8.3, 5.8.24; and *Cheshire, North and Fawcett: Private International Law*, 14th edn, 2008, pp.268, 272, 275. More ambivalently, see Magnus and Mankowski, pp.325, 445, demonstrating inconsistency within the commentary. As to case law, see *Re Jurisdiction in a Consumer Contract* (2U 1788/99) [2002] I.L.Pr. 14 Regional Court of Appeal (Koblenz) at [11].

[259] Although weaker parties must follow art.23, the content of their choice is circumscribed for their own benefit by arts 14, 17, 21.

[260] i.e. as provided for by arts 12, 16.2, 20.

[261] See arts 13.1, 17.1, 21.1.

[262] Jenard Report, p.34.

[263] But not as to choice of law—for Rome I Regulation art.6 still will apply, conferring special protection.

[264] See, e.g J.J. Fawcett (ed.), *Declining Jurisdiction in Private International Law* (Oxford: Clarendon Press, 1995); R. Schuz, "Controlling Forum Shopping: The Impact of *MacShannon v Rockware Glass Ltd*" (1986) 34 I.C.L.Q. 374; Verheul, "The Forum (Non) Conveniens in English and Dutch law and Under Some International Conventions" (1986) 35 I.C.L.Q. 413; Prince, "Bhopal, Bogainville and OK Tedi: Why Australia's forum non conveniens Approach is Better" (1998) 47 I.C.L.Q. 573; H. Zhenjie, "*Forum non conveniens*: An Unjustified Doctrine", 2001 NILR 143; J. Harris, "Stays of Proceedings and the Brussels Convention" (2005) 54 I.C.L.Q. 933; and B.J. Rodger, "*Forum non conveniens* Post-*Owusu*" (2006) 2(1) J. Priv. Int. L. 71.

law is taken to be the famous dictum by Lord Kinnear in *Sim v Robinow*,[265] where his Lordship said:

> ". . . the plea can never be sustained unless the Court is satisfied that there is some other tribunal, having competent jurisdiction, in which the case may be tried more suitably for the interests of all the parties and for the ends of justice."

This form of words was quoted with approval by Lord Goff in *Spiliada Maritime Corp v Cansulex Ltd*,[266] which decision of the House of Lords represents the acceptance by English law that its position in this area is indistinguishable from the Scots plea.[267] Useful consideration of the subject in Scotland is found in *De Mulder v Jadranska Linijska (Jadrolinija)*,[268] where the considerations appeared to be relatively straightforward or neutral, for example, convenience of witnesses, and language difficulties. Conflicting interests may present acutely or controversially and the question for the forum is how, if at all, judicial discretion should weigh these interests.

---

[265] *Sim v Robinow* (1892) 19 R. 665, 668. Later notable Scottish cases are *Longworth v Hope* (1865) 3 M. 1049 (where the court noted the infelicity of the formerly used term *forum non competens*; still, *conveniens* should not be translated as convenient, but rather as appropriate, fit for, or suitable); *Société du Gaz de Paris v Armateurs Francais*, 1926 S.C. (H.L.) 13; *Argyllshire Weavers Ltd v A Macaulay (Tweeds) Ltd (No.1)*, 1962 S.C. 388; *Crédit Chemique v James Scott Engineering Group Ltd*, 1979 S.C. 406; *De Mulder v Jadranska Linijska (Jadrolinija)*, 1989 S.L.T. 269; *Shell (UK) Exploration and Production Ltd v Innes*, 1995 S.L.T. 807; *FMC Corp v Russell*, 1999 S.L.T. 99; *Compagnie Commerciale Andre SA v Artibell Shipping Co Ltd (No.1)*, 1999 S.L.T. 1051; and *Banks v CGU Insurance Plc*, 2005 S.C.L.R. 556.

[266] *Spiliada Maritime Corp v Cansulex Ltd (The Spiliada)* [1986] 3 All E.R. 843 at 853.

[267] The trend of English judicial thinking can be traced to *The Spiliada* [1986] 3 All E.R. 843, from the strict or avid *St Pierre v South American Stores (Garth & Chaves) Ltd* [1936] 1 K.B. 382; through *Owners of the Cressington Court v Owners of the Marinero (The Marinero)* [1955] P. 68; *The Soya Margareta* [1961] 1 W.L.R. 709; *Owners of the Atlantic Star v owners of the Bona Spes (The Atlantic Star)* [1973] 2 All E.R. 175; *MacShannon v Rockware Glass Ltd* [1978] A.C. 795 (the "natural forum"); *Castanho v Brown & Root (UK) Ltd* [1981] A.C. 557; *Trendtex Trading Corp. v Credit Suisse* [1982] A.C. 679; *Smith Kline & French Laboratories v Bloch* [1983] 2 All E.R. 72; *Astro Exito Navegacion SA v WT Hsu (The Messiniaki Tolmi)* [1983] 1 Lloyd's Rep. 666; *The Biskra* [1983] 2 Lloyd's Rep. 59; *RA Lister & Co Ltd v EG Thomson (Shipping) Ltd and PJ Djakarta Lloyd (The Benarty) (No.1)* [1983] 1 Lloyd's Rep. 361; *The Atlantic Song* [1983] 2 Lloyd's Rep. 394; *Owners of the Las Mercedes v Owners of the Abidin Daver* [1984] 2 W.L.R. 196 HL. Post-*Spiliada* cases include: *The Nordglimt* [1988] 2 All E.R. 531; *Roneleigh Ltd v MII Exports* [1989] 1 W.L.R. 619; *Cleveland Museum of Art v Capricorn Art International SA* [1990] 2 Lloyd's Rep. 166; *Banco Atlantico SA v British Bank of the Middle East* [1990] 2 Lloyd's Rep. 504; *Connelly v RTZ Corp Plc (No.2)* [1998] A.C. 854 HL; *Europs Ltd v Sunshine Lifestyle Products Ltd* [1998] C.L.Y.B. 750; *Carlson v Rio Tinto Plc* [1999] C.L.Y.B. 718; *Berezovsky v Forbes Inc* [1999] C.L.Y.B. 717; *Radhakrishna Hospitality Service Private Ltd v EIH Ltd* [1999] 2 Lloyd's Rep. 249; *Askin v Absa Bank Ltd* [1999] I.L.Pr. 471; *International Credit & Investment Co (Overseas) Ltd v Adham* (Share Ownership) [1999] I.L.Pr. 302; *Lubbe v Cape Plc (No.2)* [2000] 1 W.L.R. 1545; *XN Corp Ltd v Point of Sale Ltd* [2001] I.L.Pr. 35; *Ceskoslovenska Obchodni Banka AS v Nomura International Plc* [2003] I.L.Pr. 20; *Owusu v Jackson (t/a Villa Holidays Bal-Inn Villas)* [2005] Q.B. 801; *Shekar v Satyam Computer Services Ltd* [2005] I.C.R. 737; *Dornoch Ltd v Mauritius Union Assurance Co Ltd* [2006] EWCA Civ 389; *Ark Therapeutics Plc v True North Capital Ltd* [2006] 1 All E.R. (Comm) 138; *Novus Aviation Ltd v Onur Air Tasimacilik AS* [2009] EWCA Civ 122; and *Pacific International Sports Clubs Ltd v Soccer Marketing International Ltd* [2009] EWHC 1839 (Ch).

[268] 1989 S.L.T. 269.

The onus of proof is shared in the following manner: the case having been properly laid in Scotland, the onus is on the defender[269] making the plea, to show that there is a competent and more appropriate forum elsewhere. If this be established to the satisfaction of the original forum, in terms of expense and convenience of witnesses, etc.[270] the onus shifts to the pursuer to show "objectively by cogent evidence"[271] that to require him to litigate abroad would remove from him a personal or juridical advantage of such importance that it would be unjust to him to deprive him of it[272]:

> ". . . a general principle may be derived, which is that, if a clearly more appropriate forum overseas has been identified, generally speaking the plaintiff will have to take that forum as he finds it, even if it is in certain respects less advantageous to him than the English forum".[273]

"Only if the plaintiff can establish that substantial justice cannot be done in the appropriate forum will the court refuse to grant a stay."[274] Availability in England of legal aid, or the benefit of a conditional fee agreement (i.e. availability of financial assistance absolutely necessary, and absolutely lacking in Namibia in *Connelly v RTZ Corp Plc (No.2)*)[275] was held, in two House of Lords cases, to be good reason not to defer to the jurisdiction of the objectively natural forum.[276]

Levels of damages, nature of the system of discovery of evidence, and content of the rules of evidence will not normally be suitable factors to be taken into account. Expiry of a limitation period in the alternative forum is an ambivalent factor, the weight attributed depending on circumstances, especially the court's assessment of the conduct of the party potentially disadvantaged by it, for example degree of culpability or motive or excuse in failing to act expeditiously.[277] The court may take into account the amount of legal and technical work done in one jurisdiction, or in one jurisdiction in relation to a similar case (the "Cambridgeshire factor").[278] The existence of a jurisdiction

---

[269] A pursuer having selected a forum will not normally be permitted, upon a change of mind, to plead *forum non conveniens* with a view to having his chosen Scots court defer to another court: *Marodi Service de D Mialich v Mikkal Myklebusthaug Rederi A/S*, 2002 G.W.D. 13–398.

[270] If this is not established (see, e.g. *Banks v CGU Insurance Plc*, 2005 S.C.L.R. 556), the argument will not continue.

[271] *De Mulder v Jadranska Linijska (Jadrolinija)*, 1989 S.L.T. 269, per Lord Kincraig at 274.

[272] The principles which govern the identification of the appropriate forum in non-Brussels consistorial cases are similar: see Ch.12, below.

[273] *Connelly v RTZ Corp Plc (No.2)* [1998] A.C. 854, per Lord Goff at 872.

[274] *Connelly v RTZ Corp Plc (No.2)* [1998] A.C. 854, per Lord Goff at 853.

[275] [1998] A.C. 854.

[276] *Lubbe v Cape Plc* [2000] 1 W.L.R. 1545; and *Connelly v RTZ Corp Plc (No.2)* [1997] 4 All E.R. 335 (Lord Hoffman dissenting).

[277] *The Spiliada* [1986] 3 All E.R. 843 at 860. In *Banks v CGU Insurance Plc*, 2005 S.C.L.R. 556, Lady Smith declined to accede to the plea of *forum non conveniens* in respect of the English court, taking the view that the connections with England were no stronger than with Scotland. However, had the first stage plea been accomplished successfully for the defender, her Ladyship then would have had to consider whether the interests of justice required that the plea be not sustained, given that the pursuer was time-barred in England. The onus would have been on the pursuer to persuade the court of this, and the hint was given that the onus in the circumstances might not have been discharged.

[278] At the time of the *Spiliada* decision, litigation was ongoing in England concerning a similar action for damage to a cargo of sulphur, involving the same defendant shippers, but a different ship, *The Cambridgeshire* (hence, this factor has become known as the "Cambridgeshire factor"), and many of the same lawyers and expert witnesses.

clause in favour of the forum will render it unlikely that the forum would accede to a plea of *forum non conveniens*.[279]

Hence, assessment by the forum of what constitutes personal or juridical advantage is the crucial and most difficult issue,[280] but there arises also the question *when* particular factors ought to be considered, i.e. at the first, or second, stage of the plea.[281] It is thought that at the first stage availability of alternative forum means availability in principle; at the second stage, it will be open to the claimant to seek to establish that, in reality, the alternative forum is not open to him, by reason for example of: time bar; absence of public funding; or that for political or other reasons the claimant will not be afforded a fair hearing, or any hearing at all, or will be in danger of his life in the alternative forum.[282]

The court may grant or refuse the sist; and if the former, it may dismiss or sist[283] the Scottish proceedings.

When may the plea be used?

Section 49 of CJJA 1982, enacts that: **7–55**

> "Nothing in this Act shall prevent any court in the United Kingdom from staying, sisting, striking out or dismissing any proceedings before it, on the ground of forum non conveniens or otherwise, where to do so is not inconsistent with the 1968 Convention, or as the case may be, the Lugano Convention."

Generally, a stay will be inconsistent with the Brussels/Lugano regime, but the question which has arisen in England is whether the plea can be used in an English/Scottish (CJJA 1982 Sch.4) context. There are two conflicting decisions of the same judge on the question, the later decision favouring the continuing competence of the plea within the UK being preferred,[284] and so far uncontradicted. Lady Smith gave no indication that the plea would not be competent within the UK, in her judgment in *Banks v CGU Insurance Plc*.[285]

Subject to the UK situation in Sch.4, it can be said that the plea of *forum non conveniens* is not available within the Brussels/Lugano regime.[286] But a

---

[279] *Horn Linie GmbH & Co v Panamericana Formas e Impresos SA (The Hornbay)* [2006] EWHC 373 (Comm).

[280] Per Lord Goff in his classic judgment in *The Spiliada* [1986] 3 All E.R. 843, and in *Connelly v RTZ Corp Plc (No.2)* [1997] 4 All E.R. 335 at 345.

[281] See L. Merrett, "Uncertainties in the First Limb of the Spiliada Test" (2005) 54 I.C.L.Q. 211.

[282] *Askin v Absa Bank Ltd* [1999] I.L.Pr. 471; and *Mohammed v Bank of Kuwait and the Middle East KSC* [1996] 1 W.L.R. 1483.

[283] *De Mulder v Jadranska Linijska (Jadrolinija)*, 1989 S.L.T. 269: litigation in Scotland was sisted, in case the alternative forum (in the former Yugoslavia) should cede to the Scots court.

[284] *Foxen v Scotsman Publications, The Times*, February 17, 1994 and *Cumming v Scottish Daily Record, The Times*, June 8, 1995, both per Drake J., the latter in favour of use of the plea as not inconsistent with CJJA 1982 s.49.

[285] 2005 S.C.L.R. 556. See also *Ennstone Building Products Ltd v Stanger (No.1)* [2002] C.L.Y.B. 624; and *Lennon v Scottish Daily Record & Sunday Mail Ltd* [2004] EWHC 359 (QB).

[286] Brussels I Regulation arts 27–30; *Arkwright Mutual Insurance Co v Bryanston Insurnace Co Ltd* [1990] 2 All E.R. 335; *S&W Berisford Plc v New Hampshire Insurance Co Ltd* [1990] 2 All E.R. 321; and *Aiglon Ltd v Gau Shan Co Ltd* [1993] 1 Lloyd's Rep. 164.

doubt which had arisen[287] about availability of the *forum non conveniens* discretion where it is attempted to use the plea in the court of a Member State, where the alternative forum is in a non-EU/non-EFTA state,[288] has been resolved by the ECJ (in the negative) in *Owusu v Jackson (t/a Villa Holidays Bal Inn Villas) (q.v.)*,[289] a decision which is of assistance in understanding the reach of the Brussels regime. The decision is a notable, if not necessarily welcome, contribution to our understanding of the relationship between the Brussels regime and the legal systems of Third States.

Owusu v Jackson (t/a Villa Holidays Bal Inn Villas)[290]

7–56   The claimant, a "UK domiciliary", who rented from the first defendant, also domiciled in "the UK", a holiday villa in Jamaica with access to a private beach, suffered severe injuries following a diving accident. Mr Owusu walked into the sea and, diving under the water when it was at waist level, struck his head against a submerged sandbank, sustaining grave injuries rendering him tetraplegic. A similar accident, with the same outcome, allegedly occurred two years earlier to another English holidaymaker.

In 2000, Mr Owusu brought an action in England against Mr Jackson, the owner of the holiday villa, in contract; and against several Jamaican companies, including the owner and licensed users of the beach, in tort. The ground of argument in contract was that there was an implied term that the beach would be reasonably safe, or free from hidden dangers; and in tort, that it was the duty of the owner/occupier of the beach to warn swimmers of the unseen hazard constituted by the submerged sandbank.

Proceedings were commenced in Sheffield District Registry of the High Court, served on Jackson in the UK, and leave granted to serve the proceedings out of the jurisdiction on the other defendants in Jamaica. In response, a number of the six defendants, including Jackson, applied to the English court for a declaration that it should not exercise its jurisdiction in relation to them, on the argument that the case had closer links with Jamaica, and that Jamaica constituted a competent forum in which the case might be tried more suitably for the interests of all the parties and the ends of justice.[291]

Is it competent for an English/Scots court to accede to the plea of *forum non conveniens* in these circumstances?[292] How "European" must a case be before the plea is incompetent? In an entirely European case[293] (which, however, it seems, does not include an intra-UK case) the plea is inappropriate.

---

[287] *Re Harrods (Buenos Aires) Ltd (No.2)* [1992] Ch. 72 (in which appeal to the ECJ was abandoned).

[288] *BP International Ltd v Energy Infrastructure Group Ltd* [2003] EWHC 2924; *Navigators Insurance Co v Atlantic Methanol Production Co LLC* [2004] Lloyd's Rep. I.R. 418; *Bristow Helicopters Ltd v Sikorsky Aircraft Corp* [2004] 2 Lloyd's Rep. 150; *Royal & Sun Alliance Insurance Plc v Retail Brand Alliance Inc* [2005] Lloyd's Rep. I.R. 110; and *OT Africa Line Ltd v Magic Sportswear Corp* [2005] EWCA Civ 710.

[289] *Owusu v Jackson (t/a Villa Holidays Bal Inn Villas)* [2005] Q.B. 801. Decided under the 1968 Brussels Convention, even though a 2005 decision. See para.7–56, below.

[290] *Owusu v Jackson (t/a Villa Holidays Bal Inn Villas)* [2005] Q.B. 801.

[291] [2005] Q.B. 801 at [15].

[292] cf. *Lubbe v Cape Plc* [2000] 1 W.L.R. 1545, per Lord Bingham at 1563.

[293] Which, for present purposes, could be taken to be one where each available contending court is a court in an EU Member State.

The matter had been in doubt in the UK since the case of *Re Harrods (Buenos Aires) Ltd (No.2)*,[294] in which the Court of Appeal, seised as the seat of a company registered in England, but conducting its business in Argentina, held itself entitled, within the terms of s.49, to stay its proceedings in favour of Argentina as the more appropriate forum for trial of the issues. In *Owusu*, the judge at first instance, having no power to refer the question to the ECJ, ruled that the application to a dispute of the jurisdictional rules in the 1968 Brussels Convention depended, in principle, on whether the defendant had its seat or was domiciled in a Contracting State, and that the Convention applied to a dispute between a defendant domiciled in a Contracting State and a claimant domiciled in a non-Contracting State[295]; and on the facts that it was not open to him to stay the action because Jackson was domiciled in a Contracting State. Similarly, he held that he could not stay the action in relation to the other defendants, notwithstanding the fact that they were Jamaican domiciled, because of the risk of conflicting decisions in related actions.[296] On that basis of reasoning, he held (using non-Brussels terminology) that a court in the UK was a more appropriate forum than one in Jamaica.

Jackson and the other defendants appealed to the Court of Appeal, which stayed its proceedings in order to refer the following question to the ECJ for a preliminary ruling[297]:

> "(1) Is it inconsistent with the Brussels Convention, where a claimant contends that jurisdiction is founded on article 2, for a court of a contracting state to exercise a discretionary power, available under its national law, to decline to hear proceedings brought against a person domiciled in that state in favour of the courts of a non-contracting state, (a) if the jurisdiction of no other contracting state under the 1968 Convention is in issue, (b) if the proceedings have no connecting factors to any other contracting state? (2) If the answer to question 1(a) or (b) is yes, is it inconsistent in all circumstances or only in some and if so which?"

In relation to the first question, the ECJ held that on the interpretation and applicability of art.2, nothing in the wording of art.2 suggested that application of the general rule of jurisdiction there laid down on the basis of the defendant's domicile in a Contracting State is subject to the condition that there should be a legal relationship involving only the courts of Contracting

---

[294] *Re Harrods (Buenos Aires) Ltd (No.2)* [1992] Ch. 72. The decision was followed in *Owners of the Bowditch v Owners of the Po (The Po)* [1991] 2 Lloyd's Rep. 206 (where the HL referred the question to the ECJ, but again the case settled) and *Hamed el Chiaty & Co (t/a Travco Nile Cruise Lines) v Thomas Cook group Ltd (The Nile Rhapsody)* [1994] 1 Lloyd's Rep. 382. See also *Ace Insurance SA-NV v Zurich Insurance Co* [2001] 1 All E.R. (Comm) 802; *American Motorists Insurance Co (AMICO) v Cellstar Corp* [2003] I.L.Pr. 22; and *Travelers Casualty & Surety Co of Europe Ltd v Sun Life Assurance Co of Canada (UK) Ltd* [2004] I.L.Pr. 50. The ECJ position as expressed in *Owusu* was foreshadowed in relation to the Lugano Convention in *Mahme Trust Reg v Lloyds TSB Bank Plc* [2004] 2 Lloyd's Rep. 637.

[295] *Owusu v Jackson (t/a Villa Holidays Bal Inn Villas)* [2005] Q.B. 801 at [16].

[296] The potentially conflicting Jamaican and English judgments producing a difficult hybrid situation in terms of enforcement.

[297] This being competent in relation to the Brussels Convention; questions of interpretation with regard to the Brussels I Regulation may be requested only by the House of Lords/Supreme Court.

States. Article 2 is mandatory in nature (meaning that the English court cannot stay its proceedings against a defendant domiciled in a Contracting/Member State when it takes the view that another forum in a non-Contracting/Member State is more appropriate),[298] and there can be no derogation from the principle it lays down, except in the cases expressly provided for by the Convention. No exception on the basis of *forum non conveniens* was provided by the authors of the Convention. Respect for the principle of legal certainty would not be fully guaranteed if the court having jurisdiction under the Convention were allowed to apply the *forum non conveniens* doctrine. Application of the doctrine would undermine predictability, and affect the uniform application of the rules within the Community since the doctrine of *forum non conveniens* is recognised only in a limited number of Member States. The ECJ held that to permit any incursion of judicial discretion into the system would undermine the legal protection of persons established in the Community (although it is notable that the UK-domiciled defendant wished to have the case proceed in Jamaica in this instance).

In summary, it was held in *Owusu* that the Brussels Convention (and henceforth, by inference, the Regulation) precludes a court of a Contracting State from declining the jurisdiction conferred on it by art.2, on the ground that the court of a non-Contracting/Member State would be a more appropriate forum for the trial of the action, even if the jurisdiction of no other Contracting/Member State is in issue, or the proceedings have no connecting factors to any other Contracting/Member State.

Owusu raises complex questions about the applicability of the Brussels regime given different permutations of circumstance and identity of parties. The decision resolves, in a negative way, points of dubiety. Strictly, the decision is concerned with the ambit of authority of art.2, the key provision of in personam jurisdiction under Brussels. But to suggest faintly[299] that the plea might still be utilised in a future case in which jurisdiction has been founded on a special jurisdiction such as art.5.1, seems to invite disappointment.[300]

At a simple level, if the claimant sues a defendant on the basis of art.2,[301] it is his legitimate expectation that all the rules and principles of the Brussels regime should apply. However, to ascribe to the defendant a similar expectation seems at times inappropriate and disingenuous. There are many reasons, some of them to do with factual evidence, why *Owusu* arguably would have been more appropriately dealt with in Jamaica. On the other hand, for a claimant so grievously injured, speed of resolution of the dispute in some reasonably appropriate court is most desirable. But the Brussels system cannot

---

[298] *Owusu v Jackson (t/a Villa Holidays Bal Inn Villas)* [2005] Q.B. 801 at [20].

[299] But less faintly when there is evidence of an exclusive jurisdiction clause: *Konkola Copper Mines Plc v Coromin Ltd* [2006] EWCA Civ 5, per Rix L.J. at [71]–[73]. See re reflexive effect, para.7–63, below; also *Viking Line ABP v International Transport Workers Federation* [2006] I.L.Pr. 4.

[300] This case and these matters are treated by J. Harris, "Stays of Proceedings and the Brussels Convention" (2005) 54 I.C.L.Q. 933. Where Aberdeen Sheriff Court was seised on art.5 grounds, the sheriff refused to accede to a plea of *forum non conveniens*, considering himself to be bound by *Owusu* reasoning: *Oceanfix International Ltd v AGIP Kazakhstan North Caspian Operating Co NV*, 2009 G.W.D. 17–266. See also *Skype Technologies SA v Joltid Ltd* [2009] EWHC 2783 (Ch); *Equitas Ltd v Allstate Insurance Co* [2009] Lloyd's Rep. I.R. 227; and *Jefferies International Ltd v Landesbanki Islands HF* [2009] EWHC 894 (Comm).

[301] Or art.60: *889457 Alberta Inc v Katanga Mining Ltd* [2009] I.L.Pr. 14.

guarantee that litigation allocated, or provisionally allocated, to Member State courts will be disposed of with dispatch.

THE ANTI-SUIT INJUNCTION: RESTRAINT OF FOREIGN PROCEEDINGS

By way of contrast with *forum non conveniens*, the plea for restraint of foreign 7–57 proceedings or, as it has come to be known, the grant of an anti-suit injunction, relates to the common law power of a Scots[302] or English court to prevent a person who is subject to its jurisdiction from raising, or proceeding with, an action in a foreign court between the same parties and relating to the same subject matter as that before the Scots court. Although the Scots/English courts have no power to restrain a foreign court from proceeding to hear any action, they have power to restrain a person subject to their jurisdiction from proceeding with an action in a foreign court. This power will be exercised generally[303] if the foreign proceedings are considered to be vexatious and oppressive.

If an order is granted restraining foreign proceedings, the foreign court, nevertheless, may still hear the action (for it is part of its sovereignty so to do), but if the party against whom the order of restraint is granted proceeds with the action abroad, he will be acting in contempt of the British court and will receive no assistance in attempting to enforce the resultant decree.

Generally, the court will not exercise this power if to do so would deprive a party of an advantage in the foreign court which the Scots forum considers legitimate. There is greater likelihood of the power being exercised in a case in which the pursuer in Scotland is also the pursuer abroad.[304] Further, if no choice of forum is open to the claimant in that in only one (foreign) court is a remedy available, the claimant remaining also amenable to the home court, the English court has shown that it will hesitate before making an order to restrain the party: it would have to be shown that the defendant's being sued in the foreign forum would infringe a legal or equitable right of the defendant not to be sued.[305] An

---

[302] *Young v Barclay* (1846) 8 D. 774; *Dawson's Trustees v Macleans* (1860) 22 D. 685; *Pan American World Airways Inc v Andrews*, 1992 S.L.T. 268, per Lord Kirkwood at 271; *Shell UK Exploration & Production Ltd v Innes*, 1995 S.L.T. 807; and *FMC Corp v Russell*, 1999 S.L.T. 99. See Brown, "Interdict Proceedings in Scotland to Prevent or Restrain Court Actions in the United States", 1995 S.L.T. (News) 253 (quoting Lord Denning in *Smith Kline & French Laboratories Ltd v Bloch* [1983] 2 All E.R. 72 at 74: "As a moth is drawn to the light, so is a litigant drawn to the United States").

[303] *Deutsche Bank AG v Highland Crusader Offshore Partners LP* [2009] EWCA Civ 725.

[304] *Australian Commercial Research & Development Ltd v ANZ McCaughan Merchant Bank Ltd* [1989] 3 All E.R. 65. In *Cohen v Rothfield* [1919] 1 K.B. 410 (where the test vexatious or oppressive is used) Scrutton L.J. at 414 said: "It is not prima facie vexatious for the same plaintiff to commence two actions relating to the same subject-matter, one in England and one abroad. The applicant must prove a substantial case of vexation resulting from the identity of proceedings, remedies, and benefits, or from the existence of some motive other than a bona fide desire to determine disputes."

[305] *British Airways Board v Laker Airways Ltd* [1984] 3 All E.R. 39; *Midland Bank Plc v Laker Airways Ltd* [1986] 1 All E.R. 526; *South Carolina Insurance Co v Assurantie Maatschappij De Zeven Provincien NV* [1986] 3 All E.R. 487; *Societe Nationale Industrielle Aerospatiale (SNIA) v Lee Kui Jak* [1987] 3 All E.R. 510; *Channel Tunnel Group Ltd v Balfour Beatty Construction Ltd* [1993] A.C. 334; *Donohue v Armco Inc* [2002] 1 All E.R. 749; *Yachya v Levi* [2002] C.L.Y.B. 640 Royal Court of Jersey; *Royal Bank of Canada v Cooperatieve Centrale Raiffeisen-Boerenleenbank BA* [2004] 1 Lloyd's Rep. 471; and *Morgan Stanley & Co International Plc v China Haisheng Juice Holdings Co Ltd* [2009] EWHC 2409 (Comm).

injunction will not be granted by a UK court if that court has no sufficient interest in, or connection with, the matter in question, such as would be sufficient to justify the interference, having been seised only on a quirk of jurisdiction. Comity requires restraint.[306]

The reported cases fall into three classes:

    (a) bankruptcy[307];
    (b) consistorial actions[308]; and
    (c) commercial.[309]

The modern interest arises principally in commercial matters.[310] In *SNIA v Lee Kui Jak*,[311] on appeal from Brunei, the Privy Council ordered a party to desist from her suit in Texas because Brunei was the natural forum and the defendants would be unfairly disadvantaged if prevented from presenting their defence in Brunei. The leading opinion was given by Lord Goff who said that the principles governing an order by the English court to restrain foreign proceedings were not the same as those which govern the decision whether or not to accede to a plea under *forum non conveniens*. The restraint, it was said, will be ordered only if the parallel double procedure is regarded as vexatious and oppressive,[312] a rigorous test, once applied,[313] but now abandoned in English law in relation to *forum non conveniens*.

In an important judgment in *Deutsche Bank AG v Highland Crusader Offshore Partners LP*[314] Toulson L.J. reviewed the authorities and revisited the

---

[306] *Airbus Industrie GIE v Patel* [1999] I.L.Pr. 238.

[307] e.g. *Lindsay v Paterson* (1840) 2 D. 1373. See para.17–38, below.

[308] *Thornton v Thornton* (1886) L.R. 11 P.D. 176; *Armstrong v Armstrong* [1892] P. 98; *Vardopulo* (1909) 25 T.L.R. 518; *Orr Lewis v Orr Lewis* [1949] P. 347; *Sealey v Callan* [1953] P. 135; cf. in consistorial proceedings, the cognate subjects of mandatory and discretionary sists, and *Hemain* injunctions: para.12–16, below.

[309] *Bushby v Munday* (1821) 5 Madd. 297; *Carron Iron Co v McLaren* (1855) 5 H.L. Cas. 416; *Dawson's Trustees v Macleans* (1860) 22 D. 685; *McHenry v Lewis* (1883) L.R. 22 Ch. D. 397; *Liquidators of California Redwood Co Ltd v Walker* (1886) 13 R. 810; *Liquidators of Pacific Coast Mining Co Ltd v Walker* (1886) 13 R. 816; *Gill v Culter* (1895) 23 R. 371; *Cohen v Rothfield* [1919] 1 K.B. 410; *The Marinero* [1955] P. 68; *The Soya Margareta* [1961] 1 W.L.R. 709; *Settlement Corp v Hochschild (No.1)* [1966] Ch. 10; and *Smith Kline & French Laboratories Ltd v Bloch* [1983] 2 All E.R. 72.

[310] *SNIA v Lee Kui Jak* [1987] 3 All E.R. 510; *El Du Pont de Nemours & Co v Agnew (No.2)* [1988] 2 Lloyd's Rep. 240 CA; *Sohio Supply Co v Gatoil (USA) Inc* [1989] 1 Lloyd's Rep. 588; *Re Maxwell Communications Corp Plc (No.2)* [1992] B.C.C. 757; *Société Commerciale de Reassurance v Eras International Ltd (No.2)* [1995] 2 All E.R. 278; *Airbus Industrie GIE v Patel* [1999] I.L.Pr. 238; *Bannerton Holdings Pty Ltd v Sydbank Soenderjylland A/S (Australia)* (1997) 5 C.L. 102; *Banque Cantonale Vaudoise v Waterlily Maritime Inc* [1997] 5 C.L. 103; *General Star International Indemnity Ltd v Stirling Cooke Brown Reinsurance Brokers Ltd* [2003] I.L.Pr. 19; *West Tankers Inc v RAS Riunione Adriatica di Sicurta SpA (The Front Comor)* [2005] 2 Lloyd's Rep. 257; and *Horn Linie GmbH & Co v Panamericana Formas e Impresos SA (The Hornbay)* [2006] EWHC 373 (Comm).

[311] [1987] 3 All E.R. 510.

[312] The Court of Appeal in *Deutsche Bank AG v Highland Crusader Offshore Partners LP* [2009] EWCA Civ 725 held that there is no general presumption that where there is a non-exclusive jurisdiction clause, parallel proceedings in a different jurisdiction are to be regarded as vexatious or oppressive. Where non-exclusive jurisdiction has been agreed, parties must be taken to have accepted the possibility of parallel proceedings, and the grant of anti-suit injunction is a matter within the court's discretion.

[313] *St Pierre v South American Stores (Gath & Chaves) Ltd* [1936] 1 K.B. 382.

[314] [2009] EWCA Civ 725 at [49] et seq.

criteria upon which English judicial discretion ought to be exercised in the grant or withholding of anti-suit injunctions, producing eight "key principles" in relation to anti-suit injunctions (and *forum non conveniens*). His Lordship's second and third guidelines are as follows:

> "(2) It is too narrow to say that such an injunction may be granted only on grounds of vexation or oppression, but, where a matter is justiciable in an English and a foreign court, the party seeking an anti-suit injunction must *generally*[315] show that proceeding before the foreign court is or would be vexatious or oppressive. (3) The courts have refrained from attempting a comprehensive definition of vexation or oppression . . .".

Significantly, Toulson L.J. was of the view that: "(6) The prosecution of parallel proceedings in different jurisdictions is undesirable but not necessarily vexatious or oppressive."

English courts "cheerfully" used the tool of the anti-suit injunction in order to hold parties to their choice of court bargain[316]: if a contracting party should renege on the choice of court agreement, such an injunction seemed to the UK courts to be the appropriate remedy, on the basis that *pacta sunt servanda*. However, the advent of the ECJ decisions in *Gasser* and *Turner v Grovit* were to reinforce the strict operation of the *lis pendens* system, and the unavailability within the Brussels regime of the anti-suit injunction.

Turner v Grovit[317]

Opportunity arose in *Turner v Grovit* for the ECJ to consider whether or not **7–58** the use by one EU forum of an anti-suit injunction to seek to restrain a party from litigating in the court of another Member State is acceptable.

Turner, an English solicitor, was an employee of Harada Ltd, a company incorporated in Ireland and having its place of central management in England, and under the control of a group of companies of which Grovit was the director. The companies carried on the business of operating *bureaux de changes* in Spain. In 1997, Turner was sent to work in Madrid at the office of Changepoint SA, a Spanish company in the same group of companies as Harada. Turner remained employed by Harada Ltd, though Changepoint paid Harada for his services. Shortly after commencing work in Madrid, Turner resigned because he alleged his work involved collusion in illegal conduct (tax fraud). Having returned to England, Turner brought constructive unfair dismissal proceedings against Harada Ltd before an English employment tribunal (which considered that it had jurisdiction under arts 2, 5.1 and 5.5 of the 1968 Brussels Convention). In response, Grovit (in the name of Changepoint) sued Turner in Spain for substantial damages for "unjustified departure" and for professional misconduct. On the basis that the litigation brought in Spain was vexatious and oppressive, the Court of Appeal, at the request of Turner, granted an anti-suit injunction against Grovit. Grovit appealed to the House of Lords, which, in turn, referred the matter to the ECJ for a preliminary ruling on the following question:

---

[315] Emphasis added.
[316] *Continental Bank NA v Aekos Compania Naviera SA* [1994] 1 W.L.R. 588.
[317] *Turner v Grovit* (C-159/02) [2005] 1 A.C. 101. See also *Research in Motion UK Ltd v Visto Corp* [2008] EWCA Civ 153.

"Is it inconsistent with the Convention on Jurisdiction and the Enforcement of Judgments in Civil and Commercial Matters signed at Brussels on 27 September 1968 (subsequently acceded to by the United Kingdom) to grant restraining orders against defendants who are threatening to commence or continue legal proceedings in another Convention country when those defendants are acting in bad faith with the intent and purpose of frustrating or obstructing proceedings properly before the English courts?"

The decision of the ECJ was that a prohibition issued by one Member State court upon the commencement or continuation of legal proceedings in another is tantamount to interference with the jurisdiction of the foreign court and, with regard to the 1968 Brussels Convention, incompatible with the principle of mutual trust between legal systems of Contracting States, and the general prohibition of review of the jurisdiction of the court of one Contracting State by the court of another.

Therefore the Brussels Convention, and by implication, the Regulation, precludes the grant by a court in a Contracting/Member State of an injunction prohibiting a party to proceedings pending before it, from commencing or continuing proceedings before a court of another Contracting/Member State,[318] even where that party is acting in bad faith.

This decision, like *Gasser*, has provoked comment and criticism in the UK,[319] although its content was not unexpected, and the two decisions are consistent inter se, and coherent. Concerns may be expressed, however, about the natural justice consequences of the unrelenting rigidity of the ECJ's approach.

Somewhat surprisingly, in view of the stern disapproval shown by the ECJ to the remedy of anti-suit injunction and its prohibition "within the Brussels regime" (*q.v.*), the Court of Appeal in *Samengo-Turner v J&H Marsh & McLennan (Services) Ltd*[320] acceded to the request for the grant of an anti-suit injunction to require parties to desist from proceedings undertaken in New York, in order that the employee protection provisions contained in section 5 of the Brussels I Regulation (jurisdiction over individual contracts of employment) might be engaged. This action was alleged to be justified because it was thought the only way to give effect to the Brussels-endowed employee rights (over employees who were domiciled in England) was to seek to restrain the New York proceedings. The New York court had already decided in accordance with its own law that it had jurisdiction, but clearly, that court was neither entitled, nor bound to give effect to the Brussels I Regulation. There is irony in using a "non-Brussels" tool to achieve a "Brussels end".

ARBITRATION

7-59 In *The Angelic Grace*,[321] the Court of Appeal held that there was no difference in principle between restraining a party from commencing/

---

[318] Presumably, the grant of anti-suit injunctions by Scots or English courts remains competent in respect of proceedings in a non Contracting/Member State; though after *Owusu v Jackson (t/a Villa Holidays Bal Inn Villas)* [2005] Q.B. 801 no British lawyer can state with confidence the extent of the EU's reach (see para.7–62, below).

[319] e.g. Hartley, "The European Union and the Systematic Dismantling of the Common Law of Conflict of Laws" (2005) 54 I.C.L.Q. 813.

[320] [2007] EWCA Civ 723.

[321] *Aggeliki Charis Compania Maritima SA v Pagnan SpA (The Angelic Grace)* [1994] 1 Lloyd's Rep. 168.

continuing foreign proceedings in breach of an exclusive jurisdiction clause and doing likewise in respect of foreign proceedings raised in contravention of an arbitration clause: the restraint should be effected as promptly as possible and without diffidence.[322] The unfolding of events has revealed, however, that just as there may be no difference in principle between these two instances, neither is there any difference in practice in the grant of such a remedy by the UK courts in support of an arbitration clause or in support of a choice of court clause; each is *verboten* "within the Brussels regime".[323]

West Tankers[324]

The charterparty between West Tankers, the owner of a vessel (*The Front Comor*), and the charterer, Erg Petroli SpA, contained a clause providing that any disputes were to be resolved by arbitration in London. *The Front Comor* collided with a jetty in Syracuse, Sicily, which was owned by Erg. Erg claimed upon its insurers, RAS Riunione Adriatica di Securta, up to the limit of its insurance cover, and began arbitration proceedings in London against West Tankers for the excess. West Tankers counterclaimed that it was not liable for any of the damage caused by the collision. Adriatica, having been subrogated to Erg's claim, brought a delictual action in Italy against West Tankers, seeking to recover the amount which had been paid to Erg in terms of the insurance policies. In response, West Tankers disputed the jurisdiction of the Italian court on the ground of the existence of the arbitration agreement, and in a parallel action raised in London sought declaration that the dispute was to be settled by arbitration pursuant to the agreement, and an order requiring Adriatica to desist from pursuing the Italian action. The English High Court granted the orders sought, and on appeal by the insurers, the House of Lords, noting that art.1.2(d) of the Brussels I Regulation excludes arbitration from its scope, referred for a preliminary ruling from the ECJ the question whether an anti-suit injunction to give effect to an arbitration agreement was incompatible with the Brussels I Regulation.

7–60

The Advocate General's opinion[325] was that although art.1.2(d) specifically excluded arbitration, the decisive question was not whether the English proceedings concerning the anti-suit injunction in support of arbitration fell within the scope of the Regulation, but rather whether the Italian proceedings against which the anti-suit injunction was directed, did so.[326] In the circumstances, the subject matter of the litigation in Italy was a claim in tort, and possibly in contract, jurisdiction being founded therefore on art.5 of the Brussels I Regulation. The existence and applicability of the arbitration clause merely constituted a preliminary issue which that court had to address when examining whether it had jurisdiction. In the opinon of the Advocate General, the use of the anti-suit injunction would amount to an interference with

---

[322] *Through Transport Mutual Insurance Association (Eurasia) Ltd v New India Assurance Co Ltd (The Hari Bhum) (No.1)* [2004] 1 Lloyd's Rep. 206; [2005] 1 Lloyd's Rep. 67.

[323] *Transfield Shipping Inc v Chiping Xinfa Huayu Alumina Co Ltd* [2009] EWHC 3629 (QB); and *Midgulf International Ltd v Groupe Chimiche Tunisien* [2009] 2 Lloyd's Rep. 411.

[324] *West Tankers Inc v RAS Riunione Adriatica di Securta SpA (The Front Comor)* [2007] UKHL 4, and *West Tankers Inc v Allianz SpA* [2009] 1 A.C. 1138.

[325] *Allianz SpA (formerly Riunione Adriatica di Sicurta SpA) v West Tankers Inc* (C-185/07) [2008] 2 Lloyd's Rep. 661.

[326] See also *Youell v La Reunion Aerienne* [2009] EWCA Civ 175.

proceedings falling within the scope of the Regulation, and following *Turner v Grovit*[327] was proscribed.

The decision of the ECJ, handed down in February 2009,[328] adhered to the opinion of Advocate General Kokott, that it is incompatible with the Brussels I Regulation for the court of a Member State to make an order to restrain a person from commencing or continuing proceedings before the courts of another Member State on the ground that such proceedings would be contrary to an arbitration agreement.

Arbitration is selected by parties for reasons of speed, confidentiality and practicality. An additional merit, it had been thought, was its capacity to allow parties to circumvent, deliberately or inadvertently, the Brussels regime of jurisdiction. The decision of the ECJ in *West Tankers*, though anticipated, precludes the potential use of an arbitration clause as a device to remove parties and their disputes from the reach of the Brussels regime. It has been greeted in the UK with dismay, and has been regarded as a decision destabilising the practice of favouring London as an arbitration venue. Lord Hoffmann, in his speech in the House of Lords,[329] gives voice to the commercial concerns of the English legal system in the matter of loss of arbitration business, a matter summarily dismissed by the ECJ.[330]

The reasoning employed en route to the ECJ's decision is true to type, encapsulated in the following statement:

"Nor is it a prerequisite of infringement of the principle of mutual trust, on which the judgment in *Turner v Grovit* was substantially based, that both the application for an anti-suit injunction and the proceedings which would be barred by that injunction should fall within the scope of the Regulation. Rather, the principle of mutual trust can also be infringed by a decision of a court of a Member State which does not fall within the scope of the Regulation obstructing the court of another Member State from exercising its competence under the Regulation."[331]

It was not long before the ramifications of the *West Tankers* decision were felt in the UK. Before the Court of Appeal in *National Navigation Co v Endesa Generacion SA (The Wadi Sudr)*,[332] the implications of *West Tankers* were felt in the matter of recognition of the judgment of a Spanish court, i.e. whether a Spanish judgment on the particular point of whether or not an arbitration clause had been incorporated into a contract gave rise to an issue estoppel in arbitration proceedings in the Commercial Court in London. The Spanish judgment had ruled that the arbitration clause had not been incorporated in the contract. Reversing the decision of the judge of first instance, the Court of Appeal held

---

[327] (C-159/02) [2005] 1 A.C. 101.

[328] *West Tankers Inc v Allianz SpA* [2009] 1 A.C. 1138.

[329] *West Tankers Inc v RAS Riunione Adriatica di Securta SpA (The Front Comor)* [2007] UKHL 4 at [21], [22]; and per Lord Mance at [29], [30]. See also expert evidence from the Ministry of Justice to the House of Lords European Union Committee, *Green Paper on the Brussels I Regulation: Report with Evidence*, 2009, HL Paper No.148 (Session 2008/09), paras 98 et seq.

[330] *West Tankers Inc v Allianz SpA* [2009] 1 A.C. 1138 at [66]: "To begin with it must be stated that aims of a purely economic nature cannot justify infringements of Community law".

[331] *West Tankers Inc v Allianz SpA* [2009] 1 A.C. 1138 at [34].

[332] [2009] EWCA Civ 1397.

that the English court was bound by the Spanish decision on the incorporation or not of the clause. The Court of Appeal took the view that the decision on incorporation of an arbitration clause into a contract, in most instances, would be very closely tied to the merits of a contractual dispute; the situation therefore was comparable with the *West Tankers* decision, in which the Italian court was seised under the art.5 special jurisdiction. This decision of the Court of Appeal stems directly from the ECJ decision in *West Tankers* (a *jurisdiction* case), that a preliminary ruling as to the applicability of an arbitration clause in proceedings in which the main subject matter was within the Regulation was itself to be categorised as within the Regulation. *The Wadi Sudr* concerns the extent to which the ratio of *West Tankers* can affect decisions in national courts at the *enforcement* stage. In sum, the Court of Appeal held that a judgment of a Member State court on the preliminary issue of whether an arbitration clause is validly incorporated is a judgment under the Brussels I Regulation, despite the arbitration exception in art.1.2(d), if that judgment formed part of proceedings, the main scope of which fell within the Regulation.

To date, the use of anti-suit injunctions to order parties to desist from pursuing proceedings in the courts of a non-Member State, that is to say geographically "outside the regime", in such a way as to flout an exclusive jurisdiction clause, or an agreement to arbitrate, remains available.[333]

Future position

The European Commission has acknowledged the difficulties which have **7–61** arisen on the interface between the Brussels I Regulation and arbitration.[334] The rationale behind the exclusion of arbitration from the scope of the Brussels I Regulation was that the recognition and enforcement of such agreements is governed by the New York Convention on the Recognition and Enforcement of Foreign Arbitral Awards 1958,[335] to which all Member States are parties.[336] Though that Convention is thought to operate satisfactorily, the Commission considered that anomalies and conflicts of jurisdiction may still arise. It is difficult to avoid overlap and consequent doubt concerning the remit of arbitral and judicial tribunals, respectively, e.g. typically, where the validity of the arbitration clause is upheld by the arbitral tribunal, but not by a court, or there is a question of enforcement or not of court judgments made in disregard of an arbitration clause. The Green Paper[337] suggests that deletion of the exclusion of arbitration from the Regulation's scope might effect an improvement, in that court proceedings in support of arbitration thereby might come within the regime and all the provisions in the Regulation concerning provisional measures (not only art.31, *q.v.*) would be available. It could be that exclusive jurisdiction for such proceedings should be granted to the courts of the Member State of the place of arbitration, subject to party agreement. Moreover, bringing arbitration within the Regulation's scope would allow

---

[333] *Shashoua v Sharma* [2009] EWHC 957 (Comm) (India), per Cooke J. at [717], [718].
[334] Report on the Application of Regulation 44/2001 COM(2009)174 final, para.3.7.
[335] The effective operation of which is highlighted in, e.g. *IPCO (Nigeria) Ltd v Nigerian National Petroleum Corp* [2008] EWCA Civ 1157.
[336] See also, in Scotland, Arbitration (Scotland) Act 2010: para.9–51, below.
[337] Green Paper on the Review of Regulation 44/2001 COM(2009)175 final, para.7.

recognition, within the Regulation rules, of judgments deciding on the validity of arbitration agreements. This might prevent parallel proceedings where an arbitral agreement is held valid in one Member State and invalid in another. Finally, to strengthen the force of arbitral awards, it has been suggested that a rule could be inserted in the Regulation permitting refusal of enforcement of a Member State judgment which is irreconcilable with an arbitral award.

The Report of the House of Lords EU Committee[338] concluded that a blanket exclusion of arbitration from the scope of the Regulation does not provide the best solution; on the other hand, whilst the underlying approach of the Regulation, which is to exclude arbitration from the rules applicable to courts, in the interests of the autonomy of arbitration, is right, some changes could usefully be made, the better to facilitate the resolution of disputes through arbitration. In particular, the committee considered as promising the idea of giving exclusive jurisdiction to the courts of the Member State of the seat of the proposed arbitration to determine issues relating to the existence (including validity), scope and applicability of the agreement. To that end, it may be necessary to consider introducing in the Regulation rules to identify the seat of the arbitration. The introduction of a provision whereby judgments in court proceedings pursued in breach of an arbitration agreement would be refused recognition in other Member States would be welcome.

(Much) more detailed rules in the form of articles in a proposed Regulation to amend the Brussels I Regulation are awaited.

DELINEATION OF THE EUROPEAN LEGAL SPACE[339]

The ambit of the Brussels regime

7–62   Even though the growing jurisprudence of the ECJ continues to enlarge our understanding of the Brussels system and its reach, commensurate with the enlargement of the system itself, there still exist situations which can be envisaged as realistic possibilities in respect of which the outcome is in doubt. For example, where parties, one or more of whom is domiciled in a Member State, have agreed that the court of a non-Member State is to have jurisdiction in any dispute arising between them, and one party reneges and has resort to an EU Member State court on a ground such as art.5, art.23 is silent. It may be thought that the rationes of *Gasser* and *Owusu*, in combination, would result in preference being shown to the EU Member State court first seised. Such speculation would lead to the view that the Brussels system would insist on its own operation, shutting its eyes to proceedings ongoing outside the regime.

Similarly, if parties, one or more of whom is domiciled in a Member State, have agreed that the courts of, say, Spain, are to have jurisdiction in any dispute arising between them, and one party reneges, having resort to a non-EU court on a ground available in the circumstances, the Regulation makes no provision. One could expect that the Spanish proceedings would continue,

---

[338] *Green Paper on the Brussels I Regulation: Report with Evidence*, 2009, HL Paper No.148 (Session 2008/09), paras 86–98.
[339] See E.T. Winter, "Measuring the extent of the Brussels regime", 2010 J.R. 163. See also para.9–42, below re extent of operation of Brussels regime of recognition and enforcement.

possibly concurrently with the non-EU proceedings, leading potentially to irreconcilable judgments. Whilst the Regulation system of *lis pendens* is geared to avoiding irreconcilable judgments within the European legal space, it cannot operate so as to avoid such irreconcilability as between a court in Europe, and a non-EU court. The Brussels rules, therefore, may impinge on litigation outside Europe, e.g. so as to preclude it. Concurrent litigation between the same parties, about the same matter, conducted in an EU State and a non-EU State, is likely to run in parallel, without touching, except perhaps if it should come to a question of enforcement of the resultant decree(s) within an EU State, at which point art.34.4 might be relevant. The manner of development of ECJ interpretative authority will have a negative effect on the popularity of the choice of the UK, and London in particular, under exclusive choice of court or arbitration clauses.

Therefore a subject which is engaging the attention of courts and writers is the delineation of the area of operation, respectively, of the Brussels regime, and of the system established by pre-existing, national rules of jurisdiction. For example, when assessing the respective merits and demerits of the opposing systems of rules for dealing with cases of conflicting jurisdiction (*lis pendens* and *forum non conveniens*), a crucial debate concerns the delimitation of the area of operation of each system: where does one system end and the other begin? *Owusu* has taught us that the plea of *forum non conveniens* may not be used by a UK court in a hybrid case, involving as a putative alternative forum a court in a non-Member State, if the UK court has been seised on a Brussels ground, even though no Member State other than the UK has an interest.

One key to understanding the extent of the Brussels regime is appreciation of the special status of persons domiciled in Member States. It is axiomatic within the regime that such persons, in their litigation, as claimants or defendants, are bound by and have the benefit of the Brussels I Regulation. The 1968 Convention applied, and the Regulation applies, even where the claimant was/is domiciled in a non-Contracting/Member State, so long as the defendant was/is domiciled within a Contracting/Member State[340] (or a special or exclusive ground of jurisdiction is available). To date, a Member State-domiciled defendant has been the favourite of the regime. The terms of the Green Paper evidence a growing concern for the Member State-domiciled claimant, particularly in his dealings with Third State defendants.

In the face of desire on the part of the defendant to transfer the case to a non-EU forum, the ECJ in *Owusu*, as part of its insistence upon maintaining the coherence of the Brussels system, relied upon principles such as legal certainty, predictability, and the legal protection of persons established in the Community:

> ". . . a defendant, who is generally better placed to conduct his defence before the courts of his domicile, would not be able [were the principles of *forum non conveniens* permitted a place in the regime], in circumstances such as those of the main proceedings, reasonably to foresee before which other court he may be sued."[341]

---

[340] *Universal General Insurance Co (UGIC) v Group Josi Reinsurance Co SA* (C-412/98) [2001] Q.B. 68.
[341] *Owusu v Jackson (t/a Villa Holidays Bal Inn Villas)* (C-281/02) [2005] Q.B. 801 at [42].

An EU domiciliary, however, may utilise "non-Brussels" grounds of jurisdiction against a non-EU domiciliary (or in a non-qualifying EU case, per art.1 of the Regulation) and in such instances, would operate outside the Brussels regime—albeit that he may enforce any resulting EU judgment in any EU Member State in which the defendant has assets, using the Brussels enforcement scheme (subject to bilateral international arrangements made under art.59/72 of the Brussels Convention/Regulation). However, *Owusu* reveals that even a defendant domiciled in a non-EU Member State may require to submit to the Brussels rules, as a result of a combination of circumstances (e.g. desire to consolidate actions), even though he would prefer not to do so.

In addition to the determining factor of domicile of the defendant is the indefeasible claim to jurisdiction put forward in art.22, namely that based upon irrefutable territorial connection, regardless of domicile, e.g. most importantly, in geographical terms, land situated within the territorial bounds of the EU. In the case of *Choudhary v Bhatter*,[342] which arose before the Court of Appeal on the matter of interpretation of art.22, an important question, inter alia, concerned jurisdiction of the English court under art.22.2,[343] in proceedings regarding the affairs of a company incorporated in England, but conducting its business in India. The opening of art.22 states that: "The following courts shall have exclusive jurisdiction, regardless of domicile." The court decided that it would be wrong to interpret the words "regardless of domicile" in art.22 as having any application to a case where the person to be sued is not domiciled in a Member State.[344] The court, allowing the appeal, declined to hold that the English court was properly seised. Sir John Chadwick[345] sought to distinguish the case from the decision in *Owusu*, on the basis that *Owusu* provides:

> ". . . no direct authority on the question whether a court of a contracting state is precluded from declining the jurisdiction (if any) conferred on it by art.22 of the Judgments Regulation in respect of a person not domiciled in a Member State on the ground that a court of a non-contracting state would be a more appropriate forum for the trial of the action."

The decision in *Choudhary* exemplifies another attempt to break free from the shackles of *Owusu*, and to limit its application. But the attempt was ill founded and based on misunderstanding of the Regulation[346] and, if appealed, is unlikely to succeed (either on the interpretative point or on the *Owusu* conjecture).

To measure the full extent of the Brussels regime, therefore, it is necessary to include in the computation temporal and subject matter scope, territorial boundaries,[347] the personal law connecting factor of domicile, "deemed domicile" created through branches or agencies, and those binding ECJ/CJEU

---

[342] [2010] I.L.Pr. 8.
[343] An unsuccessful argument was run that the case fell outside the subject matter scope of the Brussels I Regulation, per art.1.2(b).
[344] *Choudhary v Bhatter* [2010] I.L.Pr. 8, per Sir John Chadwick at [38].
[345] *Choudhary v Bhatter* [2010] I.L.Pr. 8, per Sir John Chadwick at [52].
[346] Article 22 operates to override art.4, and therefore, transcends the residual national rules of jurisdiction.
[347] *Orams v Apostolides* [2010] I.L.Pr. 20.

decisions interpretative of the provisions of the Brussels I Regulation, which have a bearing on patent and latent extent. The UK, being an EU Member State but having, in conflict of laws terms at least, a generally Anglo-American legal background and preference for the use of judicial discretion in matters of jurisdiction, and being a favoured place of resort for commercial litigation and arbitration involving parties from the USA and the Far East, inevitably finds itself cast as Janus, the vigilant gatekeeper, looking in two directions.

Effet réflèxe

The possible reflexive effect of the Brussels Convention has been under **7–63** discussion since 1972,[348] but with growing interest in the UK in recent years, in keeping with the increasing avidity of the Brussels regime, as interpreted, in arrogating authority in areas previously unimagined. The theory is that where, for example, proceedings before an EU Member State court concern a question of title to land in a Third State, or where an EU Member State court is seised (second) in a matter which already is the subject of litigation before the courts of a Third State—both of the above being situations in respect of which the Brussels I Regulation has a bespoke rule of jurisdiction—"it is most improbable" that the EU Member State court is obliged to exercise its jurisdiction in the face of a stay sought by the defendant on the ground that the Third State is the *forum conveniens*.

In such situations, it is perplexing to decide whether a Member State court which cedes jurisdiction in such a case to a Third State court (thereby "reflecting" the rationale and practice of the regime, like the beam of a torch, into the dark regions which, geographically, are beyond the purlieu of the EU) pays full obeisance to the Brussels regime; or, on the other hand, if a Member State court which proves amenable to reflexive reasoning, causing it to yield to the Third State court, is being duped by sophistry, and is unjustifiably deprived of its prima facie jurisdiction. Certainly, the concept has been seised upon with enthusiasm in the common law camp, as a means of turning to its own advantage the rules of the civilian game; using the ideology of the Brussels regime in order to evade the regime.

The silence of the Regulation on this matter has been taken by some to serve as justification for employing the device; to turn traditional ECJ reasoning against itself, by drawing an inference from the observation that, "nothing in the Regulation forbids reflexive reasoning". But a stronger case can be made, on the argument that the relevant articles of the Regulation can be read in such a way as to provide positive justification for a Member State court staying its proceedings in such cases.[349] Article 2, although the foundation article of the instrument, is required to defer to arts 22, 23, 27 and 28. Why then should it not be argued that a court seised under art.2 is under a duty to defer to a Third State court where the circumstances equate to those covered by arts 22, 23, 27 and 28? It has been seen in *Samengo-Turner v J&H Marsh & McLennan (Services) Ltd*[350] that the Court of Appeal granted the non-Brussels remedy of

---

[348] G.A.L. Droz, '*La competence judiciaire et effet de jugements dans le Marché Commun (Etude de la Convention de Bruxelles du 27 septembre 1968), Bibliothèque de droit international privé*, Dalloz, Vol.XIII, 1972, pp.429–453.

[349] Winter, "Measuring the extent of the Brussels regime", 2010 J.R. 163.

[350] [2007] EWCA Civ 723.

anti-suit injunction to ensure that parties, who had been drawn into proceedings in New York, were given the opportunity to enforce in England the protective provisions with which, as "qualifying employees", they were endowed by the Brussels I regime (an inverse reflex).

Such authority as can be discerned to be in favour of application of reflexive effect is fragmentary and fragile, and perhaps is best monitored by category. It may be that the strongest case for application of *effet réflèxe* is in relation to Third State proceedings where jurisdiction is taken on grounds comparable to those covered by art.22 (exclusive jurisdiction). Secondly, a fairly strong case might be made out in favour of upholding an exclusive choice of court clause for a Third State,[351] although this in itself is odd, since *Gasser* shows that there can be no such guarantee *within* the regime. However, greater doubt attends the strength of the reflexive argument in the plain operation of the *lis pendens* rules[352]; with regard to the latter, the outcome of a reference from the Irish Supreme Court to the ECJ (the Irish High Court judge having been unwilling to stay, on this ground, litigation commenced in Ireland in face of an action earlier commenced on the same matter in USA) in *Goshawk Dedicated Ltd v Life Receivables Ireland Ltd*,[353] is uncertain, and it is possible that the reference has been abandoned.

The English court in *Catalyst Investment Group Ltd v Lewinsohn*[354] was not well disposed to reflexive effect argument. The court having been properly seised under art.2, Barling J. was not persuaded that, by reason of the existence of litigation pending in the USA, the appropriate reflexive application of art.27.2 was that the English forum was entitled to apply its national rules on *forum conveniens* in order to decide whether to stay proceedings in favour of those in the Third State. The English forum was not prepared to take so bold a step in the matter of interpretation of art.27, and distinguished the situation from that in which an EU court might defer to a Third State court by reflexive effect of art.23. It is difficult not to agree with Barling J. that the argument proferred was strained.

The arguments may be ingenious, and the self-serving motive which presumably lies at their root, understandable. It may be that before we can see whether the reflexive effect theory and its consequences will flourish, a revised Brussels I Regulation resolving many of the grievances produced by application of the regime's rules (both within what the reasonably well-informed man would judge to be the ambit of the rules, and outside it) will stunt their development.

Residual (or subsidiary) jurisdiction

7–64   As against non-EU domiciliaries (or in cases against EU domiciliaries which fall outside the subject matter scope of Brussels, per art.1), residual national rules, i.e. for Scotland, CJJA 1982 Sch.8,[355] can be utilised. Moreover, use of residual national rules opens the way to the plea of *forum non*

---

[351] *Konkola Copper Mines Plc v Coromin Ltd* [2006] EWHC 1093, per Colman J.
[352] See Richard Fentiman *International Commercial Litigation* (Oxford: Oxford University Press, 2010), paras 11.127 et seq.
[353] [2009] I.E.S.C. 7.
[354] [2009] EWHC 1964 (Ch).
[355] See para.7–69 re Sch.8 (Scotland) and English Civil Procedure Rules.

conveniens,[356] with the result that when a Scots or English court is seised under residual national rules of jurisdiction, it might find itself deferring sub nom. *forum non conveniens* to a court in another EU Member State.[357]

The Nuyts Study was commissioned by the European Commission to produce a comparative analysis of the current national rules of jurisdiction of Member States (operative in civil and commercial areas, and in matrimonial and parental responsibility proceedings)[358]; and to make recommendations for possible harmonisation of the rules.[359] The study considered whether the absence of common rules determining jurisdiction against defendants domiciled in Third States could jeopardise the application of mandatory Community legislation, or the objectives of the Community.

Of the five options identified as possible solutions to the alleged problem, the one favoured in the Nuyts Study is extension of the existing jurisdictional rules contained in the Brussels I Regulation to claims against defendants domiciled in Third States; blatant aggrandisement by the Brussels regime. The main advantage of such an option is said to be ease of implementation, and convenience for judges and lawyers. Nuyts recommended that such a change should be accompanied by the creation of additional grounds of jurisdiction to balance the necessary unavailability of the court of the defendant's domicile; and the crafting of new rules concerning declining jurisdiction in favour of the courts of Third States. Nuyts does not suggest "sanctifying" exorbitant national rules by introducing them into Community law, but advances three additional grounds of jurisdiction,[360] viz.: a jurisdiction based on the carrying out of activities in the forum by the Third State domiciled defendant, provided that the dispute relates to such activities; the location of assets belonging to such a defendant within the territory of an EU Member State, provided the claim relates to such assets; and the so-called *forum necessitatis*, permitting proceedings to be brought against such a defendant when there is no other jurisdiction available in the EU or outside the EU.

Taking account of the Nuyts Study, the Commission, in its Report,[361] under the heading "the operation of the [Brussels I] Regulation in the international legal order", states that the absence of harmonised rules on subsidiary jurisdiction gives rise to, "unequal access to justice for Community citizens". Consequently, the Green Paper[362] seeks views on the principle of creating special jurisdiction rules to be applied against Third State defendants; and on the detail, makes mention of the Nuyts Study suggestions.

The Report of the House of Lords EU Committee[363] says that clarification is necessary on the point whether possible rules on the exercise of jurisdiction

---

[356] See art.4.
[357] *Sarrio SA v Kuwait Investment Authority* [1999] 1 A.C. 32; and *Haji-Iannou v Frangos* [1999] 2 Lloyd's Rep. 337. See Morris, *Conflict of Laws*, 7th edn, 2009, para.5–046.
[358] The study concluded that recommendations for proposed harmonisation of residual jurisdiction would require to distinguish between the Brussels I and Brussels II *bis* regimes: Executive Summary, p.7.
[359] The Nuyts Study, see fn.66, above.
[360] Executive Summary, p.9.
[361] Report on the Application of Regulation 44/2001 COM(2009)174 final, para.3.2.
[362] Green Paper on the Review of Regulation 44/2001 COM(2009)175 final, para.2.
[363] *Green Paper on the Brussels I Regulation: Report with Evidence*, 2009, HL Paper No.148 (Session 2008/09), paras 86–98.

against Third State defendants will be intended to apply only where the claimant is domiciled in a Member State, or in all cases, regardless of the claimant's domicile as EU or non-EU; it is difficult to conceive how the Community is competent to regulate issues of jurisdiction between litigants neither of whom is domiciled in an EU Member State. More generally, the committee takes an English law perspective; it does not mention the residual national rules of Scotland, contained in CJJA 1982 Sch.8. As it happens, the rules of allocation of jurisdiction in Sch.8 are closer, than are the English residual rules, to those of the Brussels I Regulation. Over many decades, the English rules have developed to meet perceived needs relating to the position of London as a centre of commerce and finance, and it can be predicted that there will be alarm at the prospect of the entirety of the English courts' bases of jurisdiction, long established and discretionary in nature, being dictated from Brussels.

LUGANO II CONVENTION

7–65   A parallel scheme of rules of jurisdiction and judgment enforcement was brought into force for the European Free Trade Association (EFTA) area[364] by the 1988 Lugano ("Parallel") Convention on Jurisdiction and Enforcement of Judgments in Civil and Commercial Matters, which was extended to operate in the UK by means of the Civil Jurisdiction and Judgments Act 1991. To a large extent, the Lugano Convention repeated the text of the 1968 Brussels Convention, but the provisions, though similar, are not identical. In the matter of appeal to the European Court of Justice on points of interpretation of the Lugano Convention, there was a difference. While the Luxembourg Protocol permitted a reference to the ECJ on a matter of interpretation of the Brussels Convention by a court from which there is no further domestic appeal, there was no such provision in relation to Lugano. Nor did the Lugano Convention benefit from such advantages of speed and certainty which followed in the Brussels regime from the transformation of the Brussels Convention into a Regulation.

It was necessary therefore to effect equivalent changes to the Lugano regime. "Lugano II" refers to the Convention on jurisdiction and the recognition and enforcement of judgments in civil and commercial matters, between the European Community and the Republic of Iceland, the Kingdom of Norway, the Swiss Confederation and the Kingdom of Denmark, signed on behalf of the European Community on October 30, 2007.[365] It replaces the 1988 Lugano Convention in terms which, in general, are parallel to those contained in the Brussels I Regulation. Lugano II entered into force for the European Community, including Denmark, and Norway on January 1, 2010. It will come into effect with regard to Switzerland on January 1, 2011. With

---

[364] Now comprising, for the purposes of Lugano II, Iceland, Norway and Switzerland. The principality of Liechtenstein, an EFTA Contracting State, did not ratify the Lugano I or II Conventions.

[365] See Decision 2007/712/EC on the signing, on behalf of the Community, of the Convention on jurisdiction and the recognition and enforcement of judgments in civil and commercial matters [2007] OJ L339/1; and Decision 2009/430/EC concerning the conclusion of the Convention on jurisdiction and the recognition and enforcement of judgments in civil and commercial matters [2009] OJ L147/1. See Civil Jurisdiction and Judgment Act 1982, as amended by the Civil Jurisdiction and Judgments Regulations 2009 (SI 2009/3131).

regard to Iceland, the Convention shall enter into force three months after ratification by that country.[366]

Lugano II is accompanied by an Explanatory Report.[367] The Pocar Report stresses the importance of simplification of procedures for judgment enforcement, as a necessary contribution to the development of the single judicial area, an area which, "lends itself so well to extension to the EFTA countries".[368] Everything possible must be done to facilitate the free movement of judgments, and further reduce the obstacles which still exist.

With regard to interpretation of Lugano II, reference should be made to Protocol 2 on the Uniform Interpretation of the Convention and on the Standing Committee. As a result of Lugano II having become part of Community rules (the Convention having been signed and ratified by the Community), the CJEU has jurisdiction to give interpretative rulings on its provisions upon application to the Court by the courts of EU Member States.[369] States bound by Lugano II which are not EU Member States (i.e. the EFTA States of Iceland, Norway and Switzerland), though not entitled to make application to the CJEU for interpretative rulings on Lugano II, are entitled, in terms of art.2 of the Protocol to submit statements of case or written observations to that Court where the court of an EU Member State has made such an application. Article 1 of Protocol 2 requires any court applying and interpreting Lugano II to pay due account to relevant jurisprudence upon Lugano I, Lugano II, and the Brussels I Regulation, handed down by the ECJ/CJEU and courts bound by these instruments, respectively.

Jurisdiction provisions of Lugano II[370]

Title II of Lugano II deals with jurisdiction. The provisions have been almost completely aligned with those in the Brussels I Regulation, except for differences seen in arts 5.2 (maintenance) and 22.4 (exclusive jurisdiction in relation to the registration of patents, etc.). In relation to the former, the Brussels I Regulation is soon to be overtaken by implementation of Regulation 4/2009 in matters relating to maintenance obligations,[371] the provisions of which are similar to, but more generous than, Lugano II art.5.2. As concerns art.22.4, the words "whether the issue is raised by way of an action or as a defence" appear in Lugano II, but are absent from the Brussels I Regulation.   **7–66**

Relationship between Lugano II and the Brussels I Regulation

This subject is addressed in Lugano II Title VII art.64. In this difficult area of delimitation of ambit of the Brussels I Regulation and Lugano II,[372] the   **7–67**

---

[366] Lugano II art.69.5. Until such time as Lugano II enters into force in Switzerland and Iceland, the 1988 Lugano Convention continues to apply.

[367] Fausto Pocar, Explanatory Report [2009] OJ C319/1 ("Pocar Report").

[368] Pocar Report, para.128.

[369] While the position is clear, and the reason for CJEU jurisdiction convincing insofar as the Lugano II and Brussels I Regulation texts have been aligned, rendering divergent interpretations undesirable, the immediate authority rests only on the preamble to Protocol 2, and is not visible anywhere in the text of the articles. See also Pocar Report, para.196.

[370] Title III of Lugano II is concerned with recognition and enforcement of judgments. There is little change in this section of the instrument as compared with the 1988 Lugano Convention. See para.9–45, below.

[371] See Ch.13, below.

[372] Pocar Report, para.18.

courts of EFTA States are obliged always to apply Lugano II. Courts in Member States bound by the Regulation may find themselves having to apply both instruments.

Article 64.1 in principle provides that the scope of the Brussels I Regulation and amendments, and of the EC-Denmark Agreement, remains unaltered, not limited by Lugano II. Hence, with regard to persons domiciled in states bound by the Brussels I Regulation, or the EC-Denmark Agreement, the jurisdiction of EU Member State courts continues to be exercised in accordance with the rules contained in those instruments; these rules also continue to apply with regard to persons domiciled in Third States, which are not party to Lugano II.[373]

In matters of jurisdiction, by art.64.2, Lugano II is applicable:

> ". . . in all cases, by the courts of any State bound by the Convention, including the courts of States bound by the Brussels I Regulation, if the defendant is domiciled in the territory of a State where the Convention applies and the Regulation does not."

Essentially, therefore, if the defendant in proceedings in Scotland is domiciled, e.g. in Iceland, the Scots court shall apply Lugano II.[374] Likewise, Lugano II shall apply where, by arts 22 (exclusive jurisdiction) or 23 (prorogation), jurisdiction is conferred on a Lugano State, e.g. a Scots court seised on the ground of domicile under art.2 of the Brussels I Regulation, in proceedings concerning rights in rem in immoveable property in Iceland, must cede jurisdiction to the Icelandic courts on the basis of the respect due to the exclusive jurisdiction principle, but this would be done in terms of art.22 of Lugano II, not art.22 of the Brussels I Regulation. In terms of art.64.2(b), Lugano II shall apply in a situation where proceedings are instituted in a Lugano State, say, Norway, and proceedings in respect of the same or a related cause of action are instituted in Scotland; if, in terms of the *lis pendens* system, the Scots court must or may defer to the Norwegian court, this shall be done under Lugano II arts 27 and 28, and not under the corresponding provisions of the Brussels I Regulation.

CIVIL JURISDICTION AND JUDGMENTS ACT 1982 SCHEDULE 4[375]

7–68 By s.16 of CJJA 1982, the provisions set out in Sch.4, which contain a modified version of the Brussels I Regulation, shall have effect for determining, for each part of the UK, whether the courts of that part, or any particular court in that part, have/has jurisdiction, where the subject-matter is within the scope of the Brussels I Regulation, and the defendant is "domiciled" in the "UK", or where special jurisdiction can be established under rr.3–10, or the proceedings come under the exclusive jurisdiction rules contained in r.11, or jurisdiction is prorogued under r.12.

Schedule 4, therefore, has two main functions: first, where, under the Brussels I Regulation, jurisdiction is allotted to the "UK" generally, but not to

---

[373] Pocar Report, para.19.
[374] Pocar Report, para.20.
[375] As amended by CJJO 2001 Sch.2.

a particular territorial unit thereof,[376] Sch.4 supplies the lack. Secondly, it is utilised in cases which arise within the UK, but are related to more than one territorial unit within the UK.

The provisions of Sch.4 follow those of the Brussels I Regulation, and in approach and detail are frequently the same, or similar. Amendment of Sch.4 was effected by the CJJO 2001, so as to mirror, so far as appropriate,[377] the changes made to the jurisdiction provisions of the Brussels I Regulation. In one instance (special jurisdiction in delict), the re-cast rule in art.5.3 of the Brussels I Regulation, extending jurisdiction in the case of anticipated wrongs, provides for Regulation cases a rule which, from the outset, was the rule in Sch.4.

However, there are certain differences between the detail of the Brussels I Regulation and Sch.4. For example, the Community definition of "place of performance" of a contract provided in art.5.1 of the Regulation was not extended by the CJJO 2001 to Sch.4 r.3(a). Similarly, the presumption of exclusivity of choice of court clauses, inserted into the prorogation provision of the Regulation (art.23), is not found in Sch.4 r.12 (prorogation).

Certain "national" rules of jurisdiction of Member States were proscribed by the 1968 Brussels Convention, and now by the Regulation, and may not be used against persons domiciled in a Member State, or in a territorial unit within a Member State. This means that a Scots rule such as arrestment to found jurisdiction can be utilised only if the property sought to be arrested is situated in Scotland, and the owner/defender is not domiciled in Scotland, elsewhere in the UK or in any other Member State. There remains one ground of jurisdiction which does not feature in the Brussels I Regulation, but yet is not a proscribed ground, and therefore deserves mention as an example of a distinction in the rules between Schs 1 and 4, namely, the special jurisdiction conferred on the parts of the UK qua *lex situs*, where the proceedings concern a debt secured on immoveable property, or which are brought to assert, declare, or determine proprietary or possessory rights, or rights of security, in or over moveable property, or to obtain authority to dispose of moveable property.[378]

Recourse cannot be had to the ECJ for interpretation of the provisions of Sch.4.[379]

CIVIL JURISDICTION AND JUDGMENTS ACT 1982 SCHEDULE 8

Schedule 8 (the "residual" Scottish rules) takes effect, subject to the Brussels **7–69** I Regulation, and Lugano II (allocating jurisdiction among EU/EFTA Member States), and to Sch.4 (the "Modified Convention", allocating jurisdiction within the UK).

---

[376] e.g. for the provision of jurisdiction on the basis of the defendant's domicile under art.2 of the Brussels I Regulation, the international allocation of jurisdiction per the Regulation is satisfied by a finding that the defendant is domiciled in the UK. Thereafter, identification of the domicile of the defendant as, e.g. between Scotland, and England and Wales, is determined by Sch.4: *Daniel v Foster*, 1989 S.C.L.R. 378; and *Parkes v Cintec International Ltd* [2006] CSIH 30 Extra Division.

[377] e.g. consumer protection rules; cf. the introduction by the Brussels I Regulation of rules to protect employees, which is carried through by CJJO 2001 into Sch.4 r.10. On the other hand, protective rules for insured parties and beneficiaries, equivalent to those found in the Regulation are not present in Sch.4.

[378] See Sch.4 r.3(h).

[379] EC Treaty art.234; and now TFEU art.267, re jurisdiction of the CJEU. See *Kleinwort Benson Ltd v Glasgow City Council (No.2)* [1997] 4 All E.R. 641.

The introduction of a set of rules for Scotland was advocated by the Maxwell Committee,[380] which recommended that the grounds of jurisdiction in use in Scotland be rationalised and set out in a single code.[381] The scheme of jurisdiction for Scotland introduced by the CJJA 1982, as now amended[382] supersedes all existing rules of jurisdiction in matters covered by the Act, subject to retention of the *nobile officium* of the Court of Session. Although Sch.8 contains the "Scottish rules", the key to operation of these rules is not the Scottish location of the putative litigation, but rather the legal characteristic of the defender, or the subject matter of the litigation. The provisions of Sch.8 are termed "rules", not "articles".

Schedule 8 contains those native or idiosyncratic rules of Scots law which are capable of being utilised against persons not domiciled in an EU or EFTA Member State. A defence which can be offered for retention of these native grounds is that their effect may be mitigated by the plea of *forum non conveniens*, where it remains available and competent. There is another, unexceptional ground available at Scots common law (in cases concerning moveable property, jurisdiction being based on the situation thereof),[383] which may be used not only against persons domiciled in a non-Member State, but also against persons domiciled in any part of the UK.

Some rules in Sch.8 are identical to their counterpart in the Brussels I Regulation[384]; some rules in Sch.8 remain in the original Brussels Convention form, unamended to reflect the modifications effected internationally by the Regulation[385]; and some rules in Sch.8 are similar to those in Brussels I Regulation, but not identical.[386]

Where the rules in Sch.8 are derived from provisions contained in the Regulation, the Scottish courts must have regard to relevant principles and decisions handed down by the ECJ, and to the expert reports (Jenard and Schlosser, etc.).[387]

It is particularly important to be clear as to the ground upon which a Scots court has taken jurisdiction, given the growing jurisprudence derived from the ECJ, to the effect that if jurisdiction is laid on a Brussels ground, no other system (for example the discretionary plea of *forum non conveniens*) may be adopted by the court.

English law—Civil Procedure Rules[388]

7–70   Unlike the Scottish "residual" rules, the English "residual" rules are not contained in a Schedule to the Civil Jurisdiction and Judgments Act 1982.

---

[380] *Report of the Scottish Committee on Jurisdiction and Enforcement*, 1980 ("Maxwell Report").
[381] Maxwell Report, paras 2.16(h), 2.23, 2.24.
[382] Civil Jurisdiction and Judgments Order 2001 (SI 2001/3929) ("CJJO 2001"); Civil Jurisdiction and Judgments Regulations 2009 (SI 2009/3131).
[383] cf. Corresponding provision in Sch.4 r.3(h).
[384] e.g. Sch.8 r.2(c) (special jurisdiction in matters relating to a delict) and r.2(o) (multiple defenders), as to which see *Compagnie Commerciale Andre SA v Artibell Shipping Co Ltd (No.1)*, 1999 S.L.T. 1051.
[385] e.g. Sch.8 r.2(b) (special jurisdiction in matters relating to a contract).
[386] e.g. Sch.8 r.5 (exclusive jurisdiction). Notably, Sch.8 r.6 (prorogation) does not include a presumption of exclusivity.
[387] Civil Jurisdiction and Judgments Act 1982 s.20(5).
[388] See *Cheshire, North and Fawcett: Private International Law*, 14th edn, 2008, pp.353–454.

Rather, the pre-existing rules remain operative wherever the Brussels regime does not apply. In such cases, jurisdiction is assumed on a wide and liberal basis, namely presence of the defendant within the jurisdiction; submission of the defendant to the jurisdiction of the court; and "service out" of the English jurisdiction in cases in which the Civil Procedure Rules permit such service at the discretion of the court.[389]

PRE-TRIAL MEASURES AND PREVENTIVE MEASURES AND SAFEGUARDS

The reason for the existence of such rules and remedies in any legal system is, first, to obtain and preserve evidence for the litigation and, secondly, to preserve the defender's assets for satisfaction of the claim and expenses.   7–71

Preservation of evidence

Evidence may be obtained under authority of a commission and diligence authorised by the Scots court at common law. Further, the Administration of Justice (Scotland) Act 1972 s.1,[390] permits the Scots court in its discretion to order commission and diligence[391] for the inspection, photographing, etc. and custody of documents or other property, including land, which appear to the court to be property in respect of which a question may arise in civil proceedings (i.e. the process of "recovery" in Scots law, or "discovery" in English law).   7–72

The First Division of the Court of Session in *Iomega Corp v Myrica (UK) Ltd (No.2)*,[392] overruling *Dailey Petroleum Services Corp v Pioneer Oil Tools Ltd*,[393] permitted material so recovered to be used in foreign proceedings.[394] While the party recovering evidence was impliedly restricted in his use of the evidence to the proceedings in respect of which it had been recovered, the court had power to permit such evidence to be used in other proceedings in Scotland or elsewhere, provided it was satisfied that such use was in the interests of justice.[395]

---

[389] CPR r.6.36 (ex-6.20), and CPR PD 6B (Service out of the Jurisdiction). See, e.g. *Seaconsar (Far East) Ltd v Bank Markazi Jomhouri Islami Iran* [1993] 1 Lloyd's Rep. 236. See also *Konamaneni v Rolls Royce Industrial Power (India) Ltd* [2002] 1 W.L.R. 1269; *Morin v Bonhams & Brooks Ltd* [2003] 2 All E.R. (Comm) 36; *Apple Corps Ltd v Apple Computer Inc* [2004] EWHC 768; *Ophthalmic Innovations International(UK) Ltd v Ophthalmic Innovations International Inc* [2005] I.L.Pr. 10; *Marconi Communications International Ltd v PT Pan Indonesia Bank TBK* [2005] 2 All E.R. (Comm) 325; *Ark Therapeutics Plc v True North Capital Ltd* [2006] 1 All E.R. (Comm) 138; and *Masri v Consolidated Contractors International Co SAL* [2009] 4 All E.R. 847.
[390] See, in cases of urgency, s.1(3), the "dawn raid": *British Phonographic Industry Ltd v Cohen*, 1983 S.L.T. 137 (application for such remedy granted ex parte where there is danger that the possessor is likely to remove or destroy the property).
[391] See *Union Carbide Corp v BP Chemicals Ltd*, 1995 S.L.T. 972. As to human rights challenge, see *Narden Services Ltd v Inverness Retail and Business Park Ltd*, 2006 S.L.T. 338.
[392] 1999 S.L.T. 796.
[393] 1994 S.L.T. 757.
[394] See now extension of powers of Court of Session by Civil Jurisdiction and Judgments Act 1982 (Provisional and Protective Measures) (Scotland) Order 1997 (SI 1997/2780), as amended.
[395] *Iomega Corp v Myrica (UK) Ltd (No.2)*, 1999 S.L.T. 796, per Lord President Rodger at 804, admitting the lack of precedent.

By s.19 of the Law Reform (Miscellaneous Provisions) (Scotland) Act 1985, the court is empowered to order a party to disclose such information as he possesses as to the identity of possible witnesses or defenders.

Preservation of assets

7–73   By virtue of art.24 of the 1968 Brussels Convention,[396] and art.31 of the Brussels I Regulation (and art.31 of Lugano II), application may be made to the court in Scotland for such provisional, including protective, measures as may be available under Scots law, even if the court of another Member/Contracting State has jurisdiction as to the substance of the matter. Hence, not only does the Brussels system provide an effective procedure for enforcing judgments, it provides also a system of safeguarding the claimant's interests before and during litigation or arbitration.

In accordance with the decision of the ECJ in *Van Uden Maritime BV (t/a Van Uden Africa Line) v Kommanditgesellschaft in Firma Deco-Line*,[397] authorisation of provisional measures under art.31 of the Regulation must be founded upon a real connection between the subject matter of the action in respect of which the measures are sought and the territorial jurisdiction of the requested forum. Article 31 refers to such measures as may be available prior to judgment on the merits. Article 47 pertains to such remedies as may be available after the foundation judgment has been given, and during the grant of declaration of enforceability process. As far as the UK is concerned, such provisional, including protective measures, signify the remedies, outlined below, offered by Scots and English law.[398] The "worldwide freezing order" which may be made by an English court (*q.v.*) is authorised by the terms of art.47.1, but it has been held that if the EU Member State forum in question is England, its power does not extend in this circumstance to the grant of a worldwide freezing order.[399] Since art.47 provides remedies pending a final decision on declarator of enforceability, the provision will require to be adapted if the *exequatur* process is eliminated.

Future position

7–74   The European Commission Report[400] has stated that it is unclear how the "real connecting link" should be interpreted. In the Green Paper,[401] views are invited as to the improvement of the Regulation's provisions in this area. It is suggested that a different approach might be adopted, with the effect that the Member State whose courts have jurisdiction as to substance should be empowered to discharge, modify or adapt a provisional measure granted by the courts of the Member State having ancillary jurisdiction on the basis of art.31.

---

[396] See CJJA 1982 s.25.

[397] (C-391/95) [1998] E.C.R. I-7091; and *Mietz v Intership Yachting Sneek BV* (C99/96) [1999] I.L.Pr. 541.

[398] cf. *Reichert v Dresdner Bank* [1992] E.C.R. I-2149 (measures "intended to preserve a factual or legal situation so as to safeguard rights").

[399] *Banco Nacional de Comercio Exterior SNC v Empresa de Telecommunicationes de Cuba SA* [2007] EWCA Civ 662.

[400] Report on the Application of Regulation 44/2001 COM(2009)174 final, para.3.6.

[401] Green Paper on the Review of Regulation 44/2001 COM(2009)175 final, para.6.

In this way, the latter court would be seen as "lending remedies", which, when no longer needed, might be set aside by the court having jurisdiction on substance. This would remove the current focus on the imprecise "real connecting link" requirement. Evidence to the House of Lords EU Committee on this point was that, although there is a neatness to this solution, it has the potential to create uncertainties.[402] In addition, if the court of State A were able to vary or discharge orders granted by the courts of State B, this would be in conflict with the ECJ-recognised principle of non-interference by one national court in the affairs of another national court; and also would remove the incentive to apply for relief in any State other than that seised of the substance. The advice, which the committee accepted, was to favour maintenance of the status quo with regard to these rules.

Where the national procedural law allows a protective measure to be ordered ex parte, without prior service on the defendant, the ECJ held in *Denilauler v SNC Couchet Freres*[403] that such a measure falls outside the scope of the Brussels I Regulation, but the Commission notes that it is not clear that enforcement could be taken on the basis of the Regulation if the defendant had the opportunity to contest the measure subsequently. In response to these queries, evidence offered to the House of Lords EU Committee suggested that the current rules on provisional measures do not routinely give rise to significant problems in practice.[404]

Further, there is ECJ authority in *St Paul Dairy Industries NV v Unibel Exser BVBA*[405] that where, by national rules, it is possible for an applicant to order the hearing of a witness, in order to decide whether or not to bring a case, such a right is not covered by the notion of "provisional, including protective measures". The Commission has noted that it is not entirely clear to what extent such orders, as a general matter, are excluded from the scope of art.31 of the Brussels I Regulation. It would be desirable for the court at the situation where the evidence is located[406] to have jurisdiction in addition to that enjoyed by the court having jurisdiction over the substance of the matter.

Remedies afforded by Scots and English law

Scots law offers the remedies of attachment (in respect of corporeal move-   7–75
able property which is in the possession of the debtor, rather than a third party),[407] land attachment and residual attachment,[408] inhibition[409] (which prevents a defender from disposing of, or burdening, his heritable property to the prejudice of the inhibitor), diligence on the dependence[410]; interdict

---

[402] *Green Paper on the Brussels I Regulation: Report with Evidence*, 2009, HL Paper No.148 (Session 2008/09), paras 83, 84.
[403] (125/79) [1980] E.C.R. 1553.
[404] *Green Paper on the Brussels I Regulation: Report with Evidence*, 2009, HL Paper No.148 (Session 2008/09), para.82.
[405] (C104/03) [2006] E.C.R. I-3481.
[406] Report on the Application of Regulation 44/2001 COM(2009)174 final, para.3.6.
[407] Debt Arrangement and Attachment (Scotland) Act 2002 Pt 2. On interim attachment, see Bankruptcy and Diligence etc. (Scotland) Act 2007 Pt 7.
[408] 2007 Act Pt 4.
[409] 2007 Act Pt 5.
[410] 2007 Act Pt 6. See, previously, *Marie Brizard et Roger International SA v William Grant & Sons Ltd (No.1)*, 2001 G.W.D. 33–1302; and *China National Star Petroleum Co v Tor Drilling (UK) Ltd*, 2002 G.W.D. 12–348.

(interim or permanent) granted, like the English injunction,[411] against reasonable apprehension of wrong; money attachment[412]; diligence against earnings[413]; arrestment in execution[414]; and arrestment (which attaches only assets held by a third party arrestee, such as a bank or financial institution). By arrestment, a litigant may restrain the payment to his opponent of money or property, in the hands of a third party, due to the opponent.[415] Arrestment of the defender's property in the hands of a third party, to await the outcome of litigation, is a provisional security measure, frequently manifested in the attaching of a credit balance held by the defender at a bank, to the amount sought in the decree. There is a triangular relationship among arrester, arrestee and debtor. The arrestee (e.g. bank) must not permit operation on the account by the defender, and will be liable to the arrester should this occur.[416] While the debtor at the outset may be unaware that the creditor intends to effect, or has effected, arrestment on the dependence,[417] it is open to the debtor to apply to the court for recall of any arrestment made, on the ground that it is nimious and oppressive.[418] Diligence is strict law; formalities must be observed.[419] Arrestment on the dependence depends upon litigation having commenced. *Dramgate Ltd v Tyne Dock Engineering Ltd*[420] demonstrates that, in a conflict of laws case, the provisional safeguard of arrestment on the dependence cannot be sought or granted unless and until the jurisdiction of the Scots court over the defender is properly founded. The safeguard sought was premature and contained an inherent vice. Absence of malice made no difference.

English remedies, available from the High Court and above, of freezing orders (formerly "Mareva injunctions")[421] and search warrants (formerly "Anton Piller orders"),[422] exist respectively to prevent dissipation or removal

---

[411] See recourse to comity by Lord Marnoch in *G v Caledonian Newspapers Ltd*, 1995 S.L.T. 559, to ensure that Scots law could lend its aid to match an injunctive remedy granted by an English court in parallel proceedings.

[412] 2007 Act Pt 8.

[413] 2007 Act Pt 9.

[414] 2007 Act Pt 10.

[415] e.g. *Hydraload Research & Developments Ltd v Bone Connell & Baxters Ltd*, 1996 S.L.T. 219; *Dramgate Ltd v Tyne Dock Engineering Ltd*, 1999 S.L.T. 1392; and *China National Star Petroleum Co v Tor Drilling (UK) Ltd*, 2002 S.L.T. 1339; cf. in English law the making of a third party debt order (ex-garnishee order): *Cheshire, North and Fawcett: Private International Law*, 14th edn, 2008, pp.1238–1240.

[416] cf. Duty of care owed by a bank in terms of an English freezing order: *Customs and Excise Commissioners v Barclays Bank Plc* [2004] EWCA Civ 1555.

[417] i.e. a court order granting (until a final court decision) a temporary security over goods, or funds, e.g. in a bank account, held on behalf of the defender by a third party (Debt Arrangement and Attachment (Scotland) Act 2002 Appendix 2).

[418] *Fab Tek Engineering Ltd v Carillion Construction Ltd*, 2002 S.L.T. (Sh. Ct.) 113.

[419] *Anglo-Dutch Petroleum International Inc v Ramco Energy Plc*, 2006 S.L.T. 334.

[420] 1999 S.L.T. 1392.

[421] *Mareva Compania Naviera SA v International Bulk Carriers SA (The Mareva)* [1975] 2 Lloyd's Rep. 509. Also *Z Ltd v A-Z* [1982] 1 All E.R. 556; *Babanaft International Co SA v Bassatne* [1989] 2 W.L.R. 232; *Rosseel NV v Oriental Commercial & Shipping Co (UK) Ltd* [1990] 1 W.L.R. 1387; *S&T Bautrading v Nordling* [1997] 3 All E.R. 718; *Maimann v Maimann* [2001] I.L.Pr. 27; and *Bank of China v NBM LLC* [2002] 1 All E.R. 717.

[422] *Anton Piller KG v Manufacturing Processes Ltd* [1976] Ch. 55; *Haiti v Duvalier (No.2)* [1989] 1 All E.R. 456; *Derby & Co Ltd v Weldon (No.1)* [1989] 1 All E.R. 469; and *Balkanbank v Taher (No.2)* [1995] 2 All E.R. 904. This is a burgeoning area of development in English commercial and conflict rules. See e.g. *Camdex International Ltd v Bank of Zambia (No.2)* [1997] 1 All E.R. 728; *A/S D/S Svenborg v Wansa* [1997] 1 C.L. 122.

of a defendant's assets, i.e. to preserve them in order to satisfy the anticipated judgment and expenses; and to permit inspection of premises to discover documents relevant to the forthcoming litigation.

There must be shown to the court to be a risk of dissipation before a defendant will be ordered not to remove his assets from the jurisdiction.[423] An upper limit is set on the value of the assets frozen. The claimant normally must give an undertaking to compensate any third party who suffers damage as a result of the injunction, but where a third party holding the defendant's property, and having notice of the injunction,[424] knowingly aids and abets the defendant to breach the injunction, he is guilty of contempt of court. The claimant may be required to guarantee that he will not seek to litigate abroad with regard to the defendant's assets without the court's permission, i.e. the English court may seek to control the proliferation of foreign proceedings by the terms in which it grants its order.[425]

The "worldwide Mareva", has grown from an injunction preventing the defendant from disposing of his assets wherever situated, granted in the discretion of the English forum in a case where, in its view, the remedy was merited, and where the principal litigation was to take place in England or, if the litigation were to take place abroad, the case was justiciable in England. But the reach of the remedy has proceeded apace, in an attempt to keep abreast of defendant ingenuity and electronic advances.[426] The point has been reached now where the English court has power to make such an order in support of foreign arbitral[427] or judicial[428] proceedings, where the defendant is personally subject, on some ground,[429] to the jurisdiction of the English court, even though the issue is not justiciable in England.[430] The English court may grant an injunction restraining a party from leaving the country pending proceedings.[431]

---

[423] *Congentra AG v Sixteen Thirteen Marine SA (The Nicholas M)* [2008] 2 Lloyd's Rep. 602.

[424] See, in England, the safeguard known as the "Babanaft proviso" to identify and guide third parties: *Babanaft International SA v Bassatne* [1988] 2 Lloyd's Rep. 435. Also *Derby & Co Ltd v Weldon (Nos 3 and 4)* [1990] Ch. 65, per Lord Donaldson at 84; and *Bank of China v NBM LLC* [2002] 1 W.L.R. 844.

[425] *Dadourian Group International Inc v Simms* [2006] 1 W.L.R. 2499.

[426] See *Derby & Co Ltd v Weldon (Nos 3 and 4)* [1989] 2 W.L.R. 412, per Lord Donaldson at 420: "We live in a time of rapidly growing commercial and financial sophistication and it behoves the courts to adapt their practices to meet the current wiles of those defendants who are prepared to devote as much energy to making themselves immune to the courts' orders as to resisting the making of such orders on the merits of their case." Also *El-Ajou v Dollar Land Holdings Plc (No.1)* [1994] 2 All E.R. 685; and *Eliades v Lewis (No.9)* [2005] EWHC 2966.

[427] Arbitration Act 1996 s.2; *ETI Euro Telecom International NV v Bolivia* [2008] EWCA Civ 880.

[428] Article 31, in combination with CJJA 1982 s.25 (interim relief in England and Wales and Northern Ireland in the absence of substantive proceedings): *United States Securities & Exchange Commission v Manterfield* [2009] EWCA Civ 27. See also s.24 (interim relief and protective measures in cases of doubtful jurisdiction).

[429] The jurisdiction *in personam* is the justification for this extraordinarily powerful remedy; an element of controversy may arise where the connection of the defendant with the English jurisdiction is tenuous: *Haiti v Duvalier (No.2)* [1989] 1 All E.R. 456; *Motorola Credit Corp v Uzan (No.6)* [2004] 1 W.L.R. 113.

[430] *Credit Suisse Fides Trust SA v Cuoghi* [1997] 3 All E.R. 724, departing from the decision in *Owners of the Cargo Lately Laid on Board the Siskina v Distos Compania Naviera SA* [1979] A.C. 210 which had been followed in *Mercedes-Benz AG v Leiduck* [1995] 3 All E.R. 929. See in development of the topic, *Channel Tunnel Group Ltd v Balfour Beatty Construction Ltd* [1993] A.C. 334; and *Haiti v Duvalier (No.2)* [1989] 1 All E.R. 456.

[431] *Morris v Murjani* [1996] 2 All E.R. 384; and *B v B (Injunction: Restraint on leaving Jurisdiction)* [1997] 3 All E.R. 258 (consistorial).

War-like metaphors often are employed in this branch of the subject. While the use of negative declarations within the Brussels regime has been compared to the use of a torpedo, the English remedy of granting a worldwide freezing injunction has been termed the nuclear weapon in the litigation armoury. It is acknowledged that the injunction is a powerful remedy, and the English court will not always grant it.[432] The metaphor is not apt in a vital respect: a wrongly obtained freezing order will be discharged on appeal.[433]

SUMMARY 7

7–76
1. Allocation of jurisdiction
    There are four regimes regulating the rules in use in Scotland concerning civil and commercial jurisdiction, namely:

    (a) The Brussels regime, comprising the 1968 Brussels Convention, the Brussels I Regulation, and the EC-Denmark Agreement, with auxiliary primary legislation in the UK in the form of the Civil Jurisdiction and Judgments Act 1982, as amended by the Civil Jurisdiction and Judgments Order (SI 2001/3929);
    (b) The Lugano II Convention, with auxiliary primary legislation in the UK in the form of the Civil Jurisdiction and Judgments Act 1991, as amended by the Civil Jurisdiction and Judgments Order (SI 2009/3131);
    (c) Civil Jurisdiction and Judgments Act 1982 Sch.4: the Modified Convention, allocating jurisdiction within the UK; and
    (d) Civil Jurisdiction and Judgments Act 1982 Sch.8, being the residual, "national", Scottish rules.

2. Allocation of international jurisdiction among EU Member States is governed by the Brussels I Regulation:

    (a) The main ground of jurisdiction is "domicile" of the defendant (art.2), which, for this purpose, for the UK, is defined in CJJO 2001 Sch.1 para.9 (amending CJJA 1982 s.41).
    (b) There are alternative "special" grounds of jurisdiction, most importantly in matters relating to contract and delict (art.5).
    (c) There are protective jurisdictional rules for disadvantaged parties (arts 9–21) (insured parties, consumers and employees).
    (d) Article 22 contains rules conferring exclusive jurisdiction on a court of a Member State in specified cases, most importantly on the court of the *situs* in proceedings which have as their object rights *in rem* in immoveable property.

---

[432] *Mobil Cerro Negro Ltd v Petroleos de Venezuela SA* [2008] EWHC 532 (no English connection and no risk of dissipation).

[433] *Fourie v Le Roux* [2007] 1 W.L.R. 320: HL held that though the judge who had granted the freezing order had had jurisdiction in the strict sense to do so, the subject of the grant of such an order resting upon a combination of legislation, rules of court and judicial precedent, it was difficult to visualise a case where the grant of such an order, without notice, could be said to have been properly made in the absence of any formulation by the applicant of a case for substantive relief. It was right therefore to discharge the freezing order, i.e. the application was premature. The remedy will not be granted in the absence of evidence that litigation is in active contemplation.

(e) Article 23 permits prorogation of jurisdiction by parties.
(f) Article 24 endows with jurisdiction the court of a Member State before which a party has entered appearance, provided appearance was not solely for the purpose of contesting the jurisdiction.
(g) The *lis pendens* system of priority of process (arts 25–30) regulates "intra-EU" problems of conflicting jurisdiction.
(h) The hierarchy of provisions is as follows: art.22 takes precedence over arts 23 and 24. Article 24 takes precedence over art.23. Articles 9–21 take precedence over art.23, but are subordinate to art.24. The effect of the ECJ decision in *Gasser* is to subordinate art.23 to art.27. In terms of personal jurisdiction, art.2 is the pre-eminent ground to which all others are derogations.
(i) Cases handed down by the ECJ since 2004 have the effect of strictly guarding (with the result of extending) the Brussels system, with the aim of avoiding irreconcilable judgments within the EU area of freedom, security and justice. Most important are *Owusu; Turner v Grovit; Gasser v Misat*; and *West Tankers*.

3. The Hague Conference in 2005 concluded the Convention on Choice of Court Agreements. The Convention was signed by the EU in 2009, but is not yet in force.
4. Resolution of conflicts of jurisdiction occurring "outside the Brussels regime" are treated by Scots and English courts as a matter arising within judicial discretion, expressed in the acceding to, or refusing of, a plea by the defender of *forum non conveniens*.
5. "Outside the Brussels regime", the Scots/English courts have power to order a party who is subject to Scots/English jurisdiction to desist from commencing or continuing proceedings abroad. This power is expressed by means of grant of an anti-suit injunction.
6. Scots and English law provide (different) mechanisms to safeguard the defender's assets pending litigation, and for preserving evidence.

CHAPTER 8

EVIDENCE AND PROCEDURE

INTRODUCTION

8–01 There is a basic and crucial distinction in the conflict of laws between *substance* or *right* and *procedure* or *remedy*.

Substance is governed by the *lex causae*, the law which governs the right, such as the applicable law of contract or delict, the *lex successionis*, etc. For example, in *Re Cohn*,[1] though both the German and the English rules of succession in the case of *commorientes* (deaths in a common calamity) were held to be substantive, the English court, applying the English conflict rule, deferred to the German rule of the *lex successionis* qua *lex causae*. In the case of *In the Estate of Fuld (Deceased) (No.3)*[2] any requirement that a testator have "a free view" and that he be not unduly influenced by others as to the terms of his will, was regarded as a substantive rule, and therefore the German rule of the domicile (probably at the date of testing rather than at death, though this cannot be affirmed beyond doubt, because Fuld was held to be domiciled at all material times in Germany) was applied. Scarman J. assigned the topic of burden of proof in this instance to the category of procedure: the English Probate Court, "must in all matters of burden of proof follow scrupulously its own *lex fori*",[3] though this is not a characterisation about which all authorities agree.

Procedure is governed by the *lex fori*. Foreign rules of procedure are ignored by a Scots forum. The reason for this rule was explained in *De la Vega v Vianna*[4] by Lord Tenterden, who said that if a person comes to raise an action in England he must take the procedural law as he finds it; he cannot enjoy a (procedural) advantage over a native-born or resident litigant, nor should he be deprived of such advantages as are normally available. Further, it is feared that if a Scots or English forum should attempt to apply foreign procedural law, it may tear it out of context, misunderstand and misapply it. It would not be suitable to have litigations proceeding in Scotland according to a variety of legal systems' rules of evidence and procedure. Moreover, how "foreign" would a case have to be before application of foreign procedure seemed appropriate to apply? Hence, although a party sometimes may be able to choose the forum to his perceived best advantage, he is not entitled to choose the procedure which that forum will use to resolve the dispute.[5]

---

[1] [1945] Ch. 5.
[2] [1968] P. 675.
[3] *Fuld (No.3)* [1968] P. 675 at 697.
[4] (1830) 1 B. & Ad. 284.
[5] Even though he may try to do so: *Hamlyn and Co v Talisker Distillery* (1894) 21 R. (H.L.) 21, per Lord Herschell L.C. at 24.

There is a danger that a forum may be too quick to categorise a foreign rule as procedural. This is one means of justifying disapplication of a rule of the *lex causae*, clearing the way for application of the *lex fori*. The wording of a foreign rule may be deceptive, and the forum must look to the true nature of the rule. The worst cases of rough justice may be eliminated by a careful delimitation of what is procedural.[6] Sometimes Parliament has intervened to insist upon a characterisation as, for example, in the case of foreign limitation of actions rules, where the English and Scottish courts are directed to apply the prescription/limitation rule of the *lex causae* without attempting to classify its nature either by Scots law or by the foreign law.[7]

Frequently, European Regulations, in particular the Rome I and Rome II Regulations,[8] contain provisions which impinge upon this subject area.[9] Although, in the case of each of these instruments, in terms of their subject-matter scope, it is provided that the Regulation shall not apply to evidence and procedure,[10] nonetheless this general exclusion is qualified by particular provisions, discussed at appropriate points in this Chapter.

MEANING OF "PROCEDURE"

There are few definitions of procedure. One which may serve is per Lush L.J. **8–02** in *Poyser v Minors*,[11] which is as follows: " 'Practice' ... like 'procedure' ... denotes the mode of proceeding by which a legal right is enforced, as distinguished from the law which gives or defines the right."[12] Lord Murray in *Naftalin v London Midland & Scottish Railway Co*[13] described procedure thus:

> "No doubt procedure is a term of somewhat indefinite connotation but in his [Dicey's] opinion the true view is that any rule of law which affects, not the enforcement of a right, but the nature of the right itself, does not come under the head of procedure; or, in other words, is not governed by the lex fori."

Writers are sceptical of the possibility of making a definitive categorisation between matters of substance and matters of procedure.[14] The term "procedure" is used in a wide sense to cover forms of action and remedies, including the laws of evidence, and diligence; of this one can be confident. However, subjects such as actionability, and title to sue, have a mixed quality, and with regard to other topics, for example onus of proof and presumptions, opinions vary as to the proper categorisation.

---

[6] Anton, *Private International Law*, 1st edn, 1967, p.542.

[7] See para.8–06, below.

[8] See paras 15–38 and 16–40, below.

[9] Rome I Regulation arts 12, 17, 18; and Rome II Regulation arts 15, 22.

[10] Rome I Regulation art.1.3; and Rome II Regulation art.1.3.

[11] (1881) L.R. 7 Q.B.D. 329 at 333.

[12] Another explanation can be found per Lord Brougham in *Don v Lippmann* (1837) 5 Cl. & F. (HL) 13 at 13, 14.

[13] 1933 S.L.T. 193 at 200.

[14] See W.W. Cook, "Substance and Procedure in the Conflict of Laws" (1932–1933) 42 Yale L.J. 333; and Janeen M. Carruthers, "Substance and Procedure in the Conflict of Laws: A Continuing Debate in relation to Damages" (2004) 53 I.C.L.Q. 691, 694.

MISCELLANEOUS MATTERS PERTAINING TO LITIGATION

ACTIONABILITY

8–03 The question whether an action may be raised at all is determined by the *lex fori*. This can be seen, for example, from the Scottish and English prohibition upon suits for damages for breach of promise of marriage, no matter the identity and content of the law governing the promise.[15] This is a matter of policy of the forum, not procedure.

The preliminary, procedural side of an issue soon may become substantive. Thus, a rule providing for inter-spousal immunity from suit, if a rule of the *lex causae* as determined per the Rome II Regulation, will preclude an action in delict in Scotland, unless re-characterised as, for example, a matter of family law, or judged contrary to public policy.[16] Similarly, where the Scots applicable law of contract confers a *jus quaesitum tertio*, the party so entitled by the *lex causae* may enforce his right against a contracting party in England (or elsewhere), whether or not he would be so entitled under the domestic law of England[17] (or elsewhere), so long as the defendant was subject to the jurisdiction of the courts of England (or elsewhere), and assuming that that foreign *lex fori* classifies the point as one of substance in contract,[18] that its public policy is not outraged, and that no other conflict rule of its own intervenes.[19]

Actionability in the broader sense, therefore, of whether a cause of action arises between claimant and defender, is a substantive matter for decision by the *lex causae*, as identified by the choice of law rules of the forum, and proved to the forum.

FORM OF ACTION

8–04 This is purely a matter of procedure to be decided by the *lex fori*.[20]

TITLE TO SUE/PARTIES

8–05 Title to sue and liability to be sued each contain elements both of the substantive and the procedural; the law governing the right indicates the party who has the right or title to sue and the party who should be called as defender.[21] It is necessary, of course, to comply with the procedural requirements of the

---

[15] Law Reform (Husband and Wife) (Scotland) Act 1984 s.1; and Law Reform (Miscellaneous Provisions) Act 1970 s.1 (England).

[16] Such an immunity was removed from Scots domestic law by the Law Reform (Husband and Wife) Act 1962.

[17] As to which, see Contract (Rights of Third Parties) Act 1999.

[18] See also, e.g. *Re Bonacina* [1912] 2 Ch. 394.

[19] As, for example, where its own conflict rules of contract and property might collide in a "Romalpa" question: see para.17–18, below.

[20] *Hansen v Dixon* (1906) 23 T.L.R. 56; *Phrantzes v Argenti* [1960] 2 Q.B. 19.

[21] cf. *FMC Corp v Russell*, 1999 S.L.T. 99. See Elizabeth B. Crawford, "The Adjective and the Noun: Title and Right to Sue in International Private Law", 2000 Jur. Rev. 347. Also *Maher v Groupama Grand Est* [2009] EWCA Civ 1191.

lex fori; by the (procedural) law of the forum, certain bodies or persons may be immune from suit, or prohibited from suing.[22]

The forum's requirements on occasion may reflect anxieties about the difficulties likely to be encountered in the place of enforcement. Thus in *Brianchon v Occidental Petroleum (Caledonia) Ltd*,[23] it was thought prudent for the Court of Session to appoint a curator *ad litem* to represent the children of a victim of the Piper Alpha North Sea oil platform disaster in litigation in Scotland, where the principal litigant was their mother, in order that no question of conflict of interest should be raised later in the American courts. On the other hand, restrictions imposed by the foreign law upon a party's capacity to sue may be disregarded in Scotland as being local (of application only in the foreign jurisdiction), or penal.[24]

Unusual situations may arise, as for example, in *Toprak Enerji Sanayi AS v Sale Tilney Technology Plc*,[25] in which the plaintiff foreign company ceased to exist during the course of the proceedings. In *Bumper Development Corp v Commissioner of Police of the Metropolis*,[26] the Court of Appeal recognised, in accordance with the principle of comity of nations, the title to sue of a Hindu temple which had legal personality under its *lex situs*. Novelty was no objection since the matter remained within the discretion and power of the forum.

Certain cases may require special consideration: assignees,[27] foreign *tutrix* or "next friend",[28] ministerial representatives of foreign sovereign,[29] partnerships and companies.[30]

RULES OF PRESCRIPTION AND LIMITATION OF ACTIONS

Prescription

From a conflict of laws standpoint, the important distinction is between those **8–06** rules concerning the effect of lapse of time which extinguish the right (rules of prescription), and those which merely bar the remedy (rules of limitation).[31]

An early illustration is provided by *Huber v Steiner*[32] in which the English court interpreted the rule of the French *Code de Commerce* (that actions on promissory notes "prescribe themselves" after five years, reckoning from the day of protest if there had been no judgment or acknowledgment of the debt in that period), as no more than a limitation of the remedy and not an

---

[22] See Ch.7, above.
[23] 1990 S.L.T. 322.
[24] *Bernaben and Co v Hutchison* (1902) 18 Sh. Ct. Rep. 72.
[25] [1994] 3 All E.R. 483. See also *Kamouh v Associated Electrical Industries International Ltd* [1980] 1 Q.B. 199.
[26] [1991] 4 All E.R. 638.
[27] *Tayler v Scott* (1847) 9 D. 1504; *O'Callaghan v Thomond* (1810) 3 Taunt. 82.
[28] *Jones v Somervell's Trustees*, 1907 S.C. 545.
[29] *Yzquierdo v Clydebank Engineering and Shipbuilding Co Ltd* (1902) 4 F. (H.L.) 31.
[30] *Muir v Collett* (1862) 24 D. 1119; *Von Hellfeld v Rechnitzer* [1914] 1 Ch. 748; *Etablissement Baudelot v RS Graham & Co* [1953] 2 Q.B. 271; *Bullock v Caird* (1875) L.R. 10 Q.B. 276; and *General Steam Navigation Co v Guillou* (1843) 11 M. & W. 877.
[31] *Westminster Bank v McDonald*, 1955 S.L.T. (Notes) 73; and *Rodriguez v Parker* [1967] 1 Q.B. 116.
[32] (1835) 2 Bing. N.C. 202, Tindal C.J.; also [1835–42] All E.R. 159.

extinction of the contract, and therefore concluded that the enforceability of the French contract in England was governed by the limitation rule of the *lex fori*.[33]

In Scots domestic law, the rules on prescription were rationalised by the Prescription and Limitation (Scotland) Act 1973, as amended by the Prescription and Limitation (Scotland) Act 1984 s.4.[34] The choice of law rule contained in s.23A requires the Scots forum to apply, subject to public policy,[35] any relevant rules upon extinction of obligations of the *lex causae*, in preference to domestic rules of the *lex fori*.

Section 23A of the 1984 Act in turn was amended to take account of the European harmonisation instruments in the law of obligations. Section 23A(4) provides that that section shall not apply in any case where the law of a country other than Scotland falls to be applied by virtue of any choice of law rule contained in the Rome I (contractual obligations)[36] or Rome II (non-contractual obligations)[37] Regulations.[38] No change, however, is substantively effected because the relevant rules in the Rome I and Rome II Regulations[39] are to the effect that the rules of prescription and limitation of actions are subsumed under the scope (remit) of the law applicable per the Regulation, and governed therefore by the *lex causae*, subject as at common law to the public policy of the forum.[40]

Classification, therefore, in a conflict of laws case in the law of obligations, is effected by the Rome I and Rome II Regulations, so as to place the matter into the substantive category. It should be noted, however, that the 1973 Act for Scotland, unlike its English counterpart, the Foreign Limitation Periods Act 1984, is limited to "obligations" and does not include "property rights".[41] Clearly, the Rome I and Rome II Regulations concern contractual and non-contractual obligations. Equally clearly, the contractual and the proprietary may be commixed in any question. With regard to property questions, from a Scottish domestic perspective, the classification, so far as it continues to be relevant, appears to be as follows:

---

[33] Contrast the modern position under Foreign Limitation Periods Act 1984 (England and Wales) and Prescription and Limitation (Scotland) Act 1973, as amended.

[34] Inserting into the 1973 Act s.23A.

[35] cf. In England *OJSC Oil Co Yugraneft v Abramovich* [2008] EWHC 2613 (Comm); and *Harley v Smith* [2010] EWCA Civ 78.

[36] See also the Law Applicable to Contractual Obligations (Scotland) Regulations 2009 (SSI 2009/410); Ch.15, below. For England, Foreign Limitation Periods Act 1984 s.8, modified by the Law Applicable to Contractual Obligations (England and Wales and Northern Ireland) Regulations 2009 (SI 2009/3064).

[37] See also the Law Applicable to Non-contractual Obligations (Scotland) Regulations 2008 (SSI 2008/404); Ch.16, below. For England, Foreign Limitation Periods Act 1984 s.8, added by the Law Applicable to Non-Contractual Obligations (England and Wales and Northern Ireland) Regulations 2008 (SI 2008/2986).

[38] See tentative discussion of European harmonisation of foreign limitation periods in EU Commission Consultation Paper on the Compensation of Victims of Cross-border Road Traffic Accidents in the European Union (MARKT/H2/RM markt.h.2 (2009) 61541).

[39] Rome I Regulation art.12.1(d); Rome II Regulation art.15(h).

[40] Rome I Regulation art.21; Rome II Regulation art.26.

[41] See Carruthers, *Transfer of Property in the Conflict of Laws*, 2005, para.8.55. Also David M. Walker, *The Law of Prescription and Limitation of Actions in Scotland*, 6th edn (Edinburgh: W. Green, 2002).

Positive prescription

This involves acquisition of title to, or interest in, property (usually land) **8–07**
and is a matter of substance governed by the *lex situs*.[42]

Negative prescription[43]

The long negative prescription extinguishes an obligation. Hence, it is a **8–08**
matter of substance and is governed by the proper law of the right. The 1973
Act replaced a variety of earlier short prescriptions with a short negative
prescription which, being substantive in nature, will apply where the *lex
causae* is Scots.

Limitation

At common law, the nature of the limitation had to be ascertained by the **8–09**
forum by referring to the (foreign) statute or rule in question to find out
whether it affected the substance (and therefore the existence of the right) no
matter where a party might seek to vindicate it, or whether it was merely a rule
of procedure, effective only within the territory covered by the statute in question.[44] However, as noted above, since the coming into effect of the
Prescription and Limitation (Scotland) Act 1984, the matter has been governed
by statute, as amended, as explained above,[45] and assigned to the category of
the substantive, insofar at least as concerns obligations.

CITATION AND SERVICE OF WRITS

Service of documents within the EU

Service of documents within the EU is governed by Regulation 1393/2007 **8–10**
on the service in the Member States of judicial and extrajudicial documents in
civil or commercial matters (service of documents), and repealing Regulation
1348/2000.[46] The aim of Regulation 1348/2000 was to improve efficiency
and speed in the transmission of such documents, in order to aid the proper
functioning of the internal market. Following a study upon implementation
of that instrument,[47] the Commission adopted a Report on the application

---

[42] See Carruthers, *Transfer of Property in the Conflict of Laws*, 2005, paras 8.52–8.66.
[43] *Alexander v Badenoch* (1843) 6 D. 322; *Low v Low* (1893) 1 S.L.T. 43; *Re Low* [1894] 1 Ch.
147; *Higgins v Ewing's Trustees*, 1925 S.C. 440; and *Stirling's Trustees v Legal & General
Assurance Society Ltd*, 1957 S.L.T. 73.
[44] *Huber v Steiner* (1835) 2 Bing. N.C. 202; *British Linen Co v Drummond* (1830) 10 B.C. 903;
Don v Lippmann (1837) 2 Sh. & Macl. 682; *Harris v Quine* (1869) L.R. 4 Q.B. 653; *Goodman
v LNWR* (1877) 15 S.L.R. 449; *McElroy v McAllister*, 1949 S.C. 110.
[45] Foreign Limitation Periods Act 1984 (England) and Prescription and Limitation (Scotland) Act
1984, as amended.
[46] In accordance with art.3.2 of EC-Denmark Agreement, Denmark, by letter of November 20,
2007, notified the Commission of its decision to implement Regulation 1393/2007. In accordance with art.3.6 of the Agreement, the Danish notification creates mutual obligations between
Denmark and the EC. Regulation 1393/2007 is considered to be annexed to the EC-Denmark
Agreement [2008] OJ L331/21.
[47] Study on Application of Council Regulation (EC) No 1348/2000 (FINAL REPORT – 1348 –
B5 – 03052204, May 2004).

thereof,[48] concluding that while Regulation 1348/2000 generally had improved the transmission and service of documents between Member States, nevertheless the application of certain provisions was not fully satisfactory.[49] Following consultation, a revised proposal was issued, and the resulting instrument is Regulation 1393/2007, which applies from November 13, 2008. The Regulation takes precedence over the 1965 Hague Convention on the Service Abroad of Judicial and Extra-Judicial Documents in Civil and Commercial Matters, to which the UK is a party.[50]

In terms of the Regulation, the transmission of documents is effected directly between "local bodies" (termed the transmitting and receiving agencies), rather than through the medium of "central bodies", as provided in the 1965 Convention. While in Scotland the central body is the Constitution, Law and Courts Directorate of the EU and International Law Branch of the Scottish Government, the transmitting agencies (i.e. local bodies) are the messengers-at-arms.[51] The central body shall supply information and assist the transmitting agencies.

The document to be transmitted must have appended to it a form completed in the language of the Member State addressed, or in another language indicated by that Member State to be acceptable.[52] The use of all appropriate means of transmission are permitted,[53] provided that the content of the document received is true and faithful to that of the document forwarded, and that all information in it is legible. The receiving agency (which must send a receipt within seven days to the transmitting agency)[54] will serve, or have served, the document in accordance with the law of the Member State addressed, or by a particular form requested by the transmitting agency, unless such a method is incompatible with the law of that Member State.[55] The receiving agency shall take all necessary steps to effect the service of the document as soon as possible, and in any event within one month of receipt.[56] The receiving agency must inform the addressee that s/he may refuse to accept the document if it is in a language other than the official language of the Member State addressed, or a language of the transmitting state which the addressee understands.[57] When service has been effected, a certificate of completion will be sent to the transmitting agency.[58] If it does not prove possible to effect service within one month of receipt, the receiving agency shall inform the transmitting agency by means of a standard form certificate.[59]

---

[48] Report on the application of Regulation 1348/2000 on the service in the Member States of judicial and extrajudicial documents in civil or commercial matters COM(2004) 603 final.

[49] Regulation 1393/2007 recital (5).

[50] See recital (23) and art.20.

[51] Information communicated by Member States under Article 23 of Regulation (EC) No 1393/2007 of the European Parliament and of the Council of 13 November 2007 on the service in the Member States of judicial and extrajudicial documents in civil or commercial matters (service of documents), and repealing Council Regulation (EC) No 1348/2000 (*http:ec.europa.eu/justice_home/judicialatlascivil/html/pdf/vers_consolide_en_1393.pdf* [Accessed July 3, 2010]).

[52] See art.4.3.

[53] See art.4.2.

[54] See art.6.1.

[55] See art.7.1.

[56] See art.7.2.

[57] See art.5; see also art.8.

[58] See art.10.

[59] See art.7.2(a).

The date of service shall be the date on which it is served in accordance with the law of the Member State addressed.[60] However, where a document must be served within a particular period the date to be taken into account with respect to the applicant shall be that fixed by the law of that Member State.[61]

Other means of service remain competent: by consular or diplomatic channels,[62] post,[63] or direct service through the judicial officers, officials or other competent persons of the Member State addressed.[64]

Where a writ of summons has been transmitted under the provisions of the Regulation, and the defendant has not appeared, judgment shall not be given until it is established that the document was served by a method prescribed by the internal law of the Member State addressed for the service of documents in domestic actions upon persons within its territory; or the document was actually delivered to the defendant, or to his residence, by another method provided for by the Regulation; and that in either case, service or delivery was effected in sufficient time to enable the defendant to defend.[65] However, each Member State shall be free to make it known to the Commission that the judge, notwithstanding art.19.1, may give judgment, even if no certificate of service or delivery has been received, if three conditions have been fulfilled, namely: (a) the document was transmitted by one of the methods provided for in the Regulation; (b) a period of not less than six months, considered adequate by the judge in the particular case, has elapsed since the date of the transmission; and (c) no certificate of any kind has been received, even though every reasonable effort has been made to obtain it through the competent authorities of the Member State addressed.[66]

Extrajudicial documents may be transmitted for service in another Member State in accordance with the Regulation.[67]

Service of documents outside the EU

As regards service of documents in non-EU states, citation "furth of **8–11** Scotland" is governed by the Rules of Court,[68] assuming that the method of service does not contravene the local law or contradict the 1965 Hague Convention, where applicable.

---

[60] See art.9.1.

[61] See art.9.2.

[62] See arts 12, 13.

[63] See art.14. The Regulation does not establish any hierarchy between the method of transmission and service under arts 4–11 and that in art.14. It is therefore possible to serve a judicial document by one or other or both of those methods: *Plumex v Young Sports NV* (C473/04) [2006] E.C.R. I-1417 ECJ.

[64] See art.15.

[65] See art.19.1.

[66] See art.19.2. See also art.19.4 concerning expiry of time for appeal after non-appearance by the defendant. Consider also the inevitable interrelationship between the detail of Regulation 1393/2007, and the Brussels I Regulation art.34.2 (defence to enforcement on grounds of natural justice).

[67] See art.16.

[68] See Act of Sederunt (Rules of the Court of Session 1994) 1994 (SI 1994/1443) r.16.2 (service furth of UK) and r.16.2A (service under the EC Service Regulation). For rules concerning service, intimation and diligence generally, see RCS Ch.16. For sheriff court actions, see Act of Sederunt (Sheriff Court Ordinary Cause Rules) 1993 (SI 1993/1956) r.5.5 (service on persons furth of Scotland), as amended.

EVIDENCE

8–12 All questions as to the requirements, extent and sufficiency of evidence are determined by the *lex fori* alone, irrespective of the governing law of the matter.

Article 18.2 of the Rome I Regulation, and art.22.2 of the Rome II Regulation, which are in the same terms, mutatis mutandis, provide that a contract or an act[69] intended to have legal effect may be proved by any mode of proof recognised by the law of the forum, or by any of the laws identified by either instrument to govern issues of formal validity[70] under which that contract or act is formally valid, provided such mode of proof can be administered by the forum.

As noted above, the province of the governing law extends to all matters which involve substance rather than procedure. A distinction must be drawn between "the facts to be proved" (determined by the *lex causae*) and "the proof of the facts" (governed by the *lex fori*).[71]

The "whole point" of an evidential rule was said in *Fuld (No.3)*[72] to be one "concerned with the approach required of the court to the evidence submitted for its consideration".

In *Immanuel v Denholm and Co*[73] the question for the Scots court was whether the information contained in a bill of lading pertaining to a contract with a Danish proper law was conclusive on this matter, a point on which the *lex causae* and the *lex fori* differed. Since that point was classified by the forum as one of evidence, the Scots rule prevailed. There are many other cases which illustrate the rule.[74]

The following are particular aspects of the rule, the question in each case being whether the point truly involves substance or procedure[75]:

> (a) the *lex fori* determines whether or not a document is admissible in evidence, irrespective of whether or not it may be so under any other law[76];
>
> (b) the *lex fori* determines whether extrinsic evidence will be allowed with a view to varying the terms of a contract, irrespective of the governing law, but its admissibility to interpret the terms of a contract is determined by the proper/applicable law of the contract[77];
>
> (c) at common law, proof of a death abroad was a matter of fact to be decided by the *lex fori*,[78] but in terms of the Presumption of Death

---

[69] Falling, respectively, within the scope of the Rome I or Rome II Regulation.

[70] Rome I Regulation art.11; Rome II Regulation art.21.

[71] *The Gaetano and Maria* (1882) L.R. 7 P.D. 137: "Now the manner of proving the facts is matter of evidence, and, to my mind, is matter of procedure, but the facts to be proved are not matters of procedure; they are the matters with which the procedure has to deal", per Brett L.J. at 144.

[72] [1968] P. 675, per Scarman J. at 697.

[73] (1887) 15 R. 152.

[74] *Leroux v Brown* (1852) 12 C.B. 801; *Bain v Whitehaven and Furness Junction Railway Co* (1850) 3 H.L. 1; *Bristow v Sequeville* (1850) 5 Ex. 275; *Mahadervan v Mahadervan* [1964] P. 233; *Fuld (No.3)* [1968] P. 675; and *Caltex Singapore Pte Ltd v BP Shipping Ltd* [1996] 1 Lloyd's Rep. 286.

[75] cf. *Mahadervan* [1964] P. 233.

[76] cf. *Henaff v Henaff* [1966] 1 W.L.R. 598.

[77] cf. At common law *Thomson* (1917) 33 Sh. Ct. Rep. 84. See now Rome I Regulation art.12.1(a).

[78] *Simpson's Trustees v Fox*, 1951 S.L.T. 412. See also *In the Goods of Spenceley* [1892] P.255; *Re Schulhof* [1948] P. 66; *In the Estate of Arthur Dowds* [1948] P. 256; and *Kamouh v AEI International* [1980] 1 Q.B. 199.

(Scotland) Act 1977 s.10, where a foreign judgment of presumed death emanates from a court in a foreign country in which the person was domiciled or habitually resident on the date when he was last known to be alive, this raises a (rebuttable) presumption of death.

Professional conduct investigation/disciplinary procedure in respect of the medical profession has been held by the Privy Council[79] to be governed by English law (even though in the case in question the disciplinary committee sat in Glasgow), with the aim of having a single set of rules of evidence no matter where the committee might sit.[80] Similarly, British Army discipline by court-martial, wherever held, is governed by specialised UK rules.[81]

TAKING OF EVIDENCE ABROAD

(i) Taking of evidence within the EU

The matter is regulated by Regulation 1206/2001 on cooperation between **8–13** the courts of the Member States in the taking of evidence in civil or commercial matters. Regulation 1206/2001 entered into force on July 1, 2001,[82] creating a new system for the rapid transmission and execution of requests for the taking of evidence between Member State courts (except Denmark) and laying down precise criteria as to the form and content of such requests. The Regulation applies in civil and commercial cases where a court of a Member State requests the competent court of another Member State to obtain evidence, or asks to take evidence directly in another Member State.[83] A list of such courts competent for the purpose must be drawn up by each Member State. A request shall not be made to obtain evidence which is not intended for use in judicial proceedings, commenced or contemplated.[84]

As an aid to the working of the new scheme, Member States shall designate a "central body".

(a) Taking of evidence by request[85]

Where evidence is to be taken by request, the request must be made using a **8–14** specific form[86] and must contain certain specific details such as details of the

---

[79] *McAllister v General Medical Council* [1993] 2 W.L.R. 308 PC.
[80] cf. *Prescription Pricing Authority v Ferguson*, 2005 S.L.T. 63, concerning the jurisdiction of an industrial tribunal.
[81] Army Act 1955, as amended: see *R. v Martin (Alan)* [1998] 1 All E.R. 193.
[82] See Report on the Application of Regulation 1206/2001 on cooperation between the courts of Member States in the taking of evidence in civil or commercial matters COM(2007) 769 final. The Report concluded that Regulation 1206/2001 has achieved, to a satisfactory extent, its two main objectives, viz. simplification of co-operation between Member States, and acceleration of the performance of taking evidence; and that accordingly, no modfications of the Regulation are required (para.3). See, however, Resolution 2008/2180(INI) on cooperation between the courts of the Member States in the taking of evidence in civil or commercial matters [2010] OJ C87E/21.
[83] *Dendron GmbH v University of California* [2004] I.L.Pr. 35.
[84] See art.1.2.
[85] See Ch.II sections 1–3.
[86] See art.4.

parties, and the nature of the case. The request and all documents accompanying it shall be exempted from authentication or any equivalent formality.[87] The request must be presented in one of the official languages of the Member State requested, or in another language indicated by that state to be acceptable.[88] It is an aim of the new legislation that the taking of evidence should be done without delay. If it is not possible for the request to be executed by the requested court within 90 days of receipt of the request, the requested court should inform the requesting court, stating reasons. Representatives of the requesting court and of the parties may be physically present at the taking of evidence, but if this is not possible, aids such as video conferencing may be used to permit their participation.

Communications pursuant to the Regulation shall be transmitted by the swiftest possible means, and may be carried out by any appropriate means provided that the document received accurately reflects the content of the document forwarded, and that all information in it is legible.[89]

Within seven days of receipt of the request, the requested competent court shall send by means of a particular form, an acknowledgment of receipt to the requesting court.[90] Where the request does not fall within the jurisdiction of the court to which it was transmitted, the latter shall forward the request to the competent court of its Member State, and shall inform the requesting court.[91] If the request cannot be executed because it does not contain all information required by art.4, the requested court shall inform the requesting court thereof without delay, and at the latest within 30 days of receipt, using a particular form, and shall request it to send the missing information.[92] Similarly, if a request cannot be executed because a deposit or advance is necessary, the requested court shall inform the requesting court without delay, and at the latest within 30 days of receipt, using a particular form and informing the requesting court how the deposit or advance should be made.[93] With regard to the time limit (of execution of the request without delay and at the latest within 90 days of receipt) contained in art.10, such time limit shall begin to run when the requested court receives the request duly completed.[94] The requested court shall execute the request in accordance with the law of its Member State, although if the requesting court calls for execution in accordance with a special procedure provided for by the law of its Member State, the requested court shall comply unless this procedure is incompatible with its law, or would raise major practical difficulties.[95]

The requesting court may ask the requested court to use communications technology at the taking of evidence, in particular by using video conferencing and tele-conferencing.[96]

---

[87] See art.4.2.
[88] See art.5.
[89] See art.6.
[90] See art.7.1.
[91] See art.7.2.
[92] See art.8.1.
[93] See art.18.
[94] See art.9.
[95] See art.10.2, 10.3.
[96] See art.10.4

If, by the law of the requesting court, the parties and their representatives have the right to be present at the taking of evidence this shall be facilitated by the requested court.[97] If it is compatible with the law of the requesting court, representatives of the requesting court (including judicial personnel or experts), have the right to be present at the taking of evidence. If participation of such representatives is requested by the requesting court, the conditions under which such participation may take place shall be determined by the requested court.[98] Where necessary in executing a request, the requested court shall apply the appropriate coercive measures to the extent provided for by its law.[99]

With regard to refusal to give evidence, the Regulation provides in art.14 that the request for the hearing of a person shall not be executed where s/he claims the right to refuse to give evidence, or to be prohibited from giving evidence, under the law of the requested court, or under the law of the requesting court (subject to confirmation by the requesting court).

The execution of a request may be refused by the requested court only in exceptional circumstances, namely[100]:

(a) the request does not fall within the scope of the Regulation; or
(b) under the law of the requested court the execution of the request does not fall within the function of the judiciary; or
(c) the requesting court does not comply within 30 days with the request by the requested court to complete the request pursuant to art.8; or
(d) a deposit or advance asked for in accordance with art.18.3 has not been made within 60 days.[101]

Importantly, art.14.3 provides that execution may not be refused by the requested court solely on the ground that under the law of its Member State a court of that state has exclusive jurisdiction over the subject matter of the action, or that the law of that Member State would not admit the right of action on it.[102] If execution of the request is refused on any of the grounds in art.14.2, the requested court shall notify the requesting court thereof within 60 days of receipt.[103]

In terms of art.16, the requested court shall send without delay to the requesting court the documents establishing the execution of the request, and where appropriate return documents received.

---

[97] See art.11.
[98] See art.12.4.
[99] See art.13.
[100] See art.14.2.
[101] Article 18 concerns costs: the execution of the request shall not give rise to a claim for any reimbursement of taxes or costs. However, the requested court may require that the requesting court ensure the reimbursement without delay of experts' and interpreters' fees, and costs associated with special procedures used, including use of communications technology. Where expert opinion is required, the requested court may, before executing the request, ask the requesting court for an adequate deposit or advance towards costs. But in other cases, a deposit or advance shall not be a condition for the execution of a request, though a deposit or advance shall be made by the parties if that is a provision of the law of the requesting court.
[102] Note the subservient position of the requested court in this regard.
[103] See art.15.

8–15 *(b) Direct taking of evidence*[104]

Where a court requests to take evidence directly in another Member State, it shall submit a request to the central body, or competent authority.[105] Direct taking of evidence may take place only if it can be performed on a voluntary basis without the need for coercive measures, and the requesting court shall inform participating persons that their performance shall take place on a voluntary basis.[106]

The taking of such evidence shall be performed by a member of the judicial personnel, or designated expert, of the requesting court, in accordance with that court's law. The central body of the requested Member State shall advise within 30 days of receipt if the request is accepted, and, if necessary, under what conditions the performance is to be carried out. In particular, the central body may assign a court of its Member State to take part to ensure the proper application of this provision, and compliance with conditions.[107]

The central body may refuse direct taking of evidence only if[108]:

(a) the request does not fall within the scope of the Regulation; or

(b) the request does not contain all the necessary information pursuant to art.4; or

(c) the direct taking of evidence requested is contrary to fundamental principles of law in its Member State.

Without prejudice to the conditions mentioned above, the requesting court shall execute the request in accordance with the law of its Member State.

In terms of art.21, this Regulation shall prevail over bilateral or multilateral agreements, and in particular, over the 1970 Hague Convention on the Taking of Evidence Abroad in Civil or Commercial Matters (to which the UK is a party), in relations between the Member States party thereto.

The operation of the Regulation is to be kept under review by the Commission.

8–16 **(ii) Taking of evidence outside the EU**

As regards taking of evidence from non-EU states, evidence in the form of testimony, or documents[109] or both[110] may be obtained under the authority of, and by complying with the provisions in, the Evidence (Proceedings in Other Jurisdictions) Act 1975, implementing in the UK the 1970 Hague Convention on the Taking of Evidence Abroad in Civil or Commercial Matters. The practical problem is the degree of specification rightly required, but possibly lacking.[111]

---

[104] See Ch.II section 4.
[105] See art.3.
[106] See art.17.2.
[107] See art.17.
[108] See art.17.5.
[109] *Stewart v Callaghan*, 1996 S.L.T. (Sh. Ct.) 12; *Panayiotou v Sony Music Entertainment (UK) Ltd* [1994] 1 All E.R. 755; *Refco Capital Markets Ltd v Credit Suisse First Boston Ltd* [2001] EWCA Civ 1733; and *APA Excelsior v Premiere Technologies Inc* [2002] EWHC 2205 (QB).
[110] *Rio Tinto Zinc Corp v Westinghouse Electric Corp (Nos 1 and 2)* [1978] 1 All E.R. 434; *Boeing Co v PPG Industries* [1988] 3 All E.R. 839; and *Charman v Charman* [2006] 1 W.L.R. 1053.
[111] See *Union Carbide Corp v BP Chemicals Ltd*, 1995 S.L.T. 972.

Under the 1975 Act, the Court of Session, at the instance of a foreign court/tribunal, by "letter of request"[112] may order witnesses in Scotland to give evidence to be remitted abroad to aid foreign litigation.[113] The Extra Division has refused to accede to four incoming letters of request from a Texas court, on the ground that the material sought related to pre-trial discovery which might lead to a line of inquiry ultimately resulting in deposition testimony, and did not relate directly to evidence for use at a trial.[114]

Outside the scope of the EU Regulation, there is precedent for use of video conferencing[115] and the sitting of a Scots court abroad. The former is an acknowledgment of the benefit in suitable cases of advances in technology; the latter is an exceptional event.[116]

PROOF OF FOREIGN LAW[117]

Where foreign law arguably is applicable in a British court, its content **8–17** requires to be pleaded and proved to the court as a matter of fact by the party who seeks to rely upon it. The content of foreign law may be proved, or accepted to have been proved,[118] by the methods of admission on

---

[112] The leading case is *Re Norway's Application (Nos 1 and 2)* [1989] 1 All E.R. 745, in which the House of Lords held, inter alia, that for the process to be initiated under the 1975 Act, the proceedings for which evidence was sought to be gathered must be regarded as concerning a "civil or commercial matter" in the view of both the requesting and the requested court, since there was no internationally acceptable classification. Contrast *Lufttransportunternehmen GmbH & Co KG v Organisation Europeene pour la Securite de la Navigation Aerienne (Eurocontrol)* [1976] E.C.R. 1541, at 1552. See also *Pharaon v Bank of Credit and Commerce International SA (In Liquidation)* [1998] 4 All E.R. 455 as regards limits of disclosure; and *Cambridge Gas Transport Corp v Official Committee of Unsecured Creditors of Navigator Holdings Plc* [2007] 1 A.C. 508.

[113] *Lord Advocate, Petitioner*, 1994 S.L.T. 852 but see *Lord Advocate, Petitioner*, 1998 S.L.T. 835; *Minnesota v Philip Morris Inc* [1998] I.L.Pr. 170 (request refused because terms of letter of request from Minnesota District Court too wide ranging); *Smith v Phillip Morris Companies Inc* [2006] EWHC 916 (QB).

[114] *Lord Advocate, Petitioner*, 1998 S.L.T. 835. Contrast *Lord Advocate, Petitioner*, 1994 S.L.T. 852. And see in England, refusal to accede to letter of request from US District Court of Columbia, on the ground that the width of the questions made the letter oppressive. A balance had to be struck between international co-operation and oppression of witnesses: *First American Corp v Al-Nahyan* [1999] 1 W.L.R. 1154.

[115] As to which in English law, see *R. v Horseferry Road Magistrates' Court Ex p. Bennet (No. 3)*, *The Times*, January 14, 1994; *R. v Forsyth*, *The Times*, April 8, 1997 CA (evidence from abroad through television link).

[116] e.g. in 1992, when the Court of Session, in recognition of the age and frailty of witnesses, removed to Vilnius, Lithuania in order to hear a trial of alleged war crimes. More recently the Scots High Court removed to Camp Zeist in the Netherlands for the purposes of the Lockerbie trial, the territory being deemed part of Scotland for the purposes of the trial; cf. *Peer International Corp v Termidor Music Publishers Ltd (No.3)* [2005] EWHC 1048.

[117] See generally, Fentiman, *International Commercial Litigation*, 2010; Fentiman, *Foreign Law in English Courts*, 1998; Sofie Geeroms, *Foreign Law in Civil Litigation: A Comparative and Functional Analysis* (Oxford: Oxford University Press, 2004); T.C. Hartley, "Pleading and Proof of Foreign Law: The Major European Systems Compared" (1996) 45 I.C.L.Q. 271; and B.J. Rodger and J. van Doorn, "Proof of Foreign Law: The Impact of the London Convention" (1997) 46 I.C.L.Q. 151.

[118] See, for England and Wales only, s.4(2) of the Civil Evidence Act 1972, which provides that where any question as to the law of any country outside the UK, or of any part of the UK other than England and Wales, with respect to any matter, has been determined in any English proceedings which have been reported or recorded in citable form, that determination shall be admissible in evidence for the purpose of proving the law of that country, unless the contrary is proved.

record[119]; submission of expert evidence, usually delivered orally to the court[120]; or remit to a foreign court or foreign lawyer for an opinion.[121] Copies of Acts of Parliament of a "British possession" may be received in evidence without further procedure in terms of the Evidence (Colonial Statutes) Act 1907. A case may be stated to a foreign court of the Commonwealth under the British Law Ascertainment Act 1859. Finally, a request for information may be made under the 1968 European Convention on Information on Foreign Law ("London Convention"). Though the UK has ratified the London Convention, it has never been implemented in primary legislation, nor have there been any ensuing UK rules concerning court practice thereunder. According to Fentiman,[122] resort to the Convention is unlikely and may even be pointless, for it does not eliminate the need for expert evidence to be submitted, and even if an opinion is received, its content will not take into account the circumstances of the individual case, and may introduce a degree of unreality into its determination. Moreover, the Convention's procedures may serve to increase the cost, complexity and duration of proceedings in the UK.

By way of exception, a foreign law may be so notorious that a judge is entitled to take "judicial notice" of it[123]; for example, the fact that roulette is not unlawful in Monte Carlo.[124] Likewise, although an unusual occurrence, the court may take judicial notice of foreign law if legislation so provides.[125] In particular, a Scots court may be required by legislation to take judicial notice of a provision of English law. The UK Supreme Court, whatever its composition in a particular case, has knowledge of each and every one of the laws of the constituent jurisdictions in the UK,[126] and must develop them.[127] Hence, the Supreme Court, when dealing with the law of another part of the UK, has judicial notice of that law; that which was required to be proved as a matter of

---

[119] *Black v Black's Trustees*, 1950 S.L.T. (Notes) 32.
[120] The Civil Evidence Act 1972 s.4(1) declares that a person who is suitably qualified on account of his knowledge or experience is competent to give expert evidence as to the law of any country outside the UK, or of any part of the UK other than England and Wales, irrespective of whether he has acted or is entitled to act as a legal practitioner there. In Scots law, there is no statutory equivalent to the 1972 Act. The question of who is competent to act as an expert witness rests on the common law, and is context-dependent. The qualification of the expert witness to testify to the point in issue is a matter for the judge's discretion in each individual case. For further details, see *Cheshire, North and Fawcett: Private International Law*, 14th edn, 2008, pp.115, 116.
[121] *Welsh v Milne* (1844) 7 D.213; a more modern and specific instance is provided by art.15 of the 1980 Hague Convention on the Civil Aspects of International Child Abduction, which permits the judicial or administrative authorities of a Contracting State, prior to the making of an order for the return of the child, to request that the applicant obtain from the authorities of the state of the child's habitual residence a decision that his removal or retention was wrongful within the meaning of art.3: *Re D (A Child) (Abduction: Rights of Custody)* [2007] 1 A.C. 619 HL.
[122] Fentiman, *International Commercial Litigation*, 2010, p.243. See also Rodger and van Doorn, "Proof of Foreign Law: The Impact of the London Convention" (1997) 46 I.C.L.Q. 151, 151.
[123] i.e. acceptance of evidence without proof. Although, in the adversarial system, a court cannot find as a fact that which has not been proved, judicial notice allows a court to declare that a fact exists even though it has not been established by evidence. See Fiona Raitt, *Evidence: Principles, Policy and Practice* (Edinburgh: W. Green, 2008), para.14–02.
[124] *Saxby v Fulton* [1909] 2 K.B. 208 at 211.
[125] e.g. Maintenance Orders Act 1950 s.22(2).
[126] *Elliot v Joicey*, 1935 S.C. (H.L.) 57, per Lord MacMillan. at 68.
[127] *Bank of East Asia Ltd v Scottish Enterprise*, 1997 S.L.T. 1213.

fact during the course of the litigation becomes a matter of law in the Supreme Court. In addition, all UK judges must take judicial notice of certain matters of European law. Section 3 of the European Communities Act 1972, as amended, provides as follows:

"3. Decisions on, and proof of, Treaties and EU instruments etc.

(1) For the purposes of all legal proceedings any question as to the meaning or effect of any of the Treaties, or as to the validity, meaning or effect of any EU instrument, shall be treated as a question of law (and, if not referred to the European Court, be for determination as such in accordance with the principles laid down by and any relevant decision of the European Court).

(2) Judicial notice shall be taken of the Treaties, of the Official Journal of the European Union and of any decision of, or expression of opinion by, the European Court on any such question as aforesaid; and the Official Journal shall be admissible as evidence of any instrument or other act thereby communicated of the EU or of any EU institution.

(3) Evidence of any instrument issued by a EU institution, including any judgment or order of the European Court, or of any document in the custody of a EU institution, or any entry in or extract from such a document, may be given in any legal proceedings by production of a copy certified as a true copy by an official of that institution; and any document purporting to be such a copy shall be received in evidence without proof of the official position or handwriting of the person signing the certificate."

In the event of failure of proof of foreign law by any of the permitted methods, there is a presumption in the UK that the law of a foreign country is the same as the *lex fori*; or, alternatively, it may be said, that on failure of proof of foreign law, the *lex fori* applies by default[128]—and the onus is on a person who maintains otherwise to aver the foreign law and to prove it.[129] If the foreign law is not pleaded and proved to the court's satisfaction, then the court will not have judicial knowledge of that law and will treat the case as a purely domestic one. Not only may the content of a foreign *lex causae* be assumed to be the same as the *lex fori*, through default of proof to the contrary, but also, rarely, an outcome may be based upon an assumption or hypothesis about the content of foreign law, for example, where the point may be said to be incidental to the

---

[128] "In default of proof . . . an English judge still has to adjudicate; and his default position is that he will apply English law, *faute de mieux*": Briggs, *Conflict of Laws*, 2nd edn, 2008, p.6.

[129] *Mostyn v Fabrigas* (1774)1 Coup. 161, per Lord Mansfield, at 174; *Lloyd v Guibert* (1865) L.R. 1 Q.B. 115; *Stuart v Potter, Choate & Prentice*, 1911 1 S.L.T. 377; *Ertel Bieber & Co v Rio Tinto Co Ltd* [1918] A.C. 260. *Naftalin v London Midland & Scottish Railway Co*, 1933 S.C. 259; *Faulkner (Michael Stanislaus) v Hill*, 1942 J.C. 20; *De Reneville v De Reneville* [1948] P. 100; *Pryde v Proctor & Gamble Ltd*, 1971 S.L.T. (Notes) 18; *Bonnor v Balfour Kilpatrick Ltd*, 1975 S.L.T. (Notes) 3; *Rodden v Whatlings Ltd*, 1960 S.L.T. (Notes) 96; *Scottish National Orchestra Society Ltd v Thomson's Executor*, 1969 S.L.T. 325; *Armour v Thyssen Edelstahlwerke AG*, 1989 S.L.T. 182 IH; 1990 S.L.T. 891 HL; *Bumper Development Corp v Commissioner of Police of the Metropolis* [1991] 1 W.L.R. 1362 CA; and *Kraus's Administrators v Sullivan*, 1998 S.L.T. 963.

main issue.[130] A UK court generally does not take notice of foreign laws; the judge is treated as neither knowing, nor being able to know of his own volition, the content of the foreign law to be applied, and cannot investigate and apply foreign law *ex officio*.

While Scots judges have judicial knowledge of Scots law, and English judges of English law, including their conflict rules, a court cannot of its own initiative, therefore, order a proof of the content of foreign law. Hence although the court will apply the appropriate choice of law rule (even if the parties fail to plead it), in the absence of proof of foreign law, operation of the choice of law rule of the forum effectively will be frustrated. Accordingly, this approach in Scots and English law has fundamental implications for the conduct of litigation in UK courts; by inadvertence, negligence or tacit consent between the adversaries, the conflict of laws dimension of a case may be lost. But it has to be said that the subject, as a body of law, does not seem to have been impoverished.

Yet proof of foreign law must be regarded as a matter of fact of a peculiar kind in English and Scots courts.[131] In the UK, an appellate court always is slow to interfere with a trial court's finding of fact; but where an appeal principally or subsidiarily involves a point of foreign law, the superior court is less reluctant to revisit that issue of fact.[132] Thus, when the content of the foreign law becomes the subject of an appeal to a higher court, it is treated not merely as a question of fact, but is reviewed in much the same way as if it were an issue of law.[133] However, the appeal court cannot ascertain the foreign law *ex officio* by initiating an investigation *de novo*; rather, all it can do is to review the expert evidence submitted to the lower court, and make its own assessment of whether the foreign law has been proved adequately, and which version, if any, of the foreign law it prefers.

The civilian-based practice in European countries varies, but generally stands in contrast to the UK approach. But even where the foreign law is sought to be "proved", by any method, whether initiated by the parties, or one of them, *ex officio* by the judge, or by the judge assisted by the litigants, it should not be supposed that a forum proceeds always on an accurate understanding of its content.

Role of the parties in the matter of proof of foreign law

8–18   The UK position is that the party who wishes to rely on the point of foreign law should bear the onus of pleading and proving its content. Currently in the

---

[130] See, e.g. *Duhur-Johnson v Duhur-Johnson* [2005] 2 F.L.R. 1042 (despite absence of evidence that the divorce obtained by the husband was effective by the law of Nigeria, the English court assumed, for the purposes of the application for a stay of English proceedings, that the requirements of the Family Law Act 1986 s.46(1) had been met, and that the divorce was effective by Nigerian law).

[131] *Parkasho v Singh* [1968] P. 233, per Cairns J. at 246.

[132] *Parkasho v Singh* [1968] P. 233 at 250; *Dalmia Dairy Industries v National Bank of Pakistan* [1978] 2 Lloyd's Rep. 223 CA at 286; *Att Gen of New Zealand v Ortiz* [1984] A.C. 1; *The Saudi Prince (No.2)* [1988] 1 Lloyd's Rep. 1 CA at 3; *Bumper Development Corp v Commissioner of Police of the Metropolis* [1991] 1 W.L.R. 1362 CA at 1368; and *Grupo Torras SA v Al-Sabah (No.1)* [1996] 1 Lloyd's Rep. 7 CA at 18. See Geeroms, *Foreign Law in Civil Litigation*, 2004, paras 4.49–4.54, 5.68–5.87.

[133] *Macmillan Inc v Bishopsgate Investment Trust Plc (No.4)* [1999] C.L.C. 417. See Fentiman, *Foreign Law in English Courts*, 1998, pp.201, 202.

UK, pleading foreign law is voluntary. The principle of party autonomy is influential, but in this context it stems from UK (domestic) adversarial procedure, and not from its sanction in an EU instrument, of jurisdiction[134] or choice of law.[135] Some would say it operates as a covert choice of law (even a *fraudem legis*), through passivity, ignorance, or complicity of litigants, colluded in, in effect, by the judge, perforce of the system, and to be viewed, therefore, as an excessive use of party autonomy. In mitigation, it may be that parties' conduct is motivated by a desire to reduce expense, and in that and other ways, their expectations may be met by application of domestic law. Moreover, sometimes it may be said that raising the conflict of laws issue is not worthwhile.[136]

Where a party seeks to rely on foreign law, a "best endeavours" approach may be said to apply. If the parties can agree on the content of foreign law,[137] that is a resolution which a UK judge will accept. The burden of proof of asserting foreign law lies on the party(ies) seeking to rely on it.[138] Within the limits of honesty,[139] a party may take advantage of errors or weaknesses or lacunae in the pleadings of the other party in the particular of proof of foreign law, as in any other matter.

There is no obligation of co-operation between parties (for their interests are opposed), or between judge and parties.

Role of the judge in the matter of proof of foreign law

The judge's role is that of umpire, not investigator. The foreign law must be **8–19** pleaded and proved to the court's satisfaction before the court can apply it.[140] The judge is not entitled to, "search for himself into the sources of knowledge from which the witnesses have drawn, and produce for himself the fact which is required to be proved as a part of the case before him."[141] There is no tradition, therefore, of the UK judge applying foreign law *ex officio*. The principle of *iura novit curia* is not applicable in the UK in the case of foreign law. The role of the judge with regard to the proof of foreign law is, in general, largely passive, but, in a litigation having conflict of laws potential, s/he is not *entirely* neutral or without function, for it is the task of the judge to identify the applicable law according to the pleadings and, having done so, to

---

[134] e.g. Brussels I Regulation art.23.

[135] e.g. Rome I Regulation art.3; Rome II Regulation art.14.

[136] e.g. in forced marriage cases, in which, though the parties are of Muslim religion and Pakistani culture, they are at least second generation UK residents, making judicial consideration of their domicile profitless, the likelihood being that their personal law(s) coincide(s) with the law of the forum: *Mahmood v Mahmood*, 1993 S.L.T. 589; *Mahmud v Mahmud*, 1994 S.L.T. 599; *Singh v Singh*, 1998 S.C. 68.

[137] *Beatty v Beatty* [1924] 1 K.B. 807; *Iran v Barakat Galleries Ltd* [2007] EWHC 705; *Iran v Berend* [2007] EWHC 132 (QB).

[138] *Brown v Gracey* (1821) Dow & Ry N.P. 41; *Schapiro v Schapiro* [1904] T.S. 673; *Ertel Bieber & Co v Rio Tinto Co Ltd* [1918] A.C. 260 HL at 295; *Guaranty Trust Co of New York v Hannay & Co* [1918] 2 K.B. 623 CA at 655; and *Ascherberg, Hopwood & Crew v Casa Musicale Sonzogno* [1971] 1 W.L.R. 173.

[139] *Arrow Nominees Inc v Blackledge* [2000] 2 B.C.L.C 167.

[140] For guidance on the judicial role in this context, see judgment of Purchas L.J. in *Bumper Development Corp v Commissioner of Police of the Metropolis* [1991] 1 W.L.R. 1362. See also *Gotha City v Sotheby's (No.2)* Unreported September 9, 1998 per Moses J.; and *Harley v Smith* [2010] EWCA Civ 78 (it being ultra vires the English judge to interpret Sharia law without hearing evidence).

[141] *Di Sora v Phillipps* (1863) H.L.C. 624, per Lord Chelmsford at 640.

adjudicate upon whether or not the relevant points of the *lex causae* have been sufficiently proved.[142]

Consequences of failure to prove foreign law

8–20   A distinction must be drawn between "gaps" or deficiencies in the parties' proof of the law; and gaps or lacunae in the rules of the applicable law itself for the purpose of determining the instant question. As explained, at present under the UK system, the effect of absence of proof of foreign law, or of proof being incomplete, is that the *lex fori* supplies the lack.[143]

If the litigant provides a seemingly convincing and complete account of the content of the relevant foreign law, the judge will proceed to apply that law as detailed.[144] If, however, either or both litigant(s) fail(s) to provide for the court, in the court's view, a suitably persuasive account, with the result that the judge is uncertain as to content, the forum will assume that the content of the foreign law is the same as its own domestic law.[145] This also will happen if the litigant(s) fail(s) entirely to raise and prove the relevant point.[146]

In respect of the second situation, where the forum finds the foreign *lex causae* to be defective or deficient, the forum should not supplement the foreign *lex causae* with its own domestic law solution/remedies. Parties ought to be on their guard at the pre-litigation stage as to the outcome of application of the applicable law; if it has no domestic right or remedy which suits their needs and purpose, then a party should endeavour to formulate his pleadings/submissions, so as persuade the court that a different law is applicable (i.e. at the choice of law stage, *not* the proof of law stage). If the foreign *lex causae* as a matter of policy is found *not* to contain a particular cause of action or remedy, which happens, however, to exist in the law of the forum, it would not be right for the forum to interpone the cause of action/remedy of the *lex fori*, for that would amount, in effect, to non-application or contradiction of the *lex causae*, an outcome which is not justified except under the head of public policy. This situation must be distinguished sharply from the situation where proof fails and the *lex fori* applies by default.

---

[142] The approach taken by Scarman J. in *Fuld (No.3)* [1968] P. 675 at 700–703 was commended by Purchas L.J. in *Bumper Development Corp*.

[143] *Faulkner v Hill*, 1942 J.C. 20; *Stafford Allen & Sons Ltd v Pacific Steam Navigation Co* [1956] 1 Lloyd's Rep. 104; [1956] 1 Lloyd's Rep. 166; *Winkworth v Hubbard* [1960] 1 Lloyd's Rep. 150; *Schneider v Eisovitch* [1960] 2 Q.B. 430; *Suisse Atlantique Societe d'Armement SA v NV Rotterdamsche Kolen Centrale* [1967] 1 A.C. 361; *C Czarnikow Ltd v Koufos (The Heron II)* [1969] 1 A.C. 350; *Pryde v Proctor & Gamble Ltd*, 1971 S.L.T. (Notes) 18; *R Pagnan & Fratelli v Corbisa Industrial Agropacuaria Ltd* [1970] 1 All E.R. 165; *Bonnor v Balfour Kilpatrick Ltd*, 1975 S.L.T. (Notes) 3; *Aluminium Industrie Vaassen BV v Romalpa Aluminium Ltd* [1976] 1 W.L.R. 676; *Emerald Stainless Steel Ltd v South Side Distribution Ltd*, 1983 S.L.T. 162; *Deutz Engines Ltd v Terex Ltd*, 1984 S.L.T. 273; *Armour v Thyssen Edelstahlwerke AG* [1991] 2 A.C. 339 HL; and *Parker v TUI UK Ltd* [2009] EWCA Civ 1261. See Fentiman, *Foreign Law in English Courts*, 1998, p.161.

[144] *Sed pace Neilson v Overseas Projects Corporation of Victoria Ltd* [2005] HCA 54 (Australia); and Fentiman, *International Commercial Litigation*, 2010, paras 6.09–6.12.

[145] *Lloyd v Guibert* (1865) L.R. 1 Q.B. 115; *Ertel Bieber & Co v Rio Tinto Co Ltd* [1918] A.C. 260; *Faulkner v Hill*, 1942 J.C. 20; *Rodden v Whatlings Ltd*, 1960 S.L.T. (Notes) 96; *Pryde v Proctor & Gamble Ltd*, 1971 S.L.T. (Notes) 18; *Bonnor v Balfour Kilpatrick Ltd*, 1975 S.L.T. (Notes) 3; See also *Bumper Development Corp v Commissioner of Police of the Metropolis* [1991] 4 All E.R. 638, per Purchas L.J. at 643–646. Further, Fentiman, *Foreign Law in English Courts*, 1998, pp.182–188.

[146] *De Reneville v De Reneville* [1948] P. 100.

There is a third situation, where foreign law is proved adequately, and is not found to be lacking in provision, but those provisions in some particular are offensive to the forum. In these circumstances, the effect will be that the *lex fori* will apply, either in a negative way by overruling application of the *lex causae* or, very rarely, in a positive way by supplying a remedy that the *lex causae* lacks.[147] The applicable law having been identified per the forum's choice of law rule, the forum, therefore, is entitled to exercise a public policy discretion to disapply that foreign law, as proved. *Ex hypothesis*, this can be done only after proof of what turns out to be, in the view of the forum, the unacceptable content of foreign law. There is no scope at the point of proof of foreign law (i.e. when establishing, as a matter of fact, what is the *content* of the foreign law) for the forum to "censor" the foreign law, since the task of proof is purely a "fact"-finding exercise.

It is recognised that the different approaches taken by EU Member States to the matter of proof of foreign law, and in particular the "out-of-line" UK attitude, may frustrate the desired goal of harmonisation of applicable law rules, which, typically, are framed in a mandatory form of words.[148] Article 30 of the Rome II Regulation lays down that, not later than August 20, 2011, the European Commission shall submit to the European Parliament, the Council and the European Economic and Social Committee, a report on the application of that instrument, to include a study on the effects of the way in which foreign law is treated in the different Member States, and on the extent to which courts in the Member States apply foreign law in practice pursuant to the Rome II Regulation. Preliminary work on this has commenced,[149] and it is highly likely that a proposal for a Council Regulation will emerge in due course, seeking to address the perceived anomaly of Member State courts applying their own national rules in respect of the proof of foreign law.

ONUS OF PROOF

There is doubt whether this matter truly pertains to substance or procedure. **8–21**
Writers in their earlier editions[150] favoured classification of the topic as substantive.[151] Latterly views are equivocal,[152] but art.18.1 of the Rome I

---

[147] Instances of this third situation are difficult to find, but one might cite the example of a foreign rule of spousal immunity from suit in tort, adequate proof of which has been led, but the content of which the forum chooses to reject, thereby conferring upon an injured spouse (through default application of the forum's own law) the right to sue the offending spouse.

[148] e.g. Rome II Regulation art.4.1, ". . . the law applicable to a non-contractual obligation arising out of a tort/delict shall be the law of the country . . ."; Rome I Regulation art.4.1: "To the extent that the law applicable to the contract has not been chosen . . . the law governing . . . shall be determined as follows . . .".

[149] See generally C. Esplugues Mota, J. Eglesias Buhigues, and G. Palao Moreno (eds), *The Application of Foreign Law by Judicial and Non-Judicial Authorities in Europe*, in particular, "UK National Report" by Crawford and Carruthers (forthcoming, Sellier, 2010).

[150] *Cheshire's Private International Law*, 8th edn, 1970, p.699 and 9th edn, 1974, p.693. The case of *Re Cohn* [1945] Ch. 5 supports the view that burden of proof is substantive. See also Wolff, *Private International Law*, 2nd edn, 1950, pp.234, 235.

[151] Though Graveson, *Private International Law*, 7th edn, 1974, p.602, together with the cases of *Fuld (No.3)* [1968] P. 675 and *Mackenzie v Hall* (1854) 17 D. 164, prefers to assign the topic to procedure.

[152] The 10th edn of *Cheshire and North on Private International Law*, 1979, at p.707, does not express a firm view, nor does the latest, *Cheshire, North and Fawcett: Private International Law*, 14th edn, 2008, at p.89.

Regulation, and art.22.1 of the Rome II Regulation, which are in the same terms, mutatis mutandis, support the substantive characterisation: the instruments provide that the law governing a contractual/non-contractual obligation, as identified by either instrument, shall apply to the extent that, in matters of contractual/non-contractual obligations falling within the scope of each Regulation, it contains rules which raise presumptions of law or determine the burden of proof.

PRESUMPTIONS

8–22 Graveson[153] regarded all presumptions of law and fact as procedural, governed by the *lex fori*, but, as has been seen above, this position has been overtaken, at least in relation to the particular (contractual) matter with which it deals, by art.14(1) of Rome I. It is thought that irrebuttable presumptions contained within the *lex causae* are matters of substance. As regards rebuttable presumptions it is suggested that they should also receive effect as matters involving substance unless they are clearly (foreign) rules of procedure.

DAMAGES[154]

8–23 In principle, according to the traditional approach of Scots and English conflict of laws rules, there are two elements in the assessment of damages, namely:

(a) liability,[155] a matter of substance, to be determined by the *lex causae*; and
(b) quantification of damages, a matter of procedure, to be determined by the *lex fori*.

At common law,[156] the question whether a claim for a particular head of damages is competent was governed, therefore, by the *lex causae* (in contract, delict, or restitution, etc.); and the monetary calculation of damages was a matter purely for the *lex fori*.[157]

This statement of the traditional conflict rule now is subject to the specialties introduced by the Rome I and Rome II Regulations, in respect of contractual and non-contractual obligations, as follows:

---

[153] Graveson, *Private International Law*, 7th edn, 1974, p.602.
[154] See generally Janeen M. Carruthers, "Substance and Procedure in the Conflict of Laws: A Continuing Debate in relation to Damages" (2004) 53 I.C.L.Q. 691, 694; and "Damages in the Conflict of Laws: The Substance and Procedure Spectrum: *Harding v Wealands*" (2005) J. Priv. Int. L. 1. *Harding v Wealands* [2005] All E.R. 415 (decision reversed by HL [2007] 2 A.C. 1. See also *Re T&N Ltd* [2005] EWHC 2990 (Ch).
[155] *J D'Almeida Araujo LDA v Sir Frederick Becker & Co Ltd* [1953] 2 Q.B. 329.
[156] See *Maher v Groupama Grand Est* [2009] EWCA Civ 1191 on the characterisation by an English court (before the advent of the Rome II Regulation) on the question whether or not interest is payable pre-judgment on the damages awarded to the claimant. The Court of Appeal held the matter to be one pertaining to remedy, and referable to the English *lex fori*.
[157] *Fyffe v Ferguson* (1841) 2 Rob. 267; *Kendrick v Burnett (Owners of the SS Marsden)* (1897) 25 R. 82; *pace Boys v Chaplin* [1971] A.C. 356, the ratio of which is, notoriously, a matter of individual opinion.

The Rome I Regulation art.12.1(c), within the limits of the powers conferred on the forum by its procedural law, allocates to the scope of the *lex causae* the consequences of a total or partial breach of obligations, including the assessment of damages, in so far as it is governed by rules of law.[158] As indicated in Ch.15, below this provision expands the province of the governing law, and curtails the power of the *lex fori*.

A similar, though further reaching change, has taken place in the treatment of awards of damages in non-contractual obligations, by virtue of art.15(c) of the Rome II Regulation, which allocates to the scope of the law applicable, "the existence, the nature and the assessment of damage or the remedy claimed".[159] The subtle change of wording has wrought a significant change of position for UK courts.[160] The forum is thus enjoined to apply the *lex causae* to all aspects of the award of damages, subject only to public policy and in the case of contractual (though not expressly in non-contractual) cases, to the procedural constraints of the forum.

These European provisions are extremely significant. The wide subject-matter scope of the remit of the Rome I and Rome II Regulations must be acknowledged; the majority of contentious damages claims in EU Member State courts will arise within the law of obligations, and most of those claims, though not all, will fall within the scope of either one of the Regulations. Where the claim does not fall within the technical scope of the Regulations, it will be interesting to see whether UK courts adhere to their traditional reasoning.

CURRENCY IN WHICH JUDGMENT IS TO BE GIVEN

This area concerns the answers which the conflict of laws provides to the **8–24** problem of currency value fluctuation. It is important to distinguish between the substance of an obligation, on the one hand, and, on the other, the currency which, by agreement of the parties, is to be used to make payment in respect thereof.[161] *Money of account* (which measures the substance of an obligation)[162] is a substantive matter governed by the *lex causae*, but *money of payment* (in which the debt is discharged) is procedural.[163] In modern practice

---

[158] According to the Mario Giuliano and Paul Lagarde, Report on the Convention on the Law Applicable to Contractual Obligations [1980] OJ C282/1, p.33, the phrase of significance is "by rules of law": questions of fact in assessment of damages will always be for the forum, but international conventions or the terms of the contract itself may have provided "rules" for application in the instant matter, and these would be substantive. See para.15–43, below.

[159] Including interest pre-judgment on damages ultimately awarded? See Rogerson, 2009 All E.R. Annual Review, p.104. For the pre-Rome II position on damages in delict, see para.16–44, below.

[160] Though the change was foreshadowed in the judgment of Arden L.J. in the Court of Appeal in *Harding v Wealands* [2005] All E.R. 415 (decision reversed by HL [2007] 2 A.C. 1). See full discussion at para.16–44, below.

[161] *Adelaide Electric Supply Co Ltd v Prudential Assurance Co Ltd* [1934] A.C. 122; *Mayor of Auckland v Alliance Assurance Co Ltd* [1937] A.C. 587; *Mount Albert BC v Australasian Temperance & General Mutual Life Assurance Society* [1938] A.C. 224; *Bonython v Australia* [1951] A.C. 201; *National Mutual Life Assurance of Australasia v Att Gen of New Zealand* [1956] A.C. 369.

[162] *Woodhouse v Nigerian Produce Marketing Co Ltd* [1971] 2 Q.B. 23, per Lord Denning at 54 (affirmed [1972] A.C. 741).

[163] See further para.15–41, below.

the money of account and money of payment usually are the same, agreed between the parties at the outset. A party to a contract may cover the risk of changes in the exchange rate between his own currency and the currency of payment by arranging a forward exchange contract with a third party (usually a bank) to hedge the exchange risk. In earlier decades, this aim was achieved by use of "gold clauses", linking the obligation to the value of gold, but in more recent years a substantial body of law and practice has developed in the structuring of derivatives as the basic concept of covering forward exchange risk. Parties may make a forward purchase of currency to safeguard their exposure, or if the period of time is considerable, seek, through a bank, a swap contract, if an equal and opposite risk can be found.

For centuries it had been assumed without argument in Scotland[164] and England[165] that a British court could grant a decree for payment of money only as a sum of money expressed in sterling. In 1974,[166] however, the Court of Appeal decided unanimously that within the "Common Market" a judgment might be given in the foreign currency (being the currency of the governing law of the contract in question), and that to do otherwise would be contrary to the spirit and intent of the Treaty of Rome. Lord Denning also thought that there was no reason why a court should not now grant such a judgment in the currency of the governing law, whether or not the parties were from countries within the "Common Market".

This initiative was followed in many later cases, with refinements and advances, first and notably in *Miliangos v George Frank (Textiles) Ltd.*[167] Later the same year, in *The Halcyon the Great (No.1)*,[168] the court ordered that a ship be sold and the proceeds paid in dollars into the English court.

In Scotland, these issues arose at the same point in the 1970s, first, tentatively, in *L/F Foroya Fiskasola v Charles Mauritzen Ltd,*[169] and soon thereafter in *Commerzbank AG v Large,*[170] in which the point was clearly made that there was no reason why a foreign creditor suing for an undisputed money debt in the country of his debtor's residence should be disadvantaged by fluctuations in currency. He should be entitled to have his decree expressed in the currency of the debt. If conversion be necessary, it should take place at the latest date practicable, which would be the date of extracting the decree.[171]

There has been a "moving staircase" of judicial development, and in recognition of this the Law Commission concluded that it was inappropriate to propose substantial legislation, though minor amendments might be made.[172]

---

[164] *Hyslops v Gordon* (1824) 2 Sh. App. 451.
[165] *Re United Railways of Havana and Regla Warehouses Ltd* [1961] A.C. 1007.
[166] *Schorsch Meier GmbH v Hennin* [1975] Q.B. 416; [1974] 3 W.L.R. 823.
[167] [1975] Q.B. 487.
[168] [1975] 1 W.L.R. 515.
[169] 1977 S.L.T. (Sh. Ct.) 76; 1978 S.L.T. (Sh. Ct.) 27.
[170] 1977 S.L.T. 219.
[171] See *Carnegie v Giessen* [2005] 1 W.L.R. 2510, in which the Court of Appeal stated that conversion should be made as close as practicable to the date of payment, "having regard to realities of enforcement procedures".
[172] Law Commission, *Private International Law, Foreign Money Liabilities* (HMSO, 1983), Law Com. No.124. The question of interest on foreign currency judgment debts and arbitral awards was identified as an area where procedural change was needed: see now, for England and Wales only, Private International Law (Miscellaneous Provisions) Act 1995 Pt I.

This then is one of the few areas of modern UK conflict rules in which the legislature has refrained from itself effecting change where change was deemed necessary. There are many decisions,[173] and interest in the subject, at the time of principal change, is extensive. One of the most useful guides is the conjoined contract/tort House of Lords decision, *The Folias*,[174] which held in tort (the tort aspect having been reserved by the House of Lords in *Miliangos*) that the plaintiff should have his judgment in the currency which best expressed his loss; and in contract, that the fact that payments under a contract were in a particular currency did not necessarily mean that damages for breach need be awarded in that same currency.

A significant Scottish decision is *Fullemann v McInnes's Executors*,[175] which concerned an award of damages to a Swiss pursuer injured in a road accident in Scotland as a result of the admitted fault of the other driver. The pursuer suffered physical and patrimonial loss. Solatium was valued at £42,500 but the award for patrimonial loss was expressed in Swiss francs, or the sterling equivalent at the date of payment or of extracting decree, whichever was the earlier.[176]

DILIGENCE

This is governed at present entirely by the law of the place where a decree is **8–25** to be enforced,[177] but EU intervention is expected.[178]

SET-OFF/COMPROMISE

This subject, concerning methods of extinguishing, wholly or partly, an indebt- **8–26** edness, tends to be placed in early authorities under the heading of procedure

---

[173] *Jugoslavenska Oceanska Plovidba v Castle Investment Co Inc (The Kozara)* [1974] Q.B. 292 (arbitration); *Barclays Bank International Ltd v Levin Bros (Bradford) Ltd* [1977] Q.B. 270; *Jean Kraut AG v Albany Fabrics Ltd* [1977] Q.B. 182.

[174] *Services Europe Atlantique Sud (SEAS) v Stockholms Rederi AB Svea (The Folias)* [1979] Q.B. 491; [1978] 2 All E.R. 764.

[175] 1993 S.L.T. 259.

[176] *Fullemann v McInnes's Executors*, 1993 S.L.T. 259, per Lord Cullen at 267, contrasting *North Scottish Helicopters Ltd v United Technologies Corp Inc (No.2)*, 1988 S.L.T. 778. With reference to arguments for the defender that it was illogical for the pursuer to accept decree in sterling for solatium but to seek decree in Swiss francs for the patrimonial loss, Lord Cullen at 268 said: "There is no doubt in the present case that the patrimonial loss which was and will continue to be suffered by the pursuer is one suffered in Swiss currency." (The pursuer had had to sell his business which otherwise he might have expanded.) See Blaikie, "Personal Injuries Claims: Damages in Foreign Currency", 1993 S.L.T. (News) 184.

[177] See *Stewart v Royal Bank of Scotland Plc*, 1994 S.L.T. (Sh Ct) 27. Also *Union Carbide Corp v BP Chemicals Ltd*, 1995 S.L.T. 972; *Camdex International Ltd v Bank of Zambia Ltd* [1997] 1 C.L. 123; and *Bankers Trust International v Todd Shipyards Corp (The Halycon Isle)* [1981] A.C. 221 PC. See, in Scots domestic law, Debt Arrangement and Attachment (Scotland) Act 2002, and Bankruptcy and Diligence etc. (Scotland) Act 2007.

[178] Communication on Delivering an Area of Freedom, Security and Justice for Europe's Citizens: Action Plan Implementing the Stockholm Programme COM(2010) 175 final: the Action Plan indicates that in 2010 there will be a proposal for a Regulation on improving the efficiency of the enforcement of judgments in the EU in the matter of the attachment of bank accounts. For background, see Green Paper on improving the efficiency of the enforcement of judgments in the European Union: the attachment of bank accounts COM(2006) 618 final; and Resolution 2007/2026(INI) on the Green Paper on improving the efficiency of the enforcement of judgments in the European Union: the attachment of bank accounts [2008] OJ C263E/464.

or remedy, to be governed by the *lex fori*.[179] However, instinct would suggest that an argument can be made for treating the topic as pertaining to substance, whether it be referred to the applicable law in contract,[180] property or restitution.[181] The Rome I Regulation contains, in art.17, a new rule on set-off as it affects the subject-matter scope of that Regulation.[182] In the absence of agreement of the parties, set-off shall be governed by the law applicable to the claim against which the right to set off is asserted. If the right to set-off is the subject of an agreement between or among the parties, the applicable law of that agreement arrived at through application of art.3 (or potentially arts 5–8), must govern since, in terms of art.12.1(d), "the various ways of extinguishing obligations" falls under the scope of the law applicable, as a substantive matter.

It is clear that rights in this area may be seen often to arise out of principles of property, or the fact of possession, for example lien.[183] It could be that the earlier decisions and later thoughts might meet on the rationalisation that an unpaid party's right to retain custody of an object of property pending payment for work done or a debt due, falls within the category of remedy or procedure, and frequently will be governed by the *lex fori* qua *lex situs*. Similarly, the right of a party to set off what he owes against what he is owed (as for example arising out of several contracts forming a course of dealing between two parties), arguably should be governed by the common applicable law, if there is one; and if there is not, it might be that the remedies available to the parties should be determined by the *lex fori* qua *situs* of the debt.[184]

Any confusion which has arisen under this heading probably stems from the variety of circumstances which can be subsumed under it. Some of these issues are plainly procedural, for example, whether a counterclaim may be brought by the defender in an action against the pursuer without raising separate proceedings; and whether and under what circumstances an action may be settled by compromise.

SUMMARY 8

8–27   1. Substance is governed by the *lex causae*; procedure by the *lex fori*. Classification between the two is for the forum in each instance, but certain matters are clearly procedural: form of action and of process, evidence, and diligence. There is doubt about the classification of other issues, such as onus of proof and presumptions. Some matters

---

[179] *Mitchell v Burnett and Mowat* (1746) Mor. 4468; *Robertson's Trustees v Bairds* (1852) 14 D. 1010; *Macfarlane v Norris* (1862) 2 B.J. 783; and *Meyer v Dresser* (1864) 16 C.B. (N.S.) 646. See also Anton with Beaumont, *Private International Law*, 2nd edn, 1990, pp.748, 749.

[180] At least if the circumstances involve only two parties in a matter which could be said to arise out of a contract or putative contract between them. *Finance One Public Co Ltd v Lehman Bros Special Financing Inc*, 414 F.3d 325 (2nd Cir. 2005).

[181] cf. Rome I Convention art.10(1)(c), (d).

[182] See para.15–45, below.

[183] See minority judgment of Lords Scarman and Salmon, in *The Halycon Isle* [1981] A.C. 221 PC.

[184] These suggested solutions beg several questions, chief among them being "which debt?" (if the debts had different governing laws) and "which forum?" In practice, however, the forum probably would be that of the domicile (i.e. residence) of the debtor first sued.

    (for example, damages), originally hybrid in character, have been changed by EU instrument to substantially substantive.

2. Foreign prescriptive or limitation periods: the forum must defer to the rules of the *lex causae*, at least in matters relating to obligations.

3. Service of judicial and extrajudicial documents within the EU now is governed by Regulation 1393/2007. Service furth of Scotland outside the EU is governed by Rules of Court of the Court of Session/Sheriff Court.

4. Among EU Member States evidence from another Member State may be obtained under authority of Regulation 1206/2001. Evidence from non-EU Member States, or to be remitted abroad, may be obtained/provided by the "letter of request" procedure laid down by the Evidence (Proceedings in Other Jurisdictions) Act 1975.

5. The content of foreign law, if relied upon and not admitted, must be proved. In the absence of proof, it is presumed to be the same as the *lex fori*.

6. Decrees expressed in foreign currency may be awarded by a Scots or English court.

CHAPTER 9

ENFORCEMENT OF FOREIGN DECREES

I. INTRODUCTION

9–01 The rules for enforcement in the UK of judgments from abroad depend upon the identity of the court of origin, i.e. the territory whence the judgment originated, and the necessity for enforcement varies according to type of decree. There are different classes of judicial decree, with different consequences for enforcement. Not all judicial decrees are suitable for, or require, enforcement *extra territorium*. Moreover, sometimes reliance is placed on a foreign judgment in a negative way, as a defence to an action in Scotland or England, under the heading of *res judicata*.

CLASSES OF DECREE

Decrees may be divided into the following classes:

(a) Declarators of fact

9–02   The courts in Scotland or England are not bound by findings of fact in a foreign decree. A foreign declarator which merely purports to establish a fact is not necessarily conclusive, but may be accepted in non-contentious matters.[1]

(b) Interdicts

9–03   A decree of this class is generally enforceable only within the territorial limits of the court which granted it,[2] at least at common law, and generally in cases falling outside the ambit of the Brussels/Lugano regime.[3] However, under that regime, orders for specific implement and interdict, as well as those which are purely money judgments, have the advantage of the enforcement scheme provided thereby among Member/Contracting States.[4]

---

[1] *Simpson's Trustees v Fox*, 1951 S.L.T. 412 (death abroad; see now, in relation to proof of death abroad, Presumption of Death (Scotland) Act 1977 s.10: foreign declaration of presumption of death, from the court of the domicile of the presumed deceased, or his habitual residence, on the date when he was last known to be alive, raises in Scotland a rebuttable presumption of death).

[2] *Waygood and Co v Bennie* (1885) 12 R. 615; *British Nylon Spinners v ICI* [1953] Ch. 19. See generally *Waste Systems International Inc v Eurocare Environmental Services Ltd*, 1998 G.W.D. 6-260.

[3] See Ch.7, above.

[4] *Barratt International Resorts Ltd v Martin*, 1994 S.L.T. 434, per Lord Sutherland at 437: "An interdict [granted in Scotland] therefore can be rendered effective even though the events being interdicted may occur in Spain." Also *G v Caledonian Newspapers Ltd*, 1995 S.L.T. 559 (intra-UK enforcement).

(c) Judgments in rem

Decrees of this class establish rights in property which are effective against **9–04** the world at large, not simply between the two parties to a dispute.

The test of validity of such a decree turns upon the strength of the claim to jurisdiction of the issuing court ("court of origin"), which, in turn, depends upon the presence of the *res* within the jurisdiction,[5] with the result that if the *res* was within the jurisdiction at the time of pronouncement of the judgment, it is thought that the only ground upon which the judgment may be challenged is that of fraud.[6] It follows that the title of a third party who has acquired the *res* in compliance with that *lex situs* cannot be challenged.[7]

(d) Judgments affecting status

Judgments of this class although treated separately (i.e. possessing special **9–05** statutory rules in conflict of laws, contained in the Family Law Act 1986 Pt II (non-EU decrees) and Brussels II *bis*[8] (EU decrees)) are regarded as being equivalent in many respects to decrees in rem in that they establish rights which should be recognised internationally without the aid or intervention of a foreign court, and have a status in unrelated litigation. The decision of the House of Lords in *Administrator of Austrian Property v Von Lorang*[9] is particularly instructive as it demonstrates that an annulment of marriage granted by a court in Wiesbaden, Germany, and recognised by the Scots forum, had a direct effect upon a property dispute taking place by way of multiplepoinding (diligence on assets) in Edinburgh. Viscount Dunedin in that case said: "A metaphysical idea, which is what the status of marriage is, is not strictly a *res*, but, to borrow a phrase, it savours of a *res*, and has all along been treated as such."[10]

If there is doubt as to the validity in Scotland of a foreign, non-EU consistorial judgment, a party may seek declarator of status from the Court of Session.[11] In principle, however, it follows from the decision in *Von Lorang*, above, that no such procedure should be necessary.

In relation to EU judgments affecting marital status, in terms of art.21 of Brussels II *bis*, a judgment given in a Member State shall be recognised in the other Member States without any special procedure being required. Under the head of enforceable judgments, art.28 of Brussels II *bis* provides that a judgment on the exercise of parental responsibility given in a Member State and

---

[5] Contrast *Castrique v Imrie* (1870) L.R. 4 H.L. 414 and *McKie v McKie* [1933] I.R. 464.

[6] *Ellerman Lines Ltd v Read* [1928] 2 K.B. 144.

[7] *Cammell v Sewell* (1858) 3 Hurl. & N. 617; *Castrique v Imrie* (1870) L.R. 4 H.L. 414; *Ballantyne v Mackinnon* [1896] 2 Q.B. 455; *Minna Craig Steamship Co v Chartered Mercantile Bank of India London and China* [1897] 1 Q.B. 55; *Re Trepca Mines Ltd* [1960] 1 W.L.R. 1273; *Enochin v Wyllie* (1882) 10 H.L. Cas. 1; *Orr-Ewing's Trustees v Orr-Ewing* (1885) 13 R. (H.L.) 1; and *Doglioni v Crispin* (1866) L.R. 1 H.L. 301. See Ch.17, below.

[8] Regulation 2201/2003.

[9] 1927 S.C. (H.L.) 80.

[10] *Administrator of Austrian Property v Von Lorang*, 1927 S.C. (H.L.) 80 at 92.

[11] The Family Law (Scotland) Act 2006 s.37 contains amendments to the Domicile and Matrimonial Proceedings Act 1973 s.7 (jurisdiction of Court of Session in certain consistorial causes), to the effect of conferring jurisdiction on the Court of Session in actions for declarator of recognition of a "relevant foreign decree" (meaning a decree of divorce, nullity or separation granted by a non-EU state). Shrieval jurisdiction to grant such a declarator also is conferred by s.37(3). In English law a declaration may be sought under the Family Law Act 1986 s.55.

enforceable there shall be enforceable in another Member State when, on the application of any interested party, it has been declared enforceable there.[12] Hence, a "declaration of enforceability" is required in such parental responsibility judgments; but the Regulation makes no mention of the use of such declarations in relation to any other type of judgment covered by the Regulation.[13]

(e) Judgments in personam

9–06 Judgments of this class,[14] such as claims for debts or for damages for breach of contract, establish personal rights between the litigants: a foreign decree *in personam*, if not complied with by the defender, may be enforced in Scotland only by the holder of the personal right invoking the assistance of the courts.

In Scotland, such a decree may be enforced in one of the following ways:

(1) by action for decree conform;
(2) by judgment registration ("judgment extension") under the Administration of Justice Act 1920 or the Foreign Judgments (Reciprocal Enforcement) Act 1933;
(3) by use of the system of judgment enforcement provided by the Brussels I Regulation for judgments from EU Member States, and by the Lugano Convention, for judgments from EFTA States, all per the Civil Jurisdiction and Judgments Acts 1982 and 1991.[15] There are significant differences between the rules of the Brussels/Lugano system and the rules which apply at common law and under the 1920 and 1933 Acts;
(4) Civil Jurisdiction and Judgments Acts 1982 and 1991 Schs 6 and 7 govern the enforcement of English and Northern Ireland judgments in Scotland and vice versa;
(5) European Enforcement Order for Uncontested Claims Procedure;
(6) European Order for Payment Procedure;
(7) European Small Claims Procedure.

II. LEGAL BASIS OF ENFORCEMENT

9–07 The original bases of enforcement of any foreign decree in Scotland were simply comity and reciprocity, but it is now generally accepted that comity alone is inadequate as a reason for enforcement, though reciprocity remains relevant.[16] Later arose the doctrine that a foreign judgment imposed an

---

[12] i.e. a form of *exequatur* (registration) procedure. Such a judgment shall be enforced in England and Wales, in Scotland or in Northern Ireland only when, on the application of any interested party, it has been registered for enforcement in that part of the UK.

[13] See Chs 12 and 14, below.

[14] See *Pattni v Ali* [2007] 2 A.C. 85 PC (Isle of Man).

[15] See also Civil Jurisdiction and Judgments Order 2001 (SI 2001/3929); Civil Jurisdiction and Judgments Regulations 2007 (SI 2007/1655); and Civil Jurisdiction and Judgments Regulations 2009 (SI 2009/3131), discussed in Ch.7, above.

[16] The statutory structure of foreign judgment recognition and enforcement inter-country (in terms of 1920 and 1933 Acts; and also under the Civil Jurisdiction and Judgments Act 1982) rests on reciprocity. See, e.g. Foreign Judgments (Reciprocal Enforcement) Act 1933 ss.1, 9.

obligation[17] enforceable in another jurisdiction, the burden lying on the defender to show why it should not be enforced.

Until recently in English conflict of laws, as contrasted with its domestic law, a foreign decree was not regarded as consuming the cause of action. Hence, a claimant holding a foreign decree which he wished to enforce in England might sue either upon the decree itself, or ignore the decree and sue on the cause of action (the best course being to sue on both grounds as alternatives).[18] However, this non-merger rule was abolished by the Civil Jurisdiction and Judgments Act 1982 s.34.[19] The section does not apply to Scotland, possibly because it was not required, since the rule which it effected was already the rule in Scotland.[20]

Essentially, an unimpeachable foreign judgment creates rights and imposes obligations which should be enforceable across frontiers,[21] especially where a net of reciprocity has been woven, as by the 1920 and 1933 Acts and by the Brussels regime. The aim and rationale within the EU is the free movement of judgments, thereby facilitating the operation of the internal market.

Various principles of natural justice operate in the subject of judgment enforcement. For example, there should be finality in judgments so that a person is not required to, "hawk his defence round Europe" (reputedly per Lord Braxfield). It follows from this that the "enforcing" court, known as the "court addressed", will not act as a further court of appeal from the foreign court, the "court of origin". As a general rule, under any of the systems of judgment enforcement operative in the UK, review of substance will not be undertaken, nor will allegations of error on the part of the foreign court be investigated. The one important exception to this general rule against the re-opening of proceedings is in relation to alleged fraud, and even there the opportunity to re-open on this ground is significantly more restricted under the Brussels regime. Review of jurisdictional competence is permitted under the common law rules and older statutory schemes, but under the Brussels regime only to a very limited extent[22]: the absence of a right to query the jurisdiction of the court of origin is a *leitmotif* of the Brussels regime.

A. ENFORCEMENT OF JUDGMENTS AT COMMON LAW

Enforcement via the common law route is required when a judgment emanates **9–08** from a foreign country which is not bound by the Brussels/Lugano regime, nor

---

[17] *Schibsby v Westenholz* (1870) L.R. 6 Q.B. 155.

[18] See *East India Trading Co Inc v Carmel Exporters and Importers Ltd* [1952] 2 Q.B. 439; and *Carl Zeiss Stiftung v Rayner & Keeler Ltd* [1967] A.C. 853.

[19] Section 34: "No proceedings may be brought by a person in England and Wales, or Northern Ireland on a cause of action in respect of which a judgment has been given in his favour in proceedings between the same parties, or their privies, in a court in another part of the United Kingdom or in a court of an overseas country, unless that judgment is not enforceable or entitled to recognition in England and Wales, or, as the case may be, in Northern Ireland." See *Fraser v HLMAD Ltd* [2007] 1 All E.R. 383; and *Blyth-Whitelock v de Meyer* [2009] EWHC 2839 (Ch). *Sed contra Black v Yates* [1992] Q.B. 526.

[20] See Maxwell Report, para.6.186.

[21] *Williams v Jones* (1845) 13 M. & W. 633; *Schibsby v Westenholz* (1870) L.R. 6 Q.B. 155; *Grant v Easton* (1883) L.R. 13 Q.B.D. 302.

[22] Namely, to ensure that the rules with regard to disadvantaged parties and exclusive jurisdiction have been complied with: Brussels I Regulation art.35.1.

linked by reciprocal arrangements with the UK in terms of the Administration of Justice Act 1920 or the Foreign Judgments (Reciprocal Enforcement) Act 1933.[23] Generally speaking, common law enforcement is required in respect of judgments from the USA,[24] Africa (except for Commonwealth countries), the Middle East and the Far East (including now Hong Kong).[25]

The conditions set out below must be complied with in order that a foreign decree *in personam* may be enforceable in Scotland under the common law procedure:

(a) the decree must have been granted in a judicial process: where in the judicial process? It is not clear whether the judgment must emanate from a "superior" court.[26] By inference of case law,[27] it is clear that it is no bar to enforcement of a judgment that appeal from that judgment is competent in the legal system of the court of origin. This surely must mean that a decree from a medium ranking foreign court has sufficient status to be enforced in Scotland;

(b) the foreign court of origin must have had jurisdiction in the international sense[28];

(c) the decree must be final and *res judicata*;

(d) the decree must be for payment of a definite sum of money (a foreign decree for an indefinite sum or a decree *ad factum praestandum* is not enforceable at common law in Scotland);

(e) the subject matter of the decree must not fall within any of the areas which form exclusions or exceptions to the extraterritorial effect of foreign law (revenue or penal laws, etc.).[29]

Action for decree conform

9–09   At common law, a foreign decree is enforced in Scotland by raising an action for decree conform to the decree of the foreign court. Certified translation of the foreign decree may be required. Decree conform may be granted only against a person who was party to the foreign proceedings. Such an action

---

[23] Relevant countries in respect of each Act are listed at paras 9–16 and 9–17, below.

[24] Many such actions relate to attempted enforcement of US awards, there being no reciprocal judgment extension between the UK and the United States (except in relation to reciprocal enforcement of maintenance awards under the Maintenance Orders (Reciprocal Enforcement) Act 1972 Pt II). See, e.g. *First Fidelity Bank NA v Hudson*, 1995 G.W.D. 28-1499; *Wendel v Moran*, 1993 S.L.T. 44; *Elf Caledonia Ltd v London Bridge Engineering Ltd*, 1997 G.W.D. 33-1686; and *Clarke v Fennoscandia Ltd (No.3)*, 2008 S. L.T. 33.

[25] [1997] 12 C.L. 90.

[26] It is arguable that, to found enforcement proceedings in Scotland/England, the decree must be "incapable of revision by the Court which pronounced it": *Ascot Commodities NV v Northern Pacific Shipping (The Irini A) (No.2)* [1999] 1 Lloyd's Rep. 189 (issue estoppel). Taking a purposive approach, it seems unlikely that objection would be raised to the rank of the court of origin in its own hierarchy so long as the judgment in question meets the common law requirements as to the "finality" of the judgment. In a practical sense, decisions of the lower courts are more likely to be appealed domestically before being sought to be enforced abroad.

[27] On the question of the meaning of "final" decree: see para.9–12, below.

[28] See *Wendel v Moran*, 1993 S.L.T. 44, in which Lord Cullen refused to recognise as internationally jurisdictionally competent a New York court on the sole basis of the occurrence there of the delict, without presence of defender or express or implied submission by him; Brussels principles have no application in a common law case.

[29] See Ch.3, above.

may be raised only in the Court of Session because it is regarded as falling under the *nobile officium*.[30]

If decree conform is sought in circumstances where judgment extension under the 1920 Act is available, expenses will not be awarded.[31] Under the Foreign Judgments (Reciprocal Enforcement) Act 1933 s.6, it is incompetent to proceed at common law if registration per the Act is possible.

Grounds of challenge to actions for decree conform

(a) No jurisdiction

This will always be the first challenge to be considered. In considering the suffi- **9–10** ciency of the ground of jurisdiction assumed by a foreign court, there would be no point in referring only to the law of the foreign court because clearly that court regarded itself as having had jurisdiction; nor would there be any point in considering only the grounds assumed by the court addressed because that would restrict enforceability to cases where the two laws coincided. In practice, the courts of the enforcing country test the ground of jurisdiction in the court of origin according to whether or not it complies with a broad international standard of justice. By this standard certain grounds of jurisdiction (domicile, residence,[32] presence,[33] place of performance of contract or occurrence of delict, prorogation or submission,[34] reconvention) generally are recognised,[35] whereas other bases of jurisdiction considered exorbitant (nationality,[36] arrestment to found jurisdiction, ownership of heritage in an action unrelated to the heritage)[37] are not recognised.[38]

---

[30] *O'Connor v Erskine* (1905) 13 S.L.T. 530; *Geiger v D&J Macdonald Ltd*, 1932 S.L.T. 70.

[31] Administration of Justice Act 1920 s.9(5).

[32] *Schibsby v Westenholz* (1870) L.R. 6 Q.B. 155. As to difficulties in the case of federal states, see C.M.V. Clarkson and Jonathan Hill, *The Conflict of Laws*, 3rd edn (Oxford: Oxford University Press, 2006), pp.140–142.

[33] *Adams v Cape Industries Plc* [1991] 1 All E.R. 929. See also, in that case, consideration of the application of the principle to corporations; and Clarkson and Hill, *Conflict of Laws*, 3rd edn, 2006, pp.139, 140. Further, in *Lucasfilm Ltd v Ainsworth* [2009] EWCA Civ 1328; [2010] 3 All E.R. 329, the Court of Appeal held that the presence requirement is not satisfied if the defendant's presence in the state of origin was merely through internet trading.

[34] cf. *Copin v Adamson* (1874) L.R. 9 Ex. 345; *Blohn v Desser* [1962] Q.B. 116; contrast *Emanuel v Symon* [1908] 1 K.B. 302 and *Vogel v R&A Kohnstamm Ltd* [1973] 1 Q.B. 133. In determining the question whether the judgment debtor submitted to the jurisdiction of the court of origin, and/or whether his initial objection to the jurisdiction was maintained, attention may require to be paid to the procedural rules of the court of origin, but the final decision on submission is for the court addressed: *Akai Pty Ltd v People's Insurance Co Ltd* [1998] 1 Lloyd's Rep. 90. See now for England Civil Jurisdiction and Judgments Act 1982 s.33; and, e.g. *AES UST-Kamenogorsk Hydropower Plant LLP v UST-Kamenogorsk Hydropower Plant JSC* [2010] EWHC 722 (Comm). On the specialties of s.31 (overseas judgments given against states), see *NML Capital Ltd v Argentina* [2009] 1 Lloyd's Rep.378.

[35] Though see *Wendel v Moran*, 1993 S.L.T. 44, above.

[36] *Rainford v Newell Roberts* [1962] I.R. 95; *Singh v Rajah of Faridkote* [1894] A.C. 670; though see *Ashbury v Ellis* [1893] A.C. 339.

[37] Possession of heritable property in Scotland is a general ground of jurisdiction in the Court of Session (Civil Jurisdiction and Judgments Act 1982 Sch.8 r.2(h)(ii)). Accordingly, a Scots court might be expected to recognise foreign decrees based on an equivalent ground of jurisdiction. But this ground is not recognised in England and many other countries, and English courts will not enforce a foreign judgment where it was the ground of jurisdiction, except when the action related to the property.

[38] See in English law *Emanuel v Symon* [1908] 1 K.B. 302, per Buckley L.J. at 309; see also *Re Trepca Mines Ltd* [1960] 1 W.L.R. 1273 and *Buchanan v Rucker* (1808) 9 East. 192, where the court in England refused to enforce a judgment from Tobago in respect of which service had

In the context of recognition of foreign divorces, Lord Pearce in *Indyka v Indyka*[39] said that insofar as a court limited its rules of recognition more strictly than it did its rules of taking jurisdiction, it was adding to the sum of limping marriages. In commercial matters too, it may be reasonable to ask whether a legal system's own rules of exercising jurisdiction are consonant with the rules which it applies in order to assess the jurisdictional competence of another system's courts.[40]

The case of appearance under protest to contest the jurisdiction of the putative forum is one which requires special consideration.[41] A controversy arose in England upon the question whether appearance simply to deny that the court had jurisdiction amounted to submission. The matter was settled by the Civil Jurisdiction and Judgments Act 1982 s.33 (which does not apply to Scotland), to the effect that a person shall not be regarded as having submitted to the jurisdiction of the court by reason only of the fact that he appeared (conditionally or otherwise) in the proceedings (a) to contest the jurisdiction of the court and/or (b) to ask the court to dismiss or stay the proceedings on the ground that the dispute in question should be submitted to arbitration or to the determination of the courts of another country, or to protect, or obtain the release of, property seized or threatened with seizure in the proceedings.[42]

(b) Other grounds of challenge

9–11   As a foreign decree which, on the face of it, complies with the "international" standards of jurisdiction, is regarded as conferring rights on the holder thereof, those rights generally will be recognised in Scotland, unless the other party satisfies the court that it would not be proper for it to recognise them. A Scots or English court will not act as a further court of appeal in relation to a foreign decree.[43] The foreign court must be regarded as having been able to try the case and as having pronounced a valid judgment.

The result is that, broadly speaking, the grounds upon which a foreign decree may be challenged are restricted to those cases in which the court should be deemed not to have had jurisdiction in the international sense, as explained, or where it would be contrary to public policy to recognise the decree. A foreign judgment will be subject to challenge in Scotland or England only on some ground which goes to the very root and essence:

---

been effected on the defendant by "substituted service"; namely by nailing a copy of the writ to the courthouse door, effective under that law though the defendant had never been to Tobago.

[39] [1969] 1 A.C. 33 at 78.

[40] There may attract criticism in this regard the "long-arm" English jurisdiction rules (see *Seaconsar Far East Ltd v Bank Markazi Jomhouri Islami Iran* [1994] 1 A.C. 438) contained in CPR r.6.36 (ex-r.6.20) and CPR PD 6B r.3.1 (permitting the court in its discretion to grant leave to the claimant to effect service outside the jurisdiction if he can show a good arguable case on the merits and the case falls within one of the categories specified).

[41] Common law cases in England before Civil Jurisdiction and Judgments Act 1982 s.33, demonstrating the controversy: *Guiard v De Clermont & Donner* [1914] 3 K.B. 145; *Harris v Taylor* [1915] 2 K.B. 580; *Re Dulles Settlement (No.2)* [1951] Ch. 842; *NV Daarnhouwer & Co NV, Handelmaatschappij v Boulos* [1968] 2 Lloyd's Rep. 259; finally *Henry v Geoprosco International Ltd* [1976] Q.B. 726. Post-1982, see *Tracomin SA v Sudan Oil Seeds Ltd (No.1)* [1983] 3 All E.R. 137; and *Starlight International Inc v Bruce* [2002] EWHC 374 (Ch)

[42] cf. Brussels I Regulation art.24.

[43] Contrast continental doctrine of the *exequatur*, which in some forms permitted review of the merits (*révision au fond*).

"If a judgment is pronounced by a foreign Court over persons within its jurisdiction and in a matter with which it is competent to deal, English courts never investigate the propriety of the proceedings of the foreign Court unless they offend against English views of substantial justice."[44]

The following are the only available defences in addition to that of "no juris- **9–12** diction":

(1) Judgment not final and conclusive.[45] Particular attention should be paid to the meaning at common law of this challenge. A foreign judgment will not be enforced in Scotland or England if the merits have not been exhausted,[46] but the fact that the judgment is appealable,[47] or even that an appeal is pending, will not necessarily render it unenforceable in Scotland or England at common law. However, a Scots court would be likely to sist the action for decree conform if foreign appeal was imminent.[48]

(2) Decree for an indefinite amount[49] or *ad factum praestandum*[50]; or for enforcement of a foreign revenue or penal or other public law excluded by Scots conflict rules from extraterritorial operation.[51]

(3) Judgment no longer extant (e.g. time-barred in the foreign system, or satisfied, or otherwise no longer enforceable).[52]

(4) Fraud: *fraus omnia corrumpit*. Fraud may relate to the substantive issue, or it may reside in the fraudulent quality of the behaviour of the parties (collateral fraud).[53] Within the latter, another distinction[54] may be made, namely that between *dolus praesens* (by fraudulent use of the judgment as, for example, by falsely promising not to enforce it)

---

[44] *Pemberton v Hughes* [1899] 1 Ch. 781, per Lindley M.R. at 790.
[45] *Paul v Roy* (1852) 15 Bcav. 433; *Shedden v Patrick* (1854) 1 Macq. 535; *Sheey v Professional Life Assurance Co* (1857) 2 C.B. (N.S.) 211; *Scott v Pilkington* (1862) 2 B. & S. 11; *Harris v Quine* (1869) L.R. 4 Q.B. 653; *Nouvion v Freeman* (1889) L.R. 15 App. Cas. 1; *Blohn v Desser* [1962] 2 Q.B. 116; *Colt Industries Inc v Sarlie (No.2)* [1966] 1 W.L.R. 1287; *Berliner Industriebank AG v Jost* [1971] 2 Q.B. 463; *Black-Clawson International Ltd v Papierwerke Waldhof-Aschaffenburg AG* [1975] A.C. 591.
[46] *Nouvion v Freeman* (1889) L.R. 15 App. Cas. 1, in which it was found that an attempt was being made to enforce a preliminary Spanish judgment in circumstances where the Spanish legal system provided for preliminary and plenary proceedings.
[47] *Colt Industries Inc v Sarlie (No.2)* [1966] 1 W.L.R. 1287.
[48] As to the statutory position with regard to this matter, see Administration of Justice Act 1920 s.9(2)(e) (e.g. *NML Capital Ltd v Argentina* [2010] EWCA Civ 41), and the Foreign Judgment (Reciprocal Enforcement) Act 1933 s.1(2)(a) (e.g. *Aerotel Ltd v Wavecrest Group Enterprises Ltd* [2005] EWHC 2539 (Pat)).
[49] *Sadler v Robins* (1808) 1 Camp. 253 (amount definite to the last farthing, but expenses not taxed).
[50] *Beatty v Beatty* [1924] 1 K.B. 807.
[51] See para.3–02, above.
[52] It is not an abuse of process for a judgment creditor to seek a second judgment on its original judgment with a view to avoiding difficulties in enforcing the original judgment abroad as a result of the expiry of limitation periods: *Kuwait Oil Tanker Co SAK v Al Bader* [2008] EWHC 2432 (Comm).
[53] See, e.g. *Ochsenbein v Papelier* (1873) L.R. 8 Ch. App. 695.
[54] Made in *Jacobson v Frachon* (1924) 44 T.L.R. 103: see Wolff, *Private International Law*, 2nd edn, 1950, p.268.

and *dolus praeteritus* (consisting, for example, in fraud in the getting of the judgment, as by bribing the judge or producing perjured evidence).[55]

The alleged presence of fraud (by the court; on the court; or by one party against another)[56] may vitiate a judgment. In domestic law, a judgment may be impugned only if new evidence suggestive of fraud has been discovered since the hearing. In the conflict of laws, at least in cases falling outside the Brussels/Lugano regime, there seems to be no such requirement. Indeed, a defence relating to fraud may have been kept back in the original (foreign) proceedings, to be used in the subsequent enforcement proceedings,[57] and may then be admitted to proof.

The right, or duty, of the enforcing/requested court to consider and pronounce upon the effect of some allegedly fraudulent element, brought to the notice of, and perhaps dismissed by, the court of origin, was upheld by the Court of Appeal in *Jet Holdings Inc v Patel*,[58] itself approved by the House of Lords in *Owens Bank Ltd v Bracco*.[59] But the same latitude to the defendant in permitting him to raise a defence previously held back in the foreign proceedings was not evident where the not dissimilar issue of undue influence was alleged,[60] nor in the Brussels/Lugano context does the challenge under the head of *ordre public* allow such a wide challenge.[61]

Clearly, there are warring principles of roughly equal weight: the desirability of finality of judgments is set against the undesirability of permitting a party to profit from his/her own wrongdoing. A modern understanding of comity, together with a desire for consistency, internally and in our conflict rules, may lead us,[62] when a suitable opportunity arises in the Supreme Court to place greater faith in the decision of the foreign court in such a matter.[63]

---

[55] Wolff, *Private International Law*, 2nd edn, 1950, p.268; *Macalpine v Macalpine* [1958] P. 35; *Middleton v Middleton* [1967] P.62; and more recently, *Clarke v Fennoscandia Ltd (No.2)*, 2001 S.L.T. 1311; *Clarke v Fennoscandia Ltd (No.3)*, 2005 S.L.T. 511.

[56] *Wilson v Robertson* (1884) 11 R. 893; *Price v Dewhurst* (1837) Sim. 279; *Abouloff v Oppenheimer and Co* (1882) L.R. 10 Q.B.D. 295; *Vadala v Lawes* (1890) L.R. 25 Q.B. 310; *Habib Bank Ltd v Ahmed* [2002] 1 Lloyd's Rep. 444; and *Noble v Owens* [2010] EWCA Civ 224.

[57] *Syal v Hayward* [1948] 2 K.B. 443.

[58] [1990] 1 Q.B. 335.

[59] [1992] 2 All E.R. 193 HL (enforcement sought by means of 1920 Act); [1994] 1 All E.R. 336 ECJ; though contrast *House of Spring Gardens Ltd v Waite (No.2)* [1991] 1 Q.B. 241 (*res judicata*/estoppel).

[60] *Israel Discount Bank of New York v Hadjipateras* [1984] 1 W.L.R. 137. Undue influence would be likely to be subsumed under public policy.

[61] In *Interdesco SA v Nullifire Ltd* [1992] 1 Lloyd's Rep. 180 it was held to be incompetent for the enforcing court to investigate an issue of fraud which had been subject to the scrutiny of the original EU court. Phillips J. did not favour review of the conclusions of the foreign court in a Brussels Convention case (at 187).

[62] Scots law, both conflict and domestic, seems to be the same, since *Owens Bank Ltd* is a decision upon the construction of the 1920 Act s.9(2)(d) (a provision common to Scotland and England), to the effect of upholding the availability of a conflict challenge on fraud stronger than the domestic challenge. Scots domestic law on the point (*res noviter veniens ad notitiam: Maltman v Tarmac Civil Engineering Ltd*, 1967 S.C. 177) appears to be the same as English law. Cf. *HJ Heinz Co Ltd v EFL Inc* [2010] EWHC 1203 (Comm); and *Noble v Owens* [2010] EWCA Civ 224.

[63] And see *Owens Bank Ltd v Etoile Commerciale SA* [1995] 1 W.L.R. 44 PC, e.g. per Lord Templeman at 48–51.

(5) Decree contrary to natural justice.[64] The Scottish and English courts have recognised that it is unreasonable to expect Scottish/English procedural rules[65] to be replicated abroad. Though breach of natural justice must always be one of the prime justifications for refusal to enforce a foreign decree, the requested forum must be satisfied, before refusing to enforce, that substantial justice was not done in the granting of the decree. A complaint that the defendant in the foreign court was not allowed to give evidence on his own behalf may be answered sufficiently by an explanation that neither party, in the circumstances, was entitled by the law of the forum to give evidence.[66] The ends of comity are not served if one legal system is too quick to criticise the standards of another.[67]

Procedural irregularities may result in unfairness. A proof was ordered in *Det Norske v McLaren*.[68] A Scots sea captain, whose ship had run on to the rocks off the coast of Norway, was pursued in Scotland by a Norwegian "salvor" for decree conform to a Norwegian award of salvage, or alternatively to have the case tried again in Scotland as a salvage action. The sea captain defended not only on the ground that the pursuer was not a "salvor",[69] but also because he alleged that all the proceedings took place in the Norwegian language and that he could not understand them, and further that he had not agreed to have the question of salvage settled by a Norwegian court. Notwithstanding his lack of understanding of the language of the court, he averred that the evidence led was inadequate and that the judgment was erroneous in fact and in law. Normally it is advisable to have only one excuse or defence for fear of contradicting oneself.[70]

If, in the foreign system, there is a ladder of appeal which was not used by the party then or later declaring himself aggrieved, that fact will tell against him.[71] On the other hand, force and fear imposed on a litigant to persuade him/her to seek the remedy[72] may result in non-enforcement.[73]

---

[64] *Jeannot v Fuerst* (1909) 25 T.L.R. 424; *Robinson v Fenner* [1913] 3 K.B. 835; *Re Macartney (No.2)* [1921] 1 Ch. 522; *Macalpine* [1958] P. 35; *Pemberton v Hughes* [1899] 1 Ch. 781; *Re Arbitration between the Owners of the Steamship Catalina and the Owners of the Motor Vessel Norma* (1938) 61 Ll. L. Rep. 360 (prejudice of arbitrator openly expressed).

[65] e.g. on matters such as days of notice: *Jeannot v Fuerst* (1909) 25 T.L.R. 424.

[66] *Scarpetta v Lowenfeldt* (1911) 27 T.L.R. 509.

[67] *Igra v Igra* [1951] P. 404.

[68] (1885) 22 S.L.R. 861.

[69] By which law? The claim for salvage had been authorised by a maritime court in Norway, presumably in accordance with Norwegian law as to substantive issues and amount.

[70] Remembering the unsuccessful claim of the house insured who, when challenged that he himself had set fire to his property when drunk, replied that he was entirely sober and that the bed had been on fire when he got into it.

[71] *Cooney v Dunne*, 1925 S.L.T. 22; and *Jacobson v Frachon* (1924) 44 T.L.R. 103. Moreover, the decision of the foreign court on a procedural matter may bar the raising of that issue in the enforcement proceedings: *Desert Sun Loan Corp v Hill* [1996] 2 All E.R. 847.

[72] *Re Meyer* [1971] 2 W.L.R. 401; *Hornett v Hornett* [1971] P. 255.

[73] Where a Texas court awarded a global sum of damages, to be divided among a number of plaintiffs at the discretion of the plaintiffs' lawyers, the Texan judge making no decision upon the defendants' liability to each plaintiff, this constituted one of the grounds upon which the Court of Appeal refused to enforce the judgment: *Adams v Cape Industries Plc* [1991] 1 All E.R. 929.

(6) Decree contrary to public policy.[74] At common law, there is always the possibility of a public policy challenge to meet any circumstances which arise.

Frequently, public policy defences merge with those founded on fraud, or unfair treatment of a litigant as a result of foreign rules of procedure. It is very rare in commercial circumstances for a Scots or English court qua court addressed to refuse recognition on the ground of objection to some rule of substance on which the foreign decree is founded. However, an example of an objection to the substance of a foreign decree (in family law) can be found in the case of *Re Macartney (No.2)*,[75] in which the English court refused to enforce a Maltese award of "perpetual" aliment for a posthumously born child, out of the estate of her putative father. Novelty alone would not have rendered it unenforceable on policy grounds, but it was viewed in England, at least at that time, as unfair as well as unprecedented. It has been questioned whether it is right for a British forum to direct its attention to the policy acceptability of the underlying ground of decree, rather than of the judgment. However in a case such as *Macartney* the objectionable rule gives rise to an objectionable judgment; in contractual cases there may be more distance between the rule and the judgment. In any event, the public policy challenge to a commercial judgment is rarely found.

(7) Infringements of human rights. These venerable principles which guide the court in Scotland and England in the matter of refusing enforcement of a judgment which, in the view of the court addressed, is tainted by an element of what might generally be termed, "injustice to the judgment debtor" now have to be set against[76] the background of the European Convention on Human Rights, which entails that UK courts must not permit the enforcement in the UK of a foreign judgment which is not compliant with art.6 (right to a fair and public hearing within a reasonable time by an independent and impartial tribunal established by law). Article 6 applies both to the original proceedings in another ECHR State and to the enforcement proceedings in the UK.[77] It must be asked whether the body of guidelines accumulated in UK practice in this area meets the test which the human rights jurisprudence imposes. Might it be that the protection provided by traditional conflict of laws jurisprudence falls short of what is now required?[78] Comparable with the principles of mutual trust which are applicable among EU Member States, it appears that there has emerged a presumption that proceedings which have taken place in states which are party to the ECHR are compliant with art.6.

Arguably, the UK court addressed is entitled to overlook technical breaches of art.6 if substantive justice in its view was done in the court of origin. The authority for this is a decision of the House of Lords in

---

[74] As to which, see generally Ch.3, above.

[75] [1921] 1 Ch. 522. Also *Buchler v Al-Midani* [2006] B.P.I.R. 620; *United States Securities & Exchange Commission v Manterfield* [2009] 2 All E.R. 1009.

[76] J.J. Fawcett, "The Impact of Article 6(1) of the ECHR on Private International Law" (2007) 56 I.C.L.Q. 1; G. Ward, "Protection of the Right to a Fair Trial and Civil Jurisdiction" (2008) J.R. 15.

[77] *Citibank NA v Rafidian Bank* [2003] I.L.Pr. 49.

[78] Consider the circumstances and outcome in *Jacobson v Frachon* (1924) 44 T.L.R. 103.

United States v Montgomery (No.2).[79] Montgomery's ex-husband, Barnette, was convicted on a charge of having defrauded the US Government of approximately $15 million. Shortly before conviction, Barnette transferred shares in a company, through which he had laundered the fraudulent proceeds, to his then wife. The US Government sought a tracing and confiscation order in relation to the funds, on the argument that the Government's title to the shares ante-dated Barnette's transfer of them to Montgomery, and that consequently the shares were forfeited and had to be surrendered to the Government. Barnette, being a fugitive from US justice, was not permitted under US "fugitive disentitlement" law to appear in the relevant proceedings in the United States. When the US Government sought to enforce the resultant confiscation order against Montgomery, by that date resident in the UK, Barnette argued before the English court that if the ECHR had applied in the United States, the confiscation proceedings would have breached art.6(1), and that, therefore, if the English court registered the US order, it would contravene s.6 of the Human Rights Act 1998. Lord Carswell, having referred to earlier House of Lords authority,[80] to the effect that only a case of extreme unfairness to the applicant would suffice to permit a case of indirect effect to be made out, took the view that no different proposition had yet emerged from the Strasbourg jurisprudence. The US "fugitive disentitlement" doctrine, while not in conformity strictly with art.6, was defensible, and did not fall within the "flagrant denial of justice" precept. It was not an arbitrary deprivation of a party's right to a hearing.

Unless and until the flagrant denial test is incontrovertibly rejected, the traditional approach taken in international private law jurisprudence[81] would not appear to be notably defective.

(8) Decree taken contrary to agreement. Under the Civil Jurisdiction and Judgments Act 1982 s.32,[82] a judgment given by a court in an overseas country[83] shall not be recognised or enforced in the UK if the bringing of those proceedings was contrary to an agreement,[84] by which the dispute in question was to be settled otherwise than by proceedings in the courts of that country; and those proceedings were not brought in that court by or with the agreement of the party against whom the judgment was given; and that party did not counterclaim in the proceedings or otherwise submit to the jurisdiction of that court.[85]

---

[79] [2004] 1 W.L.R. 2241. See criticism by Fawcett, "The Impact of Article 6(1) of the ECHR on Private International Law" (2007) 56 I.C.L.Q. 1, 33.

[80] *R. (on the application of Ullah) v Special Adjudicator* [2004] UKHL 26; *R. (on the application of Razgar) v Secretary of State for the Home Department* [2004] UKHL 27 (per Lord Carswell at [26]).

[81] As e.g. in *Scarpetta v Lowenfeldt* (1911) 27 T.L.R. 509.

[82] e.g. *Cavell United States Inc v Seaton Insurance Co* [2008] EWHC 876 (Comm); and *Youell v La Reunion Aerienne* [2009] EWCA Civ 175.

[83] i.e. outside UK (s.32(4)) but not a judgment falling within the Brussels regime: *Partenreederei M/S Heidberg v Grosvenor Grain & Feed Co Ltd (The Heidberg) (No.2)* [1994] 2 Lloyd's Rep. 287.

[84] So long as the agreement was not illegal, void, unenforceable or incapable of being performed for reasons not attributable to the fault of the party bringing the proceedings in which the judgment was given (s.32(2)).

[85] See *Tracomin SA v Sudan Oil Seeds Ltd (No.1)* [1983] 3 All E.R. 137 (the first case handed down on s.32).

Res judicata

9–13   A foreign decree may be founded upon as a defence to an action in Scotland[86] or England[87] if the decree was in favour of the defender in the Scottish or English action. If in such a case the pursuer maintains that the decree should not be recognised, it may still be scrutinised, but the grounds on which it may be challenged are fewer in number; for example, the pursuer in a foreign action who is suing again in Scotland can hardly plead that the court which he himself selected had no jurisdiction. The case of *Showlag v Mansour*[88] is Privy Council authority for the view that, where there are two conflicting foreign (necessarily now, non-EU) judgments on the same matter, apparently of equal standing, the first in date should be preferred.

(c) Unavailable defences

9–14   (1) Defence omitted.[89] The defender must make available all his defences in the court of origin.[90] If he fails to do so, he will not be allowed to plead them afterwards in the court addressed, i.e. the court where enforcement is requested. The only important exception to this principle concerns defences founded on fraud.[91]

   (2) Error in fact by the court of origin.

   (3) Error in law by the court of origin as to its own law.[92] Whether the error is as to the substantive law of that court, or as to its rules of jurisdiction, it does not serve as a defence against enforcement unless the "judgment" is a nullity by its own law.

   (4) Error as to Scots or English law.[93]

   (5) Defective procedure. It behoves the court addressed to pay regard to the de minimis principle. Natural justice must be secured, but the question is always whether substantial justice has been done in the instant case.[94]

---

[86] *Boe v Anderson* (1857) 20 D. 11; *Phosphate Sewage Co v Molleson* (1878) 5 R. 1125; *Comber v Maclean* (1881) 9 R. 215.

[87] *Ricardo v Garcias* (1845) 12 Cl. & F. 368; 65 R.R. 585; *Vanquelin v Bouard* (1863) 15 C.B. (N.S.) 341; *Castrique v Imrie* (1870) L.R. 4 H.L. 414; *Godard v Gray* (1870) L.R. 6 Q.B. 139; *Taylor v Hollard* [1902] 1 K.B. 676; *Jacobson v Frachon* (1924) 44 T.L.R. 103; *Kohnke v Karger* [1951] 2 K.B. 670; *Carl Zeiss Stiftung v Rayner & Keeler Ltd* [1967] 1 A.C. 853; *Air Foyle Ltd v Center Capital Ltd* [2004] I.L.Pr. 15.

[88] [1994] 2 All E.R. 129 PC.

[89] *Ellis v McHenry* (1871) L.R. 6 C.P. 228; cf. *Henderson v Henderson* (1843) 3 Hare. 100.

[90] *Clydesdale Bank Ltd v Schroder & Co* [1913] 2 K.B. 1, per Bray J. at 5: if the party "desires to prove that he is not liable to pay the money, he must defend the action which has been brought for the very purpose of deciding whether the money is payable or not. He cannot by paying under protest reserve his right to raise the question of his liability in some subsequent proceedings".

[91] See para.9–12, above.

[92] *Henderson* (1843) 3 Hare. 100; *Scott v Pilkington* (1862) 2 B. & S. 11; *Dent v Smith* (1869) L.R. 4 Q.B. 414, per Cockburn C.J. at 446; *De Cosse Brissac v Rathbone* (1861) 6 H. & N. 301; *Merker v Merker* [1963] P. 283.

[93] *Castrique v Imrie* (1870) L.R. 4 H.L. 414; *Godard v Gray* (1870) L.R. 6 Q.B. 139; cf. *Dallal v Bank Mellat* [1986] 1 All E.R. 239 (arbitration).

[94] *Pemberton v Hughes* [1899] 1 Ch. 781, e.g. per Lindley M.R. at 789–791. As to human rights implications, see para.9–12, above.

B. DIRECT ENFORCEMENT OF FOREIGN JUDGMENTS

In terms of the Judgments Extension Act 1868, and the Inferior Courts **9–15**
Judgments Extension Act 1882, a system was established of registration in
Edinburgh in a Register of English and Irish Decrees of the Supreme (and, by
the 1882 Act, the inferior) Courts of England and Ireland. After registration
these decrees were given the same effect as decrees of the Court of Session,
and might be enforced in the same way. Both Acts were repealed by the Civil
Jurisdiction and Judgments Act 1982.

There remain applicable to judgments emanating from countries outside the
geographical ambit[95] of Brussels/Lugano two Acts concerning the registration
of foreign judgments. These are the Administration of Justice Act 1920 and
the Foreign Judgments (Reciprocal Enforcement) Act 1933. The 1933 Act is
more detailed than the 1920 Act, and is much more important in terms of
geographical reach. Both Acts depend on reciprocity. Applicability of their
provisions depends on their extension by Order in Council in suitable cases[96]
to the country whence the judgment came.

The Administration of Justice Act 1920

Part II provides for the enforcement of judgments of superior courts[97] **9–16**
within Commonwealth countries,[98] by means of registration, which is a matter
of discretion and not of right. The provisions undernoted (paraphrased and
abbreviated) are those of principal importance.

A judgment[99] of a superior court of the Dominions may be enforced on
application to the High Court in England or Northern Ireland or the Court of
Session in Scotland at any time within 12 months after its date or within such
longer period as the court addressed may allow. On any such application the
court may order the judgment to be registered and enforced in the UK if it
thinks it just and convenient to do so.[100]

No judgment may be registered if[101]:

(a) the original court acted without jurisdiction; or
(b) the defender, being neither a person carrying on business nor
ordinarily resident in the jurisdiction of the court of origin, did not

---

[95] Where a judgment from an EU Member State falls outside the scope of the Brussels I
Convention Regulation, as appropriate, and likewise where a judgment from an EFTA country
falls outside the scope of the Lugano Convention or the Lugano II Convention, the 1933 Act will
continue to apply.
[96] i.e. that in such country satisfactory reciprocal provision for enforcement of UK judgments has
been made: Administration of Justice Act 1920 s.14.
[97] *Ivory, Petitioner*, 2006 S.L.T. 758.
[98] New Zealand, Falkland Islands, Jamaica, Trinidad, Ghana, Nigeria, Kenya, Tanzania, Uganda,
Zimbabwe, Zambia, Malawi, Botswana, Sri Lanka, Malaysia, Singapore. No countries will be
added to the list. Gibraltar is now governed by the Civil Jurisdiction and Judgments Act 1982
(Civil Jurisdiction and Judgments Act 1982 (Gibraltar) Order 1997 (SI 1997/2602)).
Enforcement of Hong Kong judgments, previously falling under the Administration of Justice
Act 1920, now proceeds at common law.
[99] See *Platt v Platt*, 1958 S.L.T. 94.
[100] See s.9(1).
[101] See s.9(2).

voluntarily appear or submit or agree to submit to the jurisdiction of that court[102]; or

(c) the defender was not duly served with the process of the original court and did not appear, notwithstanding that he was ordinarily resident or was carrying on business within the jurisdiction of that court or agreed to submit to the jurisdiction of that court; or

(d) the judgment was obtained by fraud; or

(e) the defender satisfies the registering court either that an appeal is pending, or that he is entitled and intends to appeal against the judgment[103]; or

(f) the judgment was in respect of a cause of action which for reasons of public policy or some other similar reason could not have been entertained by the registering court.

When registered the decree shall have as from the date of registration the same force and effect, and proceedings may be taken thereon, as if it had been a judgment originally obtained in the registering court.[104] If an action for decree conform is raised on a decree which could have been registered the pursuer shall not be entitled to expenses unless an application for registration was refused or the court orders otherwise.[105] When a judgment has been obtained in a superior court in the UK and the judgment creditor wishes to secure the enforcement of the judgment in a part of the Dominions outside the UK to which the Act extends, the court shall issue to the judgment creditor a certified copy of the judgment to enable him to enforce it.[106]

The Foreign Judgments (Reciprocal Enforcement) Act 1933

9–17   The Act applies to certain non-Commonwealth countries as well as to Commonwealth countries,[107] the hope being that ultimately it would supersede the 1920 Act. The Australian states have transferred from the 1920 to the 1933 system. European countries, in respect of which enforcement of decrees originally was governed by the 1933 Act, transferred to the Brussels system upon accession to the EU.[108] The system of reciprocity echoes that operative under s.14 of the 1920 Act.[109]

The 1933 Act governs the enforcement in the UK of judgments under certain sector-specific conventions to which the UK is party,[110] but it does not

---

[102] *Sfeir & Co v National Insurance Co of New Zealand Ltd* [1964] 1 Lloyd's Rep. 330; and *Beach Petroleum NL v Johnson* [1996] C.L.Y. 1104.

[103] Contrast common law position, and the rule under 1933 Act s.1(3).

[104] See s.9(3).

[105] See s.9(4).

[106] See s.10. *Bank of British West Africa Ltd, Petitioners*, 1931 S.L.T. 83.

[107] The list comprises Australia, Bangladesh, Canada (except Quebec), India, Isle of Man, Israel, Jersey, Guernsey, Pakistan, Surinam and Tonga. Norway was on the original list, but the Lugano Convention q.v. now applies to Norwegian judgments. See special circumstances of the Bahamas in *B v T (No.1)*, 2002 C.L.Y.B. 637.

[108] Austria, Belgium, France, Germany, Italy, Netherlands. However, where the matter falls outside the scope of the Brussels regime, the 1933 Act continues to apply.

[109] See s.9.

[110] R. Aird and N. Jameson, *Scots Dimension to Cross-Border Litigation* (Edinburgh: W. Green/ Sweet & Maxwell, 1996), para.20.23, e.g. conventions concerning carriage by rail, road, concerning oil pollution.

cover the enforcement of a judgment of a relevant foreign country if the latter was simply for the enforcement of a judgment given in a third country.[111]

The Act may not be used for the recognition or enforcement of a foreign decree which does not relate to a commercial matter.[112] The 1933 scheme of registration is mandatory: foreign decrees which can be registered under the Act are not enforceable by other means (i.e. action for decree conform is incompetent).[113]

Unlike the 1920 Act, registration is a matter of right not discretion, subject only to the provisos (s.2(1)) that registration shall not take place if at the date of the application: (a) a judgment has been wholly satisfied[114]; or (b) it could not be enforced by execution in the country of the court of origin.

The Act applies to foreign countries, specified by Order in Council,[115] which give reciprocal treatment with regard to decrees of UK courts. The Act applies only to a judgment of a recognised court which post-dates the coming into force of the relevant Order in Council and is (a) either final and conclusive[116] as between the judgment debtor and the judgment creditor, or requires the former to make an interim payment to the latter; and (b) there is payable thereunder a sum of money, not being a sum payable in respect of taxes or other charges of a like nature, or in respect of a fine or other penalty.[117]

By s.2(1), application for registration may be made by the judgment creditor to the Court of Session within six years of the date of the decree or last judgment in the appeal proceedings; and upon registration the decree has the same force and effect as a decree of the courts of this country.[118]

Section 4(1)(a) contains grounds upon which the registration shall be set aside[119] by the registering court, viz.:

(i) the Act does not apply to the judgment in question, or the judgment was registered in contravention of the above provisions of the Act; or

(ii) the courts of the country of the original court had no jurisdiction in the circumstances of the case[120]; or

---

[111] 1933 Act s.1(2A), added by Civil Jurisdiction and Judgments Act 1982 Sch.10, pertaining to judgments at one remove, e.g. judgments of the foreign court on appeal from a court which is not a recognised court, or a judgment regarded as a judgment of the foreign court but made in another country.

[112] *Maples v Maples* [1987] 3 All E.R. 188 (concerning a Jewish divorce).

[113] See s.6.

[114] If, at the date of application for registration, the judgment has been partially satisfied, judgment shall be registered only in respect of the balance remaining payable at that date (s.2(4)).

[115] See s.1(1).

[116] See s.1(3): a judgment shall be deemed to be final and conclusive notwithstanding that an appeal may be pending against it, or that it may still be subject to appeal, in the courts of the country of the original court.

[117] See s.1(2).

[118] 1933 Act s.2(2): *Re A Judgment Debtor* [1939] 1 All E.R. 1; *Ferdinand Wagner v Laubscher Bros & Co* [1970] 2 Q.B. 313.

[119] *Société Coopérative Sidmetal v Titan International Ltd* [1965] 3 All E.R. 494; *Northern Electricity Supply Corp (Private) Ltd v Jamieson*, 1971 S.L.T. 22 (expenses).

[120] Section 4(2)(a), (b), (c): recognised grounds of jurisdiction in the court of origin are in essence *in personam*—submission by voluntary appearance by the judgment debtor; or the debtor's residence or place of business in that place. In the case of a judgment given in an action in which the subject matter was immoveable property, or in an action *in rem* of which the subject matter was moveable property, jurisdiction will be held to exist if the property in question was at the time of the proceedings in the original court situated in the country of that court. In all

(iii) the defender (even if duly served in accordance with the law of the country of the original court) did not receive notice of the proceedings in sufficient time to enable him to defend the proceedings, and did not appear; or

(iv) the judgment was obtained by fraud; or

(v) the enforcement of the judgment would be contrary to public policy in the country of the registering court[121]; or

(vi) the rights under the judgment are not vested in the person by whom the application for registration was made.

Section 4(1)(b) states that the registration may be set aside if the registering court is satisfied that the matter in dispute in the proceedings in the original court had previously to the date of the judgment in the original court been the subject of a final and conclusive judgment by another court having jurisdiction in the matter (*res judicata*).

Section 5(1) provides that on an application to set aside registration, if the applicant satisfies the registering court either that an appeal is pending, or that he is entitled and intends to appeal against the judgment, the court may set aside the registration or adjourn the application until after the expiration of such period as appears to the court to be reasonably sufficient to enable the applicant to take the necessary steps to have the appeal disposed of by the competent tribunal.

The setting aside of a registered judgment shall not prejudice a further application to register the judgment when the appeal has been disposed of or if and when the judgment becomes enforceable by execution in that country.[122]

Section 8(1) provides for finality of judgment: a judgment to which Pt I applies or would have applied if a sum of money had been payable thereunder, whether it can be registered or not, or whether, if it can be registered, it is registered or not, shall be recognised in any court in the UK as conclusive between the parties thereto in all proceedings founded on the same cause of action and may be relied on by way of defence or counterclaim.[123]

The Protection of Trading Interests Act 1980

9–18   Although the 1920 and 1933 statutes provide a structure, the system of judgment enforcement thereby enacted essentially resembles that of the common law; common law authorities on matters such as fraud, natural justice or public policy therefore may be useful. All systems so far considered envisage the enforcement in the UK of fixed money judgments from courts of a foreign legal system which has jurisdiction according to an international test; and a

---

other cases, if the jurisdiction of the original court is recognised by the law of the registering court, the original court will be taken to have been competent to hear the case subject to the provision below. But the court is deemed not to have had jurisdiction if the subject matter was immoveable property outside the country of the original court, or if the defender was immune under the rules of public international law from the jurisdiction of the original court and did not submit to that jurisdiction. If the judgment debtor was the claimant in or counterclaimed in the proceedings of the original court, the court of origin will be deemed to have had jurisdiction.

[121] *SA Consortium General Textiles v Sun & Sand Agencies* [1978] 2 All E.R. 339.
[122] See s.5(2).
[123] *Black Clawson International Ltd v Papierwerke Waldhof-Aschaffenburg AG* [1975] 1 All E.R. 810. But see now for England the Foreign Limitation Periods Act 1984 s.3.

registration system caters for those countries which have entered into reciprocal arrangements with the UK.

The enforcement system described hereto, at common law and under the Acts of 1920 and 1933, is subject to the Protection of Trading Interests Act 1980 s.5, in terms whereof no judgment to which s.5 applies shall be registered under the Acts of 1920 or of 1933, nor shall common law enforcement proceedings be entertained by any UK court.[124] The judgments affected are:

Section 5(2) (paraphrased and abbreviated):

(a) a judgment for multiple damages, i.e. a judgment for an amount arrived at by doubling, trebling or otherwise multiplying a sum assessed as compensation for the loss or damage sustained by the person in whose favour the judgment is given[125];

(b) a judgment based on a provision or rule of law specified or described in an order under s.5(4)[126];

(c) a judgment on a claim for contribution in respect of damages awarded by a judgment falling within (a) or (b) above.

Section 6 applies where such a judgment for multiple damages has been made against a UK citizen, or company incorporated in the UK or person carrying on business in the UK, and where such a defendant has paid (or has yielded through process of execution (s.6(6)) an amount on account of the damages. In such circumstances, unless the party (the "qualifying defendant") was ordinarily resident in the overseas country at the time of the institution of the judgment proceedings, or is a body corporate with its principal business there, or carried on business in the overseas country and the judgment proceedings concerned activities exclusively carried on in that country, the qualifying defendant shall be entitled to recover from the judgment creditor so much of the amount as exceeds the part attributable to compensation.[127] Further, by s.6(5), a court in the UK may entertain proceedings on such a claim even though the person against whom the proceedings are brought is not within the jurisdiction of the court.

This legislation, unusual in nature, and unusually specific, is designed to protect British individuals and companies from American antitrust legislation which makes possible an award of multiple damages for losses caused by anti-competitive actings.[128] Section 5 (and consequently s.6) does not apply within

---

[124] See *British Airways Board v Laker Airways Ltd* [1985] A.C. 58.

[125] See s.5(3). Although on a literal interpretation of s.5, such a judgment would be wholly unenforceable, *Lewis v Eliades (No.2)* [2004] 1 W.L.R. 692 is authority for the segregation and enforcement of the compensatory (i.e. non-punitive) element of an award in a case where the judgment pertains to several causes of action in respect of some, but not all of which, punitive multiplication has been applied.

[126] i.e. a judgment appearing to the Secretary of State to be concerned with the prohibition or regulation of agreements, arrangements or practices designed to restrain, distort or restrict competition in the carrying on of business of any description or to be otherwise concerned with the promotion of such competition.

[127] As defined: s.6(2).

[128] For explanation of background and details, see *Cheshire, North and Fawcett: Private International Law*, 14th edn, 2008, pp.561–563.

the Brussels/Lugano ambit, nor, generally, does it appear to strike at other foreign awards of exemplary damages which do not fall within the definition provided by s.5(3).[129]

C. JUDGMENTS RENDERED IN EU MEMBER STATES OR EFTA STATES[130]

Civil Jurisdiction and Judgments Acts 1982 and 1991[131]

9–19 It falls to consider the system of "free flow of judgments" instituted by the Brussels Convention, now largely replaced by the Brussels I Regulation, and associated European Regulations and the Lugano and Lugano II Conventions.[132] Since the 1968 Convention was a double convention, concerned to reach agreement on jurisdiction and then to proceed to a relatively simple enforcement method, certain differences from the systems earlier described are apparent, one at the outset being the small scope for query as to the jurisdiction of the court of the Member State of origin. Further, the Brussels mechanism is not limited to the enforcement of money judgments, but may extend to decrees *ad factum praestandum*; it does not matter that the judgment is not final, nor is the level of the hierarchy whence the decree comes significant.

Brussels I Regulation

Introduction and general principles

9–20 The Brussels Convention laid down its own procedure for recognition and enforcement, a procedure which has been streamlined, but not in essentials changed by the Brussels I Regulation. Where the Brussels regime is operative, no other (e.g. common law) procedure is competent[133]; the Brussels system is obligatory.

The recognition and enforcement rules of the Regulation apply only to judgments[134] from Community countries,[135] and only to such judgments as fall within the scope of the Regulation, that is, judgments in civil and commercial matters, not specifically excluded by art.1.[136] The rules of recognition and

---

[129] *SA Consortium General Textiles v Sun & Sand Agencies* [1978] 2 All E.R. 339. See, however, Rome II Regulation para.16.46, below.

[130] See W. Kennett, The Enforcement of Judgments in Europe (Oxford: Oxford University Press, 2000); and Hill, *International Commercial Disputes in English Courts*, 3rd edn, 2005.

[131] As amended by the Civil Jurisdiction and Judgments Order 2001 (SI 2001/3929), and Civil Jurisdiction and Judgments Regulations 2009 (SI 2009/3131).

[132] See Ch.7, above.

[133] *De Wolf v Harry Cox BV* [1976] E.C.R. 1759.

[134] Article 32: the recognition and enforcement scheme applies to any judgment given by a court or tribunal of a Member State, whatever the judgment may be called, including a decree, order, decision or writ of execution, as well as the determination of costs or expenses by an officer of the court. For provisions in the Brussels I Regulation concerning authentic instruments and court settlements, see Ch.IV (arts 57, 58). See, under the Convention arts.31, 50, *Baden-Wurttembergische Bank AG, Petitioner*, 2009 G.W.D. 20-318 (unsuccessful challenge on public policy).

[135] There can be no "laundering" of non-EU judgments: *Owens Bank Ltd v Bracco (No.2)* [1994] 1 All E.R. 336. The Convention/Regulation enforcement procedure does not apply to judgments from a court of a non-Contracting/non-Member State (cf. exclusion of laundering in 1933 Act s.1(2A)).

[136] See art.25.

enforcement vis-à-vis all Member States except Denmark are contained in Ch.III arts 32–56 of the Regulation. The ambit of the Brussels Convention is restricted to Denmark; as regards enforcement of Danish judgments in the UK and vice versa, reference must be made to the Brussels Convention.[137]

The enforcement mechanism under both the Regulation and the Convention applies to all qualifying judgments, whether or not the defendant was "domiciled" in a Member/Contracting State, or in Denmark. This feature of the original Convention made it necessary to provide therein for the possibility of bilateral agreements between Contracting States and non-Contracting States whose nationals live in Contracting States, in order to ensure that in the former states the enforcement procedures might not be used against such nationals in the territory of Contracting States.[138] Such bilateral agreements continue to be respected under the Regulation.[139]

Henceforth in this chapter, reference shall be to the terms of the Regulation.

Scope

The scope of the Regulation encompasses civil and commercial matters. It **9–21** shall not extend, in particular, to revenue, customs or administrative matters.[140] The Regulation shall not apply to the following categories of decree[141]:

(a) the status or legal capacity of natural persons, rights in property arising out of a matrimonial relationship,[142] wills and succession;
(b) bankruptcy, proceedings relating to the winding-up of insolvent companies or other legal persons, judicial arrangements, compositions and analogous proceedings;
(c) social security;
(d) and arbitration.[143]

Recognition rules in the Brussels I Regulation

Article 33

"1. A judgment given in a Member State shall be recognised in the other **9–22** Member States without any special procedure being required.[144]

---

[137] See para.7–06, above.
[138] Brussels Convention art.59.
[139] Brussels I Regulation art.72. But see fn.162, below.
[140] See art.1.1.
[141] See art.1.2.
[142] But maintenance is included; and where a matter falls in the area of maintenance and matrimonial property, questions of classification arise, one such case being *Van den Boogaard v Laumen* (C-220/95) [1997] All E.R. (E.C.) 517 (relating to art.5.2). See also *De Cavel v De Cavel* (C-143/78) [1979] E.C.R. 1055; *De Cavel v De Cavel* (120/79) [1980] E.C.R. 731; *Farrell v Long* (C295/95) [1997] All E.R. (E.C.) 449; and *Moore v Moore* [2007] I.L.Pr. 36. See Ch.12, below concerning consistorial causes, and Ch.13, below regarding matrimonial property issues, including commentary on Regulation 4/2009.
[143] What is to happen if a foreign court takes jurisdiction and pronounces decree in a case where ordinarily it would have jurisdiction were it not for an arbitration clause, on the view that the arbitration is invalid or not incorporated in the agreement? See paras 9–51, below.
[144] Where a judgment is given against a state by a court in another state, this, to be enforceable, must be in conformity with the State Immunity Act 1978. See *NML Capital Ltd v Argentina* [2009] 1 Lloyd's Rep. 378.

2. Any interested party who raises the recognition of a judgment as the principal issue in a dispute may, in accordance with the procedures provided for in Sections 2 and 3 of this Chapter, apply for a decision that the judgment be recognised.
3. If the outcome of proceedings in a court of a Member State depends on the determination of an incidental question of recognition that court shall have jurisdiction over the question."

Article 34

9–23 "A judgment shall not be recognised:

1. if such recognition is manifestly contrary to public policy in the Member State in which recognition is sought[145];
2. where it was given in default of appearance, if the defendant was not served with the document which instituted the proceedings or with an equivalent document in sufficient time and in such a way as to enable him to arrange for his defence, unless the defendant failed to commence proceedings to challenge the judgment when it was possible for him to do so;
3. if it is irreconcilable with a judgment given in a dispute between the same parties in the Member State in which recognition is sought[146];
4. if it is irreconcilable with an earlier judgment given in another Member State or in a third State involving the same cause of action and between the same parties, provided that the earlier judgment fulfils the conditions necessary for its recognition in the Member State addressed."

Public policy

9–24 The first of the four grounds is the widest of these challenges. Significantly, it may be possible to argue that a judgment obtained in breach of a jurisdiction clause, or an arbitration clause, should be refused effect by a Member State court on the grounds of public policy.[147] Although under this heading of public policy/*ordre public* there will be subsumed allegations of fraud, the challenge is a muted version of the stronger one which is available at common law.[148]

As to the human rights dimension, is the public policy challenge as evidenced in the development of jurisprudence thereon under the Brussels

---

[145] *Viking Line ABP v International Transport Workers' Federation* [2006] I.L.Pr. 4 at [78]–[81]; and, earlier, under Brussels Convention, *Societe d'Informatique Service Realisation Organisation (SISRO) v Ampersand Software BV* [1994] I.L.Pr. 55; and *Materiel Auxiliaire d'Informatique v Printed Forms Equipment Ltd* [2006] I.L.Pr. 44.
[146] *Hoffmann v Krieg* (145/86) [1988] E.C.R. 645 (in the context of divorce).
[147] *Philip Alexander Securities & Futures Ltd v Bamberger* [1997] I.L.Pr. 73, and *National Navigation Co v Endesa Generacion SA (The Wadi Sudr)* [2009] EWHC 196 (Comm).
[148] *Interdesco SA v Nullifire Ltd* [1992] 1 Lloyd's Rep. 180. Equally, the ECJ in *Regie Nationale des Usines Renault SA v Maxicar SpA* [2000] E.C.R. I-2973 displayed disinclination to revisit alleged error in the application of Community law by the Member State court of origin; the public policy challenge under the Brussels regime is to be interpreted strictly, and for it to be invoked, there would have to exist a manifest breach of a rule of law viewed as essential, or manifest breach of a right acknowledged as fundamental in the legal order of the Member State addressed; cf at common law, para.9–12, above.

regime[149] co-extensive with the challenge which may be made to the conduct of a court process in terms of the ECHR art.6,[150] or does it fall short of what the ECHR requires?

In *Maronier v Larmer*,[151] in 1984, a Dutch national began proceedings in the Netherlands against the defendant for damages for allegedly negligent dental treatment. The defendant filed a defence, but in 1986 the proceedings were stayed on the application of the claimant. In 1991, the defendant moved to reside in the UK. In 1998, the claimant sought to reactivate the case, by which time the defendant's solicitors had lost contact with him. The claimant made no attempt to contact the defendant, and in due course he obtained decree in absence from a Dutch court. After expiry of the time period for appeal in the Netherlands, the claimant applied ex parte to enforce the Dutch judgment in the UK under the Brussels Convention. An appeal by the claimant, against a first instance decision to refuse to register the Dutch decree, failed. The Court of Appeal, holding that the defendant manifestly had been denied a fair trial within the terms of ECHR art.6 opined that the Brussels aim of simple and rapid enforcement would be frustrated if the court addressed were required to carry out a detailed review of whether the procedure in the court of origin was art.6-compliant. Rather the court addressed should apply a strong, but rebuttable presumption that the court procedures of states which are party to the ECHR are compliant with art.6. Further, the Brussels Convention itself, in art.2, expressly recognises the right of a defendant to have a fair opportunity to defend.

The Court of Appeal decision in *Maronier*[152] has been criticised for paying insufficient attention to the jurisprudence of the European Court of Human Rights,[153] in contrast with the earlier Scottish case of *SA Marie Brizzard et Roger International v William Grant & Sons Ltd (No.2)*.[154] In *Marie Brizzard*, upon registration having been granted by a Scots court of a judgment of the *Cour D'Appel de Bordeaux*, the judgment debtors appealed under art.36 of the Brussels Convention, on the argument that the judgment should not be recognised and enforced in Scotland, being contrary to public policy in terms of art.27, with particular reference to art.6.1 of the ECHR. The judgment debtors alleged that their rights under art.6 had been infringed. Their complaint pertained to the constitution of the court of first instance, the *Tribunal de Commerce de Bordeaux*, which they alleged lacked objective impartiality. Their appeal on that ground was refused. In the judgment of Lord Mackay of Drumadoon, which took proper account of Strasbourg jurisprudence, it was right to look objectively at the whole history of the French proceedings. It was

---

[149] See, e.g. see *Krombach v Bamberski* [2001] Q.B. 709; *Pordea v Times Newspapers Ltd* [2001] C.L.Y.B. 818; *Marie Brizard et Roger International SA v William Grant & Sons Ltd (No.2)*, 2002 S.L.T. 1365; *Gambazzi v DaimlerChrysler Canada Inc* (C-394/07) [2009] 1 Lloyd's Rep. 647.

[150] The right to a fair and public hearing within a reasonable time by an independent and impartial tribunal established by law. See at common law, para–9.12.

[151] [2003] Q.B. 620.

[152] *Maronier v Larmer* [2003] Q.B. 620.

[153] See Fawcett, "The Impact of Article 6(1) of the ECHR on Private International Law" (2007) 56 I.C.L.Q. 1, 27.

[154] 2002 S.L.T. 1365. See generally Fentiman, *International Commercial Litigation*, 2010, paras 18–28, 18–29.

a question of fact whether any infringement of ECHR rights at an early stage could be, and in fact had been, cured on appeal; there was no doubt that the proceedings in the *Cour D'Appel* were fully compliant with art.6. On that basis, the judgment debtors had been afforded their full rights conferred by art.6. Lord Mackay, therefore, rejected the argument by the respondents, William Grant, that the judgment sought to be enforced was tainted by the original judgment of the *Tribunal*, which was its genesis. For such cases arising in Scots courts, it may be predicted that a court will follow Lord Mackay's example, not only in the attention he paid to human rights case law, but also, importantly, in his Lordship's approach of considering the entirety of the foreign proceedings in coming to his conclusion that there had been no breach of art.6 such as to preclude recognition and enforcement of the French decree in Scotland.

Due service

9–25   In the Brussels Convention, the word "duly" preceded "served" in this context.[155] In *Pendy Plastic Products BV v Pluspunkt*,[156] the ECJ decision was that "due service" was to be tested against the law of the court of origin, and the concept of service in "sufficient time" by the law of the court addressed. Although one of the aims of the Regulation is further to streamline the system of judgment enforcement, there is no question of there being any undermining of the right to a fair trial and the opportunity to prepare a defence.[157] Hence, the omission of the adverb "duly" was probably not significant in drafting terms; rather, with the advent of the Service Regulation,[158] the question has arisen whether service which does not meet the rules set out therein can found a ground of challenge under art.34.2, i.e. whether, in effect, "duly" has been silently reinstated with more technical meaning. In *Tavoulareas v Tsavliris (The Atlas Pride)*,[159] it was argued that the defendant had to be served in accordance with the concept of service under the Service Regulation in order to forestall any challenge under art.34.2. But the view has been advanced that, "service should be widely construed, and the essential question is whether the defendant had sufficient time to arrange his defence".[160]

---

[155] See art.27.2. See *Scania Finance France SA v Rockinger Spezialfabrik fur Anhangerkupplungen GmbH* (C522/03) [2006] I.L.Pr. 1.; *Arctic Fish Sales Co Ltd v Adam (No.2)*, 1995 G.W.D. 25-1351, and *Selco Ltd v Mercier*, 1996 S.L.T. 1247; *Verdoliva v JM van der Hoeven BV* (C-3/05) [2006] I.L.Pr. 31 (interpretation of art.36 of the Convention as to due service of the decision authorising enforcement).

[156] *Pendy Plastic Products BV v Pluspunkt Handelsgesellschaft mbH* (C228/81) [1982] E.C.R. 2723. See also *Debaecker v Bouwman* [1985] E.C.R. 1779; *TSN Kunststoffrecycling GmbH v Jurgens* [2002] 1 W.L.R. 2459.

[157] e.g. *ASML Netherlands BV v Semiconductor Industry Services GmbH (Semis)*, (C-283/05) [2007] I.L.Pr. 4 ECJ; *ASML Netherlands BV v Semiconductor Industry Services GmbH* [2009] I.L.Pr. 29 Supreme Court (Austria).

[158] Regulation 1348/2000; and now Regulation 1393/2007.

[159] [2006] EWCA Civ 1772. See also *Scania Finance France SA v Rockinger Spezialfabrik fur Anhangerkupplungen GmbH & Co* (C522/03) [2006] I.L.Pr. 1.

[160] *Cheshire, North and Fawcett: Private International Law*, 14th edn, 2008, p.618.

Article 35

"1. Moreover, a judgment shall not be recognised if it conflicts with **9–26** Sections 3, 4 or 6 of Chapter II,[161] or in a case provided for in Article 72.[162]

2. In its examination of the grounds of jurisdiction referred to in the foregoing paragraph, the court or authority applied to shall be bound by the findings of fact on which the court of the Member State of origin based its jurisdiction.

3. Subject to paragraph 1, the jurisdiction of the court of the Member State of origin may not be reviewed.[163] The test of public policy referred to in point 1 of Article 34 may not be applied to the rules relating to jurisdiction."

Article 36

"Under no circumstances may a foreign judgment be reviewed as to its **9–27** substance."

Article 37

"1. A court of a Member State in which recognition is sought of a **9–28** judgment given in another Member State may stay the proceedings if an ordinary appeal against the judgment has been lodged.

2. A court of a Member State in which recognition is sought of a judgment given in Ireland or the United Kingdom may stay the proceedings if enforcement is suspended in the State of origin, by reason of an appeal."

Enforcement rules in Brussels I Regulation

Article 38

"1. A judgment given in a Member State and enforceable in that State **9–29** shall be enforced in another Member State when, on the application of any interested party,[164] it has been declared enforceable there.

2. However, in the United Kingdom, such a judgment shall be enforced in England and Wales, in Scotland, or in Northern Ireland when, on

---

[161] That is to say, jurisdiction in matters relating to insurance (3); jurisdiction over consumer contracts (4); and exclusive jurisdiction provisions (6). The sanction to contest jurisdiction contained in art.35.1 does not extend to cases falling under section 5 (jurisdiction over individual contracts of employment). It is unlikely that this occurred through simple oversight; it is probable that a distinction was drawn between employment contracts and the other cases insofar as the applicant in the former case is more likely to be the employee, and any re-visiting of the jurisdictional competence would favour the employer rather than the employee, who is the perceived weaker party, whom these rules are designed to protect. See Hill, *International Commercial Disputes in English Courts*, 3rd edn, 2005, para.13.3.5.

[162] Article 72 ensures that agreements made by Member States with third states to protect defendants domiciled or habitually resident in those third states shall not be affected by the Regulation. It does not appear, however, that such special arrangements may be made in future.

[163] But see *Continuity Promotions Ltd v O'Connor's Nenagh Shopping Centre Ltd* [2005] EWHC 3462, QBD, in which the English court declined, in view of exceptional circumstances, to set aside a default judgment which had been entered against an Irish defendant in England without jurisdiction in terms of the Brussels I Regulation.

[164] *Haji-Ioannou v Frangos* [2009] I.L.Pr. 56.

the application of any interested party, it has been registered for enforcement in that part of the United Kingdom."[165]

This is the *exequatur* procedure ("declaration of enforceability"). In terms of art.53, a party seeking recognition or applying for a declaration of enforceability shall produce a copy of the judgment, which satisfies the conditions necessary to establish its authenticity, together with a certificate. No legalisation or other similar formality shall be required in respect of the copy judgment, certificate, or translation thereof, or in respect of a document appointing a representative *ad litem*.[166]

Article 39

9–30   "1. The application shall be submitted to the court or competent authority indicated in the list in Annex II.[167]

2. The local jurisdiction shall be determined by reference to the place of domicile of the party against whom enforcement is sought or to the place of enforcement."

Article 40

9–31   "1. The procedure for making the application shall be governed by the law of the Member State in which enforcement is sought.

2. The applicant must give an address for service of process within the area of jurisdiction of the court applied to. However, if the law of the Member State in which enforcement is sought does not provide for the furnishing of such an address, the applicant shall appoint a representative *ad litem*.

3. The documents referred to in Article 53 shall be attached to the application."[168]

---

[165] For the UK, reference is to the process of registration rather than to the declaration of enforceability (*q.v.* art.41): Hill, *International Commercial Disputes in English Courts*, 3rd edn, 2005, para.13.4.10; and Jenard-Möller Report on the Lugano Convention [1990] OJ C189/79 (para.68). This difference is attributable to the lack of an *exequatur* procedure per se in the UK, but the difference is largely one of terminology.

[166] See art.56. See also arts 51 and 52 re costs.

[167] Within the UK, application shall be submitted to: (a) In England and Wales, to the High Court of Justice, or in the case of a maintenance judgment to the magistrates' court; (b) in Scotland, to the Court of Session, or in the case of a maintenance judgment to the sheriff court; and (c) in Northern Ireland to the High Court of Justice, or in the case of a maintenance judgment to the magistrates' court (per Regulation 280/2009 amending Annexes I, II, III and IV to Council Regulation (EC) No 44/2001 on jurisdiction and the recognition and enforcement of judgments in civil and commercial matters [2009] OJ l93/13).

[168] i.e. a copy of the judgment, which satisfies the conditions necessary to establish its authenticity. A party applying for a declaration of enforceability shall also produce (without prejudice to art.55) the certificate referred to in art.54: the court or competent authority of a Member State where a judgment was given shall issue, at the request of any interested party, a certificate using the standard form in Annex V to the Regulation. Article 55 provides that if such certificate is not produced, the court or competent authority (by inference, of the state addressed) may specify a time for its production, or accept an equivalent document, or if it considers that it has sufficient information before it, dispense with its production. If that latter court so requires, a certified translation of the document shall be produced.

Article 41[169]

"The judgment shall be declared enforceable immediately on completion **9–32** of the formalities in Article 53 [*q.v.*] without any review under Articles 34 and 35. The party against whom enforcement is sought shall not at this stage of the proceedings be entitled to make any submissions on the application."

Article 42

"1. The decision on the application for a declaration of enforceability **9–33** shall forthwith be brought to the notice of the applicant in accordance with the procedure laid down by the law of the Member State in which enforcement is sought.
2. The declaration of enforceability shall be served on the party against whom enforcement is sought, accompanied by the judgment, if not already served on that party."

Article 43

"1. The decision on the application for a declaration of enforceability **9–34** may be appealed against by either party.[170]
2. The appeal is to be lodged with the court indicated in the list in Annex III.[171]
3. The appeal shall be dealt with in accordance with the rules governing procedure in contradictory matters.
4. If the party against whom enforcement is sought fails to appear before the appellate court in proceedings concerning an appeal brought by the applicant, Article 26(2) to (4) shall apply[172] even where the party

---

[169] Note also art.38.2, in relation to the UK.
[170] Under the Brussels I Regulation, it must be concluded that there are very few grounds upon which the applicant shall be refused this declaration of enforceability; presumably the only possible ground would be failure to comply with the formalities of art.53. This must be contrasted with the situation which obtained under the Brussels Convention, in which (per art.34) although the party against whom enforcement was sought was not entitled at that stage to make any submissions on the application, the application might be refused for one of the reasons specified in arts 27 and 28 of the Convention (i.e. the substantive grounds of refusal of recognition—public policy, natural justice, failure to observe the jurisdictional rules with regard to disadvantaged parties, etc.). Under the Brussels I Regulation, however, the judgment shall be declared enforceable immediately on completion of the formalities, without any review under arts 34 and 35 (the equivalent non-recognition grounds). Articles 34 and 35 can be invoked only after the declaration of enforceability has been granted. Thus, it would seem that recognition under art.33.1 is provisional in nature.
[171] In the UK, as follows: (a) in England and Wales, with the High Court of Justice or (maintenance judgment) magistrates' court; (b) in Scotland, with the Court of Session, or (maintenance judgment) sheriff court; and (c) in Northern Ireland with the High Court of Justice, or (maintenance judgment) magistrates' court (per Regulation 280/2009).
[172] i.e. rules concerning the case where a defendant domiciled in one Member State is sued in a court of another Member State and does not enter an appearance: the court shall declare of its own motion that it has no jurisdiction unless its jurisdiction is derived from the provisions of the Brussels I Regulation. The court then shall stay its proceedings unless it is shown that the defendant has received sufficient intimation in sufficient time to enable him to arrange for his defence, or that all necessary steps have been taken to this end (subject to Regulation 1393/2007 (service of documents), art.19, where applicable; where Regulation 1393/2007 is not applicable, the 1965 Hague Convention art.15 shall apply).

against whom enforcement is sought is not domiciled in any of the Member States.

5. An appeal against the declaration of enforceability is to be lodged within one month of service thereof. If the party against whom enforcement is sought is domiciled in a Member State other than that in which the declaration of enforceability was given, the time for appealing shall be two months and shall run from the date of service, either on him in person or at his residence. No extension of time may be granted on account of distance."

Article 44

9–35   "The judgment given on the appeal may be contested only by the appeal referred to in Annex IV."

Article 45

9–36   "1. The court with which an appeal is lodged under Article 43 and Article 44 shall refuse or revoke a declaration of enforceability only on one of the grounds specified in Articles 34 and 35. It shall give its decision without delay.

2. Under no circumstances may the foreign judgment be reviewed as to its substance."

Article 46

9–37   "1. The court with which an appeal is lodged under Article 43 or Article 44 may, on the application of the party against whom enforcement is sought,[173] stay the proceedings if an ordinary appeal has been lodged against the judgment in the Member State of origin or if the time for such an appeal has not yet expired; in the latter case, the court may specify the time within which such an appeal is to be lodged.

2. Where the judgment was given in Ireland or the United Kingdom, any form of appeal available in the Member State of origin shall be treated as an ordinary appeal for the purposes of paragraph 1.

3. The court may also make enforcement conditional on the provision of such security as it shall determine."

Article 47

9–38   "1. When a judgment must be recognised in accordance with this Regulation, nothing shall prevent the applicant from availing himself of provisional, including protective, measures in accordance with the law of the Member State requested without a declaration of enforceability under Article 41 being required.

2. The declaration of enforceability shall carry with it the power to proceed to any protective measures.

3. During the time specified for an appeal pursuant to Article 43(5) against the declaration of enforceability and until such appeal has been determined, no measures of enforcement may be taken other

---

[173] See *Petereit v Babcock International Holdings Ltd* [1990] 1 W.L.R. 350.

than protective measures against the property of the party against whom enforcement is sought."

Article 48

"1. Where a foreign judgment has been given in respect of several matters **9–39** and the declaration of enforceability cannot be given for all of them, the court or competent authority shall give it for one or more of them.

2. An applicant may request a declaration of enforceability limited to parts of a judgment."

Summary of enforcement procedure under the Brussels I Regulation[174]

The following is an outline of the procedure to be followed by a claimant **9–40** seeking to enforce a Member State judgment in Scotland. The claimant must sue on the judgment, and not on the cause of action.[175]

(1) Application for declaration of enforceability (i.e. registration) is made ex parte to the Court of Session. The defender has no right to be heard, or even to be informed. The element of surprise is intended to lessen the possibility of removal by the defender of his property from the enforcing state.

(2) The declaration of enforceability shall be granted (i.e. registration shall be made) immediately on completion of due formalities (i.e. production of relevant documents), without any review at this stage of matters such as public policy, natural justice, and such challenges to jurisdiction as the Regulation permits. The defender at this stage shall not be entitled to make any submissions.

(3) A declaration of enforceability (i.e. registration) shall carry with it the power to proceed to any protective measures.

(4) The declaration of enforceability (i.e. registered order) shall be served on the defender.

(5) The decision on the application for a declaration of enforceability (registration) may be appealed against by either party, to the Court of Session, within a period of one month (or two months, if the party against whom enforcement is sought is domiciled in another Member State).

(6) The judgment given on the appeal may be contested only by a single further appeal on a point of law to the Inner House of the Court of Session.[176]

(7) In the case of appeal at stages (4) or (5), the grounds of appeal are limited to those specified in arts 34 and 35 (public policy, natural justice, jurisdiction (so far as permitted)), except that the proceedings may be stayed if an ordinary appeal has been lodged against the judgment in the Member State of origin or if the time for such an appeal has not yet expired.

---

[174] See, in detail, Rules of Court of Session, Ch.62—recognition, registration and enforcement of foreign judgments, etc.—Pt V—recognition and enforcement under the Civil Jurisdiction and Judgments Act 1982, or under Regulation 44/2001, or under Lugano II.

[175] *De Wolf v Henry Cox BV* [1976] E.C.R. 1759.

[176] Civil Jurisdiction and Judgments Order 2001 (SI 2001/3929) Sch.1 r.4.

Future position

9–41   The European Commission Report on the Brussels I Regulation stated that following the political mandate granted by the Tampere and Hague programmes, the "main objective of the revision of the [Brussels I] Regulation should be the abolition of the exequatur procedure in all matters covered by the Regulation."[177] On the argument that the majority of challenges to the grant of declarations of enforceability are unsuccessful, the Commission, in the Green Paper,[178] put forward the view that it is difficult to justify in an internal market without frontiers the expense occasioned to individuals and businesses by the *exequatur* procedure in asserting their rights abroad. The model for an allegedly *exequatur*-free zone exists in the area of uncontested and small claims,[179] and the Commission now proposes that *exequatur* should be removed also from contested claims.

The Report of the House of Lords EU Committee[180] indicates that the UK Government is very cautious in the support which it lends to the Commission's suggestion, while agreeing that maintaining the requirement of *exequatur* is now difficult to justify.

Extent of operation of Brussels regime of recognition and enforcement

9–42   Delimiting the extent of the Brussels regime of jurisdiction and judgments is an area of current concern and complexity, which has been addressed in Ch.7, above from the standpoint of the extent of operation of the rules of jurisdiction, and their possible reflexive effect.[181] The case of *Orams v Apostolides*,[182] which was the subject of a reference for a preliminary ruling from the ECJ,[183] addresses this difficult point from the perspective of judgment enforcement.

Apostolides, a Cypriot national, sought, from an English court, recognition and enforcement of two judgments obtained by him against Mr and Mrs Orams, British nationals, from a court in Nicosia, in the southern, Greek-controlled, Republic of Cyprus, which became part of the EU in 2004. In principle, the recognition and enforcement of its judgments by other Member States should be governed by the Brussels I Regulation, as above described. However, the orders in question concerned land situated in that part of Cyprus controlled by the Turkish Cypriot administration and not, therefore, within the area over which the Government of the Republic of Cyprus exercised effective control, and not, accordingly, within the EU. The Turkish Republic of Northern Cyprus is not recognised by the international community, with the exception of Turkey. By a protocol annexed to the act of accession by Cyprus to the EU, the application of Community law in northern Cyprus has been

---

[177] Report on the Application of Regulation 44/2001 COM(2009) 174 final, para.3.1.

[178] Green Paper on the Review of Regulation 44/2001 COM(2009) 175 final, para.1.

[179] See paras 9–53 and 9–65; cf. Regulation 4/2009 (the "Maintenance Regulation"), examined in Ch.13, below.

[180] House of Lords European Union Committee, *21st Report of Session 2008/09, Green Paper on the Brussels I Regulation: Report with Evidence* (The Stationery Office, 2009), HL Paper No.148 (Session 2008/09), paras 29, 30.

[181] See para.7–63, above.

[182] [2010] EWCA Civ 9.

[183] (C-420/07) [2010] 1 All E.R. (Comm) 950 and 992.

suspended.[184] The Orams had purchased part of the land in question from a third party, who was the registered owner under Turkish Cypriot law, and had built a villa on the plot. By the terms of the Nicosian judgment, the Orams were required to demolish the villa, and to deliver free possession of the property to Apostolides, on the basis that his family had been compelled to abandon the land in question at the time of partition of the island in 1974. Apostolides was pronounced the rightful owner of the land in the judgment of the Cypriot court. The first judgment obtained by him was given in default of appearance by the Orams, but was confirmed by a later judgment on appeal brought by them.

The English Court of Appeal, the court addressed, referred to the ECJ the question whether the fact that the judgment concerned land situated in an area over which the Government of Cyprus does not exercise effective control had an effect on the recognition and enforcement of the judgment and, in particular, whether the court of origin could be said to have had jurisdiction, and, further, what might be the effect of the public policy of the Member State addressed upon the enforceability of the judgment. There were also issues concerning procedural correctness; although the document instituting proceedings in the Nicosian court was not served on the defendants in sufficient time to enable them to arrange for their defence, the defendants, as noted above, were able to bring an appeal against the initial judgment.

The term "hybrid case" is particularly apt in these circumstances because there is presented here a judgment from an EU Member State court which in its nature is largely an *in rem* judgment, having certain *in personam* provisions, and which, in its *in rem* character, purports to affect a *res* which technically is situated outside its territory. The case was hybrid in the fact that it concerned both *in rem* and *in personam* rights, but more importantly because the court of origin and the court addressed both are of EU Member States, but the land which the decree purported to affect is outside the territorial bounds of the EU.

By use of a manner of reasoning which has become familiar, the ECJ ruled that art.35.1 of the Brussels I Regulation does not authorise the court of a Member State to refuse recognition or enforcement of a judgment given by a court of another Member State concerning land situated "therein" but over which its government does not exercise effective control. It is often the case that the ECJ in its reasoning relies upon, and draws inferences from, the silence of the instrument in question; indeed it draws succour from that silence in order to achieve an aim which is in accordance with the overarching nature and purpose of the Brussels regime.[185] The result in *Orams* seems counterintuitive, at least according to traditional thinking,[186] namely, that the court of the *lex situs* is clothed with jurisdiction in the matter of pronouncing decrees *in rem* concerning immoveable or moveable property by virtue of the property being situated within the territorial limits of that court. In *Orams*, however, the

---

[184] Article 1.1 of Protocol No.10 on Cyprus to the Act concerning Conditions of Accession to the EU of a number of States (2004).

[185] cf. The negative attitude evinced by the ECJ in relation to a reference concerning the competence of the plea of *forum non conveniens* in a case where the alternative forum was in a Third State and there were no connections with the EU apart from the first court seised being an EU Member State: *Owusu v Jackson (t/a Villa Holidays Bal Inn Villas)* [2005] Q.B. 801.

[186] *Castrique v Imrie* (1870) L.R. 4 H.L. 414; affirmed in Brussels regime thinking, e.g. Brussels I Regulation art.22.1.

matter of overriding importance, it seems, was that the court seised was that of an EU Member State.

The ECJ ruled further that, as a practical matter, the fact that the judgment concerning land could not be enforced where the land was situated did not constitute a ground for refusal of recognition or enforcement under art.34.1 of the Brussels I Regulation, nor could it be said to fail the test set in art.38.1, the wording of which begins "a judgment given in a Member State *and enforceable in that State* . . ."[187]. With regard to the natural justice aspect of the case, a default judgment could not be refused effect under art.34.2 in circumstances where the defendants had been able to commence proceedings to challenge the default judgment.

Impact of 2005 Hague Convention on Choice of Court Agreements[188]

9–43   The provisions of the 2005 Convention (which is not yet in force) seek to ensure the effectiveness of exclusive choice of court agreements between parties to commercial transactions. A judgment given by a court of a Contracting State designated in an exclusive choice of court agreement shall be recognised and enforced in other Contracting States in accordance with the rules for recognition and refusal of recognition contained in Ch.III of the Hague Convention. Given that the rules for recognition and refusal of recognition comprise not only such rules as normally are found in this area, such as notification in sufficient time, but also have particularities[189] which are peculiar to the area within which the Convention operates, the subject of recognition and enforcement under this instrument is examined alongside the prorogation of jurisdiction rules in Ch.7, above.

Future position

9–44   As a consequence of the debate initiated by the Nuyts Study on residual jurisdiction,[190] particular consideration is given in the Brussels I Green Paper[191] to the relationship between the Brussels I Regulation rules and the residual national rules of Member States concerning jurisdiction and judgment enforcement. This was prompted by concern about difficulties which might be encountered by Community citizens in pursuing and enforcing their claims against Third State domiciled-defendants. The question is raised whether there should be a common regime among Member States of recognition and enforcement of Third State judgments. This topic was received coolly by the House of Lords EU Committee,[192] and a great deal more work will be required before the Commission's aspirations can even be transformed into legislative proposals for scrutiny at Member State level. The EU Parliament Report,[193] recognising the

---

[187] Emphasis added.

[188] For background information on the 2005 Convention, see paras 7–38—7–41, above.

[189] In particular, art.20.

[190] See para.7–64, above.

[191] Green Paper on the Review of Regulation 44/2001 COM(2009) 175 final, para.2.

[192] *Green Paper on the Brussels I Regulation: Report with Evidence*, 2009, HL Paper No.148 (Session 2008/09), para.48.

[193] European Parliament, Committee on Legal Affairs, Draft Report on the implementation and review of Council Regulation (EC) No 44/2001 on jurisdiction and the recognition and enforcement of judgments in civil and commercial matters 2009/2140/INI, para.13.

true global character of this subject, has hinted that a solution should be sought in the Hague Conference, by resurrecting negotiations on an international judgments convention, "the holy grail of private international law".

Enforcement procedures under Lugano II[194]

"Lugano II" refers to the Convention on jurisdiction and the recognition and **9–45** enforcement of judgments in civil and commercial matters, between the European Community and the Republic of Iceland, the Kingdom of Norway, the Swiss Confederation and the Kingdom of Denmark signed on behalf of the European Community on October 30, 2007.[195] It replaces the 1988 Lugano Convention in terms which, in general, are parallel to those contained in the Brussels I Regulation. Lugano II (signed on behalf of the European Community, Denmark, Iceland, Norway and Switzerland) entered into force for the European Community, including Denmark, and Norway on January 1, 2010. It will come into effect with regard to Switzerland on January 1, 2011. With regard to Iceland, the Convention shall enter into force three months after ratification by that country.[196] The Convention is accompanied by an Explanatory Report.[197]

Title III of Lugano II is concerned with recognition and enforcement of judgments. There is little change in this section of the instrument as compared with the 1988 Lugano Convention, except that the Convention art.27.4,[198] contained a rule which was considered to be unnecessary in view of the extent of progress in the harmonisation of private international law in the European Community, and the fact that an equivalent provision does not feature in Brussels II *bis*. Pocar notes that this, "vestige of the review of the merits of a foreign judgment" has disappeared from the new instrument.[199]

A comparison of the Brussels I Regulation Ch.III with Lugano II Title III discloses no substantial differences between the two instruments in respect of recognition and enforcement of judgments, except in relation to the interface between Lugano II and the Brussels I Regulation. The numbering of the articles within Ch.III and Title III, respectively, is identical (arts 32–56).

Relationship between Lugano II and the Brussels I Regulation

In the midst of so much harmony, attention must be paid to the relationship **9–46** of Lugano II with the Brussels I Regulation. This subject is addressed in

---

[194] See Ch.7, above for background, scope and rules of jurisdiction.

[195] See Decision 2007/712/EC on the signing, on behalf of the Community, of the Convention on jurisdiction and the recognition and enforcement of judgments in civil and commercial matters [2007] OJ L339/1; and Decision 2009/430/EC concerning the conclusion of the Convention on jurisdiction and the recognition and enforcement of judgments in civil and commercial matters [2009] OJ L147/1. See Civil Jurisdiction and Judgments Act 1982, as amended by Civil Jurisdiction and Judgments Regulations 2009 (SI 2009/3131).

[196] Lugano II art.69.5. Until such time as Lugano II enters into force in Switzerland and Iceland, the 1988 Lugano Convention will continue to apply.

[197] Pocar, Explanatory Report [2009] OJ 2009 C319/1 ("Pocar Report").

[198] Permitting refusal of recognition if the court of origin, in order to decide a preliminary question concerning the status or legal capacity of natural persons, rights in property arising out of a matrimonial relationship, wills or succession, all matters outside the scope of the Convention, had applied a rule different from the rule of private international law of the state in which the recognition was sought.

[199] Pocar Report, para.140. But see art.64.3.

Lugano II Title VII art.64. In this difficult area of delimitation of ambit of the Brussels I Regulation and Lugano II,[200] the courts of EFTA States are always obliged to apply Lugano II. Courts in Member States bound by the Regulation may find themselves having to apply both instruments.[201]

Article 64.1 provides that the scope of the Brussels I Regulation and amendments, and of the EC-Denmark Agreement, remains unaltered, and is not limited by Lugano II. As between States bound by the Brussels I Regulation, judgments delivered in one State must be recognised and enforced in accordance with the terms of the Regulation.

In the matter of recognition and enforcement, Lugano II applies where both states are party to the Lugano Convention alone, or when only one is a party to Lugano II and the other is bound by the Brussels I Regulation. While Lugano II shall not prejudice the application by EU Member States of the Brussels I Regulation, and amendments thereof (including the EC-Denmark Agreement), Lugano II shall be applied in matters of recognition and enforcement, where either the state of origin or the state addressed is not applying the Brussels I Regulation.[202] However, in addition to the grounds of refusal of recognition set out in arts 34 and 35 of Lugano II, recognition or enforcement may be refused if the ground of jurisdiction on which the judgment has been based differs from that set out in Lugano II and the judgment debtor is domiciled in a Lugano State, unless the judgment may otherwise be recognised or enforced under any rule of law in the state addressed.[203] This arrangement is much the same as that which pertained under art.54B.3 of the 1988 Convention.[204] With regard to the retention of the non-recognition rule in art.64.3, the Pocar Report relates that the ad hoc working party on Lugano II, while noting that art.64.3 is clearly inspired by a lack of confidence among EFTA States in the states bound by the Brussels I Regulation, and despite the fact that the rule most probably will never be applied, it was thought preferable to retain it, given that Brussels States are free to amend their rules on jurisdiction through Community procedures without the consent of EFTA States.[205]

Article 68 remains, permitting bilateral arrangements to be made between a Lugano State and a Third State, whereby it is agreed not to recognise and enforce judgments given in other Lugano States against defendants domiciled or habitually resident in the Third State, where the judgment in question could be founded only on a ground of jurisdiction specified in art.3.2 (i.e. so-called exorbitant jurisdictions).[206]

---

[200] Pocar Report, para.18.
[201] See, further, para.7.67, above.
[202] See art.64.2(c).
[203] See art.64.3; as to which see Pocar Report, para.21.
[204] See Civil Jurisdiction and Judgments Order 2001 (SI 2001/3929) Sch.2 para.1(c). See Crawford and Carruthers, *International Private Law in Scotland*, 2nd edn, 2006, para.9–60.
[205] Pocar Report, para.21.
[206] However, a Lugano State may not assume an obligation towards a Third State not to recognise a judgment given in another Lugano State by a court basing its jurisdiction on the presence within that state of property belonging to the defendant or the seizure by the plaintiff of property situated there: (1) if the action is brought to assert or declare proprietary or possessory rights in that property, seeks to obtain authority to dispose of it, or arises from another issue relating to such property; or (2) if the property constitutes the security for a debt which is the subject matter of the action (art.68.2).

D. RECIPROCAL ENFORCEMENT WITHIN THE UNITED KINGDOM

The Civil Jurisdiction and Judgments Act 1982 s.18 and Schs 6 and 7, replace **9–47** those contained in the Judgments Extension Act 1868 and the Inferior Courts Judgments Extension Act 1882 in respect of intra-UK enforcement of civil and commercial judgments. They apply to money (Sch.6) and non-money (Sch.7) judgments, and include, therefore, orders of interdict and specific implement. Arbitration awards also are included.[207]

"Judgment" is defined positively in s.18(2), beginning (s.18(2)(a)), "any judgment or order (by whatever name called) given or made by a court of law in the United Kingdom", with derogations therefrom in s.18(3)–(7), excluding judgments inter alia regarding insolvency, confiscation of the proceeds of certain criminal offences, maintenance, status or capacity, management of affairs of *incapaces*, and foreign judgments which have achieved status as UK judgments by virtue of legislation under statute, for example, the 1920 or 1933 Acts.

Schedule 6 (money provisions)[208]

Any interested party who wishes to secure the enforcement in another part **9–48** of the UK of any money provisions contained in a judgment may apply for a certificate under Sch.6, in the manner prescribed by s.2(2).[209]

A certificate shall not be issued under Sch.6 in respect of a judgment unless under the law of the part of the UK in which the judgment was given either the time for bringing an appeal against the judgment has expired, no such appeal having been brought within that time, or, such an appeal having been brought within that time, that appeal has been finally disposed of, and provided further that the enforcement of the judgment is not for the time being stayed or suspended, and the time available for its enforcement has not expired.[210]

The proper officer shall issue to the applicant a certificate stating the sum payable and such other particulars as may be prescribed, and stating that the above conditions have been satisfied.[211]

Where a certificate has been issued under Sch.6 in any part of the UK, any interested party, within six months from the date of its issue, may apply in the prescribed manner to the proper officer of the superior court[212] in any other part of the UK (i.e. Court of Session or, in relation to England and Wales, or Northern Ireland, the High Court) for the certificate to be registered in that court.[213] A certificate registered under Sch.6 shall, for the purposes of its enforcement, be of the same force and effect, the registering court shall have in respect of its enforcement the same powers, and proceedings for or with respect to its enforcement may be taken, as if the certificate has been a judgment originally given in the registering courts and had (where relevant) been entered.[214]

---

[207] See s.18(2)(e).
[208] See, in detail, Rules of Court of Session Ch.62—recognition, registration, and enforcement of foreign judgments, etc.—Pt V—recognition and enforcement under the Civil Jurisdiction and Judgments Act 1982, or under the Brussels I Regulation or under Lugano II—rr.62.37, 62.41. See also *Parkes v MacGregor*, 2008 S.C.L.R. 345.
[209] See para.2.1.
[210] See para.3.
[211] See para.4.
[212] Even if the court of origin of the judgment was an inferior court.
[213] See para.5.
[214] See para.6.1.

Where a certificate in respect of a judgment has been registered under Sch.6, the registering court (if satisfied that any person against whom it is sought to enforce the certificate is entitled and intends to apply, under the law of the part of the UK in which the judgment was given, for any remedy which would result in the setting aside or quashing of the judgment) may stay/sist proceedings for the enforcement of the certificate, on such terms as it thinks fit, for such period as appears to the court to be reasonably sufficient to enable the application to be disposed of.[215]

Where a certificate has been registered under Sch.6, the registering court:

"(a) shall set aside the registration if, on an application made by any interested party, it is satisfied that the registration was contrary to the provisions of this Schedule[216];

(b) may set aside the registration if, on an application so made, it is satisfied that the matter in dispute in the proceedings in which the judgment in question was given had previously been the subject of a judgment by another court or tribunal having jurisdiction in the matter."[217]

Schedule 7 (non-money provisions)[218]

9–49   Any interested party who wishes to secure the enforcement in another part of the UK of any non-money provisions contained in a judgment may apply for a certified copy of the judgment (to the proper officer of the original court, who shall issue the certified copy, subject, however, to the same provisos as set out above regarding appeals, etc.).[219]

Where a certified copy of a judgment has been issued in any part of the UK, any interested party may apply in the prescribed manner to the superior court in any other part of the UK (i.e. Court of Session or, in relation to England and Wales, or Northern Ireland, the High Court) for the judgment to be registered in that court.[220] However, a judgment shall not be so registered by the superior court in any part of the UK if compliance with the non-money provisions contained in the judgment would involve a breach of the law of that part of the UK.[221]

The non-money provisions contained in a judgment registered under Sch.7 shall, for the purposes of their enforcement, be of the same force and effect, the registering court shall have in relation to their enforcement the same powers, and proceedings for or with respect to their enforcement may be taken, as if the judgment containing them had been originally given in the registering court and had (where relevant) been entered.[222]

---

[215] See para.9.
[216] See, for unsuccessful petition for reduction of a certificate, *Parkes v Cintec International Ltd*, 2010 GWD 12-208.
[217] See para.10.
[218] See, in detail, Rules of Court of Session Ch.62—recognition, registration, and enforcement of foreign judgments, etc.—Pt V—recognition and enforcement under the Civil Jurisdiction and Judgments Act 1982, or under the Brussels I Regulation or under Lugano II—rr.62.38, 62.42.
[219] See para.2.1
[220] See para.5.1.
[221] See para.5.5.
[222] See para.6.1.

Where a certificate in respect of a judgment has been registered, the registering court, if it is satisfied that any person against whom it is sought to enforce the certificate is entitled and intends to apply under the law of the part of the UK in which the judgment was given for any remedy which would result in the setting aside or quashing of the judgment, may stay/sist proceedings for the enforcement of the certificate, on such terms as it thinks fit, for such period as appears to the court to be reasonably sufficient to enable the application to be disposed of.[223]

Where a certificate has been registered under Sch.7, the registering court:

"(a) shall set aside the registration if, on an application made by any interested party, it is satisfied that the registration was contrary to the provisions of this Schedule;

(b) may set aside the registration if, on an application so made, it is satisfied that the matter in dispute in the proceedings in which the judgment in question was given had previously been the subject of a judgment by another court or tribunal having jurisdiction in the matter."[224]

Summary

Judgments to which s.18 applies may not be enforced except by registration **9–50** under Sch.6 or Sch.7.[225] Moreover, reasons for refusal to register are strictly limited under both Schedules. Judgments to which s.18 apply, in the matter of intra-UK recognition only, are governed by the Civil Jurisdiction and Judgments Act 1982 s.19: subject to the definition of judgment, and exclusions thereto contained in s.18, recognition of judgments in another part of the UK shall not be refused solely on the ground that the court of origin was not a court of competent jurisdiction according to the rules of private international law in force in that other part of the UK.

E. ARBITRATION

Domestically, the Arbitration (Scotland) Act 2010 came into effect on June 7, **9–51** 2010.[226] This places on a legislative basis the Scots rules of arbitration which previously were piecemeal.[227] The Act contains certain provisions of conflict of laws significance which, in itself, is notable in drafting terms. Section 2 expressly includes, under the term "arbitration", not only domestic arbitration, but also arbitration between persons residing, or carrying on business, anywhere in the UK (the intra-UK conflict of laws situation); and international arbitration (undefined). Under s.3 an arbitration is "seated" in Scotland if:

"(a) Scotland is designated as the juridical seat of the arbitration—
    (i) by the parties,

---

[223] See para.8.
[224] See para.9.
[225] See s.18(8).
[226] Arbitration (Scotland) Act 2010 (Commencement No.1 and Transitional Provisions) Order 2010 (SSI 2010/195).
[227] See Fraser P. Davidson, *Arbitration* (Edinburgh: W. Green, 2000), and Fraser Davidson, Hew Dundas and David Bartos, *Annotated Acts: Arbitration (Scotland) Act 2010* (Edinburgh: W. Green, 2010).

      (ii) by any third party to whom the parties give power to so designate, or

      (iii) where the parties fail to designate or so authorise a third party, by the tribunal, or

    (b) in the absence of any such designation, the court determines that Scotland is to be the juridical seat of the arbitration."

By s.3(2), the fact that an arbitration is seated in Scotland does not affect the substantive law to be used to decide the dispute.[228] Enforcement of arbitral awards is governed by s.12 of the Arbitration (Scotland) Act 2010.

The conflict of laws aspects of resolution of commercial disputes by arbitration is important, complex and many-faceted. The subject is of significance at various points in a conflict of laws discussion.[229]

In the matter of civil jurisdiction, following the decision of the ECJ in *West Tankers*,[230] the Green Paper on the Review of the Brussels I Regulation[231] has addressed itself to the interface between the Brussels I Regulation and arbitration.

The Brussels I Regulation excludes from its scope arbitration,[232] as does the Lugano Convention.[233] In terms of residual national rules of jurisdiction, under the Civil Jurisdiction and Judgments Act 1982, s.20, Sch.8 rule 2(m),[234] the Court of Session has jurisdiction in proceedings concerning an arbitration if it was conducted in Scotland, or if the arbitration procedure was governed by Scots law.[235]

With regard to choice of law, as a result of the exclusion from the scope of the Rome I Regulation of "arbitration agreements and agreements on the choice of court",[236] the validity of an arbitration clause in a contract is determined by its own (common law ascertained) proper law, separate from the applicable law which governs the contract of which it forms a part. Nevertheless, the existence in a contract of an arbitration clause may be an indication of the applicable law under the Rome I Regulation art.3.1[237] or art.4.4.

If, after the parties have proceeded to arbitration as agreed, an attempt is made to have the arbitral award enforced as a judgment under the Brussels regime, the attempt should fail. However, if, in the face of an arbitration clause, a court in a Member/Contracting State gives a decision—perhaps on the basis that the clause is essentially invalid or not incorporated in the agreement, or if persuaded that the matter in dispute does not fall within the arbitration clause—is this to be enforceable in accordance with the

---

[228] See para.15–21, below.
[229] See paras 7–59, above and 15–21, below.
[230] *West Tankers Inc v Allianz SpA* [2009] 1 A.C. 1138 (see para.7.60, above)
[231] Green Paper on the Review of the Brussels I Regulation COM(2009) 175 final, para.7.
[232] See art.1.2(d).
[233] See art.1.2(d).
[234] Civil Jurisdiction and Judgments Order 2001 (SI 2001/3929) art.7.
[235] See Davidson, *Arbitration*, 2000, para.15.10.
[236] See art.1.2(e), and Rome I Convention art.1.2(d).
[237] See, under the Rome I Convention, *Egon Oldendorff v Libera Corp (No.2)* [1996] 1 Lloyd's Rep. 380, where English law was identified as both the applicable law and the curial (i.e. procedural) law. The curial law of the arbitration and the applicable/proper law to be applied by the arbiter to the substance of the dispute may differ, as happened in *James Miller & Partners Ltd v Whitworth Street Estates (Manchester) Ltd* [1970] 1 All E.R. 796. The curial law will govern matters such as whether there can be an appeal to the court from the decision of the arbiter.

Brussels/Lugano enforcement procedure and with its attendant benefits? Perhaps the party against whom the judgment was made unwisely submitted to the jurisdiction, but even if so, and especially if not, what is the position? The matter has attracted debate,[238] and circularity of argument can occur.[239] Since arbitration is excluded from the scope of the Brussels I Regulation and Lugano II, it is perhaps surprising that within the UK, an arbitration award from one jurisdiction is enforceable in another in terms of the Civil Jurisdiction and Judgments Act 1982 s.18, Schs 6 and 7.[240] In relation to enforcement of foreign judgments outwith the Brussels regime, a judgment obtained in breach of an arbitration agreement is not enforceable in the UK.[241]

Until the decision in *West Tankers*, it was the hope of common lawyers that one benefit of arbitration was that it remained competent for the courts of EU Member States to seek to enforce arbitration agreements by means of anti-suit injunctions,[242] a remedy which in view of *Turner v Grovit*,[243] has ceased to be a competent policing remedy to uphold choice of court agreements in circumstances where an EU court other than that chosen by the parties has been seised first by one of them. It has become apparent, therefore, that this was too simple a view,[244] and that arbitration agreements though ex facie excluded from the scope of the Brussels and Lugano regime, nonetheless have proved not to be immune from the regime.

Enforcement of foreign arbitration awards

Although a foreign arbitral award may be enforced at common law, or under **9–52** the judgment extension legislation,[245] but a scheme for recognition and

---

[238] But see *Marc Rich & Co AG v Societa Italiana Impianti SpA* [1991] E.C.R. I-3855 ECJ; and Hill, *International Commercial Disputes in English Courts*, 3rd edn, 2005, para.3.3.26.

[239] *Alfred C Toepfer International GmbH v Société Cargill France* [1998] 1 Lloyd's Rep. 379.

[240] Section 18(2)(e): "judgment" includes an arbitration award which has become enforceable in the part of the UK in which it was given in the same manner as a judgment given by a court of law in that part.

[241] Civil Jurisdiction and Judgments Act 1982 s.32. See *Tracomin SA v Sudan Oil Seeds Co (No.1)* [1983] 1 W.L.R. 1026. But note that s.32 does not extend to authorise the non-recognition of a judgment which is required to be recognised in terms of the Brussels regime. See also *Cavell United States Inc v Seaton Insurance Co* [2008] EWHC 876 (Comm); *DHL GBS (UK) Ltd v Fallimento Finmatica SpA* [2009] EWHC 291 (Comm); *National Navigation Co v Endesa Generacion SA (The Wadi Sudr)* [2010] 1 Lloyd's Rep. 193; and *AES UST-Kamenogorsk Hydropower Plant LLP v UST-Kamenogorsk Hydropower Plant LLP JSC* [2010] EWHC 722 (Comm).

[242] *Through Transport Mutual Insurance Association (Eurasia) Ltd v New India Assurance Co Ltd (The Hari Bhum) (No.2)* [2005] 2 Lloyd's Rep. 378. Another advantage of exclusion from the Brussels regime was that the related actions rule contained in art.28 clearly would not apply where the subject matter though related or identical is being addressed by different means, judicial and arbitral, respectively. Hence, the English court was under no obligation to stay arbitration proceedings which had been brought in England later than foreign judicial proceedings upon the same matter. Arbitration clauses were perceived to have a double tactical advantage in that it was thought to be competent for an English/Scottish court to seek to enforce them by anti-suit injunction; and whatever their date they were not affected by the Brussels *lis pendens* rule. These perceptions have turned out to be ill-founded.

[243] *Turner v Grovit* [2005] 1 A.C. 101.

[244] See para.7–60, above.

[245] An arbitration award made in a country the judgments of which are enforceable under the Administration of Justice Act 1920 or the Foreign Judgments (Reciprocal Enforcement) Act 1933, but which is not a party to the New York Convention, is enforceable in Scotland in the same way as a judicial decree. See also Arbitration (Scotland) Act 2010 s.22.

enforcement of arbitration awards is contained in the New York Convention on the Recognition and Enforcement of Foreign Arbitral Awards 1958 (replacing the Geneva Protocol 1923 and Geneva Convention 1927, except in relation to awards issued in countries which are parties thereto and not party to the New York Convention, which cases remain governed by the Arbitration Act 1950 Pt III). The New York Convention was brought into UK law by the Arbitration Act 1975. The Arbitration (Scotland) Act 2010 repeals *in toto* the Arbitration Act 1975,[246] and so reference must be made, in relation to New York Convention awards, to the 2010 Act ss.18–21 and 26.

By the 2010 Act s.19(1) an award made in pursuance of a written arbitration agreement in the territory of a state which is party to the New York Convention ("a Convention award") is to be recognised as binding on the persons between whom it was made, and accordingly may be relied on by those persons in any legal proceedings in Scotland. By s.19(2), the court may order that a Convention award be enforced as if it had been granted by that court. Recognition or enforcement may be refused only in accordance with s.20, on the grounds that the defendant proves:

> "(a) that a party was under some incapacity under the law applicable to the party,
> (b) that the arbitration agreement was invalid under the law which the parties agree should govern it (or, failing any indication of that law, under the law of the country where the award was made),[247]
> (c) that the person—
>   (i) was not given proper notice of the arbitral process or of the appointment of the tribunal, or
>   (ii) was otherwise unable to present the person's case,
> (d) that the tribunal was constituted, or the arbitration was conducted, otherwise than in accordance with—
>   (i) the agreement of the parties, or
>   (ii) failing such agreement, the law of the country where the arbitration took place."

---

[246] See s.29, Sch.2. The Law Reform (Miscellaneous Provisions) (Scotland) Act 1990 s.66, Sch. 7, which gave effect in Scots law to the UNCITRAL Model Law on International Commercial Arbitration, likewise has been repealed. See, in detail, Rules of Court of Session, Ch.62—recognition, registration, and enforcement of foreign judgments, etc.—Pt IX—recognition and enforcement of arbitral awards under the Model Law on International Commercial Arbitration. For England and Wales and Northern Ireland, the 1975 Act was repealed and largely re-enacted in the Arbitration Act 1996. Part 1 of the 1996 Act applies when the "seat" of the arbitration is in England and Wales or Northern Ireland, with modifications in Pt II relating to "domestic arbitration" (to which none of the parties is a national of, or habitually resident in, a state other than the UK or a body corporate incorporated in or having central control and management exercised in a state other than the UK and under which the seat of the arbitration (if designated or determined) is in the UK). Recognition and enforcement of foreign arbitration awards under the New York Convention is governed in English law by the 1996 Act ss 99–104. See generally Morris, *Conflict of Laws*, 7th edn, 2009, paras 8.014–8.017; and *HJ Heinz Co Ltd v EFL Inc* [2010] EWHC 1203 (Comm).

[247] cf. In England *Dallah Real Estate & Tourism Holding Co Pakistan* [2010] 1 All E.R. 592.

By s.20(3) recognition or enforcement of a Convention award also may be refused if the defendant proves that the award:

"(a) deals with a dispute not contemplated by or not falling within the submission to arbitration,
(b) contains decisions on matters beyond the scope of that submission,
(c) is not yet binding on the person, or
(d) has been set aside or suspended by a competent authority."

Further, by s.20(4), recognition or enforcement of a Convention award may be refused if:

"(a) the award relates to a matter which is not capable of being settled by arbitration, or
(b) to do so would be contrary to public policy."[248]

By s.21, a party seeking recognition or enforcement of a Convention award must produce (a) the duly authenticated original award (or a duly certified copy of it), and (b) the original arbitration agreement (or a duly certified copy of it); together with a translation if the agreement is in a language other than English.

F. European Enforcement Order for Uncontested Claims

Regulation 805/2004[249] applies generally from October 21, 2005.[250]   **9–53**
Its purpose is to ensure, by laying down minimum procedural standards, that judgments, court settlements and authentic instruments on uncontested claims, can circulate freely throughout the Member States of the EU, without the need for intermediate proceedings in the Member State addressed prior to recognition and enforcement.[251] The Regulation applies to all Member States, including the UK and Ireland,[252] but excluding, at present, Denmark.[253]

Background

Whilst the Brussels I Regulation represents notable progress in the develop- **9–54**
ment of procedures for the recognition and enforcement of judgments in civil and commercial matters, it leaves in place the requirement for *exequatur* (declaration of enforceability) procedure.[254]

---

[248] e.g. as where the arbitration agreement was valid, but the contract to which it pertained was illegal by its governing law or the law of place of performance. See *Soleimany v Soleimany* [1999] Q.B. 785, decided with reference to Arbitration Act 1950 s.26.

[249] Regulation 805/2004 creating a European Enforcement Order for uncontested claims [2004] OJ L143/15.

[250] See art.33. Article 26 provides that the Regulation applies only to judgments given, settlements approved and documents formally drawn up or registered as authentic instruments after the entry into force of the Regulation.

[251] See art.1.

[252] See recital (24).

[253] See recital (25).

[254] "[The Regulation] does not remove all the obstacles to the unhindered movement of judgments within the EU and leaves intermediate measures that are still too restrictive" (Proposal for a Council Regulation creating a European Enforcement Order for Uncontested Claims, Explanatory Memorandum, COM (2002) 159 final, p.2 (henceforth "Explanatory Memorandum")).

The European Council at its Tampere meeting agreed that, to simplify and expedite procedures for the recognition and enforcement of judgments among Member States, there should be introduced a form of automatic recognition without any intermediate proceedings, or grounds for refusal of enforcement, for certain specific types of claim.[255] The abolition of *exequatur* for uncontested claims was identified as one of the Community's priorities.

The Regulation has two distinct components, first, the creation of the European Enforcement Order; and secondly, the laying down of minimum procedural standards.

Scope of instrument

9–55 The Regulation applies to judgments, court settlements and authentic instruments on uncontested claims,[256] in civil and commercial matters, whatever the nature of the court or tribunal. It does not extend, however, to revenue, customs or administrative matters or the liability of the state for acts and omissions in the exercise of state authority.[257]

Uncontested claims

9–56 An uncontested claim is one:

(a) to which the debtor has expressly agreed by admission or by means of a settlement which has been approved by a court or concluded before a court in the course of proceedings; or

(b) to which the debtor has never objected, in compliance with the relevant procedural requirements under the law of the Member State of origin, in the course of the court proceedings; or

(c) in which the debtor has not appeared or been represented at a court hearing regarding that claim after having initially objected to the claim in the course of the court proceedings, provided that such conduct amounts to a tacit admission of the claim or of the facts alleged by the creditor under the law of the Member State of origin; or

(d) to which the debtor has expressly agreed in an authentic instrument.

The concept of "uncontested claims" is intended to cover:

". . . all situations in which a creditor, given the verified absence of any dispute by the debtor as to the nature or extent of a pecuniary claim,[258] has obtained either a court decision against that debtor or an enforceable document that requires the debtor's express consent, be it a court settlement or an authentic instrument."[259]

---

[255] Explanatory Memorandum, p.2.

[256] See recital (7); and art.3.

[257] See art.2.

[258] Amplified in recital (6), to the effect that the absence of objections from the debtor may take the form of decree by default (default of appearance at a court hearing), or decree in absence (failure to comply with an invitation by the court to give written notice of an intention to defend the case).

[259] See recital (5).

In other words, a claim will be treated as uncontested if the debtor has failed to object to it in the course of court proceedings (i.e. if decree were passed in absence,[260] or by default), or if he has expressly agreed (in court proceedings, or by means of a settlement or in an authentic instrument), that the claim exists and is justified.

European Enforcement Order

Article 6 lays down the requirements for certification as a European **9–57** Enforcement Order ("EEO") by the Member State of origin,[261] of a judgment delivered in that state on an uncontested claim.[262] Such a judgment, upon application at any time to the court of origin, shall be certified as an EEO if:

(a) the judgment is enforceable in the Member State of origin; and
(b) the judgment does not conflict with the rules on jurisdiction as laid down in sections 3[263] and 6[264] of Ch.II of the Brussels I Regulation[265]; and
(c) the court proceedings in the Member State of origin meet the requirements of Ch.III of Regulation 805/2004 (minimum standards for uncontested claims procedures); and
(d) if the claim relates to a consumer contract and the debtor is the consumer, the judgment was given in the Member State of the debtor's domicile within the meaning of art.59 of the Brussels I Regulation.

By art.9, the EEO shall be issued in the standard form provided in Annex I of Regulation 805/2004, and in the language of the judgment.

Abolition of *exequatur*

By virtue of art.5, a judgment which has been certified as an EEO in the **9–58** Member State of origin shall be recognised and enforced in the other Member State (the Member State of enforcement),[266] without the need for a declaration of enforceability, and without any possibility of opposing its recognition. Thus, it can be said that the certification of a judgment as an EEO "renders obsolete" the *exequatur* procedure which, under the Brussels I Regulation, is a precondition of enforcement of a judgment in another Member State.[267] The EEO has been described as, "a comprehensive and transparent certificate of the fulfilment of all the conditions for enforcement throughout the Community without intermediate measures."[268]

---

[260] i.e. absent or without representation.
[261] Defined in art.4(4): the Member State of origin is the Member State in which the judgment has been given, the court settlement has been approved or concluded, or the authentic instrument has been drawn up or registered, and is to be certified as a European Enforcement Order.
[262] Article 8 provides that if only parts of the judgment meet the requirements laid down in art.6, a partial EEO certificate shall be issued for those parts.
[263] Insured persons.
[264] Exclusive jurisdiction.
[265] Section 5 (employees) is omitted also in the protective provisions contained in Brussels I Regulation art.35.1
[266] See art.4(5).
[267] Explanatory Memorandum, p.6.
[268] Explanatory Memorandum, p.4.

Satisfaction of minimum procedural standards

9–59   As a corollary to the abolition of *exequatur* for uncontested claims, and to ensure that the debtor is duly informed about the court action against him,[269] the Regulation lays down, in Ch.III, minimum standards with regard to the service of documents, covering admissible methods of service, the time of service enabling the preparation of a defence and the proper information concerning the debtor.[270]

Article 12 states that a judgment on an uncontested claim can be certified as an EEO only if the court proceedings in the Member State of origin satisfied the procedural requirements set out in the Regulation. It is said that due to differences among the Member States regarding their rules of civil procedure, and especially those governing the service of documents,[271] it is necessary to lay down a specific and detailed definition of those minimum standards.[272] Accordingly, arts 13 and 14 provide for methods of service which are characterised,[273] respectively, by full certainty,[274] or by a very high degree of likelihood that the document served reached its addressee.[275]

The courts competent for scrutinising full compliance with the minimum procedural standards should, if satisfied, issue a standardised EEO certificate that makes that scrutiny and its result transparent.[276] The point to note is that it is the court of the Member State of origin, rather than that of the Member State of enforcement, which is responsible for scrutiny of the judgment, and for deciding whether the judgment satisfies the conditions precedent to its being certified as an EEO.[277]

Recital (19) states that the Regulation does not imply an obligation upon Member States to ensure that their national legislation meets the minimum procedural standards set out therein, but rather it provides an incentive to that end, by making available a more efficient and rapid enforceability of judgments in other Member States only if those minimum standards are met.[278] For Scotland, provision to satisfy minimum procedural standards has been made, via secondary legislation, namely, Act of Sederunt (Rules of the Court of

---

[269] See recital (12).

[270] "Only the compliance with these minimum standards justifies the abolition of a control of the observation of the rights of the defence in the Member State where the judgment is to be enforced" (Explanatory Memorandum, p.4).

[271] Though see Regulation 1348/2000; and see para.8–10, above.

[272] See recital (13).

[273] See recital (14).

[274] Article 13: service with proof of receipt by the debtor.

[275] Article 14: service without proof of receipt by the debtor.

[276] See recital (17).

[277] Contrast the position under the *exequatur* procedure, where responsibility rests with the court of the Member State addressed, not the Member State of origin, to determine whether the conditions for a declaration of enforceability have been met; cf. Explanatory Memorandum, p.6. This characteristic of the EEO procedure is worthy of comment in that it is novel for the court addressed in effect to lose its power of scrutiny, but such a loss is inherent in the purpose of the Regulation and the mode adopted to fulfil it.

[278] "It is up to the Member States to decide whether or not to adjust their national legislation to the minimum standards of Chapter III in order to ensure the eligibility of the largest possible number of decisions on uncontested claims for certification as a European Enforcement Order" (Explanatory Memorandum, p.4).

Session Amendment No.8) (Miscellaneous) 2005,[279] whereby rules consequential upon the introduction of Regulation 805/2004 create a procedure for certifying certain judgments as EEOs,[280] and for enforcing EEOs in Scotland[281]; and Act of Sederunt (Sheriff Court European Enforcement Order Rules) 2005,[282] pertaining to applications under the Regulation where the sheriff court is the court of origin and introducing rules of equivalent procedure for applications for EEO certificates for enforcement of judgments in other Member States.

Enforcement

A judgment that has been certified as an EEO by a court of the Member **9–60** State of origin should be treated, for enforcement purposes, as if it had been delivered in the Member State in which enforcement is sought.[283] Arrangements for the enforcement of judgments should continue to be governed by national law. Hence, recital (8) specifically provides that:

> "In the United Kingdom, for example, the registration of a certified foreign judgment will therefore follow the same rules as the registration of a judgment from another part of the UK".

In terms of art.20, the creditor shall be required to provide the competent enforcement authorities of the Member State of enforcement with (a) a copy of the judgment; (b) a copy of the EEO certificate; and (c) where necessary, a transcription of the EEO certificate.

The grounds for refusal of enforcement, per art.21, are very restricted, being limited to the existence of irreconcilable judgments.[284] On application by the debtor, enforcement shall be refused by the competent court in the Member State addressed if the judgment certified as an EEO is irreconcilable with an earlier judgment given in another (Member State or non-Member State) country, provided that: (a) the earlier judgment involved the same cause of action and was between the same parties; and (b) the earlier judgment was given in the Member State of enforcement or is recognised in that state; and (c) the irreconcilability was not and could not have been raised as an objection in the court proceedings in the Member State of origin.

Under no circumstances may a judgment or its certification as an EEO be reviewed as to its substance in the Member State of enforcement.[285]

---

[279] Act of Sederunt (Rules of the Court of Session Amendment No.8) (Miscellaneous) 2005 (SSI 2005/521), amending the Rules of the Court of Session 1994 (SI 1994/1443), which entered into force on October 21, 2005. See also Rules of Court of Session, Ch.62—recognition, registration, and enforcement of foreign judgments, etc.—Pt XII.

[280] See procedure for certification under art.6(1) (judgment on uncontested claim) or art.8 (partial EEO) of decree in absence or decree by default (r.62.82); for certification under art.24 of court settlement (r.62.83); and for certification under art.25(1) of authentic instrument (r.62.84).

[281] Registration for enforcement of a judgment, court settlement or authentic instrument certified as an EEO: r.62.88.

[282] Act of Sederunt (Sheriff Court European Enforcement Order Rules) 2005 (SSI 2005/523) (entry into force October 21, 2005).

[283] See recital (8).

[284] Article 23 provides, in exceptional cases, for the stay of enforcement proceedings, or for the limitation thereof to protective measures.

[285] See art.21(2).

Relationship with other Community instruments

9–61   Regulation 805/2004 provides Member States and, in turn, creditors, with an additional, optional, rather than compulsory, means of seeking recognition and enforcement of a judgment, court settlement or authentic instrument on an uncontested claim.[286] In suitable cases, creditors can choose whether to seek a declaration of enforceability under the Brussels I Regulation, or to utilise the more expeditious procedure laid down in Regulation 805/2004. In terms of recital (9), the latter procedure should offer significant advantages as compared with the *exequatur* procedure provided for in the Brussels I Regulation, in that there is no need for approval by the judicial authorities in a second Member State, with the expense and delay which that entails.

Similarly, in terms of art.28, Regulation 805/2004 shall not affect the application of Regulation 1348/2000, and now Regulation 1393/2007, concerning service of documents.[287]

G. European Order for Payment Procedure

9–62   Regulation 1896/2006 creating a European order for payment procedure applies from December 12, 2008. The UK and Ireland have opted into this instrument,[288] but Denmark is not participating.[289]

The purpose of this Regulation is to:

"... simplify, speed up and reduce the costs of litigation in cross-border cases concerning uncontested pecuniary claims by creating a European order for payment procedure, and to permit the free circulation of European orders for payment throughout the Member States by laying down minimum standards, compliance with which renders unnecessary any intermediate proceedings in the Member State of enforcement prior to recognition and enforcement."[290]

It is said that the expeditious recovery of uncontested outstanding debts is of paramount importance to economic operators within the EU and for the proper functioning of the internal market.[291]

---

[286] See art.27; cf. recital (20).

[287] See Ch.8, above. Recital (21) provides that when a document has to be sent from one Member State to another for service there, Regulation 805/2004 should apply together with the Service Regulation.

[288] See recital (31). See Act of Sederunt (Sheriff Court European Order for Payment Procedure Rules) 2008 (SSI 2008/436).

[289] See recital (32).

[290] See recital (9).

[291] Council of the European Union, Press Release 247 (12645/05): "it is increasingly not the exception but the rule that in the verifiable absence of any dispute the creditor has to turn to the judiciary to attain an enforceable title allowing him to collect a claim by means of forced execution that the debtor is simply unwilling or unable to honour" (Proposal for a Regulation creating a European order for payment procedure COM (2004) 173 final/3, para.2.1.1).

Scope

The Regulation applies in cross-border cases,[292] in civil and commercial **9–63** matters, whatever the nature of the court or tribunal. It does not apply, however, to revenue, customs or administrative matters, or to what may be termed "standard" excluded matters.[293]

Procedure

Article 4 states the general aim and purpose of Regulation 1896/2006, viz.: **9–64** collection of pecuniary claims for a specific amount that have fallen due at the time when the application for a European order for payment is submitted. In other words, the "efficient recovery of outstanding debts over which no legal controversy exists".[294] Therefore, the context in which this operates is where the claimant has a debt or pecuniary claim, but one which, unlike the claims in Regulation 805/2004 and Regulation 871/2007 (*q.v.*), has not yet been adjudicated upon by a court, and so is not the subject of a court decision, or court settlement, or authentic instrument. This, therefore, is an effort which can only be applauded, to assist the unpaid creditor against the prevaricating debtor.

Regulation 1896/2006 provides thus a further additional, optional means for the claimant by which to seek to recover his debt. It neither replaces, nor harmonises the existing mechanisms for the recovery of uncontested claims under national law.[295]

With regard to the opaque relationship between Regulation 1896/2006 and Regulation 805/2004, the Commission indicated that:

> "The Commission has decided to pursue both objectives—the mutual recognition of decisions on uncontested claims on the one hand and the creation of a specific procedure for the attainment of decisions on the other—in two different legislative instruments. This two-tiered strategy does not entail the risk of an overlap or of contradictions between both projects since they are clearly demarcated by their strict limitation to the stages before (creation of an order for payment procedure) and after (recognition and enforcement) the delivery of the enforceable decision, respectively. Quite on the contrary, this approach offers a number of significant advantages over a legislative initiative combining both aspects. For example, it allows a broader scope of application for the abolition of *exequatur*, extending it to all judgments handed down in the verifiable absence of any dispute over the nature and extent of a debt and not only to decisions delivered in one specific procedure."[296]

---

[292] Defined in art.3 as one in which at least one of the parties is domiciled or habitually resident in a Member State other than the Member State of the court or tribunal seised, at the date when the application for a European order for payment is submitted.

[293] See art.2.2. Mention should be made, however, of art.2(d)(i) and (ii), viz. the Regulation shall not apply to claims arising from non-contractual obligations, unless: (i) they have been the subject of an agreement between the parties or there has been an admission of debt, or (ii) they relate to liquidated debts arising from joint ownership of property.

[294] *Cheshire, North and Fawcett: Private International Law*, 14th edn, 2008, p.644.

[295] See recital (10).

[296] Proposal for a Regulation creating a European order for payment procedure COM (2004) 173 final/3; Explanatory Memorandum, para.1.1.

For the purpose of applying Regulation 1896/2006, jurisdiction shall be determined according to the rules contained in the Brussels I Regulation. The court shall examine the issues of jurisdiction and evidence in order to come to a view of the prima facie merits of the claim, and to exclude clearly unfounded claims,[297] but recital (16) states that this examination need not be carried out by a judge and may take the form of an automated procedure.[298] The claimant shall declare in his application for a European order for payment, that the information provided is true to the best of his knowledge and belief and shall acknowledge that any deliberate false statement could lead to appropriate penalties under the law of the Member State of origin.[299] The procedure shall be based, to the largest extent possible, on the use of standard forms in any communication between the court and the parties.[300] The application must include such information as suffices clearly to identify and support the claim in order to allow the defendant to make a well informed choice either to oppose the claim or to leave it uncontested. The court seised of the application shall examine, as soon as possible, whether the requirements set out in arts 2 (scope), 3 (cross-border requirement), 4 (procedure), 6 (jurisdiction), and 7 (formal requirements) are satisfied.

Assuming that all requirements are fulfilled, the court shall issue expeditiously a European order for payment ("EOP"). The defendant shall be informed that the order was issued solely on the basis of the information which was provided by the claimant and was not verified by the court; and that the order will become enforceable unless a statement of opposition has been lodged with the court in accordance with art.16.[301] In the EOP, the defendant shall be advised of his options, (a) to pay to the claimant the amount indicated in the order; or (b) to oppose the order by lodging with the court of origin a statement of opposition, to be sent within 30 days of service of the order on him.[302]

If the defendant lodges a statement of opposition, the proceedings shall continue before the competent courts of the Member State of origin (i.e. the Member State in which the EOP was issued).[303] If no statement of opposition is lodged, the court of origin without delay shall declare the EOP enforceable,[304] and shall send the order to the claimant. The order from the Member State of origin shall be recognised and enforced in the other Member States without the need for a declaration of enforceability, and without any possibility of opposing its recognition.[305] Enforcement procedures shall be governed by the law of the Member State of enforcement.[306] The grounds for refusal of enforcement, listed in art.22, are minimal and lie only in the area of *res judicata*. There can be no review of substance.[307]

---

[297] See recital (16).
[298] See art.8.
[299] See art.7.3.
[300] See recital (11).
[301] See art.12.4.
[302] See art.12.3.
[303] See arts 5, 12.4.
[304] See art.18.1.
[305] See art.19.
[306] See art.21.
[307] See art.22.3.

H. EUROPEAN SMALL CLAIMS PROCEDURE

There was introduced in 2007, with effect from January 1, 2009,[308] Regulation **9–65**
861/2007.[309] The UK and Ireland have opted into this instrument,[310] but
Denmark is not participating.[311]

Objective

The objective of Regulation 861/2007 is to simplify and speed up litigation **9–66**
concerning small claims in cross-border cases, by establishing a European
procedure for small claims ("EPSC"), and to reduce the costs associated with
pursuing such a claim.[312] The Regulation is also intended to eliminate, by
means of the EPSC, the intermediate measures which currently are necessary[313] to enable recognition and enforcement in one Member State of judgments given in another Member State. The Regulation does not prejudice the
application of the Brussels I Regulation.

Scope

The Regulation applies in cross-border cases,[314] in civil and commercial **9–67**
matters, whatever the nature of the court or tribunal, where the value of the
claim (excluding interest, expenses and disbursements), does not exceed
EUR 2000 at the time when the claim form is received by the court. The small
claims limit under Scots law, at the time of writing, is £3,000.[315] The
Regulation does not apply, however, to revenue, customs or administrative
matters, or to "standard" excluded matters.[316]

Nature of the EPSC

A relatively tight timescale is set out in art.5, in accordance with which the **9–68**
claim must be served on the defendant, his response submitted, and judgment
delivered by the court or tribunal.[317] The claimant commences the claim

---

[308] See art.29.
[309] Regulation 861/2007 establishing a European Small Claims Procedure [2007] OJ L199/1. See
also Act of Sederunt (Sheriff Court European Small Claims Procedure Rules) 2008 (SSI
2008/435).
[310] See recital (37).
[311] See recital (38).
[312] See art.1. Recital (7) narrates that the, "costs, delay and complexities connected with litigation
do not necessarily decrease proportionally with the value of the claim. The obstacles to
obtaining a fast and inexpensive judgment are exacerbated in cross-border cases. It is therefore
necessary to create a European Procedure for Small Claims. The objective of such a European
procedure should be to facilitate access to justice."
[313] Except as otherwise provided for by Regulation 805/2004 (European Enforcement Order for
uncontested claims) and Regulation 1896/2006 (EU order for payment procedure).
[314] Defined in art.3 as one in which at least one of the parties is domiciled or habitually resident in
a Member State other than the Member State of the court or tribunal seised, at the date on which
the claim form is received by the court.
[315] Small Claims (Scotland) Amendment Order 2007 (SSI 2007/496).
[316] See art.2.
[317] See art.5.3. A degree of flexibility is proposed in art.14, by which, in "exceptional circumstances", the court or tribunal may extend the time limits otherwise laid down, if that is necessary in order to safeguard the rights of the parties.

procedure[318] by completing a claim form in the style provided in the Regulation, and by lodging it with relevant supporting documents at the competent court or tribunal.[319] Upon receipt of the claim form, the court or tribunal completes the answer form,[320] and the two forms will be served, within 14 days of receipt of the claim form, on the defendant. The defendant has 30 days in which to make a response, which, within 14 days of receipt thereof by the court, must be dispatched to the claimant. The claimant has 30 days in which to respond to any counterclaim by the defendant. All documents must be submitted in the language or one of the languages of the court of tribunal.[321]

Article 5 makes plain the EPSC is a written procedure, unless, for some reason, an oral hearing is deemed by the court or tribunal to be necessary.[322] In terms of art.7, the court or tribunal shall give a judgment within 30 days of receipt of the documentation, unless it demands further details, wishes to take evidence, or summons the parties to an oral hearing, which must be held within 30 days of the summons. Article 8 permits, if the parties should agree, the holding of a hearing through audio, video or email conference.[323] Article 9.3 directs that the court or tribunal shall use the simplest and least burdensome method of taking evidence, and representation by a lawyer is not mandatory. Where an oral hearing is held, the court or tribunal shall give the judgment within 30 days of the hearing.

Under art.19, the EPSC shall be governed by the procedural law of the forum.

Enforceability of judgments

9–69   Article 15 provides that a judgment rendered shall be immediately enforceable, notwithstanding any possible appeal.[324] A judgment shall be recognised and enforced without the need for a declaration of enforceability (*exequatur* procedure).[325] Moreover, there is no possibility whatsoever (even, it seems, on a public policy basis)[326] of opposing recognition of the judgment.

Enforcement procedures shall be governed by the law of the Member State of enforcement.[327] Any judgment given in the EPSC shall be enforced under the same conditions as a judgment given in the Member State of enforcement. As with Regulation 1896/2006, the grounds for refusal of enforcement, listed in art.22, are minimal and lie only in the area of *res judicata*. There can be no review of substance.

---

[318] See art.4.

[319] See art.3.1.

[320] See Annex III.

[321] See art.6.

[322] See art.5.1.

[323] cf. Article 9 by which the court or tribunal may determine the means of proof (including taking evidence via telephone, written witness statements and audio/video/email conference) and the extent to which evidence is taken, according to its discretion. It may be expected that this could give rise to certain practical problems.

[324] cf. recital (30).

[325] See art.20.1.

[326] i.e. a (negative) policy on public policy objection, attributable to the size of the claim. It is noteworthy that in recent years important public policy cases in the area of judgment enforcement have arisen: *Maronier v Larmer* [2003] Q.B. 620; and *Krombach v Bamberski* [2000] E.C.R. I-1935. But clearly small debt cases are distinguishable.

[327] See art.21.1.

SUMMARY 9

1. Decrees *in rem* establish rights in property against all comers and **9–70** stand unaided on their own strength: challenge of a foreign decree *in rem* is limited to the challenges of "no jurisdiction in the foreign court", or fraud. Jurisdiction in any court is established by the presence of the *res* within the jurisdiction of the forum at the time of pronouncement of the decree.

2. Judgments affecting status are treated as equivalent to decrees *in rem* but recognition is governed by special statutory provision, namely, the Family Law Act 1986 Pt II and Brussels II *bis*.

3. Decrees *in personam* establish personal rights. Foreign decrees of this type, if not complied with where pronounced, require the assistance of the Scottish courts in order to be enforced in Scotland (by granting of decree conform to the foreign decree or by process of registration as described below).

4. Action for decree conform is necessary if the judgment emanates from a state with which the UK has no reciprocal arrangement of judgment enforcement under the Administration of Justice Act 1920 or the Foreign Judgments (Reciprocal Enforcement) Act 1933, and which is not an EU Member State or an EFTA State.

5. A number of defences may be raised to an action for decree conform, on jurisdictional or natural justice/public policy grounds.

6. "Direct" enforcement may be effected of Commonwealth (1920 Act) or other foreign (1933 Act) judgments, by means of registration ("judgment extension"). Under the 1920 Act, registration is a matter of discretion and will not be permitted if the defender can establish any one of a number of defences of a jurisdictional or natural justice/public policy nature. Registration under the 1933 Act is of right, but may be set aside later on application by the defender if any one of a number of challenges of a jurisdictional or natural justice/public policy nature can be made. Challenges at common law and under each of these statutes are similar to each other, but care must be taken as there are differences in detail, for example, the effect of pending or possible appeal.

7. The Protection of Trading Interests Act 1980 constitutes a specialised caveat to the above.

8. Judgments rendered by the court of an EU Member State are enforced in another Member State in accordance only with the procedures laid down by the Brussels I Regulation (and subsequent Regulations per 10, below), subject to the proviso that the matter falls within the scope of the instrument. Enforcement is not limited to money judgments, nor to judgments of superior courts. See the Civil Jurisdiction and Judgments Act 1982 Sch.1, as amended by the Civil Jurisdiction and Judgments Order 2001 (SI 2001/3929) and the Civil Jurisdiction and Judgments Regulations 2009 (SI 2009/3121).

9. There is a parallel regime, contained in the Lugano II Convention, for enforcement of judgments rendered by the courts of an EFTA State.

10. Among EU Member States, specialised procedures are available under the following Regulations:

    (a) Regulation 805/2004 (European Enforcement Order for uncontested claims);

    (b) Regulation 1896/2006 (European order for payment procedure); and

    (c) Regulation 861/2007 (European procedure for small claims).

11. Reciprocal enforcement of money and non-money judgments within the UK is governed by the Civil Jurisdiction and Judgments Act 1982 s.18 and Schs 6 and 7, as amended.

12. Enforcement of arbitral awards is governed principally by the New York Convention on the Recognition and Enforcement of Foreign Arbitral Awards 1958. See, for Scotland, the Arbitration (Scotland) Act 2010, and for England, the Arbitration Act 1996.

CHAPTER 10

STATUS AND CAPACITY

STATUS

At any particular time every person has at least one status in law. Status may **10–01** be defined as a person's legal condition in society: "The status of an individual, used as a legal term, means the legal position of the individual in or with regard to the rest of a community."[1] Status may result either from a natural condition such as age or insanity, or from a legal condition such as marriage. It is a condition which has attached to it the capacity (or incapacity) of an individual to acquire and exercise legal rights and to perform legal acts and duties. The effect of allocation, by application of the forum's choice of law rules, of an individual to a particular status automatically results in the acquisition, according to the relevant applicable law, of corresponding rights and duties, powers and disabilities, and capacities and incapacities.

GENERAL POINTS AS TO STATUS

The general rule is that a natural[2] person's status is determined by his personal **10–02** law. Traditionally in the view of Scots law, the pre-eminent personal law connecting factor has been, and in places continues to be, the law of a person's domicile. In jurisdictional terms, the court of the domicile[3] has been regarded as the appropriate court to determine the existence and effects of any status, or alteration therein, and prior to the Europeanisation of the subject a Scots court exercising jurisdiction on the basis of domicile was unlikely to yield to another court its pre-eminence in this area.

The status or legal capacity of natural persons falls outside the scope of the 1968 Brussels Convention.[4] When the Brussels Convention was concluded, the rules of the Member States on jurisdiction in matrimonial matters, "were considered so disparate as to preclude their effective unification in the 1968 Convention without major change to its nature".[5] However, account now must be taken of encroachment, notably into the rules of jurisdiction in matrimonial matters and matters of parental responsibility, by the personal law factor of

---

[1] *Niboyet v Niboyet* (1878) L.R. 4 P.D. 1, per Brett L.J. at 11.
[2] With regard to non-natural persons, see para.8–05, above.
[3] Hence the Court of Session has jurisdiction to entertain a petition to determine status if the petitioner avers sufficient evidence of a Scots domicile.
[4] 1968 Brussels Convention Title 1 art.1.
[5] House of Lords European Communities Committee, *Fifth Report of the European Communities Committee*, "Brussels II: The Draft Convention on Jurisdiction, Recognition and Enforcement of Judgments in Matrimonial Matters" (The Stationery Office, 1997), Pt 1, para.1.

habitual residence.[6] Since March 1, 2001, matrimonial status[7] has been regulated by Regulation 1347/2000 ("Brussels II"), itself superseded by Regulation 2201/2003 ("Brussels II *bis*"), with effect from March 1, 2005. In terms of these instruments, an EU Member State forum is clothed with jurisdiction in matrimonial matters, and in matters of parental responsibility, principally upon the basis of habitual residence and only residually on the basis of nationality or domicile.[8] Similarly, under the 1980 Hague Convention on the Civil Aspects of International Child Abduction,[9] the habitual residence of the child is the pivotal connecting factor. This, therefore, has had the effect of reducing the hitherto central significance of a person's domicile in this regard.[10]

With regard to debtor status, Regulation 1346/2000 on insolvency proceedings applies to such proceedings, whether the debtor is a natural person or a legal person.[11] It applies so as to identify the law applicable to insolvency proceedings, and their effects. In providing rules on jurisdiction and choice of law, it presupposes the existence of a qualifying debtor,[12] but makes no provision for the determination of debtor status itself, a matter apparently left for decision by the law(s) governing the alleged debt(s).[13]

THE THEORY OF THE UNIVERSALITY OF STATUS

10-03 The ideal is that status should be universal so that a condition of status which Scots conflict rules regard as having been validly conferred in one country (particularly if it is the country of a person's domicile) should be recognised in all other countries.[14] This theory or ideal is the basis of a legal theory known as the theory of the universality of status.[15] The theory is an excellent starting point[16]: modern times still produce cases of a bizarre nature[17] and cases of international complexity which cross the boundaries of other branches of legal knowledge[18]

---

[6] Regulation 2201/2003. See Ch.12, below.

[7] Insofar as concerns the allocation of jurisdiction, and recognition of judgments, in cases concerning divorce, legal separation, and marriage annulment, but not concerning capacity to marry which remains governed by Scots conflict rules. See Ch.11, below.

[8] See in detail Ch.12, below.

[9] Brought into effect in the UK by the Child Abduction and Custody Act 1985. See generally Ch.14, below.

[10] See generally Ch.6, below.

[11] Regulation 1346/2000 recital (9).

[12] Regulation 1346/2000 recitals (12)–(14), art.3.2.

[13] See, in respect of the Cross-Border Insolvency Regulations 2006 (SI 2006/1030), *Rubin v Eurofinance SA* [2010] 1 All E.R. (Comm) 81, in which the single judge held that, having regard to the definition of "foreign proceedings" under those regulations, it would be perverse to give the word "debtor" any other meaning than that given to it by the foreign court in those foreign proceedings, i.e. the USA court in which the main proceedings took place. Therefore, the argument that, under English law, the foreign bankruptcy proceedings related to a debtor who had no legal personality, either as an individual or as a body corporate, should be discounted.

[14] *Mackie v Darling* (1871) L.R. 12 Eq. 319 (but see *Johnstone v Beattie* (1843) 10 Cl. & F. 42).

[15] *Re Luck's Settlement Trusts* [1940] Ch. 864, per Scott L.J. at 885–919, especially 889–891.

[16] cf. comments with regard to the vested rights theory: see para.3–01, above.

[17] e.g. *W v H (Child Abduction: Surrogacy)* [2002] 1 F.L.R. 1008; *Bumper Development Corp v Commissioner of Police of the Metropolis* [1991] 4 All E.R. 638.

[18] e.g. *Arab Monetary Fund v Hashim (No.3)* [1991] 1 All E.R. 871 HL; *Westland Helicopters Ltd v Arab Organisation for Industrialisation* [1995] 2 All E.R. 387; and *Re S (Hospital Patient: Foreign Curator)* [1995] 4 All E.R. 30.

where recourse to first principles is the best help. However, Viscount Simonds in *National Bank of Greece and Athens SA v Metliss*[19] attributes recognition of a foreign status to comity rather than to the universal quality of the status. Further, the theory of universality of status is now not sufficiently strong, subtle or detailed to provide solutions to modern problems of family law. Rather, resort must be had to technical rules of jurisdiction and recognition enshrined in the Family Law Act 1986 and Brussels II *bis*, the rules of which are inspired by the theory of universality.

PUBLIC POLICY

Though policy of the forum has a residual role, status and its incidents **10–04** normally are governed by an individual's personal law. By way of exception to the principle of recognition, the forum may refuse, on grounds of public policy,[20] to accept a particular status conferred by another law, or any of its incidents.

Conflict rules of status may require still to be consulted in innominate and unusual cases, one example being *Re S*[21] in the matter of a physical *incapax* whose domicile was Norway and whose then residence was England. The presence of the *incapax* in the jurisdiction, whatever his nationality or domicile, was held to clothe the English court with jurisdiction.[22] Further, even though an appointment of a guardian by the date of litigation had been made under the Norwegian personal law, the English court retained a discretion to act in the best interests of the *incapax*. However, comity suggested that the *incapax* should be returned to his country of nationality and probable domicile, the onus of proof lying on those who argued to the contrary. Surprisingly, no reference appears to have been made to the case of *Re Langley's Settlement Trusts*[23] where, after some doubt, the English court concluded that the status of "incompetent" and its concomitant capacities and incapacities, conferred by the Californian court of the domicile upon a person mentally capable but physically incapable, did not offend the forum's public policy, but rather was to be recognised by the forum as being protective of the individual, and not punitive.

Sometimes British courts have been inconsistent in their views. A century after it had been agreed that the status of slavery could not be recognised in the UK, the English court in *Santos v Illidge*[24] enforced a contract for the sale of slaves (despite the provision of the Slave Trade Act 1824 s.2 making it unlawful for "any person" to purchase, sell or contract for the purchase or sale of slaves, a provision in its nature of intraterritorial effect only), because the contract was governed by the law of Brazil, by which it was valid. Both then and now,[25] a provision valid by the proper/applicable law of the contract, but offensive to the public policy of the forum may be refused enforcement.

---

[19] [1958] A.C. 509 at 525.
[20] See paras 3–06, above.
[21] *Re S (Hospital Patient: Foreign Curator)* [1995] 4 All E.R. 30
[22] cf. Adults with Incapacity (Scotland) Act 2000, in which the jurisdiction of the Scots court is based upon habitual residence of the *incapax* (Sch.3 para.3).
[23] [1961] 1 All E.R. 78.
[24] (1860) 8 C.B. (N.S.) 861.
[25] *Grell v Levy* (1864) 16 C.B. (N.S.) 73; and Rome I Regulation art.21.

Similarly, in family law, while prohibitions on re-marriage after divorce may be rejected by Scots and English courts,[26] and those concerning marriage out of caste[27] are rejected as imposing incapacities unacceptable on public policy grounds, it is possible to cite a case of overseas nullity recognition[28] in which a ground of nullity used by the court in Jerusalem was that the Jewish faith of the woman precluded marriage with a Christian. On the other hand, Nazi-compelled divorces of marriages between Jew and Gentile, obtained by duress or coercion, were not recognised by British courts.[29] Account has to be taken this century of grounds of non-recognition contained in relevant European instruments, such as arts 22 and 23 of Brussels II *bis*, which impose a closely worked system of rules which are highly likely to impact upon a person's status.[30]

It is interesting to note the following examples, of historical interest, all of which have been denied recognition on the ground that they were penal in the sense of discriminatory, or contrary to UK public policy: slavery[31]; civil death (i.e. removal of all civil rights); monastic celibacy; conviction for treason abroad; and the prodigal status.[32]

Both at common law, and under legislation, one should be aware of the dangerous potential of the public policy discretion, insofar as it may frustrate the aims of the subject and, in the particular matter of marital status, may produce limping status. However, it is generally appreciated by courts that delicacy and scrupulousness must be exercised in relation to public policy in international private law issues ("external public policy").[33]

STATUS AND ITS INCIDENTS

10–05 Status must be distinguished from its incidents, that is, from the effects, rights and duties, powers or disabilities which attach to it or result from it. Although a condition of status may be recognised in general, consequences following from it may or may not be recognised in certain circumstances, with the result that a condition of status may be recognised for some purposes but not for others. The question is always whether it will be recognised for the particular

---

[26] *Warter v Warter* (1890) L.R. 15 P.D. 152; *Martin v Buret*, 1938 S.L.T. 479. But see *Buckle v Buckle* [1956] P. 181; *Scott v Att Gen* (1886) L.R. 11 P.D. 128. Further as to re-marriage after divorce, see Ch.12, below.

[27] *MacDougall v Chitnavis*, 1937 S.C. 390.

[28] *Corbett v Corbett* [1957] 1 W.L.R. 486.

[29] *Re Meyer* [1971] P. 298 (duress); but regard must be had to all the circumstances—*Igra v Igra* [1951] P. 404.

[30] See paras 12–29—12–30, below.

[31] cf. *Somerset v Stewart* (1772) 20 St. Tr. 1; *Knight v Wedderburn* (1778) Mor. 14545; *Santos v Illidge* (1860) 8 C.B. (N.S.) 861.

[32] *Worms v De Valdor* (1880) 49 L.J. Ch. 261; *Re Selot's Trusts* [1902] 1 Ch. 488; *Re Langley's Settlement Trusts* [1962] 1 Ch. 541; and *M v B* [2005] EWHC 1681: refusal by Sumner J. (Family Division) to permit the parents of an adult woman with severe learning disability to remove her from the jurisdiction of England and Wales, because there was a real risk that, despite the parents' declared intentions, they would arrange for her a marriage when she was in Pakistan.

[33] See Ch.3, above; N. Enonchong, "Public Policy in the Conflict of Laws: A Chinese Wall Around Little England?" (1996) 45 I.C.L.Q. 633; and R.D. Leslie, "The Relevance of Public Policy in Legal Issues Involving Other Countries And Their Laws", 1995 J.R. 477.

purpose before the court. Thus, a foreign divorce may be recognised as having terminated a marriage,[34] but nevertheless the financial consequences thereof, exceptionally, may not be recognised.[35] Further, a condition attached to divorce considered by the forum to be penal, may be regarded as *pro non scripto*.[36]

CAPACITY

Status is the basis of capacity or incapacity so that a person's capacity to have **10–06** legal rights and to perform legal acts depends upon his status. Status is a legal condition while capacity is a power, and incapacity a disability, which results from status. Although one law determines any particular status, different laws may determine different questions of capacity within the same status. Thus, although the law of first recourse in a matter of status is that of an individual's domicile, different laws may determine his capacity to marry, to enter into a contract and to purchase land (albeit that in Scots choice of law rules, domicile is the default position).[37]

A person may stand in a number of legal conditions of status at one and the same time; thus he may be in nonage, married, and bankrupt. The question whether he is in nonage for the purposes, respectively, of marriage and bankruptcy may be decided by different laws. This is so, even though strictly speaking, it is meaningless to say that a status of nonage exists except in relation to particular capacities, with regard to each of which conflict rules will provide a governing connecting factor. Thus in Scots conflict rules, the capacity of a young person to test with regard to moveables is governed by the law of his domicile at the time of testing,[38] whereas his capacity to test with regard to immoveables is referred to the *lex situs*.[39] Therefore conflict rules direct to different legal systems, by means of different connecting factors, the question of capacity in respect of each "transaction" as it may arise. Some rules are more complex and/or uncertain than others.[40]

As in the case of penal or discriminatory conditions of status, penal incapacities are not recognised.[41] An incapacity imposed by the personal law may be

---

[34] Scots conflict rules assume that this is a defining feature of a divorce decree, as opposed to an award of judicial separation. Cf. Family Law Act 1986 s.50 and *Lawrence v Lawrence* [1985] 2 All E.R. 733.

[35] *Wood v Wood* [1957] P. 254 (pre-existing English award of maintenance kept in being by English court after pronouncement of Nevada divorce recognised in England). See now Brussels II *bis* recitals (8) and (11).

[36] See *Warter* (1890) L.R. 15 P.D. 152; *Martin v Buret*, 1938 S.L.T. 479; *Buckle v Buckle* [1956] P. 181; and *Scott v Att Gen* (1886) L.R. 11 P.D. 128.

[37] *Re S (Hospital Patient: Foreign Curator)* [1995] 4 All E.R. 30; and *Ogilvy v Ogilvy's Trustees*, 1927 S.L.T. 83.

[38] See Ch.18, below. The domestic law of Scotland sets that age at 12 years: Age of Legal Capacity (Scotland) Act 1991 s.2(2).

[39] See, e.g. *Black v Black's Trustees*, 1950 S.L.T. (Notes) 32; *Bank of Africa Ltd v Cohen* [1909] 2 Ch. 129.

[40] e.g. to reach a view on a person's capacity to contract, reference might have to be made not only to the domestic rules of the Scots personal law (say), which confers capacity at 16 (Age of Legal Capacity (Scotland) Act 1991), but also to the additions made by art.13 of the Rome I Regulation (ex-art.11 of the Rome I Convention). See Ch.15, below.

[41] *Chetti v Chetti* [1909] P. 67; *MacDougall v Chitnavis*, 1937 S.C. 390.

found to have created an incapacity of strictly limited territorial extent and may not affect that person when outside the jurisdiction of his personal law.[42] The broad rule, however, is that a person's capacity to perform acts and have legal rights, depends upon the law of his domicile in relation to personal matters and matters concerning moveable property,[43] while, in general, matters relating to immoveable property depend upon the *lex situs*.[44]

SUMMARY 10

10–07

1. Status in general is determined by the law of the domicile. A condition of status conferred by that law, in principle, should be recognised everywhere, subject to public policy and to modern EU developments in consistorial and child-related jurisdiction rules, which have increased the number of courts regarded as competent to terminate a marriage and/or to pronounce on parental responsibility matters, and thereby have raised the profile and importance of habitual residence as a determinant of status.

2. Status must be distinguished from its incidents. Not all incidents of a recognised status may be recognised by the forum for the purpose in hand.

3. As a general guide, capacity is governed by the law of the domicile or habitual residence as regards matters of personal law and as regards dealings with moveable property, and by the *lex situs* as regards immoveable property. However, legal capacity to perform a particular act is determined by the law applicable to the act or transaction in question.

---

[42] See *Bernaben and Co v Hutchison* (1902) 18 Sh. Ct. Rep. 72; and *Kaye (Peter) v HM Advocate*, 1957 J.C. 55.

[43] *Doglioni v Crispin* (1866) L.R. 1 H.L. 301; *Orlando v Earl of Fingall* [1940] I.R. 281; *Sawrey-Cookson v Sawrey-Cookson's Trustees* (1905) 8 F. 157; and *Ogilvy v Ogilvy's Trustees*, 1927 S.L.T. 83.

[44] *Black v Black's Trustees*, 1950 S.L.T. (Notes) 32; *Bank of Africa Ltd v Cohen* [1902] 2 Ch. 129; and *Ogilvy v Ogilvy's Trustees*, 1927 S.L.T. 83.

CHAPTER 11

THE LAW OF MARRIAGE AND OTHER ADULT RELATIONSHIPS

A. NATURE OF THE RELATIONSHIP

MARRIAGE

In order that a decision can be made upon the validity of a marriage in the view **11–01** of Scots conflict law, it is necessary first that the relationship presented amount in its nature to the Scots conception of marriage. If that test is satisfied, the adequacy of the "marriage" in terms of its essential and formal validity must be examined.

Lord Penzance, in *Hyde v Hyde and Woodmansee*, famously stated that: "I conceive that marriage, as understood in Christendom, may for this purpose be defined as the voluntary union for life of one man and one woman, to the exclusion of all others."[1]

It follows from this famous definition, widely accepted in the common law world, that the nature of the union must be such that it is recognised as conferring the status of married persons on one man and one woman[2] in a relationship intended to be permanent.[3] As a result of the dual domicile theory[4] no Scottish or English domiciliary has capacity to enter into "same sex

---

[1] *Hyde v Hyde and Woodmansee* (1866) L.R. 1 P. & D. 130 at 133.

[2] In the domestic law of England and Scotland it is an essential of marriage that the parties be of different sexes. The Scottish Law Commission recommended in 1992 that it continue to be a ground of nullity in Scots law that the parties are of the same sex (*Report on Family Law*, 1992, Scot. Law Com. No.135, para.8.5 and recommendation 45). From *Corbett v Corbett (No.1)* [1970] 2 All E.R. 33, courts in the UK applied solely a biological test to determine a person's sex. However in *Bellinger v Bellinger* [2003] 2 A.C. 467 (cf. *Croft v Royal Mail Group Plc (formerly Consignia Plc)* [2003] I.C.R. 1425) the Court of Appeal, in the case of an individual whose gender had been reassigned by surgery, pondered what policy demanded in the then state of medical knowledge, and concluded that it was for Parliament to address whether recognition should be given to a change of gender from that which had been assigned at birth. In the instant case, the court could not recognise the purported marriage between a transsexual female and a man because as the law then stood the petitioner's status for the purposes of marriage was male. In *Goodwin v United Kingdom* (2002) 35 E.H.R.R. 18 (and cf. *B v France* (1993) 16 E.H.R.R. 1) the ECtHR found that in applying purely biological criteria, the UK had breached the Convention rights of transsexual persons under arts 8 (right to respect for private life) and 12 (right to marry), directing that the UK Government had an obligation to rectify these breaches. Consequently, the Gender Recognition Act 2004 was brought into force, providing legal recognition of the acquired gender of transsexual people. Further, see *Grant v United Kingdom* (2007) 44 E.H.R.R. 1. See also para.11–14, below in respect of same sex "marriage".

[3] Ease of dissolution does not invalidate original intention: *Nachimson v Nachimson* [1930] P. 217.

[4] Explained below at para.11–18, below. Since the effect of the dual domicile theory is not alternative but cumulative, the stricter rule prevails.

marriage",[5] no matter that the *lex loci celebrationis* or the personal law of the other party permits such a "marriage".[6] Except in the special case of the recognition, under Scots and UK rules, of polygamous marriages,[7] the relationship of married persons must be exclusive. The law will not recognise a sub-normal marriage,[8] that is, a union under which the female party does not have the status of "wife" though the issue of such a union may be recognised as legitimate, nor will it recognise a "non-marriage" which, though it may have had the apparent trappings of marriage, was not intended to be a marriage, being in the nature of a charade.[9]

Marriage must be entered into voluntarily, "with an agreeing mind". Marriage induced by coercion[10] (to be distinguished from arranged marriage), or without matrimonial intent,[11] or under error,[12] is void.[13]

One would think Lord Penzance's definition to be both classic and comprehensive. His Lordship cannot have thought it necessary to state that both parties should be alive at the date of marriage. But a marriage may be valid in French law though one of the parties is dead, if certain conditions are satisfied, in order to safeguard the succession rights of children.[14] It is probable that such marriage, though novel in the view of Scots law, would not be so offensive to Scots public policy as to preclude recognition, provided that by the personal laws of both parties such marriages are valid.[15]

---

[5] Though registered (same sex) civil partnerships are permitted by Scots and English law by virtue of the Civil Partnership Act 2004. See paras 11–29—11–32, below.

[6] Whether same sex "marriages" contracted outside the UK between parties neither of whom is domiciled in a part of the UK, but the domicile of each of whom confers capacity to enter into such a "marriage", will be recognised by Scots courts as equivalent to heterosexual marriages is a matter of conjecture and for the policy of the forum as it may view the matter at any particular date. Consider K. Norrie, "Reproductive Technology, Transsexualism and Homosexuality: New Problems for International Private Law" (1994) 43 I.C.L.Q. 757; and "Would Scots Law Recognise a Dutch Same-Sex Marriage?", 2003 Edin. L.R. 147. The introduction into UK law of same sex civil partnerships makes a successful public policy challenge to recognition of foreign same sex "marriage" less likely.

[7] And even there, the forum must decide whether the situation presented amounts to polygamy or concubinage; the forum's view will prevail over that of the *lex loci celebrationis: Lee v Lau* [1967] P. 14.

[8] Wolff, *Private International Law*, 2nd edn, 1950, p.316. The "morganatic" marriage is a term and concept derived from German law in its early treatment of legal relationships, many of which required the parties to be of equal social standing.

[9] See, e.g. *Hudson v Leigh* [2009] EWHC 1306 (Fam): in such a case, decree of nullity was neither necessary nor appropriate. See also *Gandhi v Patel* [2002] 1 F.L.R. 603.

[10] *Szechter v Szechter* [1971] P. 286; *Mahmud v Mahmud*, 1977 S.L.T. (Notes) 17; *Mahmood v Mahmood*, 1993 S.L.T. 589; *Mahmud v Mahmud*, 1994 S.L.T. 599; and *Sohrab v Kahn*, 2002 S.L.T. 1255.

[11] *Akram v Akram*, 1979 S.L.T. (Notes) 87 (marriage of expediency: no true consent); and *Hakeem v Hussain*, 2003 S.L.T. 515; and on appeal, sub nom. *SH v KH*, 2005 S.L.T. 1025.

[12] *Lendrum v Chakravarti*, 1929 S.L.T. 96; *Mehta v Mehta* [1945] 2 All E.R. 690; and *Noble v Noble*, 1947 S.L.T. (Notes) 62.

[13] See more fully at para.11–20, below and again in "choice of law" in "nullity" at paras 12–43—12–45, below.

[14] See French Civil Code art.171.

[15] The Hague Marriage Convention 1976 (not signed or ratified by the UK nor by many other countries) excludes from its scope posthumous marriage (and proxy marriage). See E.M. Clive, *The Law of Husband and Wife in Scotland*, 4th edn (Edinburgh: W. Green, 1997), pp.111, 112; and C.A. Dyer, "The Hague Convention on celebration and recognition of the validity of marriages in perspective", Grensoverschrijdend Privaatrecht Opstellen aangeboden aan J van Rijn Van Alkemade (Kluwer, 1993).

THE SPECIAL CASE OF POLYGAMOUS RELATIONSHIPS

Polygamous marriages now are recognised for practically all purposes, but **11–02** such recognition is of relatively recent origin.[16] The older view was that such "marriages" should not be recognised at all.[17] The foundation for this view is found in the judgment of Lord Penzance in *Hyde*.[18] Courts and commentators placed emphasis upon the first excerpt from his judgment cited below, to the expense of the second, viz.:[19]

> "Now, it is obvious that the matrimonial law of this country is adapted to the Christian marriage, and it is wholly inapplicable to polygamy"; but: "[t]his Court does not profess to decide upon the rights of succession or legitimacy which it might be proper to accord to the issue of the polyga- mous unions, nor upon the rights or obligations in relation to third persons which people living under the sanction of such unions may have created for themselves. All that is intended to be here decided is that as between each other they are not entitled to the remedies, the adjudication, or the relief of the matrimonial law of England."[20]

After 1945, it was realised that there was a growing case for the recognition, for some purposes, of polygamous marriages if valid by their own laws, and it began to be appreciated that the question was not whether such a marriage should be recognised in general or in the abstract, but whether it should be recognised *for the particular purpose before the court*; that is, that the problem concerns the incidents of the status, not the status itself. This change was seen first in *The Sinha Peerage Claim*,[21] in which, in a peerage claim with no prece- dent, the son of a Hindu marriage was held entitled to succeed to the title. The marriage at its inception was potentially polygamous, but was never actu- ally polygamous and had changed its nature through a change of religious sect by the parties before the birth of the son and, obviously, therefore, before the litigation.[22] From that date, polygamous marriages began to be recognised gradually over an increasingly wide field. The cases fall into the following groups:

(a) Consistorial actions

The consistorial remedies provided by Scots and English law were regarded **11–03** as being essentially adapted to the concept of monogamous marriage and

---

[16] Much of what follows describes the development of this subject in the English conflict of laws, but there is no reason to suppose that our smaller jurisdiction was not in agreement, if less often required to comment. See denial of matrimonial remedy: *Muhammed v Suna*, 1956 S.C. 366.

[17] *Hyde* (1866) L.R. 1 P. & D. 130; *Armitage v Armitage* (1866) L.R. 3 Eq. 343; *Re Bethell* (1888) 38 Ch. D. 220; *Brinkley v Att Gen* (1890) L.R. 15 P.D. 76.

[18] *Hyde* (1866) L.R. 1 P. & D. 130.

[19] *Hyde* (1866) L.R. 1 P. & D. 130 at 135.

[20] *Hyde* (1866) L.R. 1 P. & D. 130 at 138.

[21] *The Sinha Peerage Claim*, 1939, reported [1946] 1 All E.R. 348.

[22] Hence, mutability of nature of a marriage received recognition as a concept, and mutation on the facts was accepted. The importance of *tempus inspiciendum* is clearly seen. See para.11–10, below relating to mutability.

accordingly initially were not available to parties to a polygamous marriage.[23] But if the marriage had changed its character to monogamous by the date of litigation in Scotland or England, the courts would not be precluded from taking jurisdiction.[24]

Nevertheless, such a marriage was regarded as conferring upon the parties thereto the status of married persons, to the effect that such persons, being married, could not enter into subsequent monogamous unions. Hence annulments were granted of purported monogamous unions entered into by persons who previously had entered into polygamous marriages.[25] To this extent, therefore, the polygamous marriage was recognised.

The position was altered materially by the Matrimonial Proceedings (Polygamous Marriages) Act 1972,[26] s.2 of which provides that the fact that a marriage was entered into under a law which permits polygamy shall not preclude a Scots court from entertaining proceedings for:

(a) divorce;
(b) nullity of marriage;
(c) dissolution of marriage on the ground of presumed death;
(d) judicial separation;
(e) separation and aliment, adherence and aliment or interim aliment;
(f) declarator of marriage (that a marriage is valid or invalid);
(g) any other action involving a decision on the validity of a marriage.

Section 2 also states that it shall apply whether or not either party has taken an additional spouse, but that provision may be made by rules of court for requiring notice of the proceedings to be given to any such other spouse, and conferring on such a person the right to be heard.

(b) Legitimacy and succession

11–04 The children of polygamous marriages are regarded as having the status of legitimate persons for the purpose of status generally, and of succession in particular, if they have such a status by the law of their domicile (that is, in view of the circularity problem, by the law(s) of the domicile(s) of each parent).[27]

---

[23] *Mehta* [1945] 2 All E.R. 690 (court had jurisdiction to grant remedy, marriage being essentially monogamous); *Risk v Risk* [1951] P. 50; *Sowa v Sowa* [1961] P. 70; *Ohochuku v Ohochuku* [1960] 1 W.L.R. 183; *Muhammad v Suna*, 1956 S.C. 366; Webb, "Potentially Polygamous Marriages and Capacity to Marry" (1963) 12 I.C.L.Q. 672; Cohen, "A Note on Potentially Polygamous Marriages" (1963) 12 I.C.L.Q. 1407. See also A.E. Anton, "The 'Christian Marriage' Heresy", 1956 S.L.T. (News) 201.

[24] *Cheni v Cheni* [1965] P.85; and *Parkasho v Singh* [1968] P. 233.

[25] *Srini Vasan v Srini Vasan* [1946] P. 67; *Baindail v Baindail* [1946] P. 122.

[26] As amended by Divorce Jurisdiction, Court Fees and Legal Aid (Scotland) Act 1983 s.6(2); Law Reform (Husband and Wife) Act 1984 s.9(1); Family Law (Scotland) Act 1985 s.28(1). The equivalent English provisions are contained now in the Matrimonial Causes Act 1973 s.47.

[27] *Khoo Hooi Leong v Khoo Hean Kwee* [1926] A.C. 529; [1930] A.C. 346; *The Sinha Peerage* Claim, 1939, reported [1946] 1 All E.R. 348; *Bamgbose v Daniel* [1955] A.C. 107; *Coleman v Shang* [1961] A.C. 481; *Dawodu v Danmole* [1962] 1 W.L.R. 1053. See Ch.14, below; and see Ch.6, above, for current Scots rules of domicile.

(c) General

Polygamous marriages now are recognised as creating the status of marriage **11–05** in a large number of different areas of law, from criminal law to taxation.[28] Specialties arise with regard to the following matters:

Succession to titles of honour, or of an heir in intestacy to immoveables

In such cases it must be ascertained whether the law of the title, or the *lex* **11–06** *situs*, requires the heir to be legitimate. If so, he must be legitimate in the view of that law. This does not necessarily preclude claims by children of a polygamous marriage.[29]

Bigamy

In Scots law, bigamy is a crime at common law, while in English law it is a **11–07** statutory offence under the Offences Against the Person Act 1861 s.57. In both cases the crime or offence is committed if a person who already has the status of a "married person" purports to enter into a subsequent marriage. Under Scots law a charge of bigamy can be preferred only if the second "marriage" takes place in Scotland because the common law of Scotland cannot apply elsewhere, whereas in England the Act of 1861 has extraterritorial effect, so as to affect the actings of a British subject abroad, and a charge of bigamy may be preferred even if the second marriage takes place abroad.

In the case of a person who is already a party to a polygamous marriage, there is a question as to what is meant by a "married person" in this (criminal) context, that is whether a party to a polygamous marriage is to be regarded as "married" in this sense, so as to forbid (or not) a subsequent "marriage". In English civil law, at a point in the development of the conflict rules at which recognition was not generally afforded to potentially or actually polygamous marriages, the existence of a prior marriage of such a type was recognised to the extent of barring the celebration of a valid marriage in England (necessarily monogamous in nature) by one of the parties. The first marriage would be recognised therefore, as regards civil law, to the effect of making the second marriage void,[30] but criminal charges for bigamy in respect of the second "marriage" did not follow. In *R. v Sagoo*,[31] overruling *R. v Sarwan Singh*,[32] it was held that the offence of bigamy had been committed when the first (potentially polygamous) marriage had become monogamous by statute or by change of domicile before the second marriage, but there has been no decision in a case where the first marriage has remained potentially polygamous. These

---

[28] *Mawji v The Queen* [1957] A.C. 126; *Din v National Assistance Board* [1967] 2 Q.B. 213; *Alhaji Mohamed v Knott* [1969] 1 Q.B. 1; [1968] 2 All E.R. 563; *Chaudhry v Chaudhry* [1975] 3 All E.R. 687; affirmed [1976] 1 All E.R. 805; *Shahnaz v Rizwan* [1964] 2 All E.R. 993; *Nabi v Heaton* [1983] 1 W.L.R. 626 CA (husband of two concurrent wives entitled to personal relief from income tax in respect of both of them); *Rampal v Rampal* [2001] 3 W.L.R. 795 (ancillary relief on divorce); and *Ben Hashem v Ali Shayif* [2009] 1 F.L.R. 115 (ancillary relief on divorce).

[29] cf. *Bamgbose v Daniel* [1955] A.C. 107.

[30] cf. *Baindail* [1946] P. 122 (civil action).

[31] *R. v Sagoo (Mohinder Singh)* [1975] 2 All E.R. 926.

[32] *R. v Sarwan Singh* [1962] 3 All E.R. 612.

matters are subtle and confusing, and one must note the disinclination of the authorities to prosecute.[33]

Social security

11–08   Against a background in benefits regulations whereby a (potentially) polygamous marriage will be treated as monogamous for every day that the marriage remains actually monogamous,[34] it should be noted that there are more recent exceptions which operate in favour of parties to actually polygamous marriages,[35] provided that the marriages in themselves are valid by Scots and English conflict of laws, i.e. contracted abroad between parties having legal capacity by their personal law to enter into such a marriage. United Kingdom law, apparently, will recognise marriages actually polygamous in nature as marriages for the purpose of certain benefits, though social security benefits will not be paid to spouses of such marriages who are permanently resident outside the UK. Generally in this area of allowances and taxation, the landscape is complex, and any advice must be benefit-specific, but the discernible trend overall is not to discriminate against parties to polygamous marriages.

The result is therefore that a polygamous marriage now will be recognised for most purposes.[36]

Finally, attention must be paid in any conflict of laws treatment of polygamy to the interrelated matters of (a) characterisation; and (b) capacity.

---

[33] See, for Scotland, R.D. Leslie, "Polygamous Marriages and Bigamy", 1972 J.R. 113, and the case of *Shafi* Unreported August 18, 1977 Glasgow Sheriff Court. The position seems unsatisfactory, but cases are rare and there seems to be no inclination to act further in the matter or to clarify it: Law Commission and Scottish Law Commission, *Polygamous Marriages (Capacity to Contract a Polygamous Marriage and the Concept of the Potentially Polygamous Marriage)* (HMSO, 1982), Law Com. No.83; Scot. Law Com. Memo. No.56, para.4.46.

[34] e.g. Child Benefit Act 1975 s.9(2)(a); Social Security Act 1975, s.162(b), Inland Revenue Decision Makers Guides: DMG 11105; CG 22072-*Transfer of Assets between Husband and Wife: Polygamy* (to the effect that transfers between a husband and any wife with whom he is living will be at no gain/no loss); DMG 41003-*Polygamy*; and CBTM 11020-*General and supplementary provisions: Polygamous marriages.* The British fisc refused to pay widows' benefit to two widows in Decision No.R(G) 1/93; and refused to pay invalidity benefit to one wife of a marriage proved to the satisfaction of the commissioners to be polygamous in nature in Decision No.R(S) 2/92. See also *Bibi v Chief Adjudication Officer, The Times,* July 10, 1997 CA, in which one wife of an actually polygamous marriage contracted in Bangladesh was held not to be entitled to widowed mother's allowance under the Social Security Act 1975 s.25 (now Social Security Contributions and Benefits Act 1992 s.37); it would have been different if the marriage had been merely potentially polygamous. See further Social Security and Family Allowances (Polygamous Marriage) Regulations 1975 (SI 1975/561).

[35] e.g. Income Support (General Regulations) 1987 (SI 1987/1967) regs 2(3), 18, 23(3).

[36] Consider post-1972 cases in England of *Chaudhry v Chaudhry* [1975] 3 All E.R. 687 (extending to the polygamously married the remedy in English law provided by Married Women's Property Act 1882 s.17); *Re Sehota (Deceased)* [1978] 3 All E.R. 385 (permitting one of two widows of the same man to claim under the Inheritance (Provision for Family and Dependants) Act 1975 in the estate of their husband, domiciled at death in England, he having favoured the other wife in his will). Why then should not such a wife (wives), validly married to a man who died domiciled in Scotland, claim legal rights? Cf. R.D. Leslie, *Stair Memorial Encyclopaedia,* Vol.17 "Private International Law" (Edinburgh: Butterworths), para.216.

Characterisation of the nature of a marriage

Which law characterises?

According to the balance of authorities, the character of a union as monog- **11–09** amous or polygamous is determined initially by the *lex loci celebrationis*,[37] though later, for the purpose before the court, the decision upon classification is for the forum.[38] A marriage bears a mark but not an indelible mark.

The nature of a marriage celebrated in Scotland is monogamous despite scope for a wide variation in locus and form of ceremony,[39] and regardless of the personal law(s) of the parties (or their expectations).

Until the decision by the Court of Appeal in *Hussain v Hussain*,[40] the assumption always was made that the initial character of any marriage was determined by the *lex loci celebrationis* (though there was some support for the application of the matrimonial domicile),[41] but in *Hussain* the marriage was categorised as monogamous because the capacity of each party at the marriage (English male domiciliary; Pakistani female domiciliary) precluded the possibility of any other type of marriage. In other words, the test of the nature of the marriage was capacity of parties, and the capacity of neither party[42] extended to permit the entry into a potentially polygamous union,[43] notwithstanding that it was entered into in Pakistan. However, this decision may be regarded as a creative judicial solution to a problem solved shortly thereafter by Parliament by means of ss.5–7 of the Private International Law (Miscellaneous Provisions) Act 1995.

Mutability: change of character of marriage

It has been stated above that different views may be taken about the char- **11–10** acter of a marriage, and that the view of the forum in the instant case, for the purposes of that case, governs. It is also true that the nature of any marriage may *change*, from actually or potentially polygamous to monogamous[44]; less commonly the other way.[45]

A change in character may result from a change in the parties' personal circumstances, religion, religious sect, or joint change of domicile,[46] or a

---

[37] *R. v Hammersmith Superintendent Registrar of Marriages Ex p. Mir-Anwaruddin* [1917] 1 K.B. 634; *R. v Naguib (Mark Mahommed)* [1917] 1 K.B. 359; *Lendrum v Chakravarti*, 1929 S.L.T. 96; *MacDougall v Chitnavis*, 1937 S.C. 390; *Qureshi v Qureshi* [1971] 1 All E.R. 325 (obiter); cf. wording of Matrimonial Proceedings (Polygamous Marriages) Act 1972 s.2.
[38] *Lee v Lau* [1967] P. 14, per Cairns J. at 20.
[39] Extended by Marriage (Scotland) Act 2002.
[40] [1982] 3 All E.R. 369.
[41] *Warrender v Warrender* (1835) 2 Cl. & F. 488, per Lord Brougham at 535; *Harvey v Farnie* (1882) L.R. 8 App. Cas. 43, per Lord Selborne; *De Reneville v De Reneville* [1948] P. 100, per Lord Greene M.R.; *Kenward v Kenward* [1951] P. 124, per Denning LJ at 144, 146. Cf. The legal capacity issue: *Radwan v Radwan (No.2)* [1972] 3 All E.R. 1026.
[42] The personal law of the woman did not permit polyandry.
[43] See now assistance provided by Private International (Miscellaneous Provisions) Act 1995 ss.5–7.
[44] See, e.g. *Cheni* [1965] P. 85; *Parkasho v Singh* [1968] P. 233. *Quoraishi v Quoraishi* (1983) 13 Fam. Law 86.
[45] *Drammeh v Drammeh* (1970) 78 Cey. L.W. 55; *Att Gen of Ceylon v Reid* [1965] A.C. 720. Cf. *Onobrauche v Onobrauche* (1978) 8 Fam. Law 107.
[46] *Ali v Ali* [1968] P. 564 (unilateral change by husband, but a case of short-lived fame in view of the removal of the unity of domicile rule between husband and wife by Domicile and Matrimonial Proceedings Act 1973 s.1).

change by statutory provision. Such a change will not affect the marriage's validity, though in the past it would affect jurisdiction of the UK courts, and, consequently, remedies. In *Drammeh v Drammeh*,[47] a Gambian case upheld by the Privy Council, it was decided that the change from monogamous to polygamous, effected unilaterally by the husband through reversion to his original domicile and religion, did not affect the monogamous nature of the original wife's marriage.

Date of determination of character of marriage

11–11   It was held in *Cheni v Cheni*[48] that, if a question arises as to the character of a marriage, it is determined at the date, and for the purpose, of the litigation: if the marriage was monogamous at that date, it was no objection for jurisdictional purposes that the marriage was potentially polygamous when it was entered into.

These matters, although of interest, are of less importance in view of the 1972 Act which removes the necessity for the marriage to come before the court in monogamous form.

Capacity to enter into a potentially or actually polygamous marriage

Potential polygamy

11–12   The effect of s.7 of the Private International Law (Miscellaneous Provisions) Act 1995[49] is that a person of Scots domicile may enter into a *potentially* polygamous marriage, which marriage shall be treated as a monogamous marriage for every day that it remains so. This removes doubt about the validity of marriages entered into abroad by persons of British residence and uncertain domicile, where, by the *lex loci celebrationis*, the nature of all marriages at the point of celebration is potentially polygamous, i.e. giving the husband the legal entitlement to take concurrently more than one wife.[50]

Actual polygamy

11–13   No Scottish or English domiciliary has legal capacity by his or her personal law to enter an actually polygamous marriage, wherever purportedly contracted.[51] Hence, if the dual domicile theory (*q.v.*) is used, no such purported marriage by someone whose personal law is Scots can be regarded

---

[47] (1970) 78 Cey. L.W. 55.

[48] [1965] P. 85.

[49] As to England and Wales, see ss.5, 6 (retrospective effect, subject to conditions therein contained).

[50] Unlike the equivalent English provisions, the Scots rule is not retrospective: see B.J. Rodger, annotations to statute. The precursor to this provision is the Law Commissions' joint report entitled *Private International Law—Polygamous Marriages: Report on Capacity to Contract a Polygamous Marriage and Related Issues* (HMSO, 1985), Law Com. No.146; Scot. Law Com. No.96. See also *Hussain* [1982] 3 All E.R. 369.

[51] Scots law: *MacDougall v Chitnavis*, 1937 S.C. 390; Law Commission and Scottish Law Commission, *Private International Law—Polygamous Marriages*, 1985, Law Com. No.146; Scot. Law Com. No.96, paras 4.2–4.9. Marriage (Scotland) Act 1977 ss.2(3)(b), s.5(4)(b). English law: see Matrimonial Causes Act 1973 s.11(d), and *Hussain* [1982] 3 All E.R. 369. Both laws now are subject to Private International Law (Miscellaneous Provisions) Act 1995 ss.5–7.

as valid by Scots law. Authority exists for applying the intended matrimonial home theory (*q.v.*),[52] but the decision is an isolated one, and is not highly regarded. Moreover, in a Scots court, the possibility of utilising the latter theory appears to have been precluded by the Family Law (Scotland) 2006, s.38(2)(a) of which directs that the question of capacity to enter into a marriage shall be determined by the law of the place where, immediately before the marriage, that person was domiciled.[53]

SAME SEX "MARRIAGE"

It is not the policy of the Scottish Government to change the requirement of **11–14** Scots domestic law that to create a valid marriage under Scots law the participating parties must be of opposite sex.[54] However, it seems inevitable that since the laws of certain EU Member States, and other states,[55] permit "same sex marriage", questions can be expected on a number of conflict of laws issues, e.g. the capacity of Scottish parties to enter such a "marriage" abroad, the laws to regulate formal and essential validity of such "marriages", and the recognition of such "marriages" and any incidents thereof by Scots law. These problems are likely to be complicated further by the issue of recognition of the purported divorces of such purported marriages, especially within the framework of Regulation 2201/2003.[56] Discussion of these matters is speculative, given the absence of case law, but principle would direct that in accordance with the dual domicile theory outlined below, any such "marriage", purported to be entered into anywhere in the world, where one at least of the parties is of Scots domicile, will not be regarded as valid in a Scots court, by reason of lack of legal capacity. Where, however, such "marriages" are valid by the *lex loci celebrationis*, and where by his/her personal law each contracting party has legal capacity to enter into such a union, recognition is likely to be afforded in Scotland to the status, or at least to certain of the incidents thereof. This speculative view is reinforced by the existence and terms of the Civil Partnership Act 2004, which introduces the option in English and Scots law of the formation of same sex civil partnership (on condition that the parties are eligible so to do).[57] Although the 2004 Act does not introduce into the domestic laws of

---

[52] *Radwan (No.2)* [1972] 3 All E.R. 1026 in which a woman domiciled in England was found by an English court to have contracted a valid marriage to an Egyptian domiciliary, which marriage for a short time was actually polygamous. The marriage took place in the Egyptian Consulate-General in Paris. The parties intended to live in Egypt after their marriage and fulfilled that intention for a number of years before returning to England. Contrast *Lendrum v Chakravarti*, 1929 S.L.T. 96, per Lord Mackay at 99.

[53] See para.11–18, below.

[54] Marriage (Scotland) Act 1977 s.5(4)(e). Scottish Executive, *Parents and Children* (The Stationery Office, 2001), para.6.4.2. See fn.2, above, however, in relation to transsexual individuals.

[55] e.g. Belgium, the Netherlands, Sweden, certain provinces of Canada and states of the USA. A list of legal systems in which a form of same sex partnership has been introduced is contained in Civil Partnership Act 2004 Sch.20.

[56] See further, para.12–31, below.

[57] See further, paras 11–28—11–32, below.

the United Kingdom same sex marriage,[58] it is impossible to overlook the fact that the structure of rules and the provenance of many of the terms of the 2004 Act find their foundation in domestic and conflict statutes concerning marriage and divorce.

There are many technical difficulties en route to recognition of same sex marriage, before the matter of policy is addressed. The forum in which the issue of recognition is raised will choose, define and identify the applicable law to govern legal capacity to enter into such a marriage. The fact that, by the *lex loci celebrationis*, the individuals concerned possessed legal capacity so to marry is irrelevant, at least according to conflict rules in the UK.[59]

Important matters of policy are present, and they may conflict. There may be difficulties of ranking of interests. For example, in a question of succession to land in Scotland belonging to an intestate, same sex "spouse" domiciled abroad (a party to a union, the status of which is uncertain by Scots law), there may be a competition between the surviving same sex "spouse", and other relations of the deceased having a ranking in terms of the Succession (Scotland) Act 1964. The position would be more complicated if, by his date of death, the deceased "spouse" had resumed his Scottish domicile and died possessed of moveable property in Scotland requiring to be distributed. Problems such as these have not been overlooked by the Civil Partnership Act 2004.[60]

COHABITATION AND CIVIL PARTNERSHIP

11–15 Account must be taken of the incidence now of cohabitation as an alternative, or precursor, to marriage, and of the introduction into UK law of the institution of civil partnership. While *ex hypothesi* these two domestic relationships do not meet the Scots conception of marriage, the new legislative provision, especially with regard to civil partnerships, is modelled upon existing legislative provision concerning marriage. As with marriage, these forms of adult relationship may have conflict of laws implications, and are discussed at sections C and D, below.

---

[58] In terms of s.215 of the Civil Partnership Act 2004, the effect of recognition in the UK of a speci-fied overseas relationship (including "marriage" in Belgium, the Netherlands and, under the Civil Partnership Act 2004 (Overseas Relationships) Order 2005 (SI 2005/3135), Canada inter alia) qual-ifying under Sch.20 will be to treat such a union as equivalent to a UK civil partnership. The English High Court in *Wilkinson v Kitzinger* [2006] EWHC 2022 (Fam) was asked to grant a petition for a declaration as to the petitioner's marital status pursuant to the Family Law Act 1986 s.55; and if necessary, a declaration of incompatibility under the Human Rights Act 1998 s.4 in relation to the Matrimonial Causes Act 1973 s.11(c), which specifies that a marriage shall be void on the ground that parties are not respectively male and female. In dismissing the petition, the court held that the UK Parliament had passed the Civil Partnership Act 2004 as a policy choice (being unwilling to alter the deep-rooted understanding of marriage as a heterosexual relationship), thereby providing statutory recognition of a status and relationship closely modelled on marriage, and imposing and conferring every material obligation and right which arises from marriage, with the exception of form of ceremony and the actual name and status of marriage. With reference to the Human Rights Act 1998, the President of the Family Division took the view that neither art.8 nor art.12 of ECHR guaranteed the right to have a same sex "marriage" recognised as having the status of marriage in English law, nor were those articles violated by the decision in these terms. The making of a distinc-tion between marriage and civil partnership fell within the margin of appreciation accorded to ECHR signatory states. See also, *P.B. and J.S. v Austria* (Application No.18984/02), July 22, 1010).

[59] Though see para.11–29, below on civil partnership, in respect of which, in the general case, the *lex loci registrationis* applies to "eligibility".

[60] e.g. s.131.

B. MARRIAGE: THE DISTINCTION BETWEEN ESSENTIALS AND FORM

Until about 1860, marriage was regarded as a matter of contract, the rights of **11–16** the contracting parties being governed by the law of the place where the contract was entered into, that is, the *lex loci celebrationis*. The result of this was that the *lex loci celebrationis* was applied to determine all questions as to the validity of a marriage. As the rules developed, however, it was recognised that marriage involves more than contract insofar as it creates a new status, and that the law of the domicile has an interest in being applied. When, after 1860,[61] questions concerning the validity of a marriage arose, UK courts began to distinguish between essentials and form, in order to avoid making decisions inconsistent with the "Gretna Green cases",[62] applying different choice of law rules to each aspect.

Although essentials and form are quite distinct in theory, in some cases it may be difficult in practice to distinguish between them; examples are the need for parental consent,[63] and marriage by proxy. The classification of a particular matter or element as pertaining to essentials or form is determined by the *lex fori*.

ESSENTIAL VALIDITY

The term "essentials" covers matters such as whether the parties have capacity **11–17** to marry, whether they consented to marry, the incidents of marriage, i.e. the rights and duties arising during marriage.[64] The majority of problems concern capacity to marry and consent to marry.

Capacity to marry

Since May 4, 2006, much of Scots conflict law pertaining to the constitu- **11–18** tion of marriage, both formal and essential, has rested upon the statutory basis of the Family Law (Scotland) Act 2006 ("the 2006 Act").

With regard to legal capacity to marry, e.g. in matters of consanguinity, sanity and nonage,[65] the common law view that the Scottish forum defers to the law(s) of the parties' domicile(s), subject to a public policy discretion, was given legislative approval by the Marriage (Scotland) Act 1977,[66] and more

---

[61] *Brook v Brook* (1861) 9 H.L. Cas. 193; and *Mette v Mette* (1859) 1 Sw. & Tr. 416.

[62] Marriages at Gretna had become popular when Lord Hardwicke's Act 1753, which was not extended to Scotland, ended the legality of clandestine marriages. The effect in those early days was that if a couple whose personal law was English succeeded in reaching the Border, and marrying in Scotland, application of the *lex loci celebrationis* to all aspects of the validity of the marriage would hold the marriage to be good. See further Anton and Francescakis, "Modern Scots Runaway Marriages", 1958 J.R. 253; and Anton, *Private International Law*, 1st edn, 1967, pp.273, 274.

[63] *Bliersbach v McEwen*, 1959 S.L.T. 81; see also and contrast the English cases of *Simonin v Mallac* (1860) 2 Sw. & Tr. 67 and *Ogden v Ogden* [1908] P.46. See para.11–26, below.

[64] As to matrimonial property matters see Ch.13, below.

[65] *Mette* (1859) 1 Sw. & Tr. 416; *Brook* (1861) 9 H.L. Cas. 193; *Webster v Webster's Trustee* (1886) 14 R. 90; *Re De Wilton* [1900] 2 Ch. 481; *Re Bozzelli's Settlement* [1902] 1 Ch. 751; *Despatie v Tremblay* [1921] 1 A.C. 702; *Re Paine* [1940] Ch. 46; *Pugh v Pugh* [1951] P. 482; *Rojas, Petitioner*, 1967 S.L.T. (Sh. Ct.) 24.

[66] See E.M. Clive, "The Marriage (Scotland) Act 1977 2. International Private Law", 1977 S.L.T. (News) 225.

recently, and expressly, by s.38(2) of the 2006 Act.[67] By the predominant theory at common law, namely the "dual domicile" theory, each party required to have legal capacity to marry in general, and to marry the other party, in particular, according to the law of his/her domicile immediately before the marriage (the ante-nuptial domicile). This is distributive application of the personal law. It has been said that "this theoretical construct tumbles over its own heels in hilarious circularity",[68] for the reality is the cumulative application of the parties' personal laws, with the result that the stricter rule (if two rules are involved) will prevail. Taking the example of the proposed marriage of an uncle and his niece; what does it benefit the uncle if his law permits him to marry his niece, if her law does not reciprocate?

Section 38(2)(a), in stating that the question whether a person who enters into a marriage had capacity to enter into it shall be determined by the law of the place where, immediately before the marriage, that person was domiciled, affirms in statutory form the common law approach. In so doing, it appears to have excluded the possibility in Scotland of advancing an alternative argument on choice of law which might have produced an *in favorem matrimonii* result where application of the dual domicile theory would have yielded a negative. The minority approach at common law, attributed first to Cheshire,[69] and manifested by a small number of English cases, was termed the "matrimonial domicile theory". On this approach, the relevant law was argued to be the law of the place where the parties intended to live their married life, that is, the law of the intended matrimonial domicile. The intended matrimonial domicile was presumed to be the husband's domicile, but that presumption might be rebutted if it could be inferred that the parties, at the point of marriage, intended to settle in a different country, and proved that they did so within a reasonable time.[70]

According to the matrimonial domicile theory all questions of essentials arising before, as well as after, the marriage ceremony were governed by the law of the matrimonial domicile. Authority in favour of the matrimonial theory is scarce,[71] and sometimes specialised,[72] and criticism of it not hard to find.[73]

---

[67] The conflict rules of England and Wales in this area remain largely common law.

[68] C.A. Dyer, First Secretary of the Hague Conference on Private International Law, "The Hague Convention on celebration and recognition of the validity of marriages in perspective", *Grensoverschrijdend Privaatrecht*, p.102.

[69] Geoffrey C. Cheshire, *Private International Law*, 5th edn (London: Clarendon Press, 1957), pp.305–320.

[70] Cheshire, *Private International Law*, 5th edn, 1957, p.307.

[71] *De Reneville* [1948] P. 100, per Greene M.R., especially at 114; *Kenward* [1951] P. 124, per Denning L.J. at 144, 146; *Re Swan's Will* (1871) 2 V.L.R. (I.E.&M.) 47 (Victoria, Australia); *Radwan (No.2)* [1972] 3 All E.R. 1026 (polygamous marriage); *Bliersbach v McEwen*, 1959 S.C. 43, per Lord Sorn at 55; Clive M. Schmitthoff, *The English Conflict of Laws*, 3rd edn (London: Stevens & Sons Ltd, 1954), pp.312–314 (supportive of Cheshire's theory).

[72] *Radwan (No.2)* [1972] 3 All E.R. 1026 supports Cheshire's theory, but is drawn from the specialty of polygamous marriage, and is in itself not well regarded.

[73] See current evaluation in *Cheshire, North and Fawcett: Private International Law*, 14th edn, 2008, pp.897, 898. Also Graveson, *Private International Law*, 7th edn, 1974, pp.265–269; Wolff, *Private International Law*, 2nd edn, 1950, pp.335, 356; and Bresler, "Note on *Pugh v Pugh*" (1951) 4 ICLQ 478, where it is noted that the celebrated South African case in matrimonial property of *Frankel v CIR* (1950) 1 S.A.L.R. 220 is firmly against the use of the intended matrimonial home theory at least in that connection. In that case, after learned debate of the civilian authorities, the South African forum applied as *lex causae* the German domicile of the husband at marriage although the parties were settled in Johannesburg, South Africa, within four months.

There was the problem, seen too in the context of commercial contractual capacity,[74] of seeming to permit parties to confer capacity on themselves by virtue merely of their own choice. Further, there was the danger[75] of creating uncertainty: how soon after the ceremony must matrimonial domicile be established, and what was the status of the parties should they have died en route? That said, dicta to support Cheshire's view can be produced, and certain decisions can be cited in which it is difficult to say whether the law was applied qua matrimonial domicile or qua ante-nuptial domicile(s), because the two coincided.[76] A study of the case of *Lawrence v Lawrence*,[77] especially in the first instance judgment of Anthony Lincoln J.,[78] reveals approval of the intended matrimonial home theory, or at least of a criterion of "real and substantial connection" and a *favor matrimonii* approach, to the extent of expression of the view that there is equal support for each theory, but it may be that the exigencies of the case, and the state of the conflict rule principally under consideration[79] in that case contributed to the stance taken.

In sum, the balance of authority at common law favoured the traditional **11–19** dual domicile theory. Though the Law Commissions reviewed[80] the matter in the 1980s, and concluded[81] that the dual domicile test is preferable to the intended matrimonial domicile test and should be adopted as the test for all issues of legal capacity, as yet there is no statutory provision in England equivalent to s.38(2)(a) of the Family Law (Scotland) Act 2006, which latter provision appears to have the effect of excluding the operation of the matrimonial domicile theory.

The rule in s.38(2)(a) is subject to a saving, in s.38(3), to the effect that, if a marriage entered into in Scotland is void in terms of Scots domestic law, the Scots rule shall prevail over any contrary rule of the law(s) of the party/ies' domicile(s). This reflects the position under the Marriage (Scotland) Act 1977 s.2(1). The effect is to insist upon legal capacity by the Scots *lex loci celebrationis*, as well as by the law(s) of the domicile(s). Despite consideration by the Scottish Law Commission of the matter of any requirement of capacity by a

---

[74] G.C. Cheshire, "David Murray lecture on International Contracts", University of Glasgow, March 4, 1948, pp.45, 46.

[75] See, similarly, in the matrimonial property context: *Re Egerton's Will Trusts* [1956] Ch. 593; see para.13–10, below.

[76] See pre-eminently *Brook* (1861) 9 H.L. Cas. 193, in which, though it was one of the early leading authorities cited in support of the dual domicile theory, Lord Campbell, to determine the validity of a purported marriage in Denmark between a man and his deceased wife's sister, at a time when such marriages were void by English law, applied the law of England qua ante-nuptial domicile of the parties but also as the law "in which the matrimonial residence is contemplated".

[77] [1985] 2 All E.R. 733, per Sir David Cairns at 746.

[78] *Lawrence v Lawrence* [1985] 1 All E.R. 506 at 510–512 (review of authorities).

[79] Recognition of Divorces and Legal Separations Act 1971 s.7, now repealed and replaced by Family Law Act 1986 s.50.

[80] Law Commission and Scottish Law Commission, *Private International Law: Choice of Law Rules in Marriage*, 1985, Law Com. Working Paper No.89; Scot. Law Com. Memo. No.64, paras 3.3, 3.4.

[81] Law Commission and Scottish Law Commission, *Private International Law: Choice of Law Rules in Marriage* (HMSO, 1987), Law Com. No.165; Scot Law Com. No.105; *Private International Law: Choice of Law Rules in Marriage*, 1985, Law Com. Working Paper No.89; Scot. Law Com. Memo. No.64, para.3.36.

foreign lex loci celebrationis,[82] the 2006 Act is silent on the question. Accordingly, whether a Scots court reviewing the validity of a marriage celebrated abroad would require capacity by the foreign *lex loci* was, and remains, a matter of conjecture. It may be argued that the role of the *lex loci* should be confined[83] to matters of form and ceremony (including the evidencing of consent, and registration of the event), and that marriages in Scotland are a special case justifying on policy grounds the cumulative application of the Scots *lex loci* with the law(s) of the parties' domicile(s).[84]

A difficulty may arise in a foreign *lex loci celebrationis* if, by the domestic rules of that legal system, divorce is prohibited; or if that law is opposed to the re-marriage within its jurisdiction of divorced persons. Increasingly, however, such problems are more theoretical than real. The solution in these situations is that if the antecedent divorce is worthy of recognition by the conflict rules of the *lex loci celebrationis*, its domestic policy objections must yield to direction by its conflict rules.[85] A related problem of the validity of a purported re-marriage, in respect of which one or both of the parties was previously divorced from (an)other person(s) by virtue of divorce(s) not recognised by the personal law(s), will be solved now in the UK by use of the Family Law Act 1986 s.50 (*q.v.*). Where the antecedent divorce is not worthy of recognition by the conflict rules of the *lex loci celebrationis*, but is valid by the law of the domicile, an incidental question will arise for decision by the forum qua *lex loci*.[86]

From the coming into effect of the 2006 Act, the public policy exception in Scots law rests upon s.38(4) of that Act, to the effect that the capacity of a person to enter into marriage shall not be determined by the law of his/her domicile in so far as it would be contrary to public policy in Scotland for such capacity to be so determined. Thus, the Scots forum retains its discretion not to require capacity by, or not to give effect to, the provisions of the party/ies' personal law, if it is offensive to conscience[87] or common sense.

---

[82] Law Commission and Scottish Law Commission, *Private International Law: Choice of Law Rules in Marriage*, 1987, Law Com. No.165; Scot Law Com. No.105, para.2.6. Also Scottish Law Commission, *Family Law: Pre-Consolidation Reforms* (HMSO, 1990) Scot. Law Com. D.P. No.85, paras 9.5, 9.6, 9.21. Also Scottish Law Commission, *Report on Family Law*, 1992, Scot. Law Com. No.135, paras 14.5, 14.6, 14.22.

[83] See the instructive Canadian case of *Reed v Reed* (1969) 6 D.L.R. (3d.) 617, which directed the issue of consanguinity to the domicile of British Columbia, and the issue of parental consent to the *lex loci celebrationis* in the State of Washington. By this reasoning, the purported marriage of first cousins, the female party according to her personal law being under the age of marriage without parental consent, avoided all difficulties and was held to be valid in a nullity petition brought by the female party in the British Columbian court of their (common) domicile. The case illustrates the process of teasing out the issues from the skein of a legal problem and treating them in the conflict of laws to different choice of law rules: dépeçage (see para.4–08, above).

[84] A different policy is evinced in American practice. Dyer has explained the American preference for permitting the place of celebration to judge both form and substance as the natural preference of an immigrant society whose members were far from their original home and did not intend to go back there. "The idea of holding up a marriage while waiting for a certificate of marriageability to come by slow boat from Europe would hardly appeal to these frontier societies where family life was hard and sometimes was cut very short" (Dyer, "The Hague Convention on celebration and recognition of the validity of marriages in perspective", *Grensoverschrijdend Privaatrecht*, p.102).

[85] *Breen v Breen* [1964] P. 144.

[86] See *Schwebel v Ungar* (1964) 48 D.L.R. (2d.) 644, Sup.Ct. (Can); see para.4–08, above.

[87] See discussion in *Cheni* [1965] P. 85, per Sir Jocelyn Simon P. at 99.

The 2006 Act makes no reference to other exceptions which were argued to exist at common law. The most important of these[88] was termed "penal incapacity", whereby a marriage celebrated in Scotland or England was not invalid on account of any incapacity, which, although existing under the law of the domicile of either/ both party/ies, was penal in the sense of discriminatory. Penal incapacities included restrictions or incapacities attributable to colour or race, rules of caste, or religion,[89] religious rules of celibacy, or prohibitions on re-marriage. A restriction on the re-marriage of one party (usually the "guilty" party) at any time or within the lifetime of the other (usually the "innocent" party) would be regarded in Scots law as penal,[90] and therefore would not be recognised in Scotland; but a restriction upon each party's re-marriage within a certain time limit, or until certain formalities have been complied with, would be regarded as affecting the capacity of either party to remarry, and such a condition would be respected, being an integral part of the divorce proceedings (probably imposed for the avoidance of doubt about paternity) and not uneven in application or otherwise objectionable.[91] It is very likely that incapacities of this nature would fall to be treated in Scots law within the terms of s.38(4).

Parties' consent to marry[92]

While evidencing consent is a matter for regulation by the *lex loci celebrationis*, the nature and extent of free will necessary to create a valid marriage are matters of substance for decision by the parties' personal law(s). Parties might enter a marriage in mental states varying from joyful acceptance to rueful resignation, whether under the influence of ideals of family obedience and family honour, or under duress. A "sham" marriage may be entered into for non-matrimonial purposes. Scots domestic law, while requiring "a willing   **11–20**

---

[88] Others were the Royal Marriage exception and the "unknown incapacity" exception. The former of these was to the effect that a marriage was invalid if either of the parties, being a descendant (as defined) of George II, married in contravention of the Royal Marriages Act 1772, which requires the consent of the sovereign to the marriage of such persons, no matter where the purported marriage may take place. See *The Sussex Peerage Case* (1844) 11 Cl. & F. 85. But see Farran, "The Royal Marriages Act 1772" (1951) 14 M.L.R. 53, cited in Wilson, "Validation of Void Marriages in Scots Law" (1964) J.R. 199. See more recently Pugh and Samuels, "The Royal Marriages Act 1772: Its Defects and the Case for Repeal" (1994) 15 Statute Law Review 46; Cretney, "The Royal Marriages Act 1772: A Footnote" (1995) 16 Statute Law Review 195. The "unknown incapacity" exception, which probably was not part of Scots law, and which the Law Commission would like to see removed from English law (*Private International Law: Choice of Law Rules in Marriage*, 1985, Law Com. Working Paper No.89; Scot. Law Com. Memo. No.64, and *Private International Law: Choice of Law Rules in Marriage*, 1987, Law Com. No.165; Scot Law Com. No.105, para.3.48), rests upon *Sottomayor v De Barros (No.2)* (1879) L.R. 5 P.D. 94, the ratio of which is that a marriage celebrated in England, according to local form, between parties of whom one has an English domicile and the other a foreign domicile, is not invalid on account of an incapacity affecting the foreign party under the law of his/her domicile, which does not exist under English law.
[89] *Chetti v Chetti* [1909] P. 67; *MacDougall v Chitnavis*, 1937 S.C. 390. See Clive, p.126.
[90] *Beattie v Beattie* (1866) 5 M. 181 (prohibition upon any subsequent marriage by adulteress); *Scott v Att Gen* (1886) L.R. 11 P.D. 128 (prohibition upon the re-marriage of the guilty party while the innocent party remained unmarried). There was a similar prohibition in Scotland until 1964: Clive, p.130.
[91] *Warter v Warter* (1890) L.R. 15 P.D. 152; *Martin v Buret*, 1938 S.L.T. 479; but see *Buckle v Buckle* [1956] P. 181; and see *Wall v De Thoren* (1874) 1 R. 1036.
[92] See para.11–26, below, on the subject of third parties' consent to marriage.

mind" will not generally be prepared to give effect to unilateral mental reservation by subsequent grant of an annulment. On the other hand, where it is clear that one party never had any intention to marry, as for example where s/he took part in a ceremony which s/he did not understand, there will be no marriage in the Scots or English view.[93] There are many fine distinctions, which are multiplied when the case is a conflict one giving rise to a number of choice of law options within the power of the forum to select.[94] The reported cases at common law display a variety of approaches, from application by the forum of its own law without argument,[95] through application of the *lex fori* after useful argument,[96] and application of the *lex fori* as interpreted in the light of a cultural background foreign to the *lex fori*,[97] to application by the forum of the law(s) of the parties' domicile(s).[98]

The second aspect of consent is mental capacity to consent. In cases where it is alleged that an individual is not capable of understanding the nature of marriage or giving his/her consent to be married, difficult factual questions may arise, which may operate to obfuscate the choice of law process.[99]

The Family Law (Scotland) Act 2006 s.38(2)(b) provides a rule on party consent, which directs that the question whether a person who enters into a marriage consented to enter into it shall be determined (subject to s.38(3) and (4) and to s.50 of the Family Law Act 1986)[100] by that person's ante-nuptial domicile. The rule is supplemented by s.2 of the 2006 Act, which inserts, as s.20A of the Marriage (Scotland) Act 1977, a provision on void marriages. This provision shall apply in relation to marriages solemnised in Scotland; the territorial limitation of s.20A must be noted. Section 20A(2) and (3) make clear, with regard to marriages solemnised in Scotland, that where a party was capable of consenting and purported to give consent, but did not only by reason

---

[93] *Alfonso-Brown v Milwood* [2006] EWHC 642 (Fam).

[94] There is even the possibility of conflict within the forum between and among the *lex fori* (also qua *lex loci celebrationis*), the law(s) of the parties' domicile(s), and their religious laws: *Di Rollo*, 1959 S.C. 75. Cf. Decision of Tribunal Supremo (Spain) in *Re Recognition of a Canon Law Judgment* [2008] I.L.Pr. 31.

[95] *Buckland v Buckland* [1968] P. 296; *Kassim v Kassim* [1962] P. 224; or, oddly, of its own law qua *lex loci celebrationis* (or *lex loci contractus*—Davies J.), *Parojcic v Parojcic* [1958] 1 W.L.R. 1280.

[96] *H v H* [1954] P. 258.

[97] *Mahmud v Mahmud*, 1994 S.L.T. 599; *Mahmood v Mahmood*, 1993 S.L.T. 589. See also *Mahmud v Mahmud*, 1977 S.L.T. (Notes) 17.

[98] *Szechter v Szechter* [1971] P. 286 (all parties of Polish domicile at date of marriage of expediency/mercy in Poland).

[99] A modern English example is the decision of the Court of Appeal in *KC v City of Westminster Social and Community Services Department* [2008] EWCA Civ 198, where it was found that the individual whose mental capacity was under scrutiny was severely intellectually impaired, to such an extent that by the English *lex fori* he lacked capacity to consent to marry. A marriage ceremony was conducted by telephone call between that party (who was a British national of Bangladeshi descent, and an English domiciliary) and the second party, a woman of presumed Bangladeshi domicile. By Bangladeshi law, the marriage (accepted to have taken place in Bangladesh) was formally valid, but in the view of English law, since the male party lacked the mental capacity to consent, the marriage was void. While this result might have been reached by application of the *lex domicilii* of the impaired party, the decision rests expressly on the exercise of the public policy of the English forum. See also *M v B* [2005] EWHC 1681 (Fam); *Re SA (Vulnerable Adult with Capacity: Marriage)* [2005] EWHC 2942 (Fam); and *X City Council v MB* [2006] EWHC 168 (Fam).

[100] See para.12–32, below.

of duress or error, or where a party was incapable of understanding the nature of marriage and of consenting, the marriage shall be void. Section 20A(4) states that if a party purported to give consent other than by reason only of duress or error, the marriage shall not be void by reason only of that party's having tacitly withheld consent to the marriage at the time of its solemnisation. These provisions constitute mandatory rules of the Scots *lex loci celebrationis*.[101]

The subject of applicable law pertaining to matrimonial consent will be treated in detail in Ch.12, below.

Other matters of essential validity

The Family Law (Scotland) Act 2006 makes no provision on matters of essen- **11–21** tial validity beyond capacity and consent to marry. Hence it may be presumed that the common law continues to apply to the rights and duties of the spouses during the subsistence of the married relationship,[102] to the effect that those rights shall be governed by the law of the matrimonial domicile at the time in question, namely, the place where the parties have their home in the legal sense, most probably where the parties have their primary matrimonial residence. Questions of the extent of property rights in wealth inherited by one spouse during the marriage, or as to ownership of items acquired by the parties during the marriage are within the province of conflict rules of matrimonial property.[103]

FORMAL VALIDITY

Form includes not only length of residence (and how to count the days), notice **11–22** and ceremony, but also irregular forms of marriage, such as marriage by cohabitation with habit and repute,[104] proxy marriage,[105] and marriage lacking the presence of either party.[106]

The Family Law (Scotland) Act 2006 s.38(1) confirms the common law position[107] that, subject to the Foreign Marriage Act 1892 (*q.v.*, below), the

---

[101] For further discussion of their mandatory nature and effect, see para.12–45, below.

[102] e.g. selection of home and allocation of the costs of running it, and duty to adhere. Occupancy rights in the matrimonial home fall within the interest of the *lex situs*.

[103] See Ch.13, below.

[104] The 2006 Act s.3 abolished this form of irregular marriage in Scots domestic law. Older conflict cases on this matter include *Cullen v Gossage* (1850) 12 D. 633; *Rooker v Rooker* (1863) 3 Sw. & Tr. 526; *Re Green, Noyes v Pitkin* (1909) 25 T.L.R. 222. Modern instances include *Kamperman v MacIver*, 1994 S.L.T. 763; *Dewar v Dewar*, 1995 S.L.T. 467; *Walker v Roberts*, 1998 S.L.T. 1133; *Ackerman v Logan's Executors (No.1)*, 2002 S.L.T. 37; *Sheikh v Sheikh*, 2005 G.W.D. 11–183; and *S v S* Unreported March 31, 2006 OH. The transitional provisions are contained in s.3(2) and (3), and attention should be paid to the protective provisions in s.3(4).

[105] Marriage by proxy has been classified as a matter of form, with the result that such marriages have been accepted by an English forum if this form of marriage is permitted by the foreign *lex loci celebrationis*: *Apt v Apt* [1948] P. 83; *Ponticelli v Ponticelli* [1958] P. 204; and *Pazpena di Vire v Pazpena di Vire* [2001] 1 F.L.R. 460.

[106] *McCabe v McCabe* [1994] 1 F.L.R. 410.

[107] *Bliersbach v McEwan*, 1959 S.C. 43; *Simonin v Mallac* (1860) 2 Sw. & Tr. 67; *Administrator of Austrian Property v Von Lorang*, 1927 S.C. (H.L.) 80; *Pepper v Pepper* (1921) L.J. 413; *Kenward* [1951] P. 124; *Pilinski v Pilinska* [1955] 1 W.L.R. 329; *Burke v Burke*, 1983 S.L.T. 331 (in which there was an adminicle of evidence of a marriage on the Island of St Christopher (now St Kitts). It was not for the pursuer, who was seeking nullity, having "married" the

question of formal validity of a marriage shall be determined by the law of the place where it was celebrated. In order for a marriage to be valid as to form there must be, therefore, compliance with the requirements of the *lex loci cele-brationis.*[108] Conversely, as stated by Lord Dunedin in *Berthiaume v Dame Dastous*[109]:

> "If a marriage is good by the laws of the country where it is effected, it is good all the world over, no matter whether the proceeding or ceremony which constituted marriage according to the law of the place would or would not constitute marriage in the country of the domicil of one or other of the spouses".

There may be advantage in remembering that since the 2006 Act does not expressly exclude the operation of *renvoi*, a Scots court might be persuaded to apply the *lex loci celebrationis* (or the *leges domicilii*, where appropriate under the 2006 Act) in their entirety, i.e. including their choice of law rules.[110]

The temporal aspect

11–23   Section 38(1), in directing application of the *lex loci celebrationis*, does not specify the *tempus inspiciendum*. The common law position, it is presumed, continues to prevail. The House of Lords, in *Starkowski v Att Gen*,[111] held that if the formal validity of a marriage is called in issue, this falls to be determined in accordance with the content of the *lex loci celebrationis* at that date, not at the date of the marriage ceremony. The reason for this is that, although as a general rule the validity of a marriage must be determined as at the date of the ceremony (at which the formalities either have been complied with or not), in exceptional circumstances its validity may be affected for the better by subsequent legislation of the *lex loci*. Yet *Starkowski*, though long established and of high authority, is regarded as a case tied very closely to its facts: a marriage celebrated only by religious ceremony took place in Austria in 1945. At that

---

defender in ignorance of his first marriage, to prove its validity. The maxim *omnia prae-sumuntur rite et solemniter acta esse* applied). Cf. *Pazpena di Vire* [2001] 1 F.L.R. 460. Contrast *Gandhi v Patel* [2002] 1 F.L.R. 603 (Hindu ceremony performed in England did not comply with the requirements of the English Marriage Act 1949. The purported marriage was held to be a "non marriage"); *Hudson v Leigh* [2009] EWHC 1306 (Fam) (religious, but not legally binding, ceremony in South Africa); and cf. *A v H* [2009] 4 All E.R. 641. Where Scotland is the *locus celebrationis*, see requirements contained in Marriage (Scotland) Acts 1977 and 2002.

[108] On occasion identification of the *locus celebrationis* may be difficult. See, for example, *KC v City of Westminster Social and Community Services Department* [2008] EWCA Civ 198, where the alleged marriage was carried out by means of a Muslim ceremony conducted over the telephone, one party being in England and the other in Bangladesh. By agreement between the parties, it was accepted that the *locus* was Bangladesh. See also *McCabe* [1994] 1 F.L.R. 410; sed quaere R.D. Leslie, "Foreign Consensual Marriages", 1994 S.L.T. (News) 87, who argues that the *lex loci celebrationis* in such a case is the place where mutual consent was exchanged. As to marriages at sea, see Cheshire, North and Fawcett, pp.893–895.

[109] *Berthiaume v Dame Dastous* [1930] A.C. 79 at 83.

[110] See para.5–12, above; R.D. Leslie, *Stair Memorial Encyclopaedia*, para.221. And see *Taczanowska v Taczanowski* [1957] P. 301; and *Hooper v Hooper* [1959] 2 All E.R. 575.

[111] [1954] A.C. 155. See also and contrast *Pilinski v Pilinska* [1955] 1 W.L.R. 329. See Clive, pp.134, 135.

date, this was insufficient by the Austrian *lex loci celebrationis* to constitute a valid marriage. Soon afterwards, however, an Austrian law was passed, providing that such marriages might be validated (retrospectively), if they were registered. The marriage in question was not registered until 1949. By that date, following the parties' separation, each of them, originally of Polish domicile, was held by the English court to have acquired a domicile of choice in England, whatever the status of the marriage. In 1950 the woman married another man in England. The Austrian legislation was held by the House of Lords to have validated the 1945 marriage. However, had the "second" marriage in England ante-dated the rectification of the "first" marriage in Austria, and had it been celebrated validly as to form and with no incapacity as to persons by their then domicile, it is hard to see how a British court could have denied the validity of that "second" marriage. Any suggestion that the later removal, by the law(s) of the domicile(s), of incapacities existing by that/those laws at the date of "marriage" can be effected *ratione Starkowsi* would appear unwarranted, given that the decision concerns rectification of defects of form.

Religious or customary ceremonies

In giving effect to the *lex loci celebrationis* at common law, the settled posi-   **11–24** tion was that the *lex loci* required to be complied with if it demanded observance of the rules of the parties' religious denomination(s), but not if it required compliance with the rules of some other denomination. One can expect the rule to continue that compliance or non-compliance with the religious beliefs of the parties does not affect the validity of a marriage unless the *lex loci celebrationis* insists upon observance of such forms.[112] A customary marriage proved to have been carried out according to the forms of the *lex loci celebrationis* is likely to suffice.[113]

Exceptions to the rule on formal validity

Section 38(1) admits only one exception, namely, that relative to the Foreign   **11–25** Marriage Act 1892. The 1892 Act, as amended,[114] provides that marriages of service personnel and marriages at foreign embassies will be valid if they comply with formalities laid down in these Acts. In such cases it does not matter that there is no compliance with the *lex loci celebrationis*.[115]

Section 38(1) makes no reference to another exception which exists at English common law, and may have existed in Scots common law, under the headings "belligerent occupation" and "local form impossible". These operated as benevolent exceptions in qualifying cases for the purpose of upholding

---

[112] *Re Alison's Trusts* (1874) 31 L.T. 638 (compliance with parties' own religious denomination required); *Usher v Usher* [1912] 2 I.R. 445 (marriage valid by Irish law though invalid in the view of the Roman Catholic Church); *Papadopoulos v Papadopoulos* [1930] P. 55; *Hooper v Hooper* [1959] 1 W.L.R. 1021 (compliance with the requirements of parties' nationality was the rule of the *lex loci celebrationis*); *Gray v Formosa* [1963] P. 259.

[113] cf. *Alfonso-Brown v Milwood* [2006] EWHC 642 (Fam); and *McCabe* [1994] 1 F.L.R. 410.

[114] By the Foreign Marriage Act 1947, and Foreign Marriage (Amendment) Act 1988.

[115] For equivalent provision for civil partnerships, see Civil Partnership Act 2004 ss.210, 211. In respect of registration at British consulates, s.210(3) provides that the prescribed officer of HM Diplomatic Service need not permit registration if, in his opinion, the formation of such a civil partnership would be, "inconsistent with international law or the comity of nations."

the formal validity of a marriage otherwise defective. The former exception was to the effect that a marriage celebrated in accordance with the "requirements of common law"[116] in a country under the occupation of military forces and where one of the parties is a member of these forces, was formally valid.[117] The benefit of the exception was not extended to those who attempted to comply with the local law, and who failed so to do.[118]

Secondly, a number of cases stand as authority, for English law,[119] that a marriage celebrated as nearly as possible in accordance with the "requirements of common law" in a country in which the use of the local form is impossible or in which there is no such form, is formally valid.

The likelihood in Scots law is that no further exception to that specified in s.38(1) will be admitted.

Third parties' consent to marriage

11–26   Cases in which the validity of a marriage is dependent upon the consent of a third party, and of a parent in particular, require special consideration. In some countries parental consent to marriage is required up to the age of 21, in others to 25. In some, absence of consent makes a marriage void wherever it is celebrated, whilst in others, it may make a marriage voidable within a certain period, again wherever it is celebrated. In some, it may be overcome by following certain procedure; in others, lack of consent may have different effects according to whether the individual is under or above 21.

The Scots choice of law rule now is contained[120] in the Family Law (Scotland) Act 2006 s.38(5) which provides that:

> "If the law of the place in which a person is domiciled requires a person under a certain age to obtain parental consent before entering into a marriage, that requirement shall not be taken to affect the capacity of a person to enter into a marriage in Scotland unless failure to obtain such consent would render invalid[121] any marriage that the person purported to enter into in any form anywhere in the world."

---

[116] The basic minimum, one presumes, is mutual voluntary exchange of consent, in the presence of at least one witness. However, cf. the Scots irregular form of marriage by declaration *de praesenti* (removed with effect from July 1, 1940), in respect of which no witness was required, nor proof of time nor place at which consent was given, provided that the court was satisfied that the parties' true intention was to be married to each other.

[117] *Taczanowska v Taczanowski* [1957] P. 301; *Kochanski v Kochanska* [1958] P. 147; *Merker v Merker* [1963] P. 283; *Preston v Preston* [1963] P. 141.

[118] *Lazarewicz v Lazarewicz* [1962] P. 171.

[119] *Lord Cloncurry's Case* (1811), cited in 6 St. Tr. (N.S.) 87 (evidence of exchange of consent by Protestants in Rome held sufficient since local law made no provision for Protestant marriage); *Catterall v Sweetman* (1845) 1 Rob. Ecc. 304; *Beamish v Beamish* (1861) 9 H.L. Cas. 274 at 348, 352; *Lightbody v West* (1903) 19 T.L.R. 319; *Phillips v Phillips* (1921) 38 T.L.R. 150; *Wolfenden v Wolfenden* [1946] P. 61 ("a British Subject takes to a colony only so much of English law as is applicable to his situation"); *Penhas v Tan Soo Eng* [1953] A.C. 304 (in the absence of a form appropriate to both, the parties devised a composite ceremony which they used in Singapore: the English forum accepted that a valid marriage had resulted, monogamous in nature).

[120] For background see Scottish Law Commission, *Report on Family Law*, 1992, Scot. Law Com. No.135, paras 14.8–14.10, recommendation 70(a), which was to the effect that a foreign parental consent rule should be regarded as resulting in a legal incapacity if, but only if, it precluded marriage by the person affected, anywhere in the world.

[121] i.e. invalid by the law of the party's domicile.

At common law in Scotland, it appeared that the Scots courts derived assistance from the Canon law classification of impediments to marriage, viz.:

(a) irritant impediment (*impedimentum dirimens*), being one which is so fundamental that it bars a marriage altogether and makes any union void (suggestive of substance, to be referred to the personal law); and

(b) prohibitive impediment (*impedimentum impeditivum*), being one which is not so important, merely prohibiting marriage until the impediment is removed (arguably formal or procedural).

In *Bliersbach v McEwan*[122] the consent of parents required by the Dutch Civil Code was regarded as falling under class (b),[123] with the result that the proposed marriage in Scotland of a Dutch couple without such consent was permitted to proceed. The opinions in the case suggest a potentially different result if the requirement of consent were to fall within class (a). The decision as far as it goes is to the same effect as the English cases.

Of the two notable cases in English law, the foreign parental consent required by French law in the circumstances of *Simonin v Mallac*[124] was of quite a different nature from that required in *Ogden v Ogden*,[125] but in both cases it was held that the requirement was to be regarded as a foreign rule affecting form, having no effect upon the valid celebration of a marriage in England. In effect, the English courts decided that, no matter what might be the domicile of the parties, whether or not parental consent is a necessary condition for the validity of a marriage celebrated in England was a matter to be classified by English law (the *lex fori*), and was held to be a matter of form, governed by the *lex loci celebrationis*.

In future, in qualifying cases in Scotland, s.38(5) will require proof of content of the party's domiciliary law, and its intended ambit.

Presumption in favorem matrimonii

The common law presumption is that if a marriage has been celebrated, **11–27** registered and a formal certificate produced, it will be formally valid, and the onus of proving otherwise rests upon any person who so avers.[126] There is no reason to think that the Family Law (Scotland) Act 2006 has removed this presumption.

C. CIVIL PARTNERSHIP

For several years conflict lawyers in the UK have been aware of the exis- **11–28** tence in other countries of forms of registered legal relationship (usually

---

[122] *Bliersbach v McEwan*, 1959 S.L.T. 81.
[123] But see criticism by Clive, pp.113, 114.
[124] (1860) 2 Sw. & Tr. 67 (the consent requirement being in the nature merely of a delay).
[125] [1908] P. 46.
[126] *Hill v Hill* [1959] 1 W.L.R. 127; *Mahadervan v Mahadervan* [1964] P 233. See, more recently, *Pazpena di Vire* [2001] 1 F.L.R. 460. Cf. Marriage (Scotland) Act 1977 s.23A: *omnia praesumuntur rite et solemniter acta esse*. But see s.20.

homosexual) unknown in Scots and English domestic law, and have noted the need for rules governing questions of legal capacity, formal validity and recognition. Since December 2005 the laws of Scotland and England have provided a new institution of civil partnership, by virtue of the Civil Partnership Act 2004, which contains not only domestic, but also conflict of laws rules.

A civil partnership is defined as a legal relationship between two people of the same sex which is formed when they register as civil partners of each other, in accordance with the relevant provisions of the 2004 Act, and which ends only on death, dissolution or annulment.

CIVIL PARTNERSHIP ACT 2004

11–29 The Act is in eight parts and has 30 Schedules.[127] Part 1 establishes the requirements for the creation of a valid civil partnership (both formal and essential validity). Separate provision is laid down for the different jurisdictions of the UK: Pt 2 (England and Wales), Pt 3 (Scotland), and Pt 4 (Northern Ireland). Determination of when each Part shall apply appears to depend upon the place of registration (*locus registrationis*) of the civil partnership in question.[128]

Within each Part are special rules concerning formation and eligibility, registration, occupancy rights and tenancies, dissolution and financial arrangements. Part 5, containing the conflict of laws provisions, is concerned with civil partnerships formed or dissolved abroad, and is of particular relevance here.

Civil partnerships registered in Scotland: Part 3

Eligibility—section 86[129]

11–30 Legal capacity to enter a civil partnership is placed under the heading of "eligibility". Under s.86(1), two parties are not eligible to register in Scotland[130] as civil partners of each other if:

(a) they are not of the same sex;
(b) they are related in a forbidden degree[131];
(c) either has not attained the age of 16 years;
(d) either is married or already in civil partnership; or
(e) either is incapable of understanding the nature of civil partnership, or validly consenting to its formation.[132]

It appears from s.86 that eligibility to register a civil partnership in Scotland depends only upon compliance with these provisions. This means that the

---

[127] Accompanied by relevant secondary legislation making necessary consequential changes to primary law, e.g. the Civil Partnership Act 2004 (Consequential Amendments) (Scotland) Order 2005 (SSI 2005/623).

[128] See s.1(1)(a).

[129] As amended by Family Law (Scotland) Act 2006 s.33.

[130] As regards formation of partnership, and eligibility to register a partnership in England, see ss.2, 3; and in Northern Ireland, ss.137, 138.

[131] The forbidden degrees are set out in s.86 and Sch.10 to the Act in a similar manner to that found in the Marriage (Scotland) Act 1977, as amended (mutatis mutandis).

[132] Section 123 provides that absence of consent is a ground rendering the civil partnership void.

statutory rules in Pt 3 demonstrate a basic territorial approach, applicable to all registrations in Scotland, to matters of form (s.85) and matters of capacity (s.86) alike, and to all persons registering a partnership, regardless of their domicile(s).

Civil partnerships formed abroad: Part 5

Registration at British consulates, or by armed forces personnel: Chapter 1

Section 210 makes provision for the registration by persons as civil partners **11–31** in prescribed countries outside the UK, and in the presence of a prescribed officer of HM Diplomatic Service if at least one of the proposed civil partners is a UK national, the parties would have been eligible to register as civil partners in the UK, the authorities of the country in question do not object, and insufficient facilities exist for them to enter into an overseas relationship under the law of that country. Section 211 makes equivalent provision, mutatis mutandis, for the registration of a civil partnership in a country outside the UK where at least one of the proposed civil partners is a member of HM Forces serving in that country.

Registration of overseas relationships treated as civil partnerships: Chapter 2

Section 215 provides that two people are to be treated as having formed a **11–32** civil partnership as a result of having registered an overseas relationship,[133] if under the relevant law they had capacity to enter into the relationship, and met all requirements necessary per the *lex loci registrationis* to ensure the formal validity of the relationship. The "relevant law" means, in terms of s.212(2), the law of the country of registration of the relationship, including its rules of private international law. Thus, if by the *lex loci registrationis*, parties are required to have capacity also by their personal law, this will constitute an extra requirement.

It should be noted that two people shall not be treated in "UK law" as having formed a civil partnership upon the registration of an overseas relationship if, at the date of registration, they were not of the same sex under "UK law".[134]

Importantly, s.217 makes certain mandatory provision in cases where at least one of the parties to the overseas relationship was domiciled in a part of the UK at the date of registration. By s.217(3) and (4), a person domiciled in Scotland shall not be treated as having formed a civil partnership as a result of having entered into an overseas relationship, if at the date of registration (i) s/he was related to the other party in a forbidden degree; (ii) s/he had not attained the age of 16 years; or (iii) s/he was incapable of understanding the nature of civil partnership, or validly consenting to its formation. In this way, Pt 5[135] imposes upon persons domiciled in Scotland all the requirements as to eligibility which would apply to them were they to seek to register a civil partnership in Scotland. This means that a Scottish domiciliary cannot evade, for example, Scottish rules of consanguinity or nonage by going abroad to register the partnership; this safeguard has an ancient lineage.[136]

---

[133] As defined in ss.212, 213, Sch.20.
[134] See s.216.
[135] Per ss.214(a), 216(1), 217(4).
[136] See Ch.2, below, statutes personal in the writings of Bartolus. Cf. *Sussex Peerage Case* (1844) 11 Cl. & F. 85; and *Brook* (1861) 9 H.L. Cas. 193.

Although the safeguard provided by s.217 appears sufficient, s.218 further provides that two people are not to be treated as having formed a civil partnership as a result of having entered into an overseas relationship if it would be manifestly contrary to (Scots/English) public policy to recognise the capacity, of one or both of them, under the *lex loci registrationis*, to enter into the relationship.

D. DE FACTO COHABITATION

11–33 Until the Family Law (Scotland) Act 2006, there was no single body of rules in Scots domestic law governing the definition, constitution, and proprietary and other consequences, of cohabitation, although particular claims by one partner of a cohabiting couple might be recognised on occasion.[137] Provision was haphazard. As has been explained, with effect from December 21, 2005 in Scotland and England, homosexual partners have been permitted to register their relationship as a civil partnership, in terms of the Civil Partnership Act 2004. The effect of registering is that parties become subject to the rules newly provided for the institution of civil partnership; this is a *de jure* relationship having specified consequences, which will trump application of rules, current and speculative, regulating *de facto* cohabiting relationships.[138]

As regards "*de facto*" cohabitation, the 2006 Act introduces in ss.25–30 a set of rules which, after defining "cohabitant" (s.25) provides certain rights for such persons in household goods (s.26); in money and property (s.27); upon termination of the relationship otherwise than by death (s.28); and upon termination of the relationship upon death intestate of one cohabitant (s.29[139]).

The meaning of "cohabitant" is contained in the 2006 Act s.25(1), as follows: either member of a couple consisting of (a) a man and a woman who are (or were) living together as if they were husband and wife; or (b) two persons of the same sex who are (or were) living together as if they were civil partners.

A problem with regard to the definition of cohabitation generally is that of identifying the date of commencement, and possibly the date of termination; whilst both, presumably, are questions of fact, the former one might think more difficult of proof.

The Act takes the approach of providing in s.25(1) an abstract definition of those who are eligible to be regarded as "cohabitant", and of providing in s.25(2) factors which may be taken as sufficient to establish cohabitation so as to "trigger" ss.26–30. Section 25(2) states that the court shall have regard to (a) the length of the period during which A and B have been living together (or lived together); (b) the nature of their relationship during that period; and (c) the nature and extent of any financial arrangements subsisting, or which subsisted, during that period. It is therefore not possible to advise with certainty as to whether the law would regard a particular couple as being

---

[137] e.g. Mortgage Rights (Scotland) Act 2001; the claim of a partner under the Damages (Scotland) Act 1976, as amended by the Administration of Justice Act 1982 s.14(4); and the Housing (Scotland) Act 1988 s.31(4).

[138] As to conflict of laws application, see speculation below.

[139] See *Savage v Purches*, 2009 S.L.T. (Sh. Ct.) 36; and *Chebotareva v Khandro (King's Executrix)*, 2008 Fam. L.R. 66.

cohabitants for the purposes of the Act. On the other hand, it may be difficult for a couple to evade the status of cohabitant under the 2006 Act, even if that should be their choice, an outcome which is an affront to party autonomy.

Conflict problems arising from the incidence of de facto cohabitation

These notable changes in domestic family law have the potential to generate **11–34** conflict of laws problems, but in general ss.25–30 are "conflict of laws blind", except that for application to be made for succession rights under s.29 the deceased cohabitant must have been domiciled in Scotland at death. It is implicit that application may be made for the rights provided for in the Act whenever Scots law is the *lex causae*. However, since generally the Act contains no jurisdiction or choice of law rules with regard to *de facto* cohabitation, it remains uncertain, e.g. which law governs an individual's legal capacity to attain the status of cohabitant, or indeed when Scots law is to be considered to be the *lex causae*. The essential antecedent question, not addressed in the Act, is in what circumstances the Scottish courts have jurisdiction to rule on these matters in the first place.[140]

Furthermore, as conflict rules now stand, what arguments might a party approaching the Scots court deploy to persuade the court that a law other than Scots law should apply, assuming such other law is furnished with rules containing property rights for cohabitants? Arguably, the starting point might be that Scots law is the governing law where the parties have, or last had, their principal place of cohabitation in Scotland, i.e. a simple territorial basis akin to the "matrimonial domicile". There is a strong argument for application, by the court of the country in which the parties cohabit, of the law of that country, to the consequences of cessation of *de facto* cohabitation; presumably that law also would determine when, and in what circumstances, such cohabitation is deemed to have ceased.[141] The conflict dimension of cohabitants' rights is dealt with further at Ch.13, below.

SUMMARY 11

1. Nature of the relationship **11–35**

This must be tested by the indicia of marriage according to the *lex fori*.

2. Polygamous marriages

Polygamous marriages are recognised for most purposes. In particular, consistorial actions between the parties to such a marriage have been competent since the Matrimonial Proceedings (Polygamous Marriages) Act 1972. Although no Scottish or English domiciliary has legal capacity to enter into an actually polygamous marriage, the Private International Law (Miscellaneous Provisions) Act 1995 s.7 provides that such a person has legal capacity to enter into a marriage which is potentially polygamous.

---

[140] See J.M. Carruthers in K Boele-Woelki (ed.), *Perspectives for the Unification and Harmonisation of Family Law in Europe* (Antwerp/Oxford/New York: Intersentia, 2003), p.322.
[141] 2006 Act s.28 gives lengthy consideration to the types of order which may be made on cessation of cohabitation and the criteria for awarding them, but no guidance to ascertain that cessation has occurred.

298 International Private Law

3. Essential validity of marriage

In terms of the Family Law (Scotland) Act 2006 s.38(2)(a), each party must have capacity to marry by the law of his/her domicile immediately before the marriage.

Likewise, in terms of s.38(2)(b), the question whether a party has consented to enter into a marriage is to be determined by his/her ante-nuptial domicile, subject however to the provisions on void marriages inserted by s.2 of the Act

The rule in each case is subject to s.38(3) (application of Scots law where the *locus celebrationis* is Scots), and s.38(4) (public policy of the forum).

4. Formal validity of marriage

Matters of form are governed by the *lex loci celebrationis* in terms of s.38(1) of the Family Law (Scotland) Act 2006.

5. Parental consent to marriage

In terms of s.38(5) of the Family Law (Scotland) Act 2006, a requirement of the law of a party's domicile that parental consent must be obtained to his/her marriage if s/he is under a certain age shall not be taken to affect his/her capacity to enter into a marriage in Scotland unless failure to obtain such consent would render invalid by the personal law of the party any marriage that s/he purported to enter into in any form anywhere in the world.

6. *De facto* cohabitation

The Family Law (Scotland) Act 2006 sets out rules of Scots law in respect of the rights and duties of cohabitants. No jurisdiction provisions for *de facto* cohabitation disputes are contained in the Act, and only one such choice of law rule is visible.

7. Civil Partnership Act 2004

Part 3 contains rules on the formation of civil partnerships in Scotland. Part 5 contains conflict of laws provision in respect of civil partnerships formed abroad.

CHAPTER 12

CONSISTORIAL CAUSES

I. DIVORCE

The following will be considered in turn: **12–01**

(1) jurisdiction of Scots courts;
(2) choice of law in Scots courts; and
(3) recognition of foreign decrees by Scots courts.

A. THE JURISDICTION OF SCOTS COURTS

Common law grounds of jurisdiction and statutory extension

There is a natural tendency towards interdependence between the rules of **12–02**
jurisdiction in consistorial causes utilised by a forum and its approach to
the recognition of foreign decrees in that area.[1] At one time the Scots courts
assumed jurisdiction on a wide basis, including residence, but Scots decrees
were not recognised in England unless the husband was domiciled in Scotland
at the date of the action.[2] The Scots courts did not adopt such a strict view as
to (non-) recognition at that time. Between 1852 and 1895,[3] they developed a
doctrine of matrimonial domicile, that is, that the parties should be regarded as
being domiciled in the country where they resided, for the purpose of consistorial actions only, and that the courts of that country should be regarded
as having jurisdiction in such actions. In *Le Mesurier*,[4] however, the Privy
Council, on an appeal from Ceylon, held that there was no such thing for this
purpose as matrimonial domicile and that only the courts of the husband's
domicile had jurisdiction in actions of divorce. This decision was accepted as
applying both to Scotland and England, and in Scotland the doctrine of matrimonial domicile as a ground of jurisdiction subsequently was abandoned.[5] The
practical difficulties of having to go to the court of the domicile, the problem
of the deserted wife in England,[6] and the occurrence of wartime marriages to

---

[1] *Travers v Holley* [1953] P. 246; and *Indyka v Indyka* [1969] 1 A.C. 33, per Lord Pearce at 78.
[2] *Lolley's Case* (1812) Russ. & Ry. 237; and *Shaw v Gould* (1868) L.R. 3 H.L. 55.
[3] *Shields v Shields* (1852) 15 D. 142; *Jack v Jack* (1862) 24 D. 467; *Pitt v Pitt* (1864) 2 M. (H.L.)
28; *Dombrowitzki v Dombrowitzki* (1895) 22 R. 906.
[4] *Le Mesurier v Le Mesurier* [1895] A.C. 517.
[5] See J.A. Mclaren, *Court of Session Practice* (Edinburgh: W. Green & Son Ltd, 1916), pp.57, 58.
[6] In desertion cases, the English courts regarded the husband's domicile at the date of the raising
of the action as being the determinant of jurisdiction: *H v H* [1928] P. 206 and *Herd v Herd*
[1936] P. 205. In such cases in Scotland, however, the courts assumed jurisdiction if the husband
was domiciled in Scotland at the date of desertion.

"foreigners", combined to demonstrate the undue strictness of the rule in *Le Mesurier*. As a result, a number of statutory extensions were made to permit access by the wife to the Scots or English courts on the basis of her residence in the jurisdiction.[7]

Modern grounds of jurisdiction

Rules of jurisdiction up to March 1, 2001

12–03   The earlier statutory provisions were replaced by the Domicile and Matrimonial Proceedings Act 1973 ("the 1973 Act"), as now amended in light of EU harmonisation measures.

The 1973 Act specified a ground of jurisdiction additional to that of domicile. Section 7 provided that the Court of Session should have jurisdiction in actions of divorce, separation and declarators of freedom and putting to silence if and only if: (a) either party was domiciled in Scotland at the date when the action began; or (b) either party was habitually resident in Scotland throughout the period of one year ending with the date when the action is begun.[8]

Divorce jurisdiction was extended to the sheriff court by the Divorce Jurisdiction, Court Fees and Legal Aid (Scotland) Act 1983.[9] Jurisdiction to reduce a decree of divorce granted by a court in Scotland is conferred on the Court of Session whether or not at that later date the court has jurisdiction independently to pronounce on the parties' status.[10]

Regulation 1347/2000: Brussels II

12–04   From March 1, 2001, there was put in place a discrete system of allocation of jurisdiction in matrimonial matters and consistorial decree recognition among the then Member States of the EU, in the form of Regulation[11] 1347/2000 on jurisdiction and recognition and enforcement of judgments in matrimonial matters and in matters of parental responsibility for children of both spouses (colloquially known as "Brussels II").[12] Brussels II *bis* came into force fully on March 1, 2005, repealing Brussels II. The system depends, as does the Regulation's commercial law precursors, the 1968 Brussels Convention

---

[7] Indian and Colonial Divorce Jurisdiction Acts 1926 and 1940; and Colonial and Other Territories (Divorce Jurisdiction) Act 1950; Matrimonial Causes Act 1937 (A.P. Herbert's Act) (introducing residence as a ground of jurisdiction in England for a deserted wife); and Matrimonial Causes (War Marriages) Act 1944 s.1 (England) s.2 (Scotland). The last and most useful was the Law Reform (Miscellaneous Provisions) Act 1949 s.1 (England) s.2 (Scotland).

[8] Equivalent provisions were introduced in ss.5 and 13 as regards the courts of England and Northern Ireland respectively. As to jurisdiction in annulment see para.12–40, below. See further discussion of habitual residence in paras 6–44—6–49, above.

[9] And see 1973 Act s.8(1), (2). As to the interpretation of habitual residence such as to confer jurisdiction on the sheriff, see *Williamson v Williamson*, 2010 S.L.T. (Sh. Ct.) 41.

[10] Law Reform (Miscellaneous Provisions) (Scotland) Act 1980 s.20. See previously *Acutt v Acutt*, 1935 S.C. 525. Trace similarity in approach in Wills Act 1963 s.2(1)(c); Family Law Act 1986 s.47(2); and *Leon v Leon* [1967] P. 275: "once seised, always seised".

[11] The original plan had been to produce a Brussels II Convention, but this plan was superseded by the proposal for a Regulation.

[12] OJ [2000] L160/19. The secondary legislation which effected the necessary changes to domestic legislation, particularly to the 1973 Act, so as to ensure compliance with Brussels II, was the European Communities (Matrimonial Jurisdiction and Judgments) (Scotland) Regulations 2001 (SSI 2001/36); and Act of Sederunt (Ordinary Cause Rules) Amendment (European Matrimonial and Parental Responsibility Jurisdiction and Judgments) 2001 (SSI 2001/144).

("Brussels I") and Regulation 44/2001 ("Brussels I Regulation") (the latter of which provides the structure for the family law instrument) upon Member States agreeing, first, a set of rules of jurisdiction. Thereafter, if the decree in question emanates from a court of competent jurisdiction in terms of the instrument, recognition thereof is almost certain to follow in the other Member States.

Brussels II was succeeded rapidly by Regulation 2201/2003 concerning jurisdiction and the recognition and enforcement of judgments in matrimonial matters and matters of parental responsibility (colloquially known as "Brussels II *bis*").[13] Brussels II *bis* came about as a result of the view that the scope of Brussels II, as it affected children, was too narrow. The more ambitious aim of Brussels II *bis* was to create a single European instrument securing the free movement, both of matrimonial judgments and parental responsibility judgments.

The "Brussels rules" apply, with direct effect, among all Member States of the EU,[14] with the exception of Denmark.[15]

Rules of jurisdiction after March 1, 2005: Brussels II bis[16]

The starting point is the 1973 Act, as amended first by the European **12–05** Communities (Matrimonial Jurisdiction and Judgments) (Scotland) Regulations 2001 (SSI 2001/36) (taking account of Brussels II), and more recently by the European Communities (Matrimonial and Parental Responsibility Jurisdiction and Judgments) (Scotland) Regulations 2005 (SSI 2005/42) (taking account of Brussels II *bis*).

The Scottish rules of jurisdiction are contained in s.7(2A) of the 1973 Act, to the effect that the Court of Session has jurisdiction to entertain an action for divorce or separation,[17] if and only if:

(1) the Scottish courts have jurisdiction under Brussels II *bis*; or
(2) the action is an excluded action and either of the parties to the marriage is domiciled in Scotland on the date when the action is begun.

---

[13] OJ [2003] L338/1. See also Regulation 2116/2004 concerning jurisdiction and the recognition and enforcement of judgments in matrimonial matters and the matters of parental responsibility, repealing Regulation 1347/2000, as regards treaties with the Holy See [2004] OJ L367/1). The relevant Scottish secondary legislation is the European Communities (Matrimonial and Parental Responsibility Jurisdiction and Judgments) (Scotland) Regulations 2005 (SSI 2005/42); and Act of Sederunt (Rules of the Court of Session Amendment) (Jurisdiction, Recognition and Enforcement of Judgments) 2005 (SSI 2005/135).

[14] See also 1973 Act s.12(5)(b).

[15] Protocol No.5 on the position of Denmark ([1997] OJ C340/101), in terms of which Denmark shall not take part in the adoption of proposed measures pursuant to Title IIIa of the Treaty establishing the European Community; and Protocol No.22 on the position of Denmark (consolidated versions of the TEU and the TFEU: [2008] OJ C115/299).

[16] Article 65 of Brussels II *bis* requires, no later than January 1, 2012, the Commission to present a report on the application of the instrument. The Stockholm Programme (see para.1–07, above) envisages that there may be the need for a proposal amending Brussels II *bis*. The draft Brussels II Convention was accompanied by an Explanatory Report by Dr Alegria Borras, *Explanatory Report on the Convention on Jurisdiction and the Recognition and Enforcement of Judgments in Matrimonial Matters* [1998] OJ C221/27 ("Borras Report"). No separate explanatory memorandum was issued to accompany Brussels II or Brussels II *bis*, but the Borras Report can be used to shed light on certain of the provisions in the Regulation, which echo those contained in the draft Convention.

[17] There continue to be special rules of jurisdiction for actions of declarator of marriage (1973 Act s.7(3)), and in relation to declarators of nullity of marriage, where one party was dead at the date of the action, and that party was domiciled at death in Scotland, or had been habitually resident there for one year before death (1973 Act s.7(3A)).

Brussels II bis article 3

12–06   Turning first to jurisdiction under the Regulation, the bases of jurisdiction are contained in art.3, to the following effect: in matters relating to divorce, legal separation or marriage annulment, jurisdiction shall lie with the courts of the Member State:

> "(a) in whose territory:
>
> — the spouses are habitually resident, or
> — the spouses were last habitually resident, insofar as one of them still resides there, or
> — the respondent is habitually resident, or
> — in the event of a joint application, either of the spouses is habitually resident, or
> — the applicant is habitually resident if he or she resided there for at least a year immediately before the application was made, or
> — the applicant is habitually resident if he or she resided there for at least six months immediately before the application was made, and is either a national of the Member State in question or, in the case of the UK and Ireland, has his or her "domicile" there[18];
>
> (b) of the nationality of both spouses or, in the case of the UK and Ireland, of the "domicile" of both spouses."

Article 3.1(a)

12–07   Why the focus on habitual residence, and why so many bases of jurisdiction? The Borras Report explains that:

> "The grounds adopted are based on the principle of *genuine connection* between the person and a Member State. The decision to include particular grounds reflects their existence in various national legal systems and their acceptance by the other Member States or the effort to find points of agreement acceptable to all."[19]

The notion of genuine connection is one which has been accorded some recognition in England. In *Ikimi v Ikimi*, Thorpe L.J. in the Court of Appeal, reviewing the history of jurisdiction in divorce, explained that in the late 1960s the Law Commissions wished to extend consistorial jurisdiction beyond domicile on a base of jurisdiction that meets the interests of the state and of those who, "genuinely belong here, refusing access to transients and forum shoppers."[20] The Law Commissions favoured a "belonging test" which could tolerate periods of absence but which required more than occasional or casual residence. "Habitual" residence was chosen instead of "ordinary" residence in order to provide a uniform test in family law and to conform with international

---

[18] In terms of art.3.2, for the purposes of the Regulation, "domicile" shall have the same meaning as it has under the legal systems of the UK and Ireland.
[19] Borras Report, para.30.
[20] *Ikimi v Ikimi* [2002] Fam.72 at [21].

conventions, but there was not thought to be any difference between the two in this area of the law.[21] So the idea of genuine connection between a litigant and the court is apparently the rationale, both in UK law and in EC thinking.

Ikimi is an instructive case concerning the meaning of habitual residence for the purpose of divorce jurisdiction. In terms of the quality of residence required, the Court of Appeal took the view that the bodily presence required to form a basis for habitual residence, for the purposes of jurisdiction in divorce pre-Brussels, had to be more than merely token in duration, probably amounting to residence for, "an appreciable part of the relevant year".[22] The point in issue was the degree of continuity required to establish habitual residence for the purposes of divorce jurisdiction. The court had to consider whether a Nigerian wife who filed a petition for dissolution of marriage in England on the basis of habitual residence there had two such residences. The family had two matrimonial homes, of equal status, in Nigeria and in England, and the wife had spent 161 days of the year in England. The submission that it was not possible to be habitually resident in two places, England and Nigeria, simultaneously, was firmly rejected by the Court of Appeal. On the facts, the court found there was just sufficient residence in England by the wife, looking at all the comings and goings. Interestingly, having in mind the purpose of the finding on habitual residence, Thorpe L.J. favoured a *liberal* rather than a restrictive approach to the determination of habitual residence, whilst noting that one consequence of liberality might be forum shopping. If the residence test is too hard, a spouse who divides his time equally might not be able to invoke a habitual residence in either. On the other hand, setting it too low would allow the spouse to invoke the jurisdiction of both.

Habitual residence is not defined in the instrument, and is not easy to define. The term has an autonomous meaning for the purposes of Brussels II *bis*.[23] The meaning is to be derived from ECJ jurisprudence, and is not necessarily the same as the UK domestic meaning, nor the meaning for the purposes of international child abduction as developed in the UK through Hague Convention jurisprudence.

The starting point may be said to be the suggested definition in the Borras Report, viz.:

> ". . . the place where the person had established, on a fixed basis, his permanent or habitual centre of interests, with all the relevant facts being taken into account for the purpose of determining such residence."[24]

In the spirit of the Borras definition, a similar approach to habitual residence was taken by the French *Cour de Cassation* in *Moore v Moore*,[25] viz.:

---

[21] *Ikimi* [2002] Fam.72, per Thorpe L.J. at [31]; and *Armstrong v Armstrong* [2003] EWHC 777 (Fam), per Butler-Sloss L.J.

[22] *Ikimi* [2002] Fam.72, per Thorpe L.J. at [35].

[23] *Marinos v Marinos* [2007] EWHC 2047 (Fam), per Munby J. at [17], [18]; and *Z v Z (Divorce: Jurisdiction)* [2009] EWHC 2626 (Fam).

[24] Borras Report, para.32. The suggested definition was cited with approval in *Marinos v Marinos* [2007] EWHC 2047 (Fam), per Munby J. at [33].

[25] [2006] I.L.Pr. 29.

"The place where the party involved has fixed, with the wish to vest it with a stable character, the permanent or habitual centre of his or her interests."

In *Moore*, the husband brought divorce proceedings in the French court, and a question arose as to whether or not the French court had jurisdiction under Brussels II art.2,[26] on the basis of the wife's habitual residence in France. The couple were English nationals who had moved to their second home in France for a pre-determined 18-month period. The principal purpose of the move was to have their child schooled in France. The husband argued that habitual residence for the purpose of Brussels II included "temporary installation for a definite period", and required only an objective attachment to the place. The French judge at first instance declined jurisdiction. In the *Cour de Cassation*, habitual residence was defined and applied in such a way that the conclusion was reached that evidence did not show that W had transferred the "centre of her interests" to France. This French decision is demonstrably stricter than many of the English authorities, and it may be that the French court detected an inappropriate evasion of the natural forum.

An English gloss on the Borras definition was given in the case of *LK v K*.[27] The case involved a peripatetic husband and wife, both French nationals, who married in Singapore. They arrived in England in late 2004 to live in rented property, the move occasioned by the husband's employment. His work commenced in February the following year. In March 2005 the wife began divorce proceedings in England. The husband submitted that neither party was habitually resident in England. Singer J. held that the issue of habitual residence is fact dependent, to be judged against the pattern of the couple's lives. Given the husband's work patterns, neither spouse had entered England as transients, but with the settled intention of being resident in England for the duration of the husband's employment. The court was satisfied that there existed between the parties and the English forum the "genuine connection" referred to above, and both spouses were deemed to be habitually resident in England. This is a decision resting on "centre of interests", not on length of time.

An important English case is *Marinos v Marinos*,[28] in which it fell to be decided whether or not, for the purposes of Brussels II *bis*, a person can be habitually resident in two different countries at the same time. The husband was of Greek, and the wife of British, nationality. The husband went to Greece in October 2002 to work, and his wife and children followed in December that year, on something of a trial basis. The wife claimed it was temporary relocation. In fact she and the children did not return to England until January 2007, and the day after arrival she petitioned for divorce in England, relying on Brussels II *bis* art.3 indent 6. It was not disputed that she satisfied the domicile requirement of indent 6; the case turned entirely on whether she could prove that she was habitually resident in England and had resided there for the preceding six months. Munby J. held, in what was a very evenly balanced case, that the wife's centre of gravity was located in England, not Greece, and he found that she was both resident and habitually resident in England at all material times.

---

[26] Equivalent to Brussels II *bis* art.3.
[27] *L-K v K (No.2)* [2006] EWHC 3280 (Fam), per Singer J. at [35].
[28] *M v M* [2007] EWHC 2047 (Fam).

Significantly, Munby J. considered that while it was clear that, for the purposes of English domestic law, one could be habitually resident contemporaneously in two different countries,[29] "the same is not necessarily true of the law laid down by the ECJ nor, specifically, for the purposes of the Regulation".[30]

The single judge decision in *Marinos* is at odds with another single judge decision handed down four years earlier in *Armstrong v Armstrong*[31] by the then President of the English Family Division of the High Court, Dame Elizabeth Butler-Sloss. In that Brussels II case, the President accepted that, as a matter of fact a person can have two habitual residences simultaneously and she concluded that the correct approach to the degree of continuity required to establish habitual residence in a country, "cannot just be a counting of the days spent in the country. There has to be an element of quality of residence".[32] Her Ladyship, however, did count the days, and on the facts, noted that the husband had spent 171 days in South Africa as against 71 in England. Could it be said that the husband was habitually resident in South Africa *and* in England? The court found in the negative; the husband was clearly habitually resident in South Africa, but was only resident in England, and accordingly, the English court had no jurisdiction. The husband's voluntary presence in England on a regular basis did not amount to a settled intention to make England his habitual residence, or one of his habitual residences. England was merely a stopping off place for work or holidays. The character, in fact, of the residence was not sufficient to found, in law, habitual residence

Munby J. in *Marinos* suggested that the point of interpretation of art.2 of Brussels II in *Armstrong* was inadequately argued and addressed, and that the decision of Dame Elizabeth Butler-Sloss P. rested on a "frail foundation".[33] Munby J. concluded in *Marinos*,[34] that:

". . . the language of Article 3(1)(a) of the Regulation [Brussels II *bis*][35] is clear, as is the ECJ case-law. For the purposes of the Regulation, one cannot be habitually resident in more than one country at the same time."

Of the conflicting interpretations, *Marinos* is perhaps the more persuasive,[36] but even so, there is no guarantee that different forums would identify the same legal system as the habitual residence at the *tempus inspiciendum*.[37]

Study of this subject suggests that it is not safe to use a cross-fertilisation **12–08** technique, that is, to transplant authorities from one area of law for use in another. Nonetheless, it is natural that in family law litigation, child custody

---

[29] *Marinos v Marinos* [2007] EWHC 2047 (Fam) at [38].

[30] *Marinos v Marinos* [2007] EWHC 2047 (Fam) at [38].

[31] *Armstrong v Armstrong* [2003] EWHC 777 (Fam); [2003] 2 F.L.R. 375.

[32] *Armstrong v Armstrong* [2003] EWHC 777 (Fam) at [30] (the pattern of the respondent's visits to England, together with the number of days spent in the country—one-fifth of the year—did not demonstrate sufficient residence to meet the statutory requirement of habitual residence in the 1973 Act and Brussels II).

[33] *Marinos v Marinos* [2007] EWHC 2047 (Fam) at [42].

[34] *Marinos v Marinos* [2007] EWHC 2047 (Fam) at [43].

[35] Article 3 of which is in identical terms to art.2 of Brussels II.

[36] *Marinos v Marinos* [2007] EWHC 2047 (Fam) at [40].

[37] Though see Munby J. in *Marinos v Marinos* [2007] EWHC 2047 (Fam) at [17], [18], and Singer J. in *L-K v K (No.2)* [2006] EWHC 3280 (Fam) at [35].

issues and divorce issues may be intertwined, and it may not be unreasonable, therefore, to make reference in this context to authorities from the international child abduction area.

On that basis then, there may be examined *Re R (Abduction: Habitual Residence)*,[38] which prompted discussion of the implications of the not uncommon situation where one parent is seconded from one country to another for purposes of work, for a temporary period, for a particular project and for a short time. The father, a financier, was seconded from London to Germany for what the father claimed was an indefinite period intended to extend into the foreseeable future and for a minimum period of six months, while according to the mother it was a temporary posting, of short-term duration, at maximum six months. Munby J. concluded that for a person to be regarded in law as habitually resident in any country, he must have lived there for a period; but that period is not a fixed period and may be short—a month can be an appreciable period of time. On the facts, the judge concluded that the father's "temporary" posting to Germany was sufficient to confer on him, his wife and their child, an habitual residence in Germany. The family's residence there was for a settled purpose, albeit a purpose of short duration. Munby J. paid some attention[39] to the state of mind necessary to permit acquisition of a new habitual residence, in particular, the suggestion that one cannot acquire a habitual residence in a foreign country unless one has a settled intention not to return to the country from which one is departing. His considered view was that it is wrong to suggest that a person does not lose his habitual residence in a particular country unless he has a settled intention not to return there; that, in the view of Munby J., would be to confuse habitual residence with domicile. Rather, in his opinion, it was no bar to acquisition of a new habitual residence in Germany that the individual had by no means decided to abandon the English habitual residence obtaining immediately before. This comes close to suggesting that dual habitual residence may exist,[40] an awkward conclusion in child abduction cases. Lifestyles such as this are likely to raise the possibility of dual or concurrent habitual residence, assuming that the family retains a home in the state of origin. If this fairly liberal approach were to be transposed to legal issues affecting the adult community, then it could have quite significant implications for the mobile international population.

While the suggestion of rapidly and easily alternating (i.e. consecutive not concurrent) habitual residences has its attractions for the adult community,[41] one would have to assess its suitability against the family situation as a whole in circumstances such as *Re R*, and ask whether the rapid acquisition of a new habitual residence in, say, Germany extends also to the child. It will not serve if it were to lead to the situation in which divorce jurisdiction under Brussels II *bis* might be easily established, based on a new habitual residence; but that a mother who wished, on termination of the marriage, to return with the children of the family to the English jurisdiction whence they had come, would be in danger of being found to have wrongfully removed the children from their deemed habitual residence in Germany, the "new" country.

---

[38] [2003] EWHC 1968 (Fam).
[39] *Re R (Abduction: Habitual Residence)* [2003] EWHC 1968 (Fam) at [40].
[40] cf. Munby J. in *Marinos v Marinos* [2007] EWHC 2047 (Fam), para.12–07, above.
[41] See, e.g. *Z v Z (Divorce: Jurisdiction)* [2009] EWHC 2626 (Fam).

Article 3.1(b)

Article 3.1(b) confers jurisdiction on the courts of the Member State of the **12–09** nationality of both spouses or, in the case of the UK and Ireland, of the "domicile" of both spouses. Some states had wanted the condition to attach to one spouse only, but that was rejected on the ground that it would amount to pure "*forum actoris*".[42] The phrases in art.3.1(b) must be read disjunctively so as to produce one provision for the UK and Ireland, and another for all other Member States. It does not provide an additional gateway for the UK and Ireland.[43]

A difficulty of interpretation has arisen in relation to parties of dual nationality. In *Re Hadadi*,[44] the French *Cour de Cassation* referred for a preliminary ruling the question whether art.3.1(b) is to be interpreted as meaning that where spouses hold both the nationality of the court seised, and the nationality of another Member State, the nationality of the court seised must prevail. The ECJ held that the court of the Member State addressed must take into account the fact that spouses also hold the nationality of the Member State of origin and that, therefore, the courts of the latter could have had jurisdiction to hear the case. Where spouses each hold the nationality of the same two Member States, art.3.1(b) precludes the jurisdiction of the courts of one of those Member States from being rejected on the ground that the applicant does not put forward other links with that state. On the contrary, the courts of those Member States of which the spouses hold the nationality have jurisdiction under that provision and between the two the spouses may seise the court of the Member State of their choice.[45]

"Excluded action"

The Scottish courts will have jurisdiction under the 1973 Act s.7(2A) if the **12–10** action is an "excluded action"[46] and either party is domiciled in Scotland on the date when the action is begun. An understanding of this qualification requires, therefore, an examination of the meaning of "excluded action", which is defined in s.12(5)(d) of the 1973 Act,[47] as:

">... an action in respect of which no court of a Contracting State has jurisdiction under the Council Regulation and the defender is not a person who is (i) a national of a Contracting State (other than the United Kingdom or Ireland); or (ii) domiciled in Ireland."[48]

---

[42] Borras Report, para.33.
[43] *Re N (Jurisdiction)*; sub nom. *NDO v JFO* [2009] I.L.Pr. 8.
[44] *Re Hadadi*; sub nom. *Re Hadady* (C-168/08) 2008/C 158/20 [2008] OJ C158/11.
[45] *Re Hadadi* (C-168/08) 2009/C 220/17 [2009] OJ C220/11.
[46] Brussels II *bis* art.7 provides for the continuing application of residual national rules of jurisdiction. See *A v L*; sub nom. *F v F* [2009] EWHC 1448 (Fam), discussed, para.12–15, below; *contra Sundelind Lopez v Lopez Lizazo* (C-68/07) [2008] I.L.Pr. 4, in which the ECJ made clear that jurisdiction cannot be regulated by national law under art.7.1 unless no court of a Member State has jurisdiction pursuant to arts 3–5.
[47] Introduced by reg.2(5)(d) of European Communities (Matrimonial Jurisdiction and Judgments) (Scotland) Regulations 2001 (SSI 2001/36), and substituted by European Communities (Matrimonial and Parental Responsibility Jurisdiction and Judgments) (Scotland) Regulations 2005 (SSI 2005/42) reg.8.
[48] As to jurisdiction in nullity, see below.

The main point to make here is that, in connection with actions of divorce, the pre-existing (that is, pre-March 1, 2001) Scottish jurisdictional ground of one year's habitual residence of either party in Scotland, has ceased to be available.

Conflicting jurisdictions

12–11   The common law position was that if a Scots or English court had jurisdiction in consistorial proceedings brought by one party and the other party was proceeding with another action in a foreign court, that fact would not prevent the first party from proceeding with the first action unless a very strong case was submitted.[49]

The 1973 Act set out for England (in Sch.1),[50] and Scotland (Sch.3),[51] respectively, a dual system of mandatory and discretionary sists for the treatment of instances of conflicting jurisdictions in consistorial causes. In terms of Sch.3 para.7, there is a duty on the pursuer or on any other person who has entered appearance in a consistorial action, in either the Court of Session or the sheriff court, in which proof has not begun, to give notice of any proceedings relating to, or capable of affecting the validity of, that marriage in another jurisdiction, whether within or outside Great Britain.

Mandatory sists

12–12   It has been seen in Ch.7, above that there has been much debate in the commercial arena concerning the continuing competence of the plea of *forum non conveniens* among the legal systems of the UK, resulting (currently) in tacit agreement that the plea continues to be available. The same problem arises in the family law context. The question is whether the system of mandatory sists within the UK has been affected by the system of *lis pendens* put in place by Brussels II and Brussels II *bis*. Recourse must be made to relevant secondary legislation. There does not appear to have been a repeal of the mandatory stay system, but since the systems which apply under the 1973 Act Sch.3 para.8, and Brussels II *bis* art.19, respectively, do not differ in essence, the point is academic. It is in respect of discretionary sists that the differences between the Brussels and national systems are striking. The 1973 Act approach is that where, before proof has begun in an action of divorce in the Court of Session, or sheriff court, a party shows that an action of divorce or nullity relating to the same marriage is proceeding in a related jurisdiction (that is within England and Wales, Northern Ireland, Jersey, Guernsey (including Alderney and Sark) or Isle of Man)[52] and, broadly speaking, that the parties resided together after the marriage and last resided together in that other jurisdiction, and that either party was habitually resident in that other jurisdiction throughout the year ending with the date on which they last resided together before that other action was begun, the Scottish court must sist the action.[53]

---

[49] *Sealey v Callan* [1953] P. 135.
[50] 1973 Act s.5, Sch.1.
[51] 1973 Act s.11, Sch.3.
[52] 1973 Act Sch.3 para.3.
[53] 1973 Act Sch.3 para.8.

Discretionary sists

Where, before proof has begun in any consistorial action in the Court **12–13** of Session or sheriff court, it appears that there are other proceedings relating to the marriage in another jurisdiction and that the balance of fairness, including convenience, between the parties is such that it is appropriate for those other proceedings to be disposed of before further steps are taken in the Scottish action, the court may if it thinks fit sist the action.[54]

There may be cultural considerations as a result of which the Scots forum may think that the balance of fairness and convenience lies in permitting an action to proceed in Scotland, for example, if the litigant has little hope of a satisfactory remedy in the competing jurisdiction.[55] However, many cases do not exhibit a cultural clash, and in such cases the controversial issue is the extent to which personal or juridical advantage to one party ought to be taken into account.

The need for a judicial disposal with regard to heritable property within the jurisdiction may tend to dissuade that forum from sisting.[56]

The Matrimonial and Family Proceedings Act 1984[57] has changed this situation to a significant extent, in that a party may apply to a Scots or English court for financial provision despite the existence of an antecedent foreign divorce worthy of recognition in Scotland or England. Use of the 1984 Act is subject to strict jurisdictional requirements, and there have been relatively few cases. Nevertheless, the provision should result in a smaller number of cases being defended, apparently on substance, when the true motive is financial.[58] It means also that some cases which pre-date the 1984 Act and which bear upon judicial advantage are no longer a safe guide.[59]

These rules concerning sists are a manifestation in consistorial actions of a system of allocation of jurisdiction which depends on the use of judicial discretion. It stands in contrast to the continental European preference for a system of ranking concurrent proceedings on the basis of priority of process (*lis pendens*).

Lis pendens system under Brussels regime

Since the Brussels regime has been extended, in operation and influence, from **12–14** commercial law to family law,[60] it follows that the Brussels-preferred system of

---

[54] 1973 Act Sch.3 para.9. See Schuz, "The Further Implications of Spiliada in Light of Recent Case Law: Stays in Matrimonial Proceedings" (1989) 38 I.C.L.Q. 946. See operation of the plea in the following (English) cases: *Shemshadfard v Shemshadfard* [1981] 1 All E.R. 726; *De Dampierre v De Dampierre* [1987] 2 All E.R. 1; *Thyssen-Bornemisza v Thyssen-Bornemisza* [1995] 1 All E.R. 58; *Breuning v Breuning* [2002] 1 F.L.R. 888; *A v S (Financial Relief after Overseas US Divorce)* [2002] EWHC 1157 (Fam); *O v O (Appeal against Stay: Divorce Petition)* [2003] 1 F.L.R. 192; *T v M-T* [2005] EWHC 79 (Fam); and *Ella v Ella* [2007] EWCA Civ 99.

[55] e.g. *A v L* [2009] EWHC 1448 (Fam).

[56] *Mitchell v Mitchell*, 1993 S.L.T. 123; and *Butler v Butler (No.2)* [1997] 2 All E.R. 822 CA.

[57] See para.13–40, below.

[58] Consider *Quazi v Quazi* [1980] A.C. 744 and contrast *Tahir v Tahir*, 1993 S.L.T. 194 (and *Tahir v Tahir (No.2)*, 1995 S.L.T. 451).

[59] e.g. *K v K* [1986] Fam. Law 329 and *Gadd v Gadd* [1985] 1 All E.R. 58. See *forum non conveniens* argument in context of litigation under the Matrimonial and Family Proceedings Act 1984 in *Agbaje v Agbaje* [2010] 2 All E.R. 877.

[60] See para.1–08, above.

allocating jurisdiction among competing legal systems[61] now operates to solve this problem in consistorial litigation in qualifying cases. The Brussels system must apply in cases where the interested legal systems are EU Member States,[62] but on occasion difficulties may arise in delimiting the ambit of operation of each of the EU and non-EU rules.

The rules on *lis pendens* are contained in Brussels II *bis* art.19: where proceedings relating to divorce, legal separation or marriage annulment between the same parties are brought before the courts of different Member States, the court second seised shall of its own motion stay its proceedings until such time as the jurisdiction of the court first seised is established.[63] The same system applies to concurrent proceedings relating to parental responsibility concerning the same child and involving the same cause of action.[64]

Demarcation between the 1973 Act Schedule 3 paragraph 9 and Brussels II bis article 19

12–15   There is no difficulty in appreciating the differences between the Brussels system and that provided by the 1973 Act, and their respective strengths and weaknesses. Rather, the challenging task for conflict lawyers is to form a defensible view of which set of rules applies in hybrid or borderline cases, for example, where one spouse initiates a divorce action in the court of a Member State, say, Scotland, founding on a ground under art.3 of Brussels II *bis*; and in response the other spouse argues that the court of a non-EU country, say, Iowa, USA, is a more appropriate forum, and seeks a sist of the Scottish proceedings. Whilst the UK courts are experienced in using their discretion to adjudicate between contending courts on the grounds of suitability and justice, the question arises whether a Scots court would be entitled to accede to a plea for a sist in these circumstances, since it could be argued that by doing so it would be defeating the legitimate expectations of the pursuer and would be adopting a "non-Brussels" plea in litigation which the pursuer legitimately has founded as a Brussels case. This difficulty has been met with in the commercial sphere,[65] where it has been decided that it would be against the spirit of the Brussels regime for the court addressed to exercise its discretion in the

---

[61] See para.7–45, above.

[62] 1973 Act s.11(2).

[63] This is a re-working of the rule contained in Brussels II art.11. See also Brussels II *bis* art.16, providing a bifurcated autonomous definition of the date at which a court shall be deemed to be seised, in terms equivalent to art.30 of the Brussels I Regulation. A good early example of interpretation of the priority of process rule, against the background of the technicalities of French process, is *Chorley v Chorley (Divorce: Jurisdiction)*; sub nom. *C v C (Brussels II: French Conciliation and Divorce Proceedings)* [2005] EWCA Civ 68; [2005] 1 W.L.R. 1469) in which the question posed in both conflicting jurisdictions (England and France), was whether the first phase of French divorce proceedings, termed the "*requête*", was to be taken to be an initiation of "proceedings" or an entirely separate process. The Court of Appeal upheld the husband's argument that the commencement of the French "*requête* process" rendered the French court first seised in law. See also *Re N (Jurisdiction)*; sub nom. *NDO v JFO* [2009] I.L.Pr. 8.

[64] See, however, the different rule adopted with regard to children (art.15), permitting by way of exception transfer of the case to a Member State court "better placed to hear the case". See para.14–19, below.

[65] *Re Harrods (Buenos Aires) Ltd (No.2)* [1992] Ch 72; and *Owusu v Jackson (t/a Villa Holidays Bal Inn Villas)* [2005] 1 Lloyd's Rep. 452. See para.7–56, above.

manner requested; the ambit of the *lis pendens* rule has been shown to be wider than at first thought.[66]

The problem arose for determination in the matrimonial sphere in *JKN v JCN*.[67] By the date of their separation, the spouses in question were living in New York, neither having any intention to return to England. The wife's choice of English forum arose because, in the circumstances, the residence requirements for New York jurisdiction were not met. One month later, the husband issued divorce proceedings in New York, prompting his application for a stay of the English divorce proceedings brought by his wife. This presented squarely the question whether the English court competently could accede to his plea in light of *Owusu*. The judge, Theis QC, stated that:

> "If the *Owusu* doctrine applies to [Brussels II *bis*] then the discretion to order a stay on principles of *forum non conveniens* in accordance with para 9 of Schedule 1 to the Domicile and Matrimonial Proceedings Act 1973 ('DMPA 1973') is now no longer available if the jurisdiction is founded on Article 3 [Brussels II *bis*]."[68]

In face of the wife's argument[69] that it was inconceivable that the *Owusu* doctrine could apply to the Brussels I Regulation, but not apply to Brussels II *bis*, the judge nonetheless held that it is neither necessary nor desirable to extend the principle of *Owusu* to the situation of parallel matrimonial proceedings arising under Brussels II *bis*. In granting the stay, on the basis that New York was clearly the more appropriate forum, the judge proceeded on two grounds, in the alternative, namely, that if the principle of *Owusu* were extended such as to preclude the English court from granting a stay, there was a risk of irreconcilable judgments, because both sets of proceedings would continue; and, secondly, if the first conclusion was wrong, that there was no need to extend the principle of *Owusu* to Brussels II *bis* because there was no direct connection between the two Regulations, and there were differences between them, e.g. that the transfer jurisdiction with regard to children under art.15 made it plain that the plea of *forum non conveniens* was not anathema to Brussels II *bis*. The natural and preferable construction of "proceedings governed by the Council Regulation" referred to competing proceedings between Member States; consequently, the English court's discretion to stay under Sch.1 para.9 (discretionary stays) remained in place where the competing proceedings were in a non-Member State. The judge garnered support from art.19 of Brussels II *bis*, which in terms provides a mechanism to resolve conflicting consistorial proceedings arising before courts of different Member States.

---

[66] The problem was perhaps capable of arising in *Breuning v Breuning* [2002] 1 F.L.R. 888, but does not appear to have been noticed by the court; though jurisdiction was laid in England one month after the coming into force of Brussels II, no diffidence was felt about the possible incompetence of acceding to a request for a discretionary stay in favour of South Africa. It has also to be said that discussion of jurisdiction focussed in that case upon domicile in the classic sense, and upon habitual residence with reference to the 1973 Act s.5, rather than upon Brussels II art.2.

[67] [2010] EWHC 843 (Fam) See earlier, *Cook v Plummer* [2008] EWCA Civ 484.

[68] *JKN v JCN* [2010] EWHC 843 (Fam) at [126].

[69] Relying on *Cheshire, North and Fawcett: Private International Law*, 14th edn, 2008, pp.962, 963; H.H.J. Karsten QC, "The State of International Family Law Issues: A View from London" [2009] I.F.L. 35; and Baroness Hale of Richmond in *Re I (A Child) (Contact Application: Jurisdiction)* [2010] 1 A.C. 319.

It may be expected that on appeal, or in another case before another judge, a different decision is likely to be reached. The decision of Theis QC seems hardly supportable. The risk of irreconcilable judgments is no different from that which pertains in the commercial sphere. The transfer jurisdiction is particular to children, and Brussels II *bis*'s admission of the use of discretion in that context is consciously and carefully contained. The terminology of art.19 in setting down a *lis pendens* system in consistorial causes is in equivalent terms to art.27 of the Brussels I Regulation. The tenor of the judgment is that which one might imagine would have been utilised had counsel wished to distinguish a commercial case and thereby exclude it from the operation of *Owusu*, on the basis that the Brussels ground on which the case was laid was not art.2, but, for example, art.5.1 or 5.3; the futility of such an argument is evidenced by the absence of any attempt to advance it.

If, by virtue of the factual circumstances, no Member State court has jurisdiction under art.3, and for this reason, or for reasons of practical convenience, the parties (say, a "European" married couple who are not of common nationality or domicile, and who have been habitually resident in a non-EU state, say Iowa, USA) resort to the court of Iowa which, by its own rules, may take jurisdiction in the case, recognition in an EU state of the resultant Iowa decree will be governed, not by Brussels II *bis*, but by the pre-existing (residual) divorce recognition rules of that EU state.

In *A v L*,[70] a hybrid case of some complexity, the husband asked the court in England to withdraw his wife's English divorce petition on the ground of lack of jurisdiction, or alternatively to stay those divorce proceedings under the discretionary stay provisions of the 1973 Act, on the ground that the husband previously had commenced divorce proceedings in Cairo, and the balance of fairness and convenience between the parties made it appropriate for such a stay to be granted. In response, the wife asserted that the English forum had jurisdiction under Brussels II *bis* art.3, on the ground that she was habitually resident in England, having resided there for at least a year (indent 5), or on the ground that she had been habitually resident in England for six months and was of English domicile (indent 6); or, if the court was not satisfied as to the contentions in favour of application of art.3, that, in effect, the case was an excluded action[71] because no court of a Member State had jurisdiction, and the wife at the date of the petition was domiciled in England. Sir Mark Potter, having decided that it was plausible that the wife had acquired a domicile in England,[72] went on to conclude that since, on the facts, she was not habitually resident there, jurisdiction could not be established in England on the basis of art.3, and therefore the case fell to be determined by the national rules of England, which conferred jurisdiction on the court by s.5(2)(b) of the 1973 Act. That being so, on the question of conflicting jurisdiction, the law to be applied was Sch.1 para.9 of the 1973 Act (discretionary stays). Thereafter, the question became a balancing exercise as to the merits of the husband's application to stay the proceedings. Sir Mark Potter refused a stay of the English proceedings, on the argument that it would not be fair or convenient for the wife to have to litigate in Egypt, where there would be, at the outset, doubt

---

[70] [2009] EWHC 1448 (Fam).
[71] Brussels II *bis* art.7.
[72] *A v L* [2009] EWHC 1448 (Fam) at [49].

about jurisdiction, a slow court process, and a Libyan applicable law under which the wife's putative financial provision as compared with her position in England would be meagre.

It is interesting to speculate, however, what would have happened if Sir Mark Potter had found jurisdiction to be established under art.3. *A v L* pre-dates *JKN v JCN*.[73] It has been argued above that the decision in *JKN* is challengeable, and it may well be held in a later decision that the principles of *Owusu* apply equally to Brussels II *bis* as to the Brussels I Regulation. If that should be so, meaning that the plea of *forum non conveniens* is incompetent when a Member State court is seised on a Brussels II *bis* ground, then the priority of process rule in art.19 would apply. In the instant case, the husband's proceedings in Egypt were commenced before the wife petitioned for divorce in England, and so would have taken priority. It is questionable, however, whether art.19 should be invoked in such a scenario in favour of a Third State. It may be that this could be done only reflexively, i.e. that which would have been done "inside" the regime, ought to be done "outside" the regime.[74] This question is of great moment currently, and is of some subtlety, because it is unclear whether by giving effect to the *effet réflexe* of the Regulation, the Member State forum would be honouring the regime (by applying the *lis pendens* principle) or dishonouring it (by ceding jurisdiction to the court of a Third State when a Member State clearly is seised).

Hemain injunctions

In *Hemain v Hemain*,[75] a wife petitioned for divorce in England. Her **12–16** husband, having earlier petitioned for divorce in France, applied for a stay of the English proceedings. In response the wife sought from the English court an injunction to restrain her husband from pursuing legal proceedings in France until such time as his application for a stay of the English proceedings had been determined. The husband was unsuccessful in his appeal against the grant of such an injunction. The Court of Appeal held that the English court had jurisdiction to restrain a party from commencing or pursuing legal proceedings in a foreign country where such proceedings would be vexatious or oppressive. Such jurisdiction must be exercised with caution, and the court must be mindful of potential injustice to both parties. In the immediate case, the effect of the husband's continuation of the French proceedings was oppressive because, on the facts, it precluded the wife from pursuing her English proceedings. This decision was handed down at the same point in the decade of the 1980s as the cardinal decisions of the House of Lords and Privy Council, respectively, in *Spiliada Maritime Corp v Cansulex Ltd*[76] and *Societe*

---

[73] *JKN v JCN* [2010] EWHC 843 (Fam).

[74] Whilst some acceptance of this is evident in relation to art.23 of the Brussels I Regulation, in the case of *Konkola Copper Mines Plc v Coromin Ltd (No 2)* [2006] 2 Lloyd's Rep. 446, the position with regard to the application of priority of process rules contained in arts 27 and 28 is very much more doubtful: *Catalyst Investment Group Ltd v Lewinsohn* [2009] EWHC 3501, and *Goshawk Dedicated Ltd v Life Receivables Ireland Ltd* [2009] I.L.Pr. 26 Supreme Court (Ireland). See para.7–63, above.

[75] *Hemain v Hemain* [1988] 2 F.L.R. 388. See earlier *Thornton v Thornton* (1886) L.R. 11 P.D. 176; *Armstrong v Armstrong* [1892] P. 98; *Vardopulo* (1909) 25 T.L.R. 518; *Orr Lewis v Orr Lewis* [1949] P. 347; *Sealey v Callan* [1953] P. 135.

[76] *Spiliada Maritime Corp v Cansulex Ltd (The Spiliada)* [1987] A.C. 460.

Nationale Industrielle Aerospatiale (SNIA) v Lee Kui Jak,[77] and embraces the same rationale.

Further guidance emerges from *R v R (Divorce: Hemain Injunction)*,[78] a decision of Munby J. granting the application in part, on the principle that where there are parallel proceedings in different jurisdictions, fairness requires that neither party should be allowed to litigate the substantive issues until both courts, having disposed of any preliminary issues as to jurisdiction, are ready to embark upon a consideration of substance. The *Hemain* injunction, in Munby J.'s opinion, aimed to ensure that neither party could get a "head start" on the other by manipulating both sets of proceedings to his own forensic advantage. The question in *R v R* was whether the foreign proceedings unfairly delayed the English proceedings while allowing the husband actively to pursue those foreign proceedings.[79] It was not necessary for the wife in England to demonstrate at that stage that England was the natural forum (though Munby J. was prepared to say that on the matter of appropriateness of forum, the husband's pursuit of proceedings in Denmark, whilst motivated by personal advantage, was not per se vexatious, oppressive or unconscionable).

The *Hemain* injunction has been developed in the English courts. There is no reported Scots case on attempted restraint of foreign consistorial proceedings, but there is no reason in principle why the remedy should not be sought in a Scots court. Certainly in the commercial sphere, there is familiarity with the remedy, usually termed restraint of foreign proceedings or simple interdict, but more generally now referred to as anti-suit injunction.

Although available, at least in principle, in the Scots as well as English courts, it is necessary also to consider the extent to which it continues to be available in a European context, that is, where the Scots or English court is asked to restrain proceedings which have commenced in the courts of an EU Member State. This matter has been famously litigated in the commercial sphere in *Turner v Grovit*,[80] where the ECJ held that the prohibition by a Member State court of the commencement or continuation of legal proceedings in another Member State country is tantamount to interference with the jurisdiction of that foreign court, and hence, so far as concerned the Brussels regime, is incompatible with the principles of mutual trust and comity which underpin it. Accordingly, the regime precludes the grant by a court in a Member State of an injunction prohibiting a party to proceedings pending before it from commencing or continuing proceedings before a court of another Member State, even where that party was acting in bad faith with a view to frustrating the proceedings in the first state.[81] It is impossible to conceive that the CJEU would adopt a different stance in the matrimonial context.

---

[77] [1987] A.C. 871.

[78] [2003] EWHC 2113 (Fam).

[79] Contrast *B v B (Divorce: Stay of Foreign Proceedings)* [2003] 1 F.L.R. 1, also a decision of Munby J., in which he refused a husband's application for injunctive relief against his wife's divorce action in South Africa, on the basis that any disadvantage that he might suffer in South Africa fell under the *De Dampierre* rationale. The husband's conduct itself when viewed in the context of the divorce proceedings as a whole, could be described as vexatious and oppressive; and the wife would suffer substantial prejudice if the proceedings were delayed. See also *Golubovich v Golubovich* [2010] EWCA Civ 810.

[80] (C-159/02) [2005] 1 A.C. 101, discussed para.7–58, above. See also *Cheshire, North and Fawcett: Private International Law*, 14th edn, 2008, pp.962–965.

[81] See, in detail, para.7–58, above.

B. CHOICE OF LAW IN SCOTS COURTS

At common law, when only the courts of the husband's domicile had jurisdic- **12–17** tion, no problem of choice of law arose because the *lex domicilii* and the *lex fori* were the same, and so the potentially applicable laws coincided. Under statutory jurisdiction, and in view of the breaking of the unity of domicile rule, those laws may be different. It may be contrary to principle to apply the *lex fori* both to substance and procedure, but in practice, the courts in Scotland and England, once seised of jurisdiction, apply their own domestic law to grounds of divorce.[82] Divorce rules reflect the policy of the forum at any given time. There must be some connection albeit relatively insubstantial between one party at least and the forum; and it is easier and less expensive for the forum to use its own law. The situation is quite different in relation to choice of law in nullity cases, where the ground of nullity must refer back to some earlier stage of the matrimonial history, and that stage is likely to have a conflict rule of its own (e.g. an alleged defect of form, which must be referred to the *lex loci celebrationis*, or a defect of legal capacity, which must be referred to the ante-nuptial domicile of each).[83]

Rome III

In July 2006, the Commission adopted a Proposal for a Regulation **12–18** amending Brussels II *bis* as regards jurisdiction and introducing rules concerning applicable law in matrimonial matters ("Rome III").[84] The legal basis was arts 61 and 67 of the Treaty of Amsterdam.[85] The Proposal related to judicial co-operation in civil matters having "aspects relating to family law", a legal basis which required unanimity of decision-making. It became apparent by 2008, however, that there was a division of view among Member States, making it impossible for certain states to accept the proposed Regulation. This resulted from the width of the spectrum of substantive divorce law in Member States, from liberal to conservative (at the extreme end of which divorce is not possible at all).[86] At the same time, a majority of Member States favoured the inclusion of rules on applicable law within the proposed instrument. The consequence of inclusion of applicable law rules would mean that the forum may be required to apply foreign divorce law, a result which, as noted, is objectionable to some Member States, for a variety of reasons. By June 2008, it was concluded that there was no unanimity to proceed, and that insurmountable difficulties existed. Shortly thereafter nine Member States addressed a request to the Commission, indicating that they wished to establish enhanced co-operation among themselves in this area.[87] In March 2010, the Commission responded to the request by producing a

---

[82] See *Zanelli v Zanelli* (1948) 64 T.L.R. 556 and *Warrender v Warrender* (1835) 2 Cl. & F. 488.
[83] See nullity, paras 12–41—12–45, below.
[84] Green Paper on applicable law and jurisdiction in divorce matters COM (2005) 82 final.
[85] Now TFEU art.81.
[86] As in Malta.
[87] Article 20(2) of the TEU establishes that the enhanced co-operation device can be adopted by the Council only as a last resort, "when it has established that the objectives of such cooperation cannot be attained within a reasonable period by the Union as a whole, and that at least nine Member States participate in it": Proposal for a Council Decision authorising enhanced cooperation in the area of the law applicable to divorce and legal separation COM(2010) 104 final/2, para.10)

Proposal for a Council Regulation implementing enhanced cooperation in the area of the law applicable to divorce and legal separation,[88] and an accompanying Proposal for a Council Decision authorising such enhanced co-operation.[89]

The authority for the Proposal for a Council Decision rests upon art.329(1) of the Treaty on the Functioning of the European Union, and the Proposal for a Council Regulation on art.81(1) of the TFEU. The Proposal for a Council Decision admits[90] that from the institutional standpoint enhanced co-operation is a better outcome than would be the negotiating by the interested Member States of a freestanding international agreement, because even if the acts adopted in the enhanced co-operation procedure bind only the participating Member States, they fall under EU control, and specifically under the jurisdiction of the CJEU.

Of the 27 Member States of the EU, only 14 are participating states in this Proposal[91]; the UK is not one of that number. There is an option for non-participating states subsequently to accept such instruments as may be agreed. In the meantime, there is some concern that the co-existence of harmonised rules of jurisdiction and judgment recognition and enforcement, which bind all Member States (except Denmark), with harmonised rules of applicable law for divorce and separation, which bind only one-third of Member States, will lead to a twin-track area of freedom, security and justice. The British and Irish interests are always protected by their default opt-out position.[92] From the point of view of other states who do not enjoy the benefit of the opt-out position, the enhanced co-operation procedure is advantageous as it allows them to preserve their own autonomy. Hence, although the Commission has frankly conceded its own interests in this manner of proceeding, there are, it seems, advantages from the perspective of participating, and non-participating, states alike.[93]

The alleged advantages of the Proposal for a Council Regulation include the usual suspects of strengthening legal certainty and predictability, allied, it is said, with flexibility, normally the antithesis of certainty; flexibility is said to be introduced by permitting a degree of party autonomy, again a characteristic feature of recent EU harmonisation instruments in applicable law. The specific

---

[88] Proposal for a Council Regulation implementing enhanced cooperation in the area of the law applicable to divorce and legal separation COM(2010) 105 final (hereinafter "Proposal for a Council Regulation").

[89] Proposal for a Council Decision authorising enhanced cooperation in the area of the law applicable to divorce and legal separation COM(2010)104final/2 (hereinafter "Proposal for a Council Decision").

[90] See art.30.

[91] Austria, Bulgaria, France, Spain, Italy, Luxembourg, Hungary, Romania, Slovenia, Germany, Belgium, Latvia, Malta and Portugal. Greece, which had been one of the petitioners, withdrew its request in March 2010. The legal systems of those 14 Member States (with the possible exception of Malta) in their national conflict rules on divorce already accept the potential application of foreign law. On June 3–4, 2010, the JHA Council reached political agreement on the matter and referred the matter to the Parliament, in order to obtain its consent to the enhanced co-operation procedure. Following European Parliament approval, the Council adopted a decision authorising the first enhanced co-operation (Press Release 201 PR CO 9)

[92] Protocol 21 on the Position of the UK and Ireland [2008] OJ C115/295.

[93] An instructive contrast can be drawn with the negotiations to produce a Regulation on Wills and Succession. Technically, there is a difference in that the subject matter of the latter does not require unanimity in voting; in future, in practice, if enacted, the operation of Rome V among all Member States, except the UK and Ireland, is bound to give rise to "hybrid" problems not hitherto encountered in the harmonisation exercise.

apologia for the Proposal is that by reducing the possibility of one party's being prejudiced by the "random" application to the grounds of divorce of the conflict rule of any given forum (whatever it may be), under the Proposal, there would be applied to the dissolution of the marriage a law with which both spouses have some connection. This is said to increase certainty, and prevent the "rush to the court".

Summary of proposals

The Proposal concerns the law applicable to divorce and legal separation, **12–19** but only in an "international situation", viz. where the spouses are of different nationalities or live in different Member States, or in a Member State of which at least one of them is not a national. Hence it is not open to a couple divorcing in a participating state to utilise the provisions if, in these terms, their divorce is a "domestic" one.[94] The Proposal is confined to the substantive grounds of divorce, and does not extend to applicable law rules for the property consequences of divorce.

In terms of art.3, spouses may choose by agreement the law[95] applicable to the divorce or legal separation from among the following laws: the law of the state of the spouses' habitual residence at the time of conclusion of the agreement; the law of the state of the spouses' last habitual residence, if one of them still lives there at the time of conclusion of the agreement; the law of the state of nationality of one of the spouses at the time of conclusion of the the agreement; or the *lex fori*. In the normal case, an agreement as to choice of law may be concluded and modified at any time up to the seising of the court, except that such a choice may also be made during the course of the proceedings if the *lex fori* so provides. Under art.2, the law designated by the Proposal shall apply, irrespective of whether or not it is the law of a participating Member State; this would appear to include the law of a non-participating Member State, as well as the law of a Third State, and therefore is an interesting development in the operation of the principle of universal application. In the absence of choice of law, art.4 subjects the divorce or legal separation in the first place to the law of the spouses' habitual residence at the time the court is seised; failing which, the law of the spouses' last habitual residence, provided that the period of residence did not end more than one year before the court was seised, insofar as one of the spouses continues to reside in that state at the time the court is seised; failing which, the law of the common nationality at the time the court is seised; failing which, the *lex fori*. If it should be found that the applicable law under art.3 or art.4 makes no provision for divorce, or does not treat the spouses equally, art.5 provides that the *lex fori* shall apply. While art.5 is useful in allaying the misgivings of "liberal" states, art.7 (public policy) provides a more general exit route for any forum having a fundamental objection of any kind, i.e. from any perspective, to the ground of divorce which it is directed to apply by means of these choice of law rules.

The Proposal is restricted to choice of law. It is perhaps to be anticipated, however, that the scheduled report on Brussels II *bis*, and review of its operation may seek to re-visit and incorporate the suggestions aired in the 2005

---

[94] See art.1.1. Proposal for a Council Regulation, Explanatory Memorandum, para.6.
[95] Article 6 contains the "exclusion of *renvoi*" provision.

Green Paper on Rome III as to jurisdiction, viz. to allow bilateral party choice of court in divorce cases. Attention might also be paid at that stage to the virtues and vices of the *lis pendens* system itself, and consideration given to the possibility of allowing, in exceptional circumstances, transfer of jurisdiction in a divorce action to a court of another Member State.[96]

C. RECOGNITION OF FOREIGN DIVORCES

Introduction

12–20 The basic principle underlying the recognition of foreign divorces, at common law and by statute until European intervention, is universality of status, based upon the connecting factor of domicile.[97] A foreign decree of divorce granted by the court of the husband's domicile earned recognition at common law as being regarded as the court pre-eminently appropriate and, being equivalent to a decree *in rem*,[98] received extraterritorial recognition. Through operation of common law development, the grounds upon which a foreign divorce court would be regarded as competent in Scotland and England were enlarged greatly from that first basis of husband's domicile.[99]

Recognition in Scotland of a divorce granted by a court of an EU Member State (apart from Denmark) depends now upon the scheme of jurisdiction and recognition contained in Brussels II *bis*. Recognition of Danish decrees, and non-EU decrees, continues to be regulated by the Family Law Act 1986.

In the absence of any legislative initiative by the Scottish and/or Westminster Parliaments to expand on the guidance given in art.66 of Brussels II *bis*, in relation to Member States having two or more legal systems, it is presumed that the Family Law Act 1986 s.44(2) (effectively providing a system of mutual recognition) continues to regulate the matter of recognition in one part of the UK of a consistorial decree granted in another part.

Declarators

12–21 Although a decree *in rem* requires no further approbation in any legal system where recognition or application is desired, nevertheless in order to test the validity of a foreign decree of divorce in a case of doubt, the proper procedure is not to raise an action of declarator with a crave specifically directed to the validity of the foreign decree, but rather a declarator as to the status of the petitioner (e.g. that the petitioner is free to marry). A decree in such a petition achieves the same effect, but is preferable because it enables the court to grant a declarator as to the petitioner's status without pronouncing directly upon the quality of the foreign decree.[100] The Registration of Births, Deaths and Marriages (Scotland) Acts apply only to Scots births, deaths and marriages,

---

[96] cf. Article 15 relating to parental responsibility.
[97] See Ch.6, above.
[98] cf. *Salvesen (otherwise Von Lorang) v Administrator of Austrian Property* [1927] A.C. 641, per Viscount Dunedin at 662, 663 in the matter of decrees of nullity.
[99] See para.12–23, below.
[100] *Arnott v Lord Advocate*, 1932 S.L.T. 46; *McKay v Walls*, 1951 S.L.T. (Notes) 6; *Sim v Sim*, 1968 S.L.T. (Notes) 15.

but even if a marriage took place in Scotland, a foreign decree of divorce cannot be registered or made effective indirectly in such a manner.[101]

Though strictly, a foreign consistorial decree is equivalent to a decree *in rem*, for the avoidance of doubt, the Family Law (Scotland) Act 2006 has endowed the Scots courts with power to grant such declarators. In terms of s.37 of that Act, jurisdiction to grant declarator of recognition of decrees of divorce, nullity or separation granted outwith a Member State of the EU, is given to the Court of Session and sheriff court.[102]

Brussels II bis

In terms of art.21 of Brussels II *bis*, a judgment given in a Member State **12–22** shall be recognised in the other Member States without any special procedure being required; in particular, no special procedure shall be required for updating the "civil-status records" of a Member State, on the final award of a consistorial judgment from another Member State. However, any interested party may apply for a decision that the judgment be or be not recognised.[103]

Recognition of foreign decrees of divorce at common law

At common law, a foreign decree of divorce which had been granted by a **12–23** court of competent jurisdiction and was not subject to challenge on any of certain grounds (no notice, fraud, duress, ground of divorce against public policy) would be regarded as having the same effect in Scotland as a decree granted by the Court of Session. The number of courts regarded as competent increased gradually, from the court of the husband's domicile,[104] a court recognised by that of the husband's domicile,[105] through *Travers v Holley*,[106] to the decree of a court the jurisdictional basis of which was similar to that of the English or Scots court (even though the foreign court had not proceeded on that ground).[107] English and Scots courts also recognised decrees of divorce granted in the Dominions or Colonies where the courts assumed jurisdiction under the Indian and Colonial Divorce Jurisdiction Acts. The common law development culminated in the famous case of *Indyka*[108] in which the House of Lords, by a variety of lines of reasoning including wife's nationality, wife's residence, and real and substantial connection of the marriage with the court which granted the decree, recognised a Czechoslovakian decree of divorce, even though by the date of that decree and at the date of the English litigation

---

[101] *Smart v Registrar General*, 1954 S.C. 81 (contrast *Arnott v Lord Advocate*, 1932 S.L.T. 46).

[102] cf. for England, Family Law Act 1986 s.55. See, e.g. *Abbasi v Abbasi* [2006] EWCA Civ 355.

[103] This must be read subject to an understanding that the rules governing recognition under Brussels II *bis* admit few opportunities for challenge. In the light of this it is difficult to appreciate in what circumstances art.21.4 might be useful.

[104] *Le Mesurier* [1895] A.C. 517; *Shaw v Gould* (1868) L.R. 3 H.L. 55.

[105] *Armitage v Att Gen* [1906] P. 135; but not further—*Mountbatten v Mountbatten (No.1)* [1959] P. 43.

[106] [1953] P. 246.

[107] In divorce recognition the forum addressed is not concerned with the grounds upon which the foreign court assumed jurisdiction (*Robinson-Scott v Robinson-Scott* [1958] P. 71), but rather with whether the foreign court is competent in terms of UK recognition rules. The inroad made upon this principle by *Travers v Holley* [1953] P. 246, is now historical.

[108] *Indyka* [1969] 1 A.C. 33. Scots cases following this trend shortly thereafter are *Galbraith v Galbraith*, 1971 S.C. 65 and *Bain v Bain*, 1971 S.C. 146.

the husband was domiciled in England. It could be said that this decision rein-stated the so-called ground of matrimonial domicile which had been in abeyance since *Le Mesurier* in 1895. The fame and influence of *Indyka* was short-lived because deliberations on the subject of divorce recognition conducted at the Eleventh Session of the Hague Conference resulted in a degree of international agreement, implemented in the United Kingdom by the Recognition of Divorces and Legal Separations Act 1971. The 1971 Act retained the liberality of *Indyka*, but at the same time was productive of greater certainty than had obtained at common law after *Indyka*.

The 1971 Act was repealed *in toto* by the Family Law Act 1986, wherein now are contained, in ss.44–51, the relevant rules for recognition of overseas (non-EU and Danish) decrees of divorce, legal separation and annulment (and possibly also of intra-UK decrees). Certain changes to the recognition rules were made by the 1986 Act, but the later scheme of statutory rules does not differ fundamentally from the earlier one.

Recognition of divorces (annulments and legal separations) under the Family Law Act 1986

12–24   In terms of s.44(1) of the 1986 Act, no divorce or annulment obtained in any part of the British Islands shall be regarded as effective in any part of the United Kingdom unless granted by a court of civil jurisdiction. Under s.44(2), subject to s.51 of the Act, the validity of any divorce, annulment or judicial separation granted by a court of civil jurisdiction in any part of the British Islands shall be recognised throughout the United Kingdom.[109] No extrajudi-cial divorces pronounced in the UK can be recognised.

Overseas divorces, annulments and legal separations

12–25   Sections 44–51 apply only to overseas divorces obtained outside the EU, and in Denmark.[110]

In terms of s.46:

> "(1) The validity of an overseas divorce, annulment or legal separation obtained by means of proceedings shall be recognised if—
> (a) the divorce, annulment or legal separation is effective under the law of the country in which it was obtained[111]; and
> (b) at the relevant date either party to the marriage—
>   (i) was habitually resident in the country in which the divorce, annulment or legal separation was obtained; or
>   (ii) was domiciled in that country; or
>   (iii) was a national of that country.

---

[109] Note intra-UK mutual recognition (also found in 1971 Act), subject to s.51(1) and (2) (prior irreconcilable decision or "no marriage to terminate"). Contrast *Shaw v Gould* (1868) L.R. 3 H.L. 55.

[110] 1986 Act s.45(2).

[111] See *Kellman v Kellman* [2000] 1 F.L.R. 785; *Emin v Yeldag* [2002] 1 F.L.R. 956; *H v H (Validity of Japanese Divorce)* [2006] EWHC 2989 (Fam), [2007] 1 F.L.R. 1318; and *H v H (Talaq Divorce)* [2007] EWHC 2945 (Fam).

(2) The validity of an overseas divorce, annulment or legal separation obtained otherwise than by means of proceedings shall be recognised if—

    (a) the divorce, annulment or legal separation is effective under the law of the country in which it was obtained;

    (b) at the relevant date—

        (i) each party to the marriage was domiciled in that country; or

        (ii) either party to the marriage was domiciled in that country and the other party was domiciled in a country under whose law the divorce, annulment or legal separation is recognised as valid; and

    (c) neither party to the marriage was habitually resident in the United Kingdom throughout the period of one year immediately preceding that date.

(3) In this section 'the relevant date' means—

    (a) in the case of an overseas divorce, annulment or legal separation obtained by means of proceedings, the date of the commencement of the proceedings;

    (b) in the case of an overseas divorce, annulment or legal separation obtained otherwise than by means of proceedings, the date on which it was obtained."

The Family Law Act 1986, in its treatment of the recognition of non-EU consistorial decrees, differentiates between divorces and annulments obtained by means of proceedings (s.46(1)) and divorces and annulments[112] obtained otherwise than by means of proceedings (s.46(2)). A stricter test for recognition applies in the latter case because there is concern that before such divorces may be recognised in the UK, there must be a strong connection between both parties and a legal culture which provides such relatively informal methods of divorce. Hence, s.46(2) provides that the divorce must be effective under the law of the country in which it was obtained and at the relevant date (i.e. the date on which it was obtained)[113] each party must have been domiciled[114] in that country or either party domiciled in that country and the other party domiciled in a country the law of which would recognise the divorce as valid, and neither party[115] must have been habitually resident in the United Kingdom throughout the period of one year immediately preceding the date on which the divorce was obtained.

With regard to the meaning in this context of the connecting factor of domicile, s.46(5) provides that a party to a marriage shall be treated as domiciled in a country if he was domiciled in that country either according to the law of that country in family matters or according to the law of the part of the United Kingdom in which the question of recognition arises. It is unusual for the

---

[112] See para.12–46 relating to nullities.

[113] See s.46(3)(b).

[114] See s.46(5).

[115] The prior rule had withheld recognition only if both parties had been habitually resident in the UK for one year before pronouncement of divorce (1973 Act s.16) and so the current formulation of this rule is stricter.

forum to yield to any other law in the interpretation of connecting factors generally, and of this factor in particular.[116]

Conversion of judicial separation

12–26   Section 47 regulates cross-proceedings and divorces following legal separations. With regard to the conversion of legal separations into divorces, s.47(2) provides that where a legal separation, the validity of which is entitled to recognition by virtue of the provisions of s.46 of the Act, is converted, in the country in which it was obtained, into a divorce which is effective under the law of that country, the validity of the divorce shall be recognised in Scotland whether or not it would itself be entitled to recognition by virtue of that provision.[117]

Proof of facts relevant to recognition

12–27   For the purpose of ss.46 and 47 of the 1986 Act, s.48 provides that any finding of fact on the basis of which jurisdiction was assumed in the proceedings shall, if both parties to the marriage took part in the proceedings, be conclusive evidence of the fact found; and in any other case, shall be sufficient proof unless the contrary is shown.[118]

Refusal to recognise

12–28   Section 51 narrates the bases on which recognition may be refused:

> "(1) Subject to section 52 of this Act, recognition of the validity of—
>> (a) a divorce, annulment or judicial separation granted by a court of civil jurisdiction in any part of the British Islands, or
>> (b) an overseas divorce, annulment or legal separation,
>
> may be refused in any part of the United Kingdom if the divorce, annulment or separation was granted or obtained at a time when it was irreconcilable with a decision determining the question of the subsistence or validity of the marriage of the parties previously given (whether before or after the commencement of this Part) by a court of civil jurisdiction in that part of the United Kingdom or by a court elsewhere recognised or entitled to be recognised in that part of the United Kingdom.
>
> (2) Subject to section 52 of this Act, recognition of the validity of—
>> (a) a divorce or judicial separation granted by a court of civil jurisdiction in any part of the British Islands, or
>> (b) an overseas divorce or legal separation,
>
> may be refused in any part of the United Kingdom if the divorce or separation was granted or obtained at a time when, according to the law of that part of the United Kingdom (including its rules of private international

---

[116] cf. *Re Annesley* [1926] Ch. 692.

[117] See analogous provision in Brussels II *bis* art.5.

[118] "Finding of fact" includes a finding that either party to the marriage (a) was habitually resident in the country in which the divorce, annulment or legal separation was obtained; (b) under the law of that country was domiciled there; or (c) was a national of that country.

law and the provisions of this Part), there was no subsisting marriage between the parties.

(3) Subject to section 52 of this Act, recognition by virtue of section 45 of this Act of the validity of an overseas divorce, annulment or legal separation may be refused if—

    (a) in the case of divorce, annulment or legal separation obtained by means of proceedings, it was obtained—

        (i) without such steps having been taken for giving notice of the proceedings to a party to the marriage as, having regard to the nature of the proceedings and all the circumstances, should reasonably have been taken[119]; or

        (ii) without a party to the marriage having been given (for any reason other than lack of notice) such opportunity to take part in the proceedings as, having regard to those matters, he should reasonably have been given; or

    (b) in the case of a divorce, annulment or legal separation obtained otherwise than by means of proceedings—

        (i) there is no official document certifying that the divorce, annulment or legal separation is effective under the law of the country in which it was obtained; or

        (ii) where either party to the marriage was domiciled in another country at the relevant date, there is no official document certifying that the divorce, annulment or legal separation is recognised as valid under the law of that other country; or

    (c) in either case, recognition of the divorce, annulment or legal separation would be manifestly contrary to public policy."[120]

Recognition of divorces (annulments and legal separations) under Brussels II *bis*

A defining feature of any Brussels instrument, commercial or consistorial, **12–29** is the general prohibition of review of jurisdiction of the court of origin by the

---

[119] *Duhur-Johnson v Duhur-Johnson* [2005] 2 F.L.R. 1042. Cf. generally *Akhtar v Rafiq* [2006] 1 F.L.R. 27.

[120] See, e.g. *Ahmed v Ahmed*, 2006 S.L.T. 135; *Abbassi v Abbassi* [2006] EWCA Civ 355 (talaq documentation alleged by the wife to have been forged; decision of judge of first instance to remit the case to be determined by a court in Islamabad upheld by the Court of Appeal; and *Golubovich v Golubovich* [2010] EWCA Civ 810.). Older cases, decided in relation to the 1971 Act s.8 may still be helpful: *Hack v Hack* (1976) 6 Fam. Law 177; *Newmarch v Newmarch* [1978] 1 All E.R. 1; *Joyce v Joyce and O'Hare* [1979] 2 All E.R. 156; and *Kendall v Kendall* [1977] Fam. 208. The ground of a foreign divorce is potentially or in theory a ground for non-recognition, but in practice UK courts have accepted foreign divorces on grounds unknown to them (*Perin v Perin*, 1950 S.L.T. 51; *Pemberton v Hughes* [1899] 1 Ch. 781). Contrast non-recognition of Maltese annulments in *Chapelle v Chapelle* [1950] P. 134; *Gray v Formosa* [1963] P. 259; *Lepre v Lepre* [1965] P. 52. It is different if coercion is used and the will of one party is overborne by an external agency to obtain a divorce: *Re Meyer* [1971] P. 298. But possibly means and ground might merge in the case of a person divorced against his will (and against his spouse's will) for reasons such as alleged heresy or apostasy (abandonment of religious faith) in a religious country (Muslim hisbah divorces). Cf. Refusal of recognition of a dissolution of marriage in *Viswalingham v Viswalingham* (1980) 1 E.L.R. 15 CA.

legal system in which recognition is sought. Article 24 of Brussels II *bis* states that the jurisdiction of the court of the Member State of origin may not be reviewed and, further, that the test of public policy may not be applied to the jurisdiction rules set out in the Regulation. There is no opportunity for challenging the decision of the court of the Member State of origin in its application of art.3 to the facts of the case.[121] Article 24 is consonant with the overarching principle contained in recital (21), that the recognition and enforcement of judgments given in a Member State should be based on the principle of mutual trust, and that the grounds for non-recognition be kept to a minimum. Moreover, recognition of a judgment may not be refused because the law of the Member State in which recognition is sought would not allow divorce, legal separation or marriage annulment on the same facts. Further, a judgment may never be reviewed as to its substance.[122]

The grounds of non-recognition, therefore, are very limited, and are contained in art.22. They are concerned solely with public policy, natural justice, due process, and *res judicata*. The grounds of challenge available are as follows:

Article 22

12–30   A judgment relating to a divorce, legal separation or marriage annulment shall not be recognised:

(a) if such recognition is manifestly contrary to the public policy of the Member State in which recognition is sought;

(b) where it was given in default of appearance, if the respondent was not served with the document which instituted the proceedings or with an equivalent document in sufficient time and in such a way as to enable the respondent to arrange for his or her defence unless it is determined that the respondent has accepted the judgment unequivocally;

(c) if it is irreconcilable with a judgment given in proceedings between the same parties in the Member State in which recognition is sought; or

(d) if it is irreconcilable with an earlier judgment given in another Member State or in a non-Member State between the same parties, provided that the earlier judgment fulfils the conditions necessary for its recognition in the Member State in which recognition is sought.

Recognition of same sex "divorce"

12–31   It is inevitable that the question of the validity of the termination of a same sex marriage will arise for decision by a court in the UK.

Under the 1986 Act, the matter is likely to be addressed under s.51(3)(c) (public policy). It is possible, though unlikely, that the principle of *res judicata* might be relevant.[123] Assuming that the same sex marriage in question

---

[121] Therefore, for the first time in the history of this branch of conflict rules, examination of the facts of the case against the relevant jurisdictional rules is not permissible. Contrast opportunity, strictly limited, for challenge on this ground in civil and commercial matters under the Brussels I Regulation art.35(1).

[122] See art.26. Contrast *Gray v Formosa* [1963] P. 259.

[123] cf. Generally *Vervaeke v Smith* [1983] A.C. 145.

satisfied the UK conflict rules as to form and capacity,[124] the question is whether or not the "marriage" itself would be recognised in the UK. If so, the next step is recognition of the dissolution of that "marriage", by means of a divorce satisfying s.46 of the 1986 Act. If the antecedent "marriage" is not worthy of recognition by UK conflict rules, there arises the question why the parties should be anxious to have the divorce recognised in the UK.

If the dissolution of the same sex "marriage" emanates from an EU court (with the exception of Denmark), then three questions arise: (a) does such a divorce fall within the scope of Brussels II *bis*? (b) if so, to what extent do the courts of Member States have a discretion to refuse to recognise such a divorce decree?; and (c) among such cases, how is the delimitation made between application of recognition rules in Brussels II *bis?*, and those in the Civil Partnership Act 2004 Pt 5?[125] Since neither "divorce" nor "marriage" is defined in Brussels II *bis*, it can be argued that same sex divorces fall within the scope of that instrument. In turn, this would mean that a Scottish court, as the court addressed for recognition purposes being prohibited from reviewing the jurisdiction of the court of origin,[126] and similarly prohibited from refusing recognition on the ground that Scots law would not grant a matrimonial remedy on the same facts, can rely only on art.22, above, for the expression of its policy. If, on the other hand, the Scots court is the court petitioned under art.3 of Brussels II *bis*, for the award of a same sex divorce, it is clear that the Scots court cannot refuse to hear the case, but the question of the grant of the remedy, and the public policy implications thereof, will not arise unless the "marriage" itself satisfies Scots conflict rules as to essential and formal validity. But if, finally, as a hypothesis, there is requested of the Scots court the grant of a "divorce" of a same sex "marriage" of two, say, Dutch domiciliaries habitually resident in Scotland, there is a clear difficulty in that Scots domestic law makes no provision for such a decree. It may be different, in future, if as a result of the Rome III negotiations,[127] the courts of Member States are required to apply harmonised choice of law rules in divorce, which might lead to the application of a law which provides such a remedy.

Re-marriage: Family Law Act 1986 section 50

When recognition of a foreign consistorial decree depended upon the decree **12–32** having emanated from the court of the parties' (necessarily common) domicile, and capacity to marry also (as now) was governed by the law of the domicile, there would usually be a coincidence of the two laws (unless a new domicile had been acquired in the interval between the granting of a divorce and the date of re-marriage), and no conflict would arise with regard to a person's legal capacity to (re-)marry.

However, since the recognition rule in Scots and English conflict of laws has widened under the Family Law Act 1986 to accept consistorial decrees from the domicile (in either sense),[128] habitual residence, or nationality, of either party to the marriage, while the capacity to marry rule has remained the

---

[124] See para.11–14, above.
[125] See paras 12–56—12–57, below.
[126] Brussels II *bis* art.24.
[127] See choice of law, paras 12–18—12–19, above.
[128] Family Law Act 1986 s.46(5).

same (requiring of the party intending to marry capacity to marry by his/her ante-nuptial domicile),[129] a problem may arise for the forum in prioritising its own rules in this area. Tension inevitably will occur on occasion.

At common law,[130] a persuasive case was made to the effect that a person whose personal law considered him to be already married, should be regarded as legally incapable of re-marriage in the UK no matter that the Scots or English court might view as valid a purported divorce pre-dating the desired re-marriage. In other words, the forum would defer to the personal law in the matter of recognition of antecedent decrees. *Contra*, in *Perrini*,[131] with little argument, Sir George Baker, President of the Family Division, upon finding the antecedent New Jersey nullity worthy of recognition by English conflict rules, concluded that a party thereto might re-marry in England.

In a provision now repealed (Recognition of Divorces and Legal Separations Act 1971 s.7) it was enacted that the recognition rule of the forum should take precedence over the capacity to marry rule, where the antecedent decree was that of divorce and where the re-marriage took place in the UK.[132] Now the case is governed by the Family Law Act 1986 s.50, which provides that:

> "Where, in any part of the United Kingdom—
>> (a) a divorce or annulment has been granted by a court of civil jurisdiction, or
>> (b) the validity of a divorce or annulment is recognised by virtue of this Part,
> the fact that the divorce or annulment would not be recognised elsewhere shall not preclude either party to the marriage from re-marrying in that part of the United Kingdom or cause the re-marriage of either party (wherever the re-marriage takes place) to be treated as invalid in that part."

The opposite situation (where the divorce is recognised by a party's personal law but not by the forum) is not catered for, but help may be had by reference to discussions of the incidental question,[133] and in particular to *Schwebel v Ungar*,[134] in which the Canadian forum, using a *lex causae* approach, deferred to the Israeli law of the ante-nuptial domicile of the woman, where Ontarian law and Israeli law differed as to the validity of an Israeli ghet, and by this reasoning the Ontarian court held valid a re-marriage of the woman in Ontario.

There is no provision equivalent to s.50 in Brussels II *bis*, presumably because in a situation where it is intended that recognition of EU divorces among Member States will be almost automatic, such provision would be unnecessary. However, it is not impossible that a "s.50 situation" could arise in a European context; the answer in the instant case would depend upon the conflict rules of the forum in which the problem arose.

---

[129] Family Law (Scotland) Act 2006 s.38(2)(a).
[130] *Padolecchia v Padolecchia* [1968] P. 314. See *R. v Brentwood Superintendent Registrar of Marriages Ex p. Arias* [1968] 2 Q.B. 956.
[131] *Perrini v Perrini* [1979] Fam. 84.
[132] United Kingdom restriction caused difficulties in *Lawrence v Lawrence* [1985] Fam. 106.
[133] See para.4–08, above.
[134] *Schwebel v Ungar* (1964) 48 D.L.R. (2d.) 644.

Recognition of overseas extrajudicial divorces

Not all foreign divorces are judicial: it may be found rather that a divorce has **12–33** been obtained by legislative process,[135] or by religious or other divorce,[136] the most common of which are the Muslim talaq (or talak) and the Jewish ghet[137] (or gett). Initial non-recognition by the English courts of extrajudicial divorces[138] gave way quickly to a less strict attitude, which would recognise such divorces provided that they were competent by the law of the husband's domicile,[139] no matter that the marriage[140] and/or the divorce[141] had taken place in England.[142]

The test of recognition against the law of the husband's domicile was retained by ss.2–6 of the 1971 Act. As has been noted, the 1971 Act was repealed *in toto* by the Family Law Act 1986. Nevertheless, not only have some interpretative decisions[143] survived to guide later cases, but also the interpretation of the word "proceedings" handed down in two important cases decided under the 1971 Act (*Quazi*[144] and, by way of contrast, *Chaudhary*)[145] remain as the key interpretative guidance to distinguish between cases falling respectively now under the Family Law Act 1986 s.46(1) and under s.46(2). In *Chaudhary*, concerning a "bare" talaq, Oliver L.J. attempted to make such a distinction and produced a form of words which often is quoted:

> "In the context . . . of a solemn change of status, it does seem to me that the word ['proceedings'] must import a degree of formality and at least the involvement of some agency, whether lay or religious, of or recognised by the state, having a function that is more than simply probative, although *Quazi v Quazi* clearly shows that it need have no power of veto."[146]

---

[135] *Manning v Manning* [1958] P. 112.

[136] *Lee v Lau* [1964] 2 All E.R. 248 gives an example of the Chinese chop (document signed by parties agreeing to dissolve their marriage was authenticated by the "chop" or seal); *Quazi* [1979] 3 All E.R. 897 contains reference to a Thai khula; and *H v H (Validity of Japanese Divorce)* [2006] EWHC 2989 (Fam); [2007] 1 F.L.R. 1318 refers to the Japanese "kyogi rikon" administrative procedure.

[137] See Deanna Levine, "Divorce Law, the Jewish Client and the Get", 2009 S.L.T. (News) 61.

[138] *R. v Hammersmith Superintendent Registrar of Marriages Ex p. Mir-Anwaruddin* [1917] 1 K.B. 634.

[139] See, e.g. *Maher v Maher* [1951] 2 All E.R. 37 and *Russ v Russ* [1963] P.87. The decision in *Makouipour v Makouipour*, 1967 S.L.T. 101 suggests that the Scots rule was the same as the English one.

[140] *Har-Shefi v Har-Shefi (No.2)* [1953] P. 220.

[141] *Sasson v Sasson* [1924] 1 A.C. 1007.

[142] In *Qureshi v Qureshi* [1972] Fam. 173 both the marriage and the religious divorce, which was recognised by the English court, took place in England. By this point in the development of the subject area, it was felt that legislative intervention was necessary.

[143] *Hack v Hack* (1976) 6 Fam. Law 177; *Newmarch v Newmarch* [1978] 1 All E.R. 1; *Joyce v Joyce and O'Hare* [1979] 2 All E.R. 156; *Kendall v Kendall* [1977] Fam. 208.

[144] *Quazi* [1979] 3 All E.R. 897. Cf. *Ahmed v Ahmed*, 2006 S.L.T. 135; *Abbassi v Abbassi* [2006] EWCA Civ 355; and *H v H (Talaq Divorce)* [2007] EWHC 2945 (Fam).

[145] *Chaudhary v Chaudhary* [1984] 3 All E.R. 1017.

[146] *Chaudhary v Chaudhary* [1984] 3 All E.R. 1017, per Oliver L.J. at 1031 (distinguishing, at 1030, "proceedings" from "procedure" or "ritual", and the latter two terms from each other). Also *El-Fadl v El-Fadl* [2000] 1 F.L.R. 175, wherein there was sufficient to constitute proceedings for the purposes of s.46(1), on a *Chaudhary* test, with the consequence that a talaq performed in accordance with Lebanese law, and registered with a Sharia court in Lebanon, was afforded recognition by an English court, despite the fact that the wife had remained in ignorance for 16 years of the occurrence of the divorce; pragmatism was the pre-eminent policy. Cf. *Newmarch v Newmarch* [1978] 1 All E.R. 1; *Igra v Igra* [1951] P. 404; and *H v H (Validity of Japanese Divorce)* [2006] EWHC 2989 (Fam); [2007] 1 F.L.R. 1318

In *Quazi*, the House of Lords held that compliance with the Pakistan Muslim Family Laws Ordinance 1961 involving notification to the wife and to a public authority and the compulsory elapse of a 90-day reconciliation period (but with no compulsion to attempt to achieve reconciliation), amounted to "proceedings", although essentially the divorce was a unilateral act by the husband and was a remedy which no public authority could deny him.

This subject of recognition of overseas extrajudicial divorces tends to resolve itself into a consideration of whether the religious divorce can be said to be a "proceedings" divorce or an "otherwise than by means of proceedings" divorce; whether, if the latter, s.46(2) (jurisdiction) and s.51(3)(b) (authentication) can be satisfied; whether s.51(3)(c) (public policy) can be said to have any application[147]; and finally whether the Matrimonial and Family Proceedings Act 1984 has any part to play in the situation.[148] Section 51(3)(b), which applies only to non-proceedings divorces, states that recognition may be refused if there is no official document certifying that the divorce is effective under the law of the country in which it was obtained or, where either party was domiciled in another country at the relevant date, there is no official document certifying that the divorce is recognised as valid under the law of that other country.[149] Opinion in the religious communities whence such divorces spring are thought not to be convinced of the rightness of the "proceedings" distinction, nor of the feasibility of obtaining official certificates to satisfy s.51(3)(b). Section 51(3)(a), which concerns itself with challenges on grounds of lack of notice or lack of opportunity to take part in the case of "proceedings" divorces, was thought unsuitable in relation to non-judicial divorces.

The impulse behind the *Quazi* litigation was financial[150] in that, if the Pakistan talaq was recognised, the British court, as the law then stood, could not add financial provisions to it. Now, in terms of the Matrimonial and Family Proceedings Act 1984,[151] such provision may be made after any divorce or annulment in a case where the Scots or English court satisfies the strict terms of that Act. Consequently it may be that the validity of religious divorces will be less often the subject of debate.[152]

One notable development in English conflict rules in this area of religious divorces is the enactment of the Divorce (Religious Marriages) Act 2002, by s.1 of which an insertion is made (s.10A) in the Matrimonial Causes Act 1973, to the following effect: if a decree of divorce has been granted but not made absolute, and the parties to the marriage (a) were married in accordance with (i) the usages of the Jews or (ii) any other prescribed religious usages; and (b) must co-operate if the marriage is to be dissolved, then on the application of either party, the court may order that a decree of divorce is not to be made

---

[147] Bearing in mind that the public policy challenge is always potentially available.
[148] *Tahir v Tahir*, 1993 S.L.T. 194. See para.13–40, below.
[149] 1986 Act s.51(3)(b).
[150] cf. *Ahmed v Ahmed*, 2006 S.L.T. 135 (exceptional circumstances, in which the point at issue was the standing of a Scottish divorce obtained in 1994, in the face of earlier dissolution of the marriage by Pakistan law).
[151] See para.13–40, below.
[152] *Tahir v Tahir*, 1993 S.L.T. 194; and *Ahmed v Ahmed*, 2006 S.L.T. 135.

absolute until a declaration made by both parties that they have taken such steps as are required to dissolve the marriage in accordance with those usages is produced to the court. Such an order may be made by the court only if it is satisfied that in all the circumstances of the case it is just and reasonable to do so. The order may be revoked at any time.

The background to this legislation is the importance attached to religious divorce in certain religious laws, particularly those of Judaism, where if the religious divorce is not obtained, the wife, in the view of her religion, would have the status of a "chained woman" (agunah), a status which forbids her re-marriage under Jewish law, and holds any issue of a subsequent union as illegitimate unto the tenth generation.[153]

Equivalent legislation for Scotland has been implemented by the Family Law (Scotland) Act 2006 s.15,[154] which amends the Divorce (Scotland) Act 1976 s.3, to permit postponement of the grant of a decree of divorce where religious impediment to re-marry exists. If, in any Scots divorce action in which irretrievable breakdown of a marriage has been established, one party ("the applicant") is prevented from entering into a religious marriage by virtue of a requirement of the religion of that marriage [*sic*], and the other party to the divorce can act so as to remove, or enable or contribute to the removal of, the impediment which prevents that marriage, that Scots divorce court may, upon application by the applicant, and if satisfied that it is just and reasonable to do so, postpone the grant of decree until it is satisfied that the other party has so acted to remove the impediment, etc.

Transnational divorces

In terms of s.44(1) of the 1986 Act, no divorce or annulment obtained in **12–34** any part of the British Islands shall be regarded as effective in any part of the UK unless granted by a court of civil jurisdiction.[155] Should the divorce, being part of a religious and/or legal procedure, be seen to have taken place in two countries, in order to qualify for recognition in the UK, it is essential that no part of the "proceedings" have taken place in the UK.[156] Although the wording of s.46 of the 1986 Act might suggest that what matters is whether the divorce is valid where it is completed,[157] case law shows that dual location divorces do not commend themselves as complying with the Act.[158]

---

[153] Levine, "Divorce Law, the Jewish Client and the Get", 2009 S.L.T. (News) 61.

[154] See also the Divorce (Religious Bodies) (Scotland) Regulations 2006 (SSI 2006/253).

[155] *Sulaiman v Juffali* [2002] 1 F.L.R. 479: irrespective of parties' domicile(s), an informal divorce obtained in the UK otherwise than by way of proceedings in a court of civil jurisdiction is not to be recognised. The policy applies indiscriminately to all informal divorces, regardless of the parties' religious or other beliefs.

[156] *R. v Secretary of State for the Home Department Ex p. Fatima* [1984] 2 All E.R. 458 (transnational talaq).

[157] Pilkington, "Transitional Divorces under the Family Law Act 1986" (1988) 37 I.C.L.Q. 131. See, however, *Berkovits v Grinberg* [1995] 2 All E.R. 681, per Wall J. at 692–694.

[158] *Sulaiman v Juffali* [2002] 1 F.L.R. 479 and *Berkovits* [1995] 2 All E.R. 681. In both cases part of the divorce took place in England; arguably the question of recognition of transnational divorces no part of which takes place in the UK remains open.

Brussels regime

12–35   In *Maples v Maples*,[159] it was made clear that no extrajudicial divorce can be tested for recognition in the UK except by reference to the terms of the 1986 Act.[160] In view of the EU family law harmonisation programme, it is necessary to determine the extent of application, if any, of Brussels II and Brussels II *bis*, to recognition of extrajudicial divorces. This must be done by reference to the terms of the Regulations, and to their respective preambles.

Recital (9) of Brussels II stated that the scope of the Regulation should cover, "civil proceedings and non-judicial proceedings in matrimonial matters in certain States, and exclude purely religious procedures." Article 1.2 of Brussels II states that, "[o]ther proceedings officially recognised in a Member State shall be regarded as equivalent to judicial proceedings." The preamble to Brussels II *bis* omits specific reference to religious procedures, and in recital (7) advises that the scope of this Regulation covers "civil matters, whatever the nature of the court or tribunal". There has been no attempt to date to apply the Regulation to recognition of a religious divorce.[161] Article 1.1 of Brussels II *bis* (Scope) states that the Regulation shall apply, "whatever the nature of the court or tribunal, in civil matters relating to divorce, legal separation or marriage annulment." The system of recognition depends upon jurisdiction having been assumed in terms of art.3 of the Regulation, which states that jurisdiction shall lie with the courts of a Member State, broadly speaking, on the grounds of habitual residence of one or both parties. In sum, the terms of Brussels II *bis* are somewhat ambivalent, and might be apt to include divorces involving the participation by a religious court or tribunal, such as the Jewish letter of divorcement (ghet) issued by the rabbinical court. A case could be presented that art.1.1 can be interpreted so as to include religious divorces. For a ghet, for example, to fall under Brussels II *bis*, the rabbinical court would have to satisfy art.1.1 (Scope), which ex facie it would seem to do.

II. JUDICIAL SEPARATION

12–36   Judicial separation is a remedy almost extinct domestically, and a foreign judicial separation in relation to the validity of which there lingers a conflict of laws doubt is a poor remedy indeed. That said, all rules which govern in divorce, jurisdiction, choice of law (including the proposed Rome III Regulation), and recognition of foreign decrees, apply also, mutatis mutandis, to judicial separation. Note should be made of s.47(2) of the 1986 Act, concerning conversion of legal separation into divorce.[162]

---

[159] [1987] 3 All E.R. 188.

[160] As opposed to the Foreign Judgments (Reciprocal Enforcement) Act 1933. See Ch.9, above regarding enforcement of commercial judgments.

[161] But see *Sulaiman v Juffali* [2002] 1 F.L.R. 479 in which the question whether the English court had jurisdiction in the wife's petition for divorce (contested by the husband on the ground that the marriage already had been validly dissolved by bare talaq pronounced in England and registered in Saudi Arabia in the Sharia court three days later), was determined by the Family Division of the High Court according to art.2 of Brussels II. But the recognition issue was settled by application of the Family Law Act 1986 s.44(1). It was sufficient to preclude recognition that talaq had been pronounced in England (cf. *Berkovits* [1995] 2 All E.R. 681).

[162] cf. Brussels II *bis* art.5.

III. ANNULMENT OF MARRIAGE

A. THE JURISDICTION OF SCOTS COURTS

Introduction

The treatment of annulment of marriage in the conflict of laws has **12–37** been attended by greater complexity, doubt, difficulty and interest than has the treatment of divorce. One reason is the void/voidable marriage distinction which is not found in all systems or, if present, may differ in content. Some systems may have other classifications peculiar to themselves.[163] Some systems may grant an annulment where others would grant divorce, e.g. in the area of physical incapacity.[164]

While, as has been noted, the grounds of divorce available in a system at any time will reflect its policy at that time, the grounds of annulment will be linked to an earlier matter such as alleged lack of capacity, physical or legal, or an absence of consent. Each of these factors will attract the application of a conflict rule of the forum which is called upon to judge the validity of the marriage. Therefore, while reasons of cost and convenience, to say nothing of policy, may justify application by the forum of its own law in granting divorce, the subject of choice of law in nullity rightly demands a different approach.

Further, while an annulment of a void marriage merely declares the position which always has existed, legal systems will vary in the effect which they accord (prospective only, or dating back to date of purported marriage) to a nullity decree pertaining to a voidable marriage. This is a matter properly for the forum which grants the decree: the recognising court should accept the effect as an integral part of the decree.[165]

Statutory intervention in the rules of jurisdiction and foreign decree recognition, together with abolition of the unity of domicile between husband and wife, have removed many of the difficulties and sources of doubt in Scots and English conflict rules relating to nullity.

Jurisdiction at common law

A decree of nullity of a voidable marriage clearly effects a change in the **12–38** status of the parties, but a decree of nullity of a void marriage does not have any such effect because the parties never were married. For this reason, in the past, both Scots and English courts assumed jurisdiction on a wider basis in actions of nullity involving void marriages[166] than in voidable

---

[163] e.g. *Merker v Merker* [1963] P. 283; *M v M (Divorce: Jurisdiction: Validity of Marriage)* [2001] 2 F.L.R. 6; and *Ghandi v Patel* [2002] 1 F.L.R. 603.

[164] It is no longer necessary for the UK court to classify the genus of foreign consistorial decree before knowing which rules of recognition, common law or statutory, to apply, because the rules of recognition of divorces and nullities are the same, both intra- and extra-EU, resting upon Brussels II *bis* and the Family Law Act 1986 Pt II, respectively.

[165] Social Security Decision No. R (G) 1/85.

[166] e.g. in Scots law, the assumption of jurisdiction by the forum qua *locus celebrationis* was permitted only if the marriage was thought to be void (*Prawdziclazarska v Prawdziclazarski*, 1954 S.C. 98). In England that ground initially was used with regard to both void and voidable marriages, but was rejected in respect of voidable marriages by the House of Lords in *Ross Smith v Ross Smith* [1963] A.C. 280, though it continued to be used with regard to void marriages, as can be seen from *Padolecchia v Padolecchia* [1968] P. 314.

marriages.[167] The distinction between void and voidable, which might not have been present in the law of the granting country, created difficulties as to jurisdiction in that a preliminary decision had to be made upon the nature of the marriage as void or voidable (by which law?) before it could be said whether or not the Scots forum had jurisdiction.[168] This is a variation on the problem of circularity which not infrequently arises in conflict problems.[169]

Development of grounds of jurisdiction

Rules of jurisdiction up to March 1, 2001

12–39   The position was simplified by the 1973 Act which provided in ss.5 (England), 7 (Scotland), and 13 (Northern Ireland) that the only competent grounds of jurisdiction for a declarator of marriage, or a declarator of nullity of marriage, were as follows:

> (1) Domicile of either party in Scotland on the date when the action was begun; or
> (2) Habitual residence of one year of either party prior to the date when the action was begun; or
> (3) If one party has died, that he or she either—
>   (a) was domiciled in Scotland at death, or
>   (b) had been habitually resident in Scotland throughout the period of one year ending with the date of death.

This eliminated any distinction between void and voidable marriages as regards jurisdiction.

Rules of jurisdiction after March 1, 2001

12–40   As with jurisdiction in, the starting point is the 1973 Act, as amended.[170]

The rules of Scottish jurisdiction in actions of *declarator of marriage* now are contained in s.7(3) of the 1973 Act, and remain the same as the pre-March 1, 2001 position.[171]

The rules of Scottish jurisdiction in actions of *declarator of nullity of marriage*, however, now are contained in s.7(3A) of the 1973 Act, to the effect

---

[167] Scots authorities at common law include: *Miller v Deakin*, 1912 1 S.L.T. 253; *Lendrum v Chakravarti*, 1929 S.L.T. 96; *MacDougall v Chitnavis*, 1937 S.C. 390; *Prawdziclazarska*, 1954 S.C. 98; *Aldridge v Aldridge*, 1954 S.C. 58; *Woodward v Woodward*; sub nom. *AB v CD*, 1957 S.C. 415; 1958 S.L.T. 213; *Orlando v Castelli*, 1961 S.L.T. 119; *Balshaw v Kelly*, 1967 S.C. 63; Frederick P. Walton, *A Handbook of Husband and Wife According to the Law of Scotland*, 3rd edn (Edinburgh: W. Green & Son, 1951), p.410; Thomas B. Smith, *A Short Commentary on the Law of Scotland* (Edinburgh: W. Green, 1962), pp.307, 308.

[168] *Prawdziclazarska*, 1954 S.C. 98.

[169] Elizabeth B. Crawford, "The Uses of Putativity and Negativity in the Conflict of Laws" (2005) 54 I.C.L.Q. 829.

[170] See paras 12–04—12–05, above.

[171] Similarly, the rules of jurisdiction of the Scots court in a petition for declarator of death continue to be governed by the Presumption of Death (Scotland) Act 1977 s.1(3), (4).

that the Court of Session[172] has jurisdiction to entertain such an action, if and only if:

(a) the Scottish courts have jurisdiction under Brussels II *bis*[173]; or
(b) the action is an excluded action[174] and either of the parties to the marriage is domiciled in Scotland on the date when the action is begun.[175]

The action for declarator of nullity brought in *Singh v Singh*,[176] indicates that the Regulation applies notwithstanding that the defender was of Indian domicile (the pursuer being of Scots domicile).[177] The court held that it had jurisdiction under s.7(3A)(a), there being jurisdiction under art.2.1(a) of Brussels II, then applicable, on the basis of the pursuer's habitual residence in Scotland. Alternatively, if application of the Regulation were restricted to cases where both parties could found jurisdiction in a Member State, the judge held that the action would have been an excluded one and the Court of Session would have had jurisdiction under s.7(3A)(b)(a) (domicile in Scotland on the date when the action is begun).

B. CHOICE OF LAW IN SCOTS COURTS

Which law is the court to apply in determining the validity of a marriage in an **12–41** action of nullity of marriage? Principle indicates that the court should look at the defect alleged and decide whether it relates to essentials or form. If it relates to form, reference should be made to the *lex loci celebrationis*, and if it relates to essentials, the reference should be to the law of the domicile.

But which domicile is to apply if the parties do not have a common domicile? The law of the domicile of each party applies as regards capacity to marry and matters up to the date of the ceremony, but as regards essentials and matters after the ceremony (e.g. impotence), the only law which could have been applied during the days of unity of domicile was that of the domicile of the alleged husband. Such a statement elicits immediately the response that there would be no unity of domicile if the marriage was void and today the domiciles of women, married or not, are ascertained independently of the domicile of any other person. It should be borne in mind when reading the older cases that an added difficulty was that the unity of domicile rule between husband and wife required that the domicile of the wife followed that of the husband *ex lege* if the marriage was valid or voidable,[178] but not if the

---

[172] Some doubt exists as to shrieval jurisdiction. The Family Law (Scotland) Act 2006 s.4 (coupled with Act of Sederunt (Ordinary Cause Rules) Amendment (Family Law (Scotland) Act 2006 etc.) 2006 (SSI 2006/207), amending r.33.1) purports to extend the jurisdiction of the sheriff court in declarators of marriage and of nullity of marriage, but there is no reference to the requisite change in the 1973 Act s.8. See *K v S*, 2007 Fam.L.R. 141.

[173] See paras 12–06—12–09, above.

[174] See s.7(3B).

[175] There are special provisions for the situation where either party is dead at the date of raising the action.

[176] 2005 S.L.T. 749.

[177] cf. Position re parties resident in third states, discussed in para.14–16, below.

[178] And if so would not change upon pronouncement of declarator of nullity, but only upon independent acquisition thereafter of a different domicile—*De Reneville* [1948] 1 All E.R. 56. Such difficulties are to be seen in Maltese marriage cases, *Chapelle* [1950] P. 134; *Lepre* [1965] P. 52; and *Gray v Formosa* [1963] P. 259.

marriage was void, although in that case it might be found on the facts that the woman had changed her domicile upon going to live with the man.

Where the parties have different domiciles, reference should be made to the law of the domicile of the party alleged to lack capacity, but if, by that law, the marriage is valid, reference then should be made to the law of the domicile of the other party.

Particular difficulty is encountered where the defect alleged is absence of consent or physical incapacity. In these areas, there is little judicial guidance,[179] although some discussion.[180] Sometimes the forum has applied its own law without question,[181] often because the question of application of foreign law was not raised. The decisions in *Ponticelli* and *Szechter* favour the application of the personal law.[182] In *H v H* the English forum, finding the possibly applicable laws, those of England and of Hungary, to be similar, stemming from the common parentage of the canon law, explicitly chose its own law as the law with which it was familiar.

In principle there seems no reason why, subject to public policy, a Scots court should not grant the remedy of annulment on a ground unknown to it, if it is a ground of the *lex causae* (be that the common domicile, the domicile of the complainer, or possibly the domicile of the defender).

Physical incapacity

12–42   The point is well made in *Ross Smith*, per Lord Reid,[183] that the ground of wilful refusal may found an action of divorce for desertion in some systems, and in others may give rise to no remedy, and that it is wrong for the forum, applying its own law, to grant a remedy where none is available by a law of closer connection.

Generally among legal systems, impotence is likely to found an action for nullity. In Scots law it will render a marriage voidable. The two grounds of impotence and wilful refusal to consummate are different in nature and while it might be thought appropriate to have different applicable laws, it is simpler to apply one choice of law rule for all alleged defects of physical incapacity. It could be argued that a remedy should be given if such is available under the personal law of either party, notwithstanding that this may result in a larger number of annulments.

Mental element: error, lack of consent, unilateral mental reservation

12–43   In the domestic Scots law of marriage, there must be "an agreeing mind". Scots law does not favour giving legal effect to unilateral mental reservation,

---

[179] Though see discussion in *Ponticelli v Ponticelli* [1958] P.204; *H v H* [1954] P. 258; *Szechter v Szechter* [1971] P. 286.
[180] e.g. Law Commission and Scottish Law Commission, *Choice of Law Rules in Marriage*, 1985, Law Com. Working Paper No.89; Scot. Law Com. Memo. No.64 ("Choice of Law in Nullity Suits").
[181] *Buckland v Buckland* [1968] P. 296; *Kassim v Kassim* [1962] P. 224.
[182] In *Ponticelli v Ponticelli* [1958] P.204, a case of physical incapacity, that of the domicile of the aggrieved party; and in *Szechter v Szechter* [1971] P. 286, a marriage of compassionate convenience, the domicile, as it happened, of all parties at the time of the marriage. *Szechter* is less useful than at first appears because it presented no conflict of laws, English law and Polish law concurring in the conclusion that the marriage was void.
[183] *Ross Smith v Ross Smith* [1963] A.C. 280 at 306.

yet Lord Dunpark in *Akram*[184] was required by the facts of the case to grant an annulment to Muslim parties who had "married" in a civil ceremony in Glasgow, upon evidence given that neither had considered the formalities to amount to marriage from the viewpoint of their religion.

Parties may marry out of a sense of family duty if that is the pattern of their cultural background. In each of the cases of *Mahmud*[185] and *Mahmood*,[186] the Court of Session granted an annulment of a Muslim arranged marriage, at the instance of pursuers who argued that s/he had entered into marriage without the Scottish requisite of free will, and out of a sense of family loyalty or under threat of being cut off from the family.[187] It does not appear that in either case was the issue of domicile raised; nor did the Scots court make any reference to foreign law. Seemingly the Scots domestic law of the forum was used, but the court in each case was mindful of the cultural background: in both, the parties were of Pakistani culture living in Scotland, and it was appreciated that the claimants' wills would be more easily overborne as a result of the family piety which formed part of their background. Hence, the forum appears to have interpreted its own law in the light of circumstances acknowledged to be different. It did not apply the law of the domicile (which might have upheld the marriage), but in any event no query as to the possibility of domicile being other than Scots was raised. Paradoxically, the care accorded to the background may have resulted in a decision at odds with that which would have been reached in a legal system of Muslim culture. The approach is hybrid therefore in these two cases and there is no discussion of choice of law.

Similarly in *Sohrab v Kahn*,[188] Lord McEwan granted decree of nullity of a purported marriage on the ground of the woman's lack of consent, induced by duress, and for reasons of defects of formal validity. There was much evidence on the detail of the Muslim wedding ceremony, and marriage customs. Although his Lordship's decision on lack of consent was reached after careful consideration of factual evidence of Muslim practice and parties' actings and statements in relation thereto, there is no indication that Lord McEwan applied any law other than Scots to determine the quality of consent which he deemed requisite for a valid marriage.

Sham marriage

A significant decision (reversed, however, on appeal) is that of *Hakeem v Hussain*,[189] in which Lord Clarke held, at first instance, that a civil marriage was not void merely because the parties to it did not regard it as having any religious significance. A distinction was drawn between consent to marriage for **12–44**

---

[184] *Akram v Akram*, 1979 S.L.T. (Notes) 87. Cf. *Orlandi v Castelli*, 1961 S.C. 119.

[185] *Mahmud v Mahmud*, 1994 S.L.T. 599.

[186] *Mahmood v Mahmood*, 1993 S.L.T. 589.

[187] A more extreme variation is exemplified by parental wishes to take a daughter out of a UK jurisdiction in order to arrange a marriage in Pakistan: *M v B* [2005] EWHC 1681 (consent to remove refused where the adult daughter had learning difficulties such that she was incapable of understanding the meaning of consent to marry); or where the party who, it is surmised, may be coerced into marriage, is under the age of 16 years, in which event the case may present as an abduction or wardship case: *Re KR (A Child) (Abduction: Forcible Removal by Parents)* [1999] 4 All E.R. 954.

[188] 2002 S.L.T. 1255.

[189] 2003 S.L.T. 515; and on appeal, sub nom. *SH v KH*, 2005 S.L.T. 1025.

the purposes of the civil law; and the parties' private views on the relationship of a Scottish civil marriage ceremony and a religious marriage prescribed by their own faith. This distinction, while useful (e.g. when contrasted with the outcome in *Akram v Akram*)[190] in effectively preventing the exploitation of Scots civil marriage, is a fine one, some would say almost too fine to make. Reliance was placed on a statement by Professor Clive that:

> "Everything turns on the distinction between an intention to assume the legal relationship of husband and wife and an intention not to get married at all. If the parties intended to get married . . . then they will be married even if their marriage was for a limited purpose and they had no intention of living together or assuming the normal social roles of husband and wife. If they intended not to get married at all, but merely to go through an empty ceremony they will not be married."[191]

While Clive admits that parties may not draw this distinction clearly in their minds, he writes that it is the crucial distinction. But it is difficult to grasp; the difference between marrying without the intention of assuming the normal roles, on the one hand, and, on the other, merely going through a ceremony with no intention to get married at all, is one which may not convince. Perhaps the inference which could be taken from Lord Clarke's decision (which, however, was overturned) was that marriages entered into in Scotland for an identifiable purpose,[192] albeit not "matrimonial" (whatever that may mean), should be upheld. This still may be the case, but it must now be noted that in a long and careful judgment on appeal,[193] Lord Penrose, while agreeing with Lord Clarke that parties' motives on entering into marriage are not a determinative factor, nevertheless held that:

> ". . . there may be cases in which the religious convictions of the parties may affect the consent exchanged in a regular marriage ceremony to the extent of wholly undermining it."[194]

Lord Penrose was in no doubt that the parties wished it to be understood that the registry office ceremony was a formal marriage; but the critical question in an annulment is whether at the moment of seeming acceptance of, or acquiescence in, the civil ceremony, the parties intended to become husband and wife. Since, in the view of the appellate court, an agreement that the parties would not become husband and wife in any real sense until some further condition was satisfied in the indefinite future was not a marriage, the appeal was allowed, and decree of nullity granted.

---

[190] 1979 S.L.T. (Notes) 87.

[191] Eric M. Clive, *The Law of Husband and Wife in Scotland*, 4th edn (Edinburgh: W. Green, 1997), para.07.047. A further variation is that the argument is advanced that one or both parties believed that the ceremony was merely an engagement ceremony: *Alfonso-Brown v Millwood* [2006] EWHC 642 (Fam).

[192] As in, *Hakeem v Hussain*, 2003 S.L.T. 515, e.g. so that the defender's visa could be granted if the immigration authorities considered that he was married to the pursuer.

[193] The main opinion was delivered by Lord Penrose, Lords Marnoch and Macfadyen concurring (*SH v KH*, 2005 S.L.T. 1025).

[194] *SH v KH*, 2005 S.L.T. 1025 at [36]. Lord Penrose made reference to *Brady v Murray*, 1933 S.L.T. 534.

This has been an active area of consideration in Scots family law. In all cases of this type in which annulment has been granted, the forum has been conscious of the public policy aspect, in particular, of the abuse or exploitation of the Scots institution of marriage, as entered into by means of a civil ceremony, with accompanying formalities. Insofar as this most recent decision on appeal reverts to a criterion of assessing the existence of matrimonial consent on a subjective basis, it is in line with earlier Scots law marriage precedents.[195] While it is an established rule of domestic Scots law that unilateral mental reservation to marriage with a particular person cannot found an action of nullity, the court in cases such as those under discussion is required to deal with instances of bilateral mental reservation on the ground that, at best, the Scottish civil ceremony is merely a precursor to a marriage ceremony fully recognised as such by the parties in terms of their religious views.[196] This judicial stance was a retrenchment to what might be regarded as an incontrovertible meaning of consent, i.e. subjective. On the other hand, it is impossible not to sympathise with the distinction which Lord Clarke made at first instance: if the parties register themselves as married persons, having utilised Scottish marriage procedures, they have purported to consent to enter the institution for which the formalities were designed, viz. marriage in Scots law. Such marriage has public law and private law consequences. It is unreasonable that parties should hope to enjoy the public law consequences of the married status in Scotland, but should choose not to accept the private law consequences. In these cases, the parties appear to wish to have the benefit of the incidents of marriage without acquiring the status of married parties.

Notable for its raising of the conflict implications which might be expected to attend such a case is the decision of R.F. Macdonald QC in *Singh v Singh*,[197] to the effect that the law governing the issue of consent to marry is the law of the domicile of the party alleging lack of consent. The decision provides a discussion of choice of law upon the issue of duress relating to marriage. The judge declined to follow an obiter dictum of Lord Guthrie in *Di Rollo v Di Rollo*,[198] which had favoured the application of the *lex loci celebrationis* to the question of consent. In *Singh*, the pursuer, a UK citizen, had been brought up in Edinburgh and expressed the intention to live in Scotland for the foreseeable future; there was no challenge to the inference of Scots domicile. She had accompanied her mother to India to visit relations, only to be coerced into marriage at the mother's insistence during the holiday in India. The judge applied Scots law, being the law of the pursuer's domicile, in the matter of the requirement and content of consent to marry.[199] Hence this decision brought Scots law further along a path which, it is submitted, is the correct one *quoad* choice of law; but it does not afford an example of application by the Scots forum, after proof, of a foreign marriage law qua *lex causae*. In the instant case, the court was satisfied that the threat from the pursuer's mother was

---

[195] Such as *Akram*, 1979 S.L.T. (Notes) 87, per Lord Dunpark at 88; and *Brady v Murray*, 1933 S.L.T. 534.
[196] i.e. a form of betrothal or condition precedent to "full" religious marriage.
[197] 2005 S.L.T. 749.
[198] 1959 S.L.T. 278.
[199] Making reference to *Mahmood*, 1993 S.L.T. 589 and *Mahmud*, 1994 S.L.T. 599.

sufficient to cause the will of the pursuer to be overborne and to vitiate her consent to marry.

The robust English law view of consent to marriage, namely that parties of sound mind should be held to their bargain, is seen in the notable House of Lords decision of *Vervaeke v Smith*.[200]

A *statutory response*

12–45   The Family Law (Scotland) Act 2006 seeks to address the problems encountered in this area in the following manner[201]:

Section 38(2) directs the question whether a person has consented to enter into a marriage to the law of the domicile of that person immediately before the marriage. This provision will make clear the basic rule in the general case, but the inclusion in s.2 of the Act of a particular rule concerning void marriages (inserted as s.20A of the Marriage (Scotland) Act 1977) represents an attempt to address the problems which recently have troubled the Scots courts in this area. Section 2 provides a rule which insists upon its own operation, i.e. is of an overriding nature, where the marriage, the validity of which is in question, was solemnised in Scotland. Section 2 introduces a mandatory provision of the *lex loci celebrationis*, where the *lex loci* is Scottish.[202]

Such a marriage shall be void if, at the time of the marriage ceremony, a party to the marriage who was capable of consenting to the marriage purported to give consent, but did so by reason only of duress or error (i.e. coerced marriage: s.20A(2)). Error is defined for the purposes of the legislation as (a) error as to the nature of the ceremony; or (b) a mistaken belief held by a person that the other party at the ceremony with whom the first party purported to enter into a marriage was the person whom the first party had agreed to marry (s.20A(5)).

Further, the marriage shall be void if at the time of the marriage ceremony, a party to the marriage was incapable of (a) understanding the nature of marriage; and (b) consenting to the marriage (i.e. lack of understanding: s.20A(3)). However, thirdly, if a party to a marriage purported to give consent to the marriage other than by reason only of duress or error, the marriage shall not be void by reason only of that party's having tacitly withheld consent to

---

[200] [1983] 1 A.C. 145.

[201] For measures in immigration law seeking to tackle the problem of sham marriages, see the Asylum and Immigration (Treatment of Claimants etc.) Act 2004 ss.19–24, and Immigration (Procedure for Marriage) Regulations 2005 (SI 2005/15). The legislation establishes procedures where a marriage is to be solemnised in the UK and a party to the marriage is subject to immigration control. The House of Lords held in *R. (on the application of Baiai) v Secretary of State for the Home Department* [2009] 1 A.C. 287 that the "certificate of approval" scheme established by the 2004 Act s.19 involved a disproportionate interference with the exercise of the right to marry. See, however, *R. (on the application of Aguilar Quila) v Secretary of State for the Home Department* [2010] 1 F.C.R. 81.

[202] This, at least, would be the view taken by a Scots forum. One may speculate how this mandatory, but territorially limited, rule of Scots law would be regarded by a court, say, in England, if a party to the alleged marriage (say, of Pakistan domicile) were to seek an annulment there. If such a party at the point of marrying in Scotland had unilaterally reserved consent, the English forum will take account of s.20A of the 1977 Act only if it classifies that rule as a mandatory rule of form of the *lex loci*, a conclusion that seems unlikely.

the marriage at the time when it was solemnised (i.e. sham marriages: s.20A(4)).

This statutory response[203] to the courts' difficulty, outlined above, establishes a criterion of consent, objectively construed,[204] to marriage.

C. RECOGNITION OF FOREIGN DECREES OF ANNULMENT

Until 1986, recognition of foreign decrees of annulment developed at common **12–46** law, following a pattern similar to that found in relation to recognition of foreign divorces prior to 1971.[205] The only challenges were on the grounds of no jurisdiction, fraud, or that the ground on which the foreign annulment was granted was *contra bonos mores*.[206] Error by the foreign court as to its own law or any other law was not a ground of challenge.[207]

The Law Commissions concluded[208] that there was no convincing argument for retaining common law regulation of recognition of nullity decrees. As a result, the Family Law Act 1986 ss.44–54, was applied to the recognition of foreign divorces and annulments.

Since the coming into force of Brussels II and Brussels II *bis*, the 1986 Act applies only to the recognition of annulments obtained outside the EU, and in Denmark; the Brussels regime applies to recognition of all other EU annulments in the same manner as it applies to recognition of EU divorces.[209]

---

[203] See *Akram*, 1979 S.L.T. (Notes) 87, per Lord Dunpark at 89: "It must be for Parliament to decide whether this abuse should be made a statutory offence or whether legislation should preclude parties from challenging the legal effect of any formal ceremony of marriage on the ground that they knowingly but tacitly withheld their true consent to marriage."

[204] cf. commercial contracts: *Muirhead and Turnbull v Dickson* (1905) 7 F. 686 at 694 per Lord President Dunedin: "Commercial contracts cannot be arranged by what people think in their inmost minds. Commercial contracts are made according to what people say."

[205] e.g. cf. *Law v Gustin* [1976] 1 All E.R. 113 with *Indyka* [1969] 1 A.C. 33: law of close connection. See also *Perrini v Perrini* [1979] 2 All E.R. 323. Instances of foreign extrajudicial annulments are rare. See recently Spanish decision in *Re Recognition of a Canon Law Judgment* [2008] I.L.Pr. 31. *Di Rollo v Di Rollo*, 1959 S.C. 75, concerning an extrajudicial annulment, is to the effect that the validity of a marriage good by the *lex loci celebrationis* will not be affected by the decision of a church tribunal. The court held that, for the *Armitage* principle then applicable (see para.12–23, above) to apply, there would have to have been a decision of a court (not a tribunal) recognised by the court of the husband's (Italian) domicile. One must consider now the effect of Family Law Act 1986 s.46(1), (2) in relation to extrajudicial annulments, but there have been few, if any, cases. It could be that decisions of the Roman Catholic Rota might come to be adjudicated upon under the 1986 Act. Presumably such a decision would be a "proceedings" annulment, to be judged according to s.46(1). Whether a religious annulment is capable now of being governed by Brussels II *bis* is debateable. See para.12–35, above. In the case of the Roman Catholic Rota, see also Regulation 2116/2004.

[206] *Gray v Formosa* [1963] P. 259; *Lepre* [1965] P. 52; *Chapelle* [1950] P. 134. These cases provide rare instances of a successful challenge on policy grounds of the substance of the foreign ground of nullity.

[207] *Merker v Merker* [1963] P. 283.

[208] Law Commission and Scottish Law Commission, *Private International Law: Recognition of Foreign Nullity Decrees and Related Matters* (HMSO, 1984), Law Com. No.137; Scot. Law Com. No.88, Cmnd.9341.

[209] 1986 Act s.45(2).

IV. DISSOLUTION OF CIVIL PARTNERSHIP

A. JURISDICTION OF SCOTS COURTS UNDER THE CIVIL PARTNERSHIP ACT 2004

12–47 Part 3 of the Act applies to civil partnerships registered in Scotland, and Pt 5 applies to civil partnerships formed and dissolved abroad (dissolution and separation: ss.117–122; and nullity: ss.123, 124).

Part 3—dissolution in Scotland of a civil partnership: jurisdiction

12–48   In terms of s.117, an action for the dissolution of a civil partnership may be brought in the Court of Session or in the sheriff court. Though s.117 in its terms does not restrict the jurisdiction which it confers to actions concerning civil partnerships registered in Scotland, Pt 5 of the Act (ss.225–227) lays down particular rules of jurisdiction of the Scottish courts in respect of civil partnerships formed abroad, and so by inference it would seem that Pt 3 jurisdiction must be restricted to those civil partnerships registered in Scotland, or possibly in the UK.[210] The jurisdictional link, therefore, for the first time in the treatment of the subject of jurisdiction in personal status, is based on the location of the occurrence of an event, rather than upon a personal connection between one or both parties and the forum.[211]

Under s.117, the Scottish court may grant decree of dissolution if, but only if, it is established that the civil partnership has broken down irretrievably. Irretrievable breakdown is taken to be established by proof of certain factors such as unreasonable behaviour, desertion, or non-cohabitation, all on the model of the domestic divorce law of Scotland as contained in the Divorce (Scotland) Act 1976, as amended. A register of decrees of dissolution will be maintained at the General Register Office.

Part 5—civil partnerships formed or dissolved abroad

12–49   This Part makes provision for "overseas relationships", which are defined as specified relationships,[212] or as relationships which meet the general conditions,[213] *and* which are registered in a country outside the UK by two people who under the relevant law (*q.v.*) are of the same sex at the time when they do so, and neither of whom is already a civil partner or lawfully married. The Act describes in these provisions a set of factual/legal circumstances which is a sufficient approximation to the institution of civil partnership in UK law as to justify the attachment to those circumstances of (a) recognition in the UK; and (b) availability of domestic remedy. Thus:

---

[210] "Abroad" is not defined. Section 225(1)(c) confers residual jurisdiction on the Scottish courts.

[211] As has been seen, *locus registrationis* in Scotland will regulate capacity and form, but domicile safeguards are inserted where the *locus registrationis* is overseas. See para.11–32, above.

[212] Defined in s.213, and by reference to Sch.20, as augmented by the Civil Partnership Act 2004 (Overseas Relationships) Order 2005 (SI 2005/3135).

[213] Defined in s.214, thus: the general conditions are that under the relevant law (being the law of the place of registration, including its conflict rules—s.212(2)) (a) neither of the parties is already a party to such a relationship, or lawfully married; (b) the relationship is of indeterminate duration; and (c) the effect of entering into the relationship is that the parties are either treated as married, or treated as a couple either generally or for specified purposes.

Chapter 2—overseas relationships treated as civil partnerships

(i) General rule—section 215

In order to have an overseas relationship treated as a civil partnership, the **12–50** parties must have had legal capacity under the *locus registrationis*,[214] and have met all the formal requirements of the locus.

(ii) Persons domiciled in a part of the UK—section 217

By s.217 persons domiciled in Scotland will not be treated as having formed **12–51** a civil partnership if, at the came of registration, they were not eligible in terms of s.86[215] to register such a relationship in Scotland.[216] This section reinstates for parties domiciled in a part of the UK the traditional rule that the law of the domicile regulates legal capacity to enter into domestic relationships. In this way, the registration of an overseas relationship receives a different treatment from the registration of a civil partnership within the UK, in respect of the latter of which essential validity (including capacity) and formal validity are both governed by the *lex loci registrationis*.

By inference, it must be that a Scots court in seeking to establish whether parties (neither of whom was, at the point of registration, domiciled in a part of the UK) have validly created a civil partnership abroad, must apply the *lex loci registrationis*, including its rules of private international law.

(iii) Public policy—section 218

All of the above is subject to the usual public policy discretion of the forum, **12–52** which will justify non-recognition of a capacity existing under the *lex loci registrationis*.

Part 5, Chapter 3—dissolution of civil partnerships formed abroad: jurisdiction of the Scottish courts

Section 225 provides that the Court of Session and, in qualifying cases, the **12–53** sheriff court, has jurisdiction to entertain an action for the dissolution of a civil partnership formed abroad, or for separation of such partners,[217] if (and only if):

(a) the court has jurisdiction under regulations made under s.219 of the Act (that is, to correspond to Brussels II *bis* art.3)[218]; or

---

[214] Being the law of the place of registration, including its rules of private international law (ss.212, 215), although by s.216(1) the parties are not to be treated as having formed a civil partnership in such circumstances if at the time of registration they were not at that date of the same sex under UK law.

[215] See para.11–32, above.

[216] The same principle applies to English domiciliaries (s.217(2)) and Northern Irish domiciliaries (s.217(5)).

[217] For declarators of nullity, jurisdiction is restricted to the Court of Session; see s.225(3).

[218] Detailed rules, laid under s.219 of the 2004 Act, are set out in the Civil Partnership (Jurisdiction and Recognition of Judgments) (Scotland) Regulations 2005 (SSI 2005/629) reg. 4. These rules, which align the rules on jurisdiction in respect of dissolution and annulment of civil partnerships, and separation of partners, with the corresponding rules for dissolution of marriage contained in Brussels II *bis*, came into force on December 5, 2005. Equivalent rules applying in England and Wales, and Northern Ireland, are contained in the Civil Partnership (Jurisdiction and Recognition of Judgments) Regulations (SI 2005/3334).

(b) if no court has jurisdiction under (a) above, and either civil partner is domiciled in Scotland on the date when the proceedings are begun; or

(c) the following conditions are met—

(i) the two people concerned registered their partnership in Scotland,[219]

(ii) no court has jurisdiction under (a) above; and

(iii) it appears to the court to be in the interests of justice to assume jurisdiction in the case.[220]

Conflicting jurisdictions

12–54   Given that the bases of jurisdiction adopted for dissolution of civil partnerships are modelled on the rules found in Brussels II *bis*, it would have been reasonable to expect that the rule on conflicting jurisdictions would have followed the *lis pendens* system. In fact, provision is made in s.226, and accompanying secondary legislation,[221] for the resolution of cases of conflicting jurisdiction in a manner which corresponds to the system of mandatory and discretionary sists contained in Sch.3 to the 1973 Act. This is an odd amalgam of Brussels and non-Brussels rules.

B. CHOICE OF LAW RULES FOR DISSOLUTION, SEPARATION AND NULLITY OF CIVIL PARTNERSHIP

12–55   There is no direct reference in the 2004 Act to choice of law.

Currently in divorce and separation actions in Scotland, the choice of law made by the forum is always the *lex fori*. It is assumed that this approach will apply also in relation to dissolution and separation of civil partnerships.[222]

With regard to annulment,[223] in the case of civil partnerships registered in Scotland, the civil partnership is void if, and only if, the parties were not eligible to register (see s.86), or, being eligible, either of them did not validly consent to its formation.[224]

The minor differences between the body of provisions governing civil partnerships registered in England and Wales, and Northern Ireland, from those which are to obtain with regard to civil partnerships registered in Scotland, have resulted in a latent choice of law direction in s.124, viz.: where two people have registered as civil partners of each other in England and Wales, or Northern Ireland, and wish to have that relationship declared null in Scotland,

---

[219] There is a precedent for this in that at common law in Scotland *locus celebrationis* was regarded as a good ground of jurisdiction in annulment of marriage if it was averred that the marriage was void: *Prawdziclazarska*, 1954 S.C. 98.

[220] i.e. the residual rules of national jurisdiction. Cf. Brussels II *bis* art.7.

[221] See Act of Sederunt (Ordinary Cause Rules) Amendment (Civil Partnership Act 2004) 2005 (SSI 2005/638) Pt XIII (sisting of civil partnership actions) (rr.33A.79–33A.84). For equivalent rules for England and Wales, see the Family Proceedings (Civil Partnership: Staying of Proceedings) Rules 2005 (SI 2005/2921) (r.3: obligatory stays; r.4: discretionary stays).

[222] The rules of the Scots *lex fori* pertaining to grounds of dissolution and separation are contained in ss.117–122 of the 2004 Act.

[223] The rules of the Scots *lex fori* pertaining to grounds of nullity are contained in ss.123, 124 of the 2004 Act.

[224] See s.123.

it is enacted that their civil partnership is to be regarded as void (or voidable) if it would be void (or voidable) in England and Wales, or Northern Ireland, respectively.[225] This must mean that a Scottish dissolution forum must apply to a civil partnership registered in England and Wales, or Northern Ireland, those provisions in the Act which have been particularly crafted for those jurisdictions.

By the same token where (by implication of the Act) two people seek a dissolution of their partnership in a Scots court (per ss.225–227), said partnership being "an apparent or alleged overseas relationship", s.124(7) directs that the civil partnership is void if the relationship is not an overseas relationship or, being an overseas relationship, the parties are not to be regarded under Ch.2 of Pt 5 (overseas relationships treated as civil partnerships) as having formed a civil partnership. Further, s.124(8), in regard to overseas relationships, provides that the civil partnership is voidable if it is voidable under the relevant law,[226] or, either of the parties being domiciled in England and Wales or Northern Ireland, if the circumstances fall within ss.50 or 174 (grounds on which a civil partnership is voidable, in England and Wales, and Northern Ireland, respectively).

C. Recognition of Foreign Decrees of Dissolution, Separation and Nullity of Civil Partnership

Decrees obtained in the UK

By s.233,[227] no dissolution or annulment of a civil partnership obtained in one part of the UK is effective in any part of the UK unless obtained from a court of civil jurisdiction. Likewise[228] if such a judicial dissolution, etc. is obtained from a court in one part of the UK, it shall be recognised throughout the UK subject to the principles of *res judicata* and avoidance of irreconcilable judgments.   **12–56**

Decrees obtained overseas

Section 234(2) permits rules of recognition of EU decrees to be introduced, mirroring those which obtain currently in relation to matrimonial decrees under Brussels II *bis*.[229] With regard to the recognition in Scotland of judgments from EU Member States,[230] the Civil Partnership (Jurisdiction and Recognition of Judgments) (Scotland) Regulations 2005 regs 6 and 7, lay   **12–57**

---

[225] For grounds of voidability, see ss.50, 51. Cf. ss.174, 175 for Northern Ireland.

[226] Section 124(10) defines relevant law as the law of the country or territory where the overseas relationship was registered, including its rules of private international law. This therefore amounts to reference to the use of that law, including its conflict rules.

[227] cf. Family Law Act 1986 s.44(1).

[228] cf. Family Law Act 1986 s.44(2).

[229] Civil Partnership (Jurisdiction and Recognition of Judgments) (Scotland) Regulations 2005 (SSI 2005/629); and, for England and Wales, and Northern Ireland, the Civil Partnership (Jurisdiction and Recognition of Judgments) Regulations (SI 2005/3334).

[230] Defined in the Civil Partnership (Jurisdiction and Recognition of Judgments) (Scotland) Regulations 2005 (SSI 2005/629) reg.5; and the Civil Partnership (Jurisdiction and Recognition of Judgments) Regulations (SI 2005/3334) reg.6. Notably Denmark is included as a Member State for this purpose.

down rules for obtaining a declarator of recognition, and the grounds for refusal of the same. Notably, these provisions apply to all judgments even if the date of the judgment is earlier than the date on which s.219 and the 2005 Regulations came into force.

The rules of recognition of non-EU decrees[231] follow closely the provisions for recognition (and refusal thereof) of overseas consistorial decrees which are contained in the Family Law Act 1986 ss.46 and 51. The mirroring continues in ss.237 and 238,[232] but one notable novelty is contained in s.237(2)(b)(ii), which addresses the interesting issue of the proper resolution of the following situation: what is to happen where (i) a party has purported to enter into a civil partnership in a jurisdiction in which he is not domiciled; and (ii) one or both parties to the purported partnership is/are domiciled in a country which does not recognise such relationships between two persons of the same sex; (iii) this relationship, presumably legally constituted according to the *lex loci registrationis*,[233] has broken down; (iv) the parties have obtained a dissolution order from a court in the *locus registrationis*, and now seek to have that order recognised in the UK? Section 237(2) permits the Lord Chancellor or the Scottish Ministers to make provision for such cases,[234] but it is uncertain whether provision is necessary, and it is difficult to predict the nature of the modifications to be made. If the difficulty in the case described is one of capacity to enter into a new partnership, s.238 already provides a solution. If it is rather a matter of the wisdom of according recognition to such a dissolution, s.236(3)(c) permits withholding recognition on the grounds of public policy. However, if the effect of withholding recognition of a dissolution would be to recognise the continuing existence (according to Scots conflict rules) of a legal relationship which is forbidden by the domicile of one of the parties, such an outcome seems counter-productive.

Since there is to be a dual system, with provision for one set of rules for recognition of EU decrees, and another set for non-EU decrees, it will be important to delimit the scope of operation of each set of rules. Moreover, it will require to be clarified, as regards, e.g. the recognition of EU decrees, when Brussels II *bis* applies, and when s.234, of Pt 5 of the 2004 Act applies. By which law is the relationship to be characterised as "marriage" or "partnership"? Upon that categorisation rests the decision as to which set of jurisdiction and recognition rules apply. Thus, for example, if a Scottish court is called upon to recognise a Dutch dissolution of a Dutch same sex relationship, the relationship in the eyes of Dutch law amounting to "marriage" (and therefore attracting in the Netherlands application of Brussels II *bis*), but conversely the same relationship in the eyes of Scots law amounting rather to "civil partnership" (attracting application of Pt 5 of the 2004 Act)—is the Scots forum to prefer its own approach to characterisation and consequences? A further dilemma of delimitation might arise in relation to conflicting proceedings concerning the

---

[231] See s.235 (grounds for recognition); s.236 (refusal of recognition).

[232] cf. Family Law Act 1986 ss.46(5) and 50, respectively.

[233] Bearing in mind s.124(10).

[234] See, e.g. Civil Partnership (Supplementary Provisions relating to the Recognition of Overseas Dissolutions, Annulments or Separations) (Scotland) Regulations 2005 (SSI 2005/567); and Civil Partnership (Supplementary Provisions relating to the Recognition of Overseas Dissolutions, Annulments or Legal Separations) (England and Wales and Northern Ireland) Regulations 2005 (SI 2005/3104).

same relationship, in order to decide which set of conflicting jurisdiction rules should apply (i.e. those in Brussels II *bis*, or those in the 2004 Act).

This body of primary and secondary legislation, complex and voluminous as it is, nonetheless fails to deal clearly and comprehensively with the conflict of laws dimension. Much time has been spent on drafting legislation in this area, but to date there are no reported cases.

Cessation of de facto cohabitation

De facto relationships, by definition, do not require formalities at the **12–58** point of commencement, or conclusion, but a court may be asked to make proprietary and/or financial provision to a "cohabitant", during or at the cessation of the de facto relationship, and therefore must ascertain by the relevant applicable law, whether the claimant qualifies as a cohabitant. For this purpose, the length of the period, and nature, of the alleged cohabitation will be relevant.[235] The Family Law (Scotland) Act 2006 s.28, empowers the court to make certain financial provision orders, "where cohabitants cease to cohabit otherwise than by reason of the death of one (or both) of them". The test of cessation therefore is a factual one.[236] Similarly, application to the court by the survivor for provision upon intestacy will be possible upon proof of the death intestate of a predeceasing cohabitant, domiciled in Scotland.

SUMMARY 12

1. Jurisdiction **12–59**

(a) Allocation of jurisdiction

Divorce, judicial separation and nullity: Domicile and Matrimonial Proceedings Act 1973 ss.7 and 8, as amended to ensure compliance with Brussels II *bis*.

Civil partnership: Civil Partnership Act 2004 ss.117, 121, 123, and 225–227.

(b) Conflicting jurisdictions

Divorce, judicial separation and annulment:

—Outside the Brussels regime: a discretionary sist system applies (Domicile and Matrimonial Proceedings Act 1973 Sch.3).
—Under Brussels II *bis*: a *lis pendens* system operates (art.19).

Civil partnership: a discretionary sist system applies per Civil Partnership Act 2004 s.226.

---

[235] For Scots law, see Family Law (Scotland) Act 2006 ss.25–30. See Ch.11, above.
[236] The problem is that the applicability of these provisions in a conflict of laws sense is not clear. See para.11–34, above.

2. Choice of law

Divorce and judicial separation: Scots law as the *lex fori* determines grounds as well as procedure.

Annulment: grounds of annulment in a Scots forum correspond to the Scots conflict rules on constitution of marriage. Particular note should be taken of the Family Law (Scotland) Act 2006 s.2.

Civil partnership: limited guidance is contained in the Civil Partnership Act 2004 s.124.

3. Recognition of overseas decrees

Divorce, judicial separation and nullity (including extrajudicial divorces, etc.)

—Outside the Brussels regime, and within the United Kingdom: the matter is governed by ss.44–51 of the Family Law Act 1986.
—Under Brussels II *bis*: arts 21–27 apply.

Civil partnership

—Intra-UK decrees, and non-EU decrees: Civil Partnership Act 2004 ss.233 and 234(1), respectively.
—EU decrees: Civil Partnership Act 2004 s.234(2) applies.

CHAPTER 13

PROPRIETARY AND FINANCIAL CONSEQUENCES OF MARRIAGE AND OTHER ADULT RELATIONSHIPS

I. PROPRIETARY CONSEQUENCES

A. PROPERTY RIGHTS OF MARRIED PERSONS

The effect of marriage upon the property rights of parties differs from one **13–01** legal system to another. Certain systems imply that, in the absence of an express marriage contract between the parties, marriage creates a "community of goods" between the spouses.

Under domestic Scots law, marriage per se has no effect upon the property rights of spouses. The Family Law (Scotland) Act 1985 s.24 states that marriage shall not of itself affect the respective rights of parties to the marriage in relation to their property.[1]

The different approaches taken by legal systems to the effect of marriage upon the property rights of spouses have the potential to produce conflict of laws problems. Attempts to resolve such problems, and to reconcile the differences in approach, were made by the Hague Conference on Private International Law, in 1978, resulting in a Convention on the Law Applicable to Matrimonial Property Regimes, which the United Kingdom did not sign.[2] The subject of matrimonial property is the focus of renewed international harmonisation efforts, on a European basis.[3] Meanwhile, Scots conflict rules of matrimonial property have been placed on a legislative footing in terms of the Family Law (Scotland) Act 2006 s.39.

When dealing with a question of matrimonial property rights having cross-border implications, one of the first issues to ascertain is whether a "matrimonial property regime" was established upon marriage, either by operation of law, or by contract. There are three possibilities:

---

[1] There is therefore in Scots law a system of separation of property, except for (i) piecemeal legislative provision, such as the Family Law (Scotland) Act 1985 s.25 (presumption of equal share in household goods); (ii) "equalisation" provisions which obtain at termination of marriage by divorce per Family Law (Scotland) Act 1985 ss.8–17; and (iii) the modifying effect of the surviving spouse's claim for legal rights in the moveable estate of the predeceaser on his/her death intestate, a very long-established feature of Scots law.

[2] The Convention is of limited effect, entering into force (on September 1, 1992) in only three countries.

[3] Now termed "Brussels III". See para.13–17 below.

347

(1) (default) statutory system imposing some version of a community of goods regime;
(2) private marriage contract; or
(3) absence of statutory or private contractual provision.

By virtue of the 2006 Act s.39(6)(b), the Scots conflict matrimonial property rules provided thereby are subject to the spouses' contrary agreement. It is therefore apparent that these rules do not trump private marriage contract provisions. Since, as will be explained below, the traditional approach of Scots and English conflict rules has been to assimilate the effect of statutory codes to that of private marriage contracts, and since any other construction would be productive of great difficulty, it is assumed that the provisions contained in s.39 are subject also to rights which have vested under a statutory scheme (though it has to be conceded that the Act nowhere makes such a specific assertion).[4]

Marriage contracts: statutory community of goods

13–02   In certain countries there is a statutory code which, in the absence of a private marriage contract, establishes a community of goods between husband and wife. Such a code is likely to have the same legal effect as a private marriage contract. In order to avoid the operation of statutory community of goods, parties by contract may exclude the community of goods (if permitted so to do by the statutory regime).[5]

The leading case of *De Nicols v Curlier*[6] shows that failure by spouses to enter into a private marriage contract may mean that, by default, they become subject to the property regime laid down by the law in terms of which they may be presumed to have entered the marriage relationship.[7] The rights which spouses acquire under the statutory regime are thought to vest at the point of contracting; no matter where the parties subsequently may reside, their property rights are not affected by subsequent change(s) of domicile.[8] This doctrine is known as immutability of property rights. The most famous Scottish (House of Lords) case on the topic, *Lashley v Hog*,[9] appears prima facie to be inconsistent with the theory of immutability. In *Lashley*, Hog of Newliston, domiciled in Scotland, removed to England and became domiciled there. While in

---

[4] See further para.13–11, below.
[5] *Shand-Harvey v Bennet-Clark*, 1910 1 S.L.T. 133 Sh. Ct.; the parties' choice in this case was unaffected by a subsequent change of domicile.
[6] *De Nicols v Curlier (No.1)* [1900] A.C. 21 (moveables); *De Nicols v Curlier (No.2)* [1900] 2 Ch. 410 (immoveables).
[7] There may be argument about the basis on which this law, when identified, is to apply. Any given regime of community rules will provide for the extent of its own application, e.g. *De Nicols (No.1)* [1900] A.C. 21, per Lord Macnaghten at 33: "Community of goods in France is constituted by a marriage in France according to French law, not by married people coming to France and settling there. And the community must commence from the day of the marriage. It cannot commence from any other time." Cf. Clive, p.256. "Late entry" usually therefore will be precluded.
[8] At the dates when the grand illustrative cases of *Lashley v Hog* (1804) 4 Pat. 581, *De Nicols (No.1)* [1900] A.C. 21, and *Shand-Harvey v Bennet-Clark*, 1910 1 S.L.T. 133 were handed down, the conjugal unit had one conjoined domicile. This no longer being the case, the property rules are accordingly more difficult to state.
[9] (1804) 4 Pat. 581.

England he married an Englishwoman and the parties had a number of children, including Thomas Hog, and a daughter who became Mrs Lashley (the litigants). Upon his wife's death in 1760, Hog returned to Scotland where he died domiciled. Mrs Lashley then claimed not only *legitim* (due to a child of the marriage), but also a share in the *communio bonorum* of her parents' marriage to which at that date (and until (Dunlop's) Marriage Act 1855)[10] the representatives of a predeceasing wife could lay claim, standing in their mother's place.[11] The *communio bonorum* was vestigial evidence of community of property in Scots law[12]; the law of England had no equivalent. The House of Lords, in upholding Mrs Lashley's claim, might be thought to have admitted the possibility that matrimonial property rights may change upon change of domicile, since the law of England, the domicile at marriage, would have admitted no such property claim.[13] If, on the other hand, the case is regarded as a succession case, which is plausible, it was proper for Scots law, as the law of the deceased's domicile at death, to regulate Mrs Lashley's claim.[14]

If it is to be argued by one or both parties that the foreign community of property regime has extraterritorial effect, such as to purport to extend to foreign immoveable property, this, if not admitted,[15] must be proved, the onus lying on the married pair, or the survivor as the case is more likely to be.[16] The *lex situs* in its discretion may accept that the devolution of land within its territory is to be regulated by some legal system other than its own, i.e. the *lex situs* may acquiesce in a foreign community of property regime.[17]

Although it seems clear that the survivor may claim under the terms of a matrimonial regime, private or statutory, no matter that the predeceaser died domiciled in another legal system (that is to say, it can confidently be expected that the matter will be regarded as one of matrimonial property rather than succession), if, rather, the question is whether the survivor has the option to choose between the rights conferred by a matrimonial property regime, on the one hand, and rights conferred by means of succession to the deceased's estate, on the other, the point seems to be regarded as one of succession, to be determined, in principle and in detail, by the law of the deceased's last domicile.[18]

---

[10] Intestate Moveable Succession (Scotland) Act 1855 s.6.

[11] Of the surviving three children, Mrs Lashley alone claimed under this head, her brother Alexander having received advances from their father during his lifetime. In the circumstances, it was not in the succession interests of her brother Thomas to argue in favour of the application of Scots law.

[12] It was a claim by Mrs Bell's daughter for her deceased mother's share in the "goods in communion" which occasioned the House of Lords decision on continuance of domicile of origin: *Bell v Kennedy* (1868) 6 M. (H.L.) 69.

[13] There was never a matrimonial property regime in England, a fact which enabled the House of Lords 100 years later in *De Nicols* to distinguish *Lashley*.

[14] See Ch.18, below. Cf. Walton, *A Handbook of Husband and Wife according to the Law of Scotland*, 3rd edn (Edinburgh: W. Green, 1951), pp.352–354.

[15] *De Nicols (No.2)* [1900] 2 Ch. 410.

[16] *Callwood v Callwood* [1960] A.C. 659: widow unable to prove that Danish community of property regime extended to Great Thatch Island in the British Virgin Islands.

[17] *De Nicols (No.2)* [1900] 2 Ch. 410; *Chiwell v Carlyon* (1897) 14 S.C. (S.A.) 61 (South Africa) (land in Cornwall, being community property by the law of South Africa, devolved according to that law) (details to be found at *Cheshire, North and Fawcett: Private International Law*, 14th edn, 2008, p.1303).

[18] *Re Mengel's Will Trusts* [1962] Ch. 791; contrast *Re Allen's Estate* [1945] 2 All E.R. 264.

Marriage contracts: private marriage contracts

13–03   In the absence of a default system of community of goods, or even within such a system if the system itself permits, parties may enter into a private marriage contract, selecting for example a system of community of property of their choosing and on their own terms, or of separation of property.

Proper/governing law

13–04   "Obligations arising out of matrimonial property regimes, [and] property regimes of relationships deemed by the law applicable to such relationships to have comparable effects to marriage" are excluded from the Rome I Regulation.[19] Hence, marriage contracts are governed by Scots and English common law conflict rules, though a marriage contract involving trusts will be regulated by the Recognition of Trusts Act 1987.[20] Consequently, the proper law of a private marriage contract is either the law by which the parties expressly, or by implication, agree that it is to be governed, or failing any such express or implied agreement, the law with which the contract has the most real and substantial connection.[21]

Capacity to enter into a marriage contract

13–05   As regards immoveables, capacity to enter into a marriage contract is governed by the *lex situs*.[22] As regards moveables there is no recent case law, but arguing by analogy from the topic of commercial contracts, application of the putative proper law (that is, the law which would govern the contract if it were valid) commends itself.

In earlier days, an argument was adduced that a distinction could be drawn between void and voidable marriage contracts; in the former case, capacity to grant was referable to the law of the domicile of the granter at the date of the purported grant,[23] and in the latter, the question was whether by the law of the domicile of the granter at the date of the purported revocation, s/he had capacity to revoke.[24] It may still be thought best to express the matter in the form that revocability is an issue for the putative proper law of the contract, whereas capacity to revoke is an issue for the *lex domicilii* at the time of the purported

---

[19] See art.1.2(c). Cf. "Rights in property arising out of a matrimonial relationship", Rome I Convention art.1.2.6.

[20] Implementing 1986 Hague Convention on the Law Applicable to Trusts and on their Recognition; para.18–59, below.

[21] Following the common law rules of Scotland/England for commercial contracts. For marriage contract examples, see *Chamberlain v Napier* (1880) L.R. 15 Ch. D. 614; *Re Fitzgerald* [1904] 1 Ch. 573; *Re Mackenzie* [1911] Ch. 578; *Re Hewitt's Settlement* [1915] 1 Ch. 228; *Brown v Brown*, 1913 2 S.L.T. 314; *Eadie's Trustees v Henderson*, 1919 1 S.L.T. 253; *Goold Stuart's Trustees v McPhail*, 1947 S.L.T. 221; *Earl Iveagh v Inland Revenue Commissioners* [1954] Ch. 364; *Duke of Marlborough v Att Gen* [1945] Ch. 78 ("presumption" in favour of matrimonial, i.e. husband's, domicile applied); *Re Bankes* [1902] 2 Ch. 333 ("presumption" rebutted); *R v R* [1995] 1 F.C.R. 745.

[22] *Black v Black's Trustees*, 1950 S.L.T. (Notes) 32.

[23] *Re Cooke's Trusts* (1887) 3 T.L.R. 558; *Cooper v Cooper* (1888) 15 R. (H.L.) 21; *Black v Black's Trustees*, 1950 S.L.T. (Notes) 32.

[24] *Viditz v O'Hagan* [1900] 2 Ch. 87; *Sawrey-Cookson v Sawrey-Cookson's Trustees* (1905) 8 F. 157.

revocation of the party/parties wishing to revoke. Later English consensus[25] construes all cases as supporting a reference to the putative proper law, but the case of *Cooper v Cooper*[26] (in which the House of Lords held that a wife of Scots domicile was entitled, by Irish law, to repudiate an ante-nuptial contract made by her when a minor domiciled in Ireland) strictly remains authoritative in Scotland, although the decision is open to different interpretation.[27]

The case of *Sawrey-Cookson v Sawrey-Cookson's Trustees*[28] is instructive in a number of aspects: a Scotswoman granted in Scotland a unilateral ante-nuptial marriage settlement in Scots form in anticipation of her marriage to an Englishman. A few years later, she wished to revoke it. As the proper law of the deed was Scots, Scots law determined its revocability *sua natura*, but her capacity to revoke was to be referred to her English domicile at the date of proposed revocation. She also had executed in England, after her marriage, a ratification of the settlement: that deed had an English proper law, and its effect and its revocability, as well as her legal capacity to revoke, were to be determined by the law of England.

Formal validity

It is sufficient that the deed complies in form either with the proper law or with the law of the place where the marriage contract was executed.[29] **13–06**

Essential validity

Essential validity is governed by the *lex situs* as regards immoveables.[30] As regards moveable property, the proper law applies,[31] being the law with reference to which the contract was made, and which the parties intended to govern their rights and liabilities, or failing such ascertainable or deemed intention, by **13–07**

---

[25] Morris, *Conflict of Laws*, 7th edn, 2009, paras 16–011 to 16–013; *Dicey, Morris and Collins on the Conflict of Laws*, 14th edn, 2006, para.28–041; *Cheshire, North and Fawcett: Private International Law*, 14th edn, 2008, pp.1301 1306. Also Morris, "Capacity to Make a Marriage Settlement Contract in English Private International Law" (1938) 54 L.Q.R. 78.

[26] (1888) 15 R. (H.L.) 21.

[27] See Clive, p.321, and Anton with Beaumont, *Private International Law*, 2nd edn, 1990, p.579; contrast Morris, *Conflict of Laws*, 7th edn, 2009, para.16–011; *Dicey, Morris and Collins on the Conflict of Laws*, 14th edn, 2006, para.28–038.

[28] (1905) 8 F. 157.

[29] *Guepratte v Young* (1851) 4 De G. & Sm. 217; *Van Grutten v Digby* (1862) 31 Beav. 561; *Re Bankes* [1902] 2 Ch. 333.

[30] *Tezcan v Tezcan* (1992) 87 D.L.R. 503 BC CA.

[31] Scottish cases: *Countess of Findlater and Seafield v Seafield Grant*, February 8, 1814, F.C.; *Williamson v Taylor* (1845) 8 D. 156; *Scott v Sinclair* (1865) 3 M. 918; *Earl of Stair v Head* (1844) 6 D. 904; *Corbet v Waddell* (1879) 7 R. 200; *Brown's Trustees* (1890) 17 R. 1174; *Brown v Brown*, 1913 2 S.L.T. 314; *Lister's Judicial Factor v Syme*, 1914 S.C. 204; *Battye's Trustee v Battye's Administrator*, 1917 S.C. 385; *Montgomery v Zarifi*, 1918 S.C. (H.L.) 128; *Eadie's Trustees v Henderson*, 1919 1 S.L.T. 253; *Goold Stuart's Trustees v McPhail*, 1947 S.L.T. 221; *Stevenson v Currie* (1905) 13 S.L.T. 457; *Black v Black's Trustees*, 1950 S.L.T. (Notes) 32; *Lashley v Hog* (1804) 4 Pat. 581. English cases: *Van Grutten v Digby* (1862) 31 Beav. 561; *Chamberlain v Napier* (1800) L.R. 15 Ch. D. 614; *Re Hernando* (1884) L.R. 27 Ch. D. 284; *Re Fitzgerald* [1904] 1 Ch. 573; *Re Mackenzie* [1911] 1 Ch. 578; *Re Hewitt's Settlement* [1915] 1 Ch. 228; *Duke of Marlborough v Att Gen* [1945] Ch. 78. Irish case: *Re Lord Cloncurry's Estate* [1932] I.R. 687.

the law of most real and substantial connection, objectively construed.[32] Thus the proper law applies to all questions of substance such as:

(1) the validity of the provisions of the deed;
(2) the property rights of the parties; and
(3) whether the deed is revocable *sua natura*.

The meaning of the terms of the contract (including possibly identification of the property to be affected by the contract) is determined by the law governing interpretation of the contract (which might be expressed by the parties, or could be inferred from the language of the deed; failing which the putative proper law will apply).[33]

Effect of a change of domicile on a private marriage contract

13–08   A change of domicile, while it may affect the capacity of the parties to revoke an existing agreement, does not affect the contractual rights of the parties.[34] This means that the rights of third parties, for example the husband's creditors, whose claims may be good by their own laws, i.e. by the law(s) governing the debt(s), may be prejudiced by the pre-existing rights of the debtor's spouse under another law governing the debtor's marriage contract or matrimonial regime, in terms of which the spouse's rights have vested.[35]

Effect of divorce

13–09   There is a difficulty here in that it is clear that any forum, if properly seised of jurisdiction in divorce, will apply its own law to the grounds of divorce and to the rules of property distribution upon divorce.[36] Moreover, a legal system might have policy objections to agreements which envisage, or seek to regulate, ante-nuptially, the property effects of the termination of the marriage about to be entered into, though this seems unlikely in modern circumstances. A Scots court probably will endeavour to give effect to parties' wishes as expressed in their contract, provided that the contract is valid, essentially and formally, and that the parties had capacity to enter into it.[37] Alternatively, the means and property of parties, to which the court will apply its own rules of distribution, might first have been determined, i.e. diminished, by the matrimonial property provisions of a foreign law. English courts hitherto have been more dismissive than Scots courts of earlier arrangements made by private

---

[32] See para.15–18, below. Consider *Re Bankes* [1902] 2 Ch. 333, and see also *Chamberlain v Napier* (1880) L.R. 15 Ch. D. 614 (Scots and English law governed different parts of the deed).

[33] *Corbet v Waddell* (1879) 7 R. 200; *Hope Vere v Hope Vere* (1907) 13 S.L.T. 774, affirmed (1907) 15 S.L.T. 361 HL; and *Drummond v Bell-Irving*, 1930 S.C. 704.

[34] *Shand-Harvey*, 1910 1 S.L.T. 133 Sh. Ct. Contrast Belgian authority: *Duyrewaardt v Barber* (1992) 43 R.F.L. (3d.) 139 BC CA.

[35] See e.g. *Shand-Harvey*, 1910 1 S.L.T. 133 Sh. Ct.

[36] See, for Scots law, Family Law (Scotland) Act 1985 s.14(2)(h) (power to grant an incidental order, including an order setting aside or varying any term in an antenuptial or postnuptial marriage settlement—but such an order may be made only if justified by the principles set out in s.9 of the Act); also ss.16, 17 (judicial power to vary contractual terms agreed by parties to come into effect in the event of divorce or nullity).

[37] See Clive, pp.255, 321, 322.

contract.[38] This has rendered the identity of the forum, and identification of the proper law as between Scots law and English law,[39] the more significant.[40] Recently, however, in *Radmacher v Granatino*,[41] the Court of Appeal showed favour to a pre-nuptial agreement valid and enforceable by the foreign national laws of each party. The parties (of French and German nationality, respectively), at the wife's request had made a pre-nuptial agreement, valid by French and German law, waiving any claims for maintenance after divorce. The court, noting that the subject area was ripe for reform by Parliament, took the view that under the current state of the law, an English court could give weight to the existence of the marital property regime which the parties freely had chosen, as part of the wide discretion given to the court by the Matrimonial Causes Act 1973 s.25, in ordering a financial settlement upon divorce. Hence, it would appear that in England also, autonomy of parties increasingly may be recognised.

No marriage contract

At common law, where parties did not make a private marriage contract, and did not impliedly consent to be governed by a statutory code, the rights of the husband and wife in immoveables were governed by the lex situs.[42] With regard to moveables, the test was more complex. It was essential to distinguish two different issues: first, what was the touchstone against which parties' rights were to be tested?[43]; secondly, could parties' rights change through the course of their marriage, following, for example, changes of domicile?[44]

13–10

Initially, there was a presumption to the effect that the rights of parties are/were to be determined by the law of the husband's domicile at the time of the marriage, but it seems clear that this presumption, or any more modern formulation of it, might be rebutted if there was express agreement that another law would govern, or if there was implied agreement to that effect, in that there was proof that the parties intended to set up home shortly in another legal system having a distinct matrimonial property regime (or having none), and they did in fact carry out their intention reasonably promptly. The guide was *Re Egerton's Will Trust*,[45] where not only did the parties after the marriage fail to effect their proposed removal to France, from the husband's domicile in

---

[38] See *R v R* [1995] 1 F.C.R. 745; and *F v F* [1995] 2 F.L.R. 45, and discussion and criticism thereof by C.M.V. Clarkson and Jonathan Hill, *The Conflcit of Laws*, 3rd edn (Oxford: Oxford University Press, 2006), pp.441, 442. The Law Commission began a project in 2009 upon the status and enforceability of agreements made between spouses or civil partners, or persons contemplating marriage or civil partnership, concerning their property and finances. A consultation paper is expected in 2010.

[39] *R v R* [1995] 1 F.C.R. 745.

[40] See, e.g. *Drummond v Bell-Irving*, 1930 S.C. 704; and *Montgomery v Zarifi*, 1918 S.C. (H.L.) 128.

[41] [2009] EWCA Civ 649. See, to the same effect, *Ella v Ella* [2007] EWCA Civ 99.

[42] *Welch v Tennent* (1891) 18 R. (H.L.) 72.

[43] i.e. what was the first regulator of rights in moveables, at the point of marriage? Did rights "crystallise" at that point, or could the regulator, fixed or flexible, be set at some point after marriage (the *Egerton* issue: see *Re Egerton's Will Trusts* [1956] Ch. 593)?

[44] i.e. was it possible that their rights in moveables acquired at different times during the marriage were governed by different laws?

[45] [1956] Ch. 593.

England, until two years had elapsed, but it was held also that mere agreement to change to French domicile did not carry any inference that the parties had agreed to adopt French matrimonial property law. Nevertheless, Roxburgh J. left open the possibility of the use of intended matrimonial home as the base test in a suitable case.[46] In the normal case, though, the most likely applicable law would have been the matrimonial domicile (that is, in this context, the domicile of the married pair immediately after the marriage).

The question whether the rights of parties in property acquired during the marriage must be referred always and only to that law first "chosen" was something other than the *Egerton* issue. Civilian systems typically prefer the "immutability" rule, by which the law governing matrimonial property rights at the outset, whatever that law may be, continue to regulate rights in acquisitions, wherever and whenever acquired, and no matter that the parties have changed domicile once or several times since marriage. The question was argued with full and learned citation of authority in the South African case of *Frankel v The Master*,[47] in which the decision (that the German law of the husband's domicile at the date of marriage would regulate the parties' rights in property inter se at all times thereafter even though within four months of marriage they had settled in Johannesburg, South Africa) was described as, "a tribute which logic pays to certainty". Immutability is a principle which has merits and demerits: it has the merit of certainty, but the governing law thus identified may be that of the one legal system in the world to which the parties, erstwhile refugees, would not return. The South African case of *Sperling v Sperling*[48] reveals that the South African conflict rules are disposed to apply the rules of that (initial and continuing) *lex causae* as they may prevail from time to time, i.e. if retrospective changes are made in the *lex causae*, the forum, subject to public policy, would accept them. In the United States, mutability prevails, so that rights of parties in acquisitions during the course of marriage are referred to the domicile of the parties at the time of each acquisition.[49]

It is probable that a middle path was taken in England and Scotland.[50] The only House of Lords guide was the old case of *Lashley v Hog*,[51] which, on one reading, might be said to support the argument that property rights of spouses may change upon a change of domicile. It is just as likely, however, that *Lashley*, as noted,[52] is properly understood as a succession case.

---

[46] Though the legal system to which the parties remove, at whatever speed and with whatever degree of decisiveness, may not admit "late entry". Cf. fn.7, above.

[47] (1950) 1 S.A.L.R. 220 (South Africa).

[48] 1975 (2) S.A. 707.

[49] See Davie, "Matrimonial Property in English and American Conflict of Laws" (1993) 42 I.C.L.Q. 855.

[50] Clive, p. 256, seems prepared to countenance, indeed approve, mutability, subject to protection of vested rights, in any case in which the significant features of *De Nicols* are absent. See *Kennedy v Bell* (1864) 2 M. 587, per the Lord Ordinary at 588. Also *Cheshire, North and Fawcett: Private International Law*, 14th edn, 2008, pp.1299, 1300.

[51] *Lashley v Hog* (1804) 4 Pat. 581; though see also *Clarke v Newmarsh* (1836) 14 S. 488; *Duchess of Buckingham v Winterbottom* (1851) 13 D. 1129; *Roe v Roe*, 1916 32 Sh.Ct Rep. 30; *Frankel v The Master* (1950) 1 S.A.L.R. 220 (South Africa); *Chiwell v Carlyon* (1897) 14 S.C. (S.A.) 61; *Re Bettinson's Question* [1956] Ch. 67; *Re Egerton's Will Trusts* [1956] Ch. 593; cf. *Dicey, Morris and Collins on the Conflict of Laws*, 14th edn, 2006, r.158.

[52] See para.13–02.

The Scots position immediately before the 2006 Act, therefore, probably was that although (future) rights might change with a change of domicile, the domicile change must be effected by both parties, and vested rights in earlier acquired property would not be prejudiced.

Family Law (Scotland) Act 2006 section 39

The following rules are laid down in s.39 (subject, by s.39(6)(b), to the **13–11** spouses' contrary agreement):

By s.39(1), the rights of spouses to each other's immoveable property arising by virtue of the marriage shall be determined by the *lex/leges situs*.[53] Moreover, by s.39(4), any question relating to the use of the contents of a matrimonial home, or to the use or occupation of a moveable matrimonial home, shall be determined by the law of the country in which the home is situated (for the time being, it is presumed).

By s.39(2), the rights of spouses to each other's moveable property arising by virtue of the marriage shall be determined by the law of the common domicile. The relevant time at which domicile is to be ascertained is not specified: it may be a reference to the domicile of the spouses at the date of acquisition of the property in question, or possibly to the immediate post-nuptial domicile. Section 39(5) provides that a change of domicile by one or both spouses shall not affect a right in moveable property which, immediately before the change, has vested in either spouse.[54] By s.39(3), where the parties are domiciled in different countries (when?), the spouses shall be taken to have the same rights in each other's moveable property arising by virtue of the marriage as they had immediately before the marriage (by which law?). This obscure provision is also subject to the provision on vested rights contained in s.39(5). It may mean that the parties are to be taken to have adopted for the future the matrimonial property rules existing in their respective ante-nuptial domiciles; but what if these systems are mutually inconsistent?

Section 39 shall not apply in relation to the law on aliment, financial provision on divorce, transfer of property on divorce or succession.

The need to legislate on these matters, introducing, after many years of quiescence, provisions of variable clarity and completeness, was not obvious, and in any event the wisdom of so doing in Scots law is doubtful in view of imminent EU developments.

---

[53] Ex facie this appears simply to be a reiteration of the common law position. The advisability of encasing it in legislation is not beyond doubt since the phrase, "arising by virtue of the marriage" not only begs the question, but raises the spectre of an incidental question on the point whether the marriage itself is valid. Admittedly, the same could be said of the rule at common law, but the absence of case law suggests that few problems have arisen. Further, would s.39(1) be capable, by referring to the *lex situs*, to have the parties subjected to a statutory scheme of community if the reference led, for example, to a system of law which imposed such a regime?

[54] This is thought to be the common law rule of Scots and English law where there is no statutory or private regulation of matrimonial property.

B. PROPERTY RIGHTS ARISING FROM OTHER ADULT RELATIONSHIPS

Types of cohabitation—"de facto" and "de jure"

13–12 In the following discussion, de facto cohabitation is intended to mean relationships not formalised by legal ceremony or registration process, but nevertheless attracting, to a greater or lesser extent as the case may be, financial/proprietary/succession consequences which arise by operation of law where the relationship in question satisfies the definition of cohabitation laid down by the legal system purporting to regulate that relationship. Of such a type is the cohabitation relationship to which are attached property, etc. consequences by the Family Law (Scotland) Act 2006 ss.25–30.

De jure cohabitation, on the other hand, denotes a relationship which is formally registered in accordance with the legal system which creates and regulates it. Of such a type is registered partner status.

De facto cohabitants, cohabiting in Scotland

13–13 In terms of Scots domestic law, ss.25–30 of the Family Law (Scotland) Act 2006, endow "cohabitants"[55] with certain rights (e.g. in household goods, per s.26 and, per s.27, in money derived from a household allowance or property acquired out of such money). Section 28[56] states that where cohabitation ends otherwise than by death, a Scottish court may award a capital sum to the applicant, and grant an order in respect of any economic burden of caring for a child of the cohabitants. Application is permitted to the court, per s.29,[57] by the survivor for provision on the death intestate of his/her cohabitant.

It is implicit that application may be made for the rights provided for in the Act whenever Scots law is the *lex causae*. But the Act does not specify, from a conflict of laws perspective, when, or in what circumstances, the rights created therein should apply. By inference, and arguing by analogy from the use of the matrimonial domicile in marriage cases, Scots law would be the *lex causae* in relation to rights arising during the cohabitation where the cohabitation is occurring in Scotland. This immediately raises temporal issues which, given the mobility of persons, are not academic. At least it is clear that in respect of the rights of the survivor on the death intestate of the predeceaser, Scots law, if it is the *lex ultimi domicilii*, must be the *lex causae*.[58]

---

[55] "Cohabitant" means either member of a couple consisting of (a) a man and a woman who are (or were) living together as if they were husband and wife; or (b) two persons of the same sex who are (or were) living together as if they were civil partners: s.25(1). Further, per s.25(2), in determining whether a person is a cohabitant of another person, the court shall have regard to (a) the length of the period during which the parties have been living together (or lived together); (b) the nature of their relationship during that period; and (c) the nature and extent of any financial arrangements subsisting, or which subsisted during that period. It is unclear whether a Scottish forum will be prepared to take into account any period of cohabitation spent abroad (cf. and contrast *Walker v Roberts*, 1998 S.L.T 1133).

[56] e.g. *C v S*, 2008 S.L.T. 871; *Jamieson v Rodhouse*, 2009 G.W.D. 3–54; *Gow v Grant*, 2010 G.W.D. 7–125; and *Lawley v Sutton*, 2010 G.W.D. 14–257.

[57] e.g. *Chebotareva v Khandro*, 2008 Fam.L.R. 66; *Windram, Applicant*, 2009 G.W.D. 36–617; and *Savage v Purches*, 2009 S.L.T. (Sh. Ct.) 36.

[58] See s.29(1)(b)(i). In *Chebotareva*, 2008 Fam.L.R. 66 the sheriff held that the domicile requirement of s.29 was not satisfied, the applicant having failed to persuade the court that the deceased, at the date of his death, had changed his domicile to a Scots domicile. In the view of the court, the deceased's English domicile of origin remained.

If a case were to arise with an actual or potential conflict of laws dimension, e.g. as regards the property consequences of cohabitation in Scotland of one or more foreign domiciliaries, guidance in solving such problems will require to be drawn from general conflict principles governing capacity to enter into legal relationships, recognition of status and its incidents, and public policy.

The 2006 Act contains no jurisdiction or choice of law rules with regard to de facto cohabitation. Thus, it remains uncertain in Scots law which law, for example, governs an individual's legal capacity to attain the status of cohabitant (for the purposes of s.25); and in what factual circumstances a Scottish court would be entitled to apply the provisions in the Act covering the personal, financial and proprietary consequences of cohabitation. The essential antecedent question, not addressed in the Act, is in what circumstances the Scottish courts have jurisdiction to rule on the financial/proprietary rights of cohabitants (including the question as to the extent of competence of the Scottish courts to regulate the distribution of cohabitants' foreign assets upon termination of their relationship).[59]

At this point one might summarise the position by stating that the 2006 Act introduces into Scots domestic law significant new rules relating to cohabitation without enacting when those rules shall apply. The provisions are incomplete. This is not to say that Scots conflict of laws unaided cannot provide guidance and remedy, but it is regrettable to leave these important matters to speculation. Silence about jurisdiction is the most difficult to fill.[60]

De facto cohabitants, cohabiting outside Scotland

With regard to the proprietary consequences of a foreign de facto cohabitation, and in particular, the effect, if any, upon moveable and immoveable property situated in Scotland, it is likely that, in the first instance, the Scottish court would apply the "proper law of the cohabitation" (law of closest connection) to determine whether the statutory regime imposed by that law purported to have extraterritorial effect upon property belonging to the cohabitants and situated abroad. If a foreign statutory regime (say, of community of property between cohabitants), or a private contractual arrangement between the cohabitants, purported to affect all property belonging to the couple, the Scottish *lex situs* nevertheless would retain absolute control over any immoveable property situated within Scotland, and moveable property situated there from time to time, and would have an undeniable right to recognise, or not, the purported extraterritorial proprietary effects of the statutory regime, and the purported effect of the parties' contractual arrangements. It is probable that the Scottish *lex situs* would recognise the purported proprietary effects of a de facto cohabitation, *inter partes*, but possibly not in the event of a competing claim to property in Scotland by a third party such as a creditor.[61]

13–14

---

[59] See Carruthers, *The Transfer of Property in the Conflict of Laws*, 2005, paras 2.51–2.62. Also *McKie v McKie* [1933] I.R. 464.

[60] Presumably jurisdiction could be established upon the presence of property within Scotland.

[61] At least where the third party, say, the creditor, is relying on Scots law. If, however, the proper law of the debt between the creditor and the debtor (i.e. the cohabitant) were, say, Dutch law, it would not be contrary to the reasonable expectations of the creditor to apply Dutch law rather than Scots law, and therefore, to prefer the claim to moveable property in Scotland of, say, the Dutch cohabitant (cf. *North Western Bank v John Poynter, Son and MacDonalds* (1894) 22 R. (H.L.) 1; *Scottish Provident Institution v Robinson* (1892) 29 S.L.R. 733).

The question whether a Scottish court would be entitled to apply the provisions of the Family Law (Scotland) Act 2006 to cohabitants would seem to rest upon the Scottish court having jurisdiction (the basis of which is not clear), and upon the individuals satisfying the s.25 meaning of cohabitants.

Foreign "de jure" cohabitants

13–15   Scots domestic law currently does not make provision for registered heterosexual partnerships. With regard to foreign de jure cohabitants, it is likely that the attitude of the Scots court would be similar to that outlined above in relation to de facto cohabitants cohabiting outside Scotland. In both instances, the likelihood of recognition is greater now that Scots law contains provision regulating certain proprietary and financial consequences of cohabitation, and same sex civil partnership.

Civil Partnership

13–16   In the case of civil partnerships registered in England, the property and financial consequences are detailed in Civil Partnership Act 2004 Pt 2 Ch.3 (ss.65–72).

Part 3 of the 2004 Act (civil partnership: Scotland) does not contain a direct equivalent to Pt 2 Ch.3. Instead, Pt 3 Ch.3 makes provision with regard to occupancy rights and tenancies.[62] As regards the financial consequences of a civil partnership (registered in Scotland?), or of the death intestate of a civil partner (by inference, domiciled at death in Scotland), s.261(2) and Sch.28 of the 2004 Act extend to civil partners, mutatis mutandis, the rules contained in the Succession (Scotland) Act 1964 concerning intestate and testate succession; rights in moveable property and money conferred by the Family Law (Scotland) Act 1985, and also the financial relief provisions of that Act upon dissolution of a relationship; and certain other miscellaneous legislative provisions concerning, inter alia, bankruptcy, damages, and housing. The new rights will arise whenever Scots law is the governing law, though there may well be doubt as to when this will be the case.[63]

Generally, with regard both to registered partnerships and regulation of de facto cohabitation, there is little if any express guidance in the Act on choice of law, which is a serious lack.

C. PROPOSED EU HARMONISATION MEASURES

13–17 The Stockholm Programme, detailing European strategic priorities for the period 2010 to 2014,[64] identifies this area of law as one for development. It is intended in 2010 to issue a proposal for a Regulation on the conflict of laws in

---

[62] The conflict dimension is not clear: occupancy rights and tenancies in respect of properties situated in Scotland? Or in respect of Scottish domiciliaries?

[63] cf. the position in relation to de facto cohabitants under the 2006 Act.

[64] Communication on Delivering an Area of Freedom, Security & Justice for Europe's Citizens: Action Plan Implementing the Stockholm Programme COM(2010) 175 final. See also Draft Presidency Note Multiannual Programme for an Area of Freedom, Security and Justice Serving the Citizen: the Stockholm Programme 14449/09 JAI 679.

matters concerning matrimonial property rights, including the question of jurisdiction and mutual recognition, and for regulation on the property consequences of the separation of couples from other types of unions.

Such a project has been in contemplation for several years.[65] Preparatory research conducted in each Member State encompassed not only rules of matrimonial property, but also the property consequences for unmarried, cohabiting couples. While the Hague Programme referred only to matrimonial property issues, it is now clear that any proposed instrument under the Stockholm Programme will be sufficiently wide as to include not only the property of married persons, but also of cohabiting couples and those in other forms of civil union.

II. FINANCIAL CONSEQUENCES

A. MAINTENANCE OBLIGATIONS

The current situation

Jurisdiction

The allocation of jurisdiction intra-EU currently is determined by the **13–18** Brussels I Regulation. In terms of the Regulation, a person normally is sued in the country in which s/he is domiciled (art.2), but one of the derogations to that rule concerns matters relating to maintenance. Article 5.2 states that:

> "A person domiciled in a Member State may, in another Member State, be sued . . . in matters relating to maintenance, in the courts for the place where the maintenance creditor is domiciled or habitually resident or, if the matter is ancillary to proceedings concerning the status of a person, in the court which, according to its own law, has jurisdiction to entertain those proceedings, unless that jurisdiction is based solely on the nationality of one of the parties."

Thus, maintenance creditors can opt to sue either in the court for the Member State where the debtor is domiciled, or in the Member State where the creditor is domiciled or habitually resident.[66] The option is thought to confer an advantage on the maintenance creditor (the claimant payee), who is perceived as the weaker party, and is comparable to the *forum actoris* rules provided in sections 3 (insured parties), 4 (consumers) and 5 (employees) of the Brussels I Regulation.

What is a "matter relating to maintenance"? According to *Van den Boogaard v Laumen*,[67] if a court judgment is designed to enable one spouse to provide for himself or herself or if the needs and resources of each of the spouses are taken

---

[65] The multiannual programme adopted by the European Council at its meeting in the Netherlands on November 4 and 5, 2004, para.3.4.2 (Draft Multiannual Programme 13993/04-LIMITE JAI 408).

[66] e.g. *Sawicki v Sawicka* [2008] I.L.Pr. 3; *T v L* [2009] I.L.Pr. 5 (Irish Supreme Court).

[67] *Van den Boogaard v Laumen* (C-220/95) [1997] All E.R. (E.C.) 517. Also *De Cavel v De Cavel (No.1)* (143/78) [1979] E.C.R. 1055; *De Cavel v De Cavel* (No.2) (120/79) [1980] E.C.R. 731; *Farrell v Long* (C295/95) [1997] All E.R. (E.C.) 449; and *Moore v Moore* [2007] I.L.Pr. 36.

into consideration in the determination of the amount, the decision will be concerned with maintenance. On the other hand, where the provision awarded is solely concerned with dividing property between spouses, the decision will be concerned with rights in property arising out of the matrimonial relationship and will not therefore be enforceable under the Brussels regime.[68]

Where Council Regulation 44/2001 does not apply, allocation of jurisdiction in matters relating to maintenance will be governed by r.2(e) of Sch.8 of Civil Jurisdiction and Judgments Act 1982.[69]

Choice of law

13–19 Where a Scots court has jurisdiction in respect of a maintenance claim, it will apply Scots domestic law to the substance of the question.[70] This choice of law rule has been placed on a statutory basis by Family Law (Scotland) Act 2006 s.40, and is subject to the Maintenance Orders (Reciprocal Enforcement) Act 1972 (*q.v.*).

Enforcement of maintenance orders

(a) Enforcement of maintenance orders intra-UK

13–20 The Maintenance Orders Act 1950 governs the registration and enforcement of aliment or maintenance orders intra-UK.

(b) Recovery of maintenance orders under Maintenance Orders (Reciprocal Enforcement) Act 1972, as amended[71]

13–21 For many years the enforcement of foreign maintenance orders for spouses and children gave rise to such practical difficulties that in many cases it was impossible to recover any sum whatsoever. As between Great Britain and the Commonwealth there have been reciprocal statutory provisions since 1920 (Maintenance Orders (Facilities for Enforcement) Act 1920), but these were never entirely satisfactory,[72] and the 1920 Act did not apply to Scotland. The Maintenance Orders (Reciprocal Enforcement) Act 1972,[73] was intended to facilitate the recovery of maintenance by or from persons in the UK, from or by persons in other countries.

Part I of the 1972 Act provides a system of registration and enforcement in the United Kingdom of maintenance orders made in reciprocating (mainly Commonwealth) countries.[74] The 1972 Act contains both "incoming" and "outgoing" registration provisions. Incoming orders are governed by ss.6–11 (s.6: registration in Scotland, per sheriff court, of maintenance order from

---

[68] See art.1.1. See now Council Regulation 44/2001 art.1.2(a). Cf. Regulation 2201/2003 art.1.3(e), recital (8).

[69] See the Civil Jurisdiction and Judgments Order 2001 (SI 2001/3929).

[70] i.e. those rules contained in Family Law (Scotland) Act 1985 ss.1–7.

[71] By the Maintenance Orders (Reciprocal Enforcement) Act 1992.

[72] *Peagram v Peagram* [1926] 2 K.B. 165; *Harris v Harris* [1949] 2 All E.R. 318.

[73] Providing for accession by the UK to the 1956 United Nations (New York) Convention on the Recovery Abroad of Maintenance.

[74] This replaces, for England and Wales, the Maintenance Orders (Facilities for Enforcement) Act 1920.

reciprocating country; s.8: enforcement thereof; s.9: variation and revocation thereof).[75] Under these statutory rules, no provision is made to permit refusal to enforce such an order on the ground of public policy. This matter was raised in *Sethi v Sethi*,[76] in which the husband sought reduction of the 1986 registration in Scotland of a maintenance order obtained against him by his wife in India. Lord Weir refused to accede to his request, holding that the terms of s.6 were mandatory, and observing that the pursuer ought to have challenged the original order (rather than its enforcement) as contrary to public policy.

Part II of the 1972 Act provides for reciprocal enforcement of claims for the recovery of maintenance in "Convention countries", being countries party to the 1956 New York (UN) Convention on the Recovery Abroad of Maintenance. Part II provides a procedure for the transmission, not of maintenance orders (as in Pt I), but of maintenance claims.

Part III of the 1972 Act deals with countries which are neither reciprocating countries, nor "Convention countries". Special bilateral arrangements may be made with countries, and if this is done, an Order in Council may be made under Pt III, applying modified provisions of the 1972 Act to the country in question.[77]

Where the maintenance order emanates from a foreign legal system which does not fall to be regulated by the 1972 Act, the holder may seek "decree conform" from the Court of Session.[78]

(c) Recovery of maintenance orders intra-EU

At present, a maintenance order may be enforced under the Brussels regime, **13–22** in the same way as an ordinary commercial debt.[79] The main enforcement route within the EU is the general commercial enforcement procedure provided in the Brussels I Regulation, but there is an alternative European Enforcement Order for Uncontested Claims,[80] which includes claims for maintenance payments.

Where EU Member States are party also to the 1956 New York (UN) Convention on the Recovery Abroad of Maintenance and/or the 1973 Hague Convention on the Recognition and Enforcement of Decisions relating to Maintenance Obligations, questions of priority of instrument may arise. Such questions are answered at present by art.67 of the Brussels I Regulation, to the effect that the maintenance creditor may choose which regime to follow.[81] In

---

[75] *Killen v Killen*, 1981 S.L.T. (Sh. Ct.) 77.

[76] 1995 S.L.T. 104.

[77] e.g. Reciprocal Enforcement of Maintenance Orders (United States of America) (Scotland) Order 2007 (SSI 2007/354). Of particular significance are the arrangements made under this Part in relation to countries signatory to the 1973 Hague Convention on the Recognition and Enforcement of Decisions relating to Maintenance Obligations: see, e.g. Reciprocal Enforcement of Maintenance Orders (Hague Convention Countries) (Variation) Order 2002 (SI 2002/2838).

[78] See para.9–09, above.

[79] See paras 9–29—9–40, above.

[80] Regulation 805/2004. See paras 9–53—9–60, above.

[81] See Anton with Beaumont, *Private International Law*, 2nd edn, 1990, pp.562, 563; R.E. Aird and J.N. St C. Jameson, *The Scots Domension to Cross-border Litigation* (Edinburgh: W. Green, 1996), note at para.20.46; and Clarkson and Hill, *The Conflict of Laws*, 3rd edn, 2006, p.437.

many cases, proceeding under the Brussels I Regulation will be the preferred option.[82]

Future regulation

13–23   Regulation 4/2009 on jurisdiction, applicable law, recognition and enforcement of decisions and cooperation in matters relating to maintenance obligations[83] shall apply in EU Member States from June 18, 2011.[84] The Regulation is a response to the Tampere Conclusions,[85] which called on the European Council and Commission to establish common procedural rules to simplify and accelerate the settlement of cross-border disputes concerning maintenance claims.[86] According to the Commission, "[t]he recovery of maintenance claims in the Member States accounts for a vast mass of litigation as a result of the fragile state of family relationships". The Commission claimed that the recovery of maintenance claims is, "a Community problem as a result of the free movement of Community citizens." While there may be doubt about the true volume of cases, nevertheless there is an underlying economic imperative since Member States are concerned about the considerable sums which they may have to pay out to make up for the defaults of maintenance debtors. One of the underlying themes of the Regulation is that a maintenance creditor, i.e. any individual to whom maintenance is owed or is alleged to be owed,[87] should be able to obtain easily in a Member State a maintenance decision[88] which will be automatically enforceable in another Member State without further formalities.[89]

The UK position

13–24   The UK did not take part in the adoption of the Maintenance Regulation, and therefore at that point was not bound by it, or subject to its application.[90] However, in accordance with art.4 of Protocol No.4 on the position of the UK and Ireland,[91] the UK has notified its intention to accept the Regulation.[92]

---

[82] There are two valuable features of the Regulation 44/2001 enforcement route: it applies not just to court orders, but also to "authentic instruments", including registered minutes of agreement (Civil Jurisdiction and Judgments (Authentic Instruments and Court Settlements) Order 1993 (SI 1993/604); and now also Civil Jurisdiction and Judgments (Authentic Instruments and Court Settlements) Order 2001 (SI 2001/3928)); and under no circumstances can the foreign judgment be reviewed as to its substance (reg.44; art.36).

[83] [2009] OJ L7/1.

[84] Subject to the 2007 Hague Protocol, *q.v.* being applicable in the EU by that date (art.76).

[85] See para.1–07, above.

[86] See recital (4). See, for background, Green Paper on Maintenance Obligations COM(2004) 254 final; and Proposal for a Regulation on jurisdiction, applicable law, recognition and enforcement of decisions and cooperation in matters relating to maintenance obligations COM(2005) 649 final.

[87] See art.2.1.10.

[88] By art.2.1.1, "decision" shall mean a decision given by a court, which term itself is defined in art.2.2 to include administrative authorities of Member States.

[89] See recital (9).

[90] See recital (47).

[91] Protocol No.4 on the position of the UK and Ireland [1997] OJ C340/99. See now, under the Lisbon Treaty, Protocol No.21 on the Position of the UK & Ireland; para.1–07, above.

[92] Note from General Secretariat of the Council to the Council JUSTCIV 262.

Scope of instrument

The concept of maintenance obligation is to be interpreted autonomously **13–25** for the purposes of the Regulation, but is intended to cover all maintenance obligations which arise from a family relationship, parentage, marriage or affinity, in order to guarantee equal treatment of all maintenance creditors.[93]

Jurisdiction

With regard to jurisdiction, the rule contained in art.5.2 of the Brussels I **13–26** Regulation[94] shall be replaced[95] by those set out in Ch.II of the Maintenance Regulation, the most important of which are arts 3 (general jurisdiction), 4 (prorogation of jurisdiction), 5 (appearance of defendant), 6 (subsidiary jurisdiction[96] where no court of a Member State has jurisdiction pursuant to arts 3–5), 7 (*forum necessitatis*), and 8 (limit of proceedings, i.e. jurisdiction to modify a previous award). Articles 9–14 are familiar in their terms, establishing the *lis pendens* system to which we have become accustomed.[97] The Regulation may be said to adapt the standard rules of civil and commercial jurisdiction to suit the maintenance context, but also can be seen to go further than the Brussels I Regulation by appropriating jurisdiction for the application of Community rules where the defendant is habitually resident in a Third State ("subsidiary jurisdiction").

General rule

The general rule of jurisdiction is to be found in art.3, in terms of which: **13–27**

"In matters relating to maintenance obligations in Member States, jurisdiction shall lie with:
(a) the court for the place where the defendant is habitually resident, or
(b) the court for the place where the creditor is habitually resident, or
(c) the court which, according to its own law, has jurisdiction to entertain proceedings concerning the status of a person if the

---

[93] See recital (11); and art.1.
[94] See recital (44): "This Regulation should amend Regulation (EC) No 44/2001 by replacing the provisions of that Regulation applicable to maintenance obligations. Subject to the transitional provisions of this Regulation, Member States should, in matters relating to maintenance obligations, apply the provisions of this Regulation on jurisdiction, recognition, enforceability and enforcement of decisions and on legal aid instead of those of Regulation (EC) No 44/2001 as from the date on which this Regulation becomes applicable."
[95] Likewise, art.68.2 provides that the Maintenance Regulation shall replace, in matters relating to maintenance obligations, Regulation 805/2004 (European Enforcement Orders for uncontested claims), except with regard to European Enforcement Orders on maintenance obligations issued in a Member State not bound by the 2007 Hague Protocol.
[96] Recital (15) explains that: "In order to preserve the interests of maintenance creditors and to promote the proper administration of justice within the European Union, the rules on jurisdiction as they result from Regulation (EC) No 44/2001 should be adapted. The circumstance that the defendant is habitually resident in a Third State should no longer entail the non-application of Community rules on jurisdiction, and there should no longer be any referral to national law. This Regulation should therefore determine the cases in which a court in a Member State may exercise subsidiary jurisdiction."
[97] See para.7–45, above.

matter relating to maintenance is ancillary to those proceedings, unless that jurisdiction is based solely on the nationality of one of the parties, or

(d) the court which, according to its own law, has jurisdiction to entertain proceedings concerning parental responsibility if the matter relating to maintenance is ancillary to those proceedings, unless that jurisdiction is based solely on the nationality of one of the parties."

The "adaptation" which art.5.2 of the Brussels I Regulation has undergone amounts to the addition of the alternative forum of the habitual residence of the defendant, and the conferring of maintenance jurisdiction upon a court with jurisdiction to entertain proceedings concerning parental responsibility where the maintenance matter is ancillary thereto. No reference in art.3 is made to the domicile of the defendant or the maintenance creditor; the looser criterion of habitual residence is thought, presumably, to be more suitable for the purpose.

Choice of court

13–28   Article 4 permits prorogation of court by agreement of the parties, the choice falling upon the court(s) of the habitual residence or nationality, i.e. to be interpreted in a UK court as referring to domicile,[98] of either party. In the case of spouses or former spouses, the parties may choose the court having jurisdiction in matrimonial matters, or the court of the Member State of the spouses' last common habitual residence for a period of at least one year. There is a presumption of exclusivity, i.e. that jurisdiction conferred by agreement shall be exclusive unless the parties have agreed otherwise.[99] The choice of court provision in art.4 shall not apply to a dispute relating to a maintenance obligation towards a child under the age of 18.

Article 4.1 contains a useful *tempus inspiciendum* provision, laying down that the relevant time for ascertaining the personal law connecting factor is the time the choice of court agreement is concluded or the time the court is seised.

Submission

13–29   Submission by the defendant without protest as to the jurisdiction will also confer jurisdiction upon a Member State court.[100]

Subsidiary jurisdiction and jurisdiction of necessity

13–30   "Article 6
Subsidiary jurisdiction

Where no court of a Member State has jurisdiction pursuant to Articles 3, 4 and 5 and no court of a State party to the Lugano Convention which is not a Member State has jurisdiction pursuant to the provisions of that

---

[98] See recital (18); cf. in choice of law, art.9 of the 2007 Hague Protocol on the Law Applicable to Maintenance Obligations, below.
[99] See para.7–37, above.
[100] See art.5. Cf. Brussels I Regulation art.24; see paras 7–43—7–44, above.

> Convention, the courts of the Member State of the common nationality of
> the parties shall have jurisdiction."

This significant new provision can be seen as a notable step in the creation of
EU rules to treat hybrid cases, and in effect to safeguard the position of the
claimant. Recital (15) explains that the fact that the defendant is habitually
resident in a Third State should no longer rule out the application of
Community rules so as to permit application of national rules. Rather, the
Maintenance Regulation itself imposes a rule in this situation, namely, that the
courts of the Member State of the common nationality (in a UK court common
domicile) of the parties shall have jurisdiction. Admittedly, the newly created
rule insists upon a strong connection of both parties with a Member State.

Should there be no such common nationality (or domicile in the case of the
UK), and where no court of a Member State has jurisdiction under arts 3, 4 or
5, art.7 provides that the courts of a Member State, on an exceptional basis,
may hear the case if proceedings cannot reasonably be brought or conducted
or would be impossible in a Third State with which the dispute is closely
connected. Under art.7, headed *"forum necessitatis"*, the dispute must have a
close connection with the Member State of the court seised. Recital (16)
explains that the provision of jurisdiction *necessitatis* has been conferred in
order to remedy a denial of justice.

Articles 6 and 7, read together, comprise a further aggrandisement of the
EU's own jurisdiction to deal with Third States and hybrid cases, however
intrinsically unexceptionable or justifiable the provisions may appear to be.
Such provisions are clearly distinguishable from the more modest approach
seen in art.4 of the Brussels I Regulation and art.7 (residual jurisdiction) of
Brussels II *bis*.

Limit on proceedings

It is characteristic of awards of maintenance/aliment that, in their nature, **13–31**
they are subject to change. So, too, in a conflict situation, the habitual residence of the parties, in particular of the maintenance debtor, may change.
Article 8 addresses this feature as follows:

> "1. Where a decision is given in a Member State or a 2007 Hague
>   Convention Contracting State where the creditor is habitually resi-
>   dent, proceedings to modify the decision or to have a new decision
>   given cannot be brought by the debtor in any other Member State as
>   long as the creditor remains habitually resident in the State in which
>   the decision was given.
> 2. Paragraph 1 shall not apply:
>   (a) where the parties have agreed in accordance with Article 4 to the
>   jurisdiction of the courts of that other Member State;
>   (b) where the creditor submits to the jurisdiction of the courts of that
>   other Member State pursuant to Article 5;
>   (c) where the competent authority in the 2007 Hague Convention
>   Contracting State of origin cannot, or refuses to, exercise juris-
>   diction to modify the decision or give a new decision; or
>   (d) where the decision given in the 2007 Hague Convention
>   Contracting State of origin cannot be recognised or declared

enforceable in the Member State where proceedings to modify the decision or to have a new decision given are contemplated."

Article 8.1 safeguards the maintenance creditor against uncertainty or possible prejudice resulting from a change in the habitual residence of the debtor. Article 8.1 is subject to parties' agreement in accordance with art.4, submission without protest,[101] and cases where the original court refuses to modify the decision or give a new decision or where the original decision cannot be recognised or declared enforceable in the Member State where the fresh proceedings are contemplated.

Articles 9–14

13–32   The remaining provisions of Ch.II of the Maintenance Regulation replicate the familiar indicia of the system of *lis pendens* put in place in the 1968 Brussels Convention, and now contained in the Brussels I Regulation, namely, autonomous definitions of the time at which a court shall be deemed to be seised (art.9)[102]; examination by the court seised of its own jurisdiction (art.10)[103]; examination as to admissibility (art.11)[104]; and *lis pendens* (same cause of action: art.12[105]; and related actions: art.13)[106]; and art.14 (provisional, including protective measures).[107]

Applicable law

13–33   The provisions on applicable law are contained in Ch.III of the Maintenance Regulation, and are restricted to the determination of the law applicable to maintenance obligations, and should not determine the law applicable to the establishment of the family relationships on which the maintenance obligations are based.[108]

Article 15 of the Maintenance Regulation provides that, in the Member States bound by the 2007 Hague Protocol on the Law Applicable to Maintenance Obligations,[109] the law applicable to maintenance obligations shall be determined in accordance with that Protocol. The Protocol was signed and ratified by the EU on April 8, 2010. The EU is the first member of the Hague Conference to ratify the Protocol, art.25 of which provides that two

---

[101] Article 8.2 in its terms refers to submission by the creditor pursuant to art.5. Article 5, however, refers to submission by the defendant, being the maintenance debtor.

[102] cf. Brussels I Regulation art.30; see para–7.47, above.

[103] cf. Brussels II *bis* art.17; and see also Brussels I Regulation arts 25, 26, Ch.7, fn.176, above.

[104] Brussels II *bis* art.18; and see also Brussels I Regulation arts 25, 26, Ch.7, fn.176, above.

[105] cf. Brussels I Regulation art.27, para.7–45, above.

[106] cf. Brussels I Regulation art.28, para.7–46, above.

[107] cf. Brussels I Regulation art.31, para.7–73, above.

[108] Recital (21): "It needs to be made clear in this Regulation that these rules on conflict of laws determine only the law applicable to maintenance obligations and do not determine the law applicable to the establishment of the family relationships on which the maintenance obligations are based. The establishment of family relationships continues to be covered by the national law of the Member States, including their rules of private international law." See fn.125, below.

[109] See Andrea Bonomi, *Explanatory Report on the Hague Protocol of 23 November 2007 on the Law Applicable to Maintenance Obligations* (HccH, 2009) ("*Explanatory Report*").

ratifications are necessary for its entry into force. This means that the Regulation (the application of which is dependent upon the entry into force of the Hague Protocol), will become applicable in the Member States of the EU either on June 18, 2011[110] or upon the later date of entry into force of the Protocol.

The choice of law rules contained in the Protocol provide for universal application,[111] and exclusion of *renvoi.*[112] The general rule (art.3) is that maintenance obligations shall be governed by the law of the state of the habitual residence of the maintenance creditor. This is appropriate because:

> ". . . it allows a determination of the existence and amount of the maintenance obligation with regard to the legal and factual conditions of the social environment in the country where the creditor lives and engages in most of his or her activities."[113]

Temporal issues being of particular importance in this area, art.3.2 provides that where that habitual residence changes, the law of the state of the new habitual residence shall apply as from the moment when the change occurs.[114] Article 3 in its entirety is subject to an important caveat in respect of spouses and ex-spouses, contained in art.5, to the effect that art.3 shall not apply if one of the parties objects and the law of another state, in particular the state of their last common habitual residence, has a closer connection with the marriage. In such a case the law of that other state shall apply. Article 5 is intended to protect the maintenance debtor from the effects of a unilateral and self-serving change of residence by the maintenance creditor, which might lead to an outcome which is contrary to the debtor's expectations.[115]

Article 3 proves to be subject also to art.4.3, although there is no express mention of this in art.3 itself. Article 4 confers upon certain maintenance creditors, in particular, children against their parents (and vice versa), favourable rules insofar as if a creditor is unable, by virtue of the law applicable under art.3, to obtain maintenance from the debtor, the law of the forum[116] shall apply.[117] Article 4.3 is novel in that it provides that if the creditor has seised the competent authority of the state of the debtor's habitual residence,[118] the law of that state shall apply. However, if the creditor is unable thereunder to obtain maintenance, the forum shall revert to the general rule in art.3.1 of the Protocol and apply the habitual residence of the creditor. Similarly, if the creditor is unable to obtain maintenance from the debtor under any of the laws of

---

[110] See art.76.

[111] See art.2.

[112] See art.12.

[113] *Explanatory Report*, 2009, para.37.

[114] While the inclusion of a temporal provision is welcome, it is notorious that the connecting factor of habitual residence is difficult to define, and there is a particular difficulty in the temporal dimension of ascertaining at what "particular moment" a change occurs: see paras 6–44 and 6–49, above. The *Explanatory Report*, 2009, para.42 notes that change of residence of a temporary nature is not sufficient to dislodge the pre-existing habitual residence of the creditor.

[115] *Explanatory Report*, 2009, para.77. Contrast the counterbalancing provision in art.8.1 of the Maintenance Regulation.

[116] Maintenance Regulation arts 3–8 contain the rules for identification of forum.

[117] See art.4.2.

[118] Maintenance Regulation art.3(a).

the habitual residence of the creditor, or the debtor, or of the *lex fori* (whatever the forum may be), the law of the state of the common nationality, if there is one (and, in the case of the UK, common domicile)[119] shall apply.[120] This produces a complex construct which appears to be result-driven and does violence to the traditional approach to applicable law; it is not orthodox to re-visit choice of law if the outcome of applying a particular law does not result in benefit to the party favoured by the policy of the instrument.[121] A barbed comment might be that a simpler approach, achieving much the same outcome (*"favor creditoris"*), would have been to direct the forum to apply the law most beneficial to the maintenance creditor.

Choice of law by parties

13–34   Articles 7 and 8, permitting "designation" of applicable law by parties, are in line with the trend in EU modern instruments of jurisdiction and choice of law to allow party autonomy.

Article 7, the narrower provision, permits the maintenance creditor and debtor to choose the applicable law for the purpose only of a particular proceeding in a given state. The parties may choose only the law of the forum. It is anticipated that this provision would be useful in cases of legal separation and divorce, permitting the spouses to choose the *lex fori* in the matter of maintenance as well as substance.

Article 8, which is of broader compass, permits the parties,[122] notwith-standing the provisions of arts 3–6 to choose, at any time, as applicable law one of the following:

"a) the law of any State of which either party is a national (or, in the case of the UK, a domiciliary) at the time of the designation;
b)   the law of the State of the habitual residence of either party at the time of designation;
c)   the law designated by the parties as applicable, or the law in fact applied, to their property regime;
d)   the law designated by the parties as applicable, or the law in fact applied, to their divorce or legal separation."

Article 8.4 states that, notwithstanding such a choice, the question whether the creditor can renounce his/her right to maintenance shall be determined by the law of the habitual residence of the creditor at the time of the choice.

Article 8.5 appears to undo much of the value of that which precedes it by stipulating that:

". . . unless at the time of the designation the parties were fully informed and aware of the consequences of their designation, the law designated by the parties shall not apply where the application of that law would lead to manifestly unfair or unreasonable consequences for any of the parties".

---

[119] See art.9.
[120] See art.4.4.
[121] Orthodox choice of laws methodology is result-blind: see para.3–01, above.
[122] Subject to compliance with arts 8.2 (formal validity) and 8.3 (non-age).

This begs many questions and raises incidental questions. The purpose of art.8.5 seems to be to permit parties to undo a choice of law if the consequences of application of that law would lead, in the view of the forum,[123] to manifest unfairness "for any of the parties". Hence, that which can be undone is the *choice* of law. The province of art.8.5 marches closely to, and might trespass on, the territory of art.13 (public policy), which states that the application of the *law chosen* may be refused only to the extent that its effects would be manifestly contrary to the public policy of the forum. Their effects coincide in the matter of the consequences of application of the *lex causae*, by whatever process that governing law was identified. The forum could strike out a provision of the *lex causae* even where both parties were shown to have been fully informed and aware of the consequences of choice.

As a matter of (a different) policy, there is very little point in giving party autonomy if that autonomy is so hedged about with protections[124] for one or other or both contracting parties that the choice can easily be rendered nugatory. By what law(s) will the forum assess whether the parties (either or both?) were "fully informed'" and aware of the consequences of their choice?

Scope of applicable law

The non-exhaustive scope of application of the applicable law per art.11 is: **13–35**

> "a) whether, to what extent and from whom the creditor may claim maintenance;
> b) the extent to which the creditor may claim retroactive maintenance;
> c) the basis for calculation of the amount of maintenance, and indexation;
> d) who is entitled to institute maintenance proceedings, except for issues relating to procedural capacity and representation in the proceedings;
> e) prescription or limitation periods;
> f) the extent of the obligation of a maintenance debtor, where a public body seeks reimbursement of benefits provided for a creditor in place of maintenance."

It is interesting that art.11(d) assigns title to sue, except for procedural issues, to the *lex causae*.

Given that, "matters arising from the obligation to maintain" frequently may depend upon whether the parties were or are married, reference should be made to recital (21) of the Maintenance Regulation, which makes clear that the rules in the Regulation, and therefore, via art.15, the rules in the Protocol, determine only the law applicable to the maintenance obligation, and do not determine the law applicable to the establishment of the family relationships

---

[123] Bearing in mind the number of forums which are potentially available in this context: Maintenance Regulation arts 3–8.
[124] Protections are routinely inserted into instruments which allow for party choice of court or party choice of law, but to date the protections have been of a different timbre, being typically related to exclusion of choice, time of choice, formal validity of choice, and impositions upon choice, rather than displeasure at the consequences of one's choice. See, e.g. Brussels I Regulation arts 13, 17, 21, 23; Rome II Regulation arts 6, 8, 14; Rome I Regulation arts 3, 9.

on which the maintenance obligations are based.[125] In respect of the latter, the national rules of Member States, including their rules of private international law, will continue to apply.

With regard to art.11(c) of the Protocol (the basis for calculation of the amount of maintenance) it becomes apparent from the terms of art.14 of the Protocol that the applicable law is not necessarily conclusive on the amount of maintenance. Article 14 directs the forum, even if the applicable law provides otherwise, to take into account in the matter of determining the amount of maintenance the needs of the creditor and the resources of the debtor, as well as any compensation which the creditor was awarded in place of periodical maintenance payments.[126] The Explanatory Report[127] comments that art.14 is "a substantive rule", binding on Contracting States.[128] One consequence is that if the applicable law is that of the forum, the forum may be required to deny its own law.

Intra-UK conflicts

13–36   Article 15 of the Protocol permits multi-legal system Contracting States to opt out of applying the rules of the Protocol to conflicts solely between such different systems. The Maintenance Regulation itself does not contain the customary clause dealing with states with more than one legal system. As and when the Regulation enters into force, secondary legislation will be required in Scotland and England, respectively, to confirm what the position is to be intra-UK. Normally the UK does not take advantage of the opt-out concession for intra-UK conflicts.

Recognition, enforceability and enforcement of decisions

13–37   Chapter IV lays down two different sets of rules, according to whether or not the decision to be recognised and given effect was handed down in a Member State bound by the 2007 Hague Protocol. As stated above, the Protocol was signed and ratified by the EU on April 8, 2010. It was explained in Ch.1 of this book that although the EU's membership of the Hague Conference does not supplant the membership thereof of individual EU Member States, nevertheless by dint of shared competence in projects which fall within the expanding EU remit, participation by individual EU Member States in Hague Conference projects is correspondingly inhibited,[129] because

---

[125] Article 22 of the Maintenance Regulation, in providing that, "[t]he recognition and enforcement of a decision on maintenance under this Regulation shall not in any way imply the recognition of the family relationship, parentage, marriage or affinity underlying the maintenance obligation which gave rise to the decision", is consistent with the attempt to confine the applicable law of maintenance to matters strictly limited thereto. But, on the other hand, see art.23.3, which states that if the outcome of proceedings in a court of a Member State depends on the determination of an incidental question of recognition, the court shall have jurisdiction over that question. Consider *T v L* [2009] I.L.Pr. 5 (Irish Supreme Court). See fn.108, above.

[126] cf. Rome II Regulation recital (33), discussed at para.16–28, below.

[127] *Explanatory Report*, 2009, para.179.

[128] Hence, this type of provision joins the temporarily vanquished menace of "Community public policy" (see para.16–39, below) as a controlling measure by the Community on its Member States of a type or purpose similar to the device of overriding mandatory provisons which a Member State forum must apply to the parties' choice of applicable law.

[129] See para.1–09, above.

each EU Member State, as a result of opting into the European harmonisation scheme, has lost its capacity to act autonomously in any matter concerning judicial co-operation in civil law which falls within EU competence.[130] Conversely, it is not clear whether or not, the EU having ratified the Hague Protocol, EU Member States are thereby bound. The provision of a set of rules in Ch.IV section 2 for Member States not bound by the 2007 Protocol tends to indicate that individual Member States retain some autonomy in the matter and are not bound by the ratification of an instrument by the EU.

Decisions given in a Member State bound by the 2007 Hague Protocol

Chapter IV section 1 of the Maintenance Regulation provides a set of rules **13–38** governing recognition and enforcement where the decision in question was given in a Member State bound by the 2007 Hague Protocol. Such a decision shall be recognised in another Member State without any special procedure being required and without any possibility of opposing its recognition.[131] Such a decision shall be enforceable in another Member State without the need for a declaration of enforceability[132]; for this category of case *exequatur* is abolished. By art.18, protective measures existing under the law of the state of enforcement will attach to such a decision.

The right of the defendant to apply in the court of origin for a review of the decision of that court is set out in art.19. The right to apply for such a review arises[133] where the defendant (a) was not served with the document instituting the proceedings or an equivalent document in sufficient time and in such a way as to enable him to arrange for his defence; or (b) was prevented from contesting the maintenance claim by reason of force majeure or due to extraordinary circumstances without any fault on his part; unless he failed to challenge the decision when it was possible for him to do so. If the court of origin accepts the application for review, the maintenance decision shall be null and void. If, however, the decision is to the opposite effect and the court rejects the application for review, its decision on the matter of maintenance shall remain in force, and will be enforced in another Member State upon production of relevant documents specified in art.20. Article 21 lays down such grounds of refusal or suspension of enforcement under the law of the Member State addressed as are compatible with a system of virtually automatic recognition. These grounds are, first, extinction by the effect of prescription or limitation of action of the right to enforce the maintenance decision,[134] under the law either of the Member State of origin or the Member State of enforcement, whichever limitation period is the longer; secondly, irreconcilability of the decision of the court of origin with a decision given in the Member State of enforcement or with a decision given in another Member State or in a Third State which requires to be recognised by the Member State of enforcement[135];

---

[130] See para.1–09, above.
[131] Maintenance Regulation art.17.1.
[132] Maintenance Regulation art.17.2. See para.9–29, above.
[133] Subject to time limit: art.19.2.
[134] Article 21.2 of the Maintenance Regulation concerns the extinction by prescription of the *decision* of the court of orgin. By contrast art.11(e) of the Hague Protocol assigns prescription and limitation of the maintenance obligation to the scope of its applicable law.
[135] See art.21.2.

and thirdly, where the debtor shows that the substantive decision of the court of origin is subject to review or suspension in the court of origin.[136]

Decisions given in a Member State not bound by the 2007 Hague Protocol

13–39	Chapter IV section 2 of the Maintenance Regulation establishes that in cases concerning decisions on maintenance obligations given in a Member State which is not bound by the 2007 Hague Protocol, the procedures for recognition and declaration of enforceability are modelled on the procedures and the grounds for refusing recognition set out in the Brussels I Regulation.[137] Recital (26) adds that, to accelerate proceedings and enable the creditor to recover his claim quickly, the court seised should be required to give its decision within a set time, unless there are exceptional circumstances.

By art.23, a decision given in a Member State not bound by the 2007 Hague Protocol shall be recognised in another Member State without any special procedure being required. The grounds of refusal of recognition of the maintenance decision, contained in art.24, are the same as those in art.34 of the Brussels I Regulation (based on public policy, natural justice and *res judicata*), with the additional proviso that a decision which modifies an earlier decision on maintenance on the basis of changed circumstances shall not be considered an irreconcilable decision within the meaning of art.24. The significant distinction between Section 1 and Section 2 cases lies in the fact that in respect of the latter a decision given in a Member State not bound by the 2007 Protocol shall be enforceable in another Member State (only) when, on the application of any interested party it has been declared enforceable.[138] Assuming compliance with the formalities required by art.28, the maintenance decision shall be declared enforceable without any review; and this shall be done expeditiously.[139] The maintenance debtor may not make any submissions at this stage. The declaration of enforceability shall be served on the defendant (art.31). The procedures essentially are the same as those set out in Ch.III of the Brussels I Regulation.[140] The decision on the application for a declaration of enforceability may be appealed by either party.[141] The court with which an appeal is lodged shall refuse or revoke a declaration of enforceability only on one of the grounds specified in art.24.[142]

Implementation and administration of the provisions of the Regulation is assisted by a network of central authorities, amongst which cooperation is expected (Ch.VII). Conscious of the practical, as well as legal, difficulties which this subject area entails, the Maintenance Regulation seeks to remove international barriers to the successful recovery of maintenance, making provisions in Ch.V (entitled "Access to Justice"), which are concerned with laying the obligation on Member States to provide legal aid of a level which corresponds at least to that available in an equivalent domestic case.

---

[136] See art.21.3.
[137] See recital (26).
[138] See art.26.
[139] See art.30: within 30 days of the completion of art.28 formalities, barring exceptional circumstances.
[140] See para.9–40, above.
[141] See art.32.
[142] See art.34

In the subject of maintenance, therefore, instead of producing competing instruments, the harmonisation exercises initiated in Europe and at the Hague, respectively, were streamlined, so that the resulting Convention and Protocol are not contradictory, but complementary. The manner in which the Hague and the European projects on the same subject matter have been dovetailed denotes significant progress in the harmonisation of harmonisation efforts themselves. However, some violence has been done to classic conflicts methodology, and even to modern drafting, as a result of the desire to safeguard the interests of the maintenance creditor and to provide for him/her the best of all possible rules and outcome.

B. FINANCIAL PROVISION UPON TERMINATION OF MARRIAGE AND
OTHER ADULT RELATIONSHIPS

Termination of marriage by foreign divorce

Provided that a foreign divorce is recognised in Scotland as valid, any lack **13–40** in the terms of the foreign decree in the matter of property distribution/ financial provision now may be supplied,[143] provided the Scots court has jurisdiction.[144] It was not always so. There used to be a difficulty in that, if a foreign divorce was entitled to recognition in Scotland, the Scots courts could not award financial provision to one of the parties, since *ex hypothesi* the parties were no longer married to each other, and s/he had no title to ask, nor the Scottish/English court any jurisdiction to grant, an order which it thought desirable to append to the foreign decree. The problem was compounded by the proper reluctance of any foreign court otherwise competent to terminate the marriage (in the view of Scots/English law), to make an award in relation to immoveable property outside its territory. Hence, no provision would be made with regard to immoveable property in Scotland or England. As a result, as happened in *Torok v Torok*,[145] an unseemly race to the courthouse door might ensue. Law Commission discussion followed[146] and resulted in the enactment of provisions clothing the Scots and English courts with jurisdiction to make property provision in suitable cases. All were agreed that the rules must be strict, but separate legislative provision within the Matrimonial and Family Proceedings Act 1984 was made for Scotland and England, respectively, with the result that the same end was achieved by different rules. The English provisions are contained in Pt III of the 1984 Act, and the Scottish provisions in Pt IV.

The Scottish Law Commission did not believe that actions for financial provision after foreign divorce would be frequent in Scotland. The Scottish provisions are available after foreign divorce, or annulment,[147] and are

---

[143] Matrimonial and Family Proceedings Act 1984 s.29.
[144] Matrimonial and Family Proceedings Act 1984 s.28.
[145] [1973] 1 W.L.R. 1066.
[146] Law Commission, *Family Law: Financial Relief after Foreign Divorce* (HMSO, 1980), Law Com. Working Paper No.77.
[147] See s.29A, inserted by Family Law (Scotland) Act 1985.

contained in ss.28 and 29, stipulating a number of strict jurisdictional criteria,[148] and additional conditions[149] which must be satisfied before an award may be made.

The jurisdictional criteria are as follows:

"(a) the applicant was domiciled or habitually resident in Scotland on the date when the application was made; and
(b) the other party to the marriage—
  (i) was domiciled or habitually resident in Scotland on the date when the application was made; or
  (ii) was domiciled or habitually resident in Scotland when the parties last lived together as husband and wife; or
  (iii) on the date when the application was made, was an owner or tenant of, or had a beneficial interest in, property in Scotland which had at some time been a matrimonial home of the parties; and
(c) where the court is the sheriff court, either—
  (i) one of the parties was, on the date when the application was made, habitually resident in the sheriffdom; or
  (ii) paragraph (b)(iii) above is satisfied in respect of property wholly or partially within the sheriffdom."

The additional conditions are:

"(a) the divorce falls to be recognised in Scotland;
(b) the other party to the marriage initiated the proceedings for divorce;
(c) the application was made within five years after the date when the divorce took effect;
(d) a court in Scotland would have had jurisdiction to entertain an action for divorce between the parties if such an action had been brought in Scotland immediately before the foreign divorce took effect;
(e) the marriage had a substantial connection with Scotland; and
(f) both parties are living at the time of the application."

The remedy may be sought in the Court of Session or sheriff court.[150] In disposing of an application under s.28, the court shall exercise its powers so as to place the parties, in so far as it is reasonable and practicable to do so, in the financial position in which they would have been if the application had been disposed of, in an action for divorce, etc. in Scotland, on the date on which the foreign divorce took effect. In determining what is reasonable and practicable, the court shall have regard in particular to (a) the parties' resources, present and foreseeable at the date of disposal of the application; and (b) any order made by a foreign court in or in connection with the divorce proceedings for the making of financial provision in whatever form, or the

---

[148] See s.28(2).
[149] See s.28(3).
[150] See s.30.

transfer of property, by one of the parties to the other. Where jurisdiction has been exercised solely on the basis of s.28(2)(b)(iii), the Scottish court's powers are restricted to making an order relating to the former matrimonial home and its contents, or a capital sum not exceeding the value of the defender's interest therein. A rare example in Scots law of the use of these provisions is *Tahir v Tahir*.[151]

For England, the Law Commission preferred a solution which permitted the court, guided by a list of factors, to eliminate cases where an award would be inappropriate. Hence, in England, a party must first seek the leave of the court to apply for financial relief, which leave shall not be granted unless the court thinks there is substantial ground for the making of an application for such an order; further, the leave may be conditional.[152] Under the English rules, parties may apply for financial provision after foreign divorce, annulment or legal separation. A number of cases on the operation of the English provisions can be cited,[153] often to the effect that it is inappropriate to supply the remedy,[154] or that the English court should not interfere where a foreign appropriate forum has made satisfactory provision.[155] Part III of the Act was considered by the UK Supreme Court in *Agbaje v Agbaje*,[156] a case concerning a couple of dual Nigerian and British citizenship. They married in England in 1967, and were divorced in Nigeria in 2005. They had strong connections with England, the five children of the marriage having been born and educated there, and the wife having lived continuously in England since the breakdown of the marriage in 1999. The parties had assets both in Nigeria and England; two houses in London accounted for a large proportion of their wealth. The effect of the Supreme Court order, restoring the award of the High Court, was to supplement the award made to the wife by the Nigerian court by conferring upon her a proportion of the value of the sale price of the UK properties. Lord Collins makes clear that while the factors which an English court must take into account in making or withholding an award have much in common with those which would be relevant in a *forum non conveniens* enquiry, they are not directed to the question of which of two jurisdictions is appropriate, but rather whether the making of an order by an English court would be appropriate

---

[151] *Tahir v Tahir*, 1993 S.L.T. 194; and *Tahir v Tahir (No.2)*, 1995 S.L.T. 451.

[152] 1984 Act s.13.

[153] e.g. *Macaulay v Macaulay* [1991] 1 All E.R. 865; *Chebaro v Chebaro* [1987] Fam. 127; *Garcia v Garcia* [1991] 3 All E.R. 451; *M v M* [1995] 7 C.L. 64; *Jordan v Jordan* [2000] 1 W.L.R. 2010; *Emin v Yeldag* [2002] Fam. Law 419; *A v S (Financial Relief after Overseas US Divorce)* [2002] EWHC 1157 (Fam); *T v M-T* [2005] EWHC 79 (Fam); *Moore v Moore* [2007] I.L.Pr. 36; *Traversa v Freddi (Part III Application following Italian Divorce)* [2009] EWHC 3346 (Fam); and *Agbaje v Agbaje* [2010] 2 All E.R. 877.

[154] *Hewitson v Hewitson* [1995] 1 All E.R. 472: the Court of Appeal held that the purpose of the 1984 Act was to provide a remedy in exceptional cases, where persons divorced in foreign jurisdictions had been deprived of financial relief, which it would be proper for the English court to supply, not to provide financial relief claimed to arise from the status of cohabitation, even if the parties previously had been married. The sequel came before QBD in 1999, reported at [1999] Fam. Law 450, on the matter of alleged promise by the man to maintain the woman, including questions of the evidencing thereof, jurisdiction in which matter the English court yielded to the Californian court of the matrimonial domicile, which had also been the divorce forum, and which had made a clean-break order.

[155] *Holmes v Holmes* [1989] 3 All E.R. 786.

[156] [2010] 2 All E.R. 877.

when, *ex hypothesi*, there have already been proceedings in a foreign country in which financial provision may have been made.[157]

Relationship between maintenance awards and financial provision upon termination of marriage

13–41   In *Agbaje v Agbaje*,[158] Lord Collins issued a warning regarding the relationship between the Brussels regime and the 1984 Act. The Act was introduced as a national measure, in the pre-harmonisation era. The effect of the jurisdiction provisions in the 1984 Act is to render Pts III and IV subject to the Brussels I Regulation and the Lugano Convention.[159] However, his Lordship explained that if an award of maintenance[160] had been made in another EU Member State, the question might arise as to whether the application for financial provision in England under Pt III (or, Scotland under Pt IV) would be precluded on the basis that the issue of maintenance had been determined in the other jurisdiction, that determination being entitled to recognition as an EU judgment. This important point was raised obiter, and no answer given. As of June 18, 2011 (or such later date as the 2007 Hague Maintenance Protocol enters into force),[161] this will create difficulties of ranking of legislative instruments for the UK. It seems that a UK court might properly be inhibited from acting on the basis of the 1984 Act to supplement the award of an EU Member State court, at least where account has been taken in the overseas proceedings of assets in the UK.

Termination of civil partnership by foreign dissolution

13–42   In relation to financial provision available upon the foreign dissolution of a civil partnership, the Civil Partnership Act 2004 provides, in s.125 and Sch.11, that where a civil partnership has been dissolved or annulled abroad, and the dissolution or annulment is entitled to be recognised as valid in Scotland, the Scots court may entertain an application by one of the former civil partners, or former ostensible civil partner, for an order for financial provision. The jurisdictional requirements and conditions clearly are modelled upon those contained in the Matrimonial and Family Proceedings Act 1984 ss.28 and 29. In such a case, the Scots court may make property orders in terms of the provisions of the Civil Partnership Act 2004.[162] As with divorce, after taking jurisdiction in terms of s.125 of the Civil Partnership Act 2004[163] (financial provision after overseas proceedings), the court will apply its own domestic

---

[157] *Agbaje* at [50].
[158] [2010] 2 All E.R. 877.
[159] *Agbaje* [2010] UKSC 13, Lord Collins at [55], makes clear that "maintenance" is within the scope of the Brussels I Regulation (art.5.2), and that "rights in property arising out of a matrimonial relationship" are expressly excluded from the scope thereof. These are autonomous concepts: *De Cavel (No.1)* (143/78) [1979] E.C.R. 1055; *De Cavel (No.2)* (120/79) [1980] E.C.R. 731. The Brussels II *bis* Regulation does not apply to the "property consequences of the marriage or any other ancillary measures" (recital (8)), or to "maintenance obligations" (recital (11)).
[160] *Van den Boogaard v Laumen* (C-220/95) [1997] Q.B. 759.
[161] See para.13–33, above.
[162] See para.13–16, above (civil partnership).
[163] See Sch.11 Pt 3 (disposal of applications).

law, mutatis mutandis. As regards civil partnerships dissolved or annulled in Scotland, there is provision in the 2004 Act in Sch.28 Pt 2 (and s.261), in terms of which the benefits conferred upon married persons by the Family Law (Scotland) Act 1985 are extended, mutatis mutandis, to civil partners. Financial provision on termination of de facto cohabitation otherwise than by death is discussed at paras 13–13—13–14, above.

SUMMARY 13

I. Property of married persons

1. Statutory community of goods

A foreign community of goods may have the same effect as a private marriage **13–43** contract, by creating indefeasible contractual rights in moveable and immoveable property, in the latter case subject to the acquiescence of the *lex situs*.

2. Private marriage contracts

The Rome I Regulation has no application.

The proper law is the law intended by the parties either expressly or by implication and, failing that, the law with which the deed has its closest connection. This law will govern the essential validity of the contract, subject to compliance with (or acquiescence of) the *lex situs* in the case of immoveables.

A private marriage contract is formally valid if it complies with the proper law of the contract, or with the law of the place of execution.

A Scots forum properly seised of a divorce action will apply the provisions of its own domestic law to the distribution of property between the spouses upon termination of marriage, but it is likely that a Scots forum will endeavour to respect the terms of the marriage contract.

3. No marriage contract

The Family Law (Scotland) Act 2006 s.39 has laid down a statutory rule providing applicable law rules in relation to the rights of spouses to each other's immoveable and moveable property arising by virtue of the marriage.

Questions in relation to immoveable property shall be determined by the *lex situs*. Questions in relation to the contents of a matrimonial home shall be determined by the *lex situs* of the home.

Rights of a spouse in the moveable property of the other which arise by virtue of the marriage shall be determined by the law of the common domicile (without specification as to *tempus inspiciendum*); and failing such common domicile, the spouses shall be taken to have the same rights to such property as they had immediately before the marriage.

A change of domicile by one or both spouses shall not affect a right in moveable property which immediately before the change has vested in either spouse.

Section 39 shall not apply to the law on aliment, financial provision on divorce, or transfer of property on divorce or succession; nor shall it apply to the extent that spouses agree otherwise.

II. Property rights arising from other adult relationships

Provision is made in the Family Law (Scotland) Act 2006, to confer upon cohabitants certain rights in property and upon death intestate of a predeceasing cohabitant, exigible where Scots law is the *lex causae*.

III. Maintenance obligations

1. Current position

Jurisdiction of the Scots courts rests upon Regulation 44/2001 arts 2 and 5.2, and otherwise upon the Civil Jurisdiction and Judgments Act 1982 Sch.8, as amended.

Enforcement of orders intra-UK is governed by the Maintenance Orders Act 1950.

The Maintenance Orders (Reciprocal Enforcement) Act 1972, as amended, applies: Pt I to reciprocating countries; Pt II to 1956 New York Convention countries; and Pt III to countries with which the UK has made bilateral arrangements.

Enforcement of orders intra-EU is governed principally by the Brussels I Regulation, subsidiarily by Regulation 805/2004 (enforcement orders for uncontested claims), both subject to the exercise by parties of the option of proceeding under the 1972 Act, if applicable.

2. EU harmonisation programme

Regulation 4/2009 on jurisdiction, applicable law, recognition and enforcement of decisions and cooperation in matters relating to maintenance obligations shall apply from June 18, 2011, provided that the 2007 Hague Protocol on the Law Applicable to Maintenance Obligations is by then in force.

With effect from the entry into force of that Regulation, a Scottish court shall exercise jurisdiction only in accordance with arts 3–8. The applicable law will be identified in terms of art.15, applying the 2007 Hague Protocol.

Recognition and enforcement provisions are similar to those laid down in the Brussels I Regulation.

IV. Financial provision upon termination of marriage and other adult relationships

Matrimonial and Family Proceedings Act 1984 permits a Scots court to make an award of financial provision following recognition of a foreign divorce or nullity.

Section 125 of the Civil Partnership Act 2004 endows the court with an equivalent power in relation to civil partnerships dissolved overseas.

CHAPTER 14

CONFLICT RULES AFFECTING CHILDREN: STATUS, PARENTAL RIGHTS AND RESPONSIBILITIES, ABDUCTION, GUARDIANSHIP AND ADOPTION

I. STATUS

LEGITIMACY

Questions of legitimacy are most likely to arise now in relation to matters of **14–01** testate succession, where the testator's intention must first be ascertained before identification of those who are entitled to succeed.[1]

The status of legitimacy may continue to be relevant in Scots conflict cases, even though in domestic law the Law Reform (Parent and Child) (Scotland) Act 1986 began a process of removing distinctions between children on the basis of having been born within or outside marriage. This process was completed by the Family Law (Scotland) Act 2006, which, by s.21, abolished the status of illegitimacy. Section 21(2)(a)[2] enacts a substitution in the 1986 Act (s.1: legal equality of children), to the following effect:

> "No person whose status is governed by Scots law shall be illegitimate; and accordingly the fact that a person's parents are not or have not been married to each other shall be left out of account in—
> (a) determining the person's legal status; or
> (b) establishing the legal relationship between the person and any other person."

This begs the question of when a person's status is governed by Scots law. There is a mutually dependent relationship between domicile and status in this area, domicile having been ascribed at birth according to status, but (until the advent of the 2006 Act in Scotland, and still in England) the status of the individual was/is required to be identified before domicile could/can be ascribed.[3] Since in terms of s.22 of the 2006 Act, the domicile of a child at birth is

---

[1] See para.18–28, below.

[2] Section 21 is entitled "Abolition of status of illegitimacy".

[3] Domicile depended on legitimacy, but, as domicile determined status, legitimacy depended on domicile. There was, therefore, a problem of circularity of reasoning, which was apparent in theory but seemingly not often encountered in practice. See solutions suggested by Wolff, *Private International Law*, 2nd edn, 1950, p.109, and Anton, *Private International Law*, 1st edn, 1967, pp.345, 346. Leslie, *Stair Memorial Encyclopaedia*, Vol.17, "Private International Law" (Butterworths), para.239 pointed out that whether a posthumous child, or a child whose father is unknown, is legitimate, depended on the content of the mother's domicile on that matter.

ascribed according to the rules contained therein, and not according to status as having been born inside marriage or not, one must conclude that if, in terms of s.22, the child's domicile is Scots, his/her status cannot be one of illegitimacy. But if, by that section, his/her domicile is found to be other than Scots, his/her status must be determined by that other personal law, which may contain a distinction between legitimate and illegitimate.[4]

The Scots conflict rule, traditionally stated, was[5] as follows:

— a child born anywhere of a marriage valid in the view of Scots conflict law is legitimate;

— a child not born of a marriage valid by Scots conflict law[6] is legitimate if he is legitimate by the law of the domicile of each parent at the date of his birth. This rule is subject to the qualification that in the case of intestate succession to immoveables or succession to a title of honour, the child must be legitimate also by the *lex situs* or the law of the title, if such law so requires[7] (that is to say, the requirements of the *lex situs* or the law of the title, whatever they may be, must be satisfied)[8]; and

— in the case of the child of a putative marriage,[9] his/her status will depend upon the law of the domicile of the innocent "spouse"; that is, he/she will be legitimate if that law recognises such marriages, and/or concedes that the issue thereof are legitimate.[10]

The position now falls to be regulated by s.41 ("Effect of parents' marriage in determining status to depend on law of domicile") of the 2006 Act. Section 41 provides that:

"Any question arising as to the effect on a person's status of—
(a) the person's parents being, or having been, married to each other; or

---

[4] Whether the status of illegitimacy by a foreign legal system of a party's personal law would be found to be against Scots public policy would depend upon the matter being capable of being raised in a Scots forum, and upon the context in which the matter arose. The existence of 2006 Act s.41 suggests, however, that a foreign status of illegitimacy, per se, would not offend Scots public policy.

[5] See still for England, *Dicey, Morris and Collins on the Conflict of Laws*, 14th edn, 2006, r.104. Separation of the issue of status from the issue of validity of marriage was a late development in English law and was not seen until *Re Bischoffsheim* [1948] Ch. 79. Children of polygamous marriages were considered legitimate in English law in advance of changes in the law permitting full recognition of the marriages whence they sprang: *Bamgbose v Daniel* [1955] A.C. 107. See *Khoo Hooi Leong v Khoo Hean Kwee* [1926] A.C. 529; *Hashmi v Hashmi* [1971] 3 All E.R. 1253; and *Motala v Att Gen* [1990] 2 F.L.R. 261. See para.11–04, above.

[6] cf., in England, *Azad v Entry Clearance Officer (Dhaka)* [2001] Imm. A.R. 318.

[7] As to succession to, or devolution of, titles, see Legitimation (Scotland) Act 1968 s.8(4) (saving per the Family Law (Scotland) Act 2006 (Commencement, Transitional Provisions and Savings) Order 2006 (SSI 2006/212) art.11); and cf. in England *Re Barony of Moynihan* [2000] 1 F.L.R. 113.

[8] *Birtwhistle v Vardill* (1840) 7 Cl. & F. 895; *Re Don's Estate* (1857) 4 Drewry 194; and *Shedden v Patrick* (1854) 1 Macq. 535 (although this may not be necessary as regards testate succession to land: *Re Grey's Trusts* [1892] 3 Ch. 88).

[9] According to Scots law, one contracted in the bona fide, but erroneous, belief on the part of one or both parties that they are free to marry; the error must be one of fact and not of law (David M. Walker, *Principles of Scottish Private Law*, 4th edn (Oxford: Clarendon, 1988), Vol.1, p.285).

[10] *Smijth v Smijth*, 1918 1 S.L.T. 156.

(b) the person's parents not being, or not having been, married to
each other,

shall be determined by the law of the country in which the person is
domiciled at the time at which the question arises."

It would appear that this provision, though not heralded as a conflict of laws
provision, must represent the current Scots conflict rule. The status of an individual will be referred to his/her domicile, as discovered by reference to s.22
of the 2006 Act and/or common law rules of domicile, and will be determined
by the content of that law. Where the *lex situs* and/or the law of the title
require/s that an heir be legitimate by such laws, the Scots court would give
effect to such requirements, though *ex hypothesi* Scots law could be neither the
lex situs nor the law of the title,[11] and it is difficult to conceive of circumstances when it could be the *lex fori*.

Declarators of status

The Law Reform (Parent and Child) (Scotland) Act 1986 makes provision **14–02**
for declarators of status. By the 2006 Act Sch.2, the declarators which may be
sought, in terms of s.7 of the 1986 Act, in the Court of Session or sheriff court,
are those of "parentage or non-parentage". In domestic Scots law, therefore,
the concept of illegitimacy, and associated terminology, has been removed.

LEGITIMATION

Legitimation is the means by which the status of legitimacy is acquired by an ille **14–03**
gitimate person subsequent to birth. The concept is no longer relevant in Scots
domestic law, but may be relevant where there is a foreign *lex causae*. There are
two principal methods of legitimation. The Scots conflict rules are as follows:

Legitimation by subsequent marriage (*per subsequens matrimonium*)

The conflict rule of Scots common law required capacity in the father so to **14–04**
legitimate the child by the law of the father's domicile only at the date of the
marriage, and not at any earlier date.[12] What mattered therefore was whether the
law of the father's domicile at marriage contained a doctrine of legitimation.[13]

Legitimation was not part of English common law. English domestic law
was opposed to legitimation, cleaving to the doctrine of indelibility of bastardy
and being particularly hostile where the matter concerned succession to
English land. It followed that the English conflict rule was strict. A child
would be regarded as legitimated by the marriage of its parents only if the
father had capacity so to legitimate by the law of his domicile both at the date

---

[11] Given the terms of s.22 of the 2006 Act.
[12] See *Udny v Udny* (1869) M. (H.L.) 89; *Munro v Munro* (1837) 16 S. 18; confirmed on appeal
(1840) 1 Rob. 492 HL; *McDouall v Adair* (1852) 14 D. 525; *Aikman v Aikman* (1859) 21 D.
757; affirmed (1861) 23 D. (H.L.) 3; and *Blair v Kay's Trustees*, 1940 S.L.T. 464.
[13] This was confirmed by the somewhat circuitously worded s.5(2) of the Legitimation (Scotland)
Act 1968. This Act was repealed, subject to savings per the Family Law (Scotland) Act 2006
(Commencement, Transitional Provisions and Savings) Order 2006 (SSI 2006/212) art.11.

of the child's birth and at the date of the subsequent marriage.[14] This rule was altered by the Legitimacy Act 1926, which introduced legitimation into English domestic law by s.1. In terms of s.8, the father need have such capacity by the law of his domicile only at the date of the marriage.[15] The English rules now are contained in the Legitimacy Act 1976 ss.2, 2A and 3.

Legitimation by recognition (*per rescriptum principis*)

14–05   The English common law conflict rule still applies so that a child will be regarded as having been legitimated in this manner only if its father had power so to legitimate him both at the date of the child's birth and at the date of the act of recognition.[16] The Scots conflict rule, less strict, probably is the same as that which obtains in cases of legitimation by subsequent marriage, requiring capacity to legitimate only at the date of the act of recognition.

II. PARENTAL RIGHTS AND RESPONSIBILITIES

14–06   The Borras Report[17] stated that family law, including the law in relation to children, should form part of the project of European legal integration. For many years there has existed a number of international conventions dealing with child matters,[18] including: the 1961 Hague Convention concerning the Powers of Authorities and the Law Applicable in respect of the Protection of Minors (to which the UK is not a party); the 1980 Hague Convention on the Civil Aspects of International Child Abduction[19]; the 1980 Council of Europe Convention on the Recognition and Enforcement of Decisions concerning Custody of Children[20]; and the 1996 Hague Convention on Jurisdiction, Applicable Law, Recognition, Enforcement and Co-operation in respect of Parental Responsibility and Measures for the Protection of Children.[21] Arguably, no European intervention in relation to parental rights and responsibilities would have been necessary had all EU Member States at that time ratified the 1996 Hague Convention, but in September 1995 the Council of Ministers of the EU concluded that it was necessary to make provision for parental responsibility matters, in the form of measures supplementary to those laid down in the 1996 Convention.[22] The only perceived benefit of introducing special EU rules in addition to the Hague rules was that it would fill the gap where any Member State decided not to ratify the 1996 Hague Convention, and also that it would

---

[14] *Re Goodman's Trusts* (1881) L.R. 17 Ch. D. 266.

[15] cf. *Re Askew* [1930] 2 Ch. 259: since English law at the date in question would not have considered the child to be legitimate, the benefit of legitimate status was conveyed to the child through operation of the doctrine of *renvoi*.

[16] *Re Luck's Settlement Trusts* [1940] Ch. 864. See also *Kelly v Marks*, 1974 S.L.T. 118.

[17] Borras, *Explanatory Report on the Convention on Jurisdiction and the Recognition and Enforcement of Judgments in Matrimonial Matters* [1998] OJ C221/27 ("Borras Report").

[18] In *Re G (Children) (Foreign Contact Order: Enforcement)* [2003] EWCA Civ 1607, Thorpe L.J., at [32], described the area as a "treaty jungle". Peter McEleavy, "Luxembourg, Brussels and now The Hague: Congestion in the Promotion of Free Movement in Parental Responsibility" (2010) 59 I.C.L.Q. 505.

[19] See para.14–32, below.

[20] See para.14–31, below.

[21] See para.14–28, below.

[22] Borras Report, para.9.

confer jurisdiction on the European Court of Justice ("CJEU") to interpret the provisions and thereby bring some uniformity of interpretation. The Borras Report concluded in 1998 that the negotiating and drafting work had been laborious, but fruitful[23]: the result was Council Regulation (EC) No.1347/2000 on jurisdiction and the recognition in matrimonial matters and in matters of parental responsibility for children of both spouses,[24] itself succeeded rapidly by Council Regulation (EC) No.2201/2003 concerning jurisdiction and the recognition and enforcement of judgments in matrimonial matters and matters of parental responsibility, repealing Regulation (EC) No.1347/2000.[25]

BACKGROUND

Regulation 1347/2000: Brussels II

Brussels II set out rules for jurisdiction and recognition and enforcement of **14–07** judgments in matrimonial matters and matters of parental responsibility for the children of both spouses rendered on the occasion of the matrimonial proceedings. The instrument, therefore, did not cater for all children, or for all parental responsibility issues. Whilst it covered both biological and adopted children of the couple, it did not provide for the more general concept of "children of the family." It was soon apparent that a further instrument was required, with a wider remit concerning children.

French Access Initiative[26]

In summer 2000, France presented an initiative for a Council Regulation on **14–08** the mutual enforcement of judgments on rights of access to children. The initiative was to facilitate, through the abolition of (*exequatur*) procedural hurdles, the exercise of cross-border rights of access in the case of divorced or separated couples. However, the Justice and Home Affairs Council of the EU considered that work on the French initiative could proceed only in parallel with extension of the scope of Regulation 1347/2000. Therefore the Commission presented in spring 2001 a working document on the mutual recognition of decisions on parental responsibility. Ultimately, Regulation 1347/2000 was repealed by the instrument known as "Brussels II *bis*".

REGULATION 2201/2003: BRUSSELS II BIS

Since March 1, 2005,[27] jurisdiction, recognition and enforcement of **14–09** judgments on parental rights and responsibilities have been governed by

---

[23] Borras Report, para.10.
[24] Regulation 1347/2000 (henceforth "Brussels II").
[25] Regulation 2201/2003 (henceforth "Brussels II *bis*"). See Commission Services in consultation with the European Judicial Network in Civil and Commercial Matters, Practice Guide for the Application of the New Brussels II Regulation (henceforth "Practice Guide").
[26] Initiative of the French Republic with a view to adopting a Council Regulation on the mutual enforcement of judgments on rights of access to children [2000] OJ C234/7.
[27] That is to say, among states which at that date were members of the EU. The Court of Appeal in *AD v CD* [2008] I.L.Pr. 11 held that a Romanian contact order made in October 2006 was unenforceable under Brussels II *bis* because it pre-dated Romania's accession to the EU on January 1, 2007.

Brussels II *bis*.[28] The prime importance of Brussels II *bis quoad* proceedings
relating to children lies in its severing of the link with matrimonial proceedings. Brussels II *bis* covers judgments on parental responsibility over a child,
irrespective of his parents' marital status, thereby ensuring equality of treatment for all children in the matters to which the Regulation pertains. The
objective of Community action[29] in Brussels II *bis* is to protect the child's best
interests, and to give expression to the child's fundamental right to maintain
on a regular basis a personal relationship and direct contact with both parents,
as laid down in art.24 of the Charter of Fundamental Rights of the EU.[30]

Brussels II *bis* lays down rules on jurisdiction (Ch.II), recognition and
enforcement (Ch.III), and co-operation between central authorities (Ch.IV) in
the field of parental responsibility, and contains specific rules on child abduction and access rights.[31] The Regulation applies to all civil matters concerning
the, "attribution, exercise, delegation, restriction or termination of parental
responsibility."[32] The interpretation of "civil matters" arose for decision by the
ECJ in *Proceedings Brought by A*,[33] a case in which a mother, her three children and their stepfather moved from Sweden to Finland in 2005, where they
lived on campsites and with relatives. The children did not attend school. Later
in 2005, the children were taken into care in Finland on the grounds of the
stepfather's violence, and by reason of their abandonment. On application by
the mother for the care order to be lifted, the question of the jurisdiction of the
Finnish court arose, and was referred to the ECJ for a preliminary ruling.
The ECJ held that "civil matters" had to be interpreted autonomously, and to
the effect of including measures which, from the point of view of the national
law of the Member State, fell under public law.[34] Similarly, in *Re C
(Recognition and Enforcement of Decision to Take Child Into Care)*,[35] on a
reference for a preliminary ruling from the Finnish *Korkein Hallinto-Oikeus*,
the ECJ held that a single decision ordering a child to be taken into care and
placed outside his original home in a foster family is covered by the term "civil
matters" for the purposes of that provision, even though that decision was
adopted in the context of public law rules relating to child protection.

In contrast with Brussels II, Brussels II *bis* applies to all decisions on
parental responsibility issued by a court of a Member State. However, the
following matters are not included in the scope of the Regulation: criminal
aspects of child protection; criminal offences committed by children; adoption,
emancipation, the child's names; measures taken as a result of criminal offences
committed by children; and maintenance obligations.[36] The Regulation does

---

[28] Under the Stockholm Programme, the instrument is likely to be subject in 2011 to a revision
exercise: see paras 12–18—12–49.
[29] Imposing "international obligations": *Re S (A Child)* [2009] EWCA Civ 1471.
[30] Brussels II *bis* Proposal Explanatory Memo, p.2.
[31] See arts 1.1(b), 1.2, 2.7.
[32] See art 1.1(b).
[33] (C-523/07) [2009] I.L.Pr. 39.
[34] *Proceedings Brought by A* (C-523/07) [2009] I.L.Pr. 39, summary, [1], [29].
[35] (C-435/06) [2008] I.L.Pr. 1.
[36] See recitals (10), (11), art.1.3. The last is perhaps surprising since maintenance obligations and
parental responsibilities often are dealt with in the same court action (but maintenance obligations currently are covered by Regulation 44/2001 as a civil and commercial matter; see, for the
future, Regulation 4/2009 discussed at paras 13–23—13–39, above).

not apply to general public law issues concerning education, health, immigration or asylum. Nor does it apply, within private law, to paternity issues, since establishing parenthood is thought to be quite different from the matter of attributing parental responsibility.[37]

Mostly parental responsibilities relate to a child's person, but they may relate also to a child's property.[38] It may be necessary to take certain protective measures concerning a child's property, for example to appoint a person or group to assist and represent the child in relation to that property. The Regulation applies to any such protective measure that may be necessary for the administration or sale of the property, e.g. if the child's parents are in dispute about the property. Measures relating to the child's property which are not protective in nature are not covered by the Regulation. Whether or not a measure is protective will be decided on a case-by-case basis.

Parental responsibility

For the purposes of Brussels II *bis*, "parental responsibility" means: **14–10**

".... all rights and duties relating to the person or property of a child which are given to a natural or legal person by judgment, by operation of law or by an agreement having legal effect. The term shall include rights of custody and rights of access."[39]

The list of matters in art.1.2 concerning the attribution, exercise, delegation, restriction or termination of "parental responsibility" is illustrative, not exhaustive. The expression covers not only rights of custody[40] and access,[41] but also matters such as guardianship and the placement of a child in a foster family, or in institutional care (covering cases where a specific matter of parental responsibilities is a "public law" measure).[42] The holder of parental responsibilities may be a natural person, or a legal person. The term parental responsibilities is used in the 1996 Hague Convention (*q.v.*), and the Borras Report says that it has a "degree of unifying potential".[43]

Rules of jurisdiction in Brussels II *bis*

Chapter II s.2 lays down rules of jurisdiction concerning parental responsi- **14–11** bility in respect of all children. The rules listed in arts 8–15 establish a system of grounds of jurisdiction to determine the courts of which Member States are competent. The question which court is competent within a particular Member State (e.g. sheriff court or Court of Session) is answered by domestic procedural rules.[44] The grounds of jurisdiction in matters of parental responsibility

---

[37] See recital (10).
[38] See para.14–68, below.
[39] See art.2.7.
[40] See art.2.9: "Rights of custody" shall include rights and duties relating to the care of the person of a child, and in particular the right to determine the child's place of residence.
[41] See art.2.10: "Rights of access" shall include the right to take a child to a place other than his habitual residence for a limited period of time.
[42] See art.1.2. See para.14–09, above.
[43] Borras Report, para.24.
[44] Practice Guide, p.11. As to intra-UK jurisdiction, see art.66, discussed paras 14–53—14–59.

are said to be shaped in light of the best interests of the child, "in particular the criterion of proximity".[45]

Article 8—general jurisdiction[46]

14–12   "The courts of a Member State shall have jurisdiction in matters of parental responsibility over a child who is habitually resident in that Member State at the time the court is seised."[47]

"The fundamental principle of the Regulation is that the most appropriate forum for matters of parental responsibility is the relevant court of the Member State of the habitual residence of the child".[48] The concept of habitual residence is not defined, but will be determined by the judge in each case on the basis of factual elements, and in light of the objectives and purpose of the instrument. The ECJ in *Proceedings Brought by A*[49] contributed a useful description of habitual residence for the purpose of art.8, viz.:

> "Since Article 8(1) of Regulation No 2201/2003 . . . does not make any express reference to the law of the Member States for the purpose of determining the meaning and scope of the concept of 'habitual residence', the determination of that concept must be made in the light of the context of the provisions and the objective of the regulation, in particular that which is apparent from Recital 12 in the preamble, according to which the grounds of jurisdiction which it establishes are shaped in the light of the best interests of the child, in particular on the criterion of proximity. Thus, in addition to the physical presence of the child in a Member State other factors must be chosen which are capable of showing that that presence is not in any way temporary or intermittent and that the residence of the child reflects some degree of integration in a social and family environment. Therefore, the concept of 'habitual residence' under Article 8(1) of Regulation No 2201/2003 must be interpreted as meaning that it corresponds to the place which reflects some degree of integration by the child in a social and family environment. To that end, in particular the duration, regularity, conditions and reasons for the stay on the territory of a Member State and the family's move to that State, the child's nationality, the place and conditions of attendance at school, linguistic knowledge and the family and social relationships of the child in that State must be taken into consideration. It is for the national court to establish the habitual residence of the child, taking account of all the circumstances specific to each individual case."[50]

---

[45] Recital (12): "This means that jurisdiction should lie in the first place with the Member State of the child's habitual residence, except for certain cases of a change in the child's residence or pursuant to an agreement between the holders of parental responsibility."
[46] Practice Guide, p.12.
[47] See art.8.1.
[48] Practice Guide, p.12.
[49] (C-523/07) [2009] I.L.Pr. 39.
[50] *Proceedings Brought by A* (C-523/07) [2009] I.L.Pr. 39, summary, [2], [3]; also [33], [35], [38], [44].

If the forum decides that it does not have jurisdiction under art.8, it must declare this of its own motion; it is not required to transfer the case to another court.[51]

Once a competent court is seised, in principle it retains jurisdiction even if the child acquires habitual residence in another Member State during the course of the proceedings: an example of the operation of the principle of *perpetuatio fori*. This important principle is effected by art.9. The competence of jurisdiction is determined at the time the court is seised; a change of habitual residence while the action is proceeding does not generally entail a change of jurisdiction.

Article 9—continuing jurisdiction of child's former habitual residence[52]

The Practice Guide made clear that when a child moves from one Member **14–13** State to another, it is often necessary to review access or contact arrangements. Article 9, "encourages the holders of parental responsibility to agree upon the necessary adjustments of access rights before the move."[53] Any person who can no longer exercise access rights (because of the removal of the child to a new habitual residence) can apply for an appropriate adjustment of access rights by the court which granted them (i.e. the former habitual residence of the child) for a period of three months following the move. During this three-month period, the courts of the new Member State do not have jurisdiction in matters of access rights. Article 9 deals only with access rights; it does not apply to other matters of parental responsibility.

For art.9 to apply, the following conditions must be satisfied:

(1) The courts of the Member State of origin must have issued a decision on access rights (otherwise the Member State of the child's new habitual residence would have jurisdiction under art.8);

(2) The removal of the child to the new habitual residence must be lawful (otherwise, see art.10);

(3) It is operative only during the three-month period immediately following the child's physical removal;

(4) The child must have acquired habitual residence in the new Member State during the three-month period (otherwise the Member State of origin would have art.8 jurisdiction);

(5) The holder of the access rights must still be habitually resident in the Member State from which the child was removed (the Member State of origin); and

(6) The holder of the access rights must not have accepted the change of jurisdiction.[54]

Articles 10 and 11—jurisdiction in cases of child abduction; return of the child

These provide special rules requiring closer examination (*q.v.*).[55] **14–14**

---

[51] See art.17. Contrast art.15.
[52] Practice Guide, p.12.
[53] Practice Guide, p.13.
[54] Practice Guide, pp.13, 14.
[55] See paras 14–44—14–52.

Article 12—prorogation of jurisdiction

14–15   This grants very limited scope to seise a court of a Member State in which the child is not habitually resident. The basis of prorogation is that the matter of parental responsibility is connected with a related, pending consistorial proceeding,[56] or that the child has a substantial connection with that Member State.[57] Article 12 covers two quite different situations: art.12.1 and 12.(2) provide for the related consistorial proceedings ground,[58] whereas art.12.3 provides for the substantial connection ground. The reference in art.12.1(b) to the "superior interests of the child" differs from the term "best interests of the child" in art.12.3(b). However, since the non-English versions of the Regulation employ identical wording in both paragraphs, no significance is thought to attach to the difference in wording in the English text.

Parties resident in Third States

14–16   The doubts and controversies which have been seen in relation to the extent of jurisdiction and the reach of the Brussels regime in commercial matters are now visible in the family law arena. In the case of *Re I (A Child) (Contact Application: Jurisdiction)*,[59] the Supreme Court held that nothing in the wording of Brussels II *bis* art.12 (prorogation of jurisdiction) limited the jurisdiction therein conferred to children who were resident in the EU. While this interpretative approach has a familiar European ring to it,[60] support can be gleaned from the wording of art.12.4, which suggests that the article extends to children habitually resident in the territory of a Third State. In the instant case, the requirements of art.12.3 were satisfied: the child could be said to have a substantial connection with the English court since the child was a British national and both parents had been habitually resident in the UK.

On the facts, both parents had accepted the jurisdiction of the English court. On a welfare criterion (art.12.4), the jurisdiction of the English court was in the best interests of the child. It was accepted that the habitual residence of the child was in Pakistan.[61] His parents were divorced in 2003. In 2004 the father received leave of the court to take the child to Pakistan, but agreed to facilitate visits by the child to the UK to see his mother. In 2008 the mother applied in England to enforce and vary the contact order, so as to ensure that the child was in the UK to facilitate contact. The mother had invoked the jurisdiction of

---

[56] See, under Brussels II, *X v Y* [2009] I.L.Pr. 22 *Cour de Cassation* (France).

[57] Practice Guide, p.16. Cf. *C v FC (Brussels II: Freestanding Application for Parental Responsibility)* [2004] 1 F.L.R. 317.

[58] *Re S-R (Contact: Jurisdiction)* [2008] 2 F.L.R. 1741; and *Bush v Bush* [2008] EWCA Civ 865.

[59] [2009] UKSC 10.

[60] cf. *Owusu v Jackson (t/a Villa Holidays Bal Inn Villas)* [2005] Q.B. 801 at [24].

[61] The concern expressed in the Court of Appeal about any possible contradiction of the terms of the 2003 UK-Pakistan Judicial Protocol on Children Matters (*q.v.*) was allayed in the Supreme Court by Lady Hale, *Re I (A Child) (Contact Application: Jurisdiction)* [2009] UKSC 10 at [42]–[44], on the basis that the Protocol was not directly applicable to the case, there having been no abduction or wrongful retention of the child. Moreover, the terms of an agreement between the judiciaries of one Member State and a non-Member State could not affect the proper interpretation of an EU Regulation. See also Council Regulation No.664/2009 establishing a procedure for the negotiation and conclusion of agreements between Member States and third countries concerning jurisdiction, recognition and enforcement of judgments and decisions in matrimonial matters, matters of parental responsibility and matters relating to maintenance obligations, and the law applicable to matters relating to maintenance obligations.

the English court, and the father had accepted it. In Lady Hale's opinion, as a matter of fact, there must be many cases in which consistorial jurisdiction is present under art.3 of Brussels II *bis* (jurisdiction in divorce, etc.) on the basis of the connection of one spouse to the forum, while the other spouse and children are resident outside the EU. Article 12.1 permits the divorce court to exercise jurisdiction in any matter related to parental responsibility, provided that at least one of the spouses has parental responsibility and the jurisdiction of the divorce court has been accepted unequivocally by the spouses at the time the court is seised,[62] and that jurisdiction is in the superior interests of the child. In Lady Hale's view, there was nothing to differentiate art.12.3 from art.12.1; there was nothing to suggest that its provisions be restricted to children residing in a Member State.

Article 13—jurisdiction based on child's presence

If it should be impossible to determine the child's habitual residence, and if **14–17** art.12 does not apply, then art.13 allows a Member State court to decide matters of parental responsibilities in relation to a child who is present in that Member State.[63] This would be capable of applying to refugee and asylum children.[64]

Article 14—residual jurisdiction

If no court has jurisdiction pursuant to arts 8–13, then the Member State **14–18** court may found its jurisdiction on the basis of its own national rules.[65]

Article 15—transfer to a court better placed to hear the case

Exceptionally, a court which is seised of a case (the court of origin) may **14–19** transfer it, in whole or in part, to a court of another Member State if that Member State is "better placed" to hear the case. Once a case has been transferred to the second Member State, it cannot be further transferred to a third Member State (recital (13)). This admission, though tentative, of the principle of judicial discretion, at the heart of a Brussels regime instrument, is worthy of remark. The circumstances in which the discretion may be exercised, and how it shall be done, are set out in art.15.2–15.6.[66]

---

[62] The wording of article 12.3 raises a nice question of interpretation the answer to which did not affect the instant case on the facts. The Justices of the Supreme Court agreed that there might have to be a reference to the CJEU on the question whether the proper interpretation was that there required to be acceptance (by all the parties) of the jurisdiction "at the time the court is seised", or whether acceptance (at any time) of the jurisdiction had to be had of those who were parties to the proceedings at the time the court was seised.

[63] Practice Guide, p.17.

[64] cf. ss.10 and 12 of the Family Law Act 1986, and at common law in Scotland *Oludimu v Oludimu*, 1967 S.L.T. 105.

[65] i.e. Family Law Act 1986 ss.9–18, at paras 14–53—14–59, below. Cf. the operation of the 1973 Act in cases where consistorial jurisdiction cannot be exercised under art.3 of Brussels II *bis*. *Sed contra* Regulation 4/2009 art.6 (subsidiary jurisdiction).

[66] Practice Guide, pp.18–21.See Act of Sederunt (Jurisdiction, Recognition and Enforcement of Judgments in Matrimonial Matters and Matters of Parental Responsibility Rules) 2006 (SSI 2006/397); and, in England, Practice Direction (Family Proceedings: Allocation and Transfer) [2008] 1 W.L.R. 2651; *B v B (Brussels II Revised: Article 15)* [2008] EWHC 2965 (Fam); and *Re H (Abduction)* [2009] EWHC 1735 (Fam).

Conflicting jurisdictions

14–20   Generally, the treatment of allocation of jurisdiction in a case of concurrent proceedings is determined by the *lis pendens* principle.[67] Hence, where proceedings relating to parental responsibility concerning the same child and involving the same cause of action are brought before courts of different Member States, the court second seised shall of its own motion stay its proceedings until such time as the jurisdiction of the court first seised is established.[68]

Provisional, including protective, measures

14–21   In urgent cases, the courts of a Member State may take such provisional, including protective, measures in respect of persons or assets in that state as may be available under the law of that state, even if, under Brussels II *bis*, the court of another Member State has jurisdiction as to the substance of the matter.[69]

In *Proceedings Brought by A*,[70] the ECJ indicated that a protective measure, such as the taking into care of children, may be decided by a national court under art.20 if the following three conditions are satisfied: the measure must be urgent; it must be taken in respect of persons in the Member State concerned; and it must be provisional. The taking of that measure, adopted in the best interests of the child, and its binding nature are determined in accordance with national law. After the protective measure has been taken, the national court is not required to transfer the case to the court of another Member State having jurisdiction. However, since provisional or protective measures are temporary, circumstances related to the physical, psychological and intellectual development of the child may require early intervention by the court having jurisdiction in order for definitive measures to be adopted.

Protective measures shall cease to apply when the court of the Member State having jurisdiction as to substance has taken the measures it considers appropriate.[71]

Choice of law

14–22   Brussels II *bis* does not lay down choice of law rules. If a Scots court exercises jurisdiction over a parental responsibility matter, it will apply the (internal) rules of Scots law.

Recognition and enforcement of judgments

14–23   As in the case of consistorial decrees, mutual recognition is a main objective of Brussels II *bis*. In terms of art.21, a judgment given in a Member State shall be recognised in the other Member States without any special procedure being required. However, any interested party may apply for a decision that the

---

[67] See art.19. See paras 12–14—12–15, above.
[68] See para.12–15 re implications of *Owusu v Jackson (t/a Villa Holidays Bal Inn Villas)* [2005] Q.B. 801.
[69] See art.20; cf. art.31 of the Brussels I Regulation.
[70] (C-523/07) [2009] I.L.Pr. 39; see [47], [56], [59], [64], [65].
[71] See *Re S (Care Proceedings: Jurisdiction)* [2008] EWHC 3013 (Fam); and *Deticek v Sgueglia* Case (C-403/09 PPU) [2010] All E.R. (EC) 313.

judgment be or be not recognised.[72] The grounds of non-recognition of judgments relating to parental responsibility are relatively few. These are contained in art.23. A judgment relating to parental responsibility shall not be recognised:

(a) if such recognition is manifestly contrary to the public policy of the Member State in which recognition is sought taking into account the best interests of the child[73];

(b) if it was given, except in case of urgency, without the child having been given an opportunity to be heard, in violation of fundamental principles of procedure of the Member State in which recognition is sought;

(c) where it was given in default of appearance if the person in default was not served with the document which instituted the proceedings or with an equivalent document in sufficient time and in such a way as to enable that person to arrange for his or her defence unless it is determined that such person has accepted the judgment unequivocally;

(d) on the request of any person claiming that the judgment infringes his or her parental responsibility, if it was given without such person having been given an opportunity to be heard;

(e) if it is irreconcilable with a later judgment relating to parental responsibility given in the Member State in which recognition is sought;

(f) if it is irreconcilable with a later judgment relating to parental responsibility given in another Member State or in the non-Member State of the habitual residence of the child provided that the later judgment fulfils the conditions necessary for its recognition in the Member State in which recognition is sought; or

(g) if the procedure laid down in art.56 (re placement of a child in another Member State) has not been complied with.

The jurisdiction of the court of the Member State of origin may not be reviewed, nor may the test of public policy be applied to the rules relating to jurisdiction.[74]

Enforceability

Article 28: Enforceable judgments

A judgment on the exercise of parental responsibility in respect of a child **14–24** given in a Member State which is enforceable in that Member State and has been served, shall be enforced in another Member State when, on the application of any interested party, it has been declared enforceable there. However, in the United Kingdom, such a judgment shall be enforced in England and

---

[72] This must be read subject to an understanding that the rules governing recognition under Brussels II *bis* admit few opportunities for successful challenge. See *Rinau v Rinau* (C-195/08 PPU) [2008] I.L.Pr. 51.

[73] This "public policy" clause is unusual in the qualification, "taking into account the best interests of the child"; by which law are the best interests of the child to be determined? Presumably this must lie within the discretion of the forum, probably applying its own law.

[74] See art.24.

Wales, in Scotland or in Northern Ireland only when, on the application of any interested party, it has been registered for enforcement in that part of the UK.

Where application for a declaration of enforceability has been made, the court shall give its decision without delay. Submissions by the child, or by the person against whom enforcement is sought, will not be admitted at this stage. The judgment may not be reviewed as to its substance,[75] and the application may be refused only on the ground of one of the reasons specified in arts 22–24. Article 33 sets out the rules for appealing against the decision.[76]

Rights of access

14–25   The 1980 Hague Convention does not guarantee the enforcement of access rights in the same way as it seeks to uphold custody rights, but art.21 of that instrument binds Central Authorities to promote the peaceful enjoyment of access rights and the fulfilment of any conditions to which the exercise of those rights shall be subject. They shall take steps, "to remove, as far as possible, all obstacles to the exercise of such rights".[77] The French Initiative on Rights of Access[78] having expedited agreement on parental responsibilities generally, it is not surprising to find a specific provision (art.48) in Brussels II *bis*, concerned with making practical arrangements for the exercise of rights of access.

International co-operation

14–26   Implementation of Brussels II *bis* is facilitated by the provisions of Ch.IV (co-operation between Central Authorities in matters of parental responsibility).

Disconnection

14–27   Finally, it is necessary to consider the disconnection clause[79] which specifies the relationship of Brussels II *bis* with other cognate instruments, and ranks them inter se. By far the most important point to note is that while Brussels II was subordinate to the 1980 Hague Convention, Brussels II *bis* takes precedence over it.[80]

---

[75] See art.31.

[76] *Re S (A Child) (Enforcement of Foreign Judgment)* [2009] EWCA Civ 993.

[77] See art.21. Cf. *Re J (A Minor) (Abduction: Ward of Court)* [1989] 3 All E.R. 590; *C, Petitioner*, 1997 G.W.D. 23-1132; and *Donofrio v Burrell*, 2000 S.L.T. 1051. See Crawford, "'Habitual Residence of the Child' as the Connecting Factor in Child Abduction Cases" 1992 J.R. 177; and Norrie, "The Hague Convention, Rights of Contact, and s 2(3) and (6) of the Children (Scotland) Act 1995", 1997 S.L.T. (News) 173. Cf. Council of Europe Convention (*q.v.*) art.11: *Joffre v Joffre*, 1992 G.W.D. 27–1522; and *Re H (A Minor) (Foreign Custody Order: Enforcement)* [1994] 1 All E.R. 812. For a UK example, see *Clarke v Clarke*, 1993 G.W.D. 16–1030.

[78] See para.14–08, above.

[79] See arts 59–63, in particular art.60.

[80] By means of the European Communities (Matrimonial and Parental Responsibilities Jurisdiction and Judgments) (Scotland) Regulations 2005 (SSI 2005/42), appropriate amendments have been made to relevant legislation, including in this regard the Child Abduction and Custody Act 1985, the Family Law Act 1986, and the Children (Scotland) Act 1995. The purpose of the secondary legislation is to ensure that domestic legislation complies with Brussels II *bis*, to the effect that: the 1985 Act will operate so as to give precedence to relevant provisions of the Regulation over those of the 1980 Hague Convention; the 1995 Act will operate subject to the rules of jurisdiction contained in the Regulation; and under the 1986 Act, it is possible for a Scots court to sist an action when transferring jurisdiction to the court of another Member State under art.15 of Brussels II *bis*.

This means that where child abduction matters arise under international instruments, the rules of the 1980 Hague Convention are subject to the overriding direction of Brussels II *bis* in a qualifying case.[81]

1996 HAGUE CONVENTION

A further development in this area of the conflict of laws is the 1996 Hague **14–28** Convention on Jurisdiction, Applicable Law, Recognition, Enforcement and Co-operation in respect of Parental Responsibility and Measures for the Protection of Children. The 1996 Convention was signed on April 1, 2003 by the then 14 EU Member States. No further steps were taken for several years regarding ratification of the Convention,[82] but in June 2008, the EU Council adopted a decision authorising certain EU Member States to ratify or accede to the Convention.[83] In consequence, in the UK, there has been introduced the European Communities (Definition of Treaties) (1996 Hague Convention on Protection of Children etc.) Order 2010,[84] having the effect of rendering the Convention an EU Treaty, and enabling secondary legislation to be put in place in Scotland and England implementing all aspects of the Convention. For ratification to proceed, all EU Member States require to be ready to proceed *en bloc*. The projected timetable for ratification of the Convention is such that it may enter in force in the UK by the end of 2010.[85]

It is hoped that the Convention will make a valuable contribution to the protection of children in parental responsibility and child protection cases that transcend the boundaries of Europe, and will complement Community rules. Its quadruple nature as a conflict of laws instrument is notable.

One of the great merits of the Convention is its comprehensive scope in terms of subject matter, applying equally to the protection of a child's person and property. It applies to all children, from birth to 18 years, and deals with both public law and private law matters, where these are not expressly excluded from the Convention as having been covered already by other Hague Conventions. The Convention is limited to matters of child protection or child law matters, and does not cover matters of general application having some tangential child law implications which have their own private international law rules.

The provisions on jurisdiction and recognition and enforcement of judgments concerning parental responsibility are similar in design and content to those in Brussels II *bis*. The main ground of jurisdiction under the 1996 Convention is the Contracting State of the habitual residence of the child (art.5), and there are various subsidiary bases of jurisdiction (arts 7–14).

Unlike Brussels II *bis*, the 1996 Hague Convention lays down rules concerning applicable law (arts 15–22), the general rule being that the *lex fori* shall apply.

---

[81] i.e. abduction of a child from one EU Member State to another EU Member State, both of which are parties to the 1980 Hague Convention. See paras 14–44—14–45, below.

[82] Essentially due to political conflict over the position of Gibraltar.

[83] Justice and Home Affairs Council, *EU Council Factsheet: Decisions in Civil Law Matters*, June 6, 2008.

[84] European Communities (Definition of Treaties) (1996 Hague Convention on Protection of Children etc.) Order 2010 (SI 2010/232).

[85] House of Lords Grand Committee, per Lord Bach (December 15, 2009: Columns GC124–GC128).

Article 61 of Brussels II *bis* ranks that Regulation above the relevant provisions of the 1996 Convention where the child is habitually resident in an EU Member State.

III. INTERNATIONAL CHILD ABDUCTION

HISTORICAL BACKGROUND

14–29 At common law in Scotland questions of custody[86] were regarded as pertaining to status. Accordingly, the court of the father's domicile was regarded as the court of pre-eminently suitable jurisdiction,[87] and a Scots court would consider itself clothed with jurisdiction on this ground. There was also an emergency jurisdiction if the child was resident in Scotland and the protection of the court was needed in the interests of the child.[88] Likewise, custody orders made by the court of the father's domicile were accorded the greatest respect.[89] As time passed, this was tempered by an appreciation that the Scots court, in granting a custody order or withholding recognition of a foreign custody order, should regard as paramount the best interests of the child, and should be sensitive also to the need to return the child to the "natural" forum, if foreign, there to have the substantive custody issue determined.[90] This remains the approach of the Scots court in its treatment of incoming common law cases of alleged child abduction.[91]

In England the custody jurisdiction was regarded as a manifestation of the protection afforded by the state to its residents, or alternatively by the national law in exchange for the allegiance of its nationals. To this was added a measure of judicial discretion.[92] Moreover, the English courts were doubtful about the suitability of domicile as a connecting factor in these cases given that the determination of domicile is not a speedy exercise.[93] In the matter of recognition, as the law developed, the English courts too displayed great concern for the best interests of the child in preference to adherence to a rigid rule of recognition.[94] As between the courts of the neighbouring UK legal systems, it

---

[86] The terminology has changed. For English law, see the Children Act 1989. For Scotland, the Children (Scotland) Act 1995 replaced "custody" and "access" with "residence" and "contact"; the current language speaks of "parental responsibilities" and "parental rights". In the context of intra-UK custody matters, strictly one should speak of a "Part 1 Order" (under Family Law Act 1986 Pt 1).

[87] Hence the Scots court would consider itself of pre-eminent jurisdiction if the father was of Scots domicile: *Ponder v Ponder*, 1932 S.C. 233; *McLean v McLean*, 1947 S.C. 79; *Re B's Settlement* [1940] Ch. 54; *Brown v Brown*, 1948 S.L.T. 129; *Babington v Babington*, 1955 S.C. 115; *Kitson v Kitson*, 1945 S.C. 434; *McShane v McShane*, 1962 S.L.T. 221; and *Shanks v Shanks*, 1965 S.L.T. 330. Crawford, "International Child Abduction" (1990) 35 J.L.S.S. 277.

[88] *Oludimu*, 1967 S.L.T. 105.

[89] *Westergaard v Westergaard*, 1914 S.C. 977; *Radoyevitch v Radoyevitch*, 1930 S.C. 619.

[90] *McKee v McKee* [1951] A.C. 352; *Battaglia v Battaglia*, 1967 S.L.T. 49; *Sargeant v Sargeant*, 1973 S.L.T. (Notes) 27; *Kelly v Marks*, 1974 S.L.T. 118; *Lyndon v Lyndon*, 1978 S.L.T. (Notes) 7; *Campbell v Campbell*, 1977 S.L.T. 125; and *Thomson, Petitioner*, 1980 S.L.T. (Notes) 29.

[91] See para.14–63, below.

[92] *Re Kermot (An Infant)* [1965] Ch. 217; *Re P (GE) (An Infant)* [1965] Ch. 568; *Re H (Infants) (No.1)* [1966] 1 All E.R. 886; *Re E (D) (An Infant)* [1967] Ch. 287; *Re T (Infants)* [1968] Ch. 704; *Re A (Infants)* [1970] Ch. 665; and *Fabbri v Fabbri (No.1)* [1962] 1 All E.R. 35.

[93] See, e.g. *Re P (GE) (An Infant)* [1964] 3 All E.R. 977, per Lord Denning at 980, 981.

[94] *McKee* [1951] A.C. 352; *J v C* [1970] A.C. 668.

was said that neither system was avid of jurisdiction,[95] but there is no doubt that in this area of the conflict of laws there was a degree of friction.[96]

CURRENT RULES

International child abduction disputes now fall into three categories: **14–30**

(1) cases regulated by international instrument;
(2) intra-UK cases; and
(3) cases governed by common law rules.

The rules to be applied will depend largely on the identity of the country(ies) to/in and from which the child has been wrongfully removed or retained. In the context of the international instruments, not only must the circumstances fall within those covered by the particular instrument, but the date of the circumstances must post-date the coming into effect of the instrument in the relevant country(ies).[97]

CASES REGULATED BY INTERNATIONAL INSTRUMENT

Cases falling under the 1980 Hague Convention and/or the Council of Europe Convention and/or Brussels II *bis*

The 1980 Hague Convention on the Civil Aspects of International Child **14–31** Abduction,[98] and the 1980 Council of Europe Convention on Recognition and Enforcement of Decisions concerning Custody of Children and on the Restoration of Custody of Children[99] brought about great change in the civil law governing cross-border child abduction cases. The United Kingdom became party to both Conventions by virtue of the Child Abduction and Custody Act 1985. Part 1, Sch.1 to the Act implements the Hague Convention, and Pt 2, Sch.2 implements the Council of Europe Convention.

A number of countries are party to both Conventions, and if a case is capable of falling under both instruments, a litigant may choose which to invoke. Of the two, the Hague Convention is by far the more prominent.[100]

---

[95] *Re B's Settlement* [1940] Ch. 54; *Re X's Settlement* [1945] Ch. 44.

[96] e.g. *Davidson v Davidson*, 1997 G.W.D. 2-39.

[97] *Kilgour v Kilgour*, 1987 S.L.T. 568.

[98] Convention on the Civil Aspects of International Child Abduction, signed at The Hague on October 25, 1980.

[99] Convention on Recognition and Enforcement of Decisions concerning Custody of Children and on the Restoration of Custody of Children, signed by the UK and several other states (including all the other EC countries except Denmark) at Luxembourg on May 20, 1980 (sometimes called the European or Luxembourg Convention). The instrument played a useful, but subsidiary role in securing the recognition and enforcement of "custody decisions" among signatory states.

[100] Both Conventions apply to persons under 16, but the Hague Convention seeks to uphold custody rights (whether or not there has been a "custody order"), where there has been wrongful removal of a child habitually resident in a Contracting State from the legal system of his habitual residence, or wrongful retention of him outside the legal system, whereas the Council of Europe Convention is concerned with registration and enforcement of custody decisions. Under the Council of Europe Convention, a decision will be denied recognition only on

Importantly, however, both instruments now are subject to the overriding authority of Brussels II *bis* in a qualifying EU case.[101] While the Hague Convention continues to have a very important role, and is discussed in detail in this chapter, the same cannot be said of the Council of Europe Convention. Before the coming into effect of Brussels II *bis* (and its predecessor, Brussels II), the Council of Europe Convention had received substantial support from European states, but in terms of art.60 of Brussels II *bis*, the Council of Europe Convention has been subordinated to that European Regulation.[102] The already minor contribution made by the Council of Europe Convention has been reduced further by reason of the fact that Brussels II *bis*, in its application to parental responsibility matters, principally is concerned with recognition and enforcement of parental responsibility orders emanating from EU Member States. That being so, the Council of Europe Convention's ambit of operation has been limited, first, geographically, to those signatory states which are not currently EU Member States; and secondly, by reason of subject matter (custody decisions), where for some reason it was thought necessary, or advantageous, to use the European Convention rather than the 1980 Hague Convention. Since usage of the European Convention now is so rare, its detail is not recounted in this chapter, and reference should be made to the second edition of this book

Substance of the 1980 Hague Convention

14–32   By s.4 of the Child Abduction and Custody Act 1985, the courts having jurisdiction to entertain applications under the 1980 Hague Convention shall be, in Scotland, the Court of Session, and in England and Wales, or in Northern Ireland, the High Court.

The following provisions of the Convention are of prime importance[103]:

Article 3

14–33   The removal or the retention of a child is to be considered wrongful where:

---

one or more of certain stated grounds, relating to jurisdiction, natural justice, or welfare of the child. The assumption is that a custody decision given in one Contracting State should be recognised and enforced in all others. The grounds under the Hague Convention for refusing to return the child are narrower than are those available under the Council of Europe Convention to refuse recognition and enforcement of the foreign decision. See on conflict between the Conventions: *Re S (A Minor) (Custody: Habitual Residence)* [1997] 4 All E.R. 251 (Hague and Europe); *Re R* [1997] 1 F.L.R. 673 (Hague (Child's Views)) and Council of Europe Convention (A 10(1)(b)). A case illustrating conflict within the operation of one Convention is *Re O (Child Abduction: Re Abduction)* [1997] 2 F.L.R. 712. I.L.S. Balfour and E.B. Crawford, "The Hague Convention on International Child Abduction: Recent Scottish Cases" (1996) S.L.P.Q. 411.

[101] Brussels II *bis* art.60. See *Proceedings Brought by Rinau* (C-195/08 PPU) [2008] I.L.Pr. 51; and paras 14–44—14–52, below.

[102] *Re G (Children) (Foreign Contact Order: Enforcement)* [2004] 1 W.L.R.521. Proceedings to enforce a foreign contact order under the European Convention were a nullity because the foreign order fell within the remit of the Brussels II Regulation (Regulation 1347/2000), which took precedence.

[103] These footnotes contain many important authorities, but the body of case law grows daily. Reference may be made to *http://www.incadat.com* [Accessed June 24, 2010] (the international child abduction database).

(a) it is in breach of rights of custody[104] attributed to a person,[105] an institution[106] or any other body, either jointly or alone, under the law of the state in which the child was habitually resident immediately before the removal or retention[107]; and

(b) at the time of removal or retention those rights were actually exercised,[108] either jointly or alone, or would have been so exercised but for the removal or retention.

Wrongful removal[109] and retention[110]

The removal or retention of a child is wrongful, therefore, where it is in breach of custody rights attributed to any person(s) under the law of the state in which the child was habitually resident. In *Perrin v Perrin*,[111] it was held that the determination of wrongfulness means something less than a full legal determination of the custodial rights of the parents and whether they have been breached.[112] Wrongful retention is quite distinct from wrongful removal; the concepts are mutually exclusive, and a child can be wrongfully retained only if he has first been lawfully removed.[113] In *Findlay v Findlay (No. 2)*,[114] the court made clear that removal and retention, respectively, are events which occur on a specific date, and refer to the removal or retention of a child from the state in which he is habitually resident. Importantly, retention is not to be regarded as a continuing state of affairs begun on a particular day and continuing from day to day thereafter. It is necessary to establish the date of retention in order to fix the *terminus a quo* for the running of the one-year period under art.12.[115]

14–34

---

[104] See art.5.1.

[105] This could include, e.g. grandparents. See *Re O (A minor) (Child Abduction: Custody Rights), The Times*, June 24, 1997, per Cazalet J. In Scotland grandparents may seek a parental responsibilities and rights order under the Children (Scotland) Act 1995 s.11; see also *Re D (A Minor) (Contact: Interim Order)* [1995] 1 F.L.R. 495 CA.

[106] e.g. *Z, Petitioner*, 2010 S.L.T. 285. In the view of the Scots court, the claim by a Dutch public authority that it had rights of custody in terms of art.3 was not sufficiently made out. The Dutch court order allegedly conferring custody rights on the authority appeared to provide provisional guardianship rights, but the degree of specification of the nature and time limit of the powers was lacking.

[107] *Cameron v Cameron (No.1)*, 1996 S.L.T. 306; *Moran v Moran*, 1997 S.L.T. 541; *Watson v Jamieson*, 1998 S.L.T. 180.

[108] *Urness v Minto*, 1994 S.L.T. 988. See also *AJ v FJ* Unreported April 29, 2005 IH, Second Division.

[109] *Taylor v Ford*, 1993 S.L.T. 654; *McCarthy v McCarthy*, 1994 S.L.T. 743; *Perrin v Perrin*, 1995 S.L.T. 81; *Seroka v Bellah*, 1995 S.L.T 204; *Hunter v Murrow* [2005] EWCA Civ 976.

[110] *Findlay v Findlay (No.1)*, 1994 S.L.T. 709; *Findlay v Findlay (No.2)*, 1995 S.L.T. 492; *M, Petitioner*, 2000 G.W.D. 32-1242; and *Re H (Minors) (Abduction: Custody Rights)* [1991] 3 All E.R. 230.

[111] 1995 S.L.T. 81.

[112] Lord Murray was entitled to conclude that the removal was wrongful; a letter from the French Ministry of Justice stated it was wrongful as in breach of art.372 of the French Civil Code, which awarded both parents joint custody.

[113] *McCarthy*, 1994 S.L.T. 743; *Findlay (No.1)*, 1994 S.L.T. 709.

[114] 1995 S.L.T. 492.

[115] *Re H (Minors) (Abduction: Custody Rights)* [1991] 3 All E.R. 230.

Rights of custody

14–35   The rights of custody mentioned in subpara.(a) above may arise by operation of law[116] or by reason of a judicial or administrative decision, or by reason
of an agreement having legal effect under the law of that state.[117]

The Family Division of the English High Court held, in *A v H*,[118] that art.3
is not exhaustive of how rights of custody may arise. In *A v B (Abduction:
Rights of Custody: Declaration of Wrongful Removal)*,[119] the Family Division
has held that the court itself and the father had rights of custody sufficient for
the purposes of art.3 where hours before the departure of the mother and child
from the English jurisdiction the father had obtained an ex parte order granting
him parental responsibility, and prohibiting the mother from removing the
child from the jurisdiction. The court took the view that while the mother's
ignorance of the existence of the order meant that her actings in removing
herself and the child from the jurisdiction did not amount to contempt of court,
the mere making of the ex parte order constituted the conferral of rights of
custody despite the fact that it had not been served on the mother.

A question arises as to the meaning of "law" in the context of art.3. As
explained in Ch.5 of this book, it is a rule of Hague Convention drafting that
"law" includes rules of private international law and that reference to "law" is
to internal rules, only if that is explicitly stated. The Peréz-Vera Report on the
1980 Hague Abduction Convention emphasised that the applicable law
includes rules of private international law, so as to expand the potential reach
of the Convention. This opens the door to *renvoi* reasoning in child abduction
cases, as was seen in *Re JB (Child Abduction: Rights of Custody: Spain)*[120] in
which the English court, in referring to "Spanish law" as the law of the
habitual residence of the child in the matter of the existence or not of custody
rights, accepted a referral back to English law qua law of the nationality, with
the effect that the unmarried, bereft father, had no parental rights such as to

---

[116] Of the habitual residence of the child, as proved to the court: *Re D (A Child) (Abduction: Rights
of Custody)* [2007] 1 A.C. 619.
[117] *Findlay (No.1)*, 1994 S.L.T. 709; *Findlay (No.2)*, 1995 S.L.T. 492; *Perrin*, 1995 S.L.T. 81;
Seroka v Bellah, 1995 S.L.T. 204; *Bordera v Bordera*, 1995 S.L.T. 1176; *McKiver v McKiver*,
1995 S.L.T. 790; *Urness v Minto*, 1994 S.L.T. 988; *Zenel v Haddow*, 1993 S.L.T. 975; *Taylor
v Ford*, 1993 S.L.T. 654; *McCarthy v McCarthy*, 1994 S.L.T. 743; *Dickson v Dickson*, 1990
S.C.L.R. 693; *Cameron (No.1)*, 1996 S.L.T. 306; *Moran*, 1997 S.L.T. 541; *Pirrie v Sawacki*,
1997 S.L.T. 1160; *Re S (A Minor) (Custody: Habitual Residence)* [1997] 4 All E.R. 251 HL;
Fourman v Fourman, 1998 G.W.D. 32-1638; *Re H (A Minor) (Abduction: Rights of Custody)*
[2000] 2 All E.R. 1 HL; *Re G (Abduction: Rights of Custody)* [2002] 2 F.L.R. 703; *Re P
(A Child) (Abduction: Acquiescence)* [2004] 2 F.L.R. 1057; *Re D (A Child) (Abduction:
Custody Rights)* [2007] 1 A.C. 619; *F v B-F* [2008] EWHC 272 (Fam); *A v B (Abduction:
Rights of Custody: Declaration of Wrongful Removal)* [2008] EWHC 2524 (Fam); *A v H*
[2009] 4 All E.R. 641; *Re K (Children) (Rights of Custody: Spain)* [2009] EWCA Civ 986; and
Z, Petitioner, 2010 S.L.T. 285.
[118] *A v H* [2009] 4 All E.R. 641. The case involved an investigation into the status of an alleged
marriage between the parties, which resulted in a finding by the court that the relationship
between the child's parents was a "non-marriage", rendering the father an unmarried father
with attendant consequences in domestic English law in the matter of parental rights and
responsibilities.
[119] [2008] EWHC 2524 (Fam).
[120] [2004] 1 F.L.R. 796, discussed by K. Beevers and J. Perez Milla, "'Convention Rights of
Custody'—Who Decides? An Anglo-Spanish Perspective" (2007) 3 J. Priv. Int. L.201.

justify a petition for return of the child under the 1980 Hague Convention on the grounds of wrongful removal. So too in *Re K (Children) (Rights of Custody: Spain)*,[121] the English judge at first instance, following the same approach, found himself required to take a view on the content of Spanish law, as between the conflicting expert evidence produced by the contending parents. The investigation of Spanish law in this case went a stage further than that seen in *Re JB*. While it was accepted that Spanish law would refer the matter to the law of England qua nationality, it was contended successfully by the father that the result of application of English law, in depriving an unmarried father of parental responsibility and in attributing custody to the mother without taking into account the children's welfare interests, would be contrary to the public policy of Spain. This statement of Spanish law was accepted, and the Court of Appeal made no criticism of the judge's treatment of proof of foreign law. On the facts, removal of the child by the mother was, therefore, by circuitous reasoning, in breach of the father's rights of custody under art.5.

Habitual residence of the child

This connecting factor has been discussed in detail in Ch.6. In recent years, **14–36** one of the most prominent manifestations of the use of the factor has been in international child abduction cases under the Hague Convention.[122] The factor is in a state of constant refinement in the light of circumstances presenting. In *Re P-J (Children)*[123] certain principles were put forward by the Court of Appeal as "established", viz.:

(a) the expression "habitually resident" is not to be treated as a term of art with some special meaning, but is to be understood according to the ordinary and natural meaning of the two words which it contains;

(b) "habitual residence" and "ordinary residence" are interchangeable concepts.and there is no difference in the core meaning to be given to the two phrases;

(c) there is a distinction to be made between being settled in a new place or country, and being resident there for a settled purpose which might be fulfilled by meeting a purpose of short duration or one conditional upon future events; and

(d) whether or not a person is or is not habitually resident in a specified country is a question of fact to be decided by reference to all the circumstances of the particular case.

---

[121] [2009] EWCA Civ 986.

[122] e.g. *Robertson v Robertson*, 1988 S.L.T. 468; *Dickson v Dickson*, 1990 S.C.L.R. 692; *Cameron (No.1)*, 1996 S.L.T. 306; *Cameron v Cameron (No.2)*, 1997 S.L.T. 206; *Watson v Jamieson*, 1998 S.L.T. 180; *D v D*, 2001 S.L.T. 1104; *Al-H v F* [2001] EWCA Civ 186; *W v H (Child Abduction: Surrogacy)* [2002] 1 F.L.R. 1008; *W, Petitioner*, 2003 G.W.D. 28-772; *M, Petitioner*, 2005 S.L.T. 2; *Re F (Abduction: Unborn Child)* [2006] EWHC 2199 (Fam); *Re ML and AL (Children) (Contact Order: Brussels II Regulation) (No.1)* [2006] EWHC 2385 (Fam); *A v N*, 2007 G.W.D. 01-02; *B v D* [2008] EWHC 1246 (Fam); *Re P-J (Children) (Abduction: Habitual Residence: Consent)* [2009] EWCA Civ 588; *Re S (A Child) (Habitual Residence)* [2009] EWCA Civ 1021; and *Proceedings Brought by A* (C-523/07) [2009] I.L.Pr. 39.

[123] *Re P-J (Children) (Abduction: Habitual Residence: Consent)* [2009] EWCA Civ 588.

While it may be recognised that these principles, under exception perhaps of (c), have become generally accepted, or truisms, the exigencies of cases demand that they be mapped on to complex domestic living "patterns", those patterns possibly inadequately vouched by evidence. Moreover, habitual residence decisions, like domicile cases, are particular to their facts, even assuming that these facts can be established. Thus the decision by the Court of Appeal in *Re S*,[124] that habitual residence in England had been established after residence in the jurisdiction by the child's family for only seven or eight weeks, combined with some evidence of intention at the outset to remain, was said to be justified on its facts (though finely balanced), but must be confined to the particular circumstances of the case, and not elevated to a statement of general principle. Despite the assertion that the factor is a common sense one, it should never be thought that the judicial resolution of the point will be predictable.

It was established early[125] in the *corpus* of case law interpretative of the Convention that it should not be possible for a parent to effect a change in the habitual residence of a child through unilateral wrongful actings, that is to say, although as a matter of fact, the child might be residing in the legal system to which he had been removed, in law his habitual residence remained the legal system from which he had been taken.[126] This principle was reiterated in *B v D*,[127] in the form that no unilateral action by a parent can change a child's habitual residence except by agreement or acquiescence over time by the bereft parent, or by judicial determination. Further support is provided by Lord Glennie in *A v N*.[128]

The application of these rules to unborn children arose in *Re F (Abduction: Unborn Child)*,[129] in which the parents of the child in question had lived together in Wales before the mother, while pregnant with the child, left Wales in order to live in Israel, it being alleged by the father that there was an agreement between them that the mother would return in due course to live in Wales. The child was born in Israel. Although the child had never lived in Wales, it was argued, in abduction proceedings brought by the father, that England and Wales was the child's habitual residence, because she had been wrongly retained in Israel from the date when the mother (in the father's view) reneged on the agreement to return to the UK. These facts present a further challenge to the meaning in law of habitual residence. Hedley J. held that habitual residence requires some degree of physical presence; there was no wrongful retention within art.3, for it was not possible in law to abduct a foetus.[130]

---

[124] *Re S (A Child) (Habitual Residence)* [2009] EWCA Civ 1021. See also *Re P-J (Children) (Abduction: Habitual Residence: Consent)* [2009] EWCA Civ 588.

[125] *Re J (A Minor) (Abduction: Custody Rights)* [1990] 2 A.C. 562; in the House of Lords sub nom. *C v S* [1990] 2 All E.R. 961; and *Re P (GE) (An Infant)* [1965] Ch. 568.

[126] *B v D* [2008] EWHC 1246 (Fam).Though see para.6–45, above re habitual residence initially brought about by coercion of any kind; and para.14–12 re *perpetuatio fori* under Brussels II *bis*.

[127] cf. *Re ML and AL (Children) (Contact Order: Brussels II Regulation) (No.1)* [2006] EWHC 2385 (Fam).

[128] 2007 G.W.D. 01-02.

[129] [2006] EWHC 2199 (Fam).

[130] *W v H (Child Abduction: Surrogacy)* [2002] 1 F.L.R. 1008.

Article 12

Where a child has been wrongfully removed or retained in terms of art.3 **14–37**
and, at the date of the commencement of the proceedings before the judicial or
administrative authority of the Contracting State where the child is, a period of
less than one year has elapsed from the date of the wrongful removal
or retention, the authority concerned shall order the return[131] of the child
forthwith.[132]

The judicial or administrative authority, even where the proceedings have
been commenced after the expiration of the period of one year referred to in
the preceding paragraph, shall also order the return of the child, unless it is
demonstrated that the child is now settled in its new environment.

Where the judicial or administrative authority in the requested state has
reason to believe that the child has been taken to another state, it may stay the
proceedings or dismiss the application for the return of the child.

Settlement of the child

With regard to settlement, each case must be considered on its own facts.[133] **14–38**
The court must look for physical, emotional and psychological stability and
security of a non-transient nature likely to continue into the future. This will
include consideration of home, school, friends, activities, and opportunities,
and need not be wholly associated with the children's relationship with the
abducting parent.[134] The Family Division in *Re E (Abduction: Intolerable
Situation)*[135] held that a child had settled physically and emotionally in the
UK, clear evidence being given of his integration into family and school life,
despite the fact that he and his mother were overstayers in the UK, of insecure
immigration status.

Article 12 was the subject of detailed examination by the House of Lords in
Re M (Children) (Abduction: Rights of Custody).[136] The circumstances
afforded an opportunity for the House to scrutinise the operation of art.12, in
particular, the question whether, and if so under what authority (Convention or
otherwise), and in accordance with what principles, there is a discretion to
return the children to their habitual residence, if it be established that they are
settled in the new jurisdiction. The majority (Lord Rodger of Earlsferry
dissenting) held that once a child has become settled for the purposes of art.12
the court retains a discretion to return him within the Convention procedures.[137] Thereafter, the Convention discretion is "at large" and the court
is entitled to take into account the various aspects of Convention policy

---

[131] That is to say, return to the jurisdiction of the child's habitual residence, not to the custody of
the other parent; *Findlay (No.1)*, 1994 S.L.T. 709 and *Findlay (No.2)*,1995 S.L.T. 492.
[132] See *Re S (Minors) (Child Abduction; Wrongful Retention)* [1994] 1 All E.R. 237, per Wall J.
at 249.
[133] e.g. *Re F v M (Abduction: Acquiescence: Settlement)* [2008] EWHC 1525 (Fam); *C v C*, 2008
S.C. 571; *Perrin*, 1995 S.L.T. 81; *Soucie v Soucie*, 1995 S.L.T. 414; *O'Connor v O'Connor*,
1995 G.W.D. 3-113; and *Cannon v Cannon* [2004] EWCA Civ 1330 (concealment of child),
and *Re C (A Child) (Abduction: Settlement)* [2006] EWHC 1229 (Fam).
[134] *Re H (Children)* Unreported February 27, 2010.
[135] [2008] EWHC 2112 (Fam).
[136] [2008] 1 A.C. 1288.
[137] *Re M (Children) (Abduction: Rights of Custody)* [2008] 1 A.C. 1288, per Lady Hale of
Richmond at [29]–[31].

alongside the circumstances which gave the court a discretion in the first place, and the wider considerations of the child's rights and welfare.[138]

Lady Hale indicated,[139] that:

> ". . . a view has crept in that 'exceptional' is not merely a description, to be applied to the small number of exceptions in which the court has power to refuse to order a return, but also an additional test to be applied, after a ground of opposition has been made out, to the exercise of the court's discretion".

Her Ladyship concluded that:

> "I have no doubt at all that it is wrong to import any test of exceptionality into the exercise of discretion under the Hague Convention. The circumstances in which return may be refused are themselves exceptions to the general rule. That in itself is sufficient exceptionality. It is neither necessary nor desirable to import an additional gloss into the Convention."[140]

Therefore, the House of Lords, taking into account the firm views of the children (aged 13 and 10 years, respectively, at the date of appeal) that they had settled in England and wished to stay, reversed the decision of the court below, which appeared to have been taken on the basis that a judge in the court addressed required to find something exceptional in a case before he could refuse to order return under the Convention.

Defences available under arts 12 and 13 typically coalesce, and frequently the cases display a "scattergun" approach. In law, as in life, one defence may strengthen inadequacies in another defence, or indeed there may be a symbiotic relationship between or among them, as for example in *W v W*,[141] where the objections to return to Ireland expressed by a very young child were bolstered by the fact of the family having settled into life in London for nine months. Equally, during that period, the court had to assess whether the bereft father had acquiesced in the child's wrongful removal; the Court of Appeal concluded that though he had not acquiesced, nonetheless he had allowed time to pass in knowledge of the family's London address.

Article 13

14–39	Notwithstanding the provisions of the preceding article, the judicial or administrative authority of the requested state is not bound to order the return of the child if the person, institution or other body which opposed its return establishes that:

> (a)	the person, institution or other body having the care of the person of the child was not actually exercising the custody rights at the time of

---

[138] *Re M (Children) (Abduction: Rights of Custody)* [2008] 1 A.C. 1288, per Lady Hale of Richmond at [43].

[139] [2008] 1 A.C. 1288, per Lady Hale of Richmond at [37].

[140] [2008] 1 A.C. 1288, per Lady Hale of Richmond at [40].

[141] *W v W* [2010] EWHC 332 (Fam), and on appeal sub nom. *Re W (Children)* [2010] EWCA Civ 520.

removal or retention, or had consented to or subsequently acquiesced in the removal or retention; or

(b) there is a grave risk that his or her return would expose the child to physical or psychological harm or otherwise place the child in an intolerable situation.

> The judicial or administrative authority may also refuse to order the return of the child if it finds that the child objects to being returned and has attained an age and degree of maturity at which it is appropriate to take account of its views.
> In considering the circumstances referred to in this article, the judicial and administrative authorities shall take into account the information relating to the social background of the child provided by the Central Authority or other competent authority of the child's habitual residence.

Article 12 is to be read subject to art.13; hence art.13 can be invoked irrespective of the length of time which has elapsed since the alleged wrongful removal or retention.

Consent and acquiescence

These concepts, referring to the state of mind of the bereft parent, are **14–40** related. Consent[142] can be given only in advance of the wrongful removal or retention, whereas acquiescence inevitably must follow the wrongful event.

In the cases concerning the alleged consent of the non-abducting parent[143] prior to the wrongful event, much will depend on evidence and credibility of witnesses. The cases are fact-specific.[144] That which appears to be consent may be vitiated if it was based upon a delusion as to the good faith of the other parent, as where the bereft parent erroneously believed that a contact agreement would be honoured.[145]

Notable difficulties have arisen in relation to conditional consent, that is, where consent to removal is given in the event that a particular set of circumstances should transpire, such as a failed reconciliation. Consent of this type was accepted as effective consent by the majority in *Zenel v Haddow*,[146] the court holding that agreement to removal does not require to be connected in time to the actual removal, i.e. can be open-ended. A similar set of circumstances arose in *Re P-J (Children)*,[147] where the Court of Appeal accepted that consent to the removal of a child, while it must be clear and unequivocal, may be given in respect of some future, but unspecified time, or on the happening of some future event.

To be used as an art.13 defence, such advance consent requires still to be operative and in force at the time of the actual removal. Fulfilment of the

---

[142] See *Zenel v Haddow*, 1993 S.C. 612; *Robertson v Robertson*, 1998 S.L.T. 468; *Re C (Minors) (Abduction: Consent)* [1996] 1 F.L.R. 414; *C v C*, 2003 S.L.T. 793; *H v H*, 2006 G.W.D. 18-361.
[143] Consent can be given only by the party whose rights of custody are at risk of being breached: *C v H (Abduction: Consent)* [2009] EWHC 2660 (Fam).
[144] *Re L (Abduction: Future Consent)* [2007] EWHC 2181 (Fam).
[145] *M v T (Abduction)* [2008] EWHC 1383 (Fam).
[146] 1993 S.C. 612 (Lord Morton of Shuna dissenting).
[147] *Re P-J (Children) (Abduction: Habitual Residence: Consent)* [2009] EWCA Civ 588.

condition must be reasonably capable of ascertainment, and not dependent on the subjective determination of one party. Since the situation is not completely analogous with the law of contract, but rather must be viewed against the background of the disintegration of family life, consent can be withdrawn at any time before the actual removal of the child. Once consent has been acted upon, however, change of mind by the consenter comes too late.[148] The burden of proving consent rests on the party who asserts its existence.

The House of Lords decision in *Re H*[149] established for UK jurisprudence that acquiescence[150] depends on the actual state of mind and subjective intention of the bereft parent, although this approach will be subordinated to any impression that parent had given by clear and unequivocal actings. Acquiescence cannot be inferred from oral or written[151] remarks made by someone who has just suffered the wrongful removal or retention of children.

The court addressed must consider carefully the fact of delay on the part of the bereft parent in instituting proceedings under the Hague Convention, and the reasons for this delay.[152] A parent cannot be said to have acquiesced in unlawful removal/retention unless s/he was aware of the facts and of the law.[153] In a number of cases, for a number of reasons, inaction or delay on the part of the bereft parent in issuing proceedings has been held not to amount to acquiescence.[154] Acquiescence obtained by fraud, or based on misunderstanding as to fact or intention, or non-disclosure by the abducting parent, will not suffice as an art.13 defence. What is required is clear subjective acceptance of the situation, evidenced by words and actions.[155] The court will take into account the fact that the bereft parent may have difficulty ascertaining the true intention of the abducting parent, which itself may not be constant, and in obtaining legal advice.

Grave risk

14–41   Case law indicates that the courts in Scotland and England are slow to find grave risk proved.[156] The onus lies on the party averring risk, that is, the

---

[148] *K v K (Abduction: Consent)* [2009] EWHC 2721 (Fam).

[149] *Re H (Minors) (Abduction: Acquiescence)* [1997] 2 All E.R. 225.

[150] *Soucie*, 1995 S.L.T. 414; *Robertson*, 1998 S.L.T. 468. See also *Re B (Abduction) (Article 13 Defence)* [1997] 2 F.L.R. 573; *Re M (Abduction: Acquiescence)* [1996] 1 F.L.R. 315; *J v K*, 2002 S.C. 450; *T v T*, 2003 S.L.T. 1316; *M v M*, 2003 S.L.T. 330; and *Re P (A Child) (Abduction: Acquiescence)* [2004] 2 F.L.R. 1057.

[151] Contrast *Re A (Minors) (Abduction: Custody Rights)* [1992] 1 All E.R. 929.

[152] *Re W (Children)* [2010] EWCA Civ 520.

[153] *J, Petitioner*, 2002 S.C. 450; *Re F (Abduction: Rights of Custody)* [2008] EWHC 272 (Fam).

[154] *Re G (Children) (Abduction:Withdrawal of Proceedings, Acquiescence, Habitual Residence)* [2007] E.W.H.C. 2807 (Fam); *Re F (Abduction: Rights of Custody)* [2008] E.W.H.C. 272 (Fam); *Re Z (Abduction)* [2008] E.W.H.C. 3473 (Fam); and *B v D* [2008] E.W.H.C. 1246 (Fam) (attempts to effect a reconciliation or a voluntary agreement for the return of children does not amount to acquiescence).

[155] *T v T* [2008] EWHC 1169 (Fam); *B-G v B-G* [2008] EWHC 688 (Fam).

[156] *Whitley v Whitley*, 1992 G.W.D. 15-843; 1992 G.W.D. 22-1248; *Murphy v Murphy*, 1994 G.W.D. 32-1893; *Slamen v Slamen*, 1991 G.W.D. 34-2041; *Matznick v Matznick*, 1998 S.L.T. 636; *Starr v Starr*, 1999 S.L.T. 335; *I, Petitioner*, 1999 G.W.D. 21-972; *Re W (Abduction: Domestic Violence)* [2004] 2 F.L.R. 499; *Q, Petitioner*, 2001 S.L.T. 243; *D v D*, 2001 S.L.T. 1104; *I, Petitioner*, 2004 S.L.T. 972; and *S v B* [2005] EWHC 733 (Fam). The first English decision upholding the grave risk argument was as late as 1995: *Re F (A Minor) (Child Abduction: Rights of Custody Abroad)* [1995] 3 All E.R. 641, per Butler Sloss L.J. at 648. See also now *Re M (Minors)*

abducting parent. The focus is on grave risk to the child were s/he ordered to return to his/her habitual residence, not risk to the abducting parent.[157] The *tempus inspiciendum* is the time at which the case comes to the Scots court: in a Hague Convention case it is not open to the court to ponder the effect of improvements which might be made in conditions in the legal system of habitual residence.[158] The terms of art.13 mean that the child may have to be returned though conditions are not ideal.[159] The test, therefore, is high, but it can be reached.[160] The symbiosis among the art.12 and art.13 defences, observed above, is seen also in *S v S*[161] where the court found that the child was settled in his new life, and return to his habitual residence would be devastating to such an extent as to constitute an intolerable situation.

Child's objection

The judicial or administrative authority may refuse to order the return of the **14–42** child if it finds that the child objects to being returned and has attained an age and degree of maturity at which it is appropriate to take account of its views.[162]

The House of Lords in *Re M (Children) (Abduction: Rights of Custody)*[163] made clear that "taking account of a child's views" does not mean that those views are determinative. The older the child, the greater the weight a child's objections to return might carry.[164] Article 13 refers to the child's objections, rather than to the expression of a preference; preference, it seems, may be expressed only after an objection is raised.

Black J. in *W v W*[165] stated that there was no absolute threshold below which a child could not be sufficiently mature for the purposes of the child's

---

(Abduction: Psychological Harm) [1997] 2 F.L.R. 690; *Re O (A Minor)* [1996] 6 C.L. 73; *Re S (A Child) (Abduction: Custody Rights)* [2002] F.L.R. 815; *Re R (Abduction: Immigration Concerns)* [2005] 1 F.L.R. 33; *M, Petitioner*, 2007 S.L.T. 433; *F v M (Abduction: Grave Risk of Harm)* [2008] EWHC 1467 (Fam); and *M v F* [2008] EWHC 2049 (Fam).

[157] *M, Petitioner*, 2007 S.L.T. 433.

[158] *Macmillan v Macmillan*, 1989 S.L.T. 350. But contrast Brussels II *bis* art.11.4, *q.v.*

[159] *Viola v Viola*, 1988 S.L.T. 7: the principle of paramountcy of the child's best interests does not apply. But see *Re C (A Child) (Child Abduction: Settlement)* [2006] EWHC 1229 (Fam.).

[160] e.g. *Q, Petitioner*, 2001 S.L.T. 243 (sexual abuse); *K v K* [2007] EWCA Civ 533 (domestic violence); *Re E (Abduction: Intolerable Situation)* [2008] EWHC 2112 (Fam); and *Re H (Abduction)* [2009] EWHC 1735 (Fam) (the court addressed was persuaded that siblings should not be returned to their father in Spain, there being a real risk in the view of the court that the elder child, who previously had attempted suicide, would commit suicide if ordered to return, and that the younger child would suffer damage to his psychological and emotional development).

[161] *S v S (Abduction: Wrongful Retention)* [2009] EWHC 1494 (Fam).

[162] *Urness v Minto*, 1994 S.L.T. 988; *O'Connor*, 1995 G.W.D. 3-113; *Marshall v Marshall*, 1996 S.L.T. 429; *Cameron (No.2)*, 1997 S.L.T. 206; *Matznick*, 1998 S.L.T. 636; *Singh v Singh*, 1998 S.L.T. 1084; *W v W*, 2003 S.L.T. 1253; and *Re H* [2005] EWCA Civ 319. Also *Re S (A Minor) (Child Abduction: Delay)* [1998] 1 F.C.R. 17; *W v W*, 2003 S.L.T. 1253; *Re J (Children) (Abduction: Child's objections to return)* [2004] EWCA Civ 428; *Re M (Children) (Abduction: Rights of Custody)* [2008] 1 A.C. 1288; *C v C*, 2008 S.C. 571; *Re E (Abduction:Intolerable Situation)* [2008] EWHC 2112 (Fam); *M v F* [2008] EWHC 2049 (Fam); *Re Z (Children) (Abduction)* [2008] EWHC 3473 (Fam); *Re G (Abduction)* [2008] EWHC 2558 (Fam); *Re R (A Child) (Abduction: Child's Objections)* [2009] EWHC 3074 (Fam); *M v B* [2009] EWHC 3477 (Fam); and *W v W* [2010] EWHC 332 (Fam).

[163] [2008] 1 A.C. 1288.

[164] *W v W* [2010] EWHC 332 (Fam); and on appeal sub nom. *Re W (Children)* [2010] EWCA Civ 520, per Wilson L.J. at [22].

[165] *W v W* [2010] EWHC 332 (Fam); and on appeal sub nom. *Re W (Children)* [2010] EWCA Civ 520.

objections defence. The judge found it appropriate to take into account the views of children aged eight and six. On (unsuccessful) appeal by the father, the Court of Appeal, having examined the issue, concluded that it could not be said that the age of the younger child per se foreclosed the possibility that she had objections to returning. Nonetheless, Wilson L.J. expressed concern that lowering the age at which a child's objections might be taken into account might gradually have the effect of eroding the principal objective of the Convention, which is swift restoration of a child to the state of his habitual residence.

At whatever age, but especially with regard to younger children, the court must take into account the influence which the abducting parent may have exercised upon the child in the stance the child is taking, and in the expression of his views,[166] albeit being alert to the fact that it would be unnatural for a parent not to air with the child the options available in the circumstances, and the benefits and drawbacks of each. Where an older child is thought capable of expressing his view, the effect of taking account of that view may be to influence the outcome of proceedings vis-à-vis a younger sibling.[167]

In the matter of age, the Family Division in *Re Z (Children) (Abduction)*,[168] examining the views of siblings, held that the younger child, aged five years, was too young to have his view taken into consideration, whereas the views of the seven year old could be given some weight. A strong example of the court taking full account of the clearly held views of a 13 year old is provided by *Re R (A Child) (Abduction: Child's Objections)*.[169] Sir Mark Potter, President of the Family Division of the English High Court took care to categorise under four heads the manner in which the court should assess the child's views, viz.:

(i) the child's own perspective of what is in his own short, medium or long term interests;

(ii) the extent to which the reasons for objection are rooted in reality or might reasonably appear to be so grounded;

(iii) the extent to which those views have been shaped or coloured by undue parental pressure, direct or indirect; and

(iv) the extent to which the objections would be modified on return and/or the child's removal from the pernicious influence of the abducting parent.

The court must be sure it understands the child's view, and that the child understands its options: his true wish may be to stay with one parent, wherever that parent may choose to be.[170] Yet again, the reality of the situation is that it

---

[166] *C v C*, 2008 S.C. 571; *Re R (A Child) (Abduction: Child's Objections)* [2009] EWHC 3074 (Fam).

[167] *Urness v Minto*, 1994 S.C. 249; *Ontario Court v M amd M (Abduction: Children's Objections)* [1997] 1 F.L.R. 475; and *Singh*, 1998 S.C. 1084. Though see unusual decision to separate siblings in *H v H* [2010] CSOH 32.

[168] [2008] EWHC 3473 (Fam). Contrast siblings of 12 and 9 years in *M v B* [2009] EWHC 3477 (Fam).

[169] [2009] EWHC 3074 (Fam), with reference to Ward L.J. in *Re T (Children) (Abduction: Child's Objections to Return)* [2000] 2 F.L.R. 192 at 204.

[170] *Re G (Abduction)* [2008] EWHC 2558 (Fam).

will be a rare child who would choose a place over a parent.[171] A child might be more inclined to express his view in a negative way, by saying that he does not wish to return to a given place, which is the home of the less favoured parent.[172] The difficulty can readily be seen that the "child's objection to return to a country" defence is likely to segue into a more personal preference, the denial of which, in the child's view, might be to place him in an intolerable situation.[173]

As always, the court on appeal will be reluctant to disturb the weight attributed by the trial judge to the various factors considered in the exercise of his discretion, and to his view of the evidence, and will depart from the judge's decision only if it was plainly wrong in the view of the appellate court, and the reasoning aberrant: "for it is of the essence of the [trial judge's] discretion that the exercise of attributing weight is committed to her or him".[174]

Role and function of Central Authorities

Article 7 provides for the involvement of Central Authorities. Their func- **14–43** tion, in summary, is to facilitate the smooth working of the Convention by helping a parent locate a child, and obtain legal advice. The Central Authority for Scotland is the EU and International Law Branch of the Scottish Government, and for England and Wales is the Child Abduction Unit of the Office of Official Solicitor and Public Trustee.

Central Authorities exist in every Contracting State, but the speed with which applications for assistance are dealt with varies from country to country.[175] Central Authorities shall bear their own costs, and shall not require payment from applicants towards the costs and expenses of proceedings.[176] However, a Contracting State may limit its assumption of costs to those covered by its system of legal aid and advice.[177]

Abduction cases falling under Brussels II *bis*

The 1980 Hague Convention has been ratified by all EU Member States and **14–44** applies in relations between Member States. However, the 1980 Convention now is supplemented by certain provisions of Brussels II *bis*, which operate in cases of child abduction between Member States, and which take precedence over the Hague Convention in those cases. In relations between Member States, in matters covered by Brussels II *bis*, the rules of the Regulation prevail over the rules of the 1980 Hague and Council of Europe Conventions. Brussels II *bis* aims to deter wrongful removal or retention of children between Member

---

[171] Though see *W v W* [2010] EWHC 332 (Fam), and on appeal sub nom. *Re W (Children)* [2010] EWCA Civ 520, per Wilson L.J. at [20].

[172] *M v B* [2009] EWHC 3477 (Fam).

[173] *S v S (Abduction: Wrongful Retention)* [2009] EWHC 1494 (Fam).

[174] *Re W (Children)* [2010] EWCA Civ 520, per Wilson L.J. at [25]; and *Re F (A Child) (Abduction: Refusal to Order Summary Return)* [2009] EWCA Civ 416. See also, in a non-Convention case, *Re J(A Child) (Custody Rights: Jurisdiction)* [2006] 1 A.C. 80.

[175] This has led to a number of claims based on humans rights argument. See *Cheshire, North and Fawcett: Private International Law*, 14th edn, 2008, p.1122.

[176] Though they may require payment of expenses incurred or to be incurred in implementing the return of the child: art.26.

[177] See *Matznick*, 1998 S.L.T. 636.

States, and if abduction should occur, to ensure the prompt return of a child to his Member State of origin.[178] The existence of the Regulation provides another example of the "layering" of potentially relevant conflict rules, which is characteristic of many areas of international private law at this period of its development. The instant example, however, is a case of "overlay", for it leaves in place the existing, well established Hague structure, and rather operates on top of that foundation.

Recital (17) of Brussels II *bis* states that in cases of wrongful removal or retention of a child, the child must be returned without delay; to this end, it is expressly stated that the 1980 Hague Convention continues to apply, as complemented by the provisions of Brussels II *bis*, and by art.11 in particular.[179]

The courts of the Member State to/in which the child has been wrongfully removed/retained[180] should be able to oppose the child's return in specific, duly justified cases, in the normal way under the 1980 Hague Convention.

In sum, where a child is "abducted" from one Member State (Member State of origin) (henceforth "MSO") to another Member State (the requested Member State) (henceforth "RMS"), the Regulation ensures that the courts of the MSO retain jurisdiction to decide on the question of custody, notwithstanding the abduction. Once a request for the return of the child is lodged with a court in the RMS, the RMS will apply the 1980 Hague Convention as complemented by the Regulation in order to make a decision.Where the RMS decides not to return a child by reason of art.12 or art.13 of the 1980 Hague Convention, it must inform the court of the MSO (recital (18)). However, the decision not to return the child is little more than a provisional protective decision because it may be superseded by a subsequent decision of the court of the MSO. If that subsequent decision by the MSO requires that the child be returned to his habitual residence, return must take place without special procedure for decree recognition or enforcement of that decision in the court of the state to/in which the child was wrongfully removed/retained.

Article 10—Jurisdiction in cases of child abduction

14–45 The 1980 Hague Convention does not contain direct or indirect rules of jurisdiction. Article 10 of Brussels II *bis* lays down rules for intra-EU child abduction cases, to determine which EU Member State has jurisdiction to decide "custody issues".[181] As a deterrent to intra-EU child abduction, art.10 safeguards the principle of *perpetuatio fori*[182] and regulates its operation in this context by ensuring that the courts of the MSO (the state in which the child was habitually resident before the abduction) remain competent after the abduction, to decide on matters of custody.

The RMS (the state to which the child has been abducted) may exercise jurisdiction over the child only in narrowly defined circumstances, namely, if:

---

[178] Practice Guide, p.28.
[179] See *Vigreux v Michel* [2006] EWCA Civ 630, the first case governed by the Regulation to reach the Court of Appeal. Also, for Scotland, see rules in Act of Sederunt (Rules of the Court of Session Amendment) (Jurisdiction, Recognition and Enforcement of Judgments) 2005 (SSI 2005/135).
[180] Defined in art.2.11.
[181] *B v D* [2008] EWHC 1246 (Fam).
[182] cf. *Leon v Leon* [1967] P. 275: once seised, always seised.

(a) the child has acquired habitual residence in the RMS, *and* all those with custody rights have acquiesced in the abduction; *or*

(b) the child has acquired habitual residence in the RMS[183] and has resided there for at least one year after those persons with custody rights learned, or should have learned,[184] of the child's whereabouts;[185] *and* the child has settled in the new environment;

and one of the following conditions is met:

(i) the bereft parent has not lodged a request for return of the child within a year of being able to locate the child[186];

(ii) the bereft parent has lodged a request for return of the child, but has withdrawn that request;

(iii) art.11.7 (*q.v.*) has been satisfied;

(iv) the MSO has issued a decision which allows the child to remain in the RMS.

Under art.10(a), the child would require to be returned to the court of his habitual residence, meaning that the outcome is in line with the Hague regime. The terminology is more specifically tied to jurisdiction; one may even see the beginnings of an attempt to define in an international instrument the time at which one habitual residence might be said to be supplanted by another, which is one of the most problematic matters in abduction cases.

Article 10(b) is intended to keep a jurisdictional balance. It is extremely difficult to tear jurisdiction away from the courts of the child's original habitual residence, a feature which is a great help to the bereft parent. Jurisdictional competence will shift to the RMS only if the bereft parent acquiesces, or is indifferent, or does not discharge the duty of enquiry.[187] Article 10(b) enumerates rules of specificity, the sum of which appears to hint at a desire to hone the ground of jurisdiction founded on "habitual residence" of the child. While the opening words of the article uphold the claim of the court of the jurisdiction whence the child has been wrongfully removed/retained, the remaining parts of the article afford justifications for departing from that position. Article 10 recognises the conceptual difficulties which the factor of habitual residence contains, namely, that as time goes on, it may be perverse to refuse to recognise a situation which in factual terms is incontestable.

From the "abductor's" point of view, one assumes that if acquiescence is not proved for jurisdiction purposes under art.10, the matter still could be argued for larger purposes under art.13 of the 1980 Hague Convention, since Brussels II *bis*, although demoting the Hague Convention,[188] does not extinguish it.

---

[183] By inference this presupposes that wrongful removal by a parent can effect change in habitual residence of the child; but as art.10 proceeds, it can be seen that this assumption is qualified.

[184] Practice Guide, p.30.

[185] *M v F* [2008] EWHC 2049 (Fam).

[186] Note the imposition upon a parent of a duty of enquiry by this term of the Regulation.

[187] Under the Hague regime also, unexplained inactivity by the bereft parent may give rise to judicial comment, and sometimes may contribute to a defence of acquiescence. See *contra J v K*, 2002 S.C. 450.

[188] See art.60.

Article 11—Return of the child

14-46   In any case brought in an EU Member State under the 1980 Hague Convention, in respect of the wrongful removal or retention of a child to or in another Member State, the provisions of art.11.2–11.8 of Brussels II *bis* apply.

Article 11.2—child's opportunity to be heard

14-47   Brussels II *bis* reinforces[189] the child's right to be heard. Recital (19) lays down the principle that giving audience to the child plays an important role in the application of the Regulation. When a court is applying arts 12 and 13 of the 1980 Hague Convention, it may refuse to order the child's return if it finds that the child objects to being returned, and has attained an age and maturity at which it is appropriate to take account of its views. Article 11.2 of the Regulation goes further than art.13 of the Hague Convention, by "ensuring"[190] that the child is given the opportunity to be heard, "unless this appears inappropriate having regard to his or her age or degree of maturity". Hence, there can be discerned a slight shift in emphasis in favour of the rights of the child.

Article 11.3—Six-week deadline

14-48   Article 11.3 is somewhat tautological: the court "shall act expeditiously . . . using the most expeditious procedures available in national law." The RMS must issue a decision (and, implicitly, enforce that decision) no later than six weeks after the lodging of the application for return of the child.

Article 11.4—Future arrangements

14-49   This is an interesting provision, showing how strictly art.13(b) of the Hague Convention is to be construed in intra-EU cases. Brussels II *bis* reinforces the principle that the RMS shall order the immediate return of the child by restricting the art.13(b) exceptions to a minimum.[191] The Regulation requires the return of the child to the MSO even in cases where a return would expose the child to physical or psychological harm, so long as the authorities of the MSO have made "adequate arrangements" to secure the child's protection following his return. The RMS cannot refuse to return a child on art.13(b) grounds if it is shown that, "adequate arrangements have been made to secure the protection of the child after his or her return". The child should always be returned to the MSO if he can be adequately protected there.[192]

How will it be established that adequate arrangements have been made? Is this an evidentiary issue? Adequate arrangements under art.11.4 mean more than procedures existing in theory in the MSO to safeguard the child; it must be established that the authorities in the MSO have taken definite measures to

---

[189] Practice Guide, p.33.
[190] In *Re F (A Child) (Abduction: Child's Wishes)* [2007] EWCA Civ 468 the English judge erred in failing to comply with art.11.2 by neglecting to give the child (seven years old) the opportunity to be heard.
[191] Practice Guide, p.32.
[192] *S v S (Abduction: Wrongful Retention)* [2009] EWHC 1494 (Fam). *Contra* outcome in *Q, Petitioner*, 2001 S.L.T 243, and *tempus inspiciendum* approach in *Macmillan*, 1989 S.L.T. 350, fn.158 above, both Hague Convention cases.

protect the child in question. Central Authorities will play a vital role in assessing whether or not adequate protective measures are in place.

Article 11.5—Bereft parent's opportunity to be heard

As well as the child having an opportunity to be heard, so too a court cannot **14–50** refuse to return a child unless the bereft parent (the party requesting return of the child) has been given the opportunity to be heard. Arguably the application for return of the child is itself an opportunity for the parent to be heard, but art.11.5 seems to envisage something more.

Article 11.6 and 11.7—RMS's refusal to return the child

In most cases, the RMS is likely to order return of the child to the MSO (i.e. **14–51** it will not find an art.13 ground to be established). But, in exceptional cases, where the RMS decides that the child shall not be returned to the MSO, special procedures must be followed, as laid down in art.11.6 and 11.7.[193]

Within one month of the (provisional protective) decision not to return the child, the RMS must transmit a copy of its decision to the court of the MSO (either directly or via the Central Authorities). The MSO must notify the parties, and invite them to make submissions within three months, as to whether or not they wish the MSO to examine the question of custody. If no submissions are made, the MSO shall close the case. However, if one or both parties make(s) submissions, the MSO must examine the case, in which event all parties (including, if appropriate, the child) must be given an opportunity to be heard.[194] The judge in the MSO is expected to take account of the reasons of the judge in the RMS for not returning the child. This process may result in a peremptory order for return to the MSO, as explained.

Article 11.8—Subsequent decision of MSO

Article 11.8 is the crucial provision of art.11. Following the provisional **14–52** decision issued by the RMS, if the court of the MSO, upon application by the bereft parent (as described above), makes a decision which entails the child's return to that state, this decision must be directly recognised and enforced in the RMS, without need for further procedure.[195] It is not possible for the RMS to oppose the recognition and enforcement of such a judgment, which is to be directly recognised and enforceable in the other Member States. Article 11.8 allows, in effect, for the non-return order of the RMS to be subverted.

---

[193] *HA v MB (Brussels II Revised: Article 11(7) Application)* [2007] EWHC 2016 (Fam); *Re H (Abduction: Jurisdiction)* [2009] EWHC 2280 (Fam); *Re F (A Child) (Abduction: Refusal to Order Summary Return)* [2009] EWCA Civ 416; *Re N (Jurisdiction)* [2009] I.L.Pr. 8; and *Re RC (Child Abduction) (Brussels II Revised: Article 11(7))* [2009] 1 F.L.R. 574 (application under art.11.7 refused as the foreign court had made no non-return order under art.13, but rather had decided that the father's retention of the child was not wrongful in terms of art.3; the gateway to art.11.7 of Brussels II *bis* is a non-return order per art.12 or art.13 of the Convention).

[194] See art.42.

[195] See arts 40, 42.

INTRA-UK CASES

Amendments made to the Family Law Act 1986 pursuant to Brussels II *bis*

14–53   The Family Law Act 1986, when brought into force, made provision for the allocation of jurisdiction within the UK in all matters relating to children, including rules for deferring to a court more appropriate, and for mutual recognition and enforcement, after registration, of Scots parental responsibility orders in England and *vice versa*. In light of the coming into force of Brussels II *bis*, and amending secondary legislation,[196] Pt I of the Family Law Act 1986 now must be taken to apply only where jurisdiction cannot be founded under the Regulation.[197]

By the European Communities (Matrimonial and Parental Responsibility Jurisdiction and Judgments) (Scotland) Regulations 2005, the provisions of Ch.III of the 1986 Act (jurisdiction of courts in Scotland) are subject to the provisions of Brussels II *bis*, Ch.II (jurisdiction), s.2 (parental responsibilities) and s.3 (common provisions). This means that the pre-eminent provisions with regard to jurisdiction in matters of parental responsibilities, in a qualifying (i.e. intra-EU) case, are to be found in arts 8–15 of Brussels II *bis*. Those provisions set out in Ch.III of the 1986 Act (principally, ss.9–14, below) are relegated to the status of residual national rules (an important change which can be discerned only after careful examination of the European Communities (Matrimonial and Parental Responsibility Jurisdiction and Judgments) (Scotland) Regulations 2005). This view is adduced on the basis that Brussels II *bis* is to be taken to effect allocation of jurisdiction between the territorial units of a Member State, as well as between Member States.[198] In this instance, to assume the operation of Brussels II *bis* in intra-UK cases is the less complex interpretative option.

The European Communities (Matrimonial and Parental Responsibility Jurisdiction and Judgments) (Scotland) Regulations 2005 make no mention, however, of ss.27–29 of the 1986 Act, covering registration and enforcement of parental responsibility orders intra-UK, and so it is to be assumed that these provisions continue to operate intra-UK, in qualifying cases (*q.v.*), irrespective of the recognition and enforcement provisions in Brussels II *bis* (Ch.III).

Residual national rules

14–54   For the reduced number of cases to which the 1986 Act now applies, the most important provisions of the Act, paraphrased in places for brevity or clarity, are as follows:

Chapter III—Jurisdiction of court in Scotland

Section 9: Habitual residence of the child

14–55   An application for a parental responsibilities order otherwise than in matrimonial proceedings[199] may be entertained by (a) the Court of Session if, on the

---

[196] The European Communities (Matrimonial and Parental Responsibility Jurisdiction and Judgments) (Scotland) Regulations 2005 (SSI 2005/42).
[197] See Brussels II *bis* art.14 (residual jurisdiction).
[198] See N. Lowe [2002] Fam Law 39; K. Beevers and D. McClean, "Intra-UK Jurisdiction in Parental Responsibility Cases" [2005] I.F.L.129; *Cheshire, North and Fawcett: Private International Law*, 14th edn, 2008, p.1085; and A. Inglis, 2009 J.R. 285, 287, 288; and *S v D*, 2007 S.L.T. (Sh. Ct.) 37. *Contra* Maher, 2007 S.L.T. (News) 117 and *B v B*, 2009 S.L.T. (Sh. Ct.) 24.
[199] See *Dorward v Dorward*, 1994 S.C.L.R. 928. Section 13 provides for jurisdiction ancillary to matrimonial proceedings.

date of the application, the child[200] concerned is habitually resident in Scotland; or (b) the sheriff, if, on that date, the child concerned is habitually resident in the sheriffdom.

Section 10: Presence of the child

An application for a parental responsibilities order may be entertained by **14–56** (a) the Court of Session if, on that date, the child is (i) present in Scotland; and (ii) not habitually resident in any part of the UK; or (b) the sheriff if, on that date, the child is (i) present in Scotland; (ii) not habitually resident in any part of the UK; and (iii) either the pursuer or the defender in the application is habitually resident in the sheriffdom.

Section 11: Relevant matrimonial proceedings

The jurisdiction of a court to entertain an application under ss.9, 10, or 15(2) **14–57** is excluded if, on the date of the application, matrimonial proceedings in respect of the marriage of the parents of the child are continuing in a court in any part of the UK (unless that other court has made an order under the 1986 Act enabling the custody proceedings to be taken in Scotland).

Section 12: Emergency jurisdiction

Notwithstanding that any other court, within or outside Scotland, has **14–58** jurisdiction to entertain an application for a parental responsibilities order, the Court of Session or the sheriff shall have jurisdiction if—(a) the child concerned is present in Scotland or in the sheriffdom on the date of the application; and (b) the Court of Session or sheriff considers that, for the protection of the child, it is necessary to make such an order immediately.[201]

Section 14: Power to refuse application or sist proceedings

There is power in the court to refuse application or to sist proceedings[202] or **14–59** to exercise its powers under art.15 of Brussels II *bis* where the matter has been determined already in other proceedings[203]; or where concurrent proceedings regarding the same matters are continuing, and where it would be more appropriate for those matters to be determined in proceedings outside Scotland or in another court in Scotland, and such proceedings are likely to be taken there; or where it is proper to exercise its powers under art.15, Brussels II *bis*.[204]

---

[200] A person who has not attained the age of 16: s.18(1).

[201] *Carroll v Carroll* [2005] Fam. L.R. 99: the Sheriff Principal on appeal held that the Sheriff did not, in the instant case, have jurisdiction on an emergency basis, and had not made an immediate order. Proceedings having begun in Leicester County Court, and the child being habitually resident in England, the English court was the appropriate forum for determining his best interests.

[202] *Messenger v Messenger*, 1992 S.L.T. (Sh. Ct.) 29 (sist refused); contrast *Hill v Hill*, 1991 S.L.T. 189. See *B v B*, 1998 S.L.T. 1245.

[203] *Al-Najjar, Petitioner*, 1993 G.W.D. 27-1661.

[204] Inserted by European Communities (Matrimonial and Parental Responsibility Jurisdiction and Judgments) (Scotland) Regulations 2005 (SSI 2005/42) reg.4.

Section 17: Orders for delivery of child

14–60   This empowers the Court of Session or sheriff court to make an order for delivery of a child from one parent to the other when the order is not sought to implement a parental responsibility order, if, but only if, the Court of Session or sheriff would have had jurisdiction to make a parental responsibilities order.

Chapter V—Recognition and enforcement

14–61   Section 25(1): A parental responsibilities order made by a court in any part of the UK in force in respect of a child who has not attained 16 years, shall be recognised (except for its enforcement provisions) in any other part of the UK as if made by the appropriate court in that part. Section 25(3): A court in a part of the UK in which a parental responsibility order is recognised shall not enforce the order unless it has been registered in that part of the UK as if made by the appropriate court in that part.

Section 26: An order relating to parental responsibilities or parental rights in relation to a child which is made outside the UK shall be recognised in Scotland if the order was made in the country where the child was habitually resident.[205]

Section 27(1) and (2): Any person on whom rights are conferred by a parental responsibility order may apply to the court which made it for the order to be registered in another part of the UK.[206]

Section 29(1): Where a parental responsibility order has been registered under s.27, the registering court shall have the same powers to enforce the order as if it had itself made the order and had jurisdiction to make it; and proceedings for enforcement may be taken accordingly.

Section 32: "The appropriate court" in relation to England and Wales or Northern Ireland means the High Court, and in relation to Scotland, means the Court of Session.

Chapter VI—Miscellaneous and supplemental

14–62   Various miscellaneous powers are granted to safeguard the child and ensure the effective operation of the Act:

Section 33: Power to order disclosure of a child's whereabouts (from any person whom the court has reason to believe may have relevant information).[207]

Section 34: Power to order recovery of a child, including authority to enter and search any premises where the person acting in pursuance of the order has reason to believe the child may be found, and to use such force as may be necessary to give effect to the purpose of the order.[208]

---

[205] Note statutory change to common law rule of recognition of decree of domicile of father. The statutory rule now is subject to arts 21–27, 41.1 and 42.1 of Brussels II *bis*.

[206] It became clear in *Woodcock v Woodcock*, 1990 S.L.T. 848 that, in the view of the Scots court, s.29 did not deprive the court of its discretion and duty to ensure that natural justice was observed. See D. Edwards, "A Domestic Muddle: Custody Orders in the United Kingdom" (1992) 41 I.C.L.Q. 444. See also *Rellis v Hart*, 1993 S.L.T. 738; *Messenger*, 1992 S.L.T. (Sh. Ct.) 29; and *Re B (Minors) (Residence Order)* [1992] 3 All E.R. 867.

[207] *Re G (Children) (Residence: Same Sex Partner)* [2006] UKHL 43.

[208] Section 34 was enacted without prejudice to any existing power of the court. The Scots court has common law powers: *Edgar v Fisher's Trustees* (1893) 21 R. 59; *Guthrie v Guthrie*, 1954 S.L.T. (Sh. Ct.) 58; *Fowler v Fowler (No.2)*, 1981 S.L.T. (Notes) 78; and *Abusaif v Abusaif*, 1984 S.L.T. 90.

Section 35: Powers to restrict removal of a child from the jurisdiction of the court.[209]

Section 37: Where there is in force an order prohibiting or otherwise restricting the removal of a child from the UK or from any specified part of it, the court by which the order was made may require any person to surrender any UK passport which has been issued to, or contains particulars of, the child.

Section 41: Habitual residence after removal without consent, etc.

(1) Where a child who:
   (a) has not attained the age of 16, and
   (b) is habitually resident in a part of the UK, becomes habitually resident outside that part of the UK in consequence of circumstances of the kind specified in section 41(2) below, he shall be treated for the purposes of this Part II of the Act as continuing to be habitually resident in the UK for the period of one year beginning on the date on which those circumstances arise.[210]

(2) The circumstances referred to in (1) above exist where the child is removed from or retained outside, or himself leaves or remains outside, the part of the UK in which he was habitually resident before his change of residence:
   (a) without the agreement of the person or all the persons having, under the law of that part of the UK, the right to determine where he is to reside, or
   (b) in contravention of an order made by a court in any part of the UK.

(3) A child shall cease to be treated by virtue of section 41(1) as habitually resident in a part of the UK if, during the period there mentioned:
   (a) he attains the age of 16, or
   (b) he becomes habitually resident outside that part of the UK with the agreement of the person(s) mentioned in section 41(2)(a) above and not in contravention of an order made by a court in any part of the UK.

---

[209] On occasion a custodial parent may seek the court's permission to relocate with the child outside the Scottish jurisdiction (see Children (Scotland) Act 1995 s.2(3)). See *McShane v Duryea* [2006] Fam. L.R. 15; and *M v G*, 2010 G.W.D. 17-339. For England, see *Payne v Payne* [2001] C.L.Y. 596; [2005] Fam. Law 781 (permanent removal); *Re A (A Child) (Temporary Removal from Jurisdiction)* [2004] EWCA Civ 1587; *F v R* [2007] EWHC 64 (Fam); and *Re S (Removal from Jurisdiction)*; sub nom. *DS v RS* [2009] EWHC 1594 (Fam) (temporary removal). See generally *Cheshire, North and Fawcett: Private International Law*, 14th edn, 2008, pp.1127–1129. Unusually, parents may agree, by means of submitting to a judicial decree in these terms, that a child shall not be taken to a country which is not party to the 1980 Hague Convention, and agree sanctions to operate in the event of breach thereof. Such an agreement has been upheld by the Court of Appeal in *Whyte v Whyte* [2005] EWCA Civ 858. In March 2010, under the auspices of the Hague Conference, more than 50 judges from Contracting States produced the Washington Declaration on International Family Relocation agreeing desiderata in this subject area.

[210] This protection is inserted to offset the advantage of the passage of time which otherwise generally operates in favour of a parent who removes a child. This must now be read with the overlay of art.10, Brussels II *bis*, which refines the rule (para.14–45, above), while being in keeping with it. See A. Inglis, "A Muckle Midden Cleared: Brussels II bis and section 41 Family Law Act 1986", 2009 J.R. 285, written with reference to *RAB v MIB*, 2009 S.C. 58 a sequel case to *Re B (A Child) (Court's Jurisdiction)* [2004] 2 F.L.R. 741, handed down by the English court before the advent of Brussels II *bis*.

CASES GOVERNED BY COMMON LAW RULES

14–63 The facts of the case, including geography[211] and timing of events,[212] may render it one for common law regulation.

Incoming common law cases[213] are dealt with in Scotland on a fair-minded basis of return of the child to a court of closer connection, if it is obvious that such a court exists.[214] On the other hand, if not convinced of the existence of a more appropriate forum, or if unsure about the conditions which await the child on return, the Scots court will retain the child and decide the custody issue.[215] Many years have elapsed since the era when the decree of the court of the father's domicile was entitled to unquestioned acceptance.[216]

As regards outgoing common law cases, Scots law, obviously, is unlikely to be able to influence the handling of such cases, and advice to parents is of a practical nature, seeking to stop the "abductor" from removing the child beyond the jurisdiction of the Scots courts.[217] Removal of a child to a non-Convention country of a very different culture from the UK will render unlikely a foreign court order directing return of the child to Scotland.

Application of Hague Convention principles to non-Convention cases

14–64 An interesting question is whether Scots and English courts should treat "non-Convention" incoming cases with a Convention-type approach. A Scots common law case of significance is *Calleja v Calleja*,[218] where the court opined that "physical or moral injury" (the terminology of the older common law cases) might not be the best expression in modern times, preferring the "psychological harm" wording used in the Hague Convention art.13, while not applying it directly.[219]

There were some early indications that an English court in its discretion might wish to take account of as much of the Hague Convention as it felt appropriate in a particular case.[220] However, there was cautious retrenchment by the

---

[211] Abductions from and to certain parts of the world, e.g. Islamic states, are always likely to be common law cases.

[212] In judging whether any international instrument is applicable, the initial act complained of must take place after the coming into force of the relevant instrument between the countries in question (*Kilgour*, 1987 S.L.T. 568; *Re H (Minors) (Abduction: Custody Rights)* [1991] 3 All E.R. 230 HL).

[213] Involving non-Convention countries, or involving Convention countries in circumstances where the Convention(s) does/do not apply.

[214] *Lyndon*, 1978 S.L.T. (Notes) 7; *Campbell v Campbell*, 1977 S.C. 103; *Thomson, Petitioner*, 1980 S.L.T. (Notes) 29.

[215] *Sinclair v Sinclair*, 1988 S.L.T. 87 (before Germany became a Hague Convention country); and see *Basinski v Basinski*, 1993 G.W.D. 8-533.

[216] *McKee* [1951] A.C. 352 at 365. See also Family Law Act 1986 s.26.

[217] Family Law Act 1986 ss.17, 33–37; and *Robertson, Petitioner*, 1911 S.C. 1319. In Scotland the police can become involved only if a crime has been committed—in effect, only if Child Abduction Act 1984 s. 6 applies. The first source of advice if the destination is a non-Convention country is the Foreign and Commonwealth Office, and then "Reunite", a UK charity specialising in International Child Abduction.

[218] 1997 S.L.T. 579. See also *Perendes v Sim*, 1998 S.L.T. 1382.

[219] *Calleja*, 1997 S.L.T. 579 at 603.

[220] *Re F (A Minor) (Abduction; Jurisdiction)* [1990] 3 All E.R. 97: see Crawford, "'Habitual Residence of the Child' as the Connecting Factor in Child Abduction Cases" 1992 J.R. 177, 191; *D v D (Child Abdiuction: Non-Convention Country)* [1994] 1 F.L.R. 137 CA; *Re A (Minors) (Abduction: Habitual Residence)* [1996] 1 All E.R. 24; *Re S (Minors) (Abduction)* [1994] 1 F.L.R. 297; and *Re Z (Abduction: Non-Convention Country)* [1999] 1 F.L.R. 1270.

Court of Appeal in *Re A (A Minor) (Abduction: Non-Convention Country)*,[221] where the non-Convention country was the United Arab Emirates. The need for comity, and the relativist cultural approach, retreated in favour of the welfare principle. Similarly, in *Re P*[222] the Court of Appeal held that it was not bound to apply the spirit of the Convention to a non-Convention case.

In *Re J (A Child) (Custody Rights: Jurisdiction)*[223] Baroness Hale of Richmond stated firmly that:

> "There is no warrant, either in statute or authority, for the principles of the Hague Convention to be extended to countries which are not parties to it . . . This is so even in a case where a friendly foreign state has made orders about the child's future."[224]

The House of Lords held that:

> "[I]n all non-Convention cases, the courts have consistently held that they must act in accordance with the welfare of the individual child. If they do decide to return the child, that is because it is in his best interests to do so, not because the welfare principle has been superseded by some other consideration . . . the specialist rules and concepts of the Hague Convention are not to be applied by analogy in a non-Convention case".[225]

In the instant case, the House of Lords allowed the appeal, and in refusing to order the return of the child to Saudi Arabia effectively restored the decision of Hughes J.

Under any system of rules, Convention or common law, the weight given to the views of the child must increase as the child grows older. An added dimension may present in that in some legal systems girls may be of marriageable age earlier than 16 years, and parents may be in agreement that they wish to remove the child from the UK to, for example, India, in order to have the child married there.[226] In an instance of this type,[227] Singer J. in the Family Division of the High Court held that the courts in England, while not insensitive to the traditions and concepts of family authority held by minority communities, must nevertheless uphold the integrity of the individual child or young person, whose views must prevail in the:

> ". . . highly personal context of an arranged or forced marriage. Accordingly, the courts would not permit what was, at best, the

---

[221] [1998] 1 F.L.R. 231; *The Times*, July 3, 1997. But contrast the approach taken earlier in *Re S (Minors) (Abduction)* [1994] 1 F.L.R. 297 CA. See also *Osborne v Matthan (No.3)*, 1998 S.L.T. 1264; *Re A (Minors) (Abduction: Habitual Residence)* [1996] 1 All E.R. 24; *Re JA (A Minor) (Abduction: Non-Convention Country)* [1998] 2 F.C.R. 159; and *Re J (A Child) (Return to Foreign Jurisdiction: Convention Rights)* [2005] 3 All E.R. 291 HL.

[222] *Re P (A Minor: Abduction)*, *The Times*, July 19, 1996.

[223] [2006] 1 A.C. 80.

[224] *Re J (A Child) (Custody Rights: Jurisdiction)* [2006] 1 A.C. 80 at [22].

[225] [2006] 1 A.C. 80 at [25].

[226] These cases may overlap with issues of forced marriage. See paras 11–20 and 12–43, above.

[227] *Re KR (A Child) (Abduction: Forcible Removal by Parents)* [1999] 4 All E.R. 954.

exploitation of an individual, and might, in the worst case, amount to outright trafficking for financial consideration."

UK-Pakistan Consensus on Child Abduction

14–65   A protocol was reached in 2003, reflecting agreement between senior members of the UK judiciary and the Pakistan judiciary, in the matter of protection of children from the harmful effects of wrongful removal or retention, and having the aim of promoting judicial co-operation between the legal systems concerned.[228] The Protocol recognises that in normal circumstances the welfare of the child is best determined by the courts of the country of the child's habitual/ordinary residence.

THE CRIMINAL LAW ASPECT OF INTERNATIONAL CHILD ABDUCTION

14–66 The Child Abduction Act 1984 amends the criminal law of England[229] and Scotland[230] relating to the abduction of children (i.e. the taking or sending of a child under the age of 16 out of the UK without the appropriate consent, where there is in force a parental responsibility order, or a UK order prohibiting the removal of the child from the UK).

These provisions were conceived as English measures, but it was feared that their effectiveness would be weakened if a parent or other person could take a child abroad from a Scottish airport or port without fear of criminal sanction. Hence, s.6, of application to Scotland only, was inserted at a late stage into the 1984 Act. Scots law on this subject comprises, in addition to s.6 (which defines the offence, the penalties being specified in s.8), the common law crimes of plagium (child stealing) and abduction.[231] The matter was considered by the Scottish Law Commission,[232] which recommended abolition of plagium, reform of abduction, and the creation of a statutory offence of taking or detaining a child under 16 from the control of any person having lawful control of that child, but there has been no implementing legislation.

IV. GUARDIANSHIP AND ADMINISTRATION OF A CHILD'S PROPERTY

GUARDIANSHIP

14–67 At common law in Scotland, there were three classes of guardians, viz.: (1) tutors; (2) curators; and (3) curators *bonis* and/or *ad litem*. The Age of

---

[228] See [2003] Fam. Law 199. See also comments at [2004] Fam. Law 359; [2004] Fam. Law 609; and [2006] 1 F.L.R. 5, where it is reported that the Protocol, at least "in spirit", had been used as at that date in 52 cases. See *Re Z (A Child)* [2006] EWCA Civ 1219 at [31]; *A v N*, 2007 GWD 01-2; *Re I (A Child) (Contact Application: Jurisdiction)* [2010] 1 All E.R. 445, per Lady Hale at 458, 459.

[229] See Pt 1 of the Act.

[230] See Pt 2 of the Act.

[231] Both criminal and civil aspects may arise from one set of circumstances: *Deans v Deans*, 1988 S.C.L.R. 192 Sh Ct.

[232] Scottish Law Commission, *Child Abduction* (HMSO, 1985), Scot. Law Com. Memo. No.67; Scottish Law Commission, *Report on Child Abduction* (HMSO, 1987), Scot. Law Com. No.102, Cm.64.

Legal Capacity (Scotland) Act 1991 removed the common law classification of children into pupils and minors, and replaced tutors and curators with "guardians" (defined as parent-substitutes). Curators *ad litem* and curators *bonis* still may be appointed by the court.[233] Many important changes in substance and terminology were made by the Children (Scotland) Act 1995; appointment and removal of guardians came to be regulated by s.7 (appointment), s.8 (revocation and other termination of appointment), and s.11(2)(h) (judicial appointment or removal of guardians). Under the 1995 Act, an application can be made to the Court of Session or sheriff court for an order in relation to parental responsibilities and rights, by any person who claims an interest (s.11(3)(a)(i)). Such an interest may be genetic or emotional or professional and might include, therefore, a step-parent, grandparent, medical/social services professional, or even the child himself or herself.

Under Brussels II *bis*, the definition of parental responsibility, and of the holder thereof, is apt to cover a person who in Scots law would be regarded as a guardian,[234] and so the pre-existing jurisdictional rules of Scots law contained in the Family Law Act 1986 ss.9–12, now take the function, in relation to guardianship, as for other aspects of parental responsibility, of residual national rules.[235]

Jurisdiction to administer a child's property[236]

At common law, jurisdiction in the Scots courts to appoint a guardian by whatever name, was founded on the child's domicile or residence in Scotland, or on the ownership by the child of property in Scotland.[237] Section 16 of the Family Law Act 1986[238] conferred jurisdiction on the Scots court to entertain an application for guardianship, if the child in question was habitually resident in Scotland. With regard to orders concerning the administration of a child's property, the Children (Scotland) Act 1995 ss.9, 10, and 14 now apply, the last of which has conflict of laws implications. Section 14 provides that: **14–68**

"(1) The Court of Session shall have jurisdiction to entertain an application for an order relating to the administration of a child's property if the child is habitually resident in, or the property is situated in, Scotland.
(2) A sheriff shall have jurisdiction to entertain such an application if the child is habitually resident in, or the property is situated in, the sheriffdom.
(3) Subject to subsection (4) below, any question arising under this Part of this Act—
  (a) concerning—
    (i) parental responsibilities or parental rights; or
    (ii) the responsibilities or rights of a guardian,

---

[233] Age of Legal Capacity (Scotland) Act 1991 s.1(3)(f).
[234] See art.1.2(b), (e).
[235] Brussels II *bis* art.14.
[236] See Brussels II *bis* recital (9), art.1.2(e).
[237] *Hay v Hay* (1861) 23 D. 1291; as to curators *bonis* in insanity, see *Reid v Reid* (1887) 24 S.L.R. 281.
[238] Amended by Age of Legal Capacity (Scotland) Act 1991 Sch.2 para.46.

in relation to a child shall, in so far as it is not also a question such as is mentioned in paragraph (b) below, be determined by the law of the place of the child's habitual residence at the time when the question arises[239];

(b) concerning the immediate protection of a child shall be determined by the law of the place where the child is when the question arises[240]; and

(c) as to whether a person is a validly appointed or constituted guardian of a child[241] shall be determined by the law of the place of the child's habitual residence on the date when the appointment was made (the date of death of the testator being taken to be the date of appointment where an appointment was made by will), or the event constituting the guardianship occurred."

Section 14(4) subjects the choice of law rule (in favour of the application of the law of the child's habitual residence), to the discretion of the Scots forum, which, in making an order in relation to guardianship, is required, in terms of the 1995 Act, to regard the welfare of the child as the paramount consideration.

Sections 9, 11, 13 and 14 of the 1995 Act are rendered subject to the jurisdiction rules contained in Brussels II *bis*.[242]

Recital (9) of Brussels II *bis* distinguishes between (i) measures for the protection of a child concerning the designation and functions of a person or body having charge of a child's property, representing or assisting him, and measures concerning the administration, conservation and disposal of his property; and (ii) measures relating to the child's property which do not concern his protection. Whilst the former are governed by Brussels II *bis*, the latter are governed by the Brussels I Regulation (failing which as to scope, by s.14 of the 1995 Act).

V. ADOPTION

14–69 Adoption is the form of procedure by which a person (the adoptee), becomes a member of the family of another person (the adopter). It has been said that adoption is a culture-specific legal entity. In this, it is perhaps unlike anything else so far studied under the heading of personal status, for while it is true that there are different types of marriage (monogamous, polygamous, etc.), and there are different methods of divorce (judicial, extrajudicial, etc.), the status of being married, or of being divorced, arguably has an agreed core of incidents. However, when considering recognition of foreign adoption orders, one of the difficulties which arises is that some legal systems favour "full" adoption, in which an individual who has the status of adopted person thereby

---

[239] Choice of law rule regarding parental responsibilities and rights. See *S v D*, 2007 S.L.T. (Sh. Ct.) 37.

[240] Choice of law rule regarding child protection.

[241] This amounts to a rule of recognition.

[242] Section 14(5) (added by the European Communities (Matrimonial and Parental Responsibilities Jurisdiction and Judgments) (Scotland) Regulations 2005 (SSI 2005/42) reg.5). For Brussels II *bis* arts 8–15, see paras 14–12—14–19, above.

extinguishes all links of parental influence, rights of aliment, support, property and succession, with his biological family, whereas other systems favour "simple" adoption, in which the break from the biological family is less absolute. Further, there is a difference between adoption by strangers, and adoption by blood relatives. In the latter case, contact with the biological family obviously will continue. Valid adoptions frequently bring in train benefits of citizenship, meaning that the topic often is closely linked with immigration issues.[243] The area of intercountry adoption, however, requires to be closely regulated and monitored due to the clear possibilities which exist for subterfuge, dishonesty, criminal behaviour and the exploitation of vulnerable persons.[244]

Within the domestic laws of Scotland and England, the state has now a much stronger role in adoption than was the case in earlier days, and the subject of adoption straddles public and private law. The topic has an enhanced public profile in the conflict of laws, in view of the increased opportunity to "rescue" children from overseas, which may give rise to controversial cases often lacking statutory or Convention regulation.

Prior to the introduction of the Adoption and Children (Scotland) Act 2007 ("the 2007 Act"), adoption in Scots law was regulated primarily by the Adoption (Scotland) Act 1978,[245] incidentally by Pt III of the Children (Scotland) Act 1995 and also, as regards intercountry and overseas adoption, by the Adoption (Intercountry Aspects) Act 1999, an Act which made provision for giving effect in the UK to the 1993 Hague Convention on Protection of Children and Co-operation in Respect of Intercountry Adoption. The 2007 Act, which was introduced to modernise and improve adoption law in Scotland, repeals and very largely replaces the 1978 Act,[246] repeals Pt III of the 1995 Act, and repeals also very many of the provisions in the 1999 Act which applied in Scotland. Accordingly, in relation to intercountry adoptions, the relevant law now is to be found in Pt 1 Ch.6[247] of the 2007 Act, supplemented by the Adoptions with a Foreign Element (Scotland) Regulations 2009.[248]

An important distinction must be drawn between "Convention" adoptions and "non-Convention" (or overseas) adoptions. With regard to the former, the process involves a country which, like the UK, is a signatory to the 1993 Hague Convention. Non-Convention or overseas adoptions,[249] by contrast,

---

[243] *Re H (A Minor) (Adoption: Non-Patrial)* [1983] 4 F.L.R. 85; and contrast *Re B (A Minor) (Adoption Order: Nationality)* [1999] 1 F.L.R. 907.

[244] *Re F (A Minor) (Abduction: Custody Rights)* [1991] Fam. 25; and *Northumberland CC v Z* [2009] EWHC 498 (Fam).

[245] Based on the Adoption Act 1976 for England and Wales. For adoption law in England, see now the Adoption and Children Act 2002 (Ch.6 ss.83–91A re adoptions with a foreign element); the Adoptions with a Foreign Element Regulations 2005 (SI 2005/392); and the Adoptions with a Foreign Element (Amendment) Regulations 2009 (SI 2009/2563), all examined in *Cheshire, North and Fawcett: Private International Law*, 14th edn, 2008, pp.1155–1177.

[246] With the exception of Pt IV ("Status of adopted children"), which remains in force in order to ensure that the status of such children is unaffected by the repeal of the 1978 Act.

[247] As amended by the Adoptions with a Foreign Element (Special Restrictions on Adoptions from Abroad) (Scotland) Regulations 2008 (SSI 2008/303).

[248] Adoptions with a Foreign Element (Scotland) Regulations 2009 (SSI 2009/182), as amended by the Adoptions with a Foreign Element (Scotland) Amendment Regulations 2010 (SSI 2010/173). See also the Registration of Foreign Adoptions (Scotland) Regulations 2003 (SSI 2003/67).

[249] See fn.267 re. s.67(1) definition.

concern a country which is on the UK's list of designated countries, set out in the Adoption (Designation of Overseas Adoptions) Order 1973.[250] In the main, the identity of the non-UK legal system involved in the intercountry adoption, be it the state of origin of the child in question, or the receiving state, will determine the classification of the adoption as Convention or non-Convention, and in turn the body of law which will regulate the adoption process.

RECOGNITION OF ADOPTION ORDERS

Intra-UK

14–70   There is reciprocal recognition of adoption orders intra-UK.[251]

Convention adoptions

14–71   The Adoption (Intercountry Aspects) Act 1999 brought into force in the UK the 1993 Hague Convention on Protection of Children and Co-operation in respect of Intercountry Adoption. The aim of the Convention is to improve certainty, orderliness and fairness in intercountry adoption, and to attempt to stop the trafficking of children. To this end, as with the 1980 Hague Convention on international child abduction the Central Authorities of Contracting States play an important facilitating and safeguarding role.[252]

Part 3 of the Adoptions with a Foreign Element (Scotland) Regulations 2009[253] concerns Convention adoptions. Part 3 Ch.1[254] regulates the procedure which must be followed in Scotland when the UK is the receiving state, that is, for incoming adoptions, where a child is brought from outwith the British Islands to the UK for adoption, in accordance with the Convention, by a person or couple who is/are habitually resident in Britain. Part 3 Ch.2 of the 2009 Regulations regulates the procedure which must be followed in Scotland in the rarer case of an outgoing abduction, i.e. where the UK is the state of origin, and a child who is habitually resident[255] in Britain is to be adopted, in accordance with the Convention, by a person or a couple who is/are habitually resident outwith Britain.[256]

Convention framework

14–72   The 1993 Convention shall apply where a child habitually resident in one Contracting State ("the state of origin") has been, is being, or is to be, moved

---

[250] Adoption (Designation of Overseas Adoptions) Order 1973 (SI 1973/19). See also the Adoption (Designation of Overseas Adoptions) (Variation) Order 1993 (SI 1993/690) and Adoption (Designation of Overseas Adoptions) (Variation) (Scotland) Order 1995 (SI 1995/1614). Designated countries include all western European countries, most members of the Commonwealth and UK dependent territories, South Africa, and USA. See, for England and Wales, Adoption and Children Act 2002 s.87.

[251] Adoption and Children (Scotland) Act 2007 s.77; and Adoption and Children Act 2002 s.105.

[252] See Ch.3 arts 6–13.

[253] Adoptions with a Foreign Element (Scotland) Regulations 2009 (SSI 2009/182), as amended by the Adoptions with a Foreign Element (Scotland) Amendment Regulations 2010 (SSI 2010/173).

[254] See regs 10–37.

[255] cf. In England, *Greenwich LBC v S* [2007] EWHC 820 (Fam).

[256] See regs 38–52.

to another Contracting State ("the receiving state"), either after his adoption, in the state of origin, by spouses or a person habitually resident in the receiving state, or for the purposes of such an adoption in the receiving state, or in the state of origin.[257] By art.2(2), the Convention covers only adoptions which create a permanent parent-child relationship. Certain agreements, for example of Central Authorities in the state of origin and the receiving state, must be obtained; the Convention ceases to apply if these agreements have not been given before the child attains the age of 18 years.[258]

Requirements for intercountry adoptions

In terms of art.4, an adoption within the scope of the Convention shall take **14–73** place only if the competent authorities of the state of origin have established that the child is adoptable, and have determined, after giving due consideration to placement of the child within the state of origin, that an intercountry adoption is in the child's best interests. Presumably the criteria of "adoptability" (in all its aspects) and what is in the child's best interests must be tested according to the domestic law of the state of origin.

Further, the competent authorities of the state of origin must ensure that the persons, institution, and authorities whose consent is necessary for adoption have been counselled and informed of the effects of their consent, in particular on the matter whether the adoption will result in the termination of the legal relationship between the child and his family of origin; that such persons, etc. have given their consent freely in the required form, not induced by payment, and their consent has not since been withdrawn; and that the consent of the mother, where required, has been given only after the birth of the child. Further, the authorities must ensure that the child has been counselled and informed of the effects of the adoption; that consideration has been given to the child's wishes and opinions; and that his consent, where required, has been given freely in the required legal form, uninduced by payment. These latter requirements are to be given effect having regard to the age and degree of maturity of the child.

In terms of art.5, a Convention adoption shall take place only if the competent authorities of the receiving state have determined that the prospective adoptive parents are eligible and suited to adopt; have been counselled, as may be necessary; and have determined that the child is or will be authorised to enter and reside permanently in that state. Presumably "eligibility", in all its aspects, must be tested according to the domestic law of the receiving state.

Jurisdiction—applications to adopt

There is no chapter specifically devoted to jurisdiction. It would appear that **14–74** the only criterion to enable parties to utilise the intercountry adoption process provided is that the parties be habitually resident in a Contracting State, and that the child be habitually resident in another Contracting State. But perhaps this approach to jurisdiction provision is appropriate in the circumstances which the Convention seeks to address.

---

[257] See art.2(1).
[258] See art.3.

By art.14, persons habitually resident in a Contracting State who wish to adopt a child habitually resident in another Contracting State[259] shall apply to the Central Authority in the state of their habitual residence.

If that Central Authority is satisfied that the applicants are eligible, and suited to adopt, it shall prepare a background report, to be transmitted to the Central Authority of the state of origin. If that Central Authority is satisfied that the child is adoptable, it shall prepare a background report (e.g. on the child's medical history and cultural background), ensuring that consents have been obtained in accordance with art.4; and shall determine whether the envisaged placement is in the best interests of the child. This report shall be transmitted to the Central Authority of the receiving state, with proof that the necessary consents have been obtained, taking care not to reveal the identity of the natural parents, if in the state of origin these identities may not be disclosed.

In terms of art.17, any decision in the state of origin that a child should be entrusted to prospective adoptive parents, may be made only if the Central Authority of that state has ensured that the prospective adoptive parents agree; that the Central Authority of the receiving state has approved such a decision, where such approval is necessary by the law of that state or by the Central Authority [*sic*] of the state of origin; that the Central Authorities of both states have agreed that the adoption will proceed; and that, in accordance with art.5, the prospective adoptive parents are eligible and suited to adopt, and that the child is or will be authorised to enter and reside permanently in the receiving state. The Central Authorities of both states shall take all necessary steps to obtain permission for the child to leave the state of origin, and to enter and reside permanently in the receiving state.

Where the adoption is to take place after the transfer of the child to the receiving state, and it appears to the Central Authority of that state that the continued placement of the child with the prospective adoptive parents is not in the child's best interests, such Central Authority shall take the necessary measures to protect the child (which may include arranging temporary care, or a new placement, or, as a last resort, arranging the return of the child to the state of origin, if his interests so require). Having regard to the age and degree of maturity of the child, he shall be consulted, and where appropriate, his consent to these measures obtained.[260]

Recognition and effects of adoption

14–75   The main challenge for the draftsmen of the Convention was the crafting of recognition provisions which are apt to cover recognition of a status which varies from country to country, some adoption laws effecting full adoption, and others only simple adoption. An adoption certified by the competent authority of the state of the adoption (being the state of origin, or the receiving state, as the case may be), as having been made in accordance with the Convention, shall be recognised as having operation of law in the other Contracting States.[261] The recognition of an adoption may be refused in a

---

[259] This is the (only) qualifying scenario.
[260] See art.21.
[261] See art.23.

Contracting State only if the adoption is manifestly contrary to its public policy, taking into account the best interests of the child.[262]

What does recognition of an adoption connote? In terms of art.26(1), the recognition of an adoption includes recognition of (a) the legal parent-child relationship between the child and his/her adoptive parents; (b) parental responsibility of the adoptive parents for the child; and (c) the termination of a pre-existing legal relationship between the child and his/her biological parents, if the adoption has this effect in the Contracting State where it was made. By art.26(2), where an adoption has the effect of terminating a pre-existing legal parent-child relationship, the child shall enjoy in the receiving state, and in any other Contracting State where the adoption is recognised, rights equivalent to those resulting from adoptions having this effect in each such state.[263] Conversely, by art.27(1), where an adoption granted in the state of origin is less than full, it may, in the receiving state which recognises the adoption under the Convention, be converted into a full adoption (a) if the law of the receiving state so permits; and (b) if the consents referred to in art.4 have been, or are, given for the purpose of such adoption. If so, recognition of the conversion will be guaranteed by art.23 in the same way as recognition of any other qualifying adoption.

General provisions

Chapter VI contains general provisions, of an administrative or a policy[264] **14–76** nature. By art.28, the Convention does not affect any law of the state of origin which requires that the adoption of a child habitually resident within that state take place in that state, or which prohibits the child's placement in, or transfer to, the receiving state prior to adoption.

The 1993 Convention is an important contribution in an area of law which is difficult to regulate. Its provisions appear to contain many safeguards for the child, and for those whose consent to intercountry adoption is necessary. Its value will be judged according to the degree of international support which it commands.[265] The dual responsibility of the state of origin and the receiving state is a noteworthy characteristic. The Convention contains ex facie fewer conflict rules than might be expected; indeed they must be searched out, and/or inferred. The most notable absence is of any express mention of choice of law amid much facilitative and precautionary provision. There are many

---

[262] See art.24.

[263] Hence, if an adoption is carried out under a law which operates "full adoptions", then that full status shall be enjoyed in the receiving state and essentially in all other Contracting States. However, art.26(3) provides that the child shall have the benefit of any more favourable provision which is in force in a recognising Contracting State.

[264] e.g. art.32: no-one shall derive improper financial or other gain from an activity related to an intercountry adoption.

[265] As of June 1, 2010 there are 81 Contracting States to the 1993 Convention. An interesting aspect of the Convention is that recognition of adoptions from certain specified countries can be suspended because of concerns about child trafficking. Clearly this can have severe consequences in the case of adoptions which are in course when the ban is imposed. In *R. (on the application of Thomson) v Minister of State for Children* [2006] 1 F.L.R. 175 claimant British citizens unsuccessfully applied for judicial review of a decision by the Secretary of State to impose a temporary suspension on intercountry adoptions from Cambodia, and forbidding them to proceed. See, for England and Wales, Children and Adoption Act 2006 Pt 2 ss.9–14.

problems of a factual and evidential nature in this branch of the conflict of laws, e.g. location of the biological parents of a child, and obtaining sufficient evidence of their consent to removal of the child, and in any given case such problems are likely to be as, or more, acute than the legal problems.

Non-Convention adoptions[266]

14–77   As explained above, non-Convention or overseas adoptions,[267] are adoptions to or from a country which is on the UK's list of designated countries, set out in the Adoption (Designation of Overseas Adoptions) Order 1973.[268] Many countries designated for this purpose also are party to the 1993 Hague Convention, but an adoption from such a Contracting State still may be treated as an overseas adoption if, for some factual reason, the adoption does not satisfy the particular requirements of the Convention. An overseas adoption will have equivalent effect in Scotland to a Scottish adoption.

The requirements for non-Convention cases are set out in Pt 1 Ch.6 of the Adoption and Children (Scotland) Act 2007. The 2007 Act places restrictions on incoming adoptions of children to the UK, as well as on outgoing adoptions of children from the UK. Additionally, Pt 2[269] of the Adoptions with a Foreign Element (Scotland) Regulations 2009[270] makes provision for non-Convention adoptions.

Part 2 Ch.1[271] lays down rules for cases where a child is brought into the UK in circumstances where s.58 of the 2007 Act applies.[272] Regulations 3 and 4 prescribe the requirements which must be met and the conditions which must be satisfied by prospective adopters before a child may be brought into the UK. Regulation 5 imposes functions on the local authority which apply when the child has been brought into the UK and the prospective adopters have given notice of their intention to apply for an adoption order. Part 2 Ch.2 applies to the more unusual case of where a child is to be taken out of the UK for overseas adoption. Regulations 7 and 8 lay down the requirements which must be met before an order may be made under s.59[273] of the 2007 Act.[274]

---

[266] "Overseas adoptions" per s.67(1) of the 2007 Act.

[267] Section 67(1) of the 2007 Act defines an overseas adoption as one effected under the law of any country or territory outwith the British Islands (that is, the UK, Channel Islands and Isle of Man), and which is not a Convention adoption.

[268] Adoption (Designation of Overseas Adoptions) Order 1973 (SI 1973/19). See also the Adoption (Designation of Overseas Adoptions) (Variation) Order 1993 (SI 1993/690) and Adoption (Designation of Overseas Adoptions) (Variation) (Scotland) Order 1995 (SI 1995/1614). Designated countries include all western European countries, most members of the Commonwealth and UK dependent territories, South Africa, and USA. See, for England and Wales, Adoption and Children Act 2002, s.87.

[269] With the exception of reg.9.

[270] Adoptions with a Foreign Element (Scotland) Regulations 2009 (SSI 2009/182), as amended by the Adoptions with a Foreign Element (Scotland) Amendment Regulations 2010 (SSI 2010/173).

[271] See regs 3–6.

[272] That is, where a British resident brings or causes another to bring a child into the UK for the purposes of adoption or where they bring or cause another to bring a child adopted by a British resident under an external adoption effected within a period of 12 months from that adoption. Section 58(3) makes clear that the provision has no application if a child is intended to be adopted under a Convention adoption order.

[273] That is, a preliminary order vesting parental responsibilities and rights in the prospective adopters where a child is to be adopted abroad.

[274] cf. In England and Wales, *C v X Local Authority* [2008] EWCA Civ 105, applying the Adoptions with a Foreign Element Regulations 2005 (SI 2005/392) reg.10.

Section 60 of the 2007 Act makes it an offence for any person to take or send a protected child[275] out of Great Britain to any place outwith the British Islands with a view to the adoption of that child. By virtue of s.62 of the 2007 Act,[276] if Scottish Ministers have reason to believe that, because of adoption practices taking place in an overseas country, it would be contrary to public policy to further the bringing of children into the UK from such countries, special restrictions may be ordered to prevent such movement.[277]

Adoption orders at common law

Where a foreign adoption does not qualify as a Convention case under the 2009 Regulations, or as an overseas adoption under the 2007 Act, a question of recognition will arise at common law. In such a case, where the matter falls to be decided without legislative guidance, there is support for application of old principles of recognition on the basis of domicile,[278] or "recognition by"[279] the law of domicile of the adoptive parents, or one of them. Recognition of an adoption order at common law does not necessarily require giving effect to all the incidents of that adoption.[280] Moreover, a foreign adoption may be denied recognition if recognition would be contrary to public policy, or to the best interests of the child.[281] **14–78**

SUMMARY 14

1. Status

The status of legitimacy and of legitimation may continue to be relevant in Scots conflict cases. By s.41 of the Family Law (Scotland) Act 2006, any question arising as to the effect on a person's status of his/her parents being, or having been, married to each other; or not being, or not having been, married to each other, shall be determined by the law of that person's domicile at the time at which the question arises. **14–79**

---

[275] Defined in s.60(9) as a child who is habitually resident in the UK or a Commonwealth citizen.

[276] See also the Adoptions with a Foreign Element (Special Restrictions on Adoptions from Abroad) (Scotland) Regulations 2008 (SSI 2008/303); and, for England and Wales, the Adoptions with a Foreign Element (Special Restrictions on Adoptions from Abroad) Regulations 2008 (SI 2008/1807).

[277] cf. For England and Wales, suspensions on intercountry adoption per Children and Adoption Act 2006 Pt 2 ss.9–14.

[278] *Re Wilson (Deceased)* [1954] Ch. 733; *Re Wilby* [1956] P. 174; *Re Marshall* [1957] Ch. 507; *Re Valentine's Settlement* [1965] Ch. 831; and *Re N* Unreported October 23, 2009 English High Court (Fam). See *Dicey, Morris and Collins on the Conflict of Laws*, 14th edn, 2006, r.111; *Cheshire, North and Fawcett: Private International Law*, 14th edn, 2008, p.1174, queries whether it is right to concentrate exclusively on the domicile of the adopters, ignoring the domicile of the child or of the natural parents, but accepts that if domicile of adopters is the main jurisdictional criterion, the "recognition by" extension should be accepted.

[279] On analogy of *Armitage v Att Gen* [1906] P. 135 (divorce) and *Abate v Abate* [1961] P. 29 (nullity), though this principle has ceased to apply in "proceedings" divorce and nullity recognition: Family Law Act 1986 s.46(1).

[280] See Ch.10, above.

[281] *Re MN (Non-recognised Adoptions: Unlawful Discrimination: India)* [2008] EWCA Civ 38. *Contra D v D* [2008] EWHC 403 (Fam).

2. Parental rights and responsibilities

Allocation of jurisdiction and conflicting jurisdictions: Brussels II *bis* arts 8–15 apply; failing which Family Law Act 1986 ss.8–18. See also 1996 Hague Convention arts 5–14.

Choice of law: see 1996 Hague Convention arts 15–22.

Recognition and enforcement of parental responsibility orders: Brussels II *bis* arts 21 and 23 apply; failing which Family Law Act 1986 ss.27–29. See also 1996 Hague Convention arts 23–28.

3. International Child Abduction

The primary legislation in the UK is the Child Abduction and Custody Act 1985, bringing into effect the 1980 Hague Convention on the civil aspects of international child abduction and the 1980 Council of Europe Convention. In a qualifying (intra-EU) case this is complemented by Brussels II *bis* arts 10 and 11.

In incoming common law cases, the Scottish court will act in what it perceives in its discretion to be the best interests of the child.

4. Guardianship and administration of property

Brussels II *bis*, supplemented by the Children (Scotland) Act 1995 s.14.

5. Intercountry adoption

The relevant legislation for Scotland is the Adoption and Children (Scotland) Act 2007 Pt I Ch.6, supplemented by the Adoptions with a Foreign Element (Scotland) Regulations 2009 (SSI 2009/182).

The categories of foreign adoptions are:

(a) Convention adoptions (under the 1993 Hague Convention and Pt 3 of the Adoptions with a Foreign Element (Scotland) Regulations 2009 (SSI 2009/182));

(b) non-Convention or overseas adoptions (per Pt 1 Ch.6 of the Adoption and Children (Scotland) Act 2007; and Pt 2 of the Adoptions with a Foreign Element (Scotland) Regulations 2009 (SSI 2009/182); and referring to adoptions to or from a country designated in the Adoption (Designation of Overseas Adoptions) Order 1973 (SI 1973/19), as amended); and

(c) common law adoptions.

CHAPTER 15

THE LAW OF CONTRACTUAL OBLIGATIONS

I. GENERAL MATTERS AND GOVERNING LAW

CLASSIFICATION

The question whether a conflict case is to be treated as pertaining to contract, **15–01** or to some other legal category, is determined by the *lex fori*.[1] For conflict purposes it is not essential for characterisation of a problem as contractual that there be present all the domestic requirements of the *lex fori* for constitution of a contract. It is sufficient that, in the view of the forum, the elements of a contractual obligation exist.[2]

LEGISLATIVE BACKGROUND TO CHOICE OF LAW

Choice of law rules in contract are contained in Regulation 593/2008 on the **15–02** law applicable to contractual obligations (Rome I)[3] (henceforth "Rome I Regulation"). This Regulation replaces[4] the Rome Convention on the law applicable to contractual obligations, which opened for signature on June 19, 1980 (henceforth "Rome I Convention"), and applies, in situations involving a conflict of laws, to contractual obligations in civil and commercial matters.[5]

It is clear from art.24.2 of the Rome I Regulation that insofar as the Regulation replaces the provisions of the Convention, any reference to that

---

[1] *De Nicols v Curlier (No.1)* [1900] A.C. 21; *Earl of Stair v Head* (1846) 6 D. 904; and *Krupp Uhde GmbH v Weir Westgarth Ltd* Unreported May 31, 2002 Lord Eassie.

[2] *Re Bonacina* [1912] 2 Ch. 394. Cf. Private International Law (Miscellaneous Provisions) Act 1995 s.9(2).

[3] See, on the Regulation, F. Ferrari and S. Lieble (eds), *Rome I Regulation: The Law Applicable to Contractual Obligations in Europe* (Munich: Sellier, 2009); and Binchy and Ahern (eds), *Rome I Regulation: Implications for International Commercial Litigation* (Leiden: Brill, forthcoming). Also Ministry of Justice, *Guidance on the law applicable to contractual obligations (Rome I): Outline of the main provisions* (The Stationery Office, 2010).

[4] Rome I Regulation art.24.

[5] Contrast the Rome I Convention, the rules of which applied to contractual obligations "in any situation involving a choice of law between the laws of different countries" (art.1.1). The phrase "contractual obligations" may receive, in time, an autonomous meaning from decisions of the Court of Justice of the EU in the manner of interpretation of the special jurisdiction provisions in contract contained in the Brussels I Regulation art.5(1). See *Société Jakob Handte et Cie GmbH v Société Traitements Mecano-Chimiques des Surfaces* [1992] E.C.R. I-3967; and *Atlas Shipping Agency (UK) v Suisse Atlantique Societe D'Armement SA* [1995] I.L.Pr. 600 (implied promise held to fall within the scope of Lugano Convention art.5.1).

Convention shall be understood as a reference to the Regulation. It is to be assumed that, in the absence of autonomous definitions newly inserted in the Regulation, and where the provisions of the Regulation do not differ substantially in their meaning and purpose from those in the Convention, the principle of continuity of interpretation ("vertical continuity")[6] should apply, leading to the conclusion that the body of jurisprudence interpretative of the Rome I Convention may be referred to and relied on in interpretation of the Regulation. It is desirable that a related principle, "horizontal continuity" should apply in the interpretation of cognate instruments. This means that the substantive scope and content of the Rome I Regulation should be construed consistently with the Rome II Regulation, and with the relevant jurisdiction provisions in the Brussels I Regulation.[7]

In this chapter, all references to legislation, unless otherwise specified, are to the Regulation not the Convention. All case authorities, however, unless otherwise specified, have been decided according to common law or the Rome I Convention.

The Rome I Convention was brought into force in the United Kingdom, with effect from April 1, 1991, by means of the Contracts (Applicable Law) Act 1990,[8] in respect of contracts entered into after that date.[9] On January 14, 2003 the EC Commission published a Green Paper entitled, Conversion of the Rome Convention of 1980 on the Law Applicable to Contractual Obligations into a Community Instrument and its Modernisation ("Green Paper").[10] The Commission sought views on whether the Convention should be converted into a Regulation, and upon whether, in any event, the substantive provisions ought to be amended in light of experience. The Commission pointed out that at Community level, the Rome Convention was the only international private law instrument still in the form of an international treaty, and suggested that in this important commercial area, the rules of jurisdiction, on the one hand, and of choice of law, on the other, should not be governed by different types of instrument. Proceeding by way of Regulation (rather than, say, by Directive) was said to be appropriate where an entire subject area (the private international law of contractual obligations) was to be harmonised, not simply a particular aspect of that area, and being directly applicable, meant that harmonisation measures would enter into force in all Member States contemporaneously. The separate argument that a Regulation would achieve the desirable aim of clothing the Court of Justice of the EU ("CJEU") with jurisdiction to hear appeals on matters concerning the interpretation of Rome I (with the aim of having legal concepts common to Brussels and Rome interpreted in like

---

[6] i.e. from foundation instrument to current instrument. Cf. 1968 Brussels Convention and Brussels I Regulation. See, for example, discussed in *Ilsinger v Dreschers* (C-180/06 [2009] OJ C153/3). See E.B. Crawford, "The right of a consumer to seek payment of a prize apparently won" 2009 (4) *European Journal of Consumer Law*.

[7] Rome I Regulation recital (7).

[8] See Peter Kaye, *The New Private International Law of Contract of the European Community* (Aldershot: Dartmouth, 1993); Richard Plender and Michael Wilderspin, *The European Contracts Convention: The Rome Convention of the Choice of Law for Contracts*, 2nd edn (London: Sweet & Maxwell, 2001); and Peter E. Nygh, *Autonomy in International Contracts* (Oxford: Clarendon Press, 1999).

[9] Rome I Convention art.17 (no retrospective effect).

[10] Conversion of the Rome Convention of 1980 on the Law Applicable to Contractual Obligations into a Community Instrument and its Modernisation COM(2002) 654 final.

manner), was less persuasive since the entry into force of the Brussels Protocol, *q.v.*[11]

In December 2005 the Commission presented a Proposal for a Regulation of the European Parliament and the Council on the law applicable to contractual obligations (Rome I).[12] Publication of the proposal was greeted in the UK with scepticism, since it could be seen that the draft instrument went further than an updating exercise and proposed certain fundamental changes and new provisions likely, in the UK view, to introduce uncertainty in complex international contracts. Accordingly, the initial reaction of the UK government was against opting-in.[13] Nonetheless, the government continued to participate in negotiations with a view to securing improvements in the text from the UK's point of view. Eventually, an accommodation or compromise having been reached, and following consultation of interested parties,[14] a request[15] was made by the UK to permit acceptance of, and participation in, the Regulation. The Commission gave a positive opinion,[16] with the result that the Rome I Regulation entered into force in the UK on December 22, 2008.[17] The Regulation will be applied by Member State courts, including those of the UK, to qualifying cases concerning contracts concluded as from[18] (i.e. on and after) December 17, 2009.[19] The courts of Member States must apply the rules in the Rome I Regulation to any qualifying case, regardless of whether the applicable law(s) thereunder is/are that of a Member State.[20] Hence the Rome I Regulation has the characteristic, shared by the Rome II Regulation, of "universality". The Rome I Regulation applies also in the case of conflicts of laws between the different jurisdictions of the UK.[21]

Although the provisions of the Rome I Regulation and its Convention predecessor do not differ greatly from the pre-existing common law rules of Scotland and England, it would be wrong to regard the Regulation or the Convention as a codification of common law rules.[22] Where the Rome I Regulation does not apply (art.1: scope), or where it is silent on an issue, the common law continues to apply, as it does to all contracts entered into before April 1, 1991.[23] As a result, Scots and English choice of law rules in contract

---

[11] Green Paper, para.3.2.11.
[12] Proposal for a Regulation of the European Parliament and the Council on the law applicable to contractual obligations COM(2005) 650 final.
[13] See recital (45).
[14] Ministry of Justice, *Rome I—Should the UK opt in?* (The Stationery Office, 2008), Consultation Paper CP05/08.
[15] Notified under Doc.C(2008) 8554 [2008] OJ L177.
[16] Commission Opinion COM(2008) 730 final.
[17] Decision 2009/26/EC on the request of the United Kingdom to accept Regulation (EC) No 593/2008 on the law applicable to contractual obligations [2009] OJ L10/22.
[18] Corrigendum to the Rome I Regulation 13497/1/09, REV 1, JUR369 [2008] OJ L177, correcting art.28 of the Rome I Regulation.
[19] See The Law Applicable to Contractual Obligations (Scotland) Regulations 2009 (SSI 2009/410); The Law Applicable to Contractual Obligations (England and Wales and Northern Ireland) Regulations 2009 (SI 2009/3064); and The Financial Services and Markets Act 2000 (Law Applicable to Contracts of Insurance) Regulations 2009 (SI 2009/3075). Also Elizabeth B. Crawford, "Applicable Law of Contract: Some Changes Ahead", 2010 S.L.T. (News) 17.
[20] See art.2.
[21] See art.22. Cf. 1990 Act s.2(3); and Rome II art.25.
[22] *Cheshire, North and Fawcett: Private International Law*, 14th edn, 2008, pp.676, 677.
[23] *Zebrarise Ltd v De Nieffe* [2005] 1 Lloyd's Rep. 154.

are found principally in the Regulation, but subsidiarily also in the common law; the common law should be regarded as the backdrop.[24]

With regard to interpretation of the Rome Convention, reference to the Giuliano and Lagarde report on the Rome Convention[25] (henceforth "Giuliano and Lagarde") was permitted in order to ascertain the meaning and effect of any provision.[26] Questions of interpretation were required to be determined in accordance with the principles laid down by the European Court of Justice, and any relevant decision of that court. From 1990 a body of Scottish and English decisions interpretative of the Convention has accumulated. Only since March 1, 2005 have appellate courts in the United Kingdom been permitted to refer cases raising issues concerning the interpretation of the Rome I Convention to the CJEU for decision,[27] and it might have been expected, in light of the Brussels Protocol, that a body of CJEU decisions would develop, possibly demonstrating methods of purposive interpretation different from those to which the UK is accustomed. However, before this process could be said to have become established, the Rome I Regulation came into effect. The Court of Justice of the EU has jurisdiction to give preliminary rulings on interpretation of the Rome I Regulation submitted by national courts from which there is no further appeal under national law.[28]

The coming into force of the Rome I Regulation shall not prejudice the application of other international conventions to which a Member State is a party and which lay down conflict of law rules relating to contractual obligations (e.g. conventions on carriage).[29] But, as between Member States, the Regulation shall take precedence over conventions concluded exclusively between two or more of them in so far as such conventions concern matters governed by the Regulation.[30]

GOVERNING LAW OF A CONTRACT: GENERAL PRINCIPLES

15–03 Although a contract may contain elements connecting it with a number of different legal systems, if it is closely analysed, it will be found that its main elements can be localised, and that it has, or is deemed to have, a closer connection with one particular law than with any other. This law, the governing law, was known at common law as the "proper law of the contract".

---

[24] Consider, e.g. terms of the Rome I Regulation which are not comprehensive: arts 12 (scope of the applicable law) and 13 (capacity). Article 12 does not provide an exhaustive list of essential matters to which the applicable law applies. Article 13 applies only in the circumstances which the article itself lays down.

[25] Giuliano and Lagarde, Report on the Convention on the Law Applicable to Contractual Obligations [1980] OJ C282/1.

[26] 1990 Act s.3(1), (2), (3)(a).

[27] The Contracts (Applicable Law) Act 1990 (Commencement No.2) Order 2004 (SI 2004/3448). The Brussels Protocol 1998, permitting such references, could not come into force earlier as it had not been ratified by all the EC Member States. The first and only case decided by the ECJ on interpretation of the Convention is *Intercontainer Interfrigo (ICF) SC v Balkenende Oosthuizen BV* (C-133/08) [2010] I.L.Pr. 3.

[28] Information note on references from national courts for a preliminary ruling [2009] OJ C297/01.

[29] See art.25.1.

[30] See art.25.2.

Its successor under the Rome I Convention, and now under the Rome I Regulation, is termed "the applicable law". It is the legal centre of gravity of the contract, and in it there is to be found the origin and determinant of the rights and obligations of the contracting parties.

Nature of the governing law

The governing law must be determined according to the facts as they exist **15–04** at the date of making the contract, not taking into account actings after conclusion of the contract.[31] It is generally thought that a contract must have a governing law from the outset: the governing law is held to attach at the time the contract is concluded, even though it may not be explicit and may require subsequently to be identified. It has been said that the governing law cannot float[32]: a contract cannot be "anarchic" since, should a problem arise immediately upon conclusion thereof, there must be a law to determine the existence and extent of a remedy.[33]

(a) More than one governing law

There are unusual cases in which different parts of a contract may have **15–05** closer connections with different systems of law. There is no reason why the provisions of a contract should not be severable,[34] and the result, exceptionally, is that parties may choose to have different laws govern different parts of a contract.[35]

(b) Change of governing law

By agreement, the parties may change the governing law after conclusion of **15–06** the contract. This is confirmed by the Regulation, art.3.2,[36] subject to the proviso that such variation shall not prejudice the contract's formal validity, or adversely affect the rights of third parties.

---

[31] *Compagnie Tunisienne de Navigation SA v Compagnie d'Armement Maritime SA* [1970] 3 All E.R. 71; *James Miller & Partners Ltd v Whitworth Street Estates (Manchester) Ltd* [1970] 1 All E.R. 796 (though since the parties by their subsequent conduct had acquiesced in Scottish arbitration proceedings, Scots law governed the curial procedure).

[32] See *Armar Shipping Co v Caisse Algerienne d'Assurance et de Reassurance (The Armar)* [1981] 1 All E.R. 498; *EI du Pont de Nemours & Co v Agnew (No.1)* [1987] 2 Lloyd's Rep. 585 CA; and *Libyan Arab Foreign Bank v Bankers' Trust Co* [1987] 2 F.T.L.R. 509.

[33] *The Armar* [1981] 1 All E.R. 498. Though see Plender and Wilderspin, *European Contracts Convention*, 2nd edn, 2001, para.5–06, arguing that it is the purpose of art.3 of the Rome I Convention to allow maximum scope to party autonomy, and that the provision must be taken to permit that which it does not forbid; hence, in their view, a floating choice of law clause was permissible under the Rome I Convention.

[34] G.C. Cheshire, *International Contracts* (Glasgow: Jackson, Son & Co, 1948), p.42; Wolff, *Private International Law*, 2nd edn, 1950, p.422; *Greer v Poole* (1880) L.R. 5 Q.B.D. 272; *Adelaide Electric Supply Co Ltd v Prudential Assurance Co Ltd* [1934] A.C. 122 at 151; *R. v International Trustee for the Protection of Bondholders AG* [1937] A.C. 500; *Mount Albert BC v Australasian Temperance & General Mutual Life Assuarnce Society Ltd* [1938] A.C. 224; *Forsikringsaktieselskapet Vesta v Butcher* [1986] 2 All E.R. 488 at 504, 505; affirmed [1988] 1 Lloyd's Rep. 19 at 29–33, 34, 35 CA; and [1989] 2 W.L.R. 290 HL; and *Libyan Arab Foreign Bank v Bankers' Trust Co* [1987] 2 F.T.L.R. 509.

[35] Rome I Regulation art.3.1.

[36] See, under the Convention, *ISS Machinery Services Ltd v Aeolian Shipping SA (The Aeolian)* [2001] 2 Lloyd's Rep. 641.

(c)　Change in substance of governing law

15–07　　The governing law of a contract is not static and does not remain fixed or frozen according to the provisions of that law at the date of formation of the contract.[37] The applicable law, as it stands from time to time, governs. Changes in substantive law may bring private law advantages and disadvantages, respectively, to the parties.[38]

CHOICE OF LAW RULES IN CONTRACT UNDER THE ROME I REGULATION

Material scope of Rome I Regulation

15–08　　Article 1 of the Rome I Regulation provides that:

"1.　This Regulation shall apply, in situations involving a conflict of laws, to contractual obligations in civil and commercial matters.
　　It shall not apply, in particular, to revenue, customs or administrative matters.
2.　The following shall be excluded from the scope of this Regulation:
　　(a)　questions involving the status or legal capacity of natural persons, without prejudice to Article 13;
　　(b)　obligations arising out of family relationships and relationships deemed by the law applicable to such relationships to have comparable effects, including maintenance obligations[39];
　　(c)　obligations arising out of matrimonial property regimes, property regimes of relationships deemed by the law applicable to such relationships to have comparable effects to marriage, and wills and succession;
　　(d)　obligations arising under bills of exchange, cheques and promissory notes and other negotiable instruments to the extent that the obligations under such other negotiable instruments arise out of their negotiable character[40];
　　(e)　arbitration agreements and agreements on the choice of court[41];
　　(f)　questions governed by the law of companies[42] and other bodies, corporate or unincorporated, such as the creation, by registration or otherwise, legal capacity, internal organisation or winding-up of companies and other bodies, corporate or unincorporated, and

---

[37] See para.4–07, above.
[38] *Re Chesterman's Trusts* [1923] 2 Ch. 466; *Kahler v Midland Bank Ltd* [1950] A.C. 24; and *Ralli Bros v Compania Naviera Sota y Aznar* [1920] 2 K.B. 287.
[39] Maintenance obligations generally were excluded from the scope of the Rome I Convention (contrast Regulation 44/2001 art.5.2). See Giuliano and Lagarde, p.11. The exclusion has been made explicit in the Regulation. See Ch.13, above.
[40] i.e. not simply because payment under a contract was made by cheque. Characterisation as a negotiable instrument is governed by the *lex fori*. See Giuliano and Lagarde, p.11.
[41] The UK delegation did not favour this exclusion when the Rome I Convention was being negotiated. Despite discussion about the wisdom of continuing to exclude these matters from the scope of the Regulation, the exclusion remains in place.
[42] i.e. concerning internal operation of the business entity. Contracts made with such bodies and not otherwise excluded are subject to the Rome I Regulation and Convention.

the personal liability of officers and members as such for the obligations of the company or body;

(g) the question whether an agent is able to bind a principal, or an organ to bind a company or other body corporate or unincorporated, in relation to a third party[43];

(h) the constitution of trusts and the relationship between settlors, trustees and beneficiaries[44];

(i) obligations arising out of dealings prior to the conclusion of a contract[45];

(j) insurance contracts arising out of operations carried out by organisations other than undertakings referred to in Article 2 of Directive 2002/83/EC of the European Parliament and of the Council of 5 November 2002 concerning life assurance the object of which is to provide benefits for employed or self-employed persons belonging to an undertaking or group of undertakings, or to a trade or group of trades, in the event of death or survival or of discontinuance or curtailment of activity, or of sickness related to work or accidents at work.[46]

3. This Regulation shall not apply to evidence and procedure, without prejudice to Article 18.[47]

4. In this Regulation, the term 'Member State' shall mean Member States to which this Regulation applies. However, in Article 3(4) and Article 7 the term shall mean all the Member States."

Principle of universality

The Regulation employs, as did the Convention, the principle of universal **15–09** application, meaning that any law specified[48] by the instrument shall be applied by a Member State court whether or not it is the law of a Member State.

Freedom of choice of applicable law by the parties

The Regulation endorses[49] freedom of choice of applicable law by parties. **15–10** The current formulation of the rule is as follows:

---

[43] But contracts made between agent and principal are governed by the Rome I Regulation, as was the case under the Convention. See paras 15–32—15–33, below; and Giuliano and Lagarde, p.13.

[44] See Recognition of Trusts Act 1987.

[45] Recital (10) explains that such obligations are covered by art.12 of the Rome II Regulation. Such matters (e.g. standard of conduct at the pre-contractual stage, and good faith in negotiating—an area termed *culpa in contrahendo*, from German law) generally are regarded in civilian legal systems as pertaining to tort or restitution.

[46] Contrast Rome I Convention art.1.3, and see Rome I Regulation art.7, para.15–29, below. The rules of the Rome I Convention did not apply to contracts of insurance which cover risks situated in the territories of EEC Member States (though this exclusion did not apply to contracts of re-insurance).

[47] As to burden of proof, see para.15–53, below, and generally Ch.8.

[48] This means the rules of law in force in that country other than its rules of private international law, unless provided otherwise in the Regulation: art.20. See para.15.55, below.

[49] See recital (11). See also *Duarte v Black & Decker Corp* [2007] EWHC 2720 (QB).

"Article 3
Freedom of choice

1. A contract shall be governed by the law chosen by the parties. The choice shall be made expressly or clearly demonstrated[50] by the terms of the contract or the circumstances of the case. By their choice the parties can select the law applicable to the whole or to part only of the contract.

2. The parties may at any time agree to subject the contract to a law other than that which previously governed it, whether as a result of an earlier choice made under this Article or of other provisions of this Regulation. Any change in the law to be applied that is made after the conclusion of the contract shall not prejudice its formal validity under Article 11 or adversely affect the rights of third parties.

3. Where all other elements relevant to the situation at the time of the choice are located in a country other than the country whose law has been chosen, the choice of the parties shall not prejudice the application of provisions of the law of that other country which cannot be derogated from by agreement.

4. Where all other elements relevant to the situation at the time of the choice are located in one or more Member States, the parties' choice of applicable law other than that of a Member State shall not prejudice the application of provisions of Community law, where appropriate as implemented in the Member State of the forum, which cannot be derogated from by agreement.

5. The existence and validity of the consent of the parties as to the choice of the applicable law shall be determined in accordance with the provisions of Articles 10, 11 and 13."

Under the Rome I Convention, parties might choose,[51] by means of art.3, only the law of a country (i.e. a body of State law), capable of ascertainment,

---

[50] There has been a slight change of wording from that adopted in the Rome I Convention, where the following words were used: "The choice must be express or demonstrated with reasonable certainty". Where change in wording in successive instruments does not appear to be of substantive significance, but merely a matter of semantics, the CJEU prefers to adopt continuity of interpretation. See Crawford, *"Ilsinger"*, 2009 (4) *European Journal of Consumer Law*. Notable cases interpretative of the equivalent article (art.3) of the Rome I Convention include *Egon Oldendorff v Libera Corp (No.2)* [1996] 1 Lloyd's Rep. 380; *Morin v Bonham & Brooks Ltd* [2004] 1 Lloyd's Rep. 702 (express choice of law contained in general conditions of sale in an auction catalogue, deemed to have been accepted by all bidders); and *FR Lurssen Werft GmbH & Co KG v Halle* [2009] EWHC 2607 (Comm). For cases where the choice can be inferred through, for example, an earlier course of dealing or standard conditions of the trade, see Giuliano and Lagarde, p.17. It was clearly understood that under the Rome I Convention, the court might not infer a choice of law which the parties might have made, where it was apparent that they had no clear intention of making a choice. Contrast approach at common law, outlined below.

[51] The issue whether a party later may say that his consent to a contract including a choice of law and jurisdiction clause, was not real or genuine, or existent, at the time of purported conclusion of the contract, was raised in *Horn Linie GmbH & Co v Panamericana Formas E Impresos SA (The Hornbay)* [2006] EWHC 373 (Comm). Morison J. held that in the circumstances the defendants must be held to the choice which they had expressly made: "I can think of no good reason why it would be reasonable to judge the consent of the Defendants otherwise than by the law of their choice" (at [19]) (a "putativity" argument, *q.v.*). As to law governing validity of choice itself and

and capable of answering any problem which might arise concerning the contract; as at common law, adequacy of a system to answer a question arising out of a contract is an essential prerequisite. The Rome I Convention did not contemplate, or permit, choice of a non-State system of law, such as the *lex mercatoria*, nor the choice of a body of religious law,[52] though as noted by Waller L.J. in *Halpern v Halpern*[53]:

"... if parties wish some form of rules or law not of a country to apply to their contract, then it is open to them to so agree, provided that there is an arbitration clause. The court will give effect to the parties' agreement in that way."[54]

The Court of Appeal decision in *Halpern v Halpern* provides a useful elaboration of the limits of the use which can be made of non-State law within the bounds of the Rome I Convention. While the court was clear that the English applicable law of the agreement alone must govern matters of substance, Jewish law as a distinct body of law could be relied on "as part of the contractual framework",[55] with the effect of permitting it to govern questions of interpretation. There was no justification for anticipating in the instant case any change in the approach to this subject which would be brought about by the Rome I Regulation. Waller L.J. alluded to the problems of enforcing remedies granted in terms of religious rules: "remedies, if they were to be effective, would have to flow from a system of law in the sense of the law of a country."[56]

The contractual arrangement in *Halpern* is to be contrasted with that made in *Shamil Bank of Bahrain EC v Beximco Pharmaceuticals Ltd*,[57] in which the Court of Appeal had difficulty in striving to find the true intention of the parties, and in particular in construing the clause, "subject to the principles of the glorious Sharia'a, this agreement shall be governed by and construed in accordance with the laws of England". Not only was it held to be impossible for there to be two governing laws (English law and Sharia law being incapable of

---

scope of clause, see *Finance One Public Co Ltd v Lehmann Bros Special Financing Inc*, 414 F. 3d 325 (2nd cir. 2005). On the analogous question in jurisdiction, whether or not apparent consent to prorogation under Brussels I Regulation art.23 can be challenged, see *Deutsche Bank AG v Asia Pacific Broadband Wireless Communications Inc* [2009] I.L.Pr. 36.

[52] See *Shamil Bank of Bahrain EC v Beximco Pharmaceuticals Ltd* [2004] 1 W.L.R. 1784, per Potter L.J. at [48].

[53] [2008] Q.B. 195.

[54] *Halpern v Halpern* [2008] Q.B. 195 at [38] (affirming *Halpern v Halpern* [2006] EWHC 603 (Comm), Clarke J. at [51], wherein the judge added a proviso, viz. that the parties' desire to have a dispute regulated by a body of non-state law (in the instant case Jewish law) could be fulfilled by their submission to arbitration, provided that the agreement to arbitrate should itself be enforceable under a national system of law). *Musawi v RE International (UK) Ltd* [2008] 1 Lloyd's Rep. 326 demonstrates that while the arbitrator was required by agreement of the parties to apply to the subject matter of the dispute and its resolution the principles of Shia Sharia law, a distinction has to be drawn between that agreement and the identification of the governing laws of the underlying contracts. Regardless of whether the underlying contracts were made after April 1, 1991 (being subject to the Rome I Convention), or before that date (being governed by common law principles), they could be governed only by the law of a country; cf. *Jivraj v Hashwani* [2009] EWHC 1364 (Comm).

[55] *Halpern v Halpern* [2008] Q.B. 195, per Waller L.J. at [33].

[56] [2008] Q.B. 195, per Waller L.J. at [39].

[57] [2004] 1 W.L.R. 1784, per Potter L.J. at [48].

operating jointly), but also there was the problem that the reference to "principles of the glorious Sharia'a" is a phrase of very uncertain meaning when there can be different schools of thought as to what Sharia law lays down.[58] References to Sharia law were held merely to reflect the Islamic religious principles according to which the Shamil Bank did business; the form of words used did not incorporate Sharia law as the governing law of the contract. The attempt to have Sharia law apply was inept, procedurally as well as substantively.

In this important area, the Rome I Regulation has expanded party choice. By art.3.2, parties may choose as the applicable law a body of law other than a national law (e.g. UNIDROIT Principles of International Commercial Contracts), or the rules of a Convention, such as the 1980 Vienna Convention. This greater flexibility was expected, and is generally welcome in the context of adoption of "harmonised codes", though perhaps will be problematic in relation to the possible expansion of acceptance qua applicable law of bodies of religious principles. Express authority for adoption of a body of non-State law is found not in the text of the Regulation, but in recitals.[59]

A proposed presumption in a draft version of art.3, that if parties have agreed to confer jurisdiction on a court or tribunal of a Member State to hear and determine disputes that had arisen or might arise out of the contract, they should be presumed also to have chosen the law of that Member State, was abandoned during the negotiation process. However, a hint to this effect remains through the medium of recital (12):

> "An agreement between the parties to confer on one or more courts or tribunals of a Member State exclusive jurisdiction to determine disputes under the contract should be one of the factors to be taken into account in determining whether a choice of law has been clearly demonstrated".

Relegation of the proposed "rule" to the recitals is wise. If it had been implemented in the body of the Regulation, it would have operated, as a matter of practice, to undermine the contract-specific rules set out in art.4 of the Regulation.[60] On the basis of recital (12), choice of court *may* supply choice of law; but it remains the case that choice of law cannot, of itself, supply choice of court.[61]

It would not be acceptable for parties to choose, under authorisation of the Rome I Regulation, the common law of England or Scotland pertaining to contract as it stood prior to the coming into force of the Regulation, i.e. parties cannot use Rome I to contract out of Rome I.

The parties' choice of applicable law is subject to overriding provisions discussed at paras 15–24—15–25, below, namely, arts 3.3 (an anti-avoidance

---

[58] *Shamil Bank of Bahrain EC v Beximco Pharmaceuticals Ltd* [2004] 1 W.L.R. 1784 at [33].

[59] Recital (13): "This Regulation does not preclude parties from incorporating by reference into their contract a non-State body of law or an international convention"; and recital (14): "Should the Community adopt, in an appropriate legal instrument, rules of substantive contract law, including standard terms and conditions, such instrument may provide that the parties may choose to apply those rules".

[60] Though it is conceded that a contract which contains a choice of court clause is likely also to contain an applicable law clause, bringing the case under art.3 of the Regulation.

[61] Though see *Shekar v Satyam Computer Services Ltd* [2005] I.C.R. 737 (employment tribunal, per Mr PT Wallington at [52]).

provision repeating what was contained in the corresponding article of the Rome I Convention) and 3.4 (a new provision seeking to ensure the application of "mandatory Community law"), as well as to "overriding mandatory rules" (art.9) and the public policy of the forum (art.21).

Determination of applicable law in the absence of choice of law

The provisions on determination of the applicable law in the absence of **15–11** choice have been re-cast. Article 4 of the Regulation is "contract-specific", with particular rules for particular categories of contract.[62] Such a formulation has the effect of ousting from its central role the connecting factor of "habitual residence of the party who is to effect the performance which is characteristic of the contract."[63]

Where the drafting device adopts a list of contract-specific rules, it is clearly essential to include a provision governing contracts which fall outside the list, or which straddle different categories within the list. This is contained in art.4.2. Article 4.3 is the displacement rule. It is usual in modern European choice of law instruments[64] to include a displacement provision for use at the discretion of the forum in cases where the law identified by the general rule cannot be regarded, in the view of the forum, as the law of closest connection.[65]

"Article 4
Applicable law in the absence of choice

1. To the extent that the law applicable to the contract has not been chosen in accordance with Article 3 and without prejudice to Articles 5 to 8,[66] the law governing the contract shall be determined as follows:
   (a) a contract for the sale of goods shall be governed by the law of the country where the seller[67] has his habitual residence[68];

---

[62] See Z. Tang, "Law Applicable in the Absence of Choice—The New Article 4 of the Rome I Regulation", 2008 M.L.R. 785.

[63] Rome Convention art.4.2.

[64] cf. Rome II art.4.3.

[65] See recital (16): "To contribute to the general objective of this Regulation, legal certainty in the European judicial area, the conflict-of-law rules should be highly foreseeable. The courts should, however, retain a degree of discretion to determine the law that is most closely connected to the situation." Cf. Equivalent provision in Rome I Convention art.4.5: see Crawford and Carruthers, *International Private Law in Scotland*, 2nd edn, 2006, paras 15–14 to 15–16 and paras 15–12—15–15, below.

[66] Special rules pertaining to contracts of carriage; consumer contracts; insurance contracts; and individual employment contracts, explained paras 15–26—15–33, below.

[67] Recital (17) states that the concept of "sale of goods" should be interpreted in the same way as when applying art.5 of the Brussels I Regulation in so far as sale of goods are covered by that Regulation. But the effect of insertion into the Brussels I Regulation of a community definition of "place of performance" (indicating, in sale of goods contracts, the place of delivery) would appear to have the result of clothing with jurisdiction the court of the buyer's legal system. Thus the buyer's court is enjoined to apply the seller's law.

[68] Article 19 of the Regulation provides, of new, a definition of habitual residence of companies and other bodies, corporate or unincorporated, and of a natural person acting in the course of his business activitiy, and of branches or agencies: para.15–54, below. See, under the Rome Convention, *Sierra Leone Telecommunications Co Ltd v Barclays Bank Plc* [1998] 2 All E.R. 820; and *Iran Continental Shelf Oil Co v IRI International Corp* [2002] EWCA Civ 1024. Contrast *Ennstone Building Products Ltd v Stanger Ltd* [2002] 1 W.L.R. 3059. See also *Mimusa v Yves Saint-Laurent Parfums* [2008] E.C.C 30 *Cour de Cassation*, France.

    (b) a contract for the provision of services[69] shall be governed by the law of the country where the service provider has his habitual residence;

    (c) a contract relating to a right *in rem* in immovable property or to a tenancy of immovable property shall be governed by the law of the country where the property is situated[70];

    (d) notwithstanding point (c), a tenancy of immovable property concluded for temporary private usc for a period of no more than six consecutive months shall be governed by the law of the country where the landlord has his habitual residence, provided that the tenant is a natural person and has his habitual residence in the same country;

    (e) a franchise contract shall be governed by the law of the country where the franchisee has his habitual residence;

    (f) a distribution contract shall be governed by the law of the country where the distributor has his habitual residence;

    (g) a contract for the sale of goods by auction shall be governed by the law of the country where the auction takes place, if such a place can be determined;

    (h) a contract concluded within a multilateral system which brings together or facilitates the bringing together of multiple third-party buying and selling interests in financial instruments, as defined by Article 4(1), point (17) of Directive 2004/39/EC, in accordance with non-discretionary rules and governed by a single law, shall be governed by that law.[71]

2.   Where the contract is not covered by paragraph 1 or where the elements of the contract would be covered by more than one of points (a) to (h) of paragraph 1, the contract shall be governed by the law of the country where the party required to effect the characteristic performance[72] of the contract has his habitual residence.

3.   Where it is clear from all the circumstances of the case that the contract is manifestly more closely connected with a country other than that indicated in paragraphs 1 or 2, the law of that other country shall apply.

---

[69] Recital (17) states that the concept of "provision of services" should be interpreted in the same way as when applying art.5 of the Brussels I Regulation in so far as provision of services are covered by that Regulation. The same outcome of mismatch between court and applicable law can be seen as arises in relation to sale of goods: cf. fn.67, above.

[70] A parallel may be drawn here with the exclusive jurisdiction provisions contained in Brussels I Regulation art.22.1.

[71] See also recital (18).

[72] Difficulty occasionally was encountered under the Convention in ascertaining what was the "characteristic performance", or in identifying the party who was to effect it: see, e.g. *Iran Continental Shelf Oil Co v IRI International Corp* [2002] EWCA Civ 1024; *Hogg Insurance Brokers Ltd v Guardian Insurance Co Inc* [1997] I Lloyd's Rep. 412; *Ennstone Building Products Ltd v Stanger Ltd* [2002] 1 W.L.R. 3059; and *Apple Corps Ltd v Apple Computer Inc* [2004] EWHC 768.

4. Where the law applicable cannot be determined pursuant to paragraphs 1 or 2, the contract shall be governed by the law of the country with which it is most closely connected."[73]

CONTINUING RELEVANCE OF ROME CONVENTION

Insofar as cases concerning contracts concluded before December 17, 2009 **15–12** will continue to be litigated under the Rome I Convention for a number of years after the entry into force of the Rome I Regulation, the undernoted examination of such provisions of the Convention as differ from the Regulation, with accompanying case law, continues to be of relevance.

Rome Convention article 4: applicable law in the absence of choice

Article 4 provided as follows: **15–13**

"1. To the extent that the law applicable to the contract has not been chosen in accordance with Article 3, the contract shall be governed by the law of the country with which it is most closely connected. Nevertheless, a severable part of the contract which has a closer connection with another country may by way of exception be governed by the law of that other country.
2. Subject to the provisions of paragraph 5 of this Article, it shall be presumed that the contract is most closely connected with the country where the party who is to effect the performance which is characteristic of the contract has, at the time of conclusion of the contract, his habitual residence, or, in the case of a body corporate or unincorporate, its central administration.[74] However, if the contract is entered into in the course of that party's trade or profession, that country shall be the country in which the principal place of business is situated or, where under the terms of the contract the performance is to be effected through a place of business other than the principal place of business,[75] the country in which that other place of business is situated. . . .
5. Paragraph 2 shall not apply if the characteristic performance cannot be determined, and the presumptions in paragraphs 2, 3 and 4 shall be disregarded if it appears from the circumstances as a whole that the contract is more closely connected with another country."

---

[73] The precursor to art.4.3 and 4.4 of the Regulation is the Rome I Convention art.4.5. Essentially the thrust of these provisions is the same. The effect of the Convention art.4.5 was that the forum could use its unfettered discretion to identify the applicable law if the characteristic performance could not be determined, or if it appeared from the circumstances as a whole that the contract was more closely connected with another country. Changes in format in art.4.3 and 4.4 of the Regulation do not appear to be material, and two exit routes remain.

[74] *Sierra Leone Telecommunications Co Ltd v Barclays Bank Plc* [1998] 2 All E.R. 820 (performance of the obligation of repaying a sum deposited in a bank account was made through the branch where the account was kept, and therefore the applicable law was the law of the country where the account was kept); and *Iran Continental Shelf Oil Co v IRI International Corp* [2002] EWCA Civ 1024.

[75] See *Ennstone Building Products Ltd v Stanger Ltd* [2002] 1 W.L.R. 3059; and *Mimusa v Yves Saint-Laurent Parfums* [2008] E.C.C 30 *Cour de Cassation*, France.

Rome Convention article 4.2

15–14   The provisions of art.4.2, which were derived from Swiss conflict rules, excited much comment, some of it adverse. While it is true that at common law application qua "proper law" of the *lex loci solutionis* usually was preferred to the *lex loci contractus* (where they differed), and that while in identifying the place of performance, "performance" by means of manufacture or creative work was rated more meaningful than "performance" by way of payment made by the other party,[76] the Rome I Convention introduced a significant change in its choice of the connecting factor of "habitual residence of the characteristic performer". The choice was idiosyncratic.[77] The concept of "characteristic performance" itself was new to the UK in 1990. Giuliano and Lagarde explain it thus:

> "In addition it is possible to relate the concept of characteristic performance to an even more general idea, namely the idea that his performance refers to the function which the legal relationship involved fulfils in the economic and social life of any country. The concept of characteristic performance essentially links the contract to the social and economic environment of which it will form a part."

Under the Rome I Convention manufacture was more characteristic than payment; provision of a service more characteristic than payment for the service; performance by a banker of his side of a contract with a customer more characteristic than the customer's counterpart obligation.[78] The tendency was to favour the party effecting the "positive" performance rather than the reciprocal pecuniary obligation.

The relative strengths of article 4.2 and 4.5[79]

15–15   A court applying art.4 of the Convention was permitted to disregard art.4.2 if characteristic performance could not be determined[80]; and[81] if it appeared from the circumstances as a whole that the contract was more closely connected with another country.[82] It is this latter clause of art.4.5 which permitted UK courts (in their view, at least), in a qualifying case, to draw upon the pre-existing body of common law case law concerning determination of the proper law of a contract.

---

[76] Giuliano and Lagarde, p.20.

[77] See discussion by Blaikie, "Choice of Law in Contract, 'Characteristic Performance' and the EEC Contracts Convention", 1983 S.L.T. (News) 241. Also *Ophthalmic Innovations International (UK) Ltd v Ophthalmic Innovations International Inc* [2005] I.L.Pr. 10.

[78] *Bank of Baroda v Vysya Bank Ltd* [1994] 2 Lloyd's Rep. 87. See also *Ark Therapeutics Plc v True North Capital Ltd* [2006] 1 All E.R. (Comm) 138 (a "unilateral contract").

[79] See J. Hill, "Choice of Law in Contract under the Rome Convention" (2004) 53 I.C.L.Q. 325; and S. Atrill, "Choice of Law in Contract: the Missing Pieces of the Article 4 Jigsaw" (2004) 53 I.C.L.Q. 549.

[80] See *Print Concept GmbH v GEW (EC) Ltd* [2001] EWCA Civ 352, in which Longmore L.J. held that the supply of products, rather than their onward sale, was the performance characteristic of the contract. (This having been decided, there was no need to employ art.4.5.)

[81] The disjunctive "and" should be read as "or".

[82] cf. *Kenburn Waste Management Ltd v Bergmann, The Times*, July 9, 2001 (and on appeal [2002] EWCA Civ 98), concerning a negative obligation, the nature of which made it justifiable in the view of the English forum to displace art.4.2.

The relationship between art.4.2 and 4.5 (i.e. their relative strengths) was a matter of controversy. According to art.4.5, the presumptions in art.4.2, 4.3 and 4.4 were to be disregarded if it appeared from the circumstances as a whole that the contract was more closely connected with another country. The wording of art.4.5, and choice of the verb "disregard",[83] suggested that a variety of interpretative approaches might justifiably be taken.

The EU Commission favoured the approach taken in the decision of the Dutch Hoge Raad in *Société Nouvelle des Papeteries de l'Aa SA v BV Machinenfabriek BOA*,[84] which applied the Dutch law of the place of business of the sellers as the applicable law in circumstances where all other contacts were with French law. The contract for the sale of a paper press by a Dutch seller to a French buyer had been negotiated and completed in France; the press had been delivered to the buyer in France, there to be assembled by him; the order had been placed in France with the French agent of the Dutch seller; and payment was to be made in French francs. The buyer having failed to pay, the sellers elected to sue him in the Netherlands, using the special jurisdiction in contract then extant.[85] Jurisdiction was challenged by the French parties, arguing that the place of performance (being the obligation to pay) was in France. In terms of the Brussels I Convention art.5.1, it was necessary for the forum of a Contracting State first to identify the applicable law, and by that law to determine whether or not the legal system of the forum was the place of performance of the obligation in question.[86] On this rationale, the Dutch court, applying art.4.2, found Dutch law to be the applicable law. The decision represented a strong preference for the certainty which application of art.4.2 delivered, over the possible benefits of appropriateness inherent in displacement of art.4.2 by means of art.4.5 and the discretion which the latter provision conferred. In the instant case, however, the decision permitted the forum to apply its own Dutch law.

The earliest English case interpretative of art.4.2 is *Bank of Baroda v Vysya Bank Ltd*,[87] concerning a letter of credit. The contract between the issuing and the confirming banks was English law, per art.4.2. Although the applicable law of the principal contract (for which the inter-bank contract was facilitative) would have been governed by Indian law per art.4.2, Mance J. (as he then was) held that, for clarity and simplicity, it was desirable that all aspects of this contractual nexus be governed by the same applicable law (English law). Article 4.5 was the means by which to secure this result. The line of English

---

[83] See generally *Definitely Maybe (Touring) Ltd v Marek Lieberberg Konzertagentur GmbH (No.2)* [2001] 4 All E.R. 283, per Morison J. at 287, 288; *Credit Lyonnais v New Hampshire Insurance Co Ltd* [1997] 2 Lloyd's Rep. 1, per Hobhouse L.J. at 5; *Samcrete Egypt Engineers & Contractors SAE v Land Rover Exports Ltd* [2001] EWCA Civ 2019; and *Iran Continental Shelf Oil Co v IRI International Corp* [2002] EWCA Civ 1024.

[84] (1992) No.750, RvdW (1992) No.207.

[85] Brussels Convention art.5.1.

[86] Owing to the expanded wording of art.5.1 provided by the Brussels I Regulation, in supplying an autonomous definition of "place of performance of the obligation in question" in the cases of sale of goods and provision of services, there is generally no longer a need for this two-stage reasoning. See para.7–17, above.

[87] [1994] 2 Lloyd's Rep. 87. See also *Marconi Communications International Ltd v PT Pan Indonesian Bank TBK* [2005] 2 All E.R. (Comm) 325.

authority evinces a preference for use of art.4.5 in order to confer a wider discretion upon the forum in its identification of the applicable law, a discretion which, in a number of instances, resulted in the selection of English law as the applicable law.[88] In contrast, the effect of the Dutch *Papeteries* decision is that art.4.2 was to be displaced only if the factor of the habitual residence of the characteristic performer had "no real value" as a connecting factor.

The leading Scots case on the point is *Caledonia Subsea Ltd v Micoperi Srl*,[89] which at first instance and on appeal showed a clear preference for adhering to the art.4.2 presumption.[90] The circumstances revealed a factual and legal nexus with Egyptian law, but the business of the characteristic performer was situated in Scotland. Lord President Cullen's opinion gives firm dominance to the art.4.2 presumption:

> "I consider that the presumption under para 2 should not be 'disregarded' unless the outcome of the comparative exercise referred to in para 5 . . . demonstrates a clear preponderance of factors in favour of another country."[91]

The outcome in *Caledonia Subsea* of holding to art.4.2 was application of the forum's own (Scots) law. In order for the forum to "walk home", it was not necessary always to have resort to art.4.5.

The background has been narrated at length on the rationale that in the re-cast art.4 contained in the Rome I Regulation, effectively the same discretion remains for use by the forum. The enlarged appearance of the new art.4 perhaps distracts attention from the fact that where the law applicable cannot be determined pursuant to the many rules contained in art.4.1 and 4.2, or where it is clear from all the circumstances of the case that the contract is manifestly more closely connected with a country other than that indicated in art.4.1 or 4.2, it shall be the function of the forum to take a view on the identity of the law of the country of manifestly more close connection (art.4.3) or most close connection (art.4.4). In so doing, it is unlikely that a UK forum will, or can, ignore the hinterland to this provision. But it is to be expected that over time the influence of the CJEU in interpreting the Regulation will reduce the scope for individual Member State forum variation in the manner of exercise of its judicial discretion.

---

[88] e.g. *Bank of Baroda v Vysya Bank Ltd* [1994] 2 Lloyd's Rep. 87; *Definitely Maybe (Touring) Ltd v Marek Lieberberg Konzertagentur GmbH (No.2)* [2001] 4 All E.R. 283, per Morison J. at 287, 288; see also per Hobhouse L.J. in *Credit Lyonnais v New Hampshire Insurance Co Ltd* [1997] 2 Lloyd's Rep. 1, obiter at 5; *Samcrete Egypt Engineers & Contractors SAE v Land Rover Exports Ltd* [2002] C.L.C. 533; and *Marconi Communications International Ltd v PT Pan Indonesian Bank TBK* [2005] 2 All E.R. (Comm) 325. But see comments of Lawrence Collins J. in *Ophthalmic Innovations International (UK) Ltd v Ophthalmic Innovations International Inc* [2005] I.L.Pr. 10.

[89] 2002 S.L.T. 1022. Also *William Grant & Sons International Ltd v Marie Brizard Espana SA*, 1998 S.C. 536. Contrast *Ferguson Shipbuilders Ltd v Voith Hydro GmbH & Co KG*, 2000 S.L.T. 229, obiter per Lord Penrose.

[90] cf. *Krupp Uhde GmbH v Weir Westgarth Ltd* Unreported May 31, 2002 Lord Eassie.

[91] *Caledonia Subsea Ltd v Micoperi Srl*, 2002 S.L.T. 1022 at 1029G.

CONTINUING RELEVANCE OF COMMON LAW CHOICE
OF LAW RULES IN CONTRACT

In cases which fall outside the scope of the Regulation (and the Convention),[92] **15–16**
and outside the scope of any European harmonisation instrument, well-
established common law principles and approaches remain applicable in the
UK courts. Under the Convention, it was clear that the common law rules of
Scotland and England retained residual influence insofar as the Convention
was not exhaustive in its provision, and the UK forum might legitimately
resort to common law authorities where the Convention did not supply a rule,
or supplied an incomplete rule (the most obvious example being in relation to
the matter of contractual capacity in art.11). In that certain matters continue to
fall outside the scope of the Regulation, and certain rules continue to be
incomplete,[93] the same reasoning must obtain, namely, that the common law
may be permitted to supply the lack.

In the slightly different scenario demonstrated by art.4.5 of the Convention,
and arts 4.3 and 4.4. of the Regulation, in which the EU forum is entitled to
depart, at its discretion, from the general presumptions/rules contained in the
instrument, the question arises whether the forum is entitled to summon to its aid
common law authorities peculiar to its own jurisdiction. While this was thought
to be permissible under the Convention, constrained only by the terms of
art.18,[94] the correctness of this approach perhaps may be doubted with regard to
the Regulation. The very fact that the Regulation contains no provision equivalent to art.18 of the Convention admits that uniform interpretation is expected,
and reference to national common law authorities may be inappropriate.

Party autonomy: choice of proper law

At common law, the contracting parties' expressed intention determined the **15–17**
proper law of a contract.[95] The guide was taken to be provided by Lord Wright
in *Vita Food Products Inc v Unus Shipping Co Ltd (In Liquidation)*,[96] namely
that the law selected must have been (a) chosen in good faith; (b) the choice
must have been legal; and (c) the choice must not have been contrary to public
policy.[97] Opinion varied as to whether or not there required to be some factual

---

[92] e.g. obligations arising out of matrimonial property regimes (art.1.2(c) of the Regulation; cf. art.1.2(b) of the Convention).

[93] e.g. Rome I Regulation art.13 (contractual capacity).

[94] "In the interpretation and application of the preceding uniform rules, regard shall be had to their international character and to the desirability of achieving uniformity in their interpretation and application."

[95] e.g. *Earl of Stair v Head* (1844) 6 D. 904; *The Nina* (1867) L.R. 2 P.C. 38; *British Controlled Oilfields v Stagg* [1921] W.N. 319; *Jones v Oceanic Steam Navigation Co Ltd* [1924] 2 K.B. 730; *Anselme Dewavrin Fils et Cie v Wilson & North Eastern Railway Shipping Co Ltd* (1931) Ll. L. Rep. 289; *Feist v Société Intercommunale Belge d'Electricite* [1934] A.C. 161; *Vita Food Products Inc v Unus Shipping Co Ltd (In Liquidation)* [1939] A.C. 277; *Ocean Steamship Co v Queensland State Wheat Board* [1941] 1 K.B. 402; *Stirling's Trustees v Legal & General Assuarnce Society Ltd*, 1957 S.L.T. 73; *English v Donnelly*, 1958 S.C. 494. See also *Golden Acres v Queensland Estates* (1969) St. R. Qd. 738 (Australia); and *Queensland Estates v Collas* [1971] St. R. Qd. 75.

[96] [1939] A.C. 277 at 290.

[97] The requirements were readily accepted at a superficial level, but equally readily were queried: at what point does (legitimate?) self-interest extinguish or grievously impair good faith?; "legal" by which law?

connection between the choice of law and the facts of the contract.[98] The absence of reported cases where the validity of an express choice of law was disputed suggests that, in practice, the parties' agreement would rule. Parties, for their own reasons, might wish to choose a "neutral" law. A self-interested choice, lacking good faith, and/or contrary to public policy of the forum would be struck down by the court.[99] Choice, as a matter of caprice, was unlikely.

Parties' choice was limited to the choice of a law having sufficiently well developed rules on contract to serve the purpose of the choice.[100] Parties were not permitted to choose as the governing law, for example, the "rules of comity of nations", which would be insufficient to provide an answer to the problems which might arise. Particular provisions of a foreign law could be expressly incorporated as terms of a contract; this was not the same as making the whole of that foreign law the proper law.[101]

Determination of proper law in absence of express choice of law

15–18   At common law there were subjective and objective approaches to the determination of the proper law. The subjective approach sought to find the intention of the parties, albeit never expressed: "[t]he proper law is the law which the parties either expressly or impliedly have chosen to govern their contractual relations."[102] The search, therefore, was for supposed intention, the hypothesis being that the parties had entertained an intention.[103] The objective approach preferred to treat as the proper law the law with which the contract had the most real and substantial connection objectively, considering the facts of the case as a whole. The court, therefore, supplied the (reasonable) intention. An example of the latter approach is provided by *The Assunzione*[104] in which it was said that Italian law was the law which just and reasonable persons ought to have chosen as the proper law had they thought about the matter.[105] A significant common law case, in the decade preceding the 1990 Act, is the House of Lords decision in *The Al Wahab*.[106]

---

[98] See *Cheshire and North's Private International Law*, 11th edn, 1987, pp.471, 472, where the view was expressed that an unconnected choice would be ineffective.

[99] But the principal authority striking down a choice is Australian: *Golden Acres v Queensland Estates* (1969) St. R. Qd. 738 (Australia); and *Queensland Estates v Collas* [1971] St. R. Qd. 75.

[100] See para.15–10, above.

[101] *Dicey, Morris and Collins on the Conflict of Laws*, 14th edn, 2006, para.32–086. See *Amin Rasheed Shipping Corp v Kuwait Insurance Co (The Al Wahab)* [1984] A.C. 50, per Lord Wilberforce at 69, 70; and *Forsikringsaktieselskapet Vesta v Butcher* [1988] 1 Lloyd's Rep. 19; affirmed on other grounds [1989] A.C. 852; *Shamil Bank of Bahrain EC v Beximco Pharmaceuticals Ltd* [2004] 1 W.L.R. 1784, per Potter L.J. at 1798, 1799; and *Halpern v Halpern* [2008] Q.B. 195, per Waller LJ at [31].

[102] *Re United Railways of Havana and Regla Warehouses Ltd* [1958] 1 Ch. 724, per Wynn-Parry J. at 756; see also *R. v International Trustee for Protection of Bondholders AG* [1937] A.C. 500; cf. *Zebrarise Ltd v De Nieffe* [2005] 1 Lloyd's Rep. 154.

[103] Reference still may be made to this mode of thought in modern litigation, depending on the chronology of events: *Wasa International Insurance Co Ltd v Lexington Insurance Co* [2009] UKHL 40.

[104] [1954] P. 150.

[105] See too *Boissevain v Weil* [1949] 1 K.B. 482; affirmed [1950] A.C. 327, per Lord Denning: the proper law of a contract "depends not so much on the place where it is made, nor even on the intention of the parties, or on the place where it is to be performed, but on the place with which it has the most substantial connexion" (at 490).

[106] *Amin Rasheed Shipping Corp v Kuwait Insurance Co (The Al Wahab)* [1983] 2 All E.R. 884.

Where no choice was expressed, the court would derive help from certain indications or pointers such as:

(a) Locus contractus

The *locus contractus* is the place where, technically, a contract is deemed **15–19** to have been concluded, and is determined by the *lex fori*. A contract may be entered into face to face,[107] but the circumstances, especially in conflict cases, are likely to be more complex, and more physically remote. In the case of a contract entered into by exchange of documents posted in different places, the locus has been taken to be the place where the acceptance is posted,[108] but where a contract is entered into by instantaneous means of communication, the locus has been taken to be the place where the acceptance is received.[109] The latter principle was approved, in 1982, by the House of Lords in *Brinkibon Ltd v Stahag Stahl und Stahlwarenhandelgesellschaft mbH*,[110] subject to a warning that in view of technological advances, the rule might have to give way on occasion to considerations of where the risk should lie.[111]

At common law, ascertainment of the *locus contractus* was a first step to finding the proper law of the contract. However, where challenged by another contending law, the *locus contractus* rarely would prevail.[112] Where the *locus contractus* and the place of performance of the contract coincided, it would be rare for a different law to be the proper law.

(b) Submission to a particular jurisdiction

A contractual term by which the parties agreed to submit to the jurisdiction **15–20** of a particular court was considered to indicate, in general, that the law of that court was the proper law. The converse, however, was not true: choice of a particular law did not render the parties subject to the jurisdiction of the courts of that legal system if they were not otherwise subject thereto.[113]

(c) Arbitration clauses

Until 1968, an arbitration clause was held to be a very important factor in **15–21** ascertaining the proper law: if differences were to be settled by arbitration in a particular place, or by an arbiter to be appointed in such a place, it was presumed that the parties intended that their contractual rights and duties should

---

[107] *Rutherford & Son v Miln & Co*, 1941 S.C. 125.
[108] *Benaim & Co v Debono* [1924] A.C. 514.
[109] *Entores Ltd v Miles Far East Corp* [1955] 2 Q.B. 327; *Mauroux v Soc Com Abel Pereira Da Fonseca Sarl* [1972] 1 W.L.R. 962; *Brinkibon Ltd v Stahag Stahl und Stahlwarenhandelgesellschaft mbH* [1982] 1 All E.R. 293.
[110] [1982] 1 All E.R. 293.
[111] See, per Lord Wilberforce in *Brinkibon Ltd* [1982] 1 All E.R. 293 at 296: "[n]o universal rule can cover all such cases; they must be resolved by reference to the intention of the parties, by sound business practice and in some cases by a judgment where the risks should lie." With regard to electronic commerce, see para.15–57, below.
[112] See Lord Mansfield's presumptions, para.15–23, below.
[113] *NV Kwik Hoo Tong Handel Maatschappij v James Findlay & Co Ltd* [1927] A.C. 604; *Dunbee Ltd v Gilmour & Co (Australia) Pty Ltd* [1968] 2 Lloyd's Rep. 394.

be governed by the law of that place.[114] Morris, in 1968,[115] stated that, "there is an almost irrebuttable presumption that the law of that country is the proper law of the contract as a whole". Decisions of the House of Lords of 1970[116] show, however, that although an arbitration clause was still a very strong factor, it was not conclusive and might give way to other indications. Moreover, they show that the law of the arbitration was not necessarily the same as that of the proper law of the contract: the arbitral procedure might be governed by a law different from that of the proper law of the contract (which the arbiter/arbitrator was required to apply to the substance of the contractual dispute), and in that event, matters of its procedure, including review of the arbiter's award, would be governed by the (curial) law of the arbitration.[117]

(d) Language

15–22   On occasion, the court derived help from the terms or language in which the contract was framed in order to determine the proper law.[118]

(e) Presumptions

15–23   Presumptions traceable to Lord Mansfield in the 1760s sometimes were used, for example, in favour of the *lex loci contractus*, if the contract was to be performed where made; otherwise the *lex loci solutionis*[119]; the law of the flag in a contract of affreightment, if no closer connection with another law was

---

[114] *Hamlyn & Co v Talisker Distillery* (1894) 21 R. (H.L.) 21; *Girvin Roper and Co v Monteith* (1895) 23 R. 129; *Spurrier v La Cloche* [1902] A.C. 446; *Austrian Lloyd Steamship Co v Gresham Life Assurance Society Ltd* [1903] 1 K.B. 249; *Robertson v Brandes Schonwald and Co* (1906) 8 F. 815; *Johannesburg Municipal Council v D Stewart & Co (1902) Ltd*, 1909 S.C. (H.L.) 53; *Kirchner & Co v Gruban* [1909] 1 Ch. 413; *Pena Copper Mines v Rio Tinto Co Ltd* (1911) 103 L.T. 846; *Norske Atlas Insurance Co Ltd v London General Insurance Co Ltd* (1972) 43 T.L.R. 541; *Perry v Equitable Life Assurance Society* (1929) 45 T.L.R. 468; *Kennedy v London Express* [1931] I.R. 532; *National Bank of Greece and Athens SA v Metliss* [1958] A.C. 509; *Tzortzis v Monark Line A/B* [1968] 1 W.L.R. 406.

[115] Morris, *Cases on Private International Law*, 4th edn, 1968, p.280.

[116] *Compagnie Tunisienne de Navigation SA v Compagnie d'Armement Maritime SA* [1970] 3 All E.R. 71; and *James Miller & Partners Ltd v Whitworth Street Estates (Manchester) Ltd* [1970] 1 All E.R. 796.

[117] See also *Astro Vencedor Compania Naviera SA v Mabanaft GmbH (The Damianos)* [1971] 2 Q.B. 588; *Tracomin SA v Sudan Oil Seeds Co Ltd (No.2)* [1983] 2 All E.R. 129; *Astro Venturoso Compania Naviera v Hellenic Shipyards SA (The Mariannina)* [1983] 1 Lloyd's Rep. 12; *Furness Withy (Australia) Ltd v Metal Distributors (UK) (The Amazonia)* [1990] 1 Lloyd's Rep. 236. See now, as to Scots curial law, Arbitration (Scotland) Act 2010 Sch.1; certain of these rules have been designated mandatory rules of the *lex curiae* (s.8). See also paras 9–51—9–52, above.

[118] *The Industrie* [1894] P. 58 (reference to "Act of God" or "the Queen's Enemies" assisted Lord Esher M.R. to reach the conclusion that the charterparty in English form for the carriage of goods on a German ship had an English proper law. He placed reliance not on any one fact but on all of them together, but nevertheless he found it noteworthy that the terms used were applicable to English and not to German law. The case is an exception to carriage by sea cases decided at about that date, where the preference in case of doubt was for the law of the flag (though the law of the flag might be meaningless in the circumstances; *Compagnie Tunisienne de Navigation SA v Compagnie d'Armement Maritime SA* [1970] 3 All E.R. 71)). See also *Re Pilkington's Will Trusts* [1937] Ch. 574 (whole phraseology of deed indicated a Scots deed).

[119] *Chatenay v Brazilian Submarine Telegraph Co Ltd* [1891] 1 Q.B. 79; *Re Missouri Steamship Co* (1889) L.R. 42 Ch. D. 321; *Hansen v Dixon* (1906) 23 T.L.R. 56; *Mackintosh v May* (1895) 22 R. 345; *Kremezi v Ridgway* [1949] 1 All E.R. 662; *Benaim & Co v Debono* [1924] A.C. 514; *Mauroux v Soc Com Abel Pereira Da Fonseca Sarl* [1972] 1 W.L.R. 962.

demonstrated; the "more effective" law,[120] that is, the law which favours validity of the contract, or validity of a particular clause; the *lex situs* in cases concerning immoveables[121]; or the place where a professional person practises.[122]

By the mid to late twentieth century,[123] use of these presumptions had fallen from favour.

RESTRICTIONS ON CHOICE OF LAW

Mandatory rules and the Rome I Convention

The approach which the Rome I Convention adopted to the subject of party **15–24** autonomy was to allow choice of law in principle, but to circumscribe that choice by means of the compulsory application of rules of certain other laws. Reference was made in the Convention to two types of mandatory provision, internal and overriding. While the French text made clear in its use of the terms "*dispositions imperatives*" (art.3.3) and "*lois de police*" (art.7) that there was a difference between the two types of mandatory provision, this difference was not apparent in the English language text.

The phrase "mandatory rules" in relation to art.3.3 embraced, "rules which cannot be derogated from by contract" (i.e. as a matter of the forum's domestic law).[124] Article 3.3 secured application of the mandatory rules of the law of the country to which, "all the other elements [apart from the parties' choice of law] relevant to the situation at the time of the choice are connected".

Article 7, in contrast, referred to rules which, "must be applied whatever the law applicable to the contract" (i.e. as a matter of the forum's choice of law rules). The latter usage used to be termed in UK law, "overriding legislation of the forum"[125] (referring to legislation which applied no matter what the content of the foreign proper law), and therefore was a type of directory provision, which superimposed itself upon, or countermanded, normal choice of law rules.

A court of a Convention Contracting State was required to take its own view on the question whether a rule of its domestic law was an (overriding) mandatory provision for the purpose of art.7.2. Article 7.2 provided for application of the rules of the law of the *forum* in a situation where they were mandatory irrespective of the law otherwise applicable to the contract.[126] Article 7.1, which permitted "effect to be given"[127] to the (overriding) mandatory rules of

---

[120] This presumption seems to have been rarely used. The germ of the idea may be seen in *Hamlyn and Co v Talisker Distillery* (1894) 21 R. (H.L.) 21. It is potentially unfair and liable to encourage ex post facto reasoning. See May L.J. in *Monterosso Shipping Co v International Transport Workers' Federation (The Rosso)* [1982] 3 All E.R. 841 at 848, upon comments made in *Coast Lines Ltd v Hudig & Veder Chartering NV* [1972] 2 Q.B. 34. See also *P&O v Shand* (1865) 3 Moore P.C. (N.S.) 272 and *Re Missouri Steamship Co* (1889) L.R. 42 Ch. D. 321.

[121] *Mount Albert BC* [1938] A.C. 224. Exceptionally, another law was held to apply usually in situations where the cases were concerned with personal rights arising from contracts involving land, rather than real rights in land. *Cood* (1863) 33 Beav. 314; *BSA Co v De Beers* [1910] 2 Ch. 502; *Liquidator of the Salt Mines Syndicate Ltd* (1895) 2 S.L.T. 489. An unusual Scottish example is *Hamilton v Wakefield*, 1993 S.L.T. (Sh. Ct.) 30.

[122] *R. v Doutre* (1884) L.R. 9 App. Cas. 745; *Re Maugham* (1885) 2 T.L.R. 115.

[123] See *Coast Lines v Hudig & Veder Chartering NV* [1972] 2 Q.B. 34, per Lord Denning, 44.

[124] See *Caterpillar Financial Services Corp v SNC Passion* [2004] 2 Lloyd's Rep. 99.

[125] e.g. Unfair Contract Terms Act 1977 s.27 and Timeshare Act 1992. See also *Trident Turboprop (Dublin) Ltd v First Flight Couriers Ltd* [2009] EWCA Civ 290.

[126] e.g. *Société Diw v Société Unilin* [2009] I.L.Pr. 6 *Cour de Cassation*, France.

[127] See decision of Cour de Cassation in *Viol Frères v Philippe Fauveder & Co* (2010) (X 08-21.511).

the law of *another country* with which the situation had a close connection,[128] did not apply in the UK, reservation having been entered in respect of this provision. A number of delegations regarded art.7.1 with misgiving, as novel and uncertain.[129]

A point of dubiety under the Convention was the relationship in the area of consumer protection between arts 5 (mandatory rules of the law of the country in which the consumer is habitually resident) and 7. It was not clear whether or not art.7 was available to protect the consumer in a case where, in the circumstances, he failed to qualify for art.5 protection.

Rome I Regulation

15–25   It was recognised that it would clearly be desirable in the English language text to make some distinction in verbal form between the meaning of "mandatory provisions" as they had been used in art.3.3 of the Convention, and art.7, respectively.[130] Article 3.3. of the Convention is replaced by art.3.3 and 3.4 of the Regulation. Mandatory provision for the purpose of art.3 of the Regulation must be read as referring to provisions of the law of a country which cannot be derogated from by agreement, for there is no reference in art.3 to mandatory provisions per se. "Overriding mandatory provisions" under art.9 of the Regulation (replacing art.7 of the Convention) must be taken to refer to provisions which apply regardless of the content of the applicable law. Mandatory provisions operative under art.3 of the Regulation are relevant only in circumstances where a choice of law has been made by the parties, whereas overriding mandatory provisions applicable under art.9 apply regardless of whether or not the parties have exercised freedom of choice of law.

> "Article 3
> Freedom of choice . . .
>
> 3.   Where all other elements relevant to the situation at the time of the choice are located in a country other than the country whose law has been chosen, the choice of the parties shall not prejudice the application of provisions of the law of that other country which cannot be derogated from by agreement.[131]
> 4.   Where all other elements relevant to the situation at the time of the choice are located in one or more Member States, the parties' choice of applicable law other than that of a Member State shall not prejudice the application of provisions of Community law, where appropriate as implemented in the Member State of the forum, which cannot be derogated from by agreement."

---

[128] "When applying under this Convention the law of a country, effect may be given to the mandatory rules of the law of another country with which the situation has a close connection, if and in so far as, under the law of the latter country, those rules must be applied whatever the law applicable to the contract. In considering whether to give effect to these mandatory rules, regard shall be had to their nature and purpose and to the consequences of their application or non-application."

[129] Giuliano and Lagarde, p.27.

[130] See recital (37).

[131] See also recital (15). Cf. Rome II Regulation art.14 and recital (32).

It can be seen that art.3.3 of the Regulation serves essentially the same purpose as did art.3.3 of the Convention.[132] However, art.3.4 is an innovation, seeking to ensure, in cases where the choice of applicable law is that of a non-Member State, the application of provisions of Community law which cannot be derogated from by agreement. This elevates the status of Community law, ensuring that all Member State courts are mindful of it—but possibly the application of such provisions would have been safeguarded in any case by art.9.2 (and under the Convention, by art.7.2). Where the parties' choice of law falls upon the law of a Member State, art.3.4 has no application, but art.9.2 may operate in this way to ensure the application of provisions of Community law.

In relation to art.9 (overriding mandatory provisions), there are two principal points to note: first, a definition has been supplied in art.9.1 of "overriding mandatory provisions"; and secondly, that which was optional under the Rome Convention[133] has become compulsory under the Regulation—a mandatory provision in respect of mandatory provisions (which nonetheless, paradoxically, contains within its own terms discretion for the forum).

"Article 9
Overriding mandatory provisions

1. Overriding mandatory provisions are provisions the respect for which is regarded as crucial by a country for safeguarding its public interests, such as its political, social or economic organisation, to such an extent that they are applicable to any situation falling within their scope, irrespective of the law otherwise applicable to the contract under this Regulation.
2. Nothing in this Regulation shall restrict the application of the overriding mandatory provisions of the law of the forum.
3. Effect may be given to the overriding mandatory provisions of the law of the country where the obligations arising out of the contract have to be or have been performed, in so far as those overriding mandatory provisions render the performance of the contract unlawful. In considering whether to give effect to those provisions, regard shall be had to their nature and purpose and to the consequences of their application or non-application."

There has been an important change of wording between art.7.1 of the Convention and art.9.3 of the Regulation, such as partially to allay the anxiety on the part of the UK and some other Member States that the provision was unreasonably vague.[134] The outcome was regarded by the British government as an acceptable form of wording. While the introductory words of art.9.3

---

[132] See recital (15).
[133] Since Contracting States were permitted to enter a reservation under art.7.1 (the UK and six other states exercised this right).
[134] These concerns were sufficiently serious to influence the decision by the UK as to opting-in or not to the Regulation. It is, therefore, highly significant that as a result of negotiation (during which it became clear that the UK's preference for deletion of what became art.9.3 would not secure sufficient support among Member States), a compromise rule was reached that is narrower in scope than the Commission's original proposal (which resembled more closely art.7.1 of the Convention). See Ministry of Justice, *Rome I—Should the UK opt in?*, 2008, Consultation Paper CP05/08, paras 77, 78.

remain precatory (effect *may* be given), at least it is clear that the country, the law of which may be applied, is the *lex loci solutionis* alone. This is an improvement on the approach of the Convention, in terms of art.7.1 of which effect might be given to the mandatory rules, "of the law of another country with which the situation has a close connection" if and so far as under the law of that country those rules were overriding.

It would appear to be the case that characterisation of a provision of the *lex loci solutionis* (i.e. the law of the country where the obligations arising out of the contract have to be or have been performed) as an "overriding mandatory provision" in terms of art.9.3 is a task for the forum, which must heed the Community meaning supplied in art.9.1. Similarly, the characterisation of a rule of law, for the purposes of art.3.3 and 3.4, as one which cannot be derogated from by agreement, would appear also to be a task for the forum.

Though art.11.5 (formal validity of contracts concerning immoveable property) is essentially the same as art.9.6 of the Convention, the draftsmen have taken care to specify that mandatory provisions of the *lex situs*, of either type described above, must be observed.

In this commercial sphere, the exercise by the forum of its public policy is rarely seen. Nonetheless, public policy could apply to trump even mandatory provisions. In the event of a battle of policies under art.9, the forum's policy, by virtue of art.21, could prevail. Strictly this would be true also in relation to art.3.3, though such a contest seems most unlikely.

II. SPECIAL CONTRACTS

15–26 Under the Rome I Regulation, bespoke and elaborate provision is made for four categories of special contract, viz.: contracts of carriage (art.5); consumer contracts (art.6); insurance contracts (art.7); and individual employment contracts (art.8). The rationale is explained in recital (23), to the effect that parties perceived to be at a disadvantage should be protected by conflict of laws rules that are more favourable to their interests than are the general rules.

CONTRACTS OF CARRIAGE

15–27 The Rome I Regulation in art.5 makes detailed provision for the applicable law of contracts for the carriage of goods and of passengers, whereas the Rome I Convention made provision, under the aegis of art.4.4,[135] only for the carriage of goods.[136] The terms of the Rome I Regulation are subordinate to the terms of other conventions to which a Member State is, or may become a party, and

---

[135] *Intercontainer Interfrigo (ICF) SC v Balkenende Oosthuizen BV and MIC Operations BV* Case C-133/08 [2008] OJ C158/10.

[136] Contracts of carriage of persons fell within art.4.2 of the Rome Convention, and potentially, art 5.5, as "a contract which, for an inclusive price, provides for a combination of travel and accommodation". Charters by demise, where the contract was for the hire of the ship rather than for the carriage of goods, were not covered by the special presumption in art.4.4, but rather by art.4.2, the characteristic performance being delivery of the ship by the ship owner.

which lay down conflict of law rules relating to contractual obligations (art.25).[137]

The contracting parties may exercise freedom of choice of law to govern their contract, but, in the case of contracts for the carriage of passengers, that choice is limited,[138] within the terms of art.5.2.

In the absence of choice of law, the applicable law of the contract for the carriage of *goods* (art.5.1) shall be the law of the carrier's habitual residence,[139] provided that the place of receipt or of delivery or of consignor's habitual residence is also situated in that country; which failing, the applicable law shall be the law of agreed place of delivery.

In the absence of choice of law, the applicable law of the contract for the carriage of *passengers* (art.5.2) shall be the law of the passenger's habitual residence, provided that either the place of departure or the place of destination is situated in that country; which failing, the law of the carrier's habitual residence shall apply.

By virtue of art.5.3, where no choice of law has been made by the parties, and it is clear from all the circumstances of the case that the contract is manifestly more closely connected with a country other than that indicated in art.5.1 or 5.2, the law of that other country shall apply.

CONSUMER CONTRACTS

At common law, there was no such species as "consumer" for the purpose of **15–28** the conflict of laws.[140] However, prior to the Contracts (Applicable Law) Act 1990, British domestic legislation sought to recognise and compensate cases of uneven bargaining power, principally in the cases of consumers and employees. An early example of conflict of laws awareness in a domestic statute is the Unfair Contract Terms Act 1977,[141] which contains in s.27(1) a self-denying provision, and in s.27(2) an overriding provision.

Certain "qualifying" consumer contracts were singled out for special treatment in the Rome I Convention art.5. In short, the benefit resided, first, in securing for the consumer the mandatory rules of the law of his habitual residence, notwithstanding the choice by the parties of another law; and secondly, if the parties had made no express choice of law, the swift ascription to the

---

[137] Hence, for example carriage of goods by sea continues to be regulated by the Hague-Visby Rules in terms of the Carriage of Goods by Sea Act 1971. A list of countries in which the Hague-Visby Rules are in force is set out in the Carriage of Goods by Sea (Parties to Convention) Order 1985 (SI 1985/443), as amended by Carriage of Goods by Sea (Parties to Convention) (Amendment) Order 2000 (SI 2000/1103). See *Jindal Iron & Steel Co Ltd v Islamic Solidarity Shipping Co Jordan Inc* [2005] 1 Lloyd's Rep 57.

[138] The parties may choose only the law of the country where: (a) the passenger has his habitual residence; or (b) the carrier has his habitual residence; or (c) the carrier has his place of central administration; or (d) the place of departure is situated; or (e) the place of destination is situated.

[139] As to which, see art.19 (including art.19.2 concerning contracts concluded in the course of the operations of a branch or agency).

[140] Though see *English v Donnelly*, 1958 S.C. 494 (Scots hire-purchase legislation held to apply irrespective of the proper law of the contract). Cf. Generally *Stirling's Trustees v Legal & General Assurance Society Ltd*, 1957 S.L.T. 73.

[141] As amended by Contracts (Applicable Law) Act 1990 s.5, Sch.4 para.4. See also Employment Protection (Consolidation) Act 1978; Wages Act 1986.

contract of the law of the consumer's habitual residence. These benefits arose only if the circumstances of the transaction satisfied the criteria set out in art.5.2. Care was taken, for example, by oblique wording to cover such circumstances as "cross-border excursion selling".

The Rome I Regulation is less prescriptive in relation to qualifying contracts. But since it was felt that the rules of applicable law as contained in the Rome I Convention had not kept pace with the provisions contained in the Brussels I Regulation to protect consumers in jurisdictional terms, the Rome I Regulation now contains, in art.6.1, the phrase "by any means, directs" such (commercial or professional) activities to the country of the consumer's habitual residence, a form of words which matches the wording used in art.15.1(c) of the Brussels I Regulation. The insertion of this phrase at the time of drafting the Brussels I Regulation was regarded as a success for consumers. It is thought that it should cover internet purchases.[142]

Article 6 of the Rome I Regulation provides as follows:

> "1. Without prejudice to Articles 5 and 7,[143] a contract concluded by a natural person for a purpose which can be regarded as being outside his trade or profession (the consumer)[144] with another person acting in the exercise of his trade or profession (the professional) shall be governed by the law of the country where the consumer has his habitual residence, provided that the professional:
>
>   (a) pursues his commercial or professional activities in the country where the consumer has his habitual residence, or
>
>   (b) by any means, directs such activities to that country or to several countries including that country,
>
>   and the contract falls within the scope of such activities.
>
> 2. Notwithstanding paragraph 1, the parties may choose the law applicable to a contract which fulfils the requirements of paragraph 1, in accordance with Article 3. Such a choice may not, however, have the result of depriving the consumer of the protection afforded to him by provisions that cannot be derogated from by agreement by virtue of the law which, in the absence of choice, would have been applicable on the basis of paragraph 1.
>
> 3. If the requirements in points (a) or (b) of paragraph 1 are not fulfilled, the law applicable to a contract between a consumer and a professional shall be determined pursuant to Articles 3 and 4.
>
> 4. Paragraphs 1 and 2 shall not apply to:
>
>   (a) a contract for the supply of services where the services are to be supplied to the consumer exclusively in a country other than that in which he has his habitual residence;
>
>   (b) a contract of carriage other than a contract relating to package travel within the meaning of Council Directive 90/314/EEC of 13 June 1990 on package travel, package holidays and package tours;

---

[142] See, however, recital (24).

[143] Contracts of carriage; and insurance contracts.

[144] Assuming consistency of approach with the definition of consumer in the Brussels I Regulation (cf. recital (24) of the Rome I Regulation), see case law at para.7–27 above.

(c) a contract relating to a right *in rem* in immovable property or a tenancy of immovable property other than a contract relating to the right to use immovable properties on a timeshare basis within the meaning of Directive 94/47/EC;

(d) rights and obligations which constitute a financial instrument and rights and obligations constituting the terms and conditions governing the issuance or offer to the public and public take-over bids of transferable securities, and the subscription and redemption of units in collective investment undertakings in so far as these activities do not constitute provision of a financial service;

(e) a contract concluded within the type of system falling within the scope of Article 4(1)(h)."

One source of conjecture under the Rome I Convention was the matter of ranking in a case where the mandatory rules of the consumer's habitual residence were less favourable than those of the applicable law by way of the parties' choice of law per art.3. The argument that the supplier would have been prevented from setting up the less favourable rules of the habitual residence appears to be supported by the tone of recital (23) of the Regulation.

As alluded to above,[145] the relationship between arts 5 (mandatory rules of the law of the country in which the consumer is habitually resident) and 7 of the Convention was not clear. Under the Regulation, it must be asked whether or not the relationship between arts 6 and 9 is any clearer. In particular, is art.9 available to protect the consumer in a case where, in the circumstances, s/he fails to qualify for art.6 protection? It is clear from the text of art.6 that its provisions are without prejudice to arts 5 (contracts of carriage) and 7 (insurance contracts). Recital (32) explains that owing to the particular nature of these contracts, specific provisions are required to ensure an adequate level of protection of passengers and policy holders. Article 6 does not apply in the context of those particular contracts, even if the law putatively applicable under art.6 were more generous, in the circumstances, than the law applicable per arts 5 or 7. But by the same token, since there is no explicit ranking of arts 6 and 9 (nor arts 5 and 7, and 9), it may be taken that art.9 can operate in the context of a consumer (or carriage or insurance) contract, to the effect of securing for the weaker party the most advantageous outcome.

A particular rule is contained in art.11.4 (formal validity), to the effect that the form of a consumer contract shall be governed by the law of the country where the consumer has his habitual residence, overriding all other connecting factors set out in art.11. While art.11.4 is clearly intended to provide a simple rule for the benefit of consumers, the usual doubt arises viz.: what should happen if, by the law of the consumer's habitual residence, the "contract" is invalid as to form, but by the law of the country where the consumer happened to be present at the time of conclusion of the "contract" (art.11.2), the contract is formally valid? The tenor of the weaker party protections is to take an approach which favours the weaker party; it is not clear whether a court would be justified in taking an *in favorem* (upholding the contract) or *contra proferentem* (denying the contract) approach, as best suits the consumer.

---

[145] See paras 15–24 and 15–25, above.

While much effort in the process of EC private international law harmonisation has been made[146] to secure for cross-border consumers a body of rules, both of jurisdiction and of choice of law, which operate to their advantage, and to cut the costs of settling such disputes,[147] a salutary reminder has been given[148] that such persons often may seek a remedy for their grievance in extra-judicial means such as through negotiation or alternative dispute resolution, and in any event, that the monetary amount involved may not be sufficiently large to warrant the initiation of litigation.

INSURANCE CONTRACTS

15–29 The rules of the Rome I Convention did not apply to contracts of insurance covering risks situated[149] in the territories of EC Member States.[150] This was explicable as there were several sectoral Directives governing the conflict of laws aspects of insurance. Contracts of reinsurance, however, were governed by the Convention.[151] Insured parties receive protective treatment in jurisdictional terms under the Brussels I Regulation.[152] As well as its being desirable to have a comprehensive and coherent system in place as between rules of jurisdiction and those of choice of law, criticism was expressed regarding the lack of transparency of choice of law provision in the insurance area.[153] Consequently, after consultation, specific provision for insurance contracts has been made in art.7 of the Rome I Regulation.[154]

Article 7 applies to qualifying[155] insurance contracts whether or not the risk covered is situated in a Member State, and to all other insurance contracts covering risks situated inside the territory of Member States. The Regulation does not apply to reinsurance contracts, which are excluded from the scope of the instrument[156] (in contrast with the situation obtaining under the Convention).

---

[146] See also art.27.1(b), which provides that by June 17, 2013, the Commission shall submit a report including an evaluation of the application of art.6, in particular as regards the coherence of Community law in the field of consumer protection. There has been effort also in the process of harmonisation of substantive law among Member States, and in the interrelationship between conflict of laws measures and substantive measures: see, e.g. European Commission Proposal for a Directive of the European Parliament and of the Council on Consumer Rights COM(2008) 614 final.

[147] See recital (24).

[148] See generally Jonathan Hill, *Cross-Border Consumer Contracts* (Oxford: Oxford University Press, 2008).

[149] To determine whether a risk is situated in these territories, the Convention provided that the forum should apply its internal law (art.1.3). Under the Regulation, see art.7.6.

[150] Rome I Convention art.1.3.

[151] See art.1.4.

[152] Brussels I Regulation arts 8–14. This instrument also, in art.14, differentiates between the generality of risks and particular risks (including "large risks" as defined in Directive 73/239/EC, as amended), described therein.

[153] Green Paper, para.3.2.2.

[154] Article 27.1(a) provides that by June 17, 2013, the Commission shall submit a report including a study on the law applicable to insurance contracts and an assessment of the impact of any amendments proposed.

[155] Contracts covering "large risks" as defined: art.7.2. In the absence of choice of law, the applicable law for contracts covering large risks normally shall be the law of habitual residence of the insurer.

[156] See art.7.1.

In the case of insurance contracts other than those covered by art.7.2 (i.e. contracts other than those which cover "large risk"), only limited party autonomy to choose the applicable law is permitted, within the terms of art.7.3,[157] the rationale being to protect the policyholder. In the absence of choice of applicable law by the parties, the contract shall be governed by the law of the Member State in which the risk is situated at the time of conclusion of the contract.[158]

INDIVIDUAL EMPLOYMENT CONTRACTS

Article 8 of the Rome I Regulation is worded as follows: **15–30**

"1. An individual employment contract shall be governed by the law chosen by the parties in accordance with Article 3. Such a choice of law may not, however, have the result of depriving the employee of the protection afforded to him by provisions that cannot be derogated from by agreement under the law that, in the absence of choice, would have been applicable pursuant to paragraphs 2, 3 and 4 of this Article.
2. To the extent that the law applicable to the individual employment contract has not been chosen by the parties, the contract shall be governed by the law of the country in which or, failing that, from which the employee habitually carries out his work in performance of the contract. The country where the work is habitually carried out shall not be deemed to have changed if he is temporarily employed in another country.
3. Where the law applicable cannot be determined pursuant to paragraph 2, the contract shall be governed by the law of the country where the place of business through which the employee was engaged is situated.
4. Where it appears from the circumstances as a whole that the contract is more closely connected with a country other than that indicated in paragraphs 2 or 3, the law of that other country shall apply."

The provision is specific and leans towards application of the law of the place where the employee habitually carries out his work,[159] not only in securing to him the benefit of the mandatory provisions of that law,[160] but also in identifying that law as the applicable law in the absence of choice.[161]

As with consumer contracts, the weaker party (the employee) should have the best outcome from his perspective. Within the operation of art.8, if the

---

[157] Following the model of the rule in art.5.2 (contracts of carriage of passengers). See also The Financial Services and Markets Act 2000 (Law Applicable to Contracts of Insurance) Regulations 2009 (SI 2009/3075) regs 4, 5.
[158] Additional rules for situations where a Member State imposes an obligation to take out insurance are contained in art.7.4; and provision for risks situated in more than one Member State is made in art.7.5.
[159] See further explanation in recital (36).
[160] See *Duarte v Black & Decker Corp* [2007] EWHC 2720 (QB).
[161] *Shekar v Satyam Computer Services Ltd* [2005] I.C.R. 737. Consider C.J.G. Morse, "Consumer Contracts, Employment Contracts and the Rome Convention" (1993) 41 I.C.L.Q. 1.

rules of the "chosen" law confer less benefit on him in the instant case than do the rules of the laws specified in art.8.2, 8.3 and 8.4 which cannot be derogated from by agreement, then the latter should prevail.[162] As regards the relationship between arts 8 and 9, it must be asked whether art.9 can operate in the context of an employment contract, to the effect of securing for the employee the most advantageous outcome. The answer surely must be that the employee can insist upon the application of the overriding mandatory provisions of the law of the forum, per art.9.2, if they are more generous.[163] Due to the likely coincidence between the place of habitual employment (art.8.2) and the country where the obligations arising out of the contract have to be performed (art.9.3), art.9.3 is not likely to be of assistance.

INTERNATIONAL SALE OF GOODS[164]

15–31 Various international instruments make special provision for contracts for the international sale of goods. The Rome I Regulation does not follow this approach except for the particular provision in art.4.1(a).

There have been various attempts by the Hague Conference on Private International Law to regulate contracts for the sale of goods, including: 1955 Convention on the Law Applicable to International Sales of Goods; 1958 Convention on the Law governing Transfer of Title in International Sales of Goods; and 1958 Convention on the Jurisdiction of the Selected Forum in the case of International Sales of Goods.[165] Other international efforts in this area include the 1980 United Nations Convention on Contracts for the International Sale of Goods (also known as the Vienna Convention). These conventions aim to harmonise the substantive domestic laws of Contracting States in one particular area of law, and in so doing to provide an alternative to the traditional conflict of laws method of resolving disputes. None, however, has been adopted by the UK.

By the Uniform Law on International Sales Act 1967,[166] the UK implemented two Conventions, namely, the Uniform Law on the International Sale of Goods, and the Uniform Law on the Formation of Contracts for the International Sale of Goods.[167] Since art.25.1 of the Rome I Regulation saves the application of international conventions to which a Member State is, or becomes, a party, this means that, in theory, the two Uniform Law Conventions take precedence over the solution dictated by the general provisions of the Rome I Regulation.[168] But in practice hitherto, parties very rarely agreed to adopt, for application to their contract, the body of substantive rules contained

---

[162] See also recital (35).

[163] Which effectively was the outcome in 1973 in *Brodin v A/R Seljan*, 1973 S.C. 213.

[164] See James J. Fawcett, Jonathan M. Harris and Michael Bridge, *International Sale of Goods in the Conflict of Laws* (Oxford: Oxford University Press, 2005).

[165] The 1955 Convention entered into force in nine states, but not in the UK. The two 1958 Conventions did not enter into force.

[166] Amended by the Sale and Supply of Goods Act 1994 Sch.2 para.3.

[167] Both concluded at The Hague on July 1, 1964.

[168] Subject, however, to art.25.2: however, as between Member States, the Regulation shall take precedence over conventions concluded exclusively between two or more of them in so far as such conventions concern matters governed by the Regulation.

in the Uniform Laws (assuming such a choice was competent under the Rome I Convention).[169] Additionally, certain factual conditions must be fulfilled before the *corpus* of Uniform Law rules shall operate,[170] and these uniform rules, in any event, are subordinate to the mandatory provisions of the law which otherwise would have been applicable. Hence, the option is not wholly attractive. Not only is the UK party only to a minority of these instruments, but those conventions which it has implemented are not in their substantive rules comprehensive (e.g. while passing of risk is treated, passing of property is not).

AGENCY

Article 1.2(g) excludes from the scope of the Rome I Regulation the question **15–32** whether an agent is able to bind a principal, or an organ to bind a company or body corporate or unincorporated, to a third party.[171] Other contractual aspects of agency, including disputes between principal and agent, will be subject to the Regulation,[172] and identification of the applicable law for such matters is regulated by arts 3 or 4, as the case may be.[173] Since, perhaps surprisingly,[174] agency is not one of the types of contract having a bespoke rule under art.4.1, identification of the applicable law of the principal/agent contract, must be governed in the first instance by art.4.2 of the Regulation, from which one might infer that, in the majority of cases, the applicable law shall be that of the habitual residence of the agent.

Commercial Agents

The activities of commercial agents in Great Britain[175] are regulated by the **15–33** Commercial Agents Directive 1986,[176] brought into effect in Great Britain by the Commercial Agents (Council Directive) Regulations 1993.[177]

---

[169] It is clear that such a choice would be competent under the Rome I Regulation art.3, and recital (13).

[170] See Uniform Law on International Sales Act 1967 Sch.1 art.1.

[171] cf. Rome I Convention art.1.2(f); and Giuliano and Lagarde, p.13.

[172] cf. "The exclusion affects only the relationships between the principal and third parties, more particularly the question whether the principal is bound vis-à-vis third parties by the acts of the agent in specific cases . . . principal-agent, and agent-third party relationships in no way differ from other obligations and are therefore included within the scope of the Convention" (Giuliano and Lagarde, p.13). See also *Cheshire, North and Fawcett: Private International Law*, 14th edn, 2008, pp.685, 686.

[173] Consider, generally, *Presentaciones Musicales SA v Secunda* [1994] Ch. 271.

[174] An earlier proposal by the Commission to include a special rule for contracts concluded by an agent (covering (i) the applicable law governing the contractual relations between principal and agent; (ii) the relationship between the principal and third parties, whether the agent acted within or outside his powers; and (iii) the relationship between agent and third party) did not survive negotiations. See Ministry of Justice, *Rome I—Should the UK opt in?*, 2008, Consultation Paper CP05/08, para.74.

[175] Separate provision exists for Northern Ireland, and Ireland. As to the latter, see European Communities (Commercial Agents) Regulations 1994 (SI 33/1994), as to which see *Kenny v Ireland ROC Ltd* [2005] 1 E.H.C. 241.

[176] Directive 86/653 on the co-ordination of the laws of the Member States relating to self-employed commercial agents [1986] OJ L382/17.

[177] Commercial Agents (Council Directive) Regulations 1993 (SI 1993/3053), amended by Commercial Agents (Council Directive) (Amendment) Regulations 1993 (SI 1993/3173) and Commercial Agents (Council Directive) (Amendment) Regulations 1998 (SI 1998/2868).

The 1986 Directive was introduced due to differences in the national laws of EC Member States concerning commercial representation, and the resultant inhibition upon conclusion and operation of commercial representation contracts where principal and commercial agents were established in different Member States. Since conflict of laws rules in the matter of commercial representation do not remove inconsistencies in national law, some degree of harmonisation of substantive law was required. The Directive gives priority to the legal relationship between commercial agent and principal.

The 1993 Regulations, as amended, have the general effect of protecting the agent, whereas domestic Scots law might be said to have shown particular awareness of the potential liabilities of the principal, and therefore, to be more protective of the latter party.[178] A commercial agent is defined in reg.2(1) as:

".... a self-employed intermediary who has continuing authority to negotiate the sale or purchase of goods on behalf of another person (the 'principal'), or to negotiate and conclude the sale or purchase of goods on behalf of and in the name of that principal."[179]

By Schedule to the Regulations, it is made clear that the type of agent to which this applies is one who devotes, "substantially the whole of his time to representative activities". It is a complex matter to decide as regards any individual whether the Regulations apply.[180]

It has been seen that the relationship between principal and agent is subject to the Rome I Regulation (and the Convention before it). In a British forum, it is likely that the 1993 Regulations (application whereof is determined by the location of the activities of the agent, and not by personal law factors pertaining to the principal or agent) will have the status of mandatory provision of the forum for the purposes of the Rome I Regulation. In terms of reg.1, courts are directed to apply the law which the parties have agreed (i.e. under Rome I Regulation art.3) will govern their agency contract, to the extent that the choice is the law of a Member State. But it may be assumed, given the nature of the Directive, that there will be equivalent derivative/secondary legislation in each Member State, respectively, and that such legislation will share the characteristic of being mandatory in nature. Therefore, in any case where the activities of the agent are being performed in an EC state, it seems likely, regardless of the applicable law under the Rome I Regulation (be it the law of an EC Member State, or otherwise), that the contract will be subject to the mandatory rules of the (EC) forum (Rome I Regulation art.9.2), and possibly of the law of another state under arts 3.3 or 9.3. This important point (that parties whose activities take place in a Member State cannot evade the protective provisions concerning commercial representations by choosing as the applicable law under the Rome

---

[178] See generally Fraser P. Davidson and Laura J. Macgregor, *Commercial Law in Scotland*, 2nd edn (Edinburgh: W. Green, 2008). In the matter of achieving harmonisation in the calculation of compensation, see *King v T Tunnock Ltd*, 2000 S.C. 424; and, *contra, Lonsdale (t/a Lonsdale Agencies) v Howard & Hallam Ltd* [2008] 1 Lloyd's Rep 78, discussed in Macgregor, "Compensation for commercial agents: an end to plucking figures from the air?" (2008) 12 Edin. L.R. 86.

[179] Though see express exclusions from this category in reg.2. As to definition of commercial agent, see *Parks v Esso Petroleum Co Ltd* [2000] Eu. L.R. 25; contrast *Kenny v Ireland ROC Ltd* [2005] 1 E.H.C. 241.

[180] See *McAdam v Boxpak Ltd*, 2006 S.L.T. 217.

I Regulation the law of a non-EC State) was confirmed by the ECJ in *Ingmar GB Ltd v Eaton Leonard Technologies Inc.*[181]

In cases where the agent's activities are to be performed outside the EC, presumably the effectiveness of a choice of law clause in the principal-agent contract (even where those parties have Scottish connection), for application of the law of a non-EC Member State, will depend upon the choice of law rules of the *lex fori*. If ensuing litigation should take place in Scotland in respect of such a scenario, it would seem difficult as a matter of interpretation for the Scots court to hold that the Commercial Agents Regulations, which govern the activities of commercial agents in Great Britain, are mandatory under art.9.2.[182] This suggests that a rule, or provision, may be mandatory for one purpose, but not for another.

III. INCIDENTS OF A CONTRACT

In cases covered by the Rome I Regulation, as under the Convention, the applicable law will govern most issues, but another law may govern a particular incident as an alternative to the generally applicable law, in addition to it, or in substitution for it.[183] This approach reflects the position at common law. **15–34**

CONSENT AND MATERIAL VALIDITY

Article 10 of the Rome I Regulation echoes the Convention (art.8), which itself affirmed and supplemented the common law: **15–35**

> "1. The existence[184] and validity of a contract, or of any term of a contract, shall be determined by the law which would govern it under this Regulation if the contract or term were valid.
> 2. Nevertheless, a party, in order to establish that he did not consent, may rely upon the law of the country in which he has his habitual residence if it appears from the circumstances that it would not be reasonable to determine the effect of his conduct in accordance with the law specified in paragraph 1."

According to Guiliano and Lagarde, art.8 of the Convention was intended to cover all aspects of formation of the contract "other than general validity".[185] "General validity" must be taken to mean that which at common law in the UK was referred to as "essential validity" (validity of the contract as to its whole

---

[181] [2001] All E.R. (Comm) 329. See Laura J. Macgregor, "Agency and Mandate", *Stair Memorial Encyclopaedia*, Reissue, para.48. See now art.3.4 of the Rome I Regulation.

[182] But art.9.3 may apply in these circumstances.

[183] e.g. material validity (Rome I Regulation art.10); formal validity (art.11); contractual capacity (art.13).

[184] Covering, therefore, cases such as *Albeko Schuhmaschinen AG v Kamborian Shoe Machine Co Ltd* (1961) 111 L.J. 519, where the issue was the legal effect of alleged non-receipt of an acceptance.

[185] See Giuliano and Lagarde, p.29.

purpose, and/or as to particular terms thereof), as opposed to "material validity" (establishing the fact of agreement)

The reason for the inclusion of the discretionary power in art.10.2 is to guard against the consequences of operation of a rule of some legal systems that silence on the part of the offeree connotes acceptance.[186]

This rule covers the questions whether or not there has been sufficient consent to contract (i.e. sufficient by the putative applicable law), and the agreement necessary to constitute a binding bargain. Hence, questions of substance as to what constitutes acceptance, as well as "technical" questions, such as the effect of posting an unqualified acceptance (i.e. whether or not receipt by the offeror is necessary for the constitution of the contract), are referred to the putative applicable law.

At common law, the question whether a contract had been formed was governed by the law which would have been the proper law of the contract if it were held that a contract had been validly concluded (the putative proper law),[187] exemplified in *Albeko Schuhmaschinen AG v Kamborian Shoe Machine Co Ltd*.[188] This workable approach, therefore, can be seen to have been adopted by the Convention and the Regulation, subject to addition.

CAPACITY TO CONTRACT

15–36 Article 13 of the Rome I Regulation contains a provision, introduced in art.11 of the Convention, which is remarkably specific in its terms.[189]

> "Article 13
> Incapacity
>
> In a contract concluded between persons who are in the same country, a natural person who would have capacity under the law of that country may invoke his incapacity resulting from the law of another country, only if the other party to the contract was aware of that incapacity at the time of the conclusion of the contract or was not aware thereof as a result of negligence."

This topic in practice is not simple, and there are conflicting policy considerations.[190] Where the case does not fall within the complex prerequisites of art.13, the common law continues to apply.

---

[186] See Giuliano and Lagarde, p.28.

[187] See generally *Mackender v Feldia AG* [1967] 2 Q.B. 590 and *Euro-Diam Ltd v Bathurst* [1987] 2 All E.R. 113; affirmed [1990] 1 Q.B. 1.

[188] (1961) 111 L.J. 519. See also *Compania Naviera Micro SA v Shipley International Inc (The Parouth)* [1982] 2 Lloyd's Rep. 351 CA.

[189] See commentary per *Cheshire, North and Fawcett: Private International Law*, 14th edn, 2008, pp.750–753.

[190] See Morris, *Conflict of Laws*, 7th edn, 2009, paras 13–046 to 13–048; and J. Blaikie, "Capacity to Contract: *McFeetridge v Stewarts & Lloyds* Revisited", 1984 S.L.T. (News) 161. For Scottish domestic position, see Age of Legal Capacity (Scotland) Act 1991; D. Nichols, "Can They or Can't They? Children and the Age of Legal Capacity (Scotland) Act 1991", 1991 S.L.T. (News) 395, 399, 400. These domestic Scots provisions will apply where the contract has a (putative) Scottish applicable law, subject to the provisions of art.13 of the Rome I Regulation.

Early Scots and English cases at common law indicated that contractual capacity was governed by the *lex loci contractus*,[191] but preference later was shown for the putative proper law.[192] Cheshire, when he delivered the David Murray Lecture[193] at the University of Glasgow in 1948 suggested, first, that a contract is not void for incapacity if the parties are fully capable by the putative proper law (that is, the law objectively ascertained, for parties cannot confer on themselves capacity by simple choice of a law unconnected) and, secondly, that a party who is incapable by the putative proper law should not succeed in pleading incapacity if he is of full capacity by the law of his domicile.

FORMAL VALIDITY

The matter is governed by art.11 of the Regulation, in which the list of poten- **15–37** tially relevant connecting factors has been expanded from that available under the Convention, which, in turn, was more expansive than the common law. The approach throughout remains generous. The rules traditionally have taken,[194] and the Regulation continues to take, an *in favorem* approach.

"1. A contract concluded between persons who, or whose agents,[195] are in the same country at the time of its conclusion is formally valid if it satisfies the formal requirements of the law which governs it in substance under this Regulation or of the law of the country where it is concluded.

2. A contract concluded between persons who, or whose agents, are in different countries at the time of its conclusion is formally valid if it satisfies the formal requirements of the law which governs it in substance under this Regulation, or of the law of either of the countries where either of the parties or their agent is present at the time of conclusion, or of the law of the country where either of the parties had his habitual residence at that time.[196]

3. A unilateral act intended to have legal effect relating to an existing or contemplated contract is formally valid if it satisfies the formal requirements of the law which governs or would govern the contract

---

[191] *Male v Roberts* (1800) 3 Esp. 163; *McFeetridge v Stewarts & Lloyds Ltd*, 1913 S.C. 773.
[192] *Bodley Head Ltd v Alec Flegon (t/a Flegon Press)* [1972] 1 W.L.R. 680. See also, in Canada, *Bondholders Securities Corp v Manville* (1933) 4 D.L.R. 699; *Charron v Montreal Trust* (1958) 15 D.L.R. (2d.) 240.
[193] Printed as Geoffrey C. Cheshire, *International Contracts* (Glasgow: Jackson, Son & Co, 1948).
[194] At common law a contract was formally valid if it complied with the provisions of either the proper law or the *lex loci contractus*: *Guepratte v Young* (1851) 4 De G. & Sm. 217; *Van Grutten v Digby* (1862) 31 Beav. 561; *Purvis's Trustees v Purvis's Executors* (1861) 23 D. 812 (see, per Lord Justice-Clerk Inglis at 831) (testamentary writings); *Valery v Scott* (1876) 3 R. 965. See Leslie, *Stair Memorial Encyclopaedia*, Vol.17, "Private International Law" (Butterworths), pp.257, 258.
[195] Note the express addition in the Regulation of agents. Although the complex provision devoted to principal/agent and agent/third party contracts was abandoned during negotiations (see para.15–32, above), nevertheless the Regulation is more alert to the agency dimension of contracts than was the Convention.
[196] Examination of art.11.2 reveals that there has been an enlargement of potentially applicable laws through the addition of the habitual residence of either party at the time of contracting (cf. Wills Act 1963 ss.1, 2).

in substance under this Regulation, or of the law of the country where the act was done, or of the law of the country where the person by whom it was done had his habitual residence at that time.

4. Paragraphs 1, 2 and 3 of this Article shall not apply to contracts that fall within the scope of Article 6. The form of such contracts shall be governed by the law of the country where the consumer has his habitual residence.[197]

5. Notwithstanding paragraphs 1 to 4, a contract the subject matter of which is a right *in rem* in immovable property or a tenancy of immovable property shall be subject to the requirements of form of the law of the country where the property is situated if by that law:

    (a) those requirements are imposed irrespective of the country where the contract is concluded and irrespective of the law governing the contract; and

    (b) those requirements cannot be derogated from by agreement."[198]

SCOPE OF THE LAW APPLICABLE

15–38 Whereas art.10 of the Regulation concerns material validity (establishing the fact of agreement), art.12 concerns matters of general or essential validity (validity of the contract as to its whole purpose, and/or as to particular terms thereof), although, in terms, its heading is "Scope of the law applicable". Article 12 provides as follows:

"1. The law applicable to a contract by virtue of this Regulation shall govern in particular[199]:

    (a) interpretation;

    (b) performance;

    (c) within the limits of the powers conferred on the court by its procedural law, the consequences of a total or partial breach of obligations, including the assessment[200] of damages[201] in so far as it is governed by rules of law[202];

    (d) the various ways of extinguishing obligations, and prescription and limitation of actions[203];

    (e) the consequences of nullity of the contract."[204]

---

[197] Of the "weaker" parties for whom special treatment is set out in arts 6–8, the consumer alone receives special treament in relation to formal validity.

[198] With regard to contracts concerning immoveable property, art.11.5 does not differ in substance from its precursor, art.9.6 of the Convention.

[199] The list is not comprehensive.

[200] cf. Rome II art.15.1(c). See discussion at Ch.8, above.

[201] cf. at common law *J D'Almeida Araujo LDA v Sir Frederick Becker & Co Ltd* [1953] 2 Q.B. 329 (remoteness of damage).

[202] See para.8–23.

[203] See discussion at Ch.8, above.

[204] By UK reservation the equivalent provision of the Rome I Convention art.10.1(e), did not apply in a UK court since the consequences of nullity were regarded by the UK as pertaining to rules of restitution. However, no reservations to the terms of a Regulation are permissible. In any event, application of the putative applicable law of the contract in terms of art.12.1(e) does not seem unreasonable (and is in sympathy with Rome II art.10.1—relational unjustified enrichment).

Since art.12 does not provide an exhaustive list of topics falling within the scope of the law applicable, authorities residing in the common law hinterland still may be of assistance. At common law, the essential validity[205] of a contract was governed by its proper law, or putative proper law.[206] Essential validity was deemed to include all questions pertaining to substance (i.e. the provisions of the contract), and to the rights and obligations of the contracting parties generally, including matters such as: the need for consideration; liability for non-performance; interest[207]; acquiescence in allegedly inadequate performance; rejection of goods as disconform to contract[208]; retention of payment[209]; liability for damages; third party rights under the contract (*jus quaesitum tertio*); the effect of a moratorium; the effect of war; the effects of exemption and indemnity clauses, etc. The proper law therefore determined all questions as to the rights of parties and defences, subject to the qualification that contractual rights might not have been enforceable if illegal by the law of the forum or contrary to its public policy.

(a) Interpretation

Article 12.1(a) of the Regulation, in referring the matter of interpretation **15–39** entirely to the applicable law, is rather more restrictive than the common law according to which the construction or interpretation of a contract was determined by the law chosen by the parties to govern that aspect of the contract. At common law, in the absence of a clause providing for interpretation, the law indicated by the contract applied; in the majority of cases, this was the proper law, but that law did not necessarily apply and probably would not apply if the contract were written in a language different from that of the proper law.[210]

(b) Performance

Adequacy of performance of obligations due under the contract will be **15–40** governed by the applicable law. This will include the effect of partial

---

[205] i.e. "general validity" per Giuliano and Lagarde, p.29.
[206] A selection of common law cases is noted: *Jacobs Marcus & Co v Credit Lyonnais* (1884) 12 Q.B.D. 589; *The Leon XIII* (1883) L.R. 8 P.D. 121; *Hansen v Dixon* (1906) 23 T.L.R. 56; *Kremezi v Ridgway* [1949] 1 All E.R. 662; *Equitable Trust Co of New York v Henderson* (1930) 47 T.L.R. 90; *Société des Hotels Reunis v Hawker* (1913) 29 T.L.R. 578; *Re Bonacina* [1912] 2 Ch. 394; *Re Claim by Helbert Wagg & Co Ltd* [1956] Ch. 323; *McCormick v Rittmeyer* (1869) 7 M. 854; *Gow v Caledonian Scrap Co* (1893) 7 Sh.Ct Rep. 65; *Keiner v Keiner* [1952] 1 All E.R. 643; *Hamlyn and Co v Talisker Distillery* (1894) 21 R. (H.L.) 21; *St Pierre v South American Stores* [1936] 1 K.B. 382; *The Al Wahab* [1983] 2 All E.R. 884; *The Rosso* [1982] 3 All E.R. 841; *Gill & Duffus Landauer Ltd v London Export Corp* [1982] 2 Lloyd's Rep. 627; *The Mariannina* [1983] 1 Lloyd's Rep. 12; *Armour v Thyssen Edelstahlwerke AG*, 1986 S.L.T. 94 OH; 1990 S.L.T. 891 HL; *Zahnrad Fabrik Passau GmbH v Terex Ltd*, 1986 S.L.T. 84.
[207] *Parken v Royal Exchange Assurance Co* (1846) 8 D. 365.
[208] *Benaim & Co v Debono* [1924] A.C. 514; *Sellar and Sons v Gladstone and Co* (1868) 5 S.L.R. 417; *Gow v Caledonian Scrap Co* (1893) 7 Sh.Ct Rep. 65.
[209] cf. *Bank of East Asia Ltd v Scottish Enterprise*, 1997 S.L.T. 1213.
[210] *Bonython v Australia* [1951] A.C. 201; [1952] A.C. 493; *The Assunzione* [1954] P. 150; *Re Claim by Helbert Wagg & Co Ltd* [1956] Ch. 323; *Corocraft Ltd v Pan American Airways Inc* [1969] 1 Q.B. 616; *Total Societa Italiana per Azioni v Liberian Transocean Navigation Corp (The Alexandria I)* [1972] 1 Lloyd's Rep. 399; *Woodhouse AC Israel Cocoa SA v Nigerian Produce Marketing Co Ltd* [1972] A.C. 741; *WJ Alan & Co Ltd v El Nasr Export & Import Co* [1972] 2 Q.B. 189.

performance and non-performance, as well as defective or delayed performance. Cognate topics such as impossibility of performance, and excuses for non- or partial performance, are likely to arise, and equally are substantive matters to be referred to the *lex causae*.

The law applicable to the contract governs performance, but art.12.2 provides that in relation to the manner of performance and the steps to be taken in the event of defective performance, regard shall be had to the law of the country in which performance takes place. This acts as a discretionary restriction on the operation of the law applicable to the contract, and is expressed merely in precatory terms. With regard to the precursor provision of the Convention, art.10.2, the Giuliano and Lagarde Report noted the absence of any definition of the phrase "manner of performance". The report suggests that matters such as the rules governing public holidays and the manner in which goods are to be examined would fall within this rule. The law of the place of performance seems unlikely to be granted any fuller role under this article.

Money obligations

15–41 With regard to the counterpart obligation of payment, it was found to be important at various points in the common law development of the subject, in decades in which a currency crisis had arisen, to draw a distinction between the discharge of the substance of an obligation, on the one hand, and, on the other, the performance of the obligation by payment of the debt in the currency which, by agreement of the parties, was to be used.[211] Insofar as these matters still might be of importance, the "money of account of a contract" (being the amount of money due by the debtor, and representing the currency in which his obligation must first be calculated) will be governed by the applicable law, by virtue of art.12.1(b). In contrast, the "money of payment of a contract" (being the kind of money or currency which the debtor must proffer in order to discharge his obligation, that is the currency in which the money due is to be paid) traditionally was regarded as procedural, and governed by the law of the place of performance. Conceivably, the latter aspect now may be considered to fall within art.12.1(d), and so subject too to the law applicable to the contract, rendering the distinction irrelevant.

Likewise, contractual obligations may be affected by Exchange Control Regulations. Subject to the International Monetary Fund Agreement (the Bretton Woods Agreement) among members of the IMF (to respect the currency regulations of each), exchange control legislation may affect and even invalidate contractual obligations which contravene them, if the legislation forms part of the governing law of the contract,[212] or it may be regarded as an overriding mandatory provision of the forum[213] or of the place of performance.[214]

---

[211] *Adelaide Electric Supply Co Ltd v Prudential Assurance Co Ltd* [1934] A.C. 122; *Mayor of Auckland v Alliance Assurance Co Ltd* [1937] A.C. 587; *Mount Albert BC* [1938] A.C. 224; *Bonython v Australia* [1951] A.C. 201; *National Mutual Life Association of Australasia v Att Gen of New Zealand* [1956] A.C. 369.

[212] See now art.12.1(b), subject to the public policy of the forum (art.21). Cf. At common law *Re Claim by Helbert Wagg & Co Ltd* [1956] Ch. 323, where the legislation was judged to be a genuine measure to protect the German economy.

[213] See art.9.2. Since exchange control was removed from the UK in 1979, this no longer can arise where the forum is Scots or English. But see at common law, *Boissevain v Weil* [1950] A.C. 327.

[214] See art.9.3.

Revalorisation laws (laws revaluing a particular currency) apply only to contracts and debts the applicable law of which is the law of the country concerned.[215]

Effect of illegality of a contract

The Rome I Regulation, in common with the Convention, does not make **15–42** express provision regarding the matter of illegality, but a rule can be inferred by reference to art.12, namely, that a contract which in its terms breaches its own applicable law will not be enforced by any Member State court. There must be considered as potentially relevant, in addition, rules which cannot be derogated from by agreement (under art.3.3 or 3.4), and account has to be taken of the public policy of the forum (art.21).[216] Application of any of these provisions may lead to unenforceability of a contract in the UK.[217]

Under the Rome I Convention, while a provision illegal by the mandatory rules of the forum was caught by art.7.2, art.7.1 was not available to UK courts to assist in cases where, initially or subsequently, there was illegality by some law of close connection (other than the applicable law).[218]

Now, under the Rome I Regulation, reference must be made to art.9.3, which provides expressly for cases of performance illegal by the law of the country where the obligations arising out of that contract have to be or have been performed.[219] As has been noted, art.9.3 is phrased as a guide, not a direction. Its potential application can be tested conveniently against the facts which arose in an English forum in *Ralli Bros v Compania Naviera Sota y Aznar*.[220] The case concerned the carriage of jute on a Spanish ship from Calcutta to Barcelona, at a rate of freight which, en route, became illegal by the Spanish law of the nationality of the ship[221] (taken to be the law of the place of performance). The proper law of the contract of carriage was English. Since the English forum refused to enforce the contractual rate of freight, the inference was drawn that, if the proper law of a contract is English, illegality by the *lex loci solutionis* would render the contract unenforceable in England. There was debate about whether this rule was one of English domestic or English conflict law, but it seemed reasonable, and in accordance with

---

[215] cf. at common law, *Anderson v Equitable Life Assurance Co* (1926) 41 T.L.R. 123; *Re Schnapper* [1936] 1 All E.R. 322; *Kornatzki v Oppenheimer* [1937] 4 All E.R. 133.

[216] cf. At common law, *Foster v Driscoll* [1929] 1 K.B. 470 (to avoid affront to a friendly country); *Regazzoni v KC Sethia (1944) Ltd* [1958] A.C. 301; and *Lemenda Trading Co Ltd v African Middle East Petroleum Co Ltd* [1988] Q.B. 448, and see Clarkson and Hill, *Conflict of Laws*, 3rd edn, 2006, p.489.

[217] *Soleimany v Soleimany* [1999] Q.B. 785. See Clarkson and Hill, *Conflict of Laws*, 3rd edn, 2006, p.2640; and *Cheshire, North and Fawcett: Private International Law*, 14th edn, 2008, pp.658–660.

[218] cf. notable Dutch decision, *Cie européenne des pétrôles SA v Sensor Nederlands BV Hague 1982* (1983) 23 Int. Legal Mat. 66 (see *Dicey, Morris and Collins on the Conflict of Laws*, 14th edn, 2006, para.32–142).

[219] Experience suggests that identification of the place of performance of the obligation arising out of the contract will be productive of controversy. Cf. In a jurisdictional context, Brussels I Regulation art.5.1 (see para.7–17, above).

[220] [1920] 2 K.B. 287; cf. *Regazzoni v KC Sethia (1944) Ltd* [1958] A.C. 301.

[221] An example of supervening, as opposed to initial, illegality of contractual terms by the law of the place of performance.

principle, further to infer from the decision that the effect of illegality by the *lex loci solutionis* was a matter which an English court would refer to the applicable law.[222] The common law position is that a contract would not have been enforceable in Scotland if it was illegal according to the proper law of the contract[223]; or it offended against the public policy of the *lex fori*.[224]

Applying the Rome I Regulation to the facts of *Ralli Bros*, it seems that the English forum simply would exercise its discretion whether or not to give effect to the supervening Spanish law, assuming that the English forum considered the provision in question to be an overriding mandatory provision of the law of the place of performance. There are, therefore, two steps of discretion. Although this seems a satisfactory solution to the case in question, the process of reasoning involved appears to involve a shift of power to the forum.

(c) The consequences of breach

15–43   The consequences of a total or partial breach of obligations, including the assessment of damages in so far as it is governed by rules of law,[225] is referred by the Regulation to the law applicable to the contract. Questions of fact will always be matters of procedure for the forum,[226] but the wording of this provision of the Regulation denotes a shift in demarcation, in damages awards,[227] of the provinces of the *lex causae* and the *lex fori*, respectively, to the effect of enlarging the province of the *lex causae*.

(d) The various ways of extinguishing obligations

Discharge of obligations

15–44   Obligations under a contract may be affected, or even completely discharged, by subsequent events. A general discharge of obligations, or some other act purporting to discharge obligations, is effective if it is effective under the applicable law of the contract. Thus, the governing law determines the effect of supervening impossibility, war, moratorium, and confiscatory and

---

[222] cf. Reynolds, "Illegitimacy by Lex Loci Solutionis" (1992) 108 L.Q.R. 553.

[223] *Heriz v Riera* (1840) 11 Sum. 318; *Re Hope* (1857) 8 De G.M. & G. 731; *Rousillon v Rousillon* (1880) L.R. 14 Ch. D. 351; *Re Missouri Steamship Co* (1889) L.R. 42 Ch. D. 321; *Kaufman v Gerson* [1904] 1 K.B. 591; *Société des Hotels Reunis v Hawker* (1913) 29 T.L.R. 578; *Ralli Bros v Compania Naviera Sota y Aznar* [1920] 2 K.B. 287; *Trinidad Shipping and Trading Co v GR Alston & Co* [1920] A.C. 888; *Foster v Driscoll* [1929] 1 K.B. 470; *De Beeche v South American Stores(Gath & Chaves) Ltd* [1935] A.C. 148; *R. v International Trustee for the Protection of Bondholders AG* [1937] A.C. 500; *O'Toole v Whiterock Quarry Co Ltd*, 1937 S.L.T. 521; *Kahler v Midland Bank Ltd* [1950] A.C. 24; contrast *Kleinwort Sons & Co v Ungarische Baumwolle Industrie AG* [1939] 2 K.B. 678; *Addison v Brown* [1954] 1 W.L.R. 779; *Arab Bank Ltd v Barclays Bank (Dominion, Colonial and Overseas)* [1954] A.C. 495; *Prodexport State Co for Foreign Trade v ED&F Man Ltd* [1973] Q.B. 389.

[224] It might have been that the forum in refusing to enforce a contract on this ground would have sought affirmation from another law of close connection; cf. *Lemenda Trading Co Ltd v African Middle East Petroleum Co Ltd* [1988] Q.B. 448, and see Clarkson and Hill, *Conflict of Laws*, 3rd edn, 2006, p.489.

[225] See Ch.8, above.

[226] Giuliano and Lagarde, p.33. Equally, it was clear at common law that heads of damage, and questions of remoteness were substantive matters for the *lex causae*: *J D'Almeida Araujo LDA v Sir Frederick Becker & Co Ltd* [1953] 2 Q.B. 329.

[227] The shift is visible in non-contractual obligations as well as contractual obligations: cf. Rome II art.15(c).

other legislation.[228] Similarly the effects of novation, delegation,[229] and accep-
tilation must be determined by the governing law of the principal obligation
(rather than that of the derivative agreement).[230] Excuses for non-performance
or defences attributable to statutory provision which are part of the applicable
law of the contract under the Rome I Regulation will operate. Excuses and
defences which are not part of the applicable law will be effective only where
those provisions qualify as overriding mandatory provision under art.9.[231]

The same principle applies with regard to the universal discharge of all
obligations following upon insolvency proceedings conducted under the same
law as the law governing the principal obligation. Likewise, a discharge under
a trust deed will also be a complete discharge, if granted under the same law
as the law applicable to the principal obligation. If, however, the governing law
differs from the law of the insolvency proceedings or the trust deed, a
discharge would have no extraterritorial effect[232] except that under the British
bankruptcy statutes a discharge in a Scots sequestration will be effective as a
discharge in England in respect of a claim arising from any contractual obligation, regardless of its governing law.[233] Where the discharge arises in the
context of collective insolvency proceedings in relation to a debtor whose
main interests are centred in an EC Member State, account must be taken of
Regulation 1346/2000 on Insolvency Proceedings.[234] Article 4.2. of that
Regulation states that the law of the state of the opening of proceedings (the
lex concursus)[235] (regarding main or secondary proceedings, respectively)[236]
shall determine the effects of insolvency proceedings upon current contracts to
which the debtor is party (para.(e)), and on creditors' rights after closure of
such proceedings (para.(k)). As regards contracts relating to immoveable property, however, the effect of insolvency proceedings on a contract conferring the

---

[228] See, at common law, *Watson v Renton* (1792) M. 4582; *Ellis v McHenry* (1871) L.R. 6 C.P.
228; *Jacobs Marcus and Co v Credit Lyonnais* (1884) 12 Q.B.D. 589; *Gibbs and Sons v Société
Industrielle et Commerciale des Metaux* (1890) L.R. 25 Q.B.D. 399; *Re Anglo-Austrian Bank
(Vogel's Application)* [1920] 1 Ch. 69; *Swiss Bank Corp v Boehmische Industrial Bank* [1923]
1 K.B. 673; *Employers Liability Assurance Corp Ltd v Sedgwick Collins & Co Ltd* [1927] A.C.
95; *Perry v Equitable Life Assurance Society* (1929) 45 T.L.R. 468; *Mount Albert BC* [1938]
A.C. 224; *Re United Railways of Havana and Regla Warehouses Ltd* [1961] A.C. 1007; *Adams
v National Bank of Greece and Athens SA* [1961] A.C. 255.
[229] *Re United Railways of Havana and Regla Warehouses Ltd* [1961] A.C. 1007.
[230] See Leslie, *Stair Memorial Encyclopaedia*, Vol.17, "Private International Law" (Butterworths),
p.277; cf. art.17 on set-off.
[231] Or less likely, as rules that cannot be derogated from by agreement, in terms of art.3.3 and 3.4.
At common law, the general rule was that statutory provisions, whether Scottish, UK or
foreign, affected a contract only if they were part of the proper law. *Kleinwort Sons & Co v
Ungarische Baumwolle Industrie AG* [1939] 2 K.B. 678; *Vita Food Products Inc v Unus
Shipping Co Ltd (In Liquidation)* [1939] A.C. 277; *Arab Bank Ltd v Barclays Bank* [1954] A.C.
495; *English v Donnelly*, 1959 S.L.T. 2; *National Bank of Greece and Athens SA v Metliss*
[1958] A.C. 509; *Adams v National Bank of Greece and Athens SA* [1961] A.C. 255; *Rossano
v Manufacturers Life Insurance Co* [1963] 2 Q.B. 352.
[232] See *Gibbs and Sons v Société Industrielle et Commerciale des Metaux* (1890) L.R. 25 Q.B.D. 399.
[233] For Scotland, see Bankruptcy (Scotland) Act 1985 ss.54, 55(1). For England, see *Dicey, Morris
and Collins on the Conflict of Laws*, 14th edn, 2006, rr.194, 196, and comment at paras 31–054
to 31–056, 31–068 to 31–071. For intra-UK position, see generally, *Dicey, Morris and Collins
on the Conflict of Laws*, 14th edn, 2006, Ch.31.
[234] The Regulation applies only to collective insolvency proceedings where the centre of the
debtor's main interests is located in the EC; recitals (13), (14). See Ch.17, below.
[235] See recital (23).
[236] Regulation 1346/2000 art.3. See Ch.17, below.

right to acquire or use such property, is governed solely by the law of the Member State within the territory of which the property is situated (art.8).[237]

With regard to the relationship between Regulation 1346/2000 and the Rome I Regulation, reference may be made to art.23 of Rome I, which provides that, ". . . this Regulation shall not prejudice the application of provisions of Community law which, in relation to particular matters, lay down conflict-of-law rules relating to contractual obligations". It is to be presumed, therefore, that art12.1(d) is without prejudice to the particular rules contained in Regulation 1346/2000.

Set-off [238]

15–45   The Rome I Regulation contains, in art.17, a new rule on set-off, which is a method of extinguishing, wholly or partly, an indebtedness. Impliedly under the Rome Convention, the subject of set-off fell within art.10.1(d) (the various ways of extinguishing obligations). Article 17 of the Regulation, however, sets out a special rule, to the effect that where the right to set-off is not agreed by the parties, set-off shall be governed by the law applicable to the claim against which the right to set-off is asserted. This new rule aims to resolve the more complex situation where a conflict arises because more than one obligation is involved, each obligation is governed by a different law, and the substantive laws contain different rules concerning set-off. But if the right to set-off is agreed between or among the parties, the applicable law of that agreement per art.3 (or potentially arts 5–8), in combination with art.12.1(d), must govern, in the same way as before.

Multiple liability

15–46   Multiple liability now is dealt with in a freestanding article of the Regulation, art.16, but the substantive import is unchanged from art.13.2 of the Convention. The article provides that:

> "If a creditor has a claim against several debtors who are liable for the same claim, and one of the debtors has already satisfied the claim in whole or in part, the law governing the debtor's obligation towards the creditor also governs the debtor's right to claim recourse from the other debtors. The other debtors may rely on the defences they had against the creditor to the extent allowed by the law governing their obligations towards the creditor."

Prescription and limitation of actions

15–47   In terms of art.12.1(d), prescription and limitation of actions shall be governed by the law applicable to the contract. This is in accord with pre-existing Scots and English law.[239]

---

[237] cf. recital (25).

[238] See M. Hellner in Ferrari and Lieble (eds), *Rome I Regulation: The Law Applicable to Contractual Obligations in Europe*, 2009, p.251.

[239] Prescription and Limitation (Scotland) Act 1973, as amended by the Prescription and Limitation (Scotland) Act 1984. See also reg.3 of The Law Applicable to Contractual Obligations (Scotland) Regulations 2009 (SSI 2009/410). For England, see Foreign Limitation Periods Act 1984; and reg.3 of The Law Applicable to Contractual Obligations (England and Wales and Northern Ireland) Regulations 2009 (SI 2009/3064). See Ch.8, above.

(e) The consequences of nullity of the contract

By art.12.1(e) of the Rome I Regulation, the law applicable to a contract **15–48** will govern the consequences of nullity of the contract, which will include the repayment of sums[240] due under a void or nullified contract. By UK reservation the equivalent provision of the Rome I Convention, art.10.1(e), did not apply in a UK court since the consequences of nullity were regarded by Scots and English law as pertaining to rules of restitution. In many cases the applicable law identified by these two routes would be the same. While in principle there is no reason, therefore, for UK lawyers to feel unease about the inclusion of the consequences of nullity of contract within art.12, it is important to realise the extent of regulation of this area given that in Ch.III of the Rome II Regulation there are new provisions regulating the subjects of unjust enrichment, *negotiorum gestio* and *culpa in contrahendo*. The relationship between the Rome I and Rome II Regulations in this area may be productive of difficultes of demarcation.[241]

VOLUNTARY ASSIGNMENT

Articles 14–17 of the Regulation have in common the feature that the contrac- **15–49** tual circumstances which they address involve, or are capable of involving, a third or further party in addition to the original contracting parties.

Articles 14–16 of the Regulation have re-cast and amplified provisions which were to be found in arts 12 and 13 of the Convention.

Article 14

A triangular situation arises where the creditor in an original claim against **15–50** a debtor assigns his right to pursue that claim to a third party assignee. The contract between the original parties (debtor and creditor) has a governing law, ascertained by reference to arts 3 or 4 (of the Convention or the Regulation, as the case may be, provided that the contract falls within the scope of the instrument: art.1). The assignation too, from creditor to assignee, has its own law, so determined. The third side of the triangle is the relationship between assignee and debtor.

Article 14, the successor to the criticised art.12 of the Convention, in seeking to regulate this tripartite scenario, provides as follows:

> "1. The relationship between assignor and assignee under a voluntary assignment[242] or contractual subrogation of a claim against another person (the debtor) shall be governed by the law that applies to the contract between the assignor and assignee under this Regulation.
> 2. The law governing the assigned or subrogated claim shall determine its assignability, the relationship between the assignee and the debtor,

---

[240] Giuliano and Lagarde, p.33 reveals that the equivalent provision under the Rome I Convention, art.10.1(e), was inserted to make it clear that the applicable law under the Convention governed this issue.

[241] Further, paras 15–65—15–67.

[242] Or, in Scots terminology, "assignation".

the conditions under which the assignment or subrogation can be invoked against the debtor and whether the debtor's obligations have been discharged.
3. The concept of assignment in this Article includes outright transfers of claims, transfers of claims by way of security and pledges or other security rights over claims."

The non-exhaustive explanation of the concept of assignment, in art.14.3, is new, but the meaning and effect of the remainder of art.14 largely repeats art.12 of the Convention, viz.: the relationship between assignor and assignee shall be governed by the applicable law of the contract between them[243]; and the law governing the assigned or subrogated claim shall determine not only its assignability, but also the relationship between the assignee and the debtor, and the conditions under which the assignment or subrogation can be invoked against the debtor, and whether the debtor's obligations have been discharged.[244]

The problem is that art.14, like its predecessor, makes no provision for tangential or external complexities, namely, the relationship between or among two or more competing assignees. Opportunity was not taken in the Regulation, through lack of time, to select the law which shall govern the effectiveness of an assignment or subrogation of a claim vis-à-vis third parties; nor to address the problem of finding a rule to govern the priority of an assigned or subrogated claim over competing claims made by other parties. These points currently must be dealt with by each Member State according to its own conflict rules.[245] In response to art.27.2 of the Regulation,[246] consultation has been initiated with the aim of supplying this lack.[247] Given the commercial importance of assignment, in that assignation of bundles of incorporeal rights is a commonly utilised means of raising finance, consideration needs to be given to finding a European solution, whether it be a single rule, or a general rule with exceptions for specialised cases.

Subrogation

Article 14: Contractual subrogation

15–51   The title of the new art.14 makes clear that its remit concerns voluntary assignment and contractual subrogation, i.e. subrogation by means of a contract (*not* subrogation of a claim in contract). The treatment of contractual

---

[243] See art.14.1 (ex-art.12.1 of the Convention).
[244] See art.14.2 (ex-art.12.2 of the Convention).
[245] See Ch.17, below.
[246] By June 17, 2010, the Commission shall submit a report on the effectiveness of an assignment or subrogation of a claim against third parties and the priority of the assigned or subrogated claim over a right of another person. The report shall be accompanied, if appropriate, by a proposal to amend the Rome I Regulation. At the time of writing, the report is awaited.
[247] Ministry of Justice Discussion Paper, *Rome I: European Commission Review ECR of Article 14: Assignment* (The Stationery Office, 2009). Consultation, however, is restricted to voluntary assignations; the review of art.14 does not embrace the ranking of involuntary assignations inter se (in respect of which reference may require to be made to Regulation 1346/2000), or the ranking between/among involuntary and voluntary assignations.

subrogation (of a contractual or possibly of a non-contractual[248] claim), therefore, has been aligned with the treatment of voluntary assignments, discussed above, it being thought that the two claims are similar in nature.

Article 15: Legal subrogation

Article 15 of the Regulation, which replicates in effect art.13 of the **15–52** Convention, concerns legal subrogation, i.e. subrogation by operation of law,[249] as for example the subrogation of a motor insurance company to the victim's claim against the wrongdoer, where the insurer itself has compensated the victim.

> "Where a person (the creditor) has a contractual claim against another (the debtor) and a third person has a duty to satisfy the creditor, or has in fact satisfied the creditor in discharge of that duty, the law which governs the third person's duty to satisfy the creditor shall determine whether and to what extent the third person is entitled to exercise against the debtor the rights which the creditor had against the debtor under the law governing their relationship."

BURDEN OF PROOF

Rules of evidence and procedure fall within the province of the forum, for **15–53** reasons of long held tradition and convenience.[250] The Rome I Regulation upholds this by excluding such matters from its scope (art.1.3), but the exclusion is subject to art.18, as follows:

> "1. The law governing a contractual obligation under this Regulation shall apply to the extent that, in matters of contractual obligations, it contains rules which raise presumptions of law or determine the burden of proof.
> 2. A contract or an act intended to have legal effect may be proved by any mode of proof recognised by the law of the forum or by any of the laws referred to in Article 11 under which that contract or act is formally valid, provided that such mode of proof can be administered by the forum."

The exclusion of burden of proof both from the Convention and the Regulation permits the Scots and English courts to continue to apply their own rules on proof of foreign law, i.e. the "default rule", whereby the content of a foreign applicable law, if not proved, will be presumed not to differ from the law of the forum.[251]

---

[248] The transferability of which is governed by the Rome II Regulation art.15(e).
[249] The article in terms begins: "Where a person . . . has a contractual claim against another . . .". Subrogation where a person has a non-contractual claim upon another is governed by Rome II Regulation art.19.
[250] See Ch.8, above.
[251] See paras 8–17—8–20, above.

HABITUAL RESIDENCE

15–54 As indicated in Ch.6, above,[252] an innovation is contained in the Rome I Regulation, in that art.19.1 defines, for the purposes of the Regulation, the habitual residence of companies and other bodies, corporate or unincorporated, as the place of central administration.[253] Further, it defines the habitual residence of a natural person acting in the course of his business activity as his principal place of business. With regard to *tempus inspiciendum*, the relevant point in time shall be the time of conclusion of the contract.[254]

Where a contract is concluded in the course of the operations of a branch, agency or any other establishment, or if, under the contract, performance is the responsibility of such a branch, agency or establishment, the place where the branch, agency or any other establishment is located shall be treated as the place of habitual residence.

EXCLUSION OF *RENVOI* (ARTICLE 20)

15–55 The application of the law of any country specified by the Rome I Regulation means the application of the rules of law in force in that country other than its rules of private international law, unless provided otherwise[255] in the Regulation. The proviso is new.

PUBLIC POLICY OF THE FORUM (ARTICLE 21)

15–56 The application of a rule of the law of any country specified by the Rome I Regulation may be refused only if such application is manifestly incompatible with the public policy ("*ordre public*") of the forum.

IV. ELECTRONIC COMMERCE

15–57 The internet and cyberspace pose problems in many areas of civil law, including delict (particularly damage to reputation),[256] property (instantaneous property transfer and intellectual property rights),[257] but in particular with regard to electronic transacting, especially formation of contract and all the

---

[252] See para.6–48, above.

[253] Recital (39) explains the thinking behind this provision.

[254] See art.19.3.

[255] The solitary example is to be found in art.7.2 final paragraph, concerning parties' freedom to choose a governing law. In insurance contracts not covering large risks, party choice is restricted to certain specified laws. However, if those laws themselves should grant greater freedom of choice, parties may take advantage of that freedom.

[256] *Western Provident v Norwich Union* [1997] New L.J. Digest 1277; *Loutchansky v Times Newspapers Ltd (No.5)* [2001] E.M.L.R. 39; *Richardson v Schwarzenegger* [2004] EWHC 2422 (QB); *Lewis v King* [2005] I.L.Pr. 16; *Al-Amoudi v Brisard* [2007] 1 W.L.R. 113. See generally Ch.16, below.

[257] *Shetland Times Ltd v Wills*, 1997 S.L.T. 669.

consequences flowing therefrom. Technological developments also have repercussions in matters of evidence, procedure and remedies.

Electronic advances have removed the firm basis of understanding, and consequent assumptions, that the world is divided into legal systems based on territorial areas, and have thrown into confusion certain established methods of approaching and solving conflict problems. This does not mean that "traditional" rules may not be adapted to service the electronic age. The conflict of laws was able to accommodate "remote" methods of contracting such as telegrams and telexes by identifying what it deemed to be the *lex loci contractus* and the proper law.[258] United Kingdom government policy, recognising the growth of electronic commerce, is to encourage and facilitate such transactions and to attempt to safeguard UK interests. One of the main concerns is to secure the principle of "medium neutrality", i.e. to ensure that there is no difference in legal effectiveness between traditional and electronic methods of transacting. It is interesting that the EU Commission, in its 2009 Report on cross-border e-commerce in the EU,[259] notes that while the use of e-commerce is increasing on a national level, it is "still relatively uncommon for consumers to use the internet to purchase goods or services in another Member State."[260] The Commission attributes this to cross-border barriers to online trade. It must be recognised, however, that in recent years, a number of legislative responses have been made to the technological developments.

ELECTRONIC SIGNATURE: ELECTRONIC COMMUNICATIONS ACT 2000

The Electronic Communications Act 2000 is part of the legislative **15–58** framework to facilitate and encourage confidence in electronic transactions. It seeks to implement certain provisions of the EU Electronic Signatures Directive (adopted on December 13, 1999),[261] which was intended to facilitate the use of electronic signatures and to provide for their legal recognition throughout the EU. The 2000 Act is in three Parts. Part I makes arrangements for registering providers of cryptography support services, providing, e.g. electronic signature services and confidentiality services[262]; Pt II provides for the legal recognition of electronic signatures, regulating the process under which such signatures may be "generated, communicated or verified"; and Pt III deals with miscellaneous and supplemental issues.[263]

---

[258] *Entores Ltd v Miles Far East Corp* [1955] 2 Q.B. 327; *Brinkibon Ltd* [1982] 1 All E.R. 293.

[259] Commission Report on cross-border e-commerce in the EU SEC(2009) 283 final. See also Consumer Markets Scoreboard COM(2008) 31 final.

[260] Report on cross-border e-commerce in the EU SEC(2009) 283 final, executive summary.

[261] Directive 1999/93/EC on a Community framework for electronic signatures [2000] OJ L13/12.

[262] The use of cryptography can secure confidentiality, and provide a means for delivering a signature electronically. By s.7 of the 2000 Act, electronic signatures can be admitted as evidence in court. Sections 1–6, however, were repealed (never in force) on May 25, 2005, by operation of s.16(4) of the Act. The statutory scheme contained in Pt I was to be commenced only if the industry-led approvals scheme known as the "tScheme" (i.e. self-regulation) failed.

[263] Pt III ss.11, 12 have been repealed; see Communications Act 2003.

ELECTRONIC COMMERCE DIRECTIVE

15–59 The EU Electronic Commerce Directive, adopted on May 4, 2000,[264] encourages the development of electronic commerce in the internal market. There is "no overlap in the detailed provisions" of the Electronic Commerce Directive and the 2000 Act.[265] Two main areas addressed in the Directive are ensuring legal validity of electronic contracts and limiting the liability of intermediary service providers.

Recital (58) makes clear that while the Electronic Commerce Directive does not apply to services supplied by providers established in non-EU States, nevertheless, in view of the global dimension of electronic commerce, it is appropriate to ensure that European rules are consistent with international rules. Globalisation necessitates consultation between the EU and major non-EU trading entities such as the WTO, the OECD and UNCITRAL. However, development of the EU internal market requires co-ordination at EU level of regulatory measures so as not adversely to affect the competitiveness of European industry.

Article 1.4 of the Directive declares that it does not establish additional rules on private international law, nor does it deal with the jurisdiction of courts.[266] However, art.9 (treatment of contracts) begins with the requirement that Member States shall ensure that their legal systems allow contracts to be concluded by electronic means, and that their legal requirements do not create obstacles for the use of electronic contracts, nor deprive them of legal effectiveness by reason of their having been made by electronic means. Article 9.2 permits Member States to make certain exceptions[267] to this *desideratum* in respect of all or certain contracts falling into one of the following categories:

"(a) contracts that create or transfer rights in real estate, except for rental rights;
(b) contracts requiring by law the involvement of courts, public authorities or professions exercising public authority;
(c) contracts of suretyship granted and on [*sic*] collateral securities furnished by persons acting for purposes outside their trade, business or profession;
(d) contracts governed by family law or by the law of succession."

The Electronic Commerce (EC Directive) Regulations 2002

15–60 Certain provisions of the Electronic Commerce Directive have been implemented in the UK by the Electronic Commerce (EC Directive) Regulations 2002.[268] The 2002 Regulations seek to promote the internal market in Europe,

---

[264] Directive 2000/31/EC on certain legal aspects of information society services, in particular electronic commerce, in the Internal Market [2000] OJ L178/1 (henceforth "EU Electronic Commerce Directive").
[265] Explanatory note to the 2000 Act, p.6.
[266] cf. Electronic Commerce Directive recitals (23), (55).
[267] Member States which make such exceptions are required to submit to the Commission every five years a report explaining why they consider it necessary to maintain excluded category/ies of contract.
[268] Electronic Commerce (EC Directive) Regulations 2002 (SI 2002/2013) (as extended by the Electronic Commerce (EC Directive) (Extension) Regulations 2003 (SI 2003/115) and Electronic Commerce (EC Directive) (Extension) Regulations 2004 (SI 2004/1178)).

by securing the free movement of "information society services", meaning, essentially, all commercial online services.[269] The 2002 Regulations apply to those who advertise or sell goods or services online to businesses or consumers. Generally the Regulations require online service providers to comply with certain information requirements, which can be divided into three categories: (i) information requirements, which require providers to give full information about themselves to "end users"[270]; (ii) commercial communications requirements; and (iii) electronic contracting requirements, which require the online services provider to provide end users with a description of the different technical steps to be taken to conclude a contract online.

For present purposes, the principal feature of interest is the limited guidance as to choice of law applicable to online services. The 2002 Regulations direct that UK-established service providers must comply with UK laws, even if they are providing those services in another EU Member State, and they prevent the UK from restricting the provision in the UK of online services from another EU Member State. The regulatory structure is authorised by reg.4 of the 2002 Regulations, but it does not apply to those fields set out in the Schedule to the Electronic Commerce Directive (the Schedule permitting the contracting parties, in such excluded fields, freedom to choose the applicable law and not affecting the law applicable to a consumer contract, so that the consumer may not be deprived of the mandatory rules otherwise applicable to his situation by the law of the Member State in which he has his residence).[271] Otherwise parties are free to choose the law applicable to individual contracts. The 2002 Regulations do not deal with the matter of jurisdiction.[272]

CONSUMER PROTECTION (DISTANCE SELLING) REGULATIONS 2000[273]

The 2000 Regulations regulate "distance contracts", which are defined gener- **15–61** ally as any contract concerning goods or services concluded between a supplier and a consumer under an organised distance sales or service provision scheme run by the supplier, who, for the purpose of the contract, makes exclusive use of one or more means of distance communication, up to and including the moment at which the contract is concluded.[274] The Regulations are without conflict of laws content, except to the extent that reg.25(1) prohibits contracting out of the consumer protection provisions of the regulations, and reg.25(5) stipulates that the regulations shall apply if the contract has a close connection with the territory of a Member State, notwithstanding any contract term which applies or purports to apply the law of a non-Member State.[275] The

---

[269] Electronic Commerce Directive recital (18).
[270] These information requirements are in addition to existing requirements, such as contained in the Consumer Protection (Distance Selling) Regulations 2000 (SI 2000/2334).
[271] Electronic Commerce Directive recital (55).
[272] Jurisdiction must be determined according to normal commercial rules, i.e. Regulation 44/2001.
[273] Consumer Protection (Distance Selling) Regulations 2000 (SI 2000/2334), implementing Directive 97/7/EC on the protection of consumers in respect of distance contracts [1997] OJ L144/19 ("Distance Selling Directive").
[274] See reg.3(1).
[275] cf. Distance Selling Directive reg.12(2).

effect of these provisions is to secure for the consumer in his electronic dealings the same protections as have been constructed in relation to traditional forms of consumer contract.

APPLICATION OF THE ROME I REGULATION TO ELECTRONIC COMMERCE TRANSACTIONS

15–62 None of these complex modern instruments addresses systematically the conflict of laws implications of electronic contracting, and so the conclusion must be that electronic contracts, their constitution and effects are subject to the Rome I Regulation. The absence of bespoke choice of law rules regarding electronic contracts is noticeable, particularly when one considers the exponential growth of electronic contracting, and the fact that a far higher number of such contracts have international implications than has been the case with traditional contracts. This is especially true, in theory at least, of consumer contracts.[276] The challenge is to interpret the Rome I Regulation in a manner compatible with modern electronic conditions of commerce.

The questions to be answered are the same as arise with regard to "traditional" contracts. With regard to electronic contracting, conflict disputes are likely to concern: (i) pre-contractual issues[277]; (ii) evidencing that consensus has been reached between identified parties; (iii) ascertaining the identity of the governing law and assessing the substantive validity of the contract, including any choice of court and/or choice of law clauses; (iv) performance-related issues, including the main obligation and counter-obligation (supply and payment); and (v) post-contractual issues of dispute resolution, including application of relevant rules of jurisdiction (because however great the extent and rapidity of technological change, carrying with it the impression that territorial frontiers no longer are significant, it is the case that, ultimately, a remedy must be pursued in the court of some territorial law unit).

The first matter to be ascertained is whether the contracting parties have made a choice of law, express or clearly demonstrated.[278] If such a choice is evident, the body of law applicable by parties' choice to the contract will be augmented, in the usual way, by the mandatory rules of another system of law, in terms of the Rome I Regulation arts 3.3, 3.4 and 9. It may be that in the act of ordering online one party accepts the other's express choice of law. Whether the parties have reached consensus is governed, in the usual way, by the putativity principle in the Rome I Regulation art.10.

As to formal validity, the Rome I Regulation art.11.1 provides that for contracts "concluded between persons who, or whose agents, are in the same country at the time of its conclusion" it is sufficient that the contract comply with the formal requirements of the applicable law, or of the law where it is concluded. This provision demonstrates the extent to which territorial situation remains important in traditional contracts, but at the same time reveals its inappropriate-

---

[276] Hill, *Cross-Border Consumer Contracts*, 2008; and Zheng S. Tang, *Electronic Consumer Contracts in the Conflict of Laws* (Oxford: Hart, 2009). But see Report on cross-border e-commerce in the EU (SEC(2009) 283 final).

[277] Rome II Regulation art.12. See Ch.16, below.

[278] Rome I Regulation art.3.1.

ness with regard to electronic contracting.[279] The qualifications contained in art.11.1 are unlikely to be satisfied in electronic contracts, and therefore one is led to the enlarged rule of alternative reference in art.11.2, to the effect that with regard to persons who, or whose agents, "are in different countries at the time of its conclusion", it is sufficient to comply with the formal validity rules of the applicable law, or "of the law of either of the countries where either of the parties or their agent is present at the time of conclusion, or the law of the country where either of the parties had his habitual residence at that time."[280]

With regard to contractual capacity, it has been seen that art.13 supplies a specific rule, applicable in cases of "face-to-face" contracting, which rule obviously is not helpful in the case of remote transactions. The answer, for electronic commerce, should be to apply the putative applicable law to the question of capacity.

In terms of art.4.1(a) and (b) of the Rome I Regulation, in the absence of choice of law by the parties, the law governing a contract for the sale of goods, or for the provision of services, shall be the habitual residence of the seller or service provider, respectively. This is as true of an online transaction as of a conventional transaction. Articles 4.3 and 4.4 afford to the court discretion to identify the applicable law on a wider basis and could reasonably justify consideration of factors such as the location of internet service providers. If, as in many cases of online transacting, the purchaser/user is a "consumer", he will have the benefit of the Rome I Regulation art.6. Article 6.1(b) provides that a contract concluded by a natural person acting outside his trade or profession (the consumer), with another person acting in the exercise of his trade or profession (the professional), shall be governed by the law of the consumer's habitual residence, provided that the professional pursues his activities in the country of the consumer's habitual residence, or, by any means, directs[281] such activities to that country or to several countries including that country. Provided that the contract falls within the scope of the professional's commercial or professional activities, the contract will confer upon the consumer the benefit of a "consumer contract" with its attendant advantages[282] from his point of view.

V. WHERE CONTRACT MEETS OTHER AREAS OF LAW

WHERE CONTRACTUAL OBLIGATIONS MEET NON-CONTRACTUAL OBLIGATIONS

The Rome I and Rome II Regulations are intended to be interlocking instruments, furnishing for Member State courts a set of rules of applicable law governing issues arising out of contractual and non-contractual obligations. **15–63**

---

[279] See Electronic Commerce Directive recital (55).

[280] The rule though generous, is not as explicitly inclusive as the medium-neutrality rule contained in art.23.2 of the Brussels I Regulation: any communication by electronic means which provides a durable record of the agreement shall be equivalent to "writing". See para.7–36, above (prorogation).

[281] "[B]y any means, directs" employs the same choice of wording as art.15.1(c) of the Brussels I Regulation. This brings the choice of law provision into line with the jurisdiction provision. See recital (24). The conditions required for a contract to qualify as a consumer contract in terms of the Rome I Regulation are notably simpler than those employed in the Rome I Convention art.5.2

[282] See recital (25).

They are mutually consistent, and in places are interdependent.[283] For example, the applicable law rules in contract may have a part to play in identifying the law applicable to a non-contractual obligation; in other words, the applicable law under the Rome I Regulation may influence identification of the applicable law under the Rome II Regulation.

Interface between Contract and Rome II Chapter II (Delict)[284]

15–64   Symbiosis between the two instruments is observable, e.g. in Rome II art.4.3[285] (applicable law in tort and delict), in the provision conferring discretion on the forum, in effect, to override both the principal *lex loci damni* rule in art.4.1 and the rule of commonality in art.4.2, in order to secure as the governing law in delict that law which, in the view of the forum, is manifestly more closely connected with the delict. In exercising that discretion, the forum is given a hint that such a manifestly closer connection might be based upon a pre-existing relationship between the parties, *such as a contract* that is closely connected with the delict in question.[286]

Article 4.3 of the Rome II Regulation is loosely drawn, both by use of the word "might" and by the reference, at second remove, to a contract. In the employer-employee situation, or carrier-passenger situation, the provision might be relevant. For example, a claim falling within the category of economic delicts, such as inducement or procurement of breach of contract; or an accident which occurred in a work place in which the injured party/employee would not have been but for the contract of employment. One might think that the facts found in *Johnson v Coventry Churchill International Ltd*[287] would satisfy application of art.4.3 in that the relationship between the parties was the contractual one of employer/employee, and the allegedly tortious incident happened on the building site in Germany. The claimant, an English employee working as a joiner, was injured when the plank on which he was crossing a trench collapsed, in circumstances in which under English law, but not under German law, the employer would be liable for failure to provide a safe system of work. The contract of employment in that instance was expressly governed by English law.

If, in the view of the forum, the employment and carriage situations fall within art.4.3 of Rome II, reference will be made, not simply to the applicable law identified per the general rules contained in the Rome I Regulation,[288] but also to the particular rules contained in arts 5–8 thereof. This exercise would involve an incursion into the detail of the rules of the Rome I Regulation in order to arrive at a conclusion under Rome II. That said, perhaps it is implausible to suggest that the court would look beyond Rome II art.4.1 or 4.2 in this specialised situ-

---

[283] See E.B. Crawford and J.M. Carruthers, "Connection and Coherence Between and Among European Private International Law Instruments in the Law of Obligations" in Binchy and Ahern (eds), *Rome I Regulation: Implications for International Commercial Litigation* (Leiden: Brill, forthcoming).

[284] With regard to Ch.II of Rome II, see paras 16–11—16–51, below.

[285] "Where it is clear from all the circumstances of the case that the tort/delict is manifestly more closely connected with a country other than that indicated in paragraphs 1 or 2, the law of that other country shall apply. A manifestly closer connection with another country might be based in particular on a pre-existing relationship between the parties, such as a contract, that is closely connected with the tort/delict in question."

[286] The particularity of expression is important: the delict in question, seemingly, must derive from, or have a close association with the contract.

[287] [1992] 3 All E.R. 14.

[288] See arts 3, 4.

ation of employee or passenger, for it is unlikely that there will be a manifestly more closely connected country than that identified by the principal rules.

The defender may adduce a defence in contract to a claim laid in delict, and the task then for the court is to prioritise the forum's own choice of law rules in these areas, and to assess their interaction. This occurs in cases where parties engaged in litigation arising out of an allegedly delictual situation are linked by a pre-existing contractual relationship, commonly that of employer and employee, or carrier and passenger. If one considers in this connection the celebrated problem which arose at common law of a party adducing a contractual defence to a delictual/tortious claim, such as occurred in *Brodin v A/R Seljan*[289] or *Sayers v International Drilling Co NV*,[290] is it right to assume that the forum, in this new world of harmonised rules, still would look first to the applicable law of the delict in order to ascertain whether by that law a contractual defence can be offered,[291] and thereafter ascertain, by the law governing the contract as determined under the Rome I Regulation, whether the contract and the relevant term thereof are valid, apt and sufficient to provide a defence? To employ art.4.3 of Rome II in order to establish, by reference to the pre-existing contractual relationship between the parties, the applicable law in the delict at the outset would cause confusing circularity.

Similarly, after the advent of Rome II, a futher link between Rome I and Rome II can be identified, underpinning the party autonomy rule for non-contractual obligations contained in art.14 of Rome II. By that provision, parties may agree to submit non-contractual obligations to the law of their choice by an agreement entered into after the event giving rise to the damage occurred, or where all the parties are pursuing a commercial activity, by an agreement freely negotiated before that event. Two points arise: first, the contract embodying the choice of law must be governed as to its validity in all respects by the Rome I Regulation; and secondly, party choice by commercial parties before the event must refer to the exceptional situation in which wrongdoer and victim already are known to each other and are linked by employment or carriage, as mentioned above.

Where a consumer is injured by the defective product which was the subject of his consumer contract, the Rome I/Rome II borderland must be closely examined. A different outcome might be produced by application of Rome I art.6 (consumer contracts), instead of Rome II art.5 (product liability). Both provisions point initially to the law of the habitual residence of the consumer. But, especially under Rome II, there are other possibilities, which not implausibly the court might follow, such as the law of the country of acquisition of the product,[292] or the law of the country in which the damage occurred,[293] and account also would require to be taken of a general sweeper discretion available to the forum under art.5 of Rome II.[294] Moreover, party choice of law appears to be unfettered in relation to product liability under Rome II,[295] whereas it is restricted vis-à-vis consumers under the Rome I Regulation

---

[289] 1973 S.C. 213.

[290] [1971] 1 W.L.R. 1176.

[291] Reference to art.15(b) of the Rome II Regulation suggests such an approach.

[292] Rome II art.5.1(b).

[293] Rome II art.5.1(c).

[294] Rome II art.5.2. Rome I Regulation art.6 affords the forum no such discretion.

[295] Contrast Rome II arts 6.4 (unfair competition) and 8.3 (infringement of intellectual property rights).

art.6.2. It is impossible to say which instrument, in any given situation, would prove more beneficial to the consumer, but the Rome I Regulation appears to provide greater certainty as to governing law than does the Rome II Regulation. This is not to say that a claimant necessarily will have freedom to choose because he may be constrained by the special jurisdiction rules of the Brussels regime.[296]

Interface between Contract and Rome II Chapter III (Unjust enrichment, *negotiorum gestio*, and *culpa in contrahendo*)[297]

(a) Relational unjust enrichment

15–65   In many cases arising under the head of unjust enrichment, there is found to have existed an element or semblance of a contract. The first limb of the legislative solution in art.10 of the Rome II Regulation is concerned to treat this situation. By art.10.1, non-contractual obligations arising out of unjust enrichment, including payment of amounts wrongly received, *where they concern a pre-existing relationship between the parties such as one arising out of a contract or a tort* (i.e. "relational unjust enrichment") shall be governed by the law which governs that relationship, that is to say, by the applicable law identified according to the Rome I (contract) or Rome II (tort/delict) Regulation, as the case may be. Seemingly, under art.10.1 of Rome II, the applicable law in contract will govern the obligation arising out of unjust enrichment *only* if that unjust enrichment derives from, or is closely associated with, that very contract.[298]

(b) Nullity of contract

15–66   In light of the Rome I Regulation, there is pan-European agreement that the subject of nullity of contract be dealt with by the putative applicable law of the necessarily putative contract. It is possible, therefore, that the co-existence of this rule with the relatively newly created choice of law rules under the Rome II Regulation Ch.III, may prompt problems of characterisation and distribution of application of choice of law rules between the Rome I and Rome II Regulations.

In the jurisdictional aspect also, the area of void and nullified contracts is productive of doubt.[299] Difficulties of demarcation present in borderline cases.[300] Turf wars are to be expected between art.12 of Rome I[301] and art.10.1 of Rome II.[302]

---

[296] See para.7–22, above.

[297] With regard to Ch.III of Rome II, see paras 16–65—16–69, below.

[298] cf. art.11.1 (*negotiorum gestio*). See also Rome II arts 4.3, 5.2.

[299] See para.7–18, above.

[300] See S. Pitel, "Rome II and Choice of Law for Unjust Enrichment" in Binchy and Ahern (eds), *The Rome II Regulation: The Law Applicable to Non-contractual Obligations* (Leiden: Brill, 2009), p.236

[301] See art.12.1: "The law applicable to a contract by virtue of this Regulation shall govern in particular: . . . (b) performance; . . . (e) the consequences of nullity of the contract."

[302] See art.10.1: "If a non-contractual obligation arising out of unjust enrichment, including payment of amounts wrongly received, concerns a relationship existing between the parties, such as one arising out of a contract or a tort/delict, that is closely connected with that unjust enrichment, it shall be governed by the law that governs that relationship."

(c) Culpa in contrahendo

Like the consequences of nullity of contract, this subject too weaves about **15–67** on either side of the line between contractual and non-contractual obligations.[303] Article 1.2(i) of the Rome I Regulation expressly excludes from the scope of Rome I obligations arising out of dealings prior to the conclusion of a contract. Article 12.1 of the Rome II Regulation applies to what it firmly classes as a non-contractual obligation (albeit one arising out of dealings prior to the conclusion—or not—of a contract) the applicable law of the contract, or the putative applicable law. This choice of law rule applies whether or not a contract was actually concluded.[304] If, however, the law applicable cannot be determined under art.12.1 of Rome II, then the rule which must be applied under art.12.2 is in the same terms as the general rule for delict contained in art.4.

WHERE CONTRACT MEETS PROPERTY

The terms of a contract, valid by the governing law thereof, nevertheless may **15–68** contravene, in detail or in policy, the law of some other interested legal system, most frequently in practice that of the *situs* of moveable property[305] which is the subject of the contract. Thus, while title to property may have passed according to the contractual applicable law, it may not have passed according to the governing law of property, namely, the *lex situs* of the goods at the time when ownership is purported to have passed. The *situs* of the property at the time of conclusion of the contract may differ from its *situs* when dispute arises and litigation ensues. Both time and space, therefore, may be significant. In adjudicating between or among parties claiming under different heads of law, the forum in such cases may require to rank its own choice of law rules. This matter is discussed further at Ch.17, below.

An interconnection is seen also between contractual assignation of incorporeal rights, and the choice of law property principles governing the transfer of incorporeal rights. It has been noted above that art.14 of the Rome I Regulation lacks a provision to guide the court as to choice of law to determine the effectiveness of a voluntary assignation of a claim against another person (the debtor) as against third parties, and the priority of the assigned claim over the right of another person. In such cases, it is impossible to divorce the proprietary aspects of the assignation from the contractual aspects. In the leading case of *Raiffeisen Zentralbank Österreich AG v Five Star General Trading LLC (The Mount I)*,[306] Mance L.J.[307] found it impossible to conclude that the draftsmen of the Rome I Convention art.12.2 had intended to make any such

---

[303] As to the jurisdiction aspect of pre-contractual obligations, see para.7–19, above.

[304] See art.12.1. If, however, the law applicable cannot be determined under art.12.1 of Rome II, different rules set out in art.12.2 apply, in respect of which see para.16–69, below.

[305] i.e. the law of the situation of the property at the point of contracting, or more likely, the law of the subsequent situation of the property at litigation. See, e.g. *Hammer and Sohne v HWT Realisations Ltd*, 1985 S.L.T. (Sh. Ct.) 21.

[306] [2001] 1 Lloyd's Rep. 597.

[307] *The Mount I* [2001] 1 Lloyd's Rep. 597 at [45].

distinction. Consequently, both with regard to the Rome Convention, and now in relation to the Regulation, albeit that each instrument purports to deal only with contractual obligations, it is accepted that art.12 of the Convention, and art.14 of the Regulation, are intended also to encompass the property implications of voluntary assignments.

SUMMARY 15

1. General

15–69   Classification of a matter as contractual or otherwise is determined by the *lex fori*.

The Rome I Regulation shall apply, in any EU Member State court, in situations involving a conflict of laws, to regulate contractual obligations, in civil and commercial matters, when the contract was entered into on or after December 17, 2009, and the contract does not fall within an exception to the scope of the Regulation per art.1. Cases which, by type, fall outside the ambit of the Rome I Regulation, will be governed by common law rules.

Cases which, by time, fall outside the ambit of the Rome I Regulation (i.e. those entered into before December 17, 2009), will be governed by the Rome I Convention, as embodied in the Contracts (Applicable Law) Act 1990, and by the common law where the Convention is silent, incomplete or inapplicable in terms of scope.

2. Applicable Law

Identification of the applicable law is effected through application of art.3 of the Rome I Regulation where a choice of law has been made expressly, or is clearly demonstrated by the terms of the contract or the circumstances of the case; or of art.4 of that Regulation in the absence of choice.

Article 4 provides contract-specific rules to identify the applicable law, subject to a discretion afforded to the forum to select instead the law with which, in its view, the contract is manifestly more closely connected.

Restrictions on freedom of party choice are imposed through the mandatory application of rules of Community law or national law which cannot be derogated from by contract, in terms of art.3.3 and 3.4.

All contracts, whether or not there has been a choice of law by parties, are subject to art.9 (overriding mandatory provisions).

By art.21, the application of a provision of an otherwise applicable law may be refused effect if its application is manifestly incompatible with the public policy of the forum.

The operation of *renvoi* is excluded by art.20, unless provided otherwise in the Regulation.

3. Special Contracts

A revised, stand-alone applicable law rule to govern contracts of carriage of goods, and of persons, is contained in art.5.

A revised, and somewhat simplified, applicable law rule to govern consumer contracts is contained in art.6.

A new applicable law provision to govern contracts of insurance is contained in art.7.

A modestly modified applicable law rule to govern individual employment contracts is contained in art.8.

As was the case in the Convention, the question whether an agent can bind a principal, or an organ bind a company, to a third party, is excluded from the scope of the instrument. The contract between the principal and the agent, however, is governed by the Regulation.

4. Incidents of a Contract

Consent and material validity (whether or not there is deemed to be agreement such as to constitute a contract) is governed by the putative applicable law in accordance with art.10.1, subject to a forum discretion contained in art.10.2.

The rule concerning contractual incapacity is contained in art.13. It is specific in its terms, and when on the facts of the case the article has no application, common law rules will apply.

Formal validity is governed by art.11.

Scope of the law applicable is treated by means of non-exhaustive list in art.12. A change for the UK is that art.12.1(e) subjects to the applicable law the consequences of nullity of the contract, a matter which had been excluded under the Rome Convention by means of UK reservation.

While art.12.1(d) refers the various ways of extinguishing obligations to the applicable law of the contract, specific provision in the Regulation is made for multiple liability and set-off in arts 16 and 17, respectively.

Voluntary assignment and subrogation is treated in art.14.

An applicable law rule governing legal subrogation is provided by art.15.

5. Miscellaneous

Although rules of evidence and procedure are excluded from the scope of the Regulation (by art.1.3), it is provided in art.18 that the applicable law of the contract shall apply to the extent that, in matters of contractual obligations, it contains rules raising presumptions of law or determining the burden of proof.

Article 19 contains a definition, for the purpose of the Regulation, of the habitual residence of companies and other bodies, corporate or unincorporated, and of natural persons acting in the course of business.

6. Electronic commerce

The Rome I Regulation applies in tandem with special sectoral legislative provision.

7. Hybrid cases

In certain circumstances, the forum's choice of law rules in areas of private law other than contract (principally of property and of delict, respectively), may impinge upon a situation involving a conflict of laws pertaining to a contractual obligation. The forum then must prioritise and reconcile its own conflict rules in these different areas. In particular, any EC Member State forum now must apply the Rome II Regulation in respect of non-contractual obligations, including unjust enrichment, and must be aware of the interdependence of the Rome I and Rome II Regulations.

CHAPTER 16

THE LAW OF NON-CONTRACTUAL OBLIGATIONS

I. DELICT

CHOICE OF LAW THEORIES

16–01 Over the years, various theories have been developed as to the law(s) which should be applied in UK courts in cases involving delicts with foreign elements, and in particular, delicts committed in foreign countries.[1] In brief, the main theories propounded are:

(1) The *lex fori* theory

16–02 According to this theory, the court should apply only its own law, substantive as well as procedural. The objections, however, are that application of the *lex fori* encourages forum shopping, and could result in an award for damages being granted in respect of an act which did not give rise to delictual liability in the place where it was committed, an outcome which seems fundamentally unfair.

(2) The *lex loci delicti* theory

16–03 According to this theory, the court should apply only the law of the place where the (allegedly) delictual act or omission was committed. The objections are that the *locus delicti* may be entirely fortuitous and/or difficult to determine.[2] Moreover, application of that law might result in the forum having to grant a decree for damages for an act which was not delictual by its own law, something which is likely to "jar" on the conscience of the judge.

(3) The obligation theory

16–04 This theory, which originated in the judgment of Holmes J. in *Slater v Mexican National Railroad Co*,[3] was to the effect that though the conduct in question might not be struck at by the domestic law of the forum, delictual actings give rise to an *obligatio* which attaches to the person and so may be enforced wherever the alleged wrongdoer may be found. The *lex loci delicti*, the source of the obligation, determines the existence and extent of the obligation. Clearly this is only one step removed from the *lex loci delicti* theory.

---

[1] See, e.g. Morse, *Torts in Private International Law*, 1978.
[2] See para.16–18, below.
[3] 194 U.S. 120 (1904).

(4) The proper law theory

According to this theory the rights of the parties should be governed by the **16–05** proper law of the delict, that is, the law with which, objectively, it has the closest connection. Parties' rights and liabilities should be judged according to the social environment in which the delict was committed. The progenitor of the theory was Morris, writing in 1949 to 1952,[4] soon after the problematic Scots decision of *McElroy v McAllister (q.v.)*.[5]

(5) The American experience

Until the 1960s, the preferred approach in the USA was strict adherence to **16–06** the sole application of the *lex loci delicti*. When this was plainly unsuitable in the view of the forum, recourse sometimes was had to the device of manipulative characterisation to secure a different result.[6] However, from the early 1960s there emerged a new and broader approach, unorthodox in method, similar to the proper law theory.[7]

It is scarcely appropriate to dispose in a few sentences of such creativity, but for present purposes it suffices to be aware of this development, and to note that in decisions where the court has applied "non-orthodox" methodologies (that is, rule-selecting rather than jurisdiction-selecting approaches)[8] there is an identifiable homeward trend.

The Law Commission and the Scottish Law Commission in their thorough reviews of Scots and English choice of law rules in tort and delict, and in their suggestions for possible reform, thought that the American "revolution", though interesting, and having the merit of giving due warning against over-rigidity of choice of law connecting factor, was more suited to the inter-state, than the international, situation, and so decided against recommending the adoption of such approaches in the UK.[9]

(6) The double actionability theory

Until the coming into effect of the Private International Law (Miscellaneous **16–07** Provisions) Act 1995,[10] Scots and English courts applied a choice of law rule which was a combination of theories (1) and (2) above, termed the "rule of double actionability". This rule of cumulative application was prone to work adversely (in the view at least of the claimant) so as to supply an outcome which, it can

---

[4] Morris, "The Proper Law of a Tort" (1949) 12 M.L.R. 248, expanded in (1951) 64 Harv. L. Rev. 881. Lord Denning M.R., sitting in the Court of Appeal in *Boys v Chaplin* [1968] 2 Q.B. 1, supported the proper law approach.

[5] 1949 S.C. 110.

[6] See para.4–05, above.

[7] Famously in *Babcock v Jackson*, 12 N.Y. 2d. 473, 191 N.E. 2d. 279 (1963). Also *Macey v Rozbicki*, 18 N.Y.2d. 289, 221 N.E. 2d. 380 (1966); *Griffith v United Airlines Inc*, 203 A. 2d. 796 (1964); *Tooker v Lopez*, 12 N.Y. 2d. 569, 249 N.E. 2d. 394 (1969); *Reich v Purcell*, 67 Cal. 2d. 551, 423 P. 2d. 727 (1967); *Kell v Henderson*, 26 A.D. 2d. 595, 270 N.Y.S. 2d. 552 (1966); *Bernhard v Harrah's Club*, 128 Cal. Rptr. 215, 546 P.2d. 709 (1976). See Ch.3, above regarding policy evaluation methods.

[8] See para.3–01, above.

[9] Law Commission and Scottish Law Commission, *Private International Law: Choice of Law in Tort and Delict* (HMSO, 1984), Law Com. Working Paper No.87; Scot. Law Com. Memo. No.62, paras 4.35–4.54.

[10] All references in this chapter to the "1995 Act" are to this statute.

reasonably be assumed, would not have been the desire or aim of either the *lex fori* or the *lex loci delicti*,[11] and which operated in favour of the defendant.

CHOICE OF LAW BACKGROUND

16–08 The history of this area of Scots and English choice of law evidences the use of a variety of approaches. It is a subject which, in the past at least, has been more productive of academic writing than of case law. Applicable law in delict has been characterised by the use of different rules at different points of time, initially at common law, altered by legislative intervention of the UK Parliament in terms of the Private International Law (Miscellanous Provisions) Act 1995, and now contained, largely but not exclusively, in Regulation 864/2007 on the Law Applicable to Non-obligations ("Rome II"). Despite the attainment of a harmonised set of choice of law rules through the introduction of a European Regulation, it cannot yet be said that the 1995 Act, nor even the common law, is extinct. The area presents an acute example of the layering problem which is charactertistic of modern conflict of laws rules.[12] While Rome II represents the major scheme of applicable law rules to be applied by Member State courts in qualifying cases arising under the head of non-contractual obligations, account still must be taken, in a UK court, of the 1995 Act and the common law, by reason of subject matter, and/or of date.[13]

The temporal aspect

16–09 The Rome II Regulation applies to events giving rise to damage which occur after[14] its entry into force, namely, January 11, 2009.[15] Therefore the relevant date is the date of the occurrence of the event, and not any later date on which harm may become manifest.

With regard to such events which occur before January 11, 2009, the governing rules are contained in the 1995 Act, provided that the act or omission

---

[11] cf. famously *McElroy v McAllister*, 1949 S.C. 110.

[12] Account may have to be taken of sectoral provision, such as package travel, etc. regulations (as in *Gouldbourn v Balkan Holidays Ltd* [2010] EWCA Civ 372), and motor insurance legislation. In *Jacobs v Motor Insurers Bureau* [2010] EWHC 231 (QB) the first case arising in UK courts under Rome II, the question for the court was whether the case fell to be decided in terms of EC Motor Insurance Directives, or under Rome II. The claimant contended that an accident in Spain, in which he was knocked down by a vehicle, was neither a non-contractual obligation in a civil or commercial matter, nor a situation involving a conflict of laws, on the basis that the Directives provided a freestanding right to compensation. Owen J., however, held that Rome II applied on the ground that this was a tortious situation involving a conflict of laws.

[13] The Law Applicable to Non-contractual Obligations (England and Wales and Northern Ireland) Regulations 2008 (SI 2008/2986), inserting s.15A into the 1995 Act; and The Law Applicable to Non-contractual Obligations (Scotland) Regulations 2008 (SSI 2008/404), inserting s.15B into the 1995 Act, operate to restrict the application of the statutory choice of law rules contained in Pt III of the 1995 Act and give precedence to the operation of Rome II.

[14] Contrast the position under the Rome I Regulation: Corrigendum to the Rome I Regulation 13497/1/09, REV 1, JUR369 [2008] OJ L177, correcting art.28 of the Rome I Regulation, providing that that Regulation will be applied by Member State courts, including those of the UK, to qualifying cases concerning contracts concluded as from (i.e. on and after) December 17, 2009. There is no express mention in Rome II of the law to govern events which occur *on* January 11, 2009, but it is assumed that Rome II is intended to apply in such cases. See further Andrew Dickinson, *The Rome II Regulation: the law applicable to non-contractual obligations* (Oxford: Oxford University Press, 2008), paras 3.315–3.324.

[15] See arts 31, 32.

giving rise to the claim occurred on or after May 1, 1996.[16] In relation to acts
or omissions which precede May 1, 1996, the common law rules shall apply.[17]

Subject matter scope

Article 1 of Rome II lays down the scope of the Regulation. Article 1.2 lists **16–10**
the excluded matters. These comprise, in outline, non-contractual obligations
arising out of:

(a) family and comparable relationships[18];
(b) matrimonial property and comparable regimes, and wills and
    succession;
(c) bills of exchange, cheques, promissory notes and other negotiable
    instruments to the extent that the obligations under such other
    negotiable instruments arise out of their negotiable character;
(d) the law of companies and other bodies corporate or unincorporated,
    including the personal liability of officers and members and the
    personal liability of auditors to a company or its members;
(e) the relations between the settlors, trustees and beneficiaries of a trust
    created voluntarily;
(f) nuclear damage;
(g) violations of privacy and rights relating to personality, including
    defamation.

Additionally, by virtue of art.1.1, the Regulation shall not apply to revenue,
customs or administrative matters or the liability of the state for acts and omissions in the exercise of state authority.[19]

All of these excluded matters fall to be regulated, therefore, in a UK court, by
the pre-existing law, which, in almost all cases, means the 1995 Act Pt III. In the
case of the art1.2(g) exclusion (violations of privacy and rights relating to
personality, including defamation), however, reference must be made in the first
instance to the 1995 Act s.13, which preserves the application of the common
law for the determination of "issues arising in any defamation claim".

Section 13(2) of the 1995 Act defines "defamation claim" as meaning: (a)
any claim under the law of any part of the United Kingdom for libel or slander
or for slander of title, slander of goods or other malicious falsehood and any
claim under the law of Scotland for verbal injury; and (b) any claim under
the law of any other country corresponding to or otherwise in the nature of a
claim mentioned in para.(a) above. The effect of this provision is that the
determination of defamation claims having a conflict aspect must be treated by
a Scots or English court in accordance with the pre-existing common law rule
(double actionability, *q.v.*), as interpreted and applied in Scots and English law,
respectively.

The definition in s.13(2) of the 1995 Act is not coterminous with the exclusion in art.1.2(g) of Rome II, with the effect that violations of privacy and

---

[16] 1995 Act s.14(1); and the Private International Law (Miscellanous Provisions) Act 1995
   (Commencement) Order 1996 (SI 1996/995) reg.2.
[17] See *Re T&N Ltd* [2005] EWHC 2990 (Ch).
[18] See recital (10).
[19] See recital (9).

personality rights, though excluded from the scope of Rome II, do not appear to be regulated by the common law via s.13, and so must be governed by the 1995 Act. However, in order to be regulated by Pt III of the 1995 Act, such claims must be characterised by the forum, for the purposes of private international law, as issues relating to tort or delict.[20]

THE ROME II REGULATION[21]

16–11 Regulation 864/2007 ("Rome II")[22] governs the law applicable to all non-contractual obligations arising out of a tort or delict, and restitutionary claims under the heads of unjust enrichment, *negotiorum gestio* and *culpa in contrahendo*.[23]

Scope

16–12 In terms of art.1.1, Rome II shall apply in situations involving a conflict of laws, to non-contractual obligations in civil and commercial matters, including non-contractual obligations that are likely to arise.[24] It is clear from recital (11) that the concept of a non-contractual obligation varies from one Member State to another, and that, for the purposes of the Regulation, "non-contractual obligation" should be understood as an autonomous concept.[25] It becomes apparent in art.4 (general rule) that it is an assumption of the Regulation that, for its rules to apply, damage must have occurred, or be likely to occur.[26] This explains the inclusion in art.2.1 of the statement that, for the purposes of the Regulation, damage shall cover any consequence arising out of tort/delict, unjust enrichment, *negotiorum gestio* or *culpa in contrahendo*.

---

[20] 1995 Act s.9(2). See, further, para.16–30, below.

[21] See generally A. Dickinson, *The Rome II Regulation* (Oxford: OUP, 2008 & Supplement 2010); T. Kadner Graziano, *The Law Applicable to Non-contractual Obligations in Europe* (Leiden: Brill, 2010); and Ahern and Binchy (eds), *The Rome II Regulation on the Law Applicable to Non-Contractual Obligations* (Oxford: Hart, 2011). In relation to the negotiation and drafting process, see Janeen M. Carruthers and Elizabeth B. Crawford, "Variations on a Theme of Rome II. Reflections on Proposed Choice of Law Rules for Non-Contractual Obligations" (2005) 9 Edin. L.R. 65 (Pt I), and 238 (Pt II).

[22] See, earlier, European Commission Proposal for a Regulation of the European Parliament and the Council on the Law Applicable to Non-Contractual Obligations ("Rome II") COM(2003) 427 final (2003/0168(COD)), accompanying Explanatory Memorandum ("Explanatory Memorandum"); House of Lords European Union Committee, *The Rome II Regulation, 8th Report of Session 2003–04* (The Stationery Office, 2004), HL Paper No.66 (Session 2003/04) ("Scott Report"); Amended Proposal COM (2006) 83 final; Rapporteur Diana Wallis MEP, Draft Report Revised Version on the Proposal for a European Parliament and Council regulation on the law applicable to non-contractual obligations ("Rome II") COM(2003) 427-C5-0338/2003-2003/0168 (COD); and Proposal for a Regulation of the European Parliament and the Council on the law applicable to non-contractual obligations (9142/06) JUSTCIV 118 CODEC 455 ("Council Approved Version"). For background information as to the protracted negotiations, see Dickinson, *The Rome II Regulation*, 2008, para.1.44.

[23] See also Regulation 662/2009 establishing a procedure for the negotiation and conclusion of agreements between Member States and third countries on particular matters concerning the law applicable to contractual and non-contractual obligations [2009] OJ L200/25.

[24] See art.2.2.

[25] See A. Scott, "The Scope of Non-Contractual Obligations" in Ahern and Binchy (eds), *The Rome II Regulation on the Law Applicable to Non-Contractual Obligations*, 2009. Also *Jacobs v Motor Insurers Bureau* [2010] EWHC 231 (QB); and *Maher v Groupama Grand Est* [2009] 1 All E.R. 1116 (liability of driver's insurer to the victim characterised by the forum as tortious).

[26] See art.2.3(b).

Principle of universal application

The choice of law rules contained in Rome II have universal application, that is, any law specified by the Regulation must be applied in qualifying cases in any EU forum regardless of whether the contending law is that of an EU Member State or not.[27]   **16–13**

States with more than one legal system

In the case of a Member State comprising several territorial units, each having its own rules of law in respect of non-contractual obligations, each such unit shall be considered as a country for the purpose of identifying the applicable law under the Regulation.[28]   **16–14**

Exclusion of *renvoi*

Article 24 of Rome II provides that the application of the law of any country specified by the Regulation means the application of the rules of law in force in that country other than its rules of private international law.[29]   **16–15**

Applicable law

General rule

"Article 4 . . .   **16–16**

1. Unless otherwise provided for in this Regulation, the law applicable to a non-contractual obligation arising out of a tort/delict shall be the law of the country in which the damage occurs irrespective of the country in which the event giving rise to the damage occurred and irrespective of the country or countries in which the indirect consequences of that event occur.
2. However, where the person claimed to be liable and the person sustaining damage both have their habitual residence in the same country at the time when the damage occurs, the law of that country shall apply.
3. Where it is clear from all the circumstances of the case that the tort/delict is manifestly more closely connected with a country other than that indicated in paragraphs 1 or 2, the law of that other country shall apply. A manifestly closer connection with another country might be based in particular on a pre-existing relationship between the parties, such as a contract, that is closely connected with the tort/delict in question."

A difference in principle between the civilian and UK approaches is the evident preference of the former for fixed, certain rules, contrasted with the UK preference for flexibility. At common law and in application of the 1995 Act, English courts showed confidence in utilising discretion in choice of law in tort, in order

---

[27] See art.3.
[28] See art.25.1. See, in respect of intra-UK situations, para.16–52, below.
[29] See Ch.5, above.

to find what they considered to be the most appropriate law.[30] It is trite to say that in crafting a rule for choice of law in delict the draftsmen must set that rule at some point on the line between certainty and flexibility.[31] In this Regulation, the most appropriate connecting factor to achieve the objectives of securing legal certainty and the need to effect individual justice has been determined to be the law of the place of damage, subject to certain "escape clauses".

Article 4.1—*lex loci damni* rule

16–17   Article 4.1 contains a rule of general application, applicable where no choice of law has been made by the parties under art.14 (*q.v.*), designating as applicable to the obligation[32] in question the law of the country in which the damage[33] occurs[34] (termed, in recital (15),[35] the *lex loci delicti commissi*, but more accurately termed the *lex loci damni*), irrespective of the country or countries in which the indirect consequences of that event occur.

It is said that application of the *lex loci damni* strikes a fair balance between the interests of the person claimed to be liable and the person sustaining the damage, and also reflects the modern approach to civil liability and the development of systems of strict liability.[36]

In cases of personal injury or damage to property, art.4.1 should lead to application of the law of the country where the victim was when the injury was sustained, or where the property was situated when damaged.[37]

Dealing with double/multiple locality delicts[38]

16–18   Diffculties can arise where allegedly delictual conduct is spread over intervals of time and place. Is the delict to be regarded as having been committed at (i) the place where it began, or was instigated (the place of acting); (ii) the place where it ended and its effects were felt (the place of result); or (iii) either/both places (as an option of pleading).[39] In many potentially helpful

---

[30] Carruthers and Crawford, "Variations on a Theme of Rome II. Part 2" (2005) 9 Edin. L.R. 238, 254–259.

[31] See recital (14).

[32] Article 4, in contrast with s.12 of the 1995 Act, identifies the law applicable to the obligation arising out of the tort or delict, and not the law applicable to a particular issue. In other words, the Regulation excludes the possibility of dépeçage.

[33] Covering, in terms of art.2.1, "any consequence arising out of the tort or delict". Necessarily this must be construed as "any direct consequence", for otherwise the aim of art.4.1 would be subverted.

[34] Or is likely to occur: art.2.3(b).

[35] "(15) The principle of the *lex loci delicti commissi* is the basic solution for non-contractual obligations in virtually all the Member States, but the practical application of the principle where the component factors of the case are spread over several countries varies. This situation engenders uncertainty as to the law applicable."

[36] See recital (16).

[37] Though this is not necessarily without difficulty: see Dickinson, *The Rome II Regulation*, 2008, paras 4.47–4.65. See also recital (17).

[38] See Carruthers and Crawford, "Variations on a Theme of Rome II. Part 2" (2005) 9 Edin. L.R. 238, 242.

[39] *Dow Jones & Co Inc v Gutnick* [2002] HCA 56, per Kirby J. at [140]: to adopt the law of the place of the wrong as the applicable law in international tort claims, "is not the end of the inquiry, it is merely the beginning. It leads immediately to the additional question of identifying the place of the wrong . . . much controversy can exist in relation to the proper identification of where the place of the wrong is." See also *Jameel v Dow Jones & Co Inc* [2005] EWCA Civ 75.

English cases[40] the point at issue was one of jurisdiction,[41] and when that point had been settled, no further discussion of *locus* was made for the purposes of choice of law.

Not infrequently at common law such problems of ascertaining the *locus delicti* were resolved by means of the forum paying close attention to the nature of the delict or tort in question,[42] and/or to the manner in which the complaint was framed. More generally, the court sometimes resorted to a consideration of where the substance of the alleged tort took place.[43] Much depended therefore on (i) localisation of the actings which constituted the tort or delict; or (ii) the precise description in the pleadings of the wrongdoing alleged (e.g. the putting on the market of a product/medication without due warning, rather than the negligent manufacture thereof).[44] In one of the last cases to be decided at common law, *Ennstone Building Products Ltd v Stanger Ltd*[45] (in which, as to the tortious issue, it was necessary to identify the *locus delicti*, in circumstances where advice was given in England and acted upon in Scotland), Keane L.J. accepted the argument that where the tort consisted in essence in the giving of negligent advice, the tort was committed where the advice was received, i.e. in this case, England.

A great deal of the difficulty engendered in common law cases was removed by the introduction in the 1995 Act of detailed rules, in s.11(2), which defined for the choice of law purposes of the Act where the country in which the events constituting the tort or delict occurred was to be taken to be.[46]

---

[40] *R. v Peters* (1886) 16 Q.B.D. 636; *George Monro Ltd v American Cyanamid & Chemical Corp* [1944] 1 K.B. 432; *Bata v Bata* [1948] W.N. 366; *Jenner v Sun Oil Co* (1952) 2 D.L.R. 526 (defamatory broadcast in USA heard in Canada); *Cordova Land Co Ltd v Victor Bros Inc* [1966] 1 W.L.R. 793; *R. v Robert Millar (Contractors) Ltd* [1969] 3 All E.R. 247; *Distillers Co (Biochemicals) Ltd v Thompson* [1971] A.C. 458.

[41] See *Diamond v Bank of London and Montreal* [1979] Q.B. 333, in which it was accepted that an alleged misrepresentation received by instantaneous means within the jurisdiction of the English forum had been made within that jurisdiction. Cf. *Ark Therapeutics Plc v True North Capital Ltd* [2006] 1 All E.R. (Comm) 138 at [58]. See also, with regard to Council Regulation 44/2001 art.5.3, *Henderson v Jaouen* [2002] 2 All E.R. 705, where the victim suffered in England a deterioration in his condition originally brought about by an accident in France. See, for Canada, *Bangoura v Washington Post*, 2005 (25) T.L.W.D. 2522-006 (CA C Ont.) [2005] O.J. No.5428). See also para.7–20, above in relation to Brussels I Regulation art.5.3.

[42] In *Soutar v Peters*, 1912 1 S.L.T. 111, the delict alleged being that of seduction, the sheriff felt justified in noting that the defender's arts and wiles had been practised before the couple crossed the border into England (where no such tort existed, and where the act took place), so as to secure a result of coincidence of Scots *lex fori* and Scots *lex loci delicti*, whereby the conduct complained of was capable of giving rise to delictual remedy.

[43] *Metall und Rohstoff AG v Donaldson Lufkin & Jenrette Inc* [1990] 1 Q.B. 391; *Morin v Bonham & Brooks Ltd* [2004] 1 Lloyd's Rep. 702. See discussion at Carruthers and Crawford, "Variations on a Theme of Rome II. Part 2" (2005) 9 Edin. L.R. 238, 240; cf. *Protea Leasing Ltd v Royal Air Cambodge Co Ltd* [2002] EWHC 2731; and *Ashton Investments Ltd v OJSC Russian Aluminium (Rusal)* [2006] EWHC 2545 (Comm).

[44] cf. *Castree v ER Squibb & Sons Ltd* [1980] 1 W.L.R. 1248; *Distillers Co (Biochemicals) Ltd v Thompson* [1971] A.C. 458.

[45] [2002] EWCA Civ 916; cf. *Diamond v Bank of London and Montreal* [1979] Q.B. 333.

[46] e.g. *Anton Durbeck GmbH v Den Norske Bank ASA* [2002] EWHC 1173; [2006] 1 Lloyd's Rep. 93; and *Morin v Bonham & Brooks Ltd* [2004] 1 Lloyd's Rep. 702.

Section 11(2)(c) (*q.v.*) catered for residual cases, and therefore admitted judicial discretion.[47]

The solution preferred in Rome II art.4.1 is to apply the law of the country in which the damage occurs. No regard shall be paid to the location of the event which gave rise to the damage (i.e. the place of acting), or to the place of occurrence of indirect consequences of the event.[48]

The Regulation assumes that it is possible in all cases to identify the place of damage, but there will be instances in which the localisation of the place of damage will be difficult (e.g. evidentiary problems) or impossible, such as where goods in transit across a number of countries arrive damaged at their destination. While it would be possible to argue in favour of application of the law of the place of discovery of harm as the notional place of damage; or on a "mosaic" principle, *separatim*, in favour of application of the law of each of the different countries through which the goods have passed,[49] the use of art.4.3 might commend itself more readily to the forum, enabling it to apply a law of closer connection (including, presumably, the law of the place of acting/despatch).[50]

There will be other cases in which it is proved that direct damage to the same victim occurred in more than one country. In such cases, art.4.1. must be applied by the forum[51] on a distributive basis, requiring application in turn of each *lex causae* ("*mosaikbetrachtung*" principle).[52]

The indirect consequences of the event giving rise to the damage

16–19   In most cases of personal injury (physical or psychiatric) or damage to property, the country in which the injury was sustained or the property damaged will

---

[47] See also *Anton Durbeck GmbH v Den Norske Bank ASA* [2002] EWHC 1173; [2006] 1 Lloyd's Rep. 93; and *Morin v Bonham & Brooks Ltd* [2004] 1 Lloyd's Rep. 702 in which the purchaser of a classic car at auction in Monaco (his interest in the auction having been raised by an entry in a catalogue delivered to the purchaser in London), subsequently sued in tort on the basis of alleged misrepresentation in the matter of a false odometer reading. The Court of Appeal, upholding the view of Hirst, QC, considered that although elements constituting the alleged tort occurred both in England and in Monaco, the most significant elements occurred in Monaco, and accordingly, by virtue of s.11(2)(c) of the 1995 Act, the law applicable to the torts allegedly committed by Bonham & Brooks (Monaco) Ltd was Monegasque law. See Carruthers and Crawford, "Variations on a Theme of Rome II. Part 1" (2005) 9 Edin. L.R. 65, 84.

[48] In a European context, given that a claimant, as a result of the ECJ decision in *Handelswekerij GJ Bier BV v Mines de Potasse d'Alsace SA* (21/76) [1976] E.C.R. 1735, has the option to sue in the place of acting or the place of result, the outcome in choice of law terms will be that whichever forum is chosen must apply, at least under the general rule, the law of the place of direct result. Cf. Discussion of horizontal continuity between or among EU legislative instruments in Crawford and Carruthers, "Connection and Coherence between and among European PIL Instruments in the Law of Obligations", pp.1–3.

[49] *Cheshire, North and Fawcett: Private International Law*, 14th edn, 2008, p.797.

[50] cf. Under the 1995 Act, *Congentra AG v Sixteen Thirteen Marine SA (The Nicholas M)* [2008] EWHC 1615 (Comm); and in jurisdiction *Reunion Europeene SA v Spliethoffs Bevrachtingskantoor BV* (C-51/97) [1998] E.C.R. I-6511.

[51] For the sake of avoiding further complexity, it is to be hoped that the one forum (e.g. acting as domicile of the defendant under art.2 of the Brussels I Regulation), would carry out this task; it is surely undesirable from every standpoint, including the avoidance of irreconcilable judgments, to permit the application of a double mosaic principle, with several forums and several applicable laws. It is to be hoped that art.28 of the Brussels I Regulation could be called in aid to streamline proceedings.

[52] Dickinson, *The Rome II Regulation*, 2008, para.4.69. See also A. Mills, "The Application of Multiple Laws under the Rome II Regulation" in Ahern and Binchy (eds), *The Rome II Regulation on the Law Applicable to Non-Contractual Obligations*, 2009.

be relatively easily ascertained. Difficulties may emerge in cases where a victim's condition deterioriates, potentially resulting in a claim for aggravated damage.[53] In jurisdiction terms, for the purposes of special jurisdiction in tort, the decision in the circumstances presented in *Henderson v Jaouen*[54] was to deny that a fresh cause of action arose at the place of deterioration. It would seem sensible to adopt the same approach in the context of applicable law.

Where a primary victim who suffered physical harm in state A, suffers derivative economic loss in state B, the latter should be deemed to be an indirect consequence and therefore not capable of engaging the applicable law rule under art.4.1.

Rarely, though occasionally, there may be difficulty in distinguishing between primary or direct physical harm and the indirect consequences thereof. In *Edmunds v Simmonds*, Garland J. referred to the complainant's damages, particularly the major heads, costs of care and loss of future earnings as "consequences of the events constituting the tort."[55] Strictly, however, these heads are not so much (indirect) consequences of the wrongful event, as being the actual damage which occurred, or at the very least, the "direct consequences" of the wrongful event.

A more complicated situation will be where the primary loss is financial or economic.[56] What is the place of damage in such cases? The search presumably must be for the centre of the victim's loss, the place where the loss was sustained and the financial resources depleted. More difficult, perhaps, is to draw the line between direct financial damage, and the indirect consequences of such damage.[57] The crux of the matter may be the difficulty of distinguishing between primary financial loss (suffered in state A) and secondary financial loss (suffered in state B) by the same victim, and also in fixing the loss with a physical location.

By contrast, where A, in Scotland, suffers psychiatric or financial loss as a result of physical injury caused to B, in France, the country in which the damage to A occurs is Scotland, not France. This is a situation of direct harm to a secondary victim, a scenario for which art.4.1 makes no special provision. It cannot be said that the separate cause of action accruing to A is an indirect consequence of the event giving rise to the damage to B. Rather, A's situation should be viewed as a separate harm, in respect of which the applicable law will be determined, in the first instance, by art.4.1, on the basis of location. The extent of the alleged wrongdoer's liability to a secondary victim is likely to form the basis of a freestanding claim.

---

[53] An unsuccessful attempt was made in *Jacobs v Motor Insurers Bureau* [2010] EWHC 231 (QB) to persuade the court that the place of damage was the place (England) in which the compensatory body failed to compensate the claimant in respect of a motor accident which had taken place in Spain. Owen J. held that the *lex loci damni* in terms of art.4.1 was Spain.

[54] [2002] 1 W.L.R. 2971.

[55] *Edmunds v Simmonds* [2001] 1 W.L.R. 1003 at 1009C; cf. *Harding v Wealands* [2006] UKHL 32.

[56] See Dickinson, *The Rome II Regulation*, 2008, paras 4.36–4.37, 4.66–4.68; and *Cheshire, North and Fawcett: Private International Law*, 14th edn, 2008, p.798.

[57] cf. *Dumez France SA v Heissische Landesbank* [1990] E.C.R. I-49; and *Réunion Européenne SA v Spliethoff's Bevractingskantoor BV* (C-51/97) [2000] Q.B. 690; *Protea Leasing Ltd v Royal Air Cambodge Co Ltd* [2002] EWHC 2731 (Comm); and *Marinari v Lloyds Bank Plc* [1996] Q.B. 217, discussed in Carruthers and Crawford, "Variations on a Theme of Rome II. Part 2" (2005) 9 Edin. L.R. 238, 247.

The direction in art.4.1 to disregard the indirect consequences of the event giving rise to the damage is, of course, a direction limited to the process of ascertainment of applicable law.[58] The question whether or not redress can be had from the alleged wrongdoer for indirect consequences of the event will be referred under art.15(a)–(c) (*q.v.*) to the applicable law as ascertained under arts 4 or 14(*q.v.*).

Article 4.2—rule of commonality

16–20   Article 4.2 inserts an exception[59] to the general rule in art.4.1, leading to application of the law of the common habitual residence of the defendant (the person claimed to be liable)[60] and the victim (the person sustaining the damage). Article 4.1 is thereby rendered subject to a commonality clause, to the effect that the obligation shall be governed instead by the law of the common habitual residence of the alleged wrongdoer and the victim at the time when the damage occurs, if such commonality is present.

The rule of commonality in so many words is a novelty to UK lawyers, but instances can be cited of decisions by English courts under the 1995 Act in which the existence of a shared personal law was a relevant factor in the decision whether or not to displace the prima facie applicable law.[61]

The concept of habitual residence is partly defined in the Regulation:

"Article 23
Habitual residence

1. For the purposes of this Regulation, the habitual residence of companies and other bodies, corporate or unincorporated, shall be the place of central administration.
   Where the event giving rise to the damage occurs, or the damage arises, in the course of operation of a branch, agency or any other establishment, the place where the branch, agency or any other establishment is located shall be treated as the place of habitual residence.
2. For the purposes of this Regulation, the habitual residence of a natural person acting in the course of his or her business activity shall be his or her principal place of business."

The habitual residence of a natural person acting otherwise than in the course of business activity will be construed by the forum in accordance with existing ECJ jurisprudence and its own national law.[62]

---

[58] Contrast the process which operates if art.4.3 is triggered, in which case, arguably, indirect consequences of the alleged delict may be taken into account as a factor in ascertainment of the applicable law.
[59] See recital (18).
[60] See *Jacobs v Motor Insurers Bureau* [2010] EWHC 231 (QB), in which Owen J. held that the "person claimed to be liable" was the tortfeasor, not the compensation body named as defendant.
[61] *Edmunds v Simmonds* [2001] 1 W.L.R. 1003; *Harding v Wealands* [2006] UKHL 32. Before the 1995 Act, see *Chaplin v Boys* [1971] A.C. 356 ("this was a very British occurrence"). Contrast the strict approach taken to the double rule by the Court of Session in *McElroy v McAllister*, 1949 S.C. 110, where the parties had a common habitual residence.
[62] See paras 6-44—6-48 and 15-54, above.

Article 4.2 is inflexible in the sense that it *must* oust the application of art.4.1 if common habitual residence is present.[63] But art.4.2 is subservient to art.4.3.

Article 4.3—rule of displacement and forum discretion[64]

Recital (18) states that: **16–21**

> "Article 4(3) should be understood as an 'escape clause' from Article 4(1) and (2), where it is clear from all the circumstances of the case that the tort/delict is manifestly more closely connected with another country."

A degree of similarity can be traced to the 1995 Act, which in s.12,[65] conferred upon the forum discretion to displace the otherwise applicable law in favour of a law which appeared to it in all the circumstances to be substantially more appropriate. Since, as has been noted, art.4.3, in contrast with s.12 of the 1995 Act,[66] identifies the law applicable to the obligation arising out of the tort or delict, and not the law applicable to a particular issue, it is not possible for a Member State court applying art.4 to displace the law otherwise applicable in relation to only one or some of the issues presented.[67]

The height of the displacement threshold has given rise to comment. The implicit warning to the forum against over-use of its art.4.3 discretion, by the explicit setting of the bar at "manifestly more closely connected", will not necessarily deter a forum from freely exercising the discretion to which, in the UK at least, courts have become accustomed.[68] On the other hand, Fentiman suggests that since art.4.2 provides a rule based on common habitual residence, thereby taking out that important factor in the art.4.3 exercise, art.4.3 is less significant than it appears, even to the point of being redundant.[69]

Some direction, of an unusually specific nature, is given in the last sentence of art.4.3, which suggests that a manifestly closer connection with another country might be based in particular on a pre-existing relationship between the parties, such as a contract that is closely connected with the tort/delict in question.[70] A pre-existing contractual relationship is relevant only insofar as it

---

[63] Contrast the circumstance of common habitual residence of the parties under the rules of the 1995 Act which did not require the English forum to displace, in favour of that law, the otherwise applicable law: *R. (on the application of Al-Jedda) v Secretary of State for Defence* [2007] Q.B. 621.

[64] See R. Fentiman, "The Significance of Close Connection" in Ahern and Binchy (eds), *The Rome II Regulation on the Law Applicable to Non-Contractual Obligations*, 2009.

[65] See para.16–54, below.

[66] The displacement rule contained in s.12 of the 1995 Act provides that, in certain cases, the issues arising in a case, or any of those issues, may be governed by a law other than the prima facie applicable law.

[67] See Carruthers and Crawford, "Variations on a Theme of Rome II. Part 2" (2005) 9 Edin. L.R. 238, 249.

[68] Though the argument in favour of displacement was rejected by Owen J. in *Jacobs v Motor Insurers Bureau* [2010] EWHC 231 (QB).

[69] Fentiman, "The Significance of Close Connection" in Ahern and Binchy (eds), *The Rome II Regulation on the Law Applicable to Non-Contractual Obligations*, 2009, p.91.

[70] This raises interesting questions about the interdependence and mutual assistance of cognate harmonisation instruments. See Crawford and Carruthers, "Connection and Coherence between and among European PIL Instruments in the Law of Obligations", pp.20–22. Symbiosis between the Rome I Regulation and Rome II Regulation is observable, and it is evident in art.4.3 that the applicable law rules in contract may play a not insignificant part in identifying the law applicable to a non-contractual obligation.

is closely connected with the delict in question. Article 4.3, in singling out the existence of a pre-existing relationship between the parties, raises that factor to prominence. It is questionable to what extent the factor has particular significance in the evaluation process which art.4.3 necessitates. Case law can be expected to develop the point. Other factors which, one may conjecture, may be taken into account in the comparison exercise include factors relating to the parties (e.g. common domicile and/or common nationality), the events constituting the delict (including the place of acting), and even the consequences, direct and indirect, of the delict in question, for once art.4.3 is triggered, art.4.1 cannot inhibit the discretion of the forum.

The delict-specific rules[71]

16–22   Application of the general rule is modified for cases where the general rule is not thought to allow a reasonable balance to be struck between the interests at stake.[72] Accordingly, a series of delict-specific rules are contained in arts 5–9. The delict-specific rules are more familiar to civilian lawyers than to UK lawyers. The approach taken in Rome II, which never featured in Scots and English choice of law rules in delict/tort (apart from the defamation exception contained in s.13 of the 1995 Act), nonetheless presaged the contract-specific approach which has been adopted in art.4 of the Rome I Regulation.[73]

A specific-category approach has its drawbacks in that there will always be potential for argument where the categorisation is debateable in a particular case, or where the factual and legal circumstances straddle more than one category,[74] or where the categories themselves seem inadequate for the complexity of the situation. Moreover, the presence of an abundance of categories will be likely to weaken the so-called general rule.

Product liability[75]

16–23   "Article 5[76] . . .

> 1. Without prejudice to Article 4(2), the law applicable to a non-
>   contractual obligation arising out of damage caused by a product
>   shall be:

---

[71] Each choice of law rule in arts 5–9 pertains to a specialised area of the law of delict (some more familiar than others to UK lawyers, such as delicts of unfair competition and acts restricting free competition; delicts arising out of environmental damage; and delicts arising out of industrial action), in respect of which a number of modern specialised treatments exist. Detailed treatment of all rules is not feasible or appropriate for the purposes of this chapter. The content of these new rules is largely self-explanatory, and commentary has been deliberately restricted to points of importance.

[72] See recital (19).

[73] See para.15–11, above.

[74] Note the solution to this problem adopted by art.4.2, and 4.3, 4.4 of the Rome I Regulation. No such solution operates in Rome II.

[75] The term is not defined in the Regulation, but art.5.1 would suggest that it applies wherever damage is caused by a product. There is no reason to think that it is restricted to such claims as arise under the EC Product Liability Directive, Directive 85/374 on the approximation of the laws, regulations and administrative provisions of the Member States concerning liability for defective products [1985] OJ L210/29 (implemented in the UK by the Consumer Protection Act 1987).

[76] See P. Stone, "Product Liability under the Rome II Regulation" in Ahern and Binchy (eds), *The Rome II Regulation on the Law Applicable to Non-Contractual Obligations*, 2009, p.175; and Dickinson, *The Rome II Regulation*, 2008, Ch.5.

> (a) the law of the country in which the person sustaining the damage had his or her habitual residence when the damage occurred, if the product was marketed in that country; or, failing that,
>
> (b) the law of the country in which the product was acquired, if the product was marketed in that country; or, failing that,
>
> (c) the law of the country in which the damage occurred, if the product was marketed in that country.
>
> However, the law applicable shall be the law of the country in which the person claimed to be liable is habitually resident if he or she could not reasonably foresee the marketing of the product, or a product of the same type, in the country the law of which is applicable under (a), (b) or (c).
>
> 2. Where it is clear from all the circumstances of the case that the tort/delict is manifestly more closely connected with a country other than that indicated in paragraph 1, the law of that other country shall apply. A manifestly closer connection with another country might be based in particular on a pre-existing relationship between the parties, such as a contract, that is closely connected with the tort/delict in question."

Recital (20) states that:

> "The conflict-of-law rule in matters of product liability should meet the objectives of fairly spreading the risks inherent in a modern high-technology society, protecting consumers' health, stimulating innovation, securing undistorted competition and facilitating trade. Creation of a cascade system of connecting factors, together with a foreseeability clause, is a balanced solution in regard to these objectives . . .".

Article 5, which is elaborate in its drafting, is subject to the rule of commonality in art.4.2. Article 5.2 is equivalent to the displacement rule contained in art.4.3.

The sequence of rules in art.5.1 is self-explanatory, subject perhaps only to the meaning and significance of marketing.[77] Marketing includes the sale of products, as well as other commercial dealings such as hire, and promotional gift.[78]

Interesting questions arise in the case where a consumer is injured by the defective product which was the subject of his consumer contract. In such a situation, the aggrieved party may require to be advised as to his best course of action, given that a remedy, ex facie, may be available in contract and in delict. Leaving aside possible difficulties with regard to the basis of jurisdiction on which he may seise a court,[79] it will be necessary to consider on his

---

[77] See, in detail, Dickinson, *The Rome II Regulation*, 2008, para.5.18; and Stone, "Product Liability under the Rome II Regulation" in Ahern and Binchy (eds), *The Rome II Regulation on the Law Applicable to Non-Contractual Obligations*, 2009, pp.188 et seq.

[78] Online purchases seem to be included. This would be consonant with art.15.1(c) of the Brussels I Regulation, and art.6.1(b) of the Rome I Regulation.

[79] A factor possibly inhibiting of choice is raised by the special jurisdiction rules contained in the Brussels I Regulation, namely, art.5.1 (contract) and 5.3 (delict). See para.7–22, above. The problem arises because art.5, being a derogation from art.2, must be construed strictly, and it is clear that jurisdiction in contract trumps that in delict, with the effect that a claimant in the situation outlined must proceed on a contractual basis, if the circumstances reveal a contractual nexus.

behalf whether the outcome afforded to him under the favourable consumer contract provisions contained in the Rome I Regulation[80] will be better in his particular circumstances than that achieved through utilising the bespoke product liability rule in art.5 of Rome II.

Unfair competition and acts restricting free competition[81]

16–24   It is claimed in recital (21) that the special rule in art.6 is not an exception to the general rule in art.4.1, but rather a clarification of it. The aim of the provision is very widely stated, viz.to protect competitors, consumers and the general public and ensure that the market economy functions properly. It is said that the connection to the law of the country where competitive relations or the collective interests of consumers are, or are likely to be, affected generally satisfies these objectives.[82]

At the outset, there will be serious problems of characterisation in relation to this article, especially in the UK, where there is no known special category of delict, sub nom. "acts of unfair competition". There may be scope for applying art.6, however, to the economic delicts, such as inducement/procurement of breach of contract, conspiracy, or causing loss by unlawful means.[83]

> "Article 6 . . .
>
> 1. The law applicable to a non-contractual obligation arising out of an act of unfair competition shall be the law of the country where competitive relations or the collective interests of consumers are, or are likely to be, affected.
> 2. Where an act of unfair competition affects exclusively the interests of a specific competitor, Article 4 shall apply.
> 3. (a) The law applicable to a non-contractual obligation arising out of a restriction of competition shall be the law of the country where the market is, or is likely to be, affected.
>   (b) When the market is, or is likely to be, affected in more than one country, the person seeking compensation for damage who sues in the court of the domicile of the defendant, may instead choose to base his or her claim on the law of the court seised, provided that the market in that Member State is amongst those directly and substantially affected by the restriction of competition out of which the non-contractual obligation on which the claim is based arises; where the claimant sues, in accordance with the applicable rules on jurisdiction, more than one defendant in that court, he or she can only choose to base his or her claim on the law of that court if the restriction of competition on which the claim against each of these defendants relies directly and substantially affects also the market in the Member State of that court.

---

[80] Article 6, discussed at para.15–28, above. See also Crawford and Carruthers, "Connection and Coherence between and among European PIL Instruments in the Law of Obligations", p.16.
[81] Dickinson, *The Rome II Regulation*, 2008, Ch.6.
[82] See also recitals (22) and (23).
[83] *OBG v Allan* [2008] 1 A.C. 1; *Global Resources Group v MacKay*, 2009 S.L.T. 104.

4. The law applicable under this Article may not be derogated from by an agreement pursuant to Article 14."

Environmental damage[84]

"Article 7 . . .   16–25

The law applicable to a non-contractual obligation arising out of environmental damage or damage sustained by persons or property as a result of such damage shall be the law determined pursuant to Article 4(1),[85] unless the person seeking compensation for damage chooses to base his or her claim on the law of the country in which the event giving rise to the damage occurred."

This special category of delict is not known in UK jurisprudence. Recital (24) explains that "environmental damage" should be understood as meaning:

". . . adverse change in a natural resource, such as water, land or air, impairment of a function performed by that resource for the benefit of another natural resource or the public, or impairment of the variability among living organisms."[86]

It was the inclusion of a specific rule to deal with delicts under this head, rather than the content thereof, which, during Rome II negotiations, proved controversial. Although at one point the removal of this special choice of law rule was proposed, ultimately the option was preferred[87] of providing that the law applicable to a non-contractual obligation arising or likely to arise out of a violation of the environment, including damage caused to persons or property, shall be the law determined by application of the general rule in art.4.1, unless the person[88] seeking compensation elects to base his claim on the law of the country in which the event giving rise[89] to the damage occurred (i.e. the place where the harm was triggered, rather than the place where its environmental

---

[84] M. Bogdan, "The Treatment of Environmental Damage in the Regulation Rome II" in Ahern and Binchy (eds), *The Rome II Regulation on the Law Applicable to Non-Contractual Obligations*, 2009, p.219; and Dickinson, *The Rome II Regulation*, 2008, Ch.7.

[85] But not pursuant to art.4.2 and 4.3, which do not apply in the case of environmental damage.

[86] Article 1.2(f) provides that non-contractual obligations arising out of nuclear damage are excluded from the scope of the Regulation.

[87] The reason for including the rule is explained in recital (25).

[88] A question arises to what extent legal, as well as natural, persons are competent to bring or defend a claim under the Regulation. The Regulation applies to "civil and commercial matters" (art.1.1). The Brussels regime as a whole does not extend to public authorities exercising their public powers (*Lufttransportunternehmen GmbH & Co KG v Organisation Europeenne pour la Securite de la Navigation Aerienne (Eurocontrol)* (29/76) [1977] 1 C.M.L.R. 88), but if a state or local authority were to be seen to be acting in a private capacity, as for example, as the owner of land, it would appear that Rome II will apply. Dickinson, *The Rome II Regulation*, 2008, para.7.04, argues against a wider, or "green" interpretation of "civil and commercial matters" in relation to environmental law!

[89] Contrast formulation (favouring application of the law of the place of harm) used in the general rule in art.4.1. This is justified on the basis of policy, to ensure that the law of the place of acting, if it imposes the more exacting standard, shall apply.

effects were felt). This introduces a unilateral party autonomy rule, in contrast to the bilateral rule contained in art.14 (*q.v.*).

The characterisation of a non-contractual obligation as one arising out of environmental damage is a significant one for the claimant, and favours the victim in a manner consonant with the interpretation famously given by the ECJ in *Bier BV v Mines de Potasse d'Alsace SA*.[90] The question of when the claimant can make the choice of law is to be determined in accordance with the law of the Member State forum.[91] Following this line of thought, the victim has a choice in the matters both of jurisdiction and choice of law, provided that the incident qualifies as one falling under art.7, a decision which is for the forum selected, taking account of recital (24).

Although the wording of art.7 suggests that its remit is confined to identification of applicable law for *compensation claims* for damage, it is thought[92] that it is not intended that it be so limited, and there is no reason why the applicable law rules contained therein should not also extend to applications for interdict/injunctions to prevent such damage.

Infringement of intellectual property rights[93]

16–26   "Article 8 . . .

1. The law applicable to a non-contractual obligation arising from an infringement of an intellectual property right shall be the law of the country for which protection is claimed.
2. In the case of a non-contractual obligation arising from an infringement of a unitary Community intellectual property right, the law applicable shall, for any question that is not governed by the relevant Community instrument, be the law of the country in which the act of infringement was committed.
3. The law applicable under this Article may not be derogated from by an agreement pursuant to Article 14."

Article 8.1 enshrines the principle of the *lex loci protectionis*, and this, combined with the prohibition in art.8.3 upon derogation therefrom by the parties through choice of applicable law per art.14, demonstrates the strength of application of the territoriality approach.[94] The term "intellectual property rights" is to be interpreted as including copyright, related rights, the sui generis right for the protection of databases, and industrial property rights. Characterisation by the forum of the issue as one of infringement of an intellectual property right such as covered by art.8 means that the matter must be regarded as non-contractual and be regulated in an EU Member State court by the terms of art.8.[95] Though the word "damage" is not mentioned in this

---

[90] (Case 21–76) [1978] 1 Q.B. 708 ECJ.
[91] See recital (25).
[92] cf. Bogdan, "The Treatment of Environmental Damage in the Regulation Rome II" in Ahern and Binchy (eds), *The Rome II Regulation on the Law Applicable to Non-Contractual Obligations*, 2009, p.221.
[93] See Dickinson, *The Rome II Regulation*, 2008, Ch.8.
[94] See recital (26).
[95] Cheshire, North and Fawcett, *Private International Law*, 14th edn (Oxford: OUP, 2008), p.815.

article, in referring to "protection" and "infringement", it appears nonetheless to cover both bases of claim, namely, preventative measures (anticipatory and ex post facto) and compensatory.[96]

Industrial action[97]

"Article 9 . . .   **16–27**

Without prejudice to Article 4(2), the law applicable to a non-contractual obligation in respect of the liability of a person in the capacity of a worker or an employer or the organisations representing their professional interests for damages caused by an industrial action, pending or carried out, shall be the law of the country where the action is to be, or has been, taken."

No definition of "industrial action" is included in the Regulation, and the reference[98] to each Member State's internal rules is not helpful, at least in the case of the UK, where, in Scots and English law, there is no special category of delicts pertaining to industrial action. Additionally, it is not clear whether the law applicable under art.9 determines its own applicability; one cannot be as confident that characterisation falls within the province of the forum, as one can be in relation to the other delict-specific rules.

Article 9 is subject to the rule of commonality in art.4.2, but (unlike, for example, art.5.2) contains within its short terms no equivalent to the displacement rule contained in art.4.3. Therefore, it would seem that there is no possibility of displacement in favour of a law of manifestly closer connection.

Road traffic accidents[99]

The final version of Rome II does not contain a special rule for road traffic   **16–28** accidents. This being so, the general rules in art.4 (and in art.17) will apply,[100] leading to concerns that victims of road traffic accidents in Member States other than the Member State of their habitual residence ("visiting victims") may have applied to their claims a law which, in their circumstances, may be inappropriate, both with regard to the size of the award of compensation and to the limitation period within which the claim must be brought.[101] Recital (33) of Rome II contains a steer to the effect that:

---

[96] See art.15(c), (d).

[97] See Dickinson, *The Rome II Regulation*, 2008, Ch.9.

[98] Recital (27) states that: "The exact concept of industrial action, such as strike action or lockout, varies from one Member State to another and is governed by each Member State's internal rules. Therefore, this Regulation assumes as a general principle that the law of the country where the industrial action was taken should apply, with the aim of protecting the rights and obligations of workers and employers." Further, according to recital (28): "The special rule on industrial action in Article 9 is without prejudice to the conditions relating to the exercise of such action in accordance with national law and without prejudice to the legal status of trade unions or of the representative organisations of workers as provided for in the law of the Member States."

[99] See also J. von Hein, "Article 4 and Traffic Accidents" in Ahern and Binchy (eds), *The Rome II Regulation on the Law Applicable to Non-Contractual Obligations*, 2009.

[100] See also art.18 examined below.

[101] But this is true of many victims of various types of delict which occur outside their country of residence.

"According to the current national rules on compensation awarded to victims of road traffic accidents, when quantifying damages for personal injury in cases in which the accident takes place in a State other than that of the habitual residence of the victim, the court seised should take into account all the relevant actual circumstances of the specific victim, including in particular the actual losses and costs of after-care and medical attention."

As has been said elsewhere in this book, the status of the recitals is not clear, particularly in respect of a sentiment which is not supported in a specific article.

In light of these concerns, a consultative document was issued in 2009 by the European Commission,[102] seeking views on a variety of options to address this perceived problem,[103] the first of which is to await the results and impact of the application of Rome II. Of the other options, the most striking is to apply instead the law of the country of the visiting victim's residence, which would entail the obvious consequence that in certain accidents, e.g. on a coach tour, where a range of victims are of different residences, there could be multiple *leges causae*, and the defendant could be liable to different victims to varying extents, depending on the individual victim's circumstances (legal and factual). Another possibility would be to require pan-European agreement between insurance companies, in order to produce a system whereby visiting victims could settle their claims with their own third party liability motor insurer, and on the fiction that the accident took place in the victim's country of residence, in order to receive compensation in accordance with that law. The UK Government favours the status quo.[104]

An additional complexity in this subject area is the relationship between Rome II and the 1971 Hague Convention on the Law Applicable to Traffic Accidents, to which many EU Member States (though not the UK) are parties. Article 30 of Rome II requires the Commission to produce, not later than August 20, 2011, a study on the effects of art.28 (relationship with existing international conventions) with respect to the 1971 Hague Convention. In 2009, a report was published,[105] recommending, in the first place, that solutions should be proportionate to the objectives pursued; and that at the EU level solutions should be proportionate to the significance of the issues for the internal market. Specifically, the difference in compensation levels and limitation periods lead to a great amount of uncertainty, and risks of under- and over-compensation. However, it is not clear that the distortions created by these differences have a significant impact on the internal market, "visiting victims" being few in number. Therefore, given the relatively small number of people concerned, an appropriate solution would not involve overhauling the whole legal framework as it pertains to victim compensation. A "targeted" solution

---

[102] European Commission Consultation Paper on the Compensation of Victims of Cross-Border Road Traffic Accidents in the European Union MARKT/H2/RM markt.h2(2009)61541.

[103] Views were also sought on nine proposed options to address the fact that limitation periods vary among Member States. See Ch.8, above.

[104] UK Government Response to a Consultative Document issued by the European Commission dated March 26, 2009 (June 2009).

[105] Hoche (Demolin, Brulard, Barthelemy), *Compensation of Victims of Cross-Border Road Traffic Accidents in the EU: Comparison of National Practices, Analysis of Problems, and Evaluation of Options for Improving the Position of Cross-Border Victims*, Contract ETD/2007/IM/H2/116.

would be better, including an evaluation of Rome II after two years. It is notable that among the other suggestions, none has a conflict of laws dimension.

It is unclear whether the impetus to date among some Member States for the creation of a special choice of law rule for traffic accidents will maintain its momentum.

Direct action against the insurer of the person liable[106]

Although Rome II does not contain a specific rule for road traffic accidents, **16–29** of interest and relevance in this connection is art.18, which provides that:

"The person having suffered damage may bring his or her claim directly against the insurer of the person liable to provide compensation if the law applicable to the non-contractual obligation or the law applicable to the insurance contract so provides."

This is a victim-friendly rule, which may be said to amount in effect to a delict-specific rule for motor accidents. It offers the victim a choice of defendant, and clearly it may often be advantageous to proceed immediately to sue the insurer. This can be done, by virtue of art.18, if a direct claim against the insurer of the wrongdoer is permitted so to do either by the law governing the delict or by the law applicable to the insurance contract. In jurisdiction terms the victim already is assisted by interpretation of the Brussels I Regulation, case law[107] having clarified that the Regulation confers on him, in his action against the wrongdoer's insurers, the benefits provided in section 3 of the Regulation, in particular art.9.1(b).[108] Few topics demonstrate so cogently the interrelationship of applicable law rules in non-contractual and contractual obligations; and between applicable law and jurisdiction rules.

Violations of privacy and rights relating to personality

Despite lengthy and arduous negotiations, it was not possible to agree a **16–30** harmonised choice of law rule to deal with these subjects.[109] Article 30.2 of Rome II stipulates that, not later than December 31, 2008, the Commission shall submit to the European Parliament, the Council and the European Economic and Social Committee a study on the situation in the field of the law applicable to non-contractual obligations arising out of violations of privacy and rights relating to personality, taking into account rules relating to freedom of the press and freedom of expression in the media, and conflict of law issues related to Directive 95/46/EC on the protection of individuals with regard to the processing of personal data and on the free movement of such data [1995] OJ L281/31.

The timescale appears to have slipped. In February 2009, there was published the final report, entitled, *Comparative study on the Situation in the 27 Member States as regards the law applicable to non-contractual obligations*

[106] cf. *Maher v Groupama Grand Est* [2009] EWCA Civ 1191. See also, under the 1995 Act, *Knight v Axa Assurances* [2009] EWHC 1900 (QB); and *Jones v Assurances Generales de France (AGF) SA* [2010] I.L.Pr. 4.
[107] *FBTO Shadeverzekeringen NV v Odenbreit* (C-463/06) [2007] ECR I-11321; [2008] I.L.Pr. 12.
[108] See para.7–26, above.
[109] For background, see Dickinson, *The Rome II Regulation*, 2008, paras 3.217–3.228.

arising out of violations of privacy and rights relating to personality.[110] At the
time of writing, the Commission report is awaited, and in the meantime the pre-
existing national choice of law rules continue to apply.[111]

Freedom of choice

16–31   "Article 14[112] . . .

1. The parties may agree to submit non-contractual obligations to the
   law of their choice:
   (a) by an agreement entered into after the event giving rise to the
       damage occurred;
   or
   (b) where all the parties are pursuing a commercial activity, also by
       an agreement freely negotiated before the event giving rise to the
       damage occurred.
   The choice shall be expressed or demonstrated with reasonable
   certainty by the circumstances of the case and shall not prejudice the
   rights of third parties.
2. Where all the elements relevant to the situation at the time when
   the event giving rise to the damage occurs are located in a country
   other than the country whose law has been chosen, the choice of the
   parties shall not prejudice the application of provisions of the law of
   that other country which cannot be derogated from by agreement.
3. Where all the elements relevant to the situation at the time when the
   event giving rise to the damage occurs are located in one or more of
   the Member States, the parties' choice of the law applicable other
   than that of a Member State shall not prejudice the application of provisions of Community law, where appropriate as implemented in the
   Member State of the forum, which cannot be derogated from by
   agreement."

Whether, and to what extent, party autonomy should be permitted in the area
of non-contractual obligations has been the subject of much discussion.
Recital (31) of the Rome II Regulation encapsulates the rationale for art.14, as
follows:

"To respect the principle of party autonomy and to enhance legal
certainty, the parties should be allowed to make a choice as to the law

---

[110] *Comparative study on the Situation in the 27 Member States as regards the law applicable to
non-contractual obligations arising out of violations of privacy and rights relating to personality* (University of the Basque Country, 2009), JLS/2007/C4/028; see also Annex 1 Survey
Questionnaires.
[111] For Scotland and England, see para.16–54, below.
[112] See T. Kadner Graziano, "Freedom to Choose the Applicable Law in Tort—Articles 14 and
4(3) of the Rome II Regulation" in Ahern and Binchy (eds), *The Rome II Regulation on the
Law Applicable to Non-Contractual Obligations*, 2009, p.219; and Dickinson, *The Rome II
Regulation*, 2008, Ch.13.

applicable to a non-contractual obligation. . . . Protection should be given to weaker parties by imposing certain conditions on the choice."

Party choice in relation to choice of law increasingly is permitted, even encouraged—though generally it is reined in by the concept and imposition of "mandatory rules"; and in the case of choice of jurisdiction, by provisions designed to protect weaker and presumably ill-advised parties from making choices which are perceived to be against their best interests.[113] Domestically and conflictually, the UK Parliament has intervened to ensure that persons who, potentially, may be regarded as disadvantaged shall be protected.[114]

In 1984[115] the Law Commissions, when scrutinising the subject of choice of law in tort and delict, recommended that:

"It should be possible (before or after a tort or delict has occurred) to agree by means of contract what law should govern the parties' mutual liability in tort or delict. Such agreement should be effective whether or not it results in the application of the law of the forum."[116]

Oddly, the issue of party autonomy was not addressed in the ensuing report,[117] nor did it feature in Pt III of the 1995 Act.[118] Sir Peter North remarked in 1993 that it would be "prudent and practical" to legislate for party autonomy in tort and delict since it was, ". . . highly improbable that courts would feel free to develop at common law a concept of party autonomy in tort alongside a regime of statutory choice of law rules."[119] The decision in *Morin v Bonham & Brooks Ltd*[120] suggests that not only would courts have felt reluctant to develop such a concept, but also would have been powerless so to do.[121]

When may the parties exercise choice under Rome II?

Time

In most cases, delictual events are not contemplated or anticipated. Article 14 **16–32** sanctions freedom of choice *ex post*, i.e. after the event giving rise to the

---

[113] See the protective wording of arts 13 (insured persons), 17 (consumers) and 21 (employees) in Brussels I Regulation.

[114] Nygh, *Autonomy in International Contracts*, 1999, p.28.

[115] Law Commission and Scottish Law Commission, *Private International Law: Choice of Law in Tort and Delict*, 1984, Law Com. Working Paper No.87; Scot. Law Com. Memo. No.62 (followed by *Private International Law: Choice of Law in Tort and Delict* (HMSO, 1990), Law Com. No.193; Scot. Law Com. No.129).

[116] Law Commission and Scottish Law Commission, *Private International Law: Choice of Law in Tort and Delict*, 1984, Law Com. Working Paper No.87; Scot. Law Com. Memo. No.62, p.265, para.7.3.1(a).

[117] Law Commission and Scottish Law Commission, *Private International Law: Choice of Law in Tort and Delict*, 1990, Law Com. No.193; Scot. Law Com. No.129.

[118] Sir Peter North described this as the "sin of omission" ("Torts in the Dismal Swamp: Choice of Law Revisited" in *Essays in Private International Law*, 1993, p.85). The issue, he writes, "disappeared without trace" ("Choice in Choice of Law" in *Essays*, 1993, p.190).

[119] North, *Essays*, 1993, p.190. This form of words would seem to indicate that it is Sir Peter North's opinion that contracting out of the Act is not incompetent.

[120] [2003] 2 All E.R. (Comm) 36; [2003] I.L.Pr. 25.

[121] *Morin* is a single judge decision which raised the matter in reported form for perhaps the first time.

damage occurred.[122] Article 14.1 provides that the parties may agree to submit non-contractual obligations to the law of their choice by an agreement entered into after the event giving rise to the damage occurred. However, it must be appreciated that choice *ex post facto* is not necessarily *informed* choice; permission to choose the applicable law *after* the event is no guarantee that advantage will not be taken of the weaker party. The theory behind the limitation of parties to choice *ex post facto* seems to be that they will thereby be protected from inadvertently waiving their rights, or yielding to the will of the other party in advance of the dispute (by virtue perhaps of a standard form contract). Thus, in the Brussels I Regulation, parties deemed to be weak (where there is obvious inequality in bargaining power) are restricted in their exercise of free will to the making of choices after the event and within certain safeguards.[123]

Only where all the parties are pursuing a commercial activity may choice also be exercised by an agreement freely negotiated before the event giving rise to the damage occurred. It is clear that the provisions of art.14.1(b), concerning choice *ex ante*, apply only to the minority of cases in which the parties were known to each other commercially before the occurrence of the event giving rise to the damage.

In the absence of choice of law to govern any non-contractual liability which may arise, where the parties are linked by contract, the governing law of that commercial relationship may be identified by the court as the applicable law to govern the non-contractual obligation, in terms of art.4.3,[124] even if the parties had made no anterior choice of law within the contract to govern any delictual liability which might eventuate. For the applicable law of the contract to be utilised in the context of art.4.3, the delict would require to be closely connected with the contract.

Greater freedom of choice (albeit freedom restricted by overriding mandatory provisions and public policy, *q.v.*) is probably a welcome development in this area; and of particular benefit in cases lying on the cusp where there exist parallel claims in contract and in tort, and where application of a common applicable law to the contractual and non-contractual aspects of a claim would be desirable.[125]

Context

16–33   Although art.14.1 appears to apply to all non-contractual obligations, choice of law is prohibited for certain delicts, by means of the specific choice of

---

[122] See Carruthers and Crawford, "Variations on a Theme of Rome II. Pt 1" (2005) 9 Edin. L.R. 65, 82 et seq.

[123] See paras 7–25—7–33, above.

[124] Kadner Graziano, "Freedom to Choose the Applicable Law in Tort" in Binchy & Ahern (eds), *The Rome II Regulation: The Law Applicable to Non-contractual Obligations* (Leiden: Brill, 2009), p.114.

[125] As, e.g. employer/employee disputes: *Brodin v A/R Seljan*, 1973 S.C. 213; *Coupland v Arabian Gulf Oil Co* [1983] 3 All E.R. 226; and *Sayers v International Drilling Co NV* [1971] 1 W.L.R. 1176. Cf. The "proper law of the issue", as Lord Denning, alone among his peers, sought to get to the heart of the matter in the mixed contract/tort case of *Sayers v International Drilling Co NV*. It may even transpire that there will be produced, ultimately (as originally envisaged, but abandoned in the 1970s as too ambitious an aim), an harmonisation instrument which assimilates the choice of law rules in relation to contractual *and* non-contractual obligations; in this case, one would suppose that the rule on party choice would be the same across the spectrum of obligations.

law rules set out in arts 6 (unfair competition and acts restricting free competition)[126] and 8 (infringement of intellectual property rights).[127]

What may the parties choose?

Leaving aside the question of *when* parties can exercise choice, we must ask **16–34** *what* is it that parties may choose? This subject last came to the forefront of discussion in relation to the conversion of the Rome I Convention into a Regulation. It was clear in that context that parties are not permitted to choose, for example, a body of non-State law, or "the principles of right reason" or the "laws of the Medes and the Persians".[128] The choice under Rome II will be limited to the domestic, internal rules of the chosen law,[129] with no possibility of recourse to *renvoi*. Exclusion of *renvoi* is a necessary handmaid to effective choice of law where the law selected by parties is that of a Member State; were it otherwise, circularity would ensue.[130] There will be no getting away from regulation by the Regulation as, for example, by choosing national rules of applicable law in delict operating before Rome II. However, the recitals and terms of the Rome I Regulation have opened the door to a less restrictive attitude to the content of the choice which the parties may make, and to extend it to non-State rules.[131] Such extension is likely to apply also in delict.[132]

The contract by which the parties exercise their choice under article 14

The (contractual) vehicle by which the parties exercise their choice will be **16–35** subject to the Rome I Convention/Regulation. Where the agreement on choice of law is one permitted by art.14 of the Rome II Regulation, it must be referred to the Rome I Convention/Regulation, as appropriate, for assessment as to formal validity, interpretation, material validity (at least so far as demonstrating consensus), and breach. To the issue of contractual capacity in art.13 of the Rome I Regulation, however, must be added the antecedent proviso supplied by Rome II art.14, that only "parties pursuing a commercial activity" can make such an agreement before the event giving rise to the damage occurs.[133]

With regard to essential validity of the terms of the choice of law agreement, the position is less clear: for example, A and B, commercial parties, agree in advance of any potential delictual incident, that liability will be governed by the law of Evasia, by which, let it be assumed, there is no principle of vicarious liability of an employer for an employee. The contract by which A and B make this "Rome II art.14 agreement", contains a clause to the effect that the law

---

[126] See art.6.4. But see Dickinson, *The Rome II Regulation*, 2008, para.6.75.

[127] See art.8.3. See Explanatory Memorandum, p.22.

[128] *Cheshire and North's Private International Law*, 13th edn, 1999, pp.559, 560; Rome I Green Paper COM(2002) 654 final, para.3.2.3; and see European Economic and Social Committee Opinion on Rome I Green Paper [2004] OJ C108/1, para.4.5.

[129] See art.24.

[130] Elizabeth B. Crawford, "The Use of Putativity and Negativity in the Conflict of Laws" (2005) 54 I.C.L.Q. 829.

[131] See para.15–10, above.

[132] Kadner Graziano, "Freedom to Choose the Applicable Law in Tort" in Binchy & Ahern (eds), *The Rome II Regulation: The Law Applicable to Non-contractual Obligations* (Leiden: Brill, 2009), p.119, where it is suggested that a resource such as the Principles of European Tort Law, drawn up by the European Group on Tort Law, could be viewed in the same light as the Common Frame of Reference in choice of law in contract.

[133] Noting again the prohibitions upon freedom of choice contained in Rome II arts 6, 8.

governing the contract as a whole shall be Scots law (per Rome I Regulation art.3). Insofar as vicarious liability is a principle of Scots law which cannot be derogated from by agreement,[134] the question arises whether the essential validity of the delictual choice of law agreement must be judged by the applicable law of the contract (Scots law) or by the applicable law, contractually agreed by the parties, to govern the non-contractual obligation (Evasian law). Rome II appears to anticipate this problem through its mandatory rules provision in art.14.2,[135] but this will not cover all cases. In a situation in relation to which more than two laws have an interest in being applied, it is arguable that the policing mechanisms operative under the Rome I Regulation, namely, arts 8 (employment contracts), 9 (overriding mandatory provisions), and 21 (public policy of the forum) will apply so as to temper the choice of law agreement made under art.14 of Rome II. Viewed from this perspective, the extent of party autonomy in the non-contractual sphere, where it now appears for the first time, is restricted by the rules governing party autonomy in contractual obligations. This conclusion suggests that the non-contractual obligation is subjugated to the larger contractual choice of law provision. By this mode of reasoning, any attempt by parties to evade a principle such as the vicarious liability of an employer for the wrongful actings of employees in the scope of employment would be difficult to achieve. This is the same balance or distribution of power as has been observed in relation to the functioning of the special jurisdictions in art.5.1 and 5.3 of the Brussels I Regulation.[136]

Restrictions on choice of law

16–36   Parties' choice of law in terms of art.14 will be subject,[137] per art.14.2, to the provisions of the law of another country which cannot be derogated from by agreement where all the elements relevant to the situation at the time when the event giving rise to the damage occurs are located.[138] This provision is intended to deal with a situation which is "purely internal" to one Member State, and which falls within the scope of the Regulation only because the parties have agreed on a choice of foreign law.[139] It deals with a country's rules of *internal* policy, that is, rules which are mandatory in the domestic sense, but not necessarily in the international context:

> "... *internal* public policy rules are not necessarily mandatory in an international context. Such rules must be distinguished from the rules of international public policy of the forum [art.26] and overriding mandatory rules [art.16]."[140]

By reason of art.14.3, where all the elements relevant to the situation at the time when the event giving rise to the damage occurs are located in one or

---

[134] Law Reform (Personal Injuries) Act 1948, abolishing the doctrine of common employment. Cf. *Brodin v A/R Seljan*, 1973 S.C. 213.

[135] So too per art.14.3, mandatory rules of Community law.

[136] See para.7–22, above.

[137] Recital (32) provides that: "Considerations of public interest justify giving the courts of the Member States the possibility, in exceptional circumstances, of applying exceptions based on public policy and overriding mandatory provisions."

[138] cf. Rome I Regulation art.3.3. See para.15–25, above.

[139] Explanatory Memorandum, p.22.

[140] Explanatory Memorandum, p.22.

more of the EU Member States, the parties' choice of applicable law other than that of a Member State, shall not prejudice the application of provisions of Community law, where appropriate as implemented in the Member State of the forum, which cannot be derogated from by agreement. This is a novel provision, which has been replicated in art.3.4 of the Rome I Regulation.[141] In order for the provision in art.14.3 of Rome II (as in art.3.4 of the Rome I Regulation) to apply, the choice of law of the parties must be that of a non-EU Member State. Therefore the provision can be seen as having the aim of ensuring the application of "Community law". Where the parties' choice falls upon the law of a Member State, art.16, preserving overriding mandatory provisions of the (EU) forum, may operate to preserve the application of such provisions of Community law as bind Member State forums.

Overriding mandatory provisions

"Article 16 . . .   **16–37**

Nothing in this Regulation shall restrict the application of the provisions of the law of the forum in a situation where they are mandatory irrespective of the law otherwise applicable to the non-contractual obligation."

The applicable law (whether found by application of art.4, or by the delict-specific rules, or through party choice exercised in terms of art.14) is subject to the overriding mandatory provisions of the *lex fori*.[142] Characterisation of the provision in question as mandatory for the purpose of art.16 must be done by the forum according to its own law. Rome II, in contrast with art.9.1 of the Rome I Regulation, does not contain any definition of mandatory provisions which would guide or restrict the forum.

Rules of safety and conduct

"Article 17 . . .   **16–38**

In assessing the conduct of the person claimed to be liable, account shall be taken, as a matter of fact and in so far as is appropriate, of the rules of safety and conduct which were in force at the place and time of the event giving rise to the liability.

Recital (34) provides that:

"In order to strike a reasonable balance between the parties, account must be taken, in so far as appropriate, of the rules of safety and conduct in operation in the country in which the harmful act was committed, even where the non-contractual obligation is governed by the law of another country. The term 'rules of safety and conduct' should be interpreted as referring to all regulations having any relation to safety and conduct, including, for example, road safety rules in the case of an accident."

---

[141] See para.15–25, above.
[142] cf. Rome I Convention art.7.2; and Rome I Regulation art.9.1, 9.2.

In an instrument which, by its general rule, identifies the *lex loci damni* as the applicable law, art.17 requires account to be taken of certain provisions of the *lex loci delicti* ("place . . . of the event giving rise to the liability"). The wording gives rise to ambiguities of interpretation and of application. With regard to interpretation, it is not easy to understand the extent of the forum's discretion to disregard a particular rule ("in so far as appropriate") when account "shall"/"must" be taken thereof.[143] "Rules of safety and conduct", although capable of very broad interpretation, possibly will be taken to refer principally (but not exclusively)[144] to road safety rules, as recital (34) suggests.

Public policy of the forum

16–39   "Article 26[145] . . .

> The application of a provision of the law of any country specified by this Regulation may be refused only if such application is manifestly incompatible with the public policy (*ordre public*) of the forum."

According to the Commission Explanatory Memorandum, the public policy provision can be distinguished from the provision on overriding mandatory rules[146] in that with regard to the latter, "the courts apply the law of the forum automatically, without first looking at the content of the foreign law."[147] Public policy, on the other hand, may be invoked only *after* the content of the foreign law and the result of its application has been considered by the forum. Article 16 represents, in effect, a positive exercise of the forum's policy: policy operating as a sword (i.e. the strength of the forum's policy is such that it precludes the operation of a contradictory rule of any potentially applicable foreign law). Article 26, in contrast, represents a negative exercise of the forum's public policy: policy operating as a shield, i.e the strength of the forum's policy prevents application of the prima facie relevant foreign law). It is normally the case that the effect of exercise of the forum's public policy in a matter of governing law in any context is preventative of the application of the *lex causae* for some reason that is deeply important to the forum, but conceivably, in a minority of instances, a prohibition (such as an inter-spousal immunity from suit) found in the content of the *lex causae*'s rules is itself so offensive to the forum that the forum's refusal to give effect to that prohibition has the result of producing a positive effect.

By its nature, the tool of public policy is a tool of the forum, albeit for sparing use. At the negotiation stage of Rome II, the Commission Proposal[148] contained a provision which would have given strong guidance to a forum not to give effect to a provision of the *lex causae* deemed in advance to be contrary

---

[143] Nonetheless, Dickinson, *The Rome II Regulation*, 2008, suggests at para.15.33 that Member State courts have a wide margin of appreciation in deciding whether, and if so for what purpose and to what extent, to take account of any such rule. Cf. Rome I Convention art.7.1 ("effect may be given").

[144] Article 17, for example, may have particular significance in relation to claims for environmental damage under art.7.

[145] See also recital (32).

[146] See art.16 (ex-art.12).

[147] Explanatory Memorandum, p.28.

[148] See art.24, Commission Proposal COM(2003) 427 final (2003/0168(COD)).

to "Community public policy". Reference to "Community public policy" was surprising and threatening, even though the Proposal's ambit was limited to one particular point in the law of damages. In the result, such a provision does not appear in Rome II, but traces of it can be found in recital (32).[149]

Scope of the law applicable[150]

"Article 15 . . .   **16–40**

The law applicable to non-contractual obligations under this Regulation shall govern in particular:
  (a) the basis and extent of liability, including the determination of persons who may be held liable for acts performed by them;
  (b) the grounds for exemption from liability, any limitation of liability and any division of liability;
  (c) the existence, the nature and the assessment of damage or the remedy claimed;
  (d) within the limits of powers conferred on the court by its procedural law, the measures which a court may take to prevent or terminate injury or damage or to ensure the provision of compensation;
  (e) the question whether a right to claim damages or a remedy may be transferred, including by inheritance;
  (f) persons entitled to compensation for damage sustained personally;
  (g) liability for the acts of another person;
  (h) the manner in which an obligation may be extinguished and rules of prescription and limitation, including rules relating to the commencement, interruption and suspension of a period of prescription or limitation."

Once the applicable law is identified, its scope is set down in art.15. This is clearly a provision of pivotal importance, setting out the extent of the authority of the *lex causae*.

As with art.12 of the Rome I Regulation,[151] which is the basic model for art.15 of Rome II, the list of issues which are subject to regulation by the *lex causae* is not exhaustive, but the article is useful since different Member States traditionally have adopted different classifications, the same issue in one forum being treated as substantive and therefore subject to application of the *lex causae*; in another as procedural, for the *lex fori*. From a UK perspective, it is significant that listed in art.15 are matters that a UK court otherwise would characterise as procedural and thus determinable by the *lex fori*. The manner of drafting of art.15 gives the *lex causae* an expansive scope of application, conferring upon it a very wide function. The Commission's justification for this expansive approach is certainty.[152]

---

[149] See "Damages", paras 16–43—16–46.
[150] See Janeen M. Carruthers, "Has the Forum Lost its Grip?" in Ahern and Binchy (eds), *The Rome II Regulation on the Law Applicable to Non-Contractual Obligations*, 2009, p.25; and Dickinson, *The Rome II Regulation*, 2008, Ch.14.
[151] cf. Rome I Convention art.10.
[152] Explanatory Memorandum, p.23.

Paragraph (a)

16–41   By paragraph (a), "the basis and extent of liability, including the determination of persons who may be held liable for acts performed by them" shall be governed by the applicable law in delict. This provision is intended to refer to *intrinsic* factors of liability,[153] including issues such as:

> ". . . nature of liability (strict or fault-based); the definition of fault, including the question whether an omission can constitute a fault; the causal link between the event giving rise to the damage and the damage; the persons potentially liable; etc."[154]

"Extent of liability", on the other hand, is intended to refer to:

> ". . . the limitations laid down by law on liability, including the maximum extent of that liability and the contribution to be made by each of the persons liable for the damage which is to be compensated for".[155]

Article 15(a) could be construed as covering not only what was referred to, traditionally in Scots law, as *remoteness of injury* (the existence of liability), but also what was referred to as *remoteness of damage* (the extent of liability).

The phrase, "including the determination of persons who may be held liable for acts performed by them" is ambiguous. The matter of determination of persons liable in (a) arguably covers the same thing (vicarious liability) as in art.15(g) (liability for the acts of another person). The duplication is not problematic insofar as the applicable law is the same under both paragraphs, but the drafting could be more exact. Paragraph (a) probably is intended to refer to issues such as whether an *incapax* person (by reason of non-age, or mental incapacity, etc.) may be held liable for his potentially tortious acts and omissions. In order to avoid potential conflicts of characterisation, it might have been sensible expressly to include in para.(a) the matter of tortious capacity. Curiously, although the question of capacity to incur liability in tort/delict is not expressly listed in art.15, it is narrated in recital (12) as being a matter which is governed by the *lex causae*. Why this is relegated to the recitals is not apparent. The drafters' intention, at least, is that it should not be possible under Rome II to seek to characterise tortious capacity as a matter for the choice of law rules on status and capacity, and thus generally to be governed by the law of the putative wrongdoer's personal law, be that his domicile, habitual residence or nationality.

Paragraph (b)

16–42   The grounds for exemption from liability, any limitation of liability and any division of liability are governed by the applicable law in delict. These, it is said, are *extrinsic* factors of liability,[156] or "conditions for exoneration from liability".[157] The grounds for release from liability could include *force*

---

[153] Explanatory Memorandum, p.23.
[154] Explanatory Memorandum, p.23.
[155] Explanatory Memorandum, p.23.
[156] Explanatory Memorandum, p.23.
[157] *Cheshire, North and Fawcett: Private International Law*, 14th edn, 2008, p.842.

majeure; necessity; third-party fault; and fault by the victim,[158] by way of contributory negligence or voluntary assumption of risk.

Contributory negligence on the part of the victim possibly deserves an express mention in para.(b), for it, normally, is the most important reason for a division of liability. A useful case on the subject of defences is *Dawson v Broughton*.[159] A car driven by Broughton in France was involved in a collision with another vehicle driven by a French driver. Of the passengers in Broughton's car, two were injured and one was killed. Broughton's primary liability was not disputed, but a defence of contributory negligence was entered on the ground that the individual who died had not been wearing a seat belt. Under s.11 of the 1995 Act, the applicable law was French. In terms of French law, under the *Loi Badinter*, failure to wear a seat belt does not result in any reduction in damages. A question arose as to whether that provision of French law was substantive or procedural, a matter of significance because by effect of s.14(3)(b) of the 1995 Act (*q.v.*) matters of evidence and procedure were to be determined by English law. The court held that contributory negligence was relevant to the scope of a defendant's liability and the identification of actionable damage, and therefore, that the matter was substantive, and not to be regarded as merely part of the quantification of damages. On this line of reasoning, the French provision applied (subject only to displacement under s.12 of the 1995 Act, *q.v.*). If contributory negligence falls within "exemption from liability, any limitation of liability and any division of liability", Rome II requires that the rules of the *lex causae* on this matter will govern, rendering the substance/procedure debate irrelevant.

Paragraph (c)

The most contentious aspect of art.15 is para.(c). The damages debate has long been the subject of particular interest in the UK.[160]   **16–43**

Pre-Rome II

The pre-existing UK choice of law rule relating to damages was said to be   **16–44** partly substantive and partly procedural, as follows: the applicable law in delict determined what heads of damages were available, whereas the monetary assessment or quantification of damages, and the mode of calculation (e.g. by judge or jury) were governed by the law of the forum, since these were deemed to be aspects of procedure. No Scottish or English case at common law or under the 1995 Act appears to have applied the principles of a *foreign* applicable law to the task of quantification.

---

[158] Explanatory Memorandum, p.23.
[159] *Dawson v Broughton* (2007) 151 S.J.L.B. 1167. See "Case Comment", 2007 J.P.I.L. C186.
[160] Most recently in *Harding v Wealands* [2007] 2 A.C. 1. See generally *Cheshire, North and Fawcett: Private International Law*, 14th edn, 2008, pp.95–101; G. Panagopoulos, "Substance and Procedure in Private International Law" (2005) 1(1) J. Priv. Int. Law 69; Janeen M. Carruthers, "Damages in the Conflict of Laws—the Substance and Procedure Spectrum: *Harding v Wealands*" (2005) 1(2) J. Priv. Int. Law 323; C. Dougherty and L. Wyles, "*Harding v Wealands*" (2007) 56 I.C.L.Q. 443; and R. Weintraub, "Choice of Law for Quantification of Damages: A Judgment of the House of Lords makes a Bad Rule Worse" (2007) 43 Texas Int. Law J. 311.

Subject to one's preferred ratio of *Chaplin v Boys*,[161] there are two main elements in the assessment of damages[162]:

(a) determination of liability, which was deemed to be a matter of substance to be determined in accordance with the delictual *lex causae*. The applicable law would determine all matters such as remoteness of damage and the heads under which damages may be claimed; and

(b) quantification of the amount of damages, which was considered to be a matter of procedure to be determined by the *lex fori* alone.[163]

The result of s.14(2) and (3)(b) of the 1995 Act seemingly produced no change in this area, but the matter of distinguishing between issues of substance and of procedure revealed itself to be more complex than at first sight.[164] Moreover the rationale for the distinction may be subject to criticism.[165]

Opportunity for the House of Lords to revisit the "damages rule", and to review its merits arose in *Harding v Wealands*,[166] a case decided according to the 1995 Act. The claimant, Giles Harding, an English national, domiciled in England, was rendered tetraplegic as a result of a motor accident in New South Wales in February 2003. The car in which he was a front-seat passenger was being driven, at the time of the accident, by his partner Tania Wealands, an Australian national who had lived in Australia until June 2001, at which time she moved to England to live with the claimant in a settled relationship. Ms Wealands conceded liability (no other vehicle was involved in the incident), but a preliminary issue arose before Elias J. concerning the law applicable to the assessment of damages.[167]

There were two potentially applicable laws: the law of New South Wales ("NSW"), being the law of the country where the tort occurred; and English law, being the law of the forum and also, the claimant argued, the "substantially more appropriate" law to apply. New South Wales law, unlike English law, imposed various limitations on the nature and amount of damages recoverable by the claimant in terms of the Motor Accidents Compensation Act 1999 ("MACA"). It was in the claimant's interests that English law apply to the assessment of damages.

At first instance, Elias J. found in favour of the claimant on two grounds. First, it was accepted that English law should apply to all aspects of the assessment of damages in terms of s.12 of the 1995 Act. But in any event, his Lordship concluded that, even if NSW law applied under s.11, nevertheless English law,

---

[161] [1971] A.C. 356.

[162] *Kohnke v Karger* [1951] 2 All E.R. 179; *J D'Almeida Araujo LDA v Sir Frederick Becker & Co Ltd* [1953] 2 Q.B. 329 (contract); *Chaplin v Boys* [1971] A.C. 356; *Mitchell v McCulloch*, 1976 S.L.T. 2.

[163] *Maher v Groupama Grand Est* [2009] EWCA Civ 1191; *Knight v Axa Assurances* [2009] EWHC 1900 (QB).

[164] e.g. *Edmunds v Simmonds* [2001] 1 W.L.R. 1003; *Roerig v Valiant Trawlers Ltd* [2002] 1 Lloyd's Rep. 681.

[165] *Harding v Wealands* [2005] 1 All E.R. 415. Also J.M. Carruthers, "Substance and Procedure in the Conflict of Laws: A Continuing Debate in relation to Damages" (2004) 53 I.C.L.Q. 691; and J.M. Carruthers "Damages in the Conflict of Laws" (2005) 1(2) J. Priv. Int. Law 323. See *Re T&N Ltd* [2005] EWHC 2990 (Ch) at [45].

[166] [2007] 2 A.C. 1.

[167] *Harding v Wealands* [2004] EWHC 1957 (QB). All references henceforth to Elias J. are to this citation.

as master of procedure in its own house, should govern the quantification of damages qua *lex fori*. Ms Wealands appealed. Two issues arose on appeal: first, whether Elias J. was correct to disapply the general rule in s.11 of the 1995 Act (which, it was concluded, ultimately, he was not); and, secondly, whether the NSW damages provisions were to be classified as substantive or procedural, the significance being that if they were held to be rules of substance, they would apply (given the s.11 application of NSW law) even in an English forum.

The majority[168] of the Court of Appeal found in favour of Ms Wealands. This was not an appropriate case for s.12 displacement. Moreover, English law should not govern assessment of the claimant's damages. In the Court of Appeal Arden L.J., endeavoured to steer English law in a new direction, stating that the applicable law in tort (in this case, NSW law) should govern, as far as possible, the assessment of damages, including quantification of damages. The *lex fori* should apply only as a back-up or secondary provision, where it is not possible, or just, to apply the proper law. Mr Harding appealed.

The House of Lords allowed Mr Harding's appeal, restoring the judgment of Elias J., and affirming the "damages principle". Their Lordships, retreating from Arden L.J.'s statement of the law, cleaved to the traditional British view, that questions of quantification of damages are procedural, to be determined by the law of the forum. This is at odds, however, with the harmonised European solution.

Rome II

Article 15(c) of Rome II has undergone a subtle change of wording (of serious **16–45** consequence) over its various versions and now is fixed as referring to, "the existence, the nature and the assessment of damage or the remedy claimed". These are matters for the applicable law in tort. Thus, the forum's approach to quantification of damages in tort will apply *only* if the *lex fori* happens also to be the law governing substantive liability, i.e. if the *lex fori* applies qua *lex causae*. This is a significant change of position for United Kingdom courts. There is no scope under art.15 for displacing application of the pre-determined *lex causae*; the only way in which displacement is possible is to revisit the subject of identification of the *lex causae*, or to reassess the applicability of arts 16 or 26.[169]

It is well known that the distinction between substance and procedure in damages is not always as clear-cut as might be expected.[170] However, the distinction between liability and quantification has been rendered meaningless[171] now that *all* such matters are to be referred, in any event, to the *same* law, the *lex causae*.

Of course the two-pronged approach to damages was not without defect: in quantifying *novel* claims, for example, how was the forum to quantify a head of loss which was available under the *lex causae*, but which the *lex fori* did not know or recognise? This problem did not generally arise at common law because of the requirement of double actionability,[172] but that is not true of

---

[168] Arden L.J. and Sir Wm Aldous; Waller L.J., dissenting. See *Harding v Wealands* [2005] 1 W.L.R. 1539 CA, per Arden L.J. at [52].

[169] See paras 16–37 and 16–39, above.

[170] See para.8–23, above.

[171] At least for the purposes of choice of law concerning awards of damages under Rome II.

[172] See para.16–58, below.

operation of the 1995 Act. Whatever the merit of art.15(c), it short-circuits this particular problem.

If it is the aim of the Rome II Regulation to achieve uniformity and foresee-ability of outcome (in applicable law terms at least) there is a strong case for arguing that quantification should depend on the applicable law, rather than on the law of the particular forum in which the claim happens to be brought. There is certainly something to be said for applying the foreign law, and having regard to the foreign remedy if its application would be consistent with the procedural possibilities available in the forum. Trouble may be encoun-tered, however, where its application would be inconsistent with the proce-dural possibilities of the forum, e.g. where the *lex causae* prefers payment of interim or provisional damages, or damages in instalments,[173] or where the decision on quantum is one for a jury, but the *lex fori* has no such procedural device or mechanism. Article 15(c), unlike art.15(d),[174] does not, apparently, offer an escape route from this problem. The view has been expressed that:

"... common sense requires that Article 15(c) should be interpreted as being implicitly procedurally limited in the same way as Article 10(1)(c)[175] of the Rome Convention is explicitly so limited".[176]

It is to be hoped that this common sense interpretation will be adopted.

A further significant difference in wording exists between art.10(1)(c) of the Rome I Convention and its sibling, art.15(c) of Rome II. Rome I provides that the contractual *lex causae* shall determine the assessment of damages, "in so far as it is governed by *rules of law*".[177] This proviso does not feature in Rome II.[178] The wording of Rome I is intended to draw a distinction between circum-stances when the assessment of damages raises questions of fact and those when it raises questions of law. If the issue raises a question of law,[179] then the contractual *lex causae* per Rome I will apply. If, however, the question in rela-tion to assessment is one only of fact (e.g. if a jury is to calculate the amount of damages) this is a matter purely for the *lex fori*, and the applicable law under Rome I will not apply.

Rome II does not, ex facie, vouchsafe such a role for the *lex fori*. Article 15(c) apparently is less restrictive than Rome I in this respect, and a literal approach to interpretation indicates that the applicable law in tort will apply, regardless of whether the issue of assessment arising is one of fact or of law. Strictly, there-fore, and anomalously, the role of the *lex fori* is more significantly reduced in assessment of damage in *non-contractual* obligations, than in relation to

---

[173] Although these matters, potentially, could be characterised as relating to "forms of compensa-tion" and subject, therefore, to art.15(d), which is subject to the proviso that the forum is obliged to act only within the limits of powers conferred by its own procedural law.

[174] Discussed, para.16–47, below.

[175] Which is prefaced by the words, "within the limits of the powers conferred on the court by its procedural law". Cf. Rome I Regulation art.12.1(c).

[176] *Cheshire, North and Fawcett: Private International Law*, 14th edn, 2008, p.846.

[177] cf. Rome I Regulation art.12.1(c).

[178] Notably, it did feature in the corresponding provision (art.11(e)) of the original Commission Proposal for a Regulation. For detail, see *Cheshire, North and Fawcett: Private International Law*, 14th edn, 2008, p.845, fn.591.

[179] e.g. Giuliano and Lagarde, p.33.

contractual obligations. It remains to be seen whether courts applying this paragraph will adopt a strict, literal construction of the provision, or whether they will take the view that omission of the proviso from Rome II was inadvertent. As a matter of practice, the latter approach would be the more sensible.

Non-compensatory, exemplary or punitive damages

During the negotiations of Rome II, there was an attempt by the European **16–46** Parliament to include rules directing Member State courts on the manner of treatment of awards of non-compensatory, exemplary or punitive damages of an excessive nature.[180] Within the UK there was strong concern at the prospect of development of the concept of "Community public policy".[181] Ultimately, the clause as drafted in the Commission Proposal[182] did not survive. A residue remains, however, in the form of recitals (32)[183] and (33).[184]

Paragraph (d)

This paragraph is intended to refer to: **16–47**

> ". . . forms of compensation, such as the question whether the damage can be repaired by payment of damages, and ways of preventing or halting the damage, such as an interlocutory injunction, though without actually obliging the court to order measures that are unknown in its own procedural law."[185]

This caveat[186] ensures that the forum cannot be required to order measures that have no place in its procedural law.

Paragraph (e)

This provision, providing that the applicable law will govern, "the question **16–48** whether a right to claim damages or a remedy may be transferred, including by inheritance"[187] is self-explanatory. The rule should operate effectively, so

---

[180] See Carruthers and Crawford, "Variations on a Theme of Rome II. Part 1" (2005) 9 Edin. L.R. 65, 95–97.

[181] See Scott Report, Evidence, House of Lords Committee, 8th Report, e.g. Briggs, para.16: ". . . I do not see what 'Community Public Policy' is. Public policies are national, not Community, and it strikes me as very undesirable indeed that there should be any encouragement for a 'Community Public Policy' to put down roots. If the Commission wants a special rule, let it make it in clear and precise terms, without any reference to Public Policy."

[182] Ex-arts 23 and 24.

[183] Recital (32) provides that: "Considerations of public interest justify giving the courts of the Member States the possibility, in exceptional circumstances, of applying exceptions based on public policy and overriding mandatory provisions. In particular, the application of a provision of the law designated by this Regulation which would have the effect of causing non-compensatory exemplary or punitive damages of an excessive nature to be awarded may, depending on the circumstances of the case and the legal order of the Member State of the court seised, be regarded as being contrary to the public policy (*ordre public*) of the forum."

[184] See para.16–38, above.

[185] Explanatory Memorandum, p.24.

[186] Which does not (explicitly, at least) operate in relation to art.15(c).

[187] For rules of survival of action in domestic Scots law, see Crawford and Carruthers, *International Private Law In Scotland*, 2nd edn, 2006, para.16–26.

long as it is accepted that the matter is one which properly belongs to the law of delict and not to that of succession or procedure. The Commission Memorandum states that:

">... in succession cases, the designated law[188] governs the question whether an action can be brought by a victim's heir to obtain compensation for damage sustained by the victim.[189] In assignment cases, the designated law[190] governs the question whether a claim is assignable, and also the relationship between assignor and debtor."[191]

Paragraph (f)

16–49   The applicable law will govern, "persons entitled to compensation for damage sustained personally". On first sight the meaning of this clause is not clear. The wording is opaque and arguably the matter could be treated under art.15(c). The Commission Memorandum, however, explains that the concept particularly refers to the question whether a secondary victim, that is, a person other than the "direct victim", can obtain compensation for damage sustained on a "knock-on" basis, following damage sustained by the primary victim.[192] "Such damage might be non-material, as in the pain and suffering caused by a bereavement, or financial, as in the loss sustained by the children or spouse of a deceased person."[193] The heading appears to cover both the question of availability of an award of damages in principle, and the entitlement to claim such.

At common law, the subject of title and interest to sue is normally a matter of procedure to be determined by the *lex fori*, but examples of more manipulative classification in the United States have demonstrated that this largely procedural subject, which is of the first importance in every sense, may merge into a matter of substance. For example, claims within the family may be regarded as pertaining to the law of domestic relations and may be referred to the law of the domicile. While title to sue in a technical sense is procedural, interest to sue is a substantive matter; sometimes this distinction is not clearly drawn, and the expression "title to sue" may encompass both aspects.[194]

Paragraph (g)

16–50   Paragraph (g) provides that vicarious liability shall be determined by the applicable law, and not the *lex fori*. It would cover the liability of parents for their children, and of principals for their agents, and is the same as the pre-Rome II position in the United Kingdom. Article 15(g) would appear to extend to natural and to legal persons (e.g. within a corporate group, as

---

[188] i.e. the applicable law under the Rome II Regulation.
[189] The *lex successionis* will determine who benefits from survival of the cause of action.
[190] i.e. the applicable law under the Rome II Regulation, being "the proper law of the right".
[191] Explanatory Memorandum, p.24.
[192] Explanatory Memorandum, p.24. See also para.16–19, above.
[193] Explanatory Memorandum, p.24.
[194] *FMC Corp v Russell*, 1999 S.L.T. 99. See Elizabeth B. Crawford, "The Adjective and the Noun: Title and Right to Sue in International Private Law", 2000 J.R. 347. See para.8–05, above.

regards the liability of a parent company for the acts or omissions of its subsidiaries).[195]

Paragraph (h)

Lastly, para.(h) provides that, "the manner in which an obligation may be **16–51** extinguished and rules of prescription and limitation, including rules relating to the commencement, interruption and suspension of a period of prescription or limitation" shall be referred to the applicable law under the Regulation. In line with the existing UK legislation, the law designated by Rome II will govern the loss of a right following failure to exercise it, on the conditions set by that law; it is irrelevant whether such provisions are deemed substantive or procedural under the *lex causae*.[196]

Article 15 does not eliminate the difficult interface between the applicable law and the law of the forum, that is, between substance and procedure; indeed, it makes no reference as such to substance and procedure. However, by expanding the territory over which the *lex causae* explicitly extends, Rome II reduces the size of the debateable land between substance and procedure.

The range of matters set out in art.15 as falling under the governance of the *lex causae* tilts the balance in favour of the *lex causae* in a manner which is explicit. There is no overt means in art.15 by which the forum is able to inhibit the application of the *lex causae*.

INTRA-UK CASES

Typically, European conflict of laws harmonisation instruments confer **16–52** upon states with more than one legal system the opportunity not to apply the harmonised rules to conflicts solely between the laws of such units. This provision is contained in art.25.2 of Rome II. The UK has acted typically, in response, by declining to take up the opportunity not to apply Rome II to intra-UK conflicts.[197]

Under the 1995 Act, a difficulty of interpretation arose in relation to the combined effect of ss.9(6),[198] 10 and 14(2).[199] Where allegedly delictual actings took place entirely within one territorial unit of the UK, and were litigated upon in that same unit, it was unclear whether the statutory rules

---

[195] Though arguably the law governing the company/ies has a stronger interest in, and so ought to regulate this matter.

[196] cf. Rome I Convention art.10.1(d) (awareness of which led, in part, at least, to the Foreign Limitation Periods Act 1984, discussed, paras 8–06—8–09, above), and Rome I Regulation art.12.1(d).

[197] 1995 Act s.15A, and The Law Applicable to Non-Contractual Obligations (England and Wales and Northern Ireland) Regulations 2008 (SI 2008/2986) reg.6; and 1995 Act s.15B; and The Law Applicable to Non-Contractual Obligations (Scotland) Regulations 2008 (SSI 2008/404) reg.4, respectively, extend the scope of Rome II to conflicts solely between the laws of England and Wales, Scotland, Northern Ireland and Gibraltar.

[198] "This Part applies in relation to events occurring in the forum as it applies in relation to events occurring in any other country".

[199] "Nothing in this Part affects any rules of law (including rules of private international law) except those abolished by section 10".

were to be regarded as applicable. This matter is of much decreased importance now, and reference should be made to the previous edition of this work.[200]

WHERE DELICT MEETS CONTRACT[201]

16–53	Although delictual actings usually are not premeditated, it may happen that there is a pre-existing relationship between the alleged wrongdoer and the victim. As noted above, the existence of the contractual nexus may influence the identification of the applicable law in delict,[202] and indeed may lead to the conclusion that the law applicable to the contractual and non-contractual obligation, respectively, is the same.

Where, however, this is not the case, and the parties stand to each other, for example, as employer/employee, or carrier/passenger, the defender in an action founded in delict may wish to try to use a term of the contract agreed between the parties to oust or mitigate his potential delictual liability,[203] as where a Scots employee entered into an employment contract under which he agreed to waive certain provisions of Scots law regarding the law of damages for personal injuries, and agreed instead to accept the provisions of some other (presumably less favourable) law, or an exclusion or limitation of liability on the part of the employer. If such a person is injured through an act of negligence for which his employer prima facie is responsible,[204] is his right of action to be regarded as a right based on delict governed by the conflict rules stated, or as a contractual right governed (i.e. limited) by the provisions of the contract? In *Sayers v International Drilling Co NV*,[205] the judges took different views, but it is suggested that if the approach of Lord Denning M.R. in that case, and of Lord Kissen in *Brodin v A/R Seljan*,[206] is followed, the Scots courts will treat the matter, first, as one involving delict and apply the conflict rules of delict prior to those of contract.[207]

---

[200] See Crawford and Carruthers, *International Private Law In Scotland*, 2nd edn, 2006, paras 16–10, 16–23; and E.L.R 70 et seq.; see also para.16–54, below.

[201] See Crawford and Carruthers, "Connection and Coherence between and among European PIL Instruments in the Law of Obligations", pp.14 (on the RI/RII axis), 20.

[202] See arts 4.3 and 18.

[203] cf. *Matthews v Kuwait Bechtel Corp* [1959] 2 All E.R. 345. See *Coupland v Arabian Gulf Oil Co* [1983] 3 All E.R. 226.

[204] In terms of art.15(g) of Rome II, the question of vicarious liability would fall to be governed by the applicable law determined per arts 4–14.

[205] [1971] 1 W.L.R. 1176. See also *Comex Houlder Diving Ltd v Colne Fishing Co Ltd*, 1987 S.L.T. 443 (right of contribution under Law Reform (Miscellaneous Provisions) (Scotland) Act 1940 s.3(2)).

[206] 1973 S.L.T. 198. In this case no doubt an element of policy was present. Lord Kissen was not inclined to the view that the thrust of the provisions of the UK Law Reform (Personal Injuries) Act 1948 could be displaced by the Norwegian contract of employment of a sailor injured in Scotland by a fellow employee, who sued his employer in Scotland.

[207] *Coupland v Arabian Gulf Oil Co* [1983] 3 All E.R. 226; *Henderson v Merrett Syndicates Ltd (No.1)* [1994] 3 All E.R. 506 (domestic law). See Morse, *Torts in Private International Law*, 1978, pp.187 et seq.; North, "Contract as a Tort Defence in the Conflict of Laws", reprinted in *Essays*, 1993, p.89: "The availability of the contractual defence is a matter of tort law but the validity of the contract in which it is to be found is a matter of contract law" (p.108).

Hence, applying the choice of law rule in delict (under Rome II,[208] the 1995 Act, or at common law, as the case may be), the court would decide whether contractual exclusion or limitation of delictual liability on the part of the alleged wrongdoer would be permitted by the delictual *lex/leges causae*. Only if such a defence is allowed according to the delictual *lex/leges causae* would the court proceed to consider whether the contract and/or contractual term in question is valid by its own applicable law, as determined by the Rome I Regulation, and relevant in the circumstances. In so doing, it is likely that reference will require to be made to the contract-specific rules contained in arts 5–8 of the Rome I Regulation.[209]

PRIVATE INTERNATIONAL LAW (MISCELLANEOUS PROVISIONS) ACT 1995

As stated above, while Rome II represents the major scheme of applicable law rules to be applied by Member State courts in qualifying cases arising under the head of non-contractual obligations, account still must be taken, in a UK court, of the 1995 Act, by reason of subject matter, and/or of date.[210] With regard to such events giving rise to damage which occur before January 11, 2009, the governing rules are those contained in the 1995 Act, provided that the act or omission giving rise to the claim occurred on or after May 1, 1996.[211] Further, violations of privacy and personality rights are excluded from the scope of Rome II by art.1.2(g), and so fall to be regulated by Pt III of the 1995 Act, provided the claim is characterised by the forum, for the purposes of private international law, as one relating to tort or delict.[212] **16–54**

The 1995 Act[213] sprang from the work and consultation undertaken by the Law Commissions in the 1980s,[214] in turn prompted by long-running academic discussion and speculation.[215] Section 11 provided the general rule, in the following terms:

---

[208] The choice of law process under Rome II might—arts 4.3 and 18—necessitate identification of the applicable law in contract.

[209] See paras 15–27—15–30, above.

[210] The Law Applicable to Non-Contractual Obligations (England and Wales and Northern Ireland) Regulations 2008 (SI 2008/2986), inserting s.15A into the 1995 Act; and The Law Applicable to Non-Contractual Obligations (Scotland) Regulations 2008 (SSI 2008/404), inserting s.15B into the 1995 Act, operate to restrict the application of the statutory choice of law rules contained in Pt III of the 1995 Act and give precedence to the operation of Rome II.

[211] 1995 Act s.14(1); and the Private International Law (Miscellanous Provisions) Act 1995 (Commencement) Order 1996 (SI 1996/995) reg.2.

[212] 1995 Act s.9(2).

[213] C.G.J. Morse, "Torts in Private International Law: A New Statutory Framework" (1996) I.C.L.Q. 888; J. Blaikie, "Foreign Torts and Choice of Law Flexibility", 1995 S.L.T. (News) 23; J. Blaikie, "Choice of Law in delict and tort: reform at last!" (1997) 1(3) Edin. L.R. 361; B.J. Rodger, "Whisky Galore—Por Favor", 1996 S.L.T. (News) 105; B.J. Rodger, "The Halley Holed—and Now Sunk", 1996 S.L.P.Q. 397; P.J. Rogerson, "Choice of Law in Tort: A Missed Opportunity?" (1995) I.C.L.Q. 650.

[214] Law Commission and Scots Law Commission, *Private International Law: Choice of Law in Tort and Delict*, 1984, Law Com. Working Paper No.87; Scot. Law Com. Memo. No.62; *Private International Law: Choice of Law in Tort and Delict*, 1990, Law Com. No.193; Scot. Law Com. No.129.

[215] See, for detail, Crawford and Carruthers, *International Private Law In Scotland*, 2nd edn, 2006, para.16–16.

"(1) The general rule is that the applicable law[216] is the law of the country in which the events constituting the tort or delict in question occur.[217]

(2) Where elements of those events occur in different countries, the applicable law under the general rule is to be taken as being—

(a) for a cause of action in respect of personal injury caused to an individual or death resulting from personal injury, the law of the country where the individual was when he sustained the injury[218];

(b) for a cause of action in respect of damage to property, the law of the country where the property was when it was damaged[219]; and

(c) in any other case, the law of the country in which the most significant element or elements of those events occurred."[220]

The general rule is subject to the rule of displacement supplied by s.12, viz.:

"(1) If it appears, in all the circumstances, from a comparison of—

(a) the significance of the factors which connect a tort or delict with the country whose law would be the applicable law under the general rule; and

(b) the significance of any factors connecting the tort or delict with another country,

that it is substantially more appropriate for the applicable law for determining the issues arising in the case, or any of those issues, to be the law of the other country, the general rule is displaced and the applicable law for determining those issues or that issue (as the case may be) is the law of that other country.

(2) The factors that may be taken into account as connecting a tort or delict with a country for the purposes of this section include, in particular, factors relating to the parties, to any of the events which constitute the tort or delict in question or to any of the circumstances or consequences of those events."

The decision to displace was a matter for the discretion of the forum; upon the frequency and boldness of the forum's exercise of its discretion depended the

---

[216] The applicable law shall exclude any choice of law rules forming part of the applicable law: s.9(5). Cf. at common law *McElroy v McAllister*, 1949 S.C. 110, per Lord Russell at 126; and under Rome II art.24.

[217] e.g. *Equitas Ltd v Wave City Shipping Co Ltd* [2005] 2 All E.R. (Comm) 301; *Langlands v SG Hambros Trust Co (Jersey) Ltd* [2007] EWHC 627 (Ch); *R. (on the application of Al-Jedda) v Secretary of State for Defence* [2008] 1 A.C. 332; *OJSC Oil Co Yugraneft v Abramovich* [2008] EWHC 2613 (Comm); *The Nicholas M* [2008] EWHC 1615 (Comm); *Parker v TUI UK Ltd* [2009] EWCA Civ 1261; and *Jones v Assurances Generales de France (AGF) SA* [2010] I.L.Pr. 4.

[218] e.g. *Hulse v Chambers* [2002] 1 All E.R. (Comm) 812.

[219] e.g. *West Tankers Inc v RAS Riunione Adriatica di Sicurta SpA (The Front Comor)* [2005] EWHC 454 (Comm).

[220] e.g. *Protea Leasing Ltd v Royal Air Cambodge Co Ltd* [2002] EWHC 2731 (improper management and conduct of business); *Morin v Bonham & Brooks Ltd* [2004] 1 Lloyd's Rep. 702; and *Middle Eastern Oil v National Bank of Abu Dhabi* [2008] EWHC 2895 (Comm).

strength of the general rule. The words "substantially more appropriate" sounded a warning against overuse. The decision to displace would be based on the preponderance and distribution of factors. The list of factors was not exhaustive. Morse argued that, if the surrounding circumstances could include "factors relating to the parties" (s.12(2)), it might be possible to segregate pairs of parties, so that a different applicable law might apply between different pairs of litigants even where all claims arose out of the same incident. There might be displacement in respect of a particular issue as well as in respect of the whole claim, unlike the position under Rome II art.4.3. Displacement might be in favour of the forum or of a third (or conceivably more) law(s).

A number of English cases have been handed down since the entry into force of the 1995 Act.[221] Particularly useful guidance can be had from *Roerig v Valiant Trawlers Ltd*.[222] The decision of Waller L.J. served as a useful guide to the steps which a court ought to take in deciding whether or not to displace the general rule. His Lordship stated that: "The first exercise [was] to identify the issue in relation to which it might be suggested that the general rule should not be applicable."[223] Thereafter, the next task was to identify the factors which connected the tort with the countries whose laws were competing for application. An important task for the forum was to assess the significance of the contacts, requiring the court to make a value judgment. The general rule in s.11 was not to be dislodged easily. "Substantially" was to be strictly construed, courts being careful not to displace the general rule too readily, particularly where they were displacing in favour of the *lex fori*.[224]

The *lex causae* identified under the 1995 Act governed all questions of liability, available defences,[225] and heads of damages.[226] Quantification of damages under the Act, as at common law, was a matter for the forum.

---

[221] *Hamill v Hamill* Unreported July 24, 2000, QBD; *Edmunds v Simmonds* [2001] 1 W.L.R. 1003; *Glencore International AG v Metro Trading International Inc (No.2)* [2001] 1 Lloyd's Rep. 284; *Hulse v Chambers* [2002] 1 All E.R. (Comm) 812; *Protea Leasing Ltd v Royal Air Cambodge Ltd* [2002] EWHC 2731; *Anton Durbeck GmbH v Den Norske Bank ASA* [2002] EWHC 1173 (Comm); [2006] 1 Lloyd's Rep. 93; *Morin v Bonham & Brooks Ltd* [2004] 1 Lloyd's Rep. 702; *Equitas Ltd v Wave City Shipping Co Ltd* [2005] 2 All E.R. (Comm) 301; *Trafigura Beheer BV v Kookmin Bank Co* [2006] EWHC 1450 (Comm); *Harding v Wealands* [2006] UKHL 32; *Dornoch Ltd v Mauritius Union Assurance Co Ltd* [2006] EWCA Civ 389 CA (Civ Div); *Ark Therapeutics Plc v True North Capital Ltd* [2006] 1 All E.R. (Comm) 138; *Langlands v SG Hambros Trust Co (Jersey) Ltd* [2007] EWHC 627 (Ch); *Dawson v Broughton* Unreported July 31, 2007 Manchester County Court; *Hornsby v James Fisher Rumic Ltd* [2008] EWHC 1944 (QB); *Middle Eastern Oil v National Bank of Abu Dhabi* [2008] EWHC 2895 (Comm); *B v B* Unreported, but see: (2008) 105 (39) L.S.G 20; *R. (on the application of Al-Jedda) v Secretary of State for Defence* [2008] 1 A.C. 332; *OJSC Oil Co Yugraneft v Abramovich* [2008] EWHC 2613 (Comm); *Parker v TUI UK Ltd* [2009] EWCA Civ 1261; and *Jones v Assurances Generales de France (AGF) SA* [2010] I.L.Pr. 4.

[222] [2002] 1 Lloyd's Rep. 681; cf. *Hornsby v James Fisher Rumic Ltd* [2008] EWHC 1944 (QB); and *B v B* Unreported, but see: (2008) 105 (39) L.S.G. 20.

[223] *Roerig v Valiant Trawlers Ltd* [2002] 1 Lloyd's Rep. 681 at [12](ii).

[224] cf. Rome I Convention art.4.2, 4.5; and Rome I Regulation art.4.1, 4.3, discussed at paras 15–11 and 15–15, above. Cf. *Dornoch Ltd v Mauritius Union Assurance Co Ltd* [2006] EWCA Civ 389; *Hornsby v James Fisher Rumic Ltd* [2008] EWHC 1944 (QB); and *B v B* Unreported, but see: (2008) 105(39) L.S.G. 20.

[225] i.e. defences of a substantive nature. Defences under the *lex fori*, of a procedural nature, also were available.

[226] For claims under the 1995 Act arising after January 11, 2009, Rome II art.15(c) (in terms of which assessment/quantification is for the *lex causae*) does not affect the position.

The 1995 Act generated, in its short life, a body of case law, and a concomitant expertise, at least in English courts. The approach to identification of applicable law in non-contractual matters in terms of Rome II is not fundamentally dissimilar to that employed in the Act.

DEFAMATION AND RELATED CLAIMS

16–55 As explained above,[227] non-contractual obligations arising out of violations of privacy and rights relating to personality, including defamation, are excluded from the scope of Rome II by virtue of art.1.2(g), and therefore in litigation arising under this head, Member State courts must continue to apply their own national choice of law rules. The difficulty of striking a balance between respect for private life and preservation of reputation, on the one hand, and the upholding of freedom of expression on the other, and the fact that legal systems vary in where they strike that balance, mean that the task of designing an acceptable choice of law rule defeated the draftsmen of Rome II, as it had defeated the draftsmen of the 1995 Act. At the time of UK Parliamentary debate in the 1990s, particular disquiet[228] was felt by the British Press that, as a result of loss of forum control which was a defining feature of the changes introduced by the 1995 Act, its freedom might be compromised if, following publication of material in a UK newspaper, it were possible for a suit for defamation for a delict "unknown", or as yet unknown, to the forum, to be brought in the UK[229] by a party aggrieved by the incidental dissemination of the material elsewhere. This lobby was successful at a late stage, resulting in s.13 (defamation claims) of the 1995 Act, viz.:

> "(1) Nothing in this Part applies to affect the determination of issues arising in any defamation claim.
> (2) For the purposes of this section 'defamation claim' means—
>   (a) any claim under the law of any part of the United Kingdom for libel or slander or for slander of title, slander of goods or other malicious falsehood and any claim under the law of Scotland for verbal injury; and
>   (b) any claim under the law of any other country corresponding to or otherwise in the nature of a claim mentioned in paragraph (a) above."

Consequently, liability for allegedly delictual actings under the head of defamation claims continues to be judged by the double actionability rule.[230]

---

[227] See paras 16–10 and 16–30, above.
[228] misplaced: Morse, (1996) I.C.L.Q. 888, n.53, p.892.
[229] As to the jurisdictional rules in this area, see Ch.7, above.
[230] *Skrine & Co v Euromoney Publications Plc* [2002] E.M.L.R. 15; *Vassiliev v Amazon.Com Inc* [2003] EWHC 2302 (Comm); *Metropolitan International Schools Ltd (t/a SkillsTrain and t/a Train2Game) v Designtechnica Corp (t/a Digital Trends)* [2009] EWHC 1765 (QB). Cf. Early example of *Maclarty v Steele* (1881) 8 R. 435.

Few (if any) cases have been litigated upon the point whether s.13, in principle, applies to a given claim, but the limits of the category of "defamation claims" are not free from doubt. The circumstances which allegedly give rise to a claim for verbal injury may raise related issues, for example, of privacy and confidentiality. Not only would such issues be excluded from the scope of s.13, but they might be excluded altogether from treatment as delictual issues.[231] It has been noted above[232] that since the definition in s.13(2) of the 1995 Act is not coterminous with the exclusion in art.1.2(g) of Rome II, violations of privacy and personality rights, though excluded from the scope of Rome II, do not appear to be regulated by the common law via s.13.

The common law rule

The choice of law rules which were applied, and must continue to be **16–56** applied with regard to "defamation claims", by the Scots courts at common law vary according to the place where the delict was committed:

Delicts committed within Scotland

As regards delicts committed within Scotland but having foreign elements **16–57** (e.g. through connection of parties), Scots law applies, irrespective of whether there is a right of action in delict under the personal law of the alleged wrong-doer and/or victim.[233] The English courts apply an equivalent rule.[234] One might say of such cases simply that the *lex fori* applied, or alternatively that, since there was a coincidence of the *lex fori* and *lex loci delicti*, this was an example of operation of the double actionability rule (*q.v.*).

Where the opposing parties share the same personal law, it might be thought that the occurrence of allegedly delictual conduct in a different country (which also happens to be the *lex fori*) should result at least in the possibility of displacement of the *lex fori* by a law of closer connection to the parties, for it could be said that the parties were walking in a bubble of their own law, or, more elegantly, that they were, "politically and psychologically insulated from their geographical environment."[235] Nevertheless, in *Szalatnay-Stacho v Fink*[236] the English court applied English law to the substantive issue (libel), stating that the principle of comity of nations did not compel or entitle the court to apply foreign (in this case, Czech) law to acts done in England, even though both parties to the litigation were Czech nationals. It is arguable that after *Chaplin v Boys*,[237] an English court would be entitled to use the flexible exception to achieve the aim, if it thought fit, of substituting the law of the parties' common personal law as the *lex causae*.

---

[231] cf. *Douglas v Hello! Ltd (No.6)* [2005] EWCA Civ 595; [2005] 4 All E.R. 128; and *Campbell v Mirror Group Newspapers Ltd* [2004] 2 A.C. 457; [2005] UKHL 61.

[232] See para.16–10.

[233] *Convery v Lanarkshire Tramways Co* (1905) 8 F. 117.

[234] *Szalatnay-Stacho v Fink* [1947] 1 K.B. 1; cf. *Al-Fayed v Al-Tajir* [1987] 3 W.L.R. 102.

[235] D. McLean and K. Beevers, *Morris: The Conflict of Laws,* 6th edn (London: Sweet & Maxwell, 2005), para.14–012.

[236] [1947] 1 K.B. 1.

[237] [1971] A.C. 356.

Delicts committed furth of Scotland (other than on the high seas)

Scots law[238]

16–58 As explained above, there was no suggestion or possibility at common law of giving effect to any choice of law expressed by the parties to an action.[239] The applicable law therefore was determined independently of the parties' intentions.

The Scots courts referred, in the first place, to the *lex loci delicti* as the origin of the pursuer's right, if any. If, by that law, the conduct was actionable, the court referred to Scots law as the *lex fori* to ensure that it was actionable also by that law.[240] The rule of Scots common law was that an act committed outside Scotland would be actionable as a delict in the Scots courts if:

(a) it was actionable[241] as a delict by the *lex loci delicti* at the date of the action; and
(b) it was actionable as a delict by the *lex fori* at the date of the action; and
(c) both systems of law conferred a right of action on the same person in the same capacity for substantially the same remedy.

In defamation claims, there may be particular difficulties in ascertaining the *locus delicti*. In *Evans & Sons v Stein & Co*,[242] a useful common law authority, the allegedly defamatory letters, while in transit from Scotland to their destination in England were, "as safe as if they were still locked up in the defender's desk". The *locus delicti* was the place of receipt, but the content of the letters was not actionable, because of the lack of "publication" to a third party as required by English domestic law. Clear favour was shown to the place of harm, being the place where the aggrieved person saw or heard the allegedly defamatory material or broadcast. By the same token, as regards online defamation, it was held in *Dow Jones & Co Inc v Gutnick*,[243] a decision

---

[238] The following is a selection of leading Scottish cases at common law: *Goodman v LNWR* (1877) 14 S.L.R. 449; *Rosses v Bhagvat Sinhjee* (1891) 19 R. 31; *Evans and Sons v John G Stein and Co* (1904) 7 F. 65; *Thomson v Kindell*, 1910 2 S.L.T. 442; *Soutar v Peters*, 1912 1 S.L.T. 111; *Naftalin v London Midland & Scottish Railway Co*, 1933 S.C. 259; *McElroy v McAllister*, 1949 S.C. 110; *Mackinnon v Iberia Shipping Co*, 1955 S.C. 20; *Rodden v Whatlings Ltd*, 1961 S.C. 132; *Mitchell v McCulloch*, 1976 S.L.T. 2; *James Burrough Distillers Plc v Speymalt Whisky Distributors Ltd*, 1989 S.L.T. 561; and *William Grant & Sons Ltd v Glen Catrine Bonded Warehouse Ltd*, 1995 S.L.T. 936. Cf. In Australia, *Breavington v Godleman* (1988) 80 A.L.R. 362; and contrast in Canada, *Tolofson v Jensen* (1994) 120 D.L.R. (4th) 289.

[239] Though see *Morin v Bonham & Brooks Ltd* [2004] 1 Lloyd's Rep. 702, a case raising issues in contract and tort, in which the court took note of the law governing the contract in the process of identifying the applicable law in tort.

[240] See J.M. Thomson, "Delictual Liability in Scottish International Private Law" (1976) 25 I.C.L.Q. 873; Law Commission and Scottish Law Commission, *Private International Law: Choice of Law in Tort and Delict*, 1984, Law Com. Working Paper No.87; Scot. Law Com. Memo. No.62.

[241] i.e. in general, and in the particular circumstances.

[242] *Evans and Sons v John G Stein and Co* (1904) 7 F. 65. And see earlier *Longworth v Hope* (1865) 3 M. 1049. See also *Parnell v Walter* (1889) 16 R. 917 and *Thomson v Kindell*, 1910 2 S.L.T. 442; cf. *Diamond v Bank of London and Montreal* [1979] 1 All E.R. 561 (fraudulent misrepresentation by telex was held to have been committed where received).

[243] [2002] HCA 56. See also *Jameel v Dow Jones & Co Inc* [2005] EWCA Civ 75.

of the High Court of Australia, that the tort of defamation is committed where the material complained of is downloaded.[244] In this area, there are many more cases dealing with jurisdiction than with choice of law.[245] If jurisdiction is established in Scotland (or England), the balance of opinion favours application qua *lex loci delicti* of the law of the place where the online material was accessed, on the basis that the publisher of the material must be taken to have known the extent of its possible dissemination given the current state of electronic communication development. If online material has been accessed in multiple countries, there would be multiple *leges loci delicti*.

This rule of double actionability continues to regulate available defences and the heads under which damages might be awarded.[246]

English law[247]

At common law, the English courts adopted a slightly different, more forum-dominant approach than that of the Scots courts, but they arrived at a similar result. In the first place, they looked for actionability according to the *lex fori*.[248] If that condition was satisfied, they referred to the *lex loci delicti*. The conflict rule which was applied for many years was based on the opinion of Willes J. (later Lord Penzance) in *Phillips v Eyre*[249] in which, after saying that in order to found a suit in England a tort must be actionable by the *lex fori*, he said that it must also be "not justifiable" according to the *lex loci delicti*. As a result, the choice of law rule of English law prior to *Chaplin v Boys*,[250] was that an allegedly tortious act committed in a foreign country would be actionable as such in England only if it was both:

16–59

---

[244] See also Law Commission, *Aspects of Defamation Procedure* (The Stationery Office, 2002), Scoping Study, and Law Commission, *Defamation and the Internet: A Preliminary Investigation* (The Stationery Office, 2002), Scoping Study No.2, Pt IV ("Jurisdiction and Applicable Law"). It was held in *Al-Amoudi v Brisard* [2006] 3 All E.R. 294 that in the case of an internet libel, it was for the claimant to prove that the material in question had been accessed and downloaded (*Loutchunsky v Times Newspapers Ltd (No.2)* [2001] E.M.L.R. 36, applied).

[245] See, with regard to jurisdiction, *King v Lewis* [2004] I.L.Pr. 31; and *Metropolitan International Schools Ltd v Designtechnica Corp* [2009] EWHC 1765 (QB) (liability of ISPs and search engines).

[246] For detail, see Crawford and Carruthers, *International Private Law In Scotland*, 2nd edn, 2006, para.16–13.

[247] The following is a selection of leading English cases at common law: *Dobree v Napier* (1839) 2 Bing. N.C. 781; *The Halley* (1868) L.R. 2 P.C. 193; *Phillips v Eyre* (1870) L.R. 6 Q.B. 1; *The Mary Moxham* (1876) 1 P.D. 107; *Machado v Fontes* [1897] 2 Q.B. 231; *Carr v Fracis Times and Co* [1902] A.C. 176; *Canadian Pacific Railway Co v Parent* [1917] A.C. 195; *Walpole v Canadian Northern Railway Co* [1923] A.C. 113; *Mcmillan v Canadian Northern Railway Co* [1923] A.C. 120; *M Isaacs & Sons Ltd v Cook* [1925] 2 K.B. 391; *Owners of the Seirstad v Hindustan Shipping Co Ltd (The Waziristan and The Seirstad)* [1953] 1 W.L.R. 1446; *Chaplin v Boys* [1971] A.C. 356; [1969] 2 All E.R. 1085; *John Walker & Sons Ltd v Henry Ost & Co Ltd* [1970] 1 W.L.R. 917; *Church of Scientology of California v Commissioner of Police for the Metropolis (No.1)* (1976) 120 S.J. 690; *MacShannon v Rockware Glass Ltd* [1978] 1 All E.R. 625; *Def Lepp Music v Stuart-Brown* [1986] R.P.C. 273; *Black v Yates* [1991] 4 All E.R. 722; *Tyburn Productions Ltd v Conan Doyle* [1991] Ch. 75; *Johnson v Coventry Churchill International Ltd* [1992] 3 All E.R. 14; *Red Sea Insurance Co Ltd v Bouygues SA* [1994] 3 All E.R. 749 PC; *Bank of Credit & Commerce International SA v Ali* [2006] EWHC 2135 (Ch).

[248] A tenacious requirement traceable to *The Halley* (1868) L.R. 2 P.C. 193.

[249] (1870) L.R. 6 Q.B. 1.

[250] [1971] A.C. 356.

(a) *actionable* as a tort according to English law; and
(b) *not justifiable* according to the law of the country where it was committed.

This is an unusual choice of law rule, concerned rather with the laying down of jurisdictional requirements in a broad sense, and placing the main emphasis on the *lex fori*, both as a gatekeeper, *and* as judge of substance if the case was allowed to proceed through the gate, in a manner not generally found in other English and Scots conflict rules. In requiring actionability by two laws, the claimant was placed at a disadvantage.

A difficulty was introduced by *Machado v Fontes*,[251] a libel case in which the words "not justifiable" were held to include an act which was wrongful in general (i.e. criminal) terms, but which did not confer a civil right of action by the *lex loci delicti*. This case, which had no influence in Scotland,[252] and was rejected in the leading and notorious case of *McElroy v McAllister*,[253] was overruled in *Chaplin v Boys*.[254] Nonetheless, it is probably true to say that the Scots courts tended to accord greater weight to the *lex loci delicti* than did the English courts.[255]

From the date of *Boys*, the English courts, unlike the Scots, displayed willingness to use discretion in applying a *flexible exception* to the double rule. While Scotland adhered to the double rule strictly, it was accepted in England[256] that the effect of the flexible exception was not only that the *lex loci delicti* might be displaced in favour of the *lex fori*, but also that the reverse process might take place, and that this could be done in relation either to the whole claim, or to one or more issues.[257] The English courts, in the years immediately preceding the 1995 Act, became rather bolder in the exercise of this discretionary exception,[258] but this willingness to make the rule more flexible was not evident in Scottish judicial practice.[259] It follows that Scottish courts operating the double rule, perforce now only in defamation claims, can be expected to apply it strictly, while the English courts will have at their disposal an element of discretion.

MARITIME DELICTS

16–60 This category of delict, provided it was not governed at common law by the double rule, was excluded by inference of s.14(2) of the 1995 Act from the scope of the Act. In such a case, the common law still applies. If, however, a maritime delict was governed at common law by the double rule, then it fell to be regulated by the 1995 Act.

---

[251] [1897] 2 Q.B. 231.
[252] See, however, earlier approach in *Maclarty v Steele* (1881) 8 R. 435.
[253] 1949 S.C. 110; see R.D. Leslie, *Stair Memorial Encyclopaedia*, p.293.
[254] *Chaplin v Boys* [1971] A.C. 356; affirming *Boys v Chaplin* [1968] 2 Q.B. 1.Though see Leslie, *Stair Memorial Encyclopaedia*, p.293.
[255] Blaikie, "Foreign Torts and Choice of Law Flexibility", 1995 S.L.T. (News) 23.
[256] *Johnson v Coventry Churchill International Ltd* [1992] 3 All E.R. 14.
[257] *Red Sea Insurance Co Ltd v Bouygues SA* [1994] 3 W.L.R. 926.
[258] *Johnson v Coventry Churchill International Ltd* [1992] 3 All E.R. 14; *Red Sea Insurance Co Ltd v Bouygues SA* [1994] 3 All E.R. 749 PC.
[259] See, e.g. *James Burrough Distillers Plc v Speymalt Whisky Distributors Ltd*, 1989 S.L.T. 561.

Incidents in foreign territorial waters

In the past the double actionability rule,[260] and the 1995 Act, in turn, **16–61** applied.[261] The *locus delicti* was the law of the country in whose territorial waters the incident occurred. Where, however, there was no significant link with the littoral state (which one might think would not infrequently be the case), use could be made of the rule of displacement in s.12 of the 1995 Act, in favour of the law of the flag (i.e. the law of the port of registry) or some other substantially more appropriate law.[262]

Turning to Rome II, the rules of which are postulated upon the occurrence of allegedly delictual events in a "country", it does not seem unreasonable to equate events occurring in territorial waters with events occurring in the country whose waters they are. On that basis, art.4 will apply to allegedly delictual incidents occurring in foreign territorial waters.

Incidents internal to a ship on the high seas

Such an incident was regarded as having occurred within the country whose **16–62** flag the ship flies. If the action were raised in Scotland, the 1995 Act is thought to have applied, and the locus was the port of registry of the ship.

With regard to Rome II, Ch.II has no application to allegedly delictual incidents occurring on the high seas.[263] Accordingly, incidents internal to a ship on the high seas will continue to be regulated by 1995 Act.

Incidents external to a ship on the high seas (including collisions)

The 1995 Act did not apply to such incidents, because in such cases the **16–63** courts always applied a general maritime law, so-called.[264] It may be doubted, however, whether such a body of law truly existed. It is perhaps rather more likely in these cases that the forum always applied its own law, whether or not by its own name.[265] A UK forum may require to apply provisions in the Merchant Shipping Act 1995 to a question, for example of the liability of the shipowner(s) within the ambit of operation laid down by that Act. There is no justification for application of Rome II in these circumstances.

---

[260] *Mackinnon v Iberia Shipping Co Ltd*, 1955 S.C. 20. This was an accident internal to a ship lying in the territorial waters of San Domingo. San Domingo, as the littoral state, was the *locus delicti*. The Scots forum applied the double rule in circumstances where arguably a proper law of delict, or rule of commonality approach would have been more suitable. *Dicey, Morris and Collins on the Conflict of Laws*, 14th edn, 2006, at para.35–076, note that the Scots forum took the *locus delicti* to be the littoral state, rather than the law of the flag.

[261] Rodger, annotations to the Private International Law (Miscellaneous Provisions) Act 1995.

[262] *Hornsby v James Fisher Rumic Ltd* [2008] EWHC 1944 (QB).

[263] *Cheshire, North and Fawcett: Private International Law*, 14th edn, 2008, p.859.

[264] *Boettcher v Carron C* (1861) 23 D. 322; *Aberdeen Artic Co v Sutter* (1862) 4 Macq. 355; (1862) 24 D. (H.L.) 4; *The Amalia* (1863) 1 Moore P.C. (N.S.) 471; *Submarine Telegraph Co v Dickson* (1864) 15 C.B. (N.S.) 759; *The Leon* (1881) L.R. 6 P.D. 148; *Chartered Mercantile Bank of India, London and China v Netherlands India Steam Navigation Co Ltd* (1883) L.R. 10 Q.B.D. 521; *Currie v McKnight* (1897) 24 R. (H.L.) 1; *Kendrick v Burnett (Owners of the SS Marsden)* (1897) 25 R. 82; *Owners of the SS Reresby v Owners of the SS Cobetas*, 1923 S.L.T. 719; *The Tubantia (No.2)* [1924] P. 78; *Sheaf Steamship Co Ltd v Compania Transmediterranea*, 1930 S.C. 660; *Chung Chi Cheung v R.* [1929] A.C. 16; *The King Alfred* [1914] P. 84.

[265] *Cox v Owners of the The Esso Malaysia (The Esso Malaysia)* [1974] 2 All E.R. 705 (applying *Davidsson v Hill* [1900–1903] All E.R. 997); see *Lally v Comex (Diving) Ltd* Unreported May 5, 1976, OH, unreported, cited in Leslie, p.299.

This subject area is difficult and unclear. So too is the subject of wrongful actings taking place aboard an aircraft during flight, and the extremely rare occurrence of collisions between aircraft. The rules applying to maritime delicts presumably would apply, mutatis mutandis. As to incidents on board an aircraft (such as assault, defamation, or personal injury, as, for example, by the provision of contaminated food), it seems that the analogy with maritime delicts is not entirely apt. In the case of wrongful actings taking place aboard an aircraft,[266] it would appear simpler to apply the law of the country with which the aircraft has the closest connection, namely, the place of registration of the aircraft/nationality of the aircraft.[267] Application of the law of the country in whose airspace the plane happens to be at the point of the allegedly delictual conduct could produce difficult problems of proof.

II. NON-CONTRACTUAL OBLIGATIONS ARISING OUT OF RESTITUTIONARY CLAIMS

16–64 From the latter part of the twentieth century this area of law in its domestic aspect was the subject of much academic exploration and discussion in England and Scotland.[268] Initially the writing was concerned with domestic law, but increasingly there was interest in its conflict dimensions.[269] Conflictually, the relative paucity of decisions[270] on jurisdiction[271] and choice of law[272] afforded

---

[266] Assuming liability does not exist under Ch.III of the 1929 Warsaw Convention on International Carriage by Air.

[267] *Dicey, Morris and Collins on the Conflict of Laws*, 14th edn, 2006, para.35–079.

[268] See Peter Birks, *An Introduction to the Law of Restitution*, revised edn (Oxford: Clarendon, 1989); Peter Jaffey, *The Nature and Scope of Restitution: vitiated transfers, imputed contracts and disgorgement* (Oxford: Hart, 2000); Alison Jones, *Restitution and European Community Law* (London: LLP, 2000); Andrew S. Burrows, *The Law of Restitution*, 2nd edn (Croydon: Butterworths, 2002); Lord Goff of Chieveley and Gareth Jones, *The Law of Restitution*, 6th edn (London: Sweet & Maxwell, 2002); and Robin Evans-Jones, *Unjustified Enrichment* (Edinburgh: W. Green, 2003), Vol.1. There are historical and essential differences between English and Scots domestic law in the area, including the presence in Scots, but not English law—with the associated potential for interesting conflict consequences—of a well developed rule of *negotiorum gestio*. How will an English forum react to a claim under a head unknown to it? Though see D. Sheehan, "Negotorium Gestio: A Civilian Concept in the Common Law?" (2006) 55 I.C.L.Q. 253.

[269] See J. Blaikie, "Unjust Enrichment in the Conflict of Laws", 1984 J.R. 112; and R.D. Leslie, "Unjustified Enrichment in the Conflict Laws" (1998) 2 Edin. L.R. 233.

[270] But see *Batthyany v Walford* (1887) L.R. 36 Ch. D. 269; *Cantiere San Rocco SA (Shipbuilding Co) v Clyde Shipbuilding & Engineering Co Ltd* [1924] A.C. 226; *Fibrosa Spolka Akcyjna v Fairbairn Lawson Combe Barbour Ltd* [1943] A.C. 32; *Re Jogia (A Bankrupt)* [1988] 1 W.L.R. 484; *Arab Monetary Fund v Hashim (No.9)* [1993] 1 Lloyd's Rep. 543; *El Ajou v Dollar Land Holdings Plc (No.1)* [1993] 3 All E.R. 717; [1994] 2 All E.R. 685; *Macmillan Inc v Bishopsgate Investment Trust Plc (No.3)* [1996] 1 W.L.R. 387; *Baring Bros & Co Ltd v Cunninghame DC*, 1997 C.L.C. 108; *Strathaird Farms v GA Chattaway & Co*, 1993 S.L.T. (Sh. Ct.) 36; *Kleinwort Benson Ltd v Glasgow City Council* (C346/93) [1995] All E.R. (E.C.) 514; and *Kleinwort Benson Ltd v Glasgow City Council (No.2)* [1997] 4 All E.R. 641.

[271] *Kleinwort Benson Ltd v Glasgow City Council (No.2)* [1997] 4 All E.R. 641; and *Strathaird Farms Ltd v GA Chattaway & Co*, 1993 S.L.T. (Sh. Ct.) 36. See paras 7–18 and 7–19, above.

[272] *Baring Bros & Co Ltd v Cunninghame DC*, 1997 C.L.C. 108; *Macmillan Inc v Bishopsgate Investment Trust Plc (No.3)* [1996] 1 W.L.R. 387 CA; *Arab Monetary Fund v Hashim (No.9)* [1996] 1 Lloyd's Rep. 589 CA; and cf. *Douglas v Hello! Ltd (No.6)* [2005] EWCA Civ 595; [2005] 4 All E.R. 128 (the issue of breach of confidence being treated as restitutionary).

opportunity for speculation as to applicable law[273] and reason for caution. Generally it was thought that the area provided an opportunity for creation of, "a principled and reasoned approach to the question of the proper choice of law rule for restitutionary issues."[274] Until the advent of Rome II, the area was a common law hybrid, governed neither by the Rome I Convention, nor by the Private International Law (Miscellaneous Provisions) Act 1995. Hence, from the UK perspective, Rome II, in providing for these topics, could be said to have stifled further development of national conflict rules when they were at an immature stage, but equally to have accelerated the process of producing clear rules.

THE ROME II REGULATION

Rome II deals in Ch.III (arts 10–13) with the law applicable to non-contractual **16–65** obligations arising out of a restitutionary claim[275] under the heads of unjust enrichment, *negotiorum gestio* and *culpa in contrahendo*.[276]

Unjust enrichment

"Article 10 . . . **16–66**

1. If a non-contractual obligation arising out of unjust enrichment, including payment of amounts wrongly received, concerns a relationship existing between the parties, such as one arising out of a contract or a tort/delict, that is closely connected with that unjust enrichment, it shall be governed by the law that governs that relationship.
2. Where the law applicable cannot be determined on the basis of paragraph 1 and the parties have their habitual residence in the same country when the event giving rise to unjust enrichment occurs, the law of that country shall apply.
3. Where the law applicable cannot be determined on the basis of paragraphs 1 or 2, it shall be the law of the country in which the unjust enrichment took place.

---

[273] Even to the extent of arguments in favour of *renvoi: Barros Mattos Junior v MacDaniels Ltd* [2005] I.L.Pr. 45, per Collins J. at [121].

[274] George Panagopoulos, *Restitution in Private International Law* (Oxford: Hart, 2000), p.111.

[275] The inference of recital (29) is that "damage" (see art.2.1) is a prerequisite for the application of the rules under Ch.III: "Provision should be made for special rules where damage is caused by an act other than a tort/delict, such as unjust enrichment, *negotiorum gestio* and *culpa in contrahendo*."

[276] See, for drafting background, Proposal for a Regulation on the Law Applicable to Non-Contractual Obligations COM(2003) 427 final (2003/0168(COD)), accompanying Explanatory Memorandum; House of Lords European Union Committee, *The Rome II Regulation*, 2004, HL Paper No.66 (Session 2003/04) ("Scott Report"); Amended Proposal COM(2006) 83 final; Draft Report Revised Version on the Proposal for a European Parliament and Council Regulation on the law applicable to non-contractual obligations ("Rome II") COM(2003) 427-C5–0338/2003–2003/0168 (COD); and Proposal for a Regulation on the law applicable to non-contractual obligations (9142/06) JUSTCIV 118 CODEC 455. Also Carruthers and Crawford, "Variations on a Theme of Rome II. Part 2" (2005) 9 Edin. L.R. 238; and S. Pitel, "Rome II and Choice of Law for Unjust Enrichment" in Ahern and Binchy (eds), *The Rome II Regulation on the Law Applicable to Non-Contractual Obligations*, 2009.

4. Where it is clear from all the circumstances of the case that the non-contractual obligation arising out of unjust enrichment is manifestly more closely connected with a country other than that indicated in paragraphs 1, 2 and 3, the law of that other country shall apply."

The rules which now are contained in art.10 are, at least ex facie, fairly straightforward, and are framed in what now are familiar drafting terms.

A substantial proportion of problems arising under the head of unjust enrichment have a foundation in a pre-existing relationship, usually contractual, between the parties. This fact was reflected in the terms in which, at common law, the embryonic choice of law rule in Scots and English law was emerging.[277] These cases are instances of "relational" unjust enrichment. While differentiation between relational and non-relational unjust enrichment was a broadly agreed approach at common law, a degree of criticism could be found, both generally and on the particular ground[278] that insofar as parties can choose the applicable law of their contract, it would follow that they can choose, indirectly (possibly inadvertently) and perhaps with inappropriate effect, the law to govern related restitutionary obligations.

It is not surprising that the first limb of the legislative solution in art.10 of Rome II is concerned to treat cases of relational unjust enrichment. By art.10.1 non-contractual obligations arising out of unjust enrichment, including payment of amounts wrongly received, *where they concern a pre-existing relationship between the parties such as one arising out of a contract or a tort*, shall be governed by the law which governs that relationship, that is to say, by the applicable law identified according to the Rome I Regulation (contract) or Rome II Regulation (tort/delict),[279] as the case may be. If an alleged non-contractual obligation can be said to "concern" such a relationship, the law of the relationship will govern, but the applicable law in contract (or delict) will govern the obligation arising out of unjust enrichment *only* if that unjust enrichment derives from, or is closely associated with, that very contract (or delict).[280]

It is notable that there is to be no express application of the *lex situs* in cases where the unjust enrichment is connected with a transaction concerning immoveable property. This is the only significant difference between the rules in Rome II and the pre-existing UK approach. Presumably, at least in the operation of art.10.1, the applicable law would be very likely to be the *lex situs*.

Under art.10.2, where the law applicable cannot be determined on the basis of identification of the law governing the relationship between the parties, i.e. "non-relational" enrichment cases, and the parties have a common habitual residence when the event giving rise to the enrichment occurs, the law of that country shall apply.

Further, in terms of art.10.3, where the law applicable cannot be determined on the basis of the rules pertaining to art.10.1 or 10.2, the law of the country in which the unjust enrichment took place shall be the applicable law. In the

---

[277] *Dicey and Morris on The Conflict of Laws*, 13th edn, 2000, r.200.
[278] See *Cheshire and North's Private International Law*, 13th edn, 1999, pp.679, 686, 691, 692.
[279] See Dickinson, *The Rome II Regulation*, 2008, paras 10.25, 10.26 on the subject of a pre-existing relationship arising out of tort/delict.
[280] cf. art.11.1 (*negotiorum gestio*). See also Rome II arts 4.3, 5.2.

common law consideration of this subject, opinion in the UK was divided as to the quality of the connecting factor of place of occurrence of the enrichment.[281] Enrichment may occur in several places, and those places may be artificial or casual. Yet, on occasion, the territorial place of enrichment may be regarded by the court as (also) the country with which the alleged obligation has its closest and most real connection, as in *OJSC Oil Co Yugraneft v Abramovich*.[282]

A tangential comment is provided by a consideration of the case of *Douglas v Hello! Ltd (No.6)*,[283] in which the Court of Appeal characterised the claimant's claim relating to invasion of privacy not as a tort, but rather as a restitutionary claim for unjust enrichment. Utilising therefore the connecting factor of "place where the enrichment occurred", the court, by inference, proceeded to hold in effect that England was the place of enrichment, based upon publication in England of the offending material.[284]

Finally, art.10.4 gives the forum discretion to identify as the applicable law the law of a country other than that indicated under the three preceding paragraphs of art.10, which it considers in the light of all the circumstances of the case to be manifestly more closely connected to the non-contractual obligation in question. The resulting article, while a familiar amalgam of European drafting devices in applicable law rules, nonetheless has a great deal in common with the choice of law approach observable in the UK before Rome II in the relatively few cases in which the question arose.

Parties may agree to subject non-contractual obligations arising out of a restitutionary claim under the head of unjust enrichment to the law of their choice under art.14 of the Regulation.[285] It is possible to envisage a situation in which the parties, under art.14, might choose a law to govern their non-contractual relations, which law might differ from the law which governs their contract, either by express choice under art.3 of the Rome I Regulation, or by operation of art.4, thereof.

Consequences of nullity of contract (Rome I) and problems of unjust enrichment (Rome II)

Although the rules in art.10 of Rome II are clear in theory, careful thought must be given to their interrelationship with those of the Rome I Regulation[286]; and to the contribution to the subject made by cases interpretative of the Brussels I Regulation. **16–67**

---

[281] Blaikie, "Unjust Enrichment and the Conflict of Laws", 1984 J.R. 112; Bird J. "Choice of Law", in Francis Rose (ed.), *Restitution and the Conflict of Laws* (Oxford: Mansfield Press, 1995); Leslie, "Unjustified Enrichment and the Conflict of Laws" (1998) 2 Edin. L.R. 233; *Cheshire and North's Private International Law*, 13th edn, 1999, Ch.20; Panagopoulos, *Restitution in Private International Law*, 2000; and Adrian Briggs, *The Conflict of Laws* (Oxford: Oxford University Press, 2002), Ch.7. See also decision of Lawrence Collins J. in *Barros Mattos Junior v MacDaniels Ltd* [2005] I.L.Pr. 45, where approval was not given to a mechanical application of the law of the place of enrichment. In *Dicey, Morris and Collins on the Conflict of Laws*, 14th edn, 2006 (preceding Rome II), r.230 retains support for the proper law, in residual cases, being the law of the country in which the enrichment occurs.

[282] [2008] EWHC 2613 (Comm).

[283] [2005] EWCA Civ 595; [2005] 4 All E.R. 128.

[284] *Douglas v Hello! Ltd (No.6)* [2005] EWCA Civ 595; [2005] 4 All E.R. 128 at [96]–[102].

[285] See paras 16–31—16–36, above.

[286] See also para.15–65, above.

By art.12.1(e) of the Rome I Regulation,[287] the law applicable to a contract will govern the consequences of nullity of the contract, which will include the repayment of sums[288] due under a void or nullified contract. By UK reservation, the equivalent provision of the Rome I Convention, art.10.1(e), did not apply in a UK court since the consequences of nullity were regarded by Scots and English law as pertaining to rules of restitution. In many cases the applicable law identified by these two routes would be the same. Now, however, since there is pan-European agreement that the subject of nullity of contract be dealt with by the putative applicable law of the necessarily putative contract, it is time to address the possibility that the co-existence of this rule with the relatively newly created choice of law rules under the Rome II Regulation Ch.III, may prompt problems of characterisation and distribution of application of choice of law rules between the Rome I and Rome II Regulations.

The area of void and nullified contracts is productive of doubt in the jurisdictional aspect too. A claim arising in restitution from a *void* contract does not fall, for the purpose of Scots and English jurisdiction rules under Sch.4, under art.5.1 special jurisdiction in contract.[289] On the other hand, matters relating to a contract can include matters relating to a *disputed* contract.[290] Arguably (especially from a European perspective), the consequences of nullity of a contract *should* be characterised as contractual for the purposes of jurisdiction, chiming with the Rome I Regulation for choice of law. It is hoped that the matter will be considered by the ECJ in such a way as to place a restitutionary claim of this sort under art.5.1. It seems not unreasonable that in all Member State courts the remedy for such claims be regulated by the content of what must be the putative applicable law of the void contract, and that the court properly seised to implement this remedy be, as it were, the "putative court" under art.5.1. To say that claims resulting from *void* contracts fall outside the ambit of art.5.1, but those which arise out of *voidable or unenforceable* contracts fall within its ambit, is not a helpful dividing line, and is one which is likely to be productive of uncertainty, and also to deprive of jurisdiction to award a restitutionary payment a forum which has just decided that the alleged contract is void.[291]

Negotiorum gestio

16–68   "Article 11 . . .

1. If a non-contractual obligation arising out of an act performed without due authority in connection with the affairs of another person

---

[287] Article 12.1: "The law applicable to a contract by virtue of this Regulation shall govern in particular: . . . (b) performance; . . . (e) the consequences of nullity of the contract."

[288] Giuliano and Lagarde, p.33 reveals that the equivalent provision under the Rome I Convention, art.10.1(e), was inserted to make it clear that the applicable law under the Convention governed this issue.

[289] See *Kleinwort Benson Ltd v Glasgow City Council (No.2)* [1999] 1 A.C. 153, discussed at paras 7–18 and 7–19, above (though *Kleinwort* is not an ECJ decision, and the ECJ might take a different view).

[290] *Boss Group Ltd v Boss France SA* [1996] 4 All E.R. 970; *Halki Shipping Corp v Sopex Oils Ltd (The Halki)* [1997] 3 All E.R. 833; *Belgian International Insurance Group SA v McNicol*, 1999 G.W.D. 22–1065.

[291] See Jonathan Hill, *International Commercial Disputes in English Courts*, 3rd edn (Oxford: Hart, 2005), para.5.6.16, paraphrasing the views of Lord Nicholls (dissenting) in *Kleinwort*.

concerns a relationship existing between the parties, such as one arising out of a contract or a tort/delict, that is closely connected with that non-contractual obligation, it shall be governed by the law that governs that relationship.

2. Where the law applicable cannot be determined on the basis of paragraph 1, and the parties have their habitual residence in the same country when the event giving rise to the damage occurs, the law of that country shall apply.

3. Where the law applicable cannot be determined on the basis of paragraphs 1 or 2, it shall be the law of the country in which the act was performed.

4. Where it is clear from all the circumstances of the case that the non-contractual obligation arising out of an act performed without due authority in connection with the affairs of another person is manifestly more closely connected with a country other than that indicated in paragraphs 1, 2 and 3, the law of that other country shall apply."

The formulation of choice of law rules by which to deal with cases of *negotiorum gestio* presents a challenge, to be relished more as an academic exercise than with any expectation that resort in practice often will have to be made to the carefully crafted rules. Within the UK such cases are exceedingly rare, and so seldom do they have a conflict dimension that one might say the subject was arcane. Moreover, controversy will arise only if the content of the potentially applicable laws varies (although variation, admittedly, is likely, and some legal systems will have no knowledge of the concept).

In relational cases of *negotiorum gestio*[292] under art.11.1, the law governing the relationship, be it contractual, delictual or other, shall apply. In non-relational cases, by art.11.2, the law of the common habitual residence at the time when the event giving rise to the damage occurs, shall apply, failing which,[293] by art.11.3, the applicable law shall be the law of the country in which the act (i.e. that performed without due authority in connection with the affairs of another person) took place. There is discretion in art.11.4 permitting recourse in both relational and non-relational cases to the law of a country of manifestly more close connection.

As with claims in unjust enrichment, parties may agree to subject non-contractual obligations arising out of a restitutionary claim under the head of *negotiorum gestio* to the law of their choice under art.14 of the Regulation.

In terms of art.15 (scope of the law applicable), the applicable law shall govern, inter alia, the basis and extent of liability, including determination of persons who may be held liable for acts performed by them; grounds for exemption from liability, any limitation, and any division of liability; and liability for the acts of another person. Points where there might be a variation among the domestic laws of potentially applicable *leges causae* include:

---

[292] One must speculate that examples of this would be, e.g. actings by a parent/guardian on behalf of a child concerning his property; or where an agent acts, on an ongoing basis, by virtue perhaps of a power of attorney.

[293] i.e. where the applicable law cannot be determined under either art.11.1 or 11.2.

(a) the circumstances which justify an individual person becoming an agent or *gestor*;
(b) the *gestor's* right to payment, or only to reimbursement, and the effect thereon of the *gestor's* efforts having proved fruitless or detrimental;
(c) the right of action by an individual reasonably employed by the *gestor* to sue the beneficiary (i.e. principal) direct;
(d) the standard of care to be exercised by the *gestor*, and liability of the *gestor* to the principal if that standard is not exhibited; and
(e) whether the *gestor*, having intervened, must attempt to bring matters to a conclusion, and the legal consequences of quitting the task prematurely.

Culpa in contrahendo

16–69   "Article 12 . . .

1. The law applicable to a non-contractual obligation arising out of dealings prior to the conclusion of a contract, regardless of whether the contract was actually concluded or not, shall be the law that applies to the contract or that would have been applicable to it had it been entered into.
2. Where the law applicable cannot be determined on the basis of paragraph 1, it shall be:
   (a) the law of the country in which the damage occurs, irrespective of the country in which the event giving rise to the damage occurred and irrespective of the country or countries in which the indirect consequences of that event occurred; or
   (b) where the parties have their habitual residence in the same country at the time when the event giving rise to the damage occurs, the law of that country; or
   (c) where it is clear from all the circumstances of the case that the non-contractual obligation arising out of dealings prior to the conclusion of a contract is manifestly more closely connected with a country other than that indicated in points (a) and (b), the law of that other country."

The phrase *culpa in contrahendo*, originating in German customary law, signifies those rules of national legal systems concerning the standard of conduct required of parties in pre-contractual negotiations. Whether a contract comes into existence or not, it can be seen that issues such as adequate disclosure, misrepresentation, and duty to display good faith and decent dealing, have a hybrid character within the law of obligations.[294] In many European systems, such questions are regarded as delictual or restitutionary. The symbiosis and order maintained between the Rome I and Rome II Regulations is evidenced by the express exclusion from the scope of Rome I, per art.1.2(i), of obligations arising out of dealings prior to the conclusion of a contract, and the

---

[294] In Scots law such circumstances often are treated purely as contractual, the issue being whether *consensus in idem* has been reached in the circumstances: e.g. *WS Karoulias SA v Drambuie Liqueur Co Ltd* [2005] CSOH 112.

express inclusion in Rome II of an applicable law provision specifically to address such obligations.

Recital (30) of Rome II states that *culpa in contrahendo* for the purposes of the Regulation is an autonomous concept:

> "... and should not necessarily be interpreted within the meaning of national law. It should include the violation of the duty of disclosure and the breakdown of contractual negotiations. Article 12 covers only non-contractual obligations presenting a direct link with the dealings prior to the conclusion of a contract. This means that if, while a contract is being negotiated, a person suffers personal injury, Article 4 or other relevant provisions of this Regulation should apply."

For the type of situation which can be characterised as pertaining to *culpa in contrahendo*, as illustrated above, a special rule is provided in art.12.1, which diverts attention from the non-contractual character of the obligation by nominating as applicable the putative applicable law of the (putative)[295] contract. The special choice of law rule formulated for such cases leads to the same result as would have eventuated had such cases of *culpa in contrahendo* been characterised as cases of relational unjust enrichment. Moreover, though the topic falls under Rome II (non-contractual obligations), the (restitutionary) choice of law rule, in its content as it applies to *culpa in contrahendo*, is indistinguishable from the "putative applicable law" solution to problems of material validity of contract contained in the Rome I Regulation art.10.

If the law applicable cannot be determined under art.12.1 of Rome II (which surely must be a very rare case),[296] then the rule which must be applied under art.12.2 is in the same terms as the general rule for delict contained in art.4.

Finally, parties may agree, though this seems highly unlikely,[297] to subject non-contractual obligations arising out of a restitutionary claim under the head of *culpa in contrahendo* to the law of their choice under art.14 of the Regulation.

SUMMARY 16

1. Choice of law in delict: sources   **16–70**

The rules are contained in three sources:

(a) Regulation 864/2007 on the law applicable to non-contractual obligations ("Rome II");

---

[295] The provision is available whether a contract has resulted or not.

[296] See *Cheshire, North and Fawcett: Private International Law*, 14th edn, 2008, pp.835, 836, where the case postulated is that during negotiations each party had tried to impose without success its preferred choice of law clause on the other, but the parties never reached consensus on the point. Or if contractual negotiations had broken off at a very early stage, it may be impossible to ascertain the applicable law—in such circumstances, art.12.2 must be intended to govern liability for any loss, though if negotiations were at a very early stage one would imagine that reparable loss such as to give rise to litigation engaging art.12.2 would be infrequently encountered.

[297] Choice of law *ex ante* is not competent unless all the parties are pursuing a commercial activity: art.14.1(b).

    (b) Private International Law (Miscellaneous Provisions) Act 1995 Pt III;
    (c) The common law rule of double actionability.

In order to ascertain which set of rules applies in an individual case, careful attention must be paid to the date of occurrence of the event giving rise to the damage, and to the subject matter of the claim.

2. Choice of law in delict: rules

Rome II comprises:

> Article 4: a *lex loci damni* rule, with one mandatory exception (rule of commonality) and one discretionary exception (rule of displacement);
> Articles 5–9: a series of delict-specific rules;
> Article 14: a party autonomy rule;
> Article 15: scope of the law applicable.

The 1995 Act comprises:

> Section 11: a *lex loci delicti* rule;
> Section 12: a discretionary rule of displacement.

The double actionability rule:
   A defamation claim (as defined in 1995 Act s.13(2)) is actionable as a delict in a Scots court if:

> (a) it was actionable as a delict by the *lex loci delicti* at the date of the action; and
> (b) it was actionable as a delict by the *lex fori* at the date of the action; and
> (c) both systems of law conferred a right of action on the same person in the same capacity for substantially the same remedy.

3. Choice of law rules in non-contractual obligations arising out of restitutionary claims

Rules are provided by Rome II Ch.III, for the particular subjects of:

> Article 10: unjust enrichment;
> Article 11: *negotiorum gestio*;
> Article 12: *culpa in contrahendo*;
> Article 14: party autonomy.

CHAPTER 17

THE LAW OF PROPERTY
(INCLUDING INSOLVENCY)

Different rules govern the transfer of property according to whether the **17–01** transfer in question is particular (or special) in nature, that is, affecting one or more specific assets, by means of gift, sale, mortgage, etc.; or universal (or general) in nature, that is, affecting an individual's entire estate, such as upon the event of marriage, insolvency or death. This chapter will examine, first, the rules governing particular transfers of property, and secondly, the rules which apply to general transfers in the event of insolvency.

I. PARTICULAR TRANSFERS OF PROPERTY

A. TERMINOLOGY AND CLASSIFICATION

That this is one of the very few areas of Scots and English international private **17–02** law which rests mainly on the common law, largely untouched by statute and convention, is both refreshing and alarming.[1]

Note should be taken of the following differences in terminology:

(a) domestic Scots law—heritage and moveables;
(b) domestic English law—real and personal property;
(c) conflict of laws—immov(e)ables and mov(e)ables.[2]

In a Scots or English forum the terms and classification immoveable and moveable are utilised, so as to accommodate differences in property categorisations adopted by different legal systems.[3] Examples can be cited of cases where the classification of property arrived at as a result of application of a legal system's conflict rules differs from that accorded by its domestic law, for

---

[1] The contributions of writers are influential. See Carruthers, *Transfer of Property in the Conflict of Laws*, 2005; P.A. Lalive, *The Transfer of Chattels in the Conflict of Laws* (London: OUP, 1955); and G. Zaphiriou, *The Transfer of Chattels in Private International Law* (London: University of London, The Athlone Press, 1956).

[2] *Macdonald*, 1932 S.C. (H.L.) 79, per Lord Tomlin at 84; cf. *Re Hoyles* [1911] 1 Ch. 179, per Farwell L.J. at 185. But see *Re Cutcliffe's Will Trusts* [1940] Ch. 565; and *Dicey, Morris and Collins on the Conflict of Laws*, 14th edn, 2006, para.22–004. The preferred Scottish spelling is "immoveable"; "immovable" is favoured in England.

[3] *Dicey, Morris and Collins on the Conflict of Laws*, 14th edn, 2006, para.22–004: the distinction is made in the conflict of laws on the basis of the factual difference between moveable and immoveable property, and not on technical nicety or historical grounds (such as, e.g. Scots law of "fixtures" where, in domestic law, a right over what is physically moveable is regarded as being a right over an immoveable).

example English leaseholds[4]; foreign land[5] and mortgages over land[6]; stocks and shares[7]; Scots bonds and dispositions in security[8]; and land held upon trust for sale.[9]

Property is always classified for the purposes of a conflict case as moveable or immoveable in accordance with the rules of the *lex situs* (*q.v.*).[10]

A different problem of classification may arise in relation to categorisation of the cause of action, for example, as between property and contract, or property and unjustified enrichment.[11] A claim for restitution of property is a claim to which, if there are foreign elements, it may be appropriate for the choice of law rules of property to be applied in preference to those of contract.[12] The characterisation proposed in the pleadings of parties may not be that which ultimately is adopted by the court in its resolution of the dispute.[13] The initial characterisation by the forum of a cause of action (e.g. as being one of intestate succession to moveable property) will indicate to that court the identity of its relevant choice of law rule, and the applicable law to apply (i.e. last domicile of the deceased). But to follow through the application of the *lex causae*, re-characterisation of the property by use of the domestic law of the *lex causae* occasionally may be necessary.[14] Thus, characterisation of the nature of property as moveable or immoveable, whether or not straightforward at the outset, conceivably may require to be revisited at a later stage.

---

[4] *Freke v Carbery* (1873) L.R. 16 Eq. 461; *Re Gentili* (1875) I.R. 9 Eq. 541; *Duncan v Lawson* (1889) L.R. 41 Ch. D. 394; *Pepin v Bruyere* [1902] 1 Ch. 24; *De Fogassieras v Duport* (1881) 11 L.R. Ir. 123.

[5] *Re Berchtold* [1923] 1 Ch. 192; *Macdonald*, 1932 S.C. (H.L.) 79.

[6] *Marquess of Breadalbane's Trustees* (1843) 15 S.L. 389; *Downie v Downie's Trustees* (1866) 4 M. 1067; and *Monteith v Monteith's Trustees* (1882) 9 R. 982.

[7] *Moss's Trustees v Moss*, 1916 2 S.L.T. 31; but see Anton, *Private International Law*, 1st edn, 1967, pp.387, 388; *Re Hoyles* [1911] 1 Ch. 179; *Macmillan Inc v Bishopsgate Investment Trust Plc (No.3)* [1996] 1 All E.R. 585 CA.

[8] The chameleon nature of these security rights has caused difficulties (e.g. *Train v Train's Executor* (1899) 2 F. 146; cf. *Moss's Trustees v Moss*, 1916 2 S.L.T. 31. See Anton, *Private International Law*, 1st edn, 1967, pp.387, 388 and explanation by Leslie, *Stair Memorial Encyclopaedia*, Vol.17, p.318). Such bonds were immoveable by the conflict rule of Scots law, although moveable in the succession of the creditor in the domestic law of Scotland in terms of the Titles to Land Consolidation (Scotland) Act 1868 s.117, as amended. The standard security, which replaced them in terms of the Conveyancing and Feudal Reform (Scotland) Act 1970 is a heritable security which forms a heritable debt in the estate of the debtor, and is not subject to legal rights in the estate of the creditor.

[9] The interest of a beneficiary in such land in Scotland or England is immoveable until the power of sale is exercised. *Murray v Champernowne* [1901] 2 I.R. 232; *Re Lyne's Settlement Trusts* [1919] 1 Ch. 80; *Re Berchtold* [1923] 1 Ch. 192; *Re Cartwright* [1939] Ch. 90; *Re Cutcliffe's Will Trusts* [1940] Ch. 565; *Re Middleton's Settlement* [1947] Ch. 583; *Re Stoughton* [1941] I.R. 166.

[10] *Ross v Ross's Trustees*, July 4, 1809, FC; *Hall's Trustees v Hall* (1854) 16 D. 1057; *Macdonald*, 1932 S.C. (H.L.) 79. Though see *Iran v Berend* [2007] EWHC 132 (QB) where the parties, by agreement, directed that the court should treat the asset in question (fragment of limestone relief) as moveable; and further *Martin v Secretary of State for Work and Pensions* [2009] EWCA Civ 1289.

[11] Leslie, *Stair Memorial Encyclopaedia*, Vol.17, p.312.

[12] Bearing in mind also that art.10 of the Rome II Regulation contains choice of law rules concerning non-contractual obligations arising out of unjust enrichment, including payment of amounts wrongly received. See Ch.16, above.

[13] See *Macmillan Inc v Bishopsgate Investment Trust Plc (No.3)* [1996] 1 All E.R. 585.

[14] As explained by Leslie, *Stair Memorial Encyclopaedia*, Vol.17, p.318.

Meaning of *lex situs*

In view of the importance which traditional conflict rules place upon the *lex* **17–03**
situs as a connecting factor in the resolution of title disputes, it is necessary to
be clear about the meaning of that factor.

Identification of "situs"

The definition of *situs* in relation to immoveable property normally gives **17–04**
rise to no difficulty, the *situs* being the law of the place where the property is
situated. No further definition or qualification is required, subject only in the
rare case of the re-drawing of territorial boundaries, and except to say that to
be true to the supremacy of the *lex situs*, the forum may have to be prepared to
include in its reference the conflict rules of the *lex situs*, and thereby to be open
to the concept of *renvoi*.[15]

With regard to moveable property, localising property in a spatial sense is not
generally difficult but, crucially, in disputes concerning moveable property,
there is an important temporal dimension in the ascertainment of the *lex situs*.
The spatial definition is of no use without a temporal qualification. Although it
is the nature of the *situs* of a moveable to change, *at any given time* the situation of a corporeal moveable normally is fixed. The *lex situs* (or *lex loci rei
sitae*) of a corporeal moveable, for the purposes of conflict of laws assessment
of title thereto, is the law of the place where the property is situated at the time
of the transaction in question,[16] i.e. when ownership or other proprietary right
is alleged to have passed.

Particular care is required in the ascertainment of the *situs* of certain types of
corporeal property,[17] including aircraft[18] and ships. This arises because it is
arguable that, though physically moveable, such assets have a quasi-permanent
situs at their place of registration. In *Air Foyle Ltd v Center Capital Ltd*,[19] Gross
J. gave firm support to the ascription as the *situs* of an aircraft of its physical
situation for the time being, at least unless it is over the high seas or over a territory which is not under the sovereignty of any state.[20] The same preference was
shown by Beatson J. in *Blue Sky One Ltd v Mahan Air*.[21] Similarly, with regard
to ships,[22] strong judicial preference for the physical *situs* of the vessel over the

---

[15] *Re Duke of Wellington* [1947] Ch. 506; affirmed [1948] Ch. 118; see para.5–18, above.
[16] See, per Staughton L.J. in *Macmillan Inc v Bishopsgate Investment Trust Plc (No.3)* [1996] 1
W.L.R. 387 at 400.
[17] The treatment of title to cultural property is noteworthy because the subject has attracted a high
public profile, and has generated interest in other branches of the law, and extra-legal solutions
also have been proposed. Yet essentially, from a conflict of laws viewpoint, the normal rules on
title to moveable property apply. See Carruthers, *Transfer of Property in the Conflict of Laws*,
2005, Ch.5; *Cheshire, North and Fawcett: Private International Law*, 14th edn, 2008, pp.1223,
1224; and *Iran v Barakat Galleries Ltd* [2009] Q.B. 22.
[18] UNIDROIT Convention on International Interests in Mobile Equipment and Aircraft Equipment
Protocol (2001), in relation to which see Decision 2009/370/EC on the accession of the
European Community to the Convention [2009] OJ L121/3.
[19] [2004] I.L.Pr. 15.
[20] *Air Foyle Ltd v Center Capital Ltd* [2004] I.L.Pr. 15 at [40].
[21] [2010] EWHC 631 (Comm) at [156].
[22] As to which the early cases dealt with the distinction between personal and proprietary rights in
ships by applying, in the usual case, the law of the flag to contractual rights, and the *lex situs* in cases
involving third parties and raising proprietary questions: *Schultz v Robinson and Niven* (1861) 24
D. 120; *Simpson v Fogo* (1863) 1 H. & M. 195; *Liverpool Marine Credit Co v Hunter* (1867) L.R.
4 Eq. 62; *Hooper v Gumm* (1867) L.R. 2 Ch. App. 282; *Castrique v Imrie* (1870) L.R. 4 H.L. 414.

notional or artifical *situs* thereof at the place of registration was shown by Tomlinson J. in *Dornoch Ltd v Westminster International BV.*[23]

In the case of goods in transit, the physical location of which is casual, fortuitous or transient,[24] a more flexible approach requires to be taken to the ascertainment of the *situs*. Property will be classified as being in transit if it has left the country of despatch without having arrived at its intended destination.

A more difficult concept is the *situs* of incorporeal moveables. Since by nature an intangible right has no physical location, the practice has been to impute to such property an artificial legal *situs*, according to the choice of law rule of the forum.[25] Rules have emerged in terms of which certain classes of intangible rights have been accorded a fictional *situs*, for example a money debt is deemed to be situated at the place where the debtor resides and, it is presumed, where the debt may be enforced[26]; registered shares generally are deemed to be situated in the country in which they can be effectively dealt with as between the shareholder and the company[27]; and rights of action in contract, delict or unjustified enrichment are deemed to be situated in the country in which they can be effectively pursued.

Interpretation of "lex" situs

17–05 Whilst it would be possible to argue, as with immoveables, so with moveables, that the reference to the law of the *situs* includes a reference to its rules of international private law, a possibility that was kept alive by Slade J. in *Winkworth v Christie, Manson & Woods Ltd,*[28] subsequent decisions tend to suggest that the argument in favour of *renvoi* is unlikely to succeed before an English court.[29]

Alienability of property

17–06 The *lex situs* decides whether or not property is alienable, and determines also the nature of any document or other thing connected with property, such as title deeds or keys.[30] In *Duc de Frias v Pichon*[31] the saleability of sacred

---

[23] *Dornoch Ltd v Westminster International BV (The WD Fairway)* [2009] EWHC 889 (Admlty) at [96], [97], [103].

[24] *Standard Chartered Bank Ltd v Inland Revenue Commissioners* [1978] 1 W.L.R. 1160; and *Hardwick Game Farm v Suffolk Agricultural Poultry Producers Association* [1966] 1 W.L.R. 287.

[25] *Smelting Company of Australia Ltd v Inland Revenue Commissioners* [1897] 1 Q.B. 175.

[26] *English, Scottish and Australian Bank Ltd v Inland Revenue Commissioners* [1932] A.C. 238; *Re Banque des Marchands de Moscou (Koupetschesky) (No.3)* [1954] 1 W.L.R. 1108; and *F&K Jabbour v Custodian of Israeli Absentee Property* [1954] 1 W.L.R. 139.

[27] *Brassard v Smith* [1925] A.C. 371; *R. v Williams* [1942] A.C. 541. If there should be more than one share register the *situs* will be the country in which the transaction, according to the ordinary course of business, would be registered. See *Macmillan Inc v Bishopsgate Investment Trust Plc (No.3)* [1996] 1 W.L.R. 387. Difficulties arise where the place of the issuer's incorporation differs from the place where the share register is maintained, and from the place where the shareholding can be dealt with effectively as between the investor and the issuer. See, further, para.17–35, below.

[28] [1980] Ch. 496 at 514.

[29] *Macmillan Inc v Bishopsgate Investment Trust Plc (No.3)* [1996] 1 W.L.R. 387 at 405; *Iran v Berend* [2007] EWHC 132 (QB); *The WD Fairway* [2009] EWHC 889 (Admlty); and *Blue Sky One Ltd v Mahan Air* [2010] EWHC 631 (Comm), all discussed at para.5–11, above.

[30] *Duc de Frias v Pichon* (1886) 13 *Journal du Droit International* 593; *Lushington v Sewell* (1827) 1 Sim. 435; *Stewart v Garnett* (1830) 3 Sim. 398; *Dominion Bridge Co v British American Nickel Co Ltd* (1925) 2 D.L.R. 138.

[31] (1886) 13 *Journal du Droit International* 593.

vessels stolen from a monastery in Spain was referred to the law of France, their situation at the time of the purported sale: by French law they could be sold, but not by Spanish law.

The assignability of incorporeal moveable property is a more complex matter, discussed at para.17–26, below.

B. IMMOVEABLE PROPERTY

Capacity and powers

Capacity and power generally to transact in relation to land are governed by the *lex situs*.[32] **17–07**

Contracts

A distinction should be drawn between an agreement to transfer an interest **17–08** in land or other immoveable property, or otherwise transact in relation to such property (i.e. a matter concerning only personal rights), and the actual transfer/conveyance of a right *in rem* in immoveable property (i.e a matter concerning real rights).[33]

As regards the essential validity of contracts in relation to immoveable property, the rights of the parties are governed by the governing law of the contract which usually,[34] but not necessarily,[35] will be the *lex situs*. This was reinforced by art.4.3 of the Rome I Convention, and more recently by art.4.1(c) of the Rome I Regulation.[36]

The formal validity of contracts the subject matter of which is a right in immoveable property or a right to use immoveable property is subject to the mandatory requirements of form of the *lex situs* by virtue of art.11.5 of the Rome I Regulation.[37]

Proprietary rights

The existence and nature of real rights in land or other immoveables are **17–09** governed by the *lex situs*.[38] The *lex situs*, besides being capable of clear identification, is generally thought to have an unassailable claim to be applied, as of right and common sense. Any question pertaining to the creation, including alienability, acquisition (including by means of prescription),[39] use, disposal,

---

[32] *Bank of Africa Ltd v Cohen* [1909] 2 Ch. 129 (but this case has been criticised: see Carruthers, *Transfer of Property in the Conflict of Laws*, 2005, para.4.04); *Ogilvy v Ogilvy's Trustees*, 1927 S.L.T. 83; *Black v Black's Trustees*, 1950 S.L.T. (Notes) 32; *Bondholders Securities Corp v Manville* (1933) 4 D.L.R. 699; *Charron v Montreal Trust* (1958) 15 D.L.R. (2d.) 240. See now rarely (in this connection) Rome I Regulation art.13.

[33] e.g. *Hamilton v Wakefield*, 1993 S.L.T. (Sh. Ct.) 30.

[34] *Cood* (1863) 33 Beav. 314; *Re Smith* [1916] 2 Ch. 206; see also *Mackintosh v May* (1895) 22 R. 345.

[35] *British South Africa Co v De Beers Consolidated Mines Ltd* [1912] A.C. 52.

[36] See, however, art.4.1(d) introducing a special choice of law rule for short-term tenancies, echoing the jurisdiction rule contained in art.22.1 of the Brussels I Regulation.

[37] Ex-art.9.6 of the Rome I Convention.

[38] *Dicey, Morris and Collins on the Conflict of Laws*, 14th edn, 2006, r.123.

[39] *Beckford v Wade* (1805) 17 Ves. Un. 87 (positive prescription); *Re Peat* (1869) L.R. 7 Eq. 302; *Pitt v Lord Dacre* (1876) 3 Ch. D. 295 (negative).

gift, or transfer of an interest in immoveable property, and its effect on the proprietary rights of any person claiming, by any law, to be interested therein, is governed by the *lex situs*.

All deeds of title must comply with the *lex situs* both as regards form[40] (including formalities of execution) and essentials.[41]

Real rights in security

17–10   The grant of a security interest over immoveable property must comply with the *lex situs* both as regards form and essentials.[42]

If, however, a security over land in Scotland is taken by a foreign creditor by way of equitable mortgage, or some other form of security not known to Scots domestic law, it cannot prevail against a valid security in Scots form, but it may confer a preference on the holder thereof over unsecured creditors in a Scots bankruptcy or liquidation. If there are no securities valid by the *lex situs*, or if after such securities have been satisfied, there are no prior claims valid by that law, there will then be a competition between purely personal rights,[43] which will be determined by the law common to the litigants, if there is one, and failing that, by the *lex situs*.[44]

C. Moveable Property

Preliminary

17–11   For the purpose of the resolution of conflict disputes, it is important to note certain distinctions concerning:

> (a) *the nature of the property in question*: different rules apply to the treatment of corporeal moveables (choses in possession/chattels, e.g. a motor vehicle, painting, etc.) from that of incorporeal moveables (choses in action, e.g. a money debt, or the interest under a life insurance policy);
> (b) *the nature of the purported transfer*: different rules govern voluntary assignations (e.g. by means of gift,[45] sale, or other consensual exchange) from those which govern involuntary assignations (by virtue of diligence or bankruptcy); and

---

[40] *Adams v Clutterbuck* (1883) L.R. 10 Q.B.D. 403. This is reinforced by Rome I Regulation art.11.5.

[41] *Norton v Florence Land and Public Works Co* (1887) L.R. 7 Ch. D. 332.

[42] For a rare illustration of the prevailing of another law over the *lex situs*: *Carse v Coppen*, 1951 S.C. 233. Also *Ballachulish Slate Quarries Co Ltd v Menzies* (1908) 16 S.L.T. 48.

[43] *Re Courtney Ex p. Pollard* (1840) Mont. & Ch. 239; *Coote v Jecks* (1872) L.R. 13 Eq. 597; *Ex p. Holthausen* (1874) L.R. 9 Ch. App. 722; *Re Anchor Line (Henderson Bros) Ltd* [1937] Ch. 483.

[44] See, in respect of insolvency, para.17–38 below.

[45] *Cochrane v Moore* (1890) L.R. 25 Q.B.D. 57; *Re Korvine's Trust* [1921] 1 Ch. 343. Whether or not a gift will be recognised as effective to transfer a real right in property, and all questions of proprietary rights, must be matters for the *lex situs* at the time of alleged donation. Personal rights as between donor and donee may be governed by the proper law of the gift, which need not necessarily be the *lex situs*: see *Shiftung v Lewis* [2004] EWHC 2589.

(c) *the basis of the dispute as contractual or proprietary*: contractual rights involve the rights of the parties to a transfer of moveables *only as between themselves*, and are purely personal in nature. Proprietary rights may, and usually do, involve questions with third parties relating to rights in the object which is the subject of the transfer and are real rather than personal, i.e. rights enforceable *against all the world* (*contra mundum*). Certain types of transfer have an existence which is independent of contract (e.g. donations), whereas other transfers are rooted in contract (e.g. conditional sale agreements). Whilst personal rights are governed by the law governing the contract, proprietary questions are referred to the applicable law in property.[46] This chapter is concerned mainly with the existence and ranking of proprietary (real) rights, rather than with contractual (personal) rights.

CORPOREAL MOVEABLES

The laws which might be applied in order to determine conflict questions **17–12** relating to the validity of the creation, acquisition, use and/or transfer of rights in corporeal moveables are:

(a) *lex domicilii* (of transferor and/or transferee)[47];
(b) *lex loci actus* (the law of the place where the transaction/transfer took place)[48];
(c) *lex actus* (proper law of the transfer, being the law of deemed closest connection); and
(d) *lex situs* (or *lex loci rei sitae*: the law of the situation of the asset at the time of the transfer alleged to have given rise to proprietary rights therein).

The development of the law to date shows the increasing influence of the *lex situs*; the *lex situs* generally[49] has final say over title to corporeal moveables and determines all questions involving proprietary rights in respect thereof.[50] Counsel for the claimant in *Winkworth v Christie, Manson & Woods Ltd*[51] failed to persuade the court of the possible existence of a proper law of property based on law of closest connection, and it seems such a suggestion is yet

---

[46] See *Glencore International AG v Metro Trading International Inc (No.2)* [2001] 1 All E.R. (Comm) 103; and *Pattni v Ali* [2007] 2 A.C. 85, per Lord Mance at [25].

[47] See suggestions in *Sill v Worswick* (1791) 1 H.B. 1 665 at 690, and *Re Ewin* (1830) 1 Cr. & J. 151 at 156. In the past, the maxim *mobilia sequuntur personam* (questions of moveable property are governed by the personal law) operated in questions relating to corporeal moveables, but now it is recognised that the principle applies only as a rule of succession on death, to the effect that succession, testate or intestate, to moveable estate is regulated by the law of the deceased's last domicile.

[48] As suggested by Kay L.J. in *Alcock v Smith* [1892] 1 Ch. 238 at 267.

[49] See para.17–16 regarding exceptions to the *lex situs* rule.

[50] *Re Anziani* [1930] 1 Ch. 407; *Bank voor Handel en Scheepvaart NV v Slatford (No.2)* [1953] 1 Q.B. 248; *F&K Jabbour v Custodian of Israeli Absentee Property* [1954] 1 W.L.R. 139; *Iran v Berend* [2007] EWHC 132 (QB).

[51] [1980] 1 All E.R. 1121.

premature, preference being shown for the more easily ascertained factor of *lex situs*.[52]

The validity of a transfer

17–13   The purported transfer of corporeal moveable assets must be considered as regards:

(a) alienability of property;
(b) legal and proprietary capacity of transferor and transferee[53];
(c) formal validity of transfer (if the transfer is by means of contract, see para.15–37, above; if otherwise than by means of contract, e.g. by gift, the governing law would be, by analogy, the *lex loci actus* or the *lex actus*, that is, the proper law of the transfer, being the law of deemed closest connection).

Rules for determining proprietary rights

17–14   As a general rule, proprietary rights in corporeal moveable property are governed by the *lex situs*. In a question between an "original" owner and a subsequent transferee, the latter will be preferred if he has acquired a title valid by the *lex situs* at the time of the purported transfer in his favour, or if he has acquired from an intermediate owner who has obtained such a title, that is, one which extinguishes the rights and title of the original owner.[54] Thus, if a valid transfer has taken place in the country in which an object was situated at that time, any proprietary rights which it confers on the transferee will be recognised in Scotland, whether the transfer took place by way of public or private sale, order of court,[55] Act of Parliament or its equivalent, donation, pledge or otherwise. Essentially, the law of the latest transfer (whether it favours the latest transferee or a party earlier in the chain)[56] will govern.

Fraud/sale by non-owner

17–15   The case of transfer "tainted" by fraud is singled out only for emphasis, and not because the choice of law rule applied differs from any other purported

---

[52] Though see Carruthers' suggested "lex proprietatis" in *The Transfer of Property in the Conflict of Laws*, 2005, Chs 5, 8, 9. Cf. *Glencore International AG v Metro Trading International Inc (No.2)* [2001] 1 All E.R. (Comm) 103.

[53] The proprietary capacity of the transferor (i.e. entitlement to deal with the property) is governed by the *lex situs*. The legal capacity of the transferor (i.e. age, insanity, etc.) could be governed by the putative applicable law (being the *lex situs*) or by the transferor's personal law. As to the capacity of the transferee, some assistance can be derived from *Republica de Guatemala v Nunez* [1927] 1 K.B. 669 CA. Compare generally, legal capacity of a beneficiary to succeed, para.18–11, below.

[54] *Todd v Armour* (1882) 9 R. 901; *Inglis v Usherwood* (1801) 1 East 515; *Cammell v Sewell* (1860) 5 H. & M. 728; *Castrique v Imrie* (1870) L.R. 4 H.L. 414; *Re Korvine's Trust* [1921] 1 Ch. 343; *Re Craven's Estate (No.1)* [1937] Ch. 423; *Princess Paley Olga v Weisz* [1929] 1 K.B. 718; *Winkworth v Christie, Manson & Woods Ltd* [1980] 1 All E.R. 1121.

[55] *Castrique v Imrie* (1870) L.R. 4 H.L. 414.

[56] *Goetschius v Brightman*, 245 N.Y. 186 (1927); *Century Credit Corp v Richard* (1962) 34 D.L.R. (2d.) 291 (discussed in *Cheshire, North and Fawcett: Private International Law*, 14th edn, 2008, p.1216)

transfer case. If he has been guilty of fraud or if he has acquired from a non-owner (e.g. a thief), a transferee will not obtain good title to the property in question unless in either case the transfer in his favour is valid according to the *lex situs* of the property at the time of that transfer.[57] The general principle is that a transferee takes the property subject to all restrictions on the right of the transferor, unless the *lex situs* at the time of the purported transfer has had an overriding effect which extinguishes any prior rights.[58]

Exceptions to the situs rule

Certain exceptions to the *situs* rule were conceded by the defendant in the **17–16** leading case of *Winkworth*, namely:

"The first 'if goods are in transit and their situs is casual or not known, a transfer which is valid and effective by its proper law will (semble) be valid and effective in England'[59] . . . The second exception . . . arises where a purchaser claiming title has not acted bona fide.[60] The third exception is the case where the English court declines to recognise the particular law of the relevant situs because it considers it contrary to English public policy. The fourth exception arises where a statute in force in the country which is the forum in which the case is heard obliges the court to apply the law of its own country . . . Fifthly . . . special rules might apply to determine the relevant law governing the effect of general assignments of movables on bankruptcy or succession."[61]

Competing claims to the same property

In this area of conflict of laws, the most difficult, though most common, **17–17** problem will be that concerning the ranking of competing claims to the same property. It is necessary therefore to consider first the validity of each particular, potentially contending claim, and the transfer upon which it is based. If all such claims are governed by the *same* law, a Scots or English forum will apply that

---

[57] *Winkworth v Christie, Manson & Woods Ltd* [1980] 1 All E.R. 1121. See also *Kurtha v Marks* [2008] EWHC 336 (QB).

[58] *Freeman v The East India Co* (1822) 5 B. & Ald. 617; *Mehta v Sutton* (1913) 108 L.T. 514; *Goetschius v Brightman*, 245 N.Y. 186 (1927); *Universal Credit Co v Marks* (1932) 163 A. 810; *Century Credit Corp v Richard* (1962) 34 D.L.R. (2d.) 291; *Winkworth v Christie, Manson & Woods Ltd* [1980] 1 All E.R. 1121.

[59] The proper law of the transfer, being the law having closest connection to the transfer, seems an appropriate contender. In ascertaining that law, account will be taken of the country of despatch, and the country of intended destination. See Carruthers, *Transfer of Property in the Conflict of Laws*, 2005, paras 3.32–3.35.

[60] However an explanatory gloss surely is needed, viz. any requirement of good faith on the part of the transferee in order that title shall pass must depend entirely on the content of the *lex situs* (see Carruthers, *Transfer of Property in the Conflict of Laws*, 2005, para.8.38). A more general point is that there is a division among legal systems between those favouring the instant transaction (*en fait des meubles, la possession vaut titre*), and those which find it impossible to disregard a *vitium reale* in the subject matter purported to be transferred (i.e. that stolen property has an ineradicable taint: *nemo dat quod non habet*). Clearly the well-informed art thief should seek to dispose of his spoils in the former.

[61] *Winkworth v Christie, Manson & Woods Ltd* [1980] Ch. 496 at 501. See also *Glencore International AG v Metro Trading International Inc (No.2)* [2001] 1 All E.R. (Comm) 103.

law to determine which claim succeeds.[62] However, in competitions between voluntary and involuntary transfers, or between transfers having *different* governing laws, competing proprietary claims are governed by the *lex situs*.

Where contract meets property[63]

17–18   The terms of a contract, valid by the governing law of the contract, may contravene the law of some other interested legal system. In a purely contractual sphere, this is regulated by the "overriding mandatory provisions" rules of the Rome I Regulation, and by that instrument's preservation of the forum's public policy. However choice of law rules of property typically may impinge, and there have been cases in Scotland[64] concerning the effect of advanced or elaborate forms of retention/reservation of title ("Romalpa") clauses,[65] which, while acceptable by the governing law of the contract of which they form part, are found to contravene the principles of the Scottish *lex situs* at the point of conclusion of the contract or at the date of subsequent litigation.Where there is a collision between a legal system's rules, conflict and/or domestic, of contract and property, the property rules have prevailed, at least if the dispute is one of proprietary right.

Much interest in this area was shown in Scotland in the 1980s and 1990s. Although it seemed that Scotland was being true to its own law, both domestic (that generally there can be no security without possession), and conflict (that the validity of security rights are judged by the *lex situs*), there was a problem of its being out of step in international commercial terms. A solution, by means of change in forms of security, was considered, originally by the Halliday Committee for Scotland in 1986,[66] and the Diamond Committee[67] for England

---

[62] *North Western Bank Ltd v John Poynter Son and MacDonalds* (1894) 22 R. (H.L.) 1: [1895] A.C. 56. In the time-honoured (but later, by the speaker, amended) words of Lord Watson, at 75: "[w]hen a moveable fund, situated in Scotland admittedly belongs to one or other of two domiciled Englishmen, the question to which of them it belongs is prima facie one of English law." The gloss is that the reference to, two domiciled Englishmen must be taken to mean "two men claiming under the same [English] law". *City Bank v Barrow* (1880) L.R. 5 App. Cas. 664; *Inglis v Robertson*; sub nom. *Irvine v Inglis*; *Irvine & Robertson v Baxter & Inglis* [1898] A.C. 616; *Connal and Co v Loder* (1868) 6 M. 1095; *Dinwoodie's Executor v Carruthers' Executor* (1895) 23 R. 234.

[63] See para.15–68, above. Background writing: see K. Reid and G. Gretton, "Retention of Title in Romalpa Clauses", 1983 S.L.T. (News) 77; "Retention of Title: Lord Watson's Legacy", 1983 S.L.T. (News) 105; Stewart, "Romalpa Clauses: Choosing the Law", 1985 S.L.T. (News) 149; P. Sellar, "Romalpa and Receivables—Choosing the Law", 1985 S.L.T. (News) 313; H. Patrick "Romalpa: the International Dimension", 1986 S.L.T. (News) 265 and 277; Clark, "All-Sums Retention of Title", 1991 S.L.T. (News) 155; C.G.J. Morse, "Retention of Title in English Private International Law" [1993] J.B.L. 168; and Gerard McCormack, *Reservation of Title*, 2nd edn (London: Sweet & Maxwell, 1995).

[64] *Hammer and Sohne v HWT Realisations Ltd*, 1985 S.L.T. (Sh.Ct.) 21; *Zahnrad Fabrik Passau GmbH v Terex Ltd*, 1986 S.L.T. 84; *Armour v Thyssen Edelstahlwerke AG*, 1986 S.L.T. 452 OH; 1990 S.L.T. 891 HL; *Emerald Stainless Steel Ltd v South Side Distribution Ltd*, 1983 S.L.T. 162; *Deutz Engines Ltd v Terex Ltd*, 1984 S.L.T. 273; *E Pfeiffer Weinkellerei-Weinenkauf GmbH v Arbuthnot Factors Ltd* [1988] 1 W.L.R. 150.

[65] So-called because of the name of the case in which such a clause was first noted: *Aluminium Industrie Vaassen BV v Romalpa Aluminium Ltd* [1976] 1 W.L.R. 676 (conflict issues not discussed).

[66] Scottish Law Commission Working Party on Security Over Moveable Property, chaired by Professor J.M. Halliday, *Report by Working Party on Security Over Moveable Property* (HMSO, 1986).

[67] Professor A.L. Diamond, *A Review of Security Interests in Property* (HMSO, 1989).

(though the growth of Romalpa clauses did not occasion an equivalent flurry of conflict cases on the point in that jurisdiction). Another solution might have been to redefine the *lex situs* in these cases to be, say, the place of despatch in terms of the contract,[68] or thirdly, to place the problem in a wider context of distribution in bankruptcy (for such was often the situation which brought the case to court). However, in *Armour v Thyssen Edelstahlwerke AG*[69] the House of Lords ruled that, in the courts below, the nature of the retention of title clause in the contract in question had been misconstrued; that it could not be offensive to Scots law as a security right without possession, because on a true construction only possession and not property was transferred before payment. There the matter rests.[70]

INCORPOREAL MOVEABLES

This is an area concerning the transfer of such rights as debts, shares and securities, funds in bank accounts, insurance policies, decrees, claims for damages and other causes of action, intellectual property rights, and interests in trust estates.[71] Assignation of bulk claims as a means of raising finance is a specialised sub-topic.[72]   **17–19**

Situs

As explained above, such rights have their *situs* at the place where the right is enforceable.[73]   **17–20**

Choice of law

The possible laws which might govern assignations[74] of incorporeal rights, and questions arising therefrom, are as follows: **17–21**

---

[68] Stewart, "Romalpa Clauses: Choosing the Law", 1985 S.L.T. (News) 149.

[69] 1990 S.L.T. 891.

[70] See Department of Trade and Industry, *Security Over Moveable Property in Scotland: A Consultation Paper* (HMSO, 1994); also commentary by Murray, "Security over Moveable Property", 1995 S.L.T. (News) 31. One of the items in the Eighth Programme of the Scottish Law Commission for the period 2010–14, carried forward from the Seventh Programme, is "Security over corporeal and incorporeal moveable property; assignation of incorporeal moveable property".

[71] *Clare & Co v Dresdner Bank* [1915] 2 K.B. 576; *N Joachimson (A Firm) v Swiss Bank Corp* [1921] 3 K.B. 110; *Swiss Bank Corp v Boechmische Industrial Bank* [1923] 1 K.B. 673; *New York Life Insurance Co v Public Trustee* [1924] 2 Ch. 101; *Richardson v Richardson* [1927] P. 228; *Sutherland v Administrator of German Property* (1934) 50 T.L.R. 107; *Arab Bank Ltd v Barclays Bank* [1954] A.C. 495; *Re Claim by Helbert Wagg & Co Ltd* [1956] Ch. 323; *Re Banque des Marchands de Moscou (No.3)* [1954] 1 W.L.R. 1108 at 1115; *Reuter v Mulhens (No.2)* [1954] Ch. 50; *Westminster Bank Execcutor & Trustee Co (Channel Islands) Ltd v National Bank of Greece SA* [1971] 2 W.L.R. 105; *Compania Colombiana de Seguros v Pacific Steam Navigation Co (The Colombiana)* [1965] 1 Q.B. 101; *Trendtex Trading Corp v Credit Suisse* [1982] A.C. 679; *Macmillan Inc v Bishopsgate Investment Trust Plc (No.3)* [1996] 1 All E.R. 585; and *Raiffeisen Zentralbank Osterreich AG v Five Star General Trading LLC (The Mount I)* [2000] 2 Lloyd's Rep. 684; [2001] 1 Lloyd's Rep. 597.

[72] As to which see para.17–32, below.

[73] See para.17–04, above; e.g. *F&K Jabbour v Custodian of Israeli Absentee Property* [1954] 1 W.L.R. 139; *Kwok Chi Leung Karl v Commissioner of Estate Duty* [1988] 1 W.L.R. 1035 PC; *Power Curber International Ltd v National Bank of Kuwait SAK* [1981] 3 All E.R. 607.

[74] Termed in English law "assignment".

    (a) *lex domicilii* of the creditor or the debtor;
    (b) *lex loci actus* (the law of the place where the transaction takes place: the law of the paper transfer);
    (c) *lex actus* (the law governing the assignation, being the law of deemed closest connection);
    (d) proper law of the right purportedly assigned, that is, the *lex situs* of the right (normally the residence of the debtor).

One difficulty in the early cases is that the reason for application by the forum of a particular *lex causae* is not always clear,[75] especially where the *lex domicilii*, the *lex loci actus* and the *lex situs* coincide. Thus, in the early leading case of *Republica de Guatemala v Nunez*,[76] which concerned both the formal validity of an assignation, and the legal capacity of the assignee to take (the flaw alleged being infancy), both issues were referred to the law of Guatemala which, on a revisionist view, has been said to be the (putative) proper law of the assignation.[77]

Triangular relationship

17–22   Typically, cases involving the assignation of incorporeal moveable rights concern a triangular scenario, where a creditor in an original claim against a debtor assigns his right to pursue that claim to a third party assignee. The relationship between the original parties (debtor and creditor) has a governing law, ascertained, it contractual, in accordance with the Rome I Regulation (so long as the contract falls within the scope of Rome I); if non-contractual, the relationship is governed by the proper law of the right purportedly assigned, being the law where the right may be enforced). Likewise, the assignation (from creditor to assignee) has its own governing law. The third side of the triangle is the relationship between assignee and debtor. It is important in any conflict case arising in this area to ascertain *which* parties the dispute in question concerns.

Effect of article 14 of the Rome I Regulation

17–23   Although the principal concern of this chapter is the proprietary, rather than the contractual, aspects of transfers, in relation to the assignation of incorporeal moveables of a contractual nature (e.g. a contractual debt),[78] it is difficult, and probably artificial, to sever the proprietary aspect from the contractual aspect, since the property right is a right arising under contract. Contractual assignations[79] of incorporeal moveable rights (whether of contractual or non-contractual nature) are governed by art.14 of the Rome I Regulation.[80]

---

[75] Contrast close discussion in more modern authorities such as *Trendtex Trading Corp v Credit Suisse* [1982] A.C. 679; *Macmillan Inc v Bishopsgate Investment Trust Plc (No.3)* [1996] 1 W.L.R. 387; and *Raiffeisen Zentralbank Osterreich AG v Five Star General Trading LLC (The Mount I)* [2000] 2 Lloyd's Rep. 684; [2001] 1 Lloyd's Rep. 597.
[76] [1927] 1 K.B. 669.
[77] An earlier and similar authority is *Lee v Abdy* (1886) L.R. 17 Q.B.D. 309 where it was clear that the putative proper law was the law of Cape Colony, South Africa.
[78] Rights which are capable of being assigned can be contractual, or non-contractual, e.g. the benefit arising under a right of copyright, or a right to sue (*Trendtex Trading Corp v Credit Suisse* [1982] A.C. 679).
[79] An assignation of property can be contractual, but might also be effected in a non-contractual manner, e.g. by gift or bequest.
[80] Ex-art.12, Rome I Convention.

Article 14: Voluntary assignment and contractual subrogation[81]

1. The relationship[82] between assignor and assignee under a voluntary **17–24** assignment or contractual subrogation of a claim against another person ("the debtor") shall be governed by the law that applies to the contract between the assignor and assignee under this Regulation.

2. The law governing the assigned or subrogated claim shall determine its assignability, the relationship between the assignee and the debtor, the conditions under which the assignment or subrogation can be invoked against the debtor and whether the debtor's obligations have been discharged.

3. The concept of assignment in this article includes outright transfers of claims, transfers of claims by way of security as well as pledges or other security rights over claims.[83]

Article 14 applies to claims assigned by means of contract *irrespective* of the nature of the claim itself, which may be contractual or non-contractual.[84] The validity of a contractual assignation falling outside the scope of the Rome I Regulation is governed by the common law rules of assignation. Likewise, non-contractual assignations, even of a contractual right such as a money debt, are not governed by the Rome I Regulation, but fall to be governed by the common law rules of assignation. It is important, therefore, to distinguish between contractual and non-contractual assignations of incorporeal moveable rights.[85]

Article 14, which very largely replicates the wording of art.12 of the Rome I Convention, defines the ambit of operation, or authority, of the law applicable; it does not seek to identify what shall be the law applicable.

Article 14.1 issues: relationship between the assignor and the assignee

In the case of contractual assignations, the relationship between the assignor **17–25** and assignee falls, as a contractual matter, within art.14.1 of the Rome I Regulation. This means that the applicable law of the assignation governs that relationship. The applicable law will be determined according to the rules in the Rome I Regulation, principally contained in arts 3 and 4. In the case of non-contractual assignations, matters of essential validity are governed at common

---

[81] See, on art.14 and art.15 (legal subrogation), paras 15–51 and 15–52, above. The remit of art.14 extends to voluntary assignments and contractual subrogations, it being thought that these transfers are similar in nature. "Contractual subrogation" refers to subrogation by means of a contract; it does not mean that the nature of the claim subrogated necessarily is contractual.

[82] Recital (38) provides that: "In the context of voluntary assignment, the term 'relationship' should make it clear that Article 14.1 also applies to the property aspects of an assignment, as between assignor and assignee, in legal orders where such aspects are treated separately from the aspects under the law of obligations. However, the term 'relationship' should not be understood as relating to any relationship that may exist between assignor and assignee. In particular, it should not cover preliminary questions as regards a voluntary assignment or a contractual subrogation. The term should be strictly limited to the aspects which are directly relevant to the voluntary assignment or contractual subrogation in question". Although the remit of the Rome I Regulation is non-contractual obligations in situations involving a conflict of laws, the wording of recital (38) is evidence that the competence of the instrument or amendments thereto to deal with the property aspects of voluntary assignment is assumed.

[83] Article 14.3 provides of new a non-exhaustive definition of the concept of assignment.

[84] For the law governing the transferability of a non-contractual claim see Rome II Regulation art.15(e).

[85] See Carruthers, *Transfer of Property in the Conflict of Laws*, 2005, Ch.6, para.6.12.

law by the proper law of the assignation,[86] but an assignation will be essentially valid also if it complies with the proper law of the right transferred.[87]

Article 14.2 issues

(a) Assignability

17–26   As regards contractual assignations, art.14.2 of the Rome I Regulation applies to the effect that assignability is governed by the law governing the assigned or subrogated claim.[88]

As regards non-contractual assignations (e.g. by means of gift), assignability is governed by the proper law of the right[89] (i.e. to the same result as art.14.2). The common law rule is clearly seen in the case of *Pender*,[90] in which the assignability of an insurance policy, taken out with reference to the English Married Women's Property Act 1882, was categorised by the Scots court as an assignation of a Scottish right, as to which assignability and the separate issue of capacity to assign were referred to Scots law qua, respectively, the law of closest connection and the domicile of the transferor. By Scots law the married woman granter was under a personal incapacity to assign the benefits of such a policy. Hence, her purported assignation to a bank was ineffective.

These facts illustrate that within the one broad heading of assignability, the issue of capacity to assign may take precedence.

> "In other words, the rule as to assignability is subordinate to the rule governing capacity to assign; personal (in)capacity to assign must be regarded as an essential component of assignability."[91]

In *Pender*, the *two leges causae* (law of closest connection and the domicile of the transferor) coincided in Scotland, but clearly this might not always be the case.

(b) Relationship between the assignee and the debtor

17–27   As between assignee and debtor (i.e. under the right transferred):

> "[I]t is easy to understand why the intrinsic validity of the assignment should be governed by the proper law of the assignation; but, when issues of validity (other perhaps than mere formal validity) arise between the

---

[86] *Scottish Provident Institution v Cohen* (1888) 16 R. 112; *Libertas-Kommerz GmbH v Johnson*, 1977 S.C. 191.

[87] *Re Anziani* [1930] 1 Ch. 407.

[88] Logically, it would have been expected that the subject of assignability would have been treated first in order. However, the drafting of art.14 follows the sequence adopted by art.12 of the Rome I Convention, and produces the odd result that the general rule comes second.

[89] *Grant's Trustees v Ritchie's Executor* (1886) 13 R. 646; *Pender v Commercial Bank of Scotland Ltd*, 1940 S.L.T. 306; *Campbell Connelly & Co Ltd v Noble* [1963] 1 W.L.R. 252; *Libertas-Kommerz GmbH v Johnson*, 1977 S.C. 191. (As to Scots domestic law on assignability of floating charges, see Lucas, "The Assignation of Floating Charges", 1996 S.L.T. (News) 203.)

[90] *Pender v Commercial Bank of Scotland Ltd*, 1940 S.L.T. 306.

[91] Carruthers, *Transfer of Property in the Conflict of Laws*, 2005, para.6.08.

assignee and the other party to the original contract, the argument in support of the application of the proper law of the assignation, in preference to the proper law both of the original contract and of the debt claimed, is in my opinion, inconsistent with both logic and equity."[92]

Assuming that the right in question is assignable, and that there is capacity on the part of the assignor to assign, and of the assignee to accept, art.14.2 of the Rome I Regulation states, in relation to contractual assignations, that the law governing the right to which the assignment relates (i.e. the proper law of the right) governs the relationship between the assignee and the debtor, as well as the conditions under which the assignment can be invoked against the debtor and any question whether the debtor's obligations have been discharged.

(c) Miscellaneous

Capacity to make (or to accept) an assignation. In the past, the *lex loci* **17–28** *actus* or the law of the domicile of the purported transferor (or transferee) was applied, but it is submitted that capacity to make (or to accept) an assignation of incorporeal moveable property should be governed by the proper law of the assignation or by the proper law of the right purportedly assigned,[93] perhaps according to whichever of these laws confers capacity earlier.[94] In the case of contractual assignations, the putative applicable law of the contract, subject to art.13 of the Rome I Regulation,[95] will apply.

Formal validity. At common law, there were three possibly applicable laws, **17–29** to the effect that an assignation, contractual or non-contractual, would be formally valid if it complied with any one of the *lex loci actus*, the proper law of the assignation, or the proper law of the right assigned.[96] In cases of contractual assignations regulated by the Rome I Regulation, art.11 governs formal validity.[97]

The effectiveness of an assignment of a claim against third parties, and priorities

That which was unregulated by the Convention, and was left unregulated by **17–30** the Regulation, is the effectiveness of a voluntary assignment vis-à-vis third parties. No guidance is given in the Regulation as to how a Member State forum should prioritise competing claims[98] over the same right, governed by

---

[92] *Bankhaus H Aufhauser v Scotboard Ltd*, 1973 S.L.T. (Notes) 87, per Lord Hunter at 89.
[93] *Lee v Abdy* (1886) L.R. 17 Q.B.D. 309; *Republica de Guatemala v Nunez* [1927] 1 K.B. 669.
[94] Since arguably "the conditions under which the assignment can be invoked against the debtor" encompasses the questions of incapacity of assignor and/or assignee, by virtue of art.14.2 these matters should be referred to the law governing the assigned or subrogated claim (i.e. "the proper law of the right").
[95] See Ch.15, above.
[96] *Republica de Guatemala v Nunez* [1927] 1 K.B. 669; *Stirling's Trustees v Legal & General Assurance Society*, 1957 S.L.T. 73.
[97] See earlier, *Scottish Provident Institution v Cohen* (1888) 16 R. 112; and *Bankhaus H Aufhauser v Scotboard Ltd*, 1973 S.L.T. (Notes) 87.
[98] Most likely to be by creditors of the assignor, who somehow managed to raise money or gain some kind of consideration by assigning or depositing the same right twice.

different laws. Consultation is ongoing with the aim of remedying this gap in provision.[99]

The current approach

17-31 Currently, these points must be dealt with by each Member State according to its own conflict rules. Questions involving competing proprietary rights must be considered as regards: (i) the debtor's liability under the right in question; (ii) the validity of each assignation, as to form and essentials; and (iii) the ranking of competing claims inter se.

In Scotland, the *lex situs* regulates the proprietary rights of the parties, and governs in particular (i) the debtor's liability to pay; and (ii) competitions between assignations valid by their own proper laws; and between voluntary and involuntary assignations and diligences. There are, however, certain qualifications to this rule: in a competition between two or more assignations having the same proper law and derived from the same debtor, or between a voluntary and an involuntary assignation both governed by the same proper law, the parties' rights are governed and regulated by that law.[100] This rule applies only to the determination of the rights of creditors inter se when they hold assignations with the same proper law.[101] However, the rights of creditors inter se holding under assignations with different proper laws are governed by the *lex situs*.[102] Any question of priority between the holders of voluntary and involuntary transfers,[103] such as arising as a result of diligence, also are governed by the *lex situs*.

In practice, questions are solved as follows:

(1) The debtor's liability will be determined by the *lex situs* of the right which is the subject of the assignation(s).

(2) Assuming the right in question is enforceable against the debtor, the following process is applied:

(a) the validity of each assignation, contractual or non-contractual, is determined by its governing law[104];

---

[99] Article 27(2) of the Rome I Regulation requires that the European Commission shall submit by June 17, 2010 a report to the European Parliament, the Council and the European Economic and Social Committee on the question of the *effectiveness of an assignment or subrogation of a claim against third parties*; and *the priority of an assigned or subrogated claim over a right of another person*. At the time of writing, the report is awaited. See, in this connection, Ministry of Justice Discussion Paper, *Rome I: European Commission Review of Article 14: Assignment* (The Stationery Office, 2009). Consultation was restricted to voluntary assignations; the review of art.14 does not embrace the ranking of involuntary assignations inter se (in respect of which reference may require to be made to Regulation 1346/2000), or the ranking between/among involuntary and voluntary assignations.

[100] cf. *North Western Bank v John Poynter Son and MacDonalds* (1894) 22 R. (H.L.) 1, per Lord Watson at 12.

[101] *Scottish Provident Institution v Robinson* (1892) 29 S.L.R. 733; *Dinwoodie's Executor v Carruthers' Executor* (1895) 23 R. 234; *Forbes v Official Receiver in Bankruptcy*, 1924 S.L.T. 522; *Republica de Guatemala v Nunez* [1927] 1 K.B. 669.

[102] *Le Feuvre v Sullivan* (1855) 10 Moo. P.C. 389; *Kelly v Selwyn* [1905] 2 Ch. 117.

[103] *Strachan v McDougle* (1835) 13 S. 954; *Donaldson v Ord* (1855) 17 D. 1053; *Re Maudslay Sons & Field* [1900] 1 Ch. 602; *Re Queensland Mercantile & Agency Co Ex p. Australian Investment Co* [1892] 1 Ch. 219; *F&K Jabbour v Custodian of Israeli Absentee Property* [1954] 1 W.L.R. 139.

[104] See e.g. *Scottish Provident Institution v Cohen* (1888) 16 R. 112.

(b) if there is more than one valid assignation, and each competing assignation has the same proper law, that law will regulate the rights of assignees inter se;

(c) if there is more than one valid assignation, and the competing assignations have different proper laws, or if there is a competition between voluntary and involuntary transfers, such as diligence, priority will be regulated by the *lex situs* of the right.

The proposed approach[105]

The reaction of the UK Government to the European Commission review is **17–32** that the general rule to govern the effectiveness of the assignation against third parties and the priority of assigned claims over the same right should be the law governing the claim assigned. It is thought that this factor being constant, and not liable to change, would promote certainty. However, in this complex area,[106] it is thought that there is a case for the creation of specific exceptions to the general rule. Special provision has been considered for the bulk assignment of debts (debt factoring).[107] In respect of special cases of this type, it has been proposed that the question of the effectiveness of the assignment against third parties and priority of the assigned claims over a right of another person should be governed by the law of the country where the assignor has his habitual residence. Despite the usual concerns with regard to habitual residence, namely, its uncertainty of meaning, and, in this context, the doubts which will arise if the habitual residence of the assignor changes during the crucial period, it is thought to be apt to deal with the bulk assignment case, in respect of which it would be awkward for the assignee (the financier) to ascertain the applicable law of each and every debt. A problem would arise, however, should there be a competition between or among claims, one or some of which fall to be regulated by the general rule, and others by the special rule; for such cases there would require to be a pre-eminent, tie-breaking rule.

BILLS OF EXCHANGE AND NEGOTIABLE INSTRUMENTS[108]

Bills of Exchange

Conflict rules in relation to bills of exchange were laid down early, by **17–33** statute, in terms of the Bills of Exchange Act 1882.[109] There are excluded from the Rome I Regulation[110]:

---

[105] See generally Ministry of Justice Discussion Paper, *Rome I: European Commission Review of Article 14: Assignment*, 2009; and for background, Conversion of the Rome Convention of 1980 on the Law Applicable to Contractual Obligations into a Community Instrument and its Modernisation COM(2002) 654 final, paras 3.2.13, 3.2.14.

[106] Epitomised by *Raiffeisen Zentralbank Osterreich AG v Five Star General Trading LLC (The Mount I)* [2000] 2 Lloyd's Rep. 684; [2001] 1 Lloyd's Rep. 597.

[107] And also for assignments by a natural person acting outside the course of his business or profession. Other areas considered in the Ministry of Justice Discussion Paper for special treatment are assignments of judgment debts; intellectual property rights; shares in companies; transferable securities; letters of credit; insurance policies; and claims in tort or delict.

[108] For specialised treatment, see Charles Proctor, *International Payment Obligations: A Legal Perspective* (London: Butterworths, 1997), Chs 27 (negotiable instruments) and 28 (letters of credit).

[109] The meaning of bills of exchange is defined in ss.3, 4.

[110] And also from Rome II Regulation, in terms of art.1.2(c).

"Obligations arising under bills of exchange, cheques and promissory notes and other negotiable instruments to the extent that the obligations under such other negotiable instruments arise out of their negotiable character."[111]

The wording of the exclusion is identical to that in art.1.2(c) of the Rome I Convention, and so by the principle of continuity of interpretation, it can be taken that, as under the Convention, so too under the Regulation the qualifying phrase "to the extent that . . . negotiable character" applies only to "other negotiable instruments". Bills of exchange, cheques and promissory notes[112] are excluded from the Rome I Regulation without reservation.[113] A commercial letter of credit is not a negotiable instrument and is not subject to exclusion as above.[114]

Conflict rules concerning bills of exchange are contained in the 1882 Act s.72[115] the general effect of which as regards foreign bills is to make the validity of each of the interdependent contracts depend upon its own law and not on the law of the bill. This "several laws" approach attracts widespread international agreement, but on the other hand, the nature and purpose of bills combine to produce conflict situations.[116] Section 72 applies well-established conflict of laws rules to bills[117] as follows:

    (1) the formal validity of a bill and of each indorsement is governed by the law of the place where it is made[118] but it will be sufficient for enforcement of payment in this country that the law of the UK is

---

[111] See art.1.2(d).

[112] *Zebrarise Ltd v De Nieffe* [2005] 1 Lloyd's Rep. 154.

[113] Giuliano and Lagarde, p.11.

[114] Conflict cases on letters of credit include the following: *Offshore International SA v Banco Central SA* [1976] 3 All E.R. 749 (Elizabeth B. Crawford, "Oil on Troubled Waters: proper law of letter of credit" (1977) 22 J.L.S. 434); *Power Curber International Ltd v National Bank of Kuwait SAK* [1981] 3 All E.R. 607; *United City Merchants (Investments) Ltd v Royal Bank of Canada (The American Accord)* [1983] 1 A.C. 168 HL; *Bank of Baroda v Vysya Bank* [1994] 2 Lloyd's Rep. 87 (with reference to art.4.2 of the Rome Convention, characteristic performance was held to be that of the confirming bank). See also *Marconi Communications International Ltd v PT Pan Indonesia Bank Ltd* [2005] 2 All E.R. (Comm) 325.

[115] Cases after the Act: *Re Marseilles Extension Railway and Land Co* (1885) L.R. 30 Ch. D. 598; *Re Commercial Bank of South Australia* (1887) L.R. 36 Ch. D. 522; *Bank of Montreal v Exhibit and Trading Co Ltd* (1906) 22 T.L.R. 722; *Guaranty Trust Co of New York v Hannay & Co* [1918] 1 K.B. 43; [1918] 2 K.B. 623; *Alcock v Smith* [1892] 1 Ch. 238; *Embiricos v Anglo Austrian Bank* [1904] 2 K.B. 870; [1905] 1 K.B. 677; *F Koechlin et Cie v Kestenbaum Bros* [1927] 1 K.B. 889; *Moulis v Owen* [1907] 1 K.B. 746; *Re Francke & Rasch* [1918] 1 Ch. 470; *Koch v Dicks* [1933] 1 K.B. 307; *Bank Polski v KJ Mulder & Co* [1941] 2 K.B. 266; [1942] 1 K.B. 497; *Cornelius v Banque Franco-Serbe* [1942] 1 K.B. 29; [1942] 1 K.B. 29; *Syndic in Bankruptcy of Khoury v Khayat* [1943] A.C. 507.

[116] *Dicey, Morris and Collins on the Conflict of Laws*, 14th edn, 2006, para.33–335.

[117] But only where there is a conflict: *Karafarin Bank v Mansoury-Dara* [2009] EWHC 3265 (Comm); [2010] 1 Lloyd's Rep. 236.

[118] A contract is made (s.21) when the instrument is delivered in order to give effect to the contract: delivery means transfer of possession, actual or constructive (*Dicey, Morris and Collins on the Conflict of Laws*, 14th edn, 2006, para.33–338). The Act has put the *lex loci contractus* in a dominant position in matters of form and interpretation and Dicey, Morris and Collins recommend that "gaps" in the Act be filled by ascribing to this law regulation of capacity and everything pertaining to the formation of the contract.

complied with. Lack of a stamp in accordance with the law of the place of issue does not make a bill invalid here;

(2) essential validity is governed by the law of the place where the bill and indorsements are made. The word used in the Act is "interpretation" of the drawing, indorsement, acceptance or acceptance supra protest of a bill[119] but it may be thought[120] that this term relates not merely to construction but to all questions of essential validity[121];

(3) procedure as to protest on dishonour, etc. is governed by the law of the place where the act is done[122];

(4) the due date is determined by the law of the place where the bill is payable.[123]

The 1882 Act does not provide conflict rules to govern all conflict questions which might arise in relation to a bill, and leaves aside, in particular, capacity, and the proprietary as opposed to the contractual aspects.[124] In their residual contractual aspect, and by dint of art.1.2(d) of the Rome I Regulation, they will be governed by common law contractual rules, and not by the Regulation.

Negotiable Instruments

The conflict rules on this subject are based on the conflict rules relating both **17–34** to the law of contract and the law of property. A negotiable instrument is an order involving a contract to pay money to a person to be named or to his order to be signified by indorsement of the document. No intimation to the debtor is required. A document recognised as being a negotiable instrument has certain privileges which do not apply to documents not recognised as such, in that a holder acquiring a document not having this characteristic does not necessarily acquire a good title even if he acquires it in good faith and for value.

The general view is that the question whether or not a particular document is to be regarded as a negotiable instrument is to be determined by the law of the place where its negotiation takes place, which will almost invariably be the *lex fori*.[125] It is suggested that for a document to be regarded as a negotiable instrument, the true test is that it must be recognised as such by the *lex fori* but possibly it should also have that quality according to the law under which it was created.[126]

---

[119] Provided that where an inland bill is indorsed in a foreign country the indorsement as regards the payer shall be interpreted according to the law of the United Kingdom (s.72(2)).

[120] Though see Anton with Beaumont, *Private International Law*, 2nd edn, 1990, p.390; and the views of Proctor to the effect that contractual questions which cannot be brought within the terms of the Act must be referred to the common law conflict rules of contract.

[121] *Alcock v Smith* [1892] 1 Ch. 238; *Embiricos v Anglo Austrian Bank* [1904] 2 K.B. 870; *F Koechlin et Cie v Kestenbaum Bros* [1927] 1 K.B. 889.

[122] See s.72(3).

[123] See s.72(5).

[124] *Dicey, Morris and Collins on the Conflict of Laws*, 14th edn, 2006, para.33–337; Proctor, *International Payment Obligations*, 1997, p.464.

[125] *Dicey, Morris and Collins on the Conflict of Laws*, 14th edn, 2006, para.33–326. It is considered that negotiability will be determined by the place of negotiation which will be the place of situation of instrument at time of delivery; cf. Anton, *Private International Law*, 1st edn, 1967, p.419 and 2nd edn, 1990, pp.387, 388. Giuliano and Lagarde at p.11 favoured the application of the conflict rules of the forum—"obiter", because characterisation as negotiable was not an issue governed by the Rome I Convention, and nor by the Rome I Regulation.

[126] *Goodwin v Robarts* (1876) L.R. 1 App. Cas. 476; *Picker v London and County Banking Co Ltd* (1887) L.R. 18 Q.B.D. 515; *London Joint Stock Bank v Simmons* [1892] A.C. 201.

Shares and other securities[127]

17-35   Questions of choice of law may arise in relation to (a) the effect of transfers as regards the issuing company; (b) the effect of transfers as between the parties themselves (i.e. issuer and investor); and (c) the situation of shares for the purposes of inheritance tax, stamp duties, income tax and other similar matters.

Choice of law rules in relation to shares and other securities traditionally were based upon the assumption of a direct relationship between the issuer and the investor, evidenced, in the case of registered securities, by registration of the investor's name in the books of the issuer, and in the case of bearer securities, by physical possession by the investor of a certificate. The following rules apply to directly-held securities[128]: normally the *situs* of shares of a company is the place where the company is registered and the share register is kept.[129] In order to divest the transferor and give the transferee a good title which will be effective as a real right against third parties, it is essential to comply with the *lex situs*. The rights of the parties merely as between themselves (that is contractual rights) are regulated by the law of the place where the transfer takes place which is usually the proper law of the transfer and may be different from the *lex situs* of the shares.

Technological developments, and market demands have led to the development of a more efficient holding pattern, namely, one which permits holding via an intermediary, and which allows for the transfer of interests by means of electronic book-entry to securities accounts. The traditional, materialised system in many instances has been replaced by a dematerialised (electronic), intermediated holding system. The choice of law rule traditionally applied to govern the proprietary aspects of a transfer of shares or other securities (namely, the law of the *situs* of those shares or other right) is not easily applied to the transfer of "intermediated securities". To meet the demands of the global financial market for certainty and predictability of securities transactions, there has been produced the 2006 Hague Convention on the Law Applicable to Certain Rights in respect of Securities Held with an Intermediary (not yet in force). The purpose of the Convention is to harmonise rules of choice of law concerning rights in respect of intermediated securities. The Convention applies in all cases where securities are held with an intermediary (i.e. where securities are credited to a securities account), but it has no application to directly held securities, which continue to be governed by pre-existing, national choice of law rules. The primary rule of choice of law is contained in art.4 of the Convention, and gives effect to an express agreement on governing law between an account holder and its immediate intermediary, subject

---

[127] See Carruthers, *Transfer of Property in the Conflict of Laws*, 2005, Ch.7.

[128] *Williams v Colonial Bank* (1888) L.R. 38 Ch.D. 388 (right to hold share certificates distinguished from substantive rights in shares); *Colonial Bank v Cady* (1890) L.R. 15 App. Cas. 267; *Brassard v Smith* [1925] A.C. 371; *Baelz v Public Trustee* [1926] Ch. 863; *London and South American Investment Trust Ltd v British Tobacco Co (Australia) Ltd* [1927] 1 Ch. 107; *Erie Beach Co Ltd v Att Gen of Ontario* [1930] A.C. 161; *R. v Williams* [1942] A.C. 541; *Re Middleton's Settlement* [1947] Ch. 583; *Re Fry (Deceased)* [1946] Ch. 312; *Macmillan Inc v Bishopsgate Investment Trust Plc (No.3)* [1996] 1 W.L.R. 387. See also *International Credit and Investment Co (Overseas) Ltd v Adham* [1994] 1 B.C.L.C. 66. But consider Stevens, "The Law Applicable to Priority in Shares" (1996) 112 L.Q.R. 198.

[129] *Macmillan Inc v Bishopsgate Investment Trust Plc (No.3)* [1996] 1 W.L.R. 387. See further, *Dicey, Morris and Collins on the Conflict of Laws*, 14th edn, 2006, para.22–044.

however to the requirement that the law chosen will apply only if the relevant intermediary has, at the time of the agreement, a qualifying office in the state the law of which has been chosen. If the applicable law is not determined under art.4, art.5 contains a series of "fall-back" rules. Article 6 deliberately severs any link with traditional *situs* thinking, insofar as it is expressly stated that in determining the applicable law under the Convention no account should be taken, inter alia, of the place where the issuer is incorporated, the place where securities certificates are located, or the place where a securities register is located or maintained.

Intellectual property rights

Though this heading encompasses a number of different types of right, **17–36** including copyright, patents, and trademarks,[130] each appears to be treated in broadly the same way, in that the *situs* is taken to be the country in which they may be effectively transferred, i.e. the legal system of their creation.[131] Intellectual property rights have a definite connection with a particular place,[132] and if created in the UK are effective only in the UK unless they receive effect in foreign countries under the conflict rules there applicable.

The goodwill of a business is deemed to be situated in the legal system of the situation of the asset to which the goodwill is attached.[133]

Governmental seizure of property

The territoriality principle applies, but this in turn may have private law **17–37** repercussions outside the territory. The topic is treated at paras 3–04 and 3–05, above.

II. UNIVERSAL TRANSFERS OF PROPERTY: INSOLVENCY[134]

Theories

In the development of this subject, favour has been shown to one or other of **17–38** two main theories or approaches, which will be outlined before attention is turned to recent international legislative development.

---

[130] Infringement thereof being subject to the applicable law rules contained in art.8 of the Rome II Regulation.
[131] See James J. Fawcett and Paul Torremans, *Intellectual Property and Private International Law* (Oxford: Oxford University Press, 1998), p.490.
[132] *Campbell Connolly & Co v Noble* [1963] 1 W.L.R. 252. But see jurisdiction of the English courts,with regard to alleged breach of a foreign statutory intellectual property right, *Pearce v Ove Arup Partnership Ltd* [1997] 3 All E.R. 31; *Tyburn Productions Ltd v Conan Doyle* [1990] 3 W.L.R. 167; and *Coin Controls Ltd v Suzo International (UK) Ltd* [1997] 3 All E.R. 45. But see Collier, *All E.R. Annual Review 1997*, pp.78–80.
[133] *Inland Revenue Commissioners v Muller & Co's Margarines Ltd* [1901] A.C. 217, per Lord Macnaghten at 224. Contrast dissenting judgment of Lord Halsbury L.C. at 240. Cf. *Reuter v Mulhens (No.2)* [1954] Ch. 50 at 95, 96.
[134] For a full treatment of this subject see Ian F. Fletcher, *Insolvency in Private International Law: national and international approaches*, 2nd edn (Oxford: Oxford University Press, 2005), *Supplement* (2007).

Unity of bankruptcy

17–39   According to this theory, a bankruptcy should be one and indivisible, and when a person is sequestrated or grants a trust deed for his creditors, the process should attach and convey to the trustee in bankruptcy all property, wherever situated, belonging to the bankrupt with the result that only one set of bankruptcy proceedings should be permissible. A separate bankruptcy in each country should not be permissible.

At common law, the Scots courts favoured the unity theory[135] and therefore would not grant a sequestration if the bankrupt already had been sequestrated in another country, unless perhaps for some reason the foreign bankruptcy was no longer effective or was of strictly limited effect.

Separate bankruptcies

17–40   This theory is the opposite of the unity theory. By it, the bankrupt's assets should be distributed separately in each jurisdiction for the benefit of creditors in that jurisdiction; hence it should be permissible to have separate bankrupt-cies.[136] This is the "territoriality" approach, favoured at common law in England.[137] The English courts declined to allow the existence of concurrent proceedings, or the factor of priority of date to be decisive in the question whether there should be a stay of English bankruptcy proceedings.[138]

Universality of bankruptcy

17–41   Under this principle, bankruptcy proceedings should receive extraterritorial effect, and therefore, unless proceedings clearly confer a territorially limited title on the trustee, they should be regarded as passing to the trustee all estate, moveable and immoveable, in the country where the bankruptcy was granted and all moveable estate abroad. Immoveable estate abroad is not included at common law. At common law, both the Scots and English[139] systems accepted this theory, which is the logical result of the unity theory. "Unity" and "universality" therefore mean, as it has been well put, "one set of proceedings (unity) effective in every jurisdiction (universality)".[140]

---

[135] See *Goetze v Aders and Co* (1874) 2 R. 100; *Bank of Scotland v Youde* (1908) 15 S.L.T. 847. See also *Home's Trustee v Home's Trustees*, 1926 S.L.T. 214.

[136] *Re Artola Hermanos Ex. p Chale* (1890) L.R. 24 Q.B.D. 640; see more recently *Re Thulin* [1995] 1 W.L.R. 165 (bankruptcy proceedings in England and Sweden).

[137] *Re Artola Hermanos Ex. p Chale* (1890) L.R. 24 Q.B.D. 640; *Felixstowe Dock & Railway Co v United States Lines Inc* [1988] 2 All E.R. 77; *Re Thulin* [1995] 1 W.L.R. 165. Smart, "Forum Non Conveniens in Bankruptcy Proceedings" [1989] J.B.L. 126.

[138] *Cheshire and North's Private International Law*, 12th edn, 1992, p.907.

[139] i.e. in England the status and claims of a foreign trustee would be accepted provided that there were no English proceedings.

[140] Donna McKenzie-Skene, "The EC Convention on Insolvency Proceedings" (1996) 4(3) E.R.P.L. 181.

EU DEVELOPMENTS: INSOLVENCY REGULATION[141]

Regulation 44/2001

Bankruptcy and similar proceedings in relation to insolvent companies do **17–42** not fall within the scope of Regulation 44/2001.[142] However, a company winding up can occur when a company is solvent, as well as when insolvent, and in the former case, Regulation 44/2001 will apply, directing the matter by way of the exclusive jurisdiction provision of art.22.2 to the one court which is defined for constitutional purposes as the "seat" of the company.[143] Company winding-up is excluded from the intra-UK allocation effected by the Civil Jurisdiction and Judgments Acts 1982 and 1991 Sch.4,[144] and must be governed by the rules contained in the Insolvency Act 1986.

Regulation 1346/2000

The Council of Europe produced in 1990 a Convention on Certain **17–43** International Aspects of Bankruptcy (the Istanbul Convention), which was not signed by the UK, perhaps in anticipation of EU intervention in this area. The Convention was overtaken by Regulation 1346/2000 on Insolvency Proceedings, which came into force on May 31, 2002.[145] The Regulation affects a number of areas pertaining to insolvency proceedings including jurisdiction and applicable law. It is directly applicable in all EU Member States except Denmark,[146] with effect from that date.[147]

The aim of the Insolvency Regulation is to put in place a framework for the administration of cross-border insolvencies within the EU, applicable to the insolvency of natural and legal persons. In the manner of many EU instruments of recent years in the conflict of laws, the scheme of the Regulation is to provide at the outset rules on jurisdiction, justifying rules of recognition and enforcement. However, the Regulation contains also provisions as to applicable law, and co-operation where there is more than one set of bankruptcy proceedings.

The Regulation is a compromise between the unity and territoriality approaches, to the effect that insolvency proceedings may be opened in more

---

[141] See Gabriel Moss, Ian Fletcher and Stuart Isaacs, *The EC Regulation on Insolvency Proceedings: A Commentary and Annotated Guide*, 2nd edn (Oxford: Oxford University Press, 2009).

[142] See art.1.2(b). See *SCT Industri AB (In Liquidation) v Alpenblume AB* (C-111/08) [2009] I.L.Pr. 43; *Byers v Yacht Bull Corp* [2010] EWHC 133 (Ch); and *German Graphics Graphische Maschinen GmbH v van der Schee* (C-292/08) [2010] I.L.Pr. 1. This repeats the position under the 1968 Brussels Convention. See earlier cases such as *Gourdain v Nadler* [1979] E.C.R. 733 at [4]. Consider *Thoars' Judicial Factor v Ramlort Ltd*, 1998 G.W.D. 29-1504; see note by Elizabeth B. Crawford, 1999 J.R. 203.

[143] Civil Jurisdiction and Judgments Acts 1982 and 1991 s.43, and Regulation 44/2001 art.60.

[144] See now Civil Jurisdiction and Judgments Order 2001 (SI 2001/3929).

[145] See McKenzie-Skene, "The EC Convention on Insolvency Proceedings" (1996) 4(3) E.R.P.L. 181, 182, 183, wherein will be found details of the predecessor Convention.

[146] See recital (33).

[147] In *Re Staubitz-Schreiber* (C-104) [2006] I.L.Pr. 30, the ECJ held that the Insolvency Regulation was applicable if no judgment opening insolvency proceedings had been delivered before the Regulation's entry into force on May 31, 2002, even if the request to open proceedings was lodged prior to that date. On the other hand, in *SCT Industri AB (In Liquidation) v Alpenblume AB* (C-111/08) [2009] I.L.Pr. 43, the Insolvency Regulation was held not to apply since the insolvency proceedings had been opened before its entry into force.

than one Member State, but only one set of proceedings may have extraterritorial effect. Any other proceedings will have only intraterritorial effect.

The Regulation applies to, "collective insolvency proceedings which entail the partial or total divestment of a debtor and the appointment of a liquidator".[148] For the purposes of the UK, this comprises winding up by or subject to the supervision of the court; creditors' voluntary winding up with confirmation by the court; administration; voluntary arrangements under insolvency legislation; and bankruptcy or sequestration.[149] Notably, the Regulation does not apply to receivership since that essentially is an action at the instance of one creditor, and is not a collective procedure. Moreover, the Regulation shall not apply to insolvency proceedings concerning insurance undertakings, credit institutions, investment undertakings[150] which provide services involving the holding of funds or securities for third parties, or to collective investment undertakings.[151]

Jurisdiction rules under Regulation 1346/2000

Main proceedings (article 3)

17–44   The Regulation applies to any debtor having the centre of his main interests in a Member State.[152] It is obvious that the connecting factor of "centre of a debtor's main interests" is the crux of the matter; the centre of main interests must first be identified, and found to be within the EU (except Denmark) before the Regulation applies.[153] The centre of main interests has an autonomous meaning, and must therefore be interpreted in a uniform way. Interpretation of "centre of a debtor's main interests" is central to the operation of the Regulation, and it can be expected that Member State variations in construction will be reduced in time as a result of the interpretative function of the CJEU.

Article 3.1 provides that the courts of the Member State within the territory of which the centre of a debtor's main interests (henceforth "COMI") is situated shall have jurisdiction to open[154] insolvency proceedings (the "main

---

[148] See art.1.1.
[149] See Annex A.
[150] In *Re Phoenix Kapitaldienst GmbH* [2008] B.P.I.R. 1082, where the parties accepted that as the proceedings concerned investment undertakings, Regulation 1346/2000 did not apply, the administrator of a German company in administration successfully sought from an English court an order recognising his appointment and seeking the right to exercise the powers conferred upon insolvency practitioners by the Insolvency Act 1986. The English court was clear that foreign insolvency office holders should be given such assistance as would be open to the equivalent English insolvency practitioner, given that there was a sufficient connection between the UK and the defendants; such an outcome would avoid the expense and delay of initiating parallel proceedings in England. A similar example of pragmatic co-operation is seen in *Re HIH Casualty & General Insurance Ltd* [2008] 1 W.L.R. 852.
[151] See art.1.2.
[152] See *Skjevesland v Geveran Trading Co Ltd (No.4)* [2003] B.P.I.R. 924; *Re BRAC Rent-A-Car International Inc* [2003] EWHC 128; [2003] 1 W.L.R. 1421; *Re Salvage Association* [2003] EWHC 1028; *Re Daisytek-ISA Ltd* [2004] B.P.I.R. 30; *Re Eurofood IFSC Ltd* (C-341/04) [2006] Ch. 508; *France v Klempka* [2006] B.C.C. 841 Cour de Cassation (France); *Hans Brochier Holdings Ltd v Exner* [2006] EWHC 2594 (Ch); *Re BenQ Mobile Holding BV (Amsterdam)* [2008] B.C.C. 489.
[153] Preamble, recital (14). Cf. *Official Receiver v Mitterfellner* [2009] B.P.I.R. 1075.
[154] See *Re Eurofood IFSC Ltd* [2006] Ch. 508.

proceedings").[155] This means that the Regulation may apply to a company incorporated outside the EU as long as the COMI is situated within the EU.[156]

Determination of the COMI will necessitate a detailed factual inquiry.[157] There is no conclusive definition of this important connecting factor but, with regard to companies and legal persons, art.3.1 provides that the place of the registered office shall be presumed to be the centre of main interests, in the absence of proof to the contrary. Where a debtor company is a subsidiary company whose registered office and that of its parent company are situated in different Member States, the presumption that the COMI of the subsidiary is situated in the Member State in which its registered office is situated can be rebutted only if factors, both objective and ascertainable by third parties, enable it to be established that the actuality is different from that which location at that registered office is deemed to reflect.[158] If a party seeks to establish that a company or legal person has its COMI at a place other than its registered office, then the court will examine the "totality of evidence",[159] including the location of the company's bank account, the place of preparation of financial statements, and the place of employment of the majority of employees.[160]

There is no presumption in relation to individuals, but recital (13) indicates that the COMI should correspond to the place where the debtor conducts the administration of his interests on a regular basis, being therefore ascertainable by third parties (i.e. potential creditors).[161]

Although a debtor reasonably may be held to have interests in one, or more than one, Member State(s), the Regulation does not apply unless one of these business bases can be said to be the "centre" of his interests. The criterion assumes that a debtor has only one centre of main business interests,[162] but this might not always be the case.

---

[155] To be interpreted widely, as conferring upon the court in which the main proceedings are opened jurisdiction to hear and determine actions which derive directly from those proceedings and are closely connected to them: *Seagon v Decko Marty Belgium NV* (C-339/07) [2009] I.L.Pr. 25 (and subsequently *Re Jurisdiction to Set Aside a Transaction on Grounds of Insolvency* [2010] I.L.Pr. 6). In *Seagon*, the German court was thereby enabled to set aside a transaction on the grounds of insolvency of the debtor against a defendant having its statutory seat in Belgium.

[156] See recital (14). Where the COMI is outside the EU, the Insolvency Regulation has no application: *HSBC Plc, Petitioner*, 2010 S.L.T. 281.

[157] e.g. *Re Ci4Net.com.Inc* [2004] EWHC 1941 (Ch).

[158] *Re Eurofood IFSC Ltd* [2006] Ch. 508. Contrast *MPOTEC GmbH* [2006] B.C.C. 681 *Tribunal de Grande Instance* (Nanterre); and *Re Energotech Sarl* [2007] B.C.C. 123 *Tribunal de Grande Instance* (France) (relevant factors included the location of board meetings and of creditors, and locus of dealings with clients). As to a global group of companies, see *Bank of America NA v Minister for Productive Industries* [2008] I.L.Pr. 25 *Consiglio di Stato* (Italy); *Re Nortel Networks SA* [2009] EWHC 1482 (Ch); and *Re Lennox Holdings Plc* [2009] B.C.C. 155.

[159] *Hans Brochier Holdings Ltd v Exner* [2006] EWHC 2594 (Ch).

[160] See, e.g. *Re Daisytek-ISA Ltd* [2004] B.P.I.R. 30, which concerned a petition for administration orders to be made in an English court in respect of the English holding company of a pan-European group of companies, many of the members of which had registered offices in France and Germany. The English court had to perform a balancing exercise, assessing the size and importance of interests administered in England and elsewhere, respectively. The court held that there was sufficient evidence to rebut the presumption that the place of the registered office was the COMI, with the result that the English forum was competent. A large majority of potential creditors by value was aware that many important functions of the group companies were carried out in England.

[161] e.g. *X v Fortis Bank (Nederland) NV* [2004] I.L.Pr. 37 Hoge Raad (NL).

[162] G. Maher and B. Rodger, "Jurisdiction in Insolvency Proceedings" (2003) 48 J.L.S.S. 26, 30.

There is no temporal element in the COMI criterion, which may generate problems given that in business life one would expect to find that the centre of main interests of an individual or company might change over time. This was recognised in *Shierson v Vlieland-Boddy*,[163] in which the English court took account of the fact that the debtor's centre of main interests had moved from England to Spain. The precise question whether the relevant date for identifying the centre is that of the request to open proceedings, was referred to the ECJ by the Bundesgerichtshof in *Re Opening of Insolvency Proceedings*.[164] In *Staubitz-Schreiber*,[165] the ECJ held that art.3.1 must be interpreted as meaning that the court of the Member State within the territory of which the centre of the debtor's main interests is situated at the time when the request is lodged to open insolvency proceedings retains jurisdiction to open those proceedings if the debtor moves the centre of his main interest to the territory of another Member State after the request has been lodged, but before the proceedings are opened.

Averments as to jurisdiction must acknowledge the primacy of the Regulation, and in a qualifying case, at the outset must aver in an insolvency petition that the COMI is in the forum petitioned.

Allocation of jurisdiction within the UK

17–45   It is said that territorial jurisdiction within a Member State must be established by the national law of the Member State concerned (recital (15)) (i.e. if the centre of the debtor's main interests is in the UK, "UK national law" must determine the further allocation). However, the effect of this is unclear in the UK or any other multi-legal system context, for there is no set of rules equivalent to the Civil Jurisdiction and Judgments Act 1982 Sch.4 to serve to allocate jurisdiction among the courts of the constituent units of the UK. It has been suggested[166] that, assuming it can be established that the COMI is in the UK, the allocation thereafter will be done according to the pre-existing (i.e. non-Regulation) domestic insolvency rules (*q.v.*).

Secondary proceedings

17–46   To protect the diversity of interests, the Regulation allows "secondary proceedings" to be opened in parallel with the main proceedings. Jurisdiction in respect of secondary proceedings is conferred upon the legal system of a Member State in which the debtor has an "establishment".[167] More than one set of secondary proceedings may take place concurrently. Secondary insolvency proceedings, as well as protecting local interests, serve a useful purpose in cases of complex estates which are difficult to administer as a unit, or where

---

[163] [2004] EWHC 2752; [2005] B.C.C. 416. Followed in *Cross Construction Sussex Ltd v Tseliki* [2006] EWHC 1056 (Ch); and *Official Receiver v Eichler* [2007] B.P.I.R 1636.
[164] *Re Opening of Insolvency Proceedings* (IX ZB 418/02) [2005] I.L.Pr. 4 Bundesgerichtshof (Germany). See *Re Staubitz-Schreiber* (C-104) [2006] I.L.Pr. 30.
[165] *Re Staubitz-Schreiber* (C-104) [2006] I.L.Pr. 30.
[166] Maher and Rodger, "Jurisdiction in Insolvency Proceedings" (2003) 48 J.L.S.S. 26, 30.
[167] Article 2(h): an "establishment" shall mean any place of operations where the debtor carries out a non-transitory economic activity with human means and goods (i.e. the mere presence of assets in a Member State will not confer jurisdiction). There must be an element of permanence to the establishment, but the existence of a branch office is not necessary.

there is wide variation in the laws of the jurisdictions in which the debtor has assets. The liquidator in the main proceedings may request the opening of secondary proceedings if it seems to him that efficient administration of the estate so requires.[168]

Effect of main and secondary proceedings

The main proceedings have extraterritorial effect, encompassing all of the **17–47** debtor's assets. Article 3.1, therefore, can be seen to enshrine the principle of universality.

The effect of secondary proceedings is limited to assets situated within the state in which they are opened (i.e. intraterritorial effect only).

Given the different consequences attaching to main and secondary proceedings, respectively, it is important for a court to make clear the capacity in which it is acting.

Relationship between main and secondary proceedings

There must be co-operation between the liquidator in the main proceedings **17–48** and the liquidator(s) in the secondary proceedings (art.31).[169] A creditor may lodge his claim both in the main proceedings and in any secondary proceedings (art.32). The main liquidator can request that the secondary proceedings be stayed (art.33). The stay will be refused only if it is manifestly of no interest to the creditors in the main proceedings. In the event of a stay, the main liquidator must guarantee the interests of creditors in the secondary proceedings. Any surplus assets in the state of secondary proceedings following payment of claims in that state must be remitted to the main liquidator (art.35).

Choice of law rules under Regulation 1346/2000 (articles 4 and 28)

The Regulation harmonises conflict rules, not substantive rules. Article 4 **17–49** directs that the applicable law shall be the law of the state in which the proceedings (main[170] or secondary,[171] respectively) are opened (the *lex concursus*, i.e. the *lex fori*). In other words, the opening, conduct and closure of the proceedings [172] will be conducted according to the law of the forum, being procedural in nature. This is the same as the pre-existing rule of Scots law.

More importantly, under art.4.2 the *lex concursus* also determines many essential matters,[173] including the ascertainment of assets and liabilities[174]; the lodging and verification of claims; the ranking of claims; distribution of

---

[168] Preamble, recital (19).

[169] Assistance from the courts of other Member States also may require to be sought: *Re Nortel Networks SA* [2009] I.L.Pr. 42.

[170] See art.4. *Also MG Probud Gdynia sp z oo* (C-444/07) [2010] B.C.C. 453.

[171] See art.28.

[172] See recital (23).

[173] Though see indirect application in an English court of Belgian insolvency rules on the basis of "justice and convenience": *Re MG Rover Beluxl SA/NV (In Administration)* [2006] EWHC 1296.

[174] See *German Graphics Graphische Maschinen GmbH v van der Schee* (C-292/08) [2010] I.L.Pr. 1.

proceedings; the debtor's and liquidator's powers; the effects of the insolvency proceedings on contracts to which the debtor is a party and on proceedings brought by individual creditors[175]; the conditions for, and effects of, closure of insolvency proceedings (in particular by composition); and creditors' rights after closure.

Articles 5–15

17–50   Importantly, account must be taken of arts 5–15 which provide, by way of exception to arts 4 and 28, that certain other laws shall take precedence over the *lex concursus*. For example, the effect of insolvency proceedings on a contract conferring the right to acquire or make use of immoveable property shall be governed solely by the law of the state in which that property is situated[176]; and their effect upon employment contracts shall be governed solely by the law of the state applicable to the contract of employment.[177]

It is obvious that the admission of a claim, if contractual, depends upon the validity of the claim according to its own (contractual) governing law, each EU forum applying to this question the relevant provisions, if applicable, of the Rome I Regulation.

More complex is art.7 (the opening of insolvency proceedings against the purchaser of an asset shall not affect the seller's rights based on a reservation of title where at the time of opening proceedings the asset is situated within the territory of a Member State other than the state of opening proceedings). This rule gives precedence, therefore, to the *lex situs*, where it differs from the *lex concursus*.[178] Similarly, in art.5 (third parties' rights *in rem*), the opening of insolvency proceedings shall not affect the rights *in rem* of creditors or third parties in respect of assets (of all types) belonging to the debtor which are situated at that date within the territory of another Member State.

Therefore arts 5–15[179] represent substantial, albeit defensible, derogations from the basic *lex concursus* rule.

Recognition rules under Regulation 1346/2000 (articles 16–26)

17–51   The principle in art.16 is that any judgment opening[180] insolvency proceedings handed down by a court of a Member State having jurisdiction under art.3 shall be recognised in all the other Member States without those other Member States being able to review the jurisdiction of the court of the "opening State".[181] Recognition of proceedings, however, shall not preclude the opening

---

[175] *Syska v Vivendi Universal SA* [2009] EWCA Civ 677.

[176] See art.8 and recital (25).

[177] See art.10 and recital (28).

[178] Contrast *German Graphics Graphische Maschinen GmbH v van der Schee* (C-292/08) [2010] I.L.Pr. 1, in which German Graphics' assets (over which a reservation of title existed) were situated at the time of opening of insolvency proceedings in the Netherlands, the Member State in which those proceedings had been opened.

[179] *Syska v Vivendi Universal SA* [2009] EWCA Civ 677.

[180] It was held by the ECJ in *Re Eurofood IFSC Ltd* [2006] Ch. 508 that the appointment of a provisional liquidator, involving the divestment of the debtor of his powers of management over his assets, amounted to the "opening" of insolvency proceedings.

[181] *Re Eurofood IFSC Ltd* [2006] Ch. 508. Any challenge to jurisdiction must be made to the court in which it is sought to open proceedings: *France v Klempka (Administrator of ISA Daisytek SAS)* [2006] B.C.C. 841. Also *MG Probud Gdynia sp z oo* (C-444/07) [2010] B.C.C. 453.

in another Member State of secondary proceedings.[182] Article 25 lays down the principle of mutual recognition of judgments[183] concerning the course and closure of insolvency proceedings. Grounds for non-recognition are minimal. In terms of art.26, a state may refuse to recognise the opening of insolvency proceedings, or a judgment from such proceedings, only if it is manifestly contrary to its own public policy.[184]

One notable exception to the "revenue law exception"[185] (that revenue collection is local and cannot be enforced extraterritorially), arising as a result of the promotion of equal treatment of creditors, is the recognition of the entitlement of tax authorities (and social security authorities) domiciled, habitually resident or having a registered office in a Member State other than the state of the opening of proceedings, to lodge claims in writing in any proceedings (art.39).

In terms of art.40, when insolvency proceedings are opened in a Member State, there is a duty upon the court of that state having jurisdiction, or the liquidator appointed by it, immediately to inform known creditors having their habitual residence, domicile, or registered office in other Member States, of the opening of such proceedings. This seems hardly capable of being satisfied. Not only in a complex case are assets and creditors, known and unknown, likely to be found in more than one Member State so that provisions such as art.40 seem unrealistic of attainment even within Europe, but also it is likely that assets and/or creditors will exist outside Europe, so that there will be an uneasy co-existence between the EU regulated area and the pre-existing national rules.

It is plain from the exceptions to be found in the Regulation that the drafting of a harmonised EU approach to the regulation of cross-(EU)-border insolvencies, has proved more difficult than harmonisation drafting in other areas.

IMPACT OF EU INSOLVENCY REGULATION ON PRE-EXISTING NATIONAL LAW

The Regulation applies only to collective insolvency proceedings opened after **17–52** May 31, 2002, but since that date, whenever the centre of the debtor's main interests is located within the UK, proceedings must be regulated by the Regulation, with attendant consequences. Proceedings opened prior to May 31, 2002 were unaffected, and were governed by the residual provisions of Scots domestic law.

As has been explained, the key to understanding the operation of the Regulation is as follows: if it can be said that the centre of a debtor's main interests lies within a Member State, collective insolvency proceedings in respect of the debtor must be governed by the Regulation (even where in a multi-legal system state such as the UK, allocation within that state, e.g. as between Scotland and England, is governed by pre-existing national rules). If, however (and only if), the centre of the debtor's main interests cannot be said to be in any Member State, "non-Regulation proceedings" still may be taken in Scotland if a ground of jurisdiction is available under the residual provisions of

---

[182] *Re Nortel Networks SA* [2009] EWHC 1482 (Ch).

[183] For discussion of relationship of art.16 with recognition provisions of the Brussels I Regulation, see *German Graphics Graphische Maschinen GmbH v van der Schee* (C-292/08) [2010] I.L.Pr. 1.

[184] *Re Eurofood IFSC Ltd* [2006] Ch. 508 at [62]–[64] and *MG Probud Gdynia sp z oo* (C-444/07) [2010] B.C.C. 453. But see *France v Klempka (Administrator of ISA Daisytek SAS)* [2006] B.C.C. 841.

[185] See Ch.3, above.

Scots domestic law.[186] In such cases, the jurisdiction of the Scots court will be founded upon the provisions of the Bankruptcy (Scotland) Act 1985, and the Insolvency Act 1986, as amended,[187] and problems of choice of law and matters of recognition will be regulated by these pre-existing national rules

If the centre of the debtor's main interests is situated in another Member State, main proceedings cannot be opened in Scotland, even though jurisdiction appears to exist in terms of the 1985 or 1986 Acts. The jurisdiction of the Member State where the debtor's main interests are centred obliterates the jurisdiction otherwise available to the Scots court under residual national legislation (but without prejudice to the jurisdiction of the Scots court in relation to secondary proceedings—which would, of course, be governed by the Regulation).

INTRA-UK SITUATION

17–53 Within the UK, early authority was to the effect that a bankruptcy should proceed in a single jurisdiction.[188] By the Insolvency Act 1986 s.426 (headed "Co-operation between courts exercising jurisdiction in relation to insolvency"), provision was made for reciprocal recognition of insolvency proceedings in the constituent parts of the UK,[189] and for an element of international co-operation.[190] There is also mutual recognition of receivers within the

---

[186] Companies Act 1985, Bankruptcy (Scotland) Act 1985, Insolvency Act 1986, and Enterprise Act 2002. See William W. McBryde, "Insolvency Jurisdiction", 2004 S.L.T. (News) 185.

[187] See Bankruptcy (Scotland) Regulations 2008 (SSI 2008/82); Insolvency (Scotland) Rules 1986 (SI 1986/1915); Insolvency (Scotland) Regulations 2003 (SI 2003/2109) (amending the 1985 Act and the 1986 Act and Insolvency (Scotland) Rules 1986 (SI 1986/1915) in light of the Insolvency Regulation); Insolvency (Scotland) Amendment Rules 2003 (SI 2003/2111) and Insolvency (Scotland) Rules 1986 Amendment Rules 2008 (SSI 2008/393) (both amending SI Insolvency (Scotland) Rules 1986 (SI 1986/1915) in light of the Enterprise Act 2002).

[188] *Cooper v Baillie* (1878) 5 R. 564: see, per Lord Gifford at 570: "[u]nless there is good cause to the contrary, a strictly English bankruptcy should go on in England and a Scotch bankruptcy in Scotland"; the place of sequestration may be a matter of indifference, but sometimes the results may be very different. Parties should not be able to take advantage of the specialties of the UK situation and may be interdicted from doing so: *Lindsay v Paterson* (1840) 2 D. 1373; *Royal Bank of Scotland v Assignees of Scott Stein and Co*, January 20, 1813, FC.

[189] A bankruptcy order made in one part of the UK must be recognised in another: Insolvency Act 1986 s.426(1), (2). Fletcher and Crabb, annotating the statute, sum up, "thus a complete intra-United Kingdom system of reciprocal enforcement is established in respect of bankruptcy, winding up, receivership and the administrative order and voluntary arrangement procedures". The scheme for mutual assistance extends to relevant countries, defined as (s.426(11)) any of the Channel Islands or the Isle of Man, or any country designated for this purpose by the Secretary of State: Co-operation of Insolvency Courts (Designation of Relevant Countries and Territories) Order 1986 (SI 1986/2123). Such help was always available at common law: e.g. *Re Kooperman* [1928] W.N. 101; *Obers v Paton's Trustees (No.3)* (1897) 24 R. 719. See, generally, *Cheshire and North's Private International Law*, 12th edn, 1992, pp.915, 916.

[190] Section 426(4) enacts that any court in the UK with jurisdiction in insolvency law shall assist a court with corresponding jurisdiction in any other part of the UK, or any relevant country (as defined: s.426(11)). Further, s.426(5) provides that for the purposes of s.426(4), a request made intra-UK, or to a court in the UK by a court in a relevant country, is authority for the requested court to apply, in relation to any matter specified in the request, the insolvency law which is applicable by either court in relation to comparable matters falling within its jurisdiction. Section 426(5) concludes, "In exercising its discretion . . . a court shall have regard in particular to the rules of private international law". See, e.g. *Re HIH Casualty & General Insurance Ltd* [2008] 1 W.L.R. 852.

United Kingdom in terms of the Insolvency Act 1986 s.72. Aside from ss.72 and 426, the general principles emphasising the supremacy of the *lex situs* apply.[191] Since April 4, 2006, account must also be taken of the Cross-Border Insolvency Regulations 2006 (reg.7).[192]

GENERAL PRINCIPLES GOVERNING "NON-REGULATION"
INSOLVENCY PROCEEDINGS IN SCOTLAND

The statutory background[193]

The internal law of Scotland pertaining to bankruptcy differs in substance and 17–54 terminology from that of England. The old law was contained in the Bankruptcy (Scotland) Act 1913, which was repealed in toto by the Bankruptcy (Scotland) Act 1985 which came fully into effect on December 29, 1986.[194]

The rules on personal insolvency are contained in the Bankruptcy (Scotland) Act 1985, as amended by the Bankruptcy and Diligence etc. (Scotland) Act 2007.[195] Of particular conflict significance is s.9—jurisdiction, which is subject to art.3 of the Insolvency Regulation. Section 9 establishes jurisdiction in Scotland, in the case of individuals, upon proof of an established place of business in the relevant sheriffdom, or proof of habitual residence there; and in the case of entities, upon proof of an established place of business in the relevant sheriffdom, or constitution or formation under Scots law and proof that at any time it carried on business in the sheriffdom.

The Insolvency Act 1986 is concerned with corporate insolvency law for Scotland and England (Pts IV and V),[196] but in relation to individual insolvency law, for England only. The Act contains jurisdiction provisions for the Scots courts in the matter of winding-up of companies registered in Scotland,[197] and for unregistered companies.[198] The exercise of jurisdiction by means of these provisions is subject to the operation of Regulation 1346/2000. Hence, where the proceedings fall outside the scope of the Insolvency Regulation, by reason of subject matter or time, it is safe to assume that the Insolvency Act provisions can operate. So long as the COMI is not situated in an EU Member State, the Scots court is justified in utilising the 1986 Act in

---

[191] *Galbraith v Grimshaw* [1910] A.C. 508 is authority for the view that the "no dating back" rule applies intra-UK as in foreign bankruptcy situations, being peculiar to each system's bankruptcy rules.

[192] Cross-Border Insolvency Regulations 2006 (SI 2006/1030); see below.

[193] See I. Fletcher, "The Genesis of Modern Insolvency Law—An Odyssey of Law Reform" [1989] J.B.L. 365.

[194] William W. McBryde, *Bankruptcy*, 2nd edn (Edinburgh: W. Green, 1995), p.11. See generally, on the subject of bankruptcy, McBryde, *Bankruptcy*, 2nd edn, 1995; Davidson and Macgregor, *Commercial Law in Scotland*, 2nd edn, 2008, Ch.8.

[195] See also Act of Sederunt (Sheriff Court Bankruptcy Rules) 2008 (SSI 2008/119).

[196] See, John St Clair and Lord Drummond Young, *The Law of Corporate Insolvency in Scotland*, 3rd edn (Edinburgh: W. Green, 2004); Greene and Fletcher, *The Law and Practice of Receivership in Scotland*, edited by I.M. Fletcher and Roy Roxburgh, 3rd edn (Haywards Heath: Tottel, 2005); Lawrence Collins, *Essays in International Litigation and the Conflict of Laws* (Oxford: Clarendon, 1993), Ch.XII, "Floating Charges, Receivers and Managers and the Conflict of Laws".

[197] See ss.120, 121.

[198] See ss.221, 225.

order to take jurisdiction, if the registered office, or principal place of business in the case of an unregistered company is in Scotland.[199]

Appointment and functions of trustee in sequestration

17–55   These matters are governed by the Bankruptcy (Scotland) Act 1985 s.2, as amended. The trustee, permanent or interim, must be an insolvency practitioner and must have given an undertaking that s/he will act as trustee. By virtue of s.7(1) of the Bankruptcy and Diligence etc. (Scotland) Act 2007, the requirement that the practitioner must reside within Scotland, or within the sheriffdom, has been removed.

Property vested in the trustee

17–56   Section 31 of the 1985 Act, as amended, confers upon the trustee in sequestration "the whole estate of the debtor" as at the date of sequestration, and wherever situated,[200] for the benefit of the creditors. There is no territorial limitation, but in respect of property situated abroad it is for the foreign *lex situs* to determine the effect which it gives to a Scottish sequestration,[201] ". . . [For] no Act of Parliament can of its own force and effect transfer property situated, e.g. in Turkey from the bankrupt to the trustee".[202]

Section 31AA of the 1985 Act provides that, in the application of the 1985 Act to insolvency proceedings under Regulation 1346/2000,[203] a reference to "estate" is a reference to estate which may be dealt with in those proceedings.

Applicable law

17–57   As noted above, any rights acquired by the trustee in sequestration are subject to the overriding provisions of the *lex situs*.[204] Otherwise, the forum applies its own domestic law qua *lex concursus*, and matters of administration also are governed by the *lex fori*.[205]

A creditor who recovers assets abroad may rank in Scotland if he makes available what he has recovered.[206] There is no difference in principle in ranking simply because the claim is foreign,[207] though ranking in general is the function of the *lex fori*.[208] If, however, such a creditor does not claim in the

---

[199] *HSBC Bank Plc, Petitioner*, 2010 S.L.T. 281.

[200] See s.31(1), (8).

[201] Or vice versa: *Murphy's Trustees v Aitken*; sub nom. *Morley's Trustees v Aitken*, 1983 S.L.T. 78; 1982 S.C. 73: English trustee in bankruptcy took Scottish heritage subject to any inhibitions registered against the bankrupt prior in date to trustee's appointment.

[202] *Dicey, Morris and Collins on the Conflict of Laws*, 14th edn, 2006, para.31–029.

[203] i.e. to the extent that Scots law is the applicable law under the choice of law provisions of Regulation 1346/2000.

[204] *Re Reilly* [1942] I.R. 416.

[205] cf. *Re Bank of Credit and Commerce International SA (In Liquidation) (No.11)* [1996] 4 All E.R. 796.

[206] This is not expressly laid down in the 1985 Act (ss.48, 49), but seems clear at common law: cf. *Clydesdale Bank v Anderson* (1890) 27 S.L.R. 493, per Lord Shand at 504.

[207] *Re Kloebe* (1884) L.R. 28 Ch. D. 175 (succession).

[208] Which may disadvantage foreign creditors, e.g. if their claims have prescribed by the law of the forum, but not by their own proper applicable law: see *Re Lorillard* [1922] 2 Ch. 638 (succession). See for Scots law as to unfair preferences Bankruptcy (Scotland) Act 1985 s.36, as amended.

Scots bankruptcy, it would seem that, if he obtained the assets before the date of that bankruptcy, he may retain them, but, if he obtained them after that date and he is subject to the jurisdiction in bankruptcy in Scotland, the Scottish trustee may recover the assets.[209] A claim in a Scots sequestration will subject a creditor to the jurisdiction of the Scots court by reconvention.[210]

Discharge

Discharge is governed by the *lex fori*. Discharge has the same effect territo-   **17–58**
rially as the original bankruptcy. However, a discharge under a "UK" bankruptcy will excuse the subject of the order from suit in the United Kingdom in respect of a foreign debt or obligation,[211] though its effect in a foreign court will be a matter for decision in accordance with the foreign bankruptcy/contract conflict rule.

Cross-Border Insolvency Regulations 2006[212]

In 1997 UNCITRAL adopted a Model Law on Cross-Border Insolvency,   **17–59**
offering a legislative framework for adoption by states. By virtue of the 2006 Regulations, this Model Law was adopted for Great Britain. To an extent this overlaps with the rules in Regulation 1346/2000, albeit that the latter governs only the co-ordination of insolvency proceedings within the EU. The Model Law is capable of providing a complementary regime of regulation and co-operation outside the EU:

> "This will place Great Britain, by virtue of the operation of section 426 of the Insolvency Act 1986 in the unique position of having a suite of statutory procedures available in cross-border insolvency cases, as well as the flexibility of common law."[213]

---

[209] *Stewart v Auld* (1851) 13 D. 1337; *Wilsons (Glasgow and Trinidad) Ltd v Dresdner Bank*, 1913 2 S.L.T. 437; *Murphy's Trustee, Petitioner*, 1933 S.L.T. 632; *Re Courtney Ex p. Pollard* (1840) Mont. & Ch. 239; *Re Oriental Island SS Co* (1874) L.R. 9 Ch. App. 557; *Ex p. Robertson* (1875) L.R. 20 Eq. 733; *Thurburn v Steward* (1871) L.R. 3 P.C. 478; *Ex p. Melbourne* (1870) L.R. 6 Ch. App. 64; *Banco de Portugal v Waddell* (1880) L.R. 5 App. Cas. 161; *Re Anchor Line (Henderson Bros) Ltd* [1937] Ch. 483; *Rousou's Trustee v Rousou* [1955] 1 W.L.R. 545. *Cheshire and North's Private International Law*, 12th edn, 1992, pp.908–911.

[210] *Wilsons (Glasgow and Trinidad) Ltd v Dresdner Bank*, 1913 2 S.L.T. 437; Anton with Beaumont, *Private International Law*, 2nd edn, 1990, p.734, and cf. generally the salutary tale of incautious greed: *Guiard v De Clermont & Donner* [1914] 3 K.B. 145 (Morris, *Conflict of Laws*, 3rd edn, 1984, p.113).

[211] See McBryde, *Bankruptcy*, 2nd edn, 1995, p.415; and *Dicey, Morris and Collins on the Conflict of Laws*, 14th edn, 2006, r.201. Cf. *Gibbs and Sons v Société Industrielle et Commercialle des Metaux* (1890) L.R. 25 Q.B.D. 399, Ch.15, above.

[212] Cross-Border Insolvency Regulations 2006 (SI 2006/1030) (entry into force April 4, 2006), and enabling legislation Insolvency Act 2000 s.14. See also Act of Sederunt (Rules of the Court of Session Amendment No.2) (UNCITRAL Model Law on Cross-Border Insolvency) 2006 (SSI 2006/199), Act of Sederunt (Sheriff Court Bankruptcy Rules 1996) Amendment (UNCITRAL Model Law on Cross-Border Insolvency) 2006 (SSI 2006/197) and Act of Sederunt (Sheriff Court Company Insolvency Rules 1996) Amendment (UNCITRAL Model Law on Cross-Border Insolvency) 2006 (SSI 2006/200).

[213] Explanatory memorandum to 2006 Regulations, para.7.4. See *Re HIH Casualty and General Insurance Ltd* [2006] EWCA Civ 732.

Henceforth, by reg.3 of the 2006 Regulations, "British insolvency law" shall apply,[214] with such modification as the context requires, for the purpose of giving effect to the provisions of the 2006 Regulations, though in the case of conflict, the provisions of the 2006 Regulations shall prevail. Less clear is the interaction between the Model Law and Regulation 1346/2000.[215]

In terms of the Model Law, the person administering a foreign insolvency may initiate an insolvency proceeding in Great Britain in relation to a debtor who is the subject of the foreign proceedings, and may participate in those British proceedings regarding that debtor.[216] The Model Law establishes criteria for deciding whether foreign insolvency proceedings are to be recognised elsewhere, and if so, whether as "main" or "non-main" proceedings (depending on whether the foreign proceedings are taking place in the country where the main operations of the debtor are located); and sets out the effects of recognition, and the relief available to a foreign representative.

A British court may grant discretionary relief for the benefit of any recognised foreign proceedings, although it must be satisfied that the interests of local creditors are adequately protected. Recognition of foreign proceedings does not prevent local creditors from initiating or continuing insolvency proceedings in Britain concerning the same debtor.

Rules also are provided to permit foreign creditors to commence and participate in insolvency proceedings in Britain. The Model Law seeks co-ordination between courts in different states in relation to concurrent insolvency proceedings concerning the same debtor, and authorises courts in one state to seek assistance from courts and representatives in another.[217]

RECOGNITION IN SCOTLAND OF NON-EU (OR DANISH) INSOLVENCY PROCEEDINGS

17–60 In the case of insolvency proceedings not governed by Regulation 1346/2000, pre-existing national rules apply. In general, such foreign insolvencies are recognised in Scotland, subject to the overriding control of the Scottish forum qua *lex situs*.[218] Such a foreign insolvency receives effect in Scotland provided that the court is regarded as having had jurisdiction, but only from the date of the bankruptcy. There is no retrospective or dating back effect in Scotland. The Scots rules as to illegal preferences apply only to Scots bankruptcies in Scotland and a foreign trustee does not have the right to cut down preferences, because the effect of a foreign bankruptcy in Scotland is prospective

---

[214] Guidance in practical matters as to the operation of the 2006 Regulations is to be found in *Re Rajapakse* [2007] B.P.I.R. 99.

[215] With regard to this difficult issue, there has been procrastination: the ranking provisions have not been included within the Model Law "for the time being", but are promised "as soon as it is practicable and possible" (explanatory memorandum to 2006 Regulations, para.7.20).

[216] With regard to definition of debtor, see *Rubin v Eurofinance SA* [2009] EWHC 2129 (Ch). Strauss QC held that it would be perverse, and parochial, to give the word "debtor" any other meaning than that given to it by the foreign court in the foreign proceedings. Therefore, a trust was a debtor for the purposes of the 2006 Regulations and the Model Law even though by English law it had no legal personality as an individual or a body corporate.

[217] Explanatory memorandum to 2006 Regulations, paras 7.7–7.17.

[218] *Murphy's Trustees v Aitken*, 1983 S.L.T. 78. Cf. Recognition in England of US bankruptcy proceedings, in *Rubin v Eurofinance SA* [2009] EWHC 2129 (Ch).

only.[219] Similarly, a Scots sequestration takes effect abroad but only from its date onwards so that it does not operate to cut down preferences already obtained there,[220] i.e. ranking or entitlement to rank is governed by the law under which the sequestration/bankruptcy order is granted.

Jurisdiction

The foreign court will be regarded as competent if it has assumed **17–61** jurisdiction on grounds similar to those assumed in Scotland provided that the bankrupt was a party to the proceedings.[221]

Scots heritage

Immoveable property in Scotland does not pass to the trustee under a foreign **17–62** bankruptcy. Nevertheless, the court may assist the trustee in such a bankruptcy to deal with heritage in Scotland,[222] and if so the Scots heritage will pass subject to any charges attaching to the property under the Scots *lex situs*.[223]

Moveables in Scotland

The Scots courts will recognise and enforce the right of a foreign trustee to all **17–63** the bankrupt's moveable property without further process,[224] with the result that all such property is attached and falls to the trustee in preference to the claims of creditors who may have attached the assets after the date of the bankruptcy.[225] The rights of Scots creditors who have taken action such as diligence in Scotland prior to the date of the foreign bankruptcy are not adversely affected because the foreign bankruptcy, assuming it is recognised, is regarded as taking effect only from its date onwards. The *lex situs* controls the situation and the Scots statutory provisions about dating back apply only to Scots bankruptcies.[226]

Competing claims

Competing claims are decided by the *lex fori* of the bankruptcy.[227]   **17–64**

Discharge

A discharge has the same effect territorially as the original award of **17–65** bankruptcy. A discharge in bankruptcy will have the effect of discharging a

---

[219] *Goetze v Aders* (1874) 2 R. 150.
[220] *Galbraith v Grimshaw* [1910] A.C. 508.
[221] *Wilkie v Cathcart* (1870) 9 M. 168; *Gibson v Munro* (1894) 21 R. 840; *Obers v Paton's Trustees (No.3)* (1897) 24 R. 719; *Re Davidson* (1873) L.R. 15 Eq. 383; *Re Lawson's Trusts* [1896] 1 Ch. 175; *Re Anderson (A Bankrupt)* [1911] 1 K.B. 896; *Re Craig*, 86 L.J. Ch. 62; *Bergerem v Marsh* (1921) 91 L.J. K.B. 80.
[222] *Rattray v White* (1842) 4 D. 880; *Araya v Coghill*, 1921 S.C. 462. The English courts apply the same principle: *Re Kooperman* [1928] W.N. 101.
[223] *Murphy's Trustees v Aitken*, 1983 S.L.T. 78.
[224] *Araya v Coghill*, 1921 S.C. 462.
[225] *Goetze v Aders* (1874) 2 R. 150; *Phosphate Sewage Co v Molleson* (1876) 3 R. (HL) 77; (1876) 5 R. 1125; (1876) 6 R. (H.L.) 113; *Obers v Paton's Trustees (No.3)* (1897) 24 R. 719; *Salaman v Tod*, 1911 S.C. 1214; *Home's Trustee v Home's Trustees*, 1926 S.L.T. 214.
[226] See now the 1985 Act ss.34–37.
[227] *Re Courteney Ex p. Pollard* (1840) Mont. & Ch. 239; *Re Anchor Line (Henderson Bros) Ltd* [1937] Ch. 483; *Scottish Union and National Insurance Co v James* (1886) 13 R. 928.

contractual obligation[228] only if it was granted under the same law as the proper law of the obligation.[229]

SUMMARY 17

17–66 *I. Particular transfers of property*

1. Classification and alienability

The nature of property as moveable or immoveable, and whether it is alienable, is determined by the *lex situs*.

2. Meaning of the *lex situs*

The *lex situs* is the law of the situation of the property in question at the time of the transfer allegedly giving rise to the proprietary claim. Recent case law suggests that reference to the *lex situs* is unlikely to include a reference to its rules of international private law.

3. Immoveable property

Proprietary rights in respect of immoveable property are governed by the *lex situs*

Contracts concerning immoveables are governed by their applicable law, usually the *lex situs* (see Rome I Regulation arts 4.1(c) and 11.5).

Security rights in respect of immoveable property must comply with the *lex situs*.

4. Moveable Property

(a) Corporeal moveables:

Care must be taken to distinguish rights *in rem* from rights *in personam*, the former being governed by choice of law rules in property, and the latter by choice of law rules in contract.

Title validly conferred by the *lex situs* at the time of the purported transfer prevails, subject to any overriding effect according to a subsequent *lex situs*. The *lex situs* generally governs competing claims.

(b) Incorporeal moveables:

The *situs* of incorporeal moveables is the place where the right may be enforced.

Assignability is governed by the proper law of the right purportedly assigned, that is, the *lex situs* of the right. In cases of contractual assignation regulated by the Rome I Regulation, by art.14.2 assignability shall be determined by the law governing the assigned claim.

---

[228] *Gardiner v Houghton* (1862) 2 B. & S. 743; *Ellis v McHenry* (1871) L.R. 6 C.P. 228.
[229] *Bartley v Hodges* (1861) 1 B. & S. 375; *Gibbs and Sons v Société Industrielle et Commercialle des Metaux* (1890) L.R. 25 Q.B.D. 399.

Capacity to make, or to accept, an assignation is governed by the governing law of the assignation, or by the proper law of the right purportedly assigned.

The formal validity of an assignation is governed by the *lex loci actus*, the proper law of the assignation, or the proper law of the right purportedly assigned. In cases of contractual assignation regulated by the Rome I Regulation, art.11 governs.

The essential validity of an assignation is governed by the proper law of the assignation, or the proper law of the right purportedly assigned. In cases of contractual assignation regulated by the Rome I Regulation, art.14.2 provides that the relationship between the assignee and the debtor, the conditions under which the assignation can be invoked against the debtor, and whether the debtor's obligations have been discharged, shall be determined by the law governing the assignation.

In cases of contractual assignation regulated by the Rome I Regulation, art.14.1 provides that the relationship between the assignor and the assignee under a voluntary assignation shall be governed by the law that applies to the contract of assignation between the parties in terms of the Regulation.

The *lex situs* of the right governs competing claims to the same right, and competitions between voluntary and involuntary transfers.

Special rules apply to bills of exchange, negotiable instruments, shares and other securities, and intellectual property rights.

II. Universal transfers of property: insolvency

1. Theories

Unity; separation; universality of bankruptcy.

2. EU Developments

Regulation 1346/2000 establishes a system to regulate cross-border insolvencies where the centre of a debtor's main interests is situated within an EU Member State (except Denmark).

It sets up a system of main proceedings (having extraterritorial effect) and secondary proceedings (limited to assets situated in the state where the secondary proceedings are opened), and directs that the applicable law, subject to arts 5–14, shall be the law of the state in which proceedings (main or secondary) are opened (the *lex concursus*).

3. "Non-Regulation" proceedings

The residual national rules are contained in the Bankruptcy (Scotland) Act 1985, as amended by the Bankruptcy and Diligence etc. (Scotland) Act 2007 (personal insolvency), and the Insolvency Act 1986, as amended (corporate insolvency).

4. Recognition of "non-Regulation" foreign insolvency proceedings

In general, such foreign insolvencies are recognised in Scotland subject to the overriding control of Scots law qua *lex situs*, but recognition will be prospective only.

CHAPTER 18

THE LAW OF SUCCESSION

I. MATTERS PERTAINING TO BOTH
TESTATE AND INTESTATE SUCCESSION

CONFIRMATION TO ESTATE IN SCOTLAND

18–01 No person is entitled to take any administrative act in the estate of any deceased person who has left assets in Scotland until he has obtained confirmation in Scotland. Confirmation constitutes title to all moveable and immoveable estate in Scotland vested in a deceased, whatever his domicile. There must be property in Scotland before confirmation will be granted. The same principles apply, mutatis mutandis, in England, where probate is granted in testate cases, and letters of administration in intestate cases.[1]

The granting of confirmation[2] confers authority on the executor to intromit with assets only in Scotland,[3] and not with assets situated elsewhere, i.e. before the executor has authority to intromit with assets he must complete title according to the Scots *lex loci rei sitae/lex situs*. Within the UK there used to be a system of resealing of the grant of authority made in one territorial unit in the other constituent parts, if there were assets to be dealt with there, but by the Administration of Estates Act 1971 s.3(1), resealing was dispensed with, provided that the deceased died domiciled in the legal system which issued the grant. Thus, confirmation or probate or letters of administration granted in any UK jurisdiction operates directly in the others, though obtaining confirmation to Scottish estate and separate probate/letters to English estate is still competent.[4]

If the deceased died domiciled in a Commonwealth country, and if probate, letters of administration or similar authority has/have already been granted there, it is not necessary to apply for confirmation to estate in Scotland. Instead the probate or letters may be resealed in Edinburgh.[5] Before resealing

---

[1] See *Currie on Confirmation of Executors*, edited by Eilidh M. Scobbie, 8th edn (Edinburgh: W. Green, 1995), para.14–33 (9th edn, forthcoming), and generally John G.Miller, *International Aspects of Succession* (Aldershot: Ashgate, 2000), Ch.2.

[2] Or in England, probate or letters of administration, as appropriate.

[3] Or, mutatis mutandis, England or the country where such title was granted.

[4] *Currie on Confirmation of Executors*, 8th edn, 1995, para.14–41; see generally, para.14–35.

[5] Resealing of probates in Scotland is competent under the Colonial Probate Act 1892 and the Colonial Probate (Protected States and Mandated Territories) Act 1927. If resealing is competent under these Acts, it does not matter that the executor could not have been appointed as executor in the country where resealing takes place. But see *Currie on Confirmation of Executors*, 8th edn, 1995, para.15–02, explaining that obtaining Scottish confirmation may be preferable, e.g. to obtain title to individual items of estate.

can take place, an inventory of the deceased's estate in Scotland must be lodged.[6] Resealing does not have any retrospective effect, with the result that a resealed confirmation or probate is effective in the country where it was resealed only from the date of resealing onwards, not from the date of the original grant. Reciprocal arrangements have been made for the resealing of Scottish confirmations in Commonwealth countries.

If the deceased died domiciled outside the Commonwealth and if probate, letters of administration or similar authority has/have already been granted abroad, the Scots courts will follow the law of the deceased's domicile as regards the appointment of the executor, and confirmation will be granted in Scotland to such person already appointed, or entitled to be appointed, under that law. Except in the case of small estates,[7] a petition for the appointment in Scotland of the (foreign appointed) administrator as executor dative will be required.

If the deceased died domiciled outside the Commonwealth, but probate, letters of administration, or similar authority has/have not been granted in the country of his domicile, and there is property to be administered in Scotland, it is necessary to prove either that the deceased's will is valid according to the law of his domicile, or that the person seeking appointment as executor dative is the person entitled by that law to the office of administrator.[8]

Some legal systems know no interposition of executor between the deceased and the heir,[9] in which case Scots law must be guided by the rules of the *lex situs* and/or the deceased's personal law. Its accommodation of the foreign law must inevitably be approximate because the connecting factor will be taken to be the law of the domicile of the deceased (even though the foreign law is likely to favour application of the law of the deceased's nationality to all property, moveable and immoveable). Moreover, the foreign system would have that property pass directly to the heir, without the intervention of the personal representative of the deceased. Whatever the rule of the deceased's personal law, property in Scotland or England cannot pass without confirmation, probate, letters of administration, or similar authority having been obtained by the party entitled. On the other hand, Scots law will accept as executor the person identified by the deceased's personal law, whether or not such a person would be entitled to act under Scots domestic law.[10]

---

[6] *Currie on Confirmation of Executors*, 8th edn, 1995, para.14–13.

[7] See Confirmation to Small Estates (Scotland) Order 2005 (SSI 2005/251), which increases from £25,000 to £30,000 the limit of value of a deceased person's estate at or below which confirmation of executors may be obtained by the simplified procedures prescribed by the Intestate Widows and Children (Scotland) Act 1875 (for small intestate estates), and by the Small Testate Estates (Scotland) Act 1876 (for small testate estates).

[8] On procedure and more complex cases, see *Currie on Confirmation of Executors*, 8th edn, 1995, para.2.37. For styles see *Currie on Confirmation of Executors, Supplement to the Eighth Edition*, edited by Eilidh M. Scobbie (Edinburgh: W. Green, 1996), paras 3–01 to 3–07.

[9] See Miller, *International Aspects of Succession*, 2000, pp.2–3. Also *Re Haji-Ioannou (Deceased)*; sub nom. *Haji-Ioannou v Frangos* [2009] EWHC 2310 (QB).

[10] *Currie on Confirmation of Executors*, 8th edn, 1995, para.2–36.

The following is a summary of the position.[11]

18–02 Where the deceased died domiciled in:

> (a) Scotland—confirmation constitutes title to assets in Scotland, England, and Northern Ireland.
> (b) England—probate or letters of administration granted in England are immediately effective in Scotland as regards title to property situated there (Administration of Estates Act 1971).
> (c) Northern Ireland—as for England above, mutatis mutandis, but a separate inventory must be lodged in Scotland of the deceased's Scottish estate.
> (d) Channel Islands and the Isle of Man—there is no procedure for resealing, and therefore confirmation to estate in Scotland is required.
> (e) Commonwealth—resealing under the Colonial Probate Act 1892 and the Colonial Probate (Protected States and Mandated Territories) Act 1927. A separate inventory must be lodged in Scotland of the deceased's Scottish estate, but separate Scottish confirmation is unnecessary.
> (f) A foreign non-EU country.[12]
>
>> (i) If probate or letters of administration or similar authority has/have already been granted in that country: an inventory must be lodged in Scotland, in which the executor refers to the probate, etc. as his title, and confirmation will be granted.
>> (ii) If no probate or letters of administration or similar authority has/have been granted in that country, an expert opinion may be required as to the validity of the will (if any), or eligibility of persons claiming appointment as executor. An inventory must be lodged in Scotland, and confirmation obtained.

---

[11] See *Currie on Confirmation of Executors*, 8th edn, 1995, Ch.15. Also *Hutchison v Aberdeen Bank* (1837) 15 S. 1100; *Marchioness of Hastings v Executors of Marquess of Hastings* (1852) 15 D. 489; *Whiffin v Lees* (1872) 10 M. 797; *Ewing v Orr-Ewing (No.1)* (1883) L.R. 9 App. Cas. 34; *Rodger v Adam's Trustees* (1885) 1 Sh. Ct Rep. 202; *New York Breweries Co Ltd v Att Gen* [1899] A.C. 62; *Re Duchess of Orleans* (1859) 1 Sw. & Tr. 253; *Re Tucker* (1864) 3 Sw. & Tr. 585; *In the Goods of Coode* (1867) L.R. 1 P. & D. 449; *Re Earl* (1867) L.R. 1 P. & D. 450; *Re Hill* (1870) L.R. 2 P. & D. 89; *In the Goods of Briesemann* [1894] P. 260; *In the Goods of Von Linden* [1896] P. 148; *Re Rea* [1902] I.R. 451; *Irwin v Caruth* [1916] P. 23; *Re Rankine (Deceased)* [1918] P. 134; *Re Achillopoulos* [1928] 1 Ch. 433; *Re Welsh* [1931] I.R. 161; *In the Estate of Leguia Ex p. Ashworth* [1934] P. 80; *In the Estate of Humphries* [1934] P. 78; *Re Dyas* [1937] I.R. 479; *Re O'Grady* (1941) 75 I.L.T.R. 119; *Re Schulhof* [1948] P. 66; *Re Wayland (Deceased)* [1951] 2 All E.R. 1041; *Burns v Campbell* [1952] 1 K.B. 15; *Re Kaufman (Deceased)* [1952] 2 All E.R. 261; *Finnegan v Cementation Co Ltd* [1953] 1 Q.B. 688; *Bowler v John Mowlem & Co Ltd* [1954] 1 W.L.R. 1445; *In the Estate of Yahunda* [1956] P. 388; *Inland Revenue Commissioners v Stype Investments (Jersey) Ltd* [1982] Ch. 456.

[12] See, generally, Pugh (ed.), *Administration of Foreign Estates* (London: Sweet & Maxwell, 1988), which is a compilation of essays on matters of death, succession and administration in France, Italy, Spain, Portugal, Jersey, Guernsey, Isle of Man and the State of Florida (selection of countries on the doleful rationale that it is not unlikely that British residents/nationals/domiciliaries may die in any of these countries while on holiday or on longer term stay, and where in addition, they may have second homes). See also David J. Hayton, *European Succession Laws*, 2nd edn (Bristol: Jordans, 2002); and B.E. Leslie, *Administration of Foreign Estates* (2009).

The Scots court may take evidence upon the question of the domicile of the deceased.[13] A foreign declarator of death is not conclusive in Scotland so that in a contested case proof of death may be necessary.[14]

The 1973 Hague Convention concerning the International Administration of the Estates of Deceased Persons was signed, but not ratified, by the UK.

(g) An EU Member State.

The 1998 Vienna Action Plan placed among its priorities the adoption of a European instrument concerning conflict rules of succession.[15] The Hague Programme called upon the EU Commission to present a Green Paper covering jurisdiction, applicable law, and recognition, together with administrative measures relating to wills.[16] Pursuant thereto, there was issued in 2009 a Proposal for a Regulation on jurisdiction, applicable law, and recognition and enforcement of decisions and authentic instruments in matters of succession and the creation of a European Certificate of Succession (sub nom. "Rome V"),[17] discussed in more detail at para.18–35, below. Until such time as such as instrument is introduced, cases where the deceased died domiciled in an EU Member State must be treated in the same way as cases at (f) above.

ADMINISTRATION AND DISTRIBUTION OF ESTATE

The *administration* of an estate comprises all steps of procedure in completion of title and all the duties of the executor or personal representative of the deceased up to the stage of bringing the estate to the point of division. It includes obtaining confirmation or equivalent, payment of inheritance tax, collection of assets, and payment of debts. In English law there is a presumption that, if a bequest is declared to be "free of duty" or is expressed in similar terms, such an expression covers only duties imposed by UK law unless the testator has indicated a contrary intention.[18] There is no such presumption in Scots law where the courts approach the matter purely as one of interpretation of the testator's intention.[19] If the will is silent generally about the matter of duties, taxes are paid out of the residue of the estate; and failing residue, out of the legacies, which will have to be abated.[20]   **18–03**

---

[13] Colonial Probate Act 1892 s.22.

[14] *Simpson's Trustees v Fox*, 1951 S.L.T. 412.

[15] See generally Ch.1, above. Also Elizabeth B. Crawford and Janeen M. Carruthers, "Conflict of Loyalties in the Conflict of Laws: The Cause, the Means and the Cost of Harmonisation", 2005 Jur. Rev. 251.

[16] Green Paper on Succession and Wills COM(2005) 65 final. See also Commission Staff Working Paper, Annex to the Green Paper on Succession and Wills SEC(2005) 270; and Opinion of the European Economic and Social Committee on the Green Paper on Succession and Wills [2006] OJ C28/1.

[17] COM(2009) 154 final (2009/0157 (COD)), at para.18–35, below. As well as initiating a debate on choice of law in succession, the Proposal deals with administrative matters, such as whether automatic recognition should be given in all EU Member States of the designation and functions of executor: should such a person be furnished with a certificate to describe his powers? Should the heir have a certificate as evidence of his status?

[18] *Re Scott* [1915] 1 Ch. 592; *Re Goetze* [1953] Ch. 96; *Re Nesbitt* [1953] 1 W.L.R. 595.

[19] *Maclean's Trustees v McNair*, 1969 S.L.T. 146; *Scottish National Orchestra Society Ltd v Thomson's Executor*, 1969 S.L.T. 325.

[20] See generally Alan Barr et al, *Drafting Wills in Scotland*, 2nd edn (Haywards Heath: Tottel, 2009).

The administration of a deceased's estate is governed by the *lex fori*, which is, in effect, the *lex situs* of the assets (not necessarily coinciding with the *lex domicilii* of the deceased).[21] Thus, in the case of debts which have prescribed by the law of the deceased's domicile, but not by the *lex fori* or vice versa, it is the *lex fori* which determines whether they may be admitted and which determines priorities among competing claimants on the estate.[22] The incidence and characterisation of debts as between moveables and immoveables probably is determined ultimately by the *lex situs* of the immoveables.

Distribution of an estate involves its division among the beneficiaries, and is governed by the *lex successionis*, that is, the *lex causae* (*q.v.*) rather than the *lex fori*. When the deceased dies domiciled abroad, his assets in Scotland may be remitted to the country of his domicile for distribution, but distribution at the Scots *situs* in accordance with the *lex successionis* is competent. In the case of dual/multiple administrations, the procedure in the *forum rei sitae* is termed the *ancillary administration*, while that in the *forum successionis* is termed the *principal administration*.

The classification between matters of administration and of distribution is determined by the *lex fori*.[23]

A decree of the court of the deceased's domicile upon a question of succession to moveables is a decree *in rem* entitled to recognition in Scotland, and conclusive against other claimants.[24]

APPLICABLE LAW: THE SCISSION PRINCIPLE

18–04   The scission principle refers to the split nature of the Scottish (and English) choice of law rule in succession, which differentiates between the law governing succession to moveables (the ultimate domicile of the deceased) and that governing succession to immoveables (the *lex situs*).

Whether this distinction should continue to be made is a matter long debated within the UK,[25] and has become more pressing in view of European proposals for a harmonised, unitary choice of law rule.[26]

---

[21] cf. *Weinstock v Sarnat* [2006] 3 C.L. 79 Sup. Ct (NSW).

[22] *Re Lorillard* [1922] 2 Ch. 638. This case is not without its critics: if the debts were still exigible by their own applicable laws, perhaps the forum overreached itself by refusing to admit the claims. See also *Re Kloebe* (1884) L.R. 28 Ch. D. 175; *Re Manifold* [1962] Ch. 1.

[23] *Ewing v Orr-Ewing (No.2)* (1885) L.R. 10 App. Cas. 453; *Grant v Gordon Falconer and Fairweather*, 1932 48 Sh. Ct Rep. 155; *Scottish National Orchestra Society Ltd v Thomson's Executor*, 1969 S.L.T. 325; *Re Kloebe* (1884) L.R. 28 Ch. D. 175; *Re Lorillard* [1922] 2 Ch. 638; *Re Achillopoulos* [1928] Ch. 433; *Re Wilks* [1935] Ch. 645; *Re Goenaga* [1949] P. 367; *Re Manifold* [1962] Ch. 1; *In the Estate of Weiss* [1962] P. 136.

[24] *Ewing v Orr-Ewing (No.1)* (1883) L.R. 9 App. Cas. 34; *Ewing v Orr-Ewing (No.2)* (1885) L.R. 10 App. Cas. 453; *Enochin v Wylie* (1862) 10 H.L. Cas. 1; *Doglioni v Crispin* (1866) L.R. 1 H.L. 301; *Re Trufort* (1887) L.R. 36 Ch. D. 600.

[25] See Morris, "Intestate Succession to Land in the Conflict of Laws" (1969) 85 L.Q.R. 839. Scottish Law Commission, *Some Miscellaneous Topics in the Law of Succession* (HMSO, 1986), Scot. Law Com. Memo. No.71, considers private international law aspects in Pt 6, and there is subsequent consideration in Scottish Law Commission, *Report on Succession* (HMSO, 1990), Scot. Law Com.No.124. Also Michael C. Meston, *The Succession (Scotland) Act 1964*, 5th edn (Edinburgh: W. Green, 2002), p.113.

[26] See para.18–39, below.

The Succession (Scotland) Act 1964 removed many differences which previously had existed in domestic Scots law between succession to heritage and succession to moveables. However, remnants of the distinction remain in domestic law, and continue to permeate Scots conflict rules of succession. This can lead to difficulty, particularly where property is chameleon in character, changing its nature according to the context in which it is encountered. The result may be seen as unfair: a widow may benefit twice.[27]

Conversion

Conversion (rules to be applied to determine the nature of property where **18–05** immoveables have been converted into money or vice versa) is determined, it would seem, by the law of the testator's domicile at the date of his death, and not by the *lex situs*.[28]

LEGAL RIGHTS

Most legal systems recognise rights of certain family members of the deceased **18–06** to claim against his will, or in intestacy, a reserved portion of the deceased's estate. These rights of indefeasible family provision, known in domestic Scots law as "legal rights", constitute both rights of succession and restrictions on the deceased's testamentary powers. The subject of protected family provision (sometimes termed forced heirship), being a matter of substance, is regulated in Scots conflict law by the law of the deceased's domicile at the date of his death as regards moveables,[29] and by the *lex situs* at the date of death, as regards immoveables.[30]

Rules of family provision per Scots law

Spouses and civil partners

Legal rights consist in Scots domestic law of the rights of a surviving spouse[31] **18–07** of the deceased (*jus relicti/relictae*) and of his children (*legitim*).[32] Legal rights in

---

[27] *Train v Train's Executor* (1899) 2 F. 146: see criticisms in Anton, *Private International Law*, 1st edn, 1967, pp.387, 388; *Re Collens (Deceased)* [1986] 1 All E.R. 611, in which, however, the scission rule was applied. See comments in Law Commission, *Intestacy and Family Provision Claims on Death: A Consultation Paper* (The Stationery Office, 2009) Law Com. C.P. No.191, paras 7.38, 7.39, and conclusion that, since the eventuality of double benefit will arise in a limited number of cases, and may not in fact be problematic in those cases, reform of the law on this point is not warranted.

[28] *Hall's Trustees v Hall* (1854) 16 D. 1057.

[29] *Bell v Kennedy* (1868) 6 M. (H.L.) 69; *Trevelyan v Trevelyan* (1873) 11 M. 516; *Train v Train's Executor* (1899) 2 F. 146; *Macdonald*, 1932 S.C. (H.L.) 79; *Re Groos* [1915] 1 Ch. 572.

[30] *Bell v Kennedy* (1868) 6 M. (H.L.) 69: consider *Lashley v Hog* (1804) 4 Pat. 581; *Re Ogilvie* [1918] 1 Ch. 492; *Re Collens (Deceased)* [1986] 1 All E.R. 611.

[31] Or civil partner: Civil Partnership Act 2004 s.131, which provides that a surviving civil partner may claim legal rights equivalent to those of a surviving spouse.

[32] The Scottish Law Commission published its *Report on Succession* (The Stationery Office, 2009), Scot. Law Com. No.215, in April 2009, following *Discussion Paper on Succession* (The Stationery Office, 2007), Scot. Law Com. D.P. No.136, proposing that major changes be made to the rules on family provision (Pt 8, recommendations 1–5, 14–36). There has been no implementing legislation.

Scots law, exigible now only out of moveable estate[33] and available therefore only where the deceased died domiciled in Scotland, can be claimed in intestate or testate succession, though in the former case, they do not arise until prior rights of the surviving spouse (*q.v.*) have been satisfied, and in the case of testacy, they cannot be taken in addition to any bequest under the will.[34] This may not be the case in all legal systems; the matter is one of substance, to be determined by the *lex successionis*. Land in Scotland is immune to any claim for legal rights, since Scots law, the *lex situs*, no longer admits such rights in respect of immoveables.[35]

Cohabitants

18–08   In terms of the Family Law (Scotland) Act 2006 s.29, a surviving cohabitant may apply to the Scots court for payment from the deceased cohabitant's net intestate estate of a capital sum, and for transfer of property, heritable or moveable, from that estate, as the court may prescribe having in view the size and nature of the estate, and any benefit received or to be received by the survivor in consequence of the death.[36] The court also will take into account any other rights against or claims on the estate. The order shall not exceed the amount to which the survivor would have been entitled had s/he been the spouse or civil partner of the deceased. In terms of s.29(10) "net intestate estate" means so much of the intestate estate as remains after satisfaction of inheritance tax and the legal rights and the prior rights of any surviving spouse or surviving civil partner. In order for claims under s.29 to be admitted, the deceased immediately before death must have been domiciled in Scotland, and cohabiting with the survivor.[37]

Collation

18–09   Collation in Scots domestic law is an equitable doctrine which requires a potential beneficiary, who has received advances from the deceased during his lifetime, notionally to throw these advances into the pot for division if he wishes to participate equally in the distribution of the legal rights fund upon the deceased's death. Since September 10, 1964, collation in Scots law[38] has been restricted to collation *inter liberos*. In England the equivalent principle, mutalis mutundis, "hotch pot", was removed from English law by the Law Reform (Succession) Act 1995 s.1(2).

In conflict law, the subject of collation/equalisation should be regarded as a matter of substantive succession law, applicable therefore in relation to moveable property only if the *lex ultimi domicilii* contains such a rule, and with regard to immoveables, only if the *lex situs* so directs.[39]

---

[33] Succession (Scotland) Act 1964 s.37(2) expressly preserves the operation of rules of law applicable immediately before the commencement of the Act insofar as they pertain to choice of law governing the administration, winding up or distribution of the estate and are not otherwise inconsistent with the terms of the Act.

[34] The claimant is "put to his election". See "approbate and reprobate", below.

[35] Meston, *The Succession (Scotland) Act 1964*, 5th edn, 2002, p.135. However, a qualifying dwelling house situated in Scotland may be subject to prior rights, *q.v.*

[36] e.g. *Savage v Purches*, 2009 S.L.T. (Sh. Ct.) 36; cf. *Windram, Applicant*, 2009 Fam. L.R. 157.

[37] See paras 11–33 and 13–13, above. Also *Chebotareva v Khandro (King's Executrix)*, 2008 Fam. L.R. 66.

[38] See Gloag and Henderson *The Law of Scotland* (ed. Coulsfield and McLaren), 12th edn (Edinburgh: Thomson / W. Green, 2007), para.39.13.

[39] *Hay-Balfour v Scotts* (1793) 3 Pat. 300; *Robertson v Robertson*, February 16, 1816, FC; *Robertson v McVean*, February 18, 1817, FC; *Dundas v Dundas* (1830) 2 Dow & Cl. 349 HL; *Hewitt's Trustees v Lawson* (1891) 18 R. 793; *Brodie v Barry* (1813) 3 Ves. B. 127; *Orrell v Orrell* (1871) 6 Ch. App. 302; *Brown's Trustees v Gregson*, 1920 S.C. (H.L.) 87.

Rules of family provision per English law

In English domestic law a person who is dissatisfied by the terms of a will, **18–10** and/or the effect of the rules of intestacy in the instant case, and who falls within the list of persons named in the relevant legislation, may apply to the court, within six months of the grant of representation, for the making of a discretionary order for payment or property transfer out of the estate, in terms of the Inheritance (Provision for Family and Dependants) Act 1975.[40] The list of parties entitled to claim has been extended by the Law Reform (Succession) Act 1995 s.2(3) to include a cohabitant[41] if the cohabitation has subsisted for at least two years prior to death. These rules, being substantive rules of English domestic succession law, apply where English law is the *lex successionis*.[42]

CAPACITY OF BENEFICIARIES

The law of the deceased's last domicile, as regards moveables, and the *lex* **18–11** *situs*, as regards immoveables, in principle determines the legal capacity of potential beneficiaries to succeed, as well as the substantive matter of the class of persons and order of persons who shall succeed. English cases, however, suggest that the legal capacity of a particular beneficiary to succeed to moveables may be governed by the law of the deceased's last domicile *or* by the law of the beneficiary's domicile, according to which of those laws he acquired capacity earlier,[43] and there seems no reason why a similar rule should not apply in Scotland.

Capacity to grant a discharge to trustees or executors is governed by the law of the domicile of the beneficiary (moveables) or the *lex situs* (immoveables).[44]

II. INTESTATE SUCCESSION

IMMOVEABLE ESTATE

All questions of intestate succession to immoveable estate are governed by **18–12** the *lex situs*.[45] The provisions of s.8 of the Succession (Scotland) Act 1964 concerning the deceased's house apply to all cases where the deceased,

---

[40] See Law Commission, *Intestacy and Family Provision Claims on Death*, 2009, Law Com. C.P. No.191 for recent examination of the 1995 Act.

[41] *Lindop v Agus* [2009] EWHC 1795 (Ch); and to civil partners in terms of the Civil Partnership Act 2004 s.71, Sch.4.

[42] e.g. *Gully v Dix* [2004] 1 W.L.R. 1399; *Robinson v Bird* [2003] EWHC 30 (Ch); *Morgan v Cilento* [2004] EWHC 188 (Ch); and *Agulian v Cyganik* [2006] EWCA Civ 129. See, however, Law Commission, *Intestacy and Family Provision Claims on Death*, 2009, Law Com. C.P. No.191, proposals 8.38, 8.39 (and paras 7.53, 7.54).

[43] *Doglioni v Crispin* (1866) L.R. 1 H.L. 301; *Re Hellman's Will* (1866) L.R. 2 Eq. 363; *Re Goodman's Trusts* (1881) L.R. 17 Ch. D. 266; *Re Hall (Deceased)* [1914] P. 1; *Re Schnapper* [1928] Ch. 420; *Re Hagerbaum* [1933] I.R. 198; in Scots law see *Seddon v Seddon* (1891) 20 R. 675; *Atherstane's Trustees* (1896) 24 R. 39; *Webb v Clelland's Trustees* (1904) 41 S.L.R. 229; and *Ogilvy v Ogilvy's Trustees*, 1927 S.L.T. 83.

[44] *Ogilvy v Ogilvy's Trustees*, 1927 S.L.T. 83.

[45] *Nisbett v Nisbett's Trustees* (1835) 13 S. 517; *Train v Train's Executor* (1899) 2 F. 146; *Fenton v Livingstone* (1859) 3 Macq. 497; *Re Gentili* (1875) L.R. 9 Eq. 541.

irrespective of his domicile, died intestate, and owning a qualifying dwelling house in Scotland.[46]

MOVEABLE ESTATE

18–13   Intestate succession to moveable estate is governed by the law[47] of the deceased's domicile at the date of his death.[48] This law shall govern irrespective of the law of the country of birth, death, or domicile of origin, or the situation of moveables. The applicable law is the law of the deceased's domicile as at the date of death, and not subsequent thereto.[49]

PRIOR RIGHTS

18–14   "Prior rights" is a reference to those rights, introduced in the 1964 Act, which are capable of arising in Scots domestic law in cases of intestacy, and which comprise the right of a surviving spouse to:

> (a) An interest in a qualifying dwelling house[50] under s.8 (or a cash equivalent under s.8(2)). Where the value of the house exceeds a certain sum (updated from time to time)[51] the survivor is entitled to receive the permitted sum in lieu of the house. This cash substitute also will be regarded as immoveable qua *surrogatum*,[52] and subject therefore to regulation by the *lex situs*, i.e. the *lex situs* not the *lex domicilii* determines entitlement. No right, qua Scottish prior right, nor any *surrogatum* arises if the (otherwise qualifying) dwelling house is situated outside Scotland.
>
> (b) A right to the furniture and plenishings.[53] This right is classified as a right to moveables, and hence is exigible only if the deceased died

---

[46] cf. Meston, *The Succession (Scotland) Act 1964*, 5th edn, 2002, p.133; Leslie, "Prior Rights in Succession: The International Dimension", 1988 S.L.T. (News) 105; Scottish Law Commission, *Some Miscellaneous Topics in the Law of Succession*, 1986, Scot. Law Com. Memo. No.71; and Miller, "Family Provision on Death—The International Dimension" (1990) 39 I.C.L.Q. 261.

[47] Necessarily civil law, not a body of religious law, unless the content of the law of the domicile is co-terminous with religious law: *Al-Bassam v Al-Bassam* [2004] EWCA Civ 857. Cf. *Halpern v Halpern* [2008] Q.B. 195.

[48] *Re Haji-Ioannou (Deceased)*; sub nom. *Haji-Ioannou v Frangos* [2009] EWHC 2310 (QB). See also *Brown* (1744) Mor. 4604; *Bruce v Bruce* (1790) 3 Pat. 163; *Lashley v Hog* (1804) 4 Pat. 581: *Nisbett v Nisbett's Trustees* (1835) 13 S. 517; *Newlands v Chalmers' Trustees* (1832) 11 S. 65; *Maxwell v McClure* (1857) 20 D. 307; affirmed 3 Macq. 852; *Lynch v Provisional Government of Paraguay* (1871) L.R. 2 P. & D. 268; *Re Rea* [1902] I.R. 451.

[49] In *Lynch v Provisional Government of Paraguay* (1871) L.R. 2 P. & D. 268, where a government sought to confiscate assets of the deceased in England and purported to alter the succession after the date of death, such provision was ineffective in England. However, it must be said that such governmental order would not be given effect in a British court for the reason also that it would fall foul of the rule that confiscations *extra territorium* have no effect. Moreover, the qualifying phrase "at death" may have been intended in *Lynch* merely to fix the date at which the domicile was to be identified.

[50] Defined in s.8(4).

[51] Presently £300,000: Prior Rights of Surviving Spouse (Scotland) Order 2005 (SSI 2005/252).

[52] Meston, *The Succession (Scotland) Act 1964*, 5th edn, 2002, p.134.

[53] Presently £24,000: Prior Rights of Surviving Spouse (Scotland) Order 2005 (SSI 2005/252).

domiciled in Scotland. Further, the furniture and plenishings must be those contained in the qualifying dwelling house which is the subject of s.8, and which must be situated, therefore, in Scotland.[54]

(c) A right to a cash sum,[55] which, though apparently moveable, is to be borne rateably out of both the heritable and moveable estate of the deceased. Hence, if the deceased died domiciled in Scotland, the sum is apportioned between his moveables *wherever situated*, and his immoveables in *Scotland*. However, if domiciled outside Scotland, then the whole sum is to be taken from any immoveables in Scotland.

CADUCIARY RIGHTS

Difficulties may arise with regard to the succession to assets in Scotland in the **18–15** estate of a person who died, intestate and without relatives, domiciled in a foreign country. The assets may be claimed both by the British Crown, on the basis of claimant to *bona vacantia*, and by the government of the country where the deceased died domiciled, qua universal successor or heir. In such a case, reference is made by the Scots forum qua *lex situs* to the law of intestate succession in the country of the deceased's domicile. The right claimed by the foreign government is analysed and classified by the *lex fori*: if it is a true right of succession, it will be recognised and its claim preferred, but if it is merely a right to *bona vacantia* the *lex loci rei sitae* will apply as a matter of property law and the claim of the foreign (non-*situs*) government will be refused,[56] the estate falling instead to the British Crown, i.e. Exchequer.

The case of *Maldonado*[57] is renowned for the unaccustomed generosity of the forum (the English Court of Appeal) in yielding to the foreign law of the domicile the power to classify the nature of its own claim, and accepting that classification, as expressed in the following words:

"There might be a case where a so-called right of succession claimed by a foreign State could be shown to be in truth no more than a claim to bona vacantia . . . but this has not been shown to be such a case. On the contrary, it has been found (and the Crown has accepted the finding) that the State of Spain is, in the eye of Spanish law, the true heir."[58]

---

[54] Leslie, "Prior Rights in Succession: The International Dimension", 1988 S.L.T. (News) 105, but making reference to the contrary view expressed in Scottish Law Commission, *Some Miscellaneous Topics in the Law of Succession*, 1986, Scot. Law Com. Memo. No.71, para.6.2. If the deceased spouse died domiciled in Scotland, is the survivor entitled to the furniture and plenishings contained in an otherwise qualifying dwelling house which is excluded by its foreign situation from forming the subject of a prior right to the house? The balance of sense of the statute suggests that the house must be in Scotland and the furniture in question must be within it, and for a successful claim to the furniture to be made by the survivor, the deceased spouse must have died domiciled in Scotland.

[55] Presently £42,000 if the deceased left issue, and £75,000 otherwise: Prior Rights of Surviving Spouse (Scotland) Order 2005 (SSI 2005/252).

[56] *Re Barnett* [1902] 1 Ch. 867; *Re Musurus* [1936] 2 All E.R. 1666; *Goold Stuart's Trustees v McPhail*, 1947 S.L.T. 221; *In the Estate of Maldonado* [1954] P. 223.

[57] [1954] P. 223.

[58] *Maldonado* [1954] P. 223, per Jenkins L.J. at 248–250.

If the foreign rule is simply to the effect of conveying ownerless property to its fisc, the Scottish forum qua *situs* would prefer that the property fall to the UK Exchequer, and can give effect to that preference. In 1986, the Scottish Law Commission proposed that the claim of the British Crown in such cases should be regarded as a claim in succession, as should the claim of a foreign state of the domicile of the deceased.[59] After consultation, it was decided not to recommend any such change, partly because there was no compelling need for it and partly because it would be undesirable to have the state succeed to such property on a different basis in Scotland from that on which it acquired it in England.[60]

III. TESTATE SUCCESSION

INTRODUCTION

18-16 The choice of law rules of testate succession are two dimensional (or three dimensional if one includes the *renvoi* aspect), in the sense that they depend both on time and place. A will is an inchoate or ambulatory document in that one cannot know a testator's final intention until the time of his death (unless he should lose mental capacity beforehand to such an extent that a later will is invalid) and, in the conflict sense, one cannot know whether the provisions of the will are essentially valid as to moveable property until the date of his death because only then can the legal system of his last domicile, the judge of the provisions, be identified.

TESTAMENTARY CAPACITY OF THE TESTATOR

Legal capacity

18-17 The conflict rule of Scots law regarding legal testamentary capacity (i.e. age, sanity, etc.) is that the law of the testator's domicile at the date of the will, as regards moveables, and the *lex situs*, as regards immoveables, governs.[61] By extension, challenges under the heads, e.g. of facility and circumvention, undue influence, or force and fear, must be referred to the law of the domicile of the testator at the time of making the instrument in question,[62] or the *lex situs*, as appropriate.

In domestic law, in the matter of mental capacity, a testator need not be of sufficient mental capacity to test at the date of death: his will made earlier, in time of lucidity, is sufficient.

---

[59] Scottish Law Commission, *Some Miscellaneous Topics in the Law of Succession*, 1986, Scot. Law Com. Memo. No.71, para.6.13.

[60] See Scottish Law Commission, *Report on Succession*, 1990, Scot. Law Com. No.124, para.10.10.

[61] The case of *Fuld (No.3)* [1968] P. 675, in which, however, the German domicile of the testator suffered no change between the date of testing and the date of death, suggests that legal testamentary capacity is governed by the law of the domicile at the date of execution of the will. The minimum age of testing in Scots domestic law is 12 years: Age of Legal Capacity (Scotland) Act 1991 s.2(2).

[62] *Fuld (No.3)* [1968] P. 675. As to English domestic law, see *Wingrove v Wingrove* (1885) L.R. 11 P.D. 81; *Couwenbergh v Valkova* [2008] EWHC 2451 (Ch); and *Key v Key* [2010] EWHC 408 (Ch).

Proprietary capacity

Proprietary testamentary capacity (i.e. entitlement to bequeath property), on **18–18** the other hand, concerns a testator's freedom of testation. This obviously is the correlative of the rule on legal rights or compulsory family provision, and is governed by the testator's domicile at death in relation to moveables, and by the *lex situs* in relation to immoveables.

The point is well demonstrated by *Re Groos*[63] in which a lady of Dutch domicile made a will before her marriage to another Dutch domiciliary. The terms of the will indicated that her intention was to make her future husband her heir or universal legatee, in preference to any children who might be born. Some years after their marriage, the couple came to England and acquired a domicile there. The testatrix died, survived by her husband and five children. The children could not dispute the terms of their mother's will because her proprietary testamentary capacity was judged in accordance with her English domicile at death, and by that law her capacity had been expanded, since English law at that date permitted freedom of testation. It was established that by Dutch law marriage itself did not revoke a will,[64] and that the estate by Dutch domestic law, had it applied, would have been distributed in the proportion three-quarters to the children as their legitimate portion, and one-quarter to the husband.

FORMAL VALIDITY OF WILLS

Common law

At common law in England, as regards immoveables, a will had to be **18–19** formally valid according to the *lex situs*, but as regards moveables, English law insisted upon compliance with the law of the testator's domicile at the date of his death.[65] As time went on, however, that law was interpreted to include a law recognised by the law of the domicile at the date of death, thereby providing the genesis of *renvoi* thinking in England.[66] In *Bremer v Freeman*,[67] a will made in Paris in English form by an Englishwoman then domiciled in England was held to be invalid because it was not also valid by the law of France which was the law of her domicile at the date of her death. The decision showed that a change of domicile could have the effect of invalidating a will as to form. In consequence, the Wills Act 1861 was passed.

The difficulty referred to in the preceding paragraph did not arise in Scotland,[68] because the conflict rule of Scots common law was that a will was

---

[63] *Re Groos*; sub nom. *Groos v Groos* [1915] 1 Ch. 572 (and earlier *In the Estate of Groos* [1904] P. 269).

[64] As to conflict rules pertaining to revocation of a will by marriage, see below.

[65] *Bremer v Freeman* (1857) 10 Moo. P.C. 306; *In the Estate of Groos* [1904] P. 269; *Re Grassi* [1905] 1 Ch. 584; *De Fogassieras v Duport* (1881) 11 L.R. Ir. 123; *Murray v Champernowne* [1901] 2 I.R. 232; *Re Moses* [1908] 2 Ch. 235; *In the Goods of Schroeder* [1949] I.R. 89.

[66] *Collier v Rivaz* (1841) 2 Curt. 855.

[67] *Bremer v Freeman* (1857) 10 Moo. P.C. 306.

[68] See generally: *Purvis' Trustees v Purvis' Executors* (1861) 23 D. 812; *Connel's Trustees v Connel* (1872) 10 M. 627; *Bradford v Young* (1884) 11 R. 1135; *Macdonald v Cuthbertson* (1890) 18 R. 101; *Chisholm v Chisholm*, 1949 S.C. 434; *Irving v Snow*, 1956 S.C. 257.

regarded as being formally valid if it had been executed in accordance with the *lex situs*, as regards immoveables; and as regards moveables, in accordance with any of the law of the place of execution,[69] or the law of the testator's domicile at the date of execution of the will or at death.[70]

The Wills Act 1861 (Lord Kingsdown's Act), introduced in response to *Bremer v Freeman* (1857), was not essential as regards Scots law, but it applied to both Scotland and England, and provided that (a) a will should not be held to be revoked nor its construction altered by reason of a change of domicile of the testator; and (b) various options against which the formal validity of a will could be tested were provided in addition to the common law rules stated above. However, there remained certain defects in the law.

Wills Act 1963

18-20 The law was altered again by the Wills Act 1963, which repealed the 1861 Act, and came into operation on January 1, 1964 as regards the will of a person who died after that date. The 1963 Act represents the current law on the subject and is the result of deliberations at the Hague culminating in the 1961 Hague Convention on the Conflict of Laws relating to the Form of Testamentary Dispositions. The Act contains the following rules as to formal validity:

(a) General rule (section 1(1))

18-21 A will is to be regarded as validly executed in form if it complies with any of the following laws[71]:

- (i) the law of the place of execution[72];
- (ii) the law of the testator's domicile at the date of execution or at his death;
- (iii) the law of the testator's habitual residence at the date of execution or at his death;
- (iv) the law of the testator's nationality at the date of execution or at his death (if he was a national of more than one country, then possibly compliance with either (any) of those laws will suffice).[73]

The list of applicable laws is long and the choice wide, but it is still possible for a testator to fall foul of the Act. In *Re Kanani*[74] an English national and domiciliary, on holiday in Switzerland, made a will written in his own handwriting on the writing paper of his hotel. His death occurred shortly

---

[69] *Purvis' Trustees* (1861) 23 D. 812 (will made by Scots domiciliary in the Dutch East Indies).

[70] cf. At later date *Chisholm*, 1949 S.C. 434: opinion, per Lord Ordinary Guthrie that a will made by a testator then domiciled in England which had been typed and signed, but not witnessed, should receive effect in Scotland if it complied with Scots law which was the law of his domicile at the date of his death.

[71] In each case the law in question is the internal law of the country: s.6(1) (pace Morris, *Conflict of Laws*, 7th edn, 2009, para.17–022, taking the view that the statutory provisions do not in terms obliterate the pre-existing law; see also *Cheshire, North and Fawcett: Private International Law*, 14th edn, 2008, p.1269).

[72] Even if the testator was on a temporary visit there. *Re Wynn (Deceased)* [1983] 3 All E.R. 310.

[73] F.A. Mann, "The Formal Validity of Wills in Case of Dual Nationality" (1986) 35 I.C.L.Q. 423.

[74] *Re Kanani (Deceased)* (1978) 122 S.J. 611.

afterwards. The will was invalid as to form because it did not comply with English requirements and, although Swiss law recognised holograph wills, such wills had to be entirely holograph and the printed heading of the hotel on the writing paper was fatal to the will's validity.

(b) Additional rules (section 2)

A will is also[75] to be regarded as validly executed in form in the following **18–22** circumstances:

(i) A will executed on board a vessel[76] or aircraft (s.2(1)(a)) is properly executed if the execution conforms to the internal law of the territory with which, having regard to its registration (if any) and other relevant circumstances, the vessel or aircraft may be taken to have been most closely connected.

(ii) A will so far as it disposes of immoveable property (s.2(1)(b)) is properly executed if the execution conforms to the internal law in force in the territory where the property was situated.

(c) Other relevant provisions (sections 2–6)

(i) **Revocation** (s.2(1)(c)). If a will purports to revoke a will valid in **18–23** form under the Act, it shall itself be regarded as valid in form and thus revoking the earlier will, if it conforms to any law by reference to which the revoked will would be valid.

(ii) **Powers** (s.2(1)(d), (2)). If a will exercises a power of appointment, it shall be regarded as valid in form if it conforms with the law governing the essential validity of the power. Further, (s.2(2)), a will which exercises a power of appointment shall not be treated as improperly executed by reason only that its execution was not in accordance with any formal requirements contained in the instrument creating the power.

(iii) **Foreign law** (s.3). Where a law in force outside the United Kingdom falls to be applied in relation to a will, any requirement of that law, whereby special formalities are to be observed by testators of a particular description, or witnesses are to possess certain qualifications, shall be treated as a formal requirement only.

(iv) **Construction of wills** (s.4). The construction of a will shall not be altered by reason of any change of domicile of the testator after the date of execution of the will.

---

[75] The rules in s.2 must be regarded as rules additionally available, over and above s.1, thereby precluding any argument that, e.g. a will purporting to dispose of immoveable property *must* comply with the formal requirements of the *lex situs*.

[76] Cases still arise concerning the privileges accorded under English domestic law, per Wills Act 1837 s.11, to wills made by soldiers in military service, and mariners or seamen, even extending to the acceptance of oral wills: *Re Servoz-Gavin (Deceased)* [2010] 1 All E.R. 410. In the alternative, the testator may comply with the law of closest connection. If the aircraft was on the ground, or the ship in territorial waters, it will be sufficient that the testator complied with the law of the place of execution (*Cheshire, North and Fawcett: Private International Law*, 14th edn, 2008, p.1267).

(v) **Interpretation of the Act**: Section 6 defines inter alia "internal law" as the law which would apply in a case where no question of the law in force in any other territory or state arose.[77]

Registration of wills and "international wills"

18–24   The Administration of Justice Act 1982 makes provision in ss.23–25 for registration of wills, and in ss.27 and 28 for international wills.

A Convention on the Establishment of a Scheme of Registration of Wills was drawn up at Basle in 1972 under the auspices of the Council of Europe, with the aim of establishing national registration schemes and providing supplementary rules governing the international co-operation which was thought to be required between the various national authorities entrusted with registration. Sections 23–25 of the 1982 Act were put in place to allow the UK to comply with the requirements of the Convention, and thereby to ratify it, but the sections have never been implemented.

Likewise, s.27, which provides that the Annex[78] to the Convention on International Wills,[79] concluded at Washington on October 26, 1973, shall have the force of law in the UK, is still not in force. The aim of the 1973 Uniform Law was to provide a new form of will, in addition to existing forms permitted by national rules of law, for use in circumstances where a will has "some international characteristics."[80] The aim was that a will which satisfied the provisions of the Uniform Law would be regarded as formally valid in the UK or any other Contracting State to the Convention, no matter that the said will had no connection with the UK or any such other Contracting State.[81]

It is now highly unlikely that these provisions of the 1982 Act will come into effect. The initiatives are a dead letter therefore. The impetus towards some type of international register of wills was resurrected in the EU Green Paper on Wills and Succession, but does not appear in the proposed Regulation Rome V.[82] However, in Chs V and VI of the proposed Regulation are to be

---

[77] i.e. there is to be no scope for *renvoi* in matters covered by the Act (in the very subject area which gave rise to *renvoi*). But see fn.71, above. Section 6(2) provides the solution where doubt arises in a multi-legal system state about which law to apply as the "internal law".

[78] Set out in Sch.2 to the 1982 Act.

[79] UNIDROIT Convention providing a Uniform Law on the Form of an International Will.

[80] J.P. Plantard Explanatory Report on the Convention providing a Uniform Law on the Form of an International Will (1974) I *Uniform Law Review* 91 at 92, p.2.

[81] Article 1 of the Annex states that a will shall be valid as regards form, irrespective particularly of the place where it is made, of the location of the assets and of the nationality, domicile or residence of the testator, if it is made in the form of an international will complying with the provisions set out in arts 2–5, viz.: the testator shall declare in the presence of two witnesses, and of a person authorised to act in connection with international wills (a solicitor or notary public: s.28), that the document is his will, and that he knows the contents thereof. The testator shall sign the will in the presence of the witnesses and of the authorised person, or acknowledge his signature. The witnesses and the authorised person shall attest the will by signing in the presence of the testator. The authorised person shall attach to the will a certificate in the form prescribed, which, in the absence of evidence to the contrary, shall be conclusive of the formal validity of the instrument as an international will. Since, however, art.13 provides that the absence, or irregularity, of a certificate shall not affect the formal validity of an international will, it is difficult to see the point of certification.

[82] See para.18–35, below.

found draft provisions on authentic instruments and on the creation of a European Certificate of Succession. Such provisions are not meaningful to the lawyer of common law background.[83]

DUTY OF A SOLICITOR TO ACT TIMEOUSLY UPON INSTRUCTIONS TO MAKE A WILL

The existence, or not, of such a duty will be characterised in a Scots forum as pertaining to delict. The conflict aspect of the subject must be governed, therefore, by the applicable law determined in accordance with the Rome II Regulation.[84]   **18–25**

ESSENTIAL VALIDITY OF WILLS

The essential validity of a will is governed by the *lex successionis*, which, in the case of immoveables is the *lex situs*,[85] and in the case of moveables is the law of the testator's domicile, both as at the date of death.   **18–26**

Essential validity is concerned with all matters pertaining to the validity and enforceability of the provisions of a will. Thus it deals with the extent to which the provisions of a will are valid, or may be affected adversely by any of the following matters:

(a) proof of survival[86];
(b) claims for legal rights[87];
(c) election, or approbate and reprobate[88];
(d) conditions attached to bequests, such as to marriage or religion[89];
(e) bequests contrary to public policy;
(f) bequests for religious or charitable purposes[90];

---

[83] A register inevitably would be incomplete and unsatisfactory. Upon whom would lie the duty, if duty there be, to register a will? What would be the effect of failure to register? Would a registered will trump a subsequent unregistered will?

[84] See, domestically, for England, House of Lords decision in *White v Jones* [1995] 2 A.C. 207 and in Scotland, *Holmes v Bank of Scotland*, 2002 S.L.T. 544.

[85] *Philipson-Stow v Inland Revenue Commissioners* [1961] A.C. 727; see earlier *Nelson v Bridport* (1846) 8 Beav. 547 and *Re Miller* [1914] 1 Ch. 511.

[86] *Re Cohn* [1945] Ch. 5.

[87] *Re Groos* [1915] 1 Ch. 572.

[88] The question whether or not a beneficiary must elect between a bequest under a will and an interest outside the will is determined by the law of the testator's domicile at the date of his death: *Re Ogilvie* [1918] 1 Ch. 492; *Hewit's Trustees v Lawson* (1891) 18 R. 793; *Re Allen's Estate* [1945] 2 All E.R. 264, subject to the view of the *lex situs* as regards foreign land: *Murray v Smith* (1828) 6 S. 690; *Alexander v Bennet's Trustees* (1829) 7 S. 817; *Hewit's Trustees v Lawson* (1891) 18 R. 793; *Brown's Trustees v Gregson*, 1920 S.C. (H.L.) 87; *Trotter v Trotter* (1829) 3 Wils. & Sh. 407; *Dundas v Dundas* (1830) 2 Dow & Cl. 349; *Douglas-Menzies v Umphelby* [1908] A.C. 224; *Re Ogilvie* [1918] 1 Ch. 492; *Re Mengel's Will Trusts* [1962] Ch. 791.

[89] *Ommanney v Bingham* (1936) 3 Pat. 448.

[90] *Boe v Anderson* (1862) 24 D. 732; *Ferguson v Marjoribanks* (1853) 15 D. 637; *Hewit's Trustees v Lawson* (1891) 18 R. 793; *Re Elliot* (1891) 39 W.R. 297; *Re De Noailles* (1916) 114 L.T. 1089; *Re Egan* (1918) L.J. 633; *Re Dawson* [1915] 1 Ch. 626.

    (g) the extent to which the provisions are affected by statutory provisions as to accumulation of capital and income, and perpetuities[91];

    (h) the extent to which provisions may be affected by considerations of inheritance tax[92];

    (i) the operation of the *conditio si testator sine liberis decesserit*[93];

    (j) lapse of bequest to spouse upon the occurrence of subsequent divorce or annulment[94]; and

    (k) rules of forfeiture ("the unworthy heir").[95]

The distinction between formal validity and essential validity is clear in theory, but in exceptional cases, it may not be easy to distinguish between them. In the case of *Re Priest*,[96] for example, the English forum classified its own rule that bequests would be rendered void if the will in which they were made was witnessed by the spouse of a beneficiary, as a rule of substance, governed, therefore, by the law of the testator's last domicile.[97]

CONSTRUCTION OR INTERPRETATION OF WILLS

18–27 Just as the distinction between formal validity and essential validity is clear in theory, but occasionally in practice the one aspect may tend to merge with the other, so too the distinction between essential validity and construction may converge.

Construction of a will answers the question—what do the provisions of the will mean?

Essential validity answers the question—to what extent are the provisions of a will valid and enforceable?

The general principle is that a will must be construed in accordance with the law by reference to which it was written, that is, the legal system contemplated

---

[91] *Fordyce v Bridges* (1848) 2 Ph. 497.

[92] *Philipson-Stow* [1961] A.C. 727; *Re Levick's Will Trusts* [1963] 1 W.L.R. 311. British inheritance tax is payable on transfers of property (unless it falls below the exemption limits): (a) made by a deceased who died domiciled in the UK no matter where the property was situated, and (b) situated in the UK no matter where the deceased died domiciled. See statutory extension of meaning of domicile (extending to residence in the UK in 17 out of the previous 20 years of assessment): Inheritance Tax Act 1984 s.267. Transfers of value between spouses or civil partners are exempt (Inheritance Tax Act 1984 s.18(1)), but if only the transferor spouse or civil partner is domiciled in the UK the transfer is only partially exempt. See D.R. Macdonald, *Succession*, 3rd edn (Edinburgh: W. Green, 2001), para.12.26.

[93] Contrast characterisation of the *conditio si institutus sine liberis decesserit* (*q.v.*).

[94] Such a provision was enacted for English domestic law in the Law Reform (Succession) Act 1995 s.3(1), and applicable where the gift was of moveable property and the deceased died domiciled in England, or where the bequest was of immoveable property situated in England. As to Scotland, see Family Law (Scotland) Act 2006 s.19, whereby a special destination is revoked upon the parties' divorce or annulment prior to the death of the predeceaser.

[95] See *Re DWS (Deceased)* [2001] 1 All E.R. 97: further, and criticism thereof Law Commission, *The Forfeiture Rule and the Law of Succession* (The Stationery Office, 2005), Law Com. No.295.

[96] *Re Priest (Deceased)* [1944] Ch. 58.

[97] Contrast *Irving v Snow*, 1956 S.C. 257, in which a will, though null and void under Scots law because of the prohibition on notarial execution by a party interested in the will, was held by a Scots court to have been validly executed since it satisfied the English legal requirements of the *lex loci actus*.

by the testator,[98] which may or may not be the same as the governing law of the essentials of the will. The testator's intention, deemed or actual, is the paramount consideration.[99] In *Philipson-Stow v Inland Revenue Commissioners*,[100] Lord Denning said:

". . . whilst I would agree that the construction of the will depends on the intention of the testator, I would say that in no other respect does his intention determine the law applicable to it".[101]

The following are working rules:

(1) If there is an express declaration as to the law to be applied for the purposes of interpretation, that law normally will regulate the construction of the will.
(2) In the absence of such a declaration, the law to be applied may be clearly inferred from the language of the will.[102] The use of technical terms of a particular legal system usually indicates that the will should be construed according to that law.[103]

    In the special case of a will dealing with a bequest of immoveables expressed in the technical terms of the law of a country other than the *lex situs*, the meaning of the will is first ascertained according to the law indicated by the will, and the court then endeavours to translate it and give effect to it in terms which will make sense and be effective according to the *lex situs*.[104]
(3) Otherwise, there is a presumption that the law of the testator's domicile at the date of the will shall apply as regards moveables[105] and probably also as regards immoveables,[106] because presumably he had that law in mind.[107] In exceptional cases, however, if the language of the will does not clearly indicate any particular law, the law of the domicile at the date of death has been applied.[108] In such a case, there

---

[98] *Dellar v Zivy* [2007] I.L.Pr. 60.
[99] *Re Nesbitt* [1953] 1 W.L.R. 595 (domestic case); *Re Scott* [1915] 1 Ch. 592 (conflict case).
[100] [1961] A.C. 727. Also *Re Levick's Will Trusts* [1963] 1 W.L.R. 311.
[101] *Philipson-Stow* [1961] A.C. 727 at 760, 761.
[102] *Re Goetze* [1953] Ch. 96; *Re Cunnington* [1924] 1 Ch. 68; *Re Price* [1900] 1 Ch. 442, per Stirling J. at 453; *Re Allen's Estate* [1945] 2 All E.R. 264.
[103] *Re McMorran* [1958] Ch. 624; *Re Manners* [1923] 1 Ch. 220; but see *Bradford v Young* (1885) L.R. 29 Ch. D. 617 in which the use of some technical terms of Scots law was held by the Court of Appeal, disapproving the court below, to be insufficient indication of the testator's intention to have the will construed by that law.
[104] *Studd v Cook* (1883) 10 R. (H.L.) 53; *Cripps' Trustees v Cripps*, 1926 S.C. 188; *Re Miller* [1914] 1 Ch. 511.
[105] *Dellar v Zivy* [2007] I.L.Pr. 60.
[106] *Mitchell and Baxter v Davies* (1875) 3 R. 208; *Smith v Smith* (1891) 18 R. 1036; *McBride's Trustees, Special Case*, 1952 S.L.T. (Notes) 59; *Re Price* [1900] 1 Ch. 442 (subject always to the ultimate practical pre-eminence of the *lex situs*).
[107] *Re Allen's Estate* [1945] 2 All E.R. 264; *Philipson-Stow* [1961] A.C. 727, per Lord Denning at 761, 762 (so long as the construction does not conflict with the rules of the *lex situs*).
[108] *Re Cunnington* [1924] 1 Ch. 68.

is Scots authority[109] suggestive that the forum may simply construe the will in accordance with its own law.

(4) The Wills Act 1963 s.4 provides that the construction of a will is not to be affected by a change of domicile by the testator after the date of execution of the will.

The width and variety of these "rules" (or guides) suggest that it is more important to be aware of the distinction between essentials and construction, to note that the *lex successionis* may not necessarily be the law which governs construction, and to be cognisant of those matters which have been assigned to the category of "interpretation", than to place great reliance on any one of the "presumptions".

Conflict problems involving the following matters are solved by the application of the rules as to construction:

(a) whether a will in general terms exercises a power of appointment (*q.v.*);

(b) application of *conditio si institutus sine liberis decesserit*.

In *Mitchell and Baxter v Davies*[110] the question was of the type to which the Scottish *conditio si institutus sine liberis decesserit* applies, and having been assigned by the Scots forum to the category of "interpretation", was referred to the Scots law governing the interpretation of the will, which had been made in Scots form, rather than to the English law of the deceased's last domicile.

(c) Accretion or intestacy as a result of the absence of a survivorship clause or a destination-over.

The question whether accretion to the survivors of a list of eight residuary legatees (as was the French rule), or whether the shares of the two predeceasers, neither of whom had left issue, should fall into intestacy (the English rule), was classified by the English forum, in the case of *Re Cunnington*,[111] as a matter of interpretation. The case illustrates also the relative weakness of the "working rules" to identify the law which should regulate interpretation since the French law of the domicile at death was taken to be the law governing construction, there being no indication to the contrary.

Construction of bequests

18–28   To determine the validity of a claim of a beneficiary in testate succession, it will be necessary to ascertain, according to the law governing interpretation of the will, the testator's intention with regard to that beneficiary or class of beneficiaries, but there may arise thereafter the separate issue of ascertaining the

---

[109] *Griffith's Judicial Factor v Griffith's Executors* (1905) 7 F. 470, where, however, the principal question was whether a will, executed in British Guiana by a testator who was a native of that country, but resident in Scotland for some years prior to death (and quite possibly domiciled there), carried Scottish heritage. In these circumstances, it is not surprising that the Scots court interpreted the will according to Scots law.

[110] (1875) 3 R. 208.

[111] [1924] 1 Ch. 68.

status of the claimant, i.e. whether he qualifies as a member of that class, e.g. of the legitimate/legitimated.

If the succession to the estate of X, domiciled in country A, opens, in terms of his will as interpreted in accordance with the rules set out above, only to the legitimate children of Y, domiciled in country B, and a question arises as to whether or not a person is a legitimate child of Y, Scots and English choice of law rules diverge. Scots conflict law favours the application of B law to determine the status of the children of Y,[112] whereas English conflict law prefers application of A law.[113]

Where, however, the bequest is to the "heirs", "children", "issue", "next-of-kin", etc. of the *testator*, the beneficiaries are to be identified by the *lex domicilii*[114] of the testator.

REVOCATION OF WILLS

It is necessary to consider the effect upon a will of a subsequent will; a subsequent marriage by the testator; or a change of domicile by the testator after making the will. **18–29**

(a) New will

The revocation of one will depends on the validity and scope of a subsequent will.[115] **18–30**

This simple and obvious statement contains within it a number of difficulties, for example, as to the scope of the new will, and its validity as to form and essence. In the case of an estate being administered abroad, it is possible that the new will may be deemed to be formally defective with regard to the testator's immoveable property, with the result that a prior will (if extant), valid by the *lex situs*, may continue to regulate the immoveable succession, while the new will regulates the succession to moveables.[116] The matter alternatively

---

[112] *Mitchell's Trustee v Rule* (1908) 16 S.L.T. 189; *Smith's Trustees v Macpherson's Trustees*, 1926 S.C. 983; *Goold Stuart's Trustees v McPhail*, 1947 S.L.T. 221; *Spencer's Trustees v Ruggles*, 1981 S.C. 289; *Wright's Trustees v Callender*, 1993 S.L.T. 556; *Salvesen's Trustees, Petitioners*, 1993 S.L.T. 1327. See Crawford, 1994 S.L.T. (News) 225 and Leslie, 1995 S.L.T. (News) 264. In *Spencer's Trustees*, 1981 S.C. 289, the question at issue was whether adopted children could succeed but since it was established that the testator did not intend to benefit adopted children, the second stage of debating by which law the validity of a foreign adoption should be judged was not reached.

[113] *Campbell v Campbell* (1866) L.R. 1 Eq. 383; *Re Fergusson's Will* [1902] 1 Ch. 483.

[114] There is also a temporal issue, in that the content of the applicable law may have changed between the date of testing and date of death, or between date of death and date of opening of the succession. *Wright's Trustees v Callender* 1993 S.L.T. 556 addressed rather the issue of the effect of time, and changes in the law, on the matter of *interpretation* of the truster's intentions. The effect of the decision was that the content of the applicable law as at the date of death, rather than the (much later) date of opening of the succession should prevail.

[115] *Cameron v Mackie* (1833) 7 W. & S. 16; *Cottrell v Cottrell* (1872) L.R. 2 P. & D. 397.

[116] *In the Estate of Alberti* [1955] 1 W.L.R. 1240, where a testator made a will in England dealing, inter alia, with real estate in England. Later he made a holograph will in Switzerland which was invalid by English law although valid by Swiss law and which purported to revoke all previous wills. It was held that the English will was still effective in relation to the English real estate because only a will valid by the *lex situs* could revoke the earlier will in that regard.

might be one of inference and interpretation, as when, without express revocation, the testator makes provision in a later will in relation to property included in an earlier one.

Further, a will may be regarded as having been revoked in one country, but not in another,[117] and so different wills may apply to assets in different countries.[118]

(b) A revocation clause

18–31 The effect of such a clause is considered in light of all the circumstances.[119] Again this seems a very broad guide, but it can happen on occasion that the circumstances reveal quite clearly what was the testator's intention. Thus, in *Re Wayland*[120] where the testator had separate wills to deal with his English and his Belgian estate, it was apparent that when he made a new English will, its revocation clause was intended to apply only to previous English wills. Before and after making that new English will, he corresponded with his Belgian lawyer about the safekeeping of his Belgian will.

(c) Acts involving revocation

18–32 The effectiveness of a purported act of revocation depends, as regards immoveables, upon the *lex situs*, and as regards moveables, upon the law of the testator's domicile at the date of the revocation. An excellent example is provided by *Velasco v Coney*[121]: the English testatrix, who had acquired Italian domicile on marriage, instructed her English solicitor to destroy her will, previously made by her in accordance with both English and Italian law. This he did, but not in her presence as required by English domestic law. The English court decided that such an act of revocation was sufficient to satisfy its conflict rules if the act amounted to revocation by the domicile of the testatrix at the date of the act of purported revocation—a practical decision, and one in accordance with the policy of the court, which was to, "lean towards giving effect to the intention of the testatrix." By Italian law, her letter or mandate containing her instructions to revoke would have been sufficient even without the physical destruction which in fact happened.

---

[117] *Richmond's Trustees v Winton* (1864) 3 M. 95.

[118] *Re Manifold* [1962] Ch. 1. A testatrix domiciled in Cyprus made two wills, the first valid by the laws of England and Cyprus, and the second valid only by the law of England. Probate was granted on the first will in Cyprus, but it was held that, as regards assets in England, the Wills Act 1861 must have an overriding effect and that probate must be granted on both wills. Thereafter, the administrators in England of the English estate were directed to distribute the assets in England according to the terms of the later will, on the basis that it had, in the English view, superseded the earlier will, and as if the assets in England were the whole estate, the legacies to abate rateably so far as necessary.

[119] cf. Australian case of *Re Barker* [1995] 2 V.R. 439: the question whether extrinsic evidence might be adduced to prove the intention of the testator with regard to the revocation of an earlier will in so far as it dealt with property in another country was a matter of evidence to be determined by the *lex fori* and a matter of construction to be determined by the law of the testator's domicile.

[120] *Re Wayland (Deceased)* [1951] 2 All E.R. 1041. Also *Lamothe v Lamothe* [2006] EWHC 1387 (Ch).

[121] [1934] P. 143.

(d) Change of domicile

This has no effect on the formal validity or construction of a will.[122] However, **18–33** change of domicile is of fundamental importance in the final outcome for, as explained, the essential validity of the will falls to be judged, vis-à-vis moveables, by the law of the testator's last domicile.[123]

(e) Subsequent marriage

The effect of the marriage of the testator upon a previous will is determined, **18–34** as regards moveables, by the law of the domicile of the testator immediately after the marriage.[124] By English domestic law, an ante-nuptial will is revoked by marriage of the testator, unless the will was made in contemplation of that marriage.[125] By Scots law, marriage per se does not revoke an earlier will, but if children subsequently are born, no provision having been made for them in the will, it will be open to them to seek to have applied the presumption *conditio si testator sine liberis decesserit.* The *conditio si testator* or equivalent in a conflict context is regarded as a matter of substance, available, therefore, in the Scots view only if such a rule forms part of the *lex successionis* (i.e. being Scots law, or any law containing an equivalent provision).

Any rule of revocation by subsequent marriage is regarded in Scots and English conflict rules as a matter of matrimonial law rather than succession law.[126] Since the domestic laws of Scotland and England differ on this matter, though their conflict rules agree, this means, in an English/Scottish context, that if a testator domiciled in England makes a will before his marriage, and is of English domicile immediately after marriage, the will is revoked and cannot revive even upon subsequent acquisition of Scots domicile. In contrast, the English courts will uphold any will made by a Scots domiciliary before marriage even though he may die domiciled in England, provided that his immediate post-nuptial domicile was Scottish.[127]

IV. EUROPEAN HARMONISATION: PROPOSAL FOR A REGULATION ON WILLS AND SUCCESSION

As has been seen, the conflict rules of Scots and English law in the area of **18–35** succession are well-settled and understood, and rest largely on the common law.

Succession conflict rules were excluded from early EU harmonisation processes. Whilst harmonisation of choice of law rules concerning formal validity of wills has been accomplished,[128] efforts to harmonise the rules

---

[122] Wills Act 1963 s.4.

[123] *Re Groos* [1915] 1 Ch. 572.

[124] *Re Martin* [1900] P. 211. Except that its effect upon any provisions in respect of immoveables must be determined by *lex situs* (*Re Caithness* (1891) 7 T.L.R. 354).

[125] Wills Act 1837 s.18 (substituted by s.18(1) of the Administration of Justice Act 1982). The same is true of civil partnerships, per s.18B of the 1837 Act (inserted by s.71 and Sch.4 of the Civil Partnership Act 2004): *Court v Despallieres*; sub nom. *Re Ikin (Deceased)* [2009] EWHC 3340 (Ch).

[126] *Westerman v Schwab* (1905) 8 F. 132; *Re Martin* [1900] P. 211; cf. *Re Groos* [1915] 1 Ch. 572.

[127] *Re Reid* (1866) L.R. 1 P. & D. 74.

[128] 1961 Hague Convention on the Conflicts of Laws Relating to the Form of Testamentary Dispositions, leading to 1963 Wills Act: see paras 18–20—18–23, above.

concerning essential validity have proved less successful: the 1989 Hague Convention on the Law Applicable to the Estates of Deceased Persons, to which the United Kingdom did not accede, proceeded on the principle of unity (i.e. of one law governing succession to all types of property), but the instrument received little support and was not acceptable to the UK.[129]

A consultation process took place in 2005 to elicit opinion in EU Member States, not only upon the scope of a possible harmonisation instrument to deal with wills and succession (choice of law and/or administration), but also on the detail of proposed rules.[130] The initiative was said to be justified by the growing mobility of European citizens in an area without internal frontiers, and the increasing frequency of personal unions between nationals of different Member States, together with the fact of acquisition by many individuals of property situated in the territories of different states.

In October 2009, the European Commission announced the publication of a Proposal for a Regulation on jurisdiction, applicable law, recognition and enforcement of decisions and authentic instruments in matters of succession and the creation of a European Certificate of Succession.[131] As its name suggests, this proposed instrument, known colloquially as "Rome V", is wide in technical scope, and aims to deal with all conflict of laws aspects of the subject of succession.[132]

Scope

18–36   At the outset, art.1, in excluding questions regarding matrimonial property regimes[133] and assets owned jointly with a right of survival, together with matters concerning the status of natural persons, and their legal capacity, must be taken to demonstrate the hope that such excluded matters are capable of being regulated independently of a scheme of harmonised conflict rules of succession. However, issues of matrimonial property, gifts and joint ownerships frequently are intertwined with issues of succession and proprietary capacity, as exemplified classically in the House of Lords decision of *De Nicols v Curlier (No.1)*,[134] and as a matter of practice, it is doubtful whether

---

[129] See Lord Chancellor's Department, Scottish Courts Administration, *Hague Convention on Succession: Consultation Paper* (HMSO, 1990); and Robertson, "International Succession Law. A Co-ordinated Approach" (1989) 34 J.L.S. 377.

[130] Green Paper on Succession and Wills COM(2005) 65 final. See also Commission Staff Working Paper, Annex to the Green Paper on Succession and Wills SEC(2005) 270, and Opinion of the European Economic and Social Committee on the Green Paper on Succession and Wills [2006] OJ C28/1.

[131] Proposal for a Regulation on jurisdiction, applicable law, recognition and enforcement of decisions and authentic instruments in matters of succession and the creation of a European Certificate of Succession COM(2009) 154 final (2009/0157 (COD)). See also Commission Staff Working Document accompanying the Proposal: Summary of the Impact Assessment SEC(2009) 411 final. For a detailed consideration, see Max Planck Institute for Comparative and International Private Law, *Comments on the EU Commission's Proposal issued by the Max Planck Institute for Comparative and International Private Law* (2010).

[132] Chapter I—scope and definitions; Ch.II—jurisdiction; Ch.III—applicable law; Ch.IV—recognition and enforcement; Ch.V—authentic instruments; Ch.VI—European Certificate of Succession; Ch.VII—general and final provisions.

[133] See, however, art.22 (special succession regimes).

[134] *De Nicols v Curlier (No.1)* [1900] A.C. 21.

the segregation of matrimonial property issues from succession issues will be as straightforward as the Proposal appears to envisage.

Jurisdiction

The majority of "international" successions, as with any succession, are **18–37** non-contentious, but insofar as litigation may arise concerning competing rights in property, presently there are no specialised or bespoke rules (national or European) of jurisdiction for matters of succession,[135] jurisdiction in such cases resting on the general rules pertaining to jurisdiction in property matters.[136] Therefore, the creation of a set of jurisdiction rules specifically for this area is at odds with common law experience and expectations.

The scheme proposed is as follows: the general rule (art.4) is that the courts[137] of the Member State of habitual residence of the deceased at death shall be competent to rule in matters of succession. Anticipating the proposal to permit limited party autonomy in the matter of applicable law, art.5 provides that where the deceased has chosen the law of a Member State to govern his succession in accordance with art.17, the court seised per art.4, at the request of one of the parties, and if it considers that the courts of the Member State whose law has been chosen are better placed to rule on the succession, may stay proceedings, and invite the parties to seise the courts of that other Member State. Assuming that the latter state court declares itself competent, the court first seised shall decline jurisdiction. If this does not happen, the court first seised shall continue to exercise its jurisdiction.

The scheme adopts (arts 10–15) the system of *lis pendens* with which we have become familiar under the Brussels regime in civil and commercial matters, and in consistorial proceedings. The supremacy of the *forum rei sitae* is recognised in art.9, which provides that where the Member State of the *situs* requires the involvement of its courts in the matter of recording or transferring in a public register the transmission of property, the courts of the *situs* shall be competent to take such measures.

---

[135] Except in relation to trusts, when art.5.6 of the Brussels I Regulation may apply. With regard to residual rules of Scots law re trusts, see Civil Jurisdiction and Judgments Act 1982 Sch.8 para.2 (special jurisdiction in certain matters pertaining to trusts domiciled in Scotland); and Sch.8 para.6(4), (5) (prorogation of jurisdiction in certain matters pertaining to trusts).

[136] In proceedings which have as their object rights *in rem* in immoveable property, or tenancies of immoveable property, art.22 of the Brussels I Regulation will apply: see Ch.7, above. With regard to residual rules of Scots law, see Civil Jurisdiction and Judgments Act 1982 Sch.8 para.1 (*general* jurisdiction: persons shall be sued in the courts for the place where they are domiciled); Sch.8 para.2 (*special* jurisdiction: (g) which confers jurisdiction in certain matters pertaining to trusts domiciled in Scotland; (h) which confers jurisdiction where the defender is not domiciled in the UK, on the courts for any place where—(ii) any immoveable property in which he has any beneficial interest is situated; . . . (i) in proceedings brought to assert, declare or determine proprietary or possessory rights, or rights of security, in or over moveable property, or to obtain authority to dispose of moveable property, the defender shall be sued in the courts for the place where the property is situated); Sch.8 para.5(1) (*exclusive* jurisdiction: in proceedings which have as their object rights *in rem* in immoveable property, the courts for the place where the property is situated shall have exclusive jurisdiction).

[137] Article 2 adopts a broad definition of "courts", in recognition of the fact that many successions are non-contentious, and therefore encompasses within its meaning any judicial authority or any competent authority in the Member States which carries out a judicial function in matters of succession.

Applicable law

18–38   Article 16 provides the proposed general rule, which is that the law applicable to the succession as a whole shall be that of the state[138] in which the deceased had his habitual residence at death.

The applicable law, meaning the rules of law in force in that state other than its rules of private international law,[139] shall govern all matters of substance, and such other matters as are narrated in art.19, which provides a long, but non-exhaustive, definition of subjects which fall within the scope of the applicable law,[140] and gives very wide scope to the *lex successionis*, extending apparently to matters of procedure and administration. Insofar as art.19.2(g) assigns to the governance of the *lex successionis* "the powers of the heirs, the executors of the wills and other administrators of the succession, in particular the sale of property and the payment of creditors", problems will arise for legal systems such as those in the UK, which interpose between the deceased and the heir, one or more personal representatives, whose appointment and powers presently are governed by the *lex fori* and not by the *lex successionis*.

The proposed unitary rule

18–39   Leaving for the moment the question of the quality of "last habitual residence" as a connecting factor, one notes the proposed replacement of the scission principle by a unitary principle. This would be a fundamental change for the UK. In recent years, however, abandonment of the *situs* rule has been mooted, at least in the law of intestate succession.[141]

Such a change to a unitary system, therefore, has been in contemplation in the UK for many years, and the unitary system has long been the civilian rule. Yet the *lex situs* must have its place, and certain ends cannot be achieved without its acquiescence. The proposed Regulation acknowledges the undeniable interest of

---

[138] Article 25 provides that any law specified by the Regulation shall apply, even if it is not the law of a Member State (the principle of "universality of application").

[139] See art.26. See Ch.5, above.

[140] Certain subjects in the proposed Regulation have bespoke rules, namely, simultanous death (i.e. common calamity) (art.23), and estate without a claimant (i.e. caduciary rights and *bona vacantia*) (art.24).

[141] See para.18–04, above. See also 1989 Hague Convention on the Law Applicable to Succession to the Estates of Deceased Persons; *Dicey and Morris on the Conflict of Laws*, 10th edn, 1980, re r.98, stating that, "The succession to the immovables of an intestate is governed by the law of the country where the immovables are situated (*lex situs*).", ". . . the rule has always been taken for granted rather than expressly laid down by judges . . . It makes no sense today when England and all other countries in the world (except Bermuda) have adopted one system of intestate succession for all kinds of property. It has, therefore, been suggested that the *lex situs* rule has outlived its usefulness and should be abandoned in favour of the law of the intestate's domicile" (p.613). This rule has appeared in identical terms in subsequent editions of *Dicey and Morris on the Conflict of Laws*, 11th edn, 1987, r.138; 12th edn, 1993, r.135; 13th edn, 2000, r.133; 14th edn, 2006, r.141. The warning was given (10th edn, 1980, p.614) that, "There is a serious risk that the retention of the *lex situs* rule will frustrate the intentions of Parliament" (p.614), as arguably in the case of *Re Collens (Deceased)* [1986] Ch. 505, in which the widow benefited *twice*, a result intended by neither the law of the domicile nor the *lex situs*. Similarly, by the end of the 1980s, the Scottish Law Commission had come to the view that the last domicile of the deceased should regulate the devolution of the whole (intestate) estate: Scottish Law Commission, *Some Miscellaneous Topics in the Law of Succession*, 1986, Scot. Law Com. Memo. No.71, para.6.4; and Scottish Law Commission, *Report on Succession*, 1990, Scot. Law Com.No.124, para.10.5. But see Law Commission, Intestacy and Family Provision Claims on Death: A Consultation Paper (The Stationery Office, 2009) Law Com. C.P. No.191, paras 7.38, 7.39 and fn.27 above.

the *lex situs*, as evidenced in arts 9 and 21, which, in turn, endow the *forum rei sitae* with jurisdiction, where required, for the transmission of property; and preserves the application of the law of the *situs* where it stipulates formalities for the purpose of acceptance or waiver of the succession of a legacy, or subjects the administration of the succession to the appointment of an administrator or executor via an authority located in the *lex situs*.

A major role for habitual residence

One of the main points of disquiet among UK lawyers is prompted by **18–40** selection as the principal connecting factor of the last habitual residence of the deceased. It is notorious within conflict of laws scholarship that habitual residence is a weasel factor, which does not always live up to its reputation as a common sense factual criterion.[142] Habitual residence has proved to be a fruitful source of discussion and litigation. In spite of this, the Proposal does not provide a definition.[143] Further, the Proposal does not address the problem of multiplicity of residences, commonly found in the type of succession case for which it is intended to cater. This is a serious flaw given that the impetus for this proposed instrument is said to be the need to meet the requirements of "international persons". There are serious doubts about the sufficiency of "habitual residence", as baldly used in the Proposal, to fulfil satisfactorily the pivotal function allocated to it in the proposed framework of rules.

Party autonomy

Article 17 of the Proposal provides an option for a testator to choose as the **18–41** law governing the succession to his estate the law of his nationality. Freedom of choice of law in the area of succession is a novelty to a UK lawyer. The fact that party autonomy is a recognised tool of choice of law in harmonisation instruments such as Rome I and Rome II does not mean that it necessarily should be included in a succession instrument. However, an article providing limited freedom of choice may be seen as a sensible counterbalance to a poorly constructed general rule. Against the background of the general rule set out in the Proposal, it is understandable that parties would wish to exercise a choice in order to align themselves with a point of permanence in their lives such as nationality (or from a UK perspective, domicile). Looking at art.17 from a technical perspective, choice of nationality, while certain, would need to be refined from a UK point of view.[144] If, for a UK citizen, art.17 were deemed to point to the legal system of habitual residence, that would render the alleged choice by the testator meaningless, the point of art.17 being to provide a real choice, that is, a choice other than the habitual residence. On this reasoning, for a UK citizen, the only satisfactory alternative to habitual residence would be domicile in some sense. It is not clear, and it ought to be clear, what option would be available to the UK citizen. Thus, a peripatetic academic of British nationality and Scottish domicile, whose work resulted in his spending three years in Italy, followed by three years in The Hague, nevertheless might, under

---

[142] See Ch.6, above.
[143] A rare example of a definition being provided is contained in art.19 of the Rome I Regulation, for the purpose of that Regulation. See para.15–54, above.
[144] See, however, art.28.

an expanded art.17, assure himself that Scots law (qua "law of nationality") would regulate the succession to his estate.

Party autonomy, increasingly permitted, normally is accompanied by mandatory rules in order to safeguard certain interests. There is no such inhibition in Rome V. However, to offset the lack of policing by way of mandatory rules, the testator's choice is limited to the law of his nationality.

There is a lack of guidance in art.17 upon temporal issues.[145] Article 17.1 permits a testator to choose the law of the state whose nationality he possesses. One would think that this choice could fall only upon the nationality of the testator at the time of testing, rather than his nationality, as it may happen to be at the time of death.

Freedom to choose the applicable law is restricted to the law to govern the succession "as a whole". Therefore, a testator could not use the Regulation to subvert the Regulation, by choosing, for example, the law of his nationality (or in the case of a UK citizen, his domicile) to govern the succession to immoveable property situated there, and the law of his habitual residence to regulate succession to moveables wherever situated. In every case the reference is to the law of a state in its internal sense (art.26).

Public policy

18–42   Article 27 provides the customary public policy safeguard for the forum, but interestingly art.27.2 has the effect of seeking to restrict the exercise of the forum's discretion by stating that the application of a rule of the *lex successionis* may not be considered to be contrary to the public policy of the forum on the sole ground that its clauses regarding the reserved portion of an estate differ from those in force in the forum. While under current rules in the UK it would be unprecedented for the forum to exclude the operation of the rules of the *lex successionis* as to family provision merely because they differ from those of the *lex fori*, nevertheless the express articulation of this principle in the Proposal is noteworthy. It recognises that one of the great difficulties of harmonisation in succession, even in the conflict of laws, far less substantive law, is that different legal systems have different attitudes to family provision. It reinforces the role and expanding province of the *lex causae*, and the very expression, and manner of expression, of ruling out in advance any exercise of public policy by the forum is indicative of a culture of control from the centre,[146] albeit that the effect, in this instance, is to protect the individuality of legal systems in their substantive succession rules. Such a provision, in curtailing the discretion of the forum, is indicative of a wider trend.

Recognition and enforcement

18–43   Chapter IV provides rules on recognition and enforcement among Member States of a decision[147] given pursuant to the proposed Regulation. The provisions

---

[145] Contrast art.18.1.

[146] cf. Rome II negotiations on the subject of non-compensatory, exemplary or punitive damages, and Rome II Regulation, recital (32), which nudges the forum towards disapproval on public policy grounds of a rule of the *lex causae* pertaining to such damages. Article 27.2 of proposed Rome V, by contrast, operates to preclude disapproval.

[147] Defined in art.2(g). See also arts 34 and 35 regarding recognition and enforceability of authentic instruments (defined in art.2(h)).

in Ch.IV are modelled on corresponding provisions contained in the Brussels I Regulation. While they are well tested and familiar in themselves, their inclusion in a scheme of rules servicing an area which is largely non-contentious is surprising.

Debate in the UK

Following publication of the Proposal, the UK Government directed that a **18–44** public consultation exercise be undertaken[148] to address the issue of whether it would be in the UK's national interests for the Government, in accordance with art.4 of the UK's Protocol on Title IV measures, to opt in to the proposed Regulation; and if so, on whether it should apply throughout the UK.[149]

The two issues of most pressing concern, identified by the House of Lords EU Committee after consideration of expert opinion,[150] are, first, the necessity for further refinement of the meaning of the connecting factor of "deceased's habitual residence at time of death", and secondly, the problem of clawback.

While the House of Lords Committee found itself in agreement with the proposed change to a unitary choice of law rule to apply to the whole of the estate of a deceased,[151] and further with the Proposal to employ the connecting factor of habitual residence,[152] it concluded that a compromise needed to be struck between appropriateness and certainty, and that it was essential to define the central criterion.

An example of the clawback problem is provided when a person who benefits from a forced inheritance rule is able to make a claim for that inheritance from lifetime gifts made by the deceased.[153] While Scots law, in contrast with English law, displays a long established system of fixed family provision, it has little knowledge, now, of clawback except in the limited area of *collation inter liberos*.

Article 19.2(j) of the Proposal, in referring to the *lex causae* any obligation to restore or account for gifts, and the taking of them into account when determining the shares of heirs, would subject clawback claims to the governance of the *lex successionis*. Clawback, therefore, would operate in the UK whenever the *lex successionis* contains such a rule. In terms of method, this approach disturbs the balance between the forum's application of its choice of law rules pertaining to lifetime transfers of moveable property, and those pertaining to succession, respectively.[154] The inclusion of art.19.2(j) as a matter within the scope of the applicable law, and hence a matter for the putatively harmonised rules of succession (as opposed to the unharmonised rules of title to moveable property) detracts from the ability of the forum to draw a

---

[148] Ministry of Justice, *European Commission proposal on succession and wills: a public consultation* (The Stationery Office, 2009), Consultation Paper CP41/09.

[149] Article 28.2 provides the usual "intra-UK" opt-out clause. Even in this difficult area of harmonisation of wills and succession, it is probably undesirable to maintain different layers of law.

[150] House of Lords European Union Committee, *6th Report of Session 2009–10, The EU's Regulation on Succession: Report with Evidence* (The Stationery Office, 2010), HL Paper No.75 (Session 2009/10).

[151] *The EU's Regulation on Succession*, 2010, HL Paper No.75 (Session 2009/10), para.58.

[152] *The EU's Regulation on Succession*, 2010, HL Paper No.75 (Session 2009/10), para.65.

[153] *The EU's Regulation on Succession*, 2010, HL Paper No.75 (Session 2009/10), para.86.

[154] cf. generally *Stiftung v Lewis* [2004] E.W.H.C. 2589 (Ch); also *Re Korvine's Trusts* [1921] 1 Ch. 343.

distinction between inter vivos gifts and problems of succession. There could be a clash of characterisation, e.g. the English *lex fori* insisting qua *lex situs* that a valid disposal, even shortly before death, has been made by the person now deceased, according to the property rules of English domestic and conflict law, whereas the opposing argument could be made that clawback rules form part of the substantive succession law of the *lex successionis*.

The practical concern in the UK is that those in receipt of gifts, pre-eminently charities, would be uncertain whether money or property donated by an individual during his lifetime could be subject to clawback by his heirs upon the donor's death. It is feared that this would inhibit the use by charitable organisations of funds transferred to them by inter vivos donation, or that it would force charities to seek to protect themselves by means of insurance. Insofar as choice of law principle dictates that such a problem is capable of arising under current choice of law rules if the *lex ultimi domicilii*, with regard to moveables, or the *lex situs* with regard to immoveables, should contain such a clawback provision, the degree of concern which this particular aspect of the Proposal has generated in England must be attributable to the width and uncertainty of the proposed new connecting factor of habitual residence.

In light of views expressed by an overwhelming number of respondents to the public consultation, the Government (with which the House of Lords EU Committee agreed) announced,[155] on December 16, 2009, that it has decided not to opt-in to the proposed Regulation, meaning (for the time being, at least) that the UK will not be bound by a resulting instrument. The Government concluded that the potential benefits of the Proposal are outweighed by the risks.[156] Nonetheless, the Government intends to:

"... engage fully with the forthcoming negotiations between Member States on the proposal, with the aim of removing the points that currently cause concern and to deliver further improvements for citizens with links and assets in more than one country. If that can be achieved, the Government could then decide to seek to adopt a final regulation."[157]

A new instance of hybridity

18–45   In the context of the Europeanisation of the conflict rules of Member States, the problem of hybridity has presented, notably, in the matter of ascertaining the geographical and subject matter scope of the Brussels I Regulation and related instruments. The puzzle has been to determine, under the diktat of the ECJ, the extent to which the rules of civil jurisdiction in the Brussels regime effectively apply beyond the physical boundaries of the EU, so as to prevent, for example, a Scots or English court granting a sist or stay of its own proceedings in favour of those later raised in a non-Member State court (the "Owusu

---

[155] Hansard, HL Vol.502, Part No.17, col.141 (December, 16 2009).

[156] cf. Earlier Press Release, October 6, 2005, Scottish Parliament: after consideration of expert opinion, the Justice 1 Committee of the Scottish Parliament concluded that the proposal was "fundamentally flawed and unnecessary", and strongly urged the UK Government not to opt-in to any draft instrument which should emerge following the conclusion of the consultation processes.

[157] (Then) Secretary of State for Justice and Lord Chancellor, Jack Straw.

problem").[158] There are many other examples of demarcation problems in jurisdiction in respect of Third States.[159]

In relation to proposed Rome V, should the UK ultimately decide not to opt-in, difficult new problems will require to be addressed, of characterisation and delimitation, and of co-existence of a European regime with national rules.[160] To this point, the opt-in mechanism for the UK and Ireland has been perceived as a safeguard to protect common law sensibilities and UK interests, and hitherto the effect of its operation vis-à-vis other Member States has not been the focus of attention. However, failure on the part of the UK and/or of Ireland to opt-in to Rome V has the potential to undermine the successful operation of the proposed rules in those Member States which will be bound by the Regulation. Great confusion is likely to result from a split among Member States between those which are bound by Rome V, and those which are not. For example: if a German national, domiciled in Germany, dies without having exercised any choice of law per art.17, habitually resident in Scotland, and leaving estate in Scotland and Germany, the German authorities, charged with the administration of estate, and applying Rome V, would have no jurisdiction in terms of art.4, or *ex hypothesi* under art.5, or under art.6 as currently drafted.[161] If, under a re-drafted art.6, the German court were competent to deal with the German estate, the question would arise as to which law the German forum would apply qua *lex successionis*. In terms of arts 16 and 26, it ought to apply domestic Scots law, qua habitual residence of the deceased at death. The Scots court, charged with administration of the estate in Scotland, would take jurisdiction under national rules, based upon the presence of property within Scotland, and would apply to the distribution thereof the German law of the deceased's domicile, even if, in the circumstances, German law did not seek to be applied. Ironically, the outcome of events suggests that the use of *renvoi* by the Scots court in this scenario would be helpful, i.e. applying German law including its rules of private international law. But in so doing, the Scots court could be said to be applying indirectly a Regulation which expressly the UK had declined to adopt, and also would be doing so by utilisation of the *renvoi* reasoning which (sub nom. "referral")[162] the proposed Regulation shuns.

More complex scenarios can be conjured up, and it is difficult to avoid the conclusion that UK and Irish ability not to opt-in is a power which potentially has repercussions beyond UK and Irish "citizens", with the capability of throwing the projected harmonised system into disarray. Perhaps this has not been so obvious until now because the historical pattern of UK behaviour with regard to EU harmonisation exercises has been to grumble extensively,

---

[158] See para.7–56, above. In the current context, a distinction must be drawn in that the UK, in pondering questions of hybridity and relations with non-Member States in matters of civil and commercial jurisdiction, is bound by the duty to adhere to the principle and detail of the Brussels I Regulation; *contra*, if the UK does not opt-in to Rome V, it is *not* bound by any of its provisions, and in particular by its jurisdiction provision.

[159] See paras 7–62—7–64; and E. Winter, "Measuring the Extent of the Brussels regime", 2010 J.R. 163.

[160] It is appropriate to ponder these matters in this chapter, but there are other subject matter areas, such as choice of law in divorce and matrimonial property, where in future similar problems may emerge.

[161] Though presumably the terms of art.6 could be altered so as to confer residual jurisdiction on the courts of a "Contracting" State if one or more Member State(s) exercises its right not to opt-in to the proposed Regulation.

[162] See art.26.

secure a measure of compromise, and then ultimately to opt-in. Such considerations emphasise the importance of other Member States working towards
a compromise solution in order that the UK and Ireland will feel inclined to
opt-in.

V. POWERS OF APPOINTMENT AND POWERS OF APPORTIONMENT[163]

18–46 A testator (in this context, termed "the donor") may confer on his executors
("the donee") power to deal with his estate or part thereof, and to allocate the
funds in question to an individual of the donee's choosing ("the appointee").
This may serve the purpose of a trust without going so far as to create a trust.[164]

General powers (powers of appointment) are to be distinguished from
special powers (powers of apportionment). A general power of appointment is
"close to full rights of ownership", though it must not be so wide as to be open
to the charge of usurping the testamentary role of the testator.[165] Special
powers in contrast, refer to the case where the donee's discretion is curtailed
by the donor, and his choice limited to selecting the appointee(s) from a particular class of potential persons. The latter is the more usual situation, since, as
noted, a wide discretion in the form of a general power might be void as a
delegation to another of the power to test.

The conflict dimension

18–47   Are the capacity of the donee to take, and the validity of the exercise of a
power in form and essentials, to be governed by the law of the will conferring
the power, or by the law of the domicile of the donee, or by the law of the deed
by which the power is exercised? Must the law conferring the power also be
the law of its exercise?[166] Lord Justice-Clerk Thomson in *Durie's Trustees v
Osborne*[167] expressed the matter as follows: the question is whether the donee
should be regarded as a free agent exercising the choice given to him by a
testament in accordance with his own law, or as "a cog in the machinery of the
donor's deed. In sheer logic there is much to be said for both views", but if
intention be the vital matter, "it seems better to look to a man's own law than
to one arbitrarily imposed on him".

The general principles to be elicited from English and Scottish authorities
are as follows.[168]

General powers: the fund is regarded as being akin to the property of the
donee, so that the same rules apply to a deed by the donee exercising the
power, as to the donee's own will.[169]

---

[163] See generally Barr et al, *Drafting Wills in Scotland*, 2nd edn, 2009.
[164] Barr et al, *Drafting Wills in Scotland*, 2nd edn, 2009, para.5.59.
[165] Barr et al, *Drafting Wills in Scotland*, 2nd edn, 2009, para.5.59.
[166] See Lord Justice-Clerk Moncrieff in *Kennion v Buchan's Trustees* (1880) 7 R. 570 at 573,
quoting in turn Lord Brougham in *Tatnall v Hankey*, 2 Moo. P.C. 342.
[167] 1961 S.L.T. 53 at 61.
[168] And see further Anton with Beaumont, *Private International Law*, 2nd edn, 1990, pp.696–698.
[169] See *Durie's Trustees v Osborne*, 1961 S.L.T. 53; following *Anderson v Collins*, 1913 1 S.L.T. 219.

Special powers: the fund is regarded as being still the property of the donor and the donee is seen as his agent so that the validity of a deed exercising the power is governed by the same rules as apply to the original will of the donor.

The *lex situs* will apply as regards immoveables. The undernoted rules state the position only as regards moveables:

Capacity

The exercise of the power will be valid if the donee has capacity by the law **18–48** of his domicile, though it may be sufficient, certainly in the case of special powers,[170] that he has capacity by the law of the deed creating the power.

Formal validity

The provisions of the Wills Act 1963 as to the various permissible forms apply **18–49** to wills exercising powers. In addition to the general rule as to formal validity contained in s.1,[171] an additional rule provides that a will so far as it exercises a power of appointment (sic), shall be treated as properly executed if its execution conformed to the law governing the essential validity of the power.[172] With regard to immoveables, the additional rule provided by s.2(1)(b), that a will disposing of immoveable property shall be treated as properly executed if its execution conformed to the internal law of the *lex situs*, is available. Section 2(2) provides that a will so far as it exercises a power of appointment shall not be treated as improperly executed by reason only that its execution was not in accordance with any formal requirements contained in the instrument creating the power.

Essential validity

General powers: the essential validity of a will (i.e. of the donee) exercising **18–50** a general power is determined by the law of the will itself, that is, the law of the testator's domicile at the date of his death, as regards moveables[173]; and the *lex situs* as regards immoveables. The law of the will conferring the power is irrelevant in this case.

Special powers: the essential validity of a will exercising such a power is determined by the law governing the deed which confers the powers.

Construction

The following presumptions apply: **18–51**

General powers: a will exercising such power is construed according to the law which governs the construction of that will,[174] and not the deed conferring

---

[170] *Gould v Lewal* [1918] 2 Ch. 391; *Re Langley's Settlement Trusts* [1962] Ch. 541.
[171] See para.18–21, above.
[172] Wills Act 1963, s.2(1)(d). See, at common law: *Kennion v Buchan's Trustees* (1880) 7 R. 570; *Anderson v Collins*, 1913 1 S.L.T. 219—ruling law that of donee; *Durie's Trustees v Osborne*, 1961 S.L.T. 53; *Re Price* [1900] 1 Ch. 442; *Barretto v Young* [1900] 2 Ch. 339; *Re Wilkinson's Settlement* [1917] 1 Ch. 620.
[173] *Pouey v Hordern* [1900] Ch. 492; *Re Pryce* [1911] 2 Ch. 286; *Re Waite's Settlement Trusts* [1958] Ch. 100; *Re Khan's Settlement* [1965] 3 W.L.R. 1291.
[174] *Durie's Trustees v Osborne*, 1961 S.L.T. 53; *Re Price* [1900] 1 Ch. 442; *Re Khan's Settlement* [1965] 3 W.L.R. 1291; *Gould v Lewal* [1918] 2 Ch. 391; *Re McMorran* [1958] Ch. 624; *Re Waite's Settlement Trusts* [1958] Ch. 100; *Re Fenston's Settlement* [1971] 1 W.L.R. 1640.

the power. The law governing construction of the donee's will determines whether a will expressed in general terms without mentioning a power in fact operates as an exercise of the power.[175]

Special powers: the rule is that the construction of a deed exercising a special power must be governed by the law conferring the power.

Revocation

18–52   A deed revoking the exercise of a power will be effective (i.e. as regards essentials) if it complies with either the law of the deed conferring the power or the law of the donee's domicile at the date of revocation.[176]

VI. TRUST ESTATES

Common law

18–53   Prior to the Recognition of Trusts Act 1987, the following rules applied:

(a) Domicile

18–54   Most matters were governed by what was known for convenience as the "domicile" of the trust, that is, the proper law of the trust deed or the law of the country with which the trust had the closest connection. Thus, it was the court of the domicile of the trust which had jurisdiction to determine an application to vary the trust purposes under the Trusts (Scotland) Act 1961.[177] Broadly speaking, the law of the domicile of a testamentary trust would be the law of the country in which the testator's will was lodged and a grant of confirmation or probate was first obtained. In exceptional cases the domicile of a trust might be changed.[178]

(b) Capacity to create a trust

18–55   The *lex situs* applied as regards heritage[179]; otherwise the law of the granter's domicile would apply.

---

[175] Though see further Anton with Beaumont, *Private International Law*, 2nd edn, 1990, p.697.

[176] *Velasco v Coney* [1934] P. 143.

[177] As to what constitutes a Scottish trust see George Duncan and D. Oswald Dykes, *The Principles of Civil Jurisdiction as Applied in the Law of Scotland* (Edinburgh: W. Green, 1911), p.213 quoted with approval by Lord President Clyde in *Clarke's Trustees, Petitioners*, 1966 S.L.T. 249 at 251. Article 60.3 of the Brussels I Regulation states that in order to determine whether a trust is domiciled in the Member State whose courts are seised of the matter, the court shall apply its rules of private international law. In respect of the UK, Civil Jurisdiction and Judgments Order 2001 (SI 2001/3929) Sch.1 para.12(3) (re Civil Jurisdiction and Judgments Act 1982 s.45) provides that a trust is domiciled in a part of the UK if and only if the system of law of that part is the system of law with which the trust has its closest and most real connection. As to definition of trust for the purposes of the Recognition of Trusts Act 1987, see Schedule to the Act, art.2.

[178] Cheshire, *Private International Law*, 8th edn, 1970, pp.577, 578; Anton, *Private International Law*, 1st edn, 1967, p.481; *Duke of Marlborough v Att Gen* [1945] Ch. 78; *Baroness Lloyd*, 1963 S.L.T. 231; *Re Seale's Marriage Settlement* [1961] Ch. 574; *Re Weston's Settlements* [1969] 1 Ch. 223; *Re Windeatt's Will Trusts* [1969] 1 W.L.R. 692.

[179] *Black v Black's Trustees*, 1950 S.L.T. (Notes) 32.

(c) Formal validity

It was sufficient that the deed comply with either the proper law of the trust **18–56**
or the law of the place of execution.[180] Where the trust was testamentary in
nature, the provisions of the Wills Act 1963 would apply, the definition of
"will" in s.6(1) thereof including "any testamentary instrument or act".

(d) Essential validity

Trustees' powers and variation of trust purposes were governed by the law **18–57**
of the domicile of the trust. So too were matters of construction.

(e) Sales of Scots heritage by English trustees

The powers of sale conferred upon Scots and English trustees by the Scots **18–58**
and English Trusts Acts applied only to Scots and English trustees and land in
Scotland and England respectively. If an English will did not confer express
power[181] of sale, power to sell land in Scotland might be obtained at the discretion of the court.[182] Retrospective sanction was not usually granted.[183] Whether
this procedure, after the advent of the Recognition of Trusts Act 1987,[184] is still
required is unclear.[185]

Recognition of Trusts Act 1987[186]

The Act applies to trusts regardless of their date of creation, subject to indi- **18–59**
vidual state reservation and to the caveat that the Act shall not affect the law
governing acts or omissions of trustees before the coming into force of the Act
on August 1, 1987.

---

[180] *Thomson* (1917) 33 Sh. Ct Rep. 84; *Re Pilkington's Will Trusts* [1937] 1 Ch. 574.

[181] If power was express, no further authorisation from a Scots court was required: *Phipps v Phipps's Trustees*, 1914 1 S.L.T. 239 (though there the trustee's power to sell Scottish heritage was not express but deduced by inference from the testator's use of the words "all other my real estate whatsoever, wheresoever").

[182] In Scotland the trustees applied to the Court of Session craving power of sale under the nobile officium (*Allan's Trustees* (1896) 24 R. 238; (1896) 24 R. 718; *Pender's Trustees, Petitioners*, (1903) 5 F. 504; 1907 S.C. 207; *Harris's Trustees, Petitioners*, 1919 S.C. 432; *Laurie's Trustees, Petitioners* 1946 S.L.T. (Notes) 31; *Campbell-Wyndham-Long's Trustees, Petitioners*, 1952 S.L.T. 43; *Prudential Assurance Co Ltd, Petitioners*, 1952 S.L.T. 121; Anton, *Private International Law*, 1st edn, 1967, pp.483, 484); and in England the trustees applied to the Court of Chancery for power to apply to the Court of Session, which would normally be granted if it was considered expedient and in the interests of the trust estate to do so (*Forrest v Forrest* (1910) 54 S.J. 737; *Georges v Georges* (1921) 65 S.J. 311).

[183] *Dow's Trustees, Petitioners*, 1947 S.L.T. 293; *Prudential Assurance Co Ltd, Petitioners*, 1952 S.L.T. 121.

[184] The Act applies within the constituent parts of the UK as well as outside the UK, though it is not comprehensive in the matter of choice of law in relation to trusts (arts 14, 15).

[185] Alexander E. Anton and Paul R. Beaumont, *Civil Jurisdiction in Scotland*, 2nd edn (Edinburgh: W. Green, 1995), p.643.

[186] See Paolo Panico, *International Trust Laws* (Oxford: OUP, 2010); *Dicey, Morris and Collins on the Conflict of Laws*, 14th edn, 2006, Ch.29; Jonathan Harris, *The Hague Trust Convention* (Oxford: Hart, 2002); and D. Hayton, "The Hague Convention on the Law Applicable to Trusts and on their Recognition" (1987) 36 I.C.L.Q. 260.

This Act gave effect in UK law to the 1986 Hague Convention on the Law Applicable to Trusts and on their Recognition, the purpose of which is to, "ensure the international recognition of trusts and to obtain the adoption by States (even those which do not themselves have the trust concept)"[187] of a uniform choice of law rule relating to the validity, and many other aspects, of trusts.

In terms of s.1(1), the provisions of the Convention as set out in the Schedule to the Act shall have the force of law in the UK. Section 1(2): those provisions shall, so far as applicable, have effect not only in relation to the trusts described in arts 2 and 3 of the Convention, but also in relation to any other trusts of property arising under the law of any part of the United Kingdom or by virtue of a judicial decision whether in the United Kingdom or elsewhere.

The definition of "trust" in art.2 of the Schedule to the Act is wide, being designed to satisfy not only the requirements of a trust in the Anglo-American legal systems, but also analogous institutions in civilian systems.

These rules apply in UK courts whether or not the trust arises under the law of a contracting state, but only to "trusts created voluntarily and evidenced in writing" (art.3).

The statutory rules are not concerned with preliminary issues relating to the testamentary instrument which purports to convey assets to a trust (art.4).

A trust shall be governed by the law chosen by the settlor, expressly or impliedly (art.6),[188] or, failing such choice, by the law of closest connection (art.7).[189] That law shall govern (art.8) the validity, construction, effects and administration of the trust, and in particular shall govern matters itemised in a list ((a)–(j)) in art.8, including appointment and removal of trustees, trustees' rights among themselves, rights to administer and dispose of trust assets, to create security interests in the trust assets[190] or to acquire new assets, powers of investment, and liability of trustees to beneficiaries.

If the law identified as a result of the application of art.6 has no knowledge of the trust concept, the Convention, according to art.5, falls away, and shall not apply. In view of the wording of arts 5 and 7, it would not appear to be justified in such a case to divert to art.7 (applicable law in the absence of choice) in order to supply a viable governing law.

Article 11 enjoins recognition of trusts falling within the scope of the Convention and the Act, and regulates the effect of such recognition.[191] In this way, the provisions are consistent with the title of the Act, albeit that the Act, despite its name, is concerned primarily with choice of law.

---

[187] R.D. Leslie, "Trusts in Private International Law: Recognition of Trusts Act 1987" (1988) 33 J.L.S.S. 27 (see also A.E. Anton, "The Recognition of Trusts Act 1987", 1987 S.L.T. (News) 377).

[188] *Re Barton (Deceased)*; sub nom. *Tod v Barton* [2002] EWHC 264 (Ch).

[189] *Re Carapiet's Trusts*; sub nom. *Manoogian (Armenian Patriarch of Jerusalem) v Sonsino* [2002] EWHC 1304 (Ch).

[190] See saving clause in favour of the *lex situs* in art.15(d).

[191] But note art.11(d), preserving the conflict rules of property of any relevant *lex situs* to determine third party rights in relation to trust assets which have passed, as a result of a trustee's breach of trust, into his hands, provided those hands were innocent and that innocence is of importance to the *lex situs*.

SUMMARY 18

I. Testate and Intestate Succession **18–60**

1. Confirmation

The Scots courts follow the law of the domicile of the deceased as regards title to administer moveables. If probate or letters of administration or similar authority has/have been granted to a person(s) under that law, confirmation is granted to the same person(s) as executor(s) for the purposes of estate in Scotland. A foreign executor must seek confirmation in Scotland in order to deal with Scottish estate. If there has been no grant of administration abroad, the person entitled to appointment under the law of the domicile shall be confirmed to deal with property in Scotland. Confirmation or probate granted in any of the UK jurisdictions operates directly in the other jurisdictions, and resealing will suffice in the case of Commonwealth countries.

2. Administration and distribution

Administration, being a matter of procedure, is governed by the *lex fori*, being the law of the situation of the asset.

Distribution, being a matter of substance, is governed by the law of the succession (*lex successionis*), being the *lex ultimi domicilii* and/or the *lex situs*, as explained below.

The *lex fori* determines classification between administration and distribution.

3. The scission principle

This principle, by which a different choice of law rule (the *lex situs*) applies to succession to immoveables, from that (law of deceased's last domicile) which applies to succession to moveables, operates in Scots and English choice of law rules. A unitary rule obtains in many other legal systems.

4. Existence and extent of legal rights

These are determined by the law of the domicile of the deceased at death as regards moveables, and the *lex situs* as regards immoveables.

II. Intestate Succession

1. The laws governing intestate succession are:

   (a) re immoveables: the *lex situs* at the date of death;
   (b) re moveables: the law of the deceased's domicile at the date of death.

2. Prior rights in moveable property available by Scots domestic law arise if the deceased died domiciled in Scotland; and the prior right to the house if the qualifying dwelling house is situated in Scotland.

3. Caducary rights—the question whether the foreign government of the domicile of the deceased at death may succeed to estate in Scotland when the deceased died intestate without relatives, depends on whether or not, in the view of the forum, under the law of the deceased's domicile, that foreign government has the right to succeed as last heir as opposed merely to acquiring right to *bona vacantia*.

III. Testate Succession

Note the two-dimensional nature of the conflict rules, that is, the relevance of time and space.

1. Capacity
   Legal testamentary capacity appears to be governed by the law of the domicile of the testator at the date of the will as regards moveable property, and by the *lex situs* at that date as regards immoveables.
   Proprietary testamentary capacity is governed by the law of the domicile of the deceased at the date of death as regards moveable property, and by the *lex situs* as regards immoveables.

2. Formal Validity
   Under the Wills Act 1963 a will is to be regarded as validly executed in form if it complies with any one of the following laws:

   (a) place of execution;
   (b) domicile of testator at date of will or death;
   (c) habitual residence of testator at date of will or death;
   (d) nationality of testator at date of will or death;
   (e) place of registration of ship/aircraft;
   (f) *lex situs* (immoveables).

3. Essential Validity
   The essential validity or legality of the substance of the provisions of a will is governed by the following laws as at the date of the death of the testator:

   (a) immoveables—the *lex situs*;
   (b) moveables—the law of the testator's domicile.

4. Construction
   The testator's intention takes precedence and there are a number of working rules to identify the law to be applied as his deemed intention in the matter of construction, if his intention is not express.

5. Revocation of Wills

   (a) new will—the extent of revocation of a previous will depends on the validity and scope of a new will;
   (b) the effect of a revocation clause is determined according to the circumstances;
   (c) the effect of a purported act of revocation depends on the law of the testator's domicile as at that date, regarding moveables; or the *lex situs* relating to immoveables;
   (d) the effect of a subsequent marriage is determined by the law of the domicile of the testator immediately *after* the marriage;
   (e) a change of domicile has no effect on a will (subject to the rule that essential validity relating to moveables is governed by the law of the testator's last domicile).

IV. Proposed reform

The 1989 Hague Convention on the Law Applicable to the Estates of Deceased Persons was not ratified by the UK.

There was published in 2009 a Proposal for a Regulation on jurisdiction, applicable law, recognition and enforcement of decisions and authentic instruments in matters of succession and the creation of a European Certificate of Succession. The UK Government has decided, for the time being, not to opt-in to the proposed Regulation, but the Government intends to remain actively engaged in negotiations.

V. *Trusts*

See Recognition of Trusts Act 1987.

INDEX

617

Index